CW01668280

LONDON *in Paint*

Oil Paintings in the Collection at the Museum of London

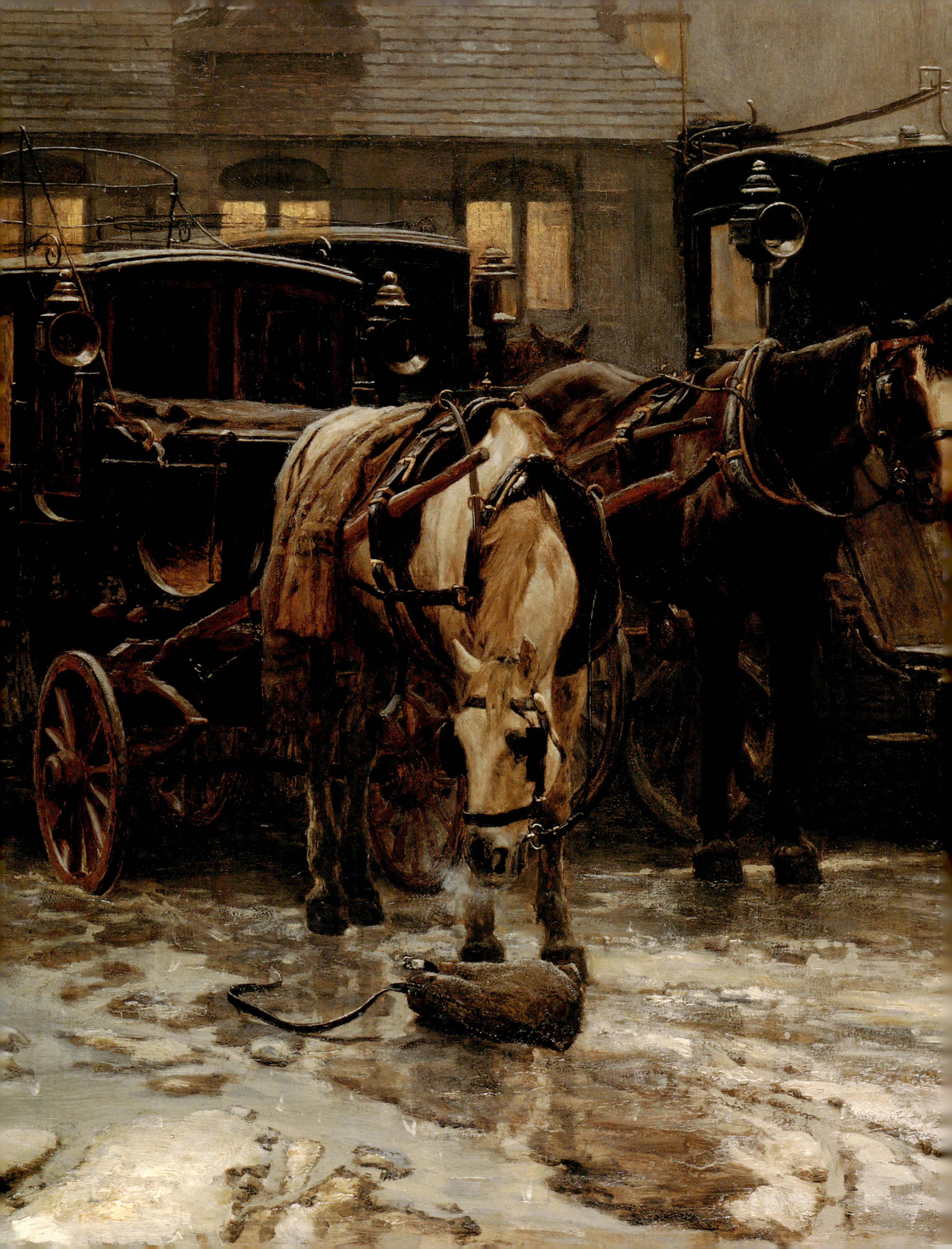

LONDON *in Paint*

Oil Paintings in the Collection at the Museum of London

MIREILLE GALINOU
AND JOHN HAYES

Foreword by Peter Ackroyd

museum of
LONDON

First published in Great Britain in 1996 by the
Museum of London, 150 London Wall,
London EC2Y 5HN

Copyright © 1996 Museum of London
Foreword copyright © 1996 Peter Ackroyd

The rights of Mireille Galinou and John Hayes
to be identified as authors of this work have been asserted
by them in accordance with the Copyright,
Designs and Patents Act, 1988.

All rights reserved. This publication may not be reproduced, stored in
a retrieval system, or transmitted, in any form or by any means,
electronic, mechanical, photocopying, recording or otherwise, without
the prior permission of the publisher.

ISBN 0 904818 51 9

Project Manager: Suzie Burt
Editorial: Penny David, Suzie Burt, Mandi Gomez, Liz Harrap
Design: Mick Keates
Photography: Torla Evans, Barrington Gray, John Chase, Richard Stroud
Index: Dorothy Frame

Formatting by Concise Artisans

Printed and bound in Great Britain by The White Dove Press

Frontispiece: A detail from *A London Cab Stand*
by John Charles Dollman

ACKNOWLEDGEMENTS

THE REVISION and expansion of John Hayes's original text published in 1970 has been a substantial task. It was achieved through the support of many experts in a wide range of fields, not only art historians such as those responsible for the most up-to-date work on individual artists such as Canaletto, William Marlow, Charles Hunt, David Roberts or the Camden Town painters, but also people whose expertise lies in lesser-known areas, such as the history of the gypsies (see cat. no. 62) or the investigation of technical aspects of London's industries (see cat. no. 135).

The following list bears witness to the richness of the expertise required to tackle the subject of London and to all these people I would like to express my deepest thanks:

W. G. M. Angliss, Edwin R. Beasley, Pat Astley Cooper from Wandsworth Museum, Di Atkinson formerly from the Museum of London, Jane Barington from the Imperial War Museum, Wendy Baron from the Government Art Collection, Xavier Baron from the University of Wisconsin, Christine Bayliss from Hammersmith and Fulham Archives, the Belgrave Gallery, John Berrington from Cheltenham Art Gallery, Oliver Bevan, Stephen Bond, M. Bradbury, Vera Brooker, Shirley Bury, Stephen Bury from Chelsea College of Art, Michael C. Buss, Beverley Carter from the Paul Mellon Collection, Margie Christian from Christie's, Samuel Clapp, Mr and Mrs Cobbe, David Cordingly, Caroline Cuthbert from the Tate Gallery, Mrs Dessau, Nick Eastaugh, Elizabeth Einberg from the Tate Gallery, Freda Elbourne, Chris Ellmers and Wendy Evans from the Museum of London, T. R. Fetherstonhaugh, Gabriele Finaldi from the National Gallery, Penelope Fussell from the Drapers Company, Kenneth Garlick, Kate Gibson, Louisa Goldsmith from the Hamilton Kerr Institute, Richard Green, Andrew Greg from Shipley Art Gallery, Helen Guiterman, Elizabeth Hamilton-Eddy from the National Maritime Museum, Caroline Hammond from the Chiswick Library, John Harris, Kate Harris from Longleat, John Harvey, Malcolm Holmes from the Swiss Cottage Library, Harold Hussey, Z. Jagodzinski from the Polish Library, Martin Kauffmann from the Bodleian Library, Michael Kenny from the City & Guilds of London Art School, Vivien Knight from the Guildhall Art Gallery, Nadine Lehni from Strasbourg Museum, Jo Links, Michael Liversidge from the University of Bristol, Roger Marijnissen, David Mayall from Sheffield Hallam University, Norman McLeod from the Royal Scottish Corporation, Sir Oliver Millar, John Mitchell who catalogued the Museum's collection of frames, Edward Morris from the Walker Art Gallery, the New Grafton Gallery, Robin Nordgreen, David Ormrod from the University of Kent, Julian Paren from the British Antarctic Survey, Michael Parkin, Hans Pearson from the Charing Cross Hotel, Viola Pemberton Piggott from the Royal Collection, Curtis Price from the Music Department of King's College, Gordon Reeves, Michael Robinson, Malcolm Rogers from the National Portrait Gallery, Natalie Rothstein, Graham Buckley Slater, David Smith, Carolyn Starren from Kensington and Chelsea Libraries, Ann Sumner from the Dulwich Picture Gallery, Peter Sutton from the Boston Museum of Fine Art, Ken Stone from the Metropolitan Police Museum, T. E. Stothard, Derek Taylor, Ken Thomas from Courage, J. C. Thorn, Ian Tyers from the Museum of London Archaeology Service, Nicholas Usherwood, Pieter Van der Merwe from the National Maritime Museum, Rozina Visram, Frances Ward from Greenwich Local History Library, Pamela Wedgwood from the Society of Antiquaries, Angela Weight from the Imperial War Museum, Lavinia Wellicome from Woburn Abbey, Nick West from Chelsea Library, Vicki White from the Kirkcaldy Museum and Art Gallery, D. C. Whitlock from the Corporation of the City of London, Mary P. Wilkinson from the Imperial War Museum, Alison Winter from Agnew's, Jenny Wood from the Imperial War Museum.

Whenever possible, I have checked new catalogue entries on contemporary works with the artists themselves and I thank them all for their co-operation.

I owe an enormous debt to the following Museum of London colleagues who have supported me through this task both in practical and also in emotional terms: most prominently Alex Werner who read, checked and suggested improvements to the text, and Shirley Waller; but also to Valerie Cumming (on all costume issues and others too), Edwina Ehrman, Hazel Forsyth and Susannah Plowright. The editor, Penny David, met the enormous task of checking the text in minute detail and I am grateful to her for remaining diligent and cheerful throughout. Liz Harrap was also unfailing at double, double-checking while Dorothy Frame tackled the task of producing a comprehensive index, for which I thank her. I am grateful to Rob Payton for co-ordinating conservation and analysis work on a number of our early paintings. The catalogue entries for these works were thus enriched and a considerable amount of data obtained, which will be very useful in the future. All of the photographs have been taken specially for this catalogue, in the Museum studio, by Barrington Gray, Torla Evans, John Chase and Richard Stroud. Macrophotography, courtesy of Nicholas Eastaugh. I am grateful to them and to the designer, Mick Keates and all the wonderful staff at the White Dove Press, for the beautiful appearance of this volume. Suzie Burt, our enthusiastic and energetic Publications Officer, brought it all together and succeeded in achieving this task in a climate not terribly propitious to large-scale undertakings. Finally the task of documenting paintings is the result of years of intelligent curating and I am deeply grateful to my predecessors who, knowingly and unknowingly, have guided my steps: John Hayes, who published the first catalogue in 1970; Joan Pollard (now Fuglesang) who was curator between 1975 and 1980 and Celina Fox between 1980 and 1993. The text was carefully double-checked by my colleague and friend at the Guildhall Library, Ralph Hyde, whose knowledge of London's topography and history provided a most valuable safety net. His colleagues John Fisher and Jeremy Smith have helped unravel many problems and their helpfulness is a constant source of delight. However, the sheer number of facts contained in this catalogue makes it impossible for anyone to master the text singlehandedly and any mistakes have to remain the responsibility of the authors.

MIREILLE GALINOU
September 1996

The Museum of London would like to thank the following galleries and institutions for granting permission to reproduce their pictures: Bodleian Library; British Library; Christie's Images; Cleveland Museum of Art; Courtauld Institute of Art, Witt Library; Dr. Nicholas Eastaugh for reproducing the macrophotographs; English Heritage; The Fine Art Society; Geffrye Museum; Guildhall Libraries and Art Gallery, Corporation of London; Harari and Johns Gallery, London; Julian Hartnoll Gallery, London; Martyn Gregory Gallery, London; Mercers' Company; Musée des Beaux Arts de Rouen; National Gallery publications; The National Trust; Richard Green Gallery, London; Rhode Island Museum; Royal Institution of Chartered Surveyors; Sotheby's; Tate Gallery; Victoria and Albert Museum.

Every effort has been made to contact the original copyright holders. The publishers would be pleased to make good any errors or omissions brought to our attention in future editions. The illustrations may not be reproduced without permission from the copyright holders.

Contents

Foreword

IN MY LIBRARY there hangs a lithograph of Wenceslaus Hollar's great panorama of London, with the date 1647 inscribed upon it; there are occasions when the sunlight seems to glance off its glass frame and actually pervade the lithograph itself, filling the old streets and houses with a familiar London light. They are, almost, reawakened to life. And here, perhaps, lies the central importance of the many paintings of London: within these bright and sometimes fiery images the city and its history are perpetually re-created by those who view them.

It has always been a city of spectacle and of display; art historians have sometimes noted the theatrical and scenic nature of many images of London, which suggests in turn that the artists have responded to the peculiar powers or properties of the city. It has remained a place of vivid contrasts, filled with the energetic display of people and institutions in apparently endless movement. Yet we need only to glance at the images of Doré or of Hogarth to realise that it has also been a dark city. In the night refuges and sick wards, the brothels and gutters, depicted by both artists, are to be found its victims. There are many paintings and drawings which display the great buildings of London but they also serve to emphasise the fact that, for more than a thousand years, it has been a city established upon money and commerce. It is built with the bricks of finance and of power, as another great London artist, William Blake, has memorably recorded.

We might take the Thames as one potent symbol of that commerce. There are many paintings depicting the river as a place of work, a thriving metropolis of its own with its wharves and barges, markets and manufactories. But it also has a more mysterious, and equally powerful, aspect which can be seen in the works of artists as diverse as Whistler and Canaletto. It is the river as enchantment or dream, the river which drifts past the opium dens of Limehouse, slinks silently by the reaches of Shadwell, and laps against Wapping Old Stairs.

But then, if we leave the riverside, we come to the streets themselves – if we think of London, we think of street scenes in the paintings of Ludgate and Oxford Circus, Cheapside and the Strand. It is a curious and not uninteresting fact that the first paintings of London streets are from the eighteenth century (in a period when the novel also became interested in the details of urban life), but in the last three hundred years there have been some wonderful evocations of London pavements from the detailed examination of George Scharf to the more expressionistic range of Leon Kossoff. There are also the darker streets, 'packed to blackness with accumulations of suffered experience' as Henry James once put it; it is the experience portrayed in Walter Sickert's London interiors, as well as in the shambling figures of Luke Fildes' engravings.

The portraits of ordinary Londoners – certainly their images in the pictures of late twentieth-century artists – show them characteristically as sad, or haunted, or somehow lost within their own city. In nineteenth-century painting, one great subject lies in the disparity between rich and poor – sometimes expressed in a moment of dramatic encounter. But in the art of our own time those contrasts are not so clearly visible; instead London has become a haunted fairground or a sad shapeless expanse of offices and homes.

It is impossible to talk of London art without mentioning the sense of place which exists everywhere within it. No city is so echoic, and so resonant with the past. Certain images, like that of London Bridge in all its incarnations, attract artists of every generation. Certain artists, like Frank Auerbach, will return to the same London scene again and again. It may also be that particular areas exert their own kind of attraction: Mornington Crescent, for example, has been the home of both Walter Sickert and Clarkson Stanfield, while around the corner, in different eras, lived George Cruikshank and Frank Auerbach.

There are other notable associations between London and London artists. There has of course been a long history of London radicalism, for example, and this spirit was most recently revived by the London artists between the wars. There has also been a history of antiquarianism in this city, which finds its avatar in John Stow. Similarly there have been artists who have deliberately attempted to retrieve images of the past in paintings of Cloth Fair or Old Southwark. But of course there have been other artists more interested in the processes of change and development within the city; it is the energy to be seen in paintings of Frith or of Ford Madox Brown. The city is at once uniquely constant and uniquely changeable, and the best artists are those who convey the sense of mystery within the immediate and temporary detail. We might mention here Samuel Scott's *Covent Garden Piazza and Market* and Joy's *Bayswater Omnibus* and Marlow's *Fresh Wharf, London Bridge*.

This is not to dismiss the actual historical significance of many paintings. Certain events, such as the Great Fire of 1666, the burning of the Houses of Parliament in 1834, and the ascent of Lunardi's balloon from St George's Fields in 1784, have all been commemorated in paintings within the collection of the Museum of London; without such vivid memorials of the past, our sense of history would be significantly weakened. In this catalogue of necessary retrieval, we must also put those painterly evocations of old fairs and street festivals; the milkmaids and chimneysweeps of May Day are now long gone, and it is unlikely that Frost Fair will ever again be celebrated on the Thames. These paintings are our inheritance in more than one sense. It is curious, in this context, how often artists have depicted fires and fires in the capital – from the burning of the Pantheon in Oxford Street and of the theatre in Drury Lane to the far greater conflagrations of the Blitz. It is a city which seems to have provoked destruction – even into the present age of terrorist bombing. As the old London alchemist once put it, 'it is the city of gold, it is the city of fire, it is the city of death'.

Yet it is wrong to end upon so stern or declamatory a note. There is no end to London, or of London painting. Now, at the end of the twentieth century, it has become the home for literally hundreds of artists who have erected studios in Bermondsey and Bethnal Green, Spitalfields and Limehouse. One thinks also of the many foreign artists who have found something of their inspiration in the streets of the city – Monet, Pissarro, Géricault, Whistler, Canaletto among them. But this is a continuing city, always building upon its past and renewing its inheritance. Here in this volume you will find the lineaments of that great tradition.

PETER ACKROYD
London, September 1996

Introduction

THE MUSEUM of London opened in December 1976, its collections merging those of the Guildhall Museum (which dated back to 1826) and the London Museum which had first opened in 1912 at Kensington Palace. The collections of paintings, prints and drawings, however, all came from the London Museum, the Corporation of the City of London retaining its collection of Paintings (Guildhall Art Gallery), Prints, Drawings and Maps, administered by the Library.

A museum to be devoted entirely to the archaeology, history and life of the capital had long been a cherished idea of Reginald, 2nd Viscount Esher (1852–1930), who was a distinguished servant of the arts and a close friend of Queen Victoria and Edward VII. He proposed it formally in a memorandum to George V in 1910. Following this initiative, the London Museum was founded by Lewis Harcourt (1863–1922), later 1st Viscount Harcourt, in 1911, with the active encouragement of Lord Esher, and of Queen Alexandra, King George V and Queen Mary. It was opened to the public on 8 April 1912; and became a National Museum under Treasury control in July 1913.

The first Keeper (1911–19) was (Sir) Guy Laking, the son of Sir Francis, one of the Court physicians. Laking, who had already published books on armour and the decorative arts, had the daunting task of putting together collections and museum within a few months. Initially pictures were often borrowed and by an interesting coincidence, the creation of the London Museum had taken place at the same time as the Whitechapel Gallery exhibition *Old London* in the winter of 1911. Requests for loans were sent to a number of owners who had lent pictures to this exhibition, and three of the pictures borrowed at this time were afterwards converted into gifts (cat. nos 21, 53 and 96), the large Deane of *Waterloo Bridge* (cat. no. 54) being the most notable example. Many pictures were also purchased, in particular a group submitted by Messrs Leggatt in 1912, which included Samuel Scott's *Covent Garden Piazza and Market*, then attributed to Canaletto (cat. no. 40). Very gradually gifts started coming in such as the primitive but lively record of Victorian rat-catching in 1917 (cat. no. 117), as well as grander works such as the rare *Interior of Henry VII's Chapel* by Canaletto in 1919 (cat. no. 33).

During the keepership of Laking's successor, Harman Oates (1919–26), the trend for gifts continued and the picture collection was increased about equally by donation and purchase. Outstanding gifts included the splendid Marlow of *The Adelphi* (cat. no. 27) presented by J. Pierpont Morgan Jr as well as for the Victorian period the imposing view of the *Houses of Parliament* by John Anderson, part of the P. A. S. Phillips gift, otherwise mostly composed of watercolours. The pair of Levins of *Covent Garden* and *Cremorne Gardens* (cat. nos 95 and 126) were among the happier purchases of the 1920s. Unfortunately, the records relating to accessions up to 1926 are often scanty, sometimes even non-existent, so that most of the information on provenance contained in the Catalogue which follows was compiled from outside sources.

A more professional attitude towards administration was introduced by (Sir) Mortimer Wheeler (Keeper, 1926–44), and from 1927 the more usual practice was adopted of numbering accessions according to the year of acquisition. Though it was in Wheeler's keepership that the first Treasury purchase grant was received (£200 for the year 1931–2), picture acquisitions at that time were entirely by gift. The Museum was thus extremely fortunate in acquiring the following paintings: Joy's *Bayswater Omnibus* (cat. no. 134, lent in 1929 and converted into a gift in 1966) which has since become one of the Museum's best loved pictures, two of the collection's best Nevinsons (cat. nos 173 and 174, in 1928 and 1930), the little known *Cab Stand* by Dollman (cat. no. 101, in 1928) as well as the splendid Hondius of *The Frozen Thames* (cat. no. 84, in 1935). One of the Nevinsons and the Hondius were acquired through the generosity of the National Art Collections Fund, thus anticipating the important role in purchases which this institution was to play in later years. Also for the first time, more recent (almost contemporary) works were presented: Holmes's *Power Station* (cat. no. 140), only thirty years after it was painted, and Atwood's *Coach Wheelwright's Shop* (cat. no. 135), acquired during the lifetime of the artist.

(Professor) W. F. Grimes, who succeeded Wheeler, brought a high degree of order into the heterogeneous collections and instituted a policy in regard to pictures which balanced the claims of aesthetic quality with those of archaeological accuracy or relevance. Clifford Hall's *Caledonian Market* fulfilled such criteria and was bought in 1951. Museum activities had virtually stopped during the war, but during Grimes's curatorship (1945–7) and directorship (1947–56) purchasing was re-introduced. In the twenty years or so after the war a number of significant purchases were made, largely the result of the two special funds which became available: the Joicey Trust Fund, received in 1943 and the Mackenzie Bell Trust Fund, received in 1956. Works acquired with the help of the Joicey Trust Fund include the Marlow of *Fresh Wharf, London Bridge* (in 1950), the O'Connor of *From Pentonville Road looking West* (in 1952), the Ritchie of *Summer Day in Hyde Park* (in 1954), the great panorama of *The Fire of London* (in 1957), the Jacob Knyff view of *Chiswick from the River* (in 1962), while the Mackenzie Bell Trust Fund was put to excellent use when purchasing the early seventeenth-century *A View of Greenwich* (in 1964). The last three works mentioned benefited from contributions from the National Art Collections Fund which increasingly played a dynamic part in the purchasing of pictures.

Up to 1959–60 the annual purchase grant received from the Treasury had never exceeded £375, and the Museum had been largely dependent on the Joicey and Mackenzie Bell Trust

Funds and on outside donations for the purchase of exhibits, but in this year the Trustees received a substantially increased Treasury grant of £1,000, a sum increased to £2,000 in 1967–8 and £3,000 in 1969–70. At the time of writing the purchase grant has increased to £51,000. Of course, this sum is not solely available for paintings and compares rather unfavourably with the resources of most fully fledged galleries, none of which really addresses the central theme of this collection and of this century: urban living. The role played by such grant-giving institutions as the National Art Collections Fund, the MGC/V&A Purchase Fund and the National Heritage Memorial Fund has simply become vital and without their support the Museum would not have been in a position to make such significant additions to its collections as Hicks's *General Post Office* in 1990 and *London from Southwark* in 1992 or, indeed, the more accessible Bomberg's *Evening in the City of London* in 1985 and MacDuff's *Lost and Found* in 1993.

In spite of the natural disinclination of donors to present pictures in a time of sharply rising prices, the collections continued to benefit from gifts and bequests. A special mention should be made of the group of Nevinsons bequeathed by the W. H. Smith director Arnold D. Power (cat. nos 183, 184, and 185, in 1959), the war works acquired through the Imperial War Museum, the Barlow Bequest of two quintessentially London works by Algernon Newton, the gift of the Bloomsbury painting by de Karlowska, and the Lady Bonham Carter bequest of the *Regalia* and Blanche's *Crystal Palace*.

When in 1976 the London Museum became the Museum of London and moved from its Kensington Palace premises to its current new home (designed by architects Powell and Moya of Festival of Britain 'Skylon' fame), the collection of paintings moved to its present purpose-built store situated alongside the Print Room housing the collection of prints and drawings. For the first time a curator dealing specifically with paintings, prints and drawings had been appointed in 1975: Joan Pollard who was effectively in charge of the collection between 1971 and 1980 and whose major contribution was to create and develop a coherent and very reliable system for storage and indexing. Acquisitions took a turning point under the curatorship of Dr Celina A. Fox (1980–91) whose informed confidence and knowledge of the art world were unprecedented.

It had previously been suggested that in view of the comparatively recent date of the Museum's foundation, and the very small funds that have been available for purchase, we should not be expected to have works by such great painters as Hogarth, Constable, Turner, Whistler, Monet or numerous other major artists who spent part of their working lives painting the London scene. Until quite recently, one of the most influential London groups of painters, the Camden Town Group, who courageously elected to paint the capital, were almost not represented in the collection. Celina Fox instigated a policy of deliberate and determined collecting to build the group now in the Museum's collection at a time when these artists were no longer 'affordable'. The Museum should continue to strive – ideally with the help of gifts and bequests – to represent the full range of paintings which have shaped the image of the capital. Contemporary collecting is, of course, of the utmost importance in this respect and recent endeavours have aimed to give the new generation of 'Capital Painters' a louder voice, through exhibitions (*Artists' London* in 1992, *Witnesses and Dreamers* in 1994, *Streets in the sky, the paintings of David Hepher* in 1996), residencies (Mao

Wen Biao in 1993, Timo Lehtonen in 1994 and Jonathan Boatfield in 1996) and acquisitions (see Modern London, cat. nos 211 to 230).

In this book, the research of Dr John Hayes, published in 1970 in *The Catalogue of Oil Paintings of the London Museum*, has been updated, expanded and reorganised chronologically and thematically. The general introductions which place our collection in context constitute, in their own right, a history of the imaging of London through oil paintings. This volume includes all paintings which entered the collection prior to the summer of 1996. The titles followed by an asterisk are the original titles for the paintings, corresponding either to artists' titles or those found in contemporary exhibitions. Within each sub category, paintings have been organised chronologically. The many people who have given such ready assistance to the authors are listed in the Acknowledgements, but a special word of thanks is due to Alex Werner, Valerie Cumming, Ralph Hyde, Xavier Baron and Penny David for reading and enhancing the typescript.

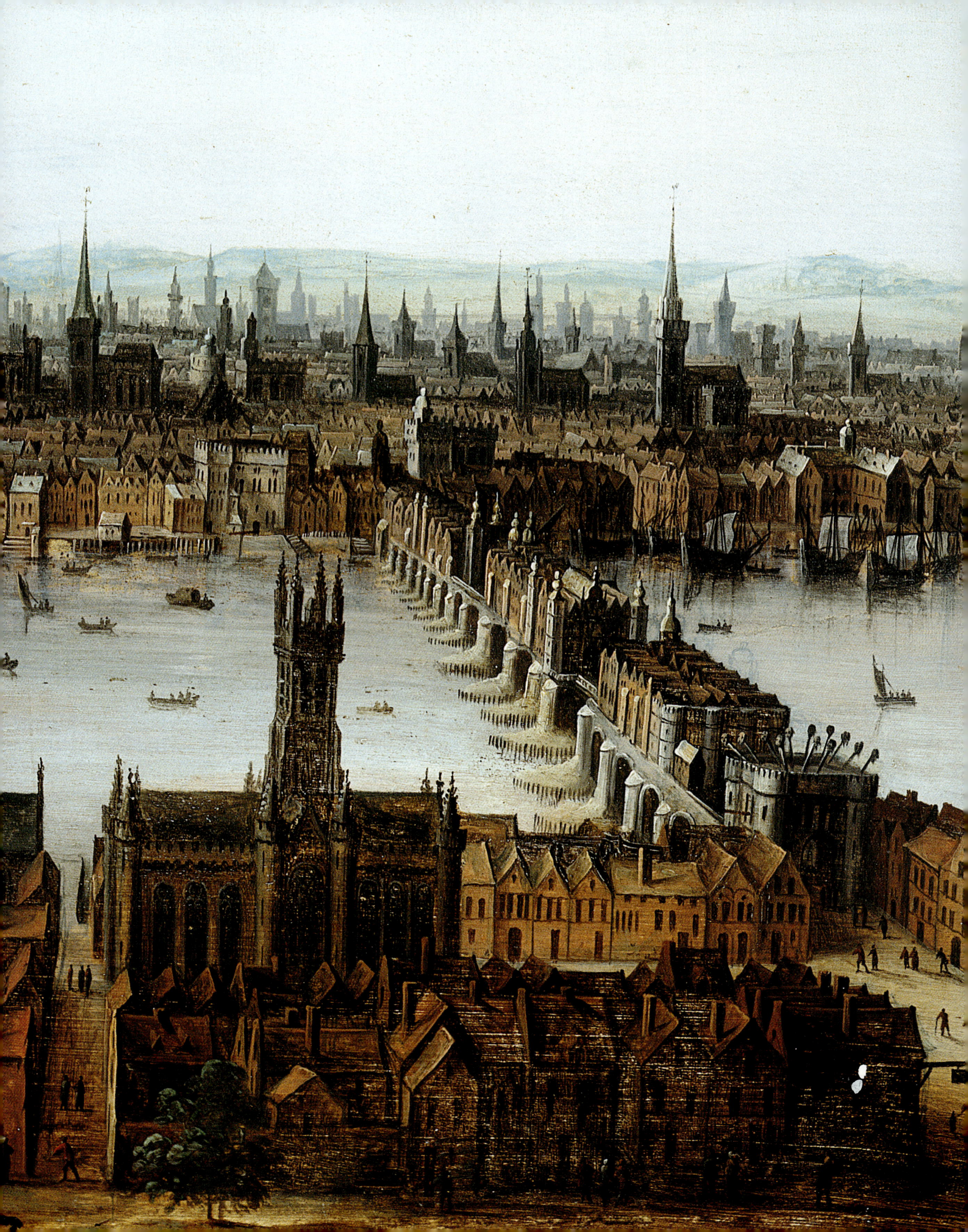

Stuart London

LONDON CITYSCAPE painting was born in the seventeenth century. It was created and developed by Netherlandish artists and most major images of the capital in the seventeenth century were therefore produced by foreigners. The first painting of London, happily in the Museum's collection, is the culmination of an artistic tradition focused on prints, drawings and maps. Showing London's topography around 1600, it marks the beginning of our study. The city it portrays, like the early Stuart monarchy, was transformed beyond recognition in mid-century. The Great Fire – depicted here in a group of vivid paintings – constitutes a watershed: the unprecedented potency of its subject matter continued to fascinate painters for centuries. After 1666 a series of fresh viewpoints emerges. The London of the later Stuarts is seen from new angles and, alongside prestigious historical occasions, popular events such as frost fairs are recorded by painters for a newly emerging art market.

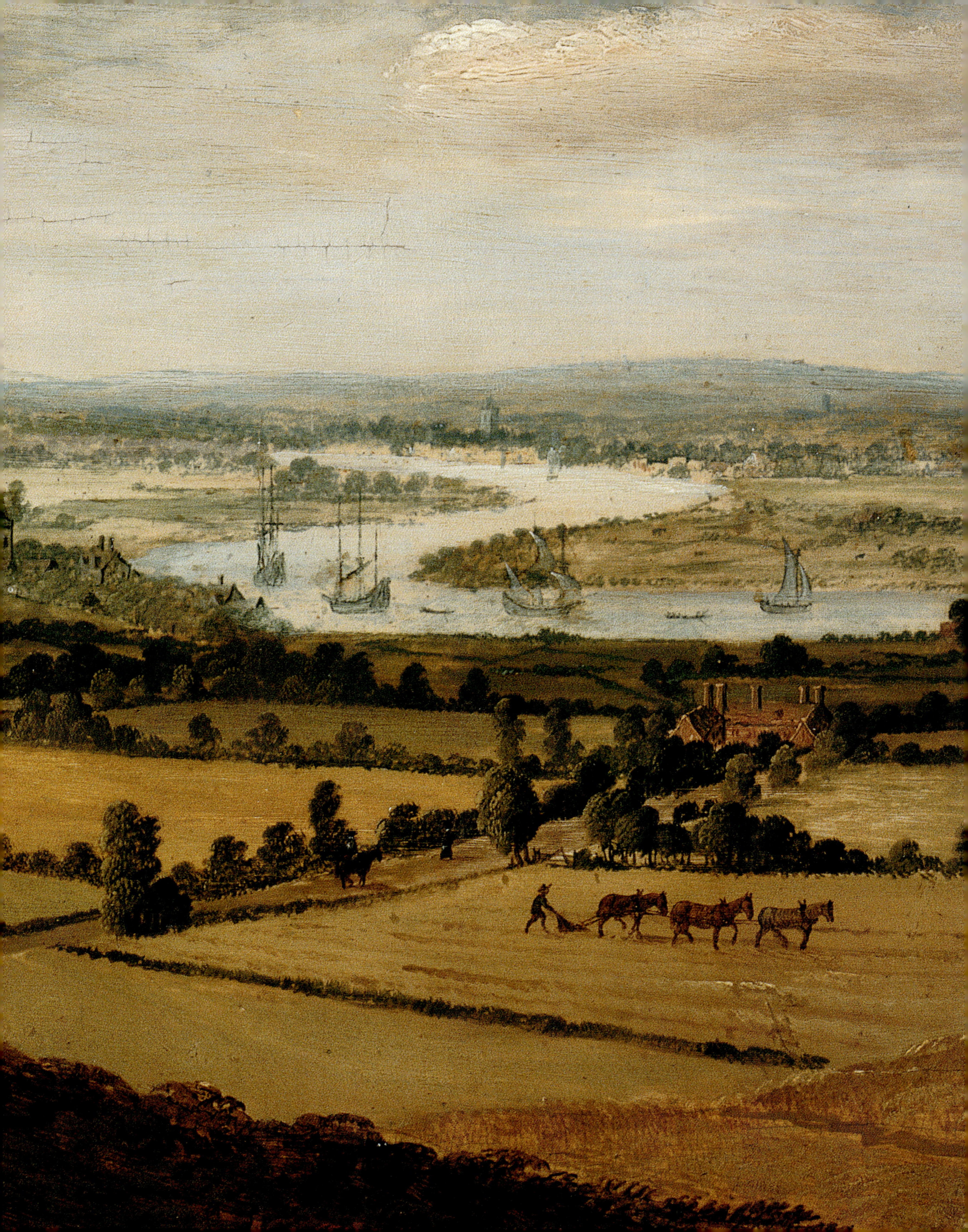

BEFORE 1666

THE PAINTING *London from Southwark* (cat. no. 3) is the earliest surviving oil painting with London as its sole subject.[1] Likely to date from the early 1630s, it marks the birth of cityscape painting in London and Britain. A limited number of prints and drawings surviving from the mid-sixteenth century onwards[2] helps us to chart early efforts to capture an image of the city, but this painting offers a particularly vivid topographical summary of the capital before it was destroyed by the Great Fire. Perhaps more importantly for subsequent generations of artists, it also developed a new pictorial formula which helped free painters from restricting earlier conventions.

This early vision of London should be considered in conjunction with the contemporary *View of Greenwich* (cat. no. 2), which affords us a glimpse of the capital's appearance from a distance. Although London had a population of some quarter of a million, nearly ten times that of Bristol or Norwich, then the most important provincial towns, it was still quite small in extent – hardly more than twice the area of the original walled city, and quite distinct from Greenwich. Artists frequently used London as a point of reference when painting Greenwich – an early manifestation of the notion of London developing as a series of villages.

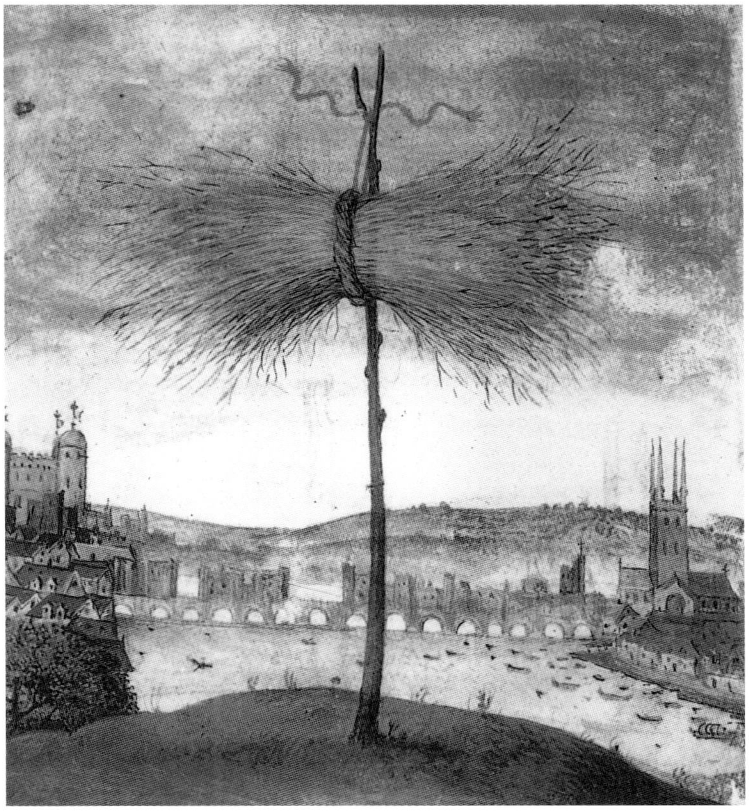

Richard Garth
London Bridge with the Tower of London and Southwark Cathedral, 1575.
Album Amicorum of Emanuel van Meteren of Antwerp.
MS Douce 68, f.47r.
The Bodleian Library, Oxford.

These two paintings offer a unique glimpse into the post-medieval city less than forty years before it burned down. They show a clean, idyllic city surrounded by an equally clean, idyllic landscape with Edmund Spenser's 'Sweete Thames' flowing softly through it.[3] This is the London William Dunbar hailed as 'Thou art the Flower of Cities all', which metaphorically blended fabric with natural environment, a blend also suggested in the late sixteenth-century watercolour drawing by Richard Garth showing a bundle of hay hanging from a pole and London Bridge in the background.[4] The medieval bridge is shown from the west, framed by London's two easterly landmarks, the church of St Mary Overy on the south bank and the Tower opposite, a viewpoint which Claude de Jongh would further develop (see below). Joris Hoefnagel's *c.*1568 *A Wedding at Bermondsey* is unequivocal about the proximity of village life to London.[5] In type it is strongly reminiscent of Flemish kermis paintings depicting village fêtes, but it is uniquely set in Bermondsey, just across the way from the Tower.

The late fifteenth-century miniature found in *The Poems of Charles, Duke of Orleans* (sometimes called the 'earliest painting of London') illustrates the imprisonment of the duke in the Tower (1415-40).[6] It draws on both traditional and new techniques to produce an image likely to have been influenced by the miniature work of Jean Fouquet.[7] The medieval tradition of multiple narrative, with Charles shown three times – imprisoned, greeted outside the White Tower and leaving through the gate – is blended with the new (Italian) interest in perspective, here most competently applied to both the cityscape and the horses. This miniature may be accepted as a good general impression of what London looked like at the end of the Wars of the Roses: beyond the Tower of London in the foreground can be seen the arcaded warehouses of Billingsgate and part of London Bridge with the swell of water beneath the arches and the chapel of St Thomas. Perhaps because its subject was specific, its size small and its circulation limited, this work stands in isolation.

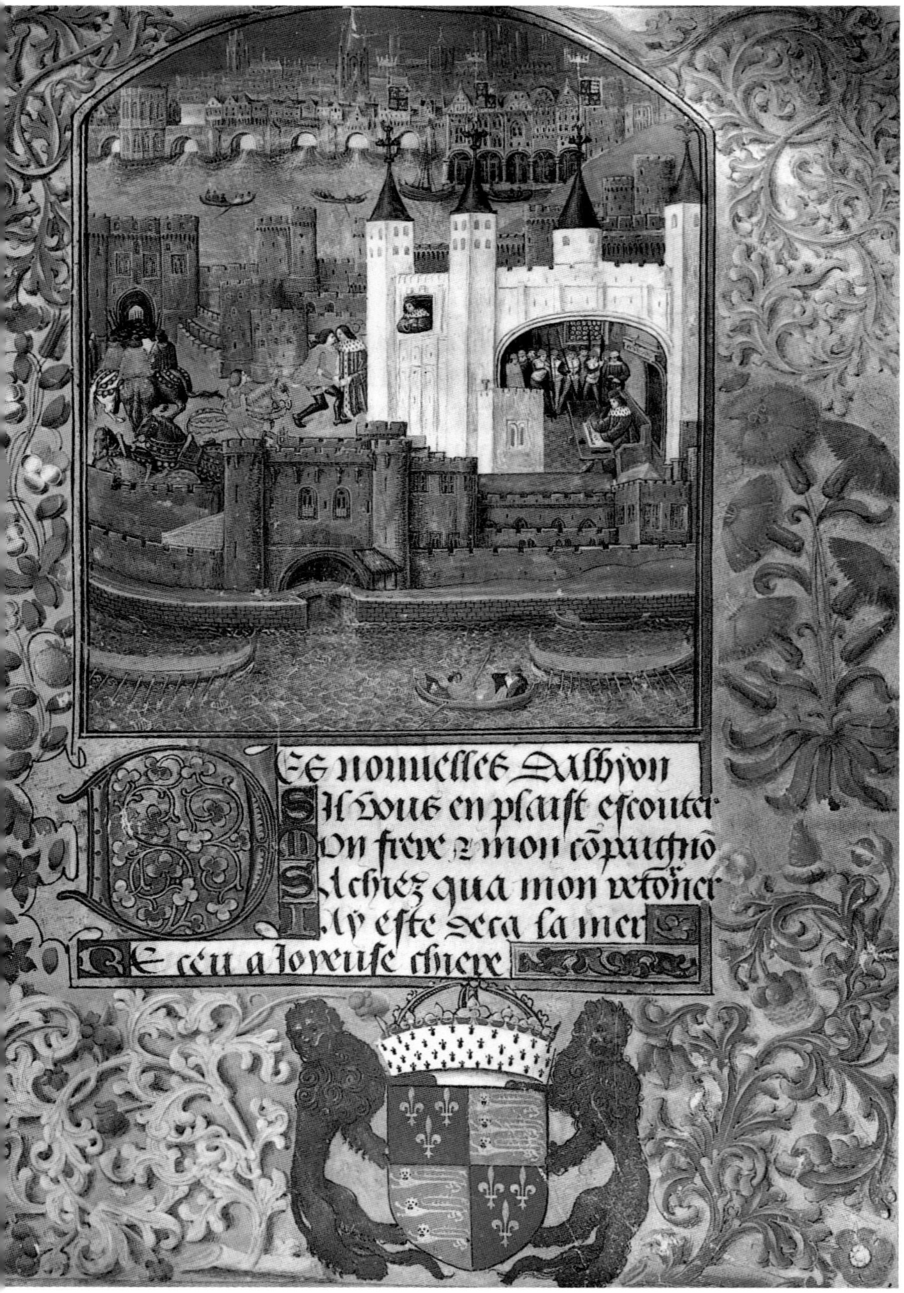

Charles d'Orleans in the Tower of London, *c.*1500.
MS drawing Royal 16. F. ii f73.
By permission of The British Library, London.

Yet another work, equally removed from public gaze, became the prototype for numerous views of London. The Antwerp artist Anthony van der Wyngaerde (active between 1510 and 1570) set the trend for the city prospects and 'long views' which finally led to the first oil paintings of London. Between 1539 and 1544 he produced fourteen large pen-and-ink sketches of London between Westminster and Greenwich, which are now in the Ashmolean Museum. His work, which was not engraved, constitutes the earliest known attempt at a detailed topographical study of London – recording, incidentally, a number of monastic foundations which were shortly to be destroyed at the Dissolution.

All these works predate one of the most dramatic episodes in the formation of London's image and identity, the Civil War (1642–60), which tore capital and country into two opposed camps, thus destroying the peaceful unity of these early images. Artists, subconsciously or not, responded to these warring factions by breaking up the city into views which no longer offered a continuous panorama. The artist, positioned near Somerset House, first looked east (to the City) and then west (to Westminster) and, moving farther east, also depicted the Pool of London beyond the old medieval bridge.

This geographical shift away from the City was also facilitated by the move of many artists, in some cases as early as the 1630s, from in and around the City, where they had established quarters, to Westminster. Two distinct studies, one focusing on artists registered with foreign churches, the other on parishes, have identified this shift to the West End.[8]

The hiring by the Earl of Arundel of Wenceslaus Hollar, London's most accurate and productive capital artist, contributes to this turning point in the imaging of London. Hollar entered the service of Arundel soon after they met in Prague in 1635 and settled at his patron's residence, Arundel House, one of the Strand palaces with a river frontage. At that time the topographical scene was still dominated by foreigners, particularly Dutch and Flemish, who favoured depicting London from the top of Southwark Cathedral. This traditional viewpoint made a great deal of artistic sense because it afforded an excellent prospect of London. Its predominance may also have been connected with the fact that Southwark was the principal point of entry into the capital for visitors approaching from the south. Statistically, the number of views taken from the south of London Bridge (London's only bridge up until 1750) is overwhelming. The first image from the west occurs with Hollar, who made the earliest panoramic view of the city from that direction standing on the roof of Arundel House (*c.*1640). This new viewpoint, foreshadowed by Richard Garth's fanciful drawing, was later consolidated in paint by the series of works by Cornelis Bol probably commissioned (*c.*1650) by John Evelyn, of which several versions survive, although not by the same hand:[9] they are the forerunners of Canaletto's famous pair of paintings (in the Royal Collection) taken from the terrace of Somerset House and, later still, of the elegant and serene Regency reworking of the theme by Charles Deane after the construction of Waterloo Bridge (see cat. no. 53). The group also introduces views of the Pool of London, east of London Bridge.

The emergence of these new viewpoints gradually changed the artist's perception of the river. Early experiments to depict London as a land- rather than a water-city were not taken up by artists.[10] By 1600 they had established an image for London as a whole which was inseparable from the river. Until the 1720s the presence of the Thames seemed so essential to painters that the majority of close-up views of the capital were centred on riverfront sites (see cat. nos 13 and 18).

Throughout the seventeenth century, the Thames remained subordinate to the image of the city itself: the long view or prospect, taken from Southwark, looking head-on to the City with London Bridge off to the right of the picture, was the archetypal image (see cat. no. 3). The river then tended to be undifferentiated and the ships were diminutive and stereotyped. When, towards 1650, the view of London was approached from three vantage points, artists became more sharply confronted with the river as a subject. By positioning themselves at Strand Lane, artists were faced for the first time with trying to animate the huge area of water which dominated the composition. The Thames easily came to life on pageant days, as is shown in the anonymous Whitehall painting (in the Royal Collection) which celebrates the 1683 Lord Mayor's Day attended by Charles II and his entourage. A century later even Canaletto, who captured the river in full glory on such days, was otherwise struggling with the vastness of the Thames.

The absence of close-up views of the people, river, streets, quarters and landmarks of the capital suggests that London's topographical tradition had not yet fully emerged. Claude de Jongh's paintings of London Bridge and the Westminster riverbank are rather exceptional.[11] The presentation of the city in the *London from Southwark*

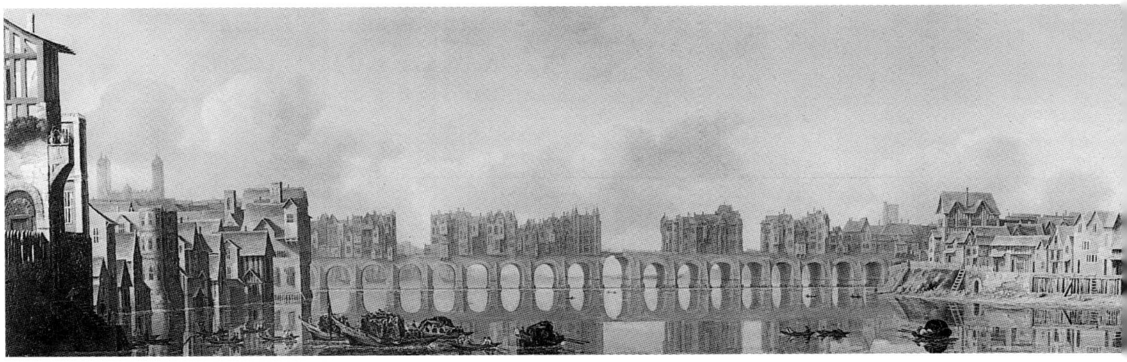

Claude de Jongh
London Bridge, 1630.
Oil on board
The Iveagh Bequest,
Kenwood House, London
© English Heritage
Photo Library.

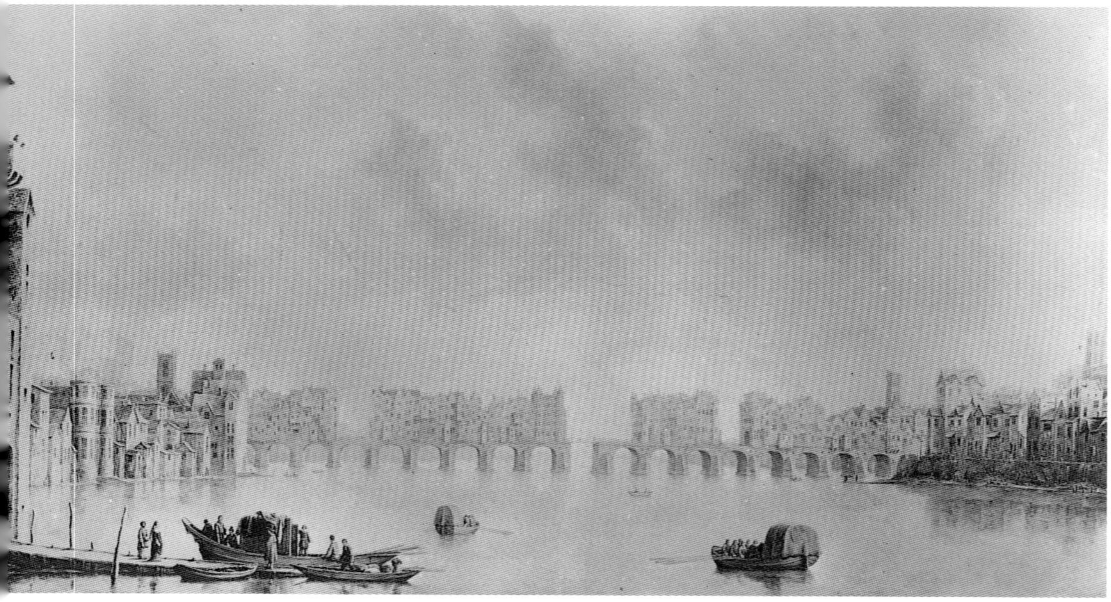

Claude de Jongh
London Bridge, 1650.
Oil on canvas
© The Board of Trustees of the Victoria and Albert Museum, London.

painting offers new possibilities for artists by breaking away from the strip presentation of previous engraved or drawn views. This is well illustrated in the career of Claude de Jongh. Two (out of the three) versions of Old London Bridge which he painted are worth examining in this respect. The first, dated 1630 (in Kenwood House), follows the early strip presentation. The second one, in the Victoria and Albert Museum and dated 1650, adopts a full sky. This simple device would later enable painters to manipulate the proportions of sky, buildings and river to create different categories of views.

We know tantalisingly little about the painters who produced these views. There are no obvious candidates for three key paintings (cat. nos 2,3 and 8) and no visual or archival references to topographical paintings hanging in houses, except for those depicting royal palaces.[12]

Admittedly, not many paintings survive from pre-Great Fire London. In the days before London's art market existed, we know little about their general availability, the proportion of commissioned works versus those sold 'off the shelf'[13] or whether they would have hung in people's houses, in public institutions or both.[14] The group below, however, offers a good cross-section of the most important historical figures and events of the first half of the seventeenth century, from the refined and delicate portrait of Henry Frederick, Prince of Wales, a keen patron of the arts, to the proud portrait of Oliver Cromwell, the not-so-glorious recording of Charles I's *memento mori*, and a key image for the Restoration, Charles II's coronation procession.

1. The 1616 diptych in the collection of the Society of Antiquaries shows a close-up view of St Paul's as well as a view of the City from the south. It was painted to encourage the restoration of the cathedral and not as a record of London. See *London Topographical Record*, vol. XXV, 1985, pp163–75.
2. See Irene Scouloudi, *Panoramic Views of London 1600–1666*, Corporation of London, 1953; Felix Barker and Peter Jackson, *London: 2000 years of a city and its people*, 1974.
3. From 'Prothalamion', 1596.
4. From the *Album Amicorum* of Emanuel van Meteren of Antwerp, Ms Douce 68, Bodleian Library, Oxford. See the exhibition catalogue *The Douce Legacy*, 1984, no. 236. Reproduced in David Piper, *Artists' London*, 1982, p15.
5. The Marquis of Salisbury, Hatfield House. Reproduced and discussed in Celina Fox, *Londoners*, 1987, p78.
6. British Museum; ms drawing; Royal 16F ii, f.73.

7. The horseriders are very similar to those in 'St Martin', *Hours of Etienne Chevalier*, in the Louvre. See Nicole Reynaud, *Jean Fouquet*, exhibition catalogue, Louvre, 1981, pp46–55.
8. Irene Scouloudi, 'Return of Strangers in the Metropolis, 1593, 1627, 1635, 1639', in *Quarto Series of the Huguenot Society*, vol. LVII, 1985, p100; Mary Edmond, 'Limners and Picture Makers – New light on the lives of miniaturists and large-scale portrait painters working in London in the sixteenth and seventeenth centuries', in *Walpole Society*, 1978–80, pp60-242.
9. The three paintings still with the Evelyn family are mentioned by George Vertue and attributed to the little-known artist Cornelis Bol. The Guildhall Art Gallery possesses another set of all three views (in poor condition) and the Dulwich Picture Gallery has the view looking towards Westminster, clearly signed CB. The drawing of the Pool of London which is in the British Museum and is currently attributed to Alexander Keirincx is almost certainly linked to these views. All these works have been the object of a postgraduate Courtauld study by Louisa Goldsmith, copies of which are both in the Courtauld Conservation Department and at the Museum of London.
10. The first known view of London by Matthew Paris in 1252 is taken from the north and so is the unique *c.*1600 *View of the Cittye of London from the North towards the Sowth* in Utrecht University Library. Both works are reproduced in Barker and Jackson, 1974, pp25 and 98.
11. See John Hayes, 'Claude de Jongh', in *The Burlington Magazine*, no. 634, vol. XCVIII, January 1956; Marten Jan Bok, 'Claude de Jongh, "Painter, Sorely Incapacitated in His Arms": A Study of His Milieu', in *Mercury*, vol. X, 1989.
12. See John Harris, *The Artist and the Country House*, 1979, pp11 and 24–5.
13. John Evelyn mentions the art dealers Michael Dahl and J. M. Wright, but London is notable for the absence of pictures sold at markets – unlike Rotterdam, Paris and Rome, which are all mentioned in his text.
14. The visual evidence is inconclusive: a number of Dutch paintings show maps, rather than views, on walls in domestic settings and perhaps it would be worth citing here the famous painting by Vermeer, *The Artist in His Studio* (*c.*1665, Vienna, Kunsthistorisches Museum), because the large map shown behind the sitter also includes a border made up of city views. A similar map survives in the Public Record Office: Jonas Moore's 1662 map of the Thames Estuary incorporates views of London, Greenwich, Woolwich, Erith and Gravesend. The only other London reference is that to John Norden's view of London. There is a 1714/15 reference to it hanging in Dulwich College staircase, in rather 'decayed' condition. See Scouloudi, 1953, p21.

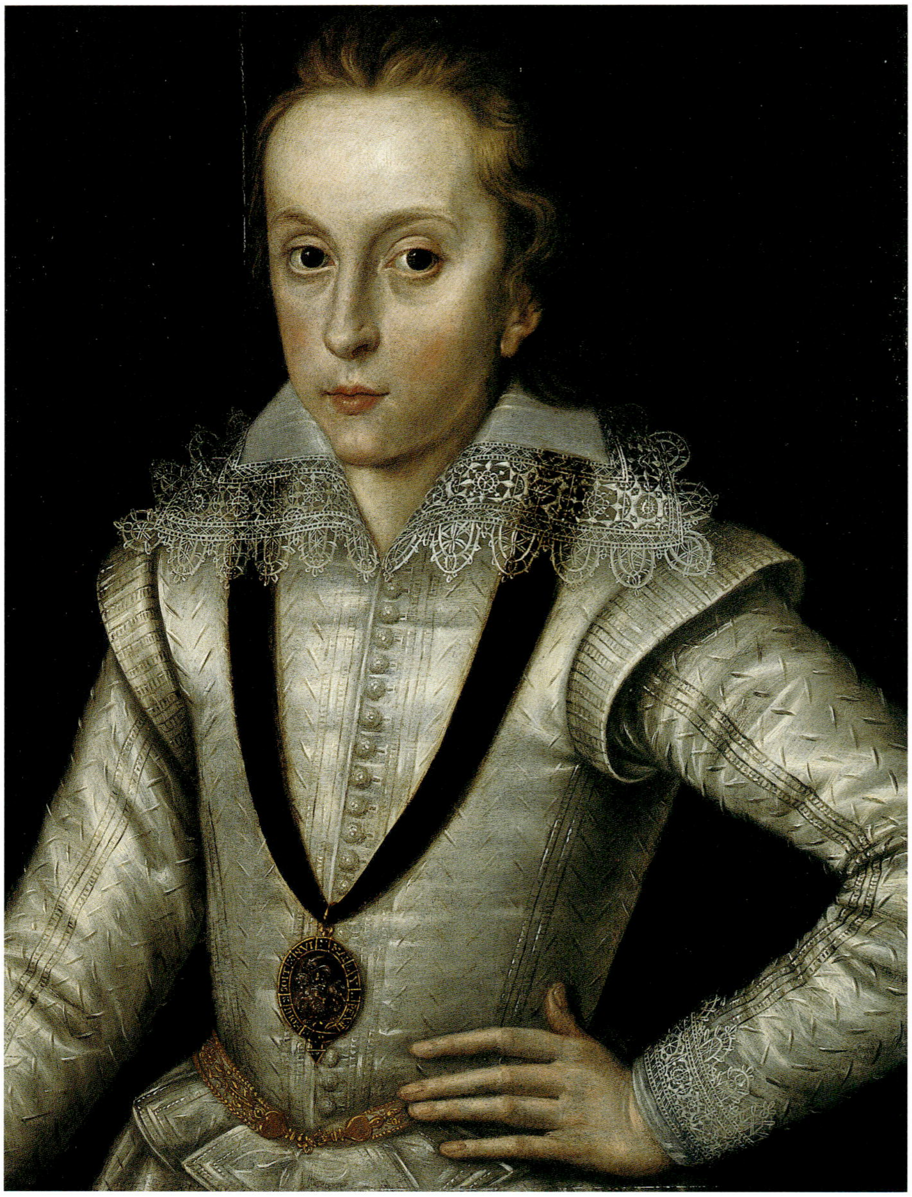

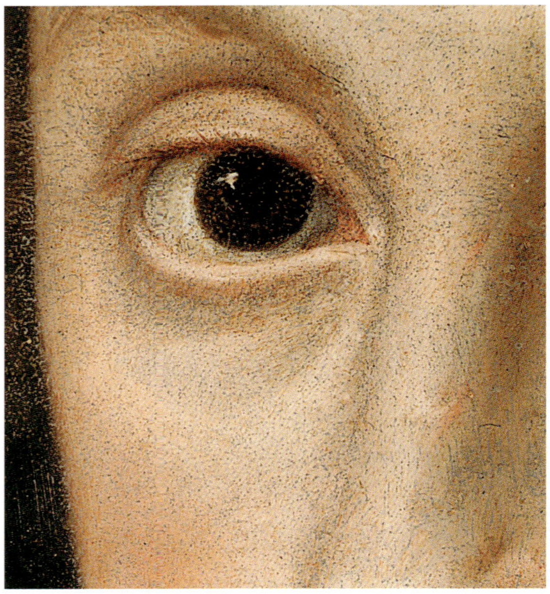

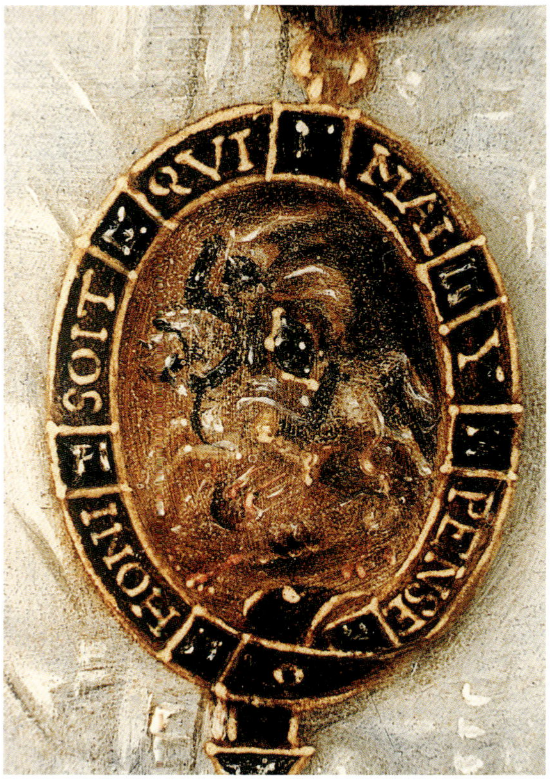
HONI SOIT QVI MAL Y PENSE

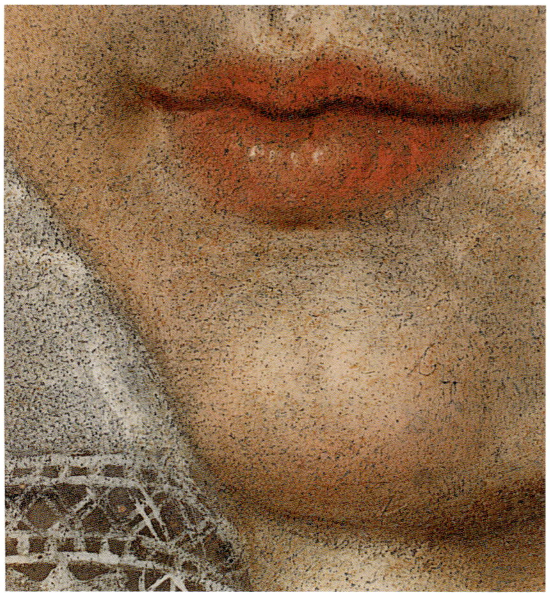

1.

ROBERT PEAKE THE ELDER

(c.1551–1619)

Portrait of Henry Frederick, Prince of Wales (1594–1612) [A 23271]

*c.*1603–5

Oil on Baltic oak, 58.1 x 48 cm

Not signed or dated

PRINCE HENRY is shown half-length, facing slightly to the left, with his left hand on his hip, wearing a silver slashed doublet, a falling lace collar and the insignia of the Order of the Garter round his neck; the background is plain.

Henry Frederick, eldest son of James I, died suddenly of typhoid fever at the age of eighteen, and was succeeded as Prince of Wales by his younger brother, later Charles I. Robert Peake was official portrait painter to Prince Henry until the latter's death in 1612. Several of his portraits of the Prince survive, of which the most important is the splendid double portrait in the Metropolitan Museum, New York, dated 1603; the present picture is closest in type and date to the half-length portrait in the Bodleian Library. The attribution is due to Sir Roy Strong. The Prince was invested with the Order of the Garter on 2 July 1603, and the falling collar suggests a date of about 1603–5. Robert Peake also carried out commission work for Prince Charles. The artist lived in the Holborn parish of St Sepulchre-without-Newgate, one of the artists' quarters of the period.

The Prince, born in the castle of Stirling, came to England in 1603, when his father James VI of Scotland inherited the English throne. This portrait would have been executed shortly afterwards, at a time when the Prince resided in a variety of places in and around London. In 1610 when he was created Earl of Chester and Prince of Wales, he became principally based at St James's Palace, where he held court.

Dendrochronology was carried out on this painting. The bracket dates obtained (1590–1620) were compatible with the dating suggested on historical, art historical and costume grounds. Radiography, infra-red reflectography and paint analysis were also carried out and the results of this investigation matched the technique for early seventeenth-century English portrait painting.

Provenance:
Bequeathed by J. G. Joicey in 1920 (as Charles I and without attribution).

Bibliography:
Hayes (cat. no. 123);
Roy Strong, *Catalogue of Tudor and Jacobean Portraits in the National Portrait Gallery*, 1969, p164 and plate 318;
Dictionary of National Biography; Mary Edmond, 'Limners and Picture Makers – New light on the lives of miniaturists and large-scale portrait painters working in London in the sixteenth and seventeenth centuries', in *Walpole Society*, 1978–80, p65.

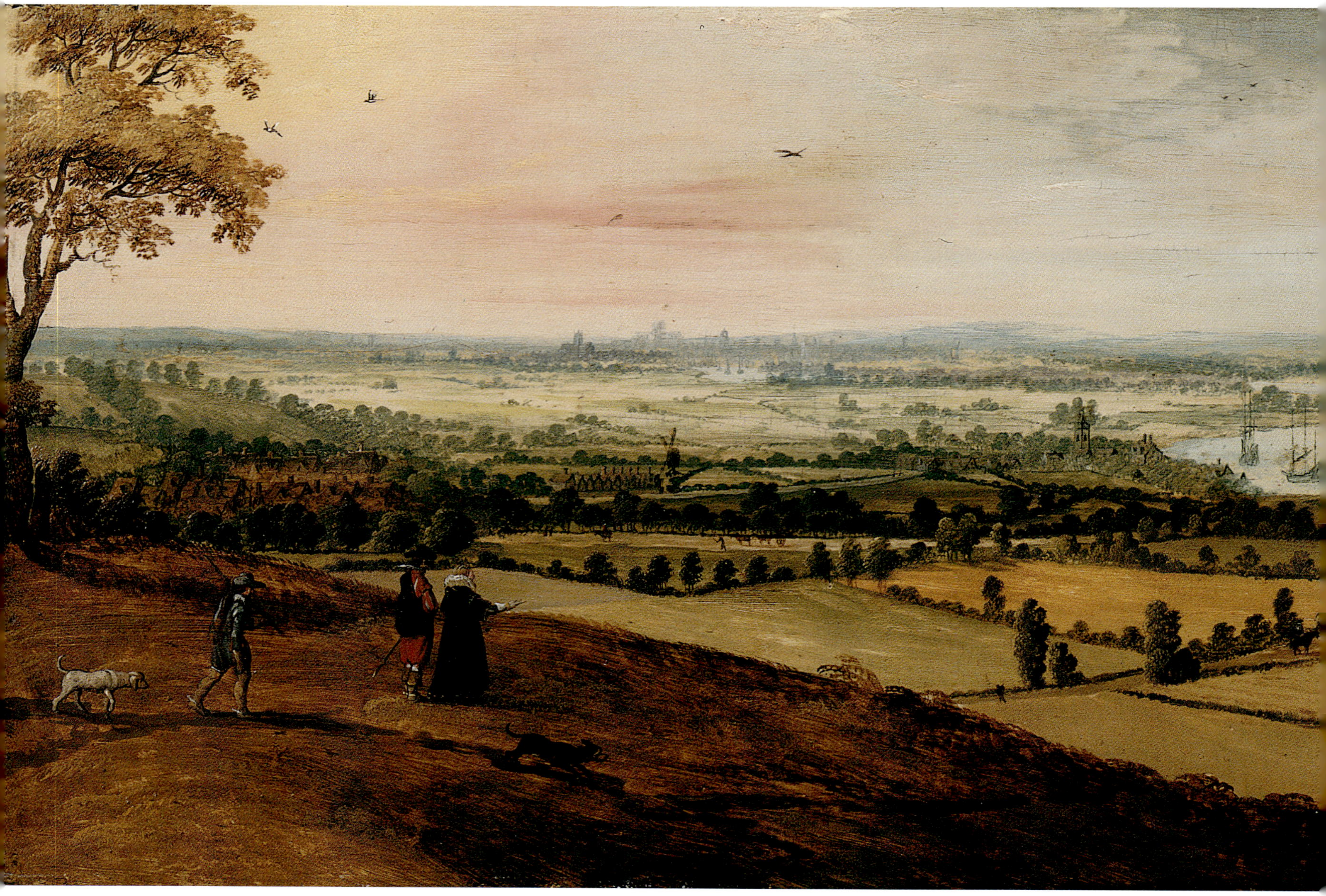

2.

FLEMISH SCHOOL

View of Greenwich [64.52]
*c.*1620–30
Oil on Baltic oak, 29.4 x 92.2 cm
Not signed or dated

THIS VIEW of Greenwich is taken from a viewpoint above Queen Elizabeth's College (Greenwich's first charitable foundation, completed in 1576) and close to the London to Dover Road. The viewpoint is similar to that used by Anthony van der

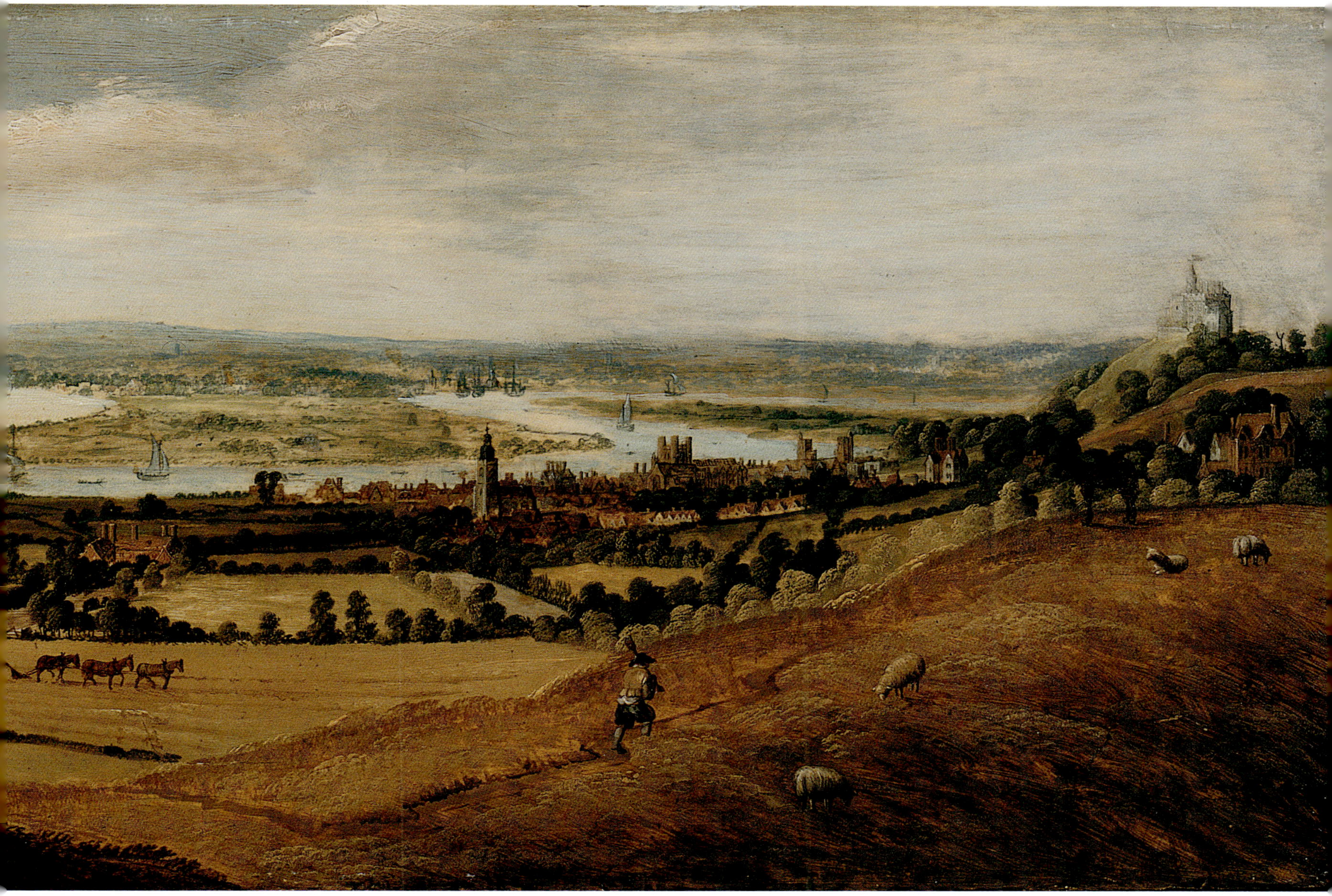

Wyngaerde in 1558. It is the earliest painted view of London from a distance showing its setting in the landscape. The extent to which Southwark Cathedral and Old St Paul's dominated the skyline is dramatically displayed.

The attribution and exact date of this painting require discussion. The matter of date is crucial to the attribution, and should be examined first. There are two clues: the costume and the Queen's House. The dress of the figures is nearer to the French or Flemish fashion than to the English, and may be dated about 1625–35; the inclusion of the Queen's House suggests a date between 1616 (when construction began) and 1640 (when it was completed by Inigo Jones); the additions which converted it into the square building we know today were designed by John Webb shortly after the Restoration, in 1661. Dendrochronological analysis confirms this evidence and offers bracket dates of 1602–30.

The style of painting is Flemish and has close affinities with Joos de Momper and

Provenance:
Janet, Countess of Eglinton (d.1923); Sir Bruce Ingram; Ingram sale, Sotheby's 11 March 1964 (12, as English school, seventeenth century), bt Colnaghi on behalf of the Museum; purchased out of the Mackenzie Bell Trust Fund, with the aid of contributions from an anonymous donor and the National Art Collections Fund.

Bibliography:
Hayes (cat. no. 43);
'The Inventories and Valuations of the King's Goods 1649–1651', in *Walpole Society*, no. 43;
Oliver Millar, *The Age of Charles I*, exhibition catalogue, Tate Gallery, 1972 (cat. no. 59);
John Harris, *The Artist and the Country House*, 1979, p11.

the Rubens circle. The figures, however, are Dutch rather than Flemish, deriving from Esaias van de Velde and Jan van Goyen. The artists Claude de Jongh and even Hollar, had he been a painter, were tentatively suggested, but do not stand under close inspection. It may be more rewarding to examine the question of patronage. Hollar, as soon as he arrived in London, produced an etching of Greenwich, published in 1637, which he dedicated to Queen Henrietta Maria. In composition, the print by Hollar and this painting are very close, despite the fact that they represent two distinct parts of Greenwich. Both works are articulated around a central landmark which, in the case of Hollar, is the Queen's House and is linked to the dedication. In our painting the central building is Queen Elizabeth's almshouses and we should consider the possibility that this was the source of the commission

Key

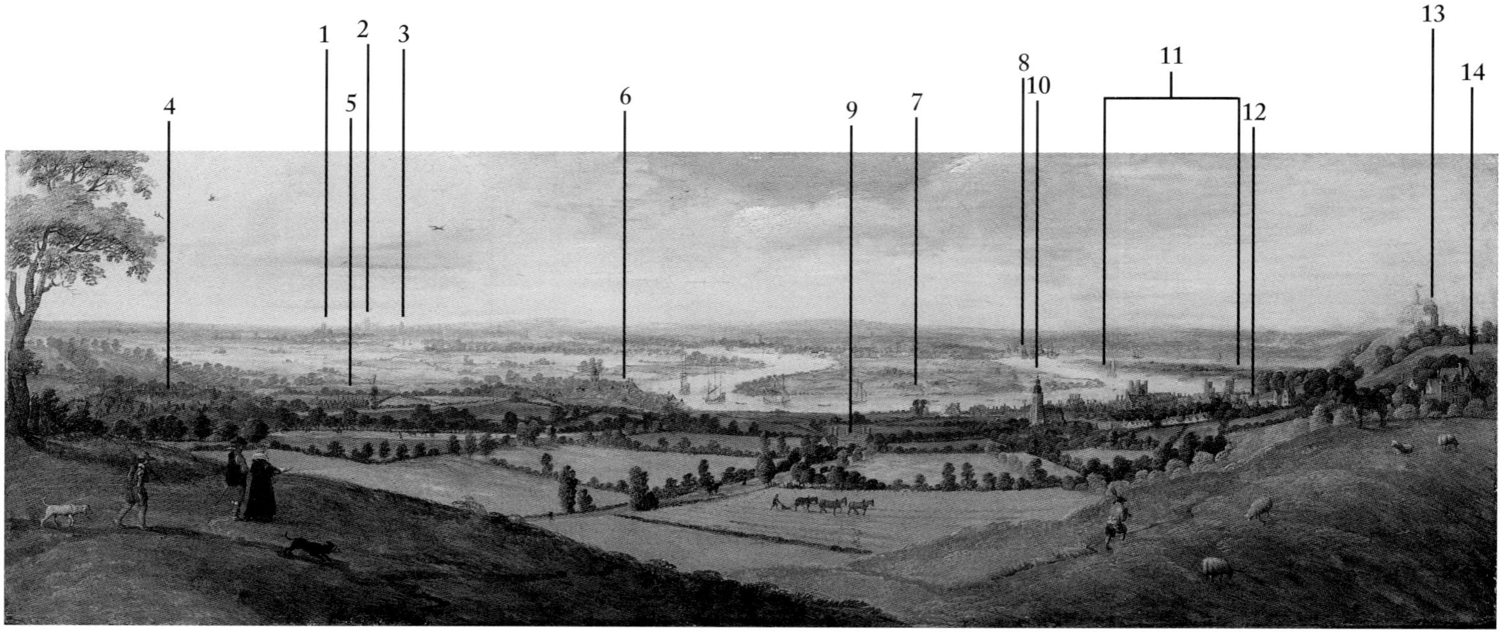

1. Church of St Mary Overy (later Southwark Cathedral)
2. St Paul's Cathedral
3. Church of St Mary-le-Bow
4. Upper Deptford: group of houses in the Deptford Bridge area
5. Mr Paget's houses (shown on the 1623 John Evelyn map of Deptford)
6. Lower Deptford
7. Isle of Dogs
8. East India Company Blackwall dockyard (built *c.*1609–12)
9. Queen Elizabeth's College
10. Church of St Alphege (pulled down 1760, replaced by Hawksmoor and Jones church)
11. Placentia Palace (post 1426 and later additions)
    Hall
    Gatehouse
    Twin towers of Henry VIII's tilt yard
12. Queen's House
13. Duke of Gloucester's castle (built early 1400s, pulled down by Charles II, became site for Royal Observatory)
14. Paternoster Croft, Croom's Hill

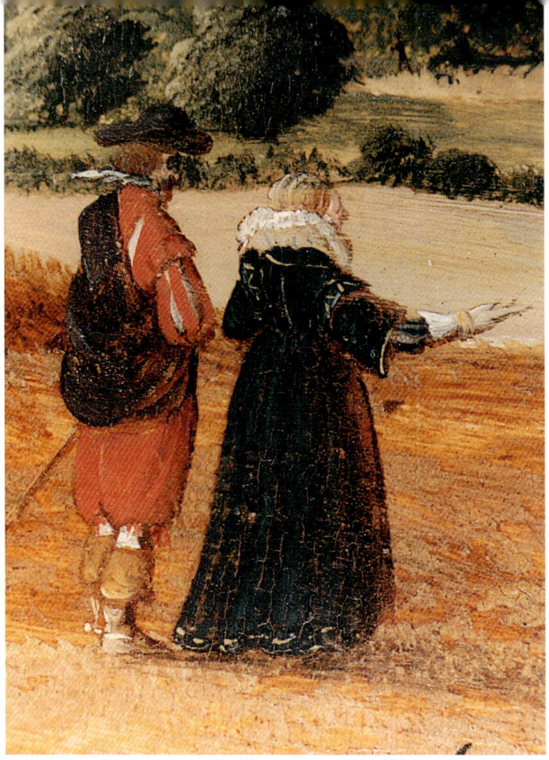

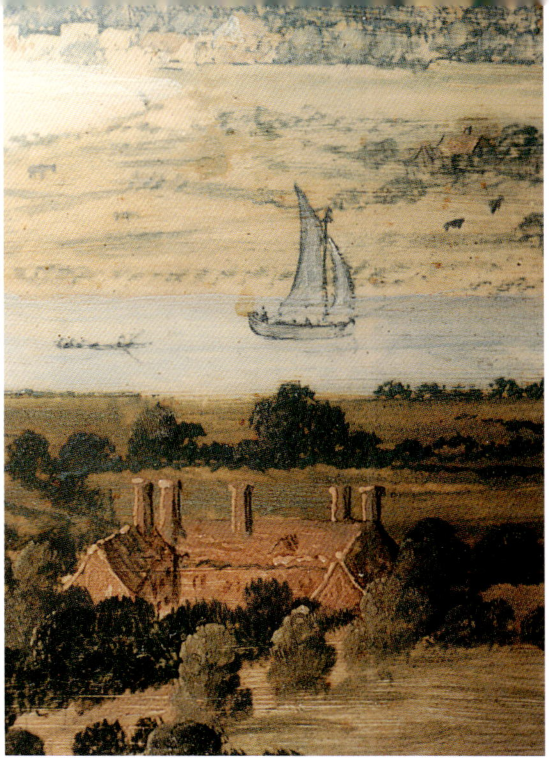

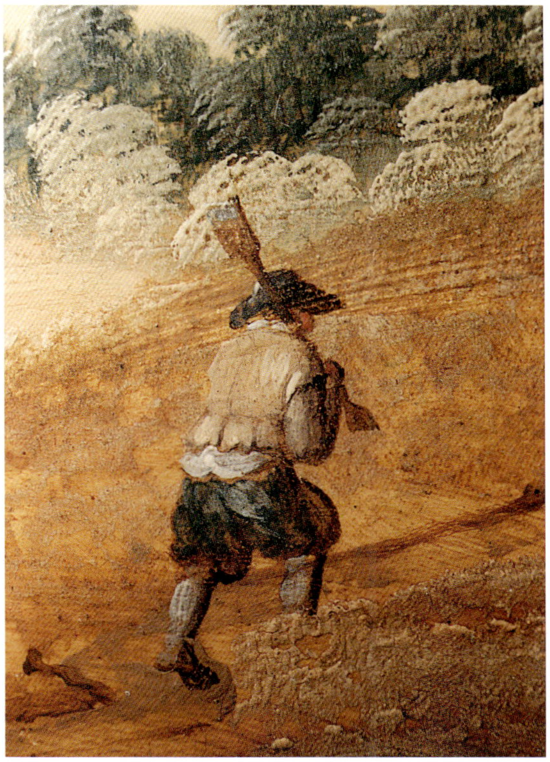

(however, their archives in the Drapers Company have been searched in vain). A number of paintings of Greenwich of the period survive and Charles I is known to have owned at least three Greenwich landscapes: two by Adrian van Stalbempt – 'Landshape(s) of Grenewch' – and a further work by the otherwise unknown George Portman – 'A landshape wth greenewich Castle in it by portman'. Oliver Millar suggests that the Museum painting may conceivably be by the latter. The emphasis on landscape rather than palace is unusual for that period, although Charles I apparently requested Balthasar Gerbier, keeper of the Duke of Buckingham's collections at York House, and Inigo Jones's successor as Court Master of ceremonies, to design a purpose-built room intended for 'exhibitions of landscapes in the manner of panoramas'. The first views of painted royal palaces, Richmond and Nonsuch by an unknown Flemish artist around 1620 (Fitzwilliam Museum, Cambridge), were clearly led by the palaces, not the landscape.

The rainbow visible in earlier photographs proved to be a later addition, and was removed during the restoration carried out by Stephen Rees-Jones in 1964–5.

A similar view of London from above Greenwich but with a viewpoint farther east, which is by the same hand though considerably less mature and probably dating from some years earlier, is in the National Maritime Museum (reproduced in colour in Barker and Jackson, 1974, p86).

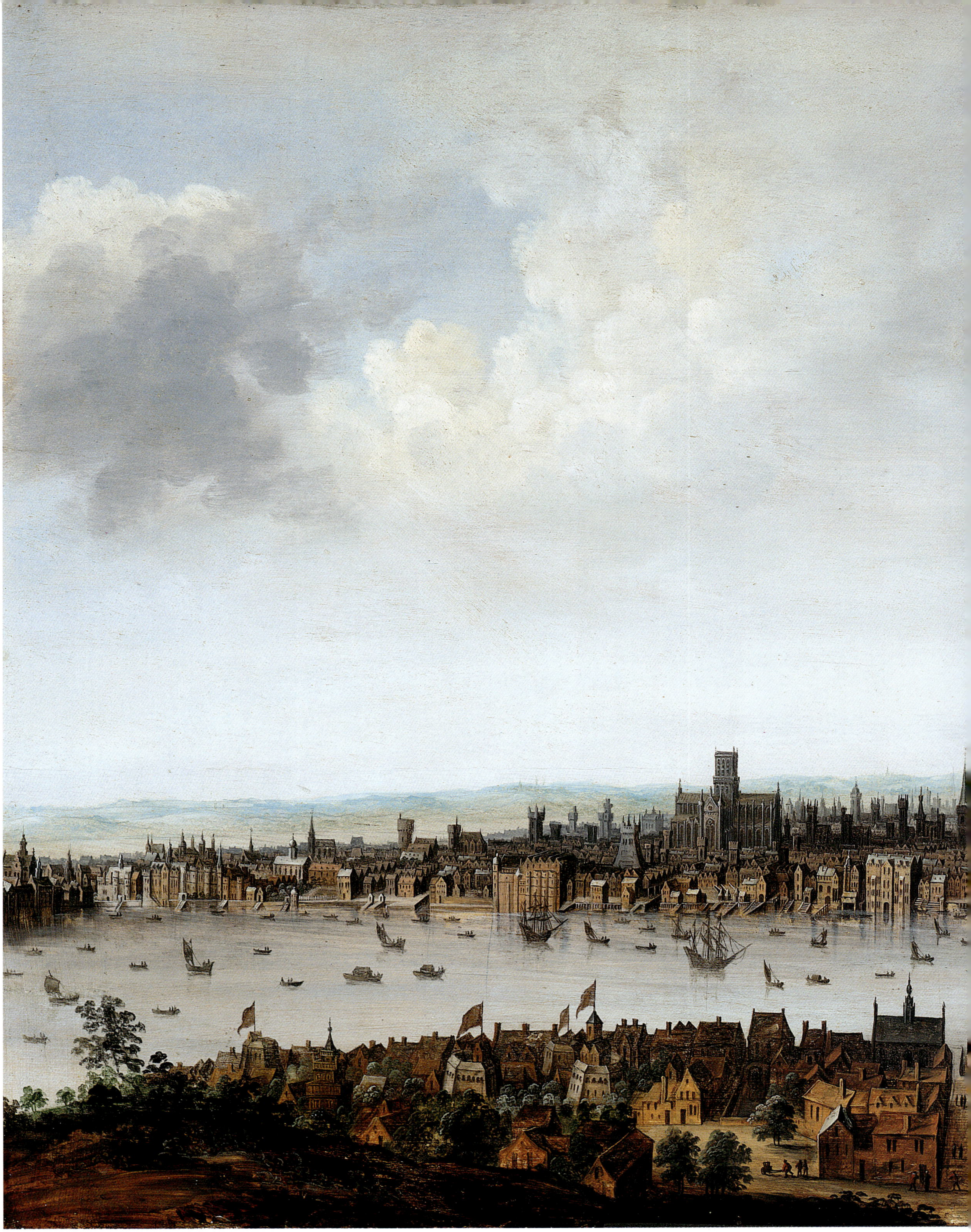

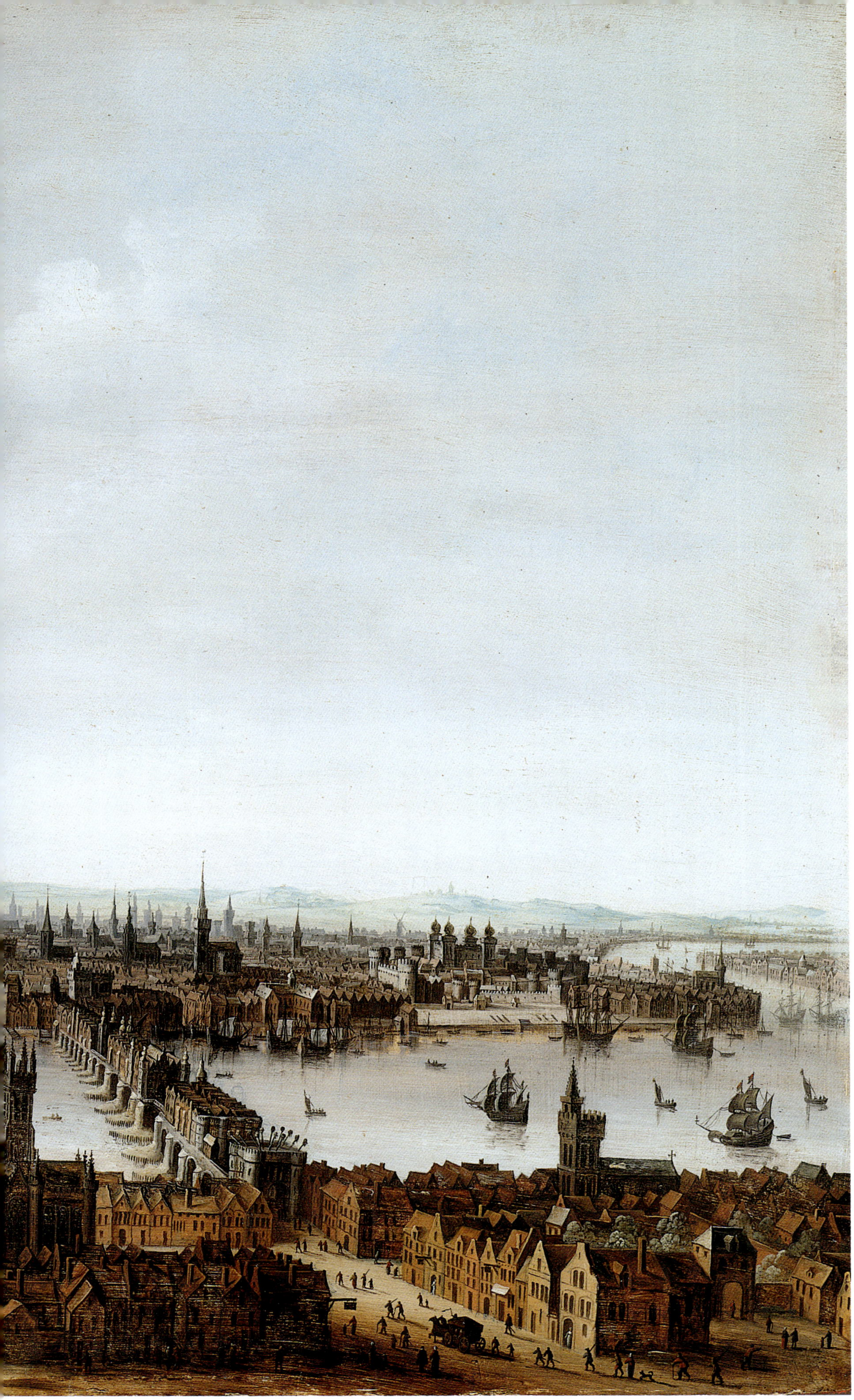

3.

DUTCH SCHOOL

London from Southwark

[92.7]

*c.*1630

Oil on oak panel,
57.7 x 85.7 cm

Not signed or dated

Back incised with
initials: D F B

Provenance:
Granville Leveson Gower (2nd Earl Granville); Earl Granville's sale, Christie's, 11 June 1892 (121), bt Colnaghi; Samuel Montague, MP; presented to Whitechapel Library Commissioners, July 1892; Council of the Metropolitan Borough of Stepney, 9 November 1900 (powers transferred from Whitechapel Library Commissioners in accordance with London Government Act 1899); London Borough of Tower Hamlets (Globe Town Neighbourhood); Christie's, 13 July 1991 (66), withdrawn from sale after sale agreement was reached between Tower Hamlets and the Museum of London, purchased with a grant from the MGC/V&A Purchase Grant Fund and with the help of the Museum's fund-raising scheme.

ONLY THREE paintings survive which show London before the Civil War. One of these, painted on canvas, is in the collection of the Duke of Devonshire at Chatsworth; another, a close composition painted on board, is the painting under review. An earlier, cruder view of the City from Southwark is in the collection of the Society of Antiquaries. However, the Antiquaries' panel does not aim to represent London (see Note 1, p8), while the support and technique of the Museum's painting point to an early date, probably the earliest (oil) painting of London. The Chatsworth painting, on the other hand, would appear to have a well documented provenance, as it was seen and described by George Vertue as in the possession of the Earl of Burlington:

> I saw, a curious painting [done before the Fire. – perhaps before the Civil Warrs.] being a View of London from the South wark side & River of Thames – where are some buildings of great houses. close to the River better expressd. and more visible than any other View – I have seen – the whole extreamly neat and curiously painted. said to be done by old ... Wyck-of Harlem. the little small figures wonderfully well. a print done from this picture. in poses̄ Mr T. West. some alteration. wants the explanation a. b. c. d. [Qu see a print, in one sheet – had been done before the fire. and the plate alterd – having flames and smoak added as on fire. dutch like work –]

It will become obvious when we examine the topographical content of this painting that the fabric depicted is that of the capital around 1600, when the public image of London was shaped – as was that of Antwerp, its closest European counterpart. London changed little between the beginning of the century and the Great Fire and what changes there were fall outside the scope of this view; one should therefore accept the painting as a fairly cogent representation of London before the Great Fire. Academic points are raised farther on to determine the influence of the painting among other artists.

All the sites that have been identified are clearly labelled on the key, so that we can concentrate here on the topographical 'problems' which this view presents. The Banqueting Hall at Whitehall is shown as a Gothic building, although it was burnt down in 1619. Salisbury and Little Salisbury Houses in the Strand are not shown, although they were partially built by 1602 and completed in 1610. Middle Temple Hall is depicted as having five instead of seven bays, and St Paul's choir is the same size as the nave instead of being shorter. Finally, and most prominently, the river bends immediately east of the Tower instead of pursuing its normal course.

These anachronisms or inaccuracies apply to a number of engravings of London which are related to this work. The historian Irene Scouloudi has recorded no less than 110 surviving panoramic views of London from between 1600 and 1666 (mostly prints), but only two rely on direct observation: the John Norden view published in 1600 and the 1647 long view by Wenceslaus Hollar. Even the famous 1616 view by John Visscher, who probably never set foot in London, was based on previous views, predominantly that of John Norden.

The print which is closest to this painting is by Clement de Jongh (fl.1640–70). The same plate was later used by two other publishers, Rombout van den

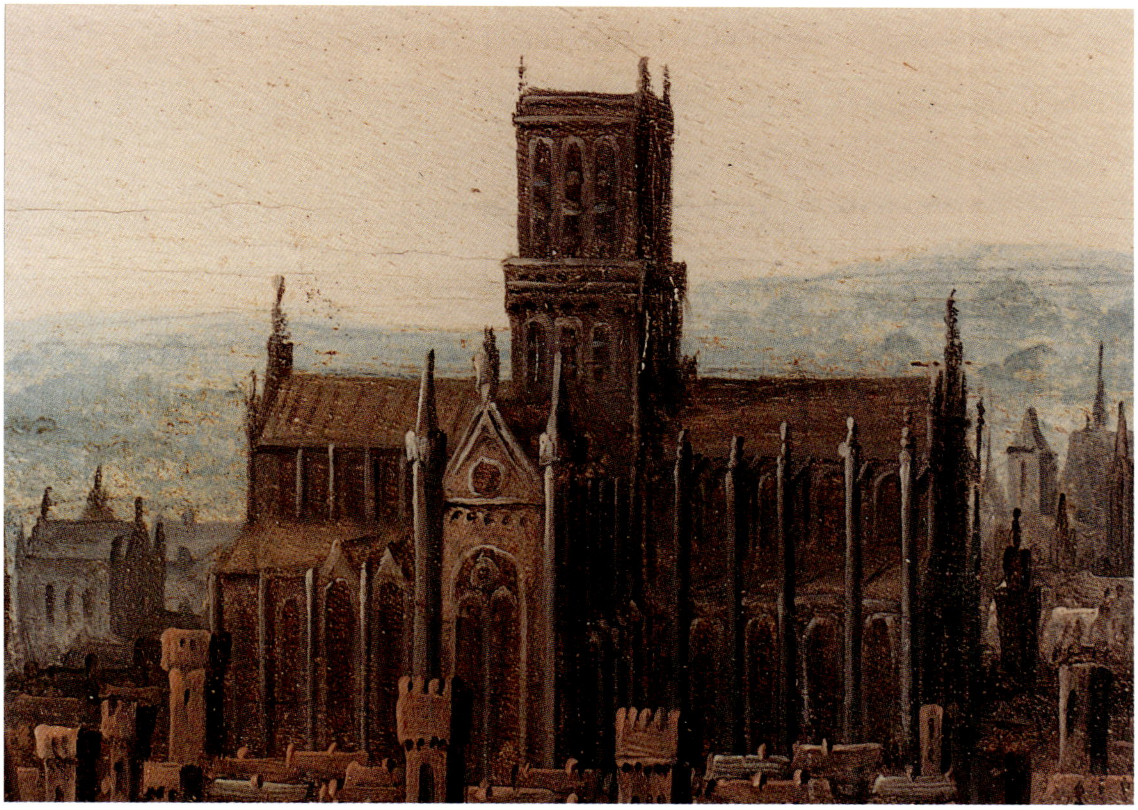

Hoeye (b.1622) and Dancker Danckerts (1634–66). None of the publication dates are known. These prints were thought to derive from the view of London by Matthew Merian which was published in the book *Neue Cosmica Archontologia* by J. L. Gottfried in 1638 (see Scouloudi). The Merian print is itself closely related to the reissue of the 1616 panoramic view produced by Visscher, which in turn derived from the John Norden prospect. In this way we are able to establish that the painting shows London as it was around 1600.

The date of the painting itself is of the utmost importance, since we still need to establish whether it came before or after the prints. The panelmaker marks on the back of the painting have been identified and are those of either Filips De Bout (d.1625) from Antwerp or his son Franchois. The latter's mark can be traced from 1637. Close scientific analysis as well as historical data revealed that the Museum's painting was probably the foundation stone for all the prints in the Merian group. Because the painting is on wood (oak), it has been possible to date this support to between 1625 and 1655. Both on stylistic and technical grounds the painting should be placed as close to the earlier date as possible. It may perhaps belong to what has been described as the 'tonal phase' in Dutch art, which lasted only during the 1620s and 1630s. Technically the painting is very close to the *View of Greenwich* (see cat. no. 2), which dates from the 1620s on costume and topographical grounds.

It should also be pointed out that the format adopted in the Museum painting is used for the first time. All previous panoramas – printed, drawn, or engraved – were composed as 'strips' with as little sky

Bibliography:
George Vertue, 'Note Books' in *Walpole Society*, vol. 5, p43; Irene Scouloudi, *Panoramic Views of London 1600–1666*, Corporation of London, 1953; Malcolm Warner, *The Image of London – Views by Travellers and Emigrés 1550–1920*, exhibition catalogue, Barbican Art Gallery, 1987, p109 (where it is misleadingly labelled 'on canvas'); Mireille Galinou and Ian Tyers, 'Portrait of London', in *Medieval World*, May/June 1992; three unpublished reports commissioned or supervised by the Museum of London: Nick Eastaugh, 'The Museum of London Project on 17th century Topographical and other Paintings on Panel' (1992), Ian Tyers's Dendrochronology Reports (DEN02/92 & REP03/91) and Louisa Goldsmith's 'Topographical painting in 17th century London' (Courtauld Institute, 1993); Valerie Cumming, 'Some observations on a recent acquisition', in *International Journal of Cultural Property*, no. 1, vol. 2, 1993; Mireille Galinou, 'Acquisition in focus', in *Apollo*, vol. 140, 1994; *Dynasties*, Karen Hearn (ed.), exhibition catalogue, Tate Gallery, 1995, no. 153.

Key

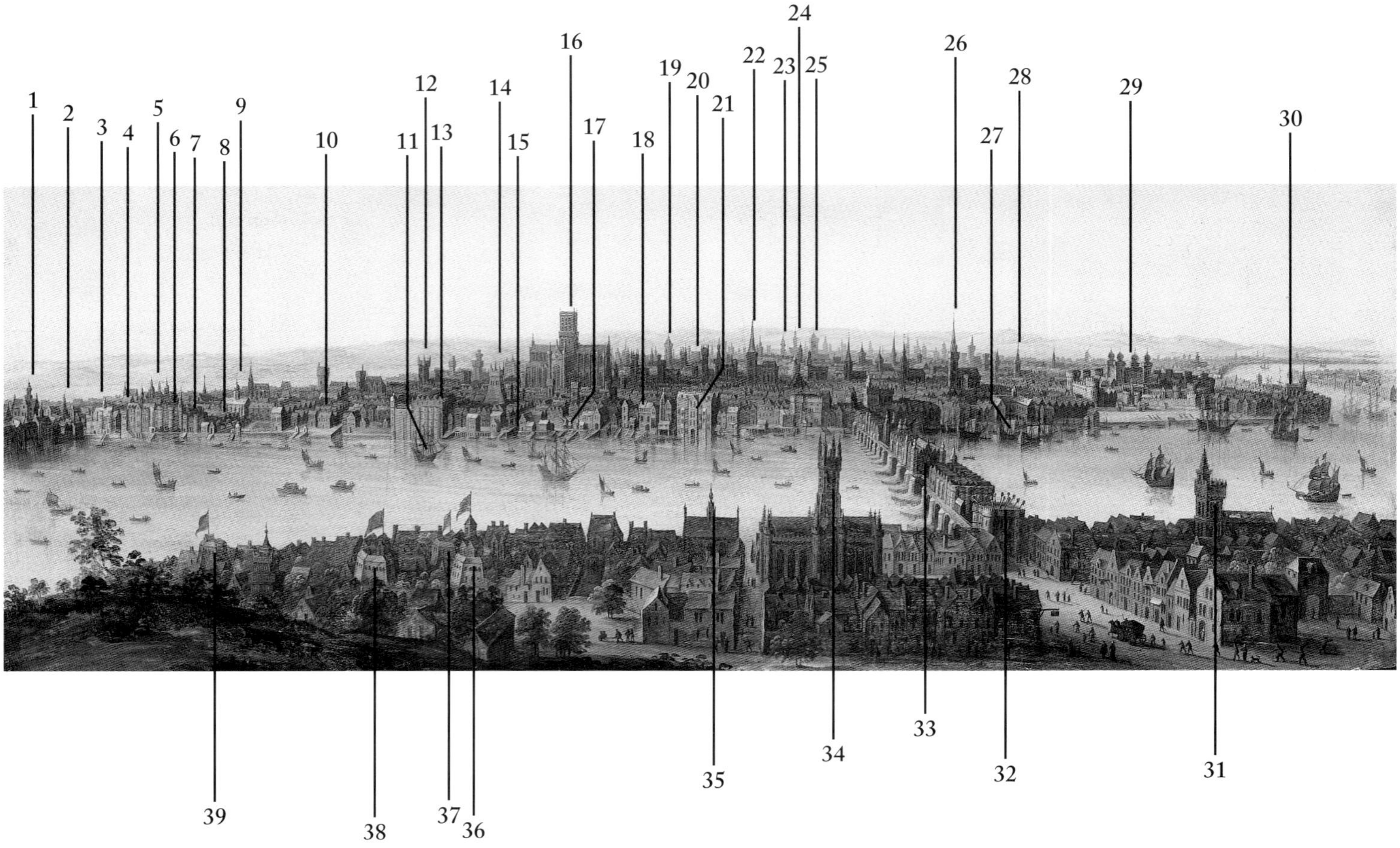

1. Whitehall Palace
2. Charing Cross
3. York House and Durham House
4. The Savoy
5. Burleigh House
6. Somerset House
7. Arundel House
8. Temple Gardens
9. Middle Temple Hall
10. Bridewell
11. Eel ships at wharf/quay Queenhithe (moved to Billingsgate *c.*1650)
12. Church of St Bride
13. Baynard's Castle
14. Bulmers Tower
15. Queenhithe
16. St Paul's Cathedral
17. Three Cranes Wharf
18. The Steelyard
19. Church of St Mary-le-Bow
20. Guildhall
21. Coldharbour
22. Church of St Lawrence Pountney
23. The Royal Exchange
24. The Dutch Church
25. Church of St Michael
26. Church of St Dunstan-in-the-East
27. Billingsgate
28. Church of All Hallows Barking
29. The Tower
30. St Katharine's Hospital
31. Church of St Olave
32. Gateway with traitors' heads
33. Nonsuch House
34. Church of St Mary Overy (later to become Southwark Cathedral)
35. Winchester House
36. Globe Theatre
37. The Rose Theatre
38. The Hope Theatre
39. The Swan Theatre

as possible, presumably in an attempt to give viewers a sense of close-up work. This painting breaks new ground because it gives London a sky and condenses the riverfront to an almost impossible degree, also almost for the first time.

The compression of the image accounts for the two main inaccuracies, Whitehall on the left and the river bend on the right, which have both been squeezed in although they could not in reality be part of this view. When looking at London from the top of Southwark Cathedral, the main seventeenth-century viewpoint for artists drawing London from the south, the river clearly curves on the right, but not as soon as the painting shows, and similarly Whitehall can be seen from Southwark tower, but the artist would have had to look over his left shoulder.

There is no obvious candidate for the authorship of this painting. Its sister version at Chatsworth is still misleadingly attributed to Thomas Wyck, whose signed works bear no resemblance to it. We should note, however, that rather surprisingly the preparation of the canvas (Chatsworth) is similar to that of the panel version (see Goldsmith) and this may suggest further links between the two paintings, although they remain clearly by different hands. The support, on the other hand, would suggest that the work on panel (Baltic oak) probably preceded the Chatsworth canvas. Board from Baltic countries was predominantly used in

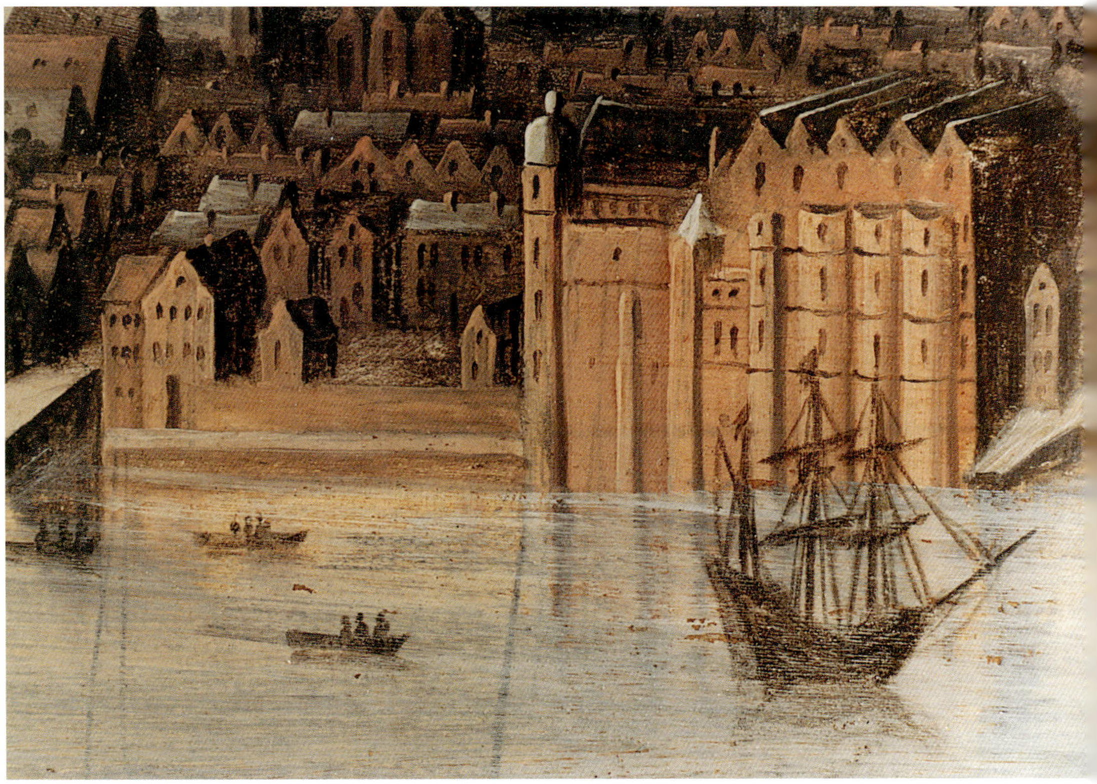

northern Europe from 1300 to 1650. In the first half of the seventeenth century, however, the Hanseatic League declined, and with it the source of supply of Baltic oak entering England. This affected the world of painters in two ways: the type of oak used changed and concurrently there was an increasing tendency to use canvas.

A third pre-Fire panoramic view of London recently emerged and was sold at Christie's (15 December 1993, Lot 43B). Its compositional formula, however, suggests that it dates from a later date, around the time of the Great Fire.

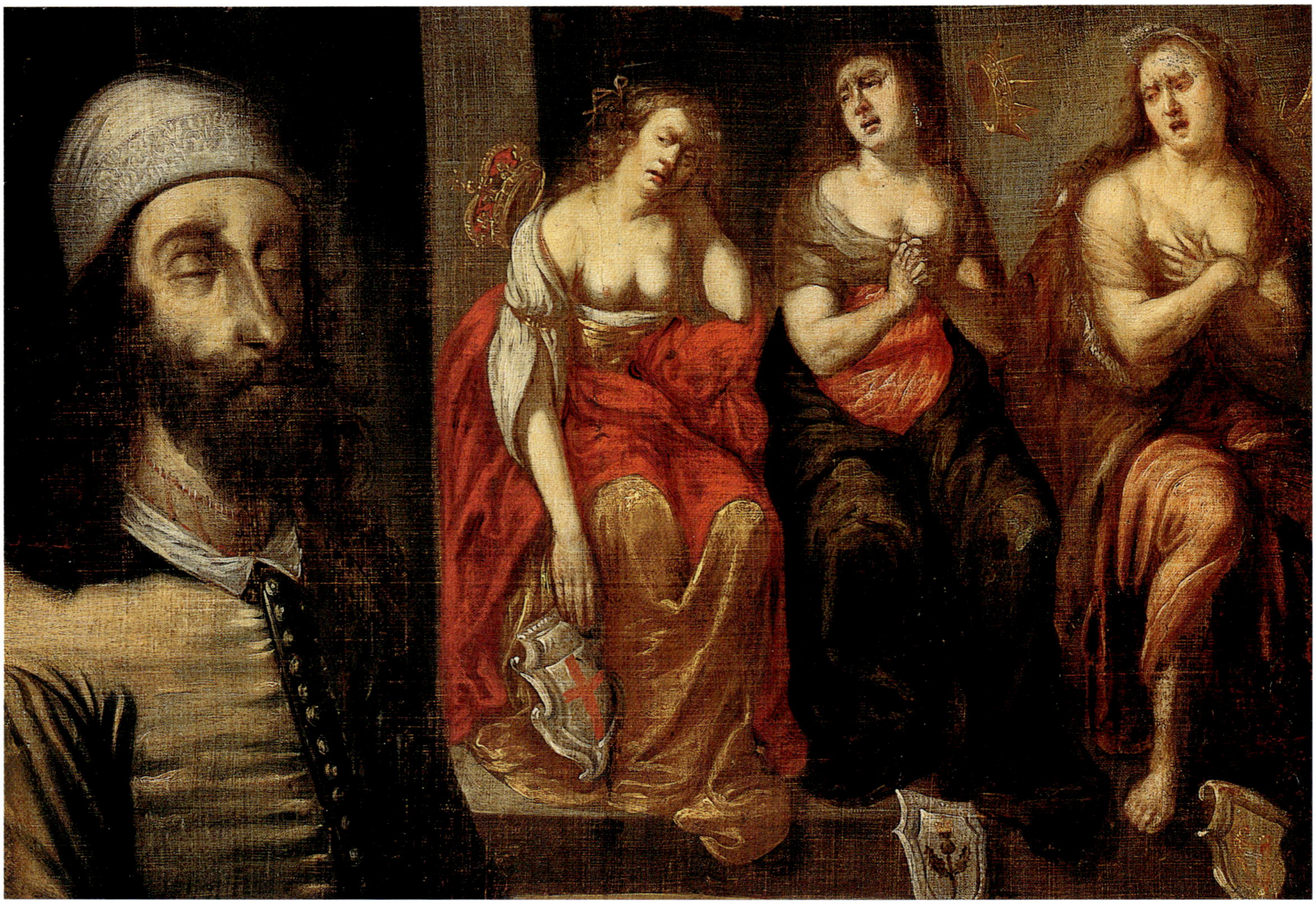

4.

BRITISH SCHOOL

Charles I after his Execution with his Head Stitched on [46.78/537]

1660s

Oil on canvas, 49.2 x 72.7 cm

Not signed or dated

THE BUST portrait of the dead Charles I is placed on the left of a rectangular niche containing three lamenting female figures representing England, Scotland and Wales.

After Charles I was publicly executed on a scaffold erected outside the Banqueting House on 30 January 1649, 'his Head and Trunk was instantly put into a Coffin covered with black Velvet, and conveyed into the Lodgings at Whitehall. There it was imbowelled by Chirurgions of their own, but a Physitian privately thrusting himself into the dissection of the body relates that Nature had designed him above the most of Mortal men for a long life... Then they bear it to St James's House, and Coffin it there in Lead' (see William Anderson).

Charles I was later buried in St George's Chapel in Windsor. The exact whereabouts of the coffin were unknown until 1813, when a workman accidentally discovered it during reconstruction work; the coffin was opened in April that year in the presence of the royal physician, Henry Halford.

The artist's choice to place the drawn but tranquil face of the dead King alongside the agitated allegorical figures representing his kingdom is uneasy (X-rays revealed this was the original composition and close observation of the edges indicated this was the original size). The arrangement detracts from the impact of this extraordinary posthumous portrait, totally free from royal pride or arrogance. The only element which deviates from the apparent authenticity of the work is the decidedly dark hair and beard of the King. The last portrait from life of Charles I, taken at his trial by Edward Bower (Royal Collection), shows very clearly that the King was going grey, particularly his beard.

Charles I is known to have worn three layers of clothing for his execution, which took place during a very harsh winter. These would probably have consisted of a linen shirt, then a vest and finally a doublet. A white embroidered cap, a lace collar and a handkerchief associated with Charles I's execution are in the Museum's collection. The cap in the painting, with its bobbin-made lace, is consistent with the 1640s, while the surviving cap of English needle lace in the Museum appears to date from a decade earlier. Logically the cap was worn for protection from the cold, but it would also have been significant for the execution since Charles's hair would have been tucked under it. This painting may record the appearance of both the execution cap and the doublet which the King would have worn over his knitted vest (in the Museum's collection). The most unusual feature in the depiction of the King's clothing, however, is the absence of an elaborate collar. This apparent omission becomes self-explanatory if we consider that the artist clearly chose to show the King's neck. It is the proof of the violence that was committed, and the display of the King's wound parallels those on the dead Christ, thus adding further weight to the theme of the martyr king.

When Charles's coffin was opened at Windsor more than a century and a half after his death, a drawing of his head was made which is in the collection of the Duke of Beaufort at Badminton (Witt Library ref.: B60/1442). The time gap and the technical nature of the record do not further the information gathered so far.

Although the artist deliberately chose to dress the female figures in the timeless draperies of allegorical representations, it is still possible to observe fashion trends that date from the Restoration rather than the late 1640s. The hairstyle of the figure on the left, the spikiness of the crowns of the other two and the low décolletage of all three are consistent with a date in the 1660s. (The Royal Collection portrait of Lady Byron by Peter Lely makes a useful comparison and dates from *c.*1663–4.)

This picture forms part of the large collection of Cromwelliana (books, pamphlets, pictures and other objects) originally collected, from 1875 onwards, by Sir Richard Tangye, and presented to the Museum by his son in 1913 (see Appendix).

Provenance:
Sir Richard Tangye (1833–1906); presented by Sir Harold Lincoln Tangye in 1913 (as by Henry Stone).

Bibliography:
Catalogue of the Cromwellian collection in the possession of Sir Richard Tangye, privately printed, 1905, no. 537;
William Anderson, *A Compleat History of the Life and Raigne of King Charles from His Cradle to his Grave*, 1658.

Provenance:
Sir Richard Tangye (1833–1906); presented by Sir Harold Lincoln Tangye in 1913 (as by Henry Stone).

Bibliography:
Catalogue of the Cromwellian collection in the possession of Sir Richard Tangye, privately printed, 1905, no. 539; *Country Life*, 10 November 1928, pp677-80.

5. BRITISH SCHOOL

Portrait of Charles I as a Martyr King

[46.78/539]
Date uncertain
Oil on canvas, 76 x 63.5 cm
Not signed or dated

THIS IS a bust portrait of the King immediately before his execution. He is shown with uplifted hands and is wearing his execution clothes. A crown is depicted on the right-hand side in the middle of a ray of sunlight, against a cloudy sky.

The composition recalls the imagery of William Marshall's frontispiece to *Eikon Basilike* (published shortly after the King's death) which shows the King kneeling and praying in a small chapel with two rays of sunlight streaming in: Charles rejects the temporal crown for a celestial one (placed in one of the light beams) and a crown of thorns. The iconography of this portrait also derives from religious art recalling the stigmatisation of those who felt close to Christ. With a gold crown floating in the sky, the painting suggests that the execution of the King would not suppress his deeper life or status.

Although the costume superficially relates to that in the previous portrait (with the addition of a lace collar), the artist has misunderstood the collar, the lace on the cap (the internal pattern may suggest it was based on an engraving rather than drawn from life) and the braiding on the doublet. This may indicate a later (nineteenth-century?) copy of a seventeenth-century idea.

There are several versions of this work (possibly the six 'Black Charles' supposed to have been painted by order of Charles II for presentation to royalist families). One is in the collection of the College Estate at Kirkoswald (see *Country Life*). The National Portrait Gallery also owns a version of this painting and another was sold at Sotheby's, 10 November 1993 (140).

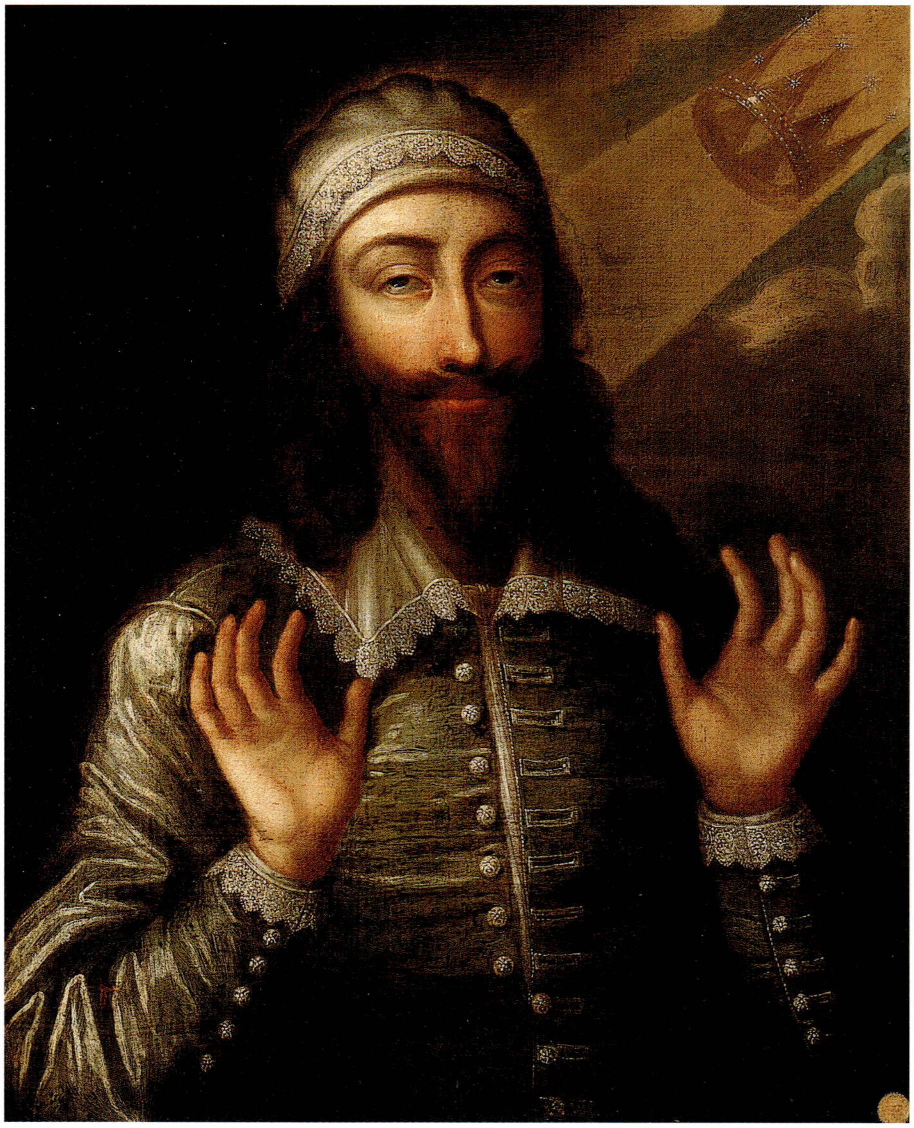

6.

AFTER SIR PETER LELY

(1618–80)

Portrait of Oliver Cromwell (1599–1658)

[46.78/526]

Date uncertain

Oil on canvas, 72.7 x 59.7 cm

Not signed or dated

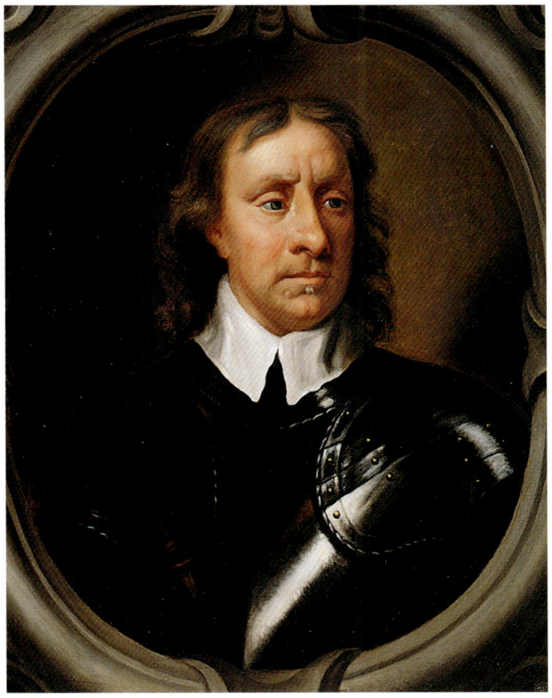

OLIVER CROMWELL is shown with his head and shoulders in armour in a feigned oval, facing the spectator, the head turned slightly to the right; the background is plain. This is one of a number of replicas, of uncertain date, of the portrait by Sir Peter Lely in Birmingham City Art Gallery, probably painted in 1653–4. The prototype almost certainly derives from the unfinished miniature sketched from the life by Samuel Cooper (?1608–72), in the collection of the Duke of Buccleuch; a finished version of this miniature signed with initials and dated 1657 is on permanent loan to the Museum (37.17/1) from Viscount Harcourt.

When he made his portrait of Cromwell, Samuel Cooper, who was born and bred in Blackfriars, lived in Henrietta Street, Covent Garden. He moved to Covent Garden King Street in 1641 or 1642 and stayed there till his death in 1672. Lely also lived in Covent Garden.

Horace Walpole recorded the uncompromising brief Cromwell was meant to have given to the painter: 'Mr Lely, I desire you would use all your skill to paint my picture truly like me, and not flatter me at all; but remark all the roughness, pimples, warts and everything, otherwise I will never pay a farthing for it.' This copy, based on Lely but not bound by the same threatening injunction, is a somewhat softened version of the original brief. Until 1654 Richard Walker was the painter responsible for Cromwell's portraits. They were essentially idealised images which strongly contrast with the realism Samuel Cooper and Peter Lely breathed into his portraits after Cromwell was made Lord Protector in 1653.

This picture forms part of the Tangye collection (see Appendix and cat. nos. 4 and 5). There are numerous versions of this particular design, notably in the National Portrait Gallery (514) and in the collection of the Earl of Sandwich.

Provenance:
Sir Richard Tangye (1833–1906); presented by Sir Harold Lincoln Tangye in 1913.

Bibliography:
Hayes (cat. no. 121); *Catalogue of the Cromwellian collection in the possession of Sir Richard Tangye*, privately printed, 1905, no. 526, p117; E. B. Powley, *The Cromwell Museum, Huntingdon, Oxford*, 1965, no. 4 (pp1–2); Mary Edmond, 'Limners and Picture Makers – New light on the lives of miniaturists and large-scale portrait painters working in London in the sixteenth and seventeenth centuries', in *Walpole Society*, 1978–80, p65; David Piper, 'The contemporary portraits of Oliver Cromwell', in *Walpole Society*, vol. XXXIV, 1958, pp31–3 and 39–40; Oliver Millar, *Sir Peter Lely 1618–80*, exhibition catalogue, National Portrait Gallery, 1978, no. 22.

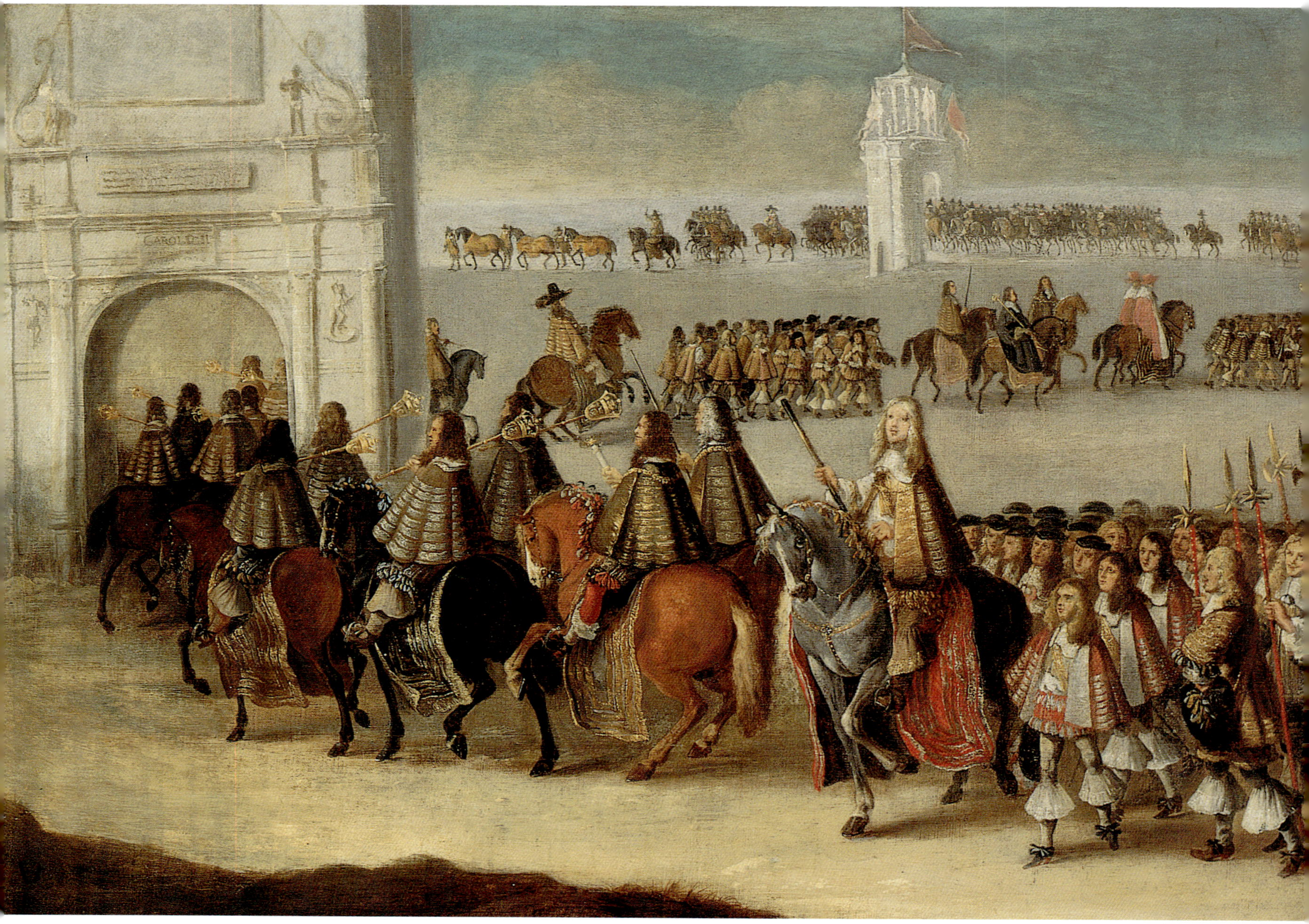

7.

DIRCK STOOP

(c.1618–86)

Charles II's cavalcade through the City of London, 22 April 1661 [79.18]
1662
Oil on canvas, 66.8 x 202.5 cm
Signed *R.S.* for Roderigo (Dirck) Stoop and dated *166(2)* bottom left
Label on the back: *Henry Graves & Co, 6 Pall Mall, 233*

THIS PAINTING depicts the state entry into the City of London of Charles II, on 22 April 1661, the day before his coronation, as part of the traditional procession between the Tower of London and Westminster. The canvas shows the earliest representation of the standing army.

In the complete absence of topographical background, the procession is guided through four huge triumphal arches which were erected by Peter Mills, the City Surveyor, and an anonymous

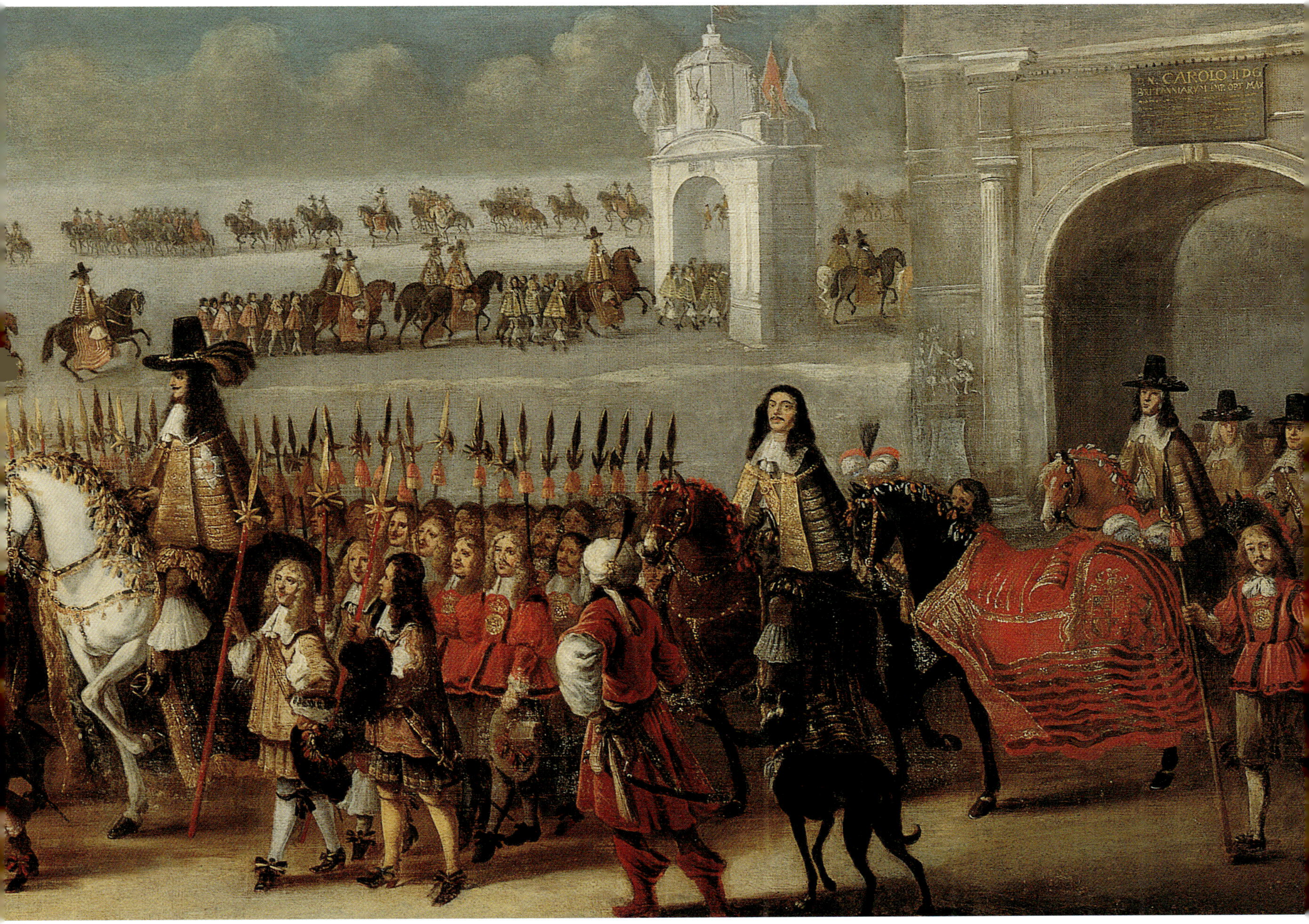

architect at the City's expense (they stood in the streets until June that year). They mark the route within City territory (original designs in the RIBA Library; the arches were also engraved by David Loggan): starting on the right, at Leadenhall Street, and moving on to Cornhill, Cheapside and Whitefriars.

Apart from the meticulous record of formal ceremonial robes worn by the King, the Officers of State and other dignitaries in the procession, including the Lord Mayor of that year (in the middle ground, second horserider below the arch), the costume shows the elaborate fashion of petticoat breeches and large periwigs introduced by the court after 1660, a brief and fantastic period of which there are few representations.

The significance of the Turk in the foreground has not been established. It is doubtful that he would, on his own, account for the 'company of men all like Turks' whom Samuel Pepys noted as following Sir George Carteret but without knowing who they were. This inclusion may have had a private meaning to the person who commissioned this painting. The artist himself certainly had a fascination for Turkish characters, who crop up in many of his works. Dirck Stoop, a Flemish artist from Utrecht who had become a court painter in Lisbon (hence the adoption of Roderigo rather than Dirck), first came to London in 1662 in the entourage of Catherine of Braganza when she came to marry the King; he stayed until 1678. Stoop would therefore not have witnessed the previous year's 'cavalcade' and coronation of Charles II. His main source of reference for this event was John Ogilby's book *The Entertainment*…,

Key

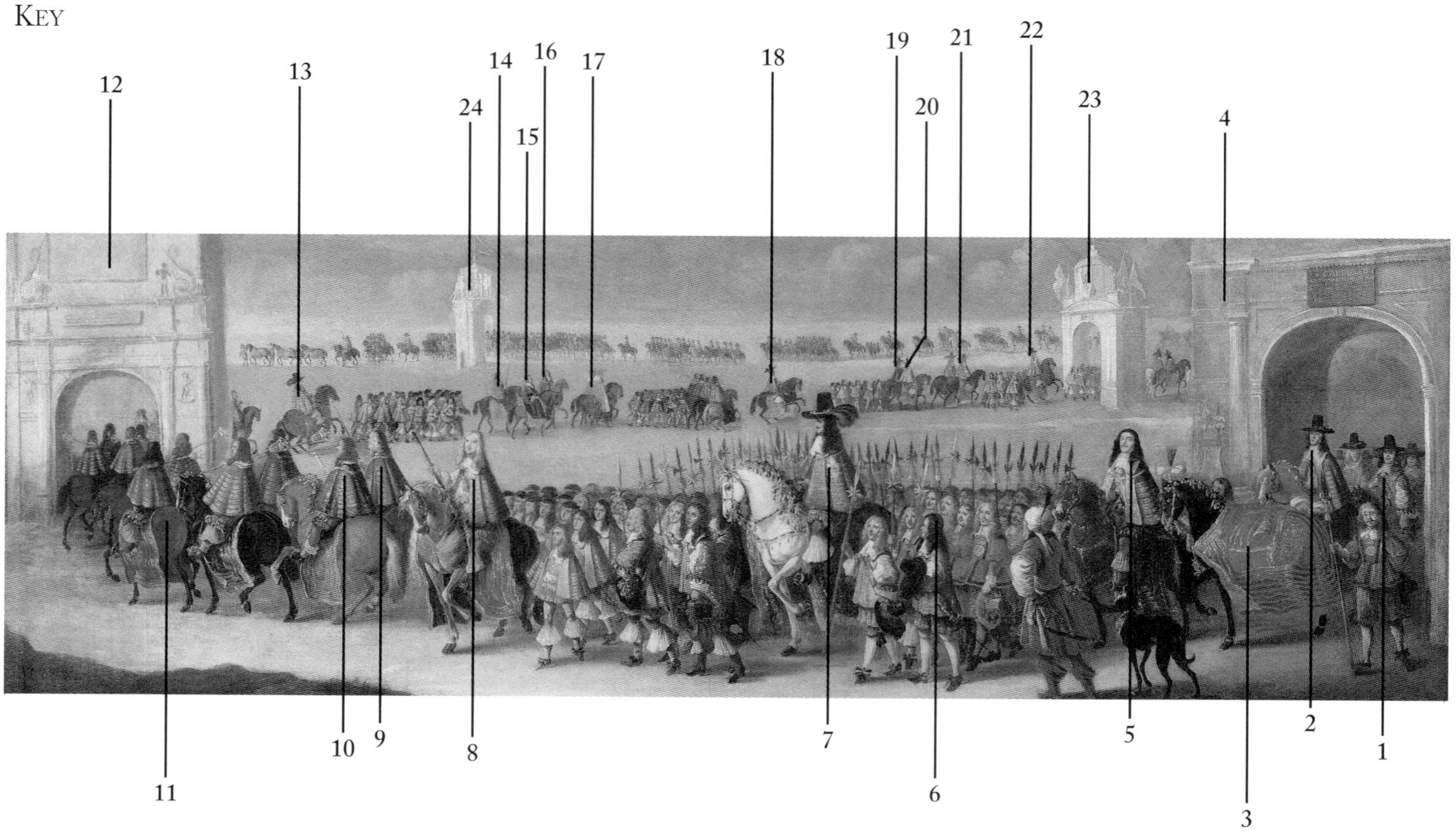

1. King's troop (second Life Guards)
2. Sir George Carteret, Vice Chamberlaine
3. King's Horse
4. Arch: Leadenhall Street (theme: the monarchy)
5. George, Duke of Albemarle (Master of the Horse)
6. Yeomen of The Guard and Gentlemen Pensioners
7. Charles II
8. James, Earl of Suffolk, Deputy Earl Marshall
9. Lord Great Chamberlain (Robert, Earl of Lindsay)
10. Lord High Constable (Algernon, Earl of Northumberland)
11. Troop of Horse Guards (the first Life Guards)
12. Arch: Cornhill (theme: Neptune, London's maritime prosperity)
13. James, Duke of York
14. Edward, Earl of Sandwich
15. Lord Mayor Sir Richard Browne
16. The Garter King at Arms
17. Representatives of Duke of Normandy and Aquitaine
18. James, Duke of Ormond
19. Lord High Chancellor
20. High Treasurer
21. Two Kings at Arms
22. Duke of Buckingham
23. Arch: Cheapside (Temple of Concord: to accommodate a choir and 24 violins)
24. Arch: Whitefriars (theme: Garden of Plenty)

published in 1662 (in the Museum's collection), in which Wenceslaus Hollar illustrated the procession in a series of etchings. The commission of this painting may well have originated from the Queen herself. Stoop recorded in a series of etchings, and possibly one painting (*Country Life*, 18 February 1949), the various ceremonial processions, in Lisbon and England, which were dictated by the royal marriage. Their compositional formula, a ribbon unfolding and receding in the background, was well established in Continental processional prints from the late sixteenth century. It was used notably in a print depicting the visit of the future Charles I to Madrid in 1623, but is used here for the first time in an English context.

The royal connections of this artist may account for the general reliability of his record. He corrects Hollar, who wrongly depicted the King's personal bodyguards with staff weapons known as partisans; Stoop shows the Gentlemen Pensioners surrounding the King armed with pole-axes and the Yeomen of the Household with partisans (these, however, are not drawn very accurately). He also successfully gains advantage over the monochrome world of engravings by recording correctly the colours of the military plumes, armours and horse trappings, as specified by Sir Edward Walker, Garter Principal King at Arms in his *Circumstantial Account of the Preparations…* (prepared in 1660 but not published before 1820).

The 1661 procession was deliberately planned by both the Crown and the City to erase memories of the interregnum and the City's anti-royal attitudes which had emerged during the Civil War. The event was therefore particularly lavish; the enthusiastic Pepys wrote: 'So glorious was the show with gold and silver that we were not able to look at it – our eyes at last being so overcome with it.'

The coronation procession through the city, which wove a symbolic link between the cities of London and Westminster, was instituted by Richard II in 1377 and finally abolished by James II in 1685. One previous painted record was made, the cavalcade of Edward VI in 1547 which unfolded on the walls at Cowdray House in Essex. It was recorded in watercolour by S. H. Grimm in 1785, eight years before the mural was destroyed by fire. Charles II's coronation was the first to be so lavishly recorded.

Two further paintings attributed to Isaac Fuller (1606–72) should be mentioned here: *Charles II's arrival at the Banqueting Hall* (in a private collection, reproduced in Barker and Jackson) and *The Restoration of Charles II*, which shows his arrival in London (in the Dugdale Collection, Warwickshire). The latter is an almost exact replica of the print later published by Romeyn de Hooghe showing the entry into London of William III. This perhaps suggests that the 'entry' iconography devised for the Restoration was later reused. The Museum of London painting remains the first and last work in oil to record the coronation cavalcade. The principle of such processions was continued in Lord Mayor's pageants but their frequency and predominantly 'local' appeal have weakened the impact.

A pen-and-ink drawing after this painting featured in Phillips's sale of 31 January 1994 (20). This may well have been the drawing executed in the workshop of Henry Graves & Co. for the purposes of engraving and publishing the work. However, no print was ever issued.

Bibliography:
'George Vertue's Note Books', in *Walpole Society*, vol. 5, 1938, pp26–8; *The Diary of Samuel Pepys*, Robert Latham and William Mathews (eds), 1971, vol. II, pp81–3; Felix Barker and Peter Jackson, *London: 2000 years of a city and its people*, 1974 pp128–9; John Ogilby, *The Entertainment of His Most Excellent Majestie Charles II in His Passage through the City of London to his Coronation*, 1662.

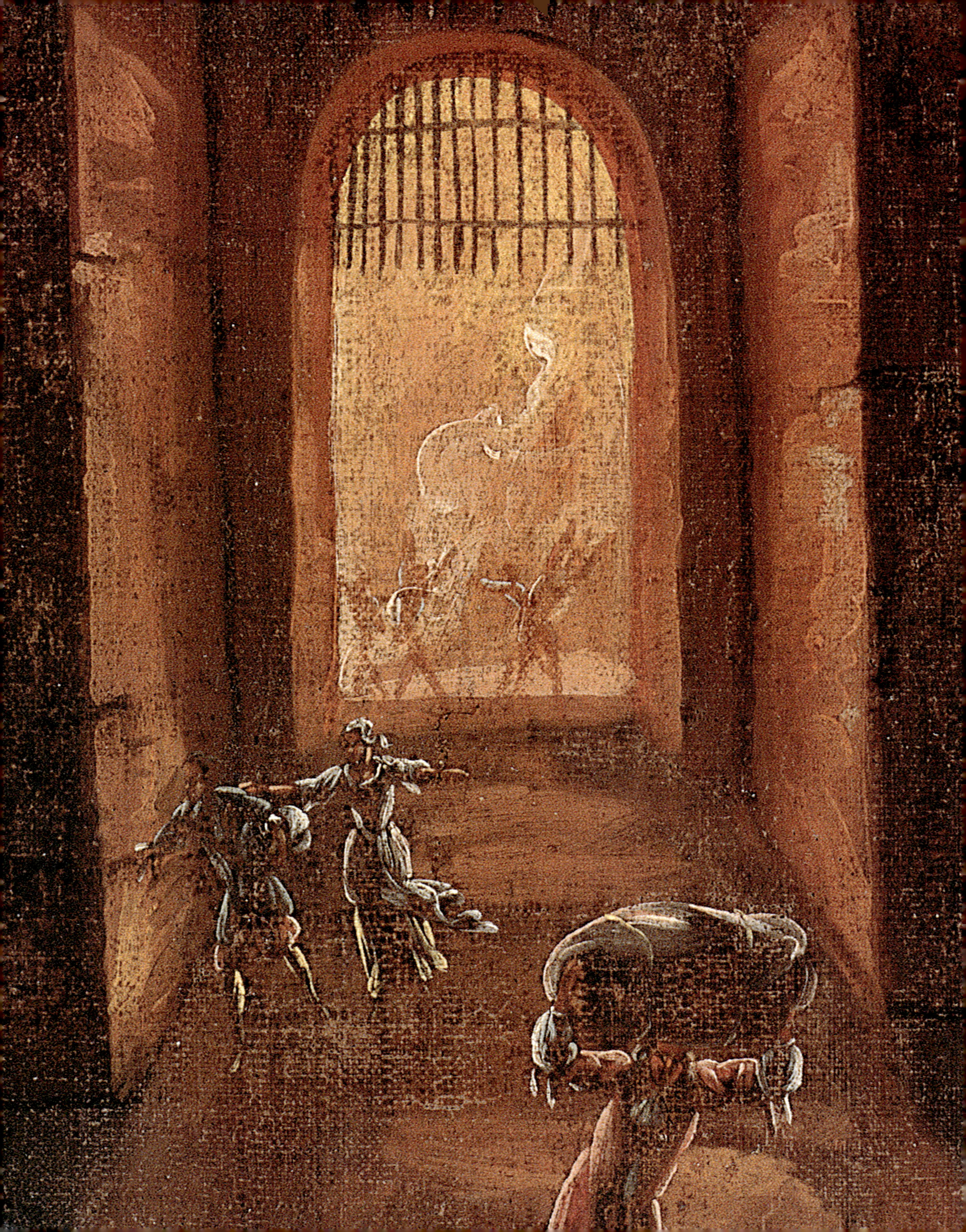

THE GREAT FIRE

THE GREAT FIRE started in a baker's shop in Pudding Lane in the early hours of Sunday morning, 2 September 1666, and raged for four successive days. The strong and relentless east wind, which was so largely responsible for the rapid spreading of the fire, is most vividly shown fanning the flames in all the paintings, and many artists chose to depict London as it appeared between eight and nine o'clock on the evening of Tuesday 4 September, when the flames finally began to reach Old St Paul's but before its roof collapsed.[1]

A number of publications on the Great Fire have given contemporary accounts, statistics, maps and, more recently, archaeological evidence[2] showing the progress of the fire over the four days it raged across the City and past its walls along Fleet Street, menacingly heading towards Westminster.

To artists and Londoners at large the Great Fire gave a final blow to the pristine city shown in cat. no. 3. The heart of London *had meant* the old walled city and as much on either side of it as could be accommodated looking from the south. The Civil War had split London into two opposed factions – the City and Westminster – and the Great Fire was now eradicating one of them. From this time on, when artists started developing close-up views of the capital, they would do so outside the City walls, except for landmarks such as St Paul's and the Tower.

How did artists tackle this most extraordinary disaster? By bringing together three distinct traditions in painting: first, the panoramic views of London (see cat. no. 3) as developed by resident foreign artists; then by drawing on the Dutch experience in conflagration painting which, headed by Egbert van der Poel and Aert van der Neer, had started towards the middle of the seventeenth century. This development must in turn have drawn inspiration from the biblical or mythical city fires which, in the fifteenth and sixteenth centuries, had driven Giorgione, Lucas de Leyden, Adam Elsheimer and others to depict Lot and his daughters with the destruction of the city of Sodom, or Aeneas and Anchises fleeing the destruction of Troy.[3]

By an interesting coincidence, from the twelfth century onwards, historians had been associating London with the New Troy (Troynovant or Trinovantum),[4] so that the ground had been well prepared for linking up the Great Fire with ancient city fires. The most explicit painting to carry this message is by the artist Cornelis Saftleven (1607–81). There are two versions, one of which is on public show at Petworth, in Sussex.[5] Against the background of burning London is set a nightmarish scene of threatening wild beasts, ruins and torture; a painting propped in the foreground shows the execution of Charles I: regicide and destruction (plague and fire) were indeed overwhelming events and we should not be surprised that many contemporaries established a direct parallel with the sinful cities of the Bible which, the prophets Isaiah and Jeremiah record, were first destroyed and then invaded by wild beasts. The paintings which derived from Jan Griffier (cat. nos 9 and 10) come closest to this vision of hell. It has been convincingly suggested that Ludgate 'stands out as a dramatic silhouette against the flames and, with its teeth-like portcullis, suggests the gaping mouth of hell'.[6]

Cornelis Saftleven (1607–1681)
Allegory of London in the 17th century.
Oil on canvas
Petworth House
(The National Trust)
Photograph:
Courtauld Institute of Art.

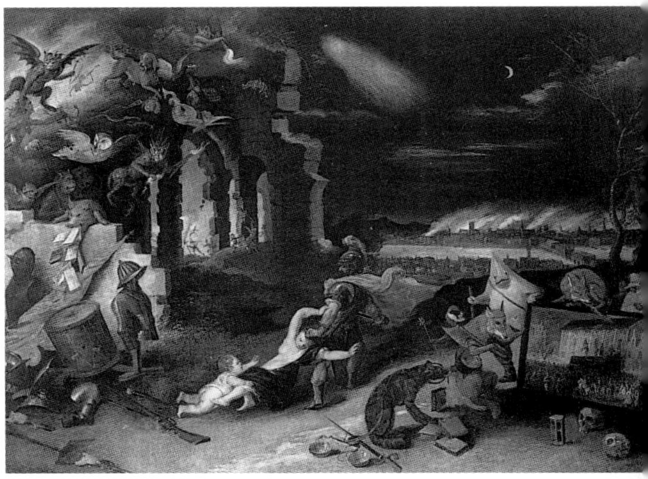

The artistic scene in London was still dominated by foreigners and most of the works, if not all, appear to have originated from Netherlandish artists or painters working in Netherlandish style. They fall into four distinct categories which are based on the viewpoints adopted, all of which were already familiar (see previous section), except for that of the Griffier (category three).

1. Taken from the river just outside the Tower of London

Cat. no. 8 is the best example in this group. The viewpoint can be linked to the Cornelis Bol painting of the Pool of London and, indeed, the medieval illumination showing Charles d'Orleans as a prisoner in the Tower (see p5).

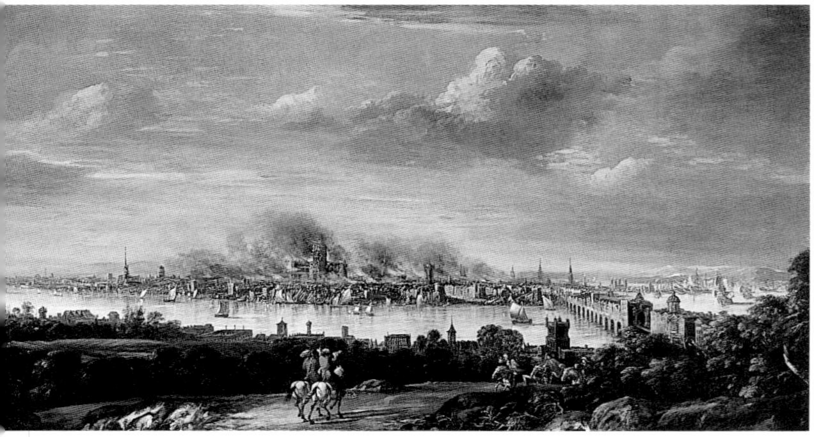

Anonymous
The Great Fire of London from Southwark, 1666.
Oil on canvas
(Sold at Sotheby's 10 July 1991, Lot 69).

2. Taken from the south – the traditional viewpoint

Thomas Wyck's version,[7] although taking considerable liberties with the topography of the south bank (St Saviour's is omitted altogether), is possibly the most striking example. The numerous prints which adopt this viewpoint, many of which were produced in Holland, were based on earlier engravings of London, mainly Hollar's 'long view' of 1647 – with the addition of the appropriate flames and smoke, and clearly have no value as literal representations of the event. The painting attributed to Thomas Wyck from the Chester Beatty Collection would seem to work along similar lines.[8] It is unusual in its representation of the Fire by day.

3. Taken from Ludgate, as close to the fire as was safely possible

See cat. nos 9 and 10 and Appendix. A rather elaborate version of this subject is in the collection of the Yale Center for British Art (B1076.7.27). This particular viewpoint is perhaps explained by the fact that the parish of St Anne, Blackfriars, was an artists' quarter in the seventeenth century.[9]

4. Taken from the west, either from Strand Lane, between Arundel and Somerset houses, or from Essex Stairs

George Vertue records Waggoner's view at Painter-Stainers' Hall,[10] which was engraved in Pennant's *Some Account of London*, 1790, facing p324. This painting seems to have been particularly praised; unfortunately it was destroyed during the Blitz, and no photographs of it were ever taken.

Several versions of the Somerset House prototype by the artist Thomas Wyck survive. Vertue notes that 'Mr. Wyke painted the View of the fire of the City of London several times very well',[11] and Richard Gough tells us further that a certain 'Mr. Granger saw in Berkshire an excellent view of London on fire by Thomas Wych'.[12] A signed canvas by Wyck is in the collection of the Duke of Beaufort; another very close to it was sold at Sotheby's;[13] and another is in the collection of Sir Oliver Millar.

A further group of four paintings represents the Essex Stairs viewpoint: one is in the collection of Barclays Bank, another with the Society of Antiquaries, another with the

Guildhall Art Gallery and the last in this collection (cat. no. 11).

Most paintings in the last two sub-groups (misleadingly) place the City of London on a hill and this alone suggests that they are related to one another. However, the Museum's painting is worth singling out for its departure from this prototype. It is the only one which does not depict the City of London on higher ground.

The Great Fire had a profound influence on British culture. Fires in London have been extensively recorded and have often been newsworthy items. At the end of the eighteenth century, Romanticism coupled with the search for the 'Sublime' put fires back on the artistic agenda (see pp179–85). Philippe Jacques de Loutherbourg produced his own version of the Great Fire over a century after the event[14] and publishers reissued prints after compositions from categories three and four.[15]

The paintings in the Museum's collection memorably represent the first, third and fourth of the viewpoints described.

1. Walter G. Bell, *The Great Fire of London*, 1920, pp130 and 133.
2. John E. N. Hearsey, *London and the Great Fire*, 1965; John Beresford Ellis, *The Great Fire of London*, 1976; Gustav Milne, *The Great Fire of London*, 1986.
3. The earliest depictions of the subject were by Lucas de Leyden for *Lot and his Daughters* (*c.*1514) and Giorgione for *Aeneas and Anchises* (this work does not survive). There are two extant versions of *The Burning of Troy* by Adam Elsheimer (*c.*1600), one of which is in the collection of the Alte Pinacotheck, Munich. In 1605 Henrick van Steenwyck the Younger (1580–1649) also painted *Aeneas and Anchises in Burning Troy* (Chicago Art Institute).
4. John Clark, 'Trinovantum – the evolution of a legend', in *Journal of Medieval History*, vol. 7, 1981, pp135-51.
5. The other, attributed to Jan Brueghel II, was sold at Christie's (Old Master pictures), 15 December 1989 (147).
6. Malcolm Warner, *The Image of London*, 1987, p115.
7. Reproduced in the *Illustrated London News*, 8 April 1950; close to it is the painting attributed to Daniel van Heil which was sold at Christie's, 24 June 1977 (103).
8. Sold at Sotheby's, 10 July 1991 (69).
9. See Mary Edmond, 'Limners and Picture Makers – New light on the lives of miniaturists and large-scale portrait painters working in London in the sixteenth and seventeenth centuries', in *Walpole Society*, 1978-80, p124.
10. 'George Vertue Note Books', in *Walpole Society*, vol. 20, 1932, p30.
11. 'George Vertue Note Books', in *Walpole Society*, vol. 18, 1930, p106.
12. Richard Gough, *British Topography*, 1780, vol. I, p705.
13. Sotheby's, 24 November 1971 (83).
14. The painting (which was engraved) is in the collection of the Yale Center for British Art. See Warner, *The Image of London*, 1987, cat. no. 45.
15. See the entries for the two paintings after Griffier for the Ludgate viewpoint; for the west viewpoint, as well as the Pennant engraving described under item four, we should add that reproduced in *Londina Illustrata*, 7 August 1811, by Robert Wilkinson.

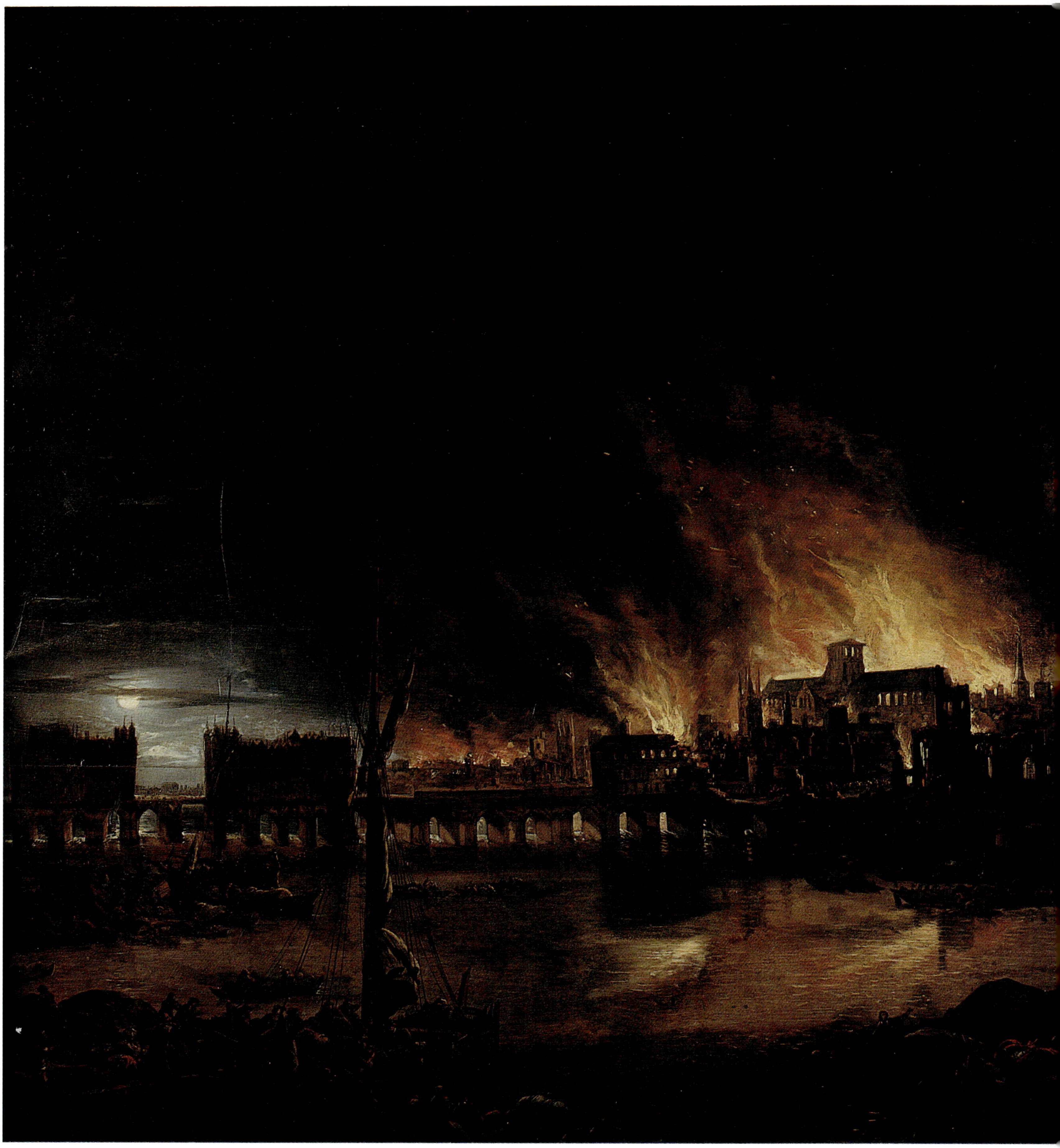

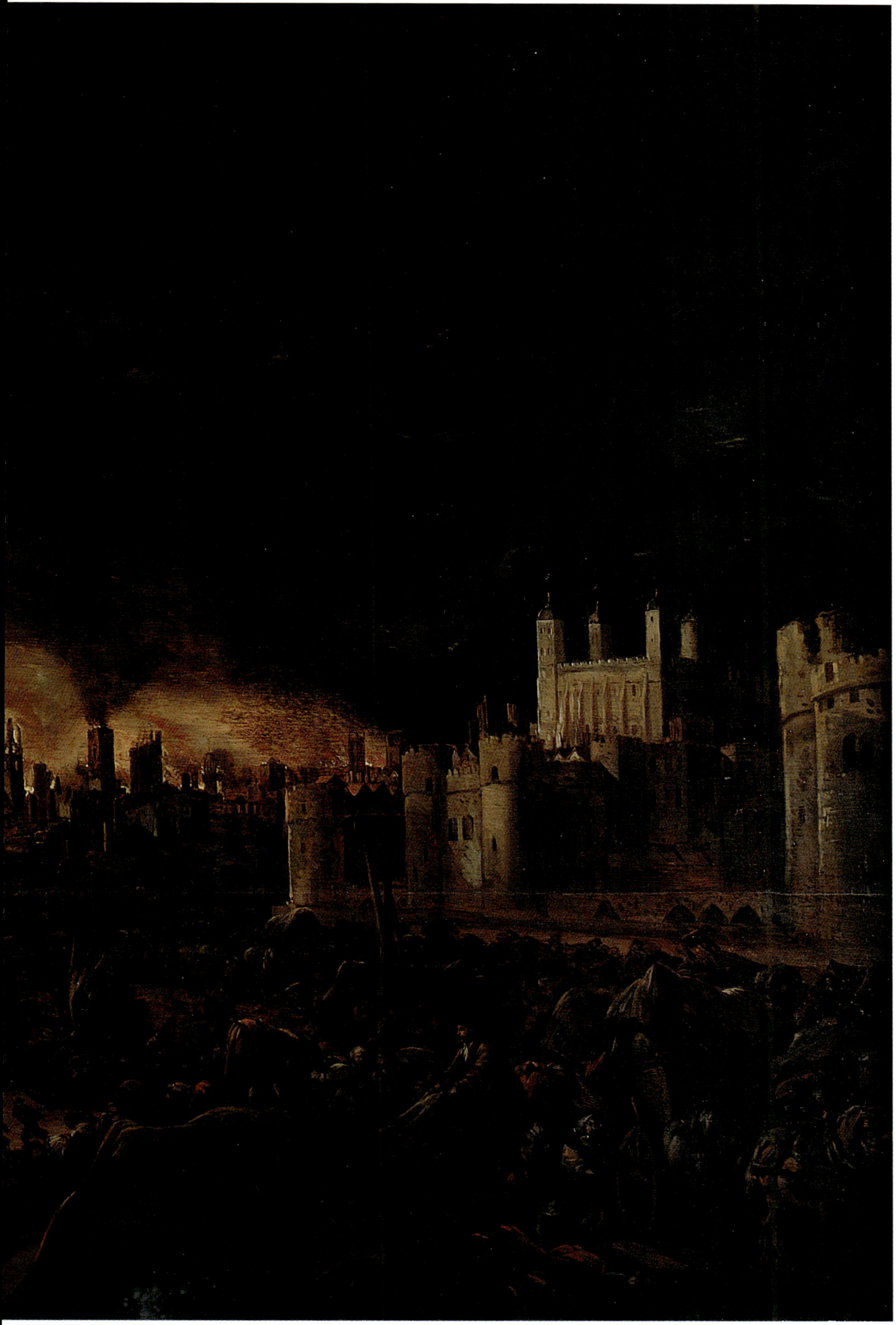

8.

DUTCH SCHOOL

The Great Fire of London, 1666 [57.54]

*c.*1666

Oil on oak,

89.7 x 151.6 cm

Not signed or dated

Provenance:
Silvertop collection, Minster Acres, near Hexham, Northumberland; Charles Silvertop sale, Anderson and Garland, Newcastle, 22 January 1957 (47, as de Loutherbourg), bt W. M. Sabin; purchased from Edward Speelman, partly out of the Joicey Trust Fund and with the aid of contributions from an anonymous donor and the National Art Collections Fund, in 1957.

Bibliography:
Hayes (cat. no. 40).

THE FIRE is here seen as it would have appeared between eight and nine o'clock on the evening of Tuesday 4 September, from a boat in the vicinity of Tower Wharf (viewpoint one on p32). In so far as it is possible to judge, both the detail and the disposition of the buildings are exceptionally accurate. The detail is notably so at points where other seventeenth-century topographers have consistently misrepresented actuality; the arches of Old London Bridge are shown pointed and of irregular width (where Claude de Jongh and many others had painted them as rounded), and the north-east turret of the White Tower is correctly represented as the one circular in shape (whereas Hollar has the north-west tower as rounded). Errors and omissions, however, there are. Old London Bridge has been given too many arches, and the burning of the tenement block on the bridge should not have been included, as this was destroyed at a much earlier stage of the conflagration (Sunday morning); the south transept of St Paul's is seen without its pinnacles; the apse of the Chapel of St John has been omitted from the south-east corner of the White Tower, and the outer bastions of the Tower are no more than approximations of the appearance of these buildings, St Thomas's Tower being foreshortened and its gateway omitted, and the complex of buildings round the Byward Tower left out; finally, the foreground wharf to the right, where we see the human drama so poignantly rendered, never existed and must be interpreted as artistic licence.

The accuracy of certain details which could not have been learned from other pictures or engravings of contemporary London demonstrates that the artist knew the city at first hand. The viewpoint selected, which would have been both the best and the safest one for sketching the fire, and such authentic observation as the live brands and sparks scattered high over the city – and the spectacular effect of their reflection in the water – suggest, further, that the artist may have been an eye-witness of the event.

The identity of the artist has proved a perplexing problem. The scene is in the tradition of Egbert van der Poel (1621–64), who specialised in conflagrations, some of them by moonlight, and painted the explosion at Delft in 1654. The painter's technical expertise in night and fire painting as well as the way in which he organised the space is reminiscent of Aert van der Neer's *Fire in Amsterdam* (the painting is now called *City Burning by Moonlight* and was once in the Borchard collection), but the work cannot be attributed to this artist on stylistic grounds.

Before the painting came into the Museum's possession, an attribution to Lieve Verschuier (*c.*1630–86) was proposed on the basis of the similar canvas of the Great Fire signed by Verschuier in the Museum of Fine Arts, Budapest (cat. no. 380), which is almost the same size and taken from the same viewpoint; subsequently doubts concerning Verschuier's authorship have been expressed. The complete unreliability of the topography in this last picture, however, rules out the possibility that the two works were executed by the same hand; moreover the handling is quite different. The similarity in tone, the liveliness of the painting of flames and the reflections in the water, as well as the closeness of the composition (down to details such as the boat on the left, which

KEY

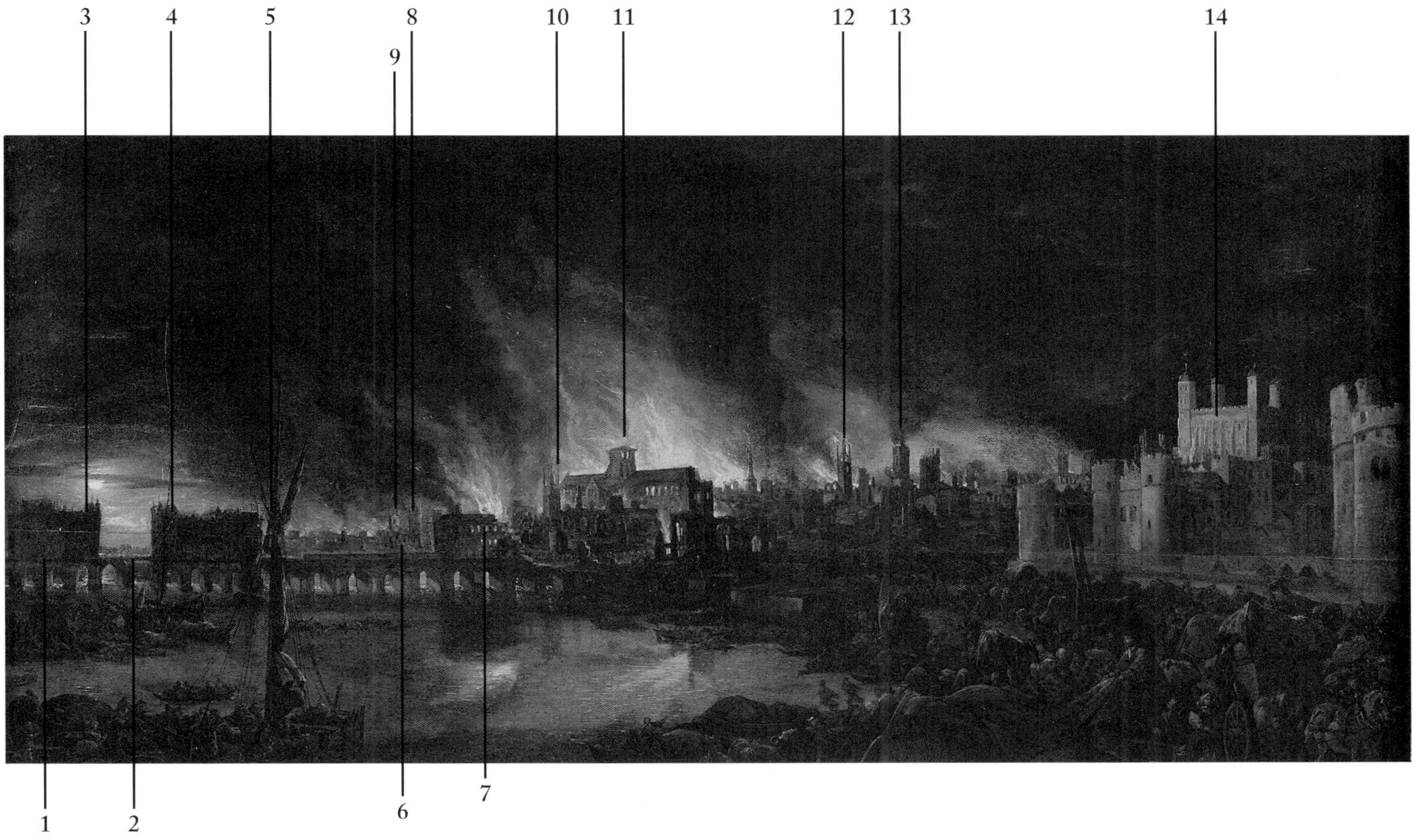

1. Old London Bridge
2. Drawbridge
3. Block of medieval buildings
4. Nonsuch House
5. Chapel House
6. Wooden parapet put up in 1635 after the 1632–3 fire which destroyed houses
7. Three-storey tenement block (erected 1645–9)
8. Church of St Dunstan-in-the-West ?
9. Church of St Bride
10. Church of St Martin – Vintry or St Andrew – Holborn
11. Old St Paul's
12. Church of St Mary-le-Bow
13. Church of St Dunstan-in-the-East (with its spire destroyed)?
14. The Tower of London

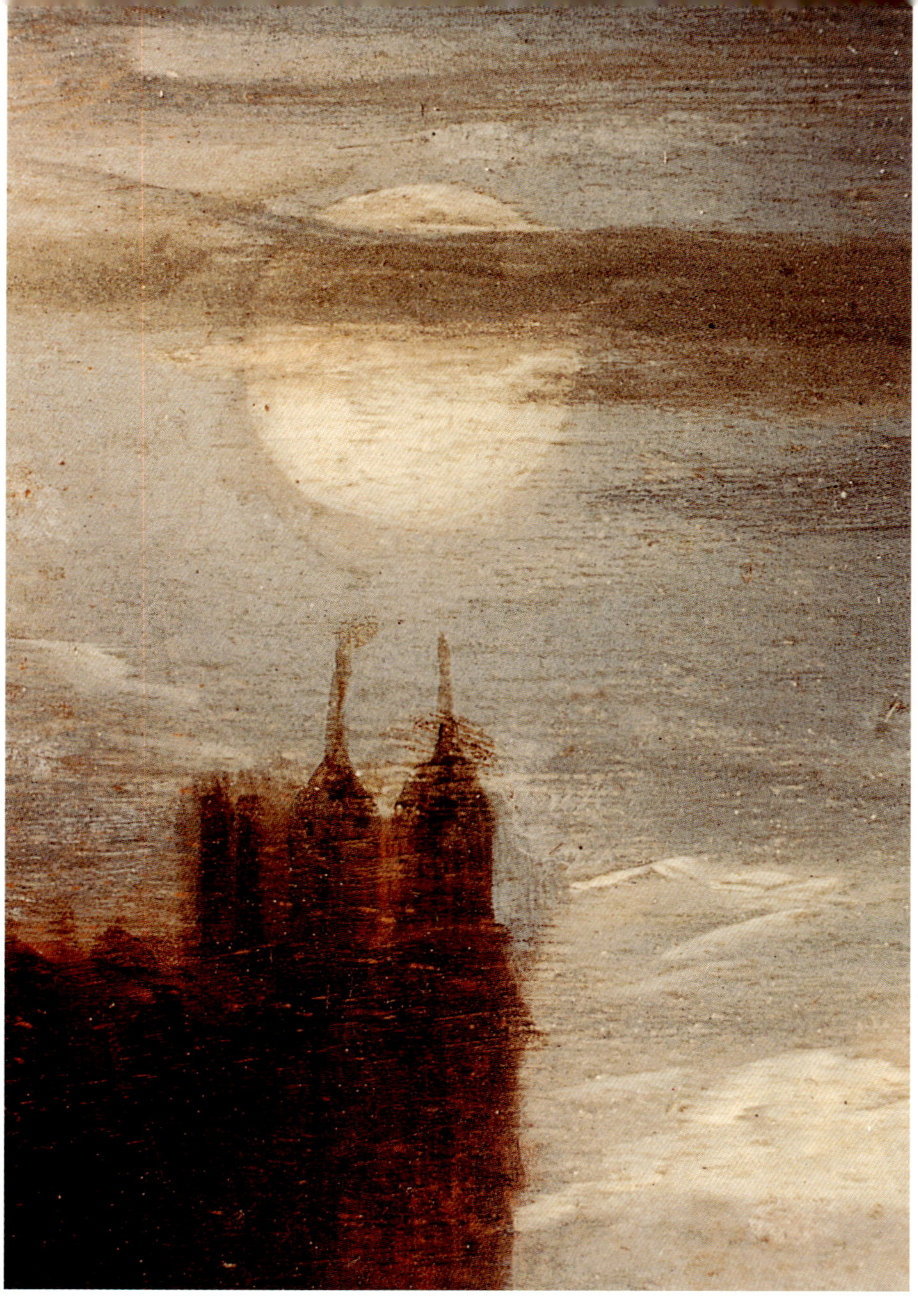

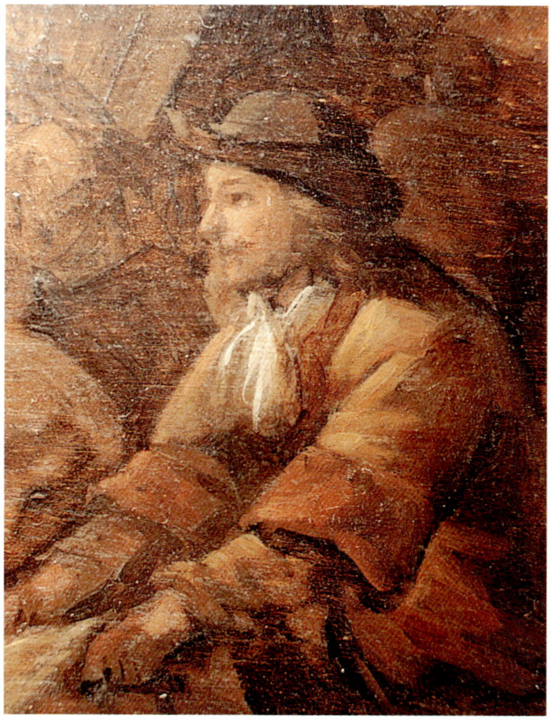

has its mast in much the same position) suggest certainly, however, that the artist of the Budapest painting was familiar with the Museum of London picture; evidently he was interested only in the pictorial possibilities of this subject, and not in delineating London as it actually was. The previous tentative attribution to William van de Welde (Hayes cat. no. 40) is unlikely to be correct.

The scientific analysis of this painting revealed a date between 1650 and 1680 for the oak panel. As expected for that date, the tree rings did not match Baltic chronologies (which stop at 1625; see p21) but matched those of a 'central European' origin. The technical and methodological differences between this painting and the two earliest paintings of London (cat. nos 2 and 3) are very marked. This work has a different ground/imprimatura layer structure and infra-red reflectography did not reveal any underdrawing. It seems that, instead, the painter was making an extensive use of a wet-in-wet painting technique. Further research into early cityscapes may help us define how and when this technical turning point occurred, between 1630 and the late 1660s.

A smaller version of the Museum painting (80.5 x 111 cm, unsigned, and painted on canvas, not panel) is in the possession of the Worshipful Company of Goldsmiths at Goldsmiths' Hall. Although the south transept of St Paul's is more correctly rendered in this version (perhaps using Hollar's engravings), at almost every other point – for instance, the blocks of medieval houses on London Bridge and the churches of St Mary-le-Bow and St Magnus the Martyr – it is more generalised and summary in its topography, while the three-storey block of tenements on London Bridge has been reduced to two storeys, and the churches of St Dunstan-in-the-West and St Bride's are omitted altogether. The absence of any of the painterly qualities of the Museum painting also suggests that the Goldsmiths' canvas is not by the same hand and perhaps somewhat later in date.

A view of the Great Fire derived from this composition (panel, 47.7 x 75 cm) is in the National Maritime Museum; this painting, though either near-contemporary or early eighteenth-century in date, has little archaeological accuracy, and was probably executed by a Dutch artist unfamiliar with London itself. The existence of a late eighteenth- or early nineteenth-century version of this composition, a watercolour in the Atlas Van Stolk collection in Rotterdam (cat. no. 2350), suggests that yet another version of this painting may have existed, recorded in this drawing.

The late seventeenth-century frame is most likely to be the original frame for the painting. It is presumably English, although such frames were also produced in Holland. It is pine, carved with running oak leaves and acorns as well as flowers bound with undulating ribbon, with acanthus leaves in the corners. It has its original oil gilding.

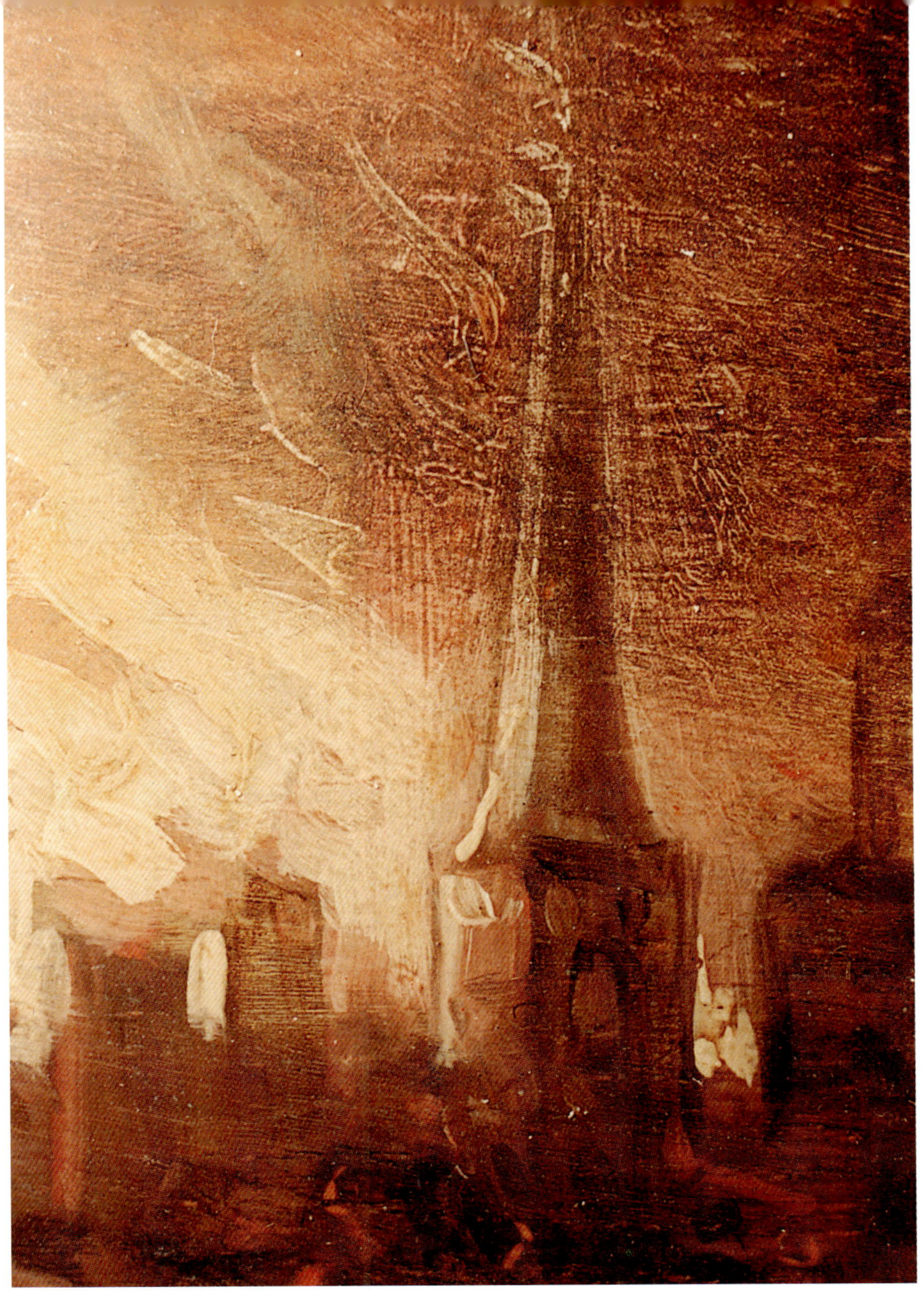

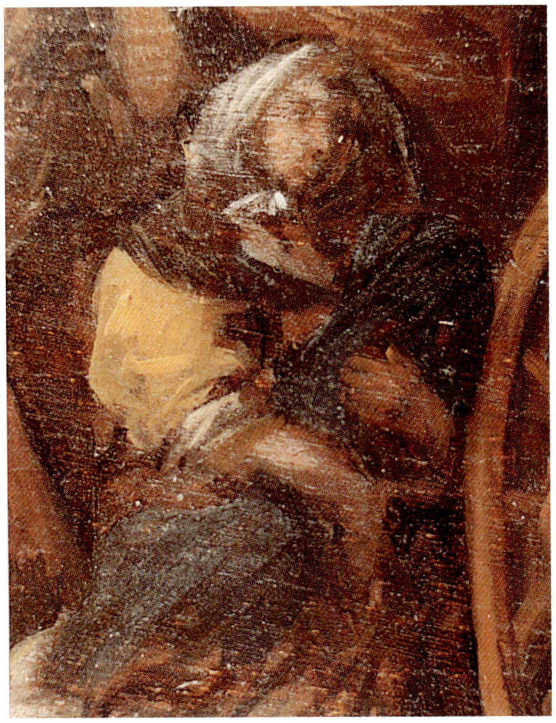

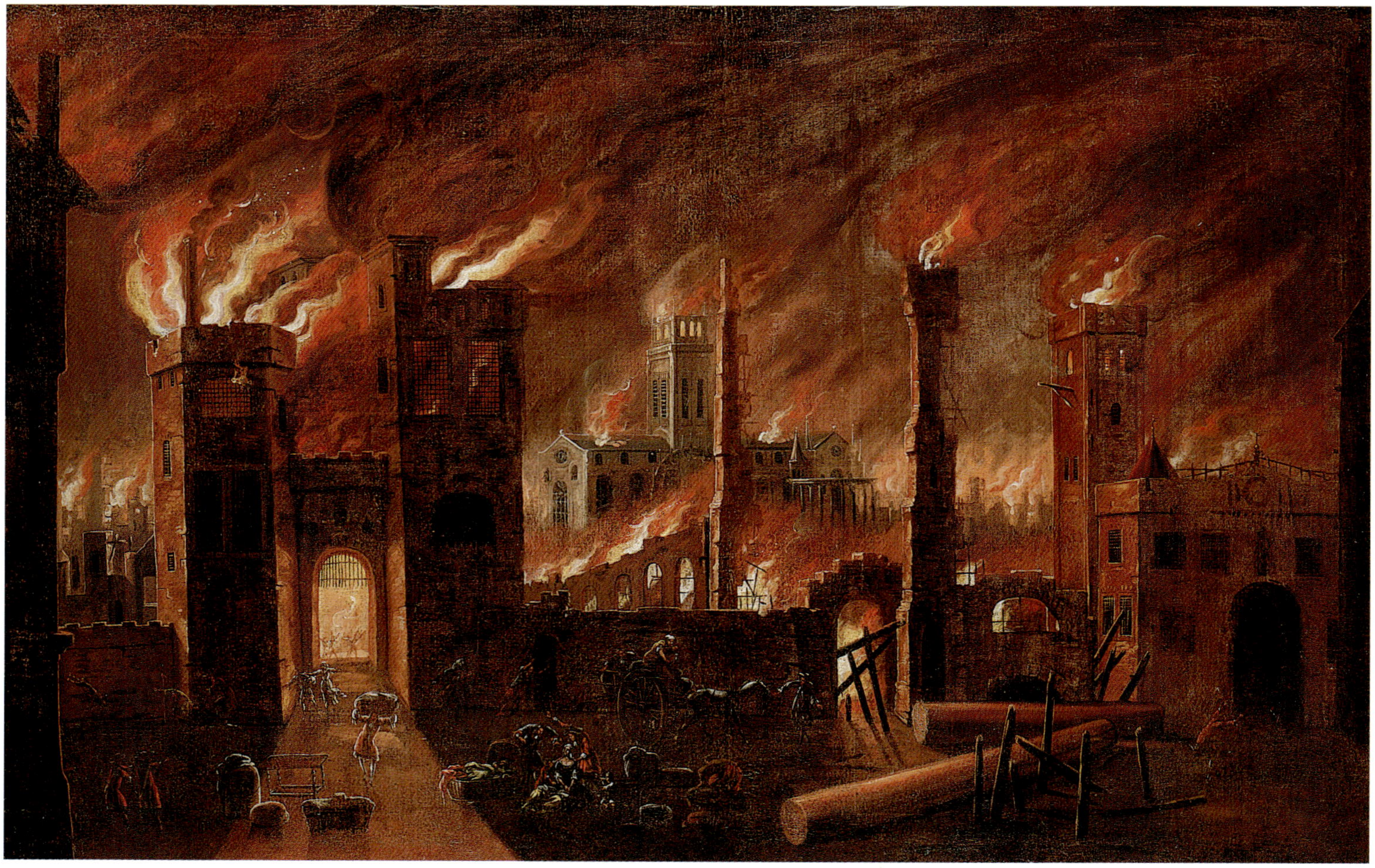

Provenance:
Mr Hollister, Cheltenham, *c.*1830–40; Hollister sale, Assembly Rooms, Cheltenham, *c.*1886 (no bid); acquired from the auctioneers in 1910 by William Jones, who presented it to the Museum in 1927 (without attribution).

Bibliography:
Hayes (cat. no. 152).

9.
AFTER JAN GRIFFIER THE ELDER
(c.1645/?52–1718)

The Great Fire of London, 1666 [27.142]
*c.*1675
Oil on canvas, 103.1 x 165 cm
Not signed or dated
Inscription recorded on the back of the canvas (which is no longer there): *Burning of London, by Lgi… A.D. Sept. 2nd 1666*

THESE TWO works derive from the painting by Jan Griffier the Elder which is mentioned in Vertue. If the original painting has survived, its present whereabouts are unknown, but it was recorded in an undated early nineteenth-century lithograph published by W. Birch after an 'original painting in the possession of Robert Golden'. It includes the signature *J. GRIFFIER* on a piece of masonry to the right. George Vertue recorded of Griffier that 'the Grandson of him. told me he had heard His Grandfather came into England. soon after the Fire of London 1666 and that he had painted some views of London

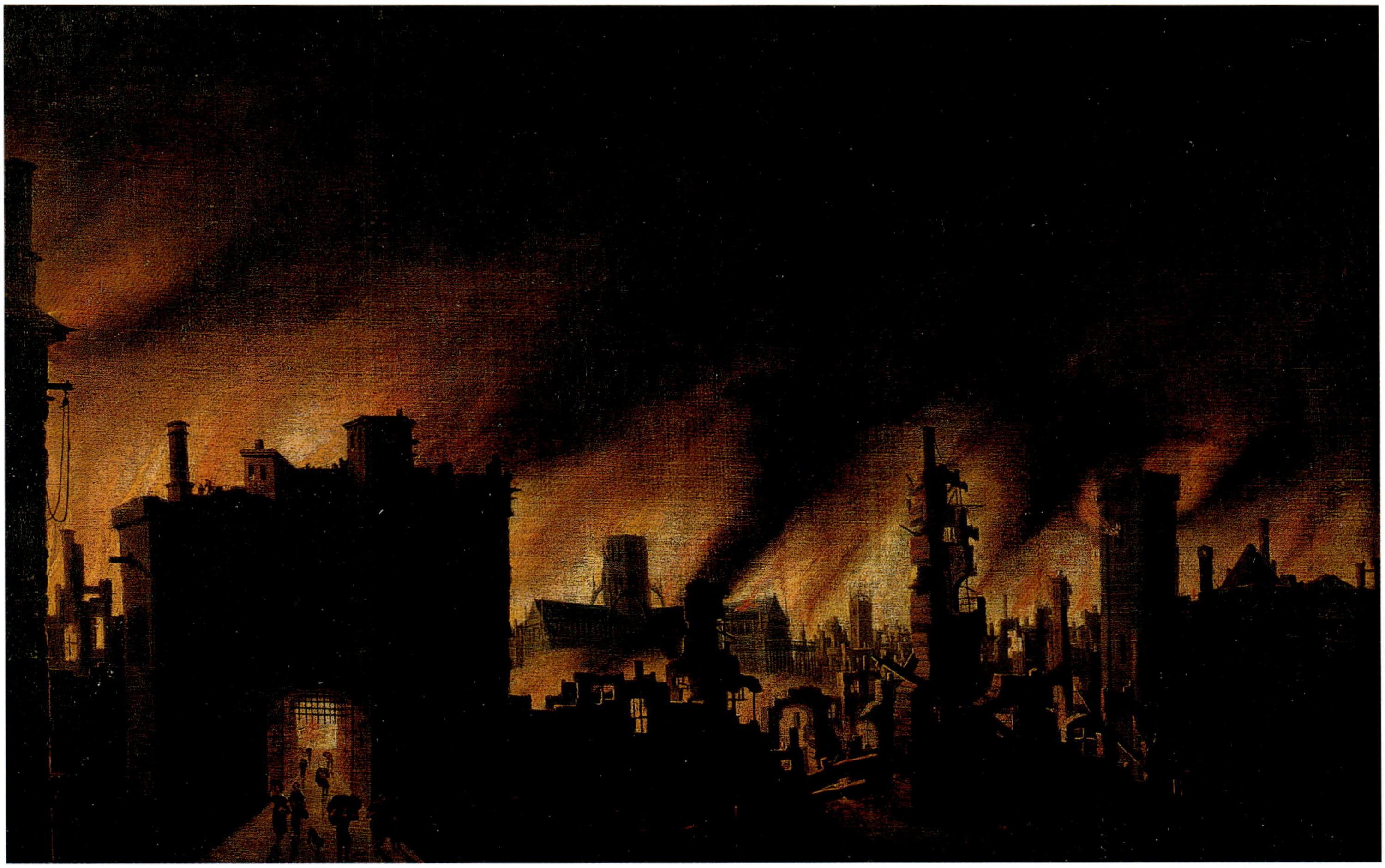

10.

AFTER JAN GRIFFIER THE ELDER

(c.1645/?52–1718)

The Great Fire of London, 1666 [51.53]

Date unknown

Oil on canvas, 74.2 x 115.3 cm

Not signed or dated

Provenance:
Miss Brougham Thompson; Thompson sale, Christie's, 2 August 1951 (101, as Jan Griffier); bt National Art Collections Fund, by whom it was presented to the Museum.

Bibliography:
Hayes (cat. no. 48); George Vertue 'Note Books', in *Walpole Society*, vol. 26, 1938, p69.

about that Time. representing the City on Fire' (George Vertue 'Note Books'). None of these views is certainly identifiable.

The topography of the Griffier image as rendered in the Birch print is most cogent (illustrated). The view is looking at St Paul's and the Great Fire and is clearly taken from a viewpoint in Blackfriars slightly south of Ludgate (the only visual record of this gate). We are therefore looking from a slightly oblique viewpoint at the west facade of St Paul's and its south transept. On the right are the ruins of the church of St Anne, Blackfriars (the ruins may show part of the friary on which it was based) and in the distance the soaring tower of St Lawrence Pountney, one of the highest in the City (also shown in the *London from Southwark* view, cat. no. 3).

The views which derive from this work are considerably less accurate: the distance between Ludgate and St Anne's has been so confusingly widened that Ludgate is mistakenly labelled Newgate and St Anne's, Ludgate; St Paul's has been turned on its axis to the point of impossibility; the south transept has been elongated and the steeple of St Lawrence now vaguely resembles that of St Mary-le-Bow, another impossibility from the angle chosen.

Probably the most important difference between the two paintings under review is the distance the artist places between himself and his subject. The 'distant' painting can be identified with the painting engraved in Robert Wilkinson's *Londina Illustrata* and published on 7 August 1811. The original work was in the possession of a Mr Lawrence of High Timber Street, Queenhithe (and later Mrs Lawrence of Thames Street) and is there described as being 'on a comparatively small scale'. No attribution is given by Wilkinson.

The other painting came into the collection badly damaged but deserves to be re-evaluated: it is probably one of the most striking images that was produced of the fire, and the sensation of being right in the middle of it breaks new ground and looks forward to the next artistic phase, when artists chose to take a closer look at London.

The figures in both paintings are small and elusively dressed, but the figures in the close-up version (acc. no. 27.142) can still be dated between *c.*1670 and 1678. Although the costume is not overly fashionable, the lines of the coats, the fullness of the breeches, the curve of the hats, the narrowness of the skirts and details such as length of sleeve and arrangement of shirts all point to a date around 1675.

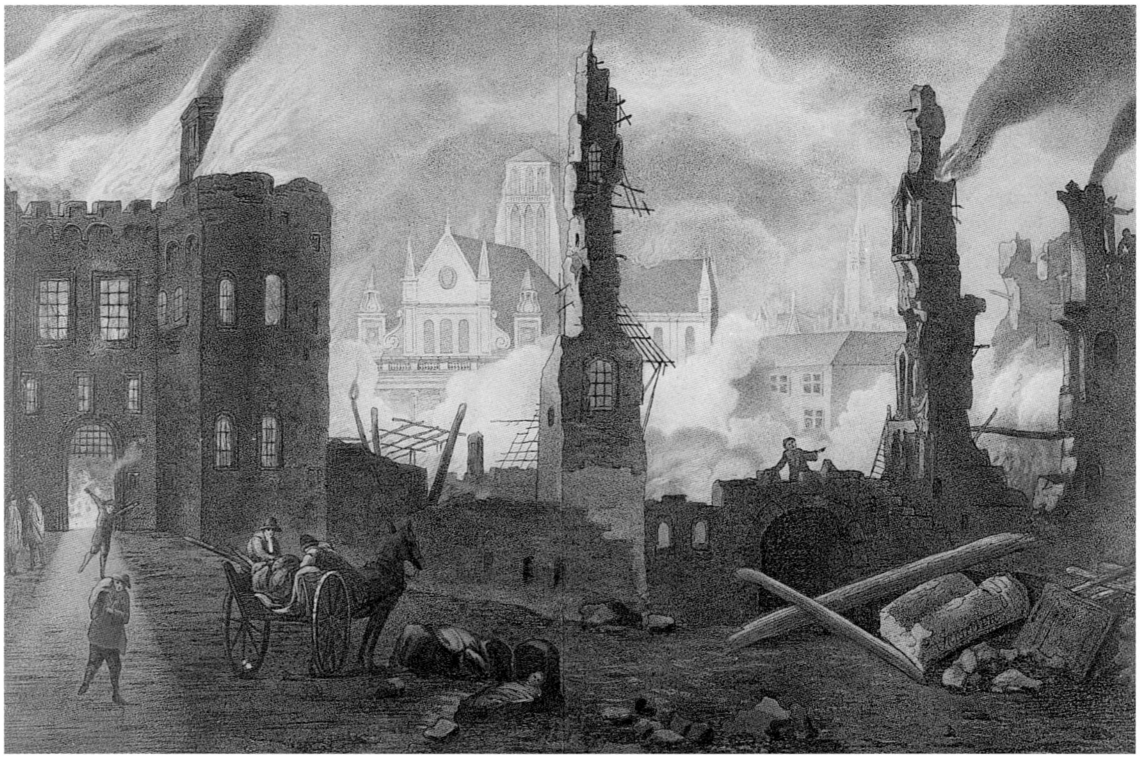

After Jan Griffier the Elder
Great Fire of London at Ludgate, 1666.
Lithograph Publ. W. Birch, early 19th century.
Museum of London.

11.

ANGLO-DUTCH SCHOOL

The Great Fire of London [95.313]
*c.*1666
Oil on canvas, 38.7 x 48.5 cm
Not signed or dated

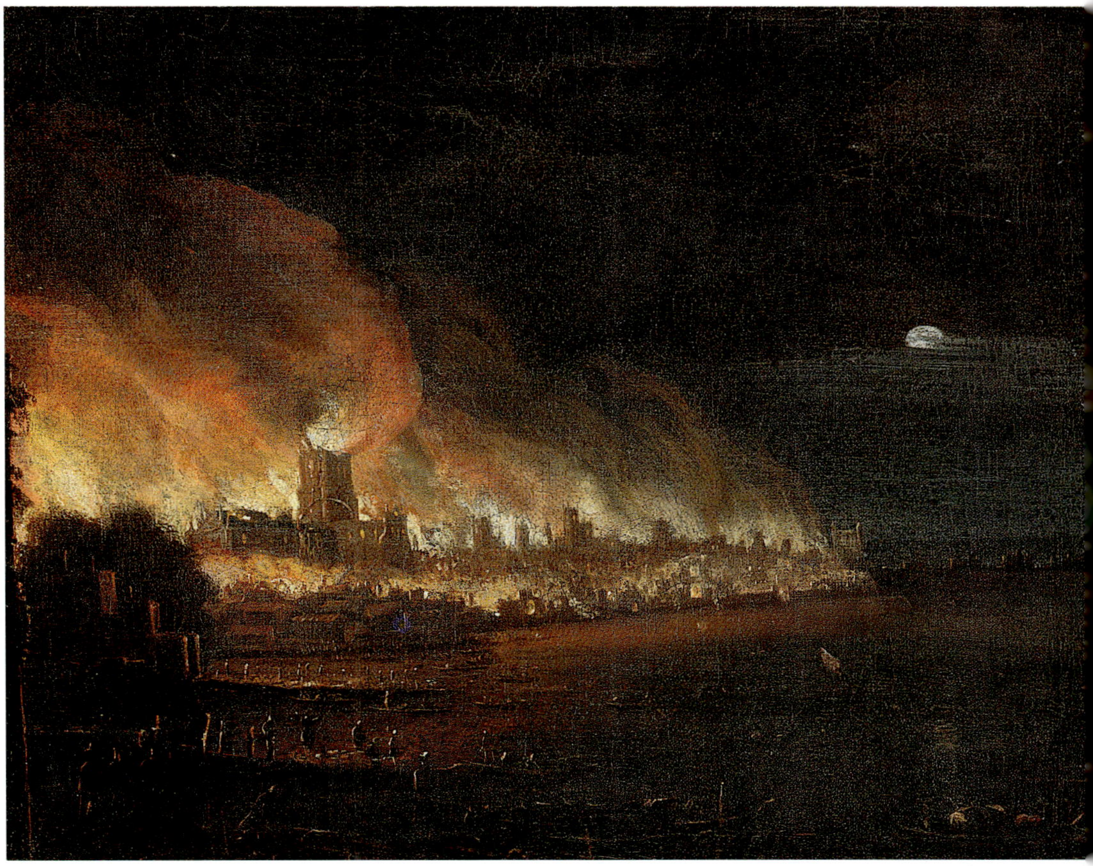

THIS PAINTING of the Great Fire belongs to the category of views taken from the west (see p32). It is taken from Essex Stairs and several landmarks may be identified from left to right. The sliver of tall balustraded wall at the edge of the painting belongs to Essex Buildings (a frontal view of these may be found in cat. no. 16) adjacent to Essex Stairs. The next stairs are Temple Stairs and they are placed in front of a dark area which represents the trees of Temple Gardens. The area of the riverbank which appears to project towards the middle of the picture may show Bridewell Dock, which had been flattened by the time of John Overton's map of 1676. London Bridge closes the perspective on the right-hand side. The ruined City does not readily match the most reliable visual records available to us, those of Hollar. For instance, the easily identifiable church spire of St Mary-le-Bow cannot be identified here and the shell of Baynard's Castle on the riverfront is missing.

This painting appears to offer an almost 'Impressionist' rendering of the subject. Although the City's buildings are represented in a two-tiered fashion, and this follows the formula adopted in all versions of this view, the artist here has not used the artificial and inaccurate device of placing the City on a hill. As a result of this and the rapid technique, we are left with the impression of its being a most vivid depiction of the Great Fire. If we combine this observation with the small size of the painting, it is possible to suggest that this may have been an almost 'on the spot' study intended to be subsequently developed in the studio, allowing the artist to introduce accurate topographical landmarks (working from published engravings) and also to 'improve' on certain compositional devices, moving away from the original rendering of the scene. Could this painting have been at the source of the views from the west that have come down to us?

This painting was analysed scientifically and showed the presence of lead tin yellow among the pigments and the use of a double ground structure, both of which are consistent with seventeenth-century techniques.

Provenance:
(...) John Gough Nichols (1806–73); J. Farthing (...); Henry Spencer (Retford, Notts), November 1984 (168, as van der Poel); Dennis Hall (Doncaster); Sotheby's 13 July 1994 (101), unsold; Sotheby's 12 July 1995 (119), bt Miles Cato; purchased by the Museum in 1995.

Bibliography:
Nicholas Eastaugh, 'A technical report on a painting depicting the Great Fire of London and its comparison to other seventeenth-century topographical paintings in the collection of the Museum of London', unpublished report commissioned by the Museum of London, 16 January 1996, ref. 95365.1.

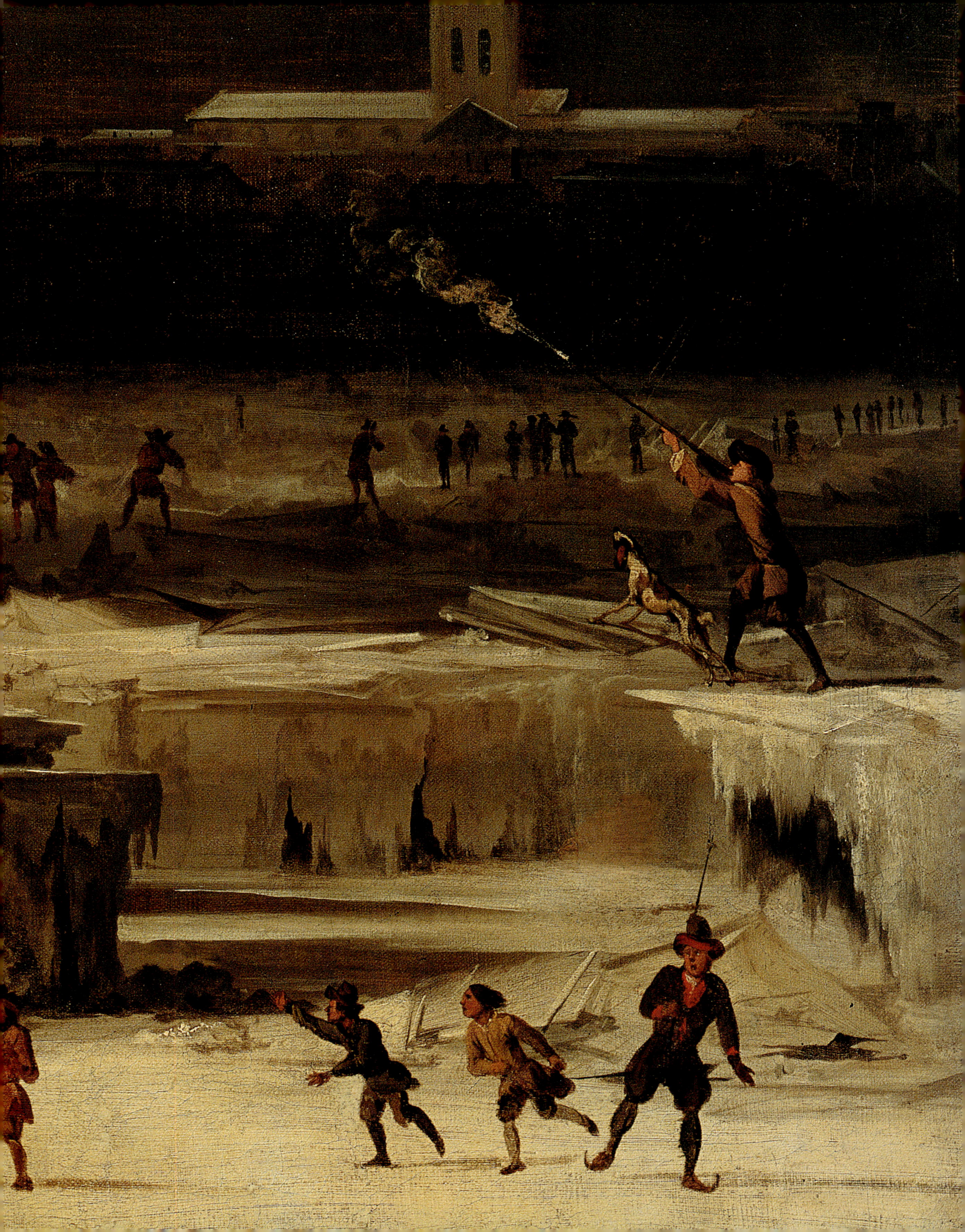

AFTER 1666

AFTER ELEVEN years of Parliamentary rule, the return of the monarchy in 1661 made a considerable impact on the artistic scene. Paintings associated with the coronation of Charles II were discussed in the first section (see cat. no. 7), but there was a second wave of grand royal paintings in the early 1670s. Perhaps prompted by the attempted theft of the crown jewels in 1671 (see cat. no. 12), Charles II appeared eager to be portrayed as a glorious monarch and painters such as John Michael Wright, Godfrey Kneller and Sir Peter Lely were employed to further the royal cause. The painting of the regalia of Charles II should be seen in that context. However, despite the ostentatious display of royal symbols, the former self-confidence of the monarchy had been profoundly shaken and Titus Oates had no difficulty convincing everyone of a 'Popish plot' and conspiracy against the King's life. His fraud lasted seven years (1678–85), during which time he was responsible for the execution of thirty-five men (cat. no. 17).

We should not therefore be surprised to find that the general trend towards reinforcing the royal principle also affected cityscape painting: a new focal point was adopted. Although Hollar once again paved the way with *The Prospect of London and Westminster taken from Lambeth* (*c*.1643), it was Jan Griffier who developed a particularly successful formula for bird's-eye views taken from the Westminster/Lambeth area, in contrast to the Southwark and Strand viewpoints. This echoed the power shift from the City of London (which 'lost' the Civil War and was virtually destroyed in the Great Fire) to the city of Westminster. Even frost fairs migrated: the frost fair held immediately outside the Temple and therefore at the doors of the City in 1683–4 shifted to Westminster the next time it took place, in 1715–16. Jan Griffier painted the latter event with considerable skill, blending detail and panorama (Guildhall Art Gallery). The experiment was, however, rather short-lived, because the only successful paintings *from* Westminster are those *of* Westminster. The City is too far away for an embracing view to be completely successful and the formula was never properly adopted by other painters, although a number of paintings include certain panoramic elements in the background (see cat. no. 18). Lambeth Palace, conveniently situated across the river and a notable landmark which had so far been neglected, became the object of many paintings, prints and drawings.

At Greenwich, the site of London's other notable river palace, Jan Vosterman and Peter Tillemans continued the tradition of painting an area which offered the rare combination of being close to London and having both a strong royal connection and a beautiful landscape. This particular group of works is well represented in the collection of the National Maritime Museum.

However, it is also important to point out that, despite the resurgence of royal interests, the nature of art patronage changed after the Restoration. Charles I and his royal entourage had acted as a powerful magnet for the arts in the first half of the seventeenth century. After the Restoration a new market emerged based on the demands of the nobility.[1] We have already observed that the art market on the Continent operated on an 'off the shelf' basis (see p7), while in England it was firmly shaped by commissions, although the rise of the dealer may be charted around this time (see below).

The Museum's collection, on the other hand, has prime examples of early close-up views of the capital. There is a strong element of landscape in these early town views. The river, countryside and gardens rather than the fabric of London dominate the production. Knyff and Griffier, the artists the aristocracy favoured for recording their country seats, adapted to an urban setting the rich tradition of country-house views which had started with the trend for depicting royal palaces in the second quarter of the century.[2]

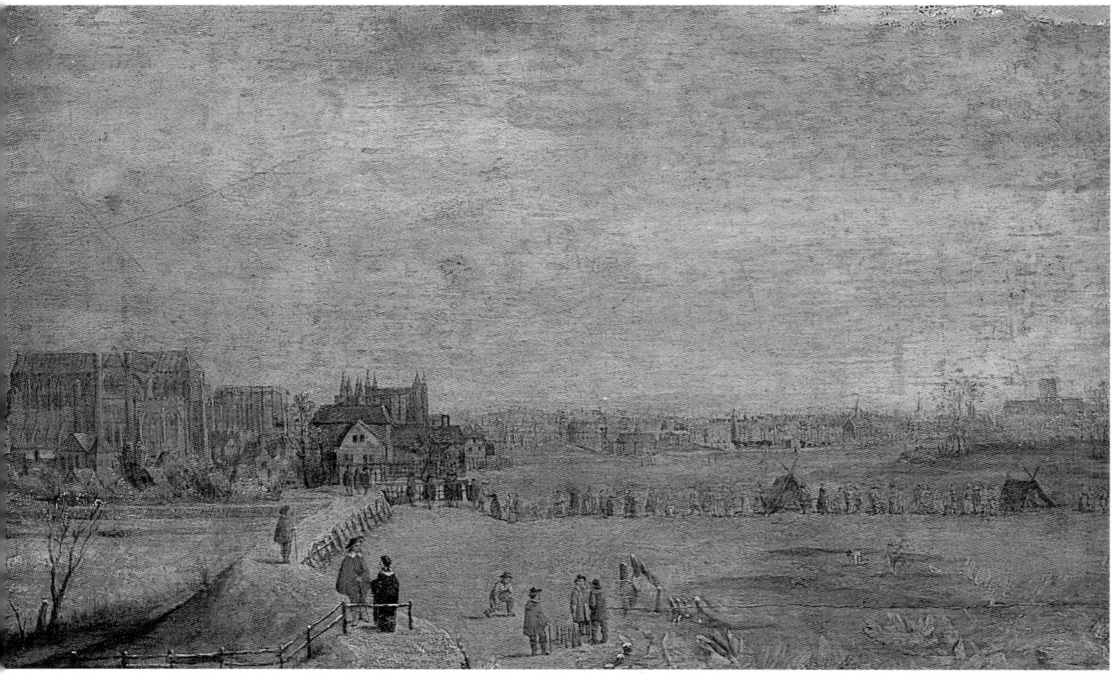

Anonymous
Frost Fair, 1649 or 1655 (?).
Oil on panel
(Sold at Sotheby's 13th April 1994, Lot 78).

Finally we should return to frost fairs, which today exercise a great deal of fascination and were particularly topical in the seventeenth century. These were among the first paintings (with those of the Great Fire) to record historical events outside royal and religious occasions. Although the first recorded frost fair – attended by Queen Elizabeth – was in 1565, painters did not attempt to tackle the theme in earnest until 1683–4 (see cat. no. 16), when the frost fair held in the second half of January was visited by Charles II and his family and commemorated in print by G. Croom, 'Printer on Ice'. However, a painting on panel recently came to light which clearly shows a pre-Fire frost fair near Westminster with Old St Paul's in the background.[3] On costume grounds the painting may be dated late 1640s or early 1650s, thus suggesting the frost fair of either 1649 or 1655. It is unexpected to find such an event during the Commonwealth, and further research would be needed to corroborate this evidence.

As was usefully pointed out,[4] these early frost fairs gave birth to a new genre in painting, the outcome of Anglo-Dutch cross-fertilisation. The generalised winter landscapes in vogue in the Netherlands gave way in London to those depicting specific events. The uniquely large depiction of the *Frozen Thames* by Hondius (see cat. no. 15), almost certainly a commissioned painting, points to the role played by patronage; the blend of genre painting and specific setting had already occurred in Joris Hoefnagel's *A Wedding in Bermondsey* (p5).

To return to the subject of fairs, we know that the river froze twenty-three times between 1620 and 1814 and that frost fairs were held on the Thames, in 1565, 1608, 1621, 1649, 1655 (see above), 1684, 1689, 1716, 1740, 1789 and 1814.[5] Since 1814 the Thames in London has never been completely frozen over; the last serious frost was recorded in paint (see cat. no. 84).

The emergence of specific views of London was undoubtedly linked to the emergence of an art market and the rise of the painter's profession. In the seventeenth century this process culminated with the staging in 1682 of the first London picture auction and the abolition in 1695 of the law banning imports of paintings.[6] The landscape painter Thomas Manby (fl.1672–95) was the first Englishman to set up as an independent dealer and in the 1670s one of Thomas Wyck's *Great Fire of London* paintings was available 'off the shelf' as part of Mr Fletcher's sale stock of thirty-six paintings.[7] London's first colourmen made their appearance in the third quarter of the seventeenth century, having broken away from their apothecary/grocer origins. 'Ye colour shop[s]' of Mr Phines could be found at Fleet Bridge, that of Mr Williams at Snow Hill and the 'Colour seller at St Luke's head without Temple Barr' was John Savage (active 1680–1700).[8]

Too little is known about the artists who shaped the production of London paintings at that time. What brought them to this country? How successful were they and what was the exact nature of their contribution to the London art scene? A recent Dutch initiative, based at the Universities of Delft and Rotterdam, may soon yield much long-awaited data.[9] It is worth pointing out here what was observed in Amsterdam inventories between the 1620s and 1670s: the decline in history and myth painting went hand in hand with the increase in landscapes and seascapes, *cityscapes* (my italics), and battle scenes from 17.2 per cent in the 1620s to 23.1 per cent in the 1630s and 34.5 per cent in the 1660s and 1670s.[10]

1. 'The Exchange of Ideas' in *Britain and the Netherlands*, Simon Groenveld and Michael Wintle (eds), Zutphen, Netherlands, 1994, vol. XI, p179.
2. John Harris, *The Artist and the Country House*, 1979.
3. Sold at Sotheby's on 13 April 1994 (78).
4. Groenveld and Wintle (eds), 1994, p169.
5. Edward Walford, *Frost Fairs on the Thames*, 1887 (privately printed); for a comprehensive list of cold winters, see H. H. Lamb, *Climate Past, Present and Future*, 1972.
6. Iain Pears, *The Discovery of Painting*, 1988, p57.
7. Ibid, p238.
8. For artists' supplies, see James Ayres, *The Artist's Craft*, 1985. In her 1992 Courtauld Institute Postgraduate thesis, Louisa Goldsmith usefully surveyed 'The Supply of Painting Materials in Seventeenth-Century London' (a copy was deposited at the Museum of London's Print Room). Rosanna Eadie also researched the subject in great detail and presented some of her findings at the 1993 Art History Conference, Tate Gallery.
9. Peter Hecht (Utrecht University) and Eric Sluijter (Leiden University) are conducting a research project on Dutch artists in England, with Leiden examining the pre-Restoration period and Utrecht the post-Restoration.
10. J. Michael Montias, *Artists and Artisans in Delft,* Princeton, New Jersey, 1982, p242; J. Michael Montias, 'Cost and value in seventeenth-century art, in *Art History*, vol. 10, December 1987.

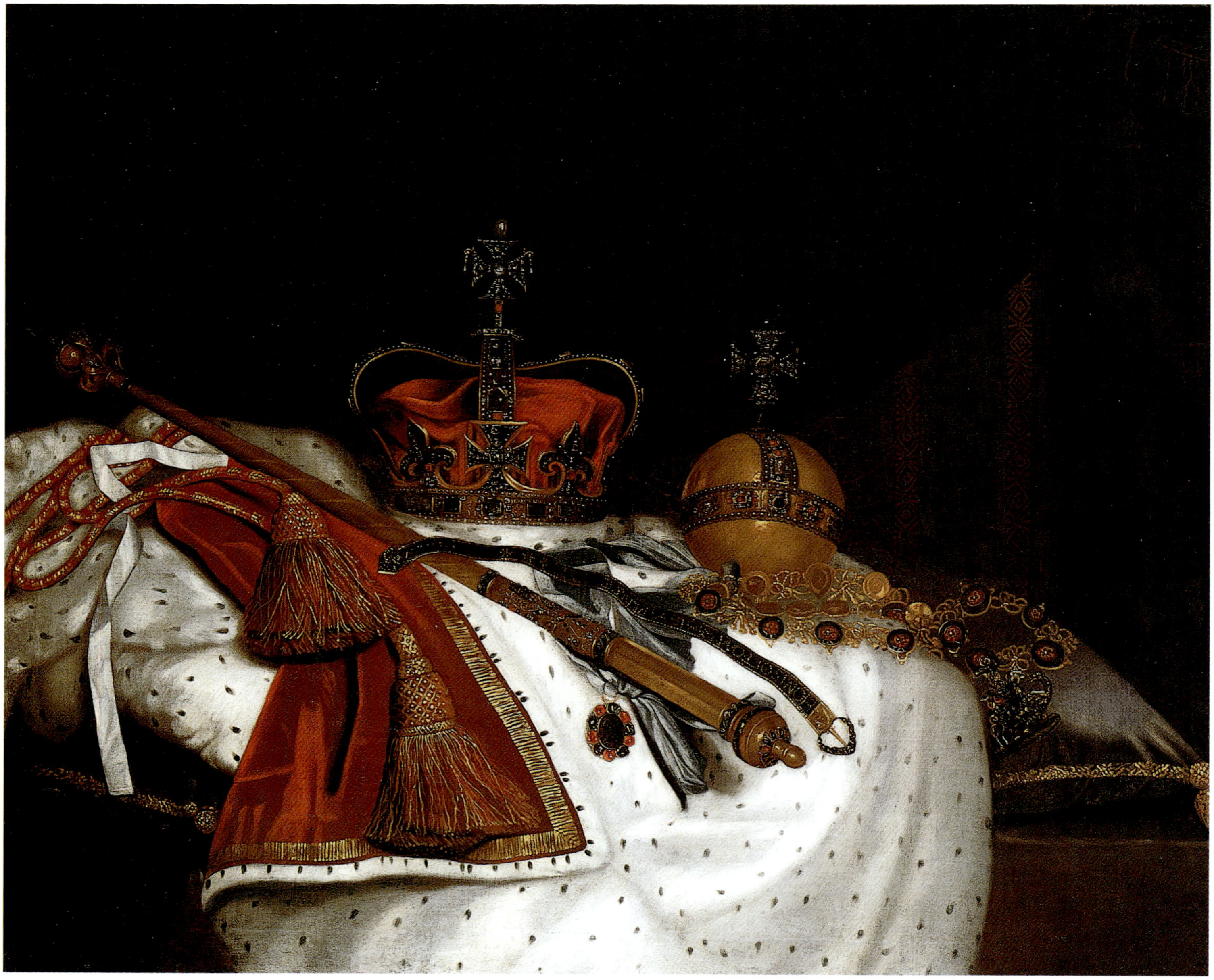

12.

BRITISH SCHOOL

Regalia of Charles II [90.344/2]
1670s
Oil on canvas, 103 x 128 cm
Not signed or dated

THIS STILL-LIFE painting shows part of the regalia of Charles II, with the Crown of State, the Royal Sceptre with its cross finial, the orb, the Garter, the Garter riband with the 'lesser George' and the Garter collar with the 'George', all resting on a cushion and what appears to be a loosely folded crimson parliamentary robe with red and gold cords ending in large tassels.

After Charles I was executed in 1649, the royal regalia was taken from Westminster Abbey to the Tower for destruction by order of Parliament. There is some evidence that this order was not entirely carried out and that St Edward's Crown, for instance, was remade from the surviving fragments of the medieval crown. Charles II commissioned the goldsmith Robert Vyner to restore the Royal Regalia to its former glory and most of the pieces shown here would have been crafted in his workshop. The sword(s), ampulla, anointing spoon (which survived the Civil War), sceptre with a dove finial, spurs and armills are missing from this still life.

The combination of the crimson robe and items of regalia worn and carried by monarchs in parliament with the insignia of the Order of the Garter is a telling one. The symbolism conveys the message that the head of state is, once more, an anointed monarch entitled by rank and inheritance to be head of one of the oldest orders of chivalry in Europe. It is no coincidence that the first chapter of the Order of the Garter for over twenty years was held shortly before Charles II's coronation on 23 April 1661. It was a positive signal that Charles II wished to reinstate all of those aspects of ceremonial monarchy associated with his father.

The ostentatious representation of royal attributes in painting was first found in Daniel Mytens's full-length portrait of Charles I (1631, National Portrait Gallery and studio copy at the National Maritime Museum). Peter Lely produced many portraits of Charles II, some of which similarly include the crown and sceptre. However, the still life under review most certainly aims to anchor or reinforce the return of the monarchy and has no connection with the contemporary royal still-life paintings of the London-based painter Evert Collier. The latter brings out the *vanitas* element in his royal compositions, often by making specific (retrospective) references to the doomed Charles I.

The objects in the Museum painting follow closely those depicted by the painter John Michael Wright in *Charles II Enthroned* (Royal Collection). Alterations and adjustments made to the actual objects for subsequent coronations would account for the differences between the objects that have come down to us and those shown in the two paintings. The significant role played by the Garter in both paintings and costume details in the Wright painting point to the 1670s rather than 1661, the year of the coronation (see the discussion on dating in the Wright catalogue). The wig, triangular and very full, with tight corkscrew curls, comes into fashion only in the early 1670s. The shoes and the cravat with its deep band of lace can only be comfortably dated *c.*1670. The cushion on which the King's feet rest can also be dated to the 1670s.

The Museum's work is also clearly associated with another still life (in the collection of the Guildhall Art Gallery): *The Insignia of the City of London* shows on a velvet cushion the collar of SS, the crystal sceptre, the pearl sword, the mace and fur cap of maintenance (acc. no. 1256). Compositionally the two paintings look as if they were meant to hang side by side. While *The Regalia* promotes the return of the monarchy, the existence of *The Insignia* would suggest that the recently opposed camps of Westminster and the City are being put on the same footing. Both paintings have been attributed to Pieter Gerritz van Roestraeten. George Vertue, when he discussed the paintings at Lord Radnor's house in St James's which were sold after his death on 28 April 172–, wrote: 'Some of Roestrate particularly the original Crown Mond & scepter, painted by him from the Regalia in the Tower'

Provenance:
Sheppard, Esq.; gift to Basingstoke Town Hall in 1765; Sotheby's 24 February 1965 (1), bt Lady Bonham Carter, who bequeathed it to the Museum in 1990.

Bibliography:
Martin Holmes, *The English Regalia*, 1972; *The King's Painter, John Michael Wright*, Scottish National Portrait Gallery exhibition catalogue, September 1982; *The Crown Jewels*, ed. Claude Blair, 2 vols, (forthcoming HMSO publication).

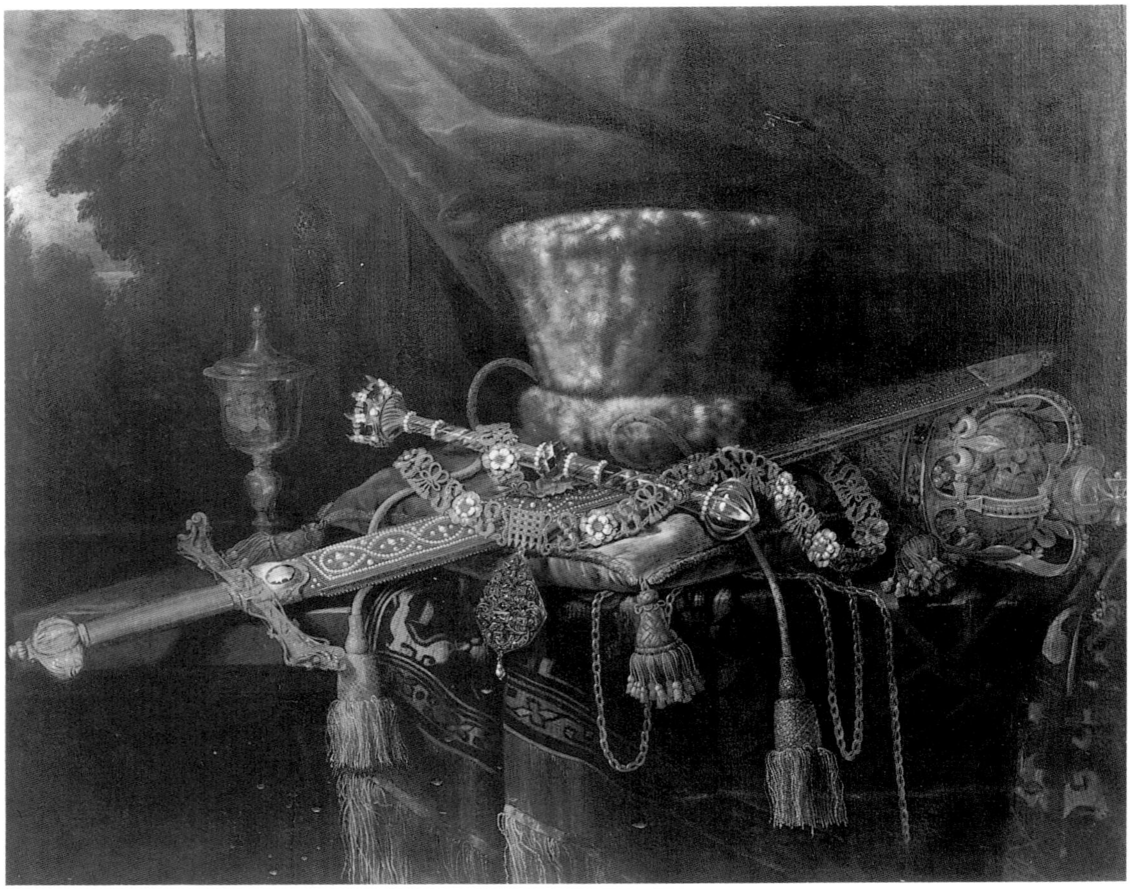

Pieter Gerritz Roestraten
(1630–1700)
The Insignia of the City of London.
Oil on canvas
Guildhall Art Gallery,
Corporation of London.

(George Vertue 'Note Books', vol. I, p132). The Museum of London and Guildhall paintings, however, are clearly by different hands. The Museum's painting, not of exceptional quality, is likely to be based on the Roestraeten prototype, perhaps the painting hanging in the ante-library at Longleat, although its format and execution differ from the *Insignia* painting; the Longleat version is an over-door painting which forms part of a complete sequence of eight over-door still-life paintings in the ante-library. Edward Harley, 2nd Earl of Oxford, is also known to have bought a 'picture of a Crown and Septer by Roostrate' before 1724.

The connection with the City is of great interest because a similar connection has also been suggested with the Wright painting. 'I am told the King will sitt to my great picture for the Citty next moneth', wrote the painter to Sir Walter Bagot on 27 July 1676. Unfortunately there are no records in the City Corporation Records Office which enable us to develop this interesting point.

It is possible that the attempted theft by Colonel Thomas Blood of the Crown Jewels on 9 May 1671 may have prompted a renewed interest in the emblems of Royalty and that both Wright's painting and this one came out of its aftermath. Maybe the Regalia painting was painted as some kind of *aide-mémoire* to help Wright with his commission without disturbing the jewels?

The early 1670s also saw the publication by Ashmole of *The Institution, Laws and Ceremonies of the Most Noble Order of the Garter* (1672), which, patronised by the King, surveyed in great detail the reformed Order. The same year Charles II's statue trampling the body of Oliver Cromwell was unveiled in the Stocks Market (a conversion of a statue of the King of Poland trampling on the Turk!). A year later, in 1673, Robert Vyner, the leading City goldsmith who made the Regalia, also commissioned John Michael Wright to paint a grand family portrait at Swakeleys, the Vyners' house in Middlesex; this work is now in the National Portrait Gallery.

We may one day be able to connect all these different strands. A later version of the painting was sold at Christie's on 18 November 1988 (93), attributed to Francis Pike or J. Arnold.

The Museum's painting was once in the collection of Basingstoke Town Council and formed part of a group of paintings associated with the Restoration (the others being portraits of Prince Rupert, Charles II, General Monck and Sir Matthew Hale) which were sold at Sotheby's in 1965. In 1864 Samuel Leech traced them to a *c.*1765 gift of 'Sheppard, Esq. who then lived at Old Basing' to the Mayor and Corporation of Basingstoke. A 1958 newspaper cutting suggested:

> 'It would appear that the original owner of the pictures was also intimately concerned in the events which led up to the restoration of the Stuart dynasty, and probably came from one of the great mansions. It has been suggested that the pictures were loot taken at the sacking of Basing House.'

Since the latter took place in 1645, the information is unlikely to be correct; the article went on attributing some of the works to Peter Lely (including *The Regalia*).

The Museum has Britain's first coronation mugs, associated with Charles II.

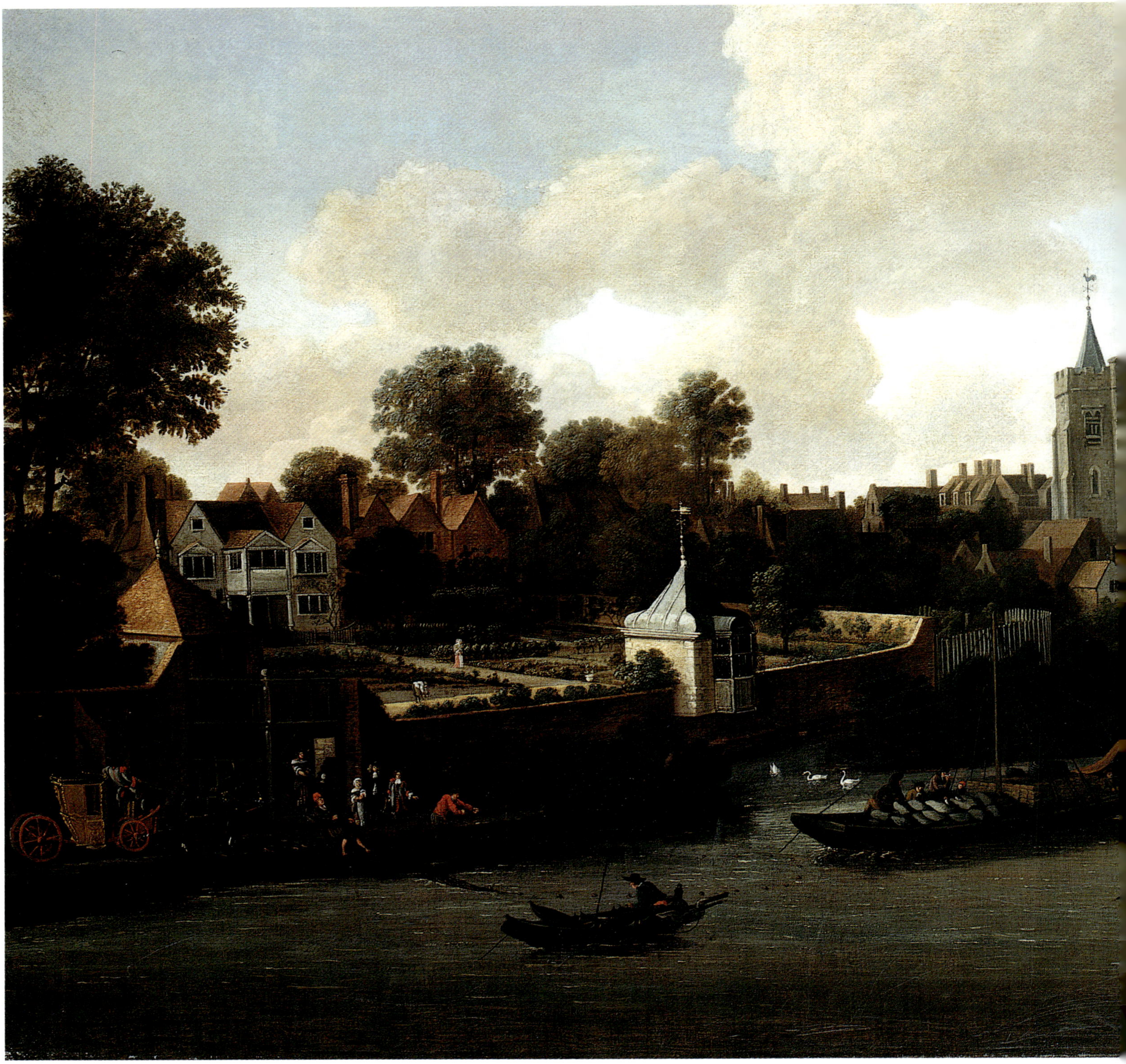

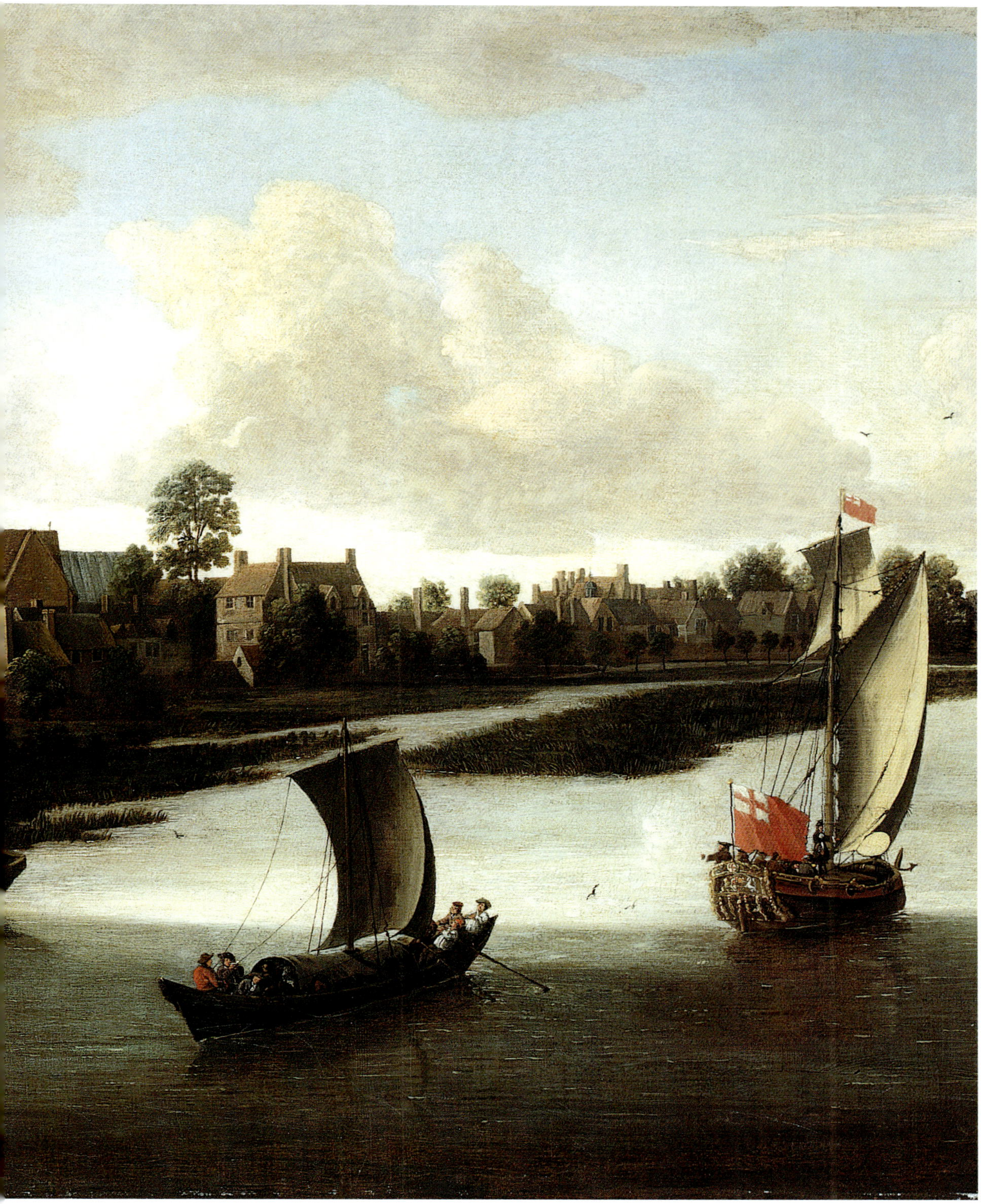

13.

JACOB KNYFF

(1639–81)

Chiswick from the River

[62.32]

*c.*1675–80.

Oil on canvas,

81.9 x 159.4 cm

Not signed or dated

Provenance:
Purchased out of the Joicey Trust Fund with a contribution from the National Art Collections Fund, from Frank T. Sabin in 1962 (as Jan Wyck).

Bibliography:
Hayes (cat. no. 61); John Harris, *The Artist and the Country House*, pp44 and 62; J. B. C. Chatelain, *Fifty Small Original and Elegant Views of the Most Splendid Churches, Villages, Rural Prospects and Masterly Pieces of Architecture Adjacent to London*, 1750.

THE EARLIEST known view of Chiswick, showing, from left to right, Old Corney House, a property acquired by John Russell, 1st Earl of Bedford, in 1542; the parish church of St Nicholas, surrounded by a cluster of sixteenth-century houses; and Chiswick Eyot, with some larger Tudor houses on the waterfront beyond. A chariot has drawn up on the left, and a group of people are watching two fishermen dragging nets. A fishing boat is close by, and a barge laden with merchandise is stationary beyond; another craft is sailing past, and on the right a barge bearing the arms of the City Corporation, and flying its flag and pennant, is firing a salute.

The painting is also important because it shows the first painted London garden. Its layout contrasts with that of John Evelyn at Sayes Court, Deptford, the major contemporary garden for this period, recorded in a detailed plan with a key. While Evelyn's garden is in the tradition of the grand, 'comprehensive' gardens of this country, this painting offers a rare early glimpse of a truly urban garden, its size adapted to a capital setting. With its Jacobean summer-house overlooking the Thames, an enduring feature for this and subsequent periods, this arrangement looks forward to eighteenth-century river schemes, for instance, the Chinese pavilion of Montagu House, also overlooking the Thames between London and Westminster bridges (see Tessa Murdoch in *Country Life*, 24 January 1991, pp58–9).

An engraving published on 29 September 1750, by J. Roberts after J. B. C. Chatelain, shows the extent to which Chiswick had already changed since Knyff's painting. Old Corney House had been replaced by New Corney House, an early Georgian mansion, and the houses beyond the Eyot had been pulled down for the formation of the Mall (many of the fine Georgian houses built along the Mall still survive there, and the name Bedford House preserves the memory of the owners of Corney House). The church was rebuilt and the tower restored and altered in 1836; today timber yards and warehouses stand upon the site of Corney House; and the Eyot is covered with thick bushes, so that hardly anything remains now of the topography recorded in this view.

Part of the site of Old Corney House was excavated by Museum of London archaeologists in the 1980s (site supervisor: John Lewis, code LEP89). Some of the house's timber-lined drains were recovered as well as a (later?) brick-built cellar.

The attribution of the painting to Jacob Knyff rests on its close similarity in style to the view of Durdans House, Epsom, signed and dated 1673, at Berkeley Castle: the darkness of tone and feeling for chiaroscuro, the coarseness of touch generally, and the minutiae of handling, are exactly alike in both works. The costume of the figures on the left indicates a date of about 1675–80.

14.
STUDIO OF WILLIAM WISSING
(1656–87)

Portrait of Mary of Modena (1658–1718)
[60.17]
1676–85
Oil on canvas, 74.4 x 62.5 cm
Inscribed bottom right: *Maria. Beatrix./Dutchess of York*

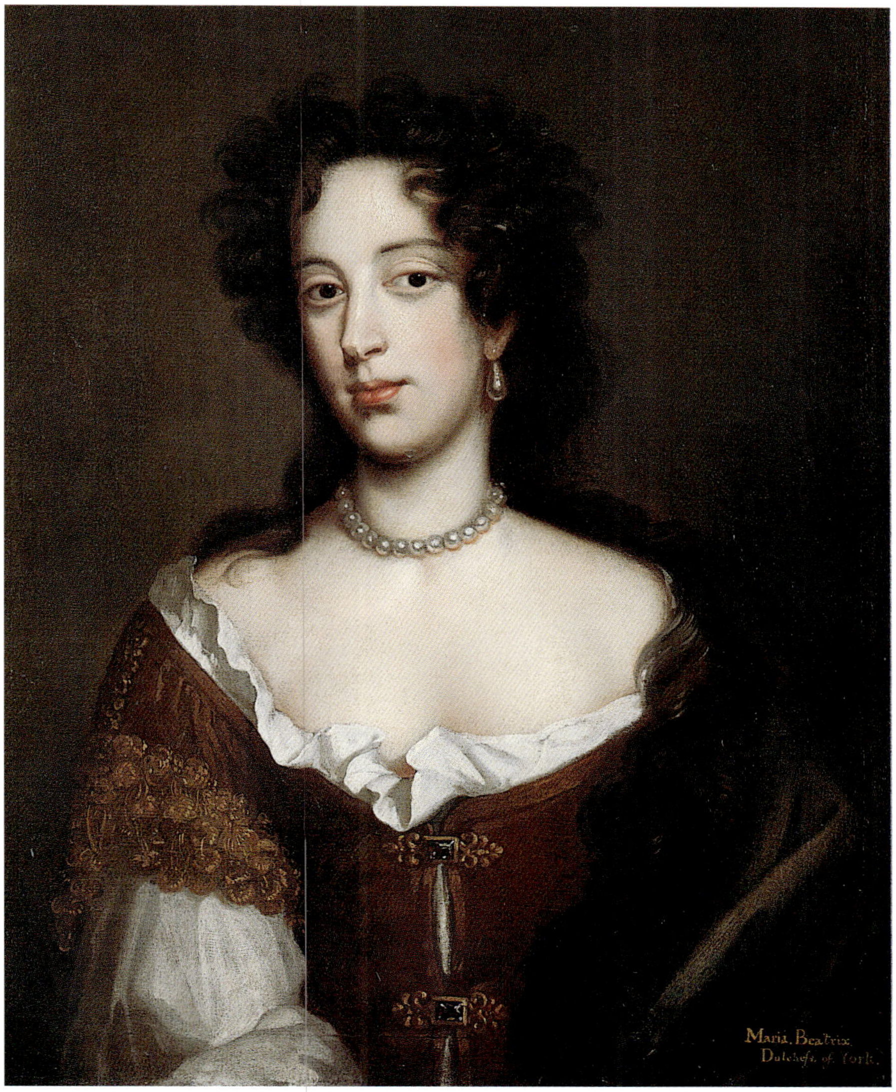

THE SITTER is shown half-length facing the spectator, with her head turned slightly to left. The background is plain. Mary of Modena, who was married by proxy to James, Duke of York (later James II) in her native city on 30 September 1673, is portrayed here as Duchess of York. The date of the Museum picture must lie between Wissing's arrival in this country in 1676 and the Duchess's accession to the throne as Queen Consort in 1685. Wissing was much employed by James both before and after his accession, and he is known to have painted several portraits of Mary of Modena, most of them following this pattern down to the earring and the fall of the hair; the version in the National Portrait Gallery is an exact repetition of the design, but extended to three-quarter length. This is the only surviving painting showing Mary of Modena as Duchess of York.

The state bed of James II and Mary of Modena is also in the Museum (36.239).

Provenance:
Presented by HRH Princess Alice, Countess of Athlone, in 1960.

Bibliography:
Hayes (cat. no. 126);
K. K. Young *National Portrait Gallery – Complete Illustrated catalogue*, 1981, no. 214.

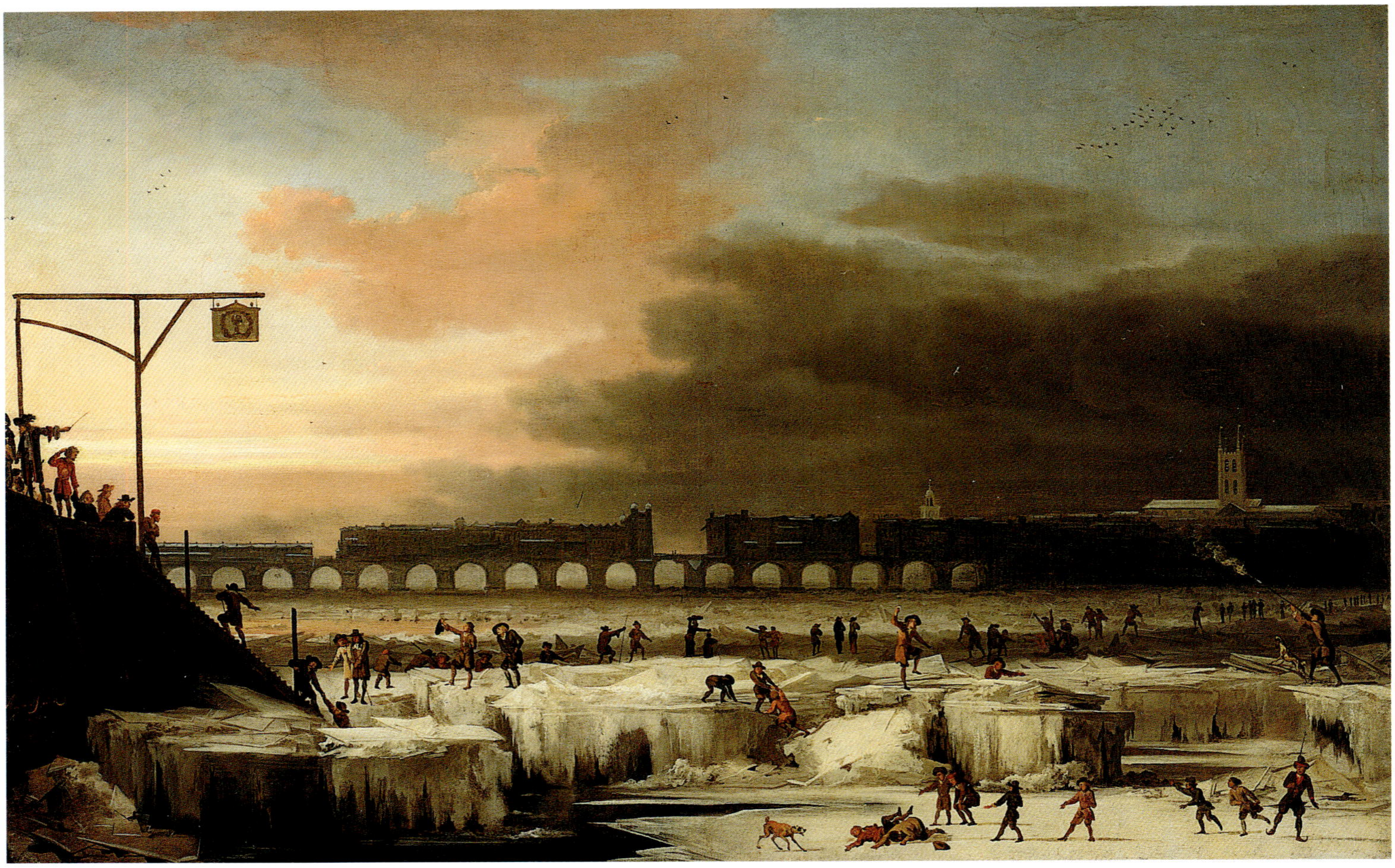

Provenance:
Sir James Rawlins, Syston Court, Mangotsfield, Bristol; J. E. Rawlins sale, Norfolk and Prior, 21 May 1935 (183, reproduced); purchased from Spink by the National Art Collections Fund with a contribution from Owen H. Smith and presented to the Museum.

15.

ABRAHAM HONDIUS

(c.1625/30–91)

The Frozen Thames [35.190]

1677

Oil on canvas, 107.8 x 175.6 cm

Signed and dated lower left:

Abraham Hondius/Ao 1677

NUMEROUS FIGURES are shown amusing themselves on the frozen river, skating (the figure on the right wears Dutch skates), sliding, snowballing and even shooting. The view is probably meant to be taken from Old Swan Stairs (with a temporarily redundant waterman standing at the top of the stairs); it is looking east and is reminiscent of the composition by Richard Garth in the Bodleian Library (see p5). The sign depicting a Dutch cup with a hop (?) wreath has not been identified but may refer to that of a tavern or brewery, many of which lined that part of the Thames. Old London Bridge is seen in the middle distance, with beyond it, part of the tower of St Olave's Tooley Street (rebuilt by Flitcroft 1738, after it had fallen into serious disrepair) and Southwark Cathedral. In common with most other seventeenth-century painters, Hondius has drawn the pointed arches of Old London Bridge incorrectly, as almost rounded and of more or less equal width; and the block of houses seen on the left, which replaced those burnt in the fire of 1632–3, should be of greater height. The stairs in the left foreground greatly exaggerate the height even of those along the City waterfront, and are presumably imaginary.

The frost depicted is evidently that of December 1676, which began to break on 3 January 1677, and the date of the scene shown here must, therefore, be the very beginning of January 1677 (since the picture is dated that year). Hondius has depicted the state of the ice with great accuracy. The tall floes with almost sheer sides, separated by narrow channels, have been exaggerated by the artist but are characteristic of an accumulation of snow on a basis of thin ice, and this was the sequence of events in 1676. A covering of thin ice had formed by 12 December, when there was a heavy fall of snow (Evelyn called it 'so great a snow, as I remember not to have ever seene the like'), followed by another on 19 December. People first began to cross the ice on 31 December, and it is recorded that on 1 January 1677 'hundreds passed over the Thames'. The ice was not thick enough, however, for any sustained activity of the kind that occurred in 1683–4 (see cat. no. 16).

The last occasions on which the Thames froze were in 1813–14 and 1895 (see cat. no. 84), and it was partly as a result of the dangers to which Old London Bridge became subject from the pressure of the ice in the freeze of 1813–14 that the bridge was finally pulled down. Its replacement was designed so that its arches did not impede the flow of water in the way that the arches of the old bridge had always done.

Hondius's *Arctic Adventure* painting in the Fitzwilliam Museum confirms this artist's interest in the depiction of frozen waters. There the treatment of the ice is reminiscent of that in his *Frozen Thames*. However, in size and mood the Fitzwilliam picture is closer to the *Frost Fair* below.

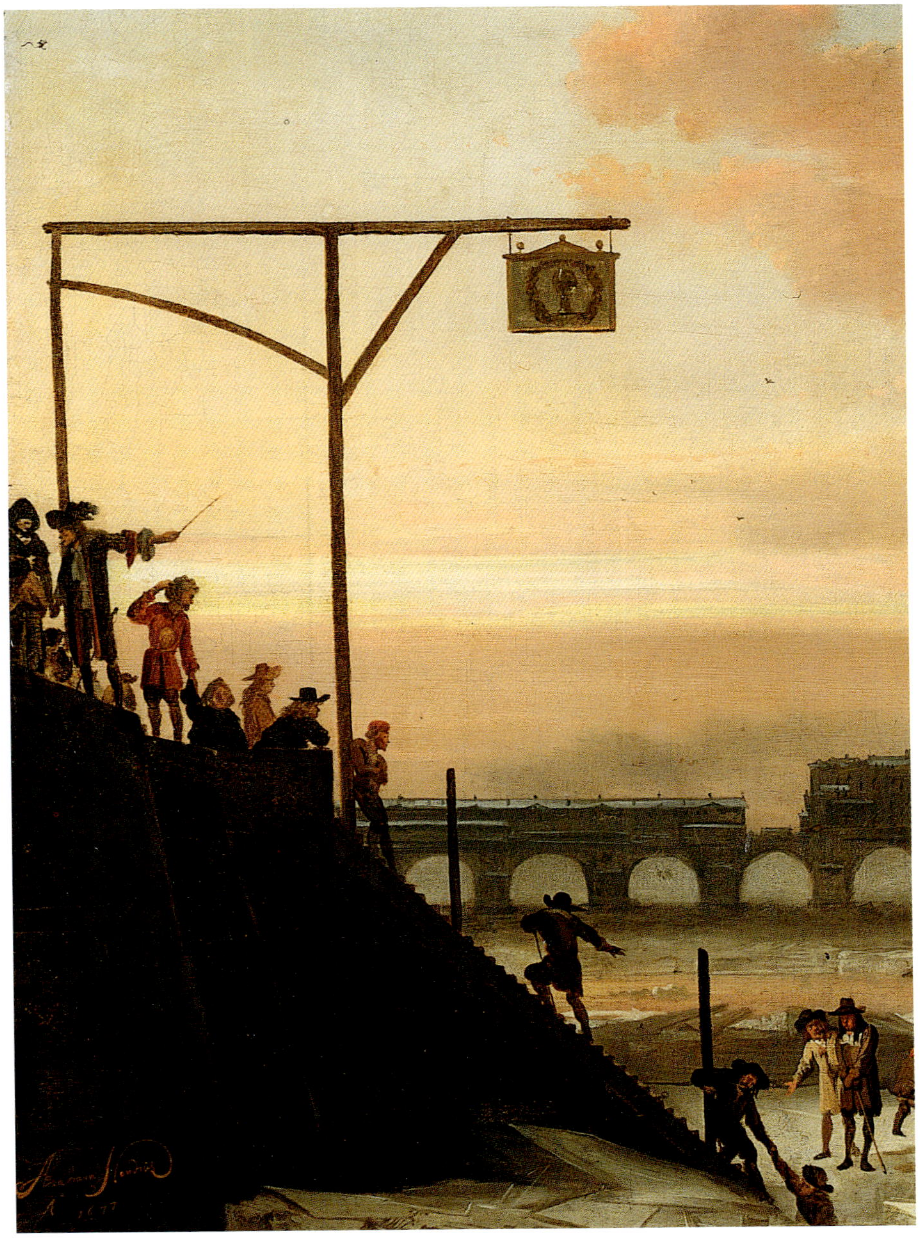

The size of the *Frozen Thames* is exceptionally large for a genre painting by both British and Dutch standards. It is unique in the oeuvre of Hondius for a genre scene. It is unlikely that a painter would produce such an ambitious work for stock, and the painting is likely to have been the result of a commission.

Bibliography:
Hayes (cat. no. 56); 'The Exchange of Ideas' in *Britain and the Netherlands*, Simon Groenveld and Michael Wintle (eds), Zutphen, Netherlands, 1994, vol. XI; Alfred Hentzen, 'Abraham Hondius', in *Jahrbuch der Hamburger Kunstammlungen*, Band 8, Hamburg, 1963, pp33-56.

Provenance:
Purchased out of the Joicey Trust Fund from Philip Moore and Spooner, Hove, in 1949 (without attribution).

Bibliography:
Hayes (cat. no. 57); Malcolm Warner, *The Image of London*, exhibition catalogue, Barbican Art Gallery, 1987, cat. no. 47.

16.
ABRAHAM HONDIUS
(c.1625/30–91)

A Frost Fair on the Thames at Temple Stairs
[49.80]
*c.*1684
Oil on canvas, 66.9 x 111.9 cm
Not signed or dated

THE THAMES was frequently frozen over during severe winters, in the years before Old London Bridge was pulled down, but the frost of 1683–4 was unparalleled in London's history. It lasted from the beginning of December 1683 until 4 February 1684, and the ice was thicker than had ever been known. There were also exceptionally bad fogs. As Evelyn tells us in his *Diary*, by New Year's Day 'streetes of Boothes were set up upon the Thames' that were like a 'Continual faire, all sorts of Trades & shops furnished, & full of Commodities, even to a Printing presse, where the People & Ladys tooke a fansy to have their names Printed & the day & yeare set downe, when printed on the Thames'. Many woodcuts of the scene were also sold as souvenirs.

In this picture the principal line of booths, which extended from Temple Stairs to the Old King's Barge-House, is shown in the centre; coaches, sledges and sedan-chairs are plying on the ice, and citizens are strolling on the frozen river; a game of ninepins is seen in progress in the foreground centre, and nearby there is a gaping hole in the ice.

The buildings represented in the background are, from left to right: St Clement Danes (before the addition of Gibbs's steeple in 1719) with Arundel Street in front of it; Essex Buildings (Nicholas Barbon's first speculative enterprise in this district) with Essex Stairs in front; Middle Temple Hall; Temple Stairs; Crown Office Row (partly hidden by the trees); the Temple church; the hall of Serjeant's Inn with, in front of it, the predecessor of Paper Buildings; and, on the extreme right, King's Bench Walk.

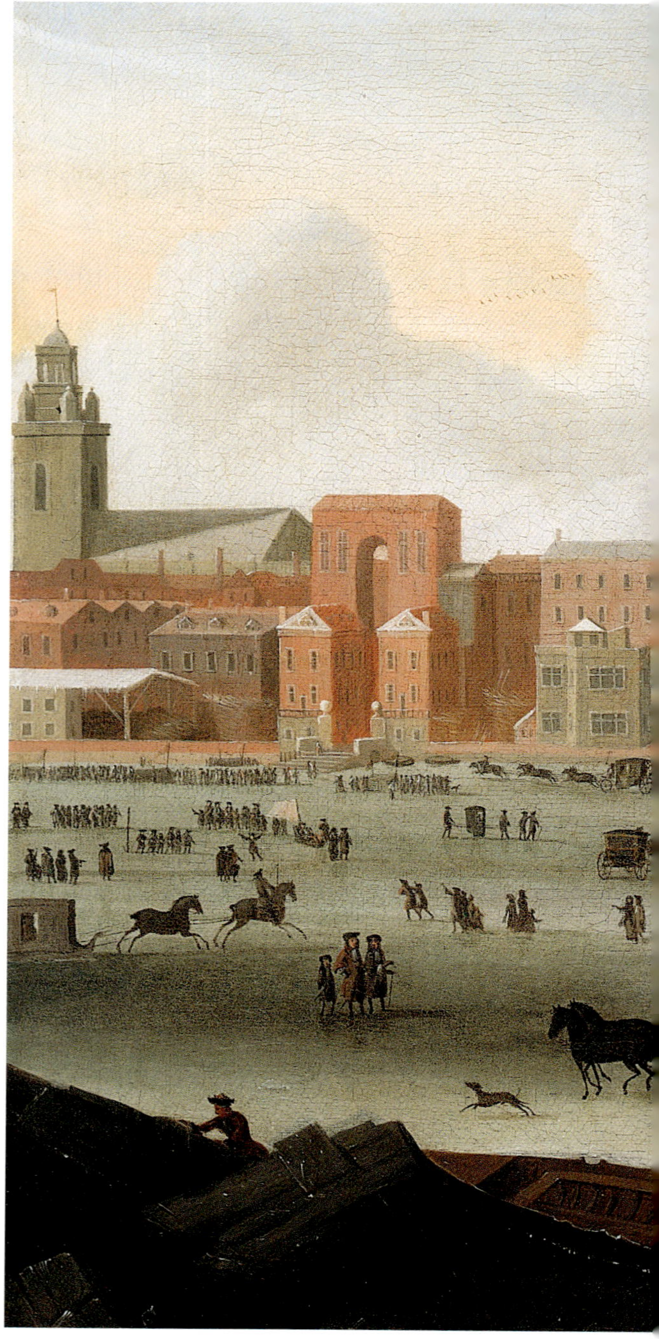

On the evidence of the booths described by Evelyn, the date of the scene depicted is January or the beginning of February 1684.

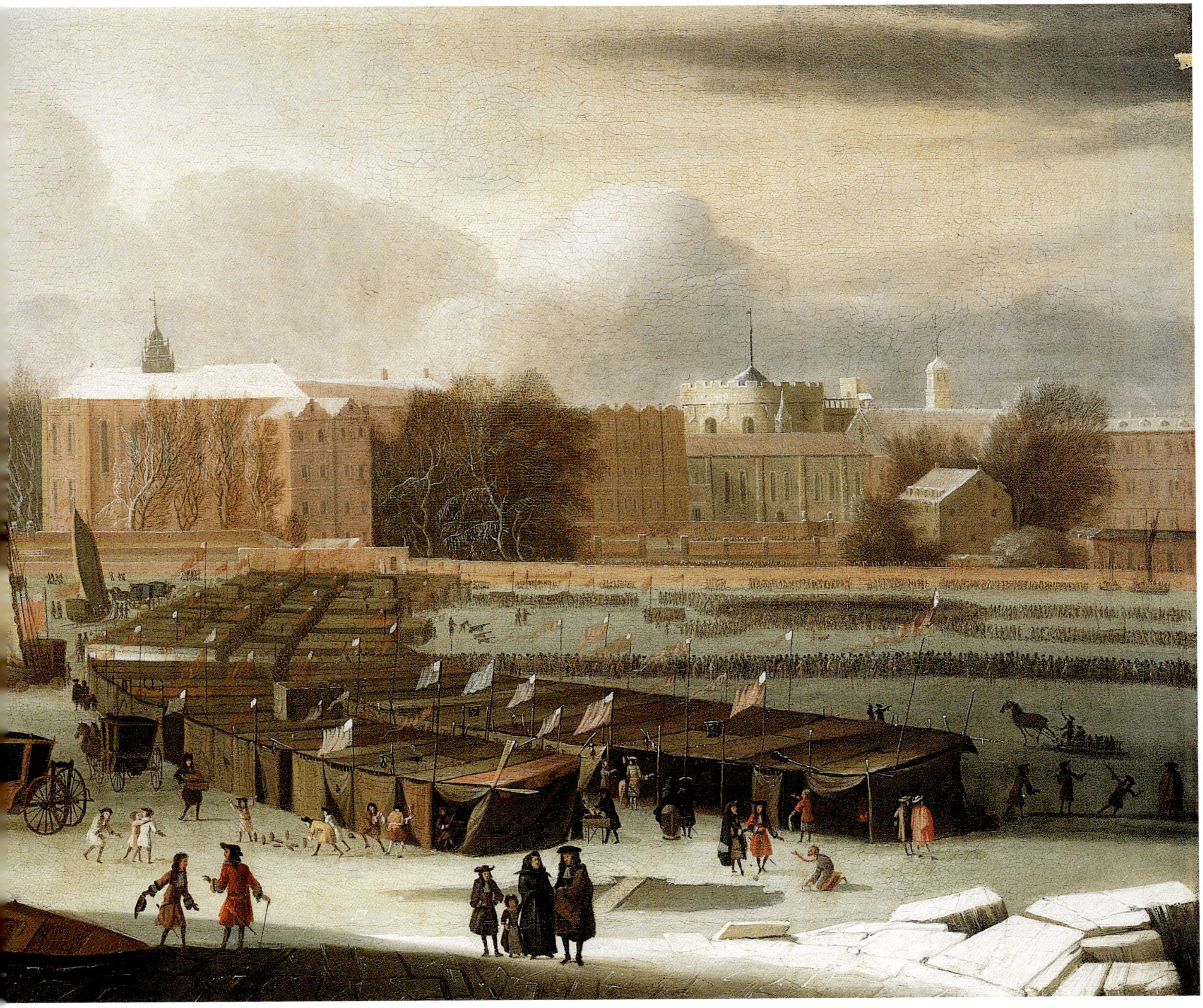

A version of this picture, differing only slightly (in the disposition of the clouds, and in some of the figures), was with Leggatt Brothers in 1926, and yet another was sold at Christie's 26 May 1989 (38).

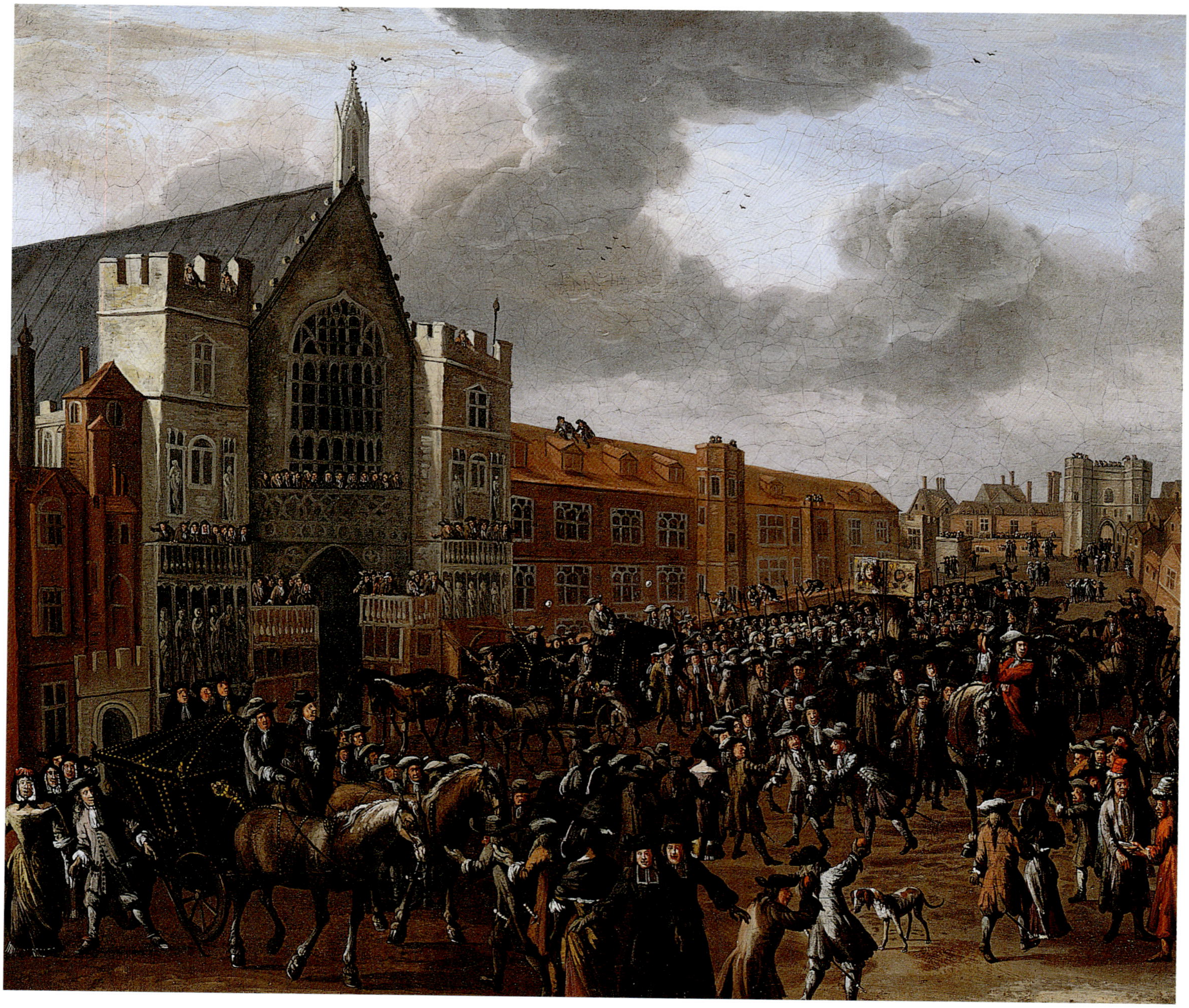

17.

IMITATOR OF JAN WYCK
(c.1645–1700)

Titus Oates in the Pillory [34.54]
*c.*1687
Oil on canvas, 62.5 x 74.7 cm
Not signed or dated

TITUS OATES (1649–1705), perhaps the most infamous of all false informers in British history, was brought to trial for perjury in May 1685. He was condemned by Judge Jeffreys to imprisonment for life, as well as to stand annually in the pillory at certain specified places and times, and, every May, to be flogged from Aldgate to Newgate, and two days later, from Newgate to Tyburn. Extraordinarily, Oates survived this ordeal, and the Museum picture shows him standing in the pillory in New Palace Yard in 1687. Westminster Hall appears on the left, with, beyond, a range of late Tudor buildings incorporating one of the towers of the Palace Gate which formerly stood at this point; in the distance is the new Palace Gate, which opened on to King Street (not to be confused with the better-known King Street gate of Whitehall Palace).

The viewpoint of the picture is identical with that adopted by Hollar for his etching of 1647, and it seems possible that the artist based his composition on Hollar's print and was not actually familiar with London at all. Support for this theory could come from the inclusion of the Palace Gate in the distance, which appears in Hollar, but which had evidently been pulled down before William Morgan published his great map of London in 1682; also the features of the many figures in the crowd are decidedly more Dutch than English. There are, however, two notable omissions *vis-à-vis* Hollar which rather undermine this theory: the water conduit, which was dismantled in 1670, and the upper part of Westminster Abbey.

Doubts have been expressed as to whether the picture represents Titus Oates (the traditional title of the picture, for which there is no known authority). There is no other portrait of him with which the head painted here may be compared; but it should not be assumed, anyway, that the latter was necessarily a good likeness of the pilloried man, or indeed a likeness at all. However, the costume of the numerous figures points in all particulars to a date of about 1685; there was no other case of the period for which such crowds could have been expected to congregate and special boxes to have been erected outside Westminster Hall; and prints of Titus Oates in the pillory seem to have been produced quite commonly in and after 1685. There is little reason to suppose, therefore, that the painting does not represent Oates; whether it is an actual record of the scene is open to considerable doubt. The treatment of the architectural detail is very generalised, and of little archaeological value.

Special mention should be made of the depiction of a London crowd. This is one of the earliest to combine successfully the general and the particular. Again, Wenceslaus Hollar did pioneering work when he first tackled the theme in his print of the execution of the Earl of Stafford in 1641. His crowd, however, remains undifferentiated. The crowds of the 1683–4 frost fair are so diminutive that they fail to have much impact. The two contemporary works which render the theme successfully are an anonymous wash drawing showing Lord Mayor's Day in 1686 (in the Museum's collection, acc. no. 81.434) and the painting under review.

The painting generally and, in particular, the very idiosyncratic stylised clouds suggest that the painter was a close follower of Jan Wyck, and the handling is identical with a view of the 1683–4 frost fair attributed to Jan Wyck, now in the collection of the Yale Center for British Art.

Conservation of this work in 1995 revealed two shining white blobs beneath the two men on the roof (there may be a link between the two). These are contemporaneous with the painting, but their significance remains a mystery.

Provenance:
Purchased from Leger Galleries by the National Art Collections Fund in 1934 and presented to the Museum.

Bibliography:
Hayes (cat. no. 112); *Dictionary of National Biography*; Celina Fox, *Londoners*, 1987, pp66–7.

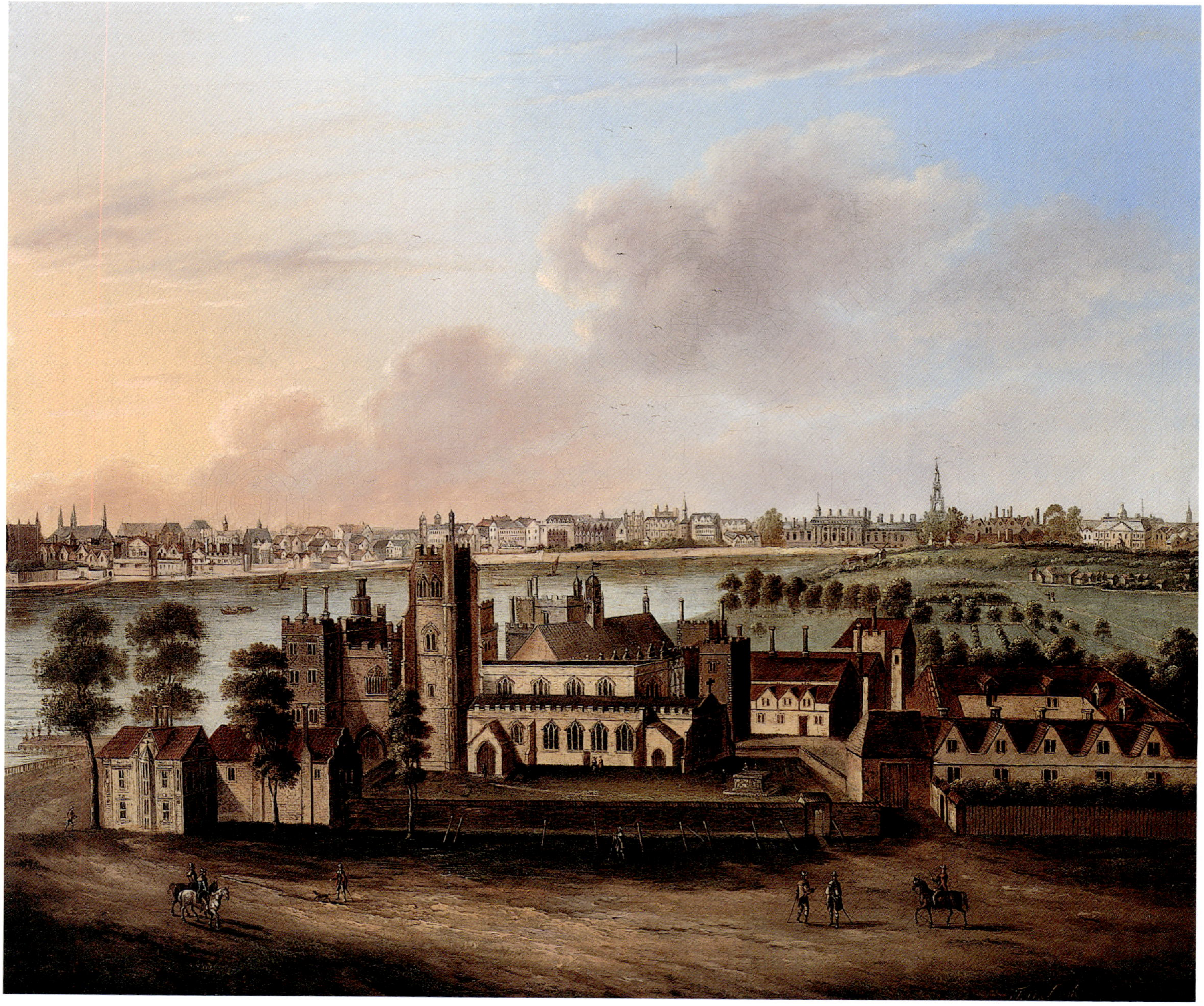

18.

F. W. SMITH

(active late seventeenth century)

Lambeth Palace [52.137]

*c.*1682–7

Oil on canvas, 62.5 x 75.3 cm

Signed bottom right: *F. W. Smith*

(the signature was revealed when the painting, previously catalogued as 'Imitator of Leonard Knyff', was conserved in 1975.)

THIS PAINTING of Lambeth Palace includes a distant view of Westminster and the Strand. The rendering of one of the most prominent features, Morton's Tower, with twice as many windows as there should be (and as appear in Knyff and Kip's view of 1697), does not suggest that the painting is very careful as regards detail, but the disposition of the various buildings is correct, and the picture is of considerable interest in showing the general appearance of this part of London towards the end of the seventeenth century. The view must date after 1682 (since it shows the steeple of St Clement Danes, completed in that year) and before 1687 (since it does not show the alterations to Whitehall Palace which were made by Wren in 1687–8). The costume indicates a date of about 1685.

The painting was engraved in the early nineteenth century (in the Museum's collection, acc. no. 48.11/437) as being by Hollar. The painting's viewpoint is that of Hollar's *Prospect of London and Westminster taken from Lambeth* (*c*.1643), but the painting is firmly focused on Lambeth Palace and makes no attempt at a comprehensive prospect in the style of Hollar.

Provenance:
Henry, 2nd Baron Melchet; purchased out of the Joicey Trust Fund from the Parker Gallery in 1952 (as Leonard Knyff).

Bibliography:
Hayes (cat. no. 62).

KEY

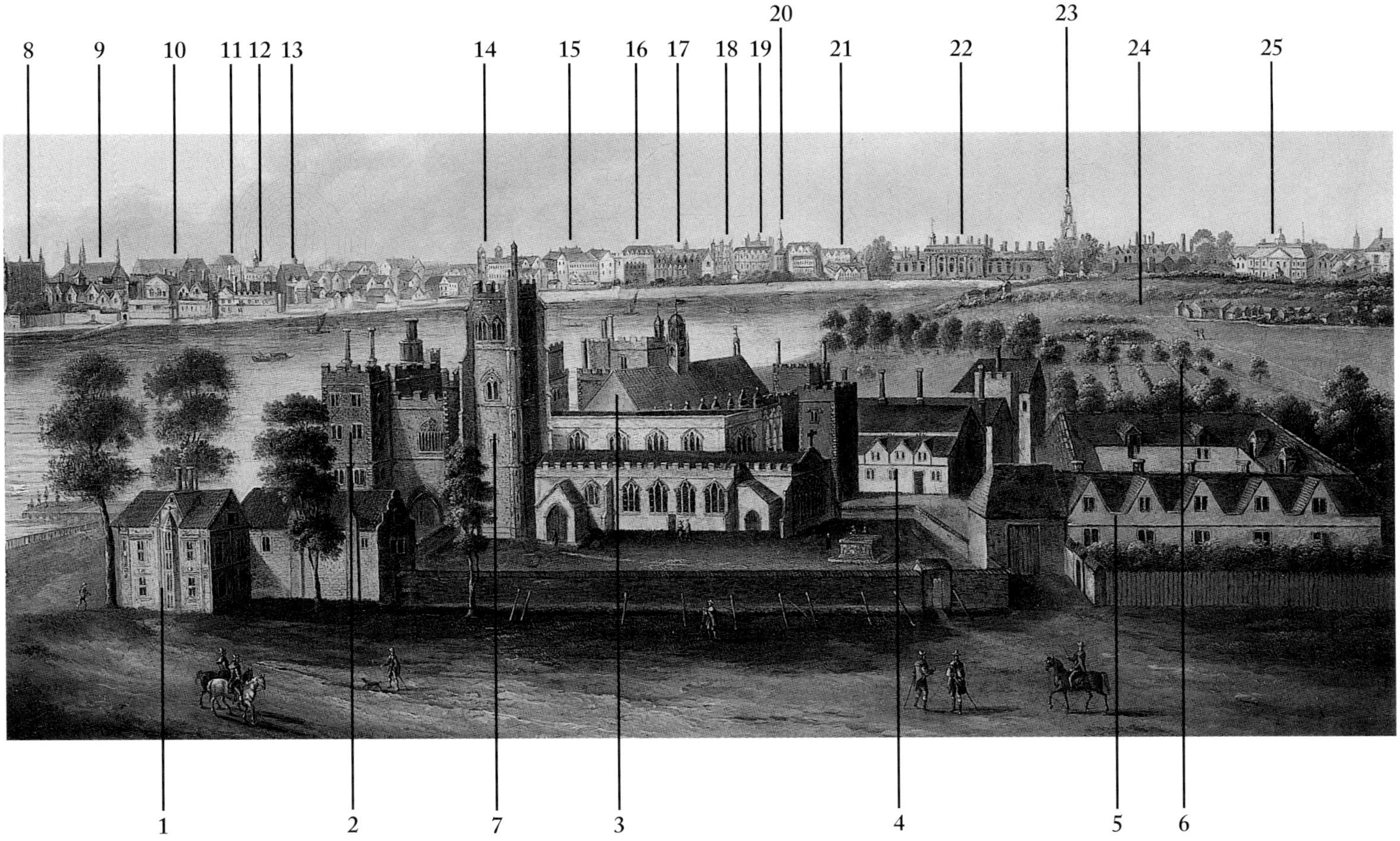

1. Rectory of St Mary
2. Gatehouse (Morton's Tower)
3. Great Hall
4. Kitchen block
5. Stables
6. Orchard
7. Church of St Mary
8. St Stephen's Chapel
9. Roof of Westminster Hall
10. Westminster Abbey
11. Banqueting House
12. Cupola of Old Horse Guards
13. Roof of Great Hall, Whitehall Palace
14. Northumberland House
15. York House
16. Durham House
17. Salisbury House
18. Exeter House
19. Worcester House
20. Spire of Church of St Giles-in-the-Fields
21. The Savoy
22. Old Somerset House
23. Spire of Church of St Clement Danes
24. Lambeth Marsh
25. Sir Thomas Fitch's House on the corner of Fleet Canal

19.
AFTER JAN GRIFFIER THE ELDER
(c.1646 or 1652–1718)

The Thames at Horseferry [54.96]
*c.*1706–10
Oil on canvas, 60.6 x 108.7 cm
Not signed or dated

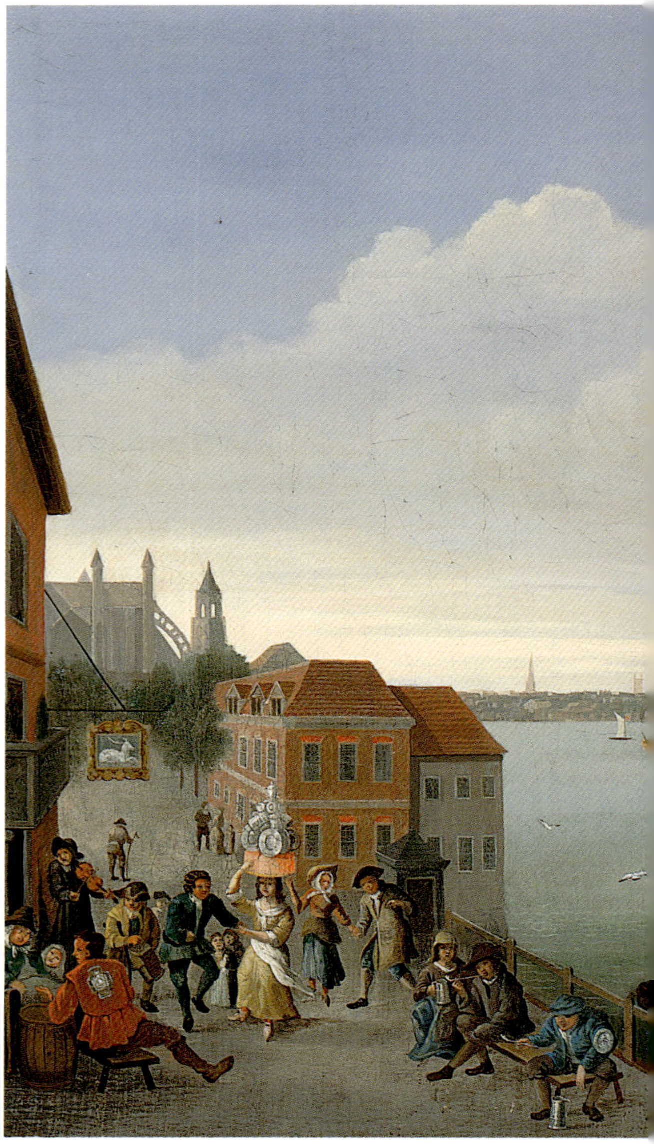

IN THIS picture a coach and pair are shown being punted across the Thames, while a naval barge close by fires a friendly salute. In the foreground left is Millbank Terrace, with a May Day procession: a milkmaid, with the traditional May Day garland of pots and pans, and three other figures are dancing outside the White Hart tavern to the accompaniment of a fiddler and concertina player. Other figures, including a royal bargeman in his scarlet coat and a Thames waterman in blue uniform, are seated on benches smoking and drinking; and three naked youths are bathing from a near-by punt. Beyond are Westminster Abbey and what is intended to be the tower of St Margaret's, Westminster, and, in the distance, the City waterfront, dominated by the spires of Wren's churches and the great mass of St Paul's Cathedral. In the middle distance are Lambeth Marsh and Lambeth Palace, where, from left to right, are visible Laud's Tower, the Great Hall, the gatehouse (Morton's Tower), Lambeth stairs, the tower of St Mary's Church and the ramp of a barge-house.

The horseferry, which plied on the site of the present Lambeth Bridge and is still recalled in the name Horseferry Road, was, until the building of Westminster Bridge in 1736–50, the only point along the entire waterfront of the capital west of London Bridge where coaches could be taken across the river. The ferry rights belonged to the See of Canterbury, but were usually leased out; at the date of this painting, they were in the possession of a Mr Leventhorp, who was accused by the parishioners of St Margaret's, Westminster, of 'usurping the whole profits of the horseferry, and neglecting to repair the roads leading thereto'. The ferry rights lapsed after the opening of Westminster Bridge.

The treatment of the architectural detail is very summary, and this picture is a generalised and abbreviated copy of the signed Griffier in the Galleria Sabauda, Turin, with fewer ships and figures, but

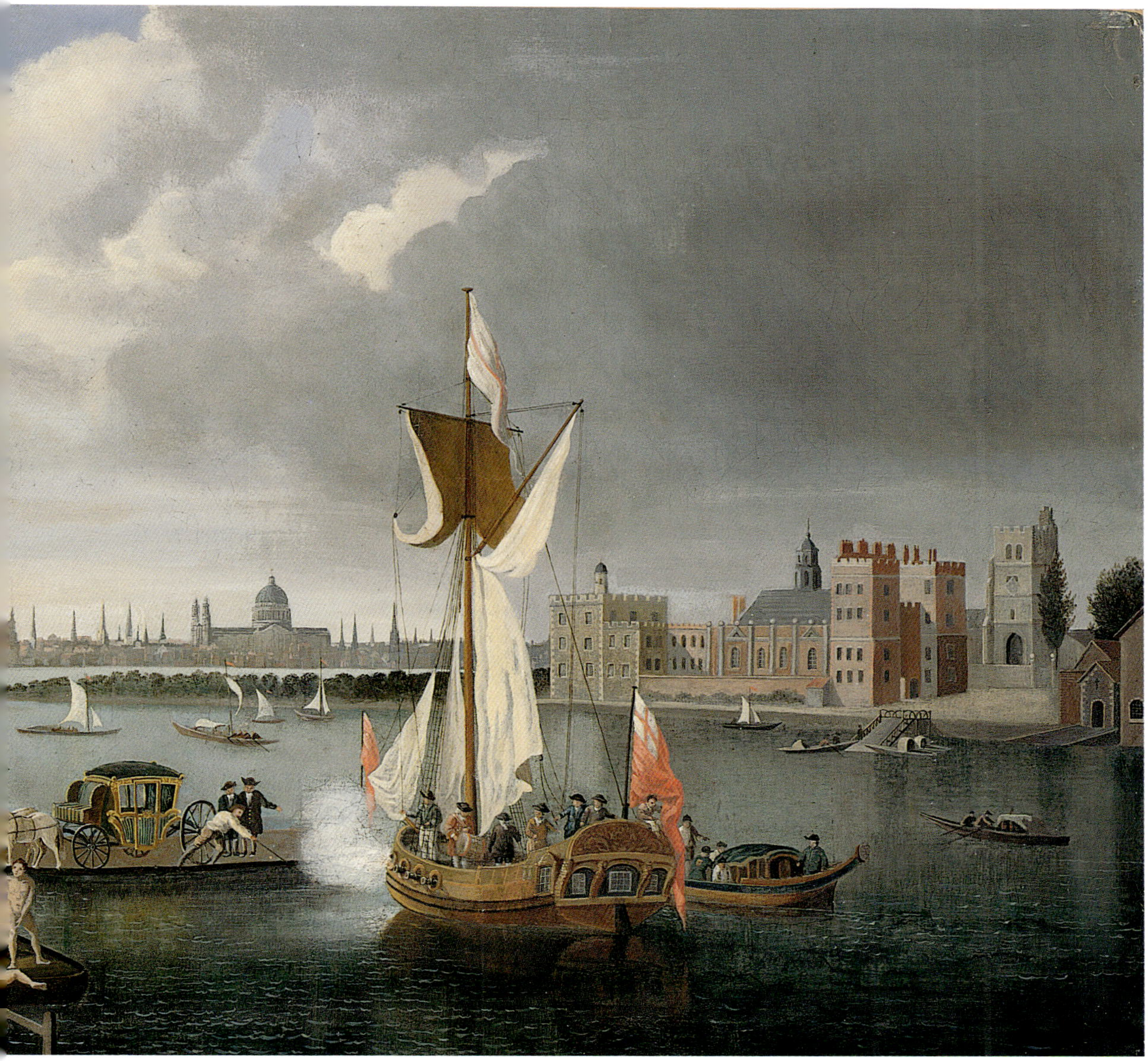

Provenance:
A. J. Pidduck; Pidduck sale, Christie's, 19 December 1908 (79, as Hayman), bt in; with M. Bernard; Christie's, 13 June 1952 (127, as Scott), bt J. Mitchell; purchased out of the Joicey Trust Fund from the Parker Gallery in 1954.

Bibliography:
Hayes (cat. no. 49).

with those that are included for the most part painted in much the same positions and poses. (The compositional formula, however, appears to hark back to Lucas van Valckenborgh's sixteenth-century *Winter Carnival* from the Cremer collection, sold at Sotheby's, New York, 22 October 1980.) The costume in both paintings suggests a date of about 1700–20. They were clearly painted either during or after the completion of the west front of St Paul's, the towers having been built in 1705–8, and the ball and cross surmounting the lantern being paid for in October 1708. But the ensign flying on the naval barge is that in use before the Union with Scotland in 1707. Either the artist showed St Paul's during completion, but without the scaffolding, as it would have been seen when finished; or else he depicted an outmoded ensign. A bracket of 1706–10 is the closest acceptable dating.

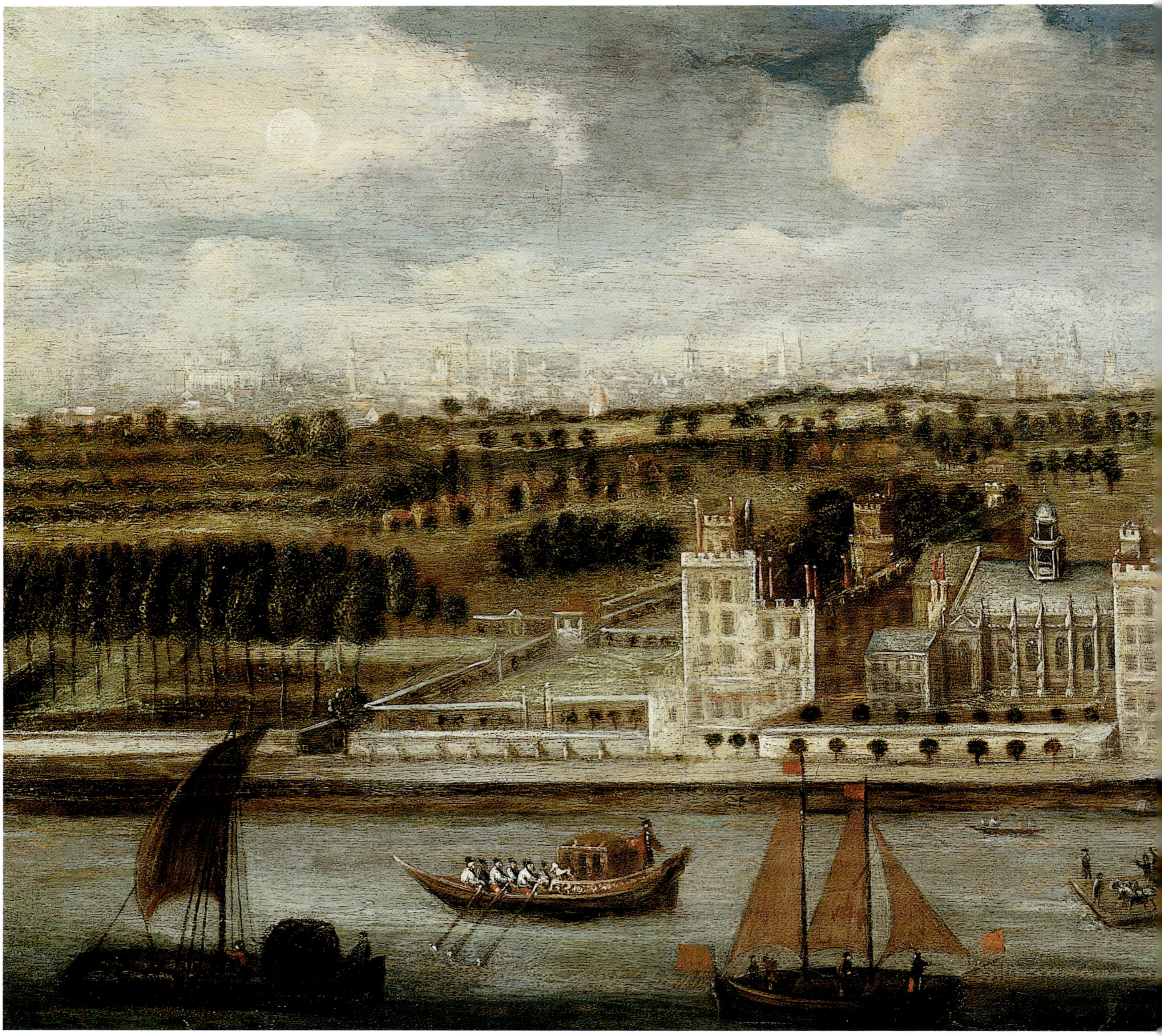

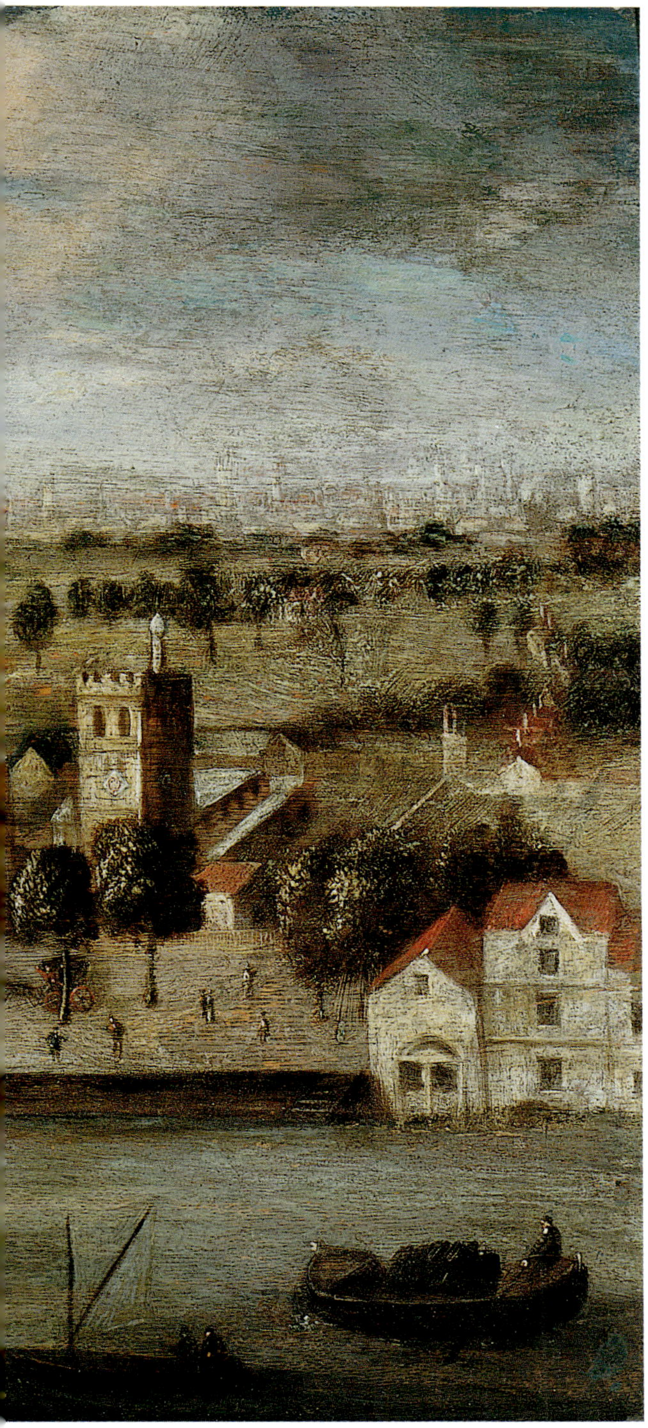

20.

BRITISH SCHOOL

Lambeth Palace [C 1256]

*c.*1715

Oil on oak panel, 32.5 x 55 cm

Not signed or dated

THIS BIRD'S-EYE view of Lambeth Palace, with the Thames in the foreground, looks north-eastwards over Lambeth Marsh, not as yet built on, towards a 'stylised' panorama of the City from St Paul's to the Tower. Dendrochronology carried out on the painting shows that its panel dates from between 1686 and 1710; the work would have been executed after 1710, as is suggested by the inclusion of St Paul's western towers.

The 1647 inventory of the Palace garden which was made after the death of Archbishop Laud throws light on the garden layout represented here. The walled garden nearest to the river is almost certainly the flower garden. At the other end, the clump of small trees may represent the orchard composed of apple, pear and plum trees. The promenade along the north wall (which should have been shown arched) and its upper walkway are visible, as is the Banqueting House in the middle of that run. John Rocque's great plan of London of 1737–46 shows the garden and terrace walls in the same positions and the garden laid out with squares of lawn (presumably) in gravel walks.

The painting, which is not meticulously executed, probably derives from the considerably more detailed view engraved by J. Kip after Leonard Knyff of around 1715. The shipping on the river has been simplified, but otherwise corresponds to that in the engraving.

Provenance:
Purchased from Richard Phillips in 1914 (as Scott).

Bibliography:
Hayes (cat. no. 130); Gladys Taylor, *Old London Gardens*, 1977, pp53–9.

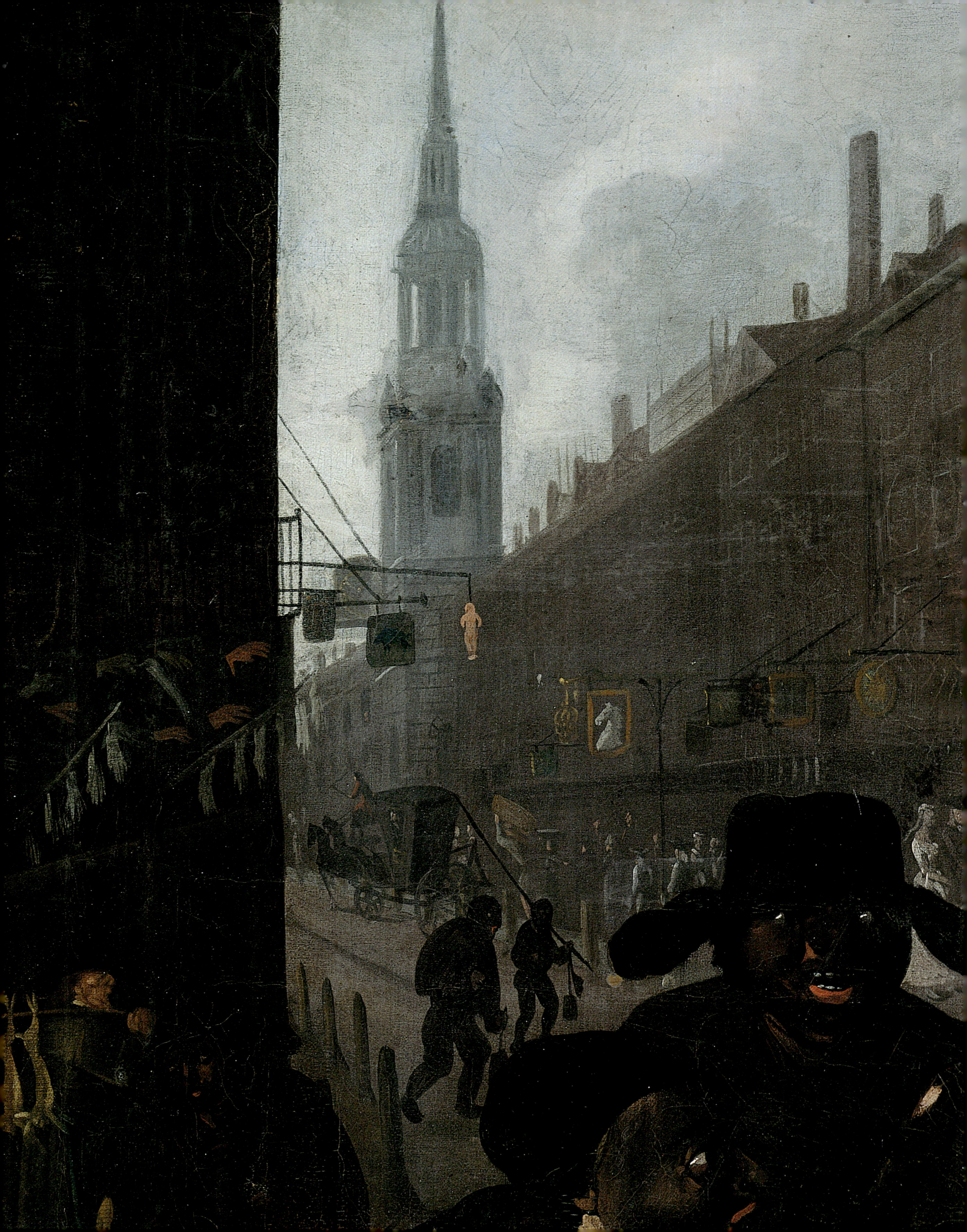

The Georgian Era

BY THE TIME George I succeeds Queen Anne in 1714 – and particularly by the reign of George II – a growing body of work is being produced by native artists, albeit often strongly influenced by Italian traditions. The emerging theme of the river displays this influence, and is immortalised by Canaletto and all the painters who follow in his footsteps. Images of architectural landmarks but also paintings of ordinary London streets are becoming commonplace. The work of the Covent Garden Group in the 1730s, which marks decisively the stylistic break with the earlier Stuart period, merits special interest. The social scene increasingly receives the attention of genre painters, oscillating between the straight commission work of the conversation piece and the caricatured approach of Hogarth and John Collet.

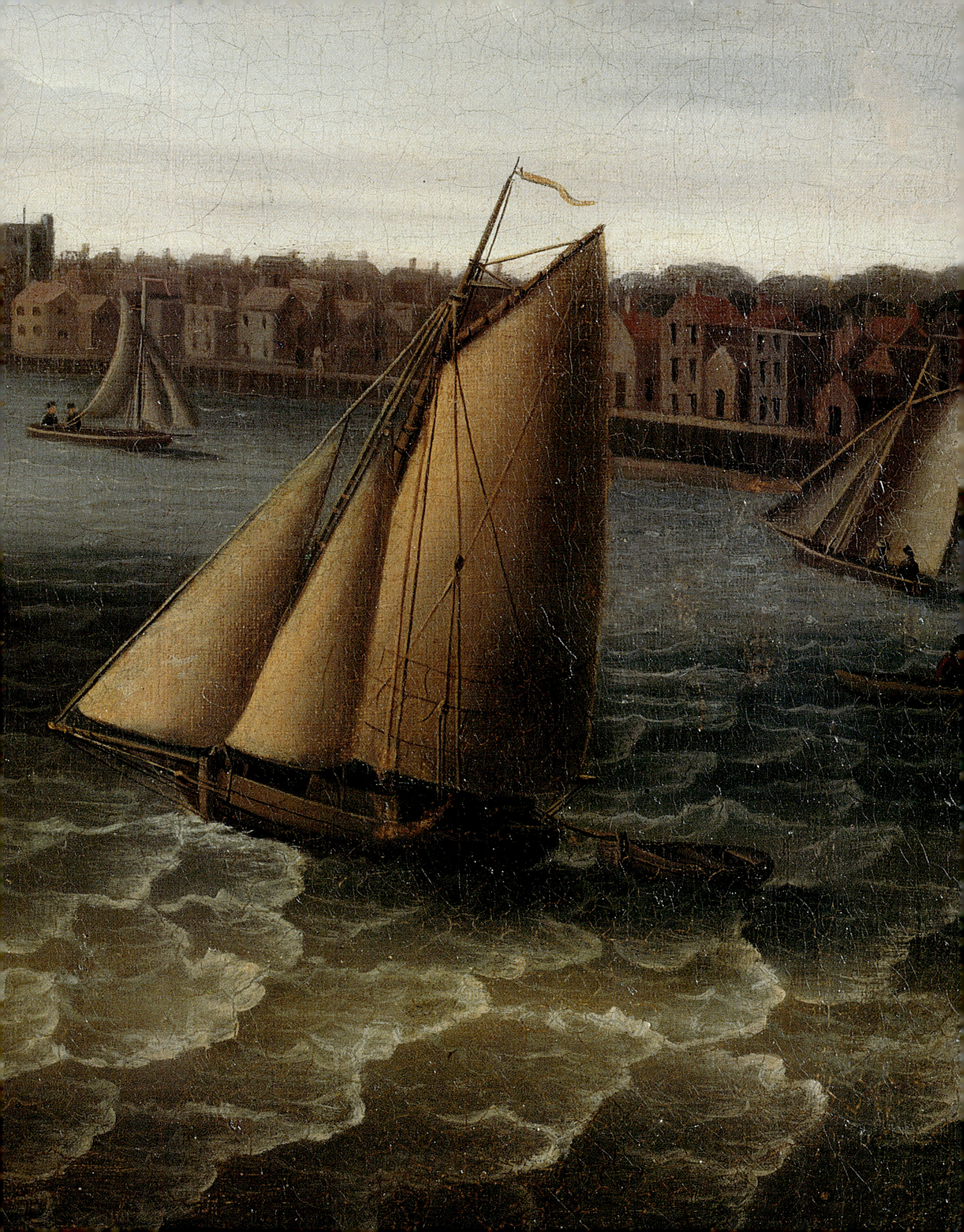

THE RIVER

WITH CANALETTO'S paintings of London from Somerset House terrace,[1] the earlier 'ribbon-like' formula for depicting the Thames finally gave way to the panoramic approach, which had been anticipated in the mid-seventeenth century in the paintings attributed to Cornelis Bol (see p6). Canaletto's arrival also coincided with the development in London of a gifted local group of topographers, notably Samuel Scott and later William Marlow, and a host of more minor painters.

What particularly focused artists' attention on the subject of the river was the construction of new bridges. Since the building of London Bridge in the twelfth century, the city had had only one crossing. In response to growing criticisms about the overcrowding of London Bridge, the capital acquired a further four bridges during the Georgian period, respectively Putney Bridge, opened in 1729; Westminster Bridge, built between 1739 and 1750; Blackfriars Bridge, between 1760 and 1769, and Battersea Bridge in 1771–2. The fascination for bridges in the eighteenth century was so unprecedented that a number of capriccio paintings and unexecuted designs based on the concept of a 'bridge of magnificence' were produced.[2]

Both the Westminster and Putney projects met with formidable opposition from the City Corporation and the Company of Watermen and Lightermen (in 1699 there were as many as seventeen plying places between Vauxhall and Limehouse). Westminster Bridge was the first stone bridge to be built over the Thames since the construction of London Bridge and constituted a major architectural and engineering achievement. It consisted of fifteen arches spanning the river, which at this point was wider than at London Bridge. The designer was the Swiss Chas Labelye. After a temporary setback when one of the piers subsided in 1748 (recorded by Canaletto, see note 4), the bridge was opened to traffic in November 1750.[3]

It is almost certain that the arrival of Canaletto in 1746 was connected with the building of Westminster Bridge, which the artist recorded in a group of memorable pictures.[4] It has also been noted that nearly all this painter's early patrons were commissioners of the bridge.[5]

By the time Canaletto came to London, Samuel Scott was a well-established marine artist who had already produced a painting of the Thames at Wapping (*c.*1740), a body of drawings of Westminster Bridge (1742–4) and also paintings of the Tower of London and Westminster from Lambeth (1746).[6] Canaletto was therefore contributing to the topographical scene in London, rather than creating it as is sometimes stated. It was previously believed that his painting of Greenwich Hospital might have partially been painted by Scott, but the collaborator on this occasion turned out to be Jacques Rigaud.[7] Scott's own composition of this subject predated Canaletto's and his version of the Thames at York Buildings may have inspired Canaletto's painting of this subject rather than the other way round.[8] As far as river painting is concerned, the scope of subject matter in Scott is considerably wider than in Canaletto, who never painted the Thames east of London Bridge. Scott's large painting *The Tower of London*[9] is a case in point. Since it was probably commissioned by the 4th Earl of Radnor as a companion picture to Canaletto's *Old Horse Guards from St James's Park* (Sir Andrew Lloyd Webber Art Foundation), both painters enjoyed the same patronage and no doubt the same status. The shipping east of London

Bridge was far larger than anything found on the west side of the bridge, and Scott uses this to his advantage by introducing strong verticals in a predominantly horizontal format and by depicting a lively foreground in a panoramic view. By comparison, Canaletto's landscape remains sternly horizontal and distant. In this case as in many others, Scott (and later his pupil William Marlow) produced a more focused and articulated view of London.

It is unfortunate that this collection should represent both artists by their most unrepresentative works – a rare interior for Canaletto (cat. no. 33) and a non-river view for Samuel Scott (cat. no. 40) – but Marlow's view of the Adelphi (cat. no. 27) is an outstanding work by this artist, which pays tribute to the two masters.

A host of minor (often anonymous) artists copied and disseminated these artists' successful formulas. The print market also contributed to popularising the painters' vision of a city on the river which became available to many classes of Londoners. As well as the classic river panorama published in 1749 by the brothers Buck – in the tradition of those of the preceding century[10] – there were three major publications which were devoted to the river: Boydell's *Collection of Views* in 1770, Ireland's *Picturesque Views of the Thames* in 1792 and Boydell's *History of the Thames* in 1794–6.[11] The recording of the river banks of London from the Thames in series was first initiated by the enterprising John Boydell (1719–1804) around 1750. His growing success as a printmaker and then as a printseller culminated in his being elected Lord Mayor of the City of London in 1790. He celebrated this event by reissuing a retrospective collection of thirty Thames prints and shortly afterwards, in 1792, he decided to publish a *History of the Thames in 76 plates* from its source to its estuary.[12] The venture proved a great success.

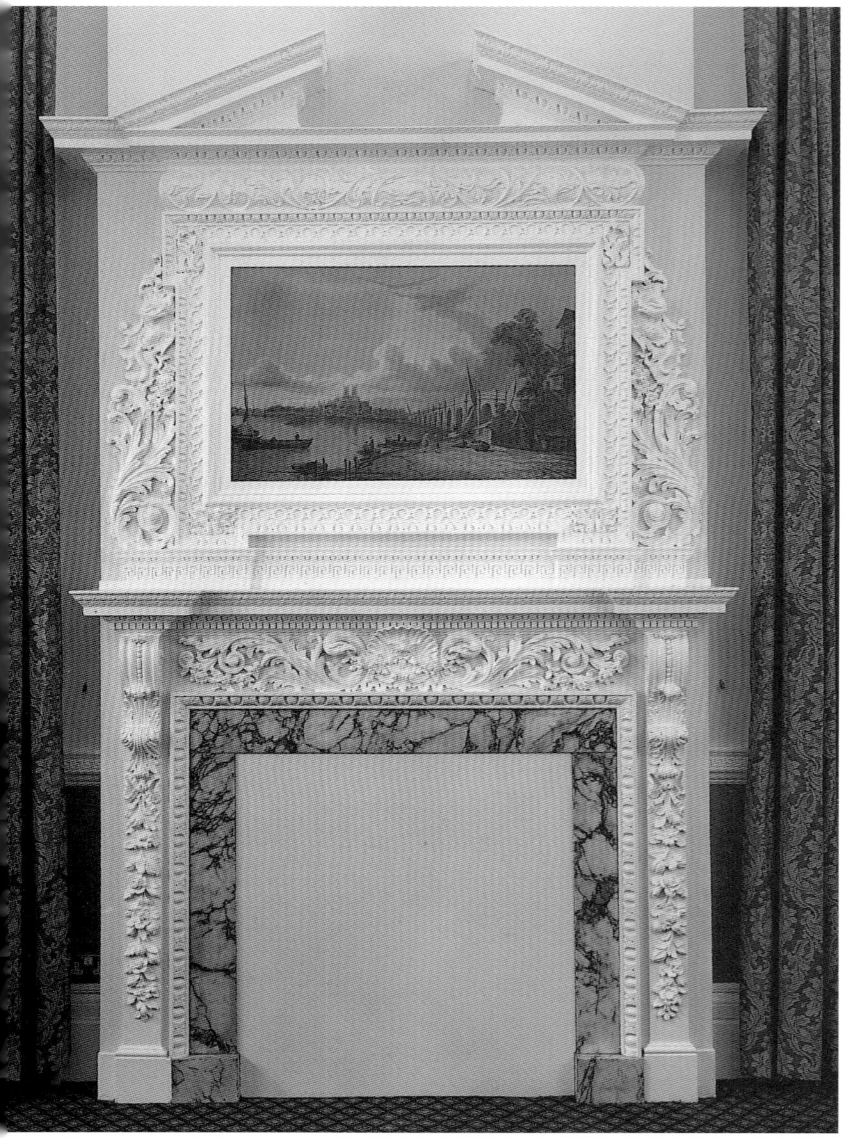

Carved wood mantelpiece, *c.*1750, in the Edinburgh Room, 12 Great George Street, showing a painting (the Thames at Westminster) forming part of a decorative architectural scheme. Photo: Museum of London by kind permission of the Royal Institution of Chartered Surveyors.

The abundance and repetitiveness of mid-eighteenth-century topographical views, notably river scenes at Lambeth and Westminster, may be explained by the developing market for displaying (predominantly) river views in fashionable interior decoration schemes. Paintings came to form an intrinsic part of carved wood mantelpieces and overmantels, for instance at 5 and 12 Great George Street.[13] At number 12 (illustrated) the view of Westminster from Lambeth is in the same spirit as the Museum's cat. no. 28. Artists responded with various degrees of expertise and originality to the great demand for paintings of London views and did not seem to hesitate to 'pirate' the engraved views (see cat. nos 23, possibly 24 and 25).

On the whole, however, painters seem to have avoided recording the working banks of the Thames. From as far back as 1558, twenty 'legal quays' were established between London Bridge and the Tower. It was in the eighteenth century that London became the world's busiest port and yet for reasons of patronage, fashion or convention, those painters who recorded this extraordinary phenomenon exerted very limited influence on the artistic scene. By the eighteenth century, when river painting emerged, the area east of London Bridge was well outside the fashionable western end of London and this may explain why it remained relatively ignored by artists. Samuel Scott and his former pupil William Marlow were almost alone[14] in recording work activities on the river, echoing the enthusiasm Daniel Defoe displayed in 1725:

> The keys or wharfs, next the river, fronting not the Custom House only, but the whole space from the Tower Stairs, or dock, to the Bridge, ought to be taken notice of as a publick building; nor are they less an ornament to the city, as they are a testimony of the vast trade carried on in it, than the Royal Exchange itself.[15]

Marlow's dedication to London's working river life was such that even when he chose a grand architectural subject such as the Adelphi (see cat. no. 27), he depicted the scheme unfinished – thereby giving us fascinating insight into the building industry and the distribution of coal in London.

The new Rome, the new Venice?

More than any other Georgian artist, William Hogarth drew attention to and even challenged the overwhelming prestige of Italian painters in England. When he heard that the Venetian painter Jacopo Amigoni was certain to obtain the mural commission for the entrance hall at St Bartholomew's Hospital, he offered to carry out the commission free of charge.[16]

John Evelyn's diary describes how at the end of the preceding century Italian pictures constituted the most valuable items in London picture collections. The early decades of the eighteenth century saw the building in Chelsea of a pseudo-Roman Pantheon – the Rotunda at Ranelagh Gardens – and witnessed the birth of Palladianism, named after the Venetian Renaissance architect Palladio; not surprisingly, perhaps, the Italian baroque painters were extremely fashionable: 'I have heard a famous painter assert that our English nobility and gentry may boast of as many good Pictures of the best Italian Masters as Rome itself.'[17] Apart from securing a great number of large-scale commissions for murals, the contribution of Venetian painters to the imaging of London is very substantial, from Marco Ricci's earliest view of Londoners promenading in the Mall,[18] to Luca Carlevaris's grandiose records of the arrival of Venetian ambassadors at the Tower of London,[19] to Francesco Zuccarelli's *The Thames at Richmond Hill*[20] and Antonio Joli's capriccios and topographical views.[21] James Ralph, the editor of the *Weekly Review*, retaliated by promoting the work of British-born painters (notably Hogarth) and by ridiculing the work of foreign painters.[22]

Yet the aspiration to re-create in London some of Italy's grandeur was the powerful motive which shaped many programmes and private collections. This process of transformation proved to be slow and too

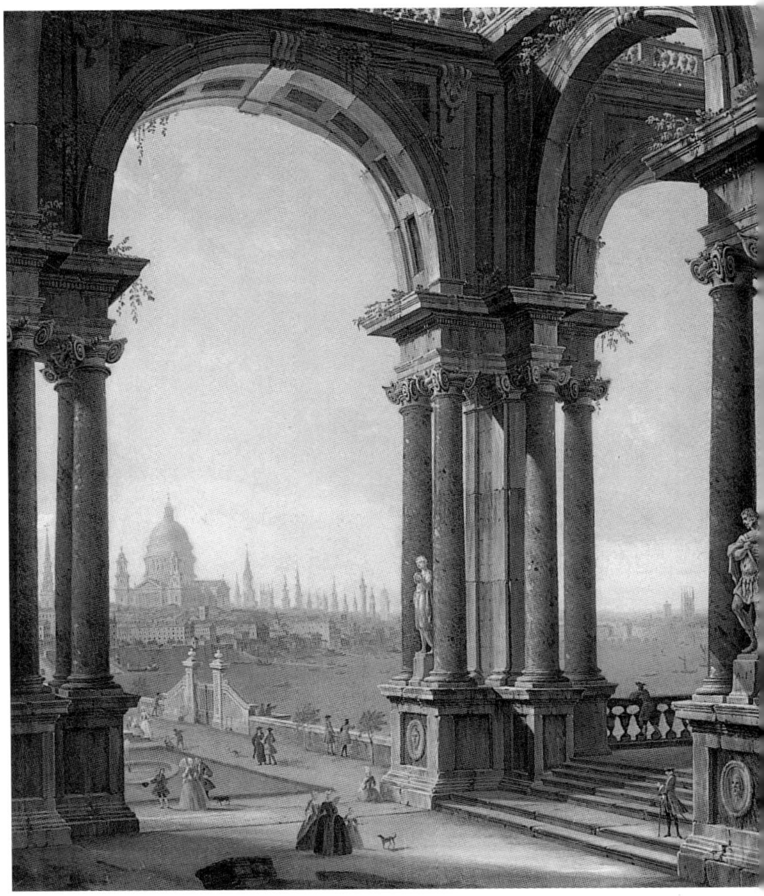

Antonio Joli (*c.*1700–1777)
Capriccio Bridge
Oil on canvas
Private Collection.

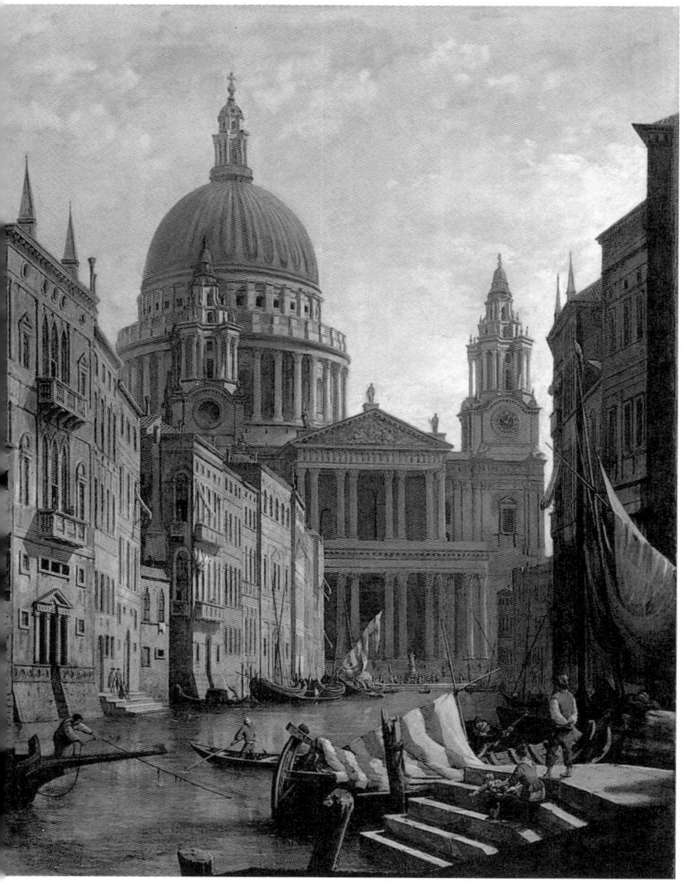

William Marlow
(1740–1813)
*Capriccio: St. Paul's and a Venetian canal, c.*1795?
Oil on canvas
Tate Gallery, London.

costly. Thomas Sandby's vision of a bridge of magnificence was no more than a dream and William Chambers's design for Blackfriars Bridge was rejected as too ambitious. The true aesthetic aspirations of the age for London are locked in capriccios: Antonio Joli breathed pictorial life into Chambers's design, thus turning London into a new Rome, and William Marlow flooded Ludgate Hill, which – after it was lined with delicate *palazzi* – turned St Paul's vista into a new Venice.[23]

1. See *Canaletto & England*, Michael Liversidge and Jane Farrington (eds), 1993, p74.
2. Thomas Sandby's watercolour *A Bridge of Magnificence over the Thames at Somerset House*, Windsor collection, Oppé 186; William Chambers's unexecuted design for Blackfriars Bridge; Antonio Joli's capriccios (see below).
3. See R. J. B. Walker, *Old Westminster Bridge*, 1979, for the complete history of this project.
4. J. G. Links, 'Canaletto and old Westminster', in *Apollo*, May 1992.
5. Walker, 1979, p237.
6. Richard Kingzett, 'A catalogue of the works of Samuel Scott', in *Walpole Society*, vol. XLVIII.
7. The attribution to Scott was made by Kingzett (see above) and the current one, to Rigaud, by Jane Dacey in 'A note on Canaletto's views of Greenwich', in the *Burlington Magazine*, 1981, pp485–8.
8. Kingzett, op. cit., p3.
9. Liversidge and Farrington (eds), 1993, p120.
10. Ralph Hyde, *A Prospect of Britain: the Town Panoramas of Samuel & Nathaniel Buck*, 1994.
11. Bernard Adams, *London Illustrated 1604–1851*, 1983, cat. nos 47, 71 and 75.
12. Ibid, p177ff; it was also in 1792 that Boydell presented the City with the river painting *The Lord Mayor's Procession by Water to Westminster, November 9 1789* by Francis Wheatley and Richard Paton (Guildhall Art Gallery, acc. no. 54).
13. Penelope Hunting, *Royal Westminster*, 1981, p103.
14. The Cleverleys (father John and sons John Jnr and Robert) recorded shipyards at Deptford, Woolwich and Gravesend; Francis Holman painted *Blackwall Yard* (National Maritime Museum).
15. Daniel Defoe, *A Tour through London about the Year 1725*, republ. 1929 by B. T. Batsford, p39.
16. *The Pool of Bethesda* and *The Good Samaritan*, *c.*1735–7, can still be enjoyed in their original setting today.
17. Iain Pears, *The Discovery of Painting*, 1988, p174.
18. See *Manners & Morals*, cat. no. 9 and Liversidge and Farrington (eds), 1993, p32.
19. This work is reproduced in Celina Fox, *Londoners*, 1987, p18.
20. Reproduced in Liversidge and Farrington (eds), 1993, p35.
21. See Malcolm Warner, *The Image of London*, 1987, p126 for capriccios; for topographical views, see Liversidge and Farrington (eds), 1993, p103 and Christie's, 9 July 1993 (100).
22. Liversidge and Farrington (eds), 1993, p34.
23. Ibid, pp102 and 146.

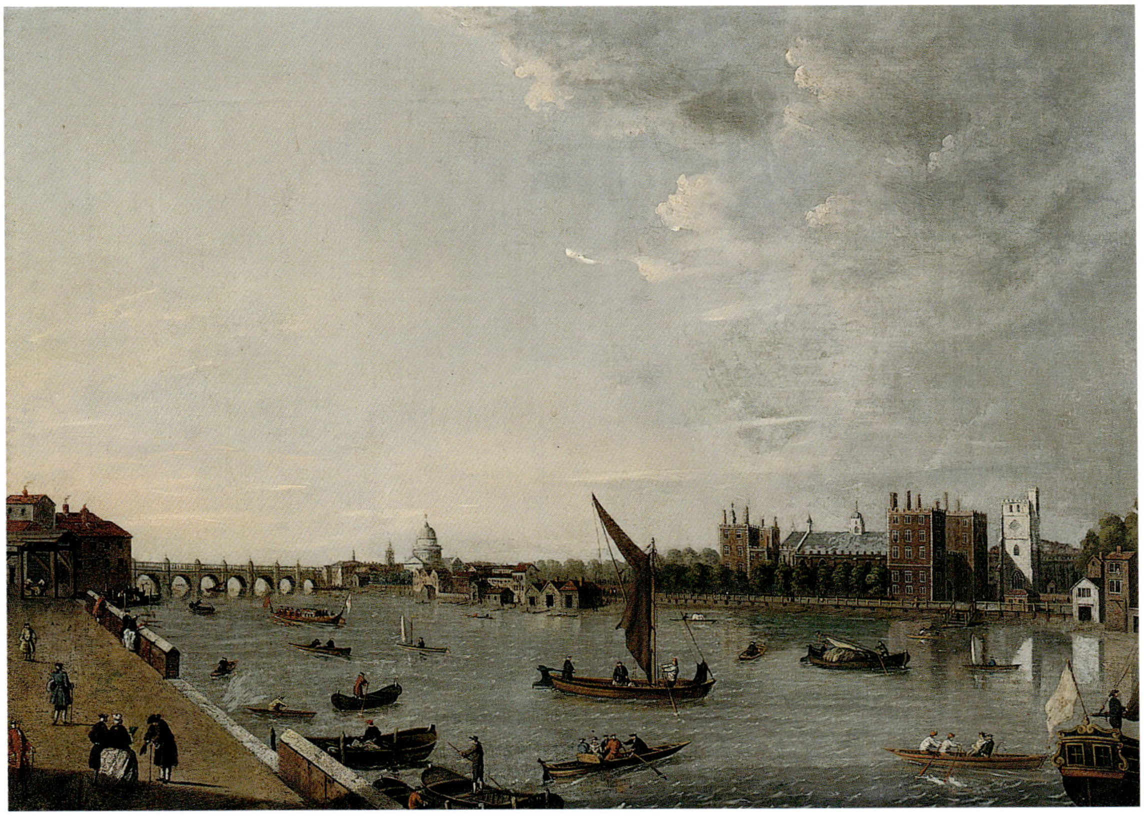

Provenance:
B. T. Batsford; Batsford sale, Christie's, 12 January 1901 (12, as Canaletto), bt Agnew; lent by Mrs C. W. Bischoffsheim in 1911 (as Boydell); by descent to Sir Arthur Fitzgerald, Knight of Kerry, who presented it in 1966.

Bibliography:
Hayes (cat. no. 14).

21.
BRITISH SCHOOL
Lambeth Palace from Horseferry [C 352]
*c.*1745–50
Oil on canvas, 48.4 x 68.4 cm
Not signed or dated

THIS VIEW is taken from much the same viewpoint on Millbank Terrace as cat. no. 19 and shows the scene some forty years later. Westminster Bridge, built between 1736 and 1750, is shown as completed, and a good deal of development has taken place on the fringe of Lambeth Marsh, between the bridge and the Palace. The barge-houses of the Archbishop of Canterbury are seen in the centre, and a tree-lined walk has been laid out in front of Lambeth Palace. Lambeth stairs and St Mary's church are seen to the right. St Paul's still dominates the distance, but less commandingly than it used to do. Some passengers are being ferried across the river in the foreground, and a ceremonial barge can be seen in the middle distance.

Various versions of this painting are known to exist. They were recorded as being with Agnew (1921), Knoedler (1931), and in a sale at Parke-Bernet (21–2 September 1962, 223) and at Christie's (22 November 1963, 32). The popularity of the view is attested to by the John Maurer engraving which was published in 1745 and from which this may derive. The costume of the figures indicates a date not later than about 1750.

Provenance:
By descent to Angus Whiteford Acworth (1898–1981), who bequeathed it to the Museum in 1981 as by Jonathan Richardson the Elder.

Bibliography:
C. J. Feret, *Fulham Old and New*, 1900, vol. I, pp55–6; W. A. Green, *Pedigree of Acworth of Bedfordshire*, 1905; R. J. B. Walker, *Old Westminster Bridge*, 1979, p39ff.

22.
BRITISH SCHOOL

Portrait of Sir Jacob Acworth as a Boy
[81.632]
*c.*1700
Oil on canvas, 61 x 74 cm
Not signed or dated

THIS THREE-QUARTER-LENGTH frontal portrait of Jacob Acworth (d.1749) shows him as a boy. He is carrying a bow in his right hand and the figure is set in a partially hidden oval with a background of landscape with trees.

In 1728 Sir Jacob Acworth, shipwright, surveyor and commissioner of the Navy, submitted a design for Putney Bridge (see cat. no. 23) which was selected and referred to a building committee which included Dr William Cheselden and Thomas Ripley. The bridge was built in 1729 and in 1730 the proprietors passed a resolution which began: 'Resolved, as the bridge is built entirely according to a scheme and principles laid down by Mr Cheselden, and as he has been very serviceable in directing the execution of the same…' Perhaps this suggests that Cheselden's rather than Acworth's proposal was adopted or alternatively that Acworth's proposal had been considerably modified by Cheselden.

A pair of portraits of Abraham Acworth (1719–81) and his wife Margaretta Mabella Acworth, née Buckeridge (1727–94) by Thomas Hudson are in the collection of the Iveagh Bequest, Kenwood. That institution holds typescript excerpts from the Acworth family papers prepared by Angus Acworth in 1944 (copies in Museum of London records).

There is no reason to doubt the family records relating to the subject of this painting and these would dictate a date of *c.*1700. However, stylistically, the painting would fit the 1720s.

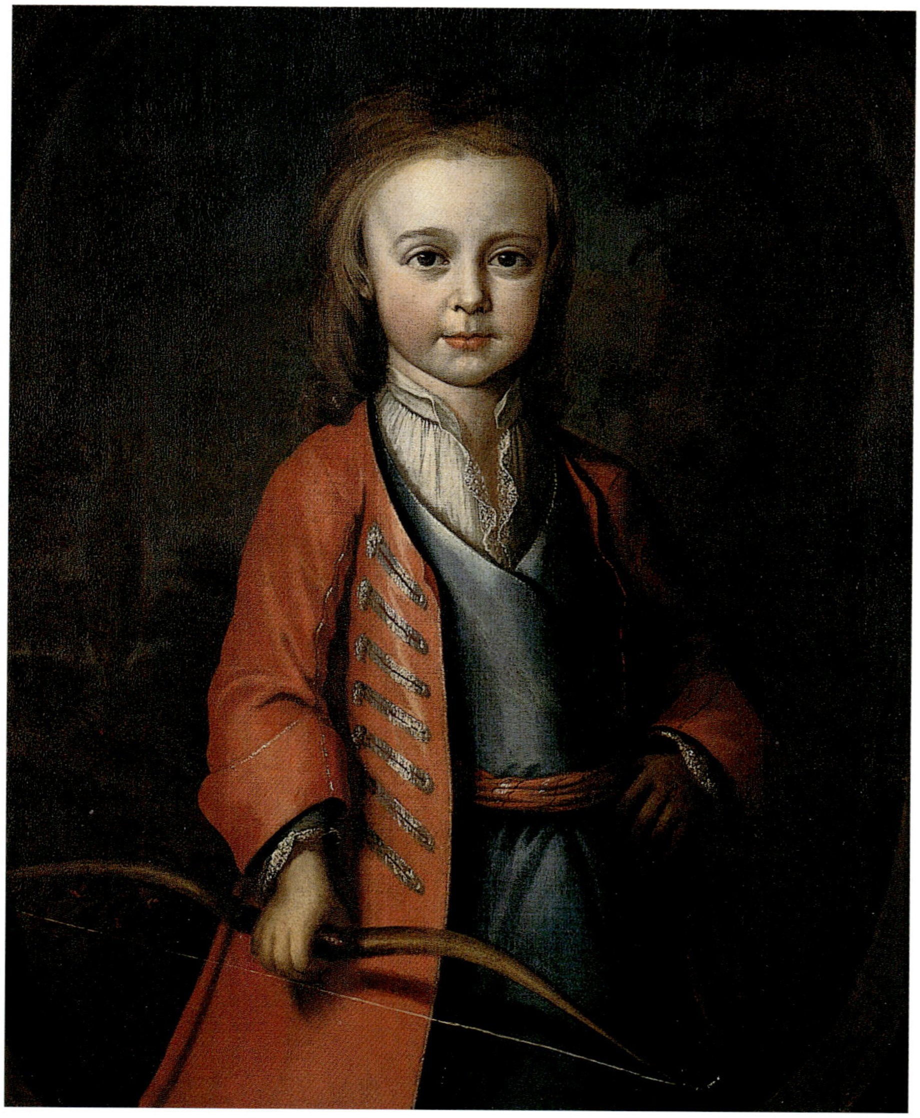

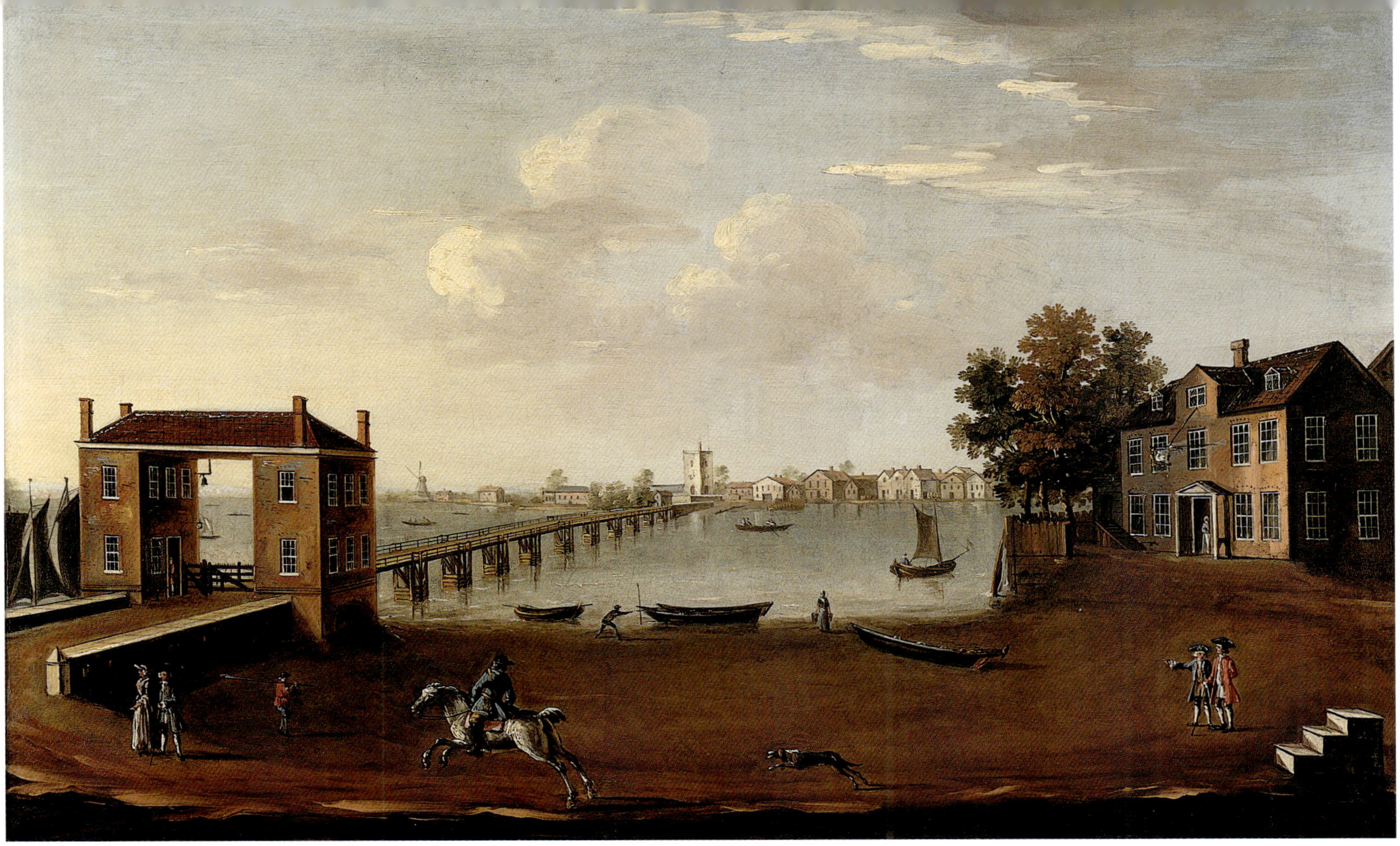

23.

BRITISH SCHOOL

Putney Bridge and Village from Fulham
[42.50/2]

*c.*1750
Oil on canvas, 61.6 x 100.2 cm
Not signed or dated

THE PAINTING shows the wooden bridge built by Cheselden, perhaps to Acworth's design (see cat. no. 22). The main toll-house, or Bridge House, depicted here, was situated at the Fulham end, and included a residence for the manager; for toll charges see cat. no. 24. The bell under the roof was used to warn of approaching highwaymen. A smaller brick toll-house stood on the Putney side after 1850. Across the river are the riverside houses of Putney grouped round the parish church of St Mary, which adjoined the approach to the bridge; the windmill was situated on the extremity of the village on the verge of North Fields, but across the parish boundary, in Wandsworth. On the right is the Swan Inn, where the bridge commissioners held their first meeting on 26 July 1726; some mounting steps are in the foreground.

The Museum picture is not painted with great care, and the distant buildings are no more than generalised. The painter may have based his canvas on the engraving after J. B. C. Chatelain published in 1750 (in *Fifty Small Original and Elegant Views of the Most Splendid Churches, Villages, Rural Prospects and Masterly Pieces of Architecture Adjacent to London*), which depicts the view from precisely the same viewpoint, and the costume indicates a date of about 1750. This remains, however, the earliest painted picture of the bridge.

A larger version, in which the huntsman and house and the two figures on the right also appear, was with Sabin Galleries in 1962; and a version with different staffage was in the collection of Sir R. G. Leon in 1970.

Provenance:
Bequeathed by Marcus R. Samuel in 1942.

Bibliography:
Hayes (cat. no. 18).

Provenance:
Bequeathed by Marcus R. Samuel in 1942 (as Boydell).

Bibliography:
Hayes (cat. no. 17).

24.
BRITISH SCHOOL
Putney and the Thames from Putney Bridge [42.50/1]
*c.*1750
Oil on canvas, 34.4 x 100 cm
Not signed or dated

THIS IS the earliest painted view of Putney; it is looking up the river from Putney Bridge, and shows the riverside village of Putney on the left. The first bridge connecting Putney and Fulham, of which only a fragment is seen here, was the wooden structure built in 1729 by Thomas Phillips, carpenter to George II after an original design by Jacob Acworth (see cat. no. 22), apparently revised by Thomas Ripley and William Cheselden. This bridge (see cat. no. 23) remained in place until the present stone bridge was built in 1882–6 by Sir Joseph Bazalgette. The charge for crossing was a penny for foot passengers and up to two shillings for vehicles, and, as this was the only bridge above London Bridge until the opening of Westminster Bridge in 1750, the proprietors who subscribed towards its cost made a good income from it.

At this date, Putney was only a small village, little more than the High Street and the riverside area, but it was already noted for the beauty of its villas and also for its orchards and market gardens. With the exception of the fifteenth-century tower, seen prominently in this view, the parish church of St Mary's was rebuilt in 1836.

The Museum picture corresponds exactly, save for the disposition of the boats, with Boydell's engraving of the scene which is undated but probably published *c.*1750. It is difficult to determine which came first and at least one, and possibly two, other versions are known to exist (see Sotheby's, 11 July 1990, 71).

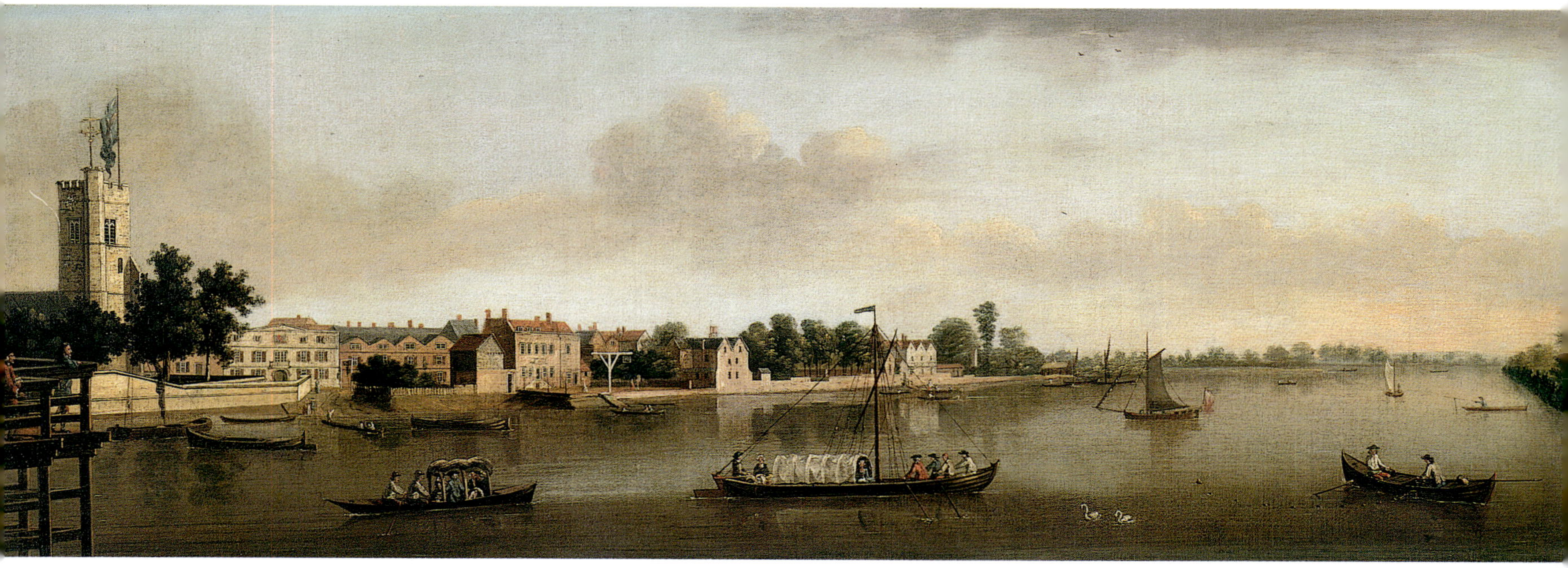

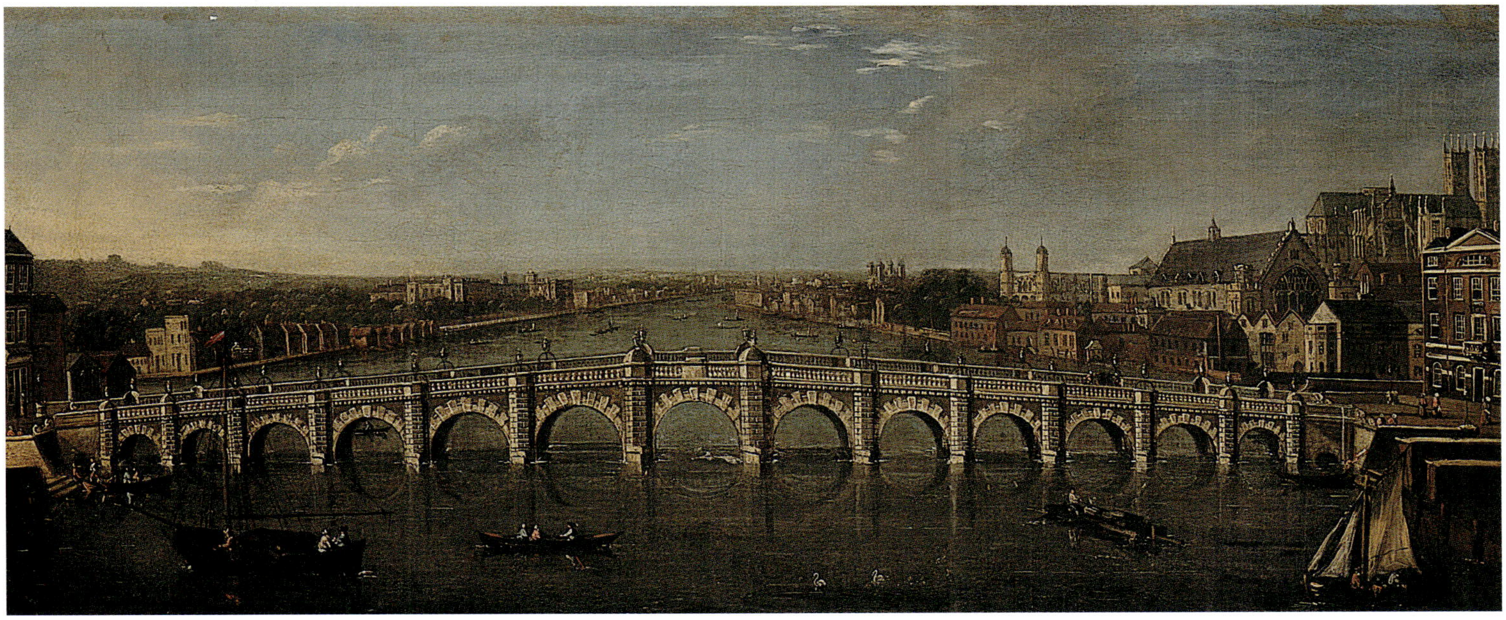

25.
BRITISH SCHOOL
Westminster Bridge from the River, Looking South [A 8079]
c.1750
Oil on canvas, 36.9 x 89.9 cm
Not signed or dated

THIS VIEW is looking at Westminster Bridge from the north. A brief history of the bridge is given on p71. Note the stone alcoves, each with lamps on top (for lighting in London, see p92), in which pedestrians could shelter in showery weather, and the broad approaches to the bridge at both ends. The problems raised by the building of the bridge passed largely unnoticed by most Londoners, who responded to this new landmark as one of the wonders of the age. Twelve days before the official opening (19 November 1750), a crowd driven by impatient enthusiasm attempted to cross the bridge and a troop of guards had to be called in.

Beyond Westminster Bridge can be seen: on the left, the bargehouses of the Archbishop of Canterbury, Lambeth Palace; and on the right, the last houses on Millbank (Mill Bank Row), the four towers of the church of St John's Smith Square, St Stephen's Chapel (meeting place of the House of Commons until its destruction by fire in 1834), Westminster Hall, Westminster Abbey and at the foot of the bridge, the Bear Inn.

The picture is crudely painted, and cannot be relied upon for detailed accuracy. It probably derives from one of the many engravings of this view. Innumerable versions of this composition exist, the prime source being Canaletto's painting of 1746, now in the collection of the Yale Center for British Art, which incorrectly shows the bridge in its completed state and also depicts the Lord Mayor's procession.

Provenance:
Purchased from Leggatt Brothers in 1912.

Bibliography:
Hayes (cat. no. 20); Hugh Phillips, *The Thames around 1750*, 1951, pp134 and 135; W. G. Constable (revised J. G. Links), *Canaletto*, 1989, cat. nos 435 and 436; J. G. Links, 'Canaletto and Old Westminster' in *Apollo*, May 1992.

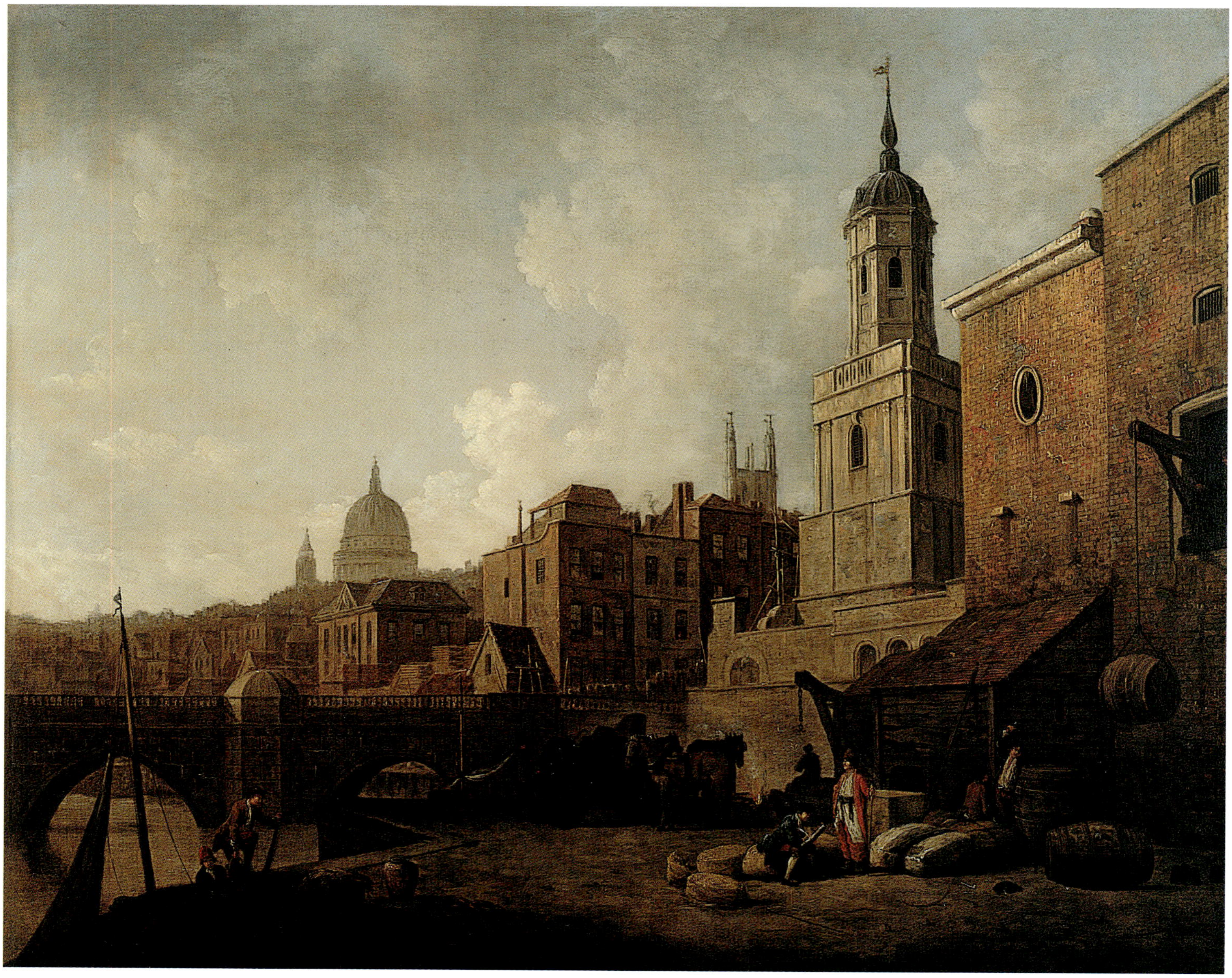

26.

WILLIAM MARLOW
(1740–1813)
Fresh Wharf, London Bridge [50.31]
*c.*1762
Oil on canvas, 99.1 x 128.7 cm
Not signed or dated

THIS PICTURE was taken from Fresh Wharf, the most westerly of the 'legal quays' between the Tower and London Bridge (see p72). The wharf was constructed after the Great Fire to facilitate the activities of the Port and this was one of the most significant improvements incorporated in the rebuilding of the city. Some barrels and bales of merchandise are being checked, and a dray with three horses is seen behind (notice also the Spanish olive jar on the left).

Old London Bridge is seen shorn of its superstructure of shops and houses, which had long been a public nuisance and obstructed the flow of traffic. The demolition, alterations and widening were carried out under the supervision of George Dance the Elder, Clerk of the City

Works, and Sir Robert Taylor, in 1756–62, the east side of the bridge being completed by 1761, and all the houses removed by 1762. Scaffolding and fencing are seen at the north end of the bridge and in front of the church of St Magnus the Martyr; the west ends of the aisles of the church were set back and openings cut through the arches of the tower to make a passageway, as part of the bridge approach widening operations, and the work was begun in 1762 and finished in June 1763. Beyond the bridge (immediately beneath St Paul's) is Fishmongers' Hall, designed by Edward Jerman, which was replaced by the present building in 1831–3. The dome of St Paul's and the tower of St Michael's, Cornhill, appear in the distance.

Marlow served his apprenticeship with Samuel Scott, and the standards of accuracy he maintained in his topographical painting were comparatively high; nevertheless, Fishmongers' Hall has been painted here with single windows (instead of three) in the side bays, St Michael's, Cornhill, could never have been seen from this viewpoint, and the waterwheels of the Bridge Waterworks have been omitted (he later exhibited, in 1780, *The Waterworks at London Bridge on Fire*, at the Society of Artists).

In spirit this painting should be affiliated to the two paintings by Samuel Scott of *The so called Custom House Quay* in the collections of the Fishmongers' Company and the Victoria and Albert Museum. One is dated 1757, the other is a reworking in the 1760s.

There are three other versions of Marlow's composition; one in the Guildhall Art Gallery, City of London, originally painted for Lord Hardwicke (acc. no. 1837), in which more activity is shown in the foreground left; one in the Royal Collection, which is closer in detail to the Museum picture but incorrectly gives Fishmongers' Hall four windows in the central bay and includes two buildings not shown in either this or the Guildhall version, namely the spire of St Antholin's (a church pulled down in 1874) and a large pedimented building in Fish Street Hill which appears never to have been erected; and one much smaller version, almost exactly corresponding to the Museum painting, which was sold at Christie's, 14 July 1994 (44).

Either the Museum painting or one of the other versions is likely to have been the picture exhibited at the Society of Artists in 1762 (under the title: *A view of a wharf, St Magnus church and part of London Bridge*). An upright variant (signed) is at Scampston Hall; and a watercolour copy by John Thirtle, with some alterations in the foreground detail, is in the Victoria and Albert Museum (no. 1272–1871).

Provenance:
Possibly Sir William Chambers, and Chambers sale, Christie's, 6 April 1799 (97), bt Taylor; Mrs Wauchope of Niddrie; Wauchope Settlement Trust Sale, Christie's, 12 May 1950 (58), bt London Museum (purchased out of the Joicey Trust Fund).

Bibliography:
Hayes (cat. no. 73); *William Marlow*, exhibition catalogue, Guildhall Art Gallery, 1956, no. 7; Hugh Phillips, *The Thames around 1750*, 1951, pp41 and 202.

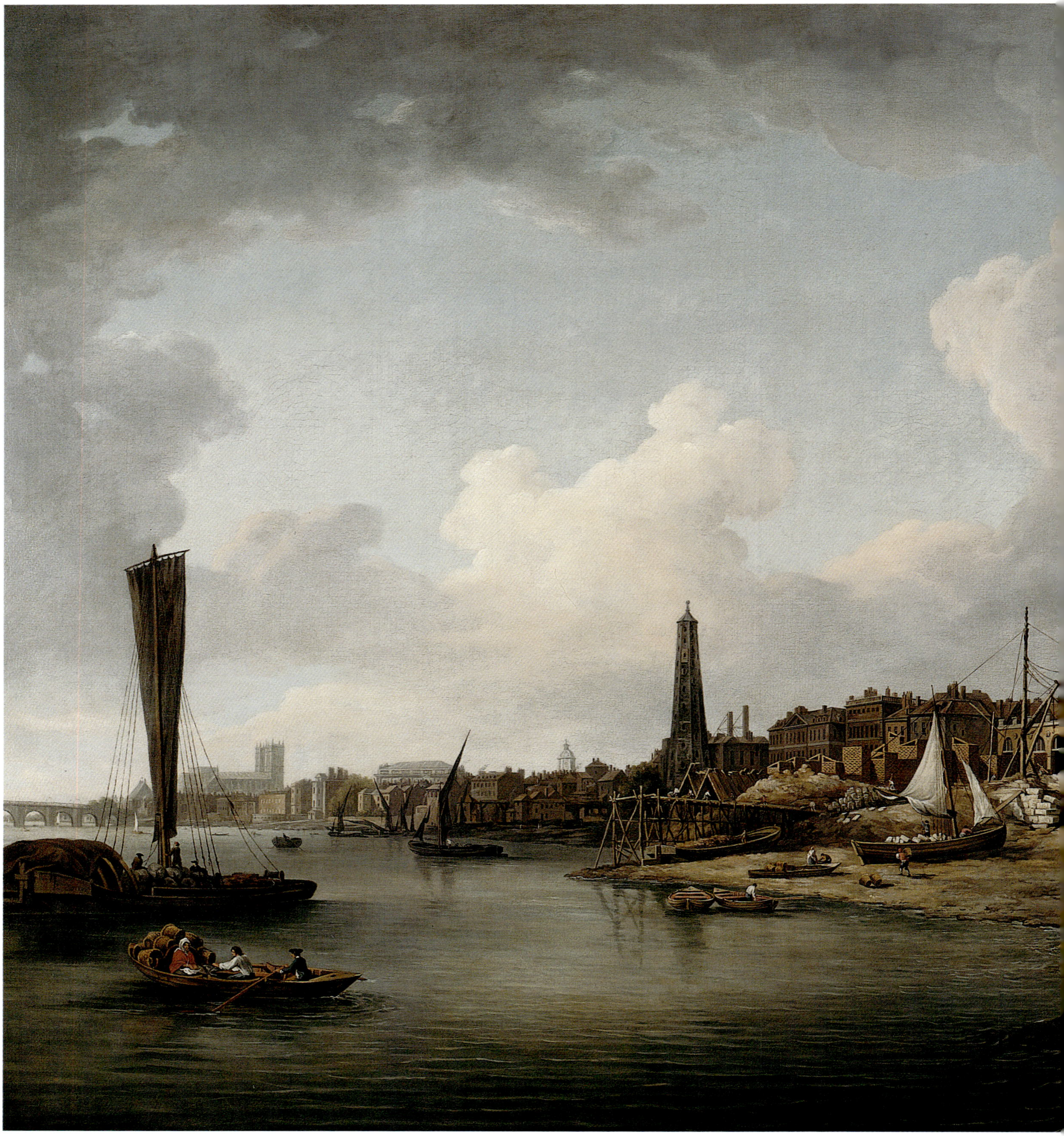

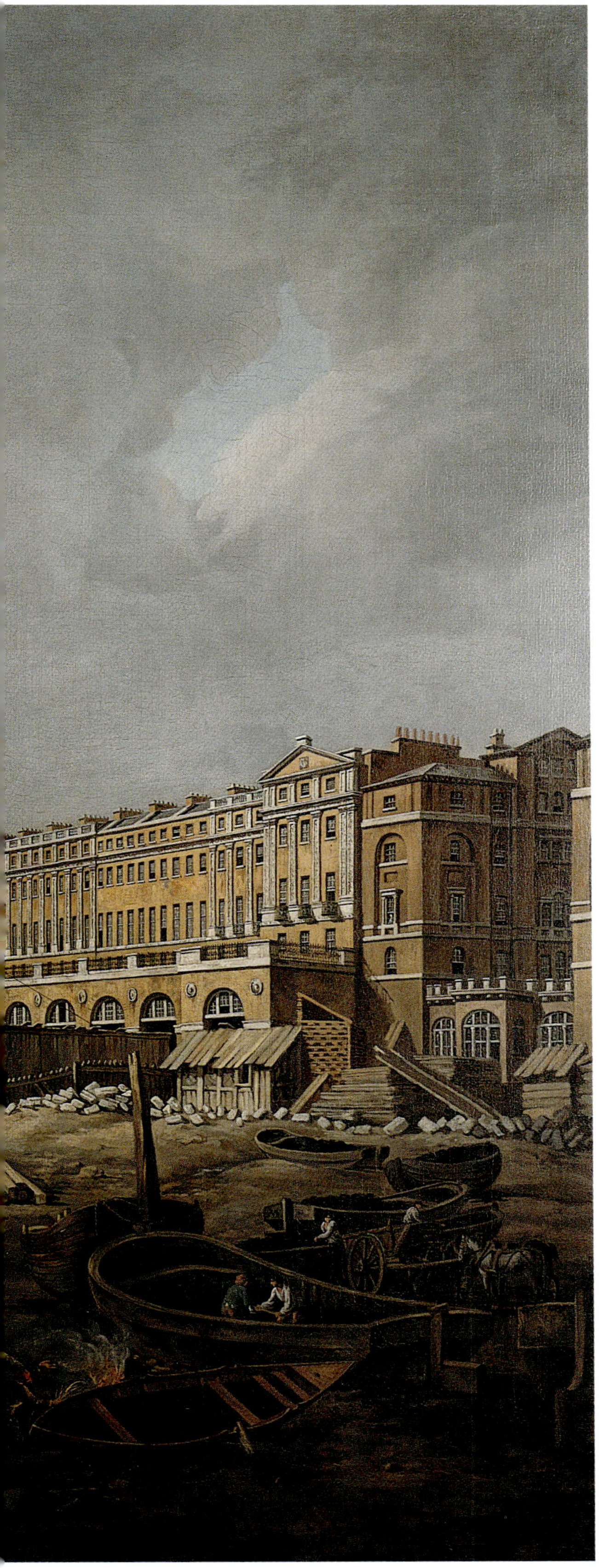

27.

WILLIAM MARLOW

(1740–1813)

The London Riverfront between Westminster and the Adelphi [A 25874]

*c.*1771–2

Oil on canvas, 135.3 x 190 cm

Signed with initials on the stern of a boat on the right: *WM*

THIS VIEW of the riverfront from the site of the present Waterloo Bridge makes an interesting comparison with the *c.*1770 watercolour looking at Westminster from Temple Gardens (sold by Aldridge's of Bath Ltd, 30 March 1993, Lot 684; Martyn Gregory, catalogue 65, no. 70). This watercolour, illustrated overleaf, undoubtedly inspired by the art of Canaletto, treats the riverfront as a distant panorama, whereas here Marlow composes a more focused view which beautifully balances foreground with background and land with water.

The Adelphi was a highly imaginative, but in the event financially disastrous, development by the brothers Adam. These architects took a lease on the site of Durham House in 1768, and obtained an Act of Parliament which enabled them to reclaim part of the river (a shallow bay) at this point. They then built, over a vast substructure of brick vaults which served as foundations, a superb terrace of private houses fronting the river. The Royal Terrace was conceived as an architectural unity with pilasters accenting the centre and ends; four of the subsidiary streets were called after their own names, Robert, John, James and William.

The Museum picture must date from about 1771–2, with the Royal Terrace and Adam Street already built, but Robert

Provenance:
Possibly Thomas Parnell, 2 Royal Terrace, Adelphi, and his sale, Foster's, 12 June 1829 (40), bt Colnaghi; Leggatt Brothers, from whom it was purchased by J. Pierpont Morgan Jr and presented in 1923.

Bibliography:
Hayes (cat. no. 74); Celina Fox, *Londoners*, 1987, pp172–3; *Canaletto & England*, Michael Liversidge and Jane Farrington (eds), 1993, p144.

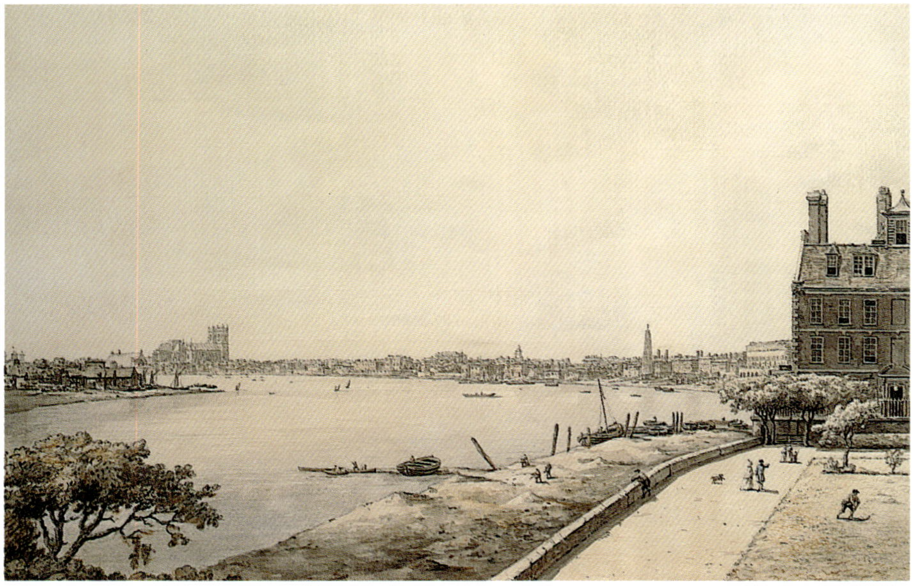

William Marlow (1740–1813)
View of the Thames looking towards Westminster from Temple Gardens *c.*1770
Watercolour reproduced by kind permission of the Martyn Gregory Gallery, London.

Street still to be constructed. Two rough preparatory sketches in pen and brown ink, and a more detailed study in pencil, all for the right half of the composition, are in the British Museum. A large watercolour of the Adelphi Wharf by an anonymous artist, dating from *c.*1810, and also in the Museum of London collection updates this scene by Marlow (acc. no. 86.148).

In Marlow's painting the Royal Terrace is shown completed (some of the houses were ready for occupation by 1772, and David Garrick had moved into number 5 by April of that year) and so is Adam Street (the street at right angles to the Terrace terminated by a house with a pediment), houses in this street being let in 1771. But the companion street to Adam Street on the west side of the Terrace, Robert Street, was not yet built – two of the houses were noted as 'not being quite finished' in 1773 – nor was Adelphi Wharf. Heaps of stone and more carefully piled stacks of timber are distributed about the site; a jetty has been constructed for rubbish disposal (the rubble would be dropped into waiting craft); and a number of barges and skiffs(?) are drawn up on the foreshore. On the extreme right is Salisbury Street, rebuilt by James Paine in 1765–9.

The presence of coal barges on the right-hand side is an early manifestation of the coal activities of Adelphi Wharf. The coal arrived from north-east England and was unloaded in mid-stream into barges to the east of London Bridge. It was then distributed to all parts of London by water to wharves, causeways and stairs. Two Regency artists, Théodore Géricault and John Augustus Atkinson, later recorded this activity most strikingly.

The whole of the Adelphi buildings (except for 7 Adam Street and one or two others) were demolished in 1936, and Colcutt and Hamp's massive office block, Adelphi House, built in 1936–8, now occupies the site.

Versions of this canvas, of approximately the same size, and differing only very slightly in detail, are in the possession of the Earl of Iveagh and the National Westminster Bank (two versions). Another view by Marlow, showing the Adelphi under construction, but from the opposite side, is in the collection of Lord Rosebery at Dalmeny. One of these pictures may be identified with the *View of the Royal Terrace, Adelph, in 1771, just before its completion* by Marlow, which was in Thomas Parnell's sale at Foster's, 12 June 1829. A painting entitled *The Adelphi* was also exhibited by Marlow at the Society of Artists in 1771. A later painting by Marlow of the Adelphi, probably the picture exhibited at the Royal Academy in 1789 (172), is in the Government Picture Collection; it is taken from a different angle showing the activity on Adelphi Wharf with the Royal Terrace much closer.

Key

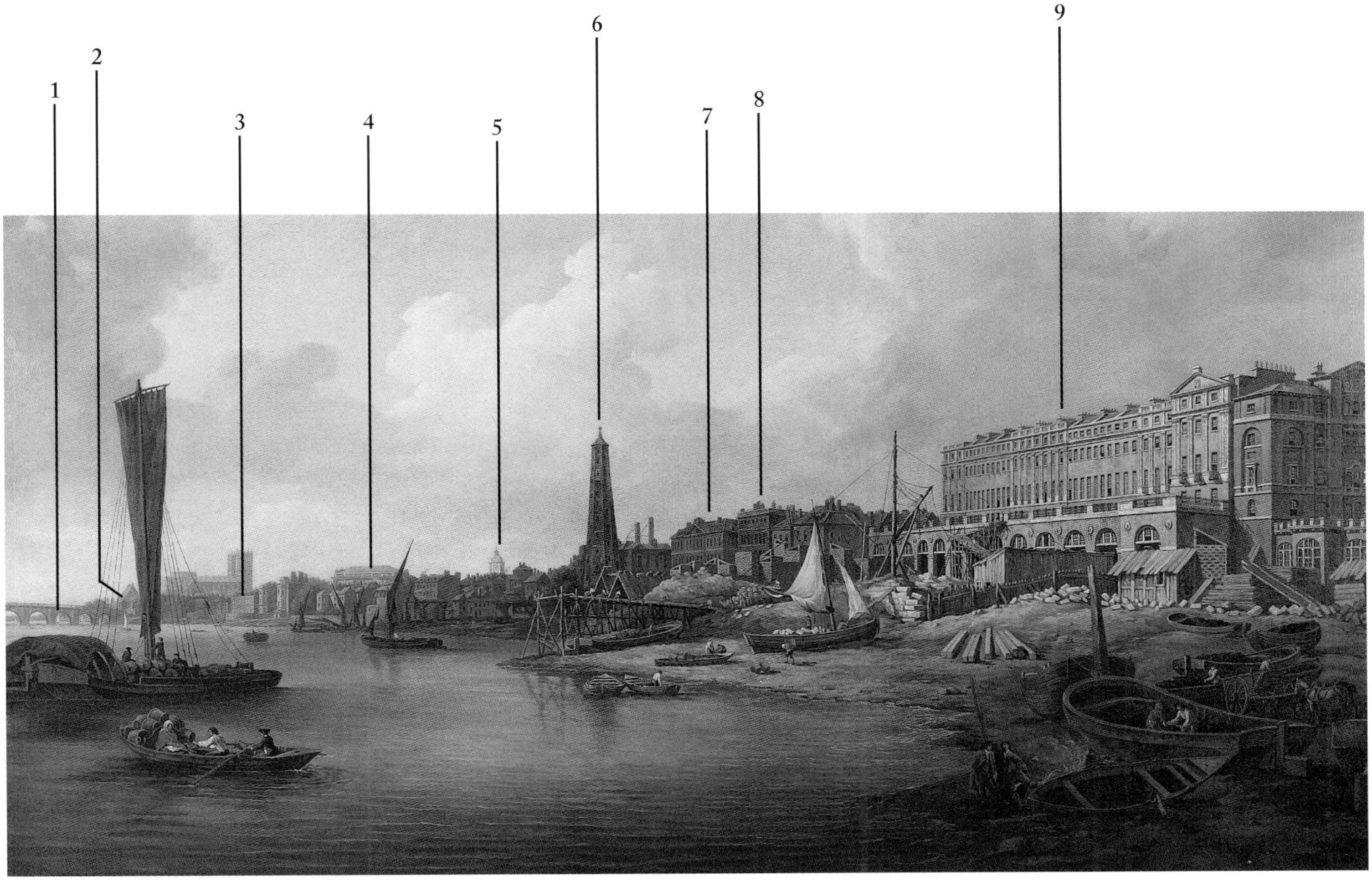

1. Westminster Bridge
2. Westminster Hall
3. Westminster Abbey
4. Banqueting House
5. Cupola of Horse Guards
6. Tower and chimneys of the York Buildings Waterworks Company
7. Salt Office (once the residence of Samuel Pepys, 1688–1701, and once of Robert Harley, Earl of Oxford, 1702–14)
8. House at SE corner of Buckingham Street owned by Sir Philip Botelier 1740–63
9. The Adelphi

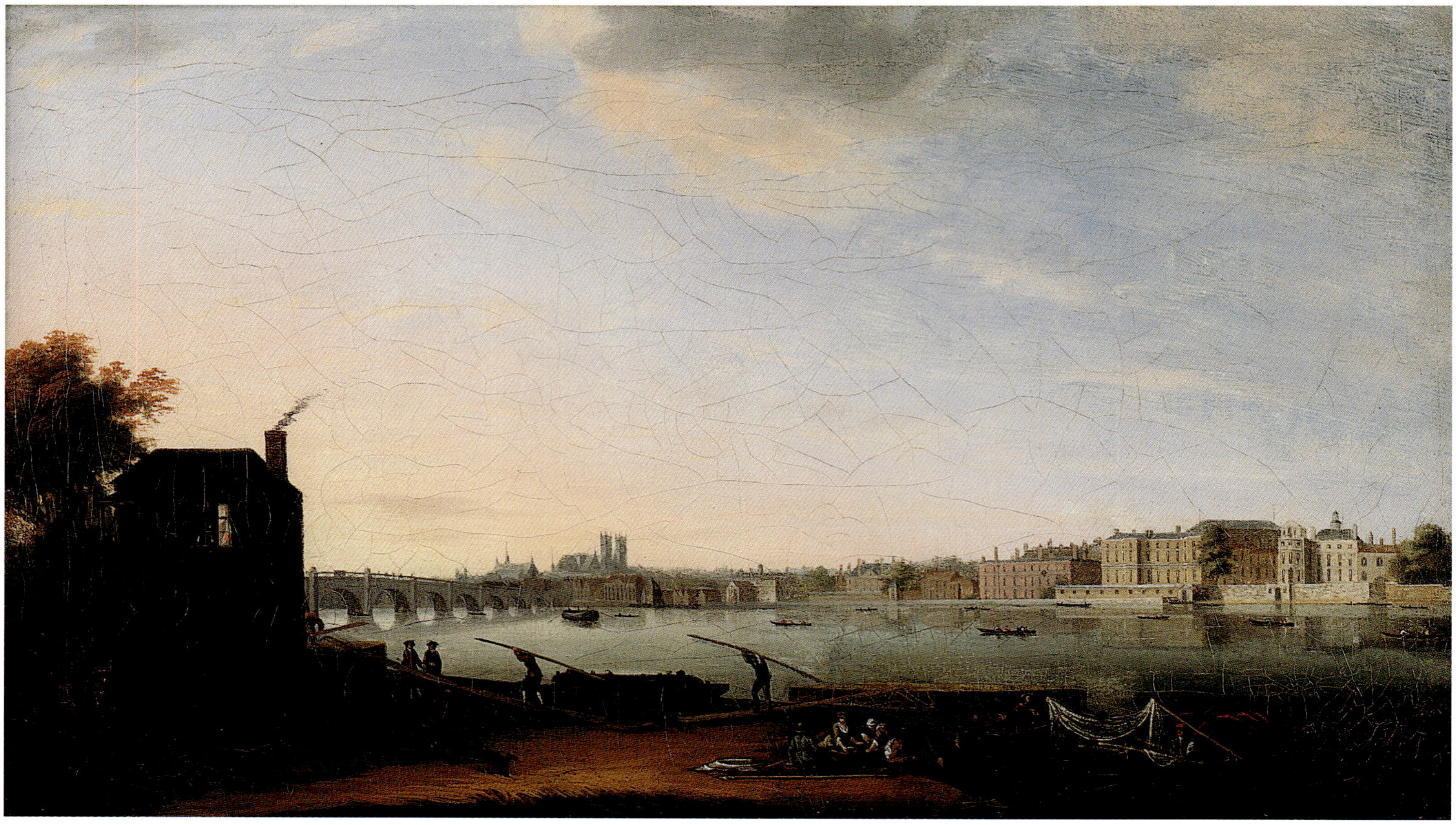

Provenance:
Unknown.

Bibliography:
Hayes (cat. no. 21; the accession number A 28583 is wrong).

28.

BRITISH SCHOOL

Westminster Bridge and Whitehall from Lambeth [A 28583]
*c.*1775
Oil on canvas, 35.6 x 72 cm
Illegibly inscribed and perhaps dated on the landing stage (the light area)

A VIEW of Westminster and the Whitehall riverfront looking south-westwards from one of the timber yards on the Lambeth shore, perhaps Mr Smith's, one of the largest on that stretch of the river, which features on Richard Horwood's 1792–9 map of London and in Samuel Leigh's 1829 *Panoramic View of London from the Adelphi* (coloured aquatint in Museum's collection, acc. no. 81.136).

Members of the nobility had occupied mansions along the Thames since medieval times, frequently with pleasant gardens running down to the water's edge, and some continued to do so until well into the nineteenth century. The houses occupied by the Dukes of Richmond and Montagu were among the grander of these town residences; and new Montagu House (built 1859–62) remained a private residence (of the Dukes of Buccleuch) until 1917.

In the foreground, fishermen are active, two women are sorting fish and some planks of timber are being carried ashore. The Surrey waterfront, from Westminster Bridge to the Old Barge House Stairs opposite the Temple, was largely composed of timber yards and wharves, the storehouse of London's flourishing building trade.

The costume indicates a date of about 1775. The work makes an interesting comparison with Samuel Scott's paintings of the building of Westminster Bridge executed some thirty years earlier (five versions: see Richard Kingzett, 'A catalogue of the works of Samuel Scott', in *Walpole Society*, vol. XLVIII). The works are taken from a similar viewpoint and they highlight the timber trade characteristic of the south bank. While the erection of Westminster Bridge monopolised the attention in Scott's painting, the work under review reverts back to a more traditional panoramic approach, which reveals much of the topography of the north bank.

KEY

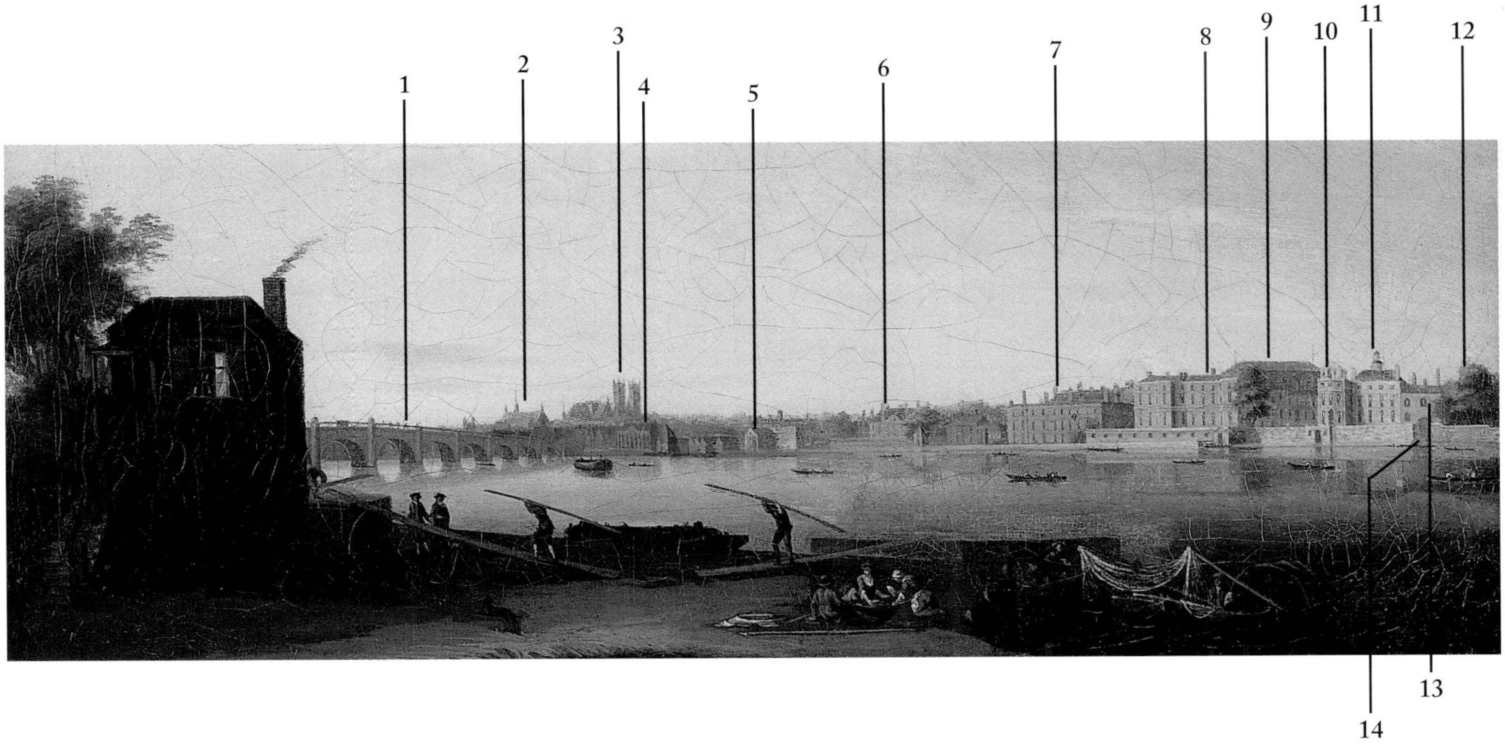

1. Westminster Bridge
2. Westminster Hall
3. Westminster Abbey (with its two western towers designed by Hawksmoor and completed in 1745)
4. Dorset Court (a mid-eighteenth century residential block)
5. Richmond House
6. Montagu House
7. The Duchess of Portland's House (with its celebrated Portland Museum)
8. Pembroke House (two bay windows and water-gate altered by William Chambers in 1757)
9. Banqueting House
10. Viscountess Townshend's House
11. Cupola of the Horse Guards
12. Trees of Whitehall Yard
13. Sir Thomas Robinson's House (Whitehall stairs in front)
14. Whitehall Stairs

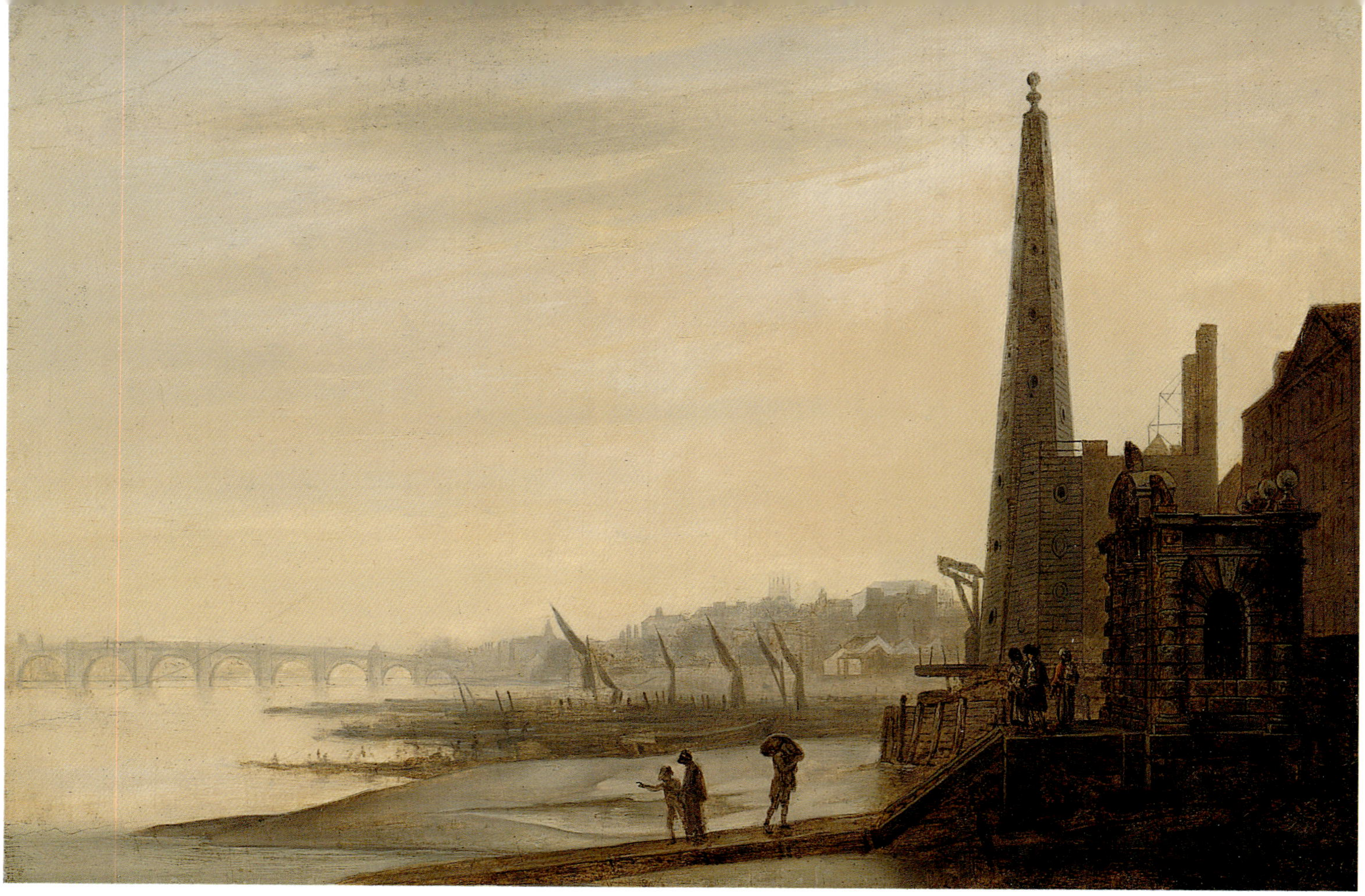

Provenance:
Purchased from Leggatt Brothers in 1912 (as Vanderstein).

Bibliography:
Hayes (cat. no. 19); Hugh Phillips, *The Thames around 1750*, 1951, pp116–17.

29.

BRITISH SCHOOL

Westminster from York Stairs [A 8083]
*c.*1780–5
Oil on panel, 29.4 x 44.1 cm
Not signed or dated

IN THE foreground is York Stairs, with the York Water Gate, which was then the means of egress to the river from the terrace of York Buildings. Behind are the tower and chimneys of the York Buildings Waterworks Company, founded at the end of the seventeenth century to supply water to houses recently built on the sites of the old riverside mansions of the nobility. On the right is the Salt Office (also shown in Marlow, cat. no. 27). In the distance is Westminster Bridge, first opened to traffic in 1750, and the riverfront of Westminster and Whitehall, with the towers of Westminster Abbey and the roof of the Banqueting House visible over the tops of the houses.

The extensive foreshore at low tide, so evident here, which was the hunting ground of mudlarks in search of nails and other small objects they could sell for a few pence, virtually disappeared with the construction of the Embankment in the 1860s; the York Water Gate also became isolated on the north side of the Embankment Gardens some hundred and fifty metres away from the river.

This small and delightful painting is remarkable for its rendering of the misty atmosphere of the Thames foreshore, perhaps at the beginning or the end of a day.

The costume of the figures indicates a date of about 1780–5.

30.

BRITISH SCHOOL

The Thames at Millbank [A 8088]
*c.*1785–90
Oil on canvas, 55.6 x 85.6 cm
Not signed or dated

THIS VIEW shows Sullivan's boat-building yard and the group of houses at Millbank stairs, whence a ferry operated to Vauxhall. At this date, Millbank was a pleasant riverside walk, extending almost as far as Chelsea Hospital. The marshy area of Tothill Fields behind was still totally undeveloped, and the most southerly house in built-up Westminster was Belgrave House, the riverside home of Earl Grosvenor, which was pulled down in 1809 to make way for the Millbank Penitentiary (in its turn destroyed, in 1890, for the building of the Tate Gallery). On the Surrey shore, houses now stretched as far as Vauxhall, and in the distance is Lambeth Palace, with the dome of St Paul's beyond.

This stretch of the Thames was popular with artists who often depicted the picturesque wind-blown trees at Millbank (here in the middle distance at the end of the river path).

Another view by the same hand, depicting the Red House at Battersea, was with Spink in the 1960s and attributed to Thomas Priest.

Provenance:
Purchased from Leggatt Brothers in 1912.

Bibliography:
Hayes (cat. no. 16).

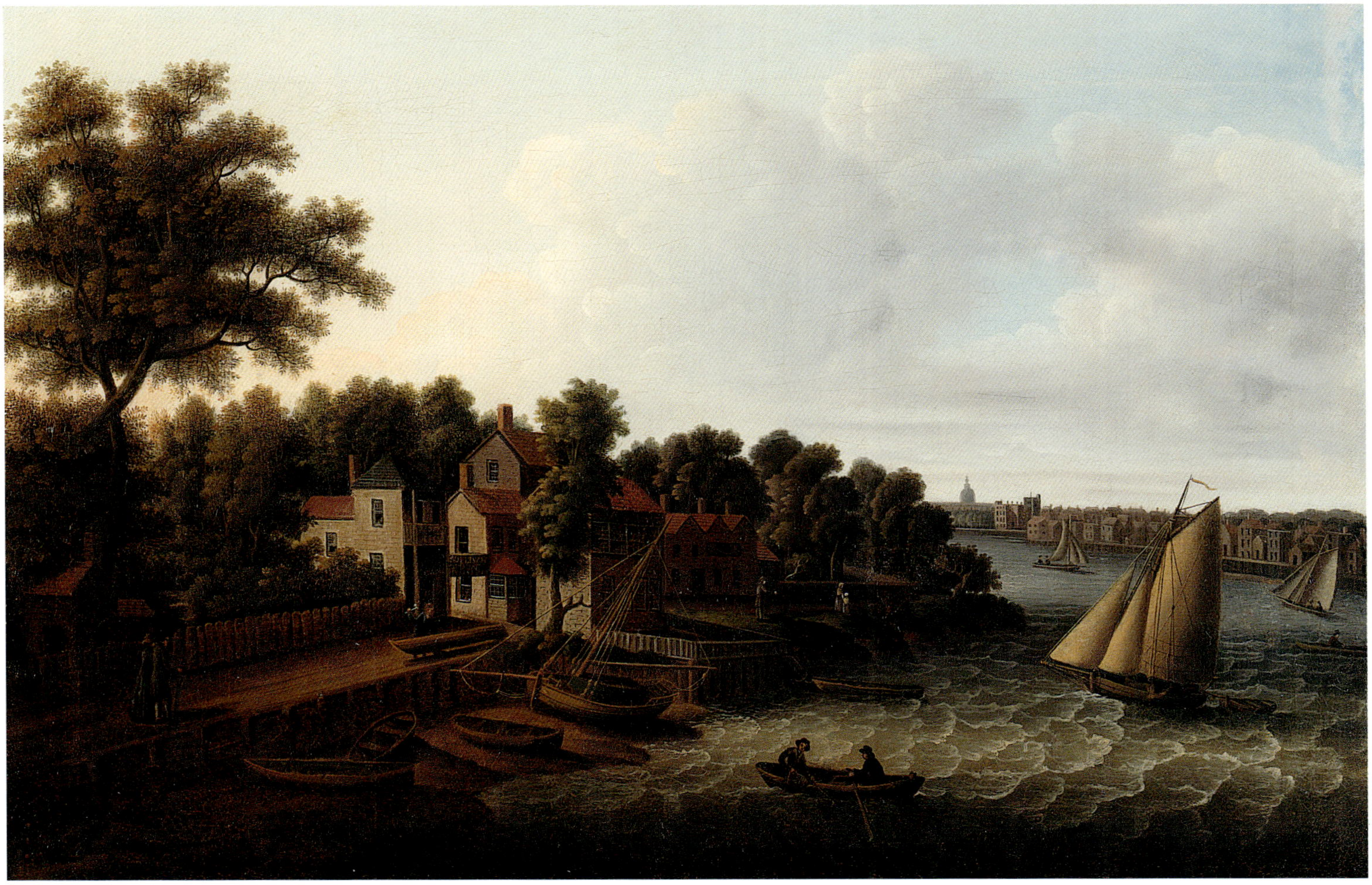

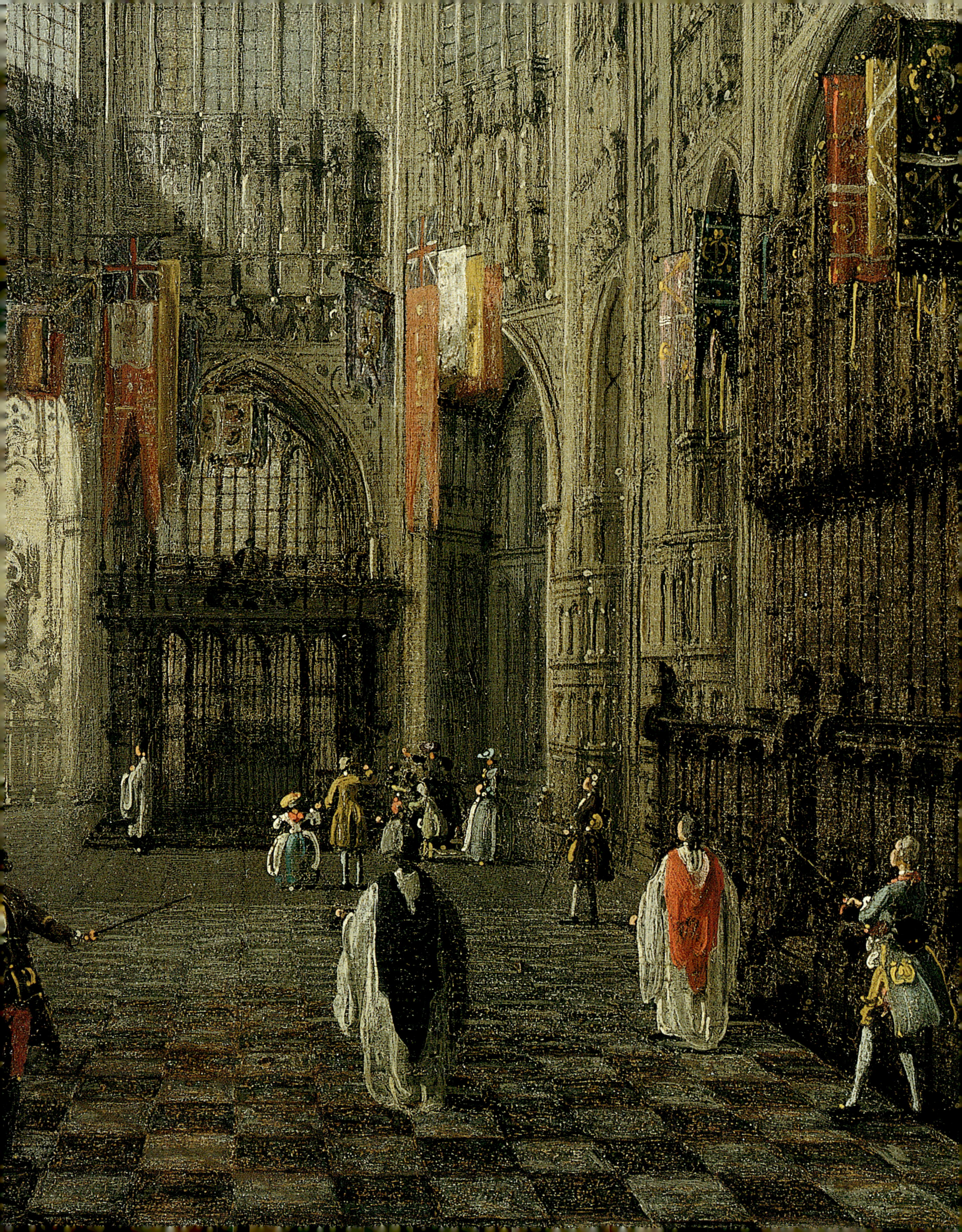

STREETS AND BUILDINGS

IT IS IN THE EIGHTEENTH century that, for the first time in British painting, we witness the visual recording of the life and fabric of London's streets.

César de Saussure's account of his 1725 visit to London[1] offers many insights against which we should measure the group of paintings under review:

> A number of [streets] are dirty, narrow and badly built; others again are wide and straight, bordered with fine houses . . . The streets of London are unpleasantly full of either dust or mud. This arises from the quantity of houses that are continually being built, and also from the large number of coaches and chariots rolling in the streets day and night. Carts are used for removing mud, and in the summer the streets are watered by carts carrying barrels or casks pierced with holes through which the water flows. Another unpleasantness of the streets is that the pavement is so bad and rough that when you drive in a coach you are most cruelly shaken, whereas if you go on foot you have a nice smooth path paved with wide flat stones, and elevated above the road . . .

See cat. no. 35 for Saussure's last point, and for as late as 1824, see cat. no. 62. Archenholtz's observations offer further insight into the complex reality of London's street life in around 1780. To encompass the vast discrepancies he found, he envisaged two Londons:

> The east end, especially along the shores of the Thames, consists of old houses, the streets there are narrow, dark and ill-paved; inhabited by sailors and other workmen who are employed in the construction of ships and by a great part of Jews. The contrast between this and the west end is astonishing: the houses here are mostly new and elegant; the squares are superb, the streets straight and open.[2]

While London's grander aspects might consistently be illustrated through paintings, its seedier sides and its poorer areas were often best recorded in caricature form – depicting, for instance, crossing a dirty street, nightwatchmen repeatedly defeated by crime, sailors ransacking houses, drunks vomiting in the streets. The only major painter to record something of the sorry state of the city was William Hogarth, but his ultimate goal for painting such vivid London scenes as *A Rake's Progress* or *Industry and Idleness* was the subsequent engraving of these works. Sadly this artist is not represented here, but the spirit of caricature in which John Collet worked owed much to Hogarth's example and these two painters provide a healthy antidote to the grand and airy views of 'Canaletto's London'.

Besides Samuel Scott's riverside paintings (see pp72–3) and the recording of ship-building activities (see note 14 on p74), there is virtually nothing to illustrate the East End and very little to bring to life the streets of the City. The shift to the West End which has already been mentioned was such that what visual evidence we have of Georgian street life is centred on the West End and more particularly on the St James's and Covent Garden areas (see below, p117), where many painters resided. Even then the coverage remained patchy: the depiction of London's squares, the capital's most elegant form of development in the West End, only very occasionally produced paintings.[3]

The introduction of the first Westminster Paving Act in 1762 may be described as the beginning of a new era.[4] Commissioners were appointed to maintain and repair streets. There were a few casualties such as the disappearance of London's dangerous but colourful signboards, those 'specimens of genius... truly English' first authorised by Charles I in 1637[5] (see cat. no. 31). Advantages outweighed disadvantages and in 1787 the whole enterprise was described as having 'introduced a degree of elegance and symmetry into the streets of the metropolis, that is the admiration of all Europe and far exceeds anything of the kind in the modern world'.[6] Even the removal of London's picturesque signs was felt to render the streets 'more airy and wholesome'.[7]

This development paralleled the improvement of street lighting under local acts. César de Saussure wrote in 1725:

> Most of the streets are wonderfully well-lit, for in front of each house hangs a lantern or a large globe of glass inside of which is a lamp burning all night. Large houses have two of these lamps suspended outside their doors by iron supports, and some have even four. [See cat. no. 35.][8]

William Hogarth
(1697–1764)
Night, from *The Four Times of Day*, *c.*1736
Oil on canvas
Upton House (The National Trust)
Photograph: The National Trust Photographic Library.

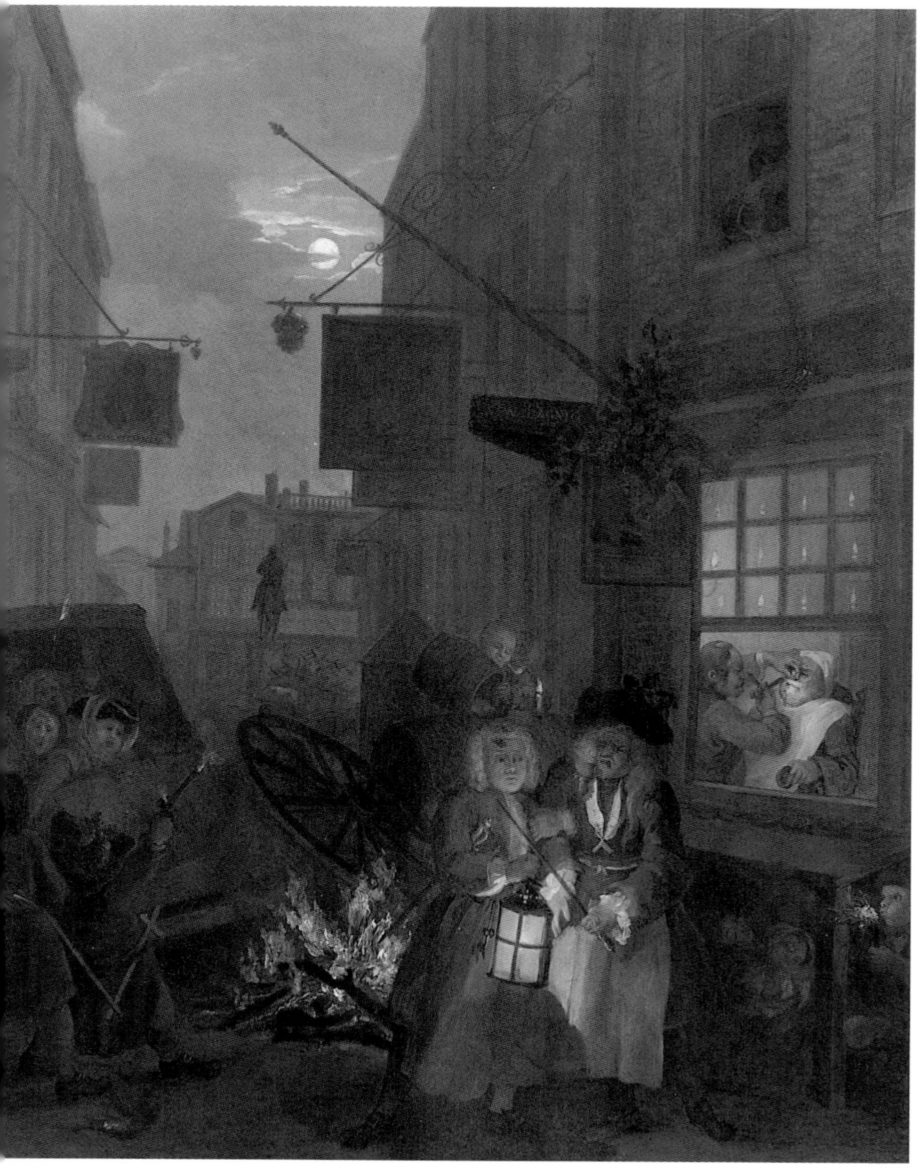

It was William and Mary who instituted a system of public lighting from Michaelmas to Lady Day, which operated from dark till midnight. Those Londoners who did not contribute to this public service were responsible for hanging lights outside their properties. The dependence on individual goodwill was not always effective, but in 1736 an act was passed in the City enabling the collection of rates to the specific end of ensuring public lighting. Other parishes followed and the lighting of the streets was so spectacular that a commentator wrote that in Oxford Street alone, 'there are more lamps than in all the city of Paris'.[9]

These developments are difficult to chart in images. The theme of night painting in art is patchy. The painter was faced with considerable technical difficulty when trying to 'light' a night painting and after a short-lived period of (foreign) night pieces to capture the Great Fire in its full horror, no English painter dared to address the theme until Hogarth in his *Four Times of the Day*. The 'Night' painting[10] is set in Charing Cross. The moon, hand-held lantern and window candles would have been insufficient to light the painting and Hogarth introduced an additional source by devising an incident involving a street fire. Not even Canaletto was prepared to tackle the subject of night painting and he settled for the (paradoxical) day depiction of Vauxhall and Ranelagh pleasure gardens, despite their essentially nocturnal vocation.

1. César de Saussure, *A foreign view of England in the reigns of George I and George II*, transl. and ed. Madame Van Muyden, London, 1902, p67.
2. Quoted in Dorothy George, *London Life in the XVIIIth century*, 1925, p66.
3. Hanover Square by the Swedish painter Elias Martin (collection Count Trolle-Bonde, reproduced in Malcolm Warner, *The Image of London*, exhibition catalogue, Barbican Art Gallery, 1987, p133) and Leicester Square, cat. no. 37.
4. These themes and many others of eighteenth-century London are well described in three key works: Dorothy George, 1925; Hugh Phillips, *Mid-Georgian London*, 1964; and Dan Cruikshank and Neil Burton, *Life in the Georgian City*, 1990.
5. From Hogarth's assistant, Philip Dawes, quoted in Celina Fox's 'Introduction' in the exhibition catalogue *Specimens of Genius Truly English*, an exhibition of eighteenth-century designs for London signboards from the collection of the late Lord Clark, 1984, The Clarendon Gallery and Niall Hobhouse.
6. Dorothy George, 1925, p100.
7. Ibid.
8. See César de Saussure, op. cit., p67.
9. Dorothy George, 1925, p102.
10. National Trust, Bearsted Collection, Upton House, Warwickshire.

Provenance:
Purchased from Julian Simon Fine Art (as attributed to Balthazar Nebot) in 1982 with a grant from the MGC/V&A Purchase Grant Fund.

Bibliography:
J. T. Smith, *London Cries*, 1817; Kenneth Rogers, *Old Cheapside and Poultry*, 1931.

31.
BRITISH SCHOOL
The Curds and Whey Seller, Cheapside
[82.338]
*c.*1730
Oil on canvas, 127.3 x 102 cm
Not signed or dated

THREE CHIMNEYSWEEPS are buying curds and whey from a blind(?) girl wearing the gown and petticoat with apron and pocket, scarf and hat that were a familiar sight in contemporary market paintings. The scene is set at the western end of Cheapside in the City, at the corner of Blowbladder Street and at the foot of the Little Conduit which, when it stopped functioning, became a haunt for chimney-sweeps.

The Little Conduit, the monumental structure behind the street seller, is a unique depiction of the post-Great Fire Cheapside conduit which replaced the fifteenth-century Gothic conduit at the east end of the church of St Michael-le-Querne shown in Ralph Treswell's 1585 drawing in the British Museum (John Schofield, *The Surveys of Ralph Treswell*, 1987, pp56–7, plate 1). The design adopted was that of the fashionable obelisk, many of which had been much admired by British visitors in Rome. Work started on 5 March 1679 but was never completed beyond the base shown here, despite the catalogue of complaints filed in the Corporation records.

There are no further references to the conduit after 1707, when the case was brought to the Court of Common Council. According to A. S. Foord in *Springs, Streams and Spas of London*, 1910, p256, the Little Conduit was pulled down in 1727. Maps did not always include the conduit, but the site is visible on George Foster's map of 1739, although by the time Rocque made his 1746 survey it had disappeared.

Ned Ward provides colourful information on the presence of chimney-sweeps at the Cheapside conduit in 1698:

> . . . at Cheapside Conduit, pallisaded with chimneysweepers' brooms and guarded with such an infernal crew of soot-coloured funnel scourers that a countryman seeing so many black attendants waiting at a stone hovel, took it to be one of Old Nick's tenements.
> [*The London Spy*, republished 1927, p74]

This is exactly the scene depicted here. According to J. T. Smith, the pudding men of Hogarth's day were still certain to congregate at Tyburn on execution days 'and indeed many articles were sold & the cries of new milk, curds and whey, spice cakes, barley sugar & hot spice gingerbread were... numerous and loud'. In John Collet's *Covent Garden Piazza and Market* (see cat. no. 41), a curds and whey seller is operating in a busy public place. In Peter Angelis's painting of the same subject (*c.*1727, Paul Mellon collection) and in Egbert van Heemskerk's *Bartholomew's Fair* (Guildhall Art Gallery) older women wearing a similar costume display a cooked version of this foodstuff. The basic wooden pail shown here is replaced by a sturdy and smart earthenware pot and the milky product has been shaped into small pancakes. By the early nineteenth century the artists' favourite food stall had become that of the saloop seller, offering a hot drink made from the powdered root of a plant imported from Turkey. Since artists have tended to depict these food stalls in the context of fairs and markets, it may be worth highlighting here the presence, very near by, of the City's main market, Newgate.

The background of the painting is a rapid but accurate record of the appearance of Cheapside in the mid-eighteenth century. This can be established by comparing it with engravings of the period and by the identification of a number of street signs, for instance The Naked Boy and Glove, in the left foreground on the corner of Blowbladder Street. It is also interesting to note that after almost a hundred years, the pair formed by the Nag's Head and its spherical companion (The Globe?), so prominent in the engraving of the procession of Marie de' Medici (1639), can be seen in the middle ground of the painting.

In composition the work may be linked to two works by Peter Angelis (1685–1734). One in the Paul Mellon collection showing a vegetable seller at Covent Garden also has a monumental figure set against an architectural base, with a glimpse of the location in the background. The other is a group of beggars and street sellers in Ludgate Street (sold at Sotheby's, 18 November 1981), where the street background is composed in an almost identical way. Although the painting under review may appear, architecturally or topographically, more competent than the Angelis, its style is much cruder. The artist may have been affiliated to the so-called Covent Garden Group (see p118–19) but he is unlikely to have been one of its main protagonists.

The painting can be dated to about 1730 on costume grounds.

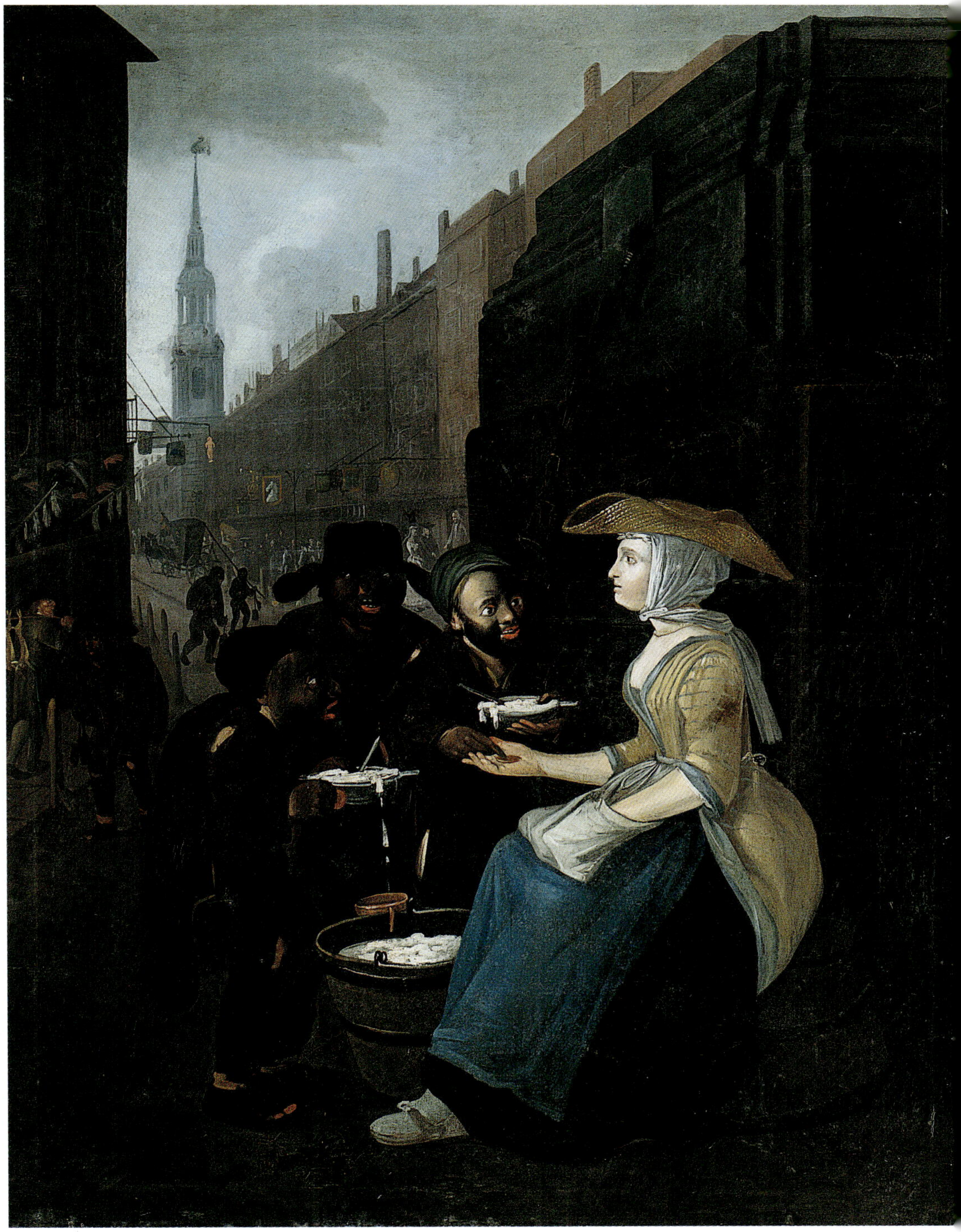

Provenance:
B. C. Creasy; Creasy sale, Christie's, 30 November 1917 (13, as Laroon), bt London Museum.

Bibliography:
Hayes (cat. no. 64); *Survey of London*, vol. XIV, 1931, pp113–41.

32.
BRITISH SCHOOL
The Garden of No. 10 Downing Street
[A 20760]
c.1736–45
Oil on canvas, 89.4 x 142.8 cm
Not signed or dated

THIS PIECE of pure landscape in an urban context shows the garden of 10 Downing Street in the foreground, surrounded by a high brick wall; two gardeners are shown at work, one of them rolling the gravel path, the other tidying the edge of the grass with a pair of shears. On the terrace are two figures which, according to a nineteenth-century label on the back of the frame, are portraits of Sir Robert Walpole (1676–1745), Prime Minister from 1722 to 1742, and George Pitt, 1st Baron Rivers (1722?–1803). The figure on the left, who is wearing the sash of the Order of the Garter, is definitely not Walpole, but, judging from portraits of him by Kneller, might well be intended to be Spencer Compton, 1st Earl of Wilmington (1673?–1743), who succeeded Walpole as First Lord of the Treasury in 1742; there is no reason to exclude the identification of the figure in profile as George Pitt, who was elected MP for Shaftesbury in 1742. Number 10 Downing Street, now the official residence of the Prime Minister, was built for the Earl of Lichfield in 1676–7. In 1732, according to Horace Walpole, George II 'offered it to... [Sir Robert] *Walpole*, but he would only accept it for his Office of First Lord of the Treasury, to which post he got it annexed for ever', (*Survey of London*, p129). The house was substantially remodelled by William Kent in the early 1730s and Walpole moved in 1735. The land for the garden was acquired, and the grounds laid out, in 1736. The garden was 'made and fitted up at the Charge... of the Crown' (*Survey of London*, p122). Both house and garden were 'meant to be annexed & united to the Office of his Majesty's Treasury & to be & remain for the Use & habitation of the first Commissioner of his Majesty's Treasury for the time being'. Samuel Milward was appointed to look after the garden.

The garden's layout is geometrical, its gravel walks, lawns and flower borders forming regular patterns, as does the flower planting scheme. Georgian town gardens appear to have remained geometrical throughout the eighteenth century, judging by the archaeological evidence gathered in Bath at number 4 Circus (*c*.1760–70) and number 19 New King Street (*c*.1766/7); by the back gardens of the Officers' Terrace at Chatham Dockyard (still in existence), their original layout recorded in a model dated 1773–4 (National Maritime Museum); and for London, by the 1791 plan for Francis Douce's garden in Upper Gower Street (Bodleian Library). However, the total absence of elaborate topiary and the irregular arrangement of shrubs or small trees add a degree of naturalness which makes it a transitional design between earlier formal tradition and the Picturesque style.

St James's Park, which was formerly meadowland dotted with trees and ponds, was laid out in the contemporary French style, but in a rather disjointed fashion, shortly after the Restoration. A mall for playing pall-mall, some quarter of a mile long, on the site of the present thoroughfare still called the Mall, was constructed immediately south of the grounds of St James's Palace, and flanked with fine avenues of trees; the path shown on the right led to the east end of this mall. The *c*.1745 painting of the Mall in the Royal Collection depicts with great success this most fashionable London location and features in the background on the left the walled garden of number 10. Also running the entire length of the park, and flanked by a double row of trees, was a long canal, which is seen on the left of this painting with some people beside it; at the farther end of this sheet of water was Rosamond's Pond, connected to it by a sluice. A formal garden was laid out north of the mall on the site of what is now Marlborough House and Carlton House Terrace. Over the tops of the trees on the right can be seen the spire of St James's Piccadilly. The park was completely remodelled in the 'Picturesque' taste by John Nash in 1828, and the canal was then replaced by the present serpentine lake.

John Kip's engraved panoramic view of St James's Park taken from the roof of Buckingham House at the beginning of the eighteenth century shows clearly the way in which adjoining gardens to the park were designed, regardless of their size, to benefit from the green vistas offered by the park. Many of the gardens were fitted with terraces, as is the one shown here, from which to enjoy the newly developed concept of *rus in urbe*.

Formerly attributed to Wilson and Hogarth, and afterwards to Marcellus Laroon, this canvas was then ascribed to George Lambert, whose views of, for example, Wotton Place, were felt to be close in style and technique. Elisabeth Einberg (who is currently compiling a catalogue of Lambert's works to be published by the Walpole Society) does not think it could possibly be by this artist: the sky and the handling of foliage are not consistent with his manner of painting, nor is the green of the grass on the left-hand side. The scale of the composition is also uncharacteristic. Einberg has tentatively suggested that this could be the work of John Griffier II, who occasionally treats foliage as neat, tiny light dots which throw shrubs and trees into higher relief. The canal here also has some analogies with the Hurstbourne Park set by Griffier which is reproduced in John Harris's *The Artist and the Country House*, 1979.

The costume indicates a date of about 1735–45, and the inclusion of the garden a date subsequent to 1736. If the principal figure could be established as Lord Wilmington, the date could be narrowed to 1742–3.

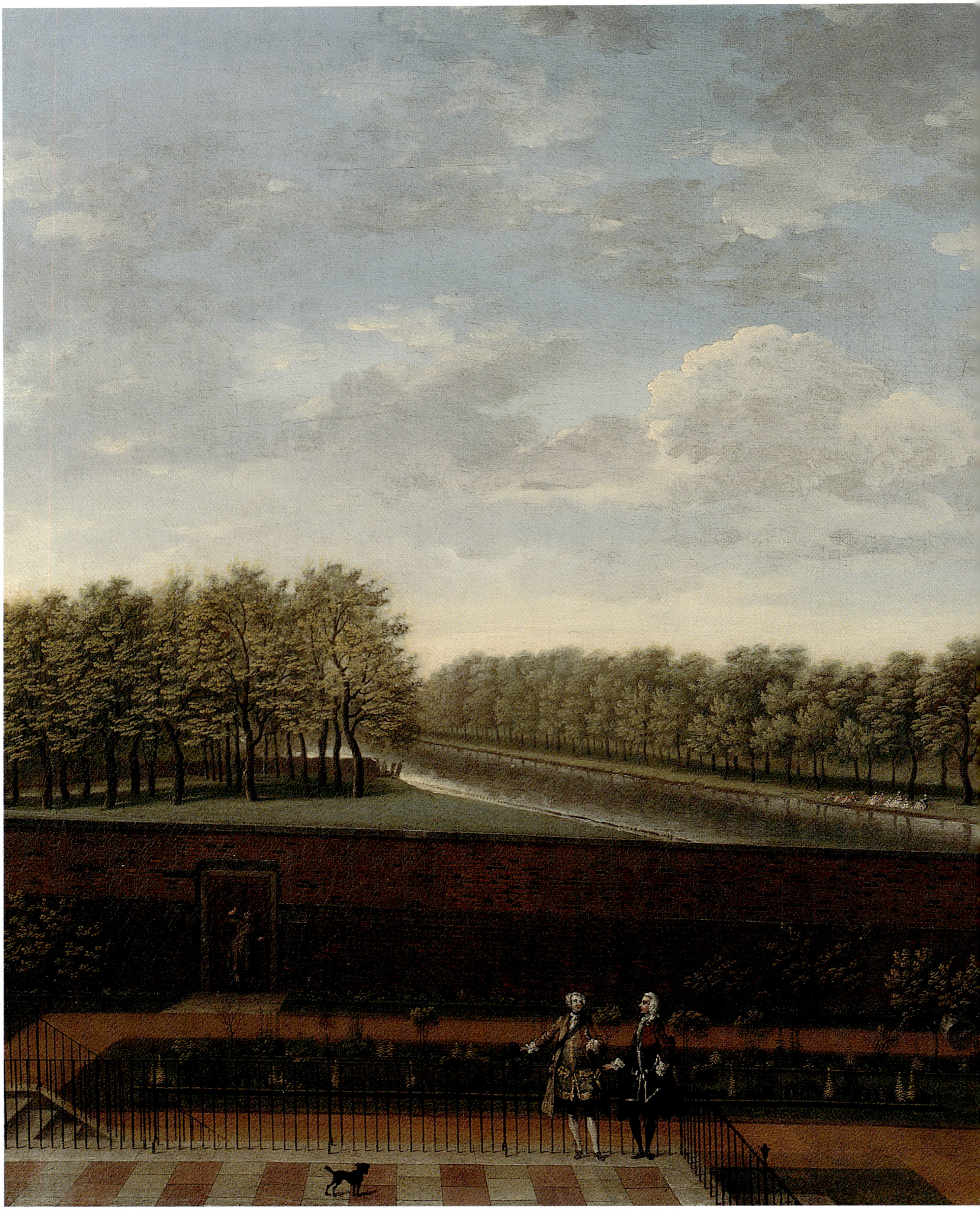

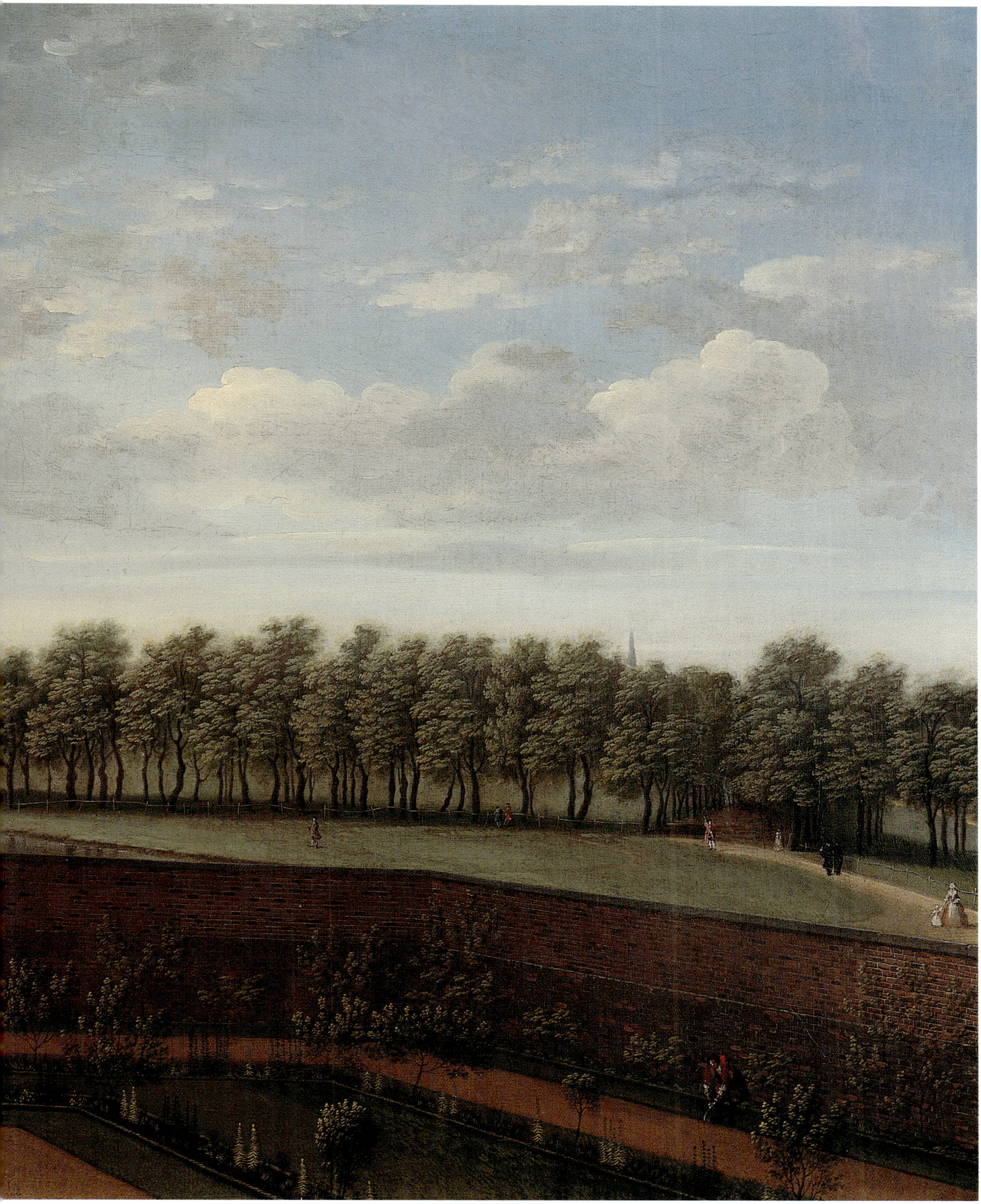

Provenance:
Sir Ralph Wilmot, Bt; Wilmot sale, Christie's, 28 February 1913 (111), bt McKay; presented by Cecil B. Harmsworth in 1919, through the National Art Collections Fund.

Bibliography:
Hayes (cat. no. 27); Bernard Adams, *London Illustrated 1604–1851*, 1983, cat. no. 27:77, p63; W. G. Constable (revised J. G. Links), *Canaletto*, 1989, no. 433.

33.

GIOVANNI ANTONIO CANAL called CANALETTO

(1697–1768)

Interior of Henry VII's Chapel, Westminster Abbey [A 20964]
*c.*1750–53
Oil on panel, 70 x 58.7 cm
Not signed or dated

THIS PANEL is one of Canaletto's very rare interior subjects, King's College Chapel, the Rotunda at Ranelagh and San Marco being other examples. The view of the chapel (built between 1503 and 1519) is taken looking eastwards, and the tomb of Henry VII, with its surrounding grille, the work of Pietro Torrigiano, is seen in the centre. To the left, in the side-chapel, is the tomb of John Sheffield, 1st Duke of Buckingham (1648–1721), by Plumier, Scheemakers and Delvaux. The banners above the stalls are those of the companions of the Order of the Bath, an order of chivalry which had been established for political reasons in 1725 (an earlier view of the chapel, *c.*1723, and showing the stalls without the banners, was drawn and engraved by James Schijnvoet as a frontispiece for vol. 2 of Dart's *Westmonasterium*).

For London this is an early example of the genre of church interior painting developed in Holland in the seventeenth century, which in Britain tended to adopt the form of engravings. Apart from some generalising of the complicated fan-vaulting of the roof, and one or two other discrepancies (the arches behind the stalls cannot be seen so clearly from the viewpoint chosen), this painting gives an accurate impression of the appearance of the chapel.

This painting is little known, for it was dismissed by the late Professor Constable as unlikely to be by Canaletto. More recent opinions now agree that the work is unquestionably by this artist. It is interesting to compare this work with that of the same subject in the collection of Ernest G. Kleinwort (with Robert Holden Ltd in 1996). The latter is a wider picture, of which the viewpoint has shifted to the side (as in the Schijnvoet print). By centralising the perspective in the Museum's picture (as in the King's College Chapel painting) and by accentuating the play of light and dark on the architectural lacework, Canaletto is able to achieve extraordinary results. The dazzling verticality of the architecture, its delicacy and the quality of the atmosphere thus created have been rendered with brilliancy. The greater number of figures – two of them, clerics, majestically draped – seems to be used by Canaletto as a device reinforcing the carefully modulated play of light and dark already observed in the architecture. (A mid-eighteenth-century view in the style of Canaletto is in the possession of the Dean and Chapter of Westminster. It is taken from the same viewpoint as this painting, using different proportions for the architectural components and different figures.)

Canaletto hardly ever painted on panel and this work belongs to the small group of only three known (London) works using this type of support, the other two being The (New) Horse Guards (Constable/Links, no. 417) and Somerset House (private collection, catalogued in a forthcoming edition of Constable/Links catalogue). It has been suggested that these last two paintings may have been conceived as a pair and the same hypothesis was raised

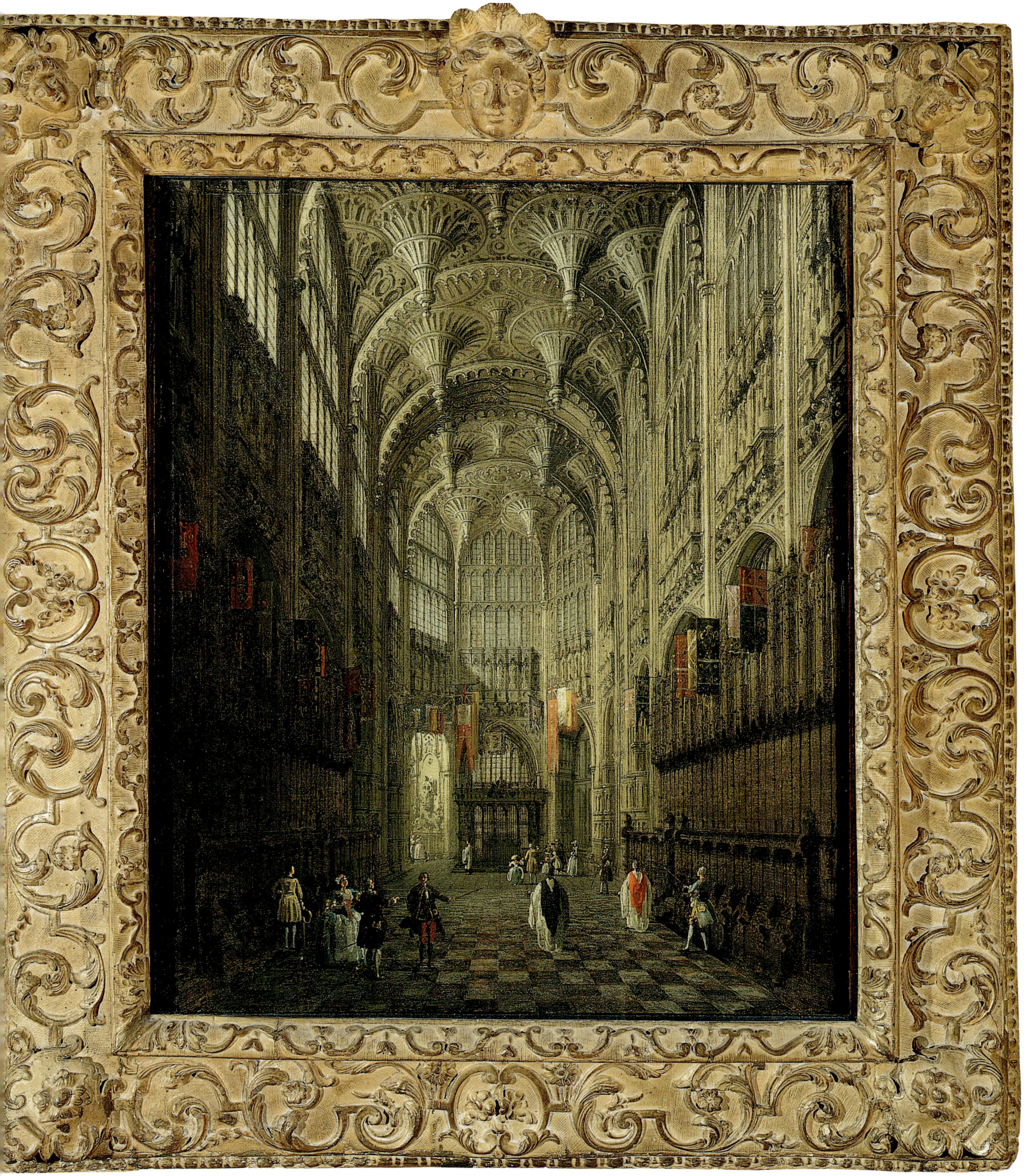

regarding Canaletto's two 'perpendicular' church interiors, Henry VII's chapel and the interior of King's College, Cambridge. The latter, apparently based on an engraved view by David Loggan, is in a private collection in America and is the only surviving work out of three that Canaletto painted of this subject (see Constable/Links, no. 411).

Since Canaletto's time a number of changes have occurred inside the chapel: an extra row of stalls (usually assumed to have been carved in 1725) was added on each side to make the number up to the requisite thirty-eight for the Knights of the Bath; the screens to the side chapels were destroyed or mutilated to make way for the extra stalls and as a result of the seating arrangements at Installation ceremonies; the tomb of Henry VII was re-orientated and a step added; an altar was built in front of the tomb in 1935; and the chapel at the east end was converted into the Royal Air Force Chapel (consecrated 1947).

The costume indicates a date of about 1750; the other two panel paintings discussed earlier, perhaps a pair, appear to date from *c*.1753.

The panel painting appears to be encased in a mahogany cradle and some damage to the surface paint has occurred. The frame, earlier than the picture, was extended to fit the painting. It is French Regency/late Louis XIV and was carved in lime and pine (the work might be Huguenot). It may have been a mirror frame and may have come from the Bordeaux region.

34.

JOHN COLLET

(1725–80)

May Morning [84.166]
c.1760
Oil on canvas, 43 x 53 cm
Not signed or dated

FOR THE first time in British painting, the artist casts a satirical eye on the traditional May Day procession. J. T. Smith would usefully summarise the changing dynamics of this event in *Vagabondiana* (published in 1817); he presented it as a run-down affair, deploring the switch from 'innocent scenes of May day gaiety' to 'the indecent conduct' of men who 'hire old dresses and join the chimney sweepers', cinder-shifters' or Bunters' Garland... to extort money from their numerous admirers'.

From left to right are the Lord and Lady of May (the 'Lady' may in fact be a man and the 'Lord' decorated with ribbons has a severe leg handicap); behind them a woman (perhaps another man) is getting ready to collect money in the bowl of a brass 'ladle'; next are two children (one with retarded looks) and next to them, a hurdy-gurdy player (with a very rough face) has replaced the fiddler found in earlier images. The facial features of the soldier observing the scene and the coachman holding a whip in the right background look equally rough. The milkmaid, normally attractive and the centre of attention (see Marcellus Lauron's *Cries* or Francis Hayman's *May Day or The Milkmaid Garland* at the Victoria and Albert Museum) has been replaced by a bunter (a low, vulgar woman, here relegated to the back row) who is a large, tall girl with crossed eyes carrying an imitation garland made up of 'an inverted basket covered with flowers and brass culinary utensils' (Judge, p8). A black servant wearing a livery (probably a slave) has joined the group. He is holding a broom, perhaps suggesting he was sweeping the pavement of his master's house when the procession walked past (see cat. no. 35). In Benjamin Haydon's reworking of the theme (*Punch or May Day*, 1829, Tate Gallery), the black servant is no longer a participant: his proud and detached looks suggest he wants no connection with the event and therefore looks straight in front of him. A chimneysweep wearing a May Day wig and two poor children, all with their toes showing through their worn out shoes, prefigure later caricatures showing handfuls of bewigged imps in attendance (for example in pictures by Samuel Collings or Robert Dighton). The posture of the couple at the back suggests shady dealings.

The painting is dateable to *c*.1760 on costume grounds, which makes it the earliest caricatured record of the May Day procession. It contrasts with the interpretations of Lauron and Hayman (mentioned above) or that of *May Day procession at Temple Bar*, currently attributed to Collet, in the collection of the Earl of Jersey.

The location represented has not been identified but the background of tall Elizabethan houses would suggest somewhere in the City of Westminster, an ancient quarter of London untouched by the Great Fire.

The bumpy street and smooth pavement noticed by foreign visitors (see p91) feature prominently.

This is the first visual record of the garland as having become an elaborate affair.

Provenance:
M. M. Collection (according to Spink records); Spink & Son Ltd 1969; Patrick Cormack; purchased by the Museum in 1984 with a grant from the MGC/V&A Purchase Grant Fund.

Bibliography:
Octagon, vol. VI, no. 1, Spring 1969; Roy Judge, *Jack-in-the-Green*, 1979.

It no longer solely consists of a pyramid of objects carried on the head since, partly hidden on the right-hand side, is a second, more monumental pyramid, resting on a stick(?) (in the artist's contemporary Temple Bar painting, it is carried by two men).

The May Day procession shown here is transitional: before the appearance of the Jack-in-the-Green (see cat. no. 86) and its associated characters, but after the original 'milkmaids only' celebration. The event developed into a varied procession when the once separate processions of milkmaids, chimneysweeps, bunters etc merged into one.

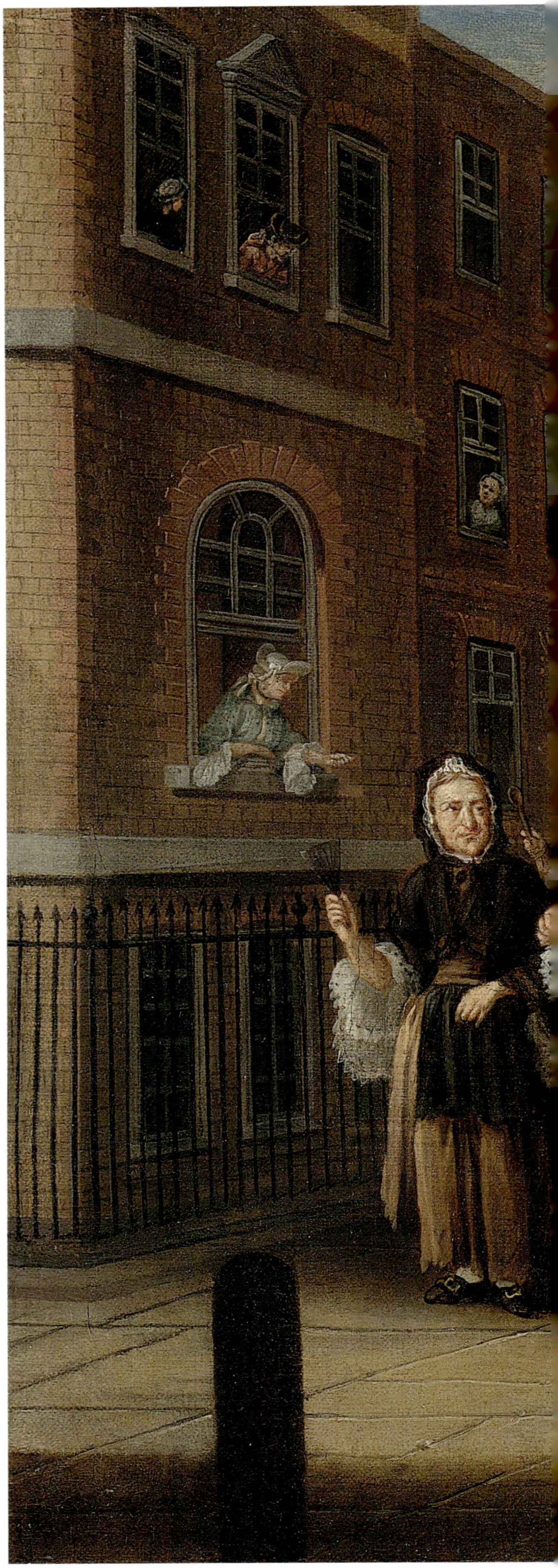

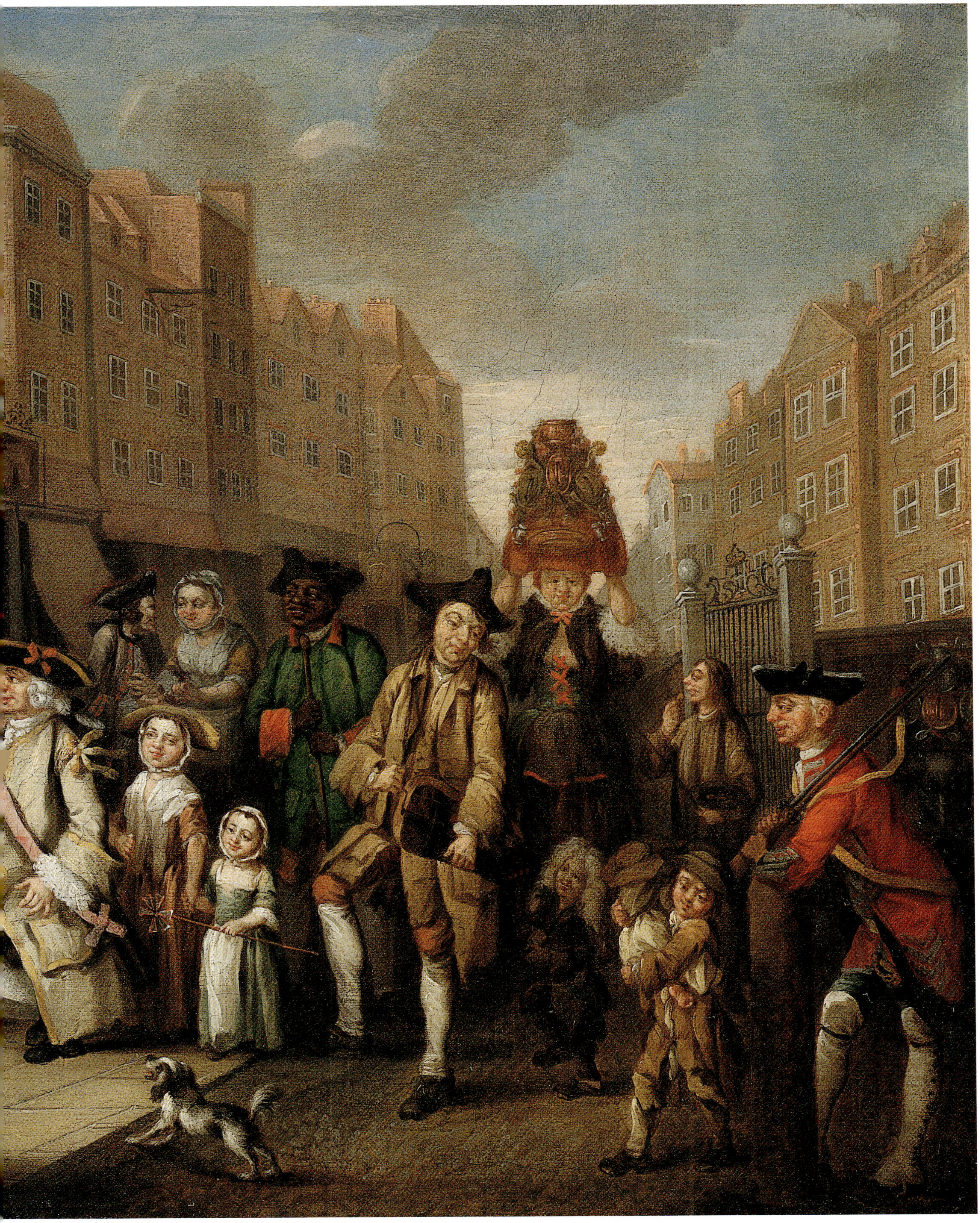

Provenance:
Sotheby's 23 November 1966 (54); purchased from Christie's 15 July 1988 (90), with the help of grants from the MGC/V&A purchase fund and the National Art Collections Fund.

Bibliography:
Celina Fox, *Londoners*, 1987: see chapter on servants.

Exhibited:
Free Society of Artists, 1764.

35.

EDWARD PENNY
(1714–91)

A City Shower [88.126]
*c.*1764
Oil on canvas, 76.5 x 64 cm
Not signed or dated

A YOUNG maid standing on the pavement outside the doorway of a wealthy house vigorously shakes her mop, spraying a male passer-by who steps back in dismay. The artist records in some detail the classical pedimented doorway, street railings, lighting (see p92) and smooth pavement, raised outside the doorway to facilitate the alighting of passengers from carriages. The artist is also very meticulous in the way he has recorded dress and its accessories: note, for instance, the maid's pretty blue petticoat (probably handed down from her mistress, a common practice in the eighteenth century), or the pattens worn by the maid to protect her feet from the street mud and dirt described in so many accounts. The man is smartly dressed and his social status is further reinforced by the presence in his pocket of a newspaper.

The painting illustrates a passage from Jonathan Swift's London poem published in the *Tatler* (14–17 October 1710):

> Such is that Sprinkling which some
> careless Quean
> Flirts on you from her Mop,
> but not so clean.
> You fly, invoke the Gods;
> then turning, stop
> To rail; she singing, still whirls
> on her Mop...

The link with the poem was made explicit in the engraving Thomas Chambers made after this painting, which he published on 7 May 1775 as 'The Mop Trundler' with the quotation from Swift. The image of the energetic London maidservant was already present in Swift's 'A Description of a Morning' (*Tatler*, 30 April 1709):

> Now Moll had whirl'd her mop with
> dextrous airs
> Prepar'd to scrub the Entry and the Stairs.

When it was exhibited at the Free Society of Artists in 1764, the painting bore the title *A scene from Jonathan Swift's description of a city shower*.

The scene blends spontaneity and theatre, in the spirit of Hogarth's paintings (see p128). Hogarth's group portrait of his servants painted in the 1750s (Tate Gallery) is the major visual statement on London servants for the eighteenth century: it is deeply humane and certainly contrasts with the traditional presentation of servants as accessories to and status symbols for their masters. Here we have a delightful reversal of roles. The maid, filled with the confidence of working for the worthy classes, is shown displaying great independence in the context of street cleaning. When Archenholz visited London in 1780 he noted that female domestic servants could be mistaken for 'gentlewomen' and his observations in *A Picture of England* in 1797 (vol. II, pp118–19) suggest that modern notions on servants may not necessarily be applicable:

> The appearance of the female domestics will, perhaps, astonish a foreigner more than any thing in London. They are in general handsome and well clothed: their dress has the appearance of some taste, and their conversation such as if they had kept the best company...

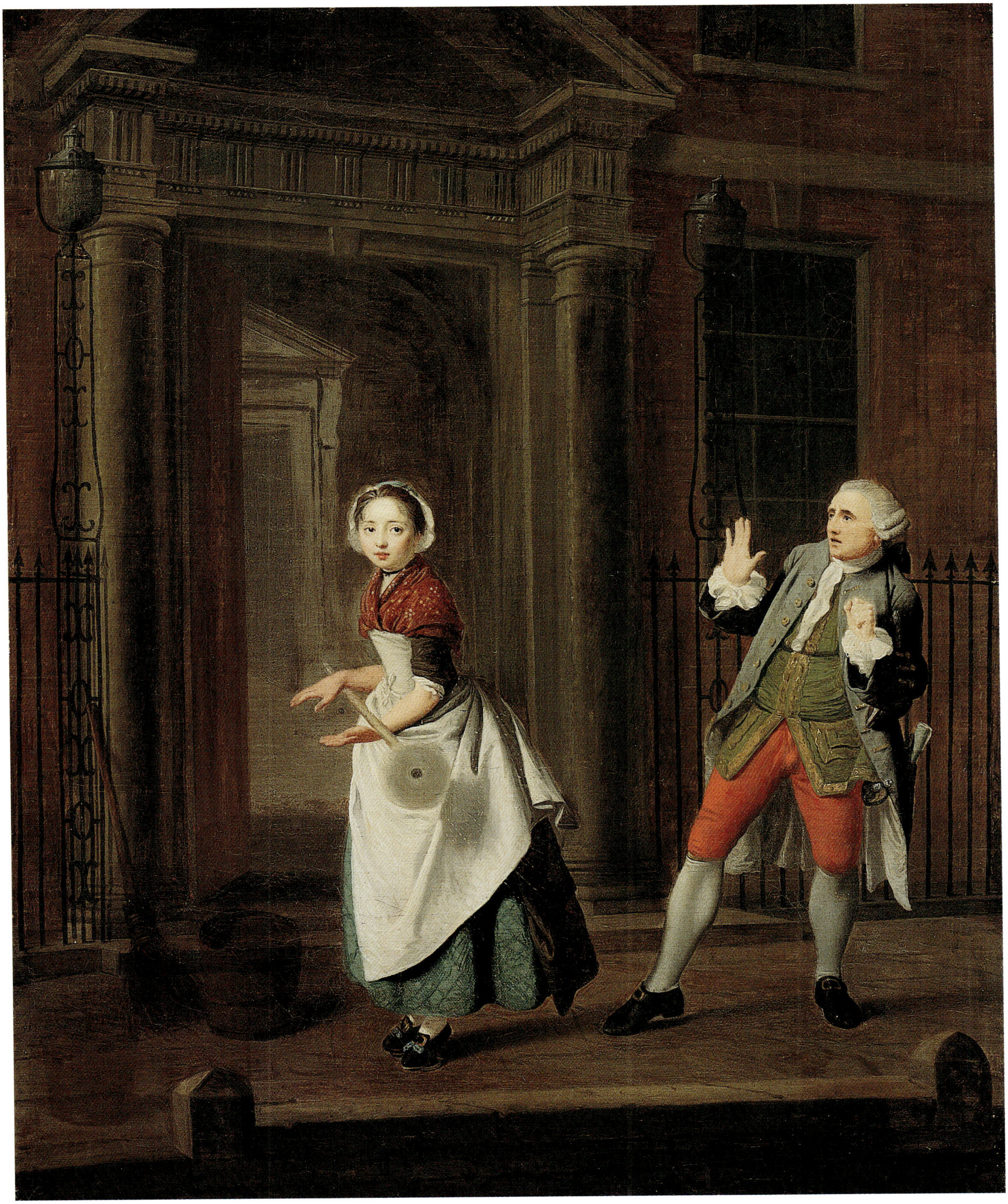

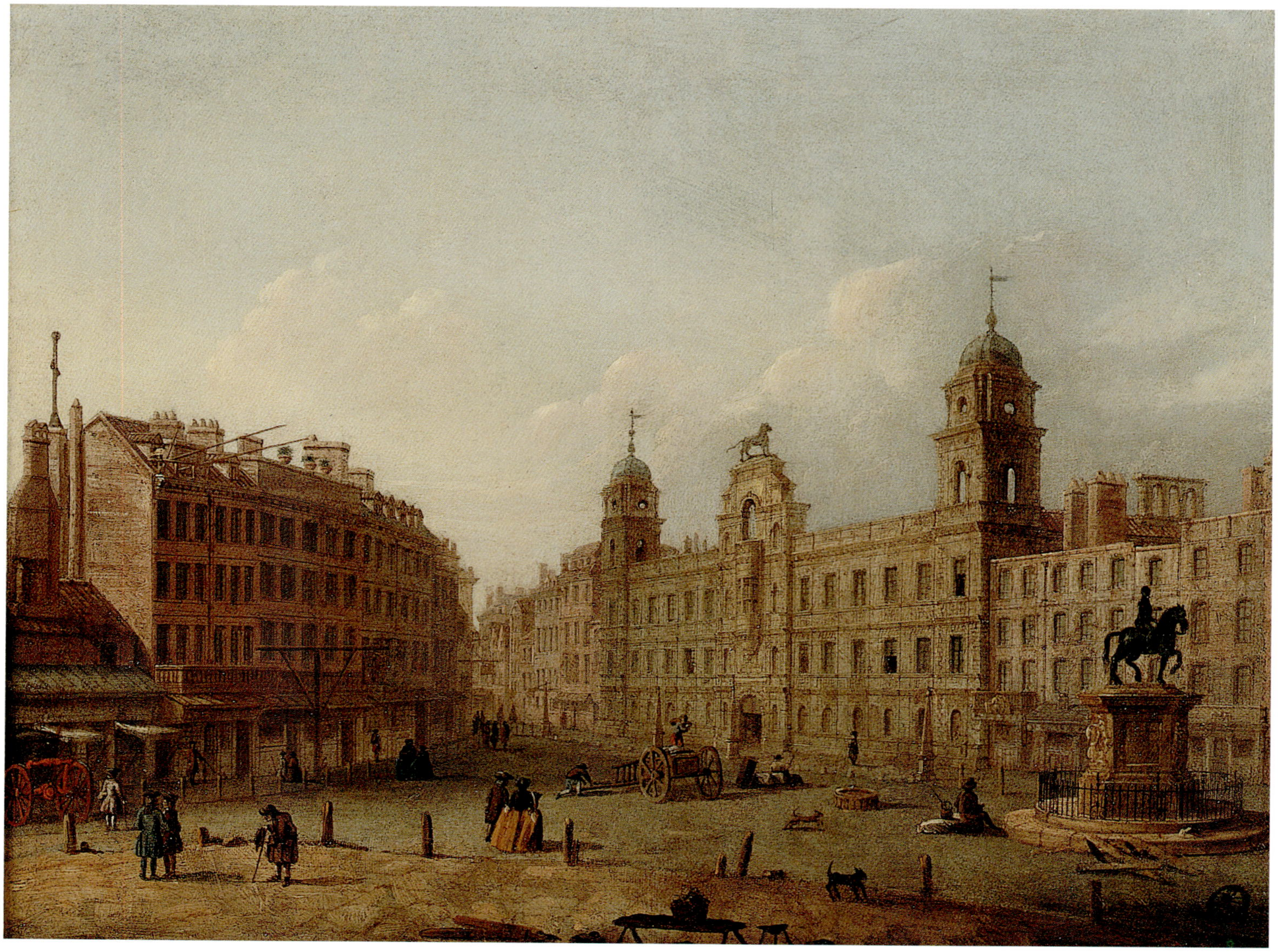

36.

BRITISH SCHOOL

Charing Cross and Northumberland House [A 28576]
Late eighteenth century
Oil on canvas, 37.5 x 49.2 cm
Not signed or dated

THE COMPOSITION and certain of the figures are derived from the painting by Canaletto executed for the Earl of Northumberland and which was engraved in 1753. The view of Northumberland House on the right, at the entrance to the Strand, is taken from Cockspur Street and also shows the Golden Cross Inn on the left and le Sueur's statue of Charles I on horseback on the right.

Northumberland House, which was known as Suffolk House in the earlier part of the seventeenth century, is seen in the centre of the picture. Built in 1605–9, it was until last century one of the principal monuments of Jacobean architecture in the metropolis, and stood on the south-east side of Charing Cross, between the Strand and Whitehall, with a garden stretching down to the river.

In 1749 the 2nd Earl (later the 1st Duke) of Northumberland, who had just succeeded to the title and later commissioned Robert Adam to rebuild Syon House, began extensive alterations to the house, including the building of a fine new gallery; the modifications in the facade, seen here, comprised the building of the turrets with their lead cupolas, the erection of the Percy lion above the parapet of the splendid frontispiece, and the replacement of the Jacobean window lights with Georgian sash windows. The house was destroyed in 1874 to make way for the formation of Northumberland Avenue, having been purchased by the Metropolitan Board of Works for just under half a million pounds; the Percy lion was then removed to Syon House.

The bronze equestrian statue of Charles I in armour by Hubert le Sueur was cast in 1633 for Lord Weston and intended for his garden in Roehampton. It later came into the possession of the Crown, and was set up at Charing Cross (on the site of the old Eleanor Cross, destroyed by the Parliamentarians in 1643) between 1675 and 1677, with a pedestal by Joshua Marshall. It still remains in the same position, facing down Whitehall.

Charing Cross was a noted shopping centre in the eighteenth century (as was the Strand, which can be seen in the distance), and among the shops seen on the left and right of this picture are jewellers, instrument makers, hosiers, trunkmakers and saddlers. The latter two were suitably located close to the Golden Cross Inn, whose sign appears on the left, and whose yard was one of the principal starting points for the mail-coach services.

A larger but less accomplished version of this view is in the Museum (see Appendix; Hayes, cat. no. 129); and a variant of the composition is also in the collection (see Appendix; Hayes, cat. no. 164). Innumerable other versions exist which show the impact Canaletto had on London topographers.

Provenance:
Purchased by an unknown buyer in Lisbon in 1872 (as Canaletto); date and source of acquisition unknown.

Bibliography:
Hayes (cat. no. 13).

Provenance:

Commissioned from the artist by R. B. O'Reilly; Mrs Sligo de Porthonier; Porthonier sale, Christie's, 26 February 1917 (85, as Canaletto), bt Knoedler; Christie's, 8 December 1919 (114), bt Scott; purchased from George de Pyre in 1920.

Bibliography:

Hayes (cat. no. 15); *Survey of London*, vol. XXXIV, 1966, pp455–64; *Getting London in Perspective*, exhibition catalogue, Barbican Art Gallery, 1984, no. 8; Curtis Price, Judith Milhous and Robert D. Hume, 'A Royal Opera House in Leicester Square (1790)', in *Cambridge Opera Journal*, vol. 2, no. 1, 1990, pp1–28.

37.

WILLIAM HODGES

(1744–1797)

Design for a Proposed New Opera House in Leicester Square [A 28577]

*c.*1790

Oil on canvas, 148.2 x 235 cm

Not signed or dated

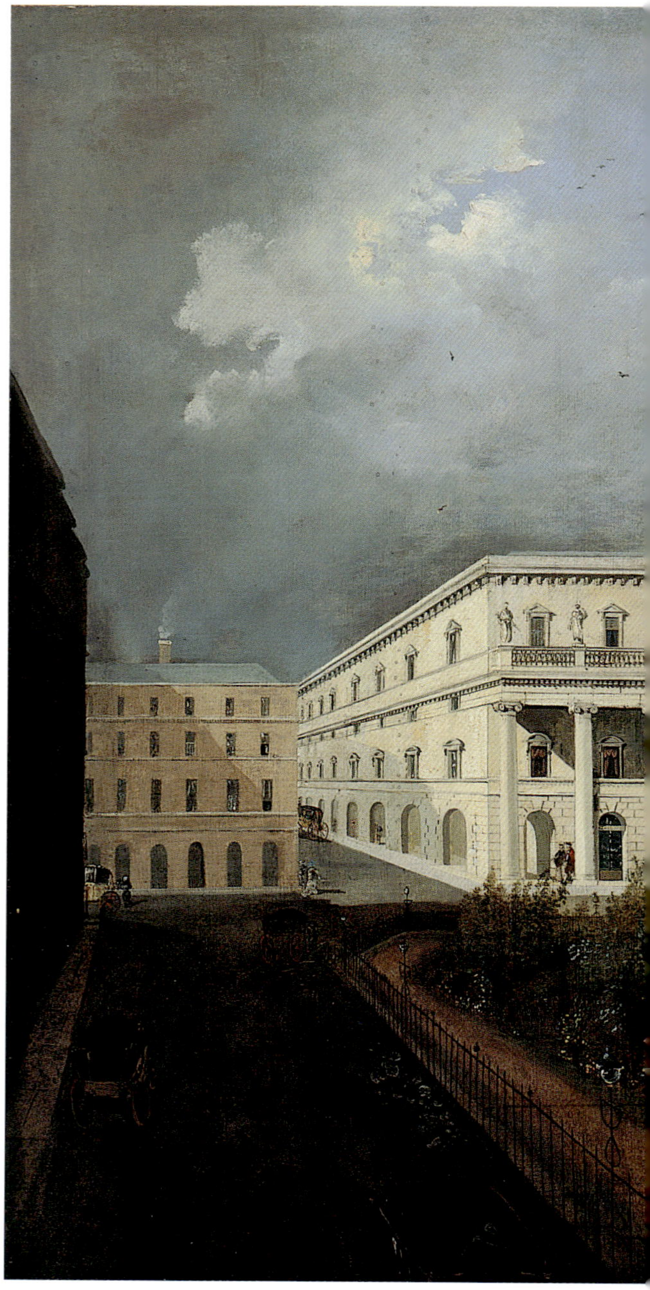

THE VIEW is taken from the south side of the square looking north across the gardens towards the site of Leicester House (pulled down in 1789). The land was purchased by Robert Bray O'Reilly in January 1790. He was a law student who had become the legal adviser of Giovanni Gallini, the mortgagee of the Haymarket Opera House. The two men had planned the construction of a magnificent new opera house, intended to replace that in the Haymarket which burned down on 17 June 1789. Initially, the scheme was powerfully backed by the Prince of Wales, the Duke of Bedford and the Marquis of Salisbury. The new theatre shown here, surmounted by the royal coat of arms, but which was never built, was to stretch from Leicester Street on the west to a new street formed out of Cranbourn Alley on the east, and from the foot-pavement of Leicester Square on the south to Gerrard Street on the north.

The scheme for the Opera House came to nothing as the promised patent was never granted, and O'Reilly took a lease of the Pantheon for the performance of Italian opera (see cat. no. 38). Three sets of designs for the Leicester Square scheme had been drawn up: by Victor Louis, architect of the new theatre in the Palais Royal, which O'Reilly had admired on his visit to Paris (two of Louis's drawings were sold by Christie's on 30 November 1983, Lots 68 and 69); by Sir John Soane, who was to have been the supervising architect; and by O'Reilly himself. There are a number of irreconcilable differences between the designs that have survived, but the features they have in common point to a glamorous and exclusive 'court' project. A contemporary source describes O'Reilly's design as including a 'piazza' (or arcade) on every side and grand fronts to north and south, 'each with a superb Ionic portico'. Although the description could be made to

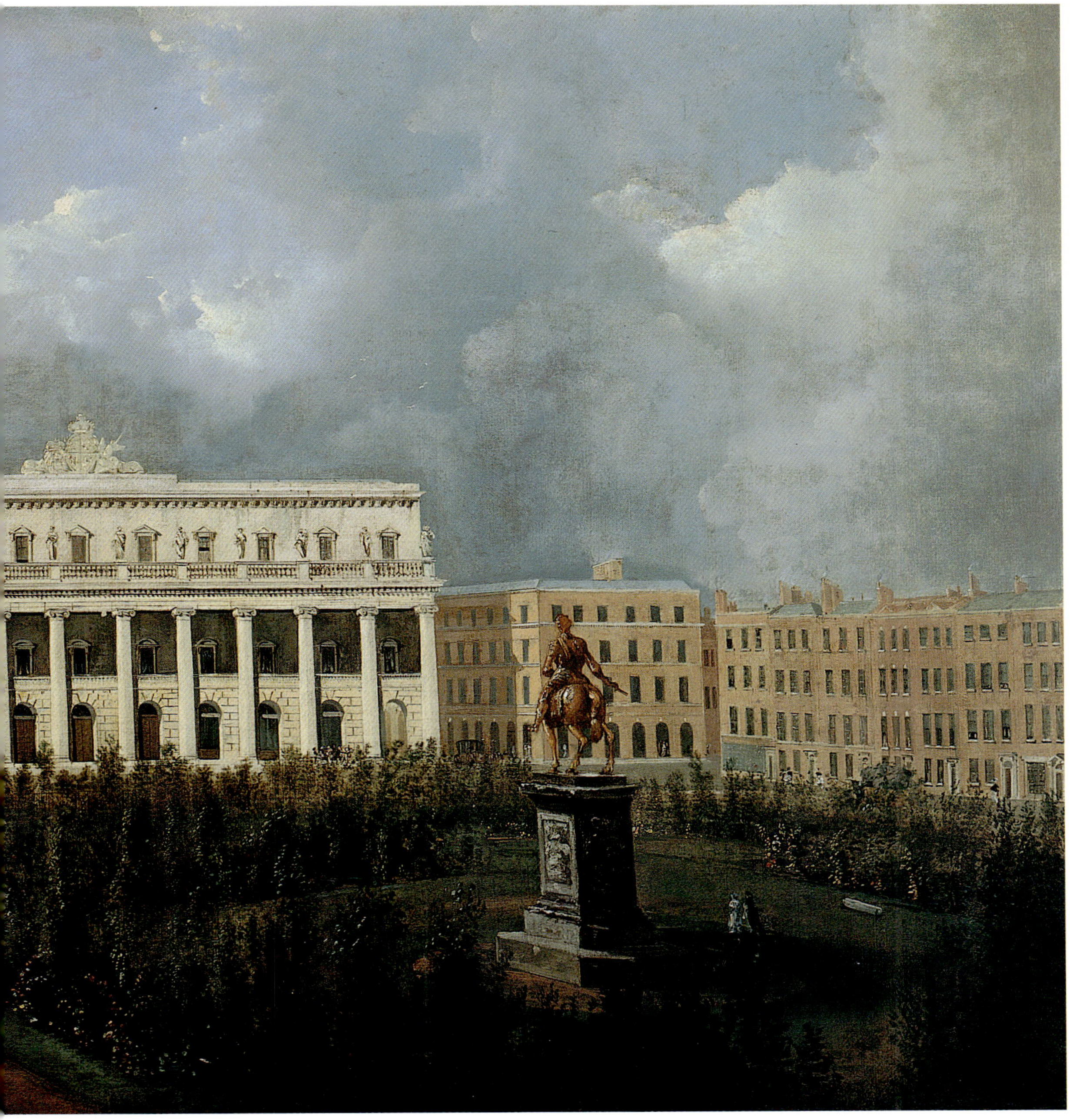

apply to a theatre design by Thomas Sandby in the Royal collection at Windsor (*Survey of London*, XXXIV, plate 29a; Oppé cat. no. 188), it also corresponds to the Museum painting. Moreover the elevation in this work is consistent with a ground plan in the Soane Museum portfolio (*Survey of London*, XXXIV, plate 28a). In character, the exterior design is almost exactly the same as that of the Grand Théâtre in Bordeaux (designed by Victor Louis and built in 1775–80), except for the domed roof. It is probable that William Hodges, who was commissioned by O'Reilly to produce 'the large picture of Leicester fields' which cost him £80, was requested to use the Louis design for Bordeaux for which contemporary engravings were available. This artist's impression therefore represents O'Reilly's vision for the scheme rather than literally his own specific design.

It is extremely unusual for such an elaborate perspective *oil* painting to have been produced. There is a precedent for this in the oeuvre of Hodges: the 1777 painting of Worksop Manor in the collection of the Duke of Norfolk at Arundel Castle. Although only one side of the manor was ever built, Hodges depicts the whole as if it was complete. The greatest exponent of the genre, Joseph Michael Gandy (1771–1843), produced comparable views, though smaller and in watercolour, of the architectural schemes devised by his patron John Soane. In a letter dated 2 May 1792 (in the Pantheon papers of the Bedford Estates Office), O'Reilly explains that the work was intended for Lord Salisbury. The wealth and rank of the opera house backers, as well as O'Reilly's own grandiose plans for the Leicester Square project, account for this late major work by Hodges, an exceptionally grand record of a scheme that was never carried out.

The beautifully painted gardens contrast with the awkward rendering of the architecture. The gardens were known to be real (rather than imaginary) only with the discovery of a drawing by Alexander Nasmyth dated 1816 (now in the Museum's collection, acc. no. 95.284). It confirmed beyond any doubt the planting shown here and also showed the development of the garden over twenty years or so. Hodges's important place in the development of English landscape painting manifests itself even in this most urban of subjects. The gardens' layout differs from that of earlier pictorial records where the space was divided into four squares with a central focus, first of a single tree, then of the statue. The geometric rigidity of this arrangement is abandoned for a unified design round the statue. In spirit this is comparable to the design devised in 1791 by Richard Twiss for Francis Douce's garden in Gower Street – a central block thickly planted with shrubs, a path going around and cut corners – but the presence of the statue as well as the difference in scale limit the comparison. The inclusion of colourful flowers at the edges may show the influence of the garden designer William Mason. Between 1788 and 1808 the maintenance of the garden was the responsibility of the Tulk family.

The lead equestrian statue of George I by John Nost, which originally stood at Canons, the seat of the 1st Duke of Chandos, was erected in Leicester Square by Frederick, Prince of Wales (who lived at Leicester House) in 1748. The base of the statue shown here differs from earlier records, which show it rounded rather than rectangular. It remained *in situ* until 1851, when it was taken down at the time of the building of James Wyld's Great Globe (for the display of geographical and historical dioramas). The Globe was demolished in 1862, and the statue was again set up in the centre of the square; it was sold in 1872, and later destroyed.

In the nineteenth century Leicester Square was principally noted for its hotels and places of entertainment, but it had previously been a fashionable residential district. Both William Hogarth and Joshua Reynolds had lived and died there. Strype, writing in 1720, called it 'a very handsome open Square, railed about, and gravelled within', adding that 'the Buildings are very good, and well inhabited, and frequented by the Gentry'. Some of the original houses built on the east side of the square are seen in this view.

38.

WILLIAM MARLOW
(1740–1813)

The Ruins of the Pantheon in Oxford Street after the Disastrous Fire of 14 January 1792 [83.359]
1792
Oil on canvas, 102.5 x 124.5 cm
Not signed or dated

THE PANTHEON stood on the site of the present Marks & Spencer store on the south side of Oxford Street, east of Oxford Circus, and this view was taken at the entrance of its large central vaulted space, looking south-east. The roof-tops of houses in Great Marlborough Street are visible from the square openings in the upper part of the architecture.

The Pantheon, which was designed by James Wyatt and built between June 1769 and January 1772, quickly became London's most fashionable entertainment venue for exhibitions (Lunardi's balloon, stained glass, models of cities, needlework paintings etc), masquerades and concerts. After the 1789 fire which destroyed the King's Theatre in the Haymarket and the failure of R. B. O'Reilly's scheme of building a new opera house in Leicester Square (see cat. no. 37), James Wyatt was commissioned by O'Reilly to convert the Pantheon into a theatre for the Italian Opera. The gardens of the houses behind the Pantheon were acquired for building the stage.

Interior views of the Pantheon have tended to focus on its 'rotunda', notably the painting by William Hodges and Johann Zoffany in Leeds City Art Gallery; Hodges was the 'Inventor and Painter of the Decorations' at the Pantheon. The architecture recalled both that of Rome (the dome was an almost exact copy of that of its Pantheon) and of Byzantium (Santa Sophia in Constantinople, now Istanbul). Nicknamed the 'Winter Ranelagh', it also drew direct inspiration from the rotunda at Ranelagh's pleasure garden in Chelsea. By contrast, the 1772 mezzotint caricature 'The Pantheon in Oxford Street' (in the Museum's collection, acc. no. P12) exposed some of the shadier goings-on in the supper rooms below. The 1792 fire destroyed the ground floor, revealing the supper rooms (in the painting the space below the base of the columns) and it is also possible to catch a glimpse of the original pale turquoise colour scheme. There are distortions, however, caused either by the fire or by Wyatt's remodelling, and the columns have a terracotta colour rather than the imitation yellow marble recorded in the Leeds painting.

The fire apparently broke out at 1.30 am on 14 January 1792 next to the Pantheon, in a building which had just been erected as a scene-painter's room. It then spread to the Pantheon itself and soon gutted the whole building, almost completely destroying it, despite the furious efforts of the firemen. This happened during one of London's severest frosts within memory and Turner's record of the scene is particularly powerful (see below). The contemporary rumours of arson have recently been confirmed by the strange discovery (by Dr Curtis Price) in the Bedford Archives of the complete records of the Pantheon's only two seasons, carefully removed from the theatre before it met its fate.

Since Wenceslaus Hollar's comprehensive survey of the desolation of London after the Great Fire of 1666, artists had not, on the whole, shown very much interest in the

Provenance:
Sotheby's, 2 March 1983 (104); Agnew's; purchased by the Museum with the help of the MGC/V&A Purchase Grant Fund.

Bibliography:
Survey of London, vol. XXXI, Part Two, pp268–83; Richard Altick, *The Shows of London*, 1978; John Davidson's 'Turner and plot that brought the house down', in the *Sunday Times*, 31 January 1988; Curtis Price, Judith Milhous and Robert D. Hume, 'A Plan of the Pantheon Opera House (1790–2)', in *Cambridge Opera Journal*, vol. 3, no. 3, pp213–46; also see bibliography for cat. no. 37.

depiction of ruins caused by fire. The subject was of no appeal either to them or to their patrons. Richard Wilson's *The Hall of the Inner Temple after the Fire of 4 January 1737* (Tate Gallery) stands out as an exception, perhaps to record the visit to the site of Frederick, Prince of Wales. In the late eighteenth century, however, the rise of Romanticism and the development of such artistic concepts as the Sublime rekindled the interest of painters in both fires and ruins; there is at that time a noticeable increase in fire painting, seen as Sublime, and the resulting ruins, deemed Picturesque. De Loutherbourg's *c.*1797 versions of the Great Fire, notably those in the Yale Center for British Art and with Baring Brothers (see *Philippe Jacques de Loutherbourg*, exhibition catalogue, Iveagh Bequest, 1973, no. 66), are a good and literal example of this fire revival. The ruins of the Pantheon also attracted the young J. M. W. Turner, who was only seventeen and had been employed as a scenery painter there in 1791. He produced a group of drawings (British Museum) including the striking watercolour with a fire engine in the left corner and icicles hanging from the burnt-out shell of the Pantheon.

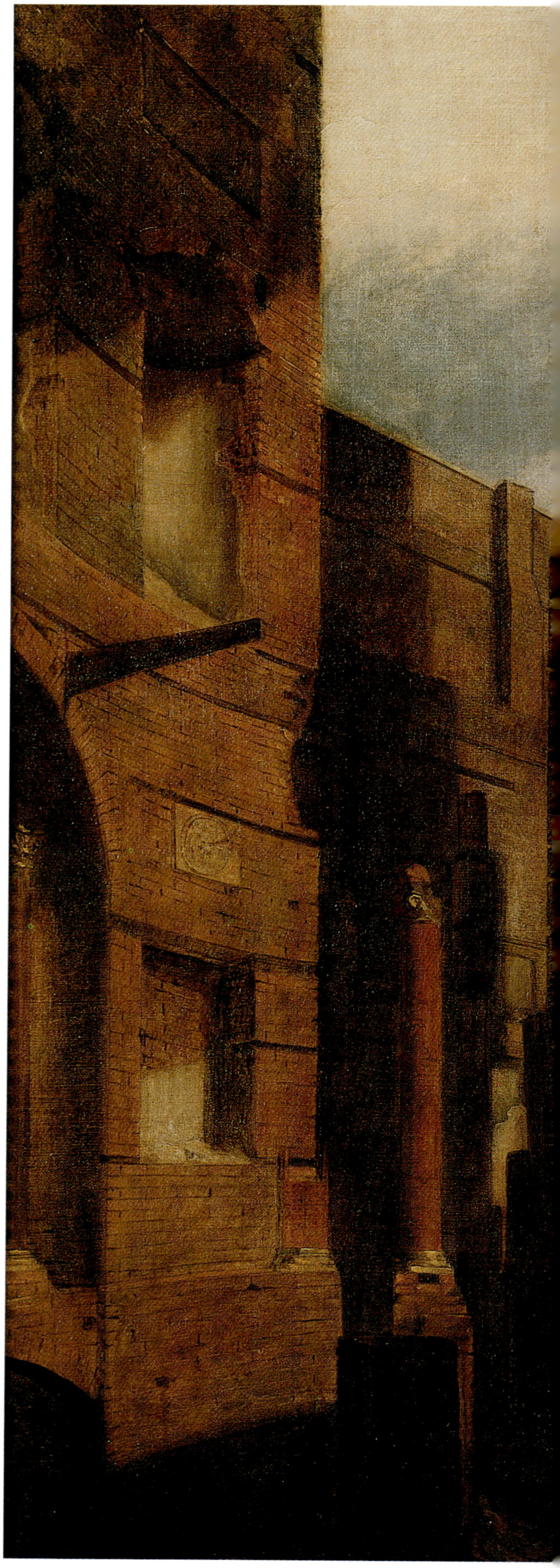

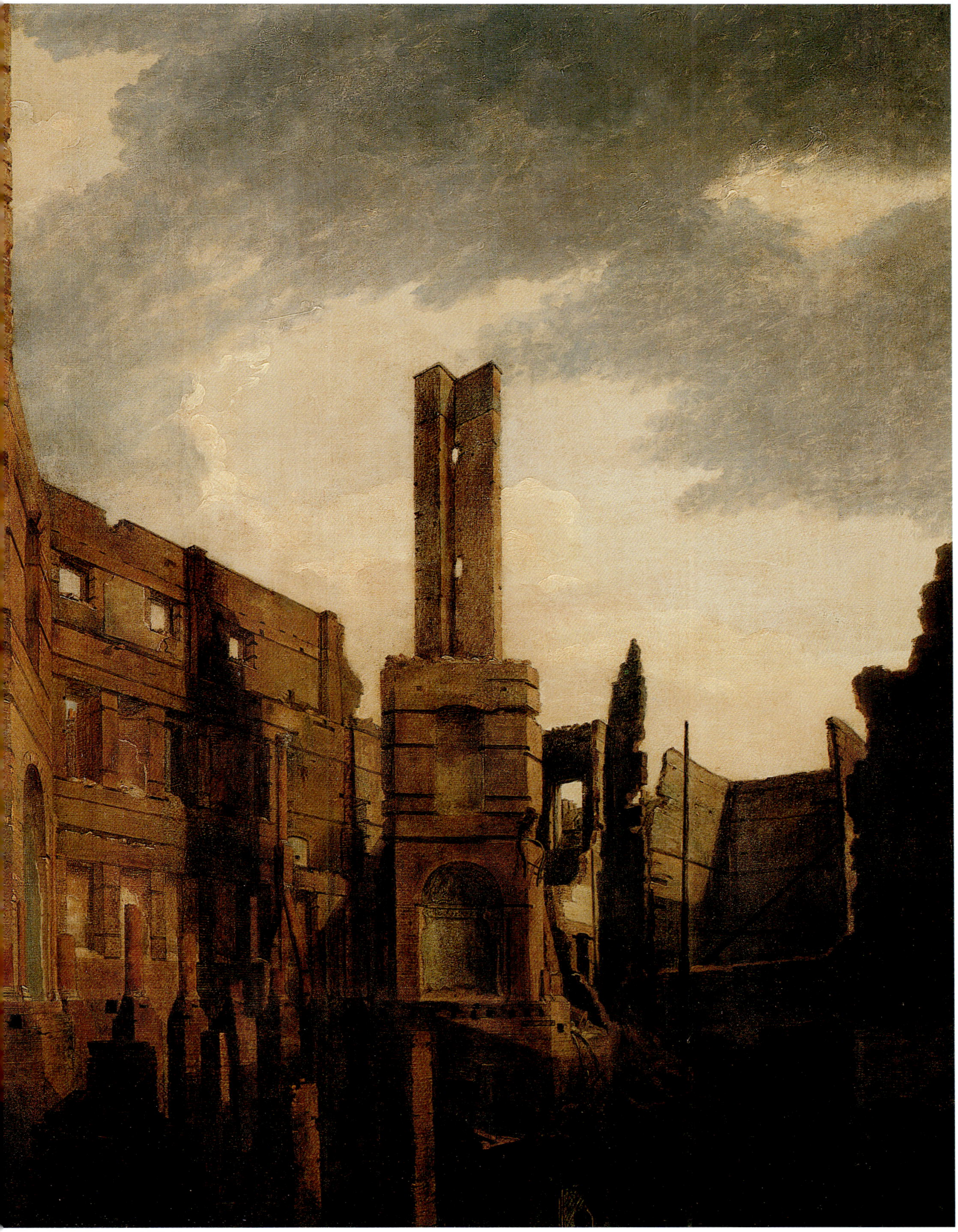

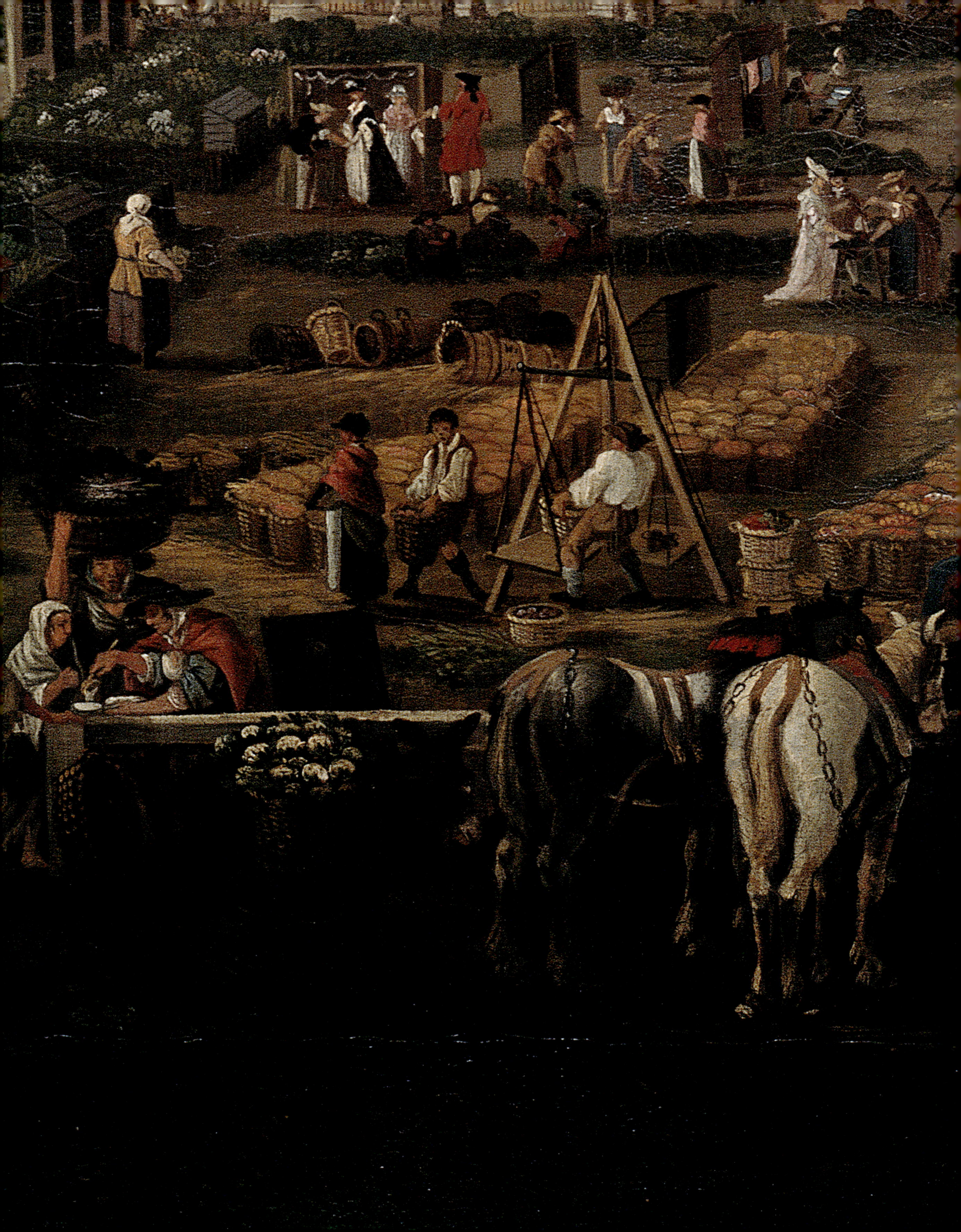

COVENT GARDEN

APART FROM the world-renowned opera house, to twentieth-century ears the words 'Covent Garden' evoke two distinct images – the square in the West End, and the market that occupied that site until the 1970s. In Georgian times the area was, in addition, the focus of artistic activity among painters who have been labelled the Covent Garden Group.

The piazza

The first London square ever planned, Covent Garden piazza[1] was laid out for Francis, 4th Earl of Bedford on the land behind his town house in the years immediately preceding the Civil War. He received his licence to build in 1631, and his architect was Inigo Jones. The houses, which were built by Isaac de Caux, were of regular width and height (something quite novel in early seventeenth-century London), with classically treated facades, and the whole square was based upon the example of the Place des Vosges, a recent development that Jones would surely have made a point of seeing when he visited Paris in 1609. By a curious misnomer, it was the arcades at street level, not the whole square, that became known to Londoners as the 'piazzas' – and it was as the piazzas that they achieved notoriety during the eighteenth century as a meeting place for gallants and their inamorata. It may seem curious that what should have continued to be the most fashionable residential square in London for many a day should so soon have declined in reputation, but the explanation is probably to be sought in the growing nuisance of the market as much as in the tendency to move ever westwards, especially marked after the Great Fire.

The story goes that when Inigo Jones laid out the square for the 4th Earl of Bedford, he was asked to make the church as simple as possible, 'not much better than a barn', to be precise. His answer to this plea for economy was that the Earl should have 'the handsomest barn in Europe', and he designed a plain but beautifully proportioned building, with a splendid portico of Tuscan columns, that cost nearly five thousand pounds. Jones's church was burnt down in 1795 (the pre-fire building is recorded in cat. nos 40 and 41), and the church that stands in its place today is an exact replica of the original by Thomas Hardwick.

The earliest views of Covent Garden date from the 1640s. Wenceslaus Hollar's small etching of 1647 is the first such record and it shows the piazza from the east. The first painting of the piazza, by an anonymous artist, represents a breakthrough in the history of London's cityscape, since it is the first close-up depiction of one of London's quarters.[2]

The market

Covent Garden market originated in the mid-1650s and an interesting painting by an unknown artist dating from within a decade of this time is in the Earl of Pembroke's collection.[3] Besides being one of the most useful illustrations of the architectural character of the square, it shows a few street sellers and their wares. The market was still a comparatively modest affair in the earlier part of the eighteenth century, though Strype referred to it in 1720 as 'a Market for Fruits, Herbs, Roots, and Flowers, every Tuesday, Thursday, and Saturday; which is grown to a considerable Account, and well served with choice Goods, which makes it much resorted unto'. An excellent impression of the bustling activity at this time is provided by Peter Angelis's painting, signed and dated 1726, which is in the Yale Centre for British Art (also see cat. no. 39) and shows the market before the sheds were built.

At the beginning of the eighteenth century Daniel Defoe listed in his *Tour of London* (1725) the capital's main flesh markets, adding that 'at all the flesh markets, there is a part set for a Fish market and a part for a herb market': Spitalfields (East End), Leadenhall, Honey Lane and Newgate (City), Clare/Newport, Westminster, Bloomsbury, St James's and Hungerford (West End), Southwark (South), Shadwell, Hoxton Brook. Under the *separate* heading 'herb markets', Defoe listed Covent Garden and the Stocks Market. These were the only two markets dealing solely in fruit and herbs, each serving very different areas of London. They are also the only two markets known to have been painted in the eighteenth century.

Further historical information on the workings of London's markets will throw light on the numerous characters and activities encountered in market scenes. Most of the produce came from market gardens alongside the Thames from Greenwich to Brentford. A range of fruit and vegetables was grown in most market gardens, but certain districts specialised – for instance, Battersea with asparagus and Deptford with onions. The county of Middlesex was an important source of supply and Hugh Middleton in his eighteenth-century *Survey of Middlesex* estimates that in around 1750, the quantity of garden ground within ten miles of the metropolis was 15,000 acres, giving employment in the fruit season to 60,000 labourers. Between ten o'clock in the evening and one o'clock in the morning, depending on how far the market gardeners were from London, they would load their carts and donkeys and set off for Covent Garden. They were a familiar sight on the western approaches to London and have been recorded by artists in landscapes of the area.[4]

A more comfortable way of transporting produce was by water and in the *Spectator* of 11 August 1742 Steele describes how a boat 'landed with 10 Sails of Apricock Boats at Strand Bridge after having put in at Nine Elms & taken in Melons consigned by Mr Cuffe of that place to Sarah Sewell & Co at their stall in Covent Garden'. The produce was carried in wicker containers, which are found in great supply in market paintings. The willow for making them was freely available on the banks of near-by streams and ditches and on the islets of the Thames. There were basket-makers' huts along the banks of the Thames all the way from Fulham to Staines, and Chiswick Eyot was a well-known centre.

The Covent Garden Group

By the eighteenth century, Covent Garden had truly become an artists' quarter. There were early signs of this process when artists started moving to the West End towards the middle of the seventeenth century (see p6). A little later, when in 1688 the City announced in the *London Gazette* that sales outside the Outroper's 'pitch' in the Royal Exchange were banned, many auctioneers chose to move out of their sites around the Exchange and to settle around Covent Garden.[5] For instance, Christopher Cock's auction house[6] was situated at the back of his house, numbers 9–10, behind the sixth and seventh arches of the north-east range of the piazza. The sign-painters, a substantial branch of the painting trade until the abolition of street signs in 1762 (see p92), also held their annual exhibition in Bow Street.

More importantly, many of London's successful painters were established in or around Covent Garden, and it is not therefore surprising to find that the birth of artists' academies in London was also focused in this area. Marcellus Lauron had owned a house in Bow Street and his son Laroon took lodgings in Covent Garden after it was sold in 1704. Before moving to Great Queen Street where he founded his Academy in 1711, Godfrey Kneller was recorded as living in Covent Garden's north-east corner in 1691; so too, between 1723 and 1734, did James Thornhill, who created his Academy of Drawing there. John Closterman, Kneller's rival, also lived in Covent Garden in 1706 and there are entries in St Paul's register for the little-documented Balthazar Nebot between 1731 and 1742. Peter Angelis lived there between 1712 and 1728 and later William James the painter also had a shop near by in Maiden Lane for selling his pictures.[7]

This concentration of the painting trade has been put forward to explain the considerable output in topographical pictures of Covent Garden in the Georgian period. In contrast, the presence in Leicester Square of William Hogarth and Joshua Reynolds did nothing to create records for this area. Covent Garden, no doubt, presented the visual artist with an unusual range of interests, from architecture to market scenes with samples of low and high life. However, one should perhaps also consider the part played by patronage in the imaging of Covent Garden. Although Bedford House, on the south side of the piazza, was demolished in 1705–6, the Earl of Bedford continued to control the licensing of the market stalls. The collection of the Bedford Estates holds a substantial group of Covent Garden paintings.[8]

The artists who painted a large number of Covent Garden pictures were Peter Angelis (1685–1734), Joseph van Aken (*c.*1699–1749), and Balthazar Nebot (fl.1730 to after 1765). They have been nicknamed the Covent Garden Group and share stylistic similarities as well as the same subject matter. To this group, however, should be appended the names of John Collet (cat. no. 41), John Griffier the Younger (see his *Covent Garden from the South* in the collection of the Bank of England), William Hogarth ('Morning' in the *Four Times of the Day*) and Samuel Scott (see cat. no. 42).

1. 'The Parish of St Paul, Covent Garden', *Survey of London*, vol. XXXVI, 1970.
2. The painting is in a private collection and is reproduced in John Harris, *The Artist and the Country House*, 1979, p39.
3. Reproduced in the Wilton House guidebook, wrongly attributed to Samuel Scott.
4. *London's Pride*, Mireille Galinou (ed.), 1990: see chapter on market gardens, pp80–99.
5. Iain Pears, *The Discovery of Painting*, 1988, p59.
6. Ibid, p142.
7. See Hugh Phillips, *Mid-Georgian London*, 1964, for most of the information relating to artists' addresses in Covent Garden; Robert Raines, *Marcellus Lauron*, 1967, p56, for Lauron and Laroon; Pears, 1988, p147 for William James.
8. Hilda F. Finberg, 'Pictures of Covent Garden in the Duke of Bedford's collection', in *Country Life*, 10 September 1921, p329.

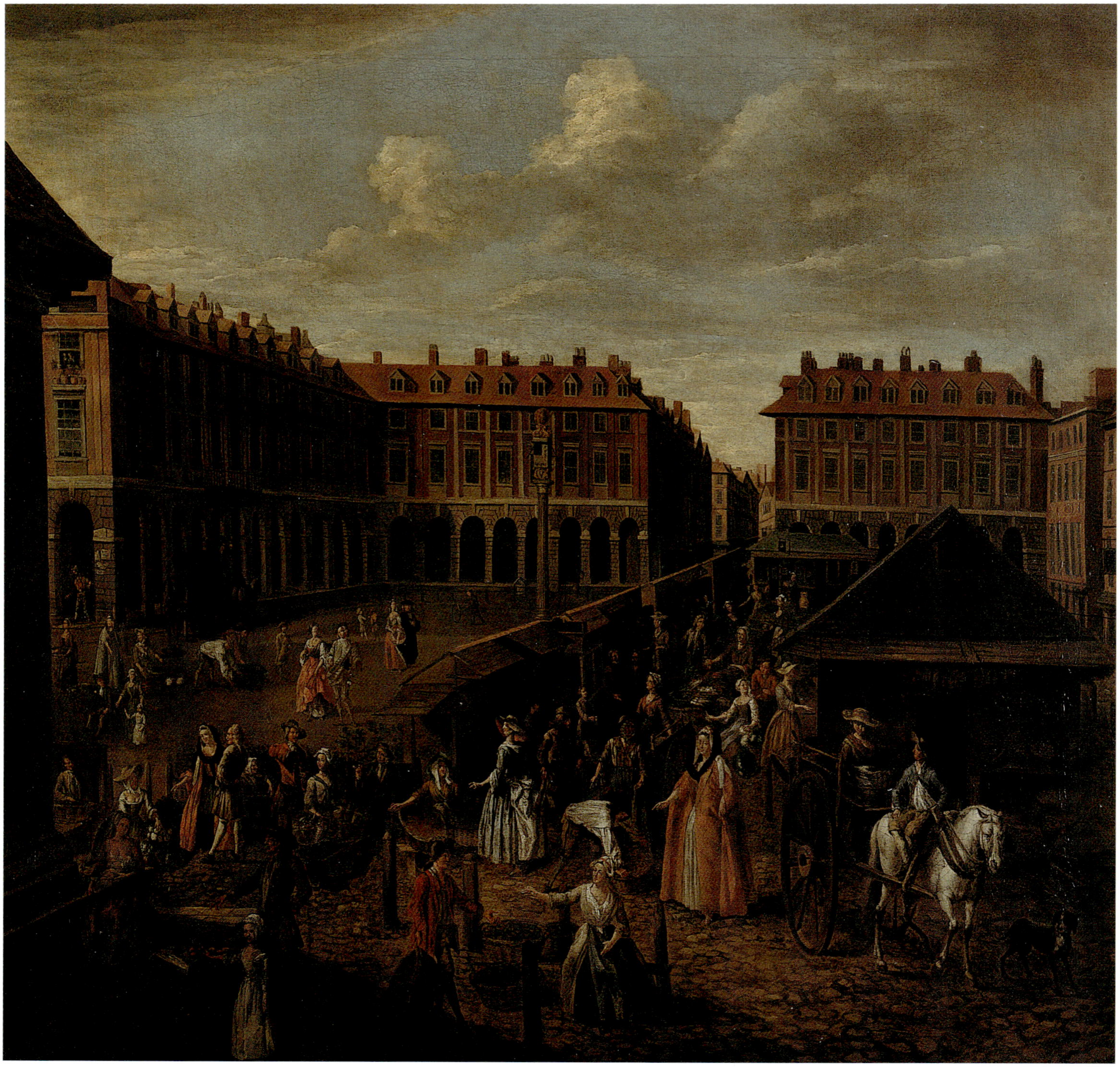

39.

JOSEPH VAN AKEN

(c.1699–1749)

Covent Garden Piazza and Market [A7466]
*c.*1720–30
Oil on canvas, 96 x 100.6 cm
Not signed or dated

THIS VIEW of the piazza and market looking east, from beside the church of St Paul's, Covent Garden (perhaps taken from the upper floor of the watch-house – see cat. no. 85) gives a good impression of the original buildings: the eastern blocks of houses were demolished, and the northern blocks extensively remodelled, during the 1880s.

This painting is the first to show market buildings on the piazza. The Angelis painting dated 1726 (see p117–18) is misleading because it does not show the row of forty-eight shops which were built in brick with slate roofs in 1705–6 inside the rails on the south side. From 1705 their lease was renewed every year. By the time the Museum picture was painted, the area occupied by the market had been paved and there was a single line of sheds, of which the nearest, seen on the right, was Tom King's celebrated coffee house (seen also in 'Morning' from Hogarth's *Four Times of the Day*), and another line of open stalls in the centre. The column supporting a sundial and gilt ball was erected in 1668 at the time when the square was enclosed with wooden railings and gravelled in (it was later cobbled, as seen here). A number of people are seen buying in the market, mostly from vendors seated beside baskets of fruit and vegetables; a horse and trap is on the right, and a hackney carriage in the distance left.

The costume indicates a date of about 1720–30.

A smaller but superior version of this picture, incorporating several of the figures (notably the lady standing in the foreground beside the trap), which is signed in monogram by Joseph van Aken, is in the Government Art Collection. A view of the Old Stocks Market in the City by the same artist is in the collection of the Bank of England. A pair of paintings showing Covent Garden piazza (with a different viewpoint) and the Stocks Market was sold at Christie's on 3 July 1996 (117 and 118 as part of the Bute Collection).

Provenance:
B. T. Batsford; Batsford sale, Christie's, 20 December 1911 (153, as Hogarth), bt Knoedler; purchased by the Museum in 1912 (as after Hogarth).

Bibliography:
Hayes (cat. no. 1); Celina Fox, *Londoners*, 1987, p142; H. F. Finberg, 'Pictures of Covent Garden in the Duke of Bedford's collection' in *Country Life*, 10 September 1921; *Manners and Morals*, exhibition catalogue, Tate Gallery, 1987, no. 43 (for related version).

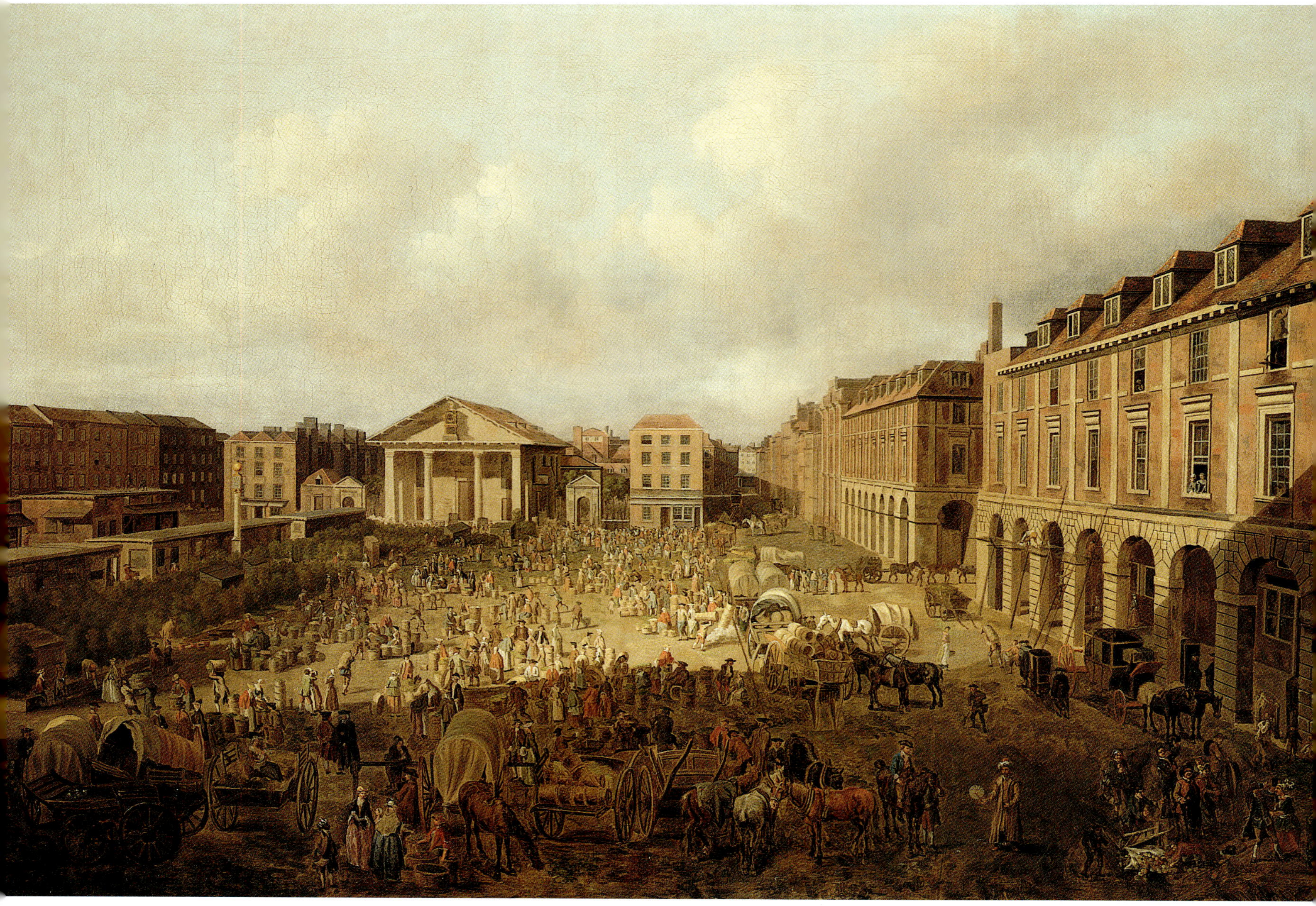

40.

SAMUEL SCOTT
(1702–72)

Covent Garden Piazza and Market
[A 80078]
*c.*1749–58
Oil on canvas, 110 x 166.7 cm
Not signed or dated

A VIEW of the piazza and market taken from a house on the east side close to the famous Bedford Coffee House, looking west towards the church of St Paul's, Covent Garden, and its symmetrically placed flanking gateways and houses.

The northern blocks of Jones's houses, with their stuccoed arcades, popularly called the 'piazzas', can be seen on the right. Beyond these is a mansion built in 1716–17 by the architect Thomas Archer (*c.*1668–1743) for Admiral Russell, the Earl of Orford (1653–1727). This house, which was carefully integrated architecturally as the string courses demonstrate, was converted into a hotel in 1774; it still stands, though completely refaced, and is now the offices of solicitors.

The south side of the square was originally occupied by the boundary wall of Bedford House, but when Wriothesley, 2nd Duke of Bedford decided to make Southampton House his London home, Bedford House was pulled down, in 1705–6, and Tavistock Row was built. Some of these early Queen Anne houses, none of which survives today, are seen on the left: note the wooden window frames flush with the brickwork – after the Building Act of 1709, they would have been required to be set back four inches, as an added safeguard against fire.

As may be seen by comparing this picture with van Aken's view, the market had expanded considerably in the space of thirty years. The line of sheds had been replaced by a row of two-storeyed buildings (the upper storeys even being used as bedrooms), and the open stalls by a row of more permanent sheds. The clock points to half-past nine, and the market is still bustling with activity; numerous carts are shown outside the railings on the north and east sides of the square, a sedan chair is seen passing by on the right, and a coach and another sedan are waiting for custom near by. An affray is taking place in the foreground as a result of an overturned vegetable barrow.

Samuel Scott was born in Covent Garden at 4 Tavistock Row and was registered as ratepayer there between 1736 and 1747. He lived at 2 Henrietta Street between 1747 and 1758, after which he moved to Twickenham, although he still retained a studio in Bedford Street. The artist painted Covent Garden four times. This painting is an unfinished version of the canvas of almost identical size in the collection of the Duke of Bedford, once attributed to Canaletto but now recognised as the work of Scott, with the help of Sawrey Gilpin for the animals (see Joseph Farington's *Diary*, 31 July 1796) and as a commission for Lord Hardwicke. The animals were no doubt put in by Gilpin in the Museum version as well, which would give a date of between 1749 and 1758, when Gilpin was apprenticed to Scott. The buildings, and the majority of the figures, have not been given Scott's detailed finish, and the cupola of St Paul's and the spire of St Martin-in-the-Fields have not been painted in. The costume indicates a date of about 1750–60. Studies for the figures of the two ladies in the foreground left are in the Oppé collection. A preliminary oil sketch in which the essentials of the composition are already worked out was given to its present owners by Mr and Mrs Paul Mellon. Finally a view with a composition different to the three already mentioned and showing Covent Garden on election day is in the collection of Charles Forte.

Provenance:
Purchased from Leggatt Brothers in 1912 (attributed to Canaletto).

Bibliography:
Hayes (cat. no. 99); *The Diary of Joseph Farington*, James Greig (ed.), vol. 1, 1923, p158 (note); Richard Kingzett, 'A catalogue of the Works of Samuel Scott', in *Walpole Society*, vol. XLVIII, pp73–5; Celina Fox, *Londoners*, 1987, p143; *Manners and Morals*, exhibition catalogue, Tate Gallery, 1987, no. 214 (for related version); *Canaletto & England*, Michael Liversidge and Jane Farrington (eds), 1993, p125.

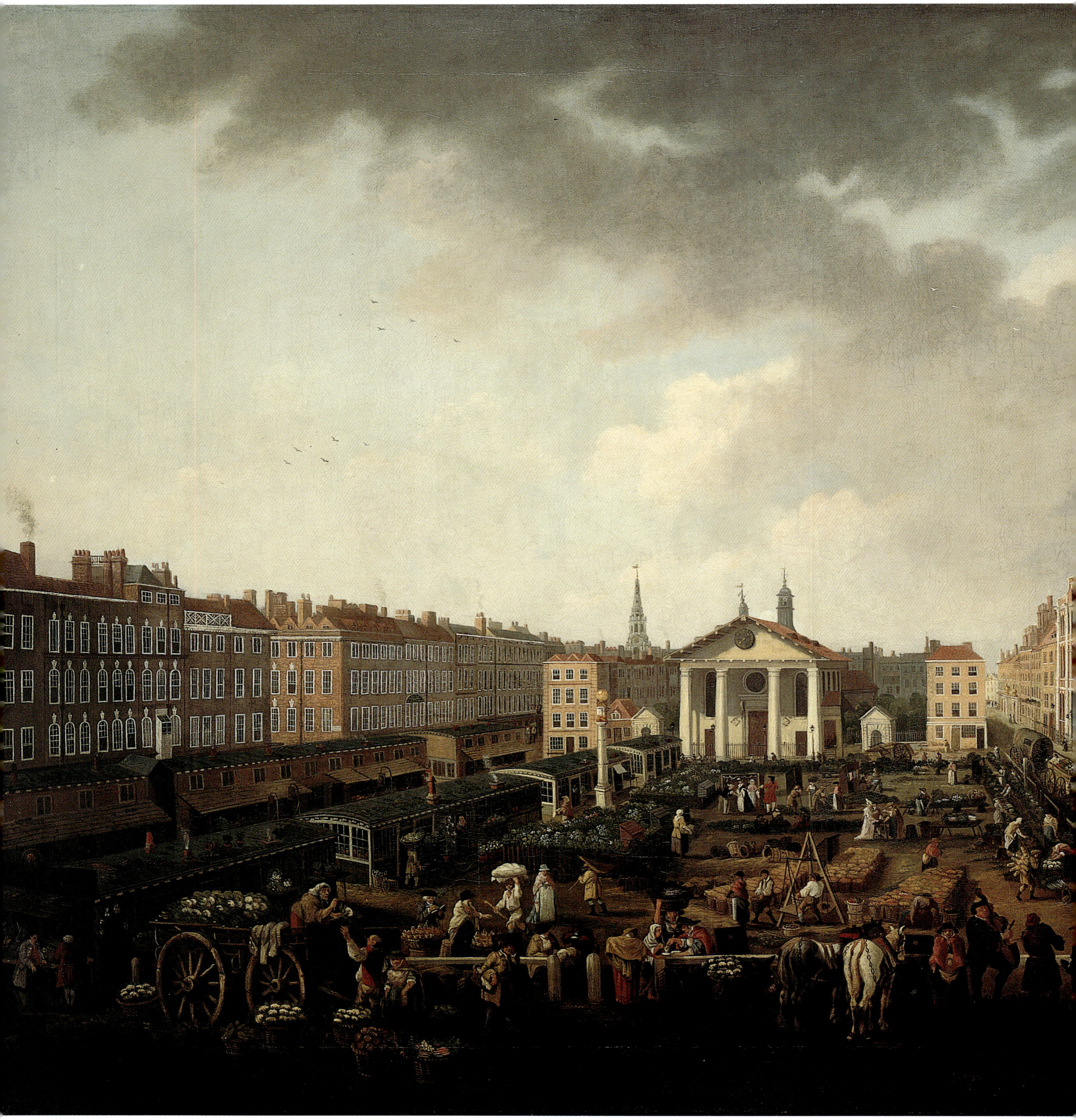

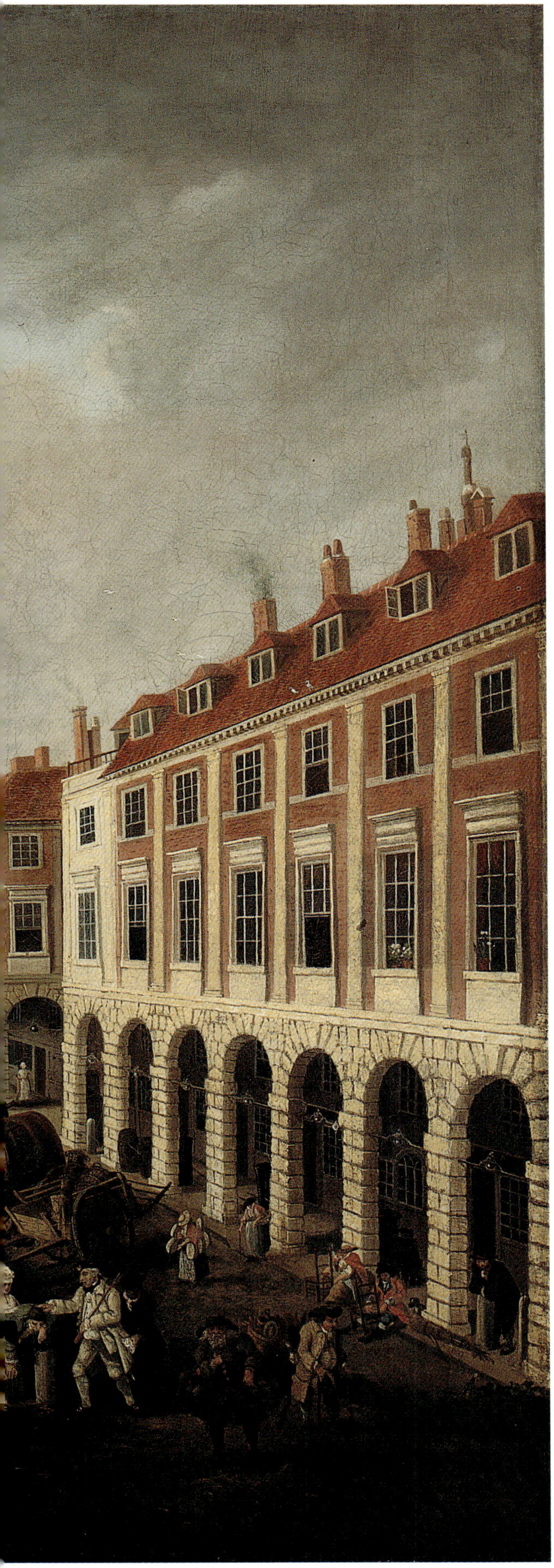

41.

JOHN COLLET

(1725–80)

Covent Garden Piazza and Market [55.72]
*c.*1770–80
Oil on canvas, 133.7 x 189.5 cm
Not signed or dated

THIS PICTURE, taken from the east side and looking towards the church of St Paul, Covent Garden, adopts the same viewpoint as Scott in his view of Covent Garden painted twenty years before. By closing in on his subject, the market, the painting becomes very successful at rendering activities, showing the full range of sheds and two-storeyed market buildings. Carts line the roadway on the north side of the market, and under the 'piazzas' are several sedan chairs. The picture is full of human activity, as one would expect from an admirer and imitator of Hogarth, and such familiar denizens of the capital as the street musician, the pickpocket and the chair mender are seen in the right foreground (see Phillips for the most famous Covent Garden characters). We should also note the presence of a curds and whey seller in the foreground (see cat. no. 31).

The architectural detail is not as accurate as in the Scott view, and St Paul's, Covent Garden, has been given quite the wrong proportions. The spire of James Gibbs's church of St Martin-in-the-Fields is visible in the distance.

The costume indicates a date of about 1770–80.

Provenance:
Ernest E. Cook, by whom it was bequeathed, through the National Art Collections Fund, in 1955.

Bibliography:
Hayes (cat. no. 30); Celina Fox, *Londoners,* 1987: see chapter on markets, pp138–53; *A Gift to the Nation: The Fine and Decorative Art Collections of Ernest E. Cook*, exhibition catalogue, Holburne Museum, Bath, 1991; Hugh Phillips, *Mid-Georgian London*, 1964, pp150–2.

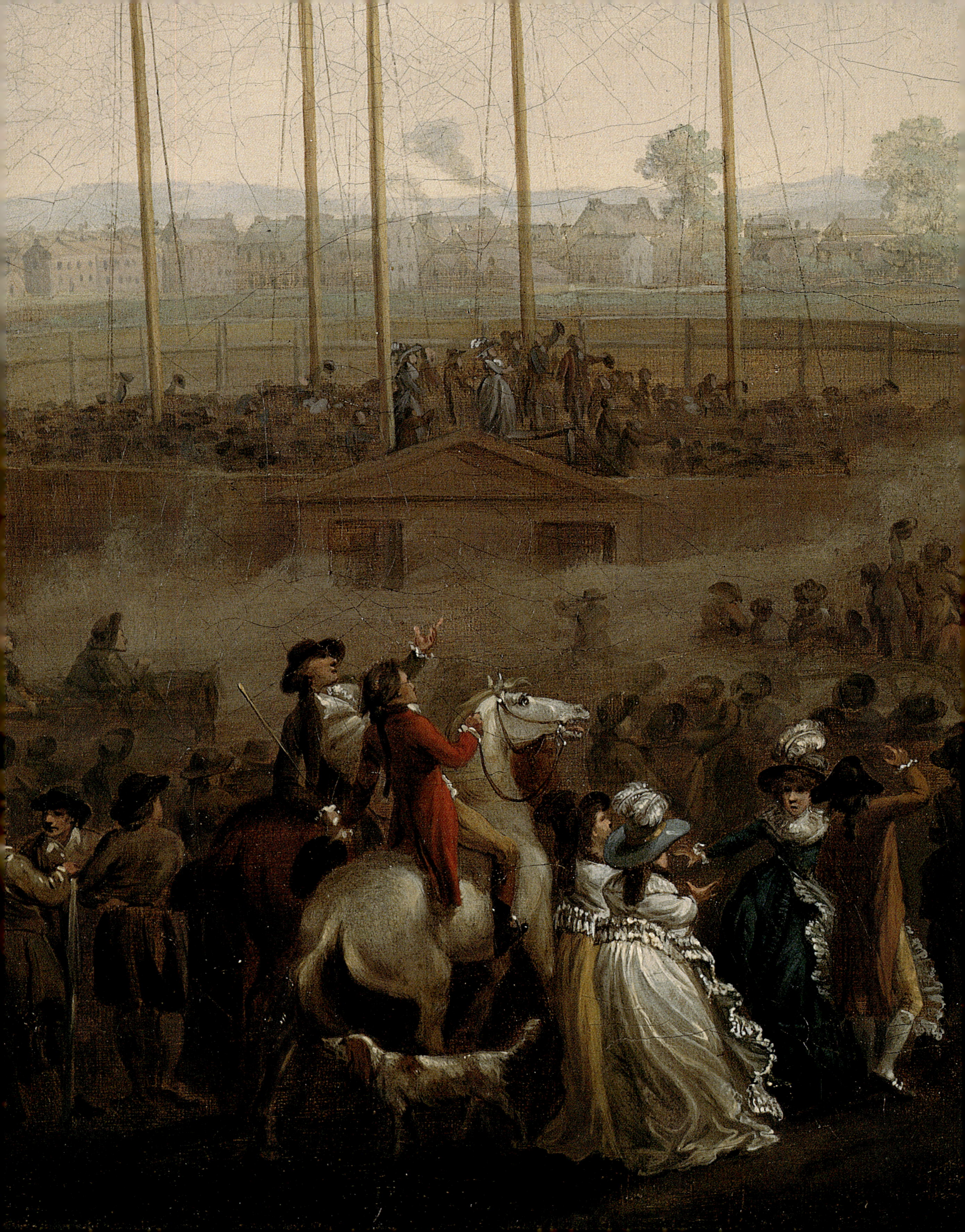

THE SOCIAL SCENE

THE CONVERSATION piece is perhaps the most representative of all manifestations of upper- and middle-class life in the eighteenth century, ranging as it does from domestic to public settings. Although the genre can be traced back to sixteenth- and seventeenth-century paintings, such as Holbein's *Sir Thomas More, his Father, his Household and his Descendants* at home in Chelsea[1] or Thomas Vyner and his family at their Swakeleys seat,[2] the formula remains firmly anchored in the eighteenth century. William Hogarth himself testifies to this fact: 'I then married [1729] and commenced painter of small conversation pieces from 12 to 15 inches high. This *having novelty* [author's italics], succeeded for a few years.'[3] Hogarth produced some of London's most memorable conversation pieces, for example the *Cholmondeley Family*, whose setting is a distillation of Lord Malpas's library and picture collection at his house in Arlington Street.[4] Even in his entertaining moral pieces, for example in plate 2 of *A Marriage à la Mode*, the interior shown may be of a house in Arlington Street, possibly Lord Granville's.[5] The Museum's example, which belongs to the end of the century, shows the Middleton family at home (cat. no. 47).

William Hogarth
(1697–1764)
The Cholmondeley Family, 1732.
Oil on canvas
Collection: The Marquess of Cholmondeley
Photograph: the Witt Library, Courtauld Institute of Art.

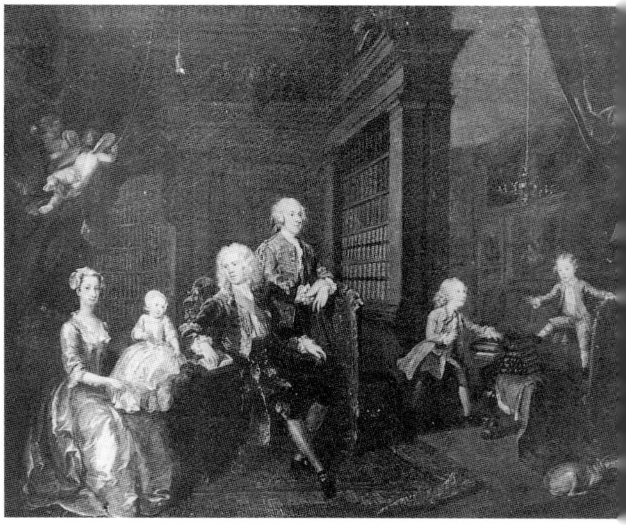

Another popular theme focused on London's social calendar. No European was more aware of a city's social life than the experienced traveller Casanova, and no one more curious to sample the delights of both high and low London than he was when he visited in the early summer of 1763, aged thirty-eight.[6] He dined, for instance, 'in all taverns of good or evil repute, so as to familiarise myself with the manners of these "great little" islanders'. His London diary is a catalogue of all that the capital had to offer then and constitutes a benchmark by which we can assess the artistic response of the day.

Casanova visited the theatres of Covent Garden and Drury Lane, went to the Stock Exchange in the mornings where he 'made many acquaintances' and in the evening 'frequented the most select bagnios where a man of quality can sup, bathe and meet well bred women of easy virtue'; dined at the house of Mrs Cornelys in Soho Square 'in which she could give a supper to 400 people at one horseshoe table... in the largest room of its kind in London'; he played cards at Lady Hamilton's (he had a letter of introduction); and he went to Ranelagh and Vauxhall.

Antonio Canaletto
(1697–1768)
Vauxhall Gardens: the Grand Walk, 1751
Oil on canvas
Collection: Lord Trevor
Photograph: the Witt Library, Courtauld Institute of Art.

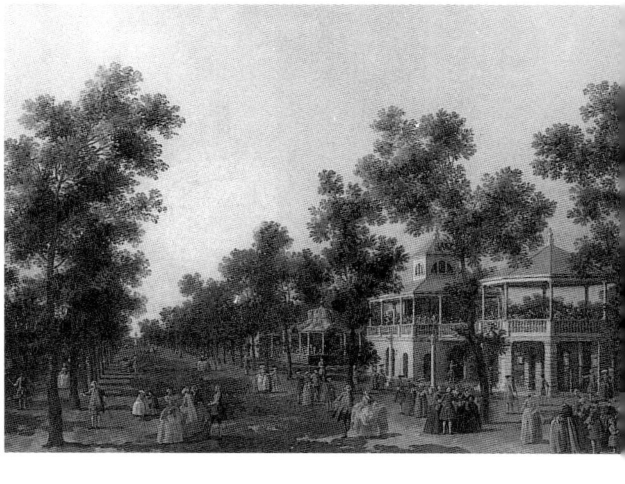

Casanova's social diary concurs with many others of the period and it is disappointing to note how little of all this painters have conveyed. Although to a certain extent prints and drawings fill some of the gaps, hardly any paintings address the themes of tavern life, bagnios and masquerades.[7] Some conversation pieces stretch into the world of party-giving and document such activities as card-playing and drinking in company, but the three most fashionable venues – Mrs Cornelys, Vauxhall and Ranelagh – have received little or no attention. Mrs Cornelys's famous establishment was never painted and only descriptive texts exist to offer any insight into her extraordinary and well-attended parties.

The mid-eighteenth-century views painted by Canaletto of the pleasure gardens are taken during the day and therefore fail to convey anything of the wonderful descriptions of their lighting. They are also treated as landscapes rather than social pieces and give no hint of what it was like to be a participant. On the other hand, the decoration of the supper rooms at Vauxhall in the 1740s, commissioned from Francis Hayman by Jonathan Tyers, encouraged the creation of a British genre painting. *May Day or the Milkmaid Garland, Sliding upon the Ice* and *The Wapping Landlady*, for instance, started three distinct trends in social painting which later produced a host of images of London folk-life, winter scenes in the parks and sailors about town.[8]

The strong theatrical content of this collection would seem unbalanced if it were not for the crucial role played by the theatre in eighteenth-century London. We are fortunate in having Hogarth's own definition of the interaction between life and theatre and its use by the artist:

> I therefore wished to compose pictures on canvas similar to representation on the stage; & farther hope, that they will be tried by the same test, & criticised by the same criterion. Let it be observed, that I mean to speak only of those scenes where the human species are actors & these, I think have not often been delineated in a way of which they are worthy and capable.[9]

In John Collet's *May Morning* (as in a number of paintings by Hogarth) the street is conceived as a receding theatrical backdrop with a triangular perspective, while Edward Penny's *A City Shower* (cat. no. 35) also has strong theatrical undertones which in concept – the visual translation of surprise – are close to those displayed in the scene from *The Suspicious Husband* with David Garrick (cat. no. 43). The interest shown in the opera houses in Leicester Square and the Pantheon (see cat. nos 37 and 38) also reinforces the centrality of this theme to life in the capital.

1. Several versions exist; perhaps the most notable are those in the National Portrait Gallery and at Nostell Priory in West Yorkshire.
2. National Portrait Gallery.
3. *Artists on Art*, R. Goldwater and M. Treves (eds), 1976, p179.
4. See *Manners and Morals*, exhibition catalogue, Tate Gallery, 1987, no. 67.
5. Hugh Phillips, *Mid-Georgian London*, 1964, p70 and plate 4.
6. *The Memoirs of Jacques Casanova de Seingalt*, London, 1922, privately printed for the Navarre Society Ltd, pp135–77.
7. Here most of the evidence is in the form of portraits. See Aileen Ribero, *The Dress Worn at Masquerades in England 1730–1790 and its relationship to fancy dress in portraiture*, New York, 1984. Also see Celina Fox and Aileen Ribero, *Masquerade*, Museum of London booklet (London Connections series), 1983.
8. See Brian Allen, *Francis Hayman*, 1987, pp107ff. For Vauxhall Gardens see David Coke, *The Muse's Bower Vauxhall Gardens 1728–1786*, exhibition catalogue, Gainsborough's House, 1978; T. J. Edelstein, *Vauxhall Gardens*, exhibition catalogue, Yale Center for British Art, Newhaven, 1983 and *Rococo, Art and Design in Hogarth's England*, Michael Snowdin and Elspeth Moncrieff (eds), exhibition catalogue, Victoria and Albert Museum, 1984, pp74–98.
9. *Artists on Art from the 14th-20th centuries*, Robert Goldwater and Marco Treres (eds), 1976 ed., p179.

42.
BRITISH SCHOOL

St Bartholomew's Fair, Smithfield [90.44]
Late 1730s/1743?
Oil on canvas, 81.5 x 109 cm
Not signed or dated

IN KEEPING with most eighteenth-century representations of St Bartholomew's Fair, this unfinished work was painted towards the end of the fair's heyday, shortly before it fell into decline. The reduction of the fair's length from a fortnight to three or four days in 1735 was the first blow and further restrictions came in 1737 when the Licensing Act limited the performance of plays, one of the fair's noted attractions, to patent theatres.

The view is taken from the north looking south-west towards St Bartholomew's Hospital (London's oldest hospital). Henry VIII's gateway, in the centre of the picture, is hidden by the theatre booths. The tower of the church of St Bartholomew-the-Less, in the hospital grounds, is visible. To its right the dome of St Paul's (incorrect position) and farther on still the square tower of St Sepulchre's church are so poorly and inaccurately represented that they may have been later additions. In the right foreground is 'Cow Lane' (now Cowcross Street) and as the eyes progress into the picture, we come across the Crown and Cushion Tavern, the Greyhound, the George Inn (the Swan Inn next door is not visible), all clearly marked on John Rocque's 1746 map of London. The theatrical booth at the end of the perspective should be situated opposite Hosier Lane.

William Hogarth's 1732 *Southwark Fair* is by far the most substantial and influential work on a London eighteenth-century fair. However, Southwark was second in importance after St Bartholomew's and it seems curious that Hogarth, who was born in Smithfield, should not depict his 'home' fair. It has been suggested that on this occasion Hogarth may have drawn inspiration from the work of other artists and that he painted Southwark because St Bartholomew's had already been illustrated (see Fox).

The unfinished state of this painting enables us to observe its technical make-up and how the artist built up his figures from sketching the outlines in thin brown lines of paint. The use of light is also very striking, since the painter is prepared to compromise the legibility of the middle ground in order to pursue the organisation according to horizontal bands of light and shade created by the cloudy sky. There is a spontaneity in the crowd and in the lighting of the painting which suggests that the work closely depends on direct observation. Unfortunately the banners advertising the shows are not sufficiently detailed and cannot be identified.

The interpretation of this work cannot be concluded without referring to the three principal pictorial records of the fair: an anonymous fan design purporting to show the fair in 1721 but probably dating from 1740 (original watercolour in the British Museum, aquatint published in 1824, see Rosenfeld, 1960, p26); a painting variously attributed to Balthazar Nebot and more convincingly to Egbert van Heemskerk (Guildhall Art Gallery); lastly, and most usefully for the purpose of identifying the booths and shows, a print published by William Dicey (in 1730?) entitled 'The Humours and Diversions of Bartholomew's Fair' (in the Museum's collection, acc. no. 49.90/8). The last two works appear to be

Provenance:
Christie's, 9 February 1990 (55).

Bibliography:
S. Rosenfeld, *Theatre of the London Fairs in the 18th century*, Cambridge, 1960; Celina Fox, 'Hogarth's Southwark Fair' in Notes, *Print Quarterly*, vol. IV, no. 4, December 1987, pp421–2.

connected: the viewpoint, the foreground details of the rope dancer and smoking monkey and the billing of the plays are identical. In essence they contain all the elements that will make up the composition of Hogarth's *Southwark Fair*: the crowd (both general *and* particular), the booths, the rope dancer and a topographical landmark. The work under observation is rather different in spirit, less descriptive (not simply because it is unfinished) and more panoramic.

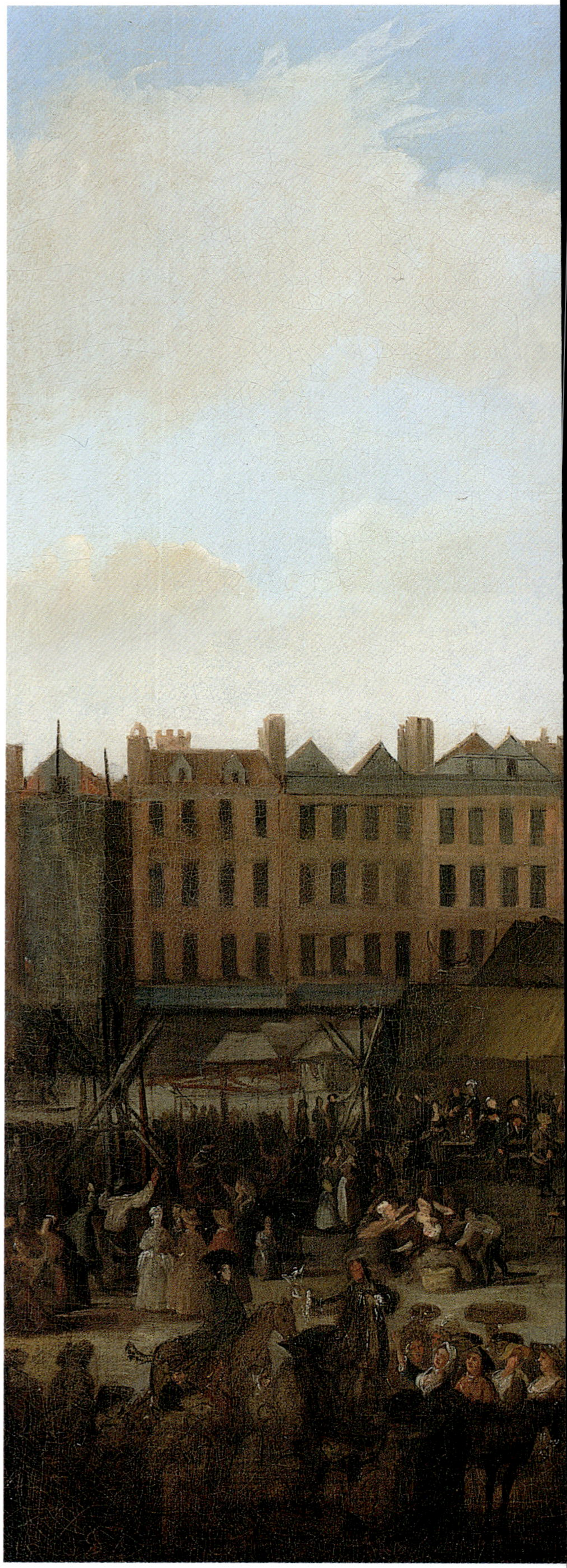

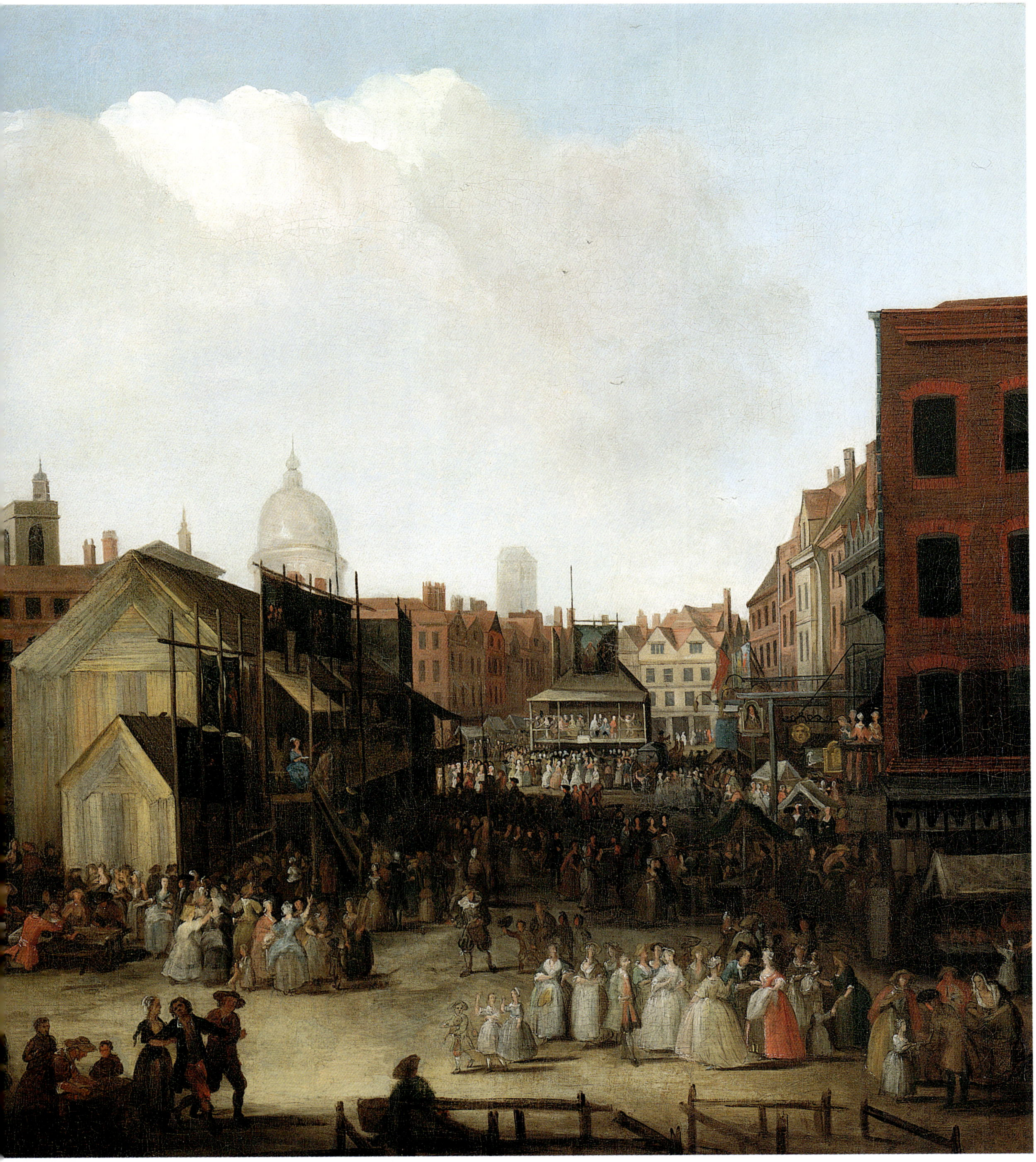

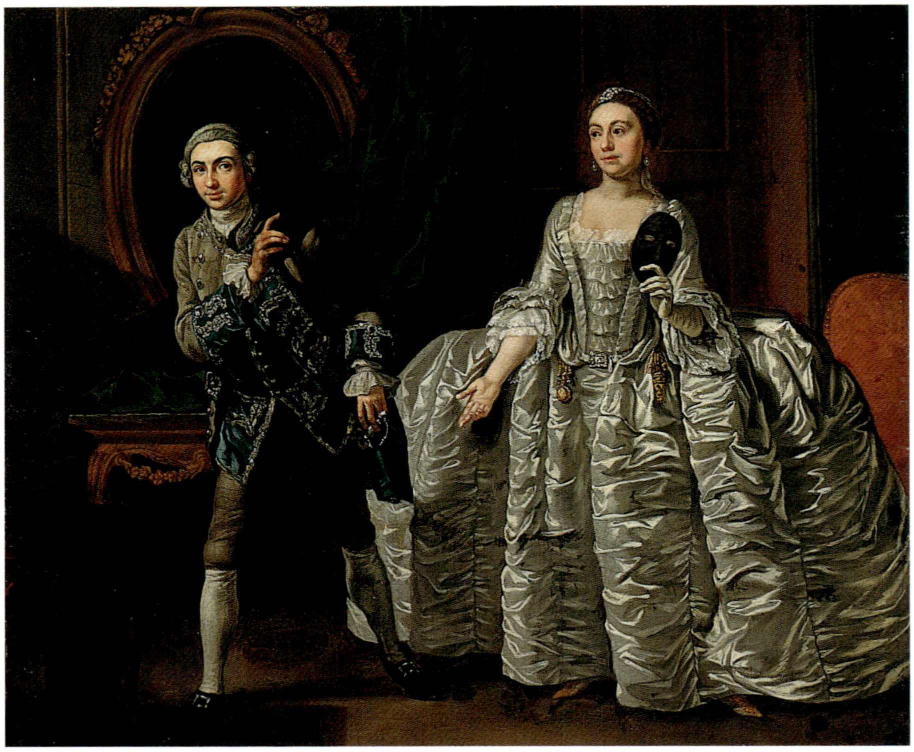

43.

FRANCIS HAYMAN
(1708–76)

David Garrick and Hannah Pritchard in a Scene from *The Suspicious Husband* [55.50]
1752
Oil on canvas, 63.7 x 76.6 cm
Not signed or dated

THIS PICTURE shows David Garrick (1717–79) and Mrs Pritchard (1711–68) as Ranger and Clarinda in Act IV, Scene iv of *The Suspicious Husband*, a comedy by Dr Benjamin Hoadly which was first produced at Covent Garden on 12 February 1747, with Garrick and Mrs Pritchard in the leading roles. Ranger has been flirting with a masked lady, unaware that she is his cousin; Hayman has chosen the moment when Clarinda is unmasked, and Ranger, much put out, declares, in an aside to the audience, 'I must brazen this out'.

Though only thirty at the time of this production, Garrick was already well established as an actor of both Shakespearean and contemporary parts, having taken the town by storm in 1741 when he appeared as Richard III at Goodman's Fields theatre. Mrs Pritchard made her début on the London stage in 1733; from 1744 until 1747 she appeared at Covent Garden, but she followed Garrick to Drury Lane when he took over the management of that theatre in 1747. She was one of Garrick's leading actresses for many years, and was held to be the greatest Lady Macbeth of her day.

Another (slightly larger) version of the Museum picture, inscribed in a contemporary hand as 'Painted by Mr Hayman 1747', previously in the Garrick Club collection (cat. no. 394), is in the Paul Mellon collection: this was executed for Dr Hoadly, the author of the play, and is identical except in one or two points of detail (eg Mrs Pritchard is shown wearing a necklace). Hayman had been a scenery painter at Drury Lane Theatre since 1736, when he carried out the commission. In May 1752 Garrick paid Hayman twenty guineas for a replica of the painting, which is the work under consideration. The fact that the Museum picture includes about 2 inches (5 cm) less of the composition on three sides, and in particular, loses part of Mrs Pritchard's dress, suggests that it has been slightly reduced at some stage, and that it was originally a 28 x 36 inch (71 x 91 cm) canvas.

Provenance:
Commissioned from the artist by David Garrick in 1752; Joseph Parkes; Parkes' Sale, Christie's, 8 May 1858 (8, as Zoffany), bt Waters; Colonel the Honble. W. H. P. Carington; Carington sale, Christie's, 11 June 1887, (50, as Zoffany), bt Parsons; T. Rogers and Co; Rogers's Sale, Christie's, 23 July 1954, (128), bt Bernard; purchased out of the Joicey Trust Fund from Frank T. Sabin in 1955.

Bibliography:
Hayes (cat. no. 119); *Royal Opera House Retrospective 1732–1982*, exhibition catalogue, Royal Academy, 1983, no. 190; Brian Allen, *Francis Hayman*, 1987, cat. no. 39.

44.

MANNER OF JOSEPH WRIGHT OF DERBY

(1734–97)

Portrait of David Garrick [56.169.2]

*c.*1770

Oil on canvas, 75 x 62.2 cm

Not signed or dated

A LATE portrait of the actor David Garrick (1717–79) shown half-length and seated, with his right hand pointing to a document on a table.

The costume indicates a date of about 1770.

A very poor portrait, and presumably a provincial work; there is nothing to suggest the style of Thomas Hudson (1701–79), to whom it was once attributed, or his school, nor is any portrait known of which this might be a copy.

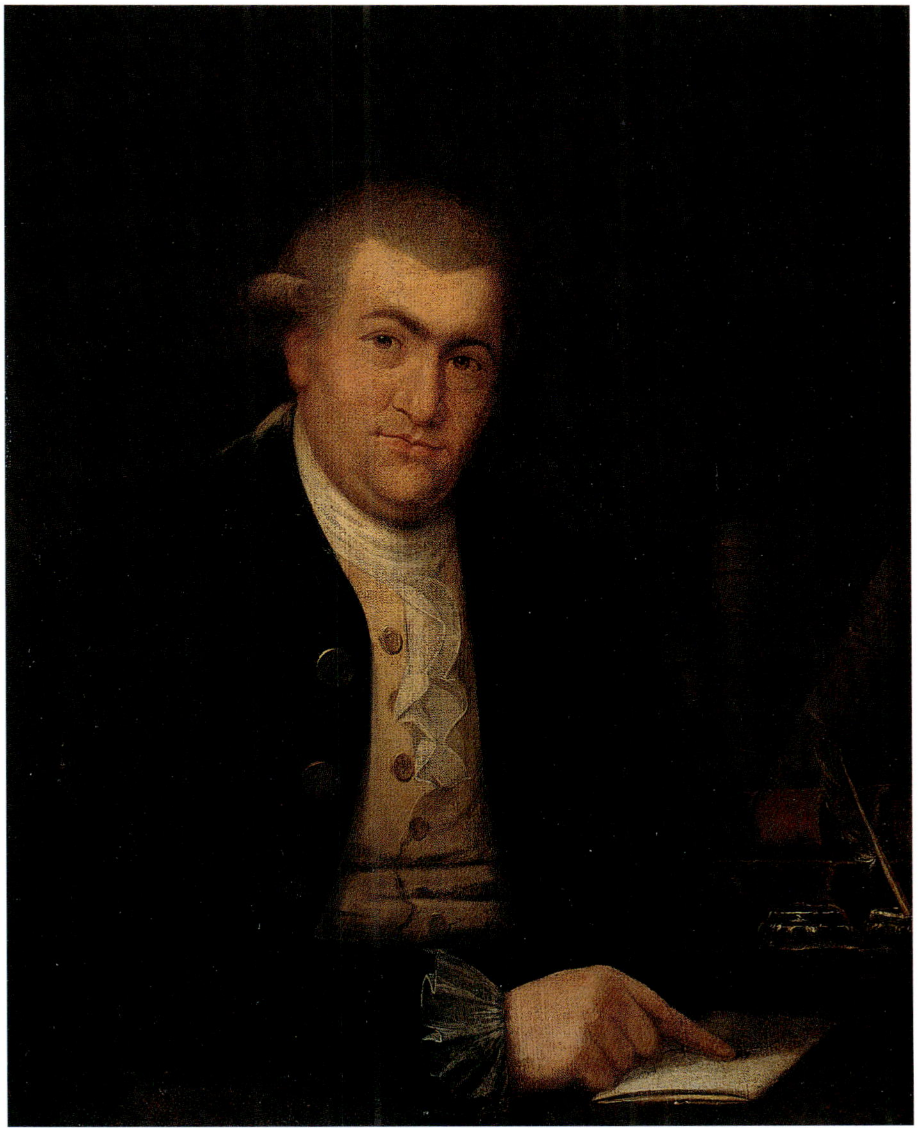

Provenance:
Presented by R. N. Green-Armytage in 1956 (as by Hudson).

Bibliography:
Hayes (cat. no. 182).

Provenance:
Purchased in 1912 (source unknown).

Bibliography:
Hayes (cat. no. 125); *The De Wildes*, exhibition catalogue, Northampton Central Art Gallery, 1971, no. 3.

45.

SAMUEL DE WILDE
(c.1751–1832)

Joseph George Holman as Chamont in Otway's *The Orphan* [A 7463]
*c.*1785
Oil on canvas, 40 x 30 cm
Not signed or dated

HOLMAN (1764–1817) is shown full length, facing slightly to the right, with his right arm outstretched; the background is plain. Joseph George Holman, one of the leading actors of his day, is portrayed here in the Windsor uniform, which he may have been entitled to wear on the stage as one of the King's Actors. This dress was instituted by George III as a private uniform for use at Court in or before 1779.

Holman made his first appearance on the stage as Romeo at the Theatre Royal, Covent Garden, in 1784. He continued to act there under Harris's management until the dispute which arose in the season of 1799–1800 over the increase in charges for a benefit and in fines for refusing a part, involving eight of the principal actors; Holman either resigned or was dismissed, and he ended his career in America. He first appeared as Chamont in Thomas Otway's play *The Orphan* (1680) at Covent Garden on 4 February 1785, and another portrait of him in this role, also by de Wilde, was in the Garrick Club collection (cat. no. 266).

The costume worn by Holman indicates a date of about 1785.

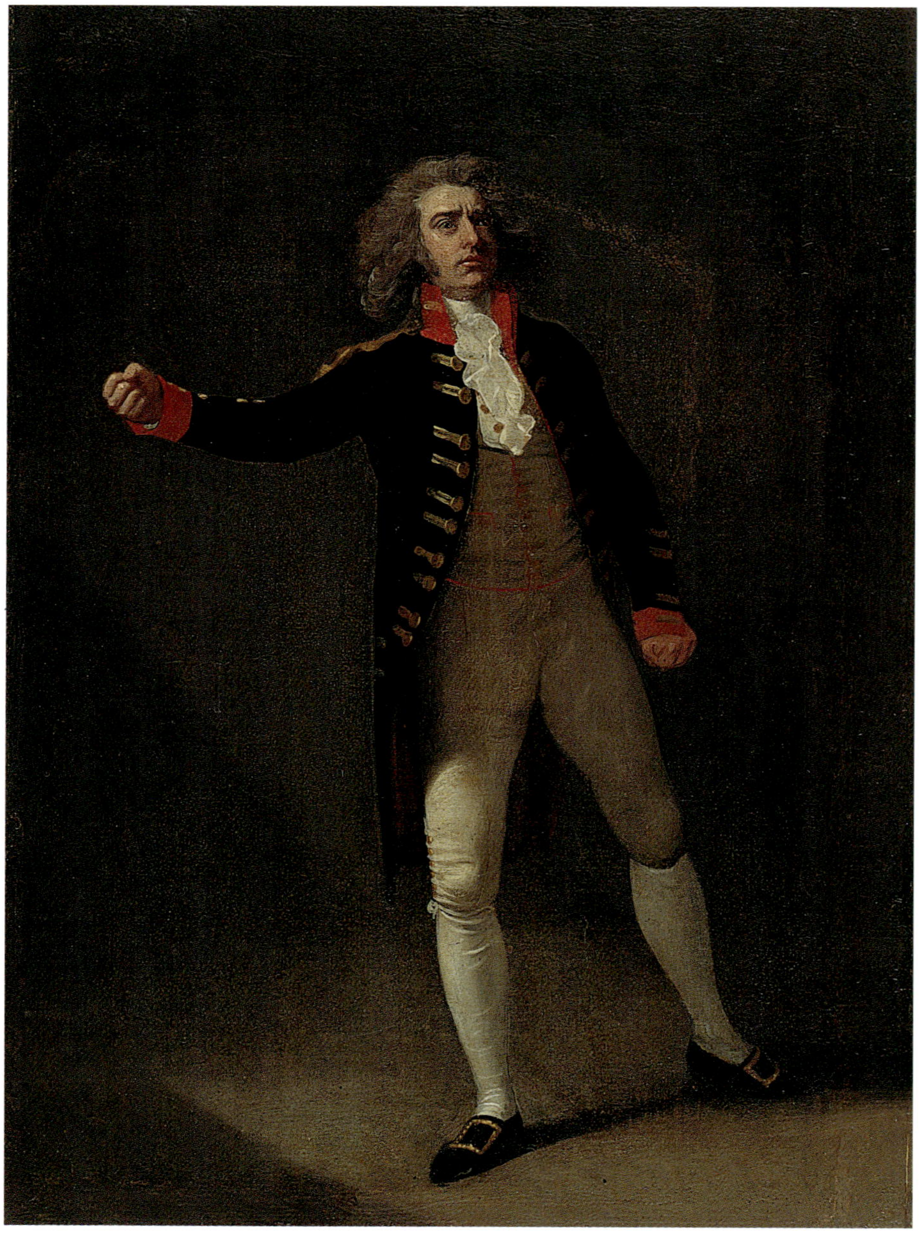

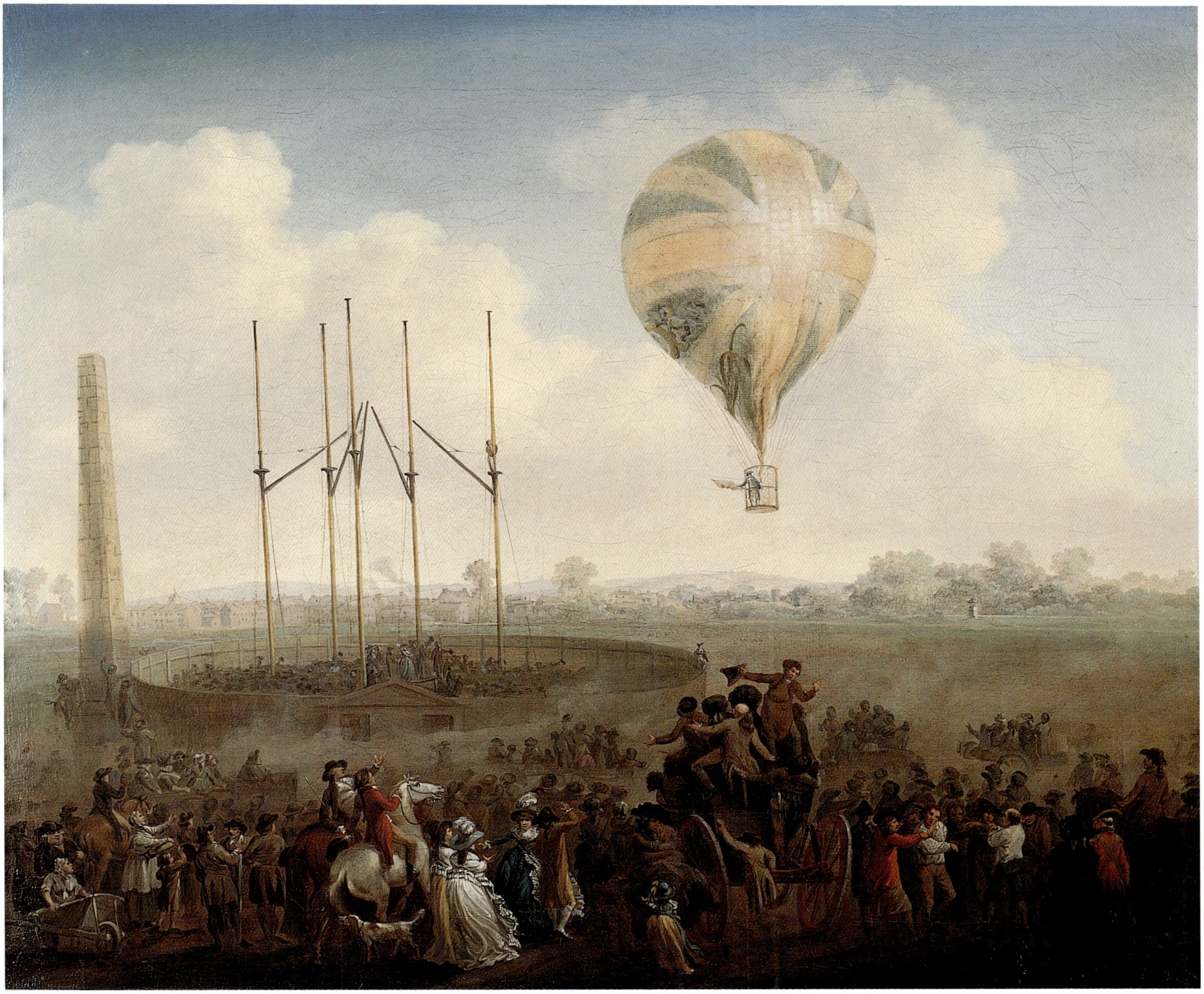

46.

JULIUS CAESAR IBBETSON
(1759–1817)
The Ascent of Lunardi's Balloon from St George's Fields [A 15491]
*c.*1788–90
Oil on canvas, 50 x 60.6 cm
Not signed or dated

IN 1784 Vincenzo Lunardi, secretary to the Neopolitan Ambassador in England, made aeronautical history with his successful ascent in a hydrogen-filled balloon when he took off from the Honourable Artillery Company's ground in Moorfields and landed at Ware.

Ibbetson's canvas is a record of the third ascent of Lunardi's balloon, from St George's Fields, Newington, on 29 June 1785. Tickets were sold for the event, and some idea of the crowd present is suggested in the foreground of the picture. Lunardi had intended to pilot the flight and take four companions with him,

Provenance:
Purchased from Willson Brothers in 1915 (without attribution).

Bibliography:
Hayes (cat. no. 59); *Julius Caesar Ibbetson*, exhibition catalogue, Iveagh Bequest, Kenwood, 1957 (cat. no. 4); Rotha Mary Clay, *Julius Caesar Ibbetson 1759–1817*, 1948, p11; Richard Altick, *The Shows of London*, 1978, p85.

but the balloon failed to rise under this load. As a result, Lunardi decided to forgo the excitement himself and two other potential aeronauts had also to be disappointed, the 'eagle's nest' being occupied only by his patron George Biggin and by Mrs Letitia Anne Sage (omitted in this picture). Though Biggin had no experience in piloting and left behind the oars used to help control the rate of ascent and descent, this flight was as successful as the first, and after floating over the Thames and Westminster, and being watched by the King from St James's Palace, the balloon eventually came down in a common field near Harrow School.

St George's Fields was an area still largely undeveloped at this time, although the new road from Blackfriars Bridge, approved by Parliament in 1769, had already been constructed and the obelisk (seen here) at the junction of this road with those from London and Westminster Bridges at St George's Circus had been raised in 1771. In this picture, Ibbetson has left out any indication of the roads which radiated from the Circus.

Next to the obelisk (which was removed to the nearby Geraldine Mary Harmsworth Park, Lambeth, in 1905) is the Royal George Rotunda, the enclosure from which the preparations for the balloon ascent were made. In the distance is Newington Butts, with the church tower of St Mary's Newington visible on the left, and beyond the hills of south London.

Following Lunardi's 1784 exploit, the balloon was exhibited at the Pantheon (recorded in a painting by F. G. Byron) and ballooning became a regular attraction at London's largest pleasure gardens.

In 1788 Ibbetson exhibited a painting of this subject at the Royal Academy. Except for the omission of Mrs Sage, the Museum picture is an exact replica of this picture (in the collection of Arthur Kauffman).

47.

BRITISH SCHOOL

John Middleton with his Family in his Drawing Room [93.28]

*c.*1796–7

Oil on canvas, 88.3 x 110.5 cm

Not signed or dated

THIS IS a group portrait showing the colourman John Middleton (probably holding a sample book) and his children, from left to right Jesse, Anna, Sarah and Joshua. The housekeeper, shown on the left, must have been a central character in the household, judging by the way everyone's eyes converge upon her. Her fine muslin apron would denote a high status in the world of servants. Her face is severe and her costume old-fashioned (late 1770s/1780s), as is John Middleton's. The older generation on the left of the painting contrasts with the younger generation on the right, both in terms of posture and costume. Allowing for the social milieu of the Middletons, Joshua's 'skeleton suit' and the waistline and neckline of the girls' muslin dresses, as well as their hairstyles, together point to a date between 1795 and 1797.

This conversation piece is set in the simply furnished drawing/music room, of mid-eighteenth-century design with a few more up-to-date touches. In the left recess of the fireplace is an English 'square piano' (developed in England by the German Johannes Zumpe, available from about 1765 and which would have been purchased from a firm such as Longman & Broderip of Cheapside) with a flute lying on it and music sheets below. On the right of the fireplace, a wine glass, knife box (*c.*1780–5) and ornamental bottles rest on a small console. The number of chairs (six) matches the number of sitters. The design of the table and chairs, made in mahogany, dates from the late 1760s.

The room's decoration is fairly plain: no patterned wallpaper (on which tax had to be paid), no patterned flooring but a close-fitted carpet and, on the wall, one painting only, set rather high above the fireplace. This, it has been suggested, may represent a landscape by the artist Julius Caesar Ibbetson, one of Middleton's clients and admirers (see Harley, p45). The work may indeed be compared to views by Ibbetson of Ullswater in the Lake District. Yet other details in the room add touches of refinement: the painted border (although not of very distinguished execution), which runs all around the fireplace and is repeated on the summer board; the fashionable glass chandeliers; the flowers informally arranged; and the smart and elaborately festooned window-curtains.

This interior could usefully be compared to that painted by Johann Zoffany in 1769 of Sir Lawrence Dundas and his grandson in the library or pillar room at 19 Arlington Street (in the Marquess of Zetland collection and illustrated on p140). The comparison highlights the difference in status between the two men but also the changes in taste that had taken place. The intensity of blue in the Zoffany was the latest fashion in the 1760s; by the 1790s the blue is still luminous but more subdued. The chocolate-brown skirting riser in the Zoffany has become white in the painting under review.

In 1784 John Middleton, from Sandys & Middleton, was trading at 8 St Martin's Lane. From 1785 when he is first listed under his own name in Bailey's *British Directory* to 1818 when he died, John Middleton lived and worked at

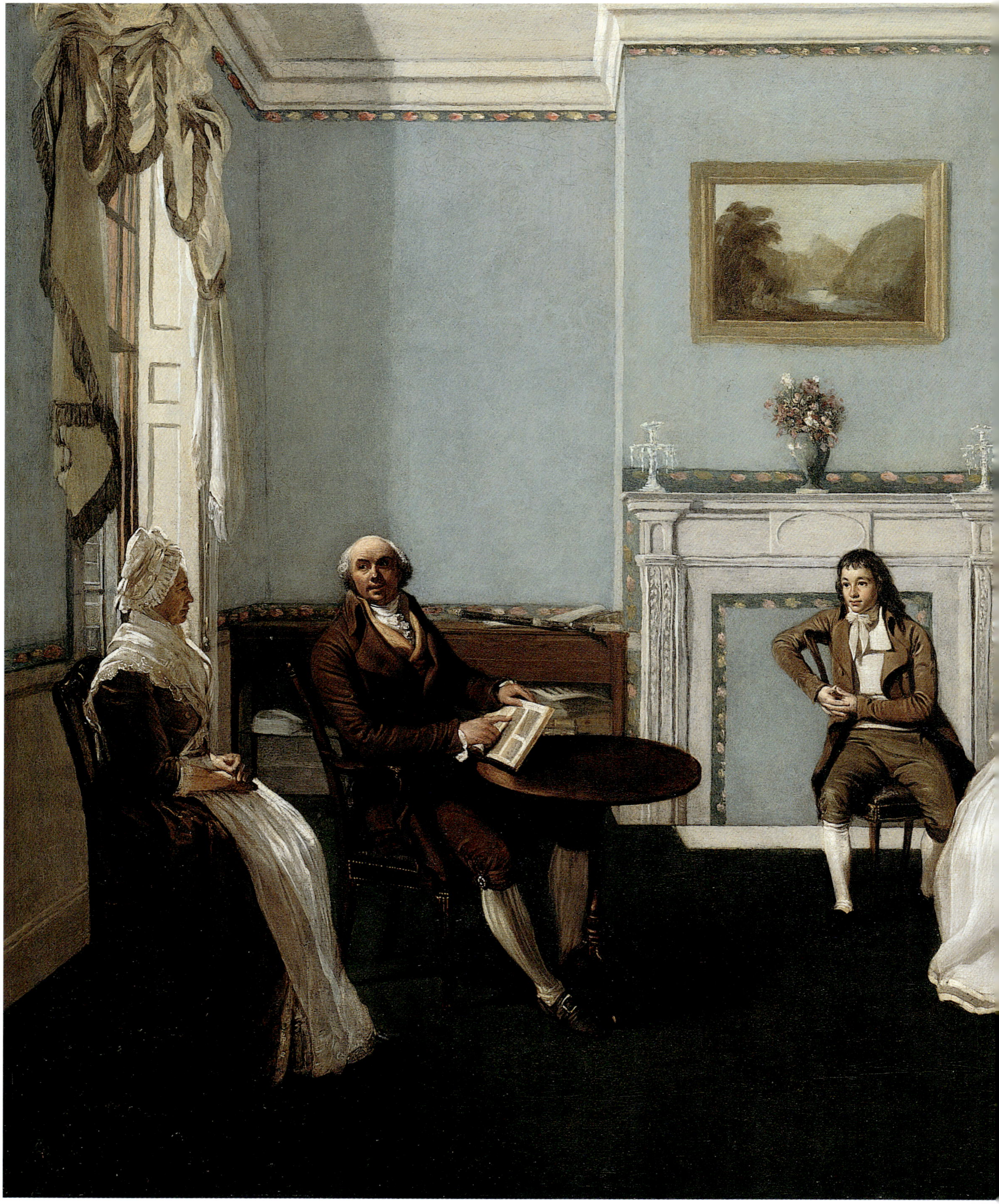

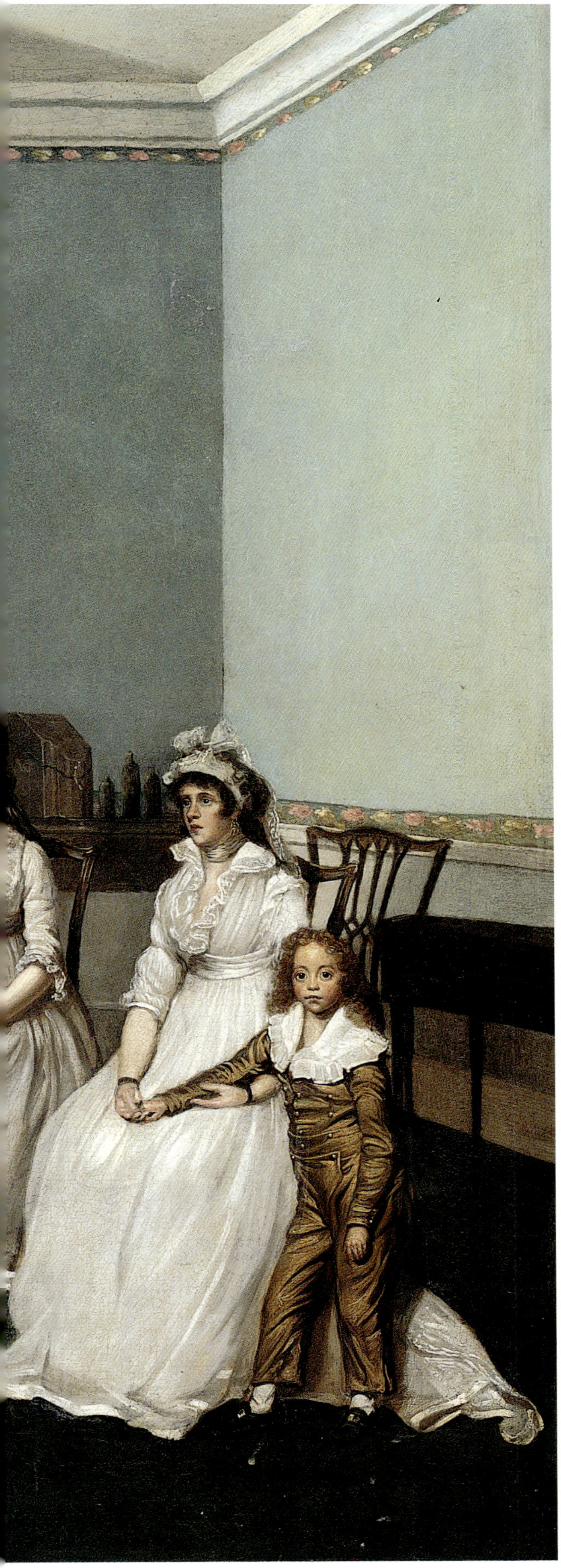

80–81 St Martin's Lane, in the heart of London's artists' quarter. A little farther down the road, on the same side, at number 96, were the premises of another colourman, Edward Powell (a British Museum 1829 watercolour by George Scharf recorded its shopfront when it had come under the ownership of Edward Prascey Allen). A little up the road stood the Old Slaughter House tavern which was or had been frequented by the painters William Hogarth, Thomas Hudson, Richard Wilson, Francis Hayman and Thomas Gainsborough and the sculptors François Roubiliac and William Cheere. Although its precise location has remained elusive, St Martin's Lane Academy was one of London's first art institutions.

The room shown here is likely to have been above the shop, on the first floor. The separation between domestic and professional quarters to which we are now accustomed took place only in the nineteenth century. At the back of Middleton's property the premises of the watchmaker Joseph Martineau were carefully recorded in a lease dated 1792 which is kept in the local history archives of Marylebone Library (ref. 72/132). The document includes a plan which shows a much more modest set-up, with Martineau's domestic quarters on the ground floor tucked into the back and side of the shop.

A colourman's manufactory (the term used in London's trade directories from the 1790s), however, required space. The eighteenth-century trade card of Joseph Emerton (later Emerton & Manby), colourman in the Strand, gives some indication of the set-up required, with a horse-driven machine to grind the pigments. J. M. W. Turner also recorded a

Provenance:
Sarah Middleton, later Mrs Robert Aspland; by descent to Robert Aspland; Sotheby's, 15 July 1987 (69, as by Philip Reinagle); Sotheby's, 6 April 1993, (37).

Bibliography:
James Ayres, *The Artist's Craft*, 1985, pp82 and 108; William T. Whitley, *Artists and their Friends in England 1700–1799*, vol. 1, pp333–4, vol. II, pp361–2; Hugh Phillips, *Mid-Georgian London*, 1964, pp106–17; Peter Jackson, *George Scharf's London*, 1987, pp19–32; *The Diary of Joseph Farington*, James Greig (ed.), 1923 (references in entry); R. D. Harley, *Artist's Pigments 1600–1835*, 2nd ed., 1982.

colourman's workshop equipped with a horse mill (Tate Gallery, ref. 5503) and it is clear from the lease mentioned above that the size of Middleton's premises was not insubstantial, with a long strip of land at the back of the house running all the way to St Martin's Court. Perhaps Middleton too had a horse mill.

John Middleton was clearly one of London's best-known colourmen, judging by the references that have come down to us in William Whitley's *Artists and their Friends* and Joseph Farington's *Diary*: in the latter we learn that he supplied materials to Benjamin West, Philippe Jacques de Loutherbourg and Thomas Lawrence (who in 1810 owed him a large sum of money) and that in 1796 he voted in the Westminster election (Farington, vol. II, p581; vol. IV, p1525; vol. V, p1983). In 1801, on the death of his competitor James Poole, he approached Farington as a prospective client (Farington, vol. IV, p1580). His main claim to fame now is that according to Paul Sandby's early biographer, he was the first to prepare watercolour cakes. However, the Society of Arts 'Great Silver Pallet' went to William Reeves in 1781 for perfecting and commercialising the process. Again, it was Middleton who had introduced William Reeves to the colourman's trade (see Ayres, 1985). At Middleton's death, the business went to his son Jesse, who concentrated his energies on the 'manufactory of paper hanging' (as listed in trade directories from around the mid-1820s). In 1806 John Middleton, a pioneer for new techniques, had won a silver medal from the Society of Arts for 'Improvements in printing paper hangings' (see its *Transactions*, vol. 24) and the manufacturing of 'paper hangings' was listed in trade directories, alongside the trade of colourman, from the 1790s.

The colourman's trade was not particularly glamorous and this group portrait is rather exceptional. The painting was with the Aspland Family until recently. (Sarah Middleton married the preacher Robert Aspland. Her son Theophilus, born in 1807 and who later became an artist, lived in the St Martin's Lane family home for part of his childhood and was taught by his aunt Anna.) A family rumour suggested that the painting might have been done in payment for artists' materials.

The Museum has a colour grinding mill (acc. no. 94.11), said to have been used by Turner, and which was donated by the firm Brodie and Middleton (there may have been a family link with John Middleton but this has not been established). The Museum's collections also hold various colourmen's signs and materials.

Johann Zoffany (1725–1810)
Sir Lawrence Dundas and his grandson, 1769–70
Oil on canvas
Collection: The Marquess of Zetland
Photograph: the Witt Library, Courtauld Institute of Art.

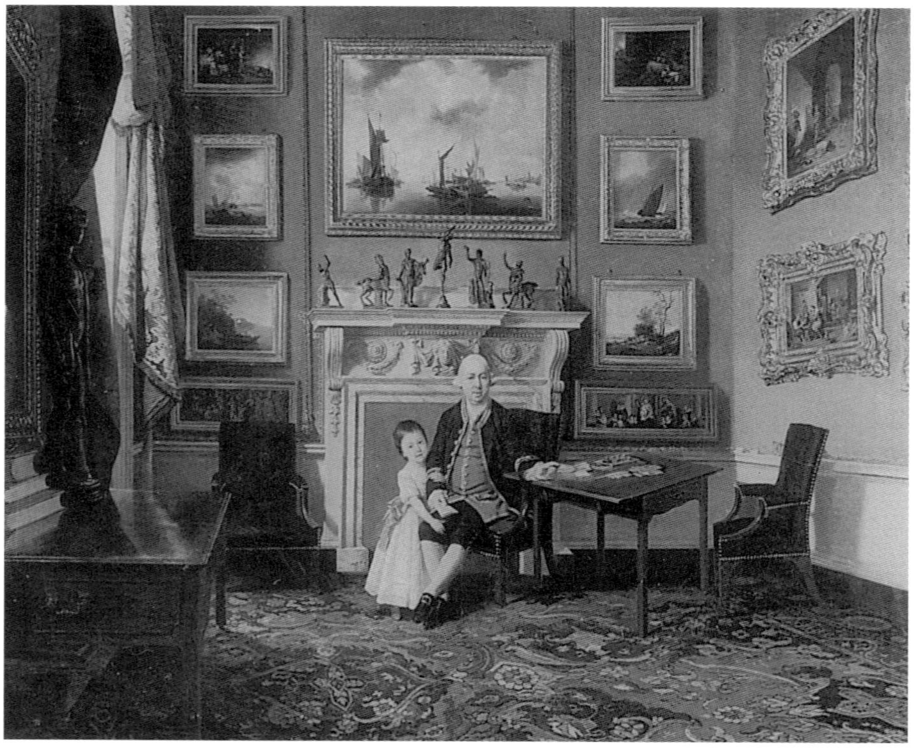

48.

AFTER SIR THOMAS LAWRENCE

(1769–1830)

Sarah Siddons as Mrs Haller in Kotzebue's *The Stranger* [56.169/3]

post 1798

Oil on canvas, 71.9 x 61.9 cm

Not signed or dated

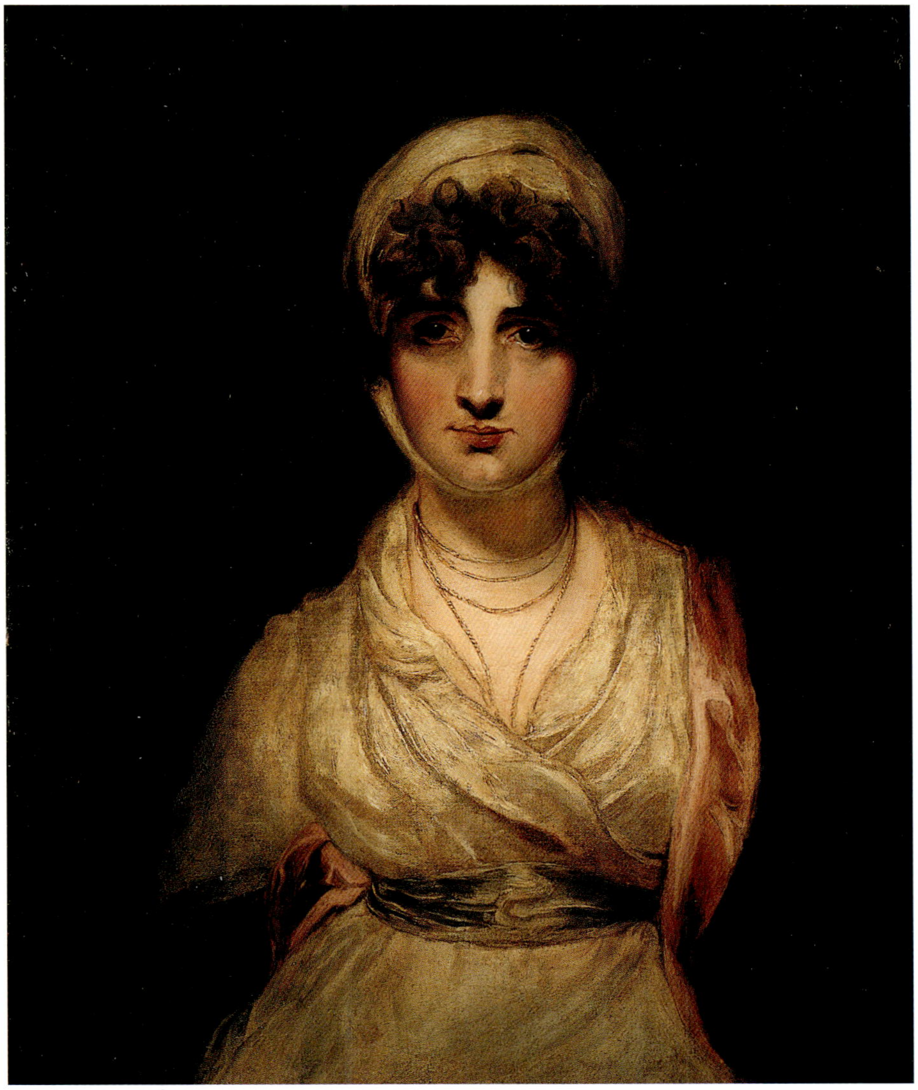

THE SITTER, Mrs Sarah Siddons, née Kemble (1755–1831), is shown half-length, facing the spectator; the background is plain. The subject of the painting, Mrs Siddons in the role she created at Drury Lane Theatre on 24 March 1798 (one of her most famous parts), is that given by Thomson in his 1820 engraving of the painting. There is, however, no corroborating evidence for this interpretation.

There are many versions of this portrait. Lawrence first drew Mrs Siddons in pastel in 1786 and first painted the composition under review in 1796 for the Kemble family, a work which has remained in private hands since that time (Garlick, no. 715d). The painting which was exhibited at the Royal Academy the following year was a second version by Lawrence and was criticised for making Mrs Lawrence look too young. The *c.*1798 portrait, which was bequeathed to the National Gallery in 1868 by Mrs Siddons's daughter Cecilia, Mrs Coombe, and is now in the Tate (no. 785) was a third version, which has been widely copied. The Museum's painting clearly derives from the Tate portrait.

Provenance:
Purchased at the Goldney House, Clifton, sale (in September 1921 at the death of Lewis Fry or in 1928 at the death of Sir George Wills); presented by R. N. Green-Armytage in 1956 (as by Lawrence).

Bibliography:
Hayes (cat. no. 158);
Kenneth Garlick, *Sir Thomas Lawrence*, 1989, p264.

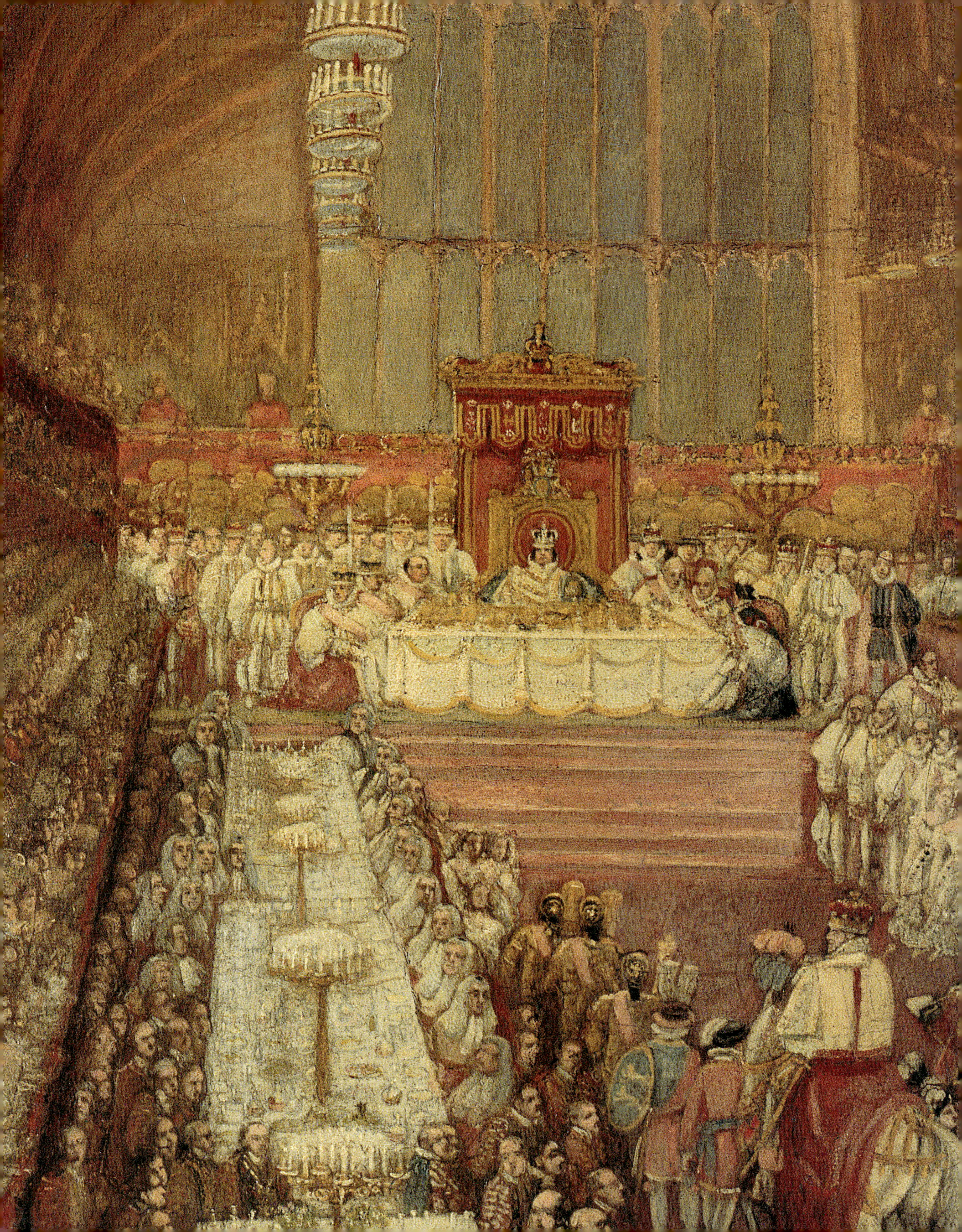

Regency London

HISTORICALLY the Regency period is very brief: it lasts from 1811, when George III becomes unable to rule, until 1821, when the Prince Regent is crowned George IV in Westminster Abbey. Here we interpret the Regency in the wider sense of spanning roughly the first four decades of the nineteenth century, a vital transitional time between Georgian and Victorian London. Artistically this period is very distinctive. The image of the Thames and of London's streets and buildings is influenced by the rediscovery of Dutch and Flemish art. From the Netherlands too, perhaps, comes the impetus to depict a new aspect of the social scene, with work and workmen adding to the human interest considered worthy of the painter's attention. A resurgence of interest in the genre of fire painting climaxes in the 1834 conflagration of the Houses of Parliament (and the disappearance of this landmark sets the scene for Victorian architectural experimentation).

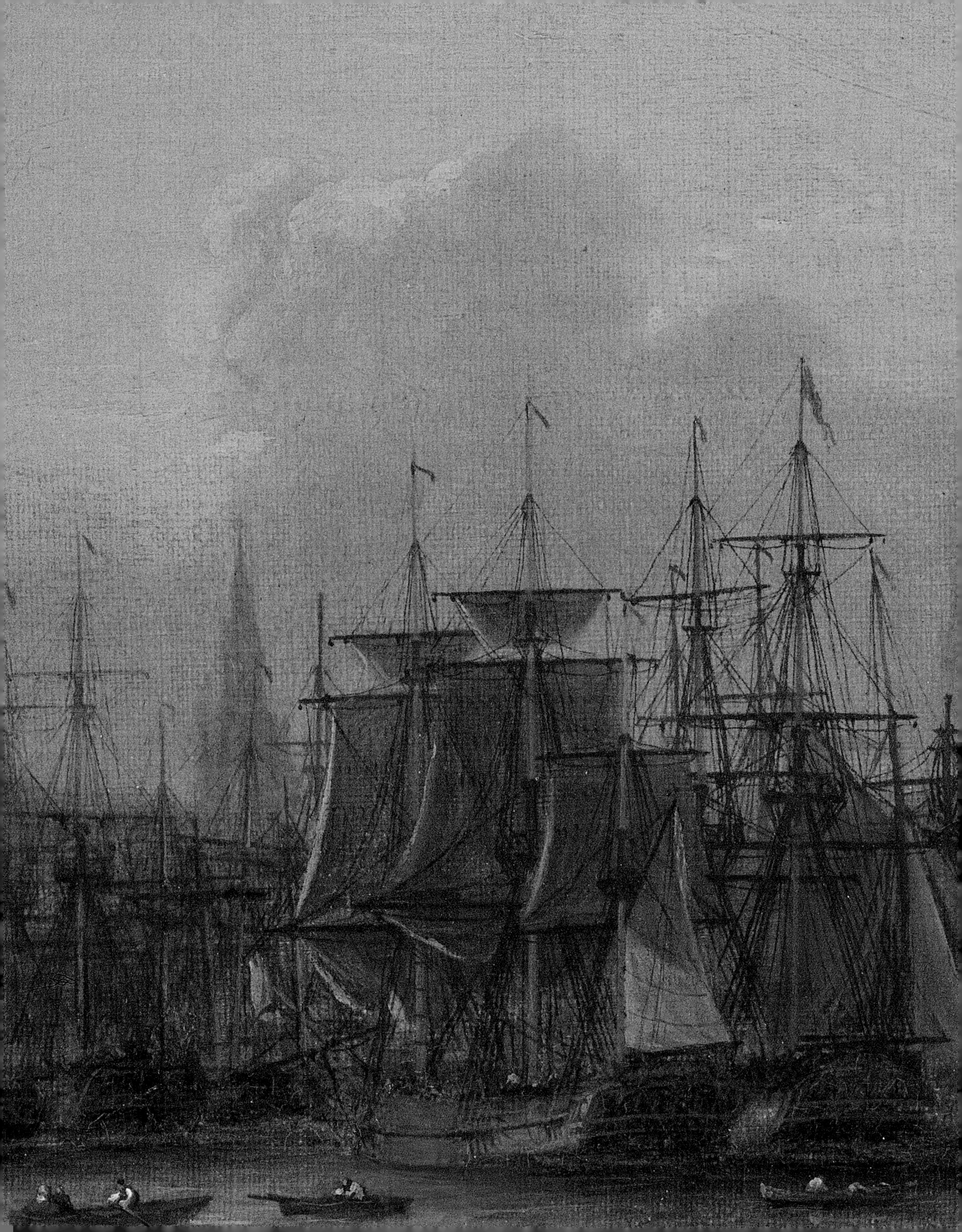

THE RIVER

THE MOST significant artistic influence on London's marine painters in the Regency period was that of Netherlandish Old Master painting. Dutch and Flemish works had been collected in London in great numbers from the seventeenth century onwards (John Evelyn in his *Diary* describes several London collections containing such Old Masters), but it was only at the turn of the eighteenth century that a succession of artistic events brought Netherlandish achievement to the fore. Although this influence does not solely manifest itself in river scenes, the impact here was particularly decisive, from the modest achievements of Daniel Turner and William Anderson to the works of J. W. M. Turner, Edward William Cooke, James Stark, Charles Deane and Augustus Wall Callcott.[1]

In his *Marriage à la Mode* series William Hogarth had ridiculed the taste of the aspiring middle classes who, in contrast with the predilection of the aristocracy for Italian paintings, collected 'vulgar' Dutch genre pieces.[2] Johann Zoffany's portrait of Sir Lawrence Dundas and his grandson[3] set in the library at 19 Arlington Street (illustrated on p140) gave a new respectability to these rising collectors. Although Zoffany used artistic licence and depicted fifteen Dutch paintings on the walls of the library when in fact only four hung in that room, he clearly brought a new dimension to his patron's collection.

London, however, had to wait until 1793 for the first exhibition of Old Masters in England, following the dismantling of the major collection of the Duc d'Orléans (catalogued in 1786 before its dispersal). The show represented half the collection (the other half had been bought by a Belgian) and was put for sale at the Royal Academy's former rooms in Pall Mall. This was soon followed in the early 1800s by (limited) access to the substantial collection of Sir Francis Bourgeois, rich in Dutch and Flemish works. In 1805–6 a purpose-built gallery was erected at Cleveland House for the Marquis of Stafford's collection, which contained a large group of Dutch and Flemish pictures. Then came the building of England's first art gallery in Dulwich to house the collection (between 1811 and 1813).

In 1806 the British Institution was opened to encourage the development of history painting. It immediately initiated a system of picture loans – from members to the institution – for art students to copy. In 1814 the Prince Regent bought the great Dutch masterpiece *The Passage Boat* by the painter Albert Cuyp, who was much admired by connoisseurs. The following year the British Institution held its first major exhibition of Dutch and Flemish Old Masters in Pall Mall so that it might

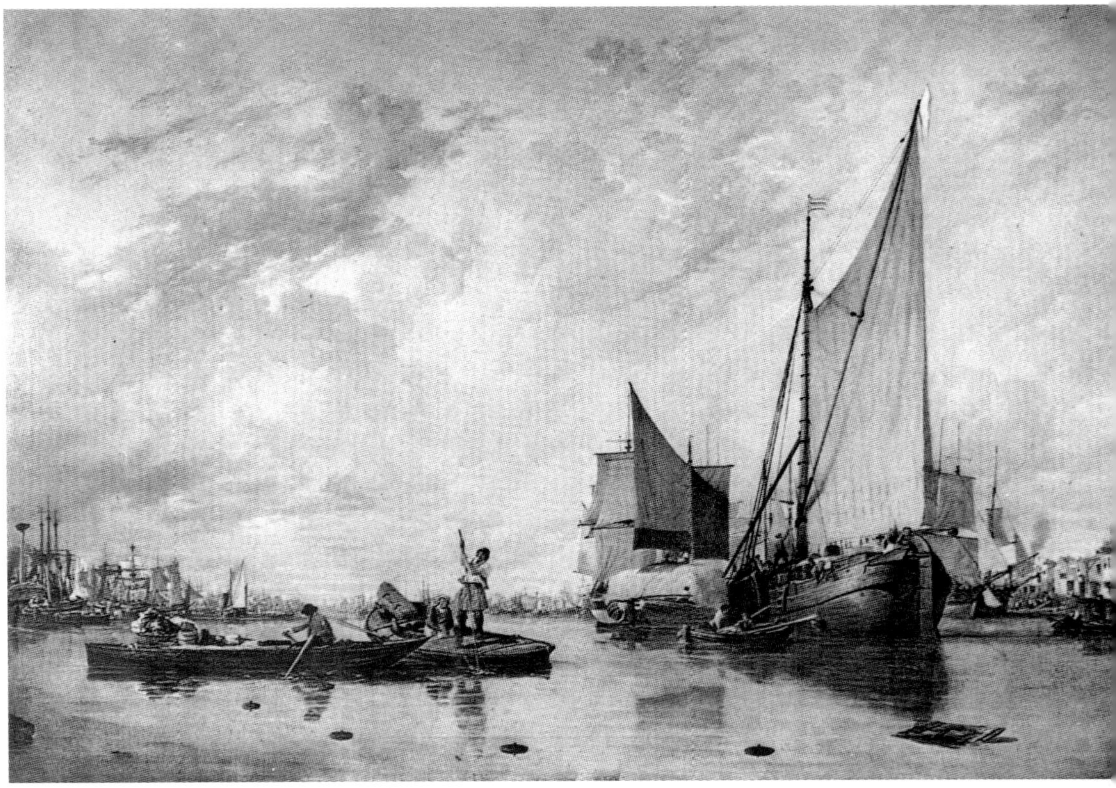

Sir Augustus Wall Callcott
(1779–1844)
The Entrance to the Pool of London, 1816
Trustee of the Bowood Collection
Photograph: the Witt Library, Courtauld Institute of Art.

'excite in the British artist the ardour of emulation', and that same year, the Dulwich Picture Gallery opened its doors to Royal Academy students.[4] In 1816 a group of six pictures from the Dulwich Gallery was selected and sent to Somerset House (notably works by Albert Cuyp). In the same year A. W. Callcott painted *The Pool of London* (Bowood collection), so reminiscent of the art of Albert Cuyp, a work which in turn influenced J. M. W. Turner's *The Pool*.[5]

In light and composition, London Thames paintings increasingly adopted the look of seventeenth-century Dutch paintings – a noticeable departure from the previous century, when Italianate influences predominated. Charles Deane's view of the Thames (cat. no. 54) is the Museum's most memorable example of this phenomenon.

The Deane painting also reveals a transformed London riverscape, with new bridges crossing the Thames. When Blackfriars Bridge was planned in the eighteenth century, artists had dreamed ambitious schemes for a 'Bridge of Magnificence' (see pp71 and 73), but John Rennie's sober design for Waterloo Bridge, around which Deane's composition is beautifully balanced, gave the river a classical dimension worthy of the large-scale classical development John Nash was devising for the city itself. Strand Bridge, as it was first named, was opened by the Prince of Wales in 1817, soon followed by Southwark Bridge in 1819 and later still by a new London Bridge to replace the medieval structure in 1831.

The new bridges furnished a considerable source of inspiration for painters: both Alexander Nasmyth and Constable placed their easels at Westminster looking east and attempted to translate the grandiose vista of that stretch of the Thames after the opening of Waterloo Bridge.[6] Clarkson Stanfield, on the other hand, tackled the opening of London Bridge in 1831 in a painting that conveys the river pageantry traditionally associated with the City or Westminster. For instance, when John Boydell became Lord Mayor in 1792, he commissioned Francis Wheatley and Richard Paton to record the Lord Mayor's water procession in painting (Guildhall Art Gallery). Even the more sombre subject of Nelson's funeral pageant was recorded in paint (see cat. no. 51).

The most historically significant transformation of life on the Thames during the Regency period was undoubtedly the building of the docks.[7] Although most artists did not draw direct inspiration from this event,[8] they seemed now to be pulled towards East London and the Pool of London in particular, often focusing their images around the Tower of London. Thomas Luny's *The Pool of London* (cat. no. 50) illustrates well the river congestion which led to the construction of the docks.

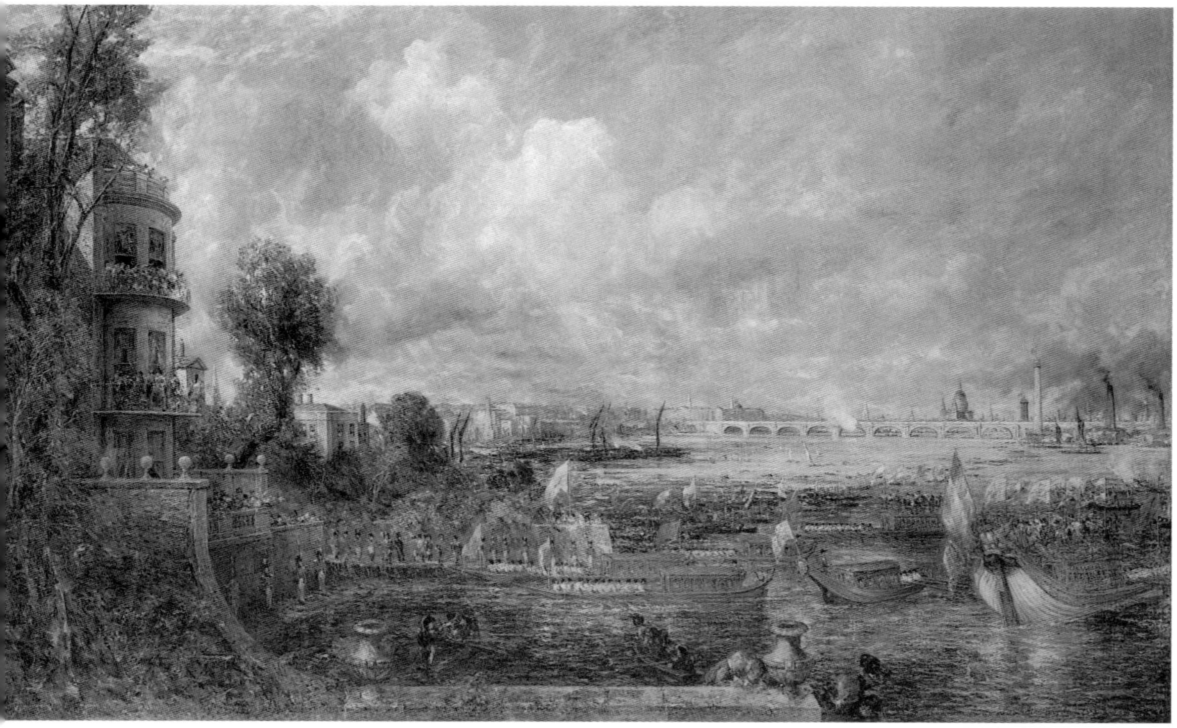

John Constable (1776–1837)
The Opening of Waterloo Bridge, Whitehall Stairs, June 18th, 1817
Oil on canvas
Tate Gallery, London.

1. Only the painters Daniel Turner (cat. nos 49, 51 and 52), William Anderson (cat. no. 53) and Charles Deane (cat. no. 54) are represented in this collection.
2. National Gallery; see number VI, the last in the series, set in the merchant's home. Background documentation in R. Paulson, *Hogarth's Graphic Works,* 1970, no. 233.
3. Painted *c.*1769–70, in the Marquess of Zetland's collection; Mary Webster, *Johann Zoffany 1733-1810,* exhibition catalogue, National Portrait Gallery, 1976, no. 56.
4. See Andrew W. Moore, *Dutch and Flemish Paintings in Norfolk*, 1988: chapter on 'Norwich and London'; Giles Waterfield, *Palaces of Art*, exhibition catalogue, Dulwich Picture Gallery, 1992.
5. *London – World City 1800–1840*, Celina Fox (ed.), 1992, no. 389.
6. *Prospect of London seen from the Earl of Cassili's Privy Garden, with Waterloo Bridge and St Paul's* by Alexander Nasmyth was sold at Sotheby's on 12 July 1989; *The Opening of Waterloo Bridge (Whitehall Stairs, June 18th 1817)* by Constable is in the collection of the Tate Gallery (see *Tate Gallery Illustrated Catalogue of Acquisitions, 1986-88,* 1996, pp12-16).
7. The best detailed summary of the series of events leading up to their construction was written by Alex Werner: 'The Port of London 1750–1806', published lecture, second North Sea History conference, Esbjerg, 1991. For a brief summary, see Chris Ellmers, *City and River*, no. 13 in the London Connection series, Museum of London, 1989.
8. Except for William Daniell's remarkable painting of Perry's Dock in Blackwall (National Maritime Museum) and his aquatint series on the docks, as well as W. Ranwell's 1828 watercolour of the construction of St Katharine's Docks (Port of London Authority).

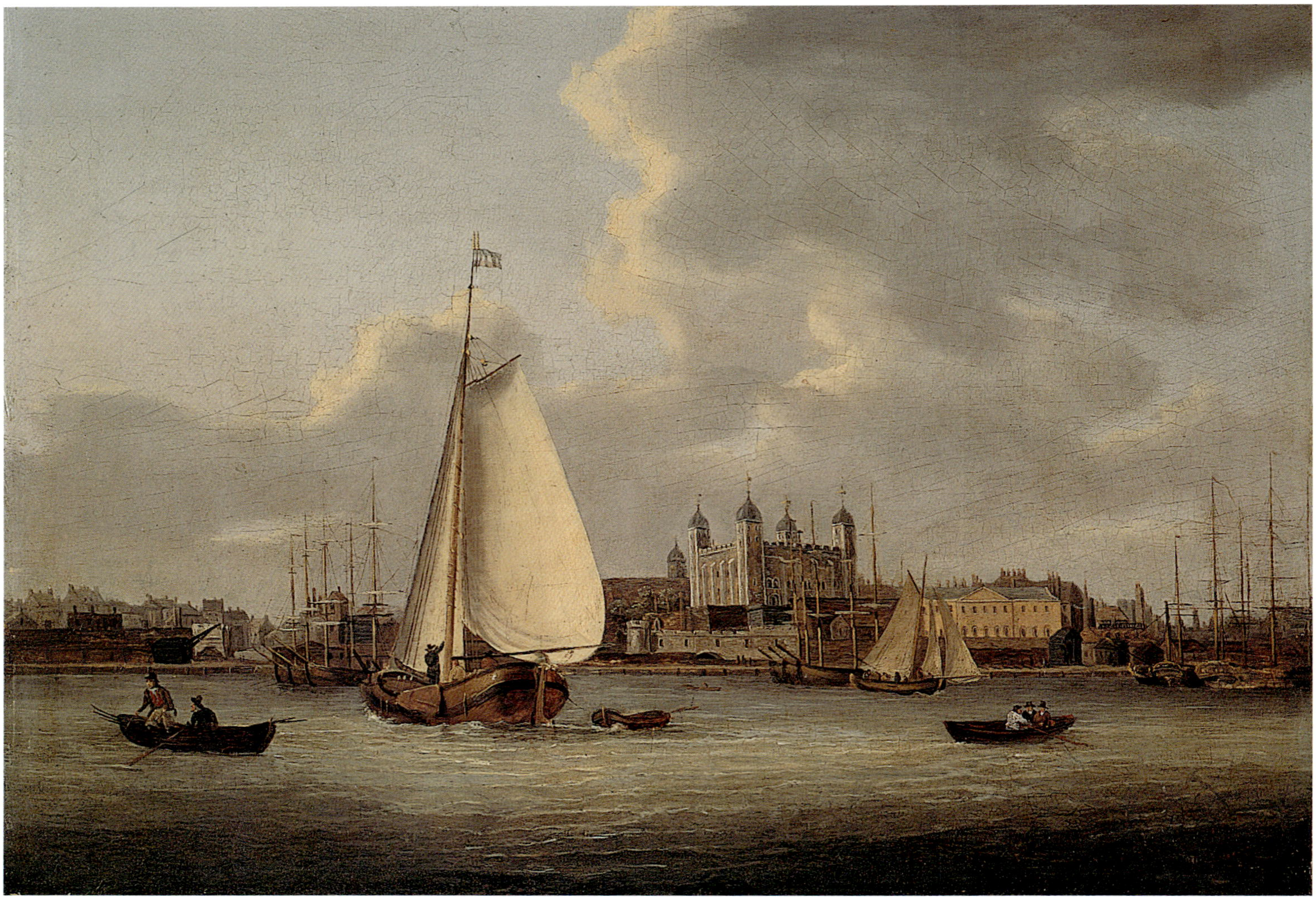

Provenance:
With Obach and Co.; Obach Sale, Christie's, 6 February 1909 (126, without attribution), bt Leggatt; purchased from Leggatt Brothers in 1912.

Bibliography:
Hayes (cat. no. 105).

49.

DANIEL TURNER

(active 1782–1806)

The Tower of London from the River

[A 8084]

*c.*1790–1810

Oil on panel, 29.4 x 40.9 cm

Not signed or dated

THIS VIEW has for its principal subject the White Tower, but makes the mistake, common among London topographers, of depicting the north-eastern tower as square instead of rounded. In front of the White Tower is St Thomas's Tower, with the Traitors' Gate just visible, but the eastern bastion is omitted. Behind it is the Great Armoury or Storehouse, which was burnt out in a fire on 30 October 1841; a barracks now occupies this position. On the right is one of the Ordnance buildings, a structure built at the end of George II's reign, in front of the old Horse Armoury.

Along the waterfront can be seen the eastern-most part of the forty-foot wide quayside that stretched past the Custom House to Queenhithe, one of the improvements carried out during the rebuilding of London after the Great Fire, replacing the clutter of wharves and warehouses that had so impeded the work of the port. A number of sailing vessels and other craft are seen on the river.

The costume indicates a date of about 1790–1810. Another version of this painting, less crudely executed, was sold at Christie's on 15 November 1991 (134).

50.
THOMAS LUNY
(1759–1837)

The Pool of London [A 8070]
*c.*1801–10
Oil on canvas, 41.6 x 63.1 cm
Signed bottom left on floating plank: *Luny*

NUMEROUS MERCHANTMEN are shown anchored near the 'legal quays', which stretched from the Tower to Old London Bridge. Part of the bridge is visible, and the great central arch, formed by removing one of the piers which was built at the time of the reconstruction work in 1756–62, is seen on the left. Behind are St Paul's and St Magnus the Martyr; the spire of St Mary-le-Bow and the Monument appear in the centre and on the right are the spires of St Dunstan-in-the-East and St Margaret Pattens.

Until the very end of the eighteenth century the City maintained a stranglehold on London's trade through its monopoly of quayside rights and customs facilities. But the value of the trade handled in the Pool had nearly trebled since 1700, and the increasing congestion of shipping in the 1790s resulted in the setting up of a parliamentary committee of inquiry in 1796. The establishment of an entirely new system of docks was approved by Parliament, and the first to be built was the West India Dock, opened in 1802.

The Union Jacks flying on several of the vessels indicate that the picture was painted after the Act of Union with Ireland was passed in 1801, but the types of ship suggest that it was painted probably before 1810.

One version of this picture, differing in the shipping, is in the collection of the Yale Center for British Art (signed and dated 1798) and another is in the collection of the Earl of Inchcape (signed and dated 1803).

Provenance:
Purchased from Leggatt Brothers in 1912.

Bibliography:
Hayes (cat. no. 70).

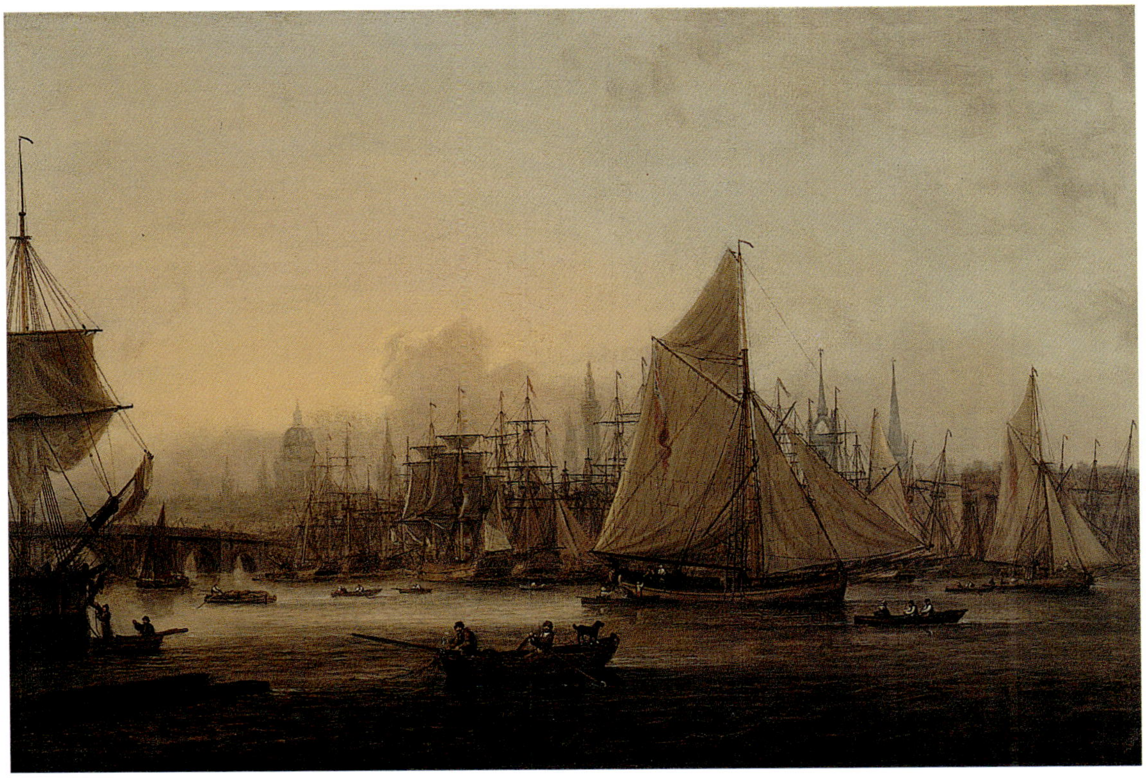

Provenance:
Purchased from Leggatt Brothers in 1912.

Bibliography:
Hayes (cat. no. 177).

51.
DANIEL TURNER
(active 1782–1806)

The Funeral Procession of Lord Nelson on the Thames [A 8081]
*c.*1806
Oil on panel, 16.2 x 24.7 cm
Signed bottom right: *D^L TURNER*

THIS IS one of a number of paintings of Nelson's funeral, which Turner depicted from various viewpoints. The flotilla of ceremonial barges and other craft is depicted from Bankside in Southwark (the particular wharf cannot be identified) with the north end of Blackfriars Bridge on the left, and St Paul's Cathedral and many of the City churches in the distance right.

The river procession, on its way from Greenwich to Whitehall, is symbolically set against St Paul's, the ultimate destination of the body. The funeral barge dressed in black is just below the first northern pier of the bridge. The different phases of this event, which spread over two weeks, between 23 December 1805 and 9 January 1806, were recorded mostly by artists working for publishers and perhaps culminated in Edward Orme's *Life and Death of Nelson* (1806). The illustrations tended to focus on the Greenwich lying-in-state, the departure from Greenwich, the return journey to Whitehall, the procession to St Paul's and the funeral service there.

Numerous versions of this event by or after Daniel Turner are known to exist (see collections of the National Maritime Museum and the Guildhall Art Gallery). Another painting showing the procession in front of the Adelphi is in this collection (see Appendix).

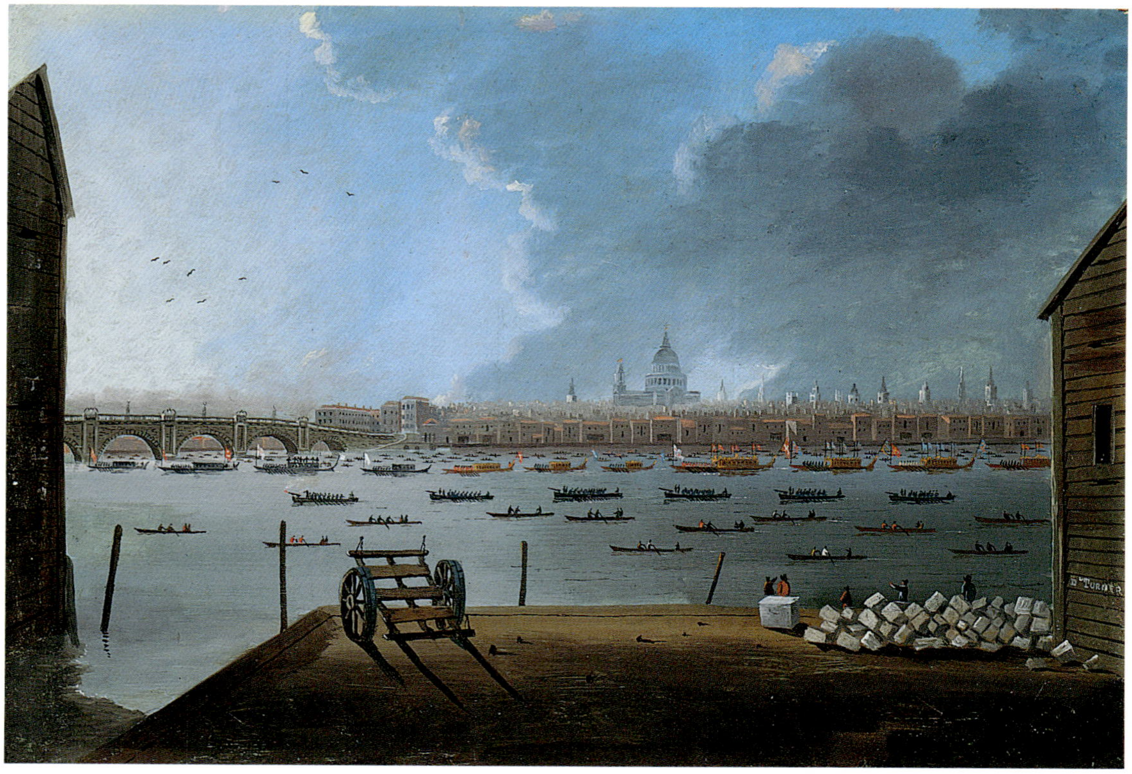

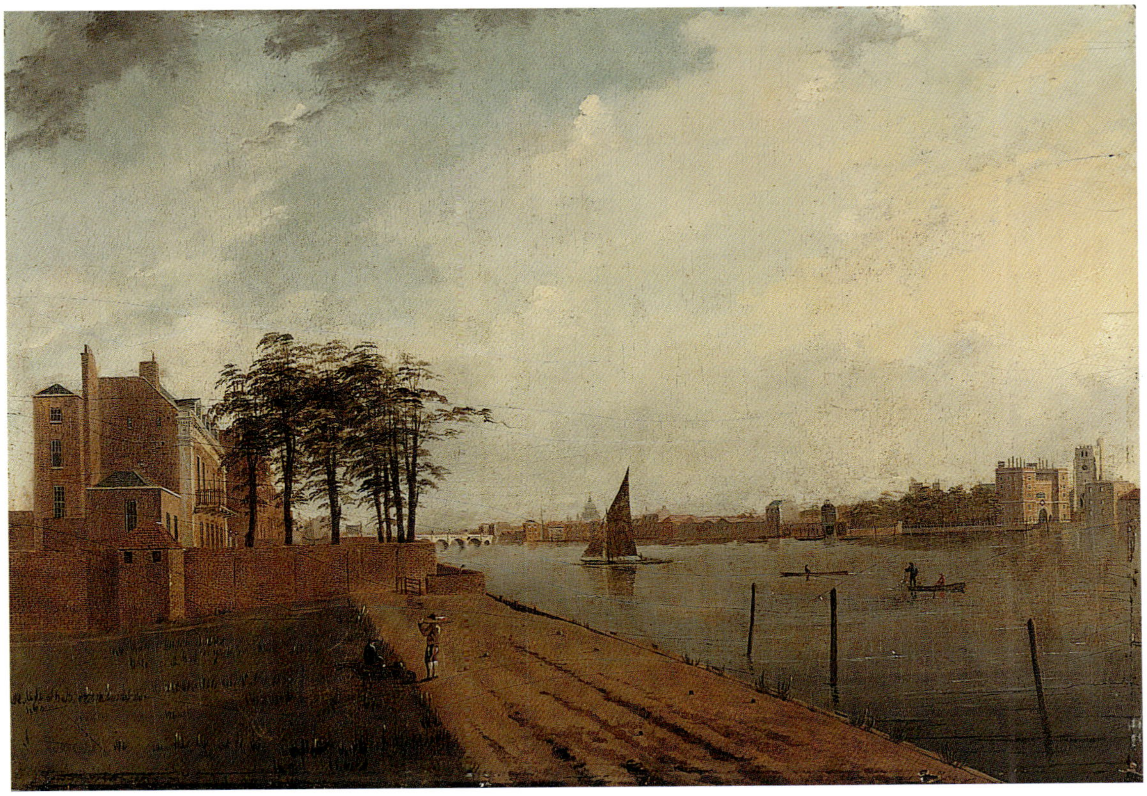

Provenance:
Presented to the Museum by Mr L. Herrick Collins in 1987.

Bibliography:
Robert Wilkinson, *Londina Illustrata*, 1819–34, vol. I, no. 104; David Pearce, *London Mansions*, 1986, pp168–9.

52.
DANIEL TURNER
(active 1782–1806)
Lambeth Palace from Millbank [87.76]
1808(?)
Oil on canvas, 41.3 x 60 cm
Signed and dated (barely legible on wheelbarrow): *DANIEL TURNER 1808*(?)

THE VIEW is taken from Millbank looking north-east to Westminster Bridge and Lambeth Palace with the dome of St Paul's visible in the middle background. The houses on the left belonged to the Grosvenor Estate on Millbank Row. This development began while the estate was owned by Alexander Davies of Ebury between 1622 and 1625. The marriage of his daughter Mary to Thomas Grosvenor in 1677 brought the Ebury estate (part of which is shown here) to the Grosvenor family. The house in the left foreground, first known as Peterborough House and from 1735 as Grosvenor House, had, according to Strype, 'a courtyard before it fronting the river, and a fine garden behind it'. It was built in the 1660s and was (with an interruption between 1755 and 1789) the London residence of the Grosvenor family until 1809, when 'it was taken down to facilitate the great improvements that have since been made in the neighbourhood' (*Londina Illustrata*); see also cat. no. 30. The front view of the house with its 'courtyard' (we would say a garden) is illustrated in *Londina Illustrata*.

The depiction of long netting for salmon is worth noting; by the 1840s the Thames had become so polluted that what was once a familiar sight had disappeared and only recently have salmon reappeared. The Corporation's River Bailiff was responsible for controlling the activities of fishermen until 1857.

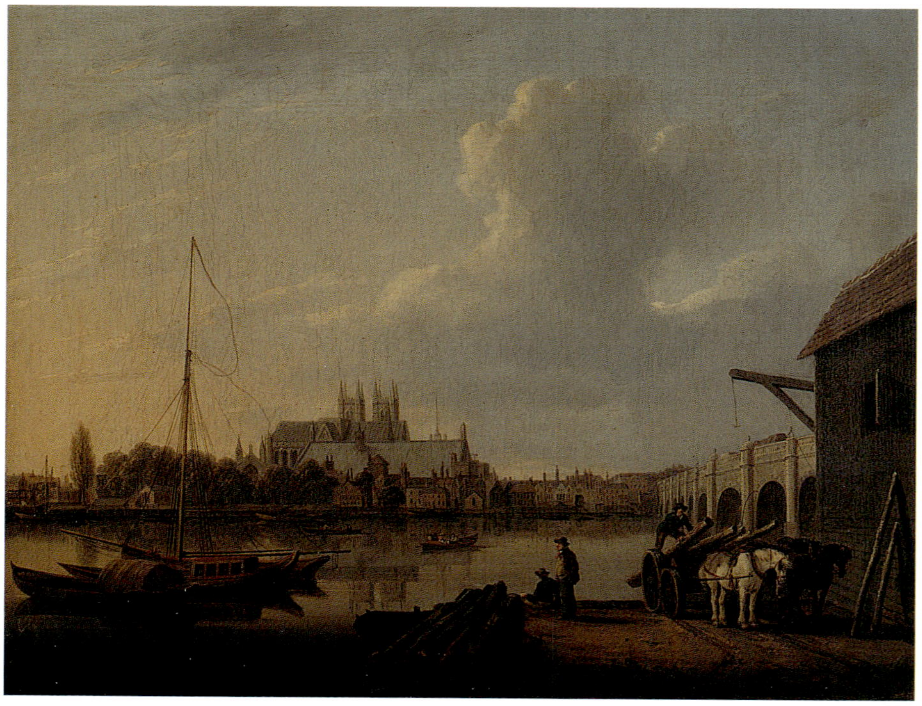

Provenance:
Bequeathed by Miss Ruth Ellam in 1985.

Bibliography:
Bernard Adams, *London Illustrated 1604–1851*, 1983, cat. no. 104:66, p240.

53.

WILLIAM ANDERSON
(1757–1837)

Westminster from the South [85.49]
1805–10
Oil on canvas 35 x 47 cm
Not signed or dated

THE VIEW is taken from Stangate Wharf, south of Westminster Bridge, looking towards Westminster Palace and Abbey. Passengers are being ferried across the Thames in a wherry.

It is interesting to bracket this painting with that found at cat. no. 69 and the painting by John Anderson (cat. no. 78), which record the major nineteenth-century architectural changes for that stretch of the river, from the demolition of the maze of buildings which composed the old Palace of Westminster to Charles Barry's Gothic extravaganza.

The prototype for this painting may have originated from the pair of paintings signed and dated 1805 and sold at Sotheby's on 26 November 1975 (129). The view of Westminster from the south bank was coupled with a view looking towards the City, also taken from the south bank, but on the other side of the bridge. Another version of the painting, signed and dated 1807, was sold at Christie's (Camperdown sale) on 27 May 1921 (120). J. Pye engraved the view, from a drawing by Anderson, for the *Beauties of England and Wales*, the twenty-five-volume serial publication (1810–16) after an idea by Edward Brailey and John Britton. The Anderson view was published on 1 August 1809 (see Bernard Adams). It is also worth pointing out more distant sources. The composition harks back to the eighteenth century, when views of the Thames were very popular in interior decoration schemes for the homes of the wealthy (see p72).

54.

CHARLES DEANE

(active 1815–51)

Waterloo Bridge and the Lambeth Waterfront from Westminster Stairs

[C 355]

1821

Oil on canvas

110 x 184.7 cm

Signed and dated bottom left: *C Deane 1821*

THIS PAINTING, one of a pair, investigates the impact of Waterloo Bridge on the London cityscape. The presence of this new bridge forced the painter to reconsider the traditional viewpoint for panoramic views of the City, which had been near Somerset House (see p7). Deane chose Westminster Stairs for the view looking east (the Museum painting) and Temple Stairs for the view looking west (this painting was with Leggatt Brothers in 1927).

Waterloo Bridge, originally called Strand Bridge, was built between 1811 and 1817 to the designs of John Rennie. It was opened by the Prince Regent on the second anniversary of the battle of Waterloo, and this picture shows it only a few years after completion. In 1924 it was found that one of the arches had become seriously weakened and, after prolonged discussion as to whether the bridge should be restored or not, it was finally decided to pull it down. This took place in 1936. Sir Giles Gilbert Scott's new Waterloo Bridge, completed in 1945, is fortunately a worthy successor to Rennie's fine structure.

Beyond Waterloo Bridge can be seen, from left to right, the spire of St Mary-le-Strand, Somerset House before the construction of the west wing, and the towers and spires of St Clement Danes, St Andrew's Holborn, St Sepulchre's and St Bride's. On the right is the Lambeth waterfront, still largely composed of timber yards and wharves (see cat. no. 28); the most prominent buildings are the slightly tapering tower of the Lambeth Waterworks in Belvedere Road, which operated from 1785 to 1853, and the square tower of the Patent Shot Manufactory east of Waterloo Bridge, erected in about 1789 and destroyed in 1937. (The more familiar round shot tower, pulled down as recently as April 1962 to make way for extensions to the Royal Festival Hall, was not built until 1826.)

Beyond is the dominating mass of St Paul's Cathedral, with, on the extreme right, the spires of (apparently) St Swithin's and St Mary Abchurch, and the tower of St Michael's, Cornhill.

Several barges are moored in the river, and in the foreground a Thames waterman in brown uniform is about to ferry a group of passengers across to Lambeth. Within a decade of the painting of this picture, the ferryboats which plied from Westminster stairs (there were landing stages adjoining Westminster Bridge on both the north and south sides) were replaced by steamboat services; the stairs were eventually superseded by Westminster Pier.

Charles Deane produced a smaller, more informal version of this painting, on panel (no. 520 in F. R. Meatyard's Summer 1938 catalogue).

Provenance:
Lent by A. L. Nicholson in 1911; afterwards presented, through the National Art Collections Fund, in 1928.

Bibliography:
Hayes (cat. no. 33); *London – World City 1800–1840,* Celina Fox (ed.), 1992, p312.

Exhibited:
British Institution, 1822 (206).

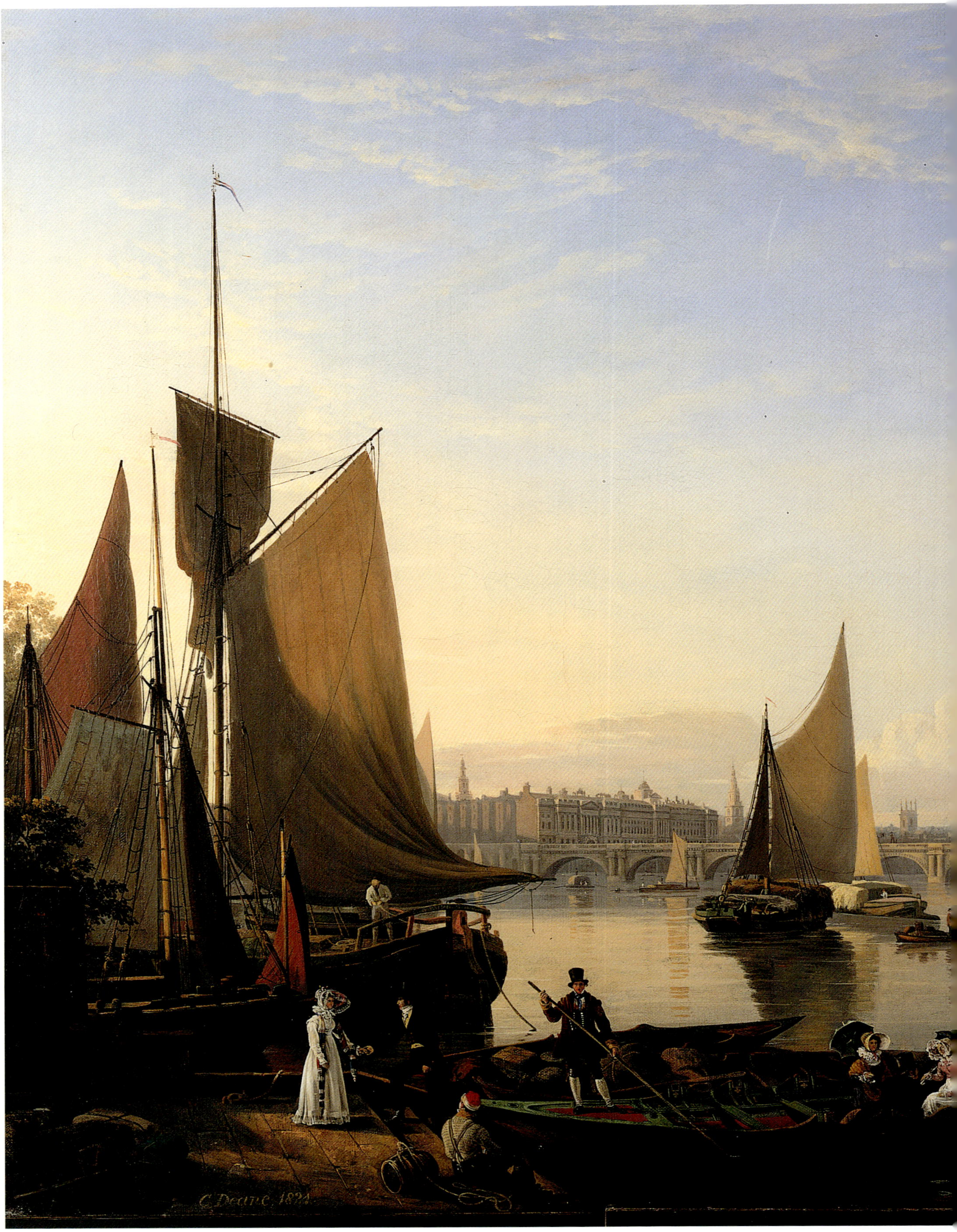
C. Deane, 1821

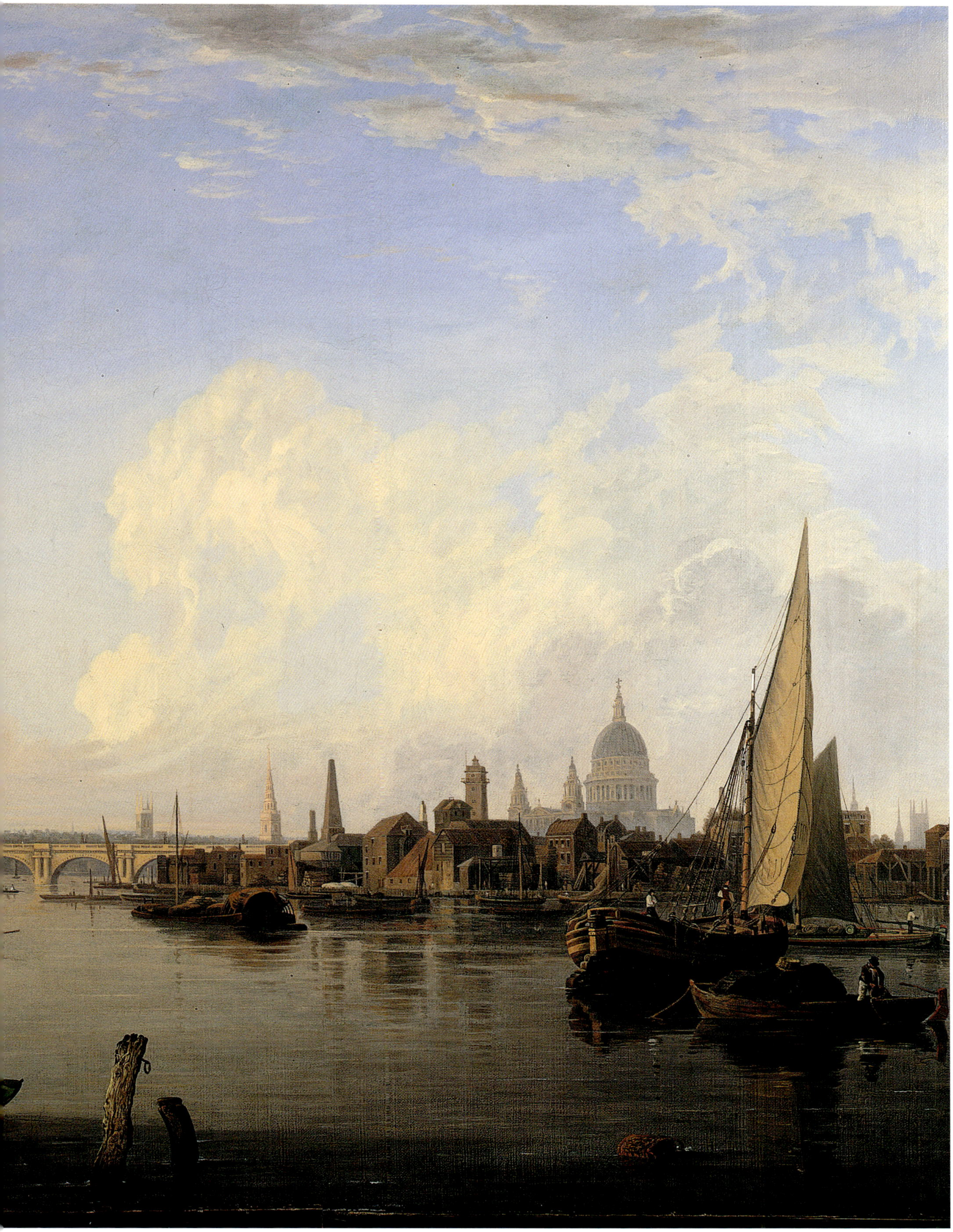

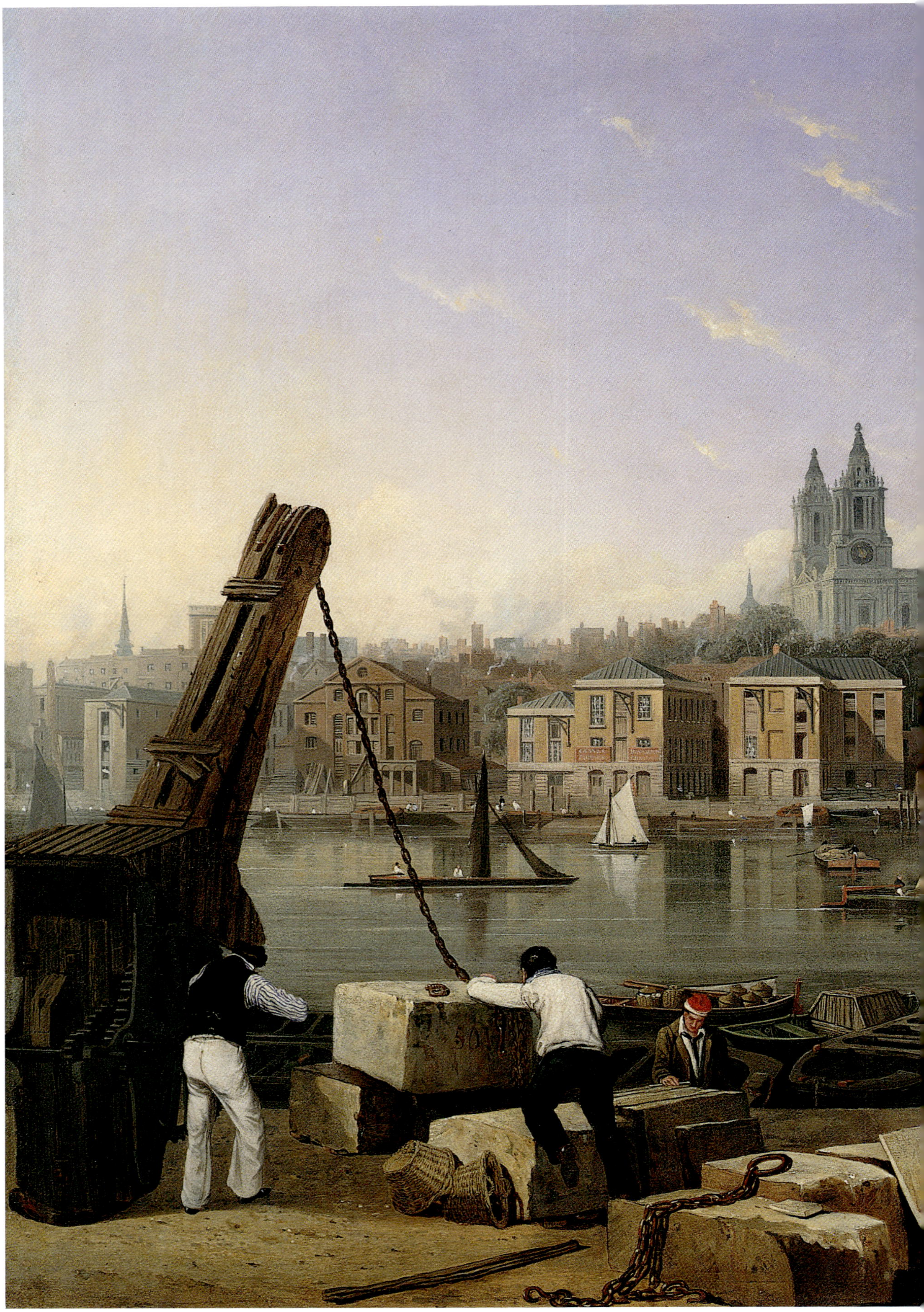

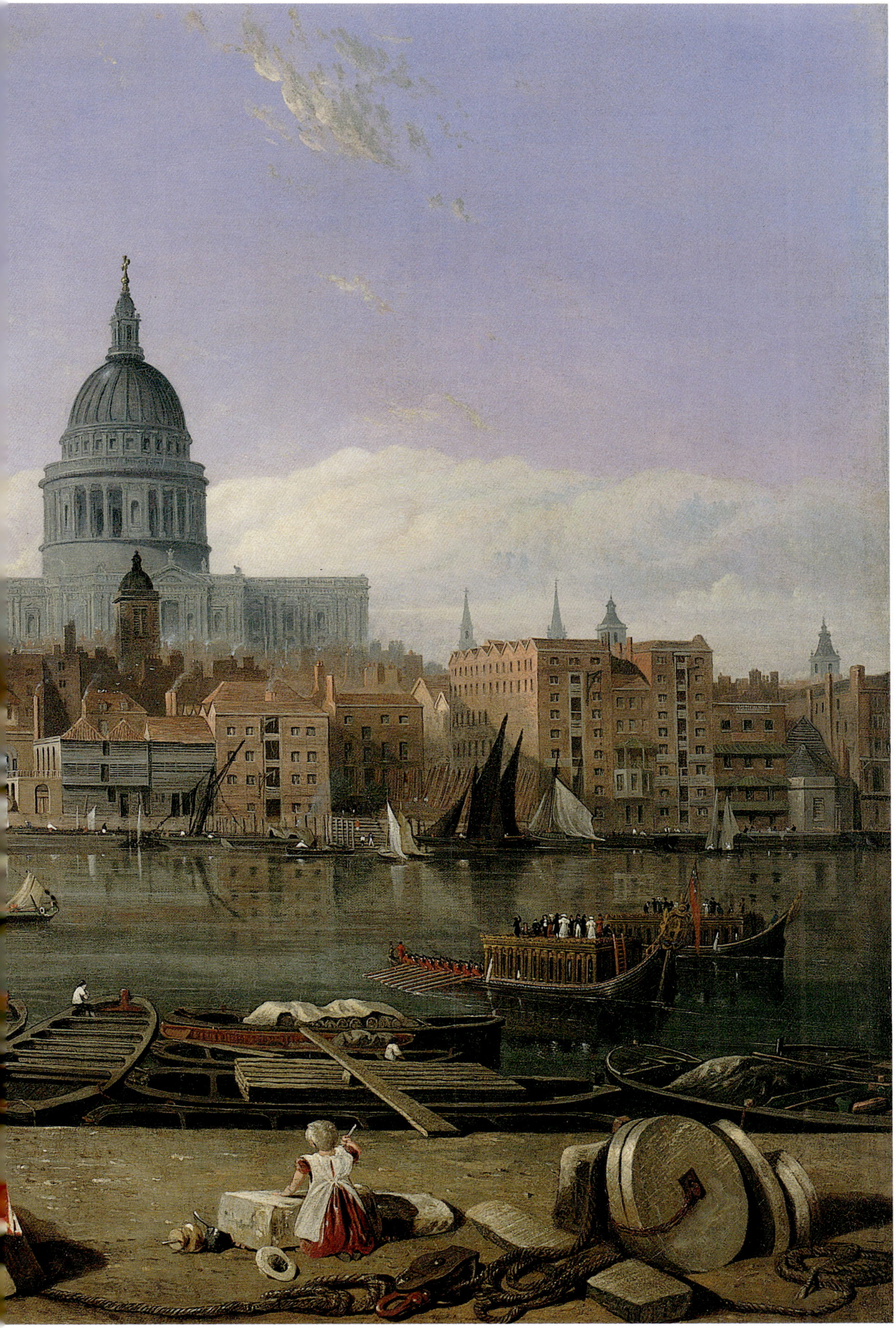

55.

THOMAS MILES RICHARDSON

(1784–1848)

The City from Bankside

[95.185]

1820s

71.5 x 92 cm

Not signed or dated

Label on the back:

R. Osmond, 90 rue de Vaugirard

Provenance:
Sold at Ader Tajan in Paris, 28 June 1994 (50), bt Spink; purchased by the Museum in 1995 with the help of the Museum of London Trust Funds.

Bibliography:
Art for Newcastle, Thomas Miles Richardson and the Newcastle Exhibitions 1822–1843, exhibition catalogue, Tyne and Wear County Council Museums, 1984; Felix Barker and Ralph Hyde, *London as it Might Have Been*, 1982, pp81–94; Roy Hutcheson, *Carron Company*, 1961.

THE PAINTING is extremely striking for the way in which it combines the aesthetic (St Paul's Cathedral) with the commercial (the Thames warehouses and the crane apparatus with loading barges in the foreground). The viewpoint adopted here, from Bankside, does not really come into its own with artists before the late nineteenth and early twentieth centuries and the Museum holds one drawing, dated 1886, taken from almost the same viewpoint as the Richardson painting (acc. no. 69.185). More familiar, perhaps, is the *c.*1897 painting of St Paul's by George Thomson in the Tate Gallery.

In the early nineteenth century several grandiose architectural schemes were proposed for a Thames Quay by such illustrious names as John Nash, Colonel Trench and John Martin, all of which attempted to rid the capital of its 'warehouse look' and to provide an aesthetically unified riverfront. None of these, however, was realised and this painting bears witness to the London that actually existed.

A series of characteristic activities for that period is depicted on the south bank and the river (at high tide), ranging from the operation of an ancient crane on the left (perhaps painstakingly drawn to pay homage to its age) by two workers colourfully dressed in blue and white striped shirts to Thames barges going up- and downriver. The men are loading barges with cut stone; grindstones may be seen on the right. In total contrast with this working environment, a child is shown playing in the foreground. Since the whole work seems very much articulated around the idea of contrast, even the cliché presence of the Lord Mayor's barge, captured on a leisure trip, adds colour and frivolity to the otherwise serious business of the working Thames.

At the beginning of the nineteenth century, most artists tended to avoid treating St Paul's from the south in a head-on view; they chose to soften the grimness of the north bank by adopting the more traditional oblique viewpoint, for instance from Blackfriars or London Bridge. David Roberts in his magnificent rendering of St Paul's and the City (Goldsmiths Company) eliminated all the warehouses by using Blackfriars Bridge as a screen and composed a strong architectural tableau entirely focused on the landmarks of the cathedral and the bridge. George F. Robson's atmospheric watercolour *St Paul's from Southwark* (1833, Yale Center for British Art) is rather exceptional and would appear to post-date the work by Richardson.

The meticulous and accurate way in which Richardson depicts the north bank suggests that the work was drawn from life and does not derive from intermediate sources, as may have been the case in relation to the Greenwich Group (*Art for Newcastle*, p64) or his son's views of Continental scenes. The topographical precision of the scene may be checked against the following sources:

1. **Panoramas of the Thames:** the Buck panorama (1749) and the MacClure and MacDonald panorama (1840s), both in the Museum's collection.
2. **360-degree panorama:** Robert Barker (1791), taken from the roof of Albion Mills in Southwark (acc. no. 65.36/1-4).

The church steeples which may be observed are also most accurately drawn and readily identifiable. Thus from left to right may be seen the following church steeples/towers: St Bride, St Andrew-by-the-Wardrobe (partly hidden by the crane), St Martin's Ludgate, St Benet in Paul's Wharf, St Vedast, St Mary-le-Bow, St Nicholas Church Abbey and St Michael in Wood Street.

Of all the warehouses lining the north bank, the nine-storey building on the right-hand side is the oldest. It clearly features, as a single-block building, in images of mid-eighteenth-century London, for instance the Buck panorama already mentioned or, indeed, the extraordinary Canaletto showing the *Thames on Lord Mayor's Day* (*c*.1747), now in Prague. By the 1790s it had been enlarged, as may be seen in the Barker panorama, and had a projecting bay in the middle. The best nineteenth-century record of this building is a photograph in the Guildhall Library and this suggests that the work under consideration was drawn from life: Richardson slightly compressed the depth of the building but otherwise painted it with great accuracy.

The painting enables us, almost for the first time, to understand visually the sequence of wharves on that stretch of the river. From left to right, Carron Wharf, St Paul's Wharf, Trig Stairs and Copper Wharf in the Baynard Castle Ward. The group of buildings on the right of the painting, part of St Paul's Wharf, are old warehouses built in dark red brick and they contrast with the group in the centre and on the left, newly built in pale golden colours and which would have been erected between 1792 and 1798. These are shown on Nathaniel Black's 1798 watercolour of Blackfriars Bridge in the Museum's collection with figures by Rowlandson (see illustration), but are not shown on the Barker panorama. The buildings in the centre of the painting form part of Carron Wharf. For the year 1819, trade directories list the English Copper Company, Fox Williams, Foster & Co, as well as the British Copper Office and Williams P. W. Crenfell & Co. This was indeed an important area for copper companies and merchants in London at this period, the Carron Company being the most famous. Although the provenance of the painting is still being investigated, it is not unreasonable to suggest that these buildings' focal prominence, the way in which they are lit (note the conspicuous highlighting of the windows with reflections) and the signs on the warehouses (Baynard Castle/Copper Company) indicate a link with the commission of the painting.

The painting is not signed, but the style and subject matter are consistent with those of Thomas Miles Richardson Senior. A Richardson watercolour, taken from a similar viewpoint, is recorded in the Witt Library as being with Trafalgar Galleries in 1973.

Nathaniel Black and Thomas Rowlandson (for the figures)
Blackfriars Bridge, 1798
Watercolour
Museum of London.

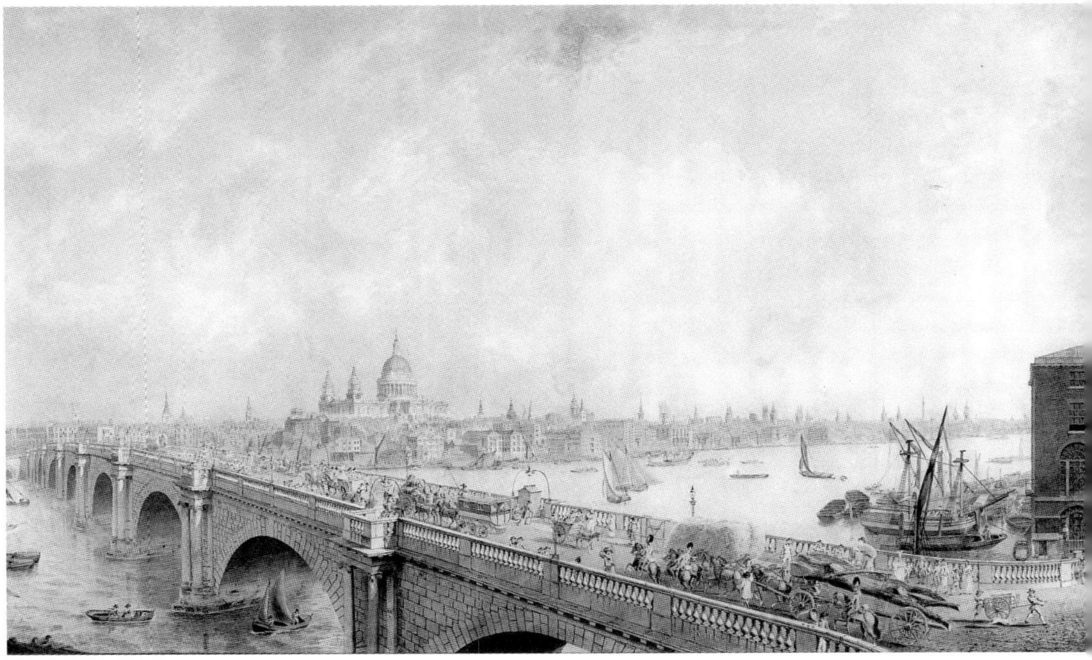

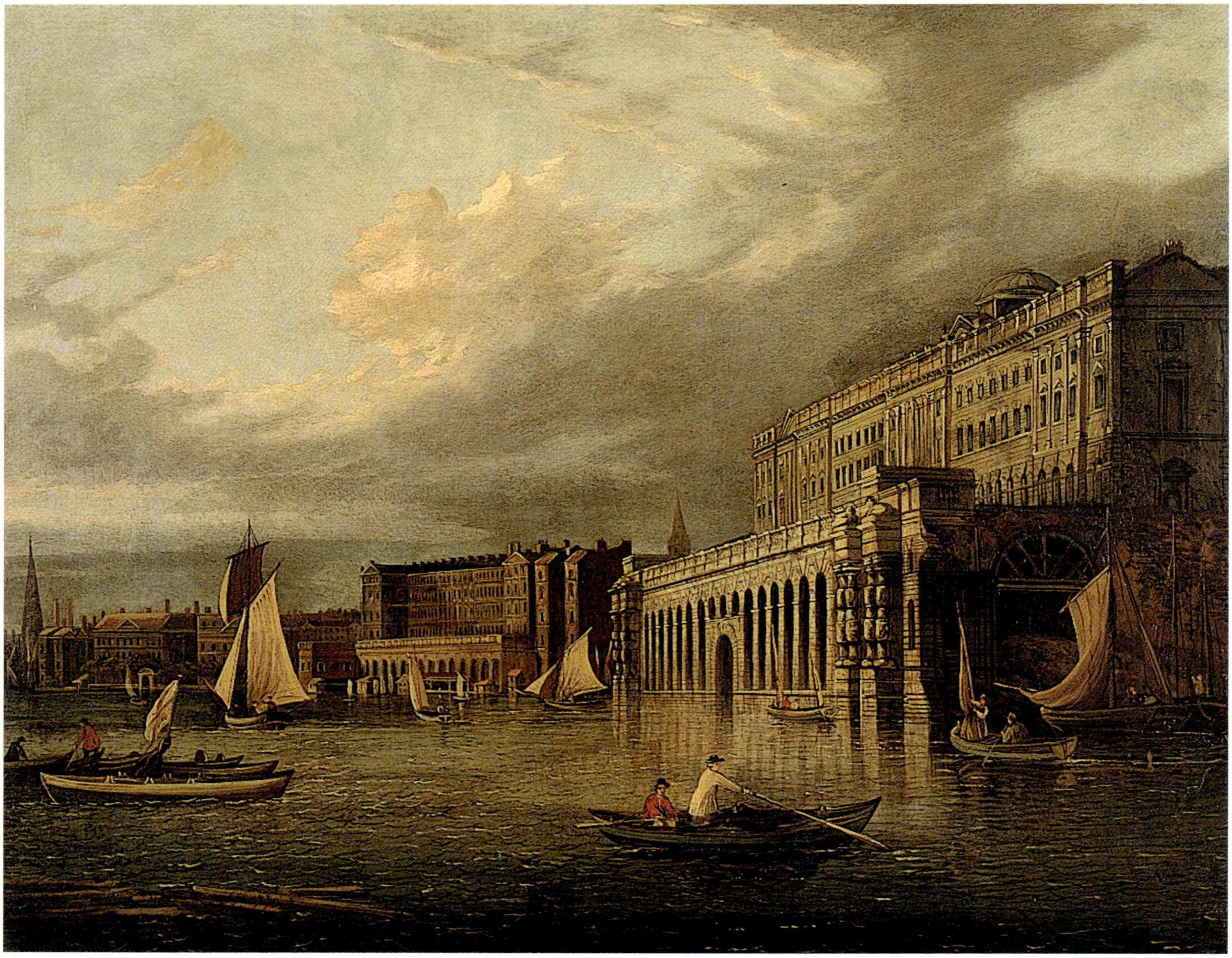

56.
JOHN PAUL
(1804–87)

Somerset House and the Adelphi from the River [C 2385]
c.1825
Oil on canvas, 69.4 x 90 cm
Signed and dated bottom left: *J F 1790*

SOMERSET HOUSE, designed by Sir William Chambers as a public building to house a number of official and learned bodies, and begun in 1776, is seen here before the river frontage was completed by the building of King's College (to the designs of Sir Robert Smirke in 1830–31), and before the arcades and watergate of its Piranesian substructure were masked by the Victoria Embankment. The Inland Revenue Office, which occupies the west wing, was added in the 1850s by Sir James Pennethorne. Beyond Somerset House is the spire of St Martin-in-the-Fields, and next to it is the Adelphi, begun by the brothers Adam in 1768 and pulled down in 1936. On the left of the picture are seen the water-tower of the York Buildings Waterworks Company, the house once owned by Samuel Pepys (see cat. no. 27) and the York Water Gate.

John Paul was principally a copyist of eighteenth-century topographical views, and this painting is identical in all but the smallest particulars with one of Farington's drawings, engraved by J. C. Stadler in 1791. That it was actually intended to pass for an original by Farington may be seen from the inscription JF 1790 which appears (as in the Stadler print) on one of the logs in the left foreground. It certainly cannot be relied upon for detailed accuracy, especially as it was done at second hand – in the case of the York Water Gate, it is no more than perfunctory – but it does, nevertheless, give a useful impression of what the riverside south of the Strand looked like before Waterloo Bridge was built and when it was dominated by two of London's most dramatic eighteenth-century buildings.

The costume indicates a date in the first quarter of the nineteenth century, and, since Paul was born in 1804, presumably towards the end of that period.

Innumerable versions of this picture exist.

Provenance:
Bequeathed by J. G. Joicey in 1919.

Bibliography:
Hayes (cat. no. 88); *Canaletto and his Influence on London Artists*, exhibition catalogue, Guildhall Art Gallery, June–July 1965 (27).

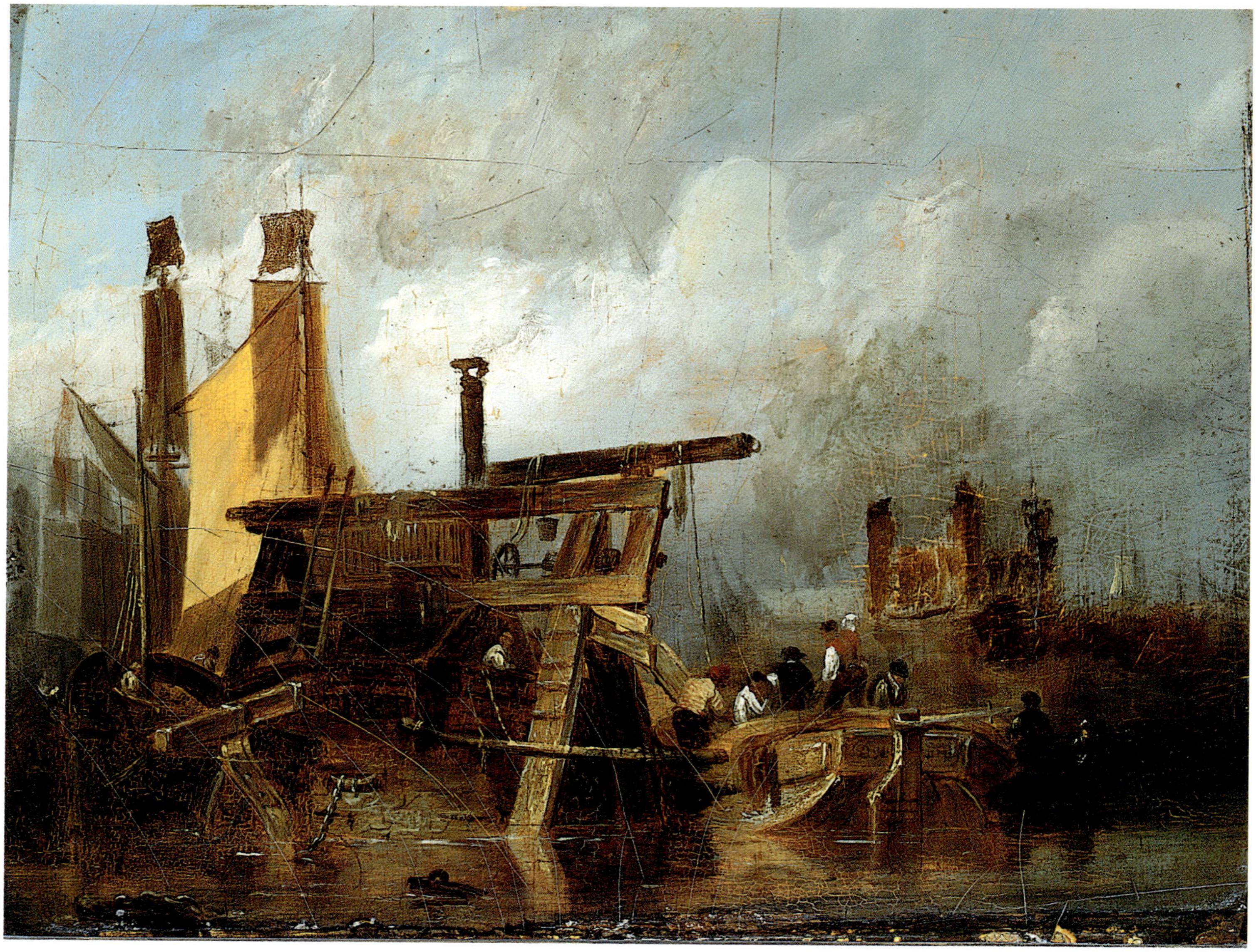

Provenance:
Presented by J. G. Joicey in 1916.

Bibliography:
Hayes (cat. no. 136); Bernard Adams, *London Illustrated 1604–1851,* 1983, cat. no. 149:5, p362; *Clarkson Stanfield,* exhibition catalogue, Tyne and Wear County Council Museums, 1979, no. 44.

57.
BRITISH SCHOOL
A Dredger on the Thames [A17588]
post 1827
Oil on panel, 22.5 x 30.5 cm
Not signed or dated

A BALLAST dredger is shown at work in the foreground; the Tower of London is seen in the middle distance right.

This work forms a pair with the next entry and was painted after an engraving published in 1827 for George Cooke's *Views in London and its Vicinity* (1826–34), from a drawing by Clarkson Stanfield of which the whereabouts are unknown (Stanfield catalogue).

58.

BRITISH SCHOOL

Westminster from Lambeth [A 17539]
post 1827
Oil on panel, 22.5 x 30.5 cm
Not signed or dated

THIS DISTANT view of Westminster shows, from left to right, the church of St John in Smith Square, Westminster Abbey, Westminster Hall and part of Westminster Bridge; four figures are seen on the shore in the foreground right, with a barge moored close by.

This work forms a pair with the previous entry and was painted after an engraving published in 1827 for George Cooke's *Views in London and its Vicinity* (1826–34), from a drawing by Samuel Prout.

Provenance:
Presented by J. G. Joicey in 1916.

Bibliography:
Hayes (cat. no. 142); Bernard Adams, *London Illustrated 1604–1851,* 1983, cat. no: 149:26, p362.

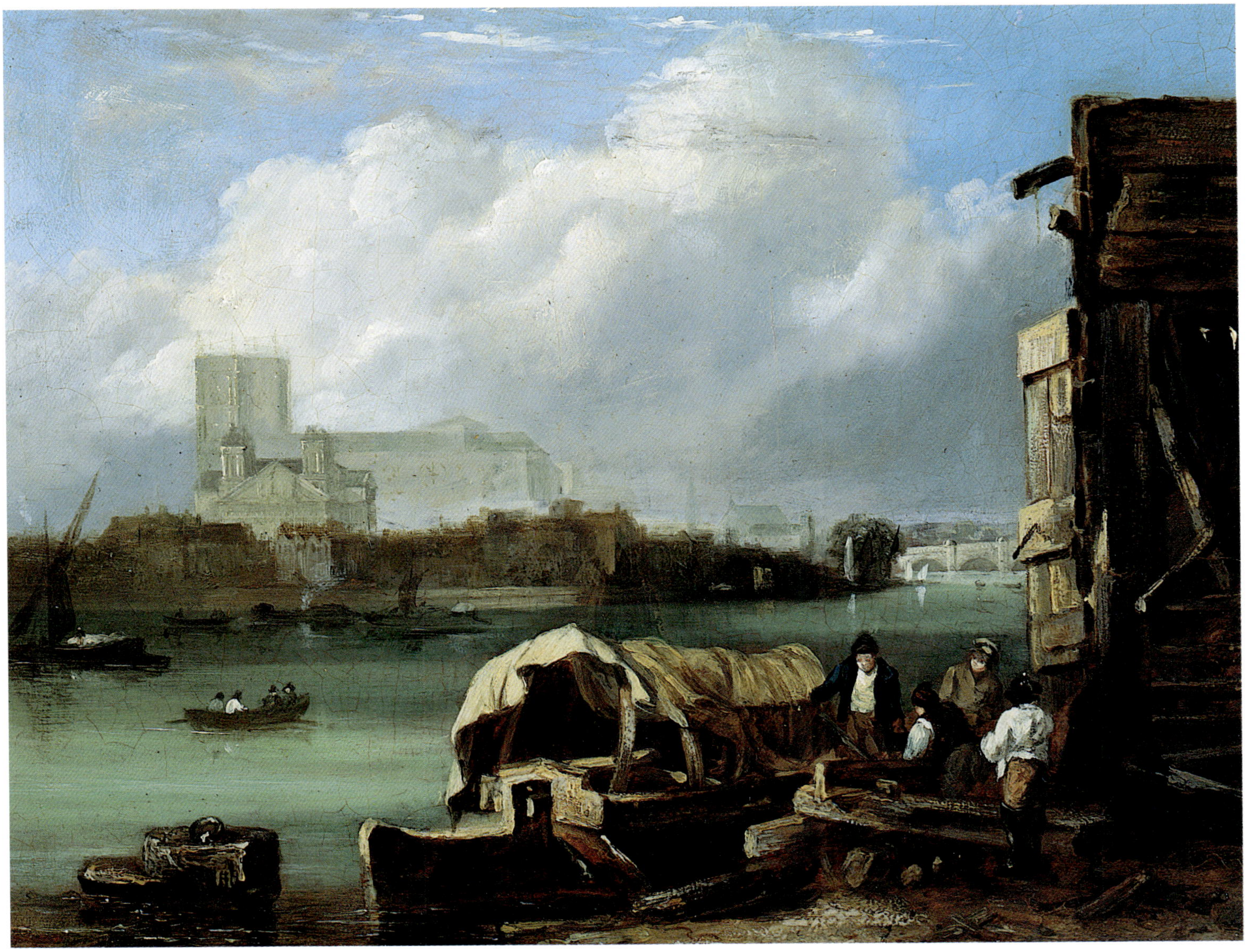

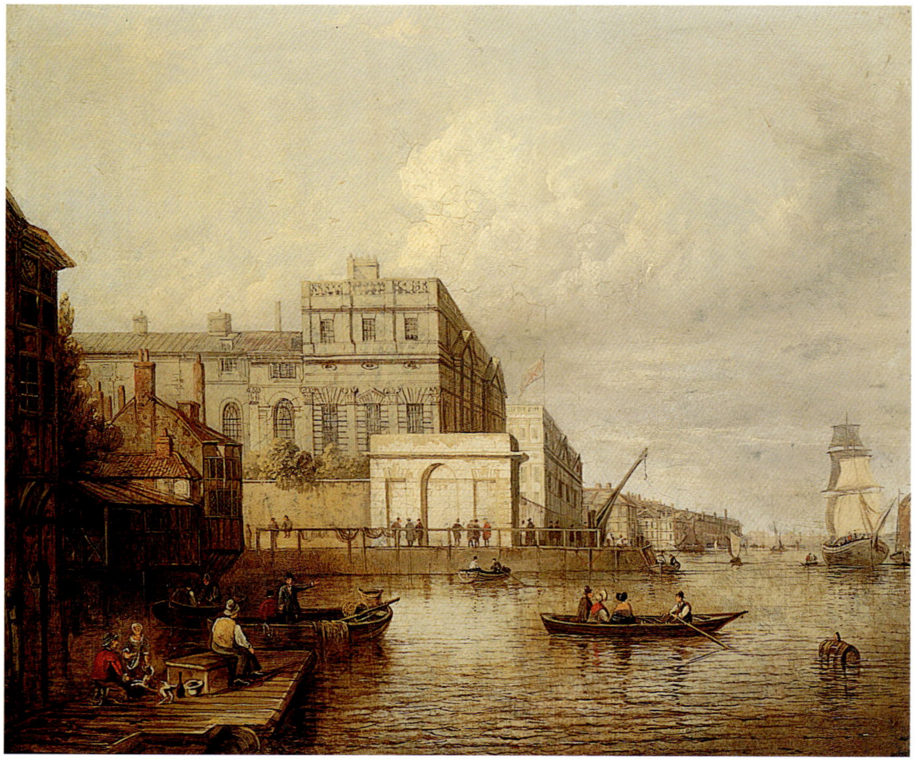

59.

JOHN PAUL

(1804–87)

Greenwich Hospital from the River

[A 13437]

*c.*1835

Oil on canvas, 62.5 x 75 cm

Not signed or dated

Provenance:
S. Girling; Girling sale, Christie's, 27 November 1909 (56, as *The Custom-House and Quay on the Thames*) bt Saunders; presented by Theodore Lumley in 1914.

Bibliography:
Hayes (cat. no. 89); Oliver Millar, *The Later Georgian Pictures in the Collection of Her Majesty the Queen*, 2 vols, 1969, no. 704.

A VIEW of the Greenwich waterfront from the old houses on the site of the Trafalgar Inn, built a year or two later in 1837. The principal features are the two riverside blocks of Greenwich Hospital (now the Royal Naval College) – Queen Anne's Block, begun by Hawksmoor in 1696 and finished by Campbell and Ripley, and King Charles's Block, the first building of all, erected to John Webb's designs in 1662–9, but extended in later years by Hawksmoor in 1712, Stuart in 1769 and Yenn in 1811–14. One of the most important buildings of its age, the Hospital remains the grandest complex of baroque architecture in London. Beyond are the Ship Tavern and the houses in Maiden Row, facing the river. Several rowing boats and other craft are seen on the river, and some figures are grouped on the landing stage in the foreground.

The Museum picture is a copy of the painting by George Chambers in the Royal Collection, which is signed and dated 1832, probably done from the engraving by J. B. Allen; the group of buildings in the middle distance has not, however, been very faithfully rendered, and the spire of St Paul's, Deptford has been omitted. A variant of Chambers's painting, signed and dated 1835, now in the National Maritime Museum (BHC1823), includes the *Dreadnought,* then anchored close to the waterfront, which served as a seamen's hospital. A watercolour of this subject by Chambers is in the Laing Art Gallery, Newcastle upon Tyne. A replica of the Museum picture, in which the boats and figures are also identical, was sold at Christie's on 19 November 1976 (30).

The costume indicates a date of about 1835, and the view dates from before the building of the Trafalgar Inn in 1837.

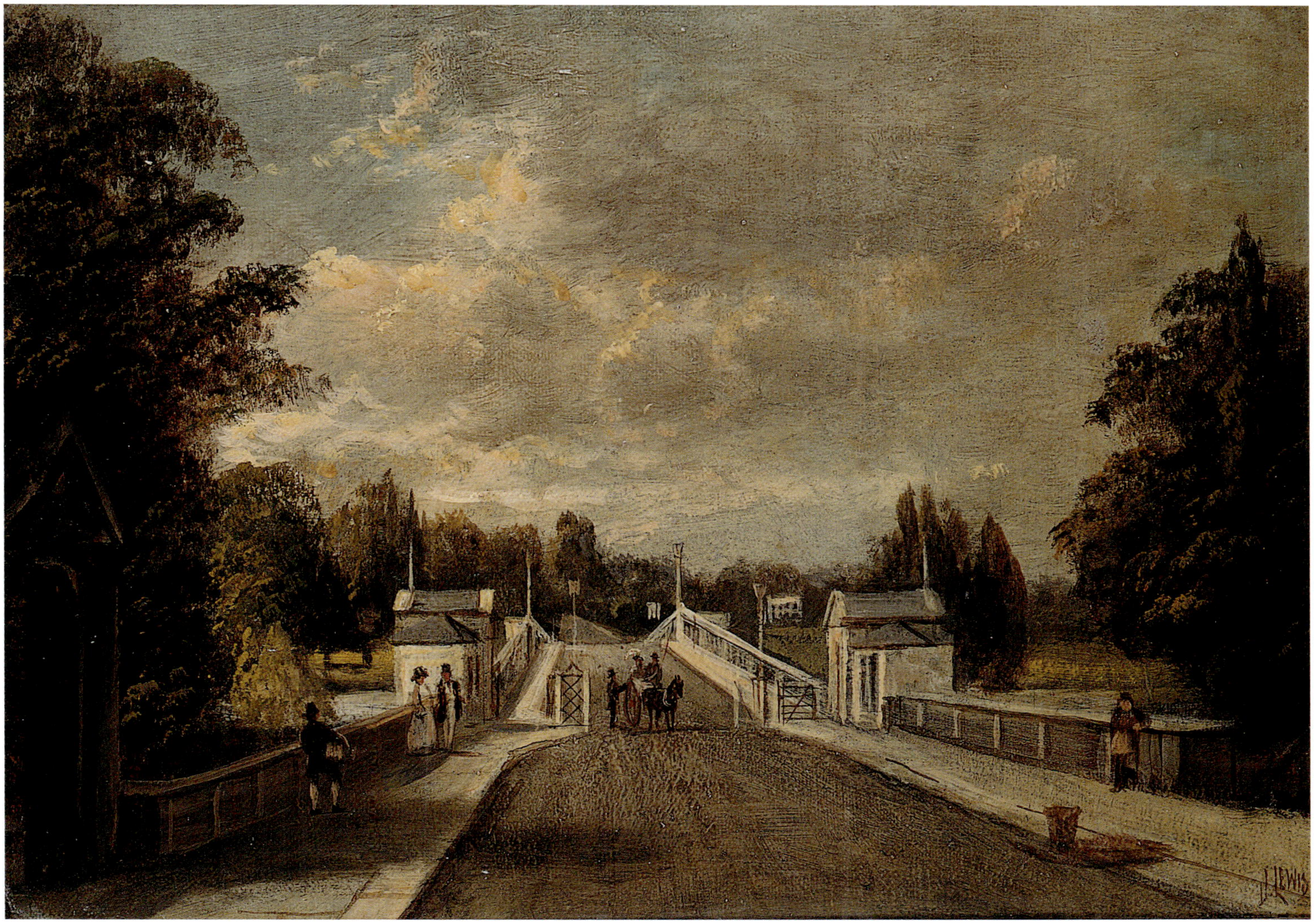

60.

JAMES ISAIAH LEWIS

(1861–1934)

Richmond Bridge [59.2/1]
Late nineteenth century
Oil on canvas, 25 x 32.8 cm
Signed bottom right: *J. Lewis*

THE VIEW shows the stone bridge (which still stands, though widened in 1937) that was built in 1774–7 to the designs of Kenton Couse and James Paine, and which replaced the ferry service between Richmond and Twickenham. The viewpoint is from the Richmond side, and shows the pair of toll-houses, with the keeper collecting the toll from a couple in a gig. On the left is seen the gate of Miss Taylor's boarding house. The picture is a copy, excluding the dogs in the foreground and the figures on the right, of the engraving by W. B. Cooke from the original drawing by J. D. Harding, published in Mrs Barbara Hofland's *Richmond and its Surrounding Scenery*, 1832.

Provenance:
Sotheby's, 14 January 1959 (141), bt London Museum.

Bibliography:
Hayes (cat. no. 159).

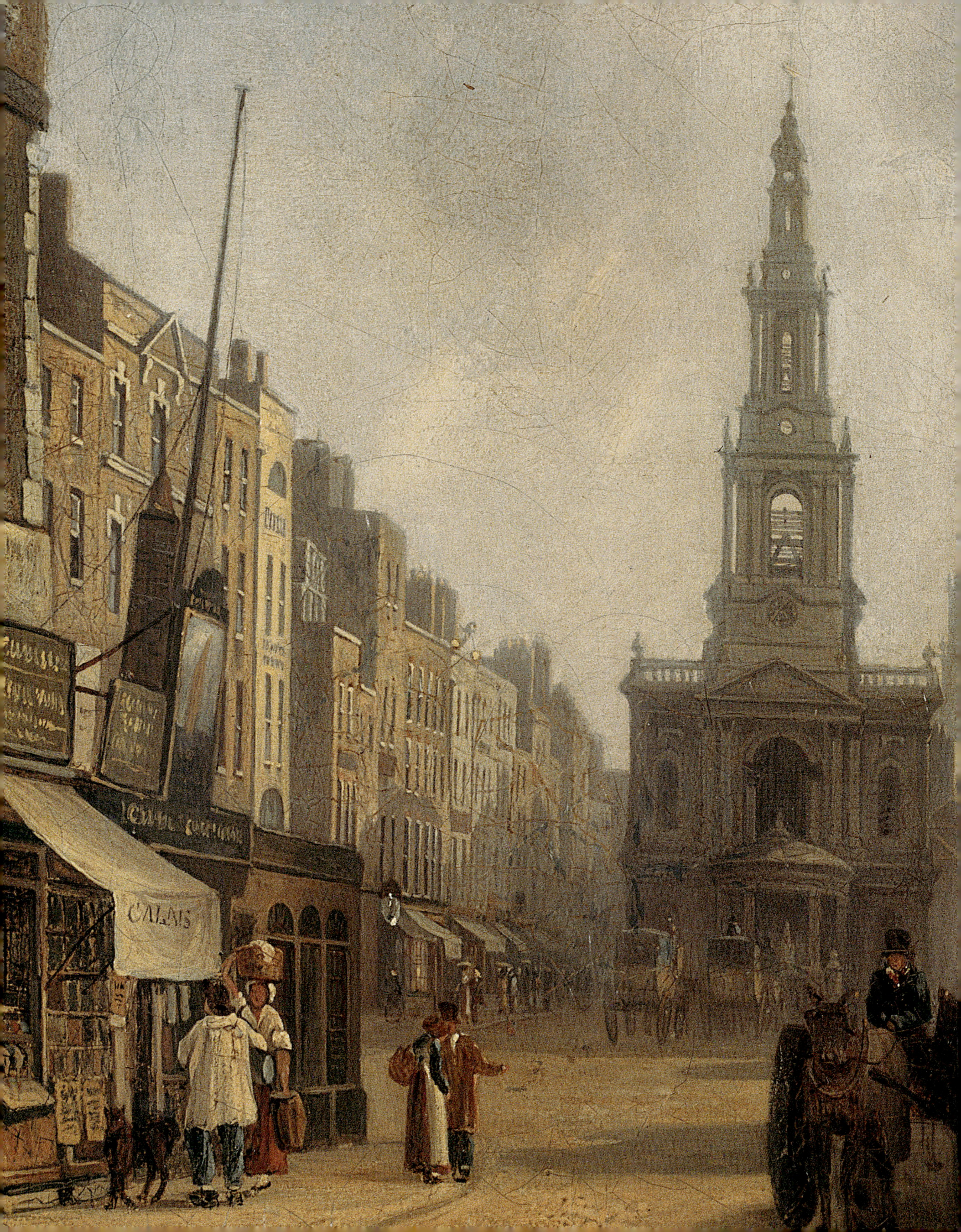
CALAIS

STREETS AND BUILDINGS

> ONCE, AND only once, has a great plan for London, affecting the development of the capital as a whole, been projected and carried to completion.

Although this almost legendary statement on the Regency 'metropolitan improvements' has been challenged recently,[1] the building programme masterminded by John Nash under the patronage of the Prince of Wales between the official start of the Regency in 1811 and the 1820s so transformed the face of London that the response of the visiting Italian General Roberto Winspeare is worth quoting. In 1818 he had felt that London 'is like the interior of a great monastery', but on returning in 1839 he was prompted to write, 'it has become an exceedingly beautiful and magnificent city; it is, in short, the leading capital of the world'.[2] By that time London had acquired Regent Street, mostly built between 1817 and 1823, an extension to the Grand Union Canal from Paddington to Limehouse (1812–20), a regular bus service (started in 1829 by George Shillibeer) and the beginning of a railway network: the first Greenwich railway was followed in 1836 by the London to Birmingham railway. The development of a public transport network in London had far-reaching consequences, but the painter's imagery for this theme emerges only in the Victorian period.

In his *Metropolitan Improvements*, published between 1827 and 1830, James Elmes described with enthusiasm the grand architectural scheme which was developed to link Carlton House, the Regent's urban residence in Waterloo Place, to Regent's Park, a beautiful garden city in which would nestle the Regent's country villa. Although the garden city of which Nash had dreamt did not materialise, enough of the scheme was built for Elmes to lyricise:

> See! the sparkling undulating line of beauty, formed by the curved neck of that swan, sailing majestically by the dark green shrubs of the Holme. The united powers of the magic pencils of Ruysdael and Claude would hardly do justice to that bit of brilliant nature.[3]

Although Elmes's words highlight not only the picturesque quality of the site but also its appeal to painters, the only images that have come down to us to illustrate the century's grandest urban scheme are those commissioned by Elmes himself from the charming draughtsman Thomas H. Shepherd. Elmes's text continued to connect the scheme with painters and he thus described Sussex Place:

> When considered with the eye of the landscape painter, it presents a variety of form, and an assemblage of picturesque outlines, which diversify the scene, and prevent a monotony of effect that might otherwise have been tedious.[4]

Yet no contemporary painting of Nash's scheme exists and, furthermore, paintings of the streets and buildings of the capital are relatively rare in the Regency period. There is a group of attractive works by the foreign artists William Seguier (1771–1843) and his brother John (1785–1856),[5] who successfully specialised in London scenes, as well as works by Louis

Pierre Spindler (1800–89)[6] and Jacques Laurent Agasse.[7] Although both Seguier brothers trained under George Morland, the style of these French and Swiss artists is decidedly Continental, sometimes in the Biedermeier tradition popular in Germany between 1815 and 1848. The works in this section, therefore, constitute a good sample of Regency street life, ranging from the view of the Strand by Caleb Robert Stanley (cat. no. 63) to James Holland's recording of grand building works in the capital (cat. no. 65). Their golden light and calm interpretation of London streets recall the cityscape work of seventeenth-century Dutch Old Masters such as Pieter Jansz Sanraedam and Jan van der Heyden.

The impact made by the rediscovery of seventeenth-century Netherlandish painting in the Regency period has been discussed in the river section (p145). James Elmes's reference to Ruysdael quoted earlier confirms this influence. It is also clearly expressed in the emergence of two genres in which the Netherlandish schools excelled, landscape and fire (see pp179–85 below for fires).

The unpretentious *Collins's Farm* by John Linnell may be seen to illustrate the unprecedented development of landscape painting in the early years of the nineteenth century. Turner and Constable, sadly not represented in the collection, epitomise the genre and both painted London extensively. The practice of pure landscape painting on the doorstep of the capital was pursued by John Varley, William Mulready, John and Alexander Nasmyth, James Pringle[8] and John Martin in a remarkable and little-known series on London parks.[9] Hampstead, of course, lent itself particularly well to such green pursuits; there William Collins, John Constable and John Linnell were neighbours. Linnell's house in particular (see cat. no. 64), became in the 1820s 'an intellectual centre of its day, a forcing house for the [rural] visionary art of [Samuel] Palmer, [Edward] Calvert and [George] Richmond as much as Linnell and Blake'.[10]

This rediscovery of landscape at the turn of the eighteenth century formed part of a wider phenomenon which is particularly well illustrated by C. R. Leslie's *Londoners Gypsying* (illustrated). The artist indulged the period penchant for nature in Epping Forest and his words bear witness to the vitality of the new craze: 'I am at present painting a picture of a party spending a day in the woods, which is a very common thing with the people of the middle class in the summer.'[11] It was also at the beginning of the nineteenth century that this popular pastime developed and that the word 'picnic' was coined.[12]

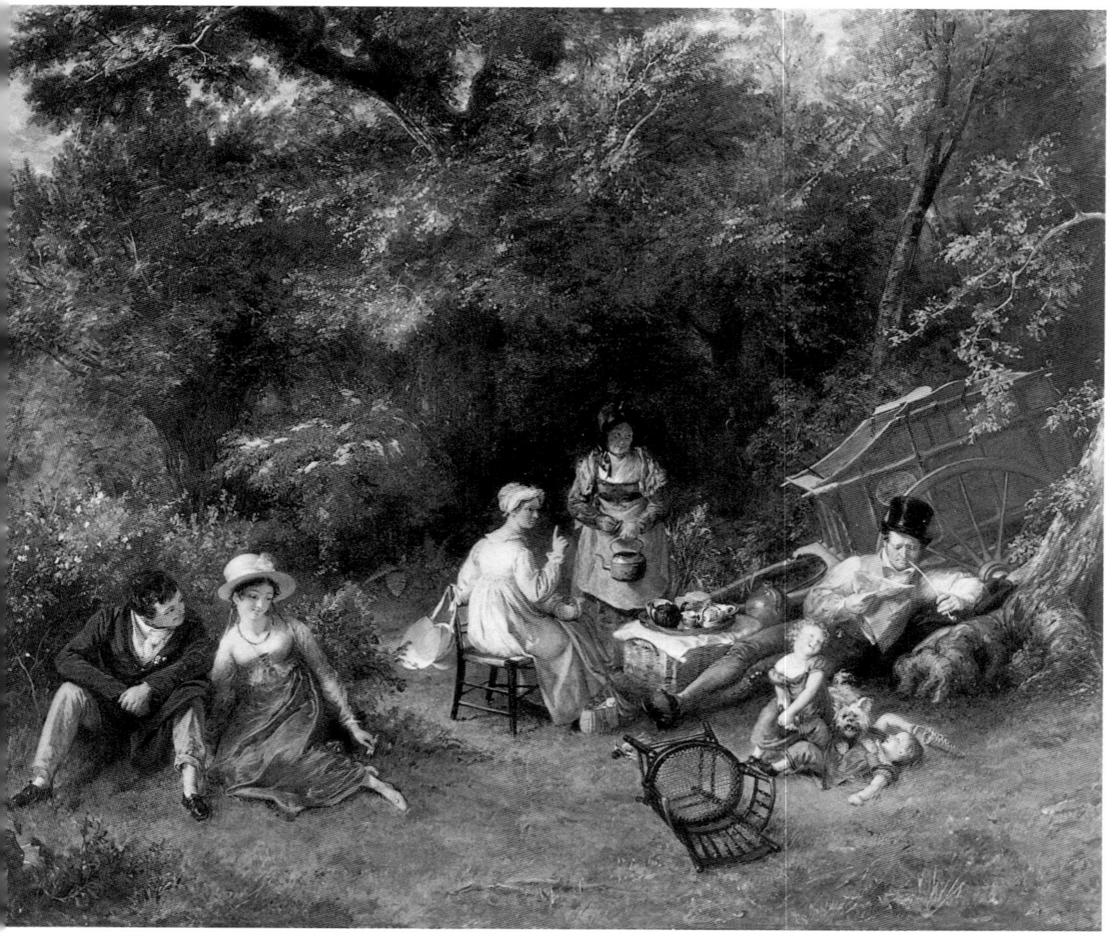

Charles Robert Leslie
(1794–1859)
Londoners Gypsying, 1820
Oil on canvas
The Geffrye Museum, London.

1. The quote comes from John Summerson, *Georgian London*, 1962. Its contents were challenged by J. Mordaunt Crook in 'Metropolitan Improvements: John Nash and the Picturesque', in *London – World City 1800–1840*, Celina Fox (ed.), 1992.
2. Quoted in Anne Pomeroy, 'An Italian in Regency England', in *Country Life*, 15 September 1983, pp696–9.
3. James Elmes, *Metropolitan Improvements; or London in the nineteenth century*, 1827–30, p29.
4. Ibid, p48.
5. See the dictionaries of painters and engravers by Bénézit and Bryan (see bibliography). John exhibited at the Royal Academy between 1811 and 1822.
6. Exhibited at the Royal Academy between 1834 and 1836. Lived at 14 Marlborough Street. See David Piper, *Artists' London*, 1982, p86.
7. See *Jacques Laurent Agasse*, exhibition catalogue, Tate Gallery, 1989. This important body of London work is little known since all the paintings are in Switzerland and rarely travel.
8. Notably in a beautiful painting of Sydenham Common, with Lane Fine Art in 1992.
9. *London's Pride*, Mireille Galinou (ed.), 1990, pp206 and 209.
10. *John Linnell*, exhibition catalogue 31, Martyn Gregory Gallery, 1982, no. 56.
11. Jeffery Daniels, 'C. R. Leslie: A Rediscovery', in *Art and Artists*, January 1977.
12. Karen Eyre and Mireille Galinou, *Picnics*, Museum of London booklet (London Connection series), 1988.

Provenance:
Inscribed on the back as purchased at Bath in 1824 (as Richard Wilson);
T. Humphry Ward; Red Cross Sale, Christie's, 23 April 1915 (1510, presented by T. H. Ward, as Wilson), bt Sir Guy Laking for the Museum.

Bibliography:
Hayes (cat. no. 25).

61.
BRITISH SCHOOL
St Mary's Church, Willesden [A 17004]
1815–24
Oil on canvas, 55.2 x 58.7 cm
Not signed or dated

A VIEW taken from the north-west showing the original thirteenth-century nave and tower before the alterations of the nineteenth century, when the south aisle was built, battlements added to the tower and the cupola removed. Some cottages are seen on the right, and through the trees on the left is a larger house, which stood on the site of the present vicarage garden (none of these buildings survives). At this date, Willesden was only a tiny village, with fewer than a hundred houses. The church is now surrounded by streets of late nineteenth-century terrace houses in the Gothic taste.

The picture must have been painted after 1815, as it shows against the church the tomb of John Methley, who died on 9 January 1815 (the monument to the left is the tomb of the Mercelin family), and before 1824, the date of its purchase in Bath.

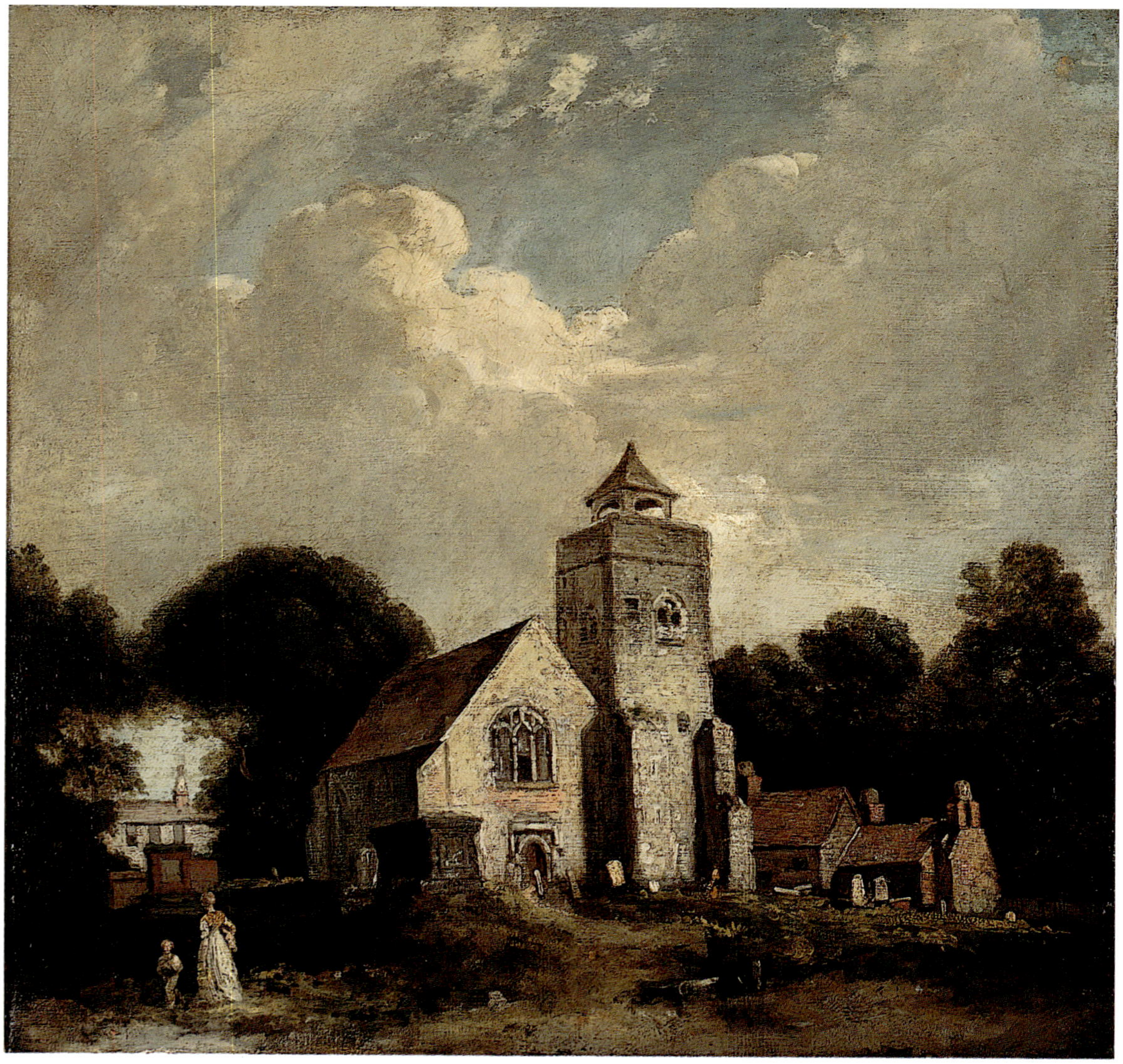

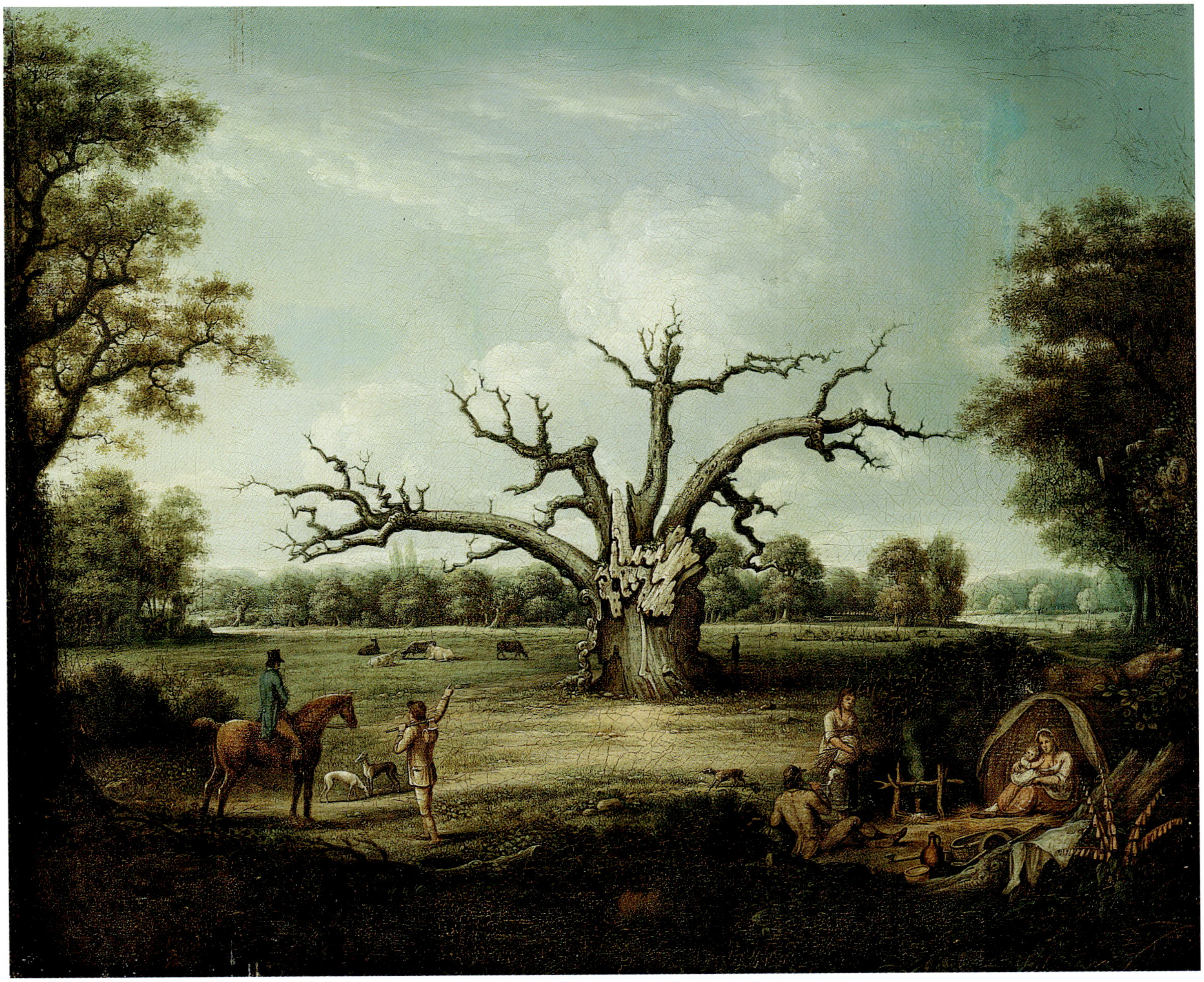

62.

HENRY MILBOURNE

(1781–c.1826)

The Fairlop Oak, Hainault Forest [59.39]
1816
Oil on canvas, 42.1 x 51.8 cm
Signed with initials and dated on the trunk of the oak: *H. M./1816*

A VIEW of the Fairlop Oak in Hainault Forest, near Ilford, which boasted a trunk 36 feet in circumference and was reputed to be nearly 2000 years old. A woodman carrying a costrel or ale barrel on his back and an axe over his left shoulder is pointing out the oak to a gentleman on a horse in the left foreground. On the right some gypsies are grouped around a camp-fire, talking to another woodman(?) with his axe by his side. The sub-commentary in this painting appears to suggest that the figures of the woodmen form a link between the two contrasting worlds of the free-spirited gypsies and the landowners.

Provenance:
Purchased from Alfred Werner in 1959 (without attribution).

Bibliography:
Hayes (cat. no. 75); Credland, 'The Fairlop Oak and Fairlop Fair' in *Essex Journal*, vol. 14, no. 3, 1979–80; *The Blasted Oak*, exhibition catalogue, Herbert Art Gallery and Museum, Coventry, 1987.

The contrast is delightfully carried through the image of the dogs.

By the late eighteenth century, the oak was noted for the fair which was held there every year on the first Friday in July. This originated in an annual dinner which Daniel Day (1638–1767), an engine- and pump-maker who had an estate near by, used to give to some of his neighbours under the shade of the old oak. By 1725, other groups had begun to gather on the same day, booths were erected, and a regular fair was in operation (it was customary to celebrate fairs and festivals beneath oak trees in many parts of England). Rowlandson is the best-known artist who has left us impressions of the Fairlop Fair during its heyday; but there is also an attractive watercolour by S. H. Grimm, which is signed and dated 1774, in the Victoria and Albert Museum (P.65–1921).

In the first half of the nineteenth century, a number of paintings dealt with the theme of gypsies, who had become more visible as enclosures restricted the places where they could camp; the paintings were also part of the attempt at that time to redefine nature and its relationship to man (see p168). Hainault Forest was a well-known resort for gypsies in the early nineteenth century (an enclosure of 1851 appears to have ended that particular tradition) and the picturesquely vaulted tent (or 'bender'), the donkey, open fire, suspended boiling pot and cooking utensils shown here would have been a familiar sight.

In 1805, as a result of the practice of lighting fires in the cavity of the trunk, the oak was badly burned, and in February 1820 it finally collapsed during a heavy gale. The fair, however, continued to be held on the site until some time after Hainault was disafforested by the Government in 1851, and took place in other parts of Ilford until the end of the century.

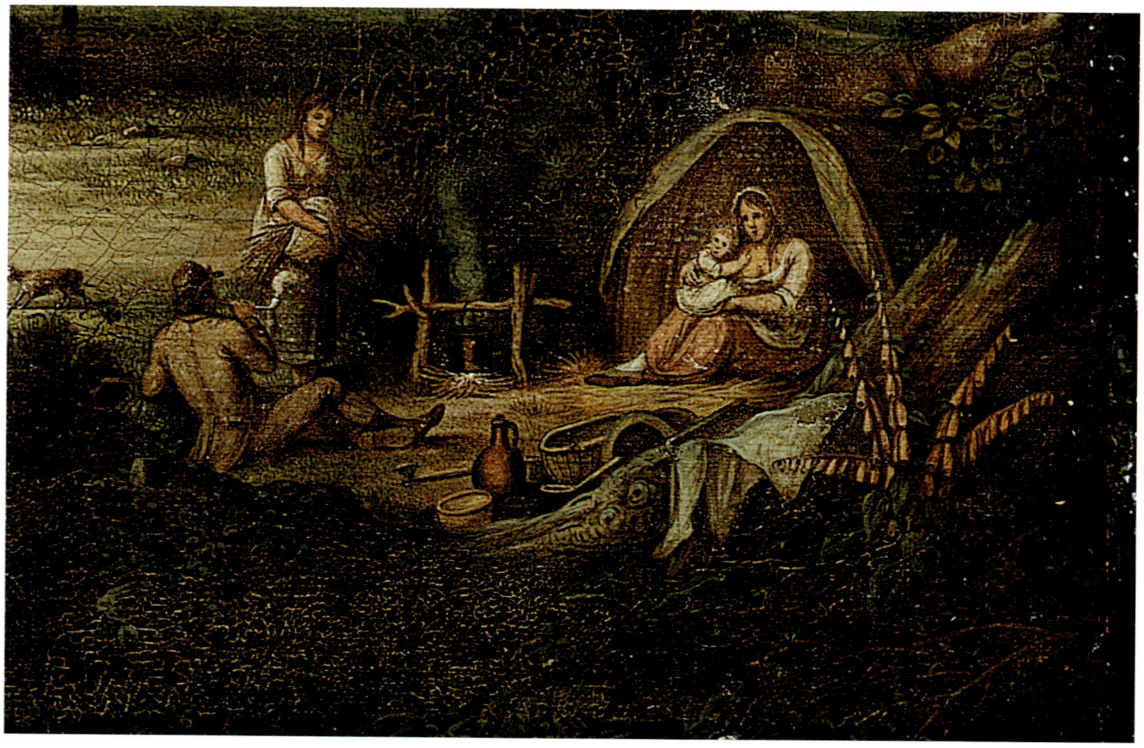

63.

CALEB ROBERT STANLEY

(1795–1868)

The Strand, Looking Eastwards from Exeter Change [60.171]

*c.*1824

Oil on canvas, 75 x 67.8 cm

Not signed or dated

A VIEW of part of the Strand, looking eastwards towards St Mary-le-Strand, built by James Gibbs in 1714–17, and St Clement Danes, a Wren church of 1680–82 with a spire added by Gibbs in 1719. Savoy Street is on the extreme right and the next turning, visible in the middle distance, is Wellington Street, which, prior to the building of the Aldwych, led to Waterloo Bridge. Exeter Change, from which the picture was taken, was an arcade of shops on two levels, built in 1676 and demolished at the time of the Strand improvements in 1829.

At this date, the Strand was still one of London's principal shopping streets. The eighteenth-century buildings seen here, with the shop windows divided into small panes, were typical of the street's general appearance throughout its length. The shop on the extreme left, at 363 Strand, belonged to Mary Arthur, snuffman; next door, at 362, were the offices of the Literary Gazette (numerous newspaper offices were then situated in this area, notably in Catherine Street). Also in this block were the offices of two steam packet navigation companies. The premises on the far right cannot be identified, although it is known that Thomas Gill, patent agent, had an office on one floor. Thomas Remnant, glover, was at 126, and the Globe and Travel office was at 127. Premises farther along the street included a boot and shoemaker and a tailor. Two street sellers are active on either side of the street; notice also the cobbled roadway, and the cab stand in front of St Mary-le-Strand, the site of the first hackney carriage stand, established in London in 1634.

The picture was painted around 1824; by the following year (when it was exhibited) the Literary Gazette had moved from 362 Strand to number 263.

Provenance:
Purchased out of the Joicey Trust Fund from M. Bernard in 1960.

Bibliography:
Hayes (cat. no. 102).

Exhibited:
British Institution, 1825 (309).

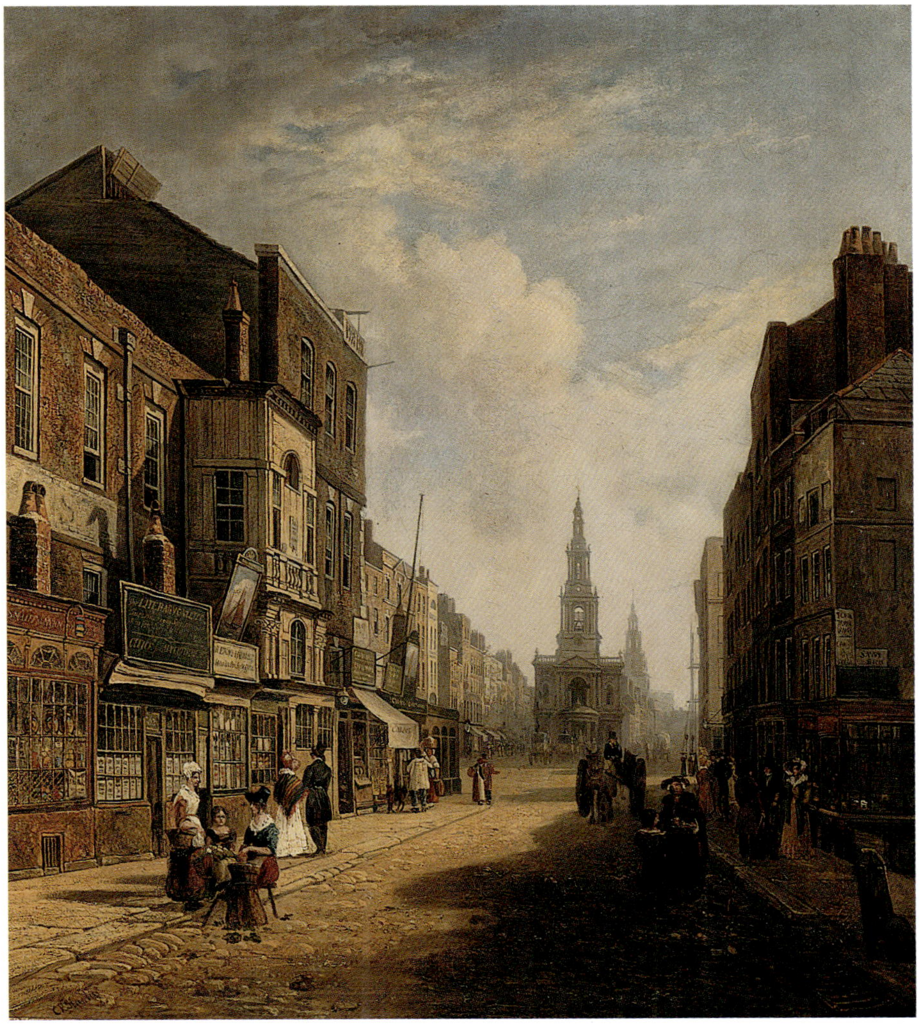

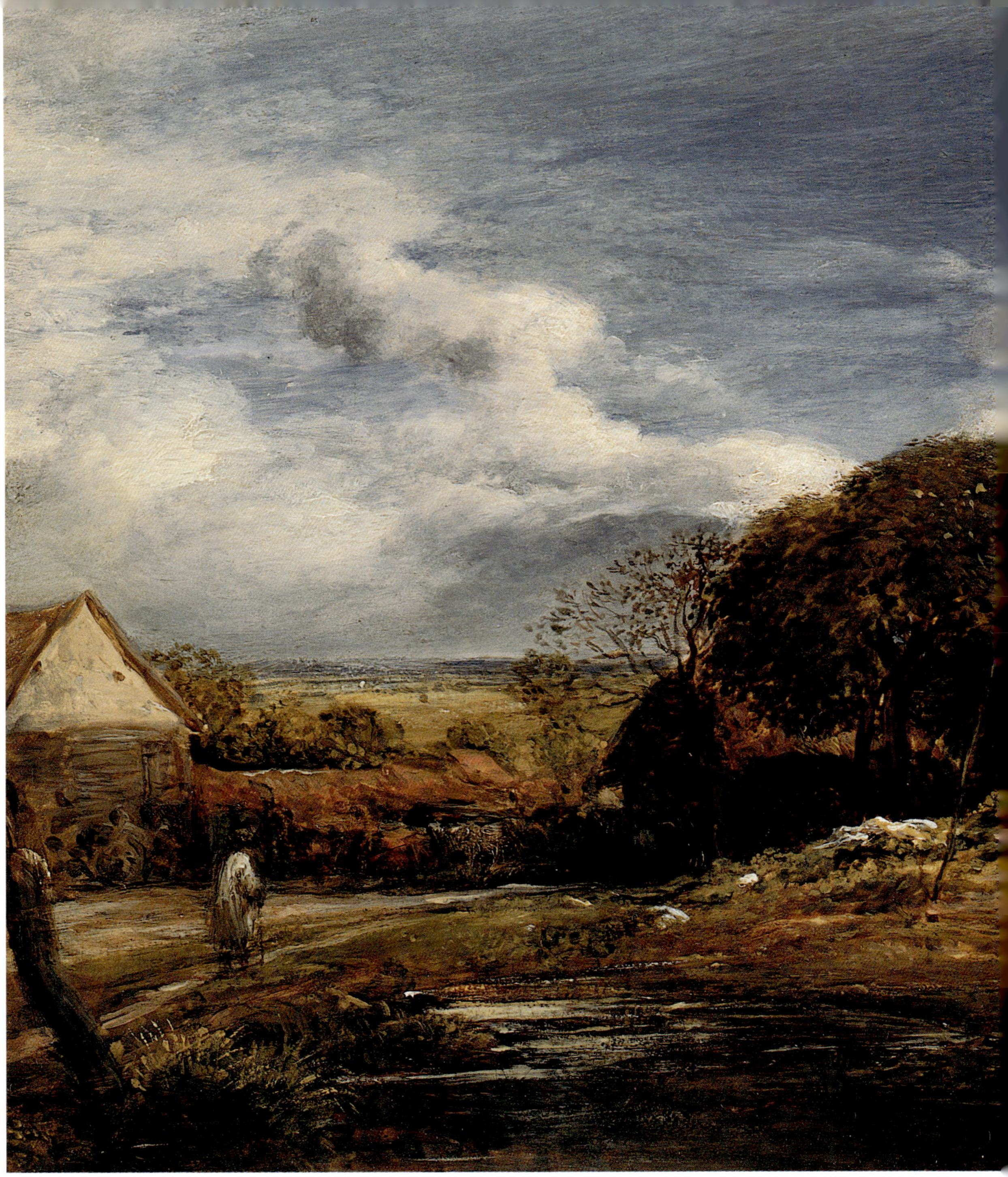

64.

JOHN LINNELL
(1792–1882)

Collins's Farm, North End, Hampstead
[63.62]
1831
Oil on panel, 15.4 x 37.5 cm
Inscribed on the back:
Collin(s's) Farm/North End/Hampstead Heath/Painted by John Linnell senr 1831

COLLINS'S FARM (now Wyldes Farm, from the name of the old estate) is a small weatherboarded house in North End, on the east side of Hampstead Way. At this date North End was no more than a cluster of houses at the foot of Hampstead Hill, on either side of North End Road which led from Jack Straw's Castle to Golders Green. Part of the hill can be seen on the right, and in the distance open fields stretch away to the horizon, on ground that is now Hampstead Garden Suburb and the built-

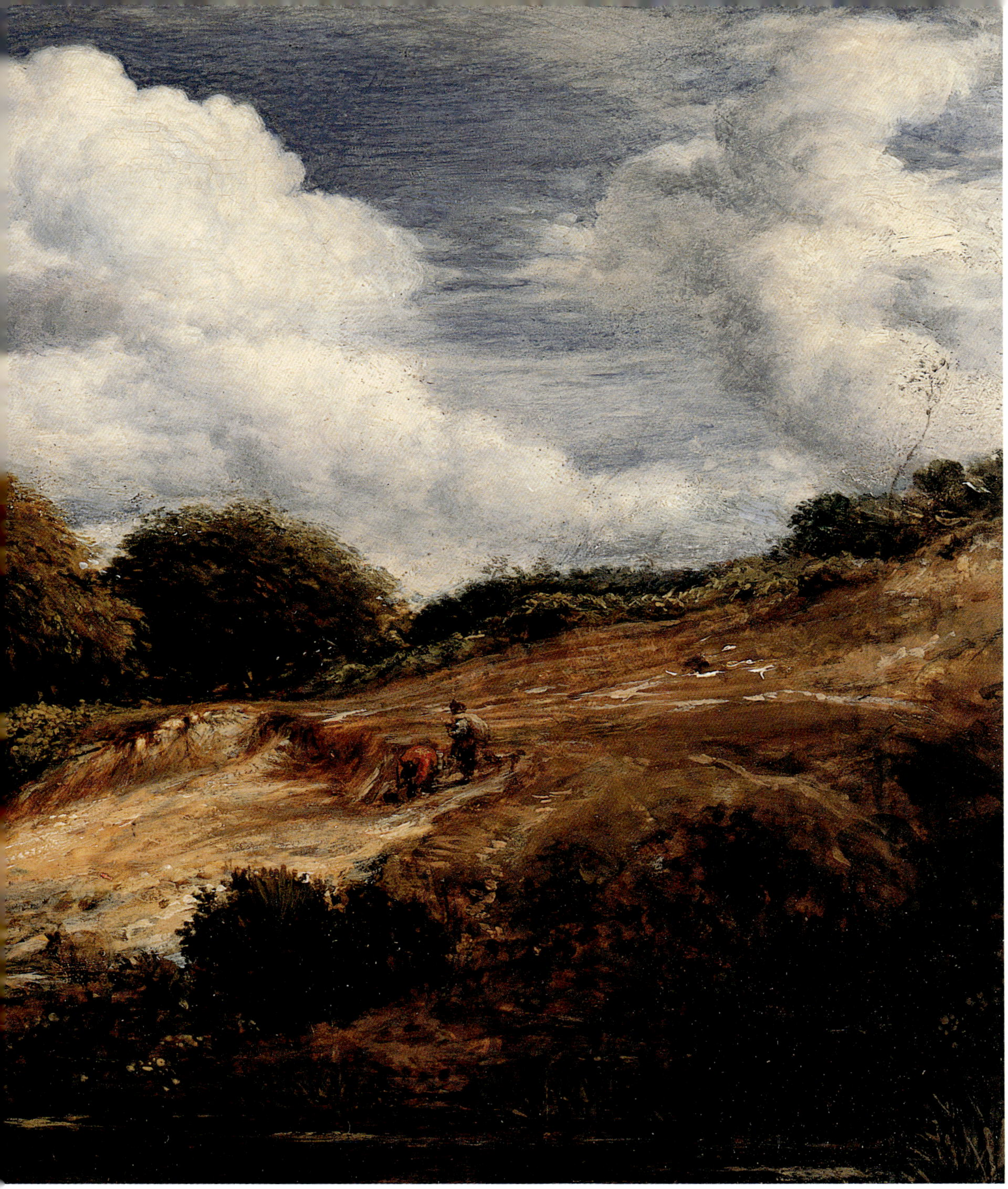

Provenance:
Purchased out of the Joicey Trust Fund from Maas Gallery in 1963.

Bibliography:
Hayes (cat. no. 69); Katharine Crouan, *John Linnell*, exhibition catalogue 32, Martyn Gregory Gallery, 1982, 'Introduction' and cat. no. 56; *John Linnell*, Fitzwilliam Museum centennial exhibition catalogue, 1982.

up area of north-west London.

In 1823 and 1824 Linnell and his family spent two summers in rented cottages on Hampstead Heath: first at Hope Cottage. From March 1824 until April 1828 they lived at Collins's Farm, though Linnell retained his studio in Cirencester Place in central London. For a short period in 1837 Charles Dickens lived at Collins's Farm, and a distinguished later occupant was Raymond Unwin, the town planner, who was responsible for the layout of Hampstead Garden Suburb.

Although Linnell later in life apparently exclaimed, 'I am not a topographer', this work is a faithful rendering of the site; by 1831 when this picture was painted, the Linnells had settled in Porchester Terrace in Bayswater, where Linnell was primarily engaged in painting a large number of genre scenes.

This picture is not included in the list of Linnell's works which Alfred T. Story appended to his *Life of John Linnell*, 1892.

Provenance:
Miss Emily J. Wood, who presented it to the National Gallery in 1888; transferred to the Tate Gallery in 1897; lent by the Tate Gallery in 1912, and transferred in 1957.

Bibliography:
Hayes (cat. no. 53).

Exhibited:
Society of British Artists Summer Exhibition, 1834.

65.

JAMES HOLLAND

(1799–1870)

Hyde Park Corner and Constitution Arch
[C 1004]
*c.*1833
Oil on canvas, 53.2 x 88.7 cm
Not signed or dated

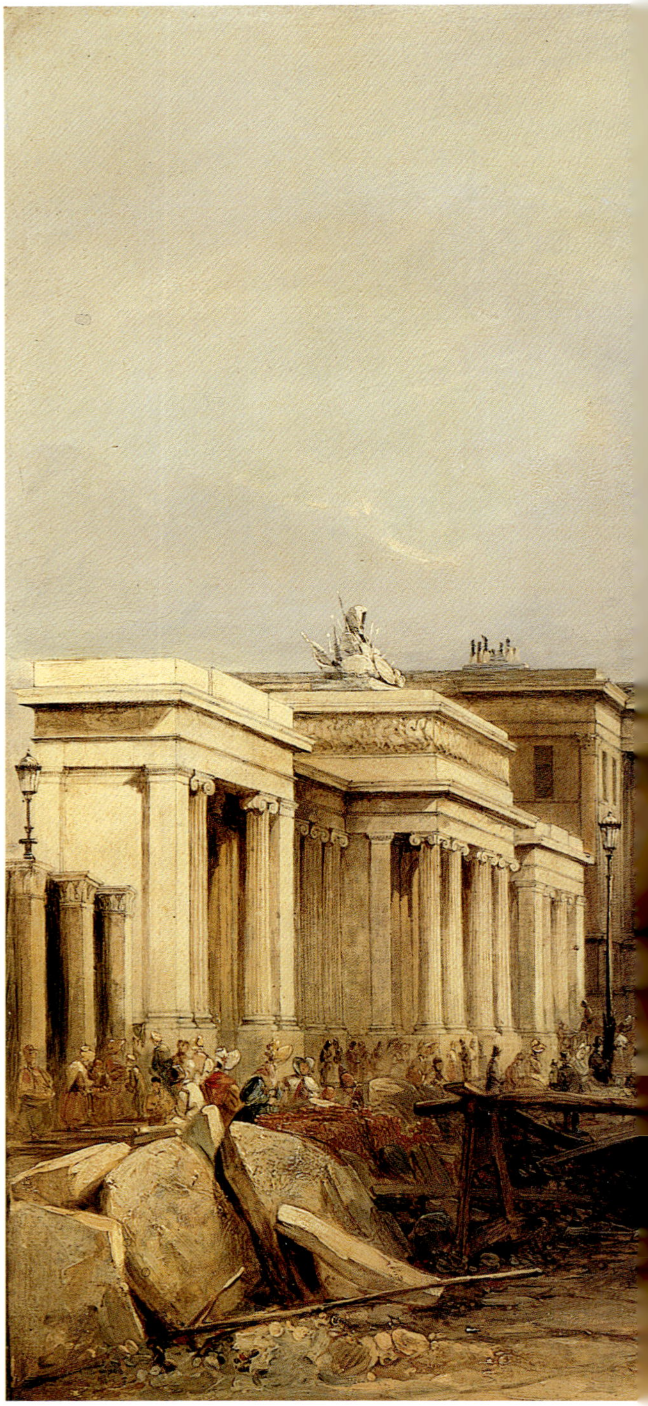

THIS VIEW shows Constitution Arch and the entrance screen to Hyde Park in alignment, as they were until the Arch was moved to its present position at the top of Constitution Hill in 1883. Several schemes for composing an entry into London at Hyde Park Corner in the grandest architectural style had been proposed in the second half of the eighteenth century, but proved abortive. In the end, the idea was turned upside down, as it were, and the grand arches actually built were not an entry into London at all, but on a totally different axis, and intended as an entrance to Nash's new Buckingham Palace, on the south (a similar triumphal entrance to the Constitution Arch, the Marble Arch, was designed by Nash for the forecourt of the Palace, and stood there until 1851). Both the Hyde Park Corner screen and the Royal Entrance (Constitution Arch) were designed by Decimus Burton, and built in 1825–8. The sculptured figure of Victory in a quadriga or four-horsed chariot surmounting the arch was replaced by a bronze equestrian statue of the Duke of Wellington by Matthew Cotes Wyatt in 1846; this in its turn was replaced, in 1912, by the bronze Victory group by Adrian Jons that still remains there.

On the right of the Hyde Park screen, Apsley House, or Number 1, London, originally an Adam House of 1771–8, is seen as it was remodelled for the Duke of Wellington by Benjamin and Philip Wyatt in 1828–9; beyond is Piccadilly. In the right foreground is part of St George's Hospital, built by William Wilkins in 1828–9. Road-mending operations are in progress in the foreground, and a crowd is watching a troop of lancers as it passes through Constitution Arch. Among the vehicles depicted are a town or dress coach,

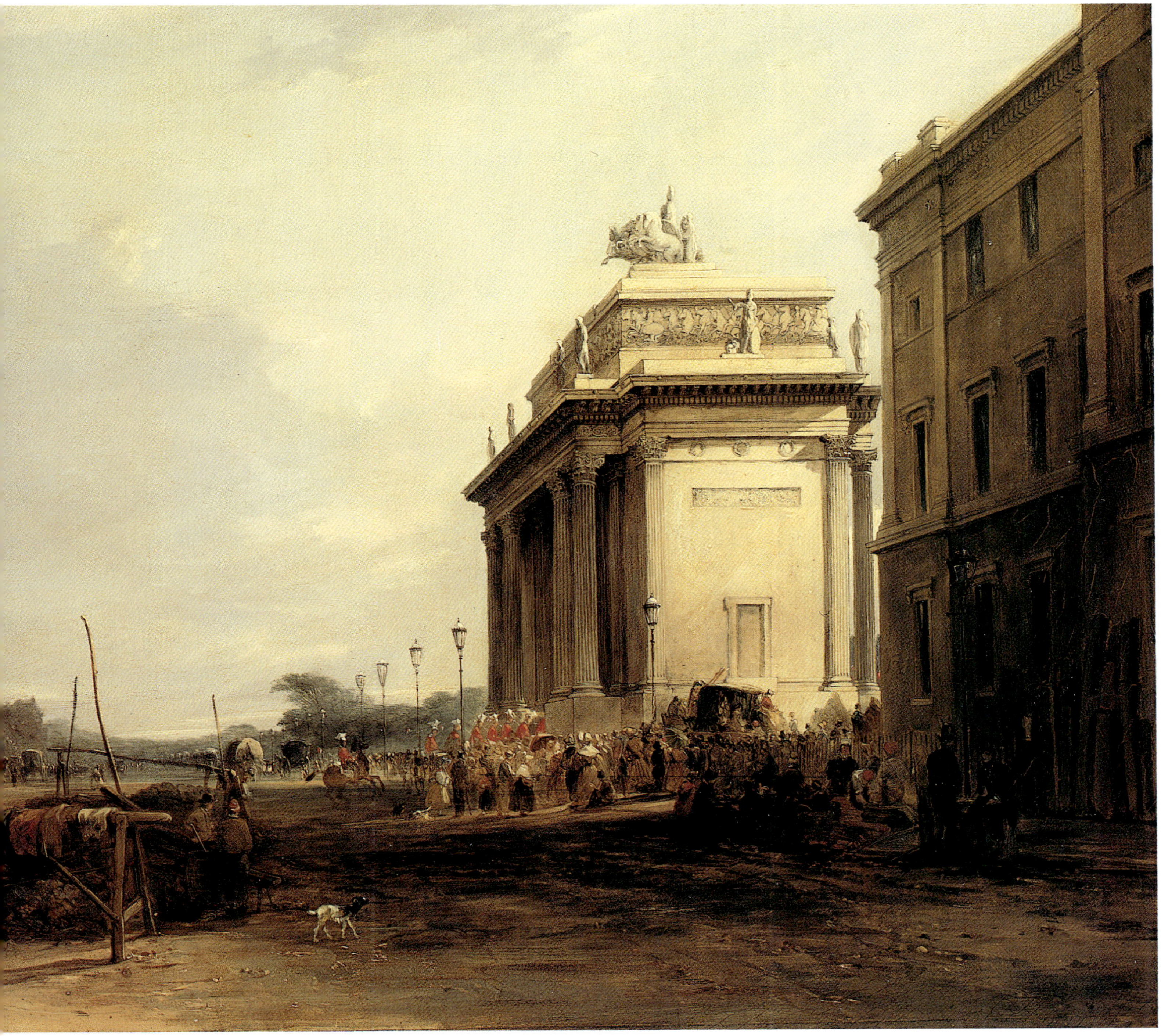

with two footmen on the platform behind, emerging from Hyde Park, a row of wagons in Piccadilly, and a dress chariot passing Constitution Arch.

The costume indicates a date of about 1829–34. The painting was exhibited at the Society of British Artists summer exhibition of 1834 and as family records show, Holland always submitted works he had newly completed. On that basis the painting should be dated 1832 or 1833 (probably the latter). After 1829, when his wife died, Holland interrupted his Continental journey to look after his young family and concentrated on painting London.

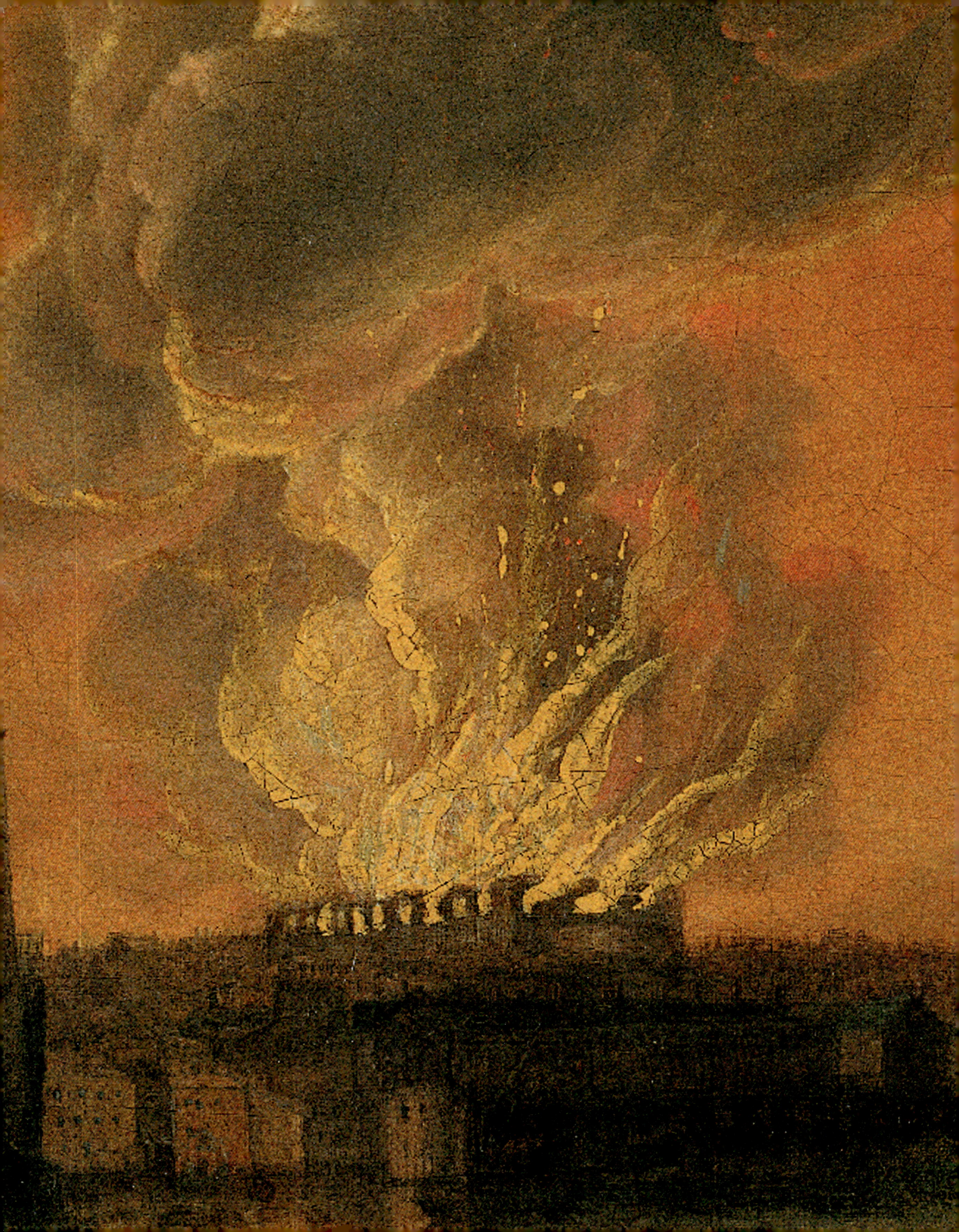

FIRES

THE ROMANTIC revival of interest in fire painting – a genre first imported into this country via London by the seventeenth-century Dutch painters – was already evident in the work of artists such as de Loutherbourg in the late eighteenth century (see pp33 and 182). The paintings grouped together here powerfully attest to the continuing fascination of this subject well into the nineteenth century.

The depiction of fires during the Regency period is not solely attributable to the painters' fancy, but seems to correspond to a real increase in their frequency. Fewer than ten fires are recorded for the whole of the eighteenth century, but for the first half of the nineteenth century the figure jumps to just under 150.[1] The fire services were not then a metropolitan brigade, but organised by the various insurance companies. It was not until 1833 that the ten leading insurance companies joined together to form the London Fire Engine Establishment.

The fire which had by far the greatest consequence for the fabric of the capital was that of the Houses of Parliament in 1834. On the night of Thursday 16 October, a furnace under the House of Lords overheated when burning a quantity of wooden Exchequer tallies, starting a fire that raced through the ancient and for the most part rotten timbers. Fanned by a brisk south-westerly wind, it resulted in the almost total destruction of the historic Palace of Westminster. *The Times* confidently noted:

> there was nothing striking, nothing picturesque in the appearance of the ruins. The devastation was too general and complete to present to the eye of the spectator any of those extraordinary combinations of shattered walls and tottering roofs which sometimes reconcile us by their terrible beauty to the very destruction which has created them.[2]

Yet the 1834 fire and its aftermath was probably the single most depicted event in nineteenth-century London (with the exception perhaps of the Great Exhibition), attracting to the scene a host of engravers, watercolourists and painters, among them Turner and Constable, both of whom recorded the scene.[3] Much attention was lavished on St Stephen's Chapel, the Gothic architecture of which had long been disguised through its use as the House of Commons. The beauty of its ruins struck public attention and there was much debate concerning its possible restoration. The Museum of London holds a remarkable series of large varnished watercolours (making them look like oil paintings), produced by Adam Lee in the 1820s and showing the chapel reconstructed in its full medieval glory.[4]

1. See Arthur Hardwick, *Memorable Fires,* 1926. The Guildhall Art Gallery exhibition catalogue *1666 and other London Fires* (1966) provides a useful survey of fire paintings.
2. Katherine Solender, *Dreadful Fire! Burning of the Houses of Parliament*, exhibition catalogue, Cleveland Museum of Art, 1984, p35.
3. See E. W. Brailey and John Britton, *The History of the Ancient Palace & late Houses of Parliament at Westminster*, 1836.
4. Mireille Galinou, 'Palace on Paper', in *Country Life*, 3 November 1988; full research published in *Transactions of the London and Middlesex Archaeological Society*, vol. 34, 1983.

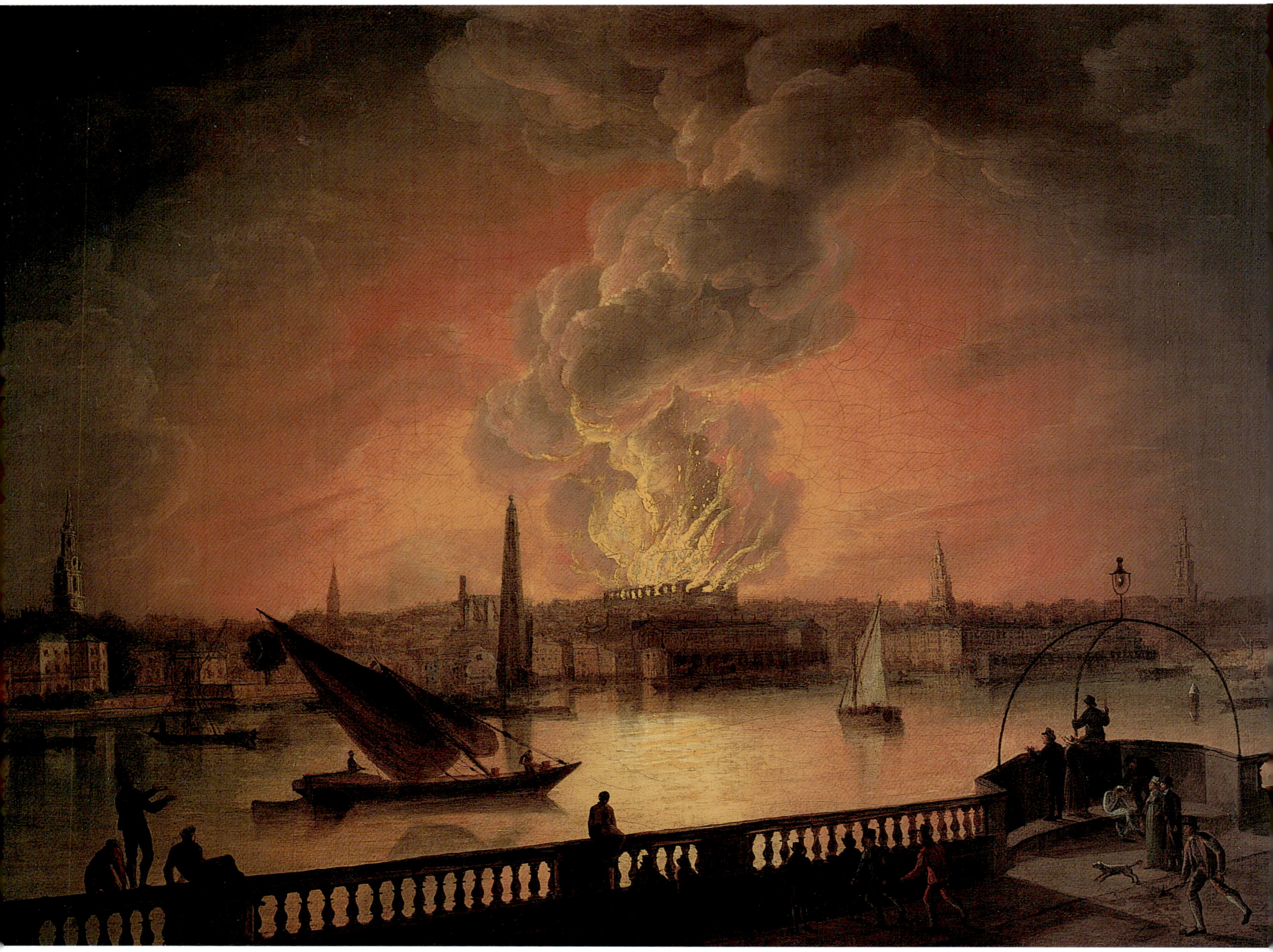

66.

THOMAS LUNY
(1759–1837)

The Burning of Drury Lane Theatre from Westminster Bridge [59.105/1]
*c.*1809
Oil on canvas, 53.4 x 75 cm
Not signed or dated

THE VIEW of the fire is taken from Westminster Bridge, and spectators can be seen in one of the alcoves and on the balustrade, while three firemen equipped with hatchets are also to be seen. In top hats and, respectively, green, red and buff uniforms, they have the badges of their companies on their left arms. The spires of St Martin-in-the-Fields, St Giles-in-the-Fields, St Mary-le-Strand and St Clement Danes, with the tower of the York Buildings Waterworks Company, are seen dominating the skyline, and the long facades of the Royal Terrace, Adelphi and Somerset House are also visible; part of the Lambeth shore appears on the extreme right.

The present Drury Lane theatre, built in 1810–12 by Benjamin Wyatt, is the fourth to stand on the site. The first was destroyed by fire in 1672. Wren's building was pulled down in 1791. And the third, Henry Holland's magnificent theatre, which opened in 1794, was burnt down on the night of 24 February 1809.

Holland's Drury Lane theatre had been constructed primarily of wood, with bricks used only for filling in this framework, so that when the fire started, just after eleven o'clock on a Friday in Lent when there was no performance or rehearsal in progress and the theatre was empty, it took less than a quarter of an hour to engulf the entire building. A vivid impression of the fantastic pillar of fire, and of the glow cast over the whole metropolis, is provided by the Museum picture.

Sebastian Pether also painted a distant view of this fire but taken from Chelsea Waterworks, near the Pumping Station. The painting was with Arthur Ackermann and Peter Johnson Ltd in January 1996.

The view was painted a few years after William Wordsworth composed 'On Westminster Bridge' and it corresponds to the panoramic vista described by the poet in 1802. The extent to which Drury Lane Theatre dominated the skyline of the West End is made explicit both in the painting and the poem:

> Ships, towers, theatres, & temples lie
> Open unto the fields, and to the sky.

A drawing by Whichelo, also taken from Westminster Bridge and giving much the same impression of the blaze, was engraved and published on 7 August 1811 for Wilkinson's *Londina Illustrata*.

The painting formed part of a considerable collection of views of fires, chiefly by Dutch artists, owned by Miss Gertrude Elbourne.

Provenance:
Miss Gertrude Elbourne; Elbourne sale, Christie's, 10 March 1950 (44, without attribution), bt in; purchased from the bookseller/printseller Stanley Crowe in 1959 (cat. 63, no. 121).

Bibliography:
Hayes (cat. no. 71); *London – World City 1800–1840*, Celina Fox (ed.), 1922, p201.

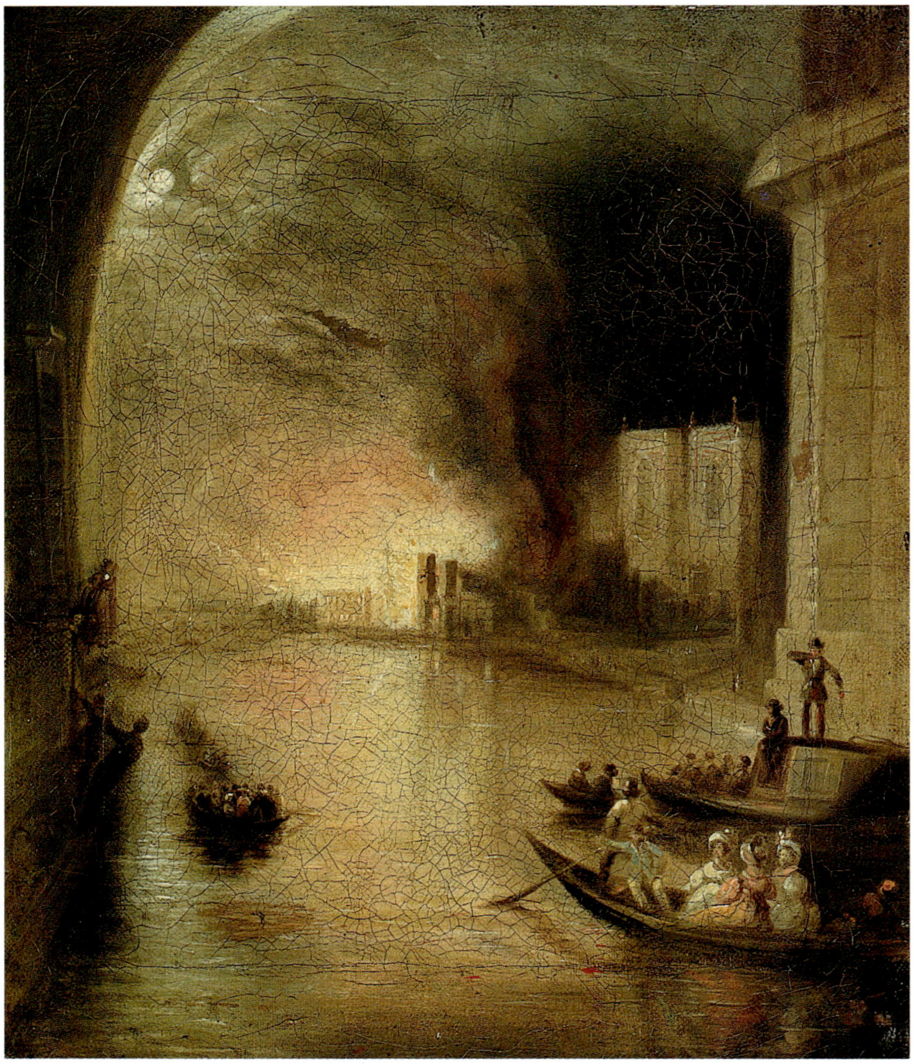

As you approach the bridge you caught a sight through its arches of a motley multitude assembled on the Strand [*sic*] below the speaker's garden, and gazing with intense eager on the progress of the flames . . . As soon as you shot through the bridge, the whole of this melancholy spectacle stood before you. [*The Times*, 17 October 1834, p3]

The composition is related to a (small) number of paintings using the same device of the arch of a bridge, first invented by Canaletto when painting Westminster Bridge. When Philippe Jacques de Loutherbourg produced his late eighteenth-century interpretation of the Great Fire (see p33), he clearly drew inspiration from the Italian master, recirculating the formula for Regency artists. At the same time as it was taken up in grand fashion by Turner (see Solender, 1984, p64), it was also used on two modest paintings by two (or one?) unknown artist(s): the Walters Art Gallery, Baltimore, version on panel (reproduced on p65 of Solender, 1984), and this one.

Provenance:
Purchased from Christie's (sale unrecorded) with the help of the Mackenzie Bell Fund.

Bibliography:
Katherine Solender, *Dreadful Fire! Burning of the Houses of Parliament*, exhibition catalogue, Cleveland Museum of Art, 1984, pp63–5.

67.

BRITISH SCHOOL

The Palace of Westminster on Fire [69.19]
1834
Oil on canvas, 35.2 x 30.1 cm
Not signed or dated

THE SCENE is depicted at night-time from a boat on the Thames looking through the first arch of Westminster Bridge to the blaze of the Palace of Westminster. The two square towers on the right are those of the western facade of Westminster Abbey. The work is of interest for its atmospheric rendering of the scene rather than for its detail or accuracy.

68.

THOMAS LUNY

(1759–1837)

Westminster Bridge and the Burning of the Houses of Parliament from Lambeth

[A 8072]

1835

Oil on canvas, 50.6 x 67.8 cm

Signed and dated bottom left: *T Luny 1835*

THIS IS another impression of the fire which destroyed most of the Palace of Westminster during the night of 16 October 1834. The strong south-westerly wind which fanned the flames is very evident, billowing the smoke over Westminster. The buildings destroyed by the blaze, and some of the spectators who watched the scene from boats on the river, are seen through the arches of Westminster Bridge. To the right are Westminster Hall and Westminster Abbey, both untouched by the flames, and the blocks of houses at the south end of Bridge Street, which were built as part of the Westminster Bridge improvements scheme following the Act of 1736; the Bridge itself, over which coaches are shown passing, was replaced twenty years after this picture was painted. In the foreground is the Lambeth shore.

Since Luny retired to Teignmouth in 1810, and suffered from a paralysis of the legs which obliged him to use a wheelchair, it is extremely unlikely that he was actually an eye-witness of the event. The painting could easily have been executed from images depicting this stretch of the river (see, for instance, cat. no. 28), slightly adapted to show the fire, well hidden behind the arches of the bridge.

Provenance:
Revd Anson Cartwright, Brimley House, Teignmouth in 1887 (presumably by descent from his grandfather, William Cartwright, who was Luny's executor); purchased from Leggatt Brothers in 1912.

Bibliography:
Hayes (cat. no. 72).

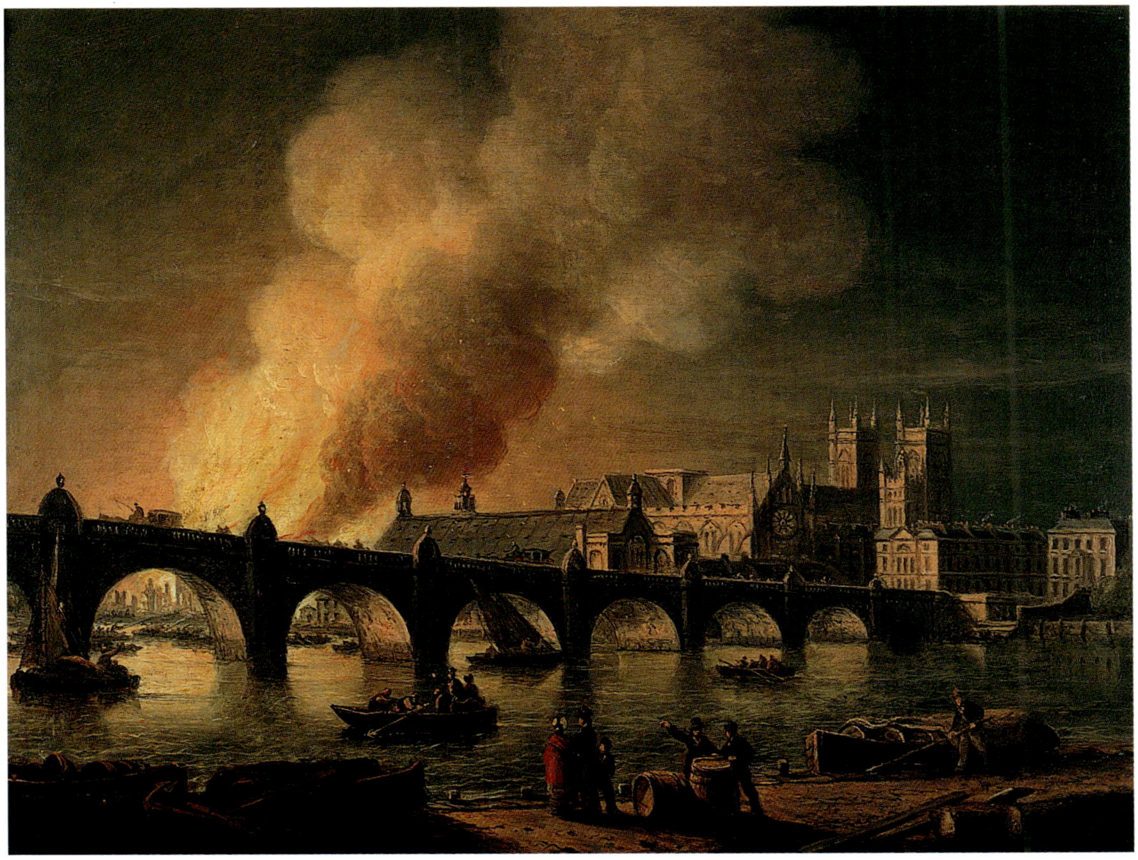

Provenance:
Purchased out of the Joicey Trust Fund from Oscar and Peter Johnson in 1963 (without attribution).

Bibliography:
Hayes (cat. no. 97); Katherine Solender, *Dreadful Fire! Burning of the Houses of Parliament*, exhibition catalogue, Cleveland Museum of Art, 1984, pp36 and 39; Helen Guiterman and Briony Llewelyn, *David Roberts*, exhibition catalogue, Barbican Art Gallery, 1986.

69.

BRITISH SCHOOL

The Palace of Westminster from the River after the Fire of 1834 [63.61]
*c.*1834
Oil on canvas, 48.2 x 68.7 cm
Not signed or dated

CROWDS CAME from all over London to watch the blaze on the night of Thursday 16 October 1834. In this picture several boats full of spectators are shown in the foreground, with two artists standing up sketching in one of them.

This view was similarly taken from a boat on the river and shows the still smouldering buildings, from left to right, a modern block containing Parliamentary offices, the thirteenth-century Painted Chamber, the Library of the House of Commons, the residence of the Clerk of the House of Commons, St Stephen's Chapel (built between 1292 and 1348, and since the mid-sixteenth century the meeting place of the House of Commons), and the Speaker's residence. All these buildings were almost completely destroyed. Behind are seen Westminster Abbey and Westminster Hall, fortunately saved from the flames.

This work was previously attributed to David Roberts but Helen Guiterman firmly de-attributed it on stylistic grounds.

A signed and dated version of the Museum picture, by David Roberts, which is rather more generalised, and differs in the boats and figures, is in the possession of the Chartered Insurance Institute (in the care of the Guildhall Art Gallery); two other unsigned versions are owned by Sir Harry Legge-Bourke and the collection of the Palace of Westminster.

A view of the new Houses of Parliament painted by John Anderson is also in the collection (see cat. no. 78).

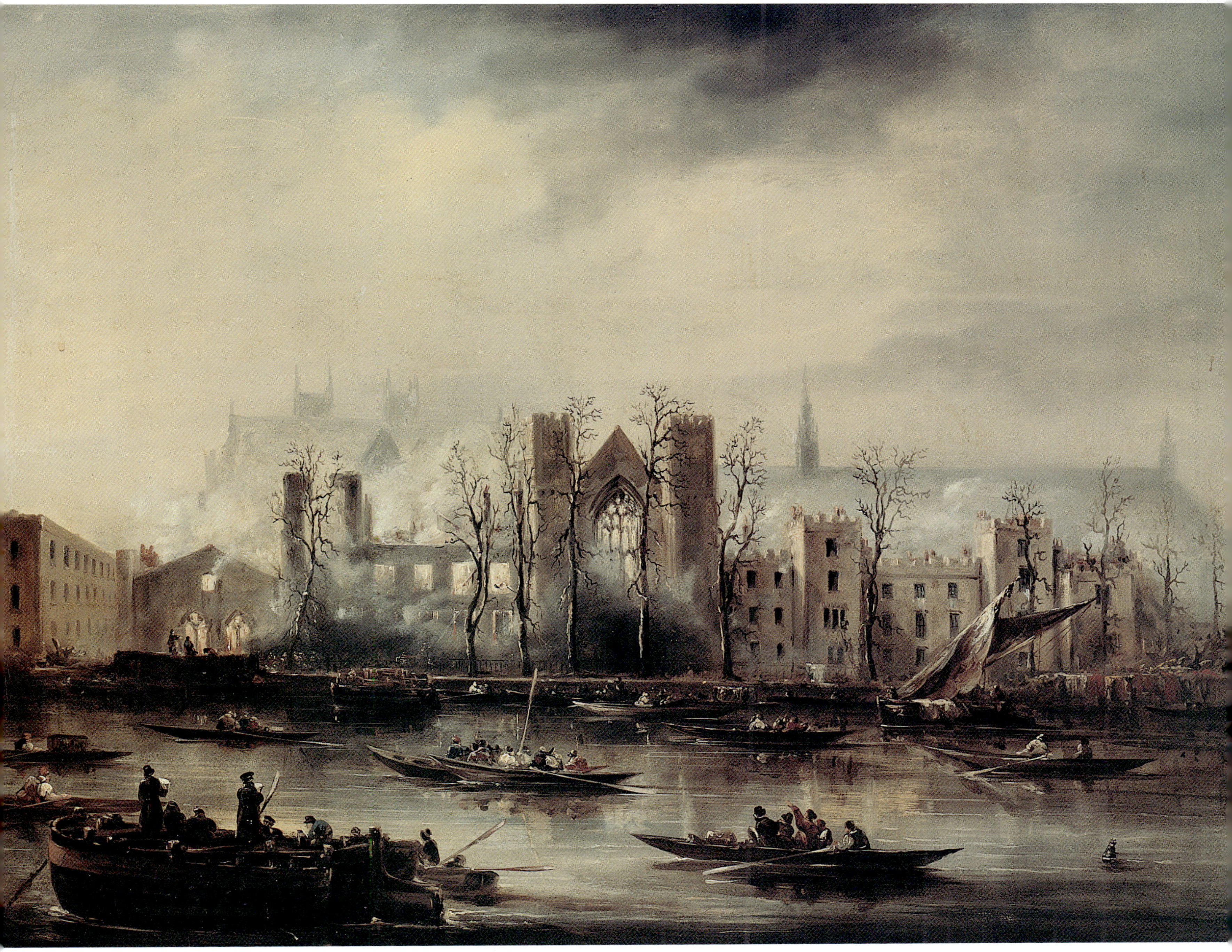

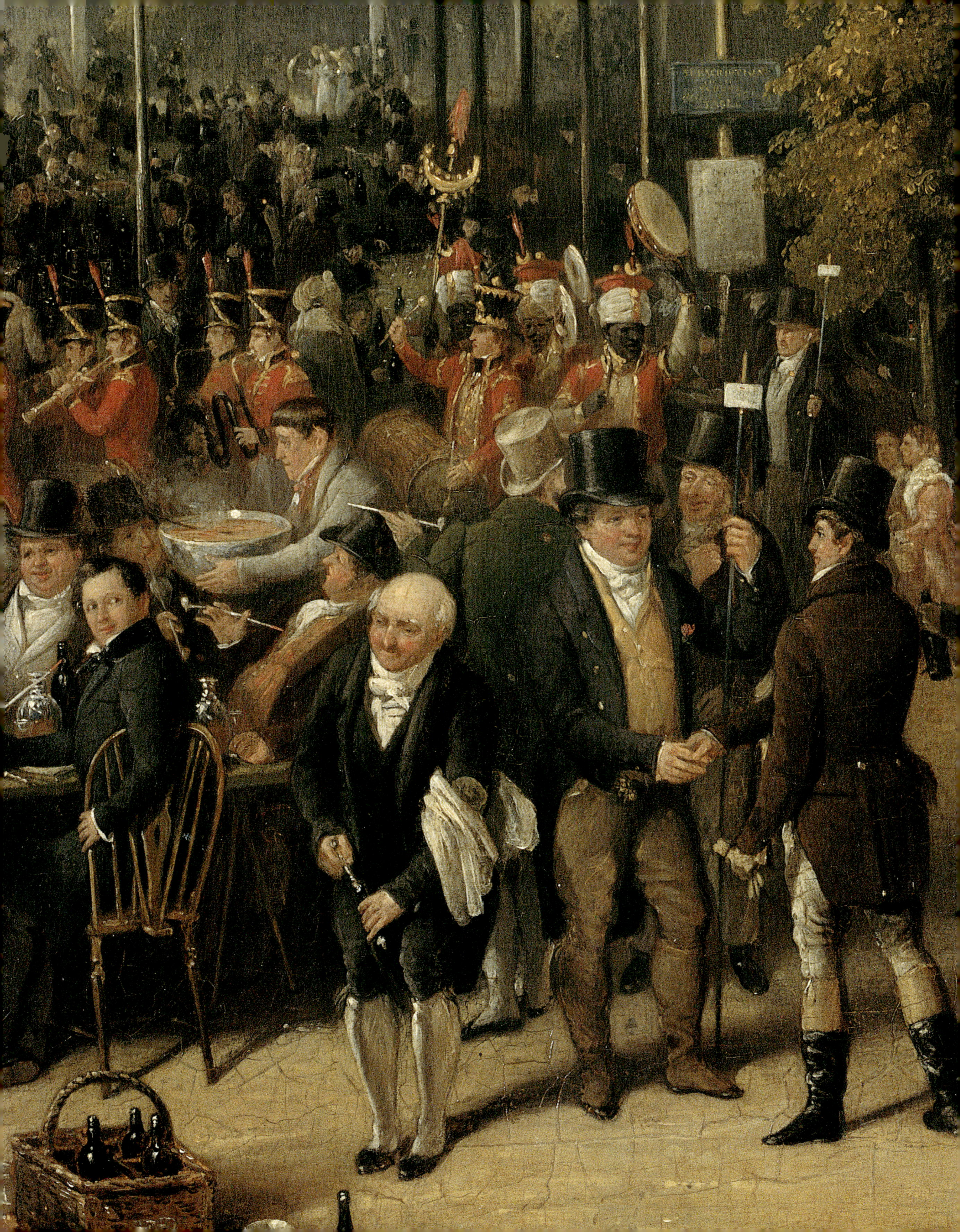

THE SOCIAL SCENE

THE PRINCE Regent played a conspicuous role in stimulating the social and artistic scenes of the early nineteenth century. Besides the great Brighton works (not directly relevant in this context) and the transformation of London's West End (discussed on p167), the Regent staged his coronation as George IV in 1821 almost as 'performance art', weaving together costume, food and pageantry on an unprecedented scale.[1] For the first time, the coronation banquet was recorded in painting (cat. no. 70).

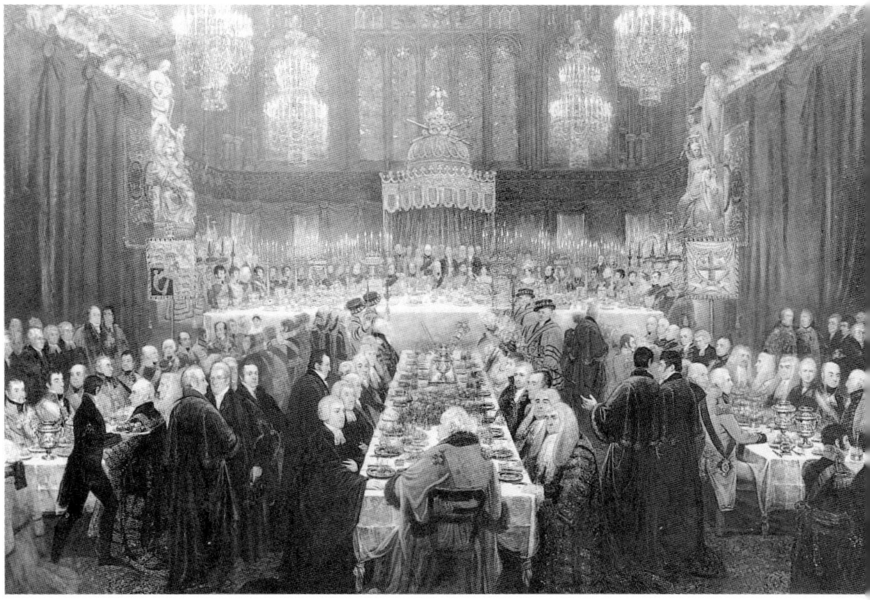

Luke Clennell (1781–1840)
Banquet given by the Corporation to the Prince Regent, the Emperor of Russia and the King of Prussia, 18 June 1814
Oil on canvas
Guildhall Art Gallery, Corporation of London.

The presence in this modest section of no less than two banquet scenes (cat. nos 70 and 74) is not accidental. The increase in public dining and the trend for recording it seems connected with the Regent[2] and the first banquet to be painted, before that of the 1821 coronation, was attended by the future George IV. Luke Clennell magnificently recorded *The Allied Sovereigns Banquet at Guildhall, 18 June 1814* (illustrated). He may have started the painting speculatively but it seems that soon after he won a premium for *The Overthrow of the French Army at Waterloo*, the 7th Earl of Bridgewater formally commissioned the painting from Clennell.[3] The occasion was exceptionally lavish and the banquet was entirely served from gold and silver plates, with the help of loans from the major Livery Companies and private individuals. The Common Council Minutes of the Corporation of London stress the central role played by the Regent, who 'as soon as he entered the Hall, pronounced it the most beautiful and magnificent spectacle he had ever seen'.[4] When working on his painting, Clennell suffered a mental breakdown from which he never recovered; nevertheless he was making history by placing on the painter's agenda a subject traditionally tackled only in prints and drawings. The Guildhall scene was unparalleled in sumptuousness, but in keeping with tradition the Corporation commissioned only a 'perspective sketch' of this extraordinary occasion and we probably owe Clennell's outstanding record to the fact that before turning his attention to the world of oil painting, he had been an engraver and watercolourist.

However, there clearly was a proliferation of social events featuring food from the late eighteenth century onwards. For example, the opening in 1768 of the London Tavern (see cat. no. 127) in Bishopsgate Street, which inspired the opening in Paris of La Grande Taverne de Londres, is well documented.[5] There, good dining was first associated with the radical politics of John Wilkes and later with the nearby East India Company, which used the tavern for their hospitality until 1834. The early years of the nineteenth century saw the rise of the importance of dining as an expression of public life, but it was not fully described until the 1850s with George A. Sala's 'A Charity Dinner'.[6] The London Tavern itself was only briefly discussed by Sala, but it was specially featured in 1851 in Dickens's weekly journal *Household Words*, where the tavern's dual public role was made explicit: 'the division of its day is less into morning, noon and night, than into Meetings and Dinners'. We should not leave the subject of banquet painting without mentioning Benjamin Robert Haydon's

The Reform Banquet,[7] painted in 1832–4 and also held in the Guildhall. Although the work 'retains considerable documentary value', it compares unfavourably with Clennell's painting, where the compositional formula is genuinely superior.

Another theme – work – emerged from the painter's brush in this period. In James Holland's painting of Hyde Park Corner (see cat. no. 65), the artist was moved to record not solely the birth of a London landmark (Constitution Arch) but also the *making* of a grand architectural scheme, with workmen and their apparatus forming part of the scene. While in the previous century Canaletto was anxious to present Westminster Bridge in its finished glory, even when the work was as yet incomplete, the celebration of London's 'improvements' in the Regency period became more spontaneous and artists seemed prepared to depict construction in progress. George Scharf's patient recording of the capital's seemingly endless works can be cited as a precedent, but his output again belongs to the freer world of drawings and prints.

Théodore Géricault
(1791–1824)
Public Hanging, *c.*1820
Pencil and wash drawing
By kind permission of the Musée des Beaux Arts in Rouen.

Anonymous
Pillory Scene at Charing Cross, 1820s
Oil on canvas
With Lane Fine Art, London, in 1992 Reproduced by courtesy of Sotheby's.

A host of paintings thus started dealing with the theme of work and workmen, from John Linnell's gravel pits,[8] to the brewery scenes of George Garrard and Dean Wolstenholme (see cat. no. 75), the timber sawyers and brickmakers of Luke Clennell[9] and the carpenter's shop of John Hill.[10]

This sudden concern among artists with what had been a hidden side of life in the metropolis may again be connected with the influence of Dutch and Flemish painting. By rediscovering the seventeenth-century Old Masters (see 'The River', pp145–6), painters were renewing interest in one of the great exponents of the golden age: genre painting, which had found poetry and beauty in the humble and the modest. This presumably led David Wilkie, John Linnell, William Mulready and others to create for Britain a contemporary genre painting, often based on rural subjects but also adaptable to urban ones, as is demonstrated in some of the paintings included here.

Significantly for this period the French artist Géricault singled out for representation the theme of work when he visited London between April 1820 and December 1821 (his passion for horses made him focus on coalmen). He also reflected a growing preoccupation with crime: his poignant lithograph of 'An Execution' must be the most powerful image ever produced on the subject in London.[11] In 1820, shortly before Géricault's arrival, the judicial system had come under an unusual amount of scrutiny. Apart from the unpopularity of the trial of Queen Caroline in that year, Lord Mayor Thorp was forced to intervene on behalf of seventeen counterfeiters wrongly condemned to death (see the commemorative watercolour in the Museum's collection, acc. no. 86.167). Furthermore, the Cato Street conspiracy of 23 February, which allegedly planned to assassinate the whole British cabinet, led to the execution at Newgate of five of the eleven men tried, despite the absence of concrete proof. Géricault's drawing of an execution (illustrated) may represent this event.[12] A contemporary painting showing a pillory scene at Charing Cross[13] (illustrated) should also be mentioned in this context, although the precise event cannot be identified. It reinforces, along with the record of the execution of Lord Fauntleroy in 1824 (see cat. no. 72), the renewed interest in crime and punishment which is notable at this time.

Perhaps the emergence of a co-ordinated police force in 1829, largely created by Sir Robert Peel to replace the inefficient nightwatchmen, acted as a calming influence on the growing fears of miscarriages of justice. After that date the treatment of crime and punishment no longer appears challenging to the authorities and is gradually replaced on the artists' agenda by the theme of poverty, which J. T. Smith and Géricault had so movingly anticipated in their prints of the London Poor.[14]

For a more complete picture of social life in London during the Regency period, readers are referred to the popular series *Life in London* and other satellite publications of the 1820s.[15] Their heroes, Tom and Jerry or Dashall and Lubin or Bob and Tom, move with ease from the refined atmosphere of a Somerset House exhibition, a levee at Carlton House or a political dinner, to the world of theatre, low-life taverns and even prisons. But the colourful scenes found in these books were not on the whole translated into oil paintings.

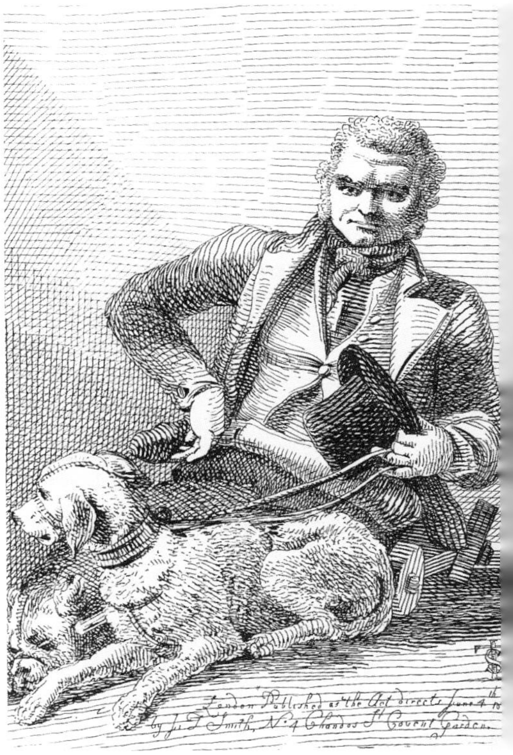

John Thomas Smith
(1766–1833)
John MacNally
Etching published in
Vagabondiana, Plate 14, 1817
Museum of London.

1. Valerie Cumming, 'Pantomime and Pageantry: The coronation of George IV', in *London – World City 1800–1840*, Celina Fox (ed.), 1992.
2. Both the Prince Regent and Lord Stewart, the British Ambassador in Vienna, promoted the work of one of Europe's greatest cooks, Antonin Carême, who worked for the Prince between 1816 and 1818 and for Lord Stewart in London in 1819 and 1820, thus setting the highest standards for gastronomy and food presentation. Further attempts to secure the services of Carême, by Lord Granville in 1823 and by George IV in 1826, were turned down (*L'art culinaire au XIXème siècle, Antonin Carême*, exhibition catalogue, Orangerie de Bagatelle, Paris, 1984).
3. Vivien Knight, 'Luke Clennell at the Guildhall', in *Apollo*, October 1993.
4. Ibid, p238.
5. John Farley, *The London Art of Cookery*, first published in 1783, new edition 1988, Ann Haly (ed.); see introduction by Stephen Medcalf.
6. In G. A. Sala, *Twice Round the Clock*, 1859.
7. Celina Fox (ed.), 1992, cat. no. 647.
8. Celina Fox, *Londoners*, 1987, pp174 and 262.
9. Ibid, pp175 and 262.
10. Ibid, pp123 and 260.
11. Ibid, pp200–21, 211 and 263.
12. Ibid, pp201 and 263.
13. Anonymous. With Lane Fine Art in 1992.
14. See J. T. Smith's *Vagabondiana*, 1817 and Celina Fox, 'Gericault's Lithographs of the London Poor', in *Print Quarterly*, vol. V, 1988, pp62–6.
15. See Celina Fox (ed.), 1992, cat. no. 671.

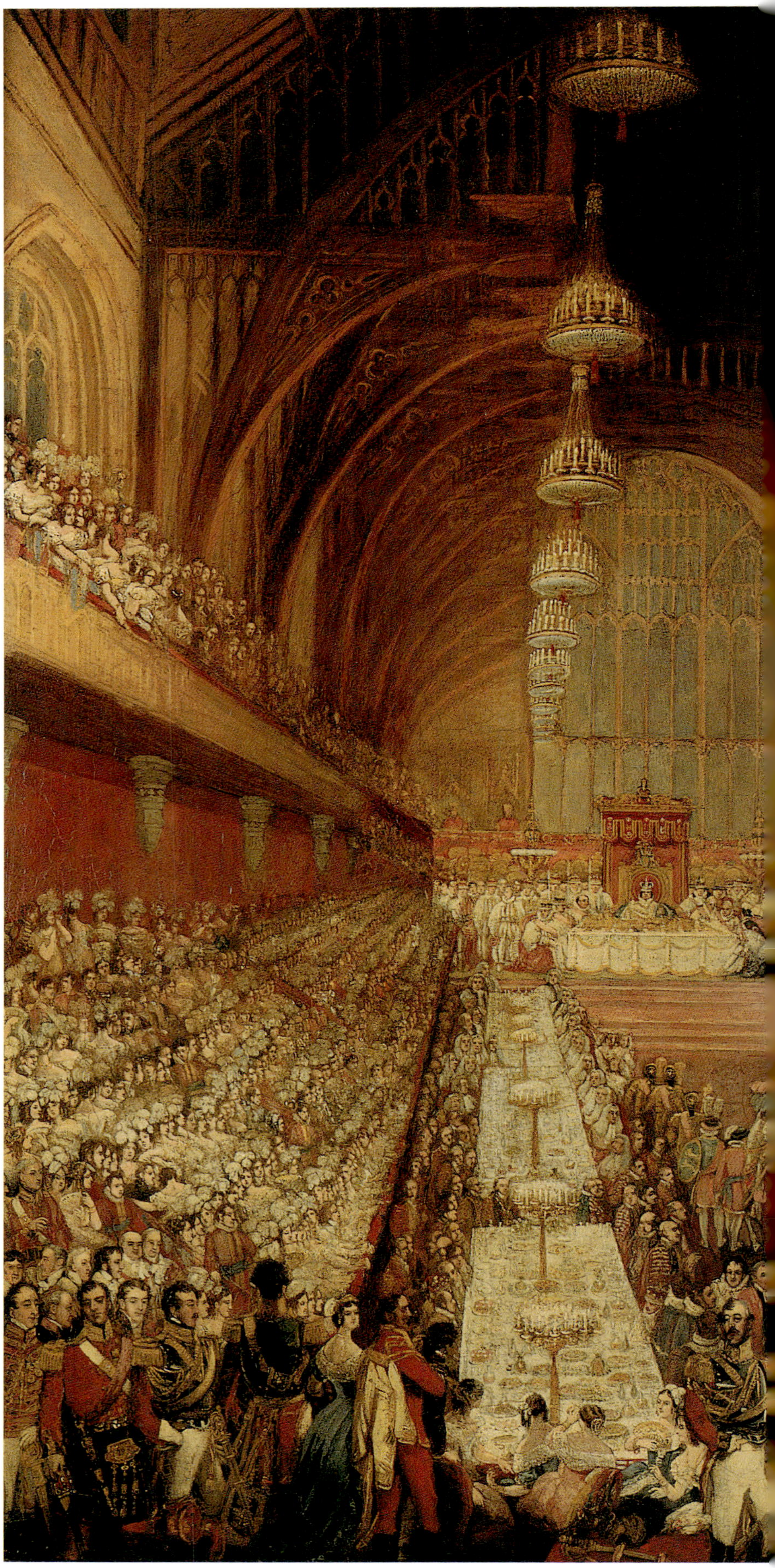

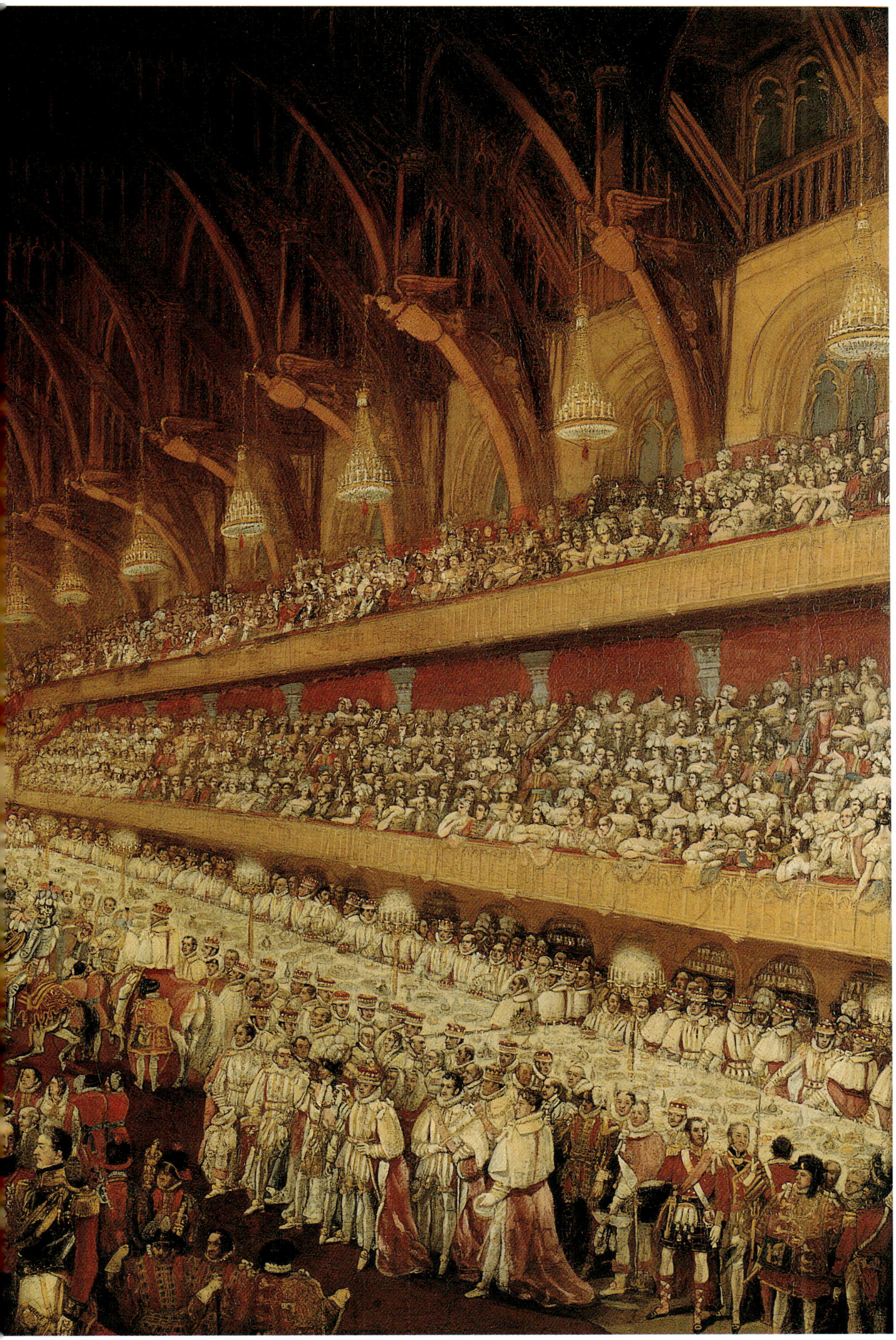

70.

BRITISH SCHOOL

The Coronation Banquet of George IV in Westminster Hall
[38.292]
1821
Oil on canvas,
99.8 x 124.5 cm
Not signed or dated

Provenance:
Presented by Bernard, 8th Earl of Granard in 1938.

Bibliography:
Hayes (cat. no. 23); Oliver Millar, *The Later Georgian Pictures in the Collection of Her Majesty the Queen*, 1969, no. 867; Valerie Cumming, 'Pantomime and Pageantry: The coronation of George IV', in *London – World City 1800–1840*, Celina Fox (ed.), 1992 and cat. no. 38.

THE CORONATION ceremony was, until 1821, customarily followed by a banquet in Westminster Hall, attended by the nobility and gentry. Between the first and second courses, the King's Champion, in full armour and on horseback, approached and challenged any comer to deny the King's right to the Crown; his fee was the armour and horse with which he was provided, and a bowl of wine proffered by the sovereign. By tradition, the office of Champion was vested in the Dymoke family, Lords of the Manor of Scrivelsby, and in this picture Henry Dymoke, deputising for his father, who was a clergyman, is seen riding up the hall between the Deputy Earl Marshal (Lord Howard of Effingham) and the Lord High Constable (the Duke of Wellington). A horse was hired from Astley's Circus for reliable docility during this performance. This was the last occasion upon which the ceremony of the challenge was performed.

The two rows of tables on either side of the Hall were occupied by the peers. The peeresses and gentry were seated in the two tiers above, and did not partake of the banquet itself. At the far end of the Hall sat the King, still wearing the Crown. The coronation of George IV was one of the most lavish and extravagant ever known, and cost approximately a quarter of a million pounds; the expenses of the banquet alone were more than twenty-five thousand pounds. Masterminding the feast from twenty-three kitchens, Jean Baptiste Watier produced 160 tureens of soup, similar quantities of fish, roast venison, beef, mutton, veal and vegetables, as well as 480 sauce boats. Some 9,840 bottles of wine and 100 gallons of iced punch were consumed and cold dishes (hams, pasties, seafood, jellies, etc) numbered 3,271. William IV made radical economies in 1831.

George Jones (1786–1869) also painted the coronation banquet (Royal Collection) and a watercolour by Denis Dighton showing Henry Dymoke in the act of issuing his challenge is in the Royal Library, Windsor Castle.

The Museum possesses the suit of Greenwich armour worn and retained by John Dymoke as King's Champion at the coronation of George III (34.121).

71.

BRITISH SCHOOL

Glassblower [80.547/1007]
1820s
Oil on canvas, 54.2 x 43.2 cm
Not signed or dated

THIS WHITEFRIARS glassblower is seated on a glassblower's 'chair' and is shaping the foot of a wineglass with tongs. By his side are an assortment of callipers and a box filled with glass products (the two ring decanters may be dated 1820s/30s) which the craftsman is using for guidance as models. Once a piece of glass was finished it would normally be placed in the annealing furnace.

The craftsman is wearing ordinary clothes which may be dated between 1800 and 1830. The heat in the glass factory is so intense that his clothing is reduced to a shirt and knee breeches, offering a rare opportunity to observe at close quarters the style of the shirt with its dropped shoulder line, its fullness and its neck fastening. The worker is wearing a leather cuff or wristlet to protect him from broken or hot glass. Despite the primitive technique, the unknown artist has rendered well the different tonalities of the worker's skin.

This is probably the earliest British painting of a glassblower. Until 1923 the Whitefriars glassworks was situated between Fleet Street and the Thames, on part of the site of the medieval Whitefriars Priory, after which they moved to Tudor Road, Wealdstone, Harrow. The glassworks, which closed in 1980, had been in operation since around 1700 (the two louvred roofs of the glasshouses are visible on Buck's engraved panorama of the Thames published in 1749) and were bought by the Powell family in 1834. Five further paintings of the Whitefriars works (dating from the 1920s) by the artist Edgar Seligman are also in the collection (see cat. no. 163 and Appendix). The Museum's Whitefriars Archive also includes images, design books, business records and glass, acquired from the Whitefriars glassworks in 1980 when their Harrow business closed.

Provenance:
From the Museum's Whitefriars Archive. Partly purchased with the aid of a grant from the Science Museum and partly a gift from the post-war business owners, Messrs Zeal.

Bibliography:
Celina Fox, *Londoners*, pp121 and 252 (note 31); George Dodd, *Days at the Factory*, 1843 pp256–78; Wendy Evans, Catherine Ross and Alex Werner, *Whitefriars Glass*, Museum of London, 1995.

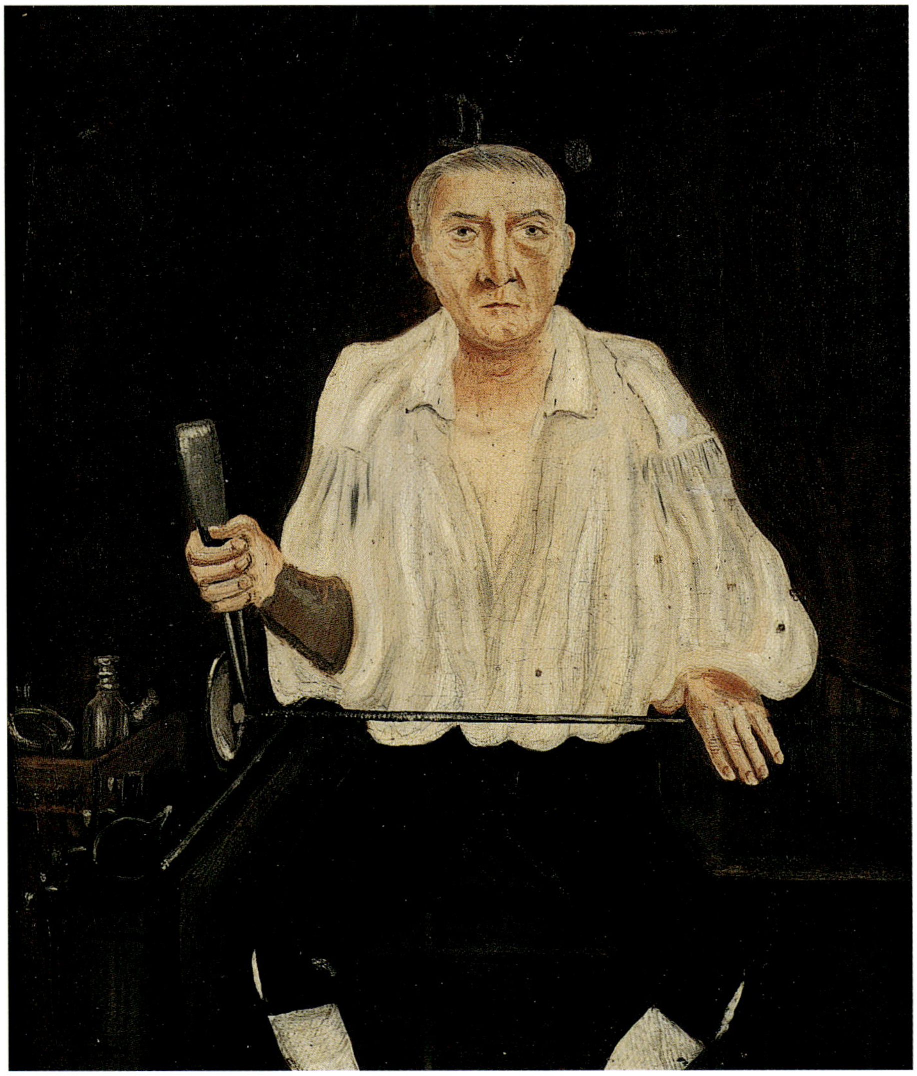

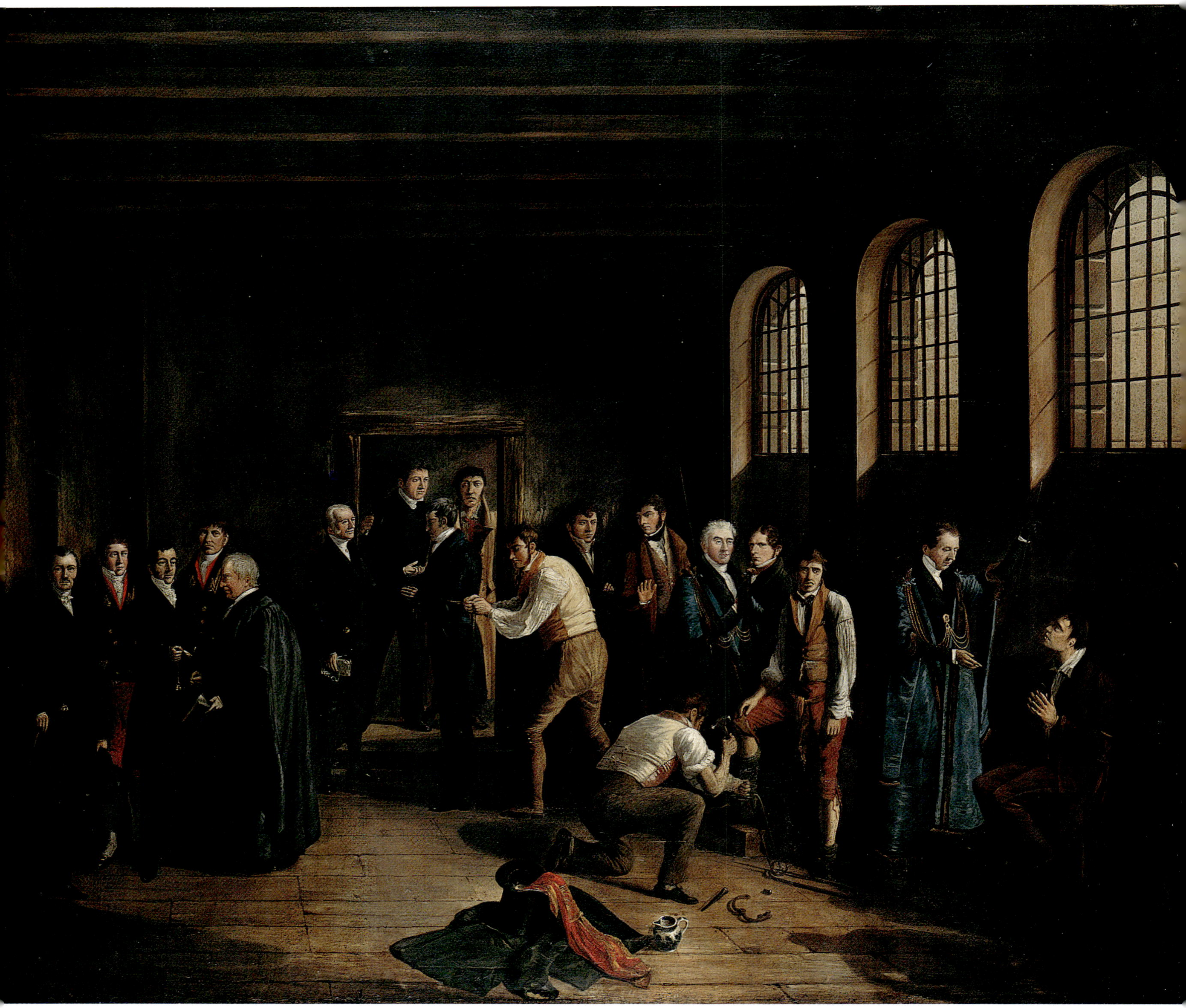

72.

W. THOMSON

(active early nineteenth century)

The Upper Condemned Cell at Newgate Prison on the Morning of the Execution of Henry Fauntleroy [A 28580]

1828

Oil on canvas, 101.9 x 127.6 cm

Signed and dated (on the chair) bottom right: *W. Thomson 1828*

HENRY FAUNTLEROY (1785–1824), a partner in the banking firm of Marsh, Sibbald and Company, was convicted of forgery in 1824 and condemned to death. Fauntleroy, while pleading guilty, declared that his actions had been forced upon him by the instability of the bank's position, and that all the sums he had raised had been used solely to improve its credit. His case aroused a great deal of sympathy, and it was said that over 100,000 people witnessed the execution on the morning of 30 November 1824.

In the scene shown here, Fauntleroy is depicted in the upper condemned cell at Newgate Prison, preparing to leave for his execution. He is seen framed against the doorway, with the executioner in the act of tying his hands. Another condemned prisoner is having his shackles removed prior to execution, and a third, with his hands already tied, is seated on the right. Among the other persons present who can be identified are the Ordinary of Newgate, the Revd Mr Cotton, fifth from the left; two friends of Fauntleroy's, the Revd Mr Springett and the Revd Mr Baker, who accompanied him to the scaffold (the former had sat with him all night), sixth and seventh from the left; Harris, the turnkey, who had been very kind to the prisoner, ninth from the left; and the Sheriffs of the City of London, Peter Laurie and G. Byrom Whittaker, third and sixth from the right respectively, who arrived at 7.45 am.

A painting by Thomson in the same genre, representing the last three pirates to be hanged receiving the death sentence from Sheriff Kelly and signed and dated 1827, was in the possession of F. W. Wheeler in 1919. In the Guildhall Library there is a print showing 'Condemned Criminals Receiving the Sacrament' and the following information is etched on to the plate: 'etching by a Prisoner – W. T. – Newgate 1828'. The composition is reminiscent of this painting and the year matches our painting too. Could W. Thomson have been a prisoner in Newgate?

Provenance:
Purchased from G. Harmsworth and Co. in 1914.

Bibliography:
Hayes (cat. no. 103); Celina Fox, *Londoners*, 1987, p212; *Turner's edition, A faithful and copious report of the Trial of H. Fauntleroy for forgery in the Bank of England*, 1824 (copy of pamphlet in Guildhall Library).

73.
WILLIAM KIDD
(1790–1863)

The Fish Stall [94.239]
*c.*1827–31
Oil on canvas, 30.5 x 25.2 cm
Not signed or dated
Labels on the back:
1. Stobo/Brook Lodge/Newton/Sudbury, Suffolk
2. . . .? Stall/by/David Wilkie BO

Provenance:
Phillips, 30 January 1987; Bourne Fine Art (Edinburgh); Private Collector; Bill Nimms (Farnham dealer); Bourne Gallery (Reigate, Surrey); purchased by the Museum in 1994.

Bibliography:
Masters of Seventeenth-century Dutch Painting, exhibition catalogue, Royal Academy, 1984, no. 92.

THE PAINTING shows a fish stall run by a young woman. The stall, a wooden table with a lead cover, is placed outside dark, unlit street-level premises. Inside may be seen, from left to right, a barrel, a water pump and a staircase lit by natural light. The fish lady stands in the street opening and is about to clean or cut a codfish. The following are depicted on the table, from left to right: two female crabs, eels, a piece of salmon, a boiled lobster, whiting, a gurnard (not very popular now), two or three haddock, a barrel of oysters and a basket of mussels. Hanging on the wall are smoked sprats at the top and saltfish (dried salt cod, consumed during Lent and sometimes at Christmas). The catch from the North Sea has not altered much over the centuries and all these fish may still be obtained from fishmongers today.

The bill stickers on the left associate the painting not only with London, but more specifically with Billingsgate, the site of the City's fish market. The larger one at the top reads:

REWARD OF. . .UINAS. . . (=GUINEAS)
We. . .n Wills (not identified)

The smaller one underneath reads:

BILLINGSGATE
BY ORDER
??
LORD MAYOR

Paintings of fishmarkets and fishmongers first appeared in the Netherlands in the 1560s, when they featured in the work of Joachim Bueckelaer. In seventeenth-century Holland such scenes were principally depicted by Hendrick Sorgh, Emanuel de Witte, Jan Steen and Adrian van Ostade. The Rijksmuseum painting of *The Fishwife* by van Ostade makes an interesting comparison with this work: the woman's gaze at the artist, her posture – ready, knife in hand, to scale or cut a large fish – are all features adopted in the painting under review. However, the Kidd work adopts a different compositional formula, substituting the rear of a shop for the street/village perspective. Yet the general formula unmistakably derives from seventeenth-century Dutch paintings which were rediscovered in London at the beginning of the nineteenth century.

The Fish Stall is very much of its time. The costume of the fish lady may be dated 1827–31, based on the style of the hair and cap, the fullness of the shoulder line and the width of the waist.

A label on the back indicates that the painting was once believed to be the work of David Wilkie. It has since been re-attributed to William Kidd and is close in subject to such paintings as *Fisher Folk* and *Bartering Fish.*

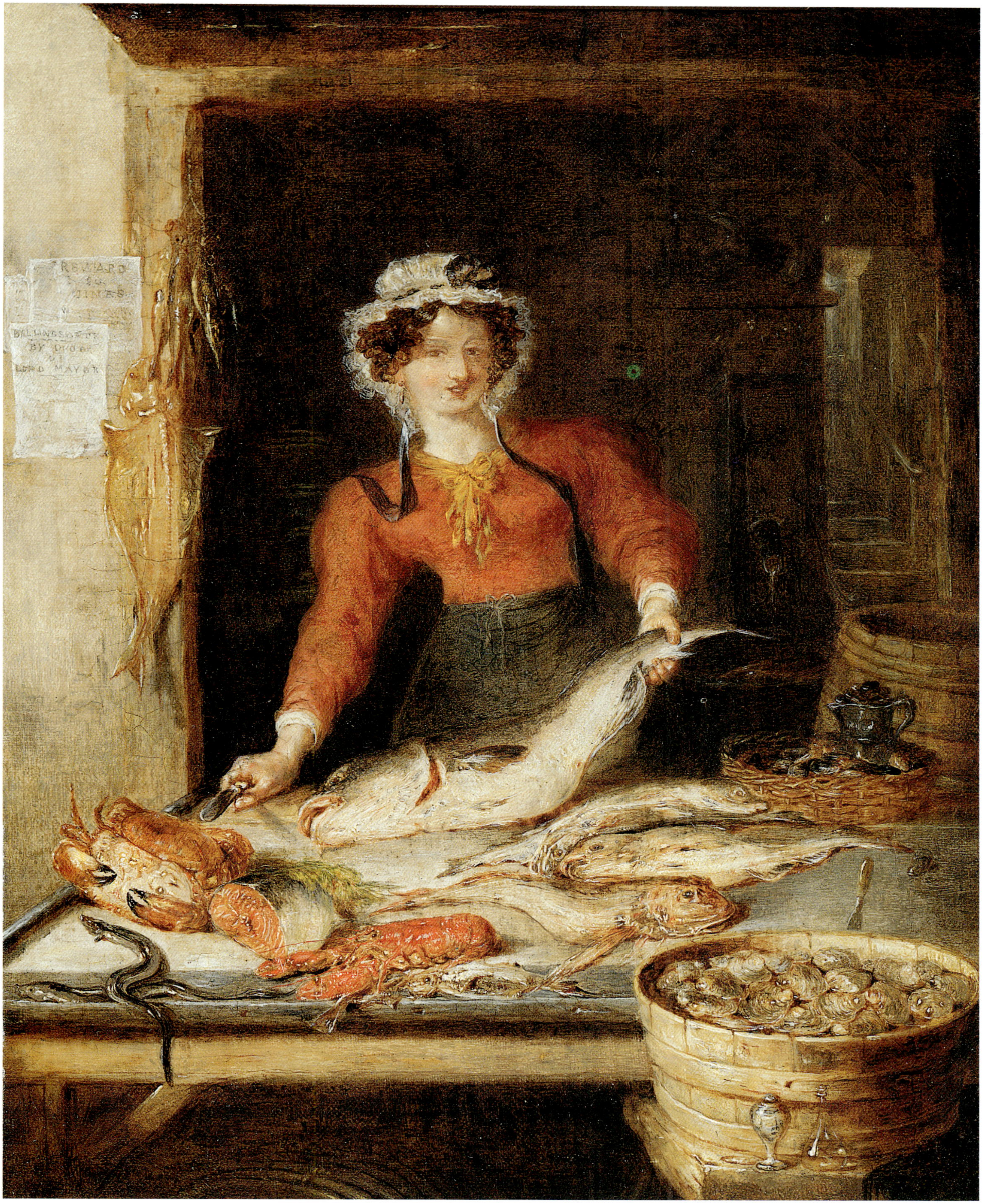
REWARD

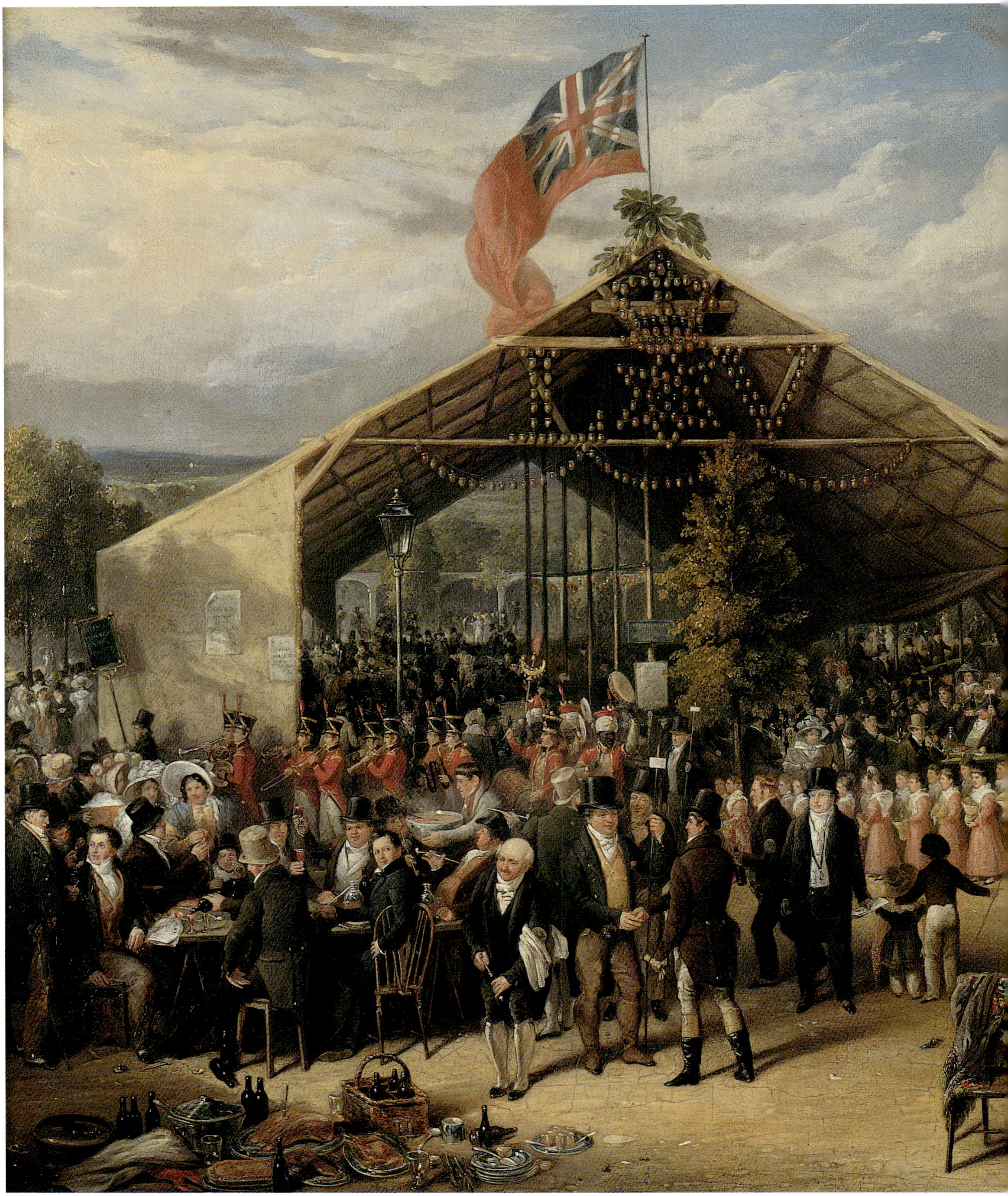

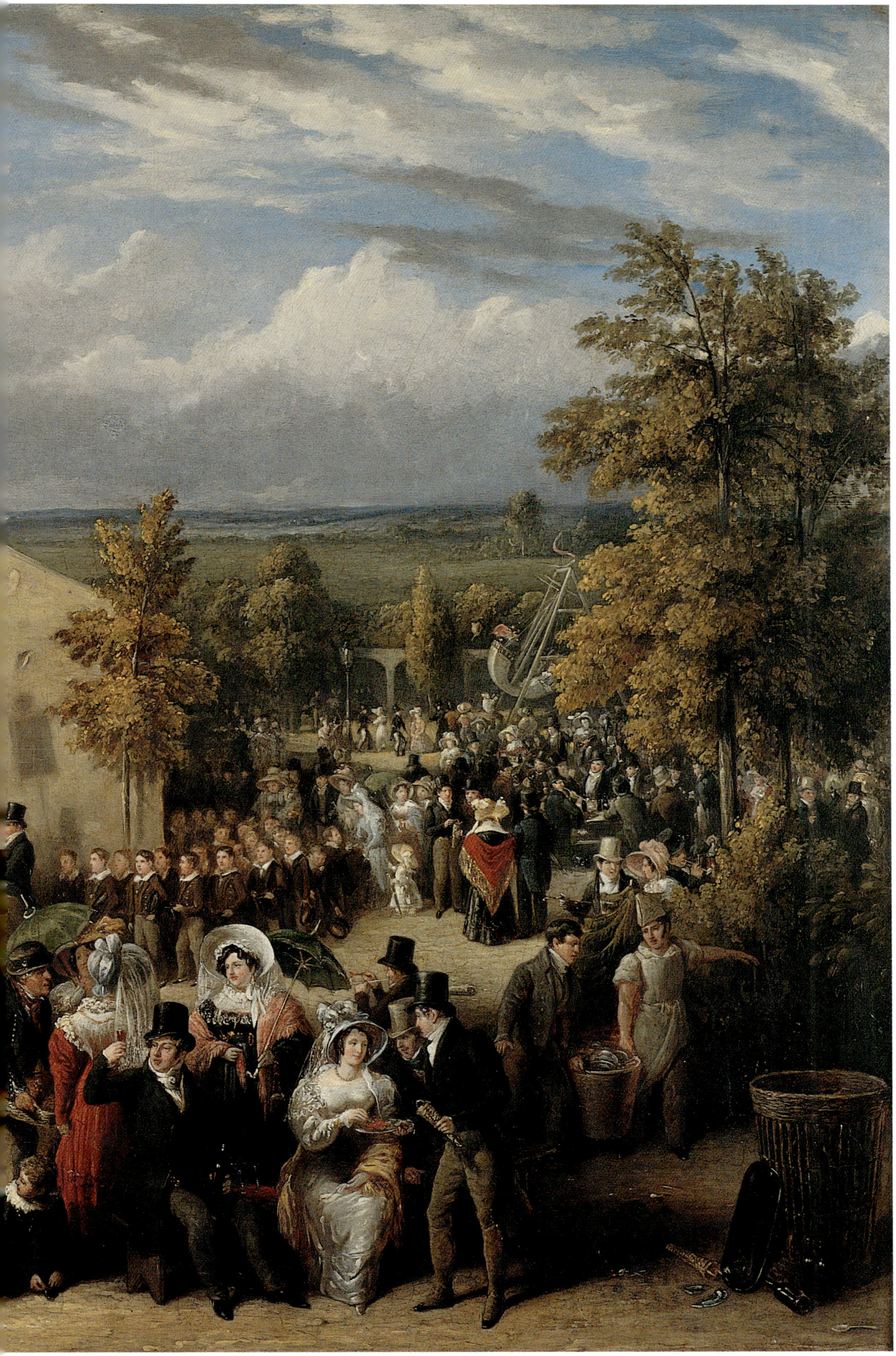

74.

E. F. LAMBERT
(active 1823–46)

The Annual Fête of the Licensed Victuallers' School [60.90]
1831
Oil on panel,
59.1 x 93.7 cm
Signed and dated bottom right:
E. F. Lambert/1831

Provenance:
Purchased out of the Mackenzie Bell Trust Fund from Leger Galleries in 1960.

Bibliography:
Hayes (cat. no. 63).

THE ANNUAL fête of the Licensed Victuallers' School was always an occasion for considerable junketing, and in 1837, when the event took place at Highbury Barn, no fewer than four thousand people sat down to dinner. The Museum picture represents the fête of 1830, which took place on 24 June at the Eyre Arms Tavern, St John's Wood (where the rehearsals for the Eglinton Tournament took place in 1839). By that date the number of school pupils had risen to 150. According to the *Morning Advertiser* (the organ of the Licensed Victuallers and the second oldest newspaper in London), nearly two thousand people were present on this occasion, being accommodated partly in the guest room and partly in a tent some two hundred feet long in the grounds. The company was entertained throughout by the Duke of Gloucester's band, and the dinner was followed by a brilliant display of fireworks in the evening.

The marquee is seen here in the middle distance, and a crowd of people is shown feasting and drinking at the tables there and in the foreground; other people are strolling about the grounds, and in the distance there are arbours, swings and people dancing. In front of the marquee is seen a procession of the children in their school uniforms, preceded by a military band.

The Society of Licensed Victuallers is the oldest charity for the drinking trade. It was inaugurated in 1793 to help members of the trade in poverty and old age. In 1803 it acquired Kennington House, on the south side of Kennington Lane, close to the Oval, which it then opened as a school for orphans and other destitute children of members of the Society: six boys and fourteen girls were admitted on 7 February of that year. The venture was evidently successful, and a new building was planned in the early 1830s, the foundation stone being laid by the Prime Minister in 1836. These premises still stand, but are now in use as the Navy, Army and Air Force Institutes, the Licensed Victuallers' School having moved out to Slough in 1921. There are now two Licensed Victuallers (independent) schools, one in Ascot (which was transferred from Slough in October 1989) and one at Ilkley in West Yorkshire (which was taken over by the Society in 1982).

In the 1840s the Victuallers took advantage of the proximity of Vauxhall Gardens and their annual fête was held there in 1841 and then between 1845 and 1849 (see vol. III of cuttings on Vauxhall Gardens, Museum of London Library).

This painting was engraved by George Hunt and published as an aquatint by J. Moore (the Guildhall Library has a copy of it which was 'republished' in 1846 under a different imprint).

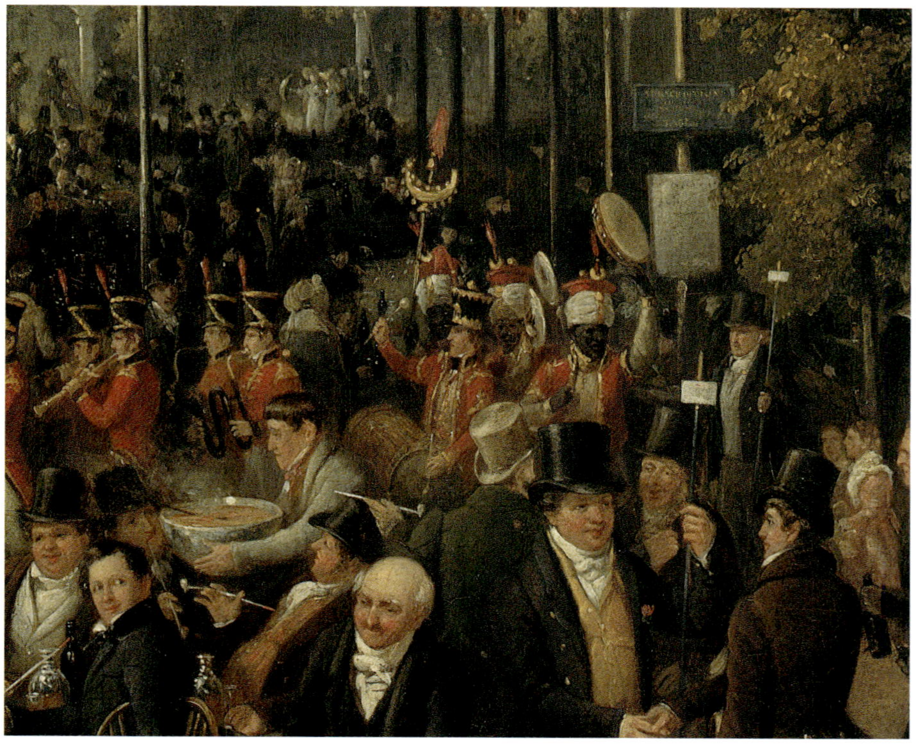

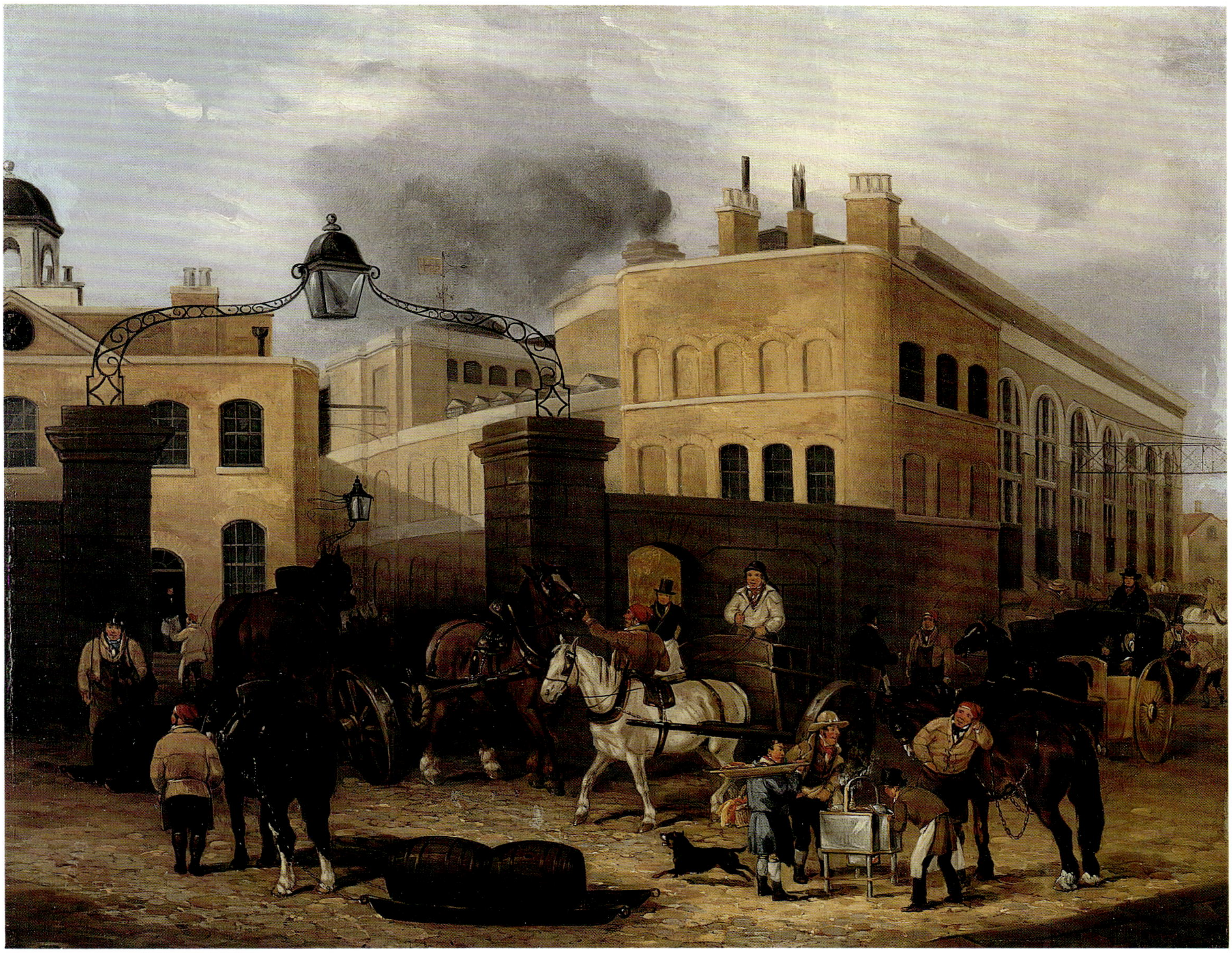

75.
BRITISH SCHOOL
Barclay and Perkins's Brewery in Southwark [A 8069]
1835–40
Oil on canvas, 50.3 x 64.7 cm
Not signed or dated

IN THE mid-nineteenth century the Anchor Brewery, owned by Barclay and Perkins, was the largest brewery in the world and covered over 12 acres on either side of Park Street, Southwark, including the site of the Globe Playhouse, and had a wharf on Bankside. It was one of the recognised sights of London, and among eminent visitors at that time were Ibrahim Ali, son of the Pasha of Egypt, and Prince Louis Napoleon, later Napoleon III. After a fire in 1832, recorded in paint by Clarkson Stanfield, the brewery was vastly extended and modernised.

This post-fire view shows the entrance to the brewery in Park Street with the office block at the rear of the yard. To the right of this is the range that housed the

Provenance:
Purchased from Leggatt Brothers in 1912 (as Shayer).

Bibliography:
Hayes (cat. no. 111); George Dodd, pp17–40, *Days at the Factories*, 1843; Blanchard Jerrold, *London: A Pilgrimage*, 1872, pp129–34; *Three Centuries*, pamphlet by B. W. Cockes and L. W. Cook on 'The Story of our Ancient Barclay, Perkins & Co.', 1951; Stephen Deuchar, *Paintings, Politics and Porter*, exhibition catalogue, Whitbread & Co., 1984; *London – World City 1800–1840*, Celina Fox (ed.), 1992, cat. no. 118; Graham Tite, 'No Beer at the Brewery', in *Country Life*, 13 November 1980.

fermenting vessels, and above the entrance wing the three windows of the head brewer's office. On the extreme right is the Great Brewhouse, with its eight huge windows, and the light suspension bridge that connected it with the buildings on the east side of the street. The brewery presented much the same appearance until the reconstruction and modernisation of 1960. The Guildhall Library has watercolours by G. Yates showing the entrance to the brewery in 1825 and 1826. In 1826 the entrance had been improved and already featured the framing low walls and pillars with the decorative ironwork above.

The picture is no less interesting for its incidental detail. A dray is seen emerging from the yard, and, to the left, other barrels are being carried on horse-drawn sleds (the sign of the anchor is clearly visible on the horses' harness). On the right a butcher's boy carrying a wooden tray, together with another customer, have stopped at a baked potato stall. Beyond, and farther to the right, two visitors are being driven to the brewery in one of the newly introduced hansom cabs (distinguished from other vehicles by its single pair of big wheels, and the seating of the driver behind; see also cat. no. 110.

Brewing became an important industry in Southwark soon after the introduction of hop growing in Kent in the fifteenth century, and the first brewhouse on the site of Barclay and Perkins's premises was established by James Monger in about 1616. In the possession of the Thrales in the eighteenth century, the brewery was sold in 1781 by the executors of Henry Thrale, one of whom was Dr Johnson, and purchased by Robert Barclay, a member of the Quaker banking family. One of Barclay's first actions was to make Thrale's enterprising manager, John Perkins, a partner in the business, and the firm continued to flourish under this name until 1955 when it was taken over by Courage (Eastern) Ltd – the neighbouring Anchor brewery had been in the Courage family since 1787.

In March 1981 beer production stopped on the Southwark site (when a new Courage brewery opened in Reading). Thirteen acres of land became available for redevelopment, enabling Museum of London archaeologists to carry out evaluations and excavations. Notably they discovered a major Roman site underneath part of the Barclay and Perkins brewery complex (ref. site code COSE 84) and the site of the Globe Theatre on the Anchor Terrace car park (ref. site code ACT 89). The area has now been redeveloped mixing commercial and residential properties (including a sheltered housing scheme built on a 1,500-square-metre site).

The costume indicates a date of about 1830–40, and the picture must have been painted after 1832, when the rebuilding operations began after the fire. The presence of a hansom cab means it should not be earlier than 1835.

This image falls within what might be termed 'the brewery genre', born at the end of the eighteenth century and which was described (by Deuchar) as 'more documentary and less essentially nostalgic than the low-life rural subjects from which [it] developed'. In addition, for urban artists attracted to horses, breweries provided a perfect outlet. In 1784 and 1789, George Garrard exhibited two *View[s] of a brewhouse and yard* at the Royal Academy, both showing the Whitbread premises in Chiswell Street. A third painting, now lost, was engraved as a

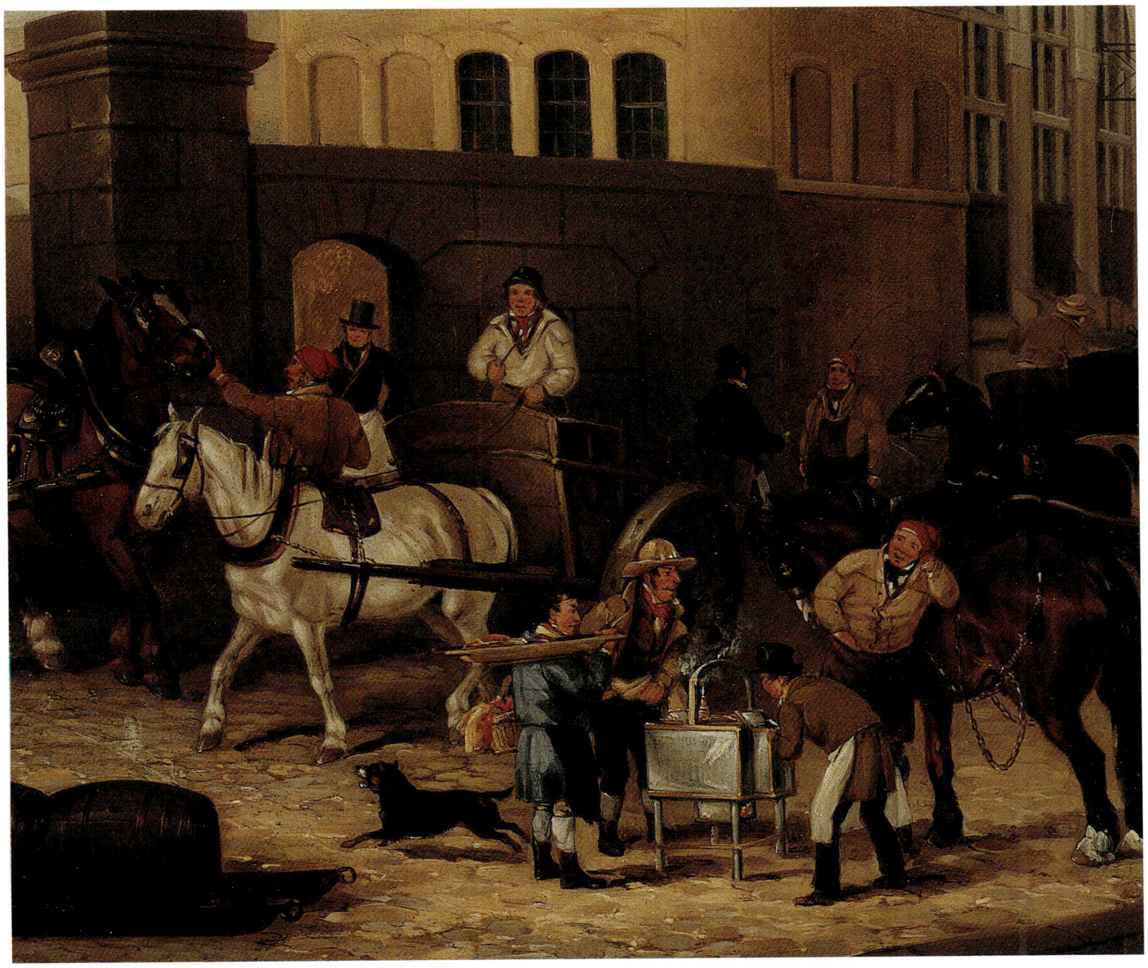

mezzotint by William Ward in 1792. Although Garrard later became the Whitbreads' protégé, none of these paintings seems to have been purchased by the family during Garrard's lifetime, which would suggest that the creation of the genre was not linked to patronage.

Dean Wolstenholme (father and son) pursued this genre into the nineteenth century and exhibited at the Royal Academy views of the Golden Lane Brewery (1807) and of the Truman Brewery (1822); the son painted Calverts' Glass House Brewery followed by Barclay and Perkins in 1840.

The message of these pictures is essentially the same as that of Hogarth in 'Beer Street', and alludes to the 'healthiness' of beer drinking. In Victorian times it was also clearly associated with work, reflecting on both the individual's and the nation's worth. Both ideas are reflected in the drayman's words collected by Jerrold in *London: A Pilgrimage* (p134): 'There's a good deal of "talkee" yet to be done, sir, before they teach English workmen that there's sin and wickedness in a pint of honest beer.'

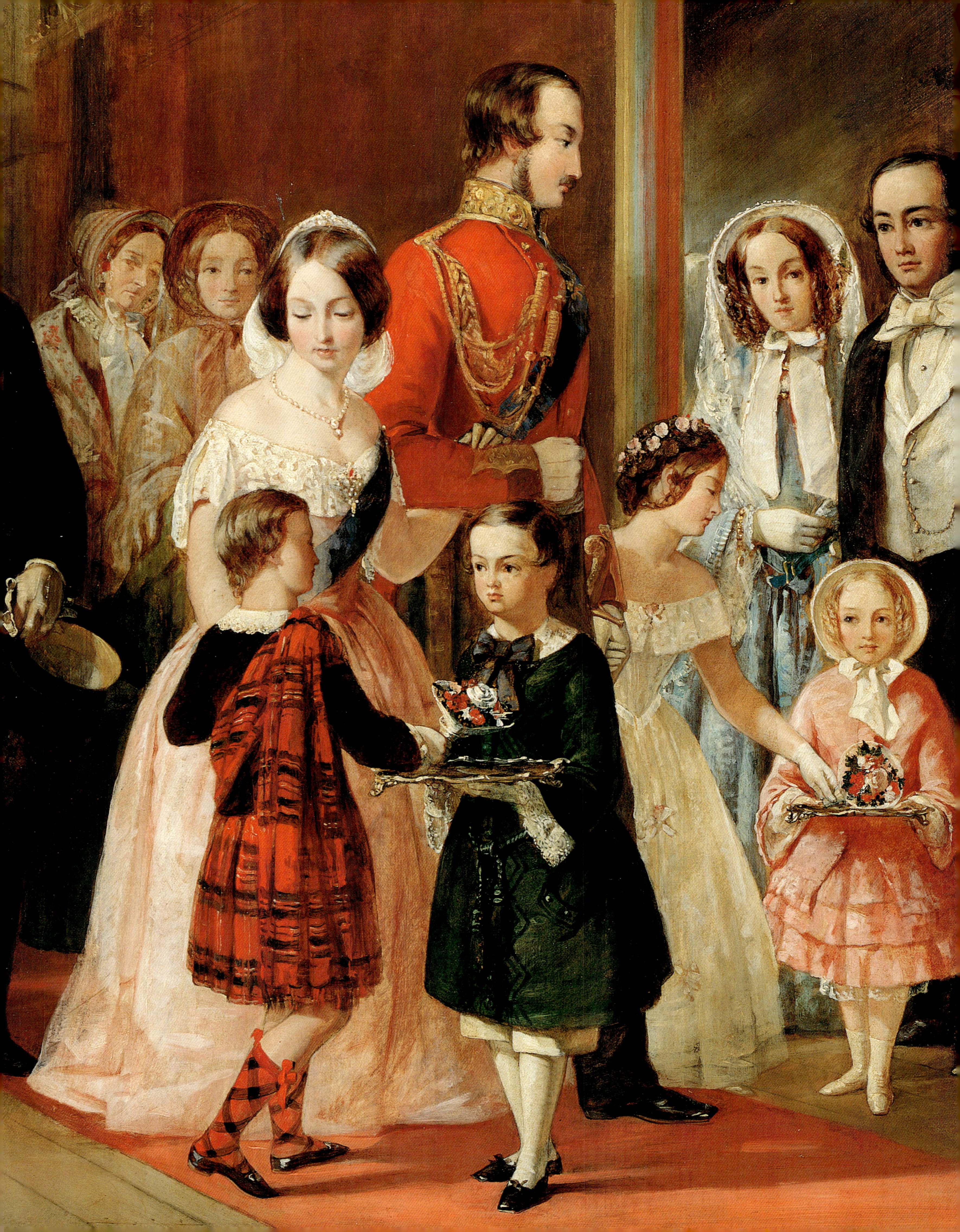

Victoria's Reign

QUEEN VICTORIA ascended the throne in 1837 and died in 1901. The large number of works in this chapter testifies to both the richness of the Museum's collection and the sheer length of the reign. The paintings are characterised by a strong sense of identity and purpose. Painters are no longer bound by the realistic (and sometimes flat) approach of a camera obscura style. There is a sense of the city as theatre in the works of John O'Connor and a heroic dimension to the social panoramas of William Powell Frith and George Elgar Hicks. Even humble subjects such as a cab stand are now handled with total confidence and even grandeur. The endless material furnished by the social scene often reflects the Victorians' sometimes philanthropic, sometimes almost voyeuristic, fascination with the urban poor. Large or small, rich or poor, the buildings and people of Victorian London are explored and magnified on the painter's palette.

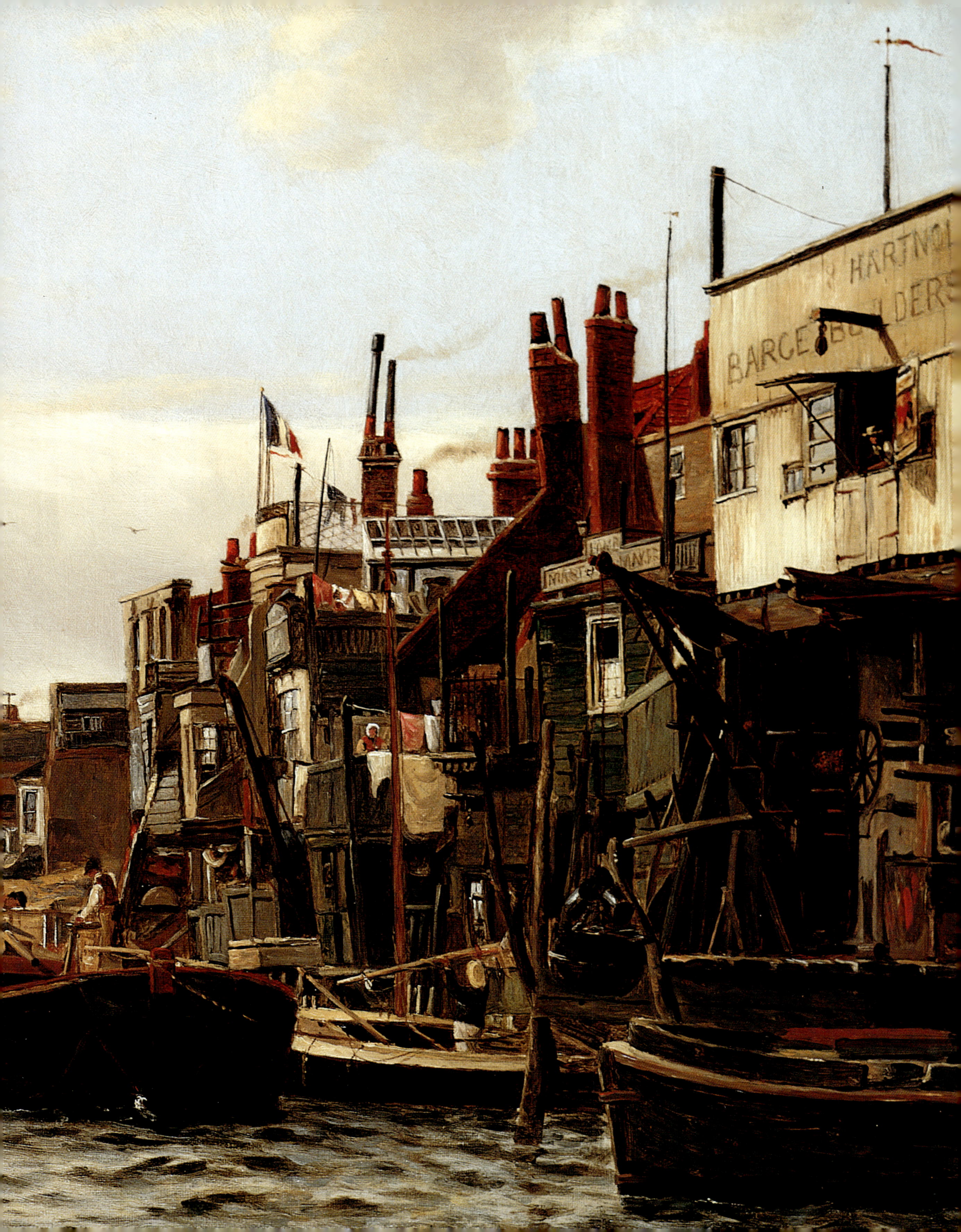
BARGE

THE RIVER

THE EARLY years of the Victorian era were dominated by the work of artists who have been discussed in the Regency period. Clarkson Stanfield (1793–1867) foreshadowed the work of late Victorian painters by introducing dynamic movement in his Thames paintings with his *Tilbury Fort – Wind against High Tide* of 1849.[1] Edward William Cooke (1811–80) displayed similar tendencies and his rendering of a violent storm in the Bay of Biscay during the transportation of Cleopatra's Needle from Egypt in 1877 is particularly dramatic.[2] David Roberts (1796–1867), on the other hand, as late as 1861 painted *A View of Waterloo Bridge, Somerset House & the Adelphi from Hungerford*[3] in the typically calm and collected style of the Regency period, and the work echoes the Museum's own version of the site by Charles Deane (cat. no. 53). By combining peaceful river scenes and genre painting in the foreground, John Wilson Carmichael (1799–1868) is completely true to the Regency vision inspired by Netherlandish Old Master paintings. His London work includes such classic pieces as *The Golden Evening: The Pool of London* (1858).[4] The Pether views of London by night, discussed below under 'Night Paintings', are almost always set by the riverside and should be seen in the context of Dutch and Flemish influence.

The second half of the nineteenth century, however, saw the emergence of new painterly concerns. The pursuit of the real led high Victorian artists to devise two opposed methods of representation. While these may be observed in the treatment of many different London subjects, the polarisation of techniques was particularly striking in relation to paintings of the Thames. Claude Monet (1840–1926) and James Tissot (1836–1902) have arguably produced some of the best works we have for illustrating these differing approaches to reality. Both were French, and their nationality carries an additional message: the considerable influence of the French artistic scene on English circles from the mid-nineteenth century onwards (see p344, note 4).

We could usefully compare two of these artists' most famous London works, *The Thames and the Houses of Parliament* by Monet and *Waiting for the Ferry* by Tissot.[5] Although the works look very different, both share the same subject – a perspective view of a London riverbank. The predominance of figures in the Tissot, to the exclusion of the waterscape, invites us to confront the total absence of this component in French Impressionist works of London. The two favoured Impressionist motifs were undoubtedly the river and the parks. The Impressionists, it should be stressed, primarily painted London and its suburbs and not, as they had in France, the regions and their town centres. These first Impressionist views set the tone for generations of painters to come, and the subsequent work of Le Sidaner, Derain and Kokoschka[6] remains linked to the early Impressionist vision of London which so focused its attention on the river.

Claude Monet (1840–1926)
The Thames below Westminster, 1871
Oil on canvas
Reproduced by courtesy of the National Gallery, London.

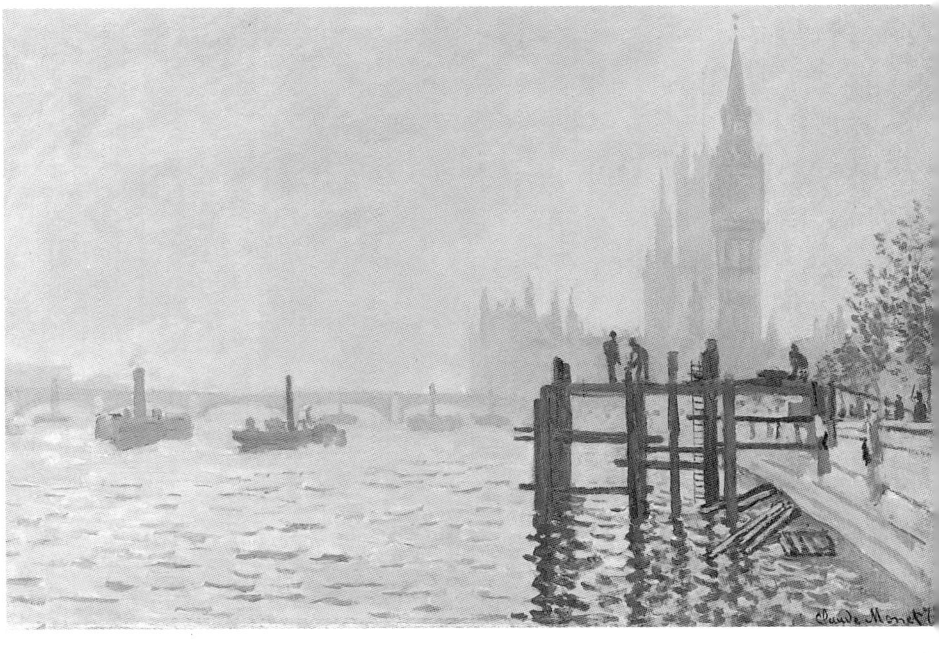

To return to our two examples, the Monet painting, intangible, is all sky, water and light, while the Tissot, linear and painstakingly descriptive, is packed with details – from costume to furniture and buildings. We obtain similar results by comparing the works of two more outsiders, James McNeill Whistler (1834–1903, the so-called Impressionist from America) and the 'linear' Atkinson Grimshaw from Leeds (1836–93), despite the latter's interest in lighting effects. Whistler's *Nocturne in Blue and Gold: Old Battersea Bridge* (illustrated on p270 and see cat. no. 109 for another version of this painting) may not be directly compared to any one composition by Grimshaw, but the latter's numerous riverside views (including Battersea Bridge, see p269) are precisely delineated to reproduce every detail of the world around us.[7]

This retrospective categorisation would not necessarily have been perceived by contemporaries. It is true that Tissot had no difficulty selling his paintings while so many of the Impressionists were living on the verge of bankruptcy, but the following commentary (probably by Frederick Wedmore) used appealing arguments to try to merge the two approaches:

> Mr Whistler and Mr Tissot have long been with us, and their work is like that of the Impressionists in two respects – it aims generally to record what the eye actually sees, and not what the mind knows the eye ought to see, and likewise it addresses itself with courage and confidence to the artistic problems of modern life, and our artificial society.[8]

There was little about the Thames in London that could be described as 'artificial'; it was predominantly a *working* river which no visionary mind had ever tried to render aesthetic. Colonel Trench's ambitious scheme for the Embankment had been received with the comment: 'Who would think of promenading along the channel of a great hazy, ague-giving river in any case?'[9]

However, London's atmospheric qualities could also totally transform the capital, including its river, as was later observed by the painter Yoshio Markino (see p342). Whistler wrote most eloquently of 'when the evening mist clothes the riverside with poetry, as with a veil, and the poor buildings lose themselves in the dim sky and the tall chimneys become campanili and the warehouses are palaces in the night and the whole city hangs in the heavens and fairy land is before us . . . '.[10] The age-long association with Italy, and with Venice in particular, dating from Georgian times was also taken up by poets, notably Symons, who in 1895 published in his *London Nights* 'Intermezzo: Venetian Nights',[11] a literary echo to Whistler's *Nocturnes* (itself a term borrowed from the world of music). The most riveting interpretation of this artist's *Nocturnes* was probably that of Henley:

> Under a stagnant sky,
> Gloom out of gloom uncoiling into gloom,
> The River, jaded and forlorn,
> Welters and wanders wearily – wretchedly – on . . . [12]

The poetic and forlorn qualities of both writings and paintings are more akin to notions of romanticism than realism. Whistler's own comments on *Nocturne in Grey and Gold: Chelsea Snow* are revealing: 'I care nothing for the past, present, or future of the black figure, placed there because the black was wanted at that spot. All that I know is that my combination of grey and gold is the basis of the picture.'[13] What a contrast with Monet's desperate attempt to capture in paint the reality of the ever-changing light of the Thames: '. . . on the Thames: what a succession of varying aspects! At the Savoy Hotel or at Saint Thomas's Hospital, from where I took my viewpoints, I had up to a hundred canvases on the go – for one single subject.'[14]

None of these approaches – the 'linear realist', the 'Impressionist' or the 'poetic' – was entirely without precedent. Early narrative painting had long adopted for London subjects a realistic and thoroughly descriptive method; we could cite as a river example George Garrard's 1796 *Mr Whitbread's Wharf*.[15] Atmospheric and poetic painting, on the other hand, had been brought to dizzy heights by Turner even if, as Pissarro angrily retorted, 'Turner and Constable, while they taught us something, showed us in their works that they had no understanding of the analysis of shadow'.[16] Turner's artistic exploits for the Thames range from the pair of paintings of the seat of William Moffatt in Mortlake Terrace to the 1834 works on the burning of the Palace of Westminster and *The Fighting 'Téméraire' tugged to her last berth* [Rotherhithe] *to be broken up, 1838*.[17] Turner's riposte when Clarkson Stanfield pointed out that the sails were too dark in *Peace – burial at sea 1842* echoes Whistler's remark quoted above: 'I only wish I had any colour to make them blacker.'[18]

The collection partly reflects the different components of this rich theme, from river workmen such as the bargeman (cat. no. 76), to riverbanks (Hemy and Anderson, cat. nos 77 and 78) and the river's shimmering light and quality (Greaves and *The Frozen Thames*, cat. nos 109 and 84). The next development is not, however, represented – the energy and speed of movement which painters such as Henry Dawson (1811–78) and W. L. Wyllie (1851–1931) introduced at the end of the century by focusing on the river's craft.[19] Life on the river becomes irresistibly dynamic in such works as Dawson's *Greenwich Hospital from the River Thames*[20] with its rocking Thames barge filled with hay or Wyllie's *Heave Away*, depicting Thames barges shooting the arches of a bridge.[21]

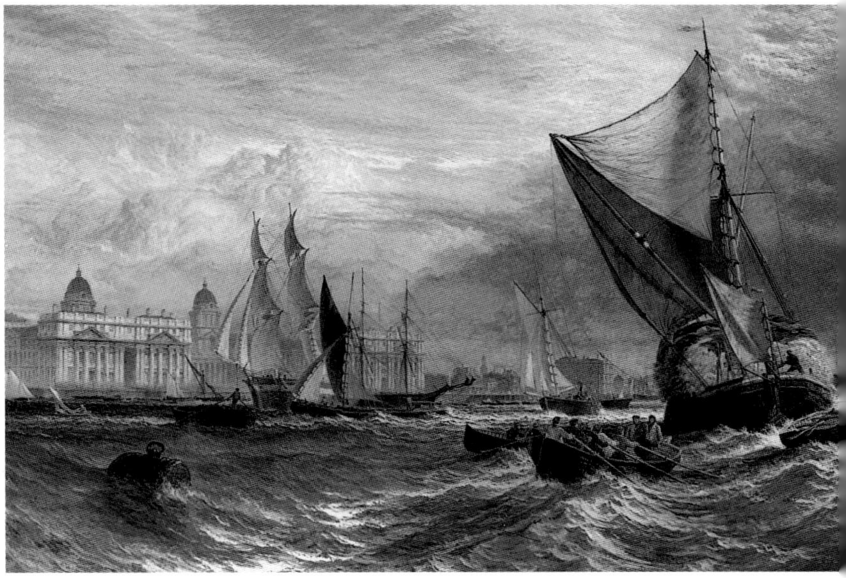

Henry Dawson (1811–1878)
Greenwich Hospital from the River Thames, 1867
Oil on canvas
Reproduced by courtesy of Richard Green, London.

1. Collection of the Port of London Authority; *Clarkson Stanfield*, exhibition catalogue, Tyne and Wear, 1979, p171.
2. Collection of the Victoria and Albert Museum; see cat. no. 165 for the story of Cleopatra's Needle.
3. In a private collection; Helen Guiterman and Briony Llewelyn, *David Roberts*, exhibition catalogue, Barbican Art Gallery, 1986, no. 45.
4. Christie's, 7 October 1983 (33).
5. The painting by Monet is in the National Gallery; that by Tissot was sold at Sotheby's on 17 June 1986 (79). A watercolour study for the background of the latter is in the collection of the Museum (acc. no. 82.423).

6. See *Henri Le Sidaner (1862–1939)*, exhibition catalogue, Musée Marmottan, Paris, 1989; for Derain see *The Fauve Landscapes*, exhibition catalogue, Royal Academy, 1991; for Kokoschka see *Oskar Kokoschka: London Views, British Landscapes*, 1972.
7. *Atkinson Grimshaw*, exhibition catalogue, Leeds City Art Gallery, 1979; also Christopher Wood and Richard Green's catalogue on this artist, 1990.
8. Review of the exhibition organised by Durand-Ruel in London in 1882 in *The Impressionists at First Hand*, Bernard Denvir (ed.), 1987, p135.
9. Quoted on p84 of Felix Barker and Ralph Hyde, *London as it Might Have Been*, 1982; also see cat. no. 80.
10. Quoted in *Atkinson Grimshaw*, 1979, p16.
11. Denys Sutton, *Nocturne: The Art of James McNeill Whistler*, Country Life Publications, 1963, p69 and note 2.
12. Ibid.
13. In the collection of the Fogg Museum, Cambridge, Massachusetts; quote from Sutton, 1963, p65.
14. *The Impressionists in London*, exhibition catalogue, Arts Council, 1973, p37.
15. Stephen Deuchar, *Paintings, Politics and Porter*, exhibition catalogue, 1984, p20, cat. no. 6.
16. Denvir (ed.), 1987, p194.
17. *Turner 1775–1851*, exhibition catalogue, Tate Gallery, 1974, nos 310 and 512; Graham Reynolds, *Turner*, 1969, pp162–5 and 176–8.
18. Ibid, p187.
19. Alfred Dawson, *The Life of Henry Dawson, Landscape Painter*, 1891; Roger Quarm and John Wyllie, *W. L. Wyllie Marine Artist (1851–1931)*, 1981.
20. *Marine Paintings*, exhibition catalogue, Richard Green Gallery, 1992, no. 39.
21. The scene, set in Rochester, would have been a familiar sight at London Bridge. The painting was with Deborah Cage Works of Art in 1992.

76.

W. R. NOBLE

(active mid-nineteenth century)

Portrait of a Royal Bargeman [38.246]

1843

Oil on canvas, 35.2 x 25.4 cm

Signed and dated bottom left:

W. R. Noble/1843

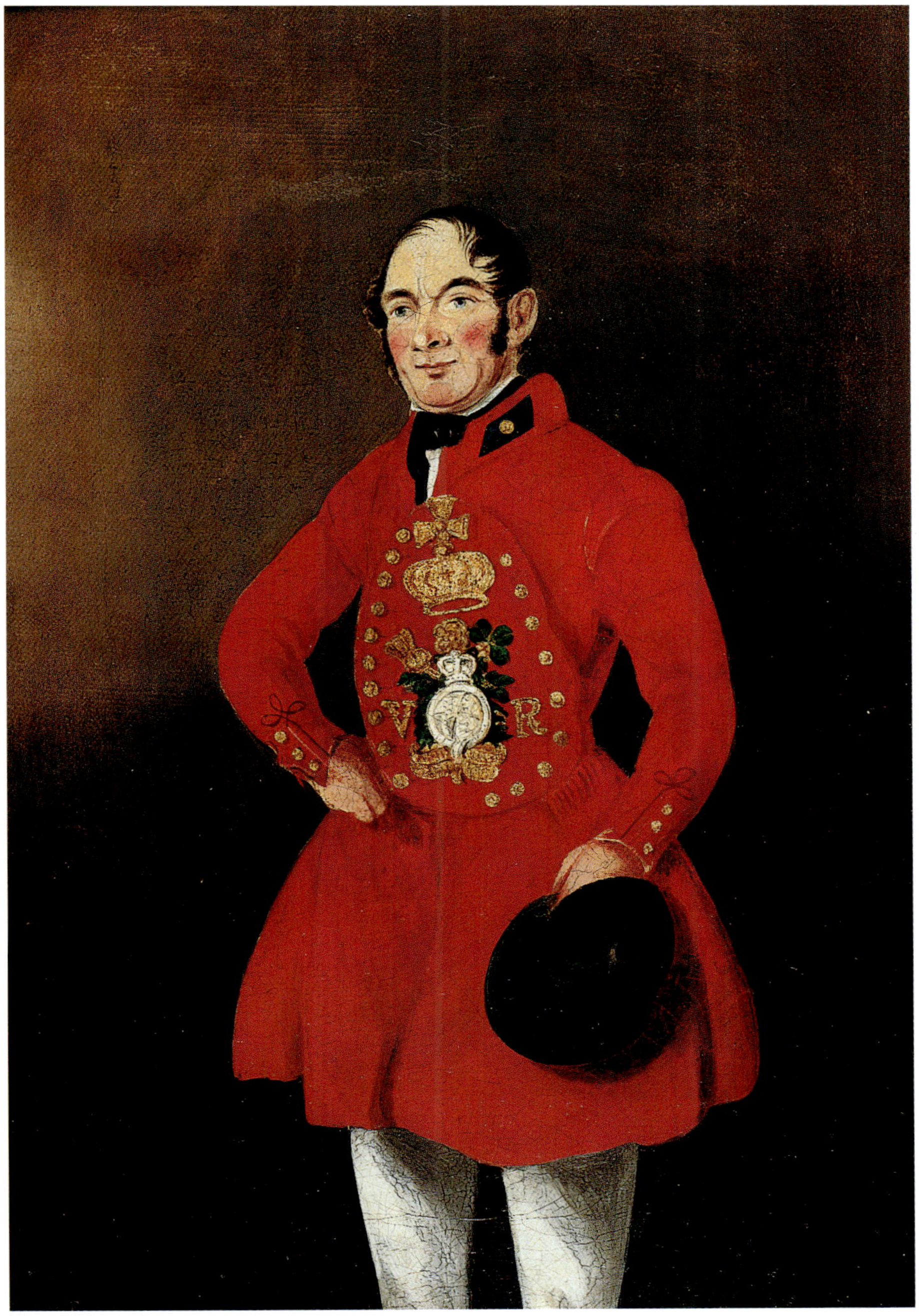

THE BARGEMAN is shown three-quarter-length against a plain background, facing slightly to the left. He is holding a top hat in his left hand and wearing the scarlet uniform of his profession, with the monogram 'VR' (Victoria Regina) and the royal arms surmounted by a crown embroidered on his breastplate.

Provenance:
Presented by Alexandre Yakovleff in 1938.

Bibliography:
Hayes (cat. no. 162).

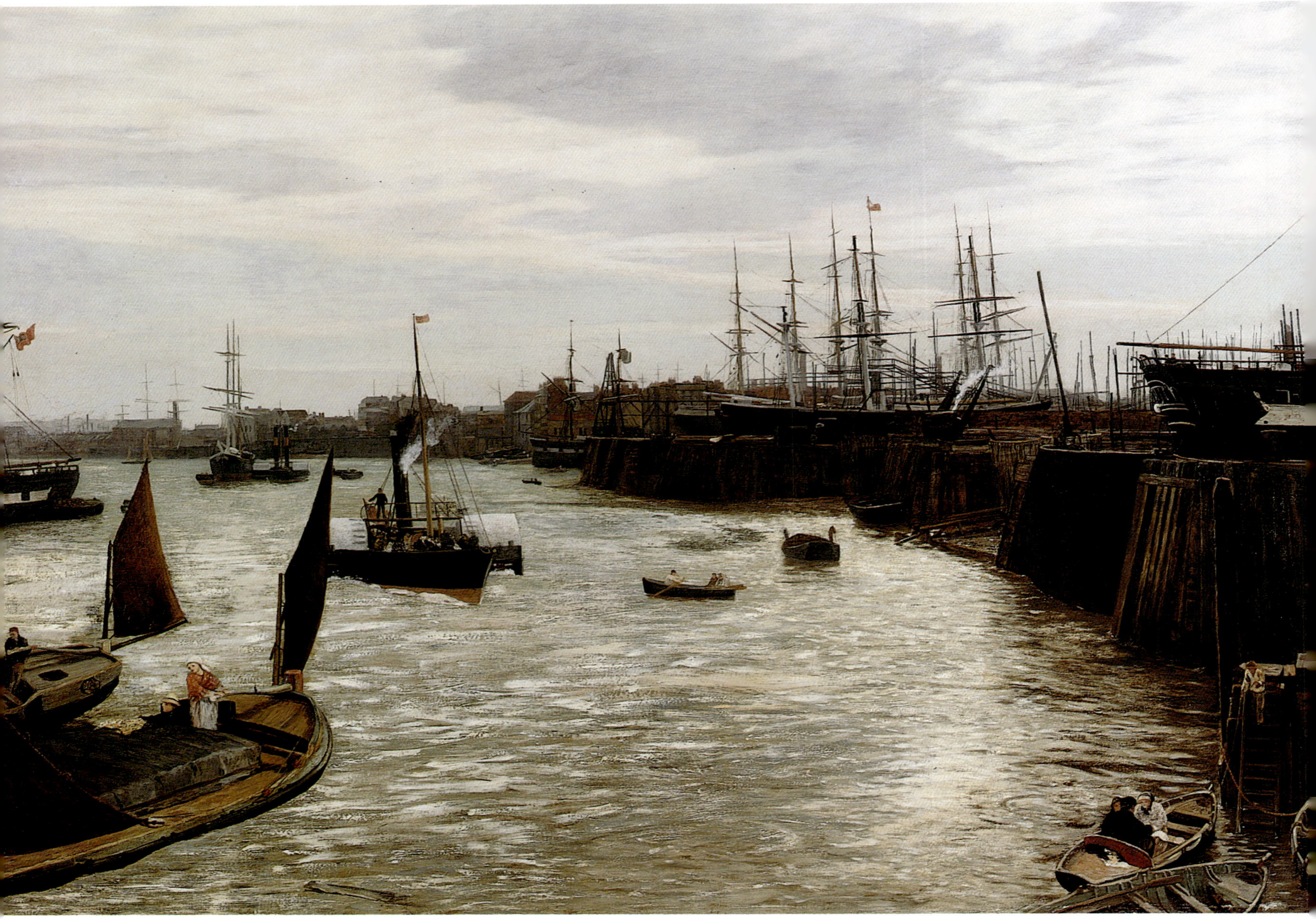

77.
CHARLES NAPIER HEMY
(1841–1917)

Blackwall [69.157]
1872
Oil on canvas, 122 x 182.7 cm
Not signed or dated

THE RIVERFRONT at Blackwall displays an impressive array of dry docks and faces south-west, looking towards Cubitt Town, Isle of Dogs. The viewpoint may be compared to that of Hemy's *London River – The Limehouse Barge-Builders* (South Shields Museum and Art Gallery), although here the painter is no longer solely concentrating on the riverbank and the perspective on to the Thames has been opened. The artist has thus depicted a couple of paddle steamers (first introduced on the Thames in the 1820s), ships moored in the river, Thames barges (often operated by a family: the one on the left is a nice example of this) and smaller vessels (note the waterman rowing passengers across from Brunswick Stairs on the right). The words which Hemy wrote about the *Barge-Builders* are partly applicable to this work: 'I painted the picture altogether from nature sitting in a barge and talking with the workmen.' Here the viewpoint is much higher, the 'barge' more likely to have been a ship moored outside the Brunswick Hotel and looking up Blackwall Reach. The distant viewpoint and the rich water reflections suggest that Hemy was attempting to capture the silvery brilliance of sky and river and might explain why less attention was paid to the depiction of rivercraft. Alternatively, this painting may represent a lesser version of the lost *Blackwall*, which Hemy is known to have considered one of his principal works (Laing, p30).

Two shipbuilding and ship-owning families, the Wigrams and the Greens, dominate the history of Blackwall Yard in the nineteenth century. They became famous for building passenger frigates that were both resilient and comfortable. From 1843, when a wall was built to divide the yard, the Wigrams operated west of it and the Greens on the east side (immediate right of the painting). This work was probably painted just before the Wigrams' part of the yard disappeared in the 1870s.

Considering that Blackwall had the most famous private shipping yard in the country, and that John Smith (1580–1631) set sail from there in 1606 to found Virginia, the first permanent English colony in America, it is surprising that the site was so little depicted. By comparison, images of Limehouse and Rotherhithe abound. This painting bears witness, with considerable accuracy, to Blackwall's little-known riverside landscape and stands out in much the same way as did its extraordinary predecessor in the eighteenth century, Francis Holman's *Blackwall Yard from the Thames* (1784) in the National Maritime Museum.

The Reuters Building, designed by Richard Rogers, now occupies most of the site shown in the painting's right-hand side. The area acquired its first tunnel shortly after this picture was painted. A second tunnel was built between 1963 and 1967 and a third tunnel is currently being envisaged.

Provenance:
Purchased from N. R. Omell in 1969.

Bibliography:
Charles Napier Hemy R. A. 1841–1917, exhibition catalogue, Laing Art Gallery, Tyne and Wear, 1984; Chris Ellmers and Alex Werner, *Blackwall Yard*, Reuters, 1989; Poplar, Blackwall and the Isle of Dogs in the *Survey of London*, vol. XLIV, 1994.

Exhibited:
Royal Academy, 1872 (198); N. R. Omell, *Old Father Thames*, 1969.

KEY

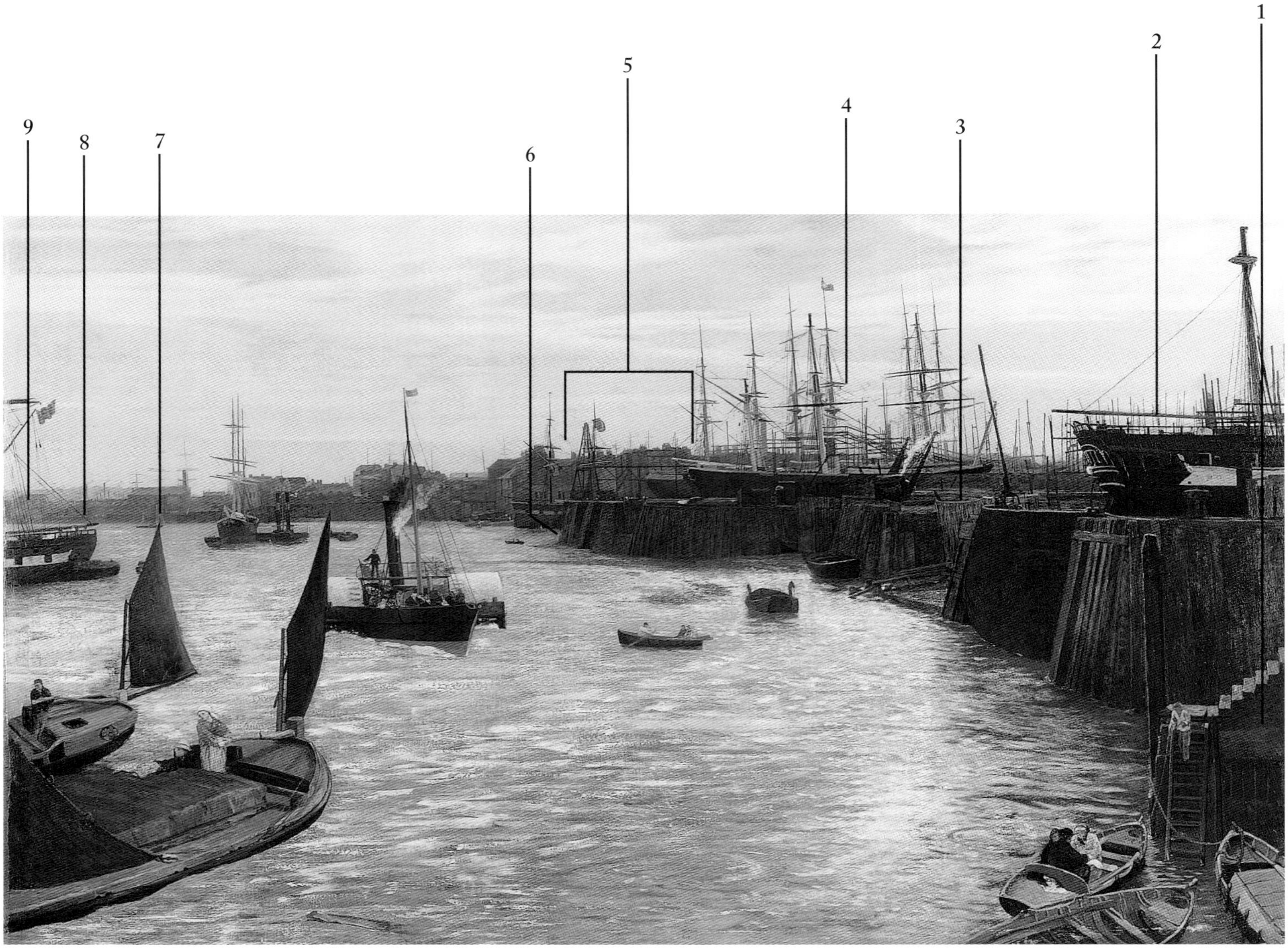

1. Brunswick Stairs
2. Blackwall Yard: Greens' side
3. Dividing wall (built 1843)
4. Blackwall Yard: Wigrams' side
5. Row of pubs and shops (western boundary of Blackwall Yard at Brunswick Street): The Ship, Shoulder of Mutton and Pig, coffee shop, bootmaker, ship's furnisher, lead- and coppersmith, the Old Hob
6. Blackwall Causeway
7. Entrance to Blackwall Basin (where the smoke is)
8. South West India Docks entrance (behind the ship moored in the river)
9. Cubitt Town

78.

JOHN ANDERSON

(1835–1919)

Westminster Bridge, the Houses of Parliament and Westminster Abbey seen from the River [A 25910]
1872
Oil on canvas, 107 x 183 cm
Signed and dated bottom left:
John Anderson/1872

THIS SUNSET view shows the Houses of Parliament from the site of the present-day Jubilee Gardens. The long river frontage of some 300 metres, designed as a main block with flanking towers and lower wings terminated by towers, is clearly seen, and behind this are the principal towers of the building: the Victoria Tower, completed in 1860, regarded at the time as a stupendous edifice, since it rose over 18 metres higher than the top of the cross on the dome of St Paul's; the Middle (ventilating) Tower, which rises above St Stephen's Hall; and the Clock Tower, finished in 1858.

Westminster Bridge, seen in the foreground, which replaced the mid-eighteenth-century structure (see cat. no. 25), was built contemporaneously with the last stages of the Houses of Parliament, in 1854–62, and was designed by Thomas Page, engineer. Beyond the bridge, on the extreme left, is the spire of Holy Trinity, Bessborough Gardens, a church built by J. L. Pearson in 1849–51, now destroyed; and on the right of the bridge are seen, from left to right, Westminster pier, the early Tudor parish church of St Margaret's (incorrectly shown with pointed windows), Westminster Abbey, and part of the Embankment. The Victoria Embankment had only recently been completed at the date of this picture, and the works connected with the building of the floating bath (operative by 1876) are seen on the right. Behind this structure are the (then) offices of the Civil Service Commission (formerly the India Board of Control) and the south-west corner of Richmond Terrace; the St Stephen's Club, which stood on the corner of Bridge Street, was not built until 1874. A steamboat is seen off Westminster pier, and several hay barges occupy the immediate foreground.

The disastrous fire of 1834 (see cat. nos 67 to 69) destroyed almost the whole of the historic Palace of Westminster save Westminster Hall. New premises had to be built for the Houses of Parliament, and the terms of the competition held in 1835 required the designs to be either Gothic or Elizabethan. This was a revolutionary requirement at the time, since no public building had been erected in anything but the classical style for a couple of centuries and more. Ninety-seven designs were submitted, nearly all of them in the Gothic style, and the winner was Charles Barry. To him is due the planning and execution of the building, but the detailing, for which literally hundreds of drawings were prepared, was entirely the work of Augustus Pugin, whom Barry called in to help him. By the time the building was finished a quarter of a century later, in 1860, Gothic was the recognised language of all leading architects in England.

A small view by Anderson, taken from Vauxhall Bridge and showing St Thomas's Hospital on the right, signed and dated 1873, was sold at Sotheby's, 15 January 1964 (188).

Provenance:
Presented by P. A. S. Phillips in 1923.

Bibliography:
Hayes (cat. no. 3); *Cast in the Mould – The origin and history of Coventry School of Art 1834–95*, exhibition catalogue booklet, City of Coventry, 1979.

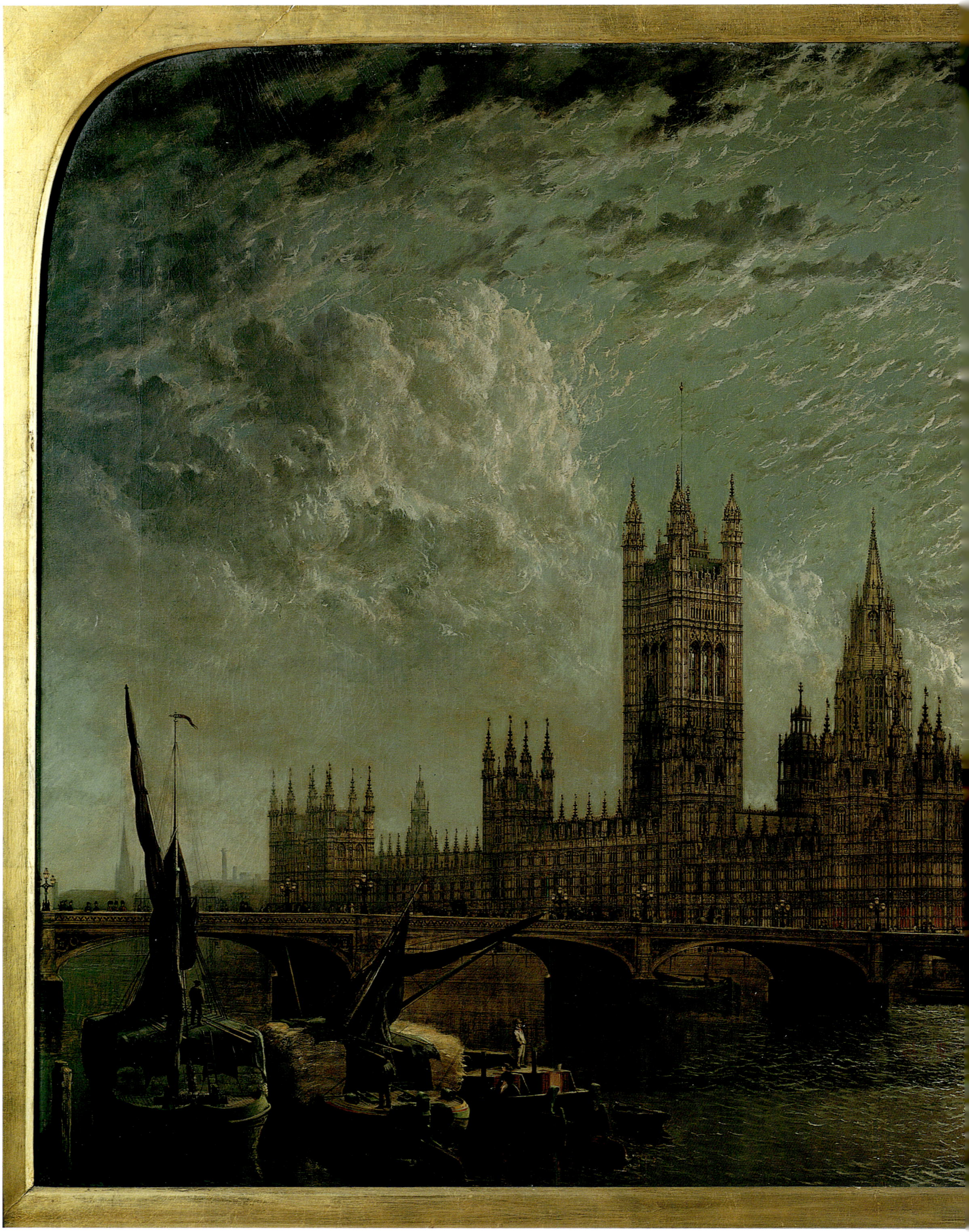

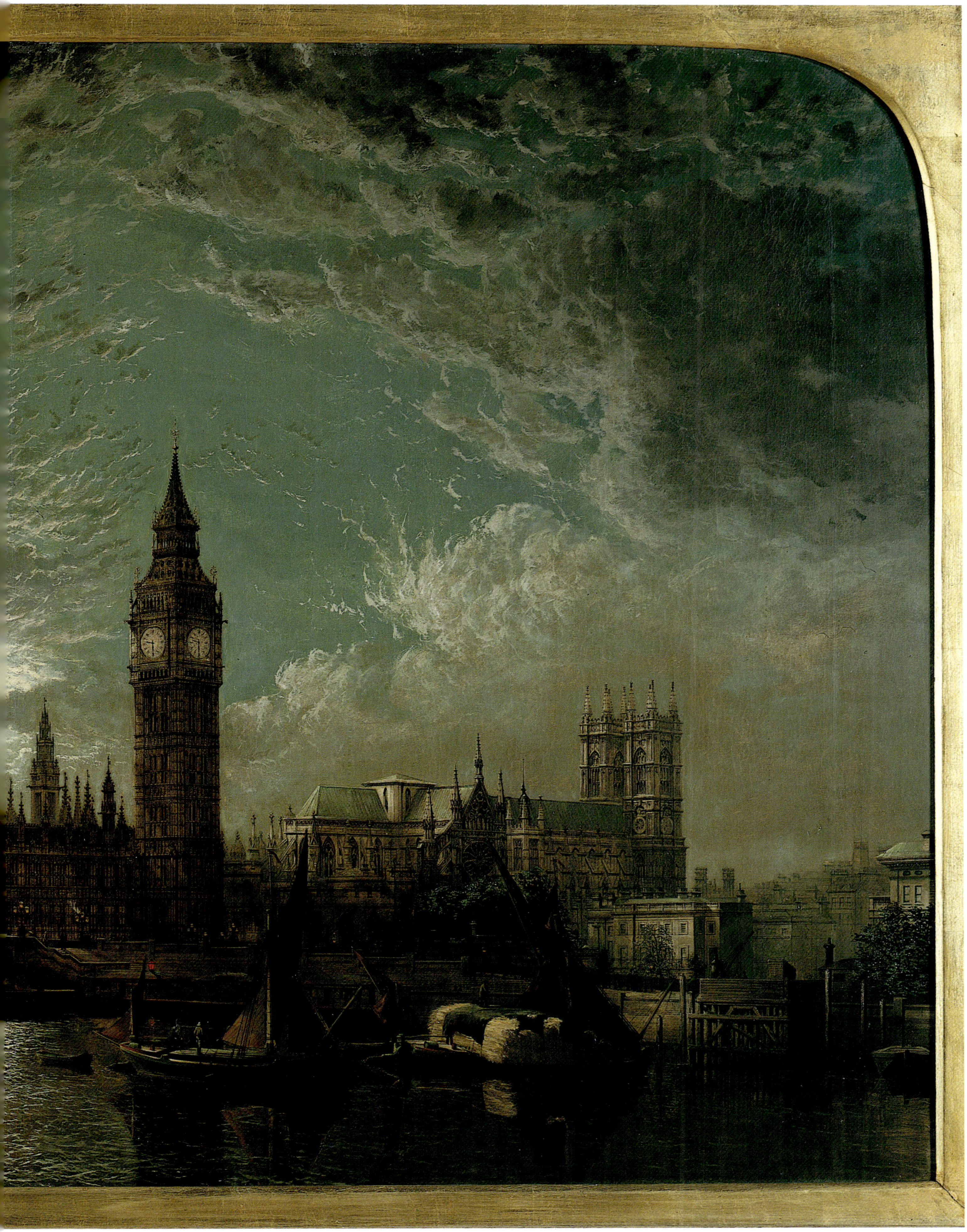

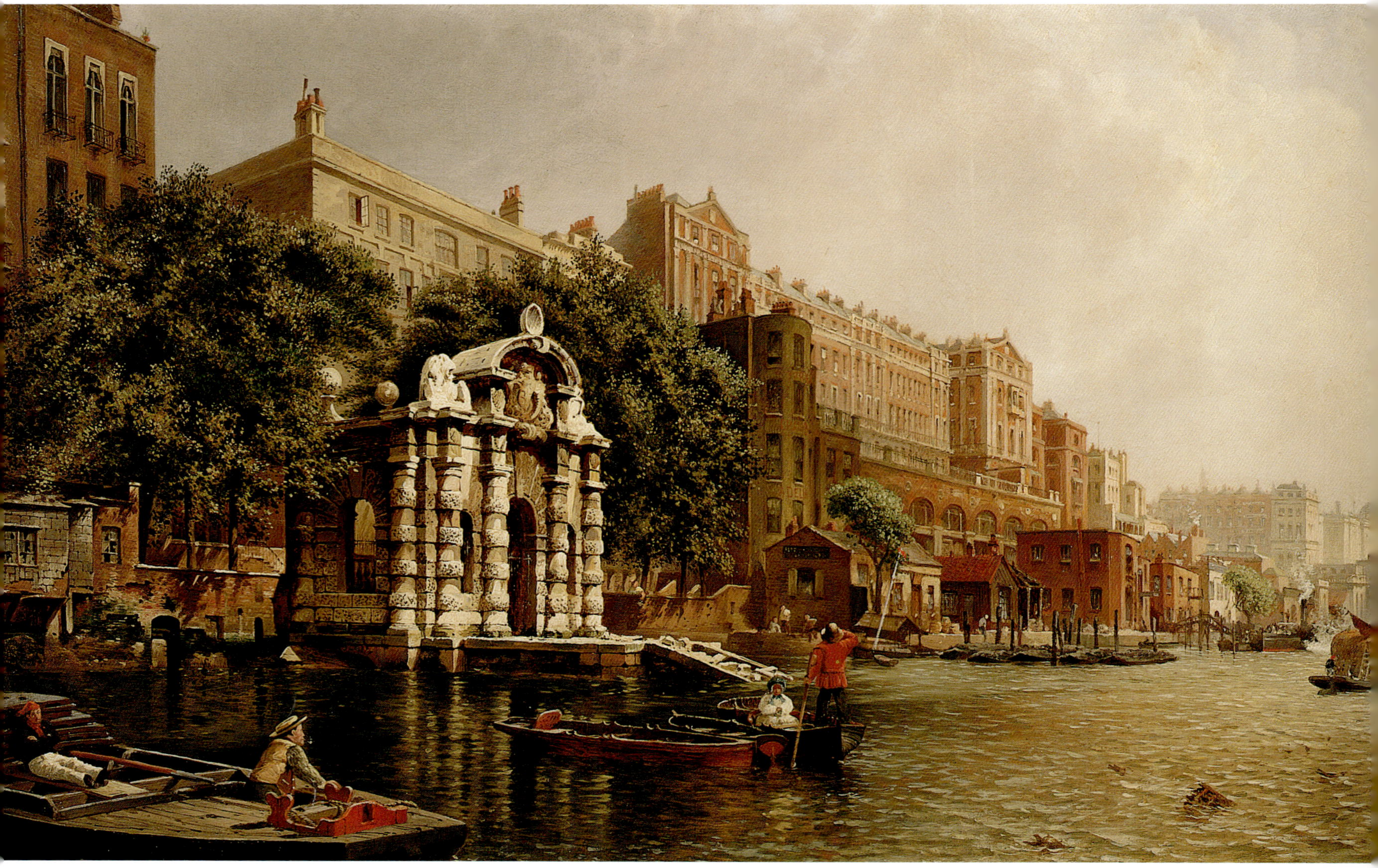

79.

JOHN O'CONNOR

(1830–89)

York Water Gate and the Adelphi from the River [A 7545]

1872

Oil on canvas, 60.8 x 101.2 cm

Not signed or dated

A VIEW of the Strand waterfront at high tide from the river, before the construction of the Embankment, looking north-eastwards and showing Somerset House and an arch of Waterloo Bridge in the distance. In the foreground is the York Water Gate, erected in 1626 by Nicholas Stone, to designs probably by Sir Balthasar Gerbier, as the stately riverside entrance to the Duke of Buckingham's mansion (built in 1626 and demolished fifty years later). It is seen here in its original position fronting the Thames; since the construction of the Embankment it has been stranded some distance inland.

Behind is the terrace of York Buildings, with the steps leading up to Buckingham Street (see cat. no. 91). To the right are the Adelphi wharves, with the Royal Terrace towering above.

The Adelphi scheme, an enterprise by the brothers Adam (see cat. no. 27) was begun in 1768 and to a large extent completed by 1772. In 1872, just a century later, the Royal Terrace was subjected to a hideous Victorian facelift (a desecration that may have prompted the painting of the present picture), and in 1936 it was totally demolished. A Thames waterman, in the traditional red uniform with arm badge, is shown staring up at the Adams' masterpiece, and barges and other craft are seen on the river.

O'Connor used his watercolour of the York Water Gate and the buildings around it, now in the National Gallery of Ireland (no. 2220), which is signed and dated 1861, for the left half of the Museum picture; the details in both are identical down to the reflections in the water, with the exception of the figure smoking a pipe, who does not appear in the watercolour. Though the picture was painted in 1872, the entry in the Royal Academy catalogue noted that it represented the scene as it had been 'ten years ago'. A pencil sketch for the composition is in the possession of Dr Michael King.

Another, more polished, version of this painting, signed and dated *J O'Connor 72* was sold by Richard Green to the Berkeley Hotel, Knightsbridge, in 1992.

Provenance:
Christie's, 2 April 1892 (27), bt Hoare; purchased in 1912, source unrecorded.

Bibliography:
Hayes (cat. no. 86).

Exhibited:
Royal Academy, 1872 (1019 as *Old York Gate, Adelphi, Ten Years Ago*), unless this was its signed and dated sister version (see text).

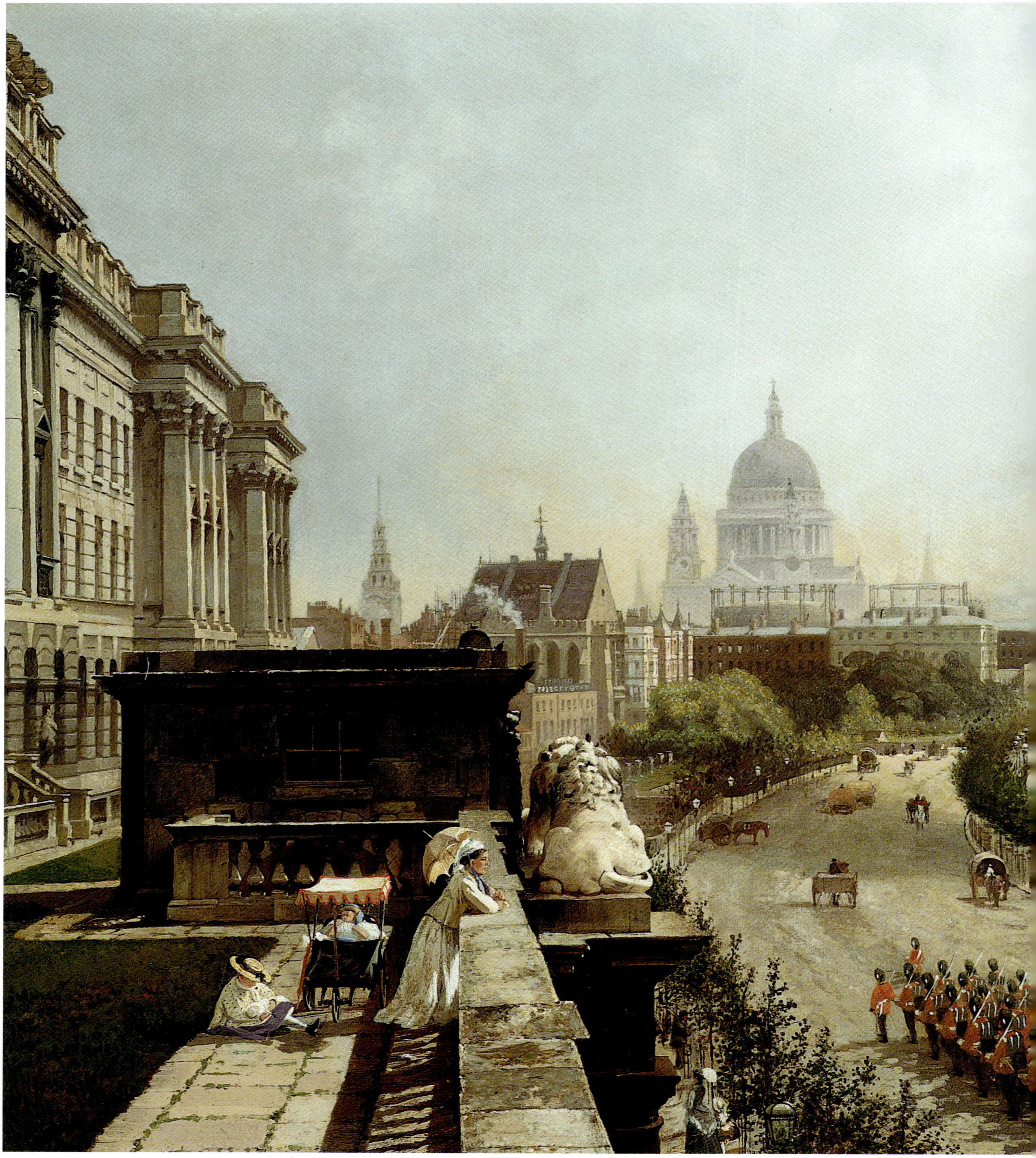

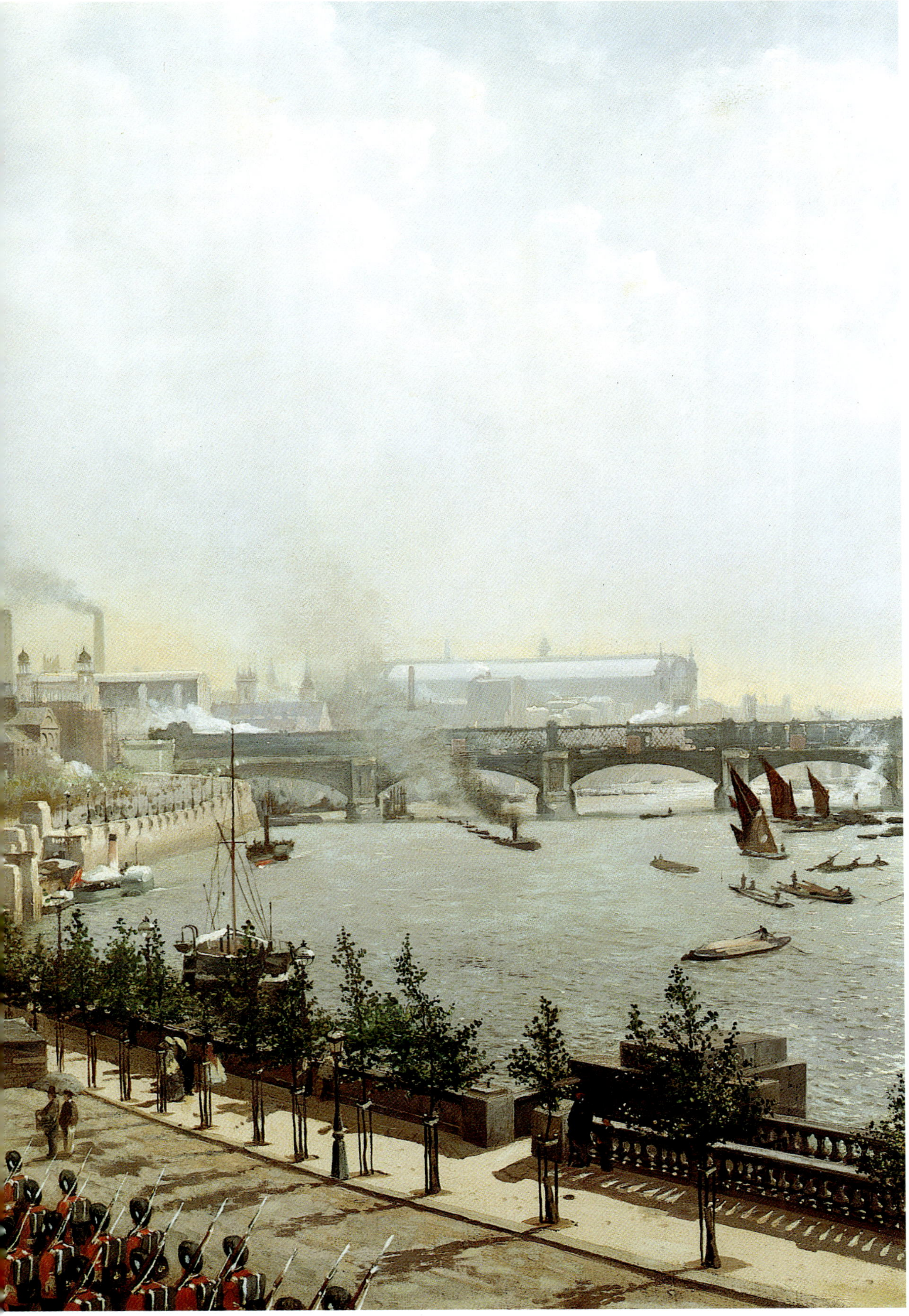

80.

JOHN O'CONNOR

(1830–89)

The Embankment

[85.552]

1874

Oil on canvas,

76.5 x 126.5 cm

Not signed or dated

Provenance:
With M. Newman Ltd in 1956 (see *Connoisseur*, March 1956); purchased by the Museum in 1985 from Cawoods Ltd, with a grant from the National Art Collections Fund.

Bibliography:
Felix Barker and Ralph Hyde, *London as it Might Have Been*, 1982, chapter 8; Felix Barker and Peter Jackson, *London – 2000 Years of a City and its People*, 1974, pp314-15; Jean Dethier, *La Ville Moderne en Europe 1870–1996*, exhibition catalogue, Museum of Contemporary Art, Tokyo, 1996, pp58–9.

Exhibited:
Royal Academy, 1874 (588).

SOME 130 years after Canaletto immortalised the view, O'Connor positioned himself on the terrace of Somerset House and depicted the new Embankment looking east towards the City, with Blackfriars Bridge framing the horizon line on the right. The regiment of Grenadiers in the foreground is probably heading for the Tower of London: it seems that when the First Battalion Grenadier Guards went on training, their duties would be undertaken by the second battalion stationed at Chelsea. (The artist, however, may simply have been fond of this motif, and a single grenadier is depicted in the foreground of his St Pancras painting – see cat. no. 99). Other noteworthy details from the painting include the vignette of the mother and her children, complete with period pram and doll, as well as the watering cart working along the Embankment.

The Victoria Embankment forms part of London's Embankment scheme masterminded by Joseph Bazalgette, Chief Engineer of the Metropolitan Board of Works, and which also includes the Albert Embankment on the South Bank (financed by the builder Thomas Cubitt and opened in 1869) and the Chelsea Embankment (opened in 1874). Discussions for a new embankment first started after the Great Fire, when grand new quays had been envisaged by Wren, Newcourt and Knight. The less grandiose scheme that was actually carried out was soon encroached upon, thus inviting further proposals in the eighteenth and nineteenth centuries: those of John Gwynn (1766), John Nash (lost) and his contemporary Colonel Trench (designs by Philip and Benjamin Wyatt with advice by John Rennie), and of John Martin (1832, with a three-level quay and grand sewer!). More proposals succeeded: in 1841, Trench again adapted the idea of an embankment to the newly arrived railways, and in 1851, W. H. Smith (of newsagent fame) produced a scheme that foreshadowed the present Victoria Embankment. In 1861, following an advertisement in *The Times*, fifty-nine schemes were produced and that of Joseph Bazalgette chosen.

The painting shows the Embankment soon after its completion in 1872. The work had started in 1864 and had temporarily come to a halt in 1869 when the Metropolitan Railway was unable to carry out its scheme through lack of funds. A total of 37 acres were claimed from the river and the project was one of the engineering feats of the period.

Henry Adlard engraved this view for *The Stationers Almanac* in 1873, after a drawing by O'Connor which may have come before the work under review and in which the river and road traffic vary slightly. The companion piece, looking west towards the Houses of Parliament, was only published in *The Stationers Almanac* for 1876, again engraved by Adlard after a drawing by O'Connor. The Museum has a small but impressive group of watercolours (by A. Swim, A. E. Goodall and E. Hull) showing the actual construction of the Victoria Embankment.

Key

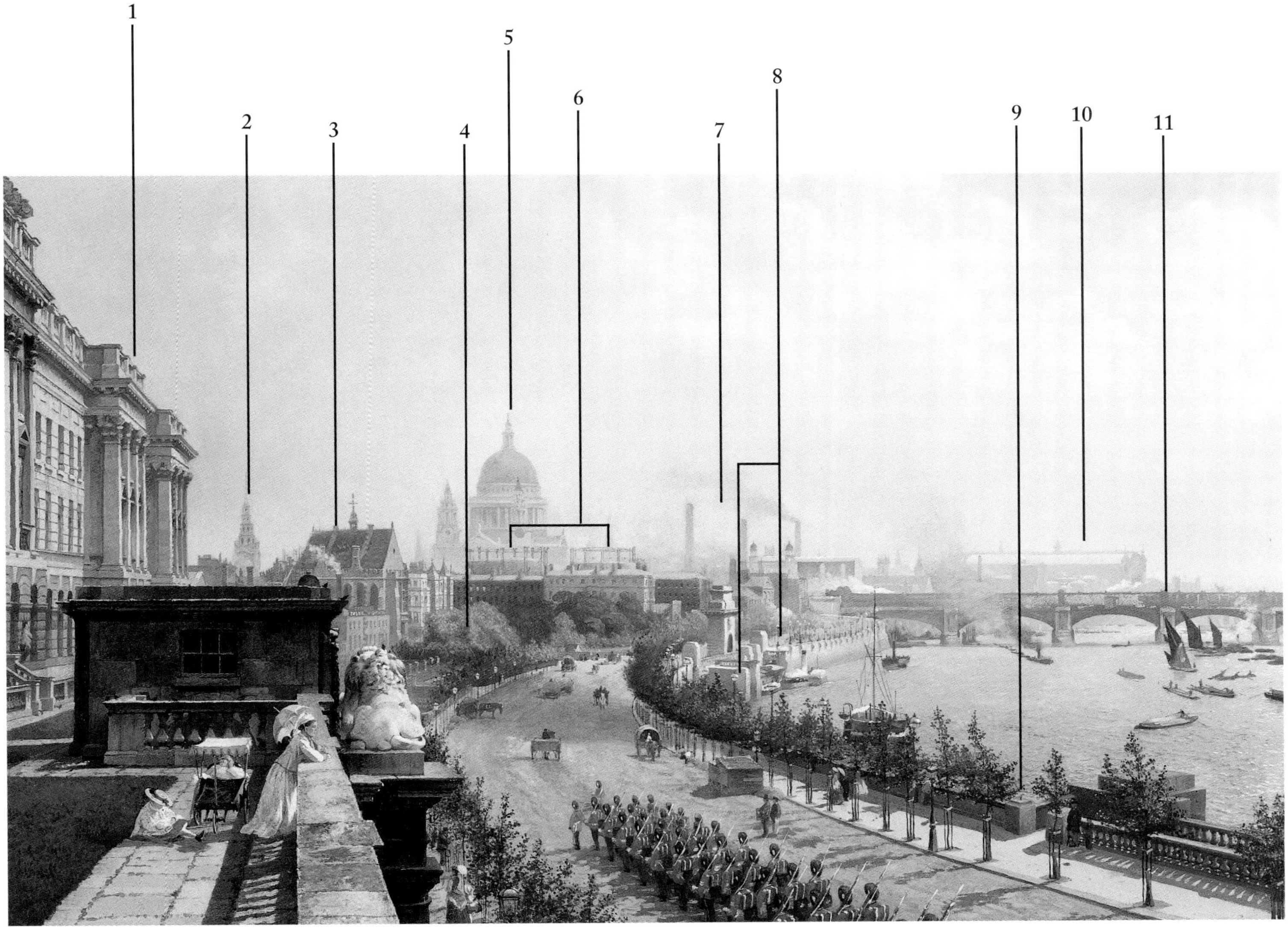

1. Somerset House
2. Steeple of St Bride
3. Middle Temple Hall
4. Temple Gardens
5. St Paul's Cathedral
6. Gasworks (twin gas holders demolished in 1873)
7. Temple Pier
8. Lamp standards in a line of lamps with dolphin bases
9. Retaining brick and granite wall (over a mile long)
10. Cannon Street Station
11. Blackfriars Bridge

Provenance:
Formerly in the collection of the Smith Art Gallery in Brighouse, Yorkshire, from the collection of Alderman William Smith (1839–1922); donated to Brighouse in 1907; purchased by the Museum from the Public Library and Art Gallery, Brighouse, in 1972.

81.
JAMES WEBB
(1825–95)

Old Kew Bridge [72.8]
*c.*1880
Oil on canvas, 112 x 87 cm
Signed bottom left: *James Webb*

THE VIEW is taken from the south-eastern end of the bridge, approximately on the site of the present Kew pier, looking north-west. Brentford Water Tower, part of the waterworks begun in 1835, dominates the view; and its size has been exaggerated to magnify the composition and reinforce its verticality. Thames barges and smaller craft are moored to the banks.

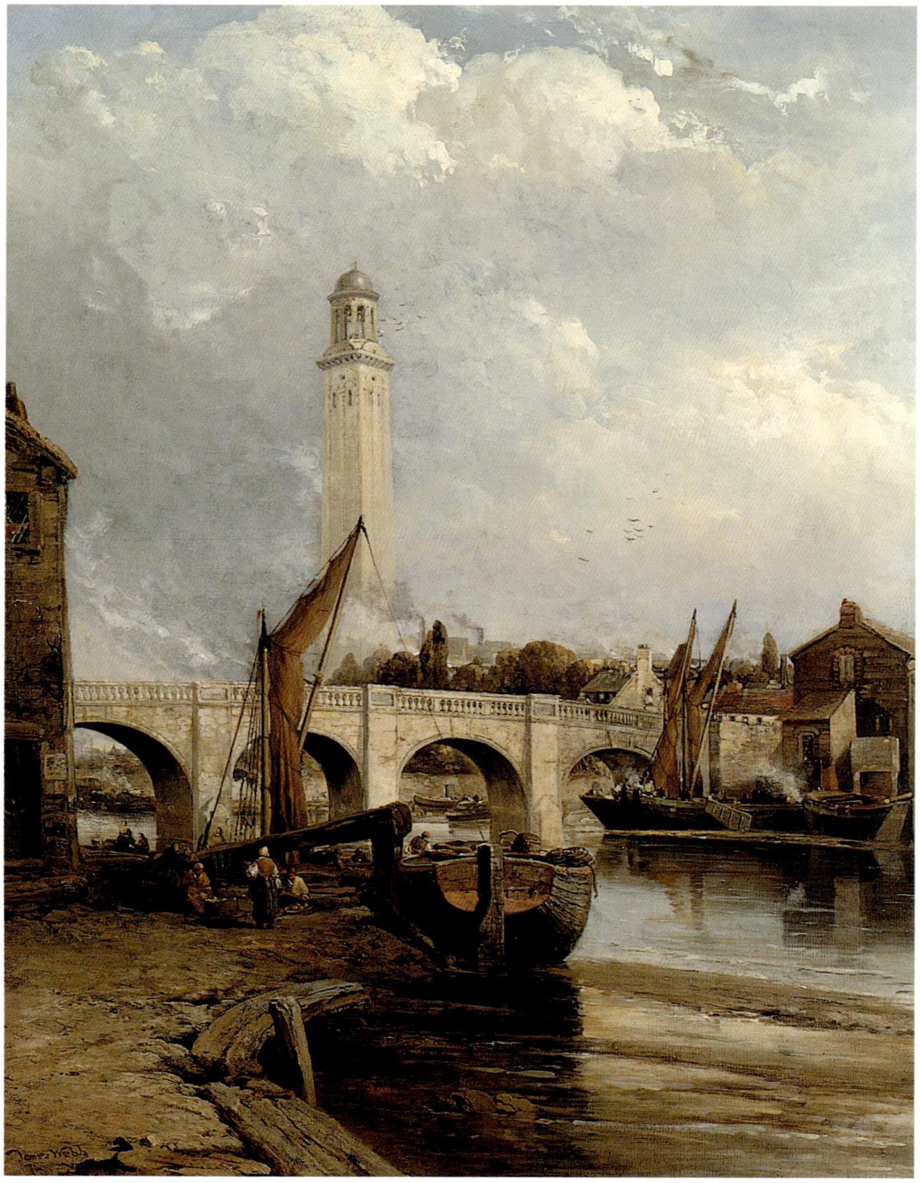

James Paine's five-arch stone bridge (built in 1784–9), shown here, has since been replaced by a squatter three-arch bridge (erected in 1903 by Sir John Woolfe-Barry and Cuthbert Brereton). The Victorian buildings on the north bank have disappeared but their modern counterparts retain the mix of housing and small industries. The blue and grey Vantage West building dominates the approach to Brentford from Kew and the accumulation of housing developments and shops on the north bank. The height of the surviving water-tower now competes with that of modern tower blocks on the site of the Victorian waterworks.

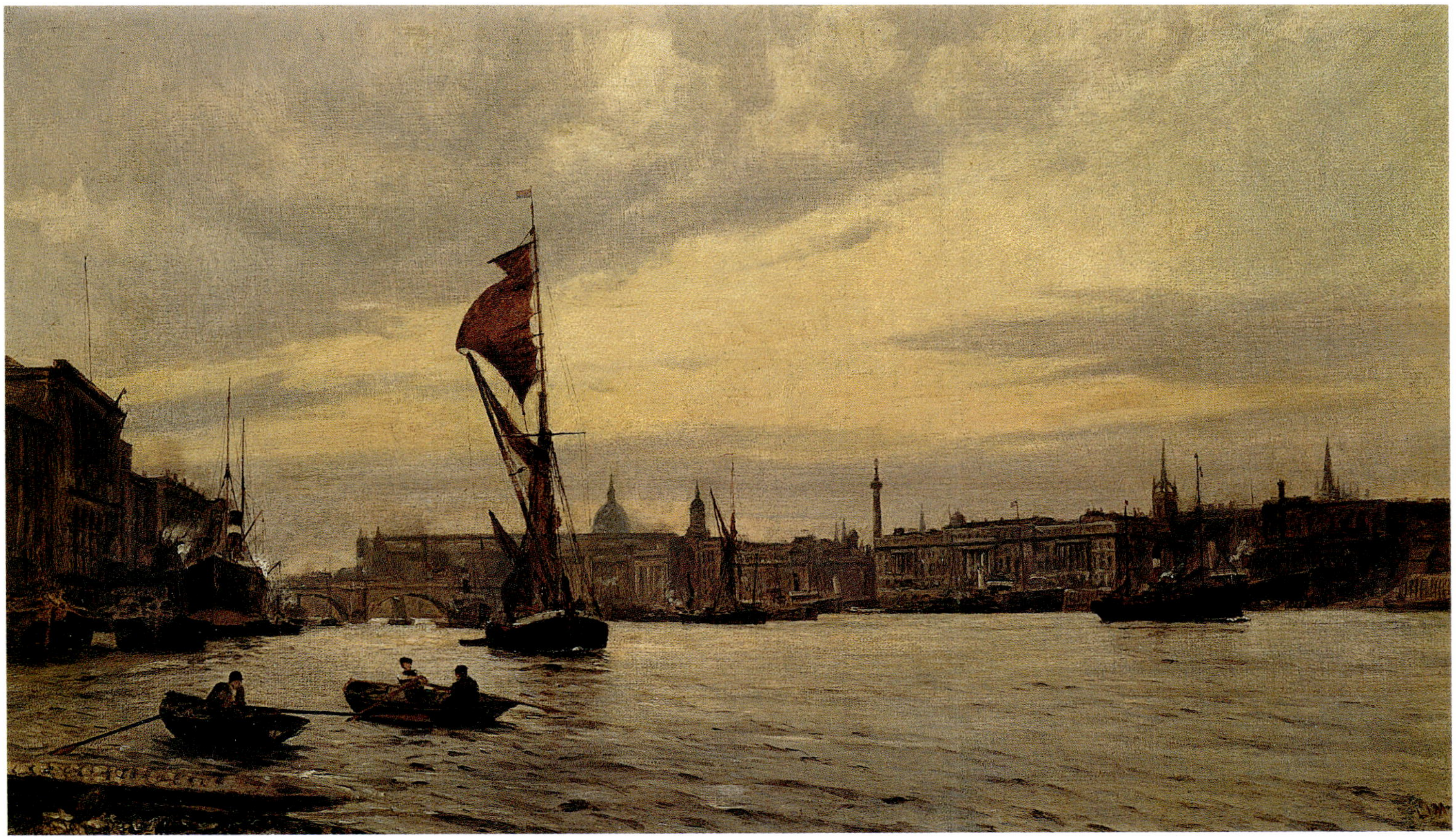

82.

FREDERICK A. WINKFIELD
(active 1873–1904, d.1920)

Evening in the Pool, River Thames
[62.187]
1887
Oil on canvas, 35.8 x 61.3 cm
Signed bottom left: *F. A. WINKFIELD*
and inscribed bottom right: *LIM*

A VIEW of the Pool from Southwark, looking westwards towards London Bridge. The buildings most clearly depicted are, from left to right: Cannon Street Station (built in 1865–6), the dome of St Paul's, St Magnus the Martyr, the Monument, the Custom House, the steeple of St Dunstan-in-the-East and the spire of St Margaret Pattens. A variety of craft is seen on the river.

It is interesting to compare this work with the Thomas Luny painting of the same scene (see cat. no. 50). The nature of the river traffic and congestion has changed and the artist here has adopted a broader landscape approach.

Winkfield also painted cat. no. 83 and a view of the Houses of Parliament (see Appendix).

Provenance:
Bonham's, 20 December 1962 (244), bt London Museum.

Bibliography:
Hayes (cat. no. 110).

Exhibited:
Royal Academy, 1997 (751).

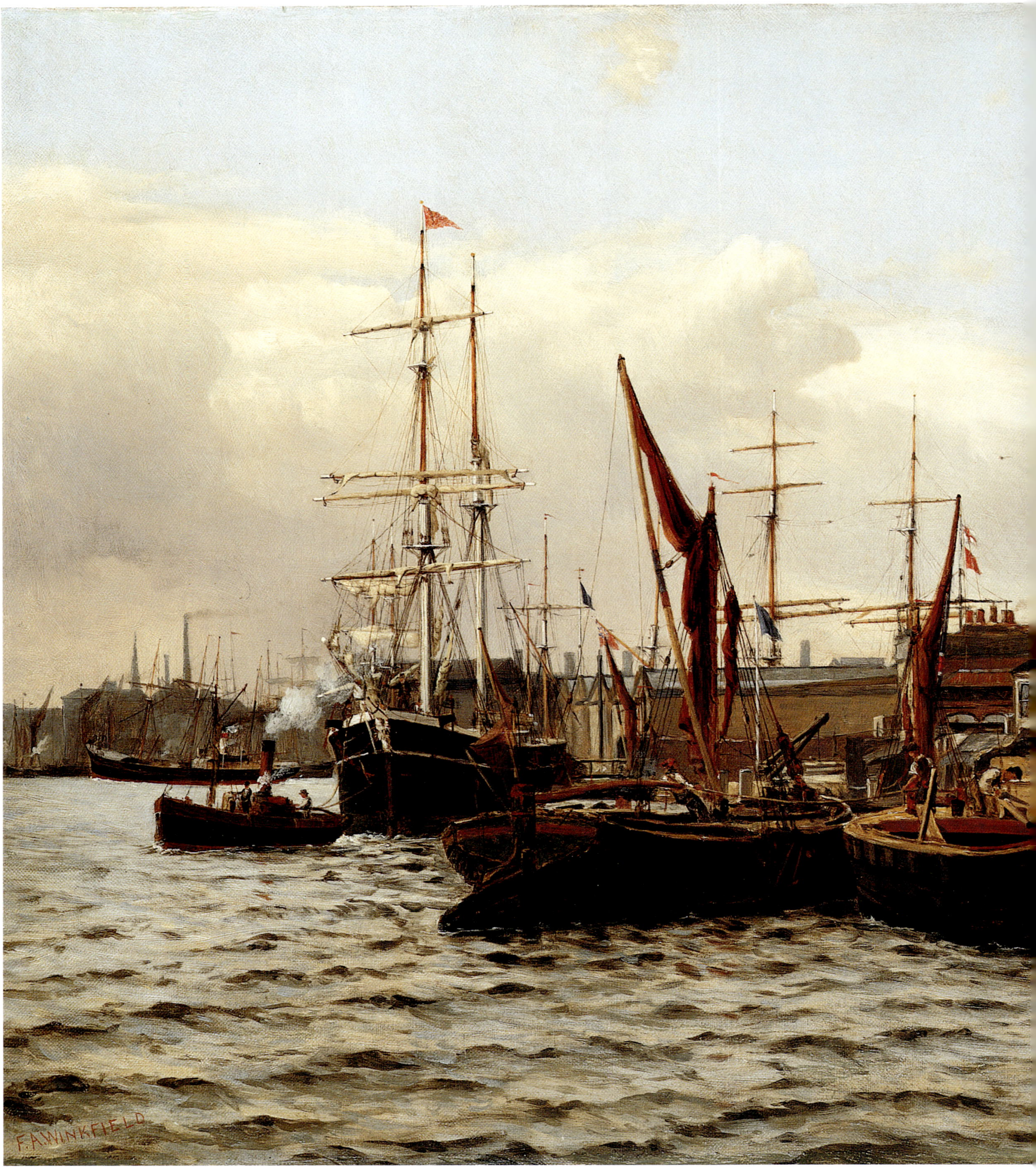
F.A.WINKFIELD

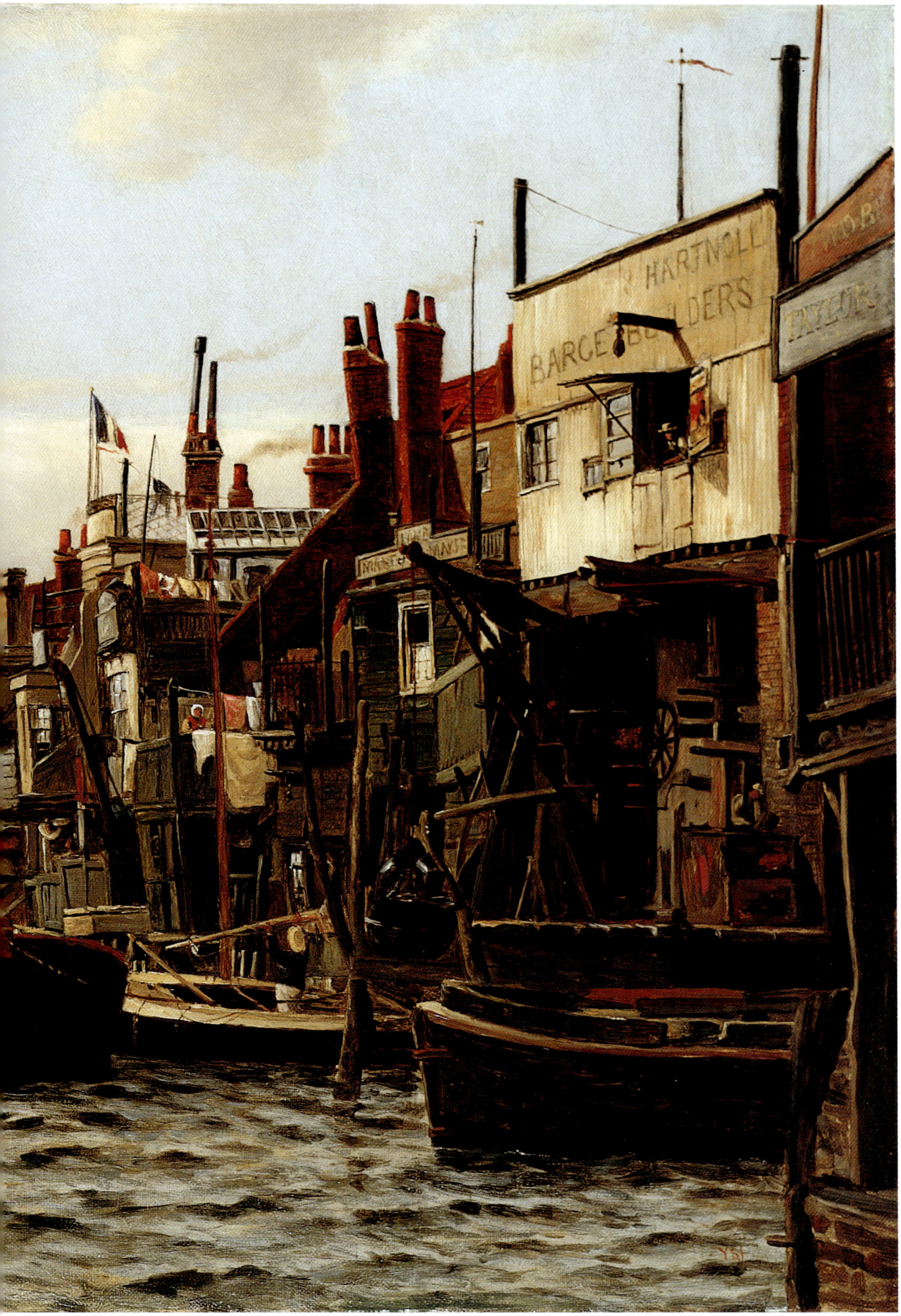

83.

FREDERICK A. WINKFIELD

(active 1873–1904, d.1920)

The Riverside at Limehouse [53.29]

*c.*1890

Oil on canvas,

45.7 x 76.8 cm

Signed bottom left:

F. A. Winkfield

Provenance:
Purchased out of the Joicey Trust Fund from the Leicester Galleries in 1953.

Bibliography:
Hayes (cat. no. 108);
Alex Werner, 'A General History of Limehouse: a London riverside parish', in *Limehouse Ware Revealed*, English Ceramic Circle, 1993, pp4–14.

THIS VIEW is taken from Duke Shore and shows the premises of George and William Lamb, mastmakers, of 92 Narrow Street, Charles John Hartnoll, barge building, at number 94, and, on the extreme right, the Two Brewers. Towards the centre of the picture may be seen the Harbour Master's office (with flags), the headquarters of the Thames police, and the Bunch of Grapes, which can just be made out in the middle distance. A barge-builder's yard is prominent among the wooden buildings characteristic of the Limehouse riverside which are seen on the right. Two barges are moored in the centre and, on the left, a tug is towing out a schooner.

Limehouse was commemorated in Dickens's *Our Mutual Friend* but in the nineteenth century it became cut off from its immediate surroundings through a succession of improvements such as the building of Limehouse Cut (1770), the West India Dock (1802), the Regent's Canal with its Limehouse dock (1820) and the London and Blackwall Railway (1840). Images of Limehouse's Chinatown date from the time of this painting, when the character of the area was increasingly influenced by its foreign populations (the Strangers' Home for Asiatics in West India Dock Road opened in 1856). Perhaps this was an added attraction to artists such as Whistler (see his 1859 *Thames Set* of etchings), Charles Napier Hemy, who produced two paintings of the Limehouse riverfront (see cat. no. 77 and Werner, 1993, p11) and Winkfield.

The picture must date from *c.*1890, after the partnership between Surridge and Hartnoll had come to an end (around 1880) as Surridge's name has been obliterated from the river frontage. Winkfield had exhibited a painting of Limehouse pier at the Royal Academy in 1879. A study for this work was sold at Christie's on 9 March 1995 (176).

Winkfield also painted cat. no. 82 and a view of the Houses of Parliament (see Appendix).

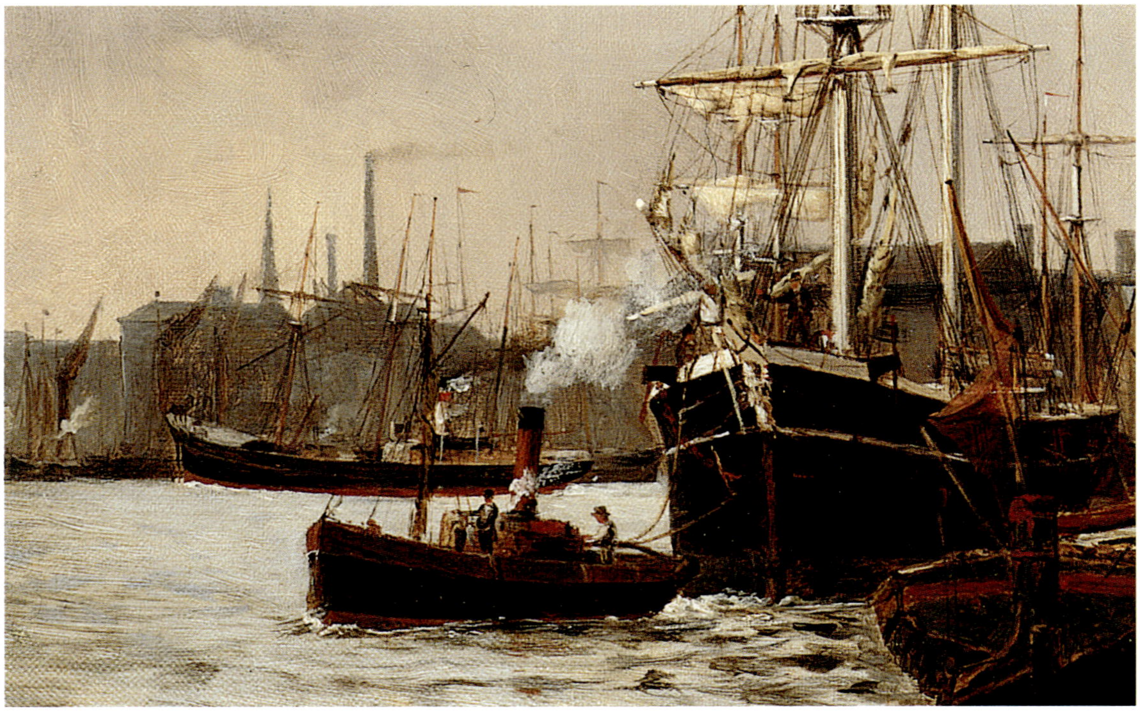

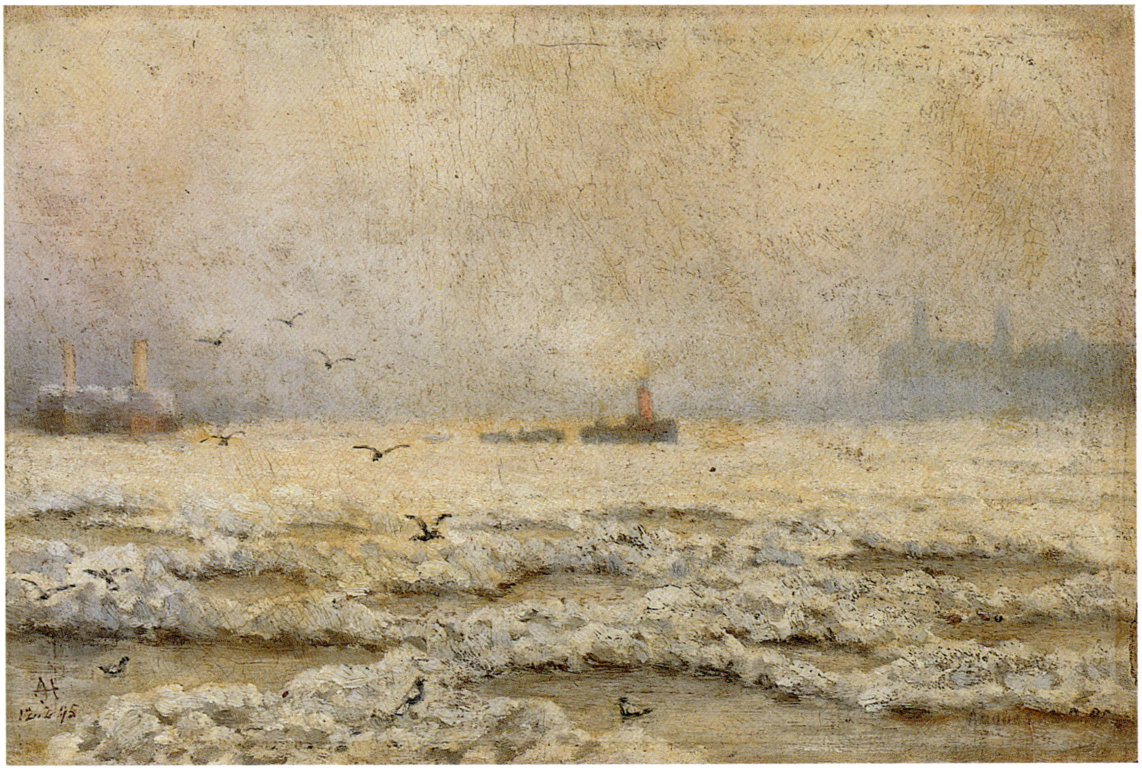

Provenance:
Mrs W. W. Hewitt; presented by Miss G. S. M. de Montmorency in 1953.

Bibliography:
Hayes (cat. no. 137); *Illustrated London News*, February 1895; J. H. Brazell, *London Weather*, 1968, p13; H. H. Lamb, *The English Climate*, 1972.

84.
BRITISH SCHOOL
The Frozen Thames at Greenwich [53.73]
1895
Oil on linoleum, 15 x 22.2 cm
Signed and dated in monogram bottom left: *AH/12.2.95*

THIS PICTURE was painted on the last occasion that the Thames froze over, in February 1895. A tug and barges are shown icebound in the middle distance centre, and some buildings are silhouetted in the distance left and right.

It was common for the Thames in London to freeze during extremely cold winters, especially before the demolition of Old London Bridge, which impeded the flow of the river, giving the ice a good grip and enabling the water to freeze solidly. After the demolition of the Old Bridge in the 1830s, there were few occasions when the Thames froze. Although the *Illustrated London News* devoted considerable picture and caption space to this event, this seems to be the only painting recording it. It is a slender but touching record if one considers that the frost made such an impression on artists. The arrival of seagulls, driven inland by hunger, was a visually spectacular event which was both noted and depicted by Nevinson (see cat. no. 173). Virginia Woolf must also have drawn inspiration from this event, which she witnessed at the age of thirteen. The Great Frost in *Orlando* (1928) is set in Elizabethan times, but the vividness of the description suggests that it was partly based on experience.

The initials A. H. on the painting may stand for A. Hewitt, as the painting originally came from a Mrs Hewitt, but nothing is known about this artist.

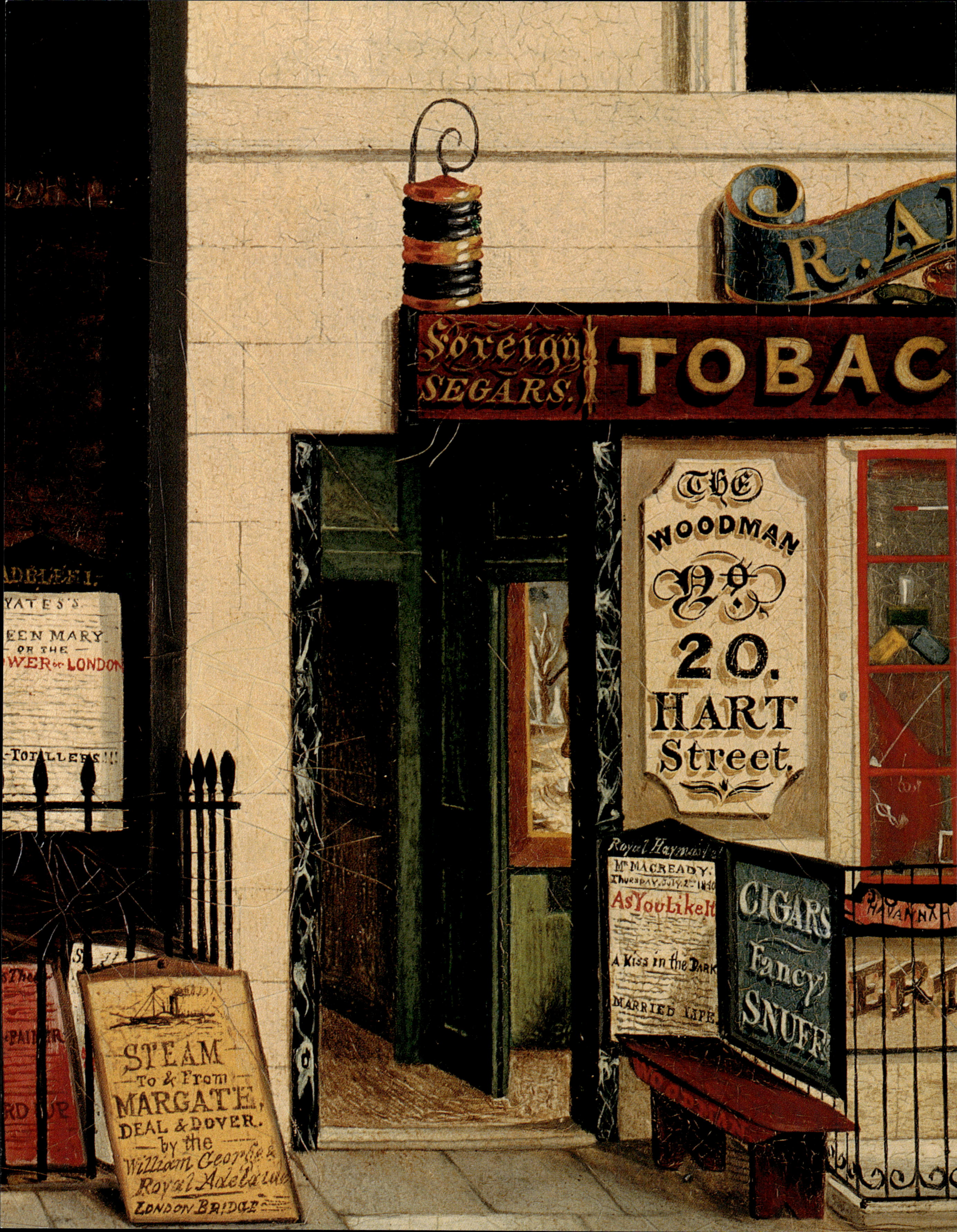
R. A
Foreign SEGARS.
TOBAC
THE WOODMAN No. 20. HART Street.
Mr MACREADY.
As You Like It
A Kiss in the Dark
MARRIED LIFE
CIGARS
Fancy
SNUFF
HAVANNAH
YATES'S
EEN MARY
OR THE
WER OF LONDON
STEAM
To & From
MARGATE,
DEAL & DOVER.
by the
William George &
Royal Adelaide
LONDON BRIDGE

STREETS AND BUILDINGS

THE DEPICTION OF VICTORIAN LONDON'S streets and buildings in the Museum's collection falls into three principal categories – grand townscape vistas, picturesque corners and transport. The first two categories recall the eighteenth-century tradition for such views, John O'Connor's paintings echoing the vistas first brushed out by Canaletto, Scott and Marlow, while the anonymous May Day group in Upper Lisson Street (cat. no. 86) recalls both its Georgian counterpart (cat. no. 34) and artists' depiction of Regency London. The little painting by Borgnis (cat. no. 88) also seems to fit more happily in the Regency spirit, its streets of a neat, pristine quality contrasting with the dark, busy thoroughfares of the Victorians. However, the context for producing views of streets and buildings had changed considerably since the Georgian period, and even since the Regency.

In Victoria's reign London's architecture fell under the influence of several historical styles. The style chosen for the rebuilding of the Houses of Parliament (see cat. no. 78) and the impact made by Ruskin's Gothic Pavilion at the Great Exhibition of 1851[1] marked the beginning of the dominant trend for Gothic fashion in design and architecture; for the next fifty years or so the many pseudo-medieval buildings which were built transformed the appearance of the streets of London. Examples include All Saints church in Marylebone (1859), the Eleanor Cross at Charing Cross (1863), Columbia Market in Bethnal Green (1869), St Pancras Station (1874), Tower House (the home of William Burges, and designed by him) in Melbury Road, Kensington (1875) and the Law Courts in the Strand (1882).

Other buildings, in contrast, followed the alternative fashion for classical architecture, and there arose a battle of styles – 'classical' Whitehall versus 'Gothic' Westminster. The Queen Anne revival followed in the 1860s, then a Tudor revival in the 1880s (the 1884 International Health Exhibition, for instance, had as its centrepiece a mock-up of a re-created Tudor street); Elizabethan style was revived in the 1890s, while Egyptian-inspired motifs reached peaks of popularity throughout the century – and this is to name only the most important trends. The single principle at work behind the eclectic styles of these successive revivals was the influence of London's past. The reinterpretation of the past by the Victorians went hand in hand with the development of a powerful antiquarian movement, which provided the backbone to all these historical styles – however far removed they may now seem to have been from their original sources.[2]

Two men, Philip Norman (1842–1931) and Henry William Brewer (d.1903), made a considerable contribution, particularly in visual terms, to the promotion and better understanding of this 'picturesque' past: Brewer (architectural draughtsman, engraver and publisher, but not painter) through his seductive but well-researched reconstructions of 'Old London', and Norman for recording the past in the present.

Brewer was the heir of Adam Lee, who had been the first to produce antiquarian reconstructions in the 1820s.[3] He regularly published these in *The Builder*, but a number of his London reconstructions were bound together with notes and published in 1921, after his death, as *London Illustrated*. In this London is shown at the time of Henry VIII and key buildings such as the Tower or Old St Paul's are reconstructed in their full medieval glory.

Norman was an indefatigable writer, researcher and draughtsman[4] whose passion for

London's past was almost unrivalled. He contributed to the emergence of what may best be described as the picturesque London cityscape. By meticulously recording historic landmarks, famous or forgotten, and often threatened with demolition, he could be seen as forging for the capital the idealised, picturesque images that Miles Birket Foster and Helen Allingham had developed for the countryside. Most of the images he produced, however, were in the form of watercolours. The Museum is fortunate in having two of his oil paintings (cat. nos 96 and 97). The existence in the Museum's collection of two versions by different artists of virtually the same view of Drury Court (cat. nos 96 and 100) is a good indicator of the popularity of this area with artists. From the 1850s onwards three principal sites emerged as 'picturesque' for artists: the back alleys of Westminster, those around the Strand, and Cloth Fair near Smithfield. A considerable number of prints and drawings relate to these sites[5] and the interest in these views was such that the subjects actually found their way into the oil medium, with good examples in this collection.

The interest in 'Old London' was no doubt encouraged by the disappearance of many historic buildings from the streets of the capital on an unprecedented scale.[6] Norman writes in his *London Vanished and Vanishing* (1905): 'Even during the writer's childhood [the 1850s] the City was still old fashioned; Kensington – the "old Court Suburb" – had somewhat the appearance of a country town, while that part of Chelsea which bordered on the Thames was a straggling riverside hamlet. But in this time of rapid change a generation makes all the difference. Growth and destruction have gone hand in hand.'[7] He adds a little later: 'Of the seventy-five illustrations here given, about sixty represent buildings which have entirely disappeared.'

There were many reasons for redevelopment in the Victorian period. Building works were linked to improved sanitation in London following the 1840s cholera epidemics, rebuilding after fires (London had to wait until 1866 for the creation of a Metropolitan Fire Brigade) and the construction of houses for a population whose number doubled in the first half of the nineteenth century. The advent of the railways was accompanied by a general improvement in London's communications network, notably the redevelopment of the Kingsway and Aldwych, the building of embankments and Holborn Viaduct, improvements carried out at Charing Cross Road and Shaftesbury Avenue (including the disappearance of Regent Circus and the creation of Piccadilly Circus) and the opening of Tower Bridge, which relieved traffic on other bridges. Major historic landmarks were lost in the process, for instance Temple Bar (see cat. no. 108), Hungerford Market and Northumberland House. The first underground railway in the world was built between 1860 and 1863 linking four major main-line termini: Paddington, Euston, King's Cross and Smithfield. In this case, however, demolition was kept to a minimum by the 'cut and cover' method, by which trenches were dug through existing routes and the road surface was rebuilt over the top.

But those *painters* anxious to recover or retain the past were in a minority. Many artists were clearly fascinated by the dramatic changes in the streets of London, and some continued to record scenes of demolition or construction, a genre already noted in the Regency section. Without passing judgement, the artist observed this massive building energy, intensified and diversified with the great building programmes of the Victorians and their consequences.[8]

This fascination with modern London was also notable in the plays of the period. As early as 1830 *The Heart of London* used the capital as a backdrop, followed by *The Scamps of London, or the Crossroads of Life* (1843), *The Streets of London* (1864), *The Great City* (1867) and *The Great Metropolis* (1874), among others.[9] This is of particular significance here since the Irish painter John O'Connor, who could almost be described as the king of topographers, created an image of London which is likely to have been derived from the theatre. His principal career was as a very successful scenery painter[10] and it is hoped that further research will be carried out into this vital link between the two professions.

Other influential painters not represented in the collection created a more socially charged vision of the London streets and buildings. The slightly enigmatic *London Visitors* by James Tissot, set in the porch of the National Gallery, is a rare glimpse of tourist London and William Logsdail's *St Martin-in-the-Fields* highlights the plight of child street sellers by contrasting an opulent part of London with one of its struggling inhabitants.[11] Niels Lund's *The Heart of the Empire*[12] (illustrated) succeeds in picturing this challenging concept by looking at the City of London from above – the centre of Britain, the Empire and, by implication, the world.

This brief survey of the fabric of Victorian London would not be complete without mentioning the extraordinary impact of transport, both on the streets of the capital and on its inhabitants. A remarkable little engraving published in Reach and Brooks's *Story with a Vengeance*[13] as early as 1852 may be seen to sum up Londoners' attitude to the emergence of a public transport network: an elderly bespectacled man sits smugly in an upholstered seat in

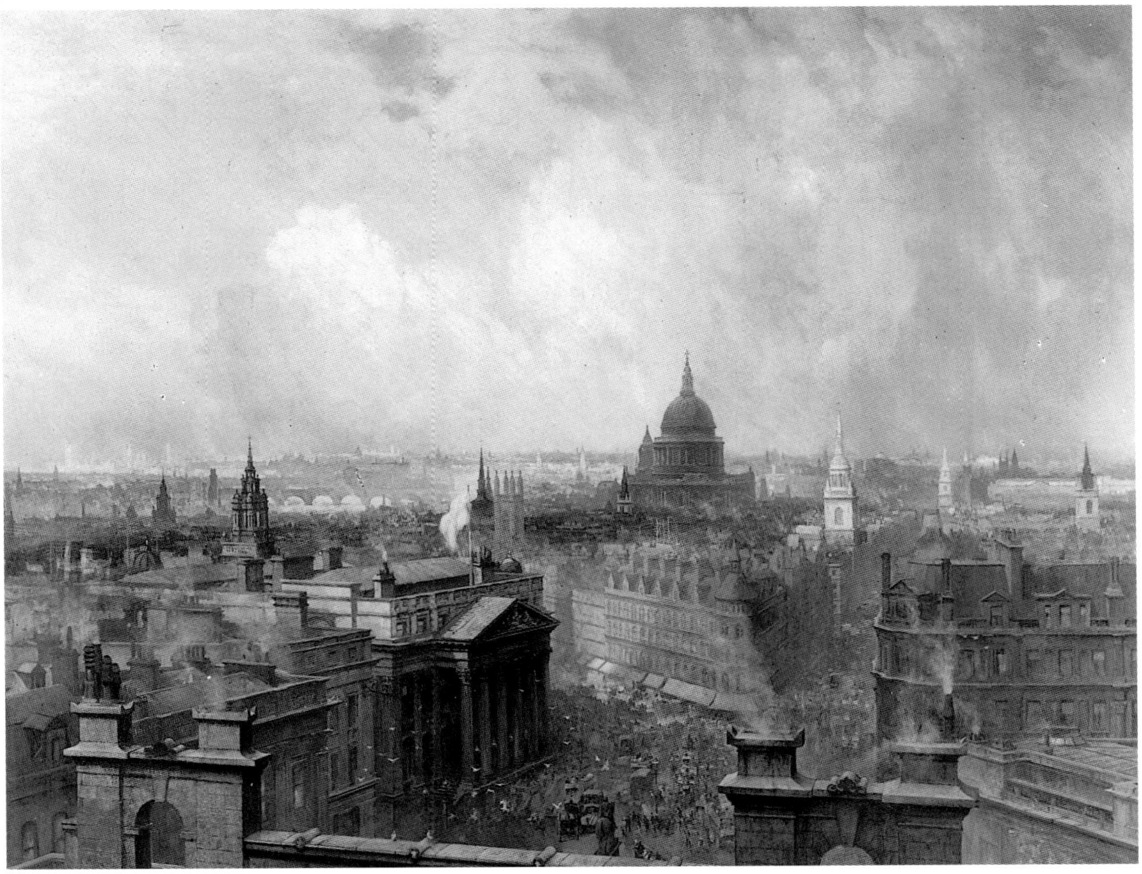

Niels Moeller Lund
(1863–1916)
The Heart of the Empire, 1904
Oil on canvas
Guildhall Art Gallery,
Corporation of London.

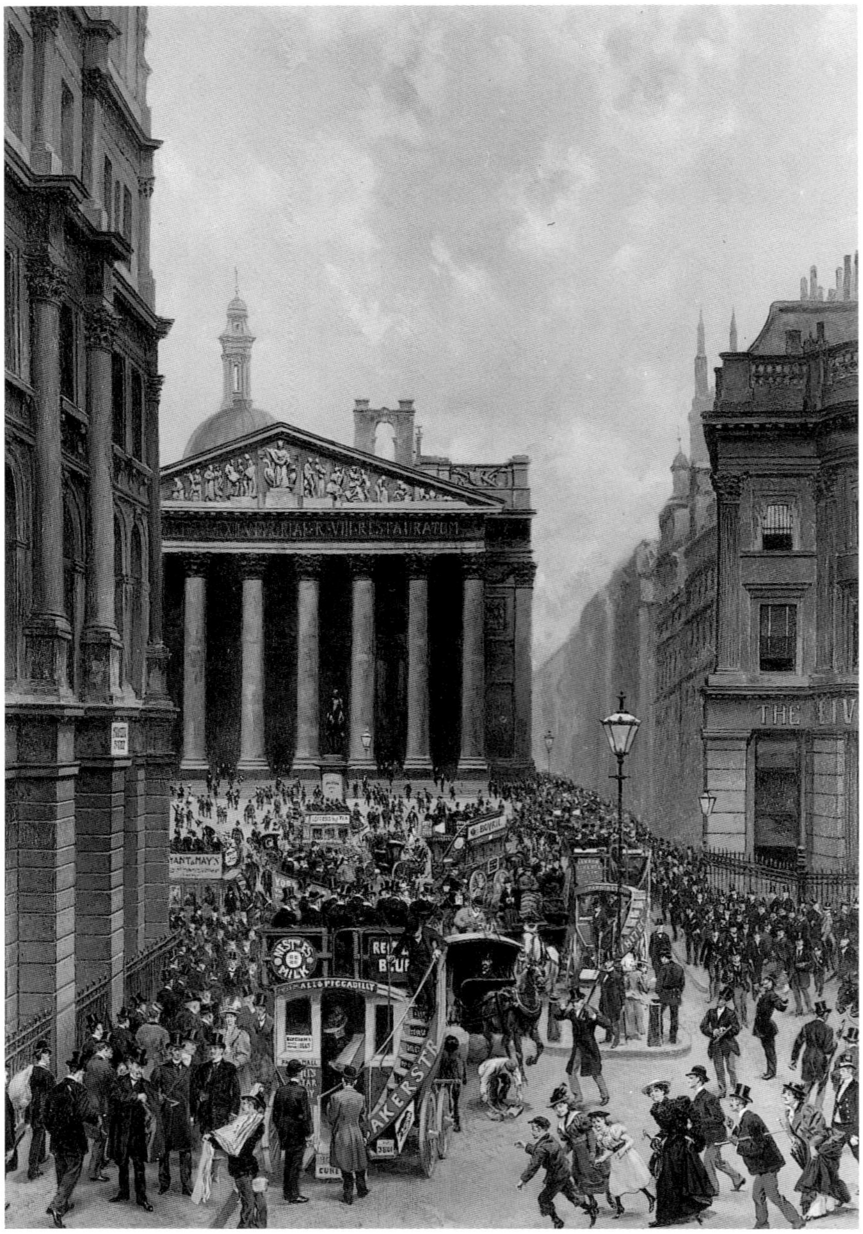

a first-class train compartment reading his paper. Save for the costume, he looks as if he could be a modern traveller with life-long commuting experience. And yet the great railway boom had only just occurred (London's first railway, the London to Greenwich line, had opened in 1836). The immediate adoption and success of new public-transport ventures in the capital was without doubt the single most revolutionary factor in the lives of Londoners. The fascination and interest of the public for railways was successfully tested when in 1862 William Powell Frith exhibited his great Paddington Station canvas *The Railway Station*. The work had to be protected by railings from enthusiastic crowds.[14] In Frith's painting and many others,[15] what artists strove to capture was not so much the architectural or engineering feats the railway projects represented but rather the impact they had on the travellers. The same was true of road transport,[16] but this collection is rather unrepresentative of the trend (apart from the magnificent Joy painting) and harks back instead to the Regency formula of 'portraiture' of vehicles. The material evidence is highlighted (cabs, coaches, buses and cab stands) and so are some of the heroes of its age (James Selby and Ted Fownes). Fritz Werner's *The Rush Hour by the Royal Exchange* (illustrated) renders well the extraordinary bustle of the capital, with its accumulation of omnibuses, cabs and people, once again meriting the title, at street level this time, of 'heart of Empire'.

Alexander Fritz Werner
(1827–1908)
The Royal Exchange from Queen Victoria Street, 1904
Oil on canvas
Reproduced by courtesy of The Mercers' Company.

1. C. H. Gibbs-Smith, *The Great Exhibition of 1851*, Victoria and Albert Museum, 1981, p85.
2. J. Mordaunt Crook, *The Dilemma of Style*, 1987.
3. Mireille Galinou, 'Adam Lee's Drawings of St Stephen's Chapel, Westminster: Antiquarianism and showmanship in early nineteenth century London', in *Transactions of the London and Middlesex Archaeological Society*, 1983, vol. 34.
4. This passion was, however, shared by a number of people and was usefully charted by Hermione Hobhouse in her historical summary, 'Ninety Years of *The Survey of London*', in *Transactions of the Ancient Monuments Society*, 1987, vol. 31.

5. The creation by artists of 'Old Picturesque London' awaits further research, but judging from the evidence in this collection based on the Aldwych site, the movement would have begun as early as the 1850s (with watercolours by the obscure W. Richardson, but also Louise Rayner) and reached a peak in the last twenty years of the century with the work of Waldo Sargeant, Hanslip Fletcher, F. L. Emanuel (much of it for the *Architectural Review*), T. R. Way (see note 6 below), C. J. Watson (see cat. no. 100), Ernest George and Howard Penton, to name but a few. Two further draughtsmen (but not painters) should be mentioned: John Crowther, whose body of work is in the Guildhall Library (see note 6 below) and J. L. Stewart, whose numerous watercolours recording old buildings (often after earlier prints) await further research; a large body of Stewart's work is in the Museum of London collection.
6. Outside the work of Philip Norman, we should also mention the topographical recordings of J. P. Emslie (1839–1913) and John Crowther (active 1876–98), both represented at the Museum of London and Guildhall Library. The following publications bear testimony to this same phenomenon: R. Paul, *Vanishing London*, 1894; T. R. Way, *Reliques of Old London*, 1897; F. Ogilvy, *Reliques and Memorials of London Town*, 1901; C. Emden, *Picturesque Westminster*, 1902; C. Gordon, *Old Time Aldwych, Kingsway & Neighbourhood*, *c.*1904; *London Past and Passing*, 1908; Hutchings, *London Town Past and Present*, 1909; and E. Beresford Chancellor, *Lost London*, 1926 (in which many of Crowther's watercolours were reproduced).
7. Philip Norman, *London Vanished and Vanishing*, 1905, pvi.
8. Apart from cat. no. 90 (Crystal Palace) and the paintings mentioned in relation to the theme of 'work' (sometimes connected with building or repairing programmes, see p232), attention should also be drawn to the following themes for painters: the building of the Thames Embankment (cat. no. 80), the transport and erection of Cleopatra's Needle (1878) and shipbuilding, for instance William Parrott's *The Great Eastern under Construction at Millwall on the Isle of Dogs in 1857* (on loan to National Maritime Museum).
9. Michael R. Booth, 'The Metropolis on Stage', in *The Victorian City*, H. J. Dyos and M. Woolf (eds), vol. I, pp211–24.
10. Martin Hardie, *Watercolour Painting in Britain*, vol. II, p189; *Theatre Notebook*, vol. 5, pp36–8, p59 (with illustrations); Joseph Harker, *Studio and Stage*, 1924, pp10–11 and 39–41.
11. Respectively in the collections of the Toledo Museum of Art (see Michael Wentworth, *James Tissot*, 1984, p117) and of the Tate Gallery (see Celina Fox, *Londoners*, 1987, p154).
12. In the collection of the Guildhall Art Gallery.
13. Felix Barker and Peter Jackson, *London: 2000 Years of a City and its People*, 1974, p270.
14. See A. Noakes, *William Frith, Extraordinary Victorian Painter*, 1978.
15. Christopher Wood, *Victorian Panorama*, 1976, pp207–15.
16. Ibid, pp216–19.

Provenance:
Sotheby's, 21 December 1957 (21, attributed to J. Pollard); purchased for the Museum of London by Appleby Brothers Ltd.

Bibliography:
Survey of London, vol. XXXVI (St Paul's, Covent Garden); Douglas G. Browne, *The Rise of Scotland Yard*, 1956, pp88–9.

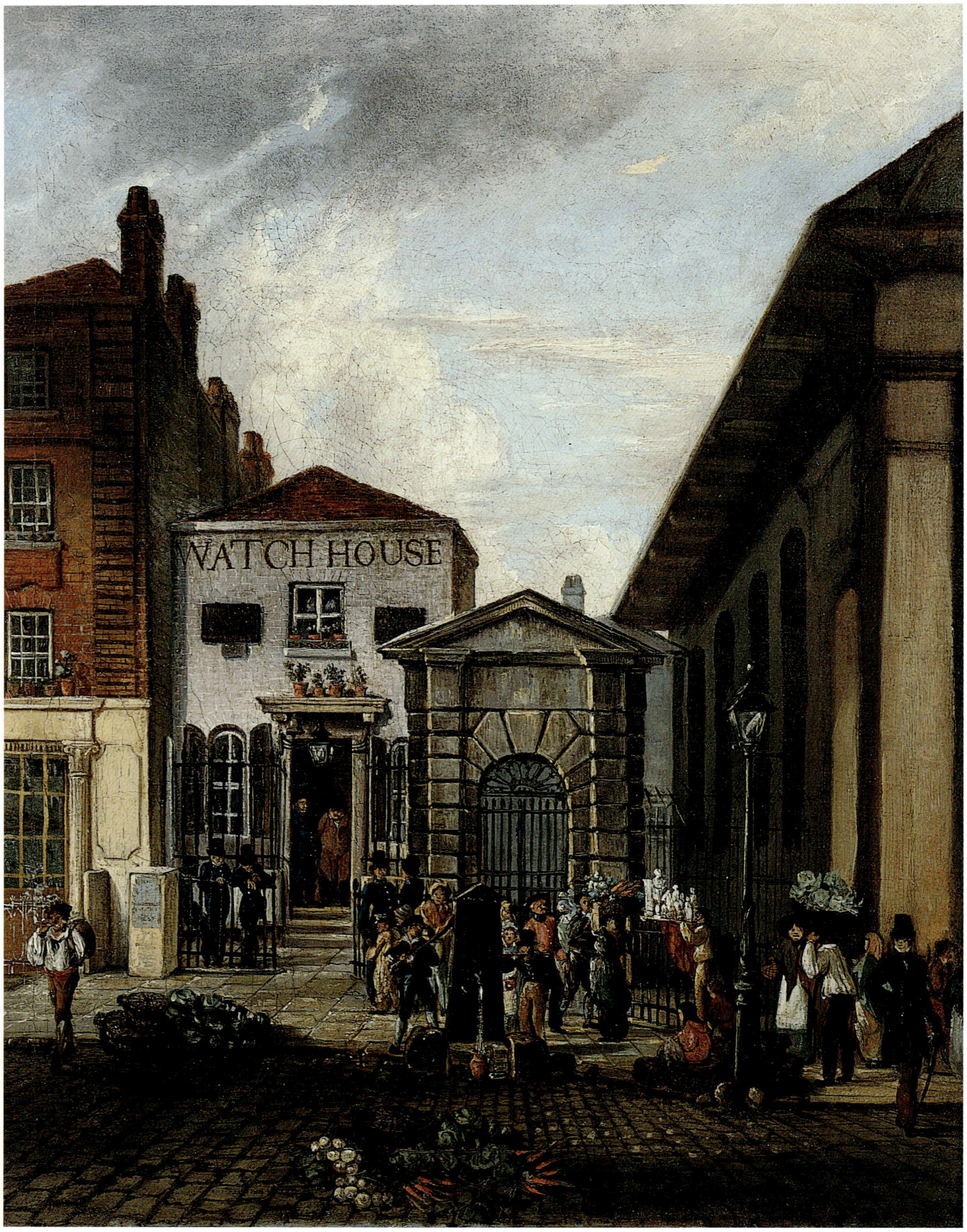

85.
BRITISH SCHOOL
Watch House, Covent Garden [68.38]
*c.*1835
Oil on canvas, 34.2 x 28.2 cm
Not signed or dated

THIS VIEW shows the watch house on the west side of Covent Garden piazza. On the right is the south side of St Paul's Church and one of its two flanking churchyard gateways. On the left is a three-storey brick house built in 1729–30, which replaced Inigo Jones's original south-west house (*Survey,* p80). In 1743, it became a tavern, the Unicorn, and it was demolished in 1888.

The painting is interesting for its street furniture detail: a gas lamp on the right, a water pump (the focal point of the painting and perhaps its true subject, despite its small size), iron railings (which replaced the original seventeenth-century high brick walls on either side of the churchyard gateway), cobbled street and raised stone pavement (contrast, for instance, with Niemann's painting, cat. no. 91).

A microcosm of street life may be observed in this view. A man draws water from the pump while another man is drinking, market workers carry baskets of vegetables, an image seller displays his board covered with statuettes; there are passers-by and, of course, the substantial presence of policemen around the watch house.

The Metropolitan Police Act had been introduced in 1829 and Covent Garden Watch House was among the first five considered fit to be taken over: it became the headquarters of Superintendent Thomas of F Division. Its underground cells apparently enjoyed 'a free current of air... to the great Advantage of the Prisoners confined there'. Soon, however, complaints were voiced and a new site had to be found. Bow Street was chosen for the new station-house, which was built and occupied by 1837.

The building which became the watch house does not appear in early views of Covent Garden (for instance, in Hollar) and probably dates from the early years of the eighteenth century (the door overhead, although very simple, looks Queen Anne). It is sometimes omitted from the views by the Covent Garden Group (see pp52–3), but clearly features in Balthazar Nebot's painting of Covent Garden in the collection of the Tate Gallery (and in a simplified form in cat. nos. 40 and 41). It may indeed have been the viewpoint for the van Aken painting (see cat no. 39), which, like the Nebot, dates from the 1730s. Unusually for this country, the ground-floor windows of the watch house have external shutters and a print by Paul Sandby (plate 15a in the *Survey of London*) also shows a shutter at the back of the building. These may have been fitted for security reasons.

In 1875 the 9th Duke of Bedford appointed the architect Henry Clutton to renovate the church and its immediate surroundings. Clutton did not regard the eastern gateways as the work of Inigo Jones and they were removed (in fact they probably were by Jones, and their rusticated Tuscan order inspired by the lowest arcade of the Roman amphitheatre at Verona). There was a proposal for re-erecting them at the ends of Henrietta Street and King Street, but this was not carried out (*Survey*, p120).

The painting may be dated between the late 1820s and 1840 on the evidence of the costume of the dandy character on the right-hand side. The latest date, however, has to predate the 1837 move to Bow Street and around 1835 is suggested.

Provenance:
Christie's, 25 March 1966 (150), bt Patten; purchased out of the Joicey Trust Fund from Richard Green (Fine Paintings) Ltd in 1966.

Bibliography:
Hayes (cat. no. 26); 'May Day is Sweeps' Day', in *Folklore*, March 1949; Roy Judge, *Jack-in-the-Green*, 1979.

86.
BRITISH SCHOOL
Sweeps' Day in Upper Lisson Street, Paddington [66.68]
Late 1830s
Oil on canvas, 37.5 x 45.6 cm
Not signed or dated

THIS VIEW of Upper Lisson Street looking north is taken from Chapel Street. A small crowd has gathered to watch a Jack-in-the-Green procession, which is seen in the centre foreground, and a number of boy chimneysweeps are collecting money. The 'Lord' wears a cross between full court dress and footman's attire with a huge cocked hat and the 'Lady' a mock court dress; she holds a long brass ladle with which to catch the coins. The pair is seen dancing on either side of Jack. The dance may have begun as a minuet and quickened into something faster before a collection was finally invited. A clown, a musician (with drum and harmonica), a man dressed in white (carrying chimneysweep brushes in each hand) and two chimneysweeps are taking part in the performance. The first depictions of a Jack-in-the-Green on May Day date from the late eighteenth century (see Judge, pp18–19) and the first appearance of the clown *à-la*-Grimaldi in pictures dates from 1820 (Judge, p20). Gradually the Jack-in-the-Green, which had first been shown by the side of the Milkmaid's plate-garland, came to replace the latter. It is interesting to compare this May Day *dance* with John Collet's May Day *procession* (see cat. no. 34): only the Lord, Lady and chimneysweeps feature in both paintings. In 1807 Robert Southey described the new character of Jack: 'the man stands in a framework which is supported upon his shoulders and is completely covered with the boughs of a thick and short-branched shrub' (Judge, p23). Jack-in-the-Green began to decline in the latter part of the nineteenth century, though one was seen as late as 1917. An unsuccessful attempt at reviving the tradition was made in the City in the 1980s and a Jack-in-the-Green was seen parading along the Barbican High Walk, paradoxically removed from the street.

Upper Lisson and Chapel Streets were largely shopping streets, and among the premises identifiable here are, from left to right, those of: Richard Hickman, ironmonger, on the corner at 11 Chapel Street; William Lamburn, grocer, a few doors up at 22 Upper Lisson Street (this shop was moved to 4 Union Street between 1844 and 1847); the Noah's Ark public house at 16 Upper Lisson Street (the tallest building seen); and on the extreme right Charles Simpson, grocer and tea dealer, at 10 Chapel Street. A butcher's shop, a boot and shoe repairer's, and a hairdressing and shaving saloon can also be seen on the right, a greengrocer's cart is being unloaded, and in front of this there is a lemonade seller (see Doré, *London A Pilgrimage*, p36). Notice also the fire insurance mark over Hickman's shop, and the tea canisters (a grocer's trade sign) over those of Lamburn and Simpson.

The fields north of New Road (Marylebone Road) and east of Edgware Road were developed in the third quarter of the eighteenth century, and Chapel Street and Upper Lisson Street were formed at this time. The east side of Upper Lisson Street remained open fields, however, until after the manor of Lisson Green was sold in 1792, and was not finally built on until 1809–12.

Lisson Street has since been rebuilt and, more recently, bisected by the arterial road connecting Marylebone Road with the west-bound Westway and A40(M) via the flyover over Edgware Road. The southern end of Lisson Street has been renamed Transept Street and most of the northern side of Chapel Street is now awaiting redevelopment.

The picture must have been painted between 1837, when the Noah's Ark was established, and 1847, by which date William Lamburn was at 4 Union Street. The costume suggests a date near the start of this timespan in the late 1830s.

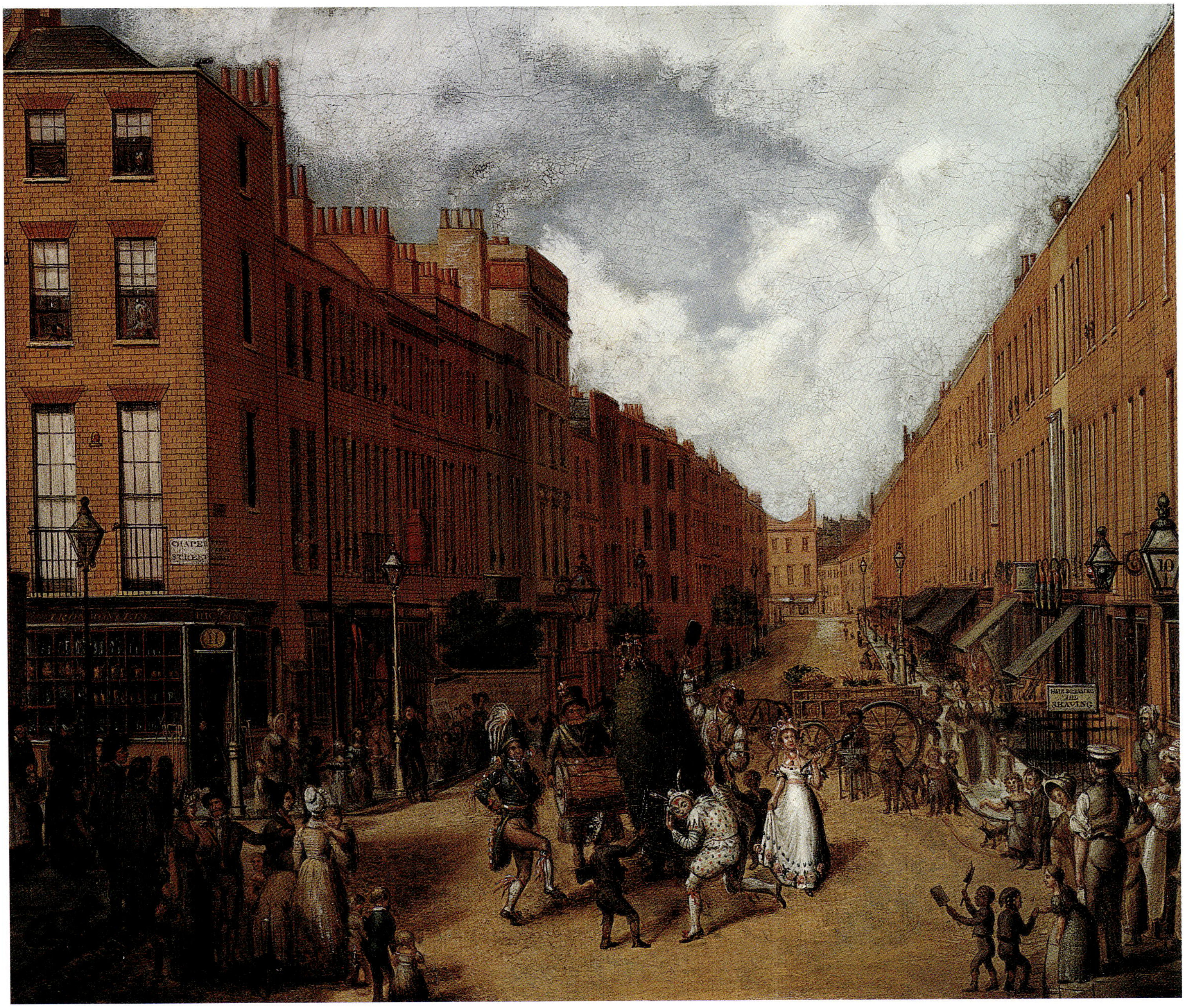

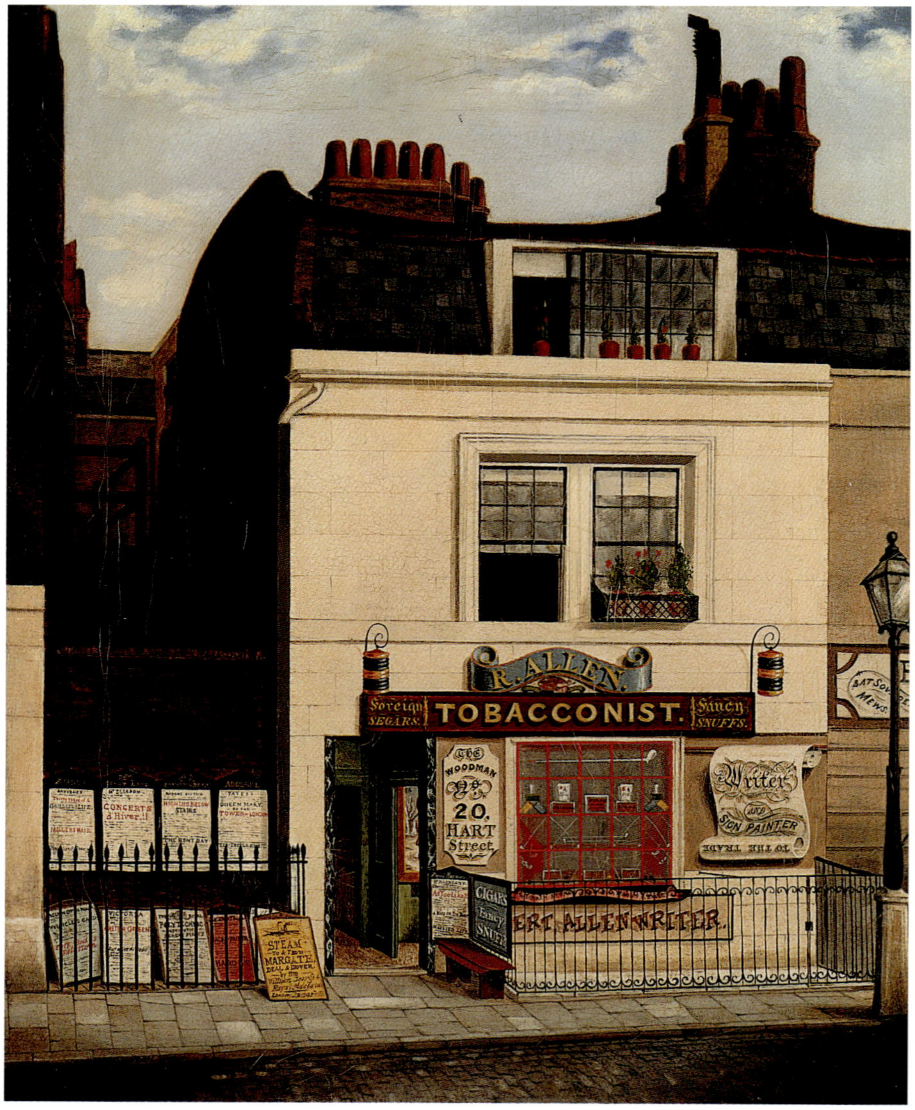

87.

ROBERT ALLEN

(active second quarter of the nineteenth century)

Allen's Tobacconist Shop, Hart Street, Grosvenor Square [39.45/1]
1841
Oil on canvas, 57.8 x 50.2 cm
Signed and dated bottom left:
Ro^{t}. Allen Feby 6.1841

Provenance:
Acquired in 1939, source unrecorded.

Bibliography:
Hayes (cat. no. 2).

THIS VIEW of the exterior of The Woodman, a tobacconist's shop at 20 Hart Street, Grosvenor Square, was painted by the proprietor, Robert Allen; as advertised outside, Allen was also a writer and sign painter. The traditional trade signs of the tobacconist surmount the fascia, and various posters are seen outside the shop: a steamer service by the *William George* and *Royal Adelaide* is advertised as operating between London Bridge and Margate, Deal and Dover; and there are placards for a number of London theatres: Macready is billed as appearing at the Royal Haymarket on 2 July 1840 in *As You Like It*, and Madame Vestris at Covent Garden in *High Life Below Stairs*.

Inside the open door can be made out part of Allen's shop sign – a copy of Thomas Barker's well-known picture, *The Woodman*, now in the Tate Gallery; this canvas, presumably executed by Allen, is also in the Museum's collections (39.45/2, see Appendix).

Hart and Brown Streets have now been replaced by Brown Hart Gardens, with flats erected in 1886–8 for four thousand artisans by the Improved Industrial Dwellings Company on ground leased by the Duke of Westminster. In the middle of Brown Hart Gardens is the London Electricity Board generating station, on top of which are the Duke Street Gardens, a bare concrete platform with a few benches but no sign of the growing plants that such a name might suggest.

88.

I. F. BORGNIS

(active mid-nineteenth century)

Shepherdess Walk, Hoxton [A 28575]

*c.*1845

Oil on panel, 62.7 x 63.1 cm

Signed bottom right: *I. F. Borgnis*

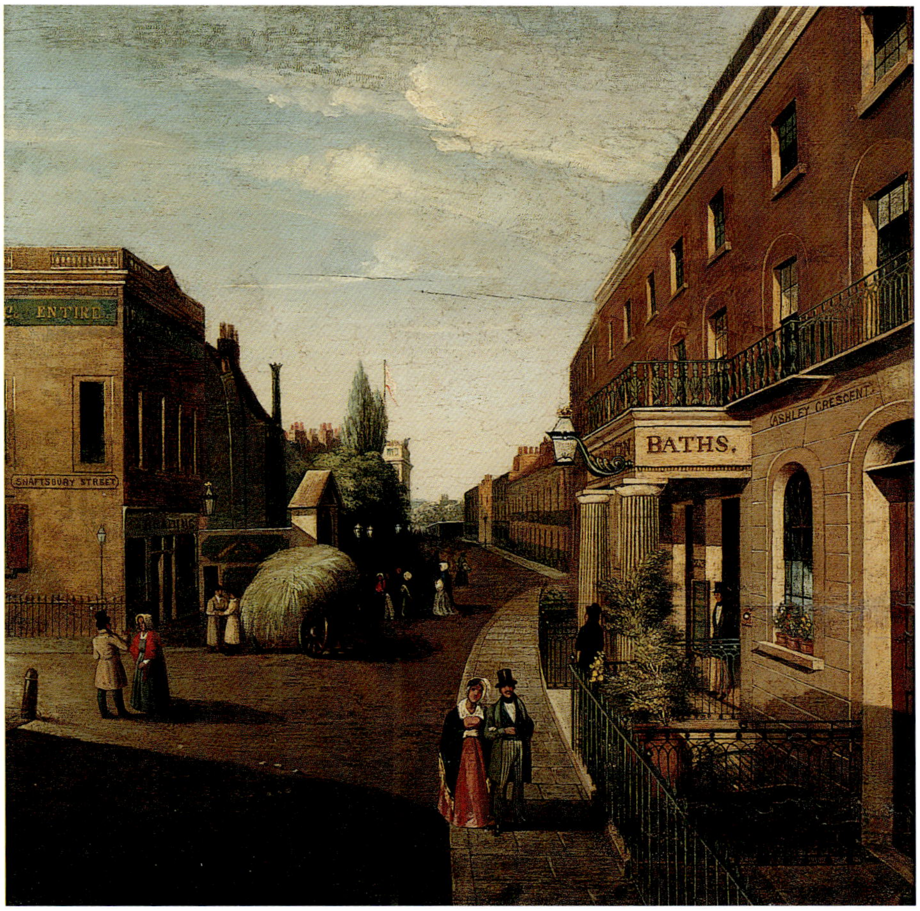

THIS VIEW of Shepherdess Walk looks south down what was then known as Vaughan Terrace towards St Luke's Workhouse, seen in the far distance. The view shows, on the right, the Metropolitan Baths at 23 Ashley Crescent (part of Shepherdess Walk). On the left is Shaftesbury Street, with the Royal Standard public house on the corner; the archway beyond, in front of which a number of people are gathered, seems to be the entrance to a Nonconformist Chapel; behind the trees is visible part of the facade of the Grecian Saloon (or theatre) attached to the celebrated Eagle Tavern (a stone eagle can be seen surmounting the parapet), shown as it was remodelled in 1837.

This part of London, which lies between City Road and Regent's Canal, began to be developed at the end of the eighteenth century. By 1795 there was a row of houses at the southern end of Shepherdess Walk, the Shepherd and Shepherdess (later known as the Eagle Tavern) had been opened, and St Luke's Workhouse constructed. Vaughan Terrace and Ashley Crescent were both finished in the early 1830s, and the houses seen here, two- and three-storey in height, partially stuccoed and with ironwork balconies, are typical of terraces of this period in the inner suburbs.

The act enabling local authorities to establish public baths and wash-houses was passed in 1846, as part of complex sanitary legislation resulting from the cholera scares of the 1840s. The Metropolitan Baths, described as a 'House with Cold, Tepid and private Baths, with Ante and Dressing Rooms and Boxes', was a more elegant private establishment opened in 1835 under the proprietorship of James Esdaile.

The costume indicates a date of about 1845.

Provenance:
Presented by Leggatt Brothers in 1912.

Bibliography:
Hayes (cat. no. 10).

Provenance:
Lent by J. G. Joicey in 1917, and afterwards bequeathed in 1919.

Bibliography:
Hayes (cat. no. 94).

89.

JAMES POLLARD

(1792–1867)

A Street Scene with Two Omnibuses
[C 2399]
1845
Oil on fibreboard, 24.7 x 32 cm
Signed and dated bottom left:
J. Pollard. 1845
An old label on the back bears the inscription:
E. & J. Wilsons[s]– *omnibuss showing/his Visiter the way to Chelsea – /on St Patricks Day March 17th 1845*

TWO EARLY London omnibuses are shown against the background of a residential square framed by four-storey eighteenth-century red-brick terrace houses, possibly Cadogan Place, Sloane Street (the building on the corner of Cadogan Place and Pont Street is reminiscent of the houses depicted by Pollard).

The foremost omnibus, painted in *Favorite* green, is labelled as one of the *Favorite* fleet, and with the owners' names E. and J. Wilson. Its terminus is marked as the Crown Inn, Holloway, and, according to the legend on a board fixed to a post above the omnibus, it plied between the Birmingham Railway (Euston) and Chelsea. Intermediate points between Holloway, Euston and Chelsea are advertised on the side of the vehicle – Islington, New Road (Euston Road), Regent Street and Knightsbridge.

The second omnibus, also green in colour, is marked as plying between Holloway and Chelsea, with Oxford Street and Knightsbridge as intermediate points; since it is further away, it offers less opportunity for the artist to include detailed lettering.

Both omnibuses are of the early single-deck type introduced by George Shillibeer in 1829. It remained the standard type up to the 1850s, until the crowds that came up to London for the Great Exhibition of 1851, and the rapidly increasing population of the metropolis itself, created a demand for more and much bigger vehicles. The earliest omnibuses were drawn by three horses (these are drawn by two, which became the norm), and the conductor stood on a plate at the back of the vehicle and held on by means of a strap; twelve seats were provided for passengers inside. Gradually, accommodation was provided on the roof as well, and at first two passengers were allowed outside, one on either side of the driver. By the mid-1840s, however, a second row of seats was often installed behind the driver, and this arrangement can be seen in the foremost omnibus here. The longitudinal roof seat (or 'knifeboard') characteristic of the 1850s and 1860s was first introduced in 1847.

At this date, there was no publicly owned transport system in London; numerous different companies operated, each with its own route and distinctive colour, and all were fiercely competitive. E. and J. Wilson, who had a licence to run eleven vehicles from Holloway, were among the leading proprietors; they also hired out horses and carriages, and their yard was called Wilson's Livery Stables. In 1855 two French speculators, Orsi and Foucauld, began to buy up the companies (the forty-eight omnibuses then owned by the Wilsons were taken over in January of that year), and out of their operations grew the London General Omnibus Company, the precursor of London Transport.

This work is one of a pair of omnibus paintings by Pollard in the Museum's collection (see Appendix).

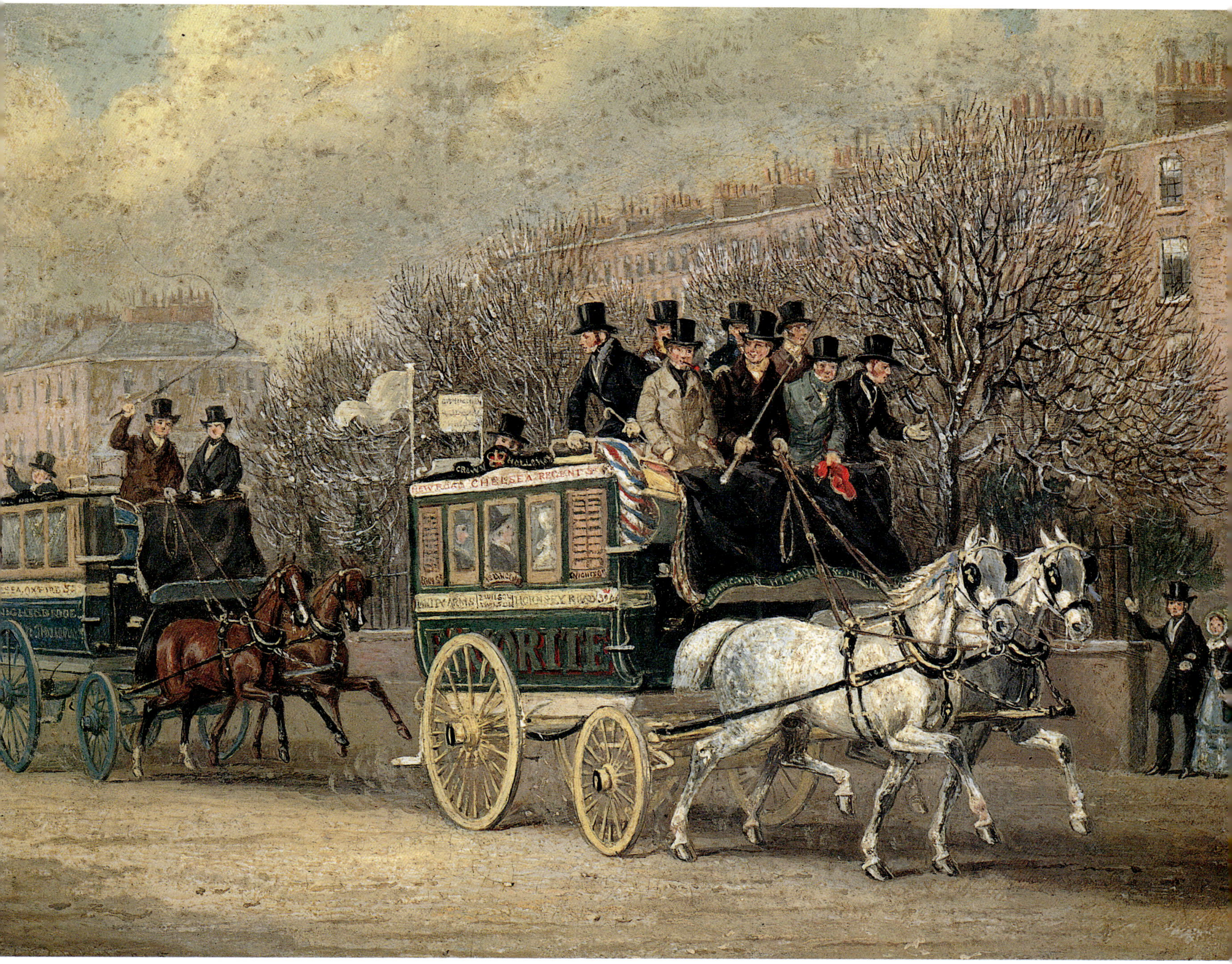
NEW ROAD CHELSEA REGENT St
HORNSEY ROAD

Provenance:
With Pulitzer Gallery in 1959; purchased from Michael Harvard in 1961.

Bibliography:
Hayes (cat. no. 34); C. H. Gibbs-Smith, *The Great Exhibition of 1851*, Victoria and Albert Museum, 1981; *The Blasted Oak*, exhibition catalogue, Herbert Art Gallery Museum, Coventry, 1987, no. 28; Hermione Hobhouse, *Prince Albert: His Life and Work*, 1983, chapter 7; Oliver Millar, *The Victorian Pictures in the Collection of Her Majesty the Queen*, 1992.

90.

THOMAS COLMAN DIBDIN

(1810–93)

Crystal Palace in Hyde Park [61.121]
1851
Oil on canvas, 68.2 x 103.5 cm
Signed and dated bottom right:
Hyde PARK 1 May 1851/T C. Dibdin.

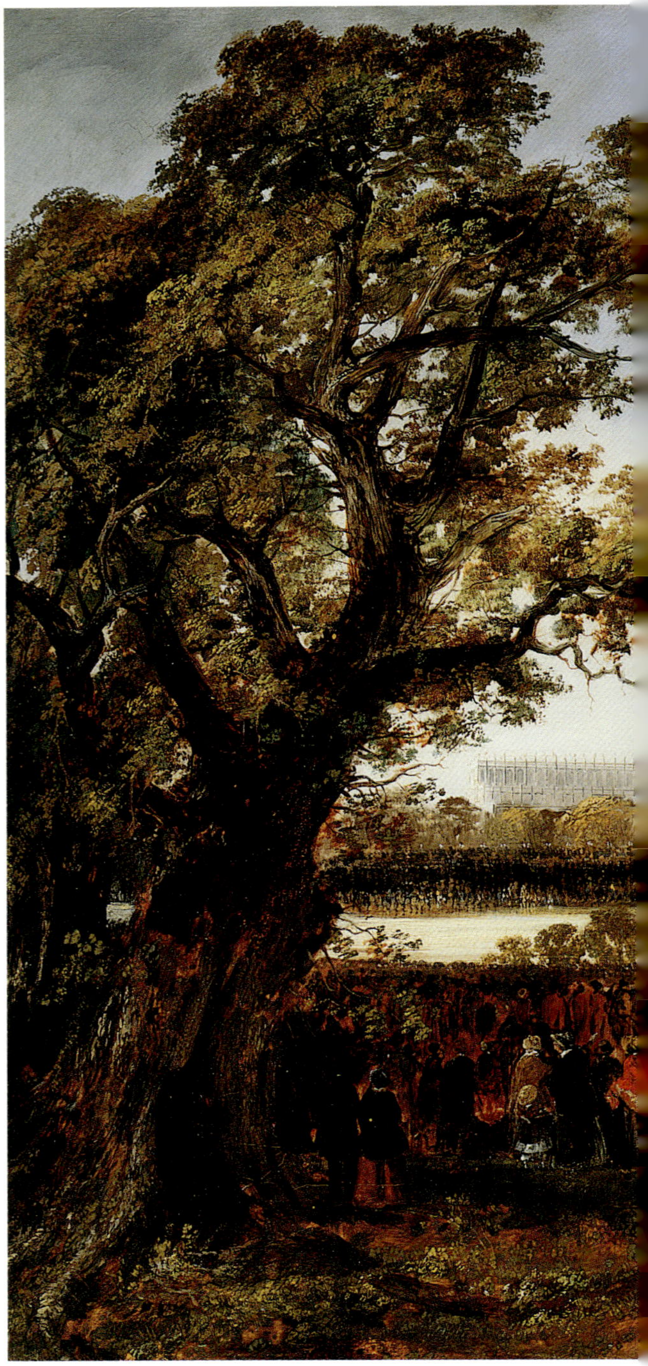

THIS PAINTING records the opening of the Great Exhibition of 1851, as is revealed by the artist's inscription and the presence of huge crowds. The scene is viewed from the north side and from beyond the Serpentine.

The exhibition was opened by Queen Victoria on 1 May 1851, exactly the day that had been decided upon sixteen months before. The Queen wrote in her journal:

> Green Park and Hyde Park were one mass of densely crowded human beings, in the highest good humour and most enthusiastic... A little rain fell, just as we started, but before we neared the Crystal Palace, the sun shone and gleamed upon the gigantic edifice, upon which the flags of every nation were flying. We drove up Rotten Row and got out of our carriages at the entrance on that side.

The plumes of the Royal Horse Guards and the canopy in front of the north transept, where the Queen entered the building, can be seen in the middle distance, across the Serpentine.

The Great Exhibition of 1851, the first international exhibition ever held, was at first intended to be simply the most important of a series of annual exhibitions of manufactures promoted by the Royal Society of Arts from 1847 onwards. It was the Prince Consort, President of the Society, who proposed that it should 'embrace foreign productions', and Henry Cole, the organiser of the exhibitions, who suggested Hyde Park as the site. From this moment, the unusual nature of the project was apparent. A Royal Commission was set up to supervise the scheme, with the Prince Consort as Chairman, and the revolutionary design for the exhibition building submitted by Joseph Paxton, then superintendent of the gardens at

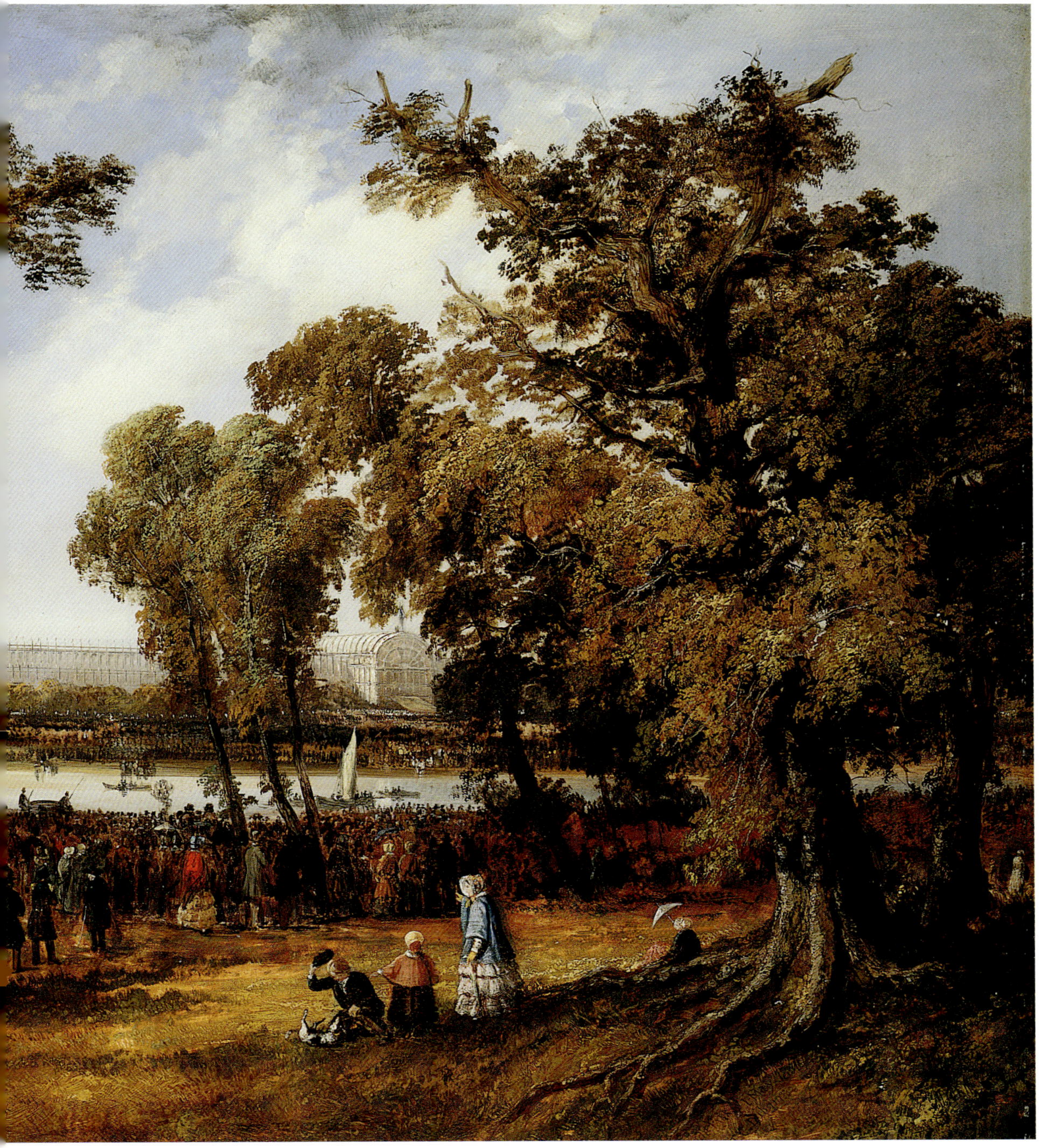

Chatsworth, was accepted. The 'Crystal Palace', as it was christened by *Punch*, was a gigantic structure of iron and glass, derived from Paxton's experience in conservatory design. Something of its vast extent, over 560 metres, stretching from the site of the present bowling green to opposite the former Hyde Park Barracks riding school, can be gauged from this view, which shows only half its length.

This painting may usefully be grouped with the two royal commissions by James Duffield Harding and William Wyld (described by Oliver Millar, 1992, cat. nos 300 and 1050). Each painter tackled the subject from a different angle; the images bear witness to the difficulties of scale and landscape encountered by artists. The Crystal Palace was dismantled in 1852 and rebuilt in Sydenham (see cat. nos 118 and 139).

Provenance:
Purchased out of the Mackenzie Bell Trust Fund from Richard Green (Fine Paintings) Ltd in 1964.

Bibliography:
Hayes (cat. no. 83).

91.

EDMUND JOHN NIEMANN
(1813–76)

Buckingham Street, Strand [64.150]
1854
Oil on canvas, 112 x 89.4 cm
Signed, dated and inscribed bottom right:
Buckingham St[t] Strand/Niemann 1854

THIS VIEW appears to be taken from the top of the street, looking south; York Place, an alleyway known until shortly before this date as Of Alley, runs off to the west a little way down. The topography is puzzling, however, as York Place also ran off to the east, and the opening of Duke Street (now John Adam Street) should be visible farther down. At the foot of the street is the York Water Gate (see cat. no. 79) which, after the construction of the Victoria Embankment, was to be stranded some 150 metres from the river. Beyond can be seen part of the Hungerford Suspension Bridge, an elegant footbridge designed by Brunel and finished in 1845; it was demolished not long after completion, in 1859–60, so that the Charing Cross Railway Bridge could be built (the chains of the old Bridge were used for the Clifton Suspension Bridge at Bristol).

On the left are the premises of Richard Stone, tallow chandler, at numbers 27 and 28, and William Crocker, boot-maker, at number 26; on the right are the Prince's Head Tavern and the shops of James Lilly, fruiterer, at number 4 and J. C. Fisher, butcher, at number 5. The premises farther down the street were still in use either as private residences or as the offices of solicitors, civil engineers and other professional people. Among the figures represented is a hurdy-gurdy player; notice also the cobbles and the absence of raised pavements, still characteristic of London's side streets.

Buckingham Street was built up in the 1670s, the whole street being complete by 1680; some of the original houses are seen here, for example, on the extreme right, but others have the set-back windows of the early eighteenth century and were clearly built later. A late seventeenth-century ceiling painting was recovered from number 15 and is now in the Museum's collection. (See Appendix/Early Period/ *Allegory of Summer*).

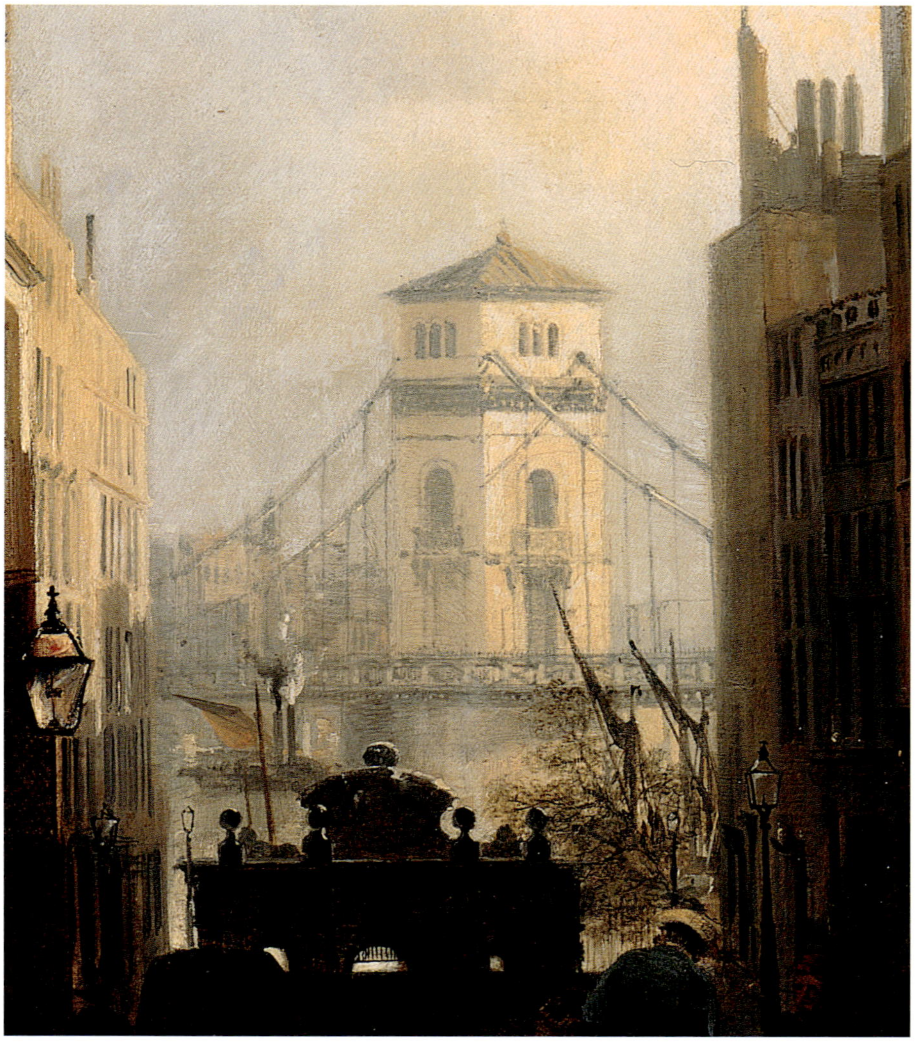

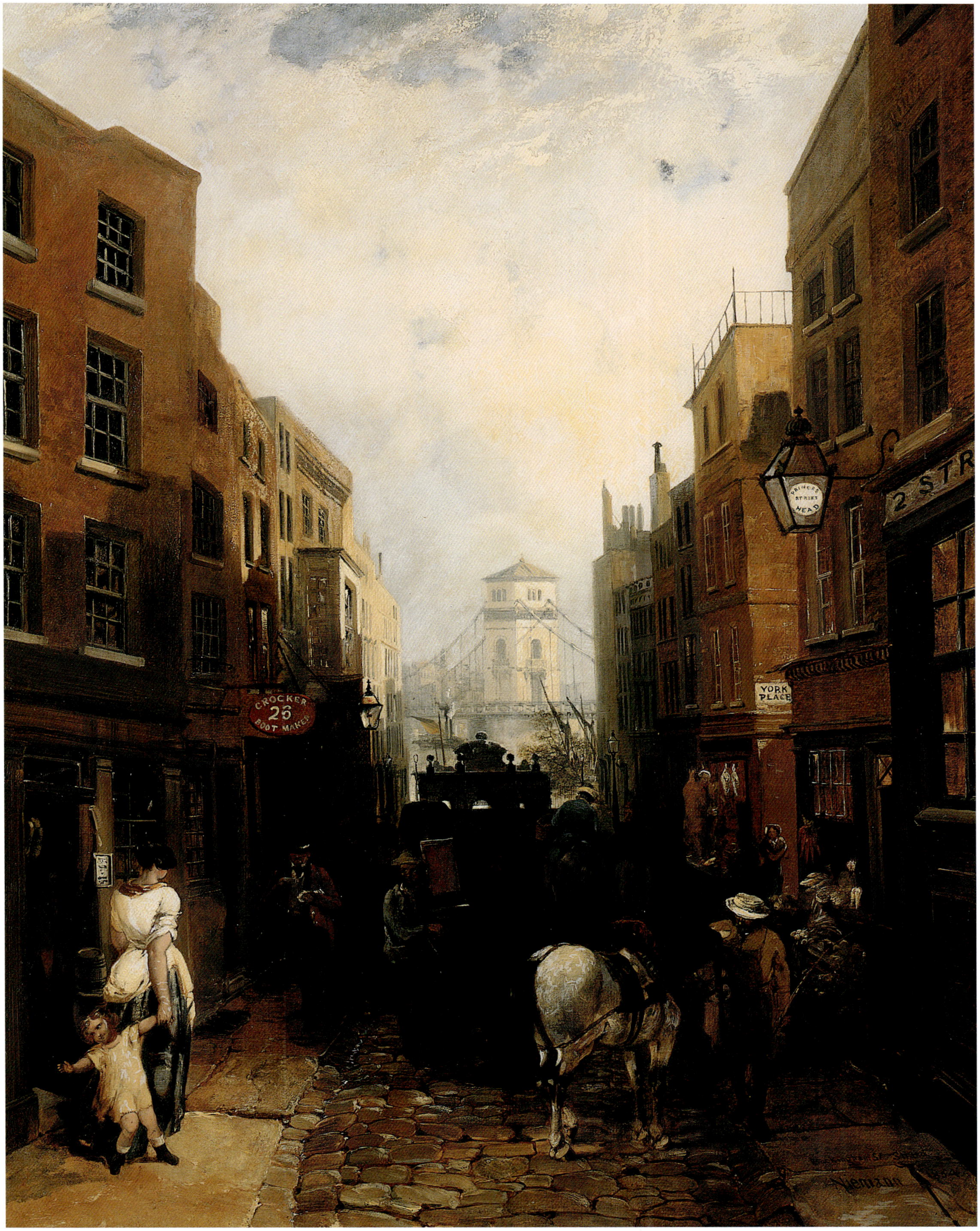
PRINCES STREET HEAD
2 STR
CROCKER
26
YORK PLACE

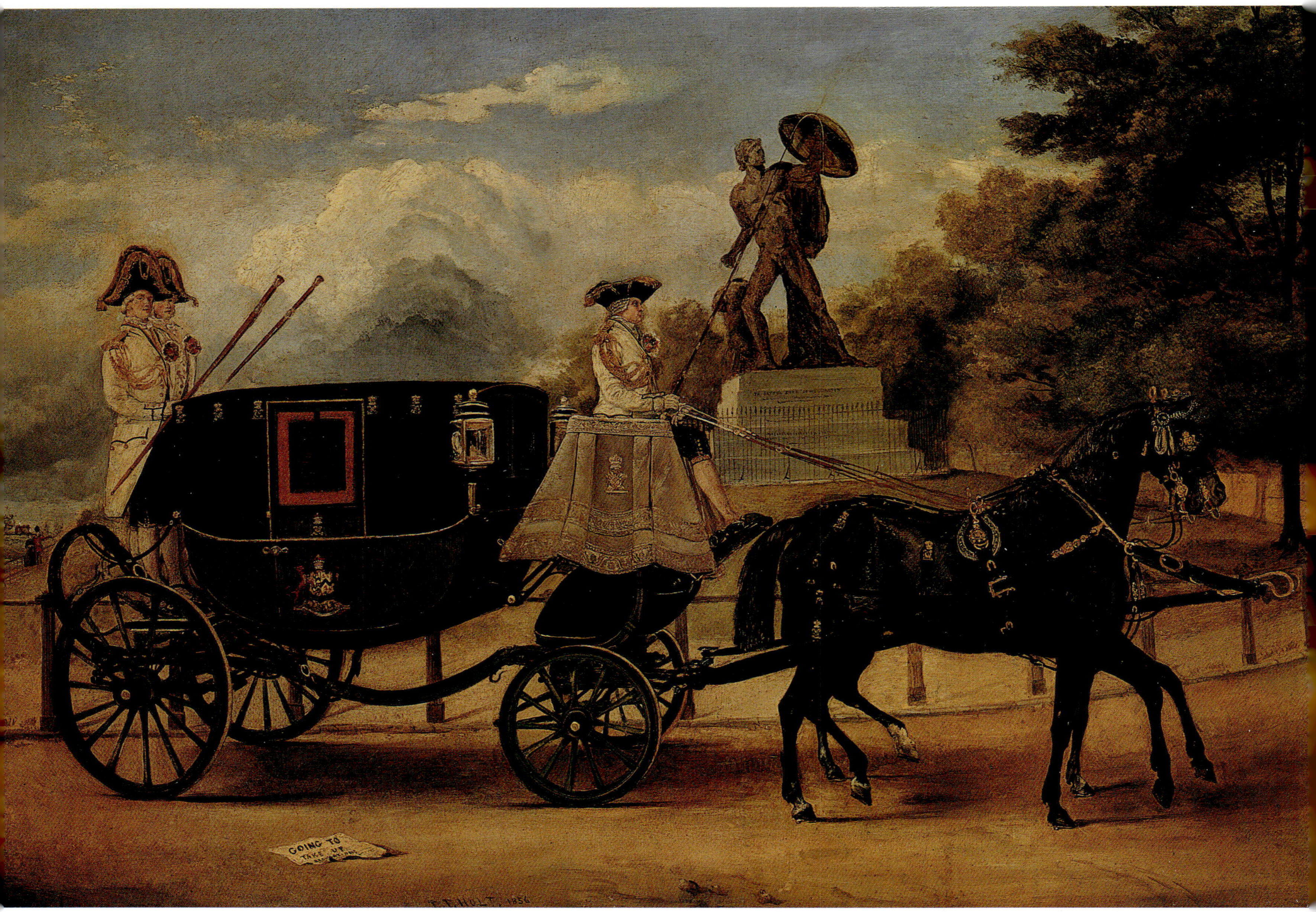
GOING TO
TAKE UP
E.F. HOLT 1856

92.

EDWIN FREDERICK HOLT

(1830–1912)

The Dress Carriage of Viscount Eversley in Hyde Park [A 20709]

*c.*1856

Oil on canvas, 60.4 x 91.3 cm

Signed and dated bottom centre:

E. F. HOLT. 1856 and inscribed *No 71*

THIS PICTURE is a 'portrait' of the dress carriage owned by Viscount Eversley, which is shown passing the Achilles monument on the Ring Road in the south-east corner of Hyde Park. Charles Shaw-Lefevre (1794–1888), Speaker of the House of Commons from 1839 to 1857, was raised to the peerage as Viscount Eversley of Heckfield on his retirement from office; the carriage may have been ordered at this time, in which case the artist dated his picture wrongly, or it may have been the vehicle Lord Eversley used as Speaker, in which case the armorial bearings were added to the canvas later.

The bodywork of the carriage is painted in two colours, black on the upper part, green with gold stripes on the lower, with the Eversley coat of arms on the door panel; the window is closed, with the blind up. On the hammer-cloth covered box sits a coachman in ivory and blue livery, wearing a tricorne hat; two footmen in similar liveries, but wearing the customary cocked hats, stand on the platform between the rear springs, carrying staves which were relics of the necessity of dealing with highwaymen or anyone else who might attempt to molest the vehicle. The carriage is drawn by two black thoroughbred horses.

Elegant dress carriages of this kind, with elaborate decorations and livery, were more common in London in the early years of Queen Victoria's reign than at any other period, and the year of the coronation, 1838, marked the peak of dress coachbuilding by London makers. By the time this picture was painted, the dress carriage was beginning to be replaced in popularity by the brougham and the landau, and the travelling carriage by the railways.

The statue of Achilles – a monument to the Duke of Wellington and his troops – was cast in bronze by Sir Richard Westmacott, from cannon taken in the battles of Salamanca, Vittoria, Toulouse and Waterloo, and erected in 1822. Hyde Park had been a fashionable venue for horse and carriage riding since the eighteenth century (see cat. no. 161). The sheet of paper in the foreground is inscribed: *GOING TO/TAKE UP REGULATIONS*; a soldier and his lass are seen in the park in the middle distance left.

Provenance:
Presented by Oliver, 3rd Viscount Esher in 1919.

Bibliography:
Hayes (cat. no. 55); Edwin R. Beasley, 'Edwin Frederick Holt Victorian Artist of Dunstable' in the *Bedfordshire Magazine*, 1982.

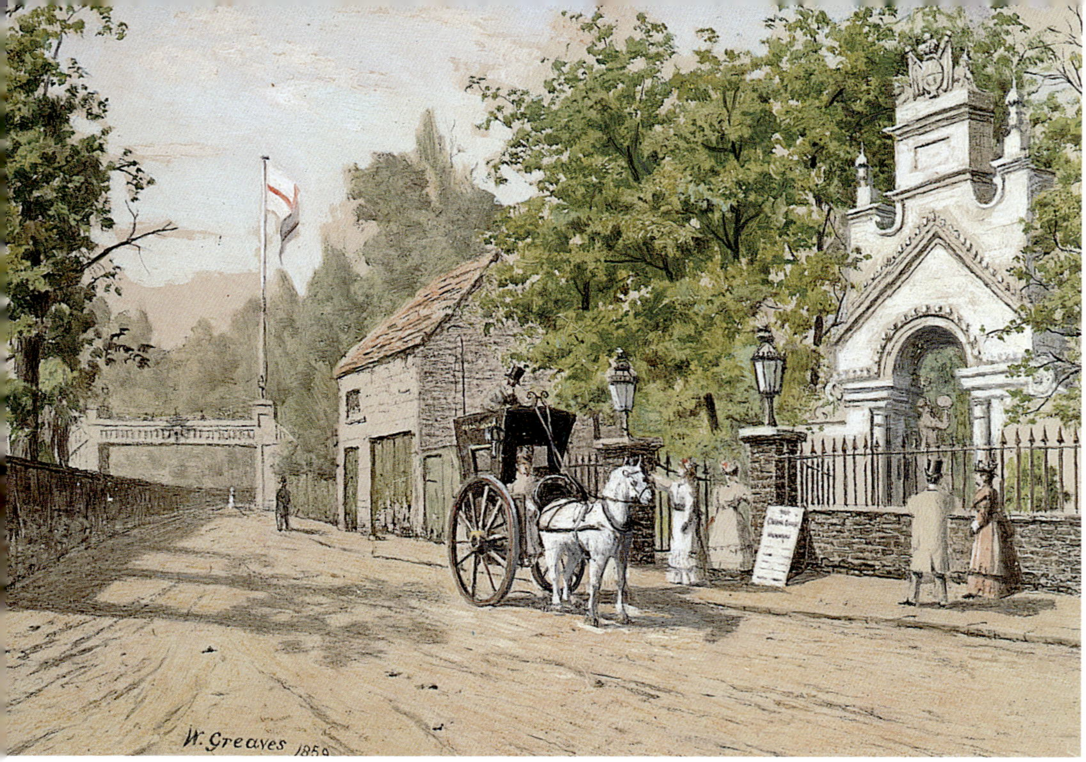

Provenance:
Purchased from Messrs P. & D. Colnaghi in 1960.

Bibliography:
Hayes (cat. no. 47); *Walter Greaves*, exhibition catalogue, Leighton House, no. 33; Warwick Wroth, *Cremorne and the later London Gardens*, 1907.

93.

WALTER GREAVES

(1846–1930)

The Waterside Entrance to Cremorne Gardens [60.68/3]

1876–79

Oil on cardboard, 22.7 x 37.5 cm

Signed and dated bottom left:

W. Greaves 1859

Inscribed in pencil on the back:

Waterside Entrance/Cremorne Gardens Chelsea

THIS VIEW shows the south-east entrance to Cremorne Gardens from Cremorne Road, close to the pier, part of which is seen in the background, with the City flag flying above it (this was one of the piers used by the City Steamship Company). A hansom cab is stopped outside the entrance; these were first introduced in 1835 (see cat. nos 101 and 110).

Cremorne House, one of Chelsea's finest riverside mansions (situated just to the north of the present Lots Road Power Station), was sold at the end of the 1820s. For a number of years it was used as a sports club, known as the Stadium, an early predecessor of Hurlingham, as well as for occasional fêtes and balloon ascents. This venture not succeeding, however, Cremorne was turned into a pleasure garden by Renton Nicholson in 1843 (see Appendix/Victoria's Reign/under Henning). Under the management of Thomas Bartlett Simpson, the grounds were laid out at the cost of five thousand pounds, and opened to the public in this form in 1846; Simpson's management lasted until 1861. One of the most notorious of the London pleasure gardens (see cat. no. 126), Cremorne was finally closed in 1877 following repeated complaints from the neighbourhood about the noise and rowdiness.

The costume indicates a date of about 1876–9, conflicting with the clearly written date of 1859. The work was bought as one of a pair (see Appendix), the other painting presenting the same dating difficulties (also see cat. no. 109).

A watercolour of this subject by Walter Greaves is in the local collection of the Royal Borough of Kensington and Chelsea; Greaves also executed a number of etchings of Cremorne Gardens, which date from 1870 and 1871.

94.

BRITISH SCHOOL

The Construction of the Charing Cross Station Hotel [61.7/12]

*c.*1863–4

Oil on canvas, 40.8 x 61.1 cm

Not signed or dated

THIS VIEW of the Charing Cross Station Hotel under construction is taken from the north-east corner (Villiers Street) with the station courtyard in the centre and with the top of the Nelson Monument (designed by William Railton, with the statue by Edward Hodges Baily) visible over the West Strand block (now destroyed and the site of South Africa House). To the right of this, in the distance, is the front of the National Gallery; the cab rank in Duncannon Street, outside St Martin-in-the-Fields, may be seen in the middle distance; and, on the extreme right, are 448 and 449 Strand. The West Strand improvements, which included the last-mentioned buildings and Charing Cross Hospital, were carried out in the early 1830s at the same time as the formation of Trafalgar Square.

The hotel was one of the first buildings in London to be faced with artificial stone and the painting shows the partial erection of the eastern portico, the hotel's main entrance.

Charing Cross Station, the terminus of the South-Eastern Railway, was built on the

Provenance:
F. Halls; Halls's sale, Christie's, 19 February 1960 (116, as C. R. W. Nevinson), bt Meatyard; purchased from Abbott and Holder in 1961.

Bibliography:
Hayes (cat. no. 22); *The Illustrated London News*, 22 May 1965, p26.

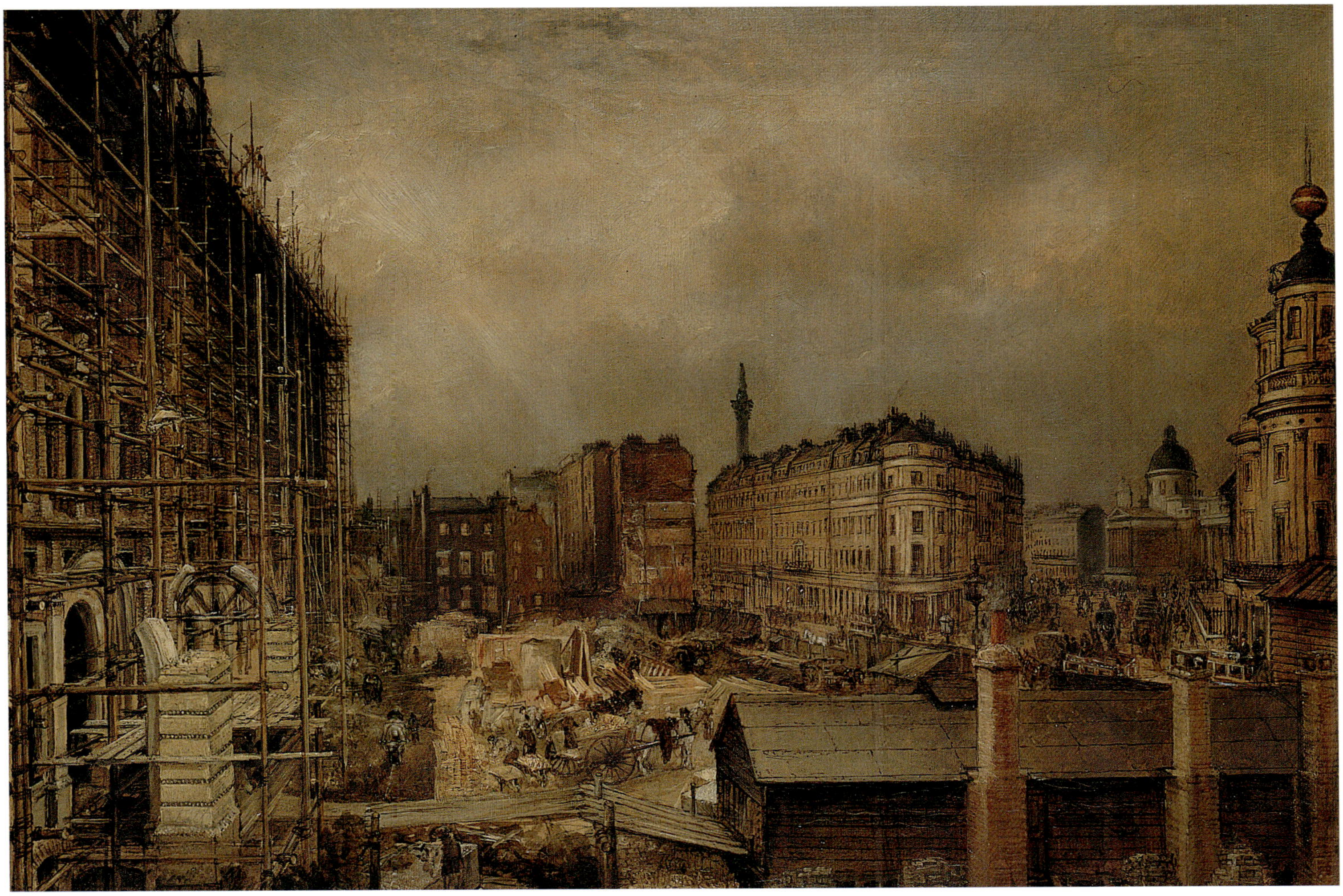

site of Hungerford Market in 1863, and the Station Hotel, seen here under scaffolding, was constructed in 1863–4 to the designs of E. M. Barry (Charles Barry's son), who had designed Covent Garden Theatre (1858). Barry's original skyline, with its red roofs and pinnacles copied from the Louvre, collapsed in 1905 and was replaced by a new flat roof.

The hotel opened on 15 May 1865 under the management of Thomas Higgs, who was previously at the Great Western Royal Hotel, Paddington. It had seven floors and 250 bedrooms. A ninety-bedroom annexe was added in 1878 on the other side of Villiers Street and connected to the main hotel by a footbridge. Barry was also responsible for the re-creation of the Eleanor Cross in the Hotel forecourt (1865).

The contemporary of the Grosvenor (1861) and Langham (1864) hotels, Charing Cross Station Hotel survived the severe competition caused by the hotel boom in the Victorian/Edwardian periods. This gathered momentum in 1881 with the opening of the Grand in Trafalgar Square; others followed: the Metropole in Northumberland Avenue and in the Strand, the Savoy, the Victoria, the Cecil, the Waldorf and the Strand Palace. The competition was intense until the 1930s, when the Depression forced many to close down. The Charing Cross Station Hotel was war-damaged in 1941, but repaired after the war.

A lithograph published by Day & Son, which shows the hotel as constructed, is in the Museum's collection (acc. no. 58.2). Although the handling of this picture has been compared to that of Edward Henry Corbould (1815–1905), the attribution of this painting has never been resolved.

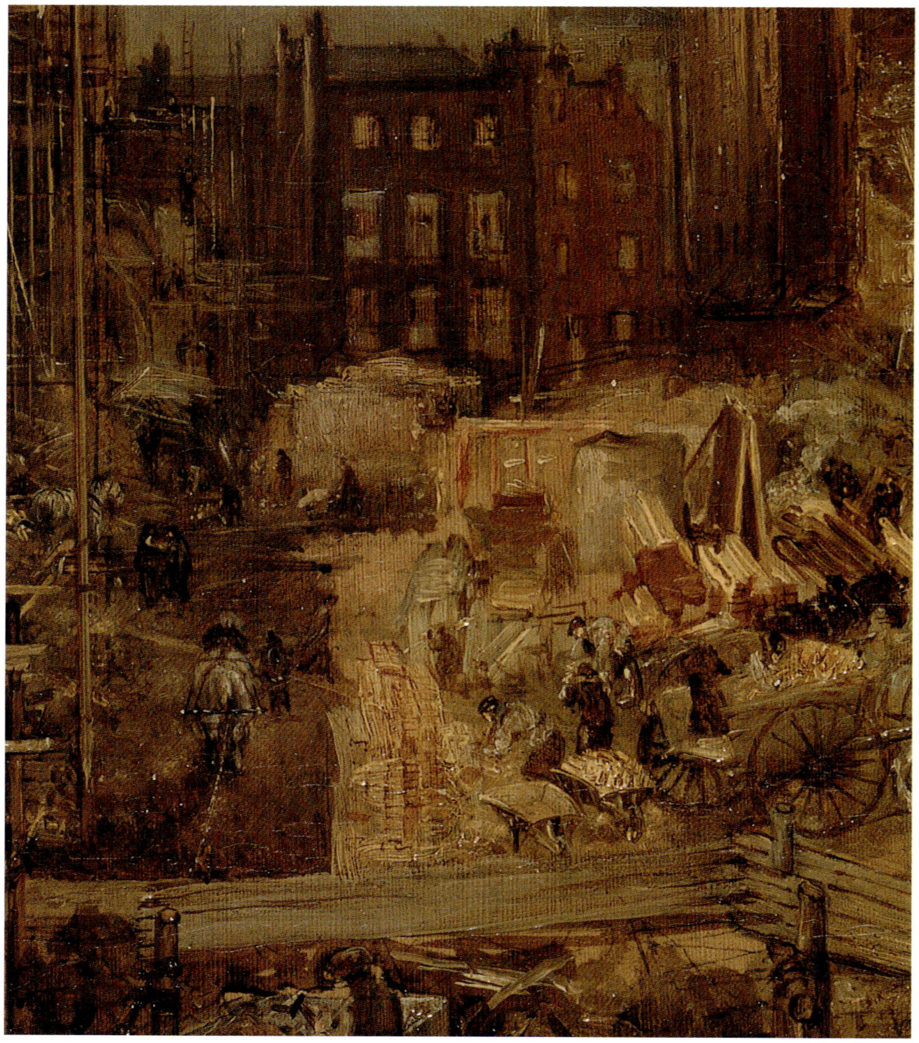

95.

PHOEBUS LEVIN

(active 1855–78)

Covent Garden Market [A 25328]
1864
Oil on canvas, 68 x 109 cm
Signed and dated bottom right:
P. Levin/1864

THIS PICTURE gives a good idea of the early-morning bustle of Covent Garden (St Paul's church clock on the right is shown at five o'clock). The view is taken from James Street on the north side of the piazza, looking south to the market building. The Tavistock Hotel on the left marks the site of the house once owned by Sir Peter Lely, which was later occupied by Richard Wilson and subsequently became auction rooms; the house opposite had become a public house – and jellied eels are advertised as well as gin and stout. The crowd is a happy blend of workers, customers and regulars; it includes, on the left, a potato seller, a flower seller and a child sleeping in one of the market baskets, while on the right may be seen a black blind man (next to a market gardener) and a porter (note the characteristic protective cushion on his head). Between the market building and the stalls filled with colourful produce, several horse-drawn carts may be seen piled high with baskets.

During the course of the eighteenth century the number of sheds and stalls in use at Covent Garden continued to grow steadily, as may be seen by comparing van Aken's view of about 1726–30 (see cat. no. 39) with Collet's view, painted some fifty years later (see cat. no. 41). As a result of this profitable expansion, John, 6th Duke of Bedford obtained an act to have the whole place cleared and rebuilt. Charles Fowler, who had designed Hungerford Market, was called in as architect, and the new premises were built in 1828–31. His sturdily designed gateways (the motto *Che Sara Sara* is that of the Dukes of Bedford) and Tuscan colonnades were a perfect match for the piazza itself, and especially for the church. Behind this classical exterior were two large market halls divided by a long glass-roofed arcade and flanked on either side by shops. Notice that the high glass roofs which now cover both the market halls had not yet been constructed. The Floral Hall, of glass and cast iron, was added in 1859 by E. M. Barry, the architect of the Royal Opera House, next door. The cupola of St Paul's, Covent Garden, has since been removed.

From late Victorian times, the situation gradually became intolerable with horse and motorised traffic congesting the narrow streets around the piazza. In 1974 the market finally moved to Nine Elms, away from the heart of the city, as had happened a few years earlier to Les Halles in Paris. The Greater London Council restored Fowler's building, converting it into shops and eating places, with offices on the first floor.

Provenance:
Jules Singer; Singer sale, Christie's, 1 May 1899 (64), bt Hamilton; G. W. Boorman; Boorman sale, Christie's, 11 December 1922 (83), bt Potter; purchased in 1923.

Bibliography:
Hayes (cat. no. 67).

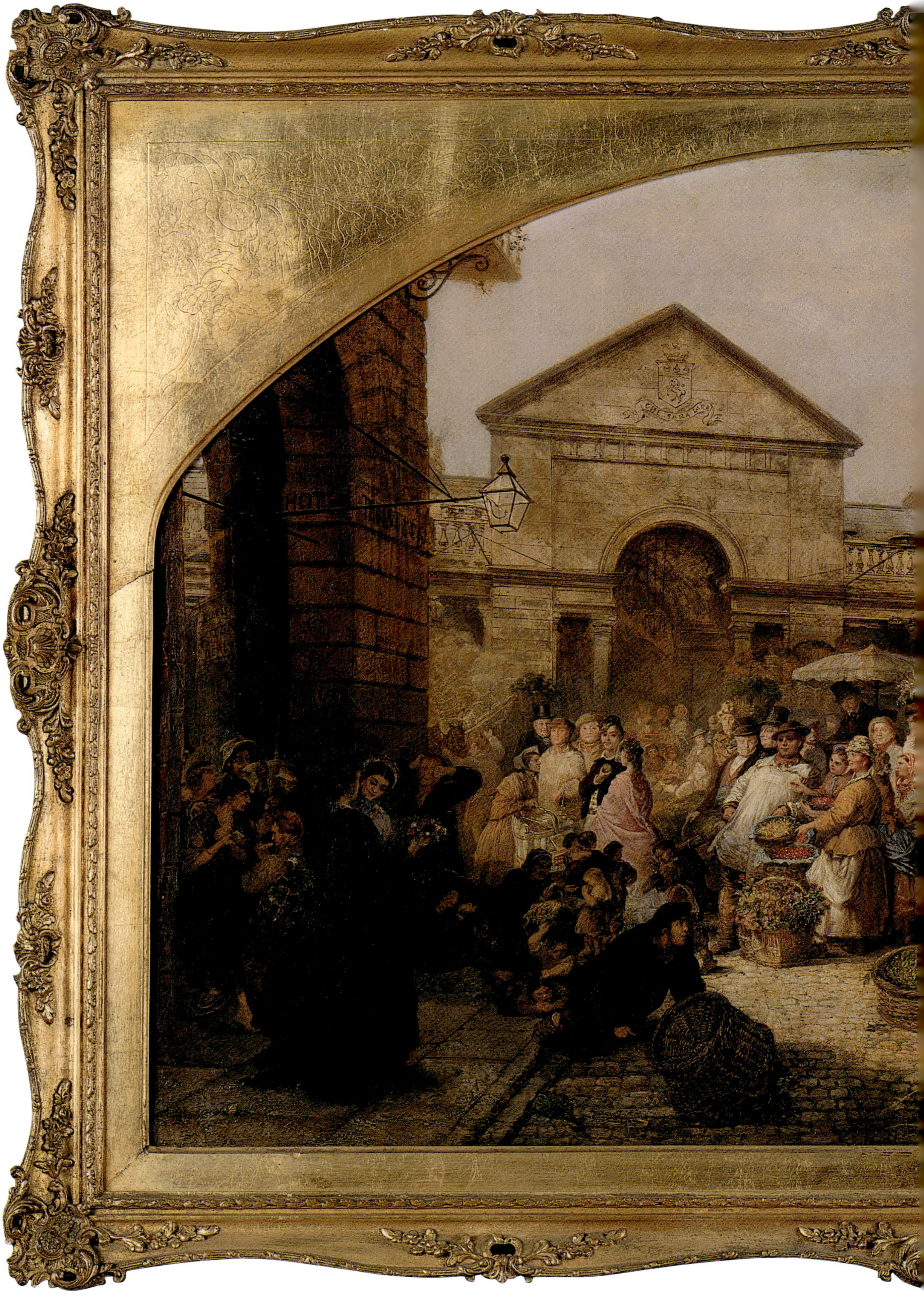

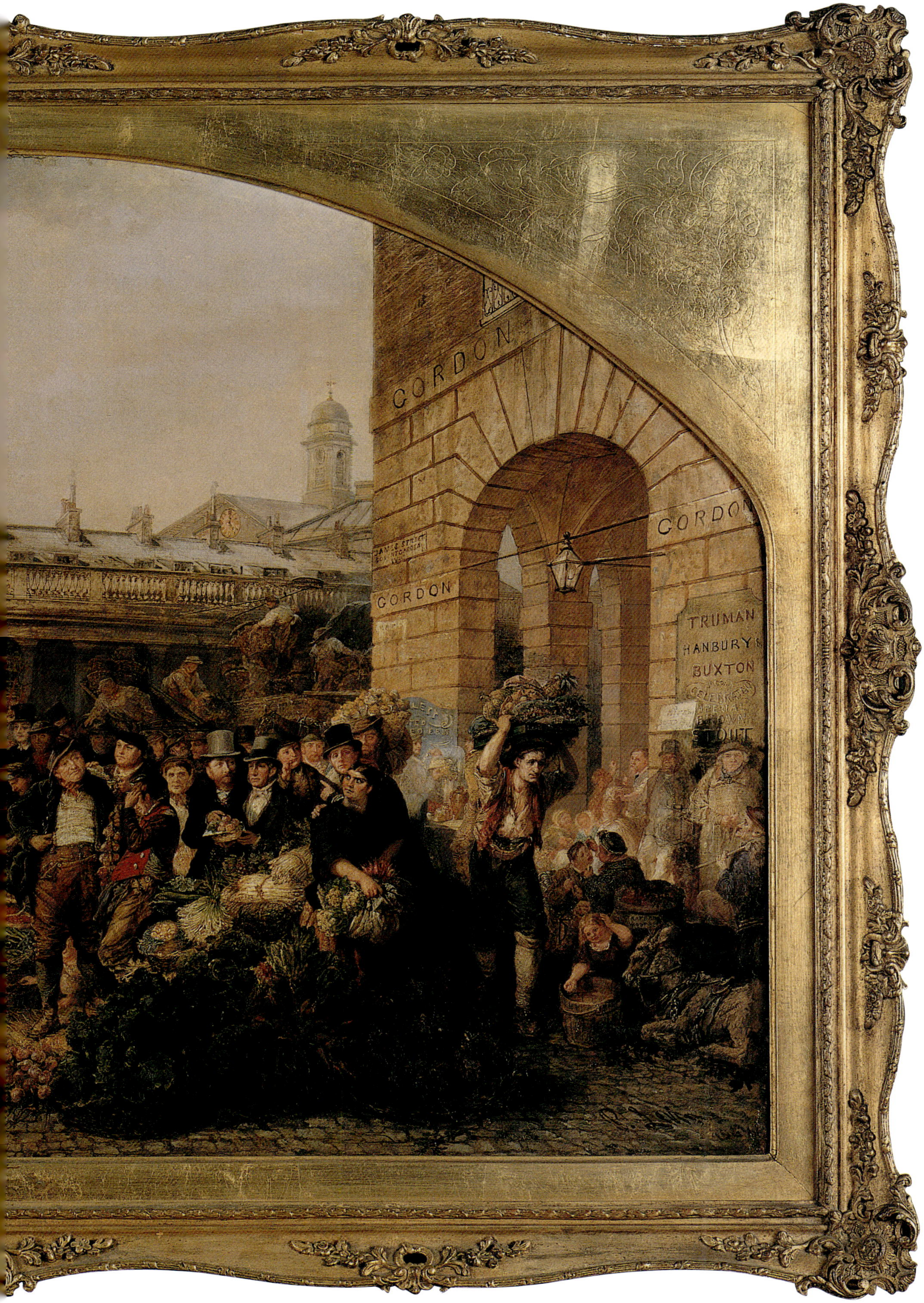
GORDON
GORDON
GORDON
TRUMAN
HANBURY &
BUXTON
STOUT

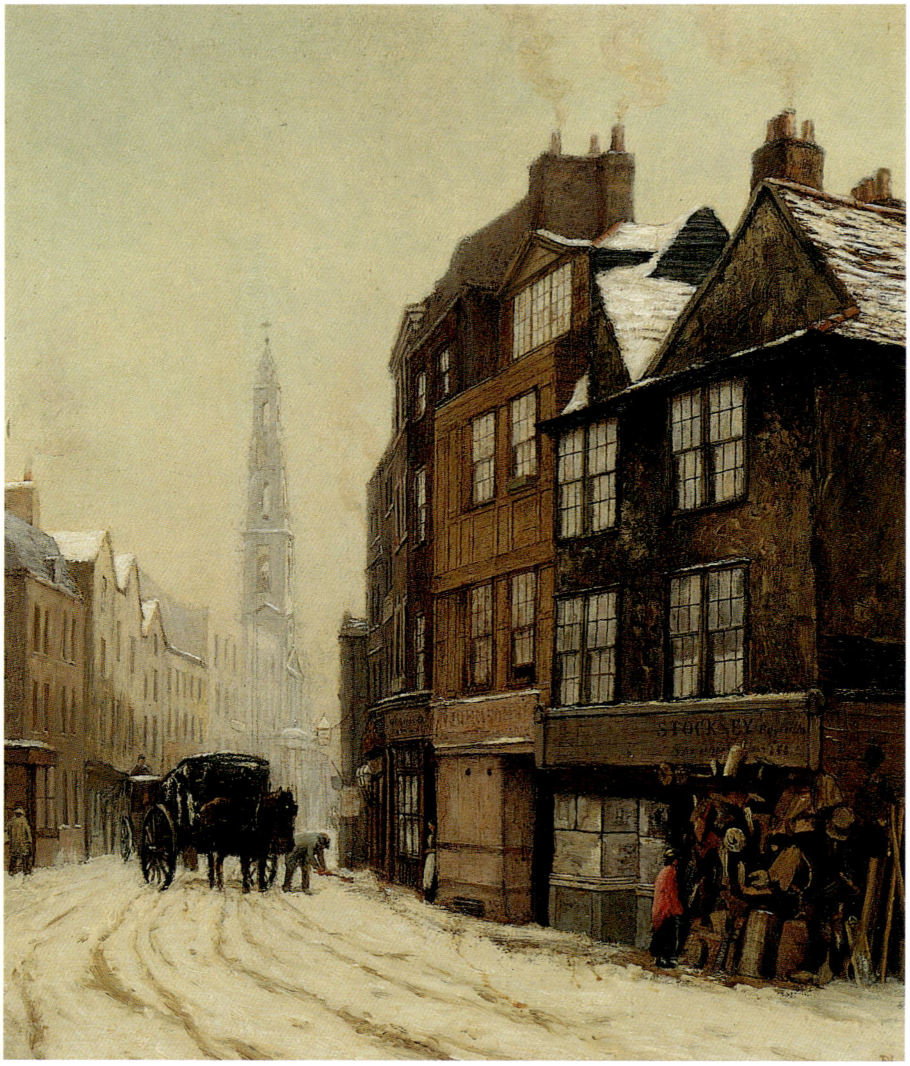

Provenance:
Lent by the artist in 1911, and afterwards purchased in 1914.

Bibliography:
Hayes (cat. no. 84); Philip Norman, *London Vanished and Vanishing*, 1905, pp246–7 (this work or its watercolour version is reproduced).

Exhibited:
Summer Exhibition, The New Gallery, 1906 (72); Old London Exhibition, Whitechapel Art Gallery, November–December 1911 (362: Lower Gallery).

96.

PHILIP NORMAN
(1842–1931)

Drury Court with the Church of St Mary-le-Strand [C 358]
1880
Oil on canvas, 52.9 x 46 cm
Signed in monogram bottom right: *PN*
Inscribed on the back by the artist as painted in 1880

THIS VIEW is taken from Drury Lane proper, and part of Bates's British Coffee House, on the corner of Wych Street, is seen on the extreme left of the picture. The seventeenth-century house on the right, the premises of E. Crafter, watchmaker, and of Stockley, bookseller, at one time the Cock and Magpye Tavern, was said to have been the house where Nell Gwyn had lodgings, and where she was seen standing at the door by Pepys in 1667. Both this and the house next door, the premises of J. Johnson, coal and coke merchant, which also dated from the seventeenth century, were pulled down in 1890. A man is seen clearing snow and piling it into a cart which would subsequently be emptied into the river.

Drury Court, the continuation of Drury Lane southwards from Wych Street to the Strand, was one of a number of streets in this area cleared away for the Aldwych and Kingsway improvements carried out in 1900–5. It was originally known as Maypole Lane, on account of its proximity to the Maypole in the Strand: the high Maypole put up shortly after the Restoration stood on the site of Gibbs's church of St Mary-le-Strand, built in 1714–17 (which is seen in the distance), but was removed by Sir Isaac Newton.

For most of the seventeenth century, Drury Court and Drury Lane had been streets of considerable distinction, with aristocratic residents, but by the beginning of the eighteenth century they had begun to acquire a more doubtful reputation. The whole district had become a seedbed of crime and vice by the mid-Victorian period, Wych Street being notorious for its brothels, ostensibly cigar shops; and extensive clearance was started in the 1880s under the provisions of the Artisans' Dwellings Act.

Another view of the street, by C. J. Watson (cat. no. 100) suggests its popularity with artists (see also pp232 and 234, note 5).

97.

PHILIP NORMAN

(1842–1931)

The Back Yard of the Queen's Head Inn, Southwark [C 407]

1884

Oil on canvas, 38.2 x 28.3 cm

Signed bottom right: *P Norman*

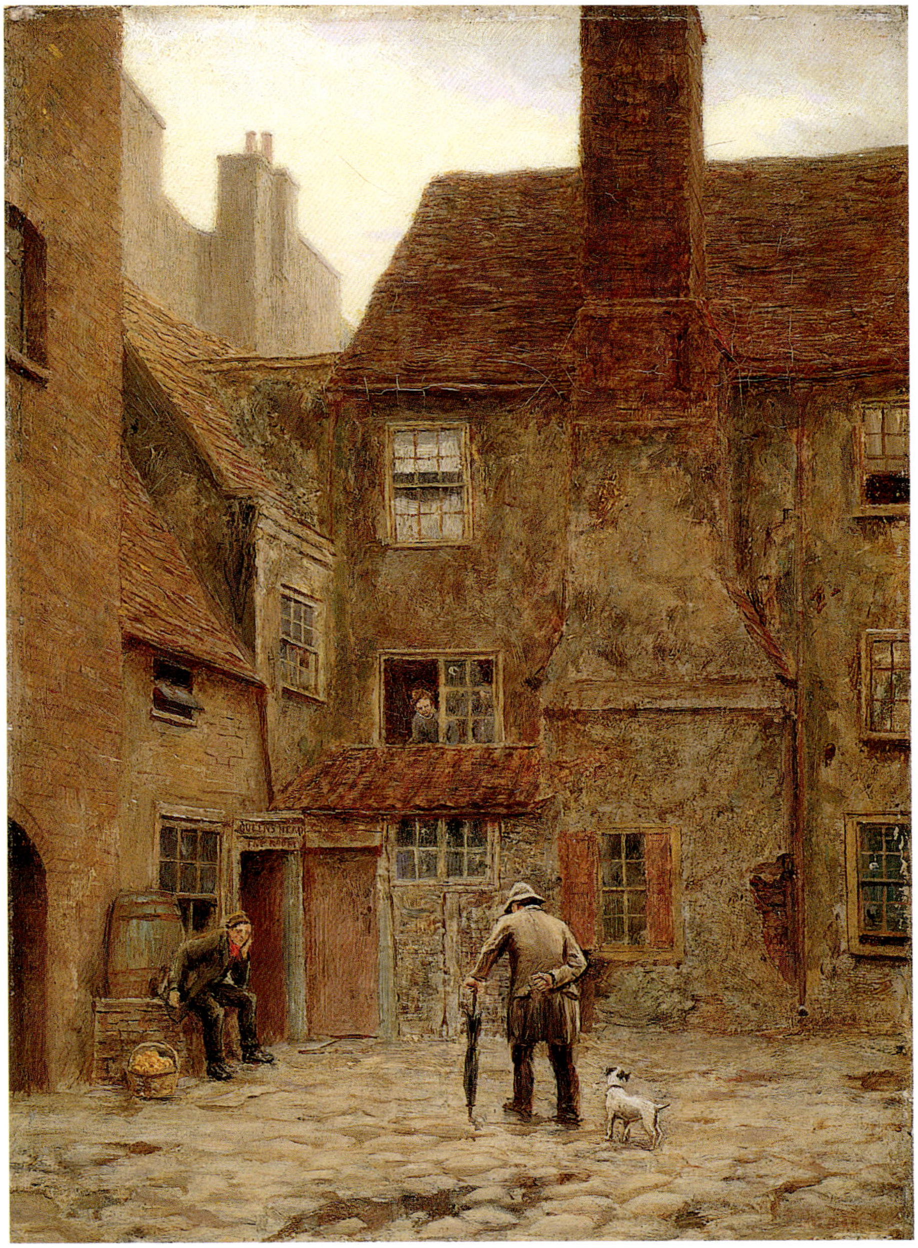

THE QUEEN'S Head Inn at 105 Borough High Street in Southwark was originally called the Cross or Crowned Keys, and was probably renamed in the sixteenth century in honour of Queen Elizabeth. Among those who have held the lease of the inn was John Harvard of Emanuel College in Cambridge, who emigrated to America where he founded Harvard University. The entrance to the tap room is seen next to the seated figure; the main entrance to the yard itself was just to the right of this view. The inn closed temporarily in 1886, when a new roof was installed. When it was finally shut up in May 1895, it was visited by Philip Norman, who described a long room on the first floor with an early seventeenth-century carved oak mantelpiece. The building gradually became dilapidated.

Two other views of the inn by Philip Norman, both in watercolour, signed and dated 1883 and 1884, are in the Victoria and Albert Museum: one (D17–1896) is identical with the Museum of London picture; the other (D16–1896) shows the main yard.

Provenance:
Lent by the artist in 1912, and afterwards purchased in 1914.

Bibliography:
Hayes (cat. no. 85); Philip Norman, *London Vanished and Vanishing*, 1905, pp18–23.

Provenance:
Painted for Richard, 6th Earl of Mayo; presented by Dermot, 7th Earl of Mayo, in 1923.

Bibliography:
Hayes (cat. no. 11).

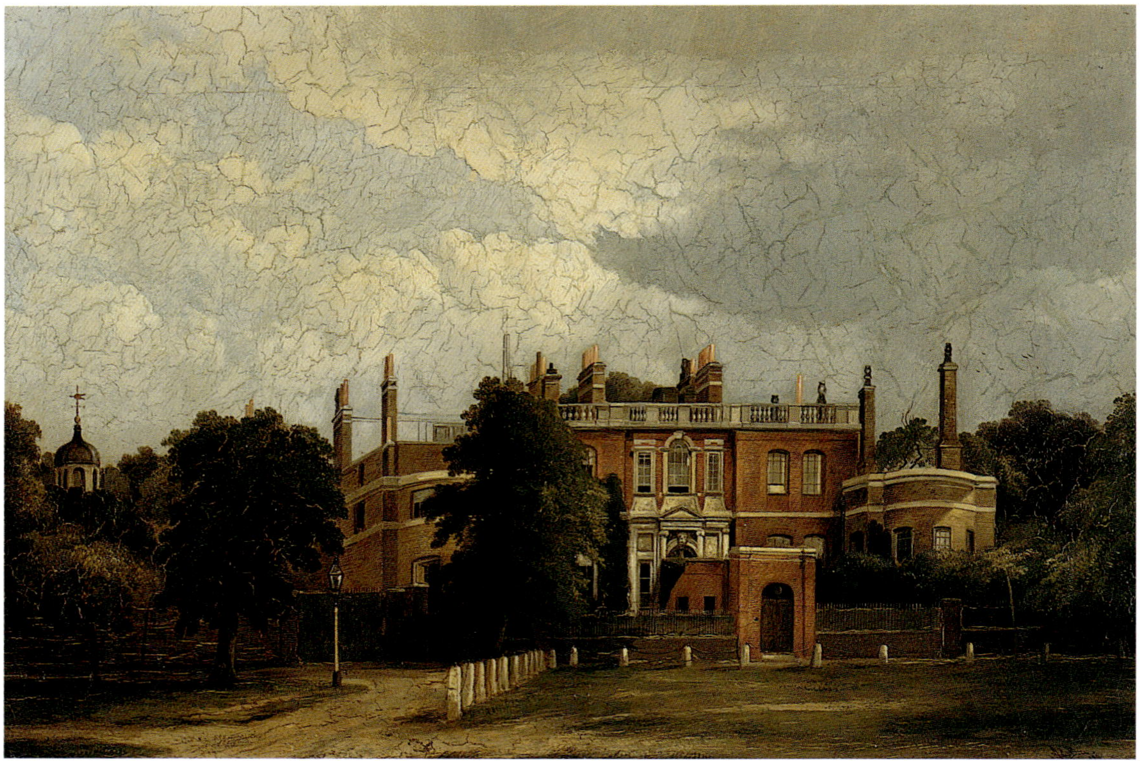

98.

ANTHONY DE BREE

(1855–1921)

Chesterfield House, Blackheath [A 25323]
1884
Oil on canvas, 30.5 x 45.8 cm
Signed and dated bottom right:
A de Bree/1884

A VIEW of the front of Chesterfield House (later Ranger's House) in Chesterfield Walk, Blackheath. The main block was built in the early eighteenth century, but the two wings, in yellow brick, were added by the 4th Earl of Chesterfield soon after he took the lease in 1753. The doorway and covered entrance seen here, which are probably Victorian (and of which this picture is the only visual record) were removed in about 1903. The cupola surmounted by a weather vane, seen between the trees on the left, which stood on the roof of one of the buildings in the stable block, was taken down in 1943 as a result of war damage. It still exists and may one day be re-erected.

Blackheath became a popular district for establishing a country retreat close to London early in the eighteenth century, and Sir Gregory Page, the South Sea millionaire, built a vast Palladian mansion there in 1721; another notable house, which still stands, is Sir John Vanbrugh's villa, Vanbrugh Castle, built in 1717–26. Chesterfield House occupies a position of advantage at the summit of Croom's Hill and has a south-westerly aspect. The house was given to the donor's mother, a Lady of the Bedchamber, by Queen Victoria, and was acquired by the London County Council in 1900; renamed Rangers House and part of English Heritage, it is now open to the public.

This work is a late example of the genre of the painted house portrait.

99.
JOHN O'CONNOR
(1830–89)

From Pentonville Road looking West: Evening* [52.87]
1884
Oil on canvas, 90.3 x 150.3 cm
Signed in monogram and dated bottom centre: *JOC 1884*

THOUGH MUCH exaggerated for the sake of pictorial effect, this picture gives an excellent impression of the varied skyline of Sir Gilbert Scott's St Pancras Hotel, one of London's 'cathedrals of the Modern Age', as seen from the hill which leads down from the Angel, Islington. The viewpoint is a rooftop on the corner of Rodney Street and Pentonville Road and the turning on the left is Penton Rise.

St Pancras Station, the London terminus of the Midland Railway, was designed by W. H. Barlow and opened in 1868. In an age of great engineering achievement, it was remarkable for its mighty barrel vault which roofed the platforms in a single span and is clearly visible here. The St Pancras Hotel, or Midland Grand Hotel, designed by George Gilbert Scott and built in 1867–76, was one of the foremost Gothic buildings in London, and fully expressed the confidence and pride of railway travel (as did the Euston Arch, pulled down in 1963). It is being restored at the time of writing to become (with Waterloo) one of the two London termini for the Channel Tunnel.

Pentonville Road, partly composed of early Victorian terrace houses and shops and partly of taller buildings dating from the third quarter of the nineteenth century, has changed considerably since the date of this picture. Some of the shops in the block on the left stood until the 1960s when they were replaced by blocks of flats (the Weston Rise Estate); a few of the buildings at the lower end of the street are still in use – even the tall lead cupola of the now Scala Cinema, at the junction of Pentonville and Gray's Inn Road, survives intact. The church on the left is the Welsh Congregational Church, now hemmed in by a block of early twentieth-century tenements. That on the right is St James's, built by Aaron H. Hurst in the Adam style in 1787; it burned down in 1983 and was rebuilt as offices for Courtaulds Textiles, now Grimaldi Park House. At the foot of the hill is the clocktower of King's Cross Station, and on the left of the picture, in the distance, are the dome of University College and the tower (inspired by the Tower of the Winds in Athens) of the parish church of St Pancras, built in 1819–22 by William and H. W. Inwood.

Numerous figures are introduced, including a policeman, a postman (notice the hexagonal pillar-box) and several sandwich-board men. Vehicles include hansom cabs, a haycart, and horse-drawn omnibuses and trams of the 'knifeboard' variety (see cat. no. 89) are seen in the roadway. Horse-drawn trams were first introduced into London by G. F. Train, an American, in 1861, but it was not until the 1870s that lines began to proliferate, chiefly in north London (only small sections were ever allowed within the City itself). The line down Pentonville Road first came into operation in 1883, and the two trams seen here, which plied between the Angel and King's Cross, are numbered 67 and coloured red – notice that three horses were used in Pentonville Road on account of the steep ascent.

Provenance:
Isaac Holden, 1887; purchased out of the Joicey Trust Fund from H. R. Cresner in 1952.

Bibliography:
Hayes (cat. no. 87).

Exhibited:
Royal Academy, 1884 (860); Royal Hibernian Academy, 1885 (39); Royal Jubilee Exhibition, Manchester, 1887 (Fine Arts Section: 1).

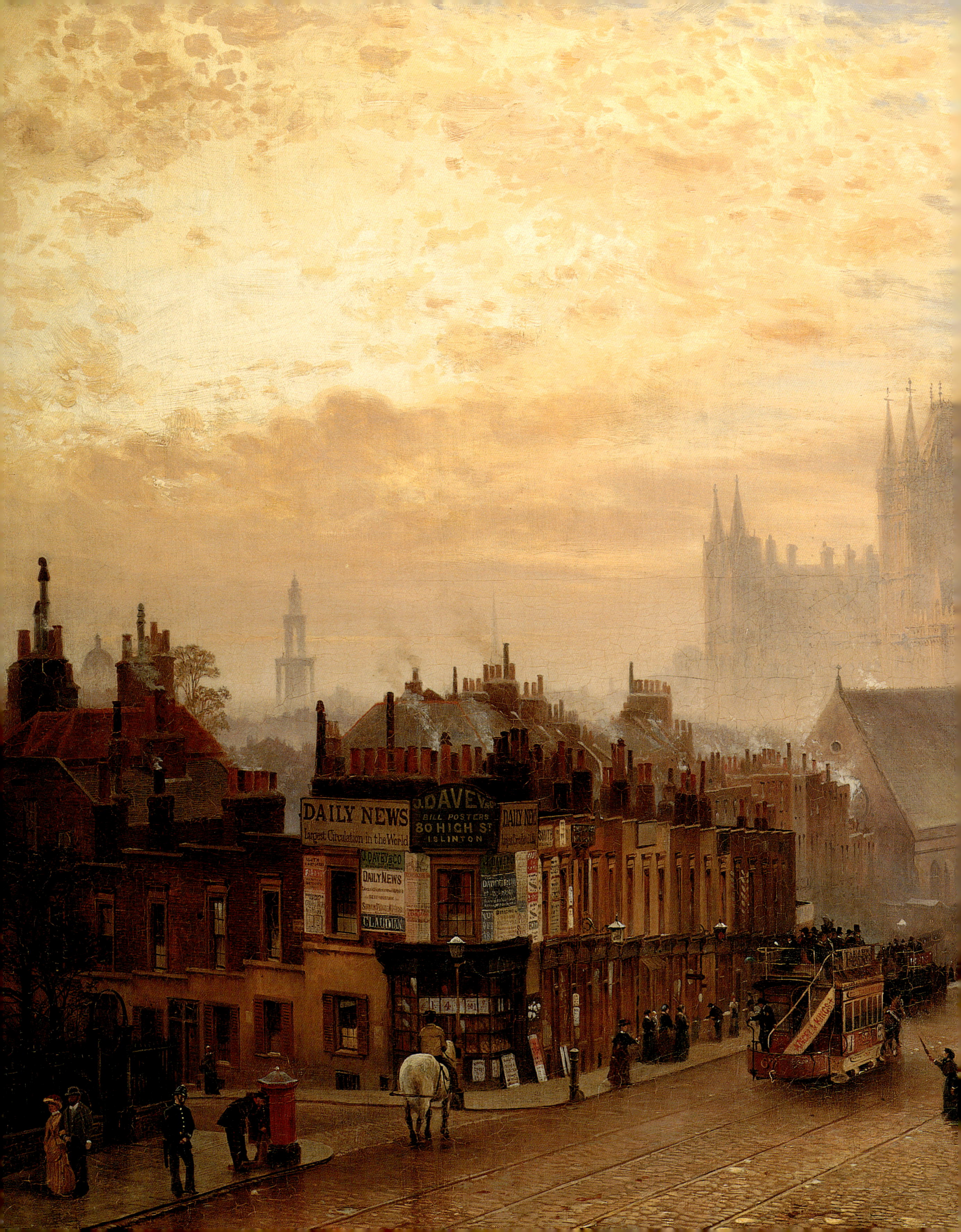
DAILY NEWS
Largest Circulation in the World
J. DAVEY & SON
BILL POSTERS
80 HIGH ST
ISLINTON
J. DAVEY AND CO
DAILY NEWS
CLAUDIAN

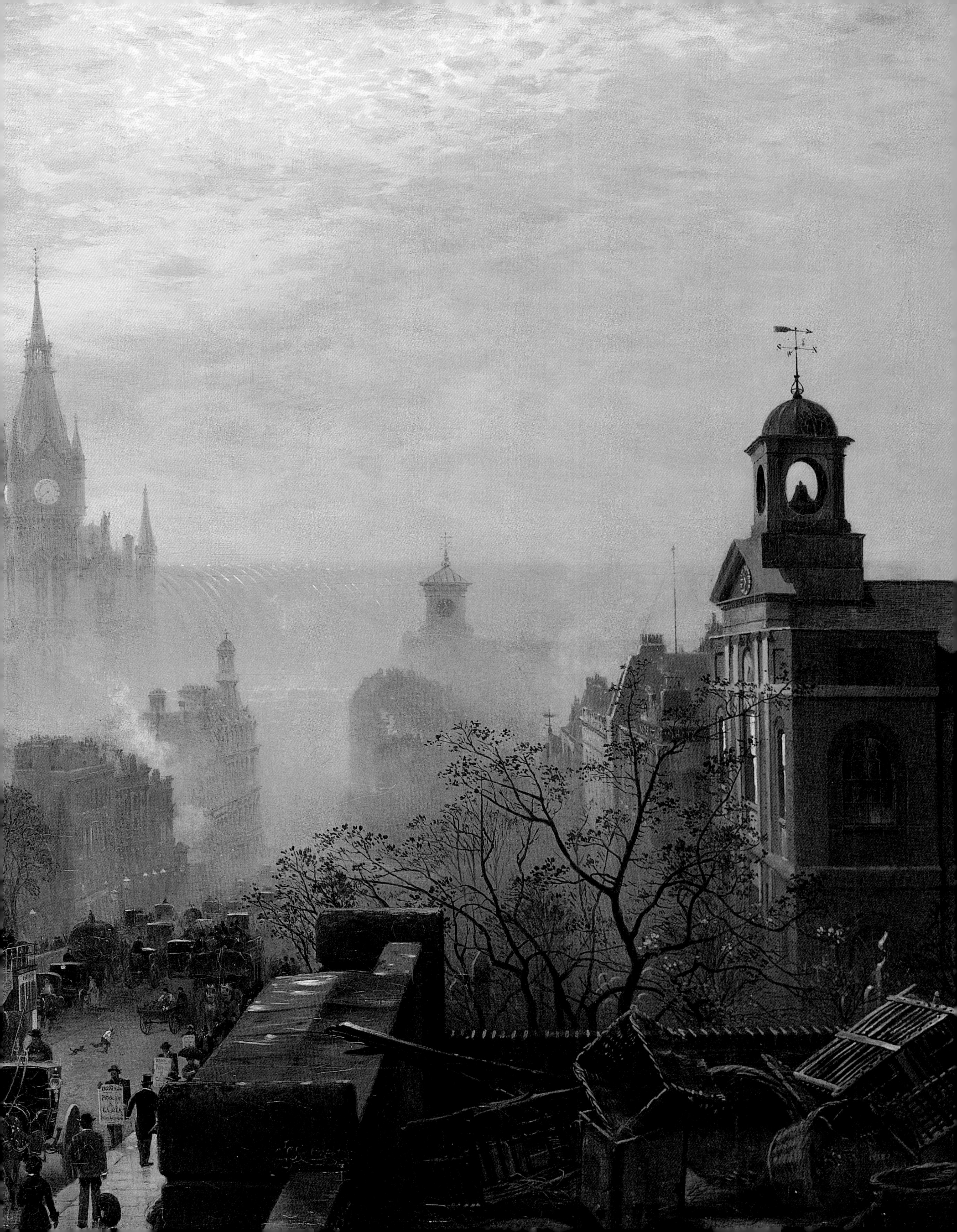

Provenance:
Mrs C. J. Watson; S. H. Dowson, by whom it was presented in 1939.

Bibliography:
Hayes (cat. no. 107).

100.

CHARLES JOHN WATSON

(1846–1927)

Drury Court with the Church of St Mary-le-Strand [39.166/3]
1886
Oil on millboard, 45.4 x 30.3 cm
Signed and dated bottom left:
C. J. Watson/1886

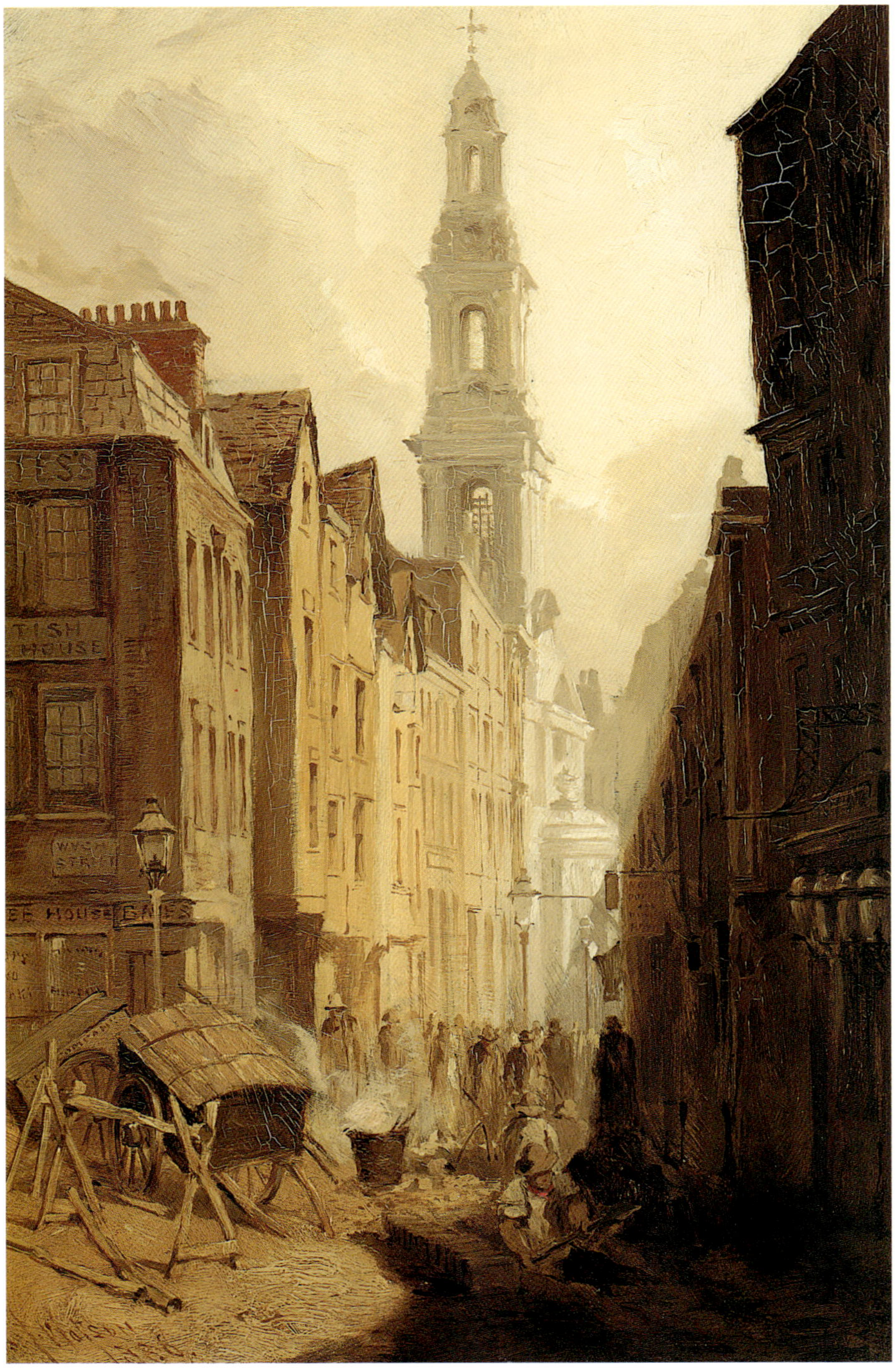

THIS VIEW is taken from a point slightly to the south of that used by Philip Norman in his painting of the same subject (cat. no. 96) and shows the beginning of Wych Street on the left, with part of the north frontage of Bates's British Coffee House. Some road-works are in progress, workmen being seen in the foreground near a brazier and a couple of carts.

The painting is based on an earlier print dated 1878 which formed part of a set of six etchings (with frontispiece) published in January 1880 by W. A. Smith under the title of the *London Thoroughfare Series* (see *Catalogue of the Etched and Engraved Works of Charles J. Watson, RE*, privately printed, 1931, no. 25, reproduced on p11).

A historical summary on Drury Court may be found under cat. no. 96 and the popularity of the site is discussed on pp232 and 234 (note 5).

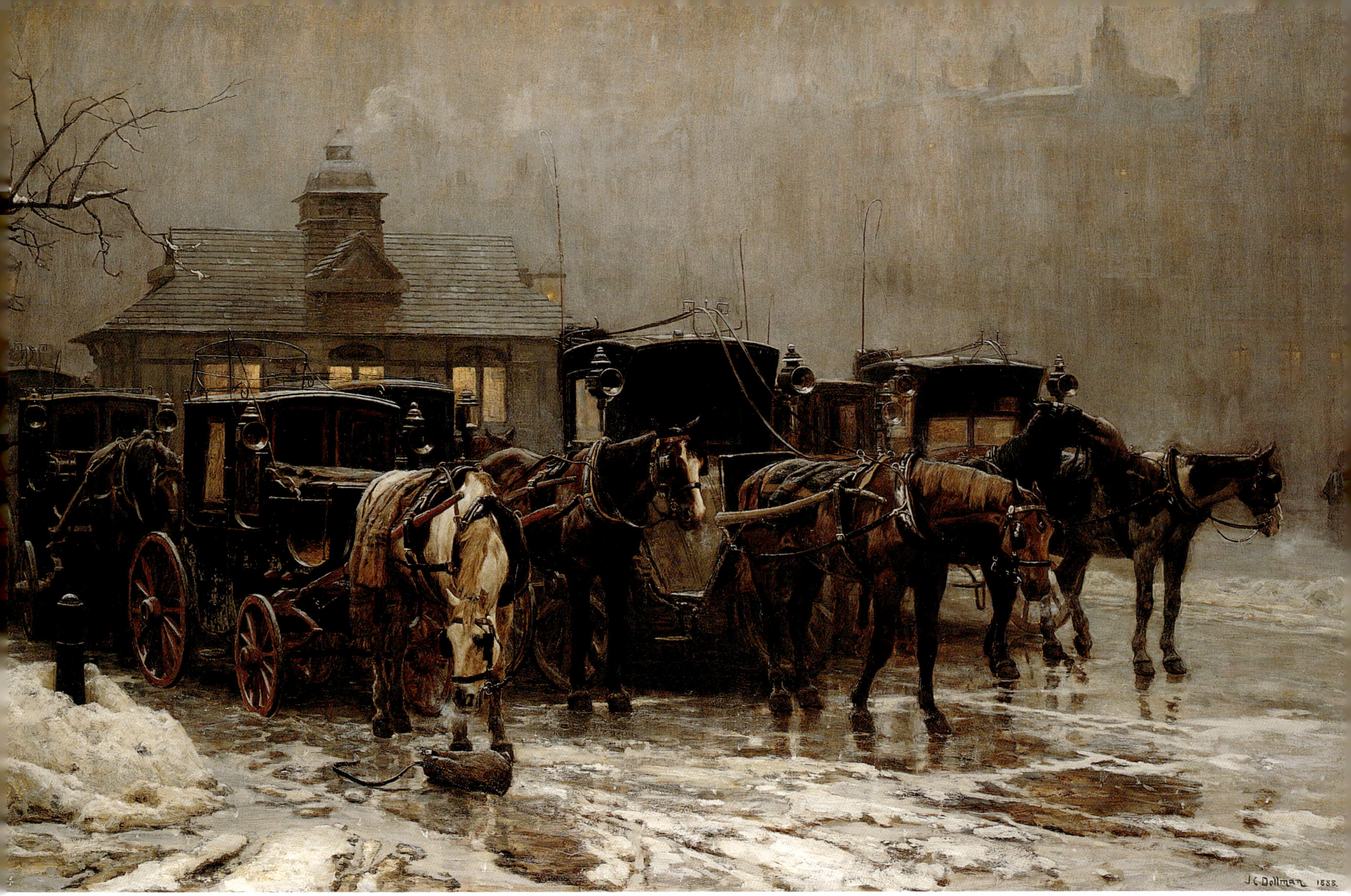

101.

JOHN CHARLES DOLLMAN

(1851–1934)

A London Cab Stand [28.35]
1888
Oil on canvas, 98.5 x 158 cm
Signed and dated bottom right:
J. C. Dollman 1888

SEVEN CABS, hansoms and 'growlers', are shown in the foreground, with a cab shelter behind on the left; a policeman is standing in the right middle distance, and some buildings are seen indistinctly beyond; the weather is wintry, with snow and slush on the ground (heavy snowstorms in many parts of England were reported for 13 and 14 February 1888)

The hansom cab was named after J. A. Hansom (1803–82), the architect, who designed and registered his 'patent safety cab' in 1834, subsequently disposing of his rights to a company for ten thousand pounds, none of which he ever received. The main innovations in the cabs as developed were the large wheels and the placing of the driver at the rear of the vehicle (see also cat. no. 110). The 'growler' was introduced in 1835 in competition with the hansoms; this was a much improved four-wheel cab with a luggage rack on the roof, initially accommodating only two people but later planned to hold four inside and one out. The law regarding cabs was regulated in 1853, when, among other provisions, it was required that a table of fares should be displayed inside all vehicles plying for hire.

Provenance:
Presented by John Scrimgeour in 1928.

Bibliography:
Hayes (cat. no. 35); Henry Mayhew, *London Labour and the London Poor*, 1861, vol. III, pp350-53.

Exhibited:
At the Royal Academy in 1888 (630) under the title *Les Miserables* and reproduced in Henry Blackburn, *Academy Notes*, 1888, p81.

Provenance:
M. W. H. Mackenzie; Mackenzie sale 1897, bt E. K. Fownes; A. Baker; purchased in 1922.

Bibliography:
Hayes (cat. no. 9).

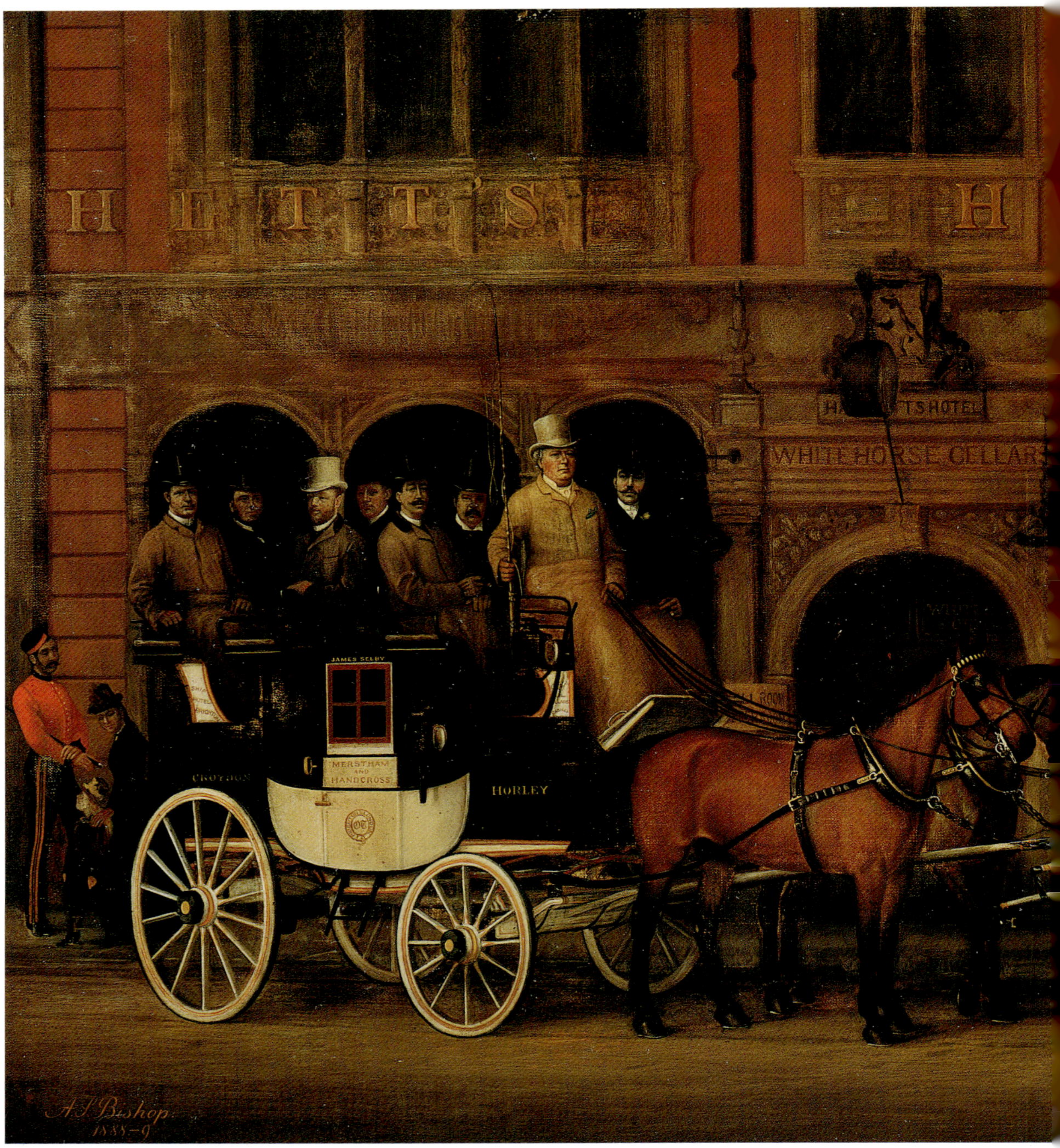

102.

A. S. BISHOP
(active 1874–89)

James Selby's Brighton Coach outside the New White Horse Cellar, Piccadilly
[A 24298]
1888-9
Oil on canvas, 60.5 x 92 cm
Signed and dated bottom left:
A. S. Bishop./1888–9

A YELLOW and black road-coach, with a coachman and a passenger on the box, and six other passengers outside, drawn by four brown horses, is shown standing outside the New White Horse Cellar, part of Hatchett's Hotel, 67–8 Piccadilly, on the corner of Dover Street. The vehicle is marked as owned by James Selby (d.1888), the best-known professional coachman of the period, and as plying between the

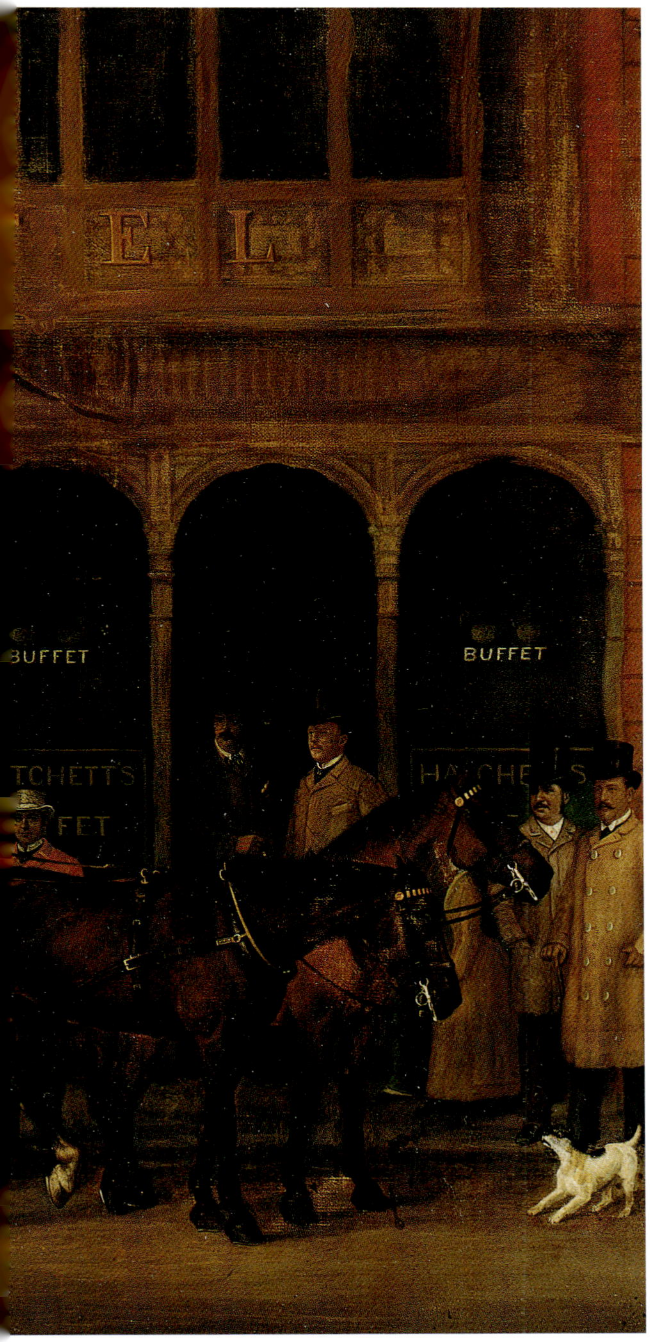

White Horse Cellar and the Ship Hotel, Brighton, with intermediate stops at Croydon, Merstham, Horley and Handcross. A woman with a little girl, and a soldier, are seen on the left, and five more people, watching the departure of the coach, are standing on the right. It seems likely that the picture was painted to commemorate James Selby's famous drive from London to Brighton and back in under eight hours, an extraordinary achievement with a regular coach and four, and which he undertook (in 1888) for a wager of a thousand pounds.

Hatchett's Hotel, Coffee House and White Horse Cellar was founded by Abraham Hatchett in 1753 following the demise of the White Horse Inn or Cellar kept by John Williams, which was situated on the south side of Piccadilly, between Duke Street and St James's Street. The 'cellar' was for the reception of parcels and luggage for the western stages, and Hatchett's was also a starting point for the mail coaches, described by Hazlitt as 'the finest sight in the metropolis'.

The New White Horse Cellar attempted to revive the taste for coaching in the mid-Victorian period, almost as a sport, and it became the starting point for many short-distance coaches, some of them driven by gentlemen (like James Selby) who were the proprietors of their own team. The coaches were often reproductions of earlier prototypes and typical destinations were Dorking, Guildford and Virginia Water. The premises shown here were probably built by Bailey and Thomas, who succeeded John Hatchett as proprietors in 1831. The hotel continued to be one of the foremost in London until its closure in 1896; Hatchett's restaurant flourished until a few years ago on the same site (now occupied by Korean Airlines).

The painting belonged for a while to E. K. Fownes, who, at the death of Selby, became the most celebrated of Victorian coachmen (see cat. nos 103 and 104). The Museum has in its collection a road-coach very similar in type to the one depicted here.

Provenance:
E. K. Fownes; purchased from the Misses Fownes, daughters of the sitter, in 1950.

Bibliography:
Hayes (cat. no. 170).

103.
THOMAS FREDERICK MASON SHEARD
(1866–1921)

Portrait of E. K. Fownes [51.16]
*c.*1900
Oil on canvas, 120.6 x 90.6 cm
Signed bottom right: *TFM Sheard*
Inscribed on the back of the stretcher in pencil:
E. K. Fownes/Brighton &/London/Coaches/ Old Times/1900/Nimrod/1911

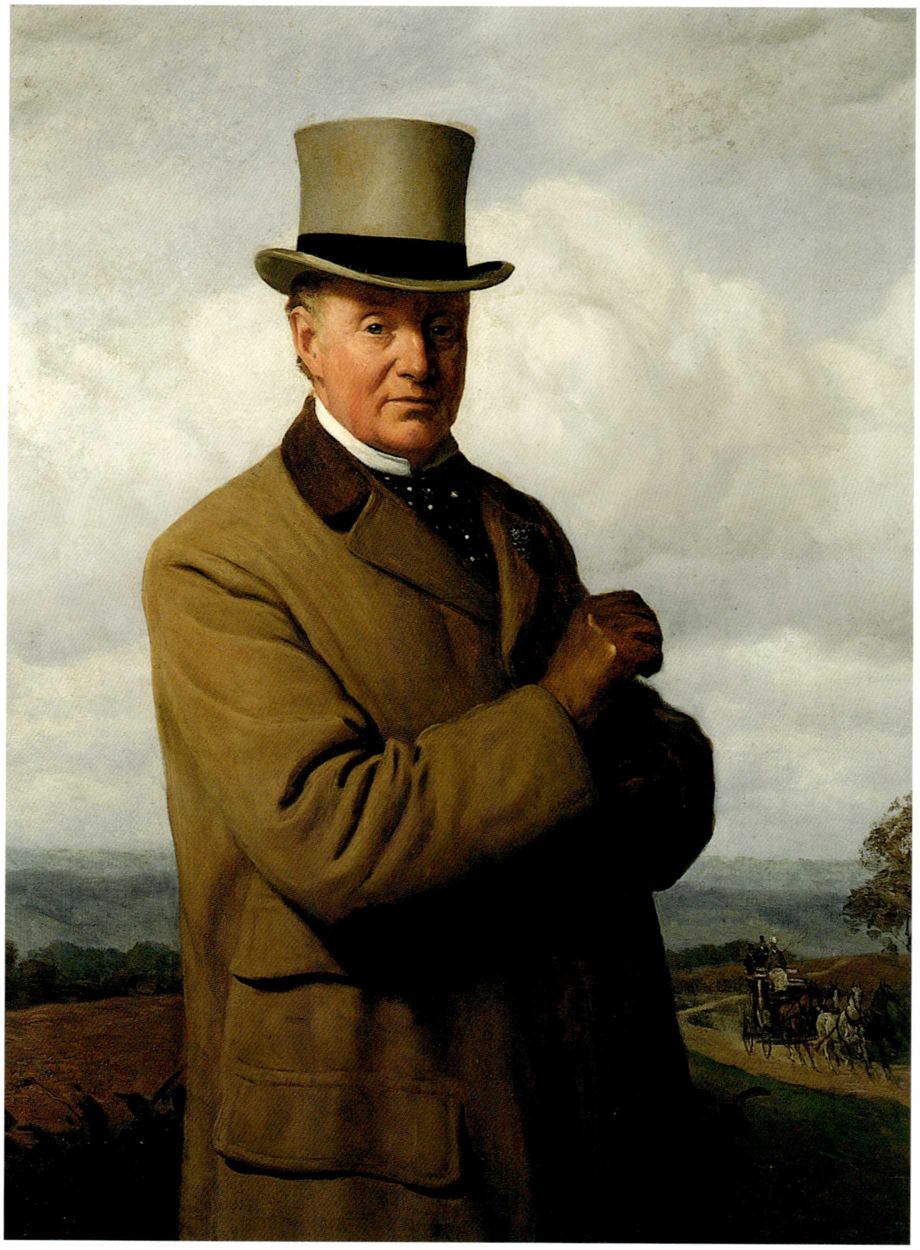

E. K. FOWNES (1850/51–1943) is shown at three-quarter length, facing half right, with his head turned to the spectator, wearing a brown overcoat and grey top hat; a coach and four is seen on the open road in the middle distance right; the background is a landscape.

Judging by the facial features of Fownes, the portrait was probably painted around the same time as the associated work by Palmer (see next entry). Although painted in the early years of the century, the work celebrates the *Victorian* career of Fownes, universally known as Ted Fownes, who was born into a coaching family; his three younger brothers were all coachmen. He was recognised as the best professional of his day from the death of James Selby in 1888 until the 1900s. He drove the *Old Times* coach for Lord Leconfield, and the *Nimrod* for Captain John Spicer.

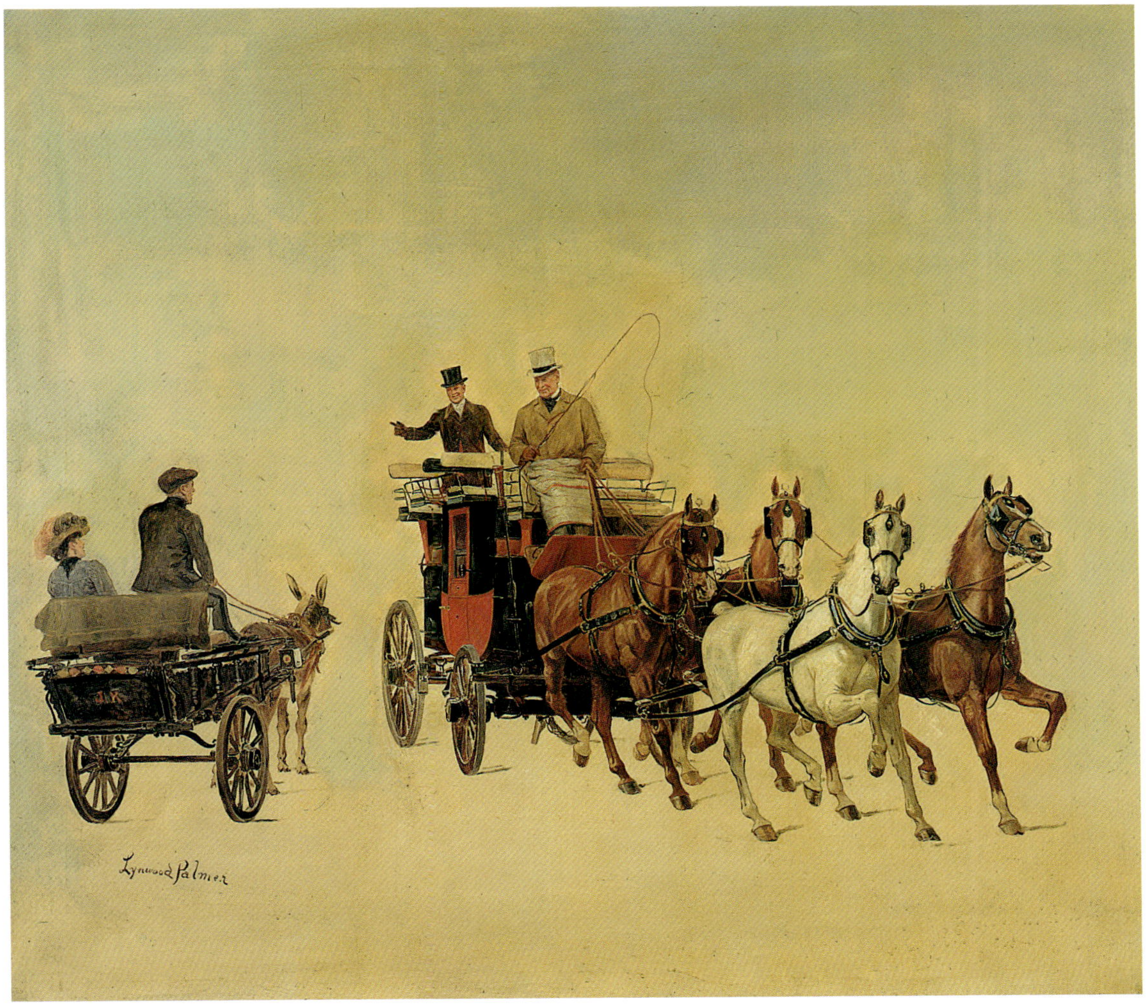

104.

JAMES LYNWOOD PALMER
(1868–1941)

A Dog Cart and Stage Coach at Olympia
[44.6/1]
*c.*1900
Oil on canvas, 101.8 x 117.2 cm
Signed bottom left: *Lynwood Palmer*

THE PAINTING shows a donkey cart on the left with the initials J. K. on the back, with a coster and a woman seated inside, entering the ring at Olympia. Leaving the ring on the right is a red stagecoach, without markings, drawn by four horses, with the well-known coachman E. K. Fownes (see previous entry) on the box and a guard standing at the back; the background is plain. This is a good example of vehicle portraiture, by a distinguished amateur coachman and collector. The costume indicates a date of about 1900.

This work belongs to the Museum's Fownes collection of coaching material, which includes various types of whips, a guard's satchel, coachman buttons, coach horns and a post-boy jacket.

Provenance:
E. K. Fownes; presented by the Misses Fownes in 1944.

Bibliography:
Hayes (cat. no. 163).

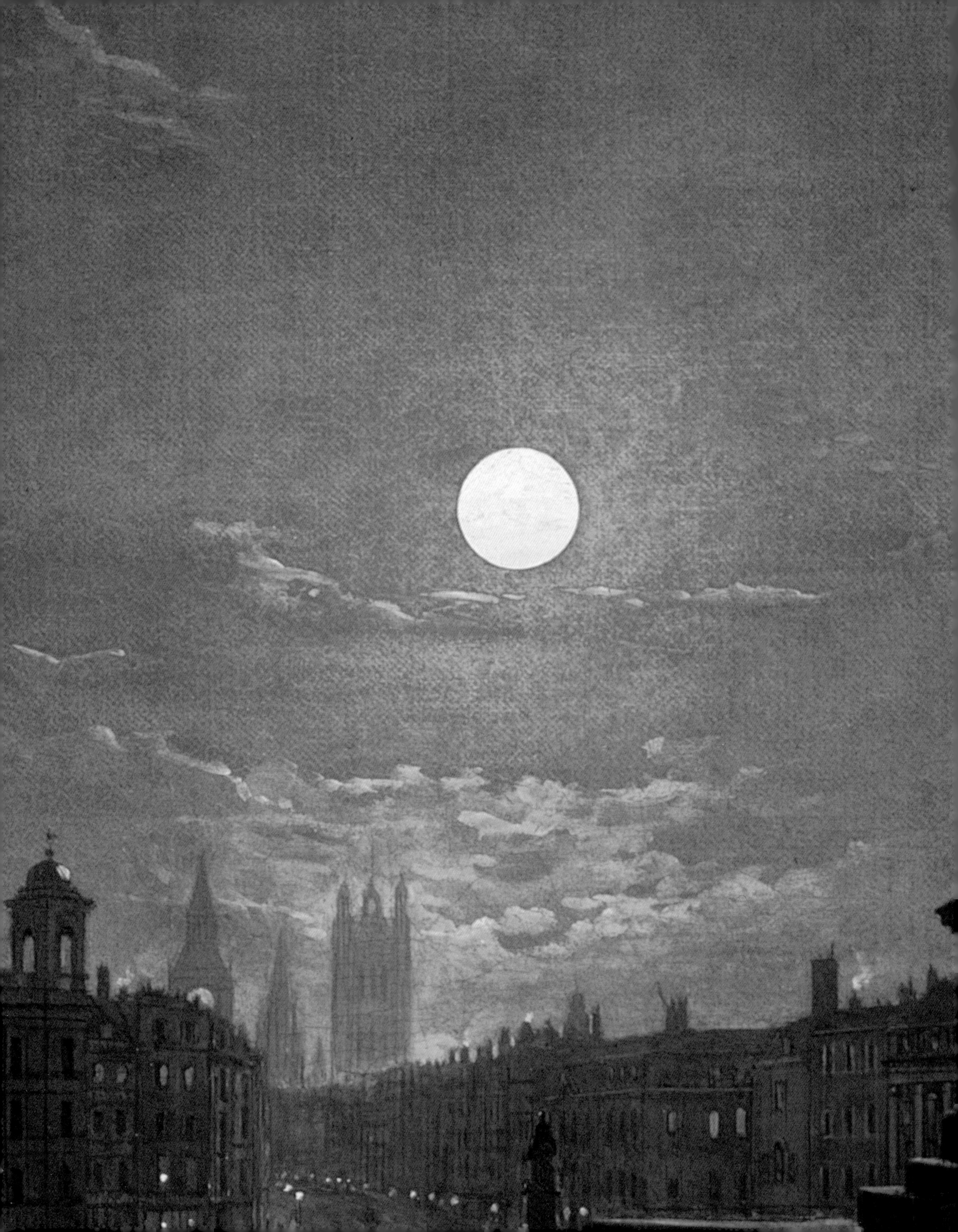

NIGHT PAINTINGS

> BUT IT IS REALLY AT NIGHT that London must be seen! London, magically lit by its millions of gas lights, is resplendent! Its broad streets disappearing into the distance; its shops, where floods of light reveal the myriad sparkling colours of all the masterpieces conceived by human industry.[1]

This enthusiastic response to London by night echoes similar comments found in Georgian texts about the capital (see p26). Its suggestion that central London was exceptionally well lit is further confirmed by an 1867 Paris guide which classified cities according to their gas consumption: London and Berlin were in the lead, followed by Paris, then Brussels; Florence and Madrid came much farther down the list.[2]

The paintings in this section fall into two groups, corresponding to two main phases in the lighting of London – first by gas, installed in many streets from the 1850s, and later by electricity, which began to supersede gas in the last quarter of the nineteenth century.

Gas lighting was first introduced in Soho in 1802 (to celebrate the peace of Amiens) and much public attention was drawn to this new technique when the outside of Carlton House was illuminated in 1807. Gas became firmly established in 1814, when it was installed in Piccadilly, Coventry Street and part of Princes Street. Artists, it seems, responded to this new, brighter illumination of London rather slowly. The Pether family of painters pioneered night painting in the late 1840s, but without taking advantage of the capital's artificial lighting: gas lights can barely be detected in Henry Pether's paintings below, except in cat. no. 107.

The emergence in the Regency period of a new form of visual entertainment based on the transformation of painted scenery from day to night would have focused attention further on the visual potential of night scenes: the Regent's Park Diorama was opened in 1823 (the building is still extant). Initially it was the discovery of fire effects at night time which caught the imagination of artists (see p179 for fire painting). In 1834 at the Regent Street Cosmorama Rooms Kenny Meadow presented his 'Grand Tableaux of the Conflagration by Day and Night with moonlight scenes in the ruins'.[3] The theatre also contributed to the general interest in night scenes: *London by Night* was produced in 1845 and *After Dark, A Tale of London Life* in 1868.[4]

Apart from the romantic image of the gas lighter, little use was made of the visual impact made by gas lighting in London, but it is interesting to note that so many moonlight scenes (with occasional gas lights) were set in London. Later on in the century, Atkinson Grimshaw made a speciality of night and twilight scenes, and a number of his paintings were set in London, where he drew his special effects from remarkable *natural* lighting – either sunsets or

John Atkinson Grimshaw
(1836–1893)
Battersea Bridge, London, 1885
Oil on canvas
Reproduced by courtesy of
Richard Green, London.

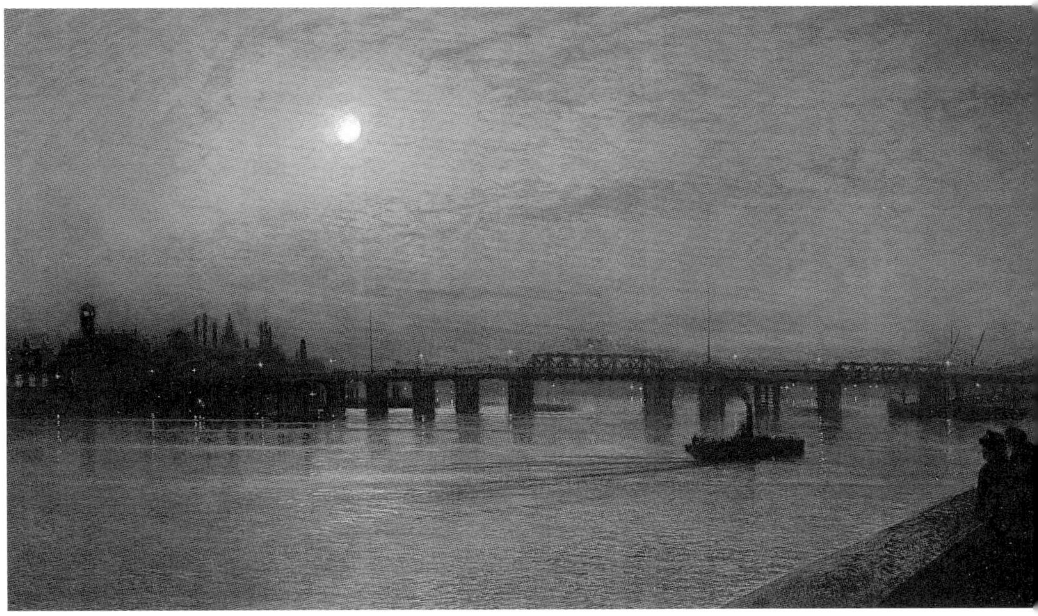

James Abbott McNeill Whistler (1834–1903)
*Nocturne in Blue and Gold: Old Battersea Bridge, c.*1872–5
Oil on canvas
Tate Gallery, London.

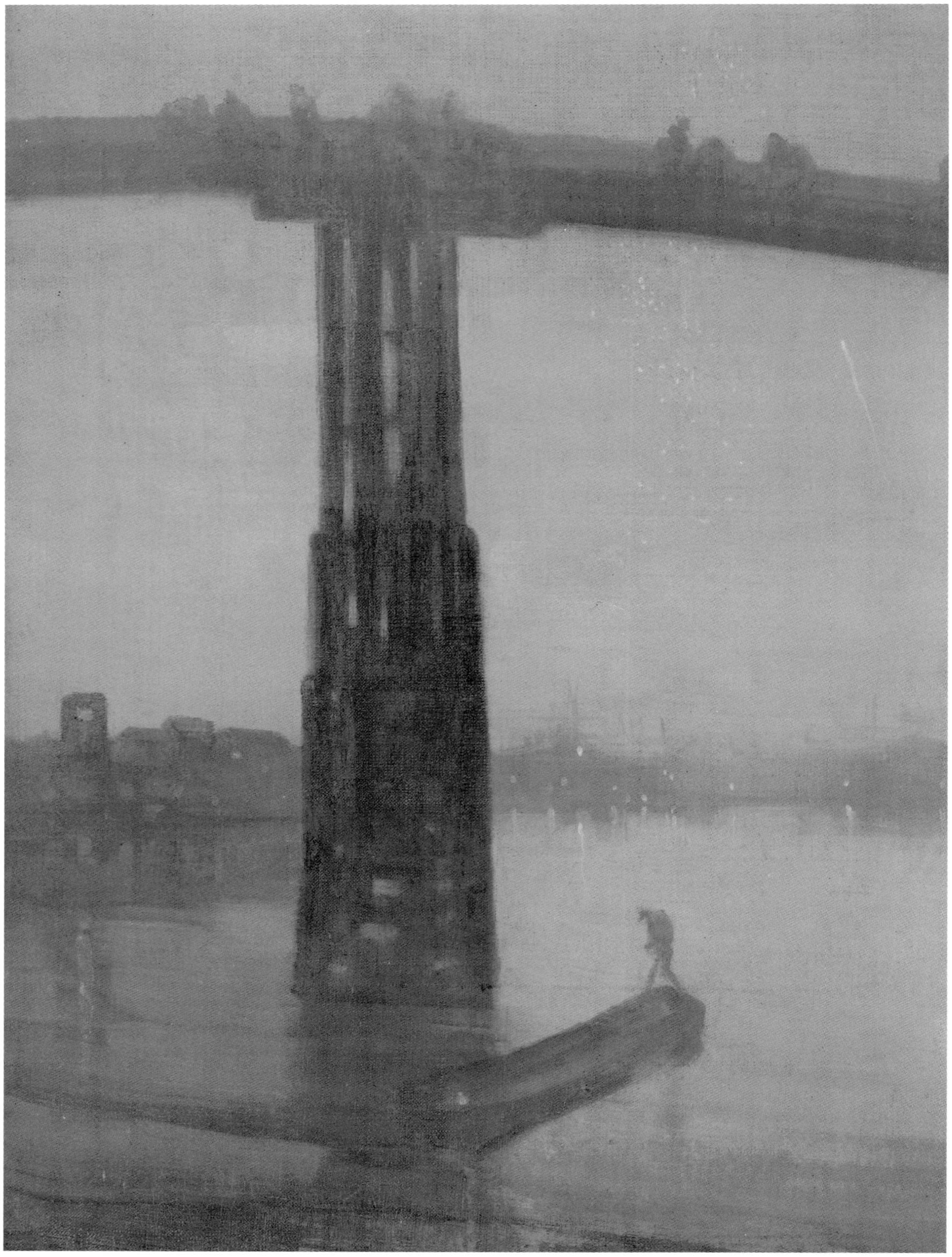

moonlight.[5] Whistler had been a late discovery in Grimshaw's life and the two men clearly responded to similar visual stimuli.

James McNeill Whistler, however, is arguably the greatest exponent of the genre of night painting with his Thames night scenes, known as *Nocturnes* (see also p208). They were mostly based around Chelsea where he lived and the artist worked largely from memory.[6] Whistler started painting his *Nocturnes* in 1871 and in 1878 fought Ruskin in court for his attack on *Nocturne in Black and Gold: the Falling Rocket*. The case eventually bankrupted Whistler but generated an interesting debate on the nature of aesthetics in a London context.

The end of the nineteenth century saw the advent of electric lighting. The first use of electricity was on the Embankment in 1878 and Atkinson Grimshaw paid tribute to its striking effect in 1880 in his *Reflections on the Thames: Westminster*.[7] This installation was followed by Billingsgate, the Savoy (the first theatre to be fitted with electric lighting, in 1881) and the Gaiety Theatre in the Strand; a little later Holborn Viaduct, the Reform Club and Langham Hotel followed suit. The first illuminated signs in Piccadilly Circus came as early as the 1890s. Dudley Heath, undeservedly little known, created images which rendered well the intensity of the new illumination process.[8]

1. Flora Tristan, *London Journal 1840*, George Prior 1980 publication, p2.
2. *La Ville, art et architecture en Europe, 1870-1993*, Jean Dethier and Alain Guiheux (eds), Pompidou Centre, Paris, 1994, p48.
3. Robert Altick, *The Shows of London*, 1978, p168.
4. *The Victorian City: Images and Reality*, H. J. Dyos and M. Woolf (eds), 1976, p212, plates 49 and 50.
5. See Atkinson Grimshaw catalogues on p210, note 7.
6. Denys Sutton, *Nocturne: the Art of James McNeill Whistler*, Country Life Publications, Malcolm Warner, 1963; *The Paintings of James McNeill Whistler*, 1980; *The Image of London*, exhibition catalogue, Barbican Art Gallery, 1987.
7. Leeds City Art Galleries; the moon remains the main source of illumination in the painting.
8. This is represented by a painting of Piccadilly Circus (cat. no. 111) but 'night' watercolours in the Museum's collection also show the British Museum and the Alhambra, Leicester Square.

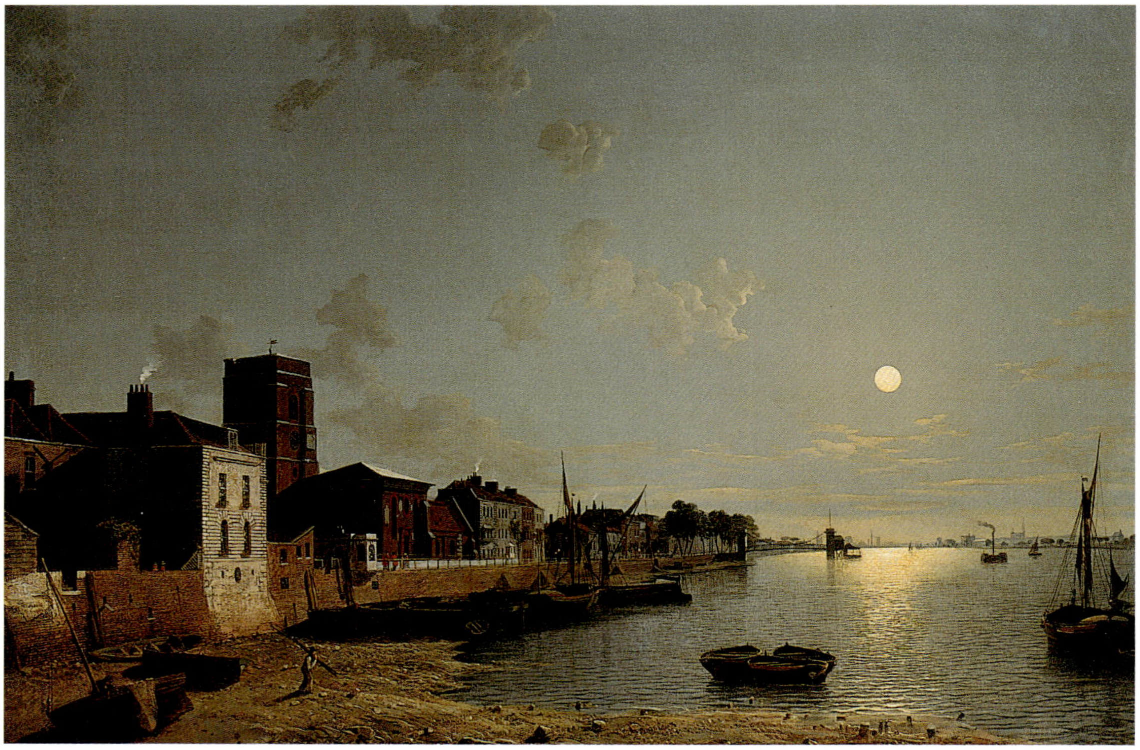

Provenance:
Possibly John Rushout, 2nd Baron Northwick (1770–1850) and Thirlestane House sale, Phillips, 29 July 1859 (311); Victor Bonney; presented by Mrs Victor Bonney in 1857.

Bibliography:
Hayes (cat. no. 90); *Illustrated London News*, 22 May 1965, p26.

105.

HENRY PETHER

(1800–80)

Cheyne Walk in Chelsea, by Moonlight

(57.68/1)

*c.*1850

Oil on canvas, 60.9 x 91.5 cm

Signed bottom left: *Henry Pether*

THIS VIEW of Cheyne Walk and the river (at low tide) looks eastwards from the foreshore just east of Battersea Bridge. It predates the construction of Chelsea Embankment, completed in 1874. In the foreground is the large house at the eastern end of Lombard Street through which an archway joined this street with Cheyne Walk. Behind this building is Chelsea Old Church, rebuilt in 1669–72, its tower dating from 1674. In the churchyard, fronting the river, stands Joseph Wilton's monument to Sir Hans Sloane (1660–1753), the distinguished naturalist whose collections are the foundation of the British Museum. Two Chelsea pensioners are standing next to the monument. Beyond the church is the row of five late seventeenth-century houses in Prospect Place (at one time called Church Row), now demolished, with Cheyne Walk extending into the distance.

In the middle distance is Cadogan pier, which a paddle steamer has just left. These had been used on the Thames since the 1820s, and by now provided a regular service between Hammersmith and London Bridge for a fare of only a few pence. In the far distance can be made out the buildings and chimneys of various works and manufactories on either side of Chelsea Reach; prominent among these is the engine house for the Southwark and Vauxhall waterworks, seen to the right of the paddle steamer.

The costume indicates a date of about 1845–50.

A version of similar size, signed and dated 1850 on the reverse, was sold at Sotheby's on 26 June 1968 (106).

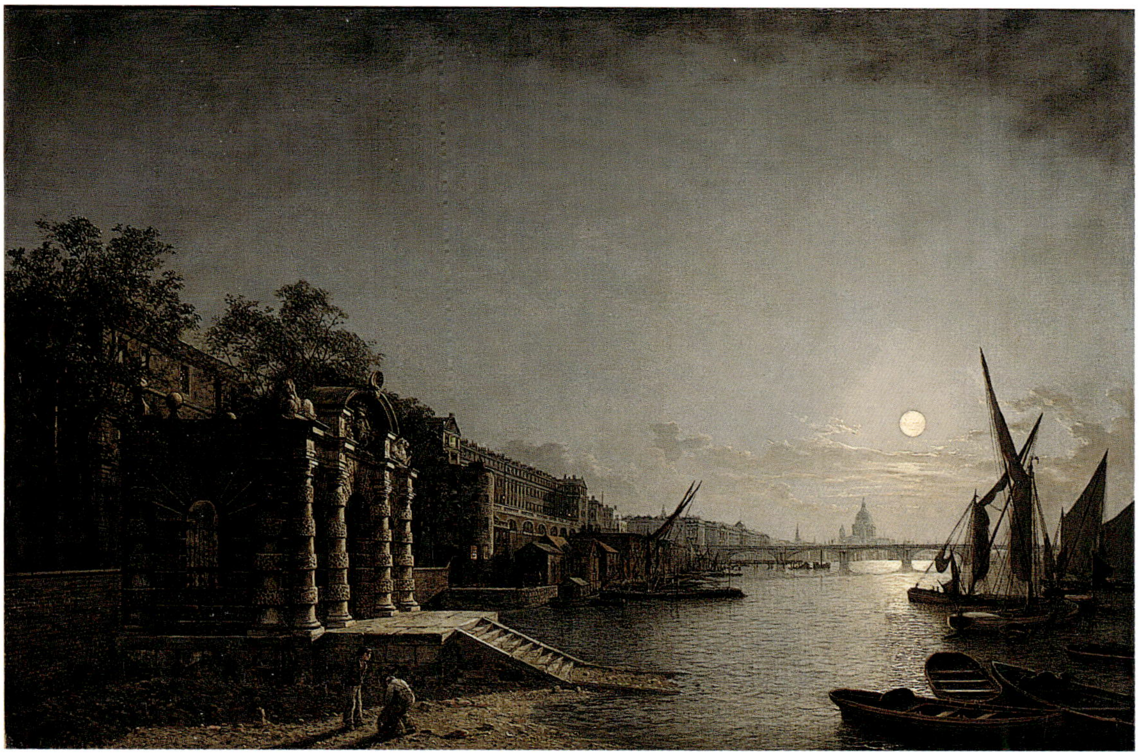

106.

HENRY PETHER

(1800–80)

York Water Gate and the Adelphi from the River by Moonlight [60.50]

*c.*1850

Oil on canvas, 58.7 x 84.1 cm

Signed bottom left: *Henry Pether*

THIS VIEW of the Strand waterfront from the river also predates the construction of the Embankment, looks north-eastwards and shows in the distance Somerset House, Waterloo Bridge, the spire of St Bride and St Paul's Cathedral. In the foreground is the York Water Gate, with the Adelphi wharves and the Royal Terrace beyond (see cat. nos 27 and 79).

Just this side of the bridge can be seen Waterloo pier, the scene of the explosion of the *Cricket* paddle steamer in 1847. A fare of one halfpenny to the City 'by the fast iron boats' was advertised at this landing stage. On the foreshore two mudlarks, as they were called, are seen gathering together what bits and pieces the tide might have washed up – coals, rope, old iron or, best of all, copper nails; these unfortunates, often aged little more than six or seven, could expect to average about threepence a day by selling their gains to the rag shops. A number of barges and rowing boats are seen in the foreground right.

Provenance:
Purchased out of the Mackenzie Bell Trust Fund from the Parker Gallery in 1960.

Bibliography:
Hayes (cat. no. 91).

Provenance:
Bonham's, 5 May 1966 (174), bt Richard Green (Fine Paintings) Ltd, from whom it was purchased out of the Mackenzie Bell Trust Fund.

Bibliography:
Hayes (cat. no. 92).

107.

HENRY PETHER
(1800–80)

Trafalgar Square by Moonlight [66.44]
1861–7
Oil on canvas, 60.4 x 91 cm
Signed bottom right: *Henry Pether*

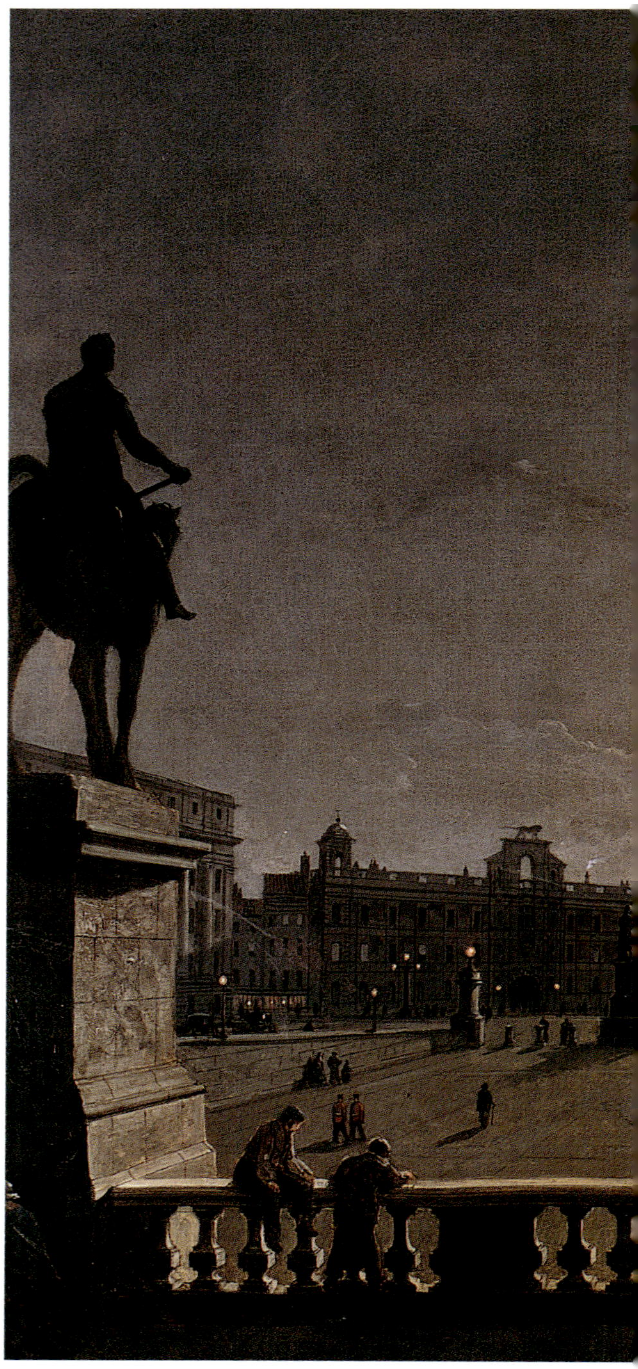

TAKEN FROM the balustrade on the north side, this moonlight view of Trafalgar Square looks south-eastwards down Whitehall; several figures are seen in the foreground, and there are two or three cabs in the distance left and right. The viewpoint is unusual, as most artists depicting Trafalgar Square tend to focus their composition on the National Gallery or St Martin-in-the-Fields. Unlike the two earlier Pethers in the collection, this picture is remarkable for the prominent inclusion of street and indoor gas lighting, as well as the partly visible lit clock-face of Big Ben.

Beyond the square are seen, from left to right: part of Morley's Hotel, built by G. L. Taylor in 1830 and destroyed in 1936 to make way for South Africa House; Northumberland House (see cat. no. 36) purchased by the Metropolitan Board of Works from the Duke of Northumberland in 1874 for five hundred thousand pounds and demolished for the construction of Northumberland Avenue; Whitehall, with Big Ben and the Victoria Tower in the distance, and Le Sueur's equestrian statue of Charles I; the offices and shops of Charing Cross and Cockspur Street; the top of the Duke of York's column, Carlton House Terrace; and the Union Club (later Canada House), built by Sir Robert Smirke in 1824–7.

Trafalgar Square was formed on the site of the King's Mews, Charing Cross, in connection with the improvements planned to link Pall Mall with St Martin's Lane, which followed the completion of Regent Street. Though the area was cleared soon after the passing of the Charing Cross Act in 1826, the layout, designed by Sir Charles Barry (but with subsequent modifications), was not finished until about 1850. The statue of Nelson by E. H. Baily was raised on its

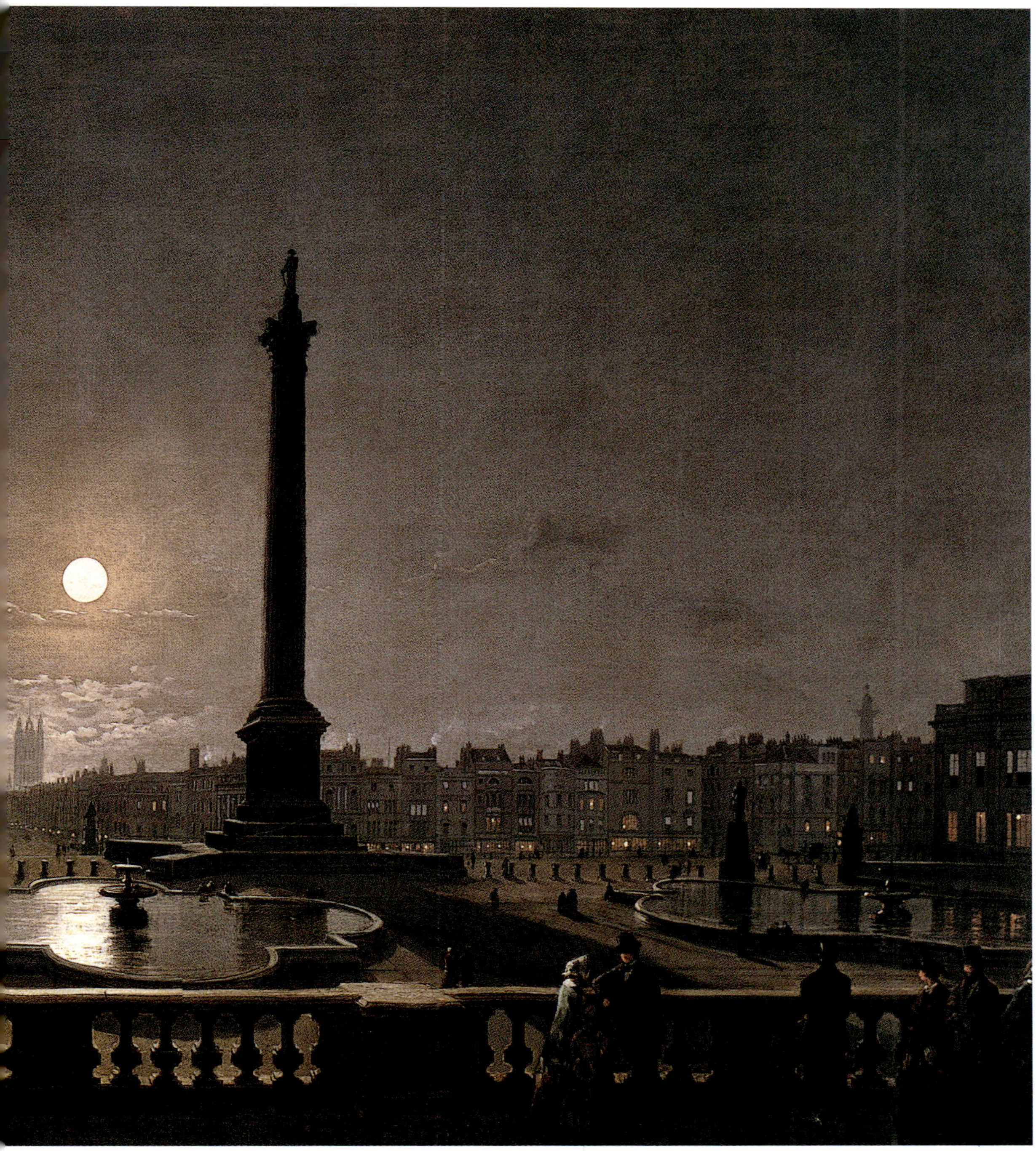

fluted Corinthian column (44 metres in height) in 1843 and the fountains and basins were in position by 1845 (these were remodelled in 1939). The four lions which now surround Nelson's column, cast from a model by Sir Edwin Landseer and set in position in January 1867, were evidently not finished at the time this picture was painted. The monuments in the square are, from left to right: George IV on horseback by Sir Francis Chantrey, put up in 1843 (this was originally intended for Marble Arch); General Havelock by W. Behnes, erected in 1861; and General Napier by G. G. Adams, erected in 1855–6. The statue seen at the far end of the western parapet wall is not known ever to have existed, and a lamp corresponding to that on the eastern parapet should occupy this position.

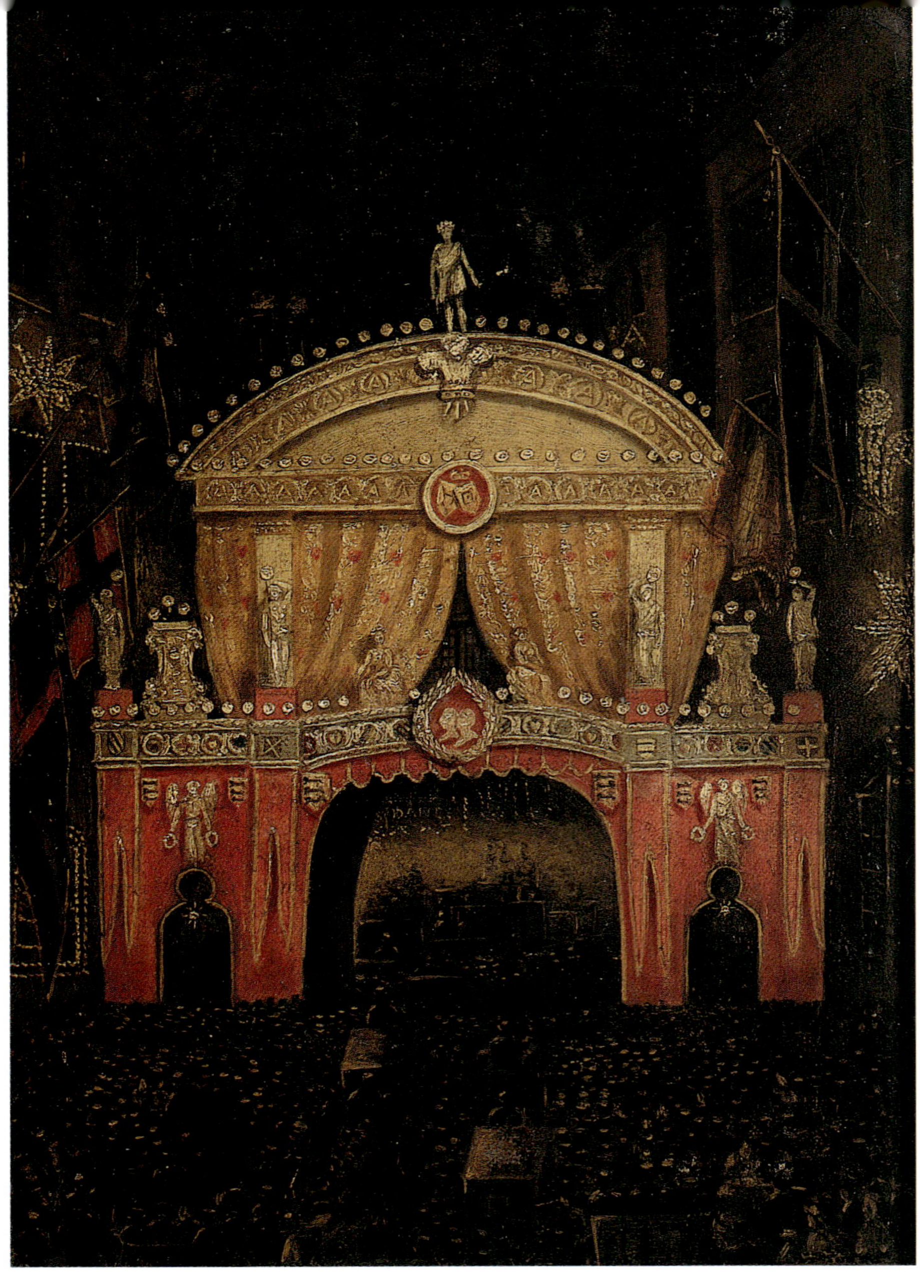

Provenance:
Purchased from R. W. Jack in 1955.

Bibliography:
Hayes (cat. no. 139); Jeremy Maas, *The Prince of Wales Wedding*, 1977; *The Illustrated London News*, 7–28 March 1863.

108.

BRITISH SCHOOL

Temple Bar Illuminated for the Marriage of the Prince of Wales, 11 March 1863 [55.79]
1863
Oil on canvas, 40.6 x 30.5 cm
Not signed or dated

TEMPLE BAR is seen at night, richly decorated in red and gold hangings, with people and vehicles thronging the Strand. Edward, Prince of Wales, later Edward VII (1841–1910), married Princess Alexandra of Denmark (1844–1925) in St George's Chapel, Windsor, on 10 March 1863.

The decoration consisted of a medallion of the Prince and Princess in the centre of Temple Bar with, above it, the arms united, the whole surmounted by a statue of Hymen carrying a torch. The entire cornice of the pediment was covered with emblematic devices in gold. Both facades of the monument were entirely enveloped with crimson cloth decorated with gold-leaf and red hearts. Angels holding orange blossoms and surmounted by tripods were placed over the footways.

The illuminations of Temple Bar for the night of the marriage took a fortnight of preparation. The *Illustrated London News* describes them: 'The front on each side was lit up with about one hundred and twenty gas-lights, under white ground-glass globes, and the effect was very beautiful. In addition to this a blaze of light from adjoining houses on each side of the bar was thrown thereon and materially heightened the effect.'

This painting is an almost exact replica of the illustration found on p352 of the *Illustrated London News* (28 March 1863) and it is likely that this work was done after it.

The marriage of the Prince and Princess of Wales was a lavish royal and public occasion. The event was officially recorded by William Powell Frith for the Queen but its impact on the London streets at night time was memorably captured by Holman Hunt in his bravura painting of London Bridge, now in the Tate Gallery (see p286).

Temple Bar itself was removed from its City site in 1878 and this event was strikingly recorded by Walter Fryer Stocks (Christie's, 15 September 1993, Lot 1). It was re-erected ten years later in Theobald Park, Cheshunt.

109.

WALTER GREAVES

(1846–1930)

Battersea Bridge – Misty Moonlight [68.137]
Late 1870s(?)
Oil on canvas, 73 x 51 cm (painting extended, presumably to fit frame)
Signed and dated bottom right:
W. Greaves 1869

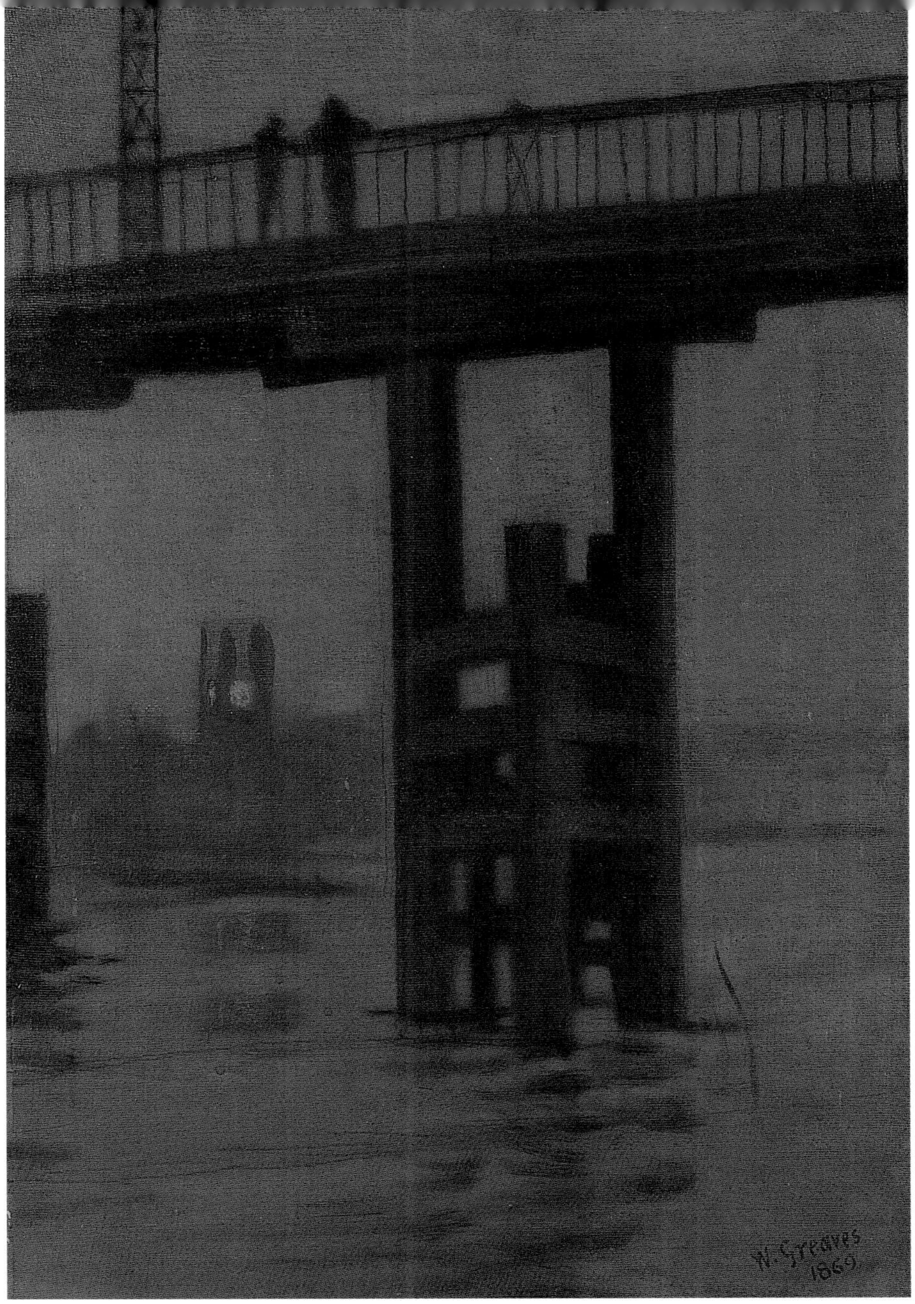

THIS NOCTURNE shows an arch of Old Battersea Bridge, probably taken from the south-east, with the moon clearly visible. The timber structure was the first bridge to be erected at Battersea and was built in 1771–2 after designs by Henry Holland. Boats often collided into the bridge when shooting the arches and that element of danger, coupled with the picturesqueness of a wooden bridge, may have appealed to artists: both the old bridges of Battersea and Putney (see cat. no. 24) were frequently depicted prior to their demolition in 1881, when they were replaced by more up-to-date structures.

This work is closely related to James McNeill Whistler's well-known painting in the Tate Gallery, *Nocturne in Blue and Gold: Old Battersea Bridge*, executed *c.*1872–5 and first exhibited in 1877 (illustrated on p270). However, in the Whistler the proportions given to the bridge are much more elongated and the composition very much in the taste of prints of bridges by the Japanese artist Hiroshige. This is quite unlike the sturdiness and relative squatness of the Greaves treatment, which is closer to Whistler's lithograph of 1878. At least two other versions of this work are known to exist, one in the Chelsea Public Library and another was with Hirschl & Adler (New York) in 1975.

As is often the case with Greaves, the date cannot be correct (also see cat. no. 93). Since the work must postdate Whistler's painting of Battersea Bridge *Nocturne*, and most probably his lithograph of the subject as well, a date in the late 1870s is suggested.

Provenance:
Purchased out of the Joicey Trust Fund from Mrs Rees, via the Fine Art Society.

Bibliography:
The Early Years of the New English Art Club, exhibition catalogue, Fine Art Society, 1968 (42); *Walter Greaves and the Nocturne*, exhibition catalogue, Parkin Gallery, 1974; *The Paintings of James McNeill Whistler*, Yale University Press, 1980, cat. nos 139 and 140; forthcoming publication on Walter Greaves by Michael Parkin and Sir John Rothenstein.

Provenance:
Babington; Sotheby's, 27 July 1960 (142), bt Colnaghi on behalf of the Museum.

Bibliography:
Hayes (cat. no. 101).

110.
P. STAHL
(active late nineteenth century)
A Hansom Cab Stand [60.114/2]
*c.*1889–90
Oil on panel, 19.7 x 25 cm
Signed bottom left: *P Stahl*
(the *PS* in monogram)

IN THIS West End night scene a couple in evening dress is approaching the foremost of two hansom cabs drawn up at the kerbside of a brightly lit street. An omnibus is passing by in the opposite direction. Hansom cabs (see cat. no. 101) first appeared on the London streets in 1835, and this painting shows the two most characteristic features of these vehicles – the exceptionally large wheels and the positioning of the driver's perch at the rear, features which ensured a high degree of balance and therefore safety. The first London taxicab, a Renault, made its début in 1907, and by the beginning of George V's reign, the hansom was in inevitable decline.

The costume indicates a date of about 1889–90.

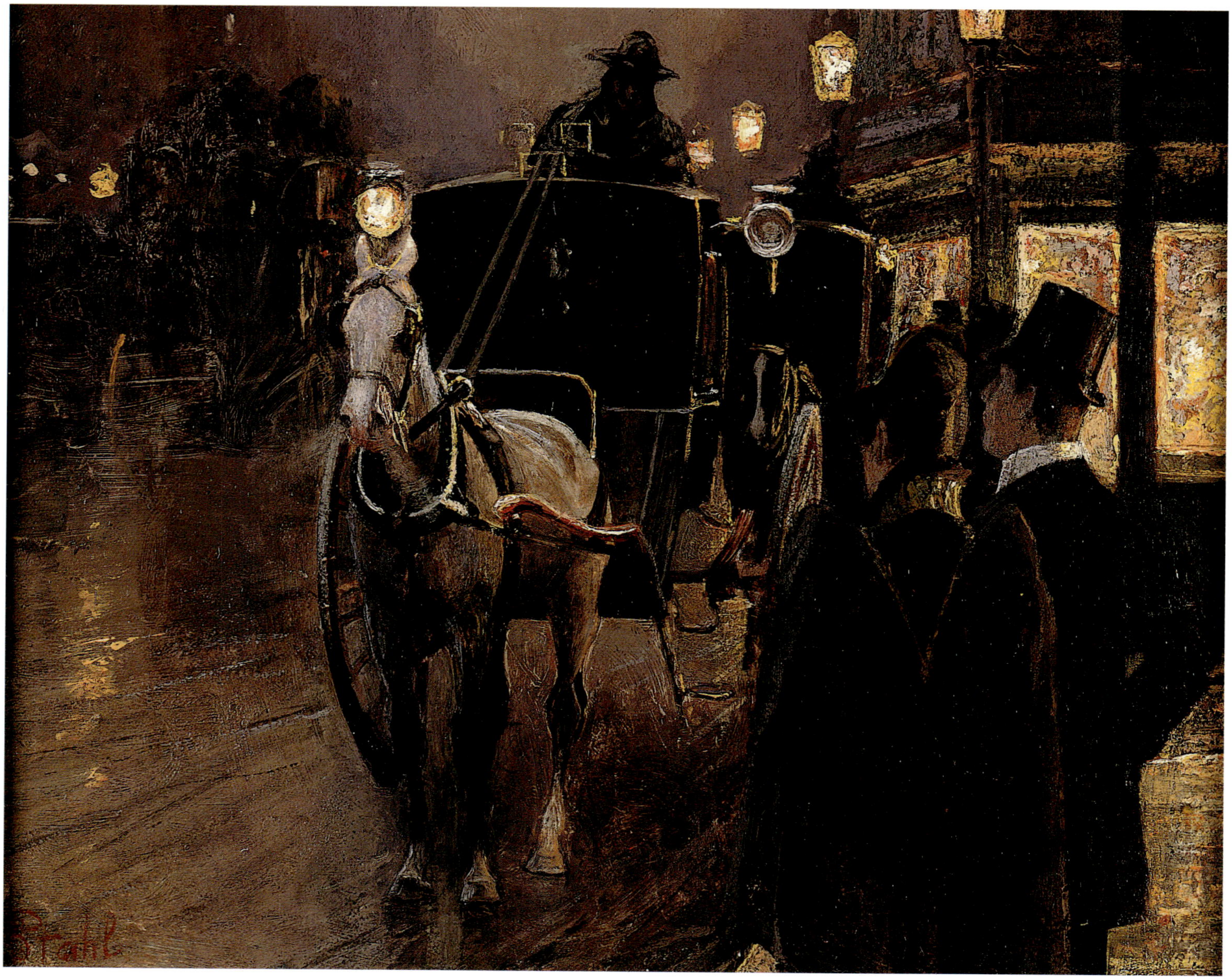

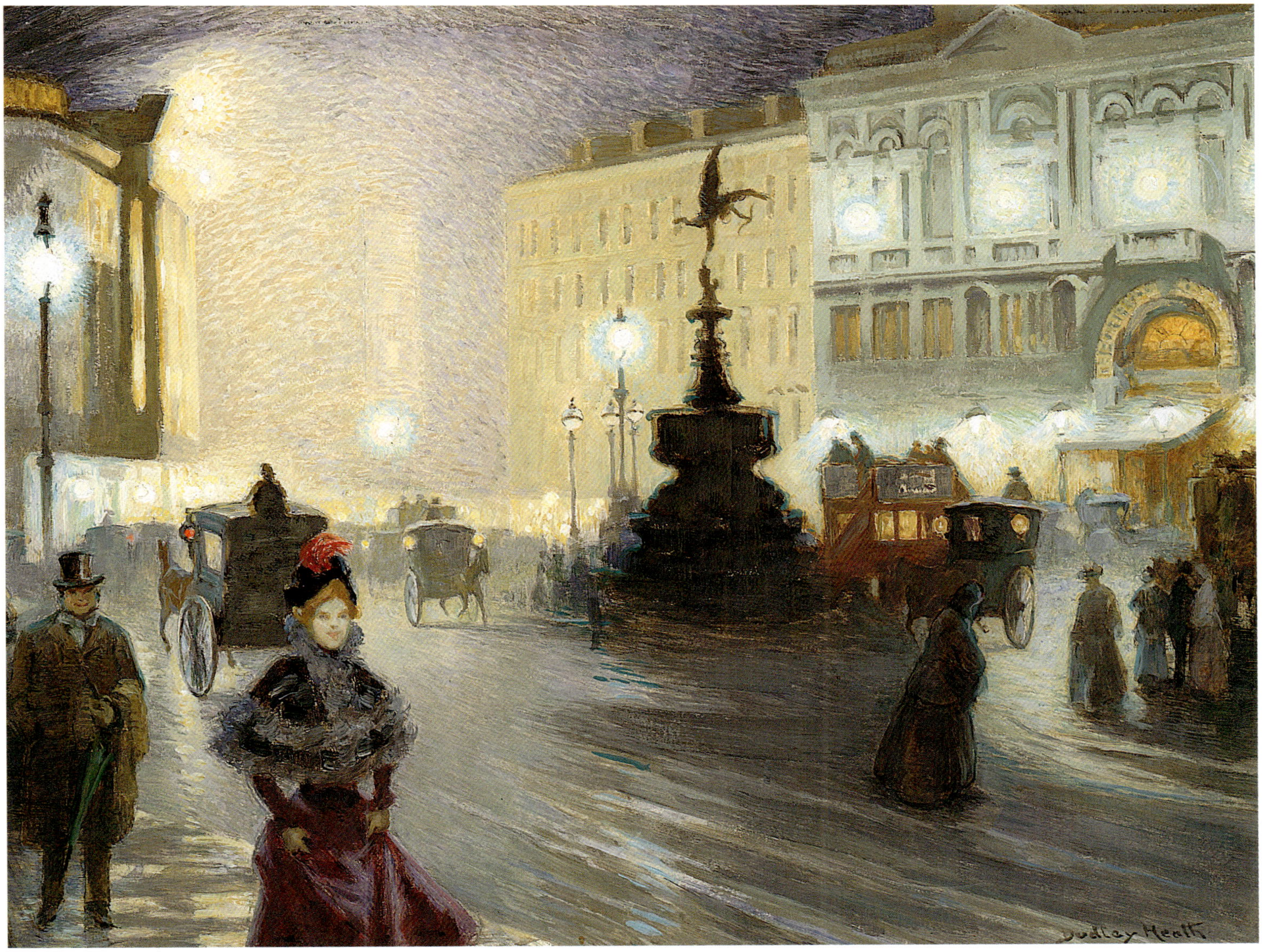

111.

ERNEST DUDLEY HEATH

(active c.1886–1940)

Piccadilly Circus at Night [41.28/1]

*c.*1893

Oil on board, 30.3 x 40.3 cm

Signed bottom right: *Dudley Heath*

THIS VIEW taken from outside the County Fire Office looks towards Haymarket and shows, from left to right: the London Pavilion, opened 1885; Sir Alfred Gilbert's Shaftesbury Memorial Fountain (Eros), unveiled on 29 June 1893; and the Criterion Restaurant and Theatre, built in 1873–4. Two omnibuses and a number of hansom cabs are seen.

The artist has successfully rendered the dazzling effect of electric lights; the intensity of lighting contrasts with the subdued and poetic lighting found in paintings by Pether.

The costume indicates a date in the early 1890s, and the picture was probably painted soon after the unveiling of Eros in 1893.

Provenance:
Presented by the artist in 1941.

Bibliography:
Hayes (cat. no. 154).

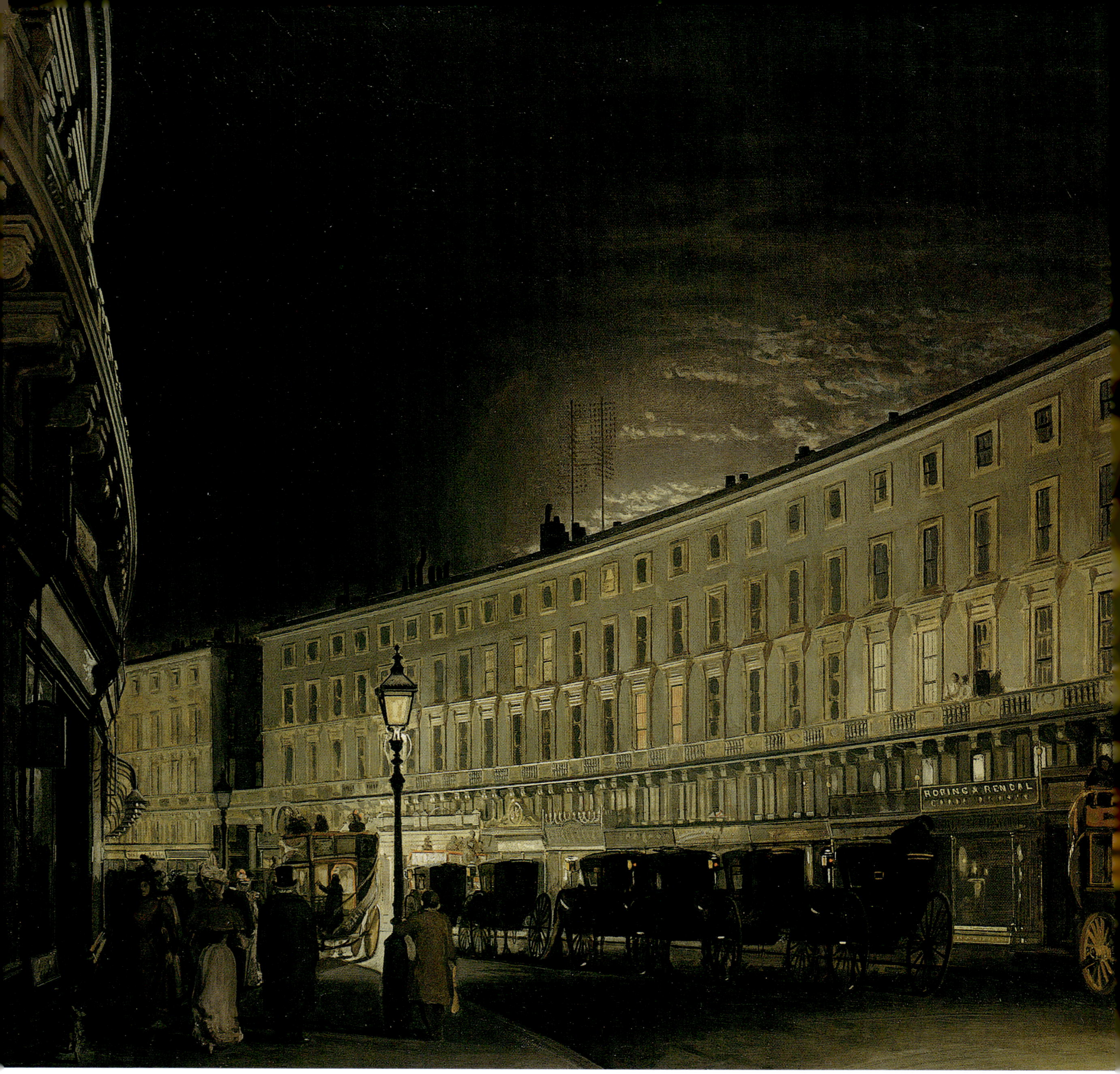

112.

FRANCIS L. M. FORSTER
(d.1916)

The Regent Street Quadrant at Night

[A 28578]

*c.*1897–8

Oil on canvas, 92 x 137.3 cm

Not signed or dated

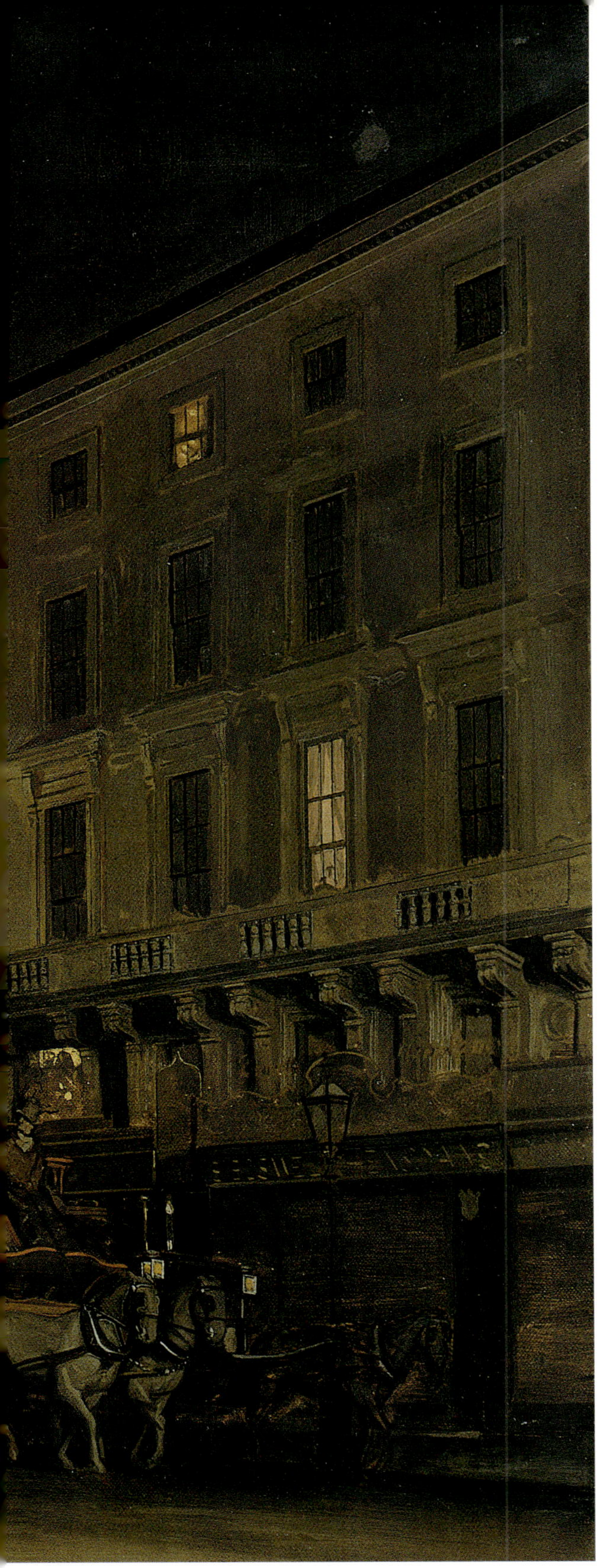

THIS VIEW of the Quadrant, which was taken from just below Glasshouse Street, looks southwards towards Piccadilly Circus, with the entrance to Swallow Street visible in the distance. It was painted only a few years before the whole character of Regent Street was drastically altered. There is very little light coming from the hidden moon and as a consequence this very dark painting relies almost entirely on the street's artificial lighting. The viewpoint is unusual as most artists have tended to position themselves looking at the Quadrant from Piccadilly Circus.

The Quadrant, which was built in 1818–20, was one of the most impressive features of the 'Royal Mile' designed by John Nash to link the Prince Regent's palace of Carlton House with Regent's Park. Its purpose was to connect Lower Regent Street, which was cut northwards from the facade of Carlton House, with Regent Street proper, which, for practical reasons, could not be placed quite in alignment. It was the only part of the street actually built by Nash himself (so important did he consider it), and the stately sweep of this once-colonnaded, uniformly designed block, contrasting with the variety and picturesque skyline of the remainder of Regent Street, constituted the essence of his architectural character. This sweep was interrupted in 1905–8 by the construction of the grandiose Edwardian facade of Norman Shaw's Piccadilly Hotel, and only partially restored in the 1920s by the rebuilding of the entire length of the Quadrant with facades in stylistic keeping with the new hotel.

Three typical late Victorian omnibuses of the garden-seat variety can be seen passing by, and six hansom cabs are waiting at a cab stand in the centre of the street. We should also note the early telegraph poles on the roof – the monopoly of the telegraph system was acquired by the Post Office in 1870. Also see cat. no. 138.

Provenance:
Presented by the artist's sister, Miss Evelyn Forster, in 1926.

Bibliography:
Hayes (cat. no. 44); *The New English Art Club*, centenary exhibition catalogue, Christie's, 1986 (66).

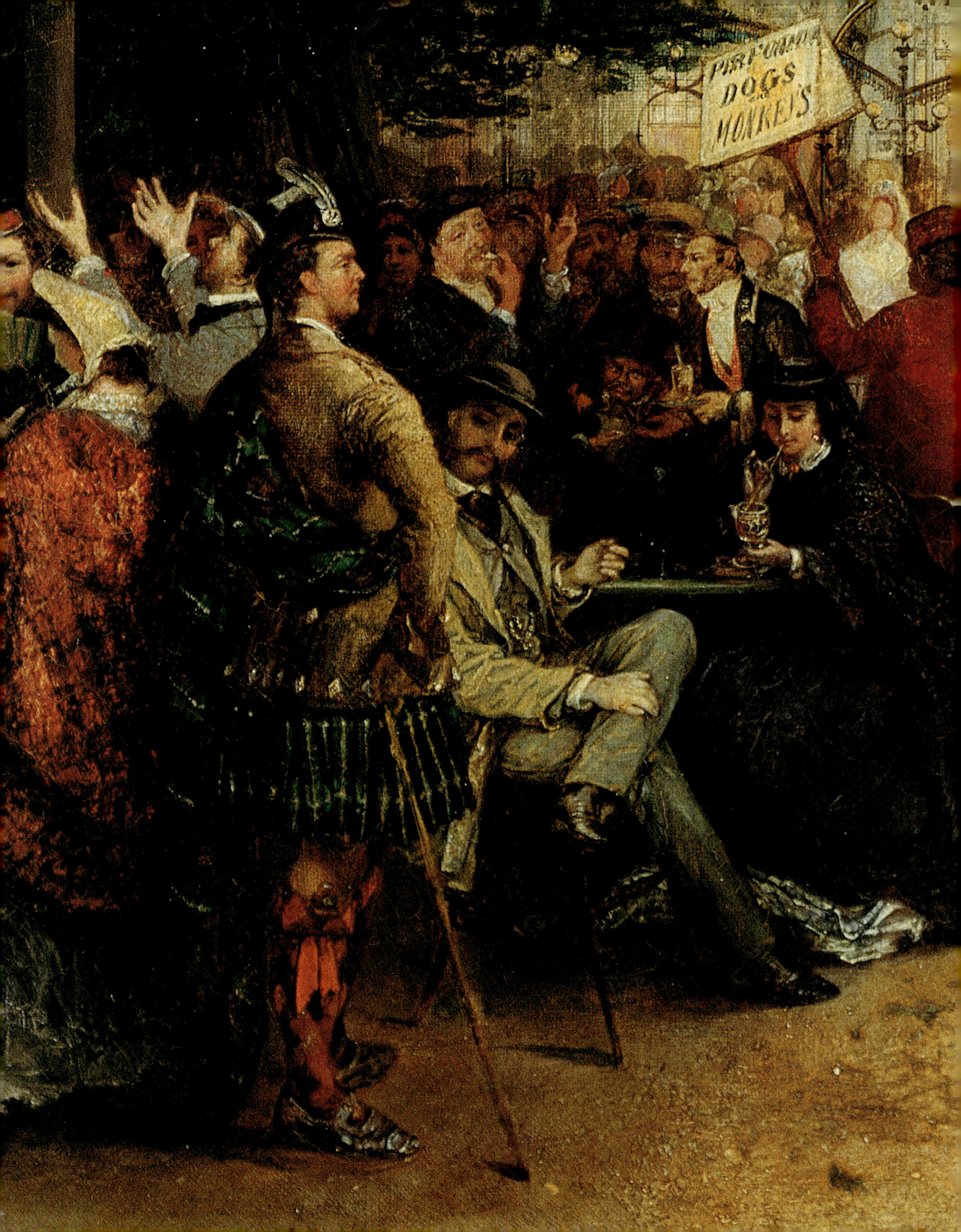
DOGS
MONKEYS

THE SOCIAL SCENE

THE VICTORIAN painters' most remarkable breakthrough was to develop a visual formula which gave the impression of representing the whole of society in a single image. John Ritchie's *Summer Day in Hyde Park* (cat. no. 120), Phoebus Levin's *Cremorne Gardens* (cat. no. 126) and *Covent Garden* (cat. no. 95) and even Charles Hunt's *Coffee Stall* (cat. no. 131) are good examples of this, showing a range of characters and classes spread across the canvas. When backgrounds such as Hyde Park, Cremorne Gardens and Covent Garden are used, the formula harks back to the eighteenth century, when society was depicted in parks and pleasure gardens (see cat. no. 161) or in attendance at market scenes.

The development of public transport in particular and of public services in general enabled Londoners to mix on an unprecedented scale. William Powell Frith, closely followed by George Elgar Hicks, are the best exponents of the new social panoramas in works such as *The Railway Station*[1] and *The General Post Office* (cat. no. 124). Arthur Boyd Houghton's lesser-known *Holborn in 1861*[2] conveys well the variety of the London crowd – the apparent freedom in the mixing of the classes makes it a rare example of true social panorama; while the Museum's collections, in addition to the works mentioned above, also include Joy's famous *Bayswater Omnibus* (cat. no. 134), which depicts the microcosm of London in a most successful composition.

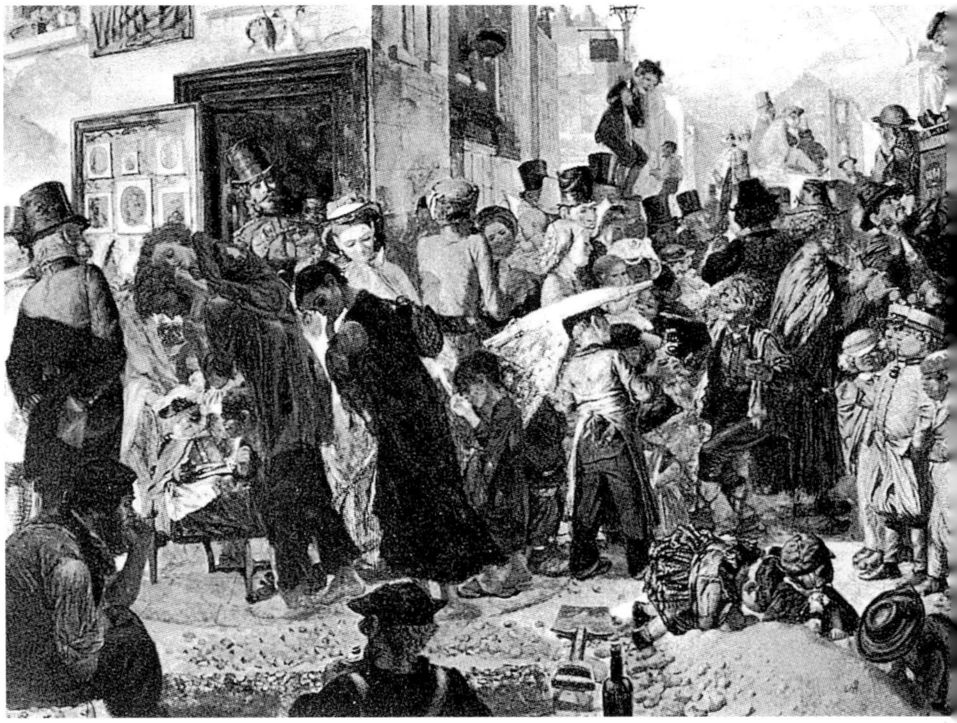

Arthur Boyd Houghton
(1836–1875)
Holborn in 1861
Oil on canvas
The Trustees of Sir Colin and Lady Anderson.

The image of Victorian London as a melting pot should not, however, be exaggerated. Most of the artistic production of the time remains as segregated when dealing with the social scene as the social scene itself. Jules Vallès's observations are rarely quoted because his text for *La Rue à Londres* (1884) is bitter and aggressive,[3] but his observations on the structure of society in London are worth quoting:

> There is not a single public place where segregation is not made explicit through labelling. Here the wretched, there the poor, the wealthy on that side. Once again, one is careful not to mix the down-trodden, not to allow the intelligence of one to provide for the ignorance of another, not to enable promiscuity between the eloquent obsolete individual and the robust craftsman, not to permit the hungry to shame those who are only thirsty.[4]

This process of segregation may be observed in Hicks's painting (cat. no. 124, particularly in relation to the preparatory drawing) and in the Macduff depiction of a 'meeting' between a shoe-black and a street arab with the 'master/protector' of street children, Lord Shaftesbury, in the form of a portrait on the other side of a glass window (cat. no. 125).

When the artist tackles the issue of movement between the classes we are quite removed from Hogarth's vision in his classic saga *Industry and Idleness*. William Powell Frith's 1878

The Road to Ruin[5] echoes Hogarth's more negative prototypes – *The Rake's Progress* and *The Harlot's Progress* – and the series is dominated by the downward social spiral. Hogarth is generally more critical of all classes of society, whereas the Victorian artists are often driven by their concern about and even fear of poverty. There were, of course, examples of human resilience in spite of adverse social conditions and *The Song of the Shirt*[6] highlighting the plight of seamstresses captured the imagination of artists and public alike. A number of images were produced to illustrate Thomas Hood's poem 'The Song of the Shirt' (published in *Punch*'s Christmas issue of 1843), the prototype and most celebrated of which was Richard Redgrave's *The Sempstress* (1844, plus replica in 1846). Anna Blunden's *For only a short hour...*[7] makes the urban environment particularly explicit – taken from the artist's lodgings at City Road, Finsbury, the picture shows Islington as its skyline. The similarities between this painting and John Roddam Spencer Stanhope's *Thoughts of the Past*[8], where the window view has become the Thames at Blackfriars, shows that the difference between a fallen woman (Stanhope) and a poor working woman (Blunden) was hardly noticeable.

There are many examples of philanthropic work with the poor classes (see cat. no. 125) which aimed to enable them only to reach a level of human dignity, not a degree of wealth (as in Hogarth's 'Good 'prentice' turned Lord Mayor). Always menacing the inhabitants of Flora Tristan's 'monster city' (see below) is the possibility of the 'fall', from wealth to ruin or from virtue to vice, as is illustrated in such paintings as Dante Gabriel Rossetti's *Found*, Augustus L. Egg's *Past and Present* and Alfred Elmore's *On the Brink*,[9] as well as by the shady goings-on in Phoebus Levin's *Cremorne Gardens* (see cat. no. 126).

Once at the bottom of the social scale, the absence of cultural life for the working classes was noted by the indefatigable Flora Tristan (Gauguin's grandmother): 'Access to libraries, museums, churches and scientific collections is practically impossible for the working class.'[10] Both Jules Vallès and Flora Tristan also noted the absence of real social life in London. Jules Vallès wrote: '... from 6 p.m., commercial London is dead. Where to go when the city has withdrawn its claws, shut its mouth, closed its eyes...? The privileged go to the Club... I have seen several of these cemeteries peopled with a world of ghosts who read, yawn or smoke...'[11] Public houses and music halls should have been seen as valid manifestations of social life for the poorer classes but before their names were partially cleared by Edwardian artists (see p374), they were seen as evil places on the 'road to ruin'. In the eyes of Vallès and Tristan, even the theatre struggled for respectability: 'In all the theatres the lobby is luxuriously appointed... but in all the theatres the lobbies have been taken over by the prostitutes whose shameless solicitations prevent women with any degree of modesty from frequenting the place.'[12]

Family life probably did benefit from this restriction on public social outlets and new categories of paintings emerged glorifying women at home (James Tissot's beloved Kathleen Newton at their home in St John's Wood), children (C. R. Leslie), and a number of ritual gatherings such as marriages (Hicks in *Changing Homes*, or Charles and Emily Floris in their Clapham wedding *Matrimony Place*),[13] and christenings.[14] These subjects were first introduced through royal patronage: weddings in particular regularly led to commissions. These were not always received with enthusiasm by painters. Frith, for instance, turned down in 1857 the commission for the marriage of Princess Alice and was uneasy about accepting that of the Prince of Wales (1863) – Landseer is quoted as saying that he would not undertake this work 'for all the money in this world, and all in the next'.[15] Only two christenings were painted, those of the first two royal children, but the Queen was disappointed with the results and the more modest medium of watercolour was adopted for later christenings.[16]

The role played by royalty in encouraging British painting was considerable, despite complaints of the excessive use of foreign painters.[17] It has been pointed out that Victoria's collection of portraits was far larger than anything of its kind amassed by her predecessors.[18] Prince Albert, on the other hand, had formulated the plan to build up a collection of contemporary British painting and although the Government imposed a reduction in the annual picture allowance, the collections thus formed were substantial.[19] It should be stressed, however, that the range of subject matter covered was anything but urban, principally dealing (portraits aside) with animals, farming, Balmoral and the Highlands, thus manifesting a strong interest in rural rather than urban issues. Was that simply the case with royal commissions or was this a more deep-rooted phenomenon?

Interestingly, when Flora Tristan tries to come to terms with the urban character of London in the 1840s, she ends up using rural imagery to deal with the issues. This extract sums up the challenge to many a Victorian painter and patron, the switch from a rural consciousness to an urban one:

> The city is several cities in one and it has grown too large for people to keep in touch or to get to know one another... Ordinary errands involve distances of five or six miles... on the average, half the day is spent striding through the streets of London... The Londoner, when he returns home in the evening, exhausted from the day's coming and going, is not disposed to gaiety or wit, nor to cultivating the pleasures of conversation, music or dancing. The intellectual faculties... are destroyed by physical fatigue carried to the extreme... thus we see that the labourer, when he returns home from the fields after twelve hours of hard work, feels only the need to eat and sleep in order to repair his strength... such is the fate of the inhabitants of the monster city![20]

The preponderance of the rural over the urban was not a mere literary device. The transposition of urban beggars to landscape settings has already been observed in the eighteenth century.[21] It is striking to note the number of cases in which Victorian London's inhabitants are presented in painting in an environment of distinctly rural character. Frith's two most famous compositions, *Derby Day* and *Ramsgate Sands*, undoubtedly depict a large number of Londoners who are presented well outside their urban setting.[22] We have already noted the social scenes set in parks and pleasure gardens by Ritchie, who also painted *Hampstead Heath* specifically as a Londoners' outing rather than as pure landscape.[23] Henry Barraud's *The London Season, Rotten Row, Hyde Park, 1864* is another example of London's society presented against a green

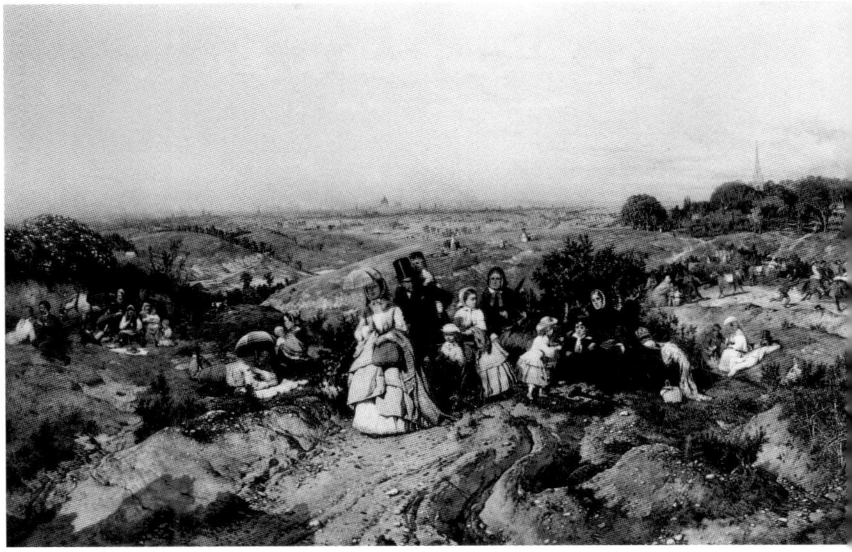

John Ritchie (active 1858–75)
Hampstead Heath, 1859
Oil on canvas
Private Collection
Reproduced by courtesy of
The Fine Art Society.

setting.[24] Tissot's substantial group of paintings dealing with his home life is dominated by scenes set in his garden rather than indoors.[25] Even the *Bayswater Omnibus* (cat. no. 134) manages to catch a glimpse of greenery as the vehicle drives along Hyde Park.

The most noteworthy of all London events in the nineteenth century was undoubtedly the Great Exhibition, but this again did little to promote true urban issues. Its architecture was revolutionary but its setting 'traditional rural', in Hyde Park. Its immense success with the public meant that the venture provided a platform for the great urban mix of people – also in this case including foreigners. The challenge proved almost too much to painters who produced images of crowds which on the whole were fairly undifferentiated and dominated by the giant size of the structure.[26]

But other crowd events, such as the marriage of the Prince of Wales, the Lord Mayor's Show or the Golden and Diamond Jubilees, encouraged artists to explore the interaction of Londoners with the urban environment, including the memorable crowded *London Bridge on the night of the Marriage of the Prince and Princess of Wales, 10 March 1863*.[27] Such official events, however, were rare occurrences in a painter's career. Where then should we look for the depiction of Londoners in truly urban settings? Among the working class and the poor.

J. T. Smith's publication *Vagabondiana* (1817) was the first work specifically devoted to London's beggars.[28] However, their context – the streets of London – was almost totally absent from Smith's etchings, as it was from Richard Beard's 1851 'studio' daguerreotypes for Henry Mayhew's *London Life and the London Poor* (republished in its full format in 1861–2). The development of a school of painting, now labelled the Social Realists,[29] meant that the true framework for such images could no longer be ignored.

Luke Fildes (1843–1927) is one of the most powerful painters of urban *Hard Times*[30] and his heroic frieze of human misery in *Applicants for Admission to a Casual Ward*[31] depicts the city's homeless, outside in the street, resigned and huddled together against the entrance and the wall of the institution which hopefully will give them a few hours of protected rest. When she describes St Giles, London's Irish quarter, Flora Tristan echoes Fildes's visual imagery: 'With my own eyes I saw children without a stitch of clothing, young girls, nursing mothers with no shoes on their feet, wearing only a tattered shift which barely covered their naked bodies . . .'[32]

The idea and composition for Fildes's painting were first worked out in a drawing published in the *Graphic* on 4 December 1869. The fantastic development, in the Victorian period, of the world of illustration, and most notably of magazine illustration, increasingly focused the artist's attention on the process of effective image making rather than questions of style. For a few years, the *Graphic*, which artistically was the best illustrated magazine on the market, was publishing drawings, which artists *subsequently* turned into oil paintings:[33] illustrations were at the cutting edge of the art world. In addition the impact on the world of painting of major print publishers such as the Graves Brothers was of great significance, directly linking the world of painting to its public in schemes which were taking further still the pioneering work of Hogarth in disseminating the artist's view.

The London Social Realists, however, were walking a tightrope and constantly ran the risk of alienating their public by the hopelessness of some of their subjects. The theme of work was, in *cities*, the (main) antidote to poverty and was presented by artists as the cement of the crumbling and troubled working classes. Most work imagery in Victorian times is centred on the lower classes. They were of course the most needy and the most reliant on work for their existence, but the artist's intention clearly goes beyond this simple logic. Ford Madox Brown's *Work* (1852–65) was set in Hampstead's Heath Street and was inspired by seeing navvies at work. As well as covering work in all its manifestations, from orphaned working children to the leisured classes (who do not need to work), the painting also includes on the right the portraits of Thomas Carlyle and F. D. Maurice, the two principal theoretical exponents of contemporary sociological concepts. These figures and others were introduced following discussions with the painting commissioner, T. E. Plint of Leeds, who wanted 'to give more fully the idea of the *head* and *heart* of work of the *mind*'.[34] A poster of the Working Men's College, founded by Maurice and where the artist taught, is included in the picture.

This most complex painting is not, however, representative of the standard production of images of work, often inextricably linked to poverty. Doré's *Poor-House* (cat. no. 128) draws much of its horror and power precisely from the absence of work. The shoe-black in *Lost and Found*, the street sellers in Mulready, Hunt and Levin, correspond more to what we should expect from Victorian artists. In contrast, the late nineteenth-century painting by Clare Atwood showing men at work in a coach-wheelwright's shop (see cat. no. 135) is most interesting as it looks forward to the dispassionate treatment of Camden Town and the work of other Edwardian painters (see p374).

1. Owned by the Royal Holloway College.
2. Owned by the Trustees of Sir Colin and Lady Anderson.
3. Jules Vallès (1832–85) was a French journalist and writer who took refuge in London during the French Commune and spent twelve years (1871–83) in the capital. His text, written in French and published in Paris, is often anti-British and has not been translated into English.
4. Jules Vallès, *La Rue à Londres*, 1884, p80.
5. See Christopher Wood, *Victorian Panorama*, 1976, pp43–8.
6. See Julian Treuherz, *Hard Times*, exhibition catalogue, Manchester City Art Galleries, 1987, pp24–6.
7. Ibid, pp30–31.
8. Dated 1858–9, in the Tate Gallery. See *The Pre-Raphaelites*, exhibition catalogue, Tate Gallery, 1984, no. 98.
9. Respectively in the Carlisle Museum and Art Gallery, the Tate Gallery (a set of three) and the Fitzwilliam Museum, Cambridge. These works illustrate various stages of fallen women, the poor mother and baby underneath the Adelphi arches in *Past and Present* being the most advanced.
10. Flora Tristan, *London Journal*, 1840, p185.
11. Vallès, 1884, pp33–4.
12. Tristan, 1840, p179.
13. The Museum has in its collection a photogravure after the painting by the Florises and published by Dawsons (acc. no. 87.148).

14. Christopher Wood's *Victorian Panorama*, 1976, usefully covers these different categories of Victorian life.
15. Oliver Millar, *The Victorian Pictures in the Collection of Her Majesty the Queen*, 1992, pxlvi.
16. Ibid, pxxi.
17. Ibid, pxxv.
18. Ibid, ppxv–xvi.
19. Ibid, pxxxi.
20. Tristan, 1840, p3.
21. Celina Fox, *Londoners*, 1987, pp185–6.
22. A. Noakes, *William Frith, Extraordinary Victorian Painter*, 1978, pp51–70. For instance, the Chief Proprietor of the animal show in Ramsgate Sands turned out to be a Mr Gwillin from Waterloo Road who posed for Frith in his London studio.
23. Private collection. Reproduced in colour on the back cover of Karen Eyre and Mireille Galinou, *Picnics*, Museum of London, 1988. Also on pp162–3 of *London's Pride*, Mireille Galinou (ed.), 1990.
24. Sold at Christie's, 19 November 1976 (92). Also the *Illustrated London News*, 18 January 1964, where it is reproduced with a key.
25. Mireille Galinou, 'Green Finger Painting', in *Country Life*, 13 July 1989. This article proposes a reconstruction of Tissot's garden at Grove End Road, St John's Wood. Also see Wentworth, *James Tissot*, 1984 and *James Tissot*, Krystyna Matyjaszkiewicz (ed.), Barbican Art Gallery, exhibition catalogue, 1984.
26. See for instance the works in the Royal Collection: Millar, 1992, nos 588 and 808.
27. By William Holman Hunt, Visitors of the Ashmolean Museum, Oxford. William Logsdail's *The Ninth of November* is a magnificent example of pageantry and London's crowd outside the Royal Exchange in the City (Guildhall Art Gallery).
28. Fox, 1987, pp188–9.
29. See Treuherz, 1987.
30. After the 'rural' painting by Sir Hubert von Herkomer (1885) in Manchester City Art Gallery.
31. Owned by the Royal Holloway College.
32. Tristan, 1840, p135.
33. Treuherz, 1987, pp53–64.
34. *The Pre-Raphaelites*, exhibition catalogue, 1984, no. 88.

113.

FREDERICK P. SHUCKARD

(active early twentieth century)

Queen Victoria Receiving the News of Her Accession at Kensington Palace, 20 June 1837 [A 25317]

1909

Oil on canvas, 90.6 x 70.3 cm

Signed and dated bottom left:

F. P. SHUCKARD/1909/AFTER WELLS

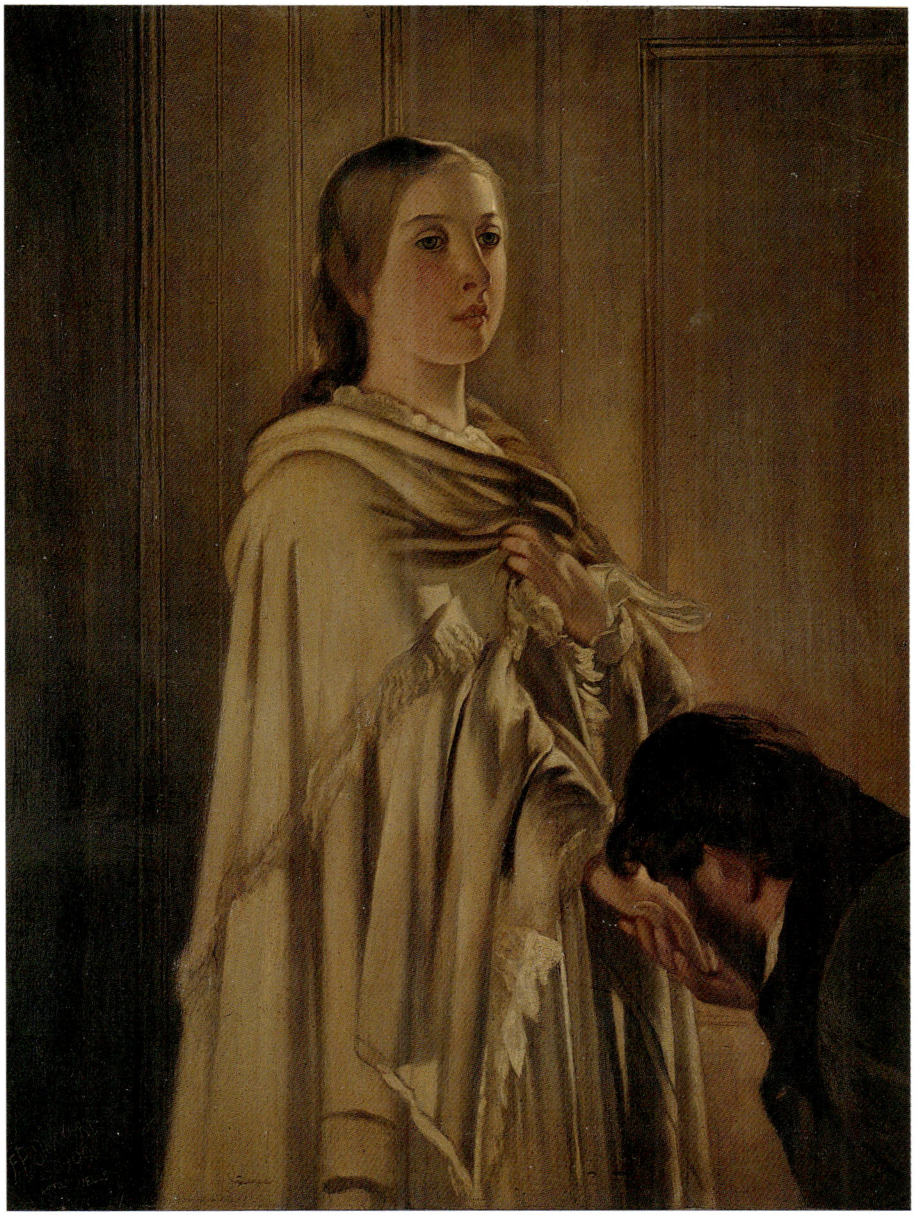

THE YOUNG Queen is shown at three-quarter length, facing half right, standing in her nightgown, with the Lord Chamberlain, Lord Conyngham, kneeling before her and kissing her hand, bottom right. The scene is copied from the central part of H. T. Wells's 1880 painting in the Tate Gallery (no. 1919). Wells made a replica of the painting which was presented to Edward VII by the artist's daughters in 1903.

Provenance:
Presented by the artist in 1923.

Bibliography:
Hayes (cat. no. 171);
Oliver Millar, *The Victorian Pictures in the Collection of Her Majesty the Queen*, 1992, cat. no. 804.

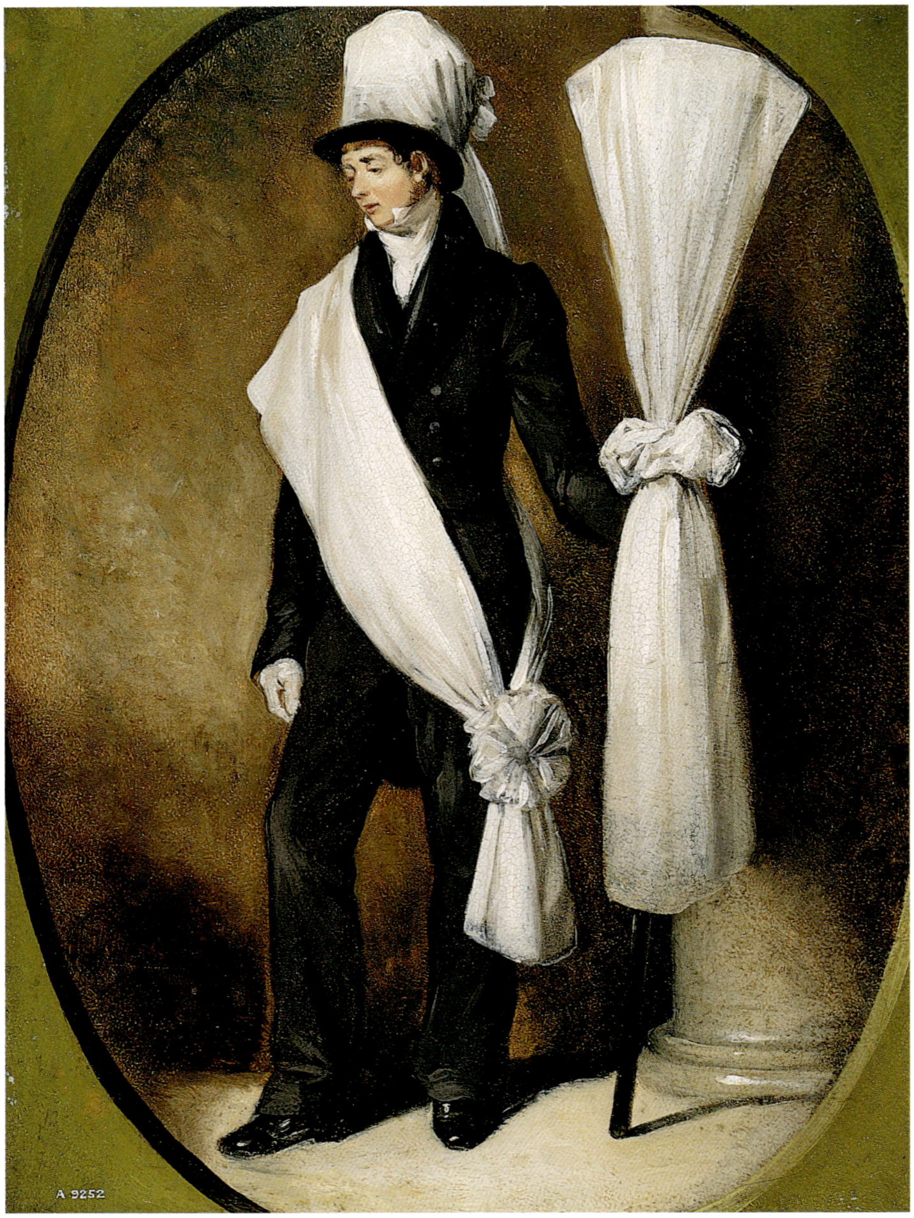

114.

ROBERT WILLIAM BUSS

(1804–74)

A Funeral Bearer [A 9252]
1830s
Oil on tinplate, 36.2 x 27.5 cm
Not signed or dated

A FUNERAL bearer, shown full length, is facing half left and looking slightly downwards, in a feigned oval; the interior background is plain with a column on the right. The bearer is wearing a grey suit, a top hat covered in white and a white sash, and is holding a staff draped in white in his left hand. The use of white indicates that the bearer is dressed to precede the funeral of a child.

Funeral bearers, or 'mutes', customarily preceded a funeral procession and were a common sight in nineteenth-century London. The costume indicates a date of about 1830–40. This work is one of a pair; the other painting shows a mute wearing a black sash and holding a staff covered in black and facing the other way (see Appendix).

Provenance:
Presented by Gerald M. Burn in 1912 (without attribution).

Bibliography:
Hayes (cat. no. 143).

115.
BRITISH SCHOOL

The Falcon Glassworks [95.279/1]
*c.*1840
Oil painting on canvas, 61.5 x 93 cm
Not signed or dated

THIS IS the earliest known detailed painting of the interior of a London glasshouse. It shows glassmaking at the Falcon Glassworks in Holland Street, at the southern end of Blackfriars Bridge. The composition focuses on the melting furnace, where a characteristically shaped melting pot may be seen in the centre and a resting groove on the right. Built around 1820, the works was the largest London glassworks in the first half of the nineteenth century.

The 'glasshouse' itself is a room of around 50 or 60 feet square with an earthen floor and an iron roof out of which rises a large tapering quadrangular chimney. There are two main furnaces with circular domes feeding into this chimney and a third auxilliary chimney in the far left corner of the room also connects to this flue. The glassblowers shown in the painting are not using moulds but are performing the more skilled operation of producing claret jugs. The different stages illustrated show the melted glass shaped with the help of a flat iron plate (the small table in the middle) and then, on the right, the worker blowing to make the glass hollow. 'The rolling and blowing having been repeated two or three times, another workman received it, and sat down in a chair having two flat parallel arms sloping downwards.' This is the operation taking place on the left- and right-hand sides, with the boy on the left blowing to keep the glass hollow while the worker shapes the mass with the use of tongs (also see cat. no. 71). The little boy in the centre would thus be attached to the workman on the right. On the right-hand side is depicted the annealing oven, the floor of which, specially fitted with a miniature railway, enabled the glass to cool slowly so as to avoid cracking. Over on the left of this oven may be glimpsed the pot room, which George Dodd compared to Ali Baba's cave filled with oil jars and thieves!

The painting is related to the engraving by M. J. Starling after Thomas Allom which was published in 1841 in Brailey's *Topographical History of Surrey*. However, a number of small changes appear to suggest the works are related, but represent distinct prototypes. Although this work is not painted with a great degree of sophistication, it is competently handled and the treatment of light, the peep at the stored pots and the inclusion of the 'coffee break' corner on the left-hand side all suggest a work carried out from direct observation rather than a copy. The two other mid-nineteenth century publications which contain illustrations of the glasshouse are quoted in the bibliography.

Provenance:
Found in the basement of Thomas Goode (who took over retailing outlets of Falcon Glassworks founder Apsley Pellatt); Neale's Auctioneers (Nottingham), 18 and 19 May 1995 (621); purchased by the Museum with the help of a grant from the Science Museum (PRISM) Fund.

Bibliography:
E. W. Brailey, *A Topographical History of Surrey*, 1841, vol. 5, Appendix p35; George Dodd, *Days at the Factory* 1843, Apsley Pellatt, *Curiosities of Glass-making*, 1849.

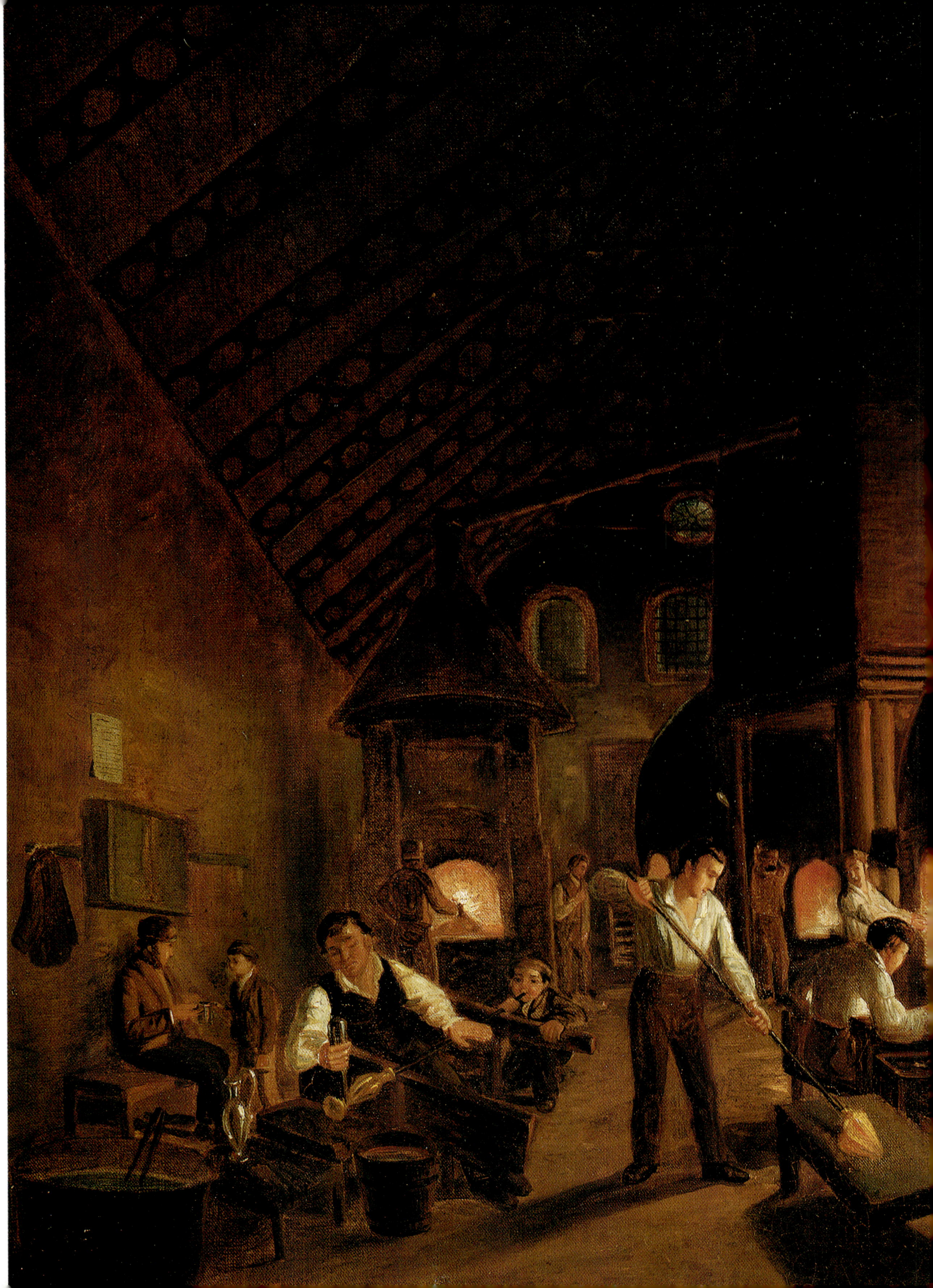

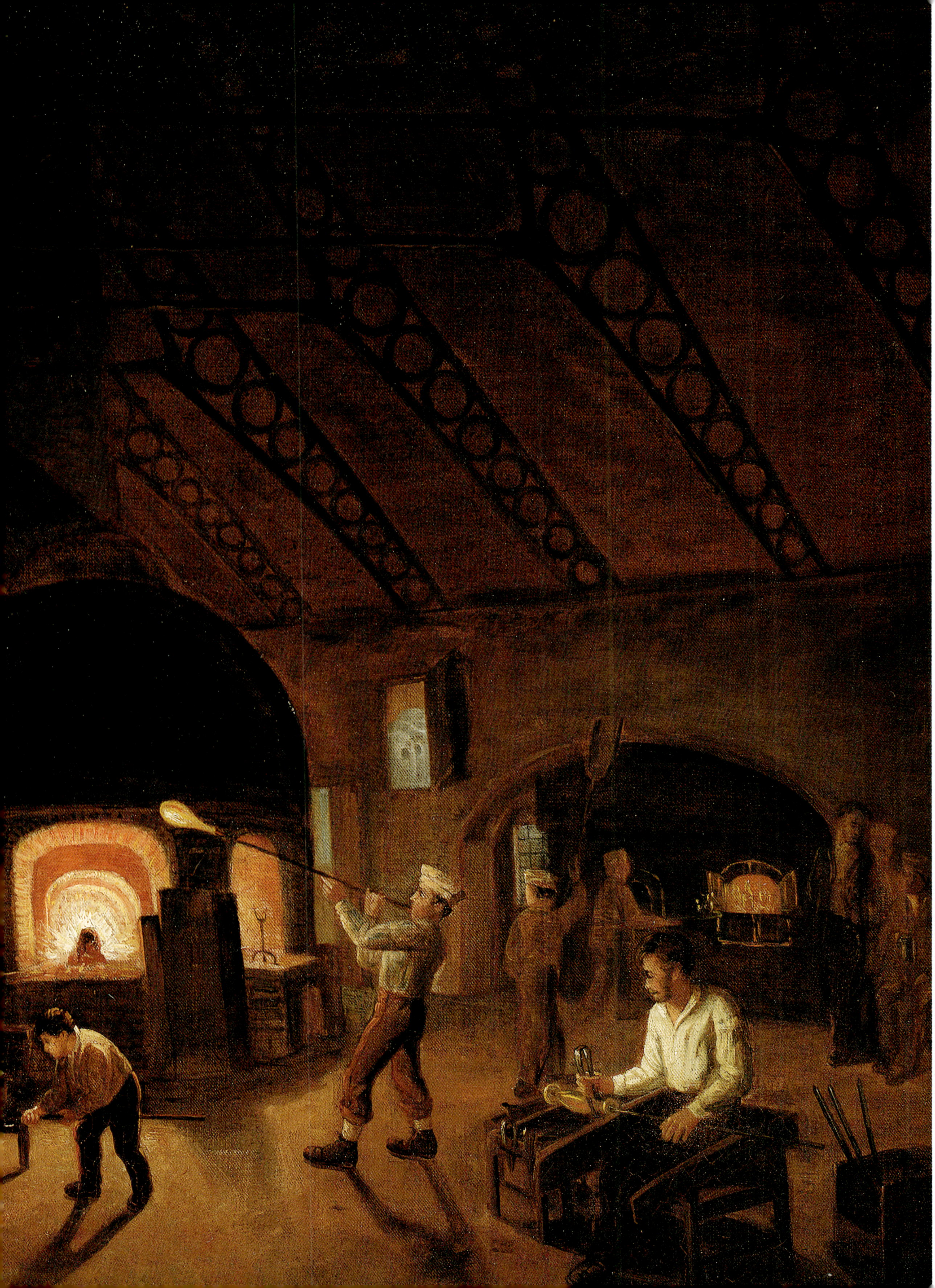

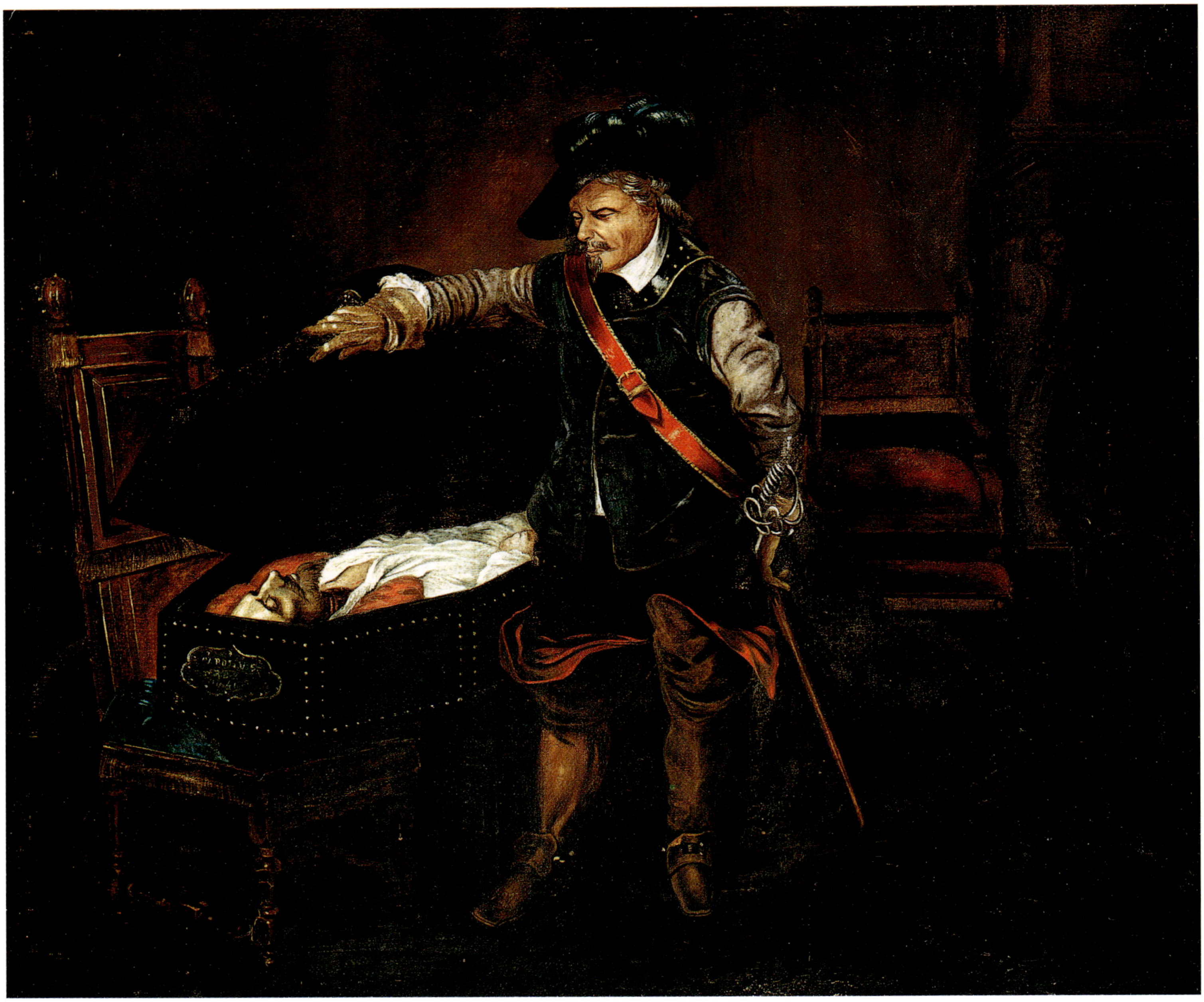

116.

AFTER PAUL DELAROCHE

(1791–1856)

Cromwell Gazing at the Body of Charles I

[46.78/531]

post 1850

Oil on canvas, 51 x 61.5 cm

Not signed or dated

THE SCENE depicted is meant to have taken place shortly after the execution of Charles I on 30 January 1649 (see cat. no. 4).

Most Victorian historians recounted the unlikely episode of Cromwell sitting up with the King's coffin:

> But there was a solemn lesson in his sovereign's lifeless corpse. He opened the coffin himself, and sadly gazed upon the cold inanimate body, without cruelty, or anger, or exultation, but reverential fear, as he thought of the judgements of God . . . [Merle d'Aubigné, quoted in Strong, p150.

It is set in an interior, with the figure of Cromwell standing by an opened coffin in which rests Charles I. With his right arm resting on the coffin lid, Cromwell contemplates the still body of Charles, who is wearing a loose white shirt. The coffin sits on two chairs, one of which is not actually visible.

This is a reduced copy of the painting by Paul Delaroche exhibited at the Paris Salon in 1831 and at the Royal Academy in 1850, and of which three copies exist, by the artist's hand (Hamburg Kunsthalle, Hermitage Museum and Sotheby's, 28 November 1979, Lot 13). This work, however, is a poor copy and clearly not by Delaroche.

Delaroche produced three paintings on the English Civil War (all in the 1830s). It may at first seem strange that a Frenchman should choose such a foreign subject, but the French Revolution did in fact generate considerable interest in this seventeenth-century prototype. Victor Hugo wrote his *Cromwell* in 1827 and in the same year Guizot published a *History of the English Revolution*. A new genre in painting, the *genre historique* made its formal appearance at the 1833 Paris Salon.

This painting is of particular interest because it illustrates the fashion for history painting in this country as well as the particular attraction the Civil War generated, culminating in the painting *When Did you Last see your Father?* by W. F. Eames (1878). British painters, perhaps stimulated by their French counterparts, started depicting episodes from the Civil War in the 1850s. One of the earliest paintings dealing with this theme, Charles Landseer's *Eve of the Battle of Edgehill* (Walker Art Gallery), was exhibited at the Royal Academy in 1845. Between the 1840s and 1870s, Cromwell was the regular subject of a number of paintings and was considered, in the wake of Carlyle's re-evaluation, as a great man. A. L. Egg's *The Night before Naseby* (1859) shows him praying in his tent at night, in an image halfway between the pure medieval knight and the Jesus of *The Agony in the Garden*.

The provenance of this painting, the Tangye collection, clearly shows the extent to which the 'cult' of the Civil War could be pursued. Towards the end of the nineteenth century Richard Tangye amassed a formidable collection of about a thousand items – books, manuscripts, pictures, miniatures, seals, medals, coins and small mementos – all relating directly or indirectly to Oliver Cromwell. Apart from a few exceptions (see, for instance, cat. nos 4 and 6), the group of pictures (paintings and prints) essentially consists of nineteenth-century reinterpretations of Civil War events.

Provenance:
Sir Richard Tangye (1833–1906); presented by Sir Harold Lincoln Tangye in 1913 (as by Paul Delaroche).

Bibliography:
Catalogue of the Cromwellian collection in the possession of Sir Richard Tangye, privately printed, 1905, p117; Roy Strong, *When Did you Last see your Father?*, 1978; also exhibition catalogue of the same title by Edward Morris and Frank Milner, Walker Art Gallery, Liverpool, 1993.

Provenance:
Presented by Norman J. Byers in 1917.

Bibliography:
Hayes (cat. no. 24); Henry Mayhew, *London Labour and the London Poor*, 1861, vol. II, pp431–3; vol. III, pp5–11; *Man's Best Friend*, exhibition catalogue, Birmingham Museum and Art Gallery, 1991, cat. no. 80.

117.
BRITISH SCHOOL
Rat-Catching at the Blue Anchor Tavern, Bunhill Row, Finsbury [A 19092]
*c.*1850–2
Oil on canvas, 42.5 x 53.5 cm
Not signed or dated

COCKPITS WERE used not only for cockfighting, but for numerous violent diversions of a similar kind; a fight between a bulldog and a prize monkey, for instance, is recorded as having taken place in a cockpit in 1822, and dogfights were quite common at this date. These male-orientated events were watched by many of the leading sportsmen of the day, and bets were placed on the contestants. An 1835 Act of Parliament banned bullbaiting and other cruel sports, but rat-catching remained legal and attained the popularity once accorded only to cockfighting. The dogs employed were always terriers, and one celebrated animal, later stuffed and exhibited at the Seven Bells in St Giles's, killed a hundred rats in five minutes.

In the scene shown here, lit with gas lamps, a terrier (a Manchester Terrier, a black and tan miniature breed) called Tiny the Wonder is attempting to kill two hundred barn rats in under an hour, a feat which he accomplished, apparently, on two separate occasions, on 28 March 1848 and 27 March 1849 'haveing on both occasions time to spare' (see handkerchief below). Mayhew describes 'A Night at Rat-Killing' and the rats used were all 'sewer and water ditch rats, and the smell that rose from them was like that from a hot drain'. Jimmy Shaw, the owner of Tiny and proprietor of the Blue Anchor Tavern, was the 'oldest caterer in rat-killing in the metropolis'. He could store up to 2,000 rats in his establishment but was against using sewer rats. Farm rats were healthier and were not poisonous like the sewer rats. He principally obtained them from Clavering (Essex) and Enfield, which was 'a kind of head quarters for rat-ketchers'. Count D'Orsay (1801–52), formerly one of the Regency dandies, is among the audience, and can be seen fourth from the left, wearing a brown coat; the figure in the centre is holding a watch in his hand, and is evidently the timekeeper.

The Museum recently acquired a cream silk printed handkerchief with a dark pink border (acc. no. 94.44) which also records the exploits of 'Tiny the Wonder'. The inscription specifies that he weighed 'only 5½ pounds'. Henry Mayhew mentions the existence of this handkerchief, framed on the wall of a tavern with weekly rat-killing 'entertainments', adding 'Tiny had been a great favorite with the proprietor, and used to wear a lady's bracelet as a collar' (Mayhew, 1861, p6). He also specified (vol. II) that Tiny had destroyed 2,525 pairs of rats in his lifetime and that in one year '17,000 pairs of rats were killed by Messrs Shaw and Sabin'.

Henry Mayhew gives us some insight into the business of rat-catching in London itself. Jack Black, the Queen's Rat-Catcher, is recorded as saying:

> Rats are everywhere about London, both in rich and poor places. I've ketched rats in 44 Portland Place, at a clergyman's house there. There was 200 and odd . . . My terms is from one guinea to five pounds per annum, besides this, I have all the rats that I ketch, and they sell for threepence each.

The rat-catchers of the sewers wore gloves to catch the rats; many house or warehouse

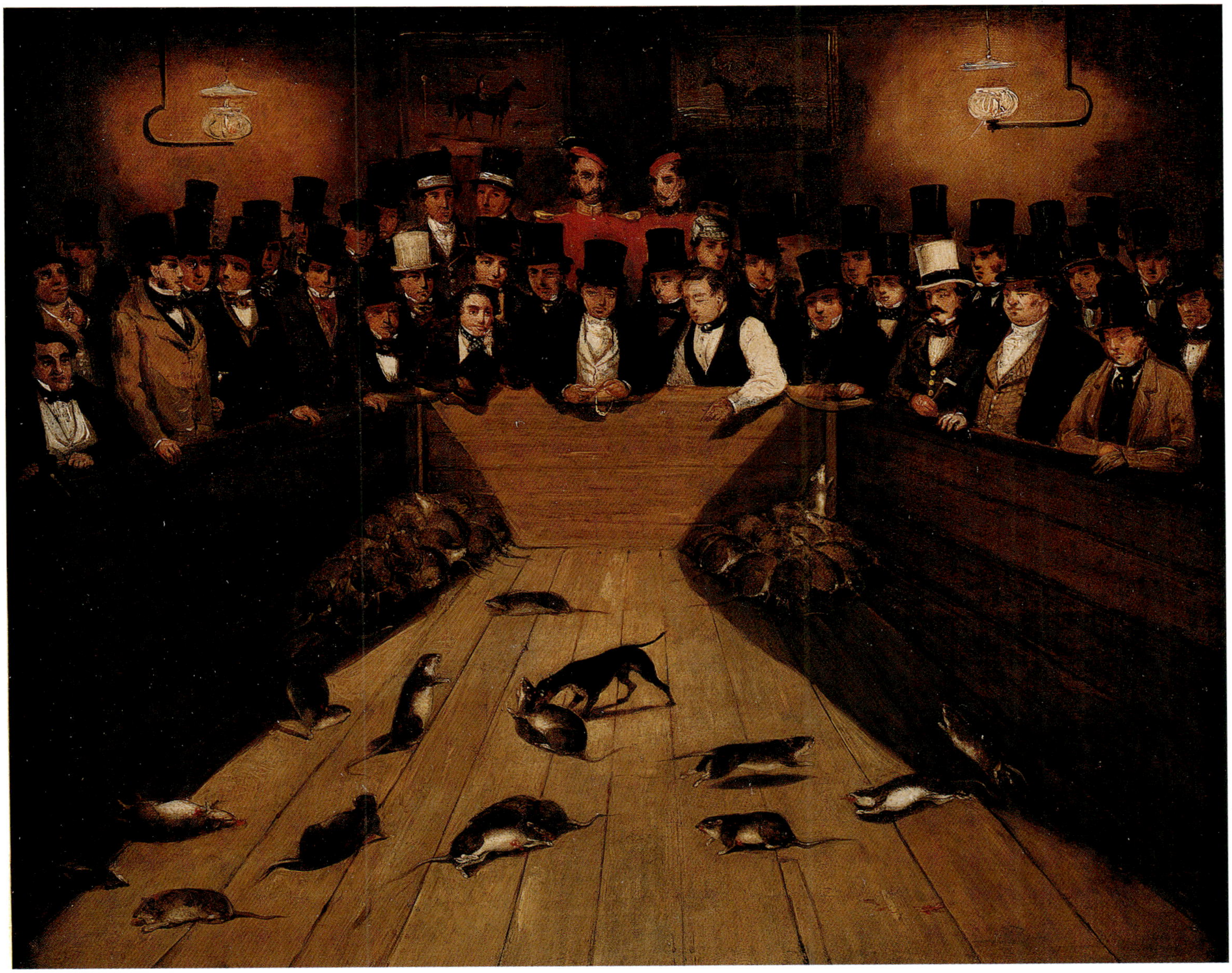

rat-catchers used ferrets, although Black, unusually, also trained a monkey and a badger to do this work.

The costume in the painting indicates a date of about 1850–55, and since the painter/sculptor and man of fashion Count D'Orsay is included, the picture must have been executed before his death in 1852.

The engraving on the handkerchief (see above) is by 'Thomson after Pasmore'. Although in composition the Museum's painting bears similarities to the print, it is unlikely, for stylistic reasons, that it is by the same artist.

Provenance:
Commissioned by Joseph Younghusband (the donor's mother's uncle) from the artist; by descent to Gordon Y. L. Crossley, MBE, ED, formerly Lieut.-Colonel in the Royal Canadian Artillery, who presented it to the Museum in 1972.

118.

C. WELLS

(active mid-nineteenth century)

Thomas Younghusband and his Family Meet Queen Victoria and her Family at Crystal Palace [72.184]

*c.*1854

Oil on canvas, 76 x 93.5 cm

Signed bottom left: *C. Wells 1851*

THE PAINTING commemorates the meeting between the royal family and the Younghusband family at Crystal Palace, Sydenham. The figures shown in the painting are, from left to right: Thomas Younghusband; Sarah, his wife: Matilda, his sister; Queen Victoria; the Prince Consort; Albert Edward, Prince of Wales; Thom Younghusband, grandson; Princess Victoria; Charlotte, daughter-in-law; Joseph, son; Charlotte, granddaughter.

Mrs T. A. Crossley, the donor's mother, recorded the circumstances attached to this painting. Gerard's Hall, in the City, the

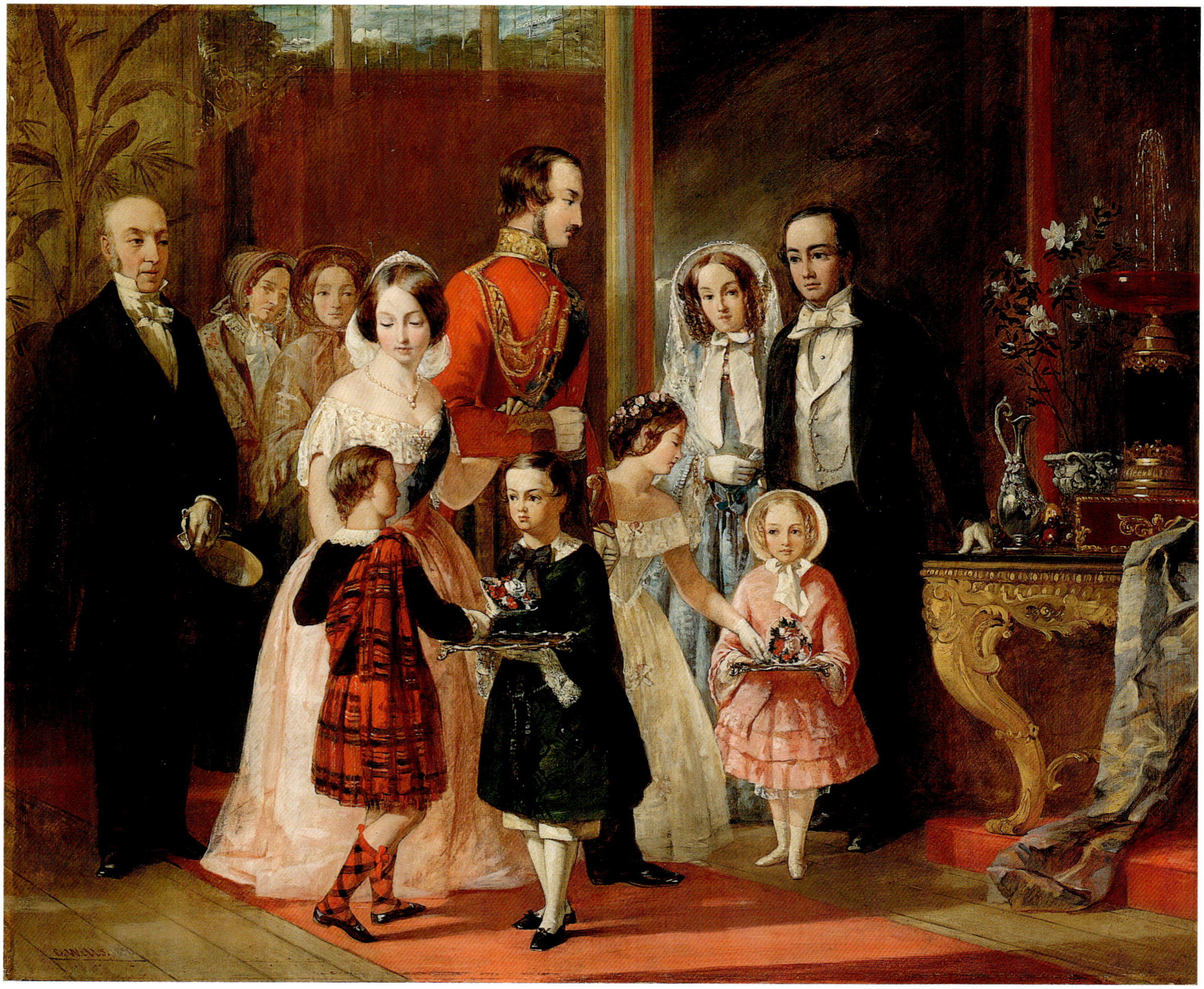

home of Thomas Younghusband, was pulled down (in 1853–4) for the construction of the Great Northern Railway, but great care was taken to remove the medieval crypt which lay beneath it to the grounds of Crystal Palace in Sydenham, where it was apparently placed underneath the rose garden. The van which Younghusband used to transport the crypt was subsequently used to move items from the Crystal Palace exhibition in Hyde Park to its new site in Sydenham. When Queen Victoria visited the new Crystal Palace, Thomas Younghusband was naturally (!) asked to conduct her. Much to the latter's surprise, his son Joseph was in attendance with his family (his children are presenting flowers to the young prince and princess). Joseph had also taken care to commission a 'Court artist' to be present to record this special occasion. The actual painting of the work was apparently carried out in the artist's studio and in the St John's Wood drawing-room of Joseph Younghusband. It is recorded to have cost either £300 or £500.

A number of details, however, do not fit this scenario. The 'Court painter', initially identified as H. T. Wells, is an unknown artist and no information is available about him. The date of 1851 on the painting would suggest an event taking place at Crystal Palace, Hyde Park, where the closing ceremony was held on 15 October 1851. The story of this painting, as recounted by the Younghusband family, states that the event was held at Sydenham. The first column of the new Crystal Palace was not erected there until 5 August 1852 and it took two years before the building was completed. The date on the painting appears to be wrong and the confusion may have arisen from the fact that the painting was a retrospective commission.

Much of the Younghusband information, however, is corroborated by official historic sources. The Post Office Directory for 1850 lists Thomas Younghusband and Sons as carriers based at 3 Basing Lane (in the City) and Thomas Younghusband at Gerard's Hall Tavern, 2 Basing Lane, on the south side of the street. The hall of John de Gisorcis (Gisors' Hall, which by corruption became Gerard's Hall) had once stood on the site. The original medieval building (pre-1290) had to be rebuilt after the Great Fire, but the crypt remained, attracting some attention in antiquarian circles at the beginning of the nineteenth century, when the centuries of accumulated debris hiding the bottom half of the columns was removed. There was outcry when the building was threatened with clearance to make way for the western extension of Cannon Street. Every stone was numbered and moved to Crystal Palace for re-erection. In the end, it must have been felt that the enterprise was not worth carrying out, and the stones were ground and re-used in the making of the model prehistoric creatures, some of which survive to this day.

Provenance:
The artist's daughter; by descent to Graham Buckley Slater *c.*1951; presented to the Museum in 1987.

119.

GEORGE BUCKLEY

(1823/4–70)

Signboard advertising the painter G. Buckley [87.38]

*c.*1858

Oil on panel, 61 x 58.8 cm

Not signed or dated

THIS SIGNBOARD provides a rare insight into the world of the capital's numerous minor Victorian painters. Their numbers grew considerably in the first half of the nineteenth-century as may be witnessed by examining the censuses of 1801 and 1851. George Buckley would have passed almost unrecorded had it not been for this charming painting.

It shows the artist at his easel, seated in an armchair, holding one brush in his right hand and a cluster of brushes in his left. His paintbox and other materials are placed on a small table by his side. On the easel is the half-length portrait of a man; the donor suggested that it was possibly John Bright (1783–1870), who was physician to the Westminster Hospital between 1822 and 1843. High on the green-painted walls of the room hang four portraits (three women and a man) with two figure compositions below. Several sculptures are also present – two busts on pedestals and three classical subjects, perhaps there for decoration or to be used as props. A number of paintings and a portfolio lean against one of the pedestals.

This scene is set in an ornate circular frame with various putti and two female classical figures holding three banderoles.

The inscription at the top reads: *PORTRAITS PAINTED From LIFE or From PHOTOGRAPHS;* in the middle: *G. BUCKLEY, PORTRAIT PAINTER, DESIGNER & GENERAL ARTIST* and at the bottom: *PAINTINGS CLEANED, RESTORED & VARNISHED.*

Buckley also apparently produced hand-coloured plates for illustrated books. From trade directories, we are able to reconstruct a few bare facts. George Buckley, painter, is recorded at 2 Broadley Terrace, Blandford Square in 1846 and 1847. And then nothing until 1858, when a George Buckley, portrait painter (presumably the same man), is at 48 Park Street, Islington.

Both William Hogarth and George Morland engraved designs advertising their activities: Hogarth's *The Battle of Pictures* was used as a bidder's ticket for the auction of his paintings in 1744 (his studio was allegorically represented on the right-hand side of the picture), while Morland designed his emblematical palette to decorate the ceiling of the 'Knights of the Palette', the society he founded; the aquatint was published in 1806.

The painting is executed on very thick board, which seems consistent with its function as a signboard. The work, however, seems in fair condition (although it was restored) and is therefore likely to have been displayed indoors rather than outdoors.

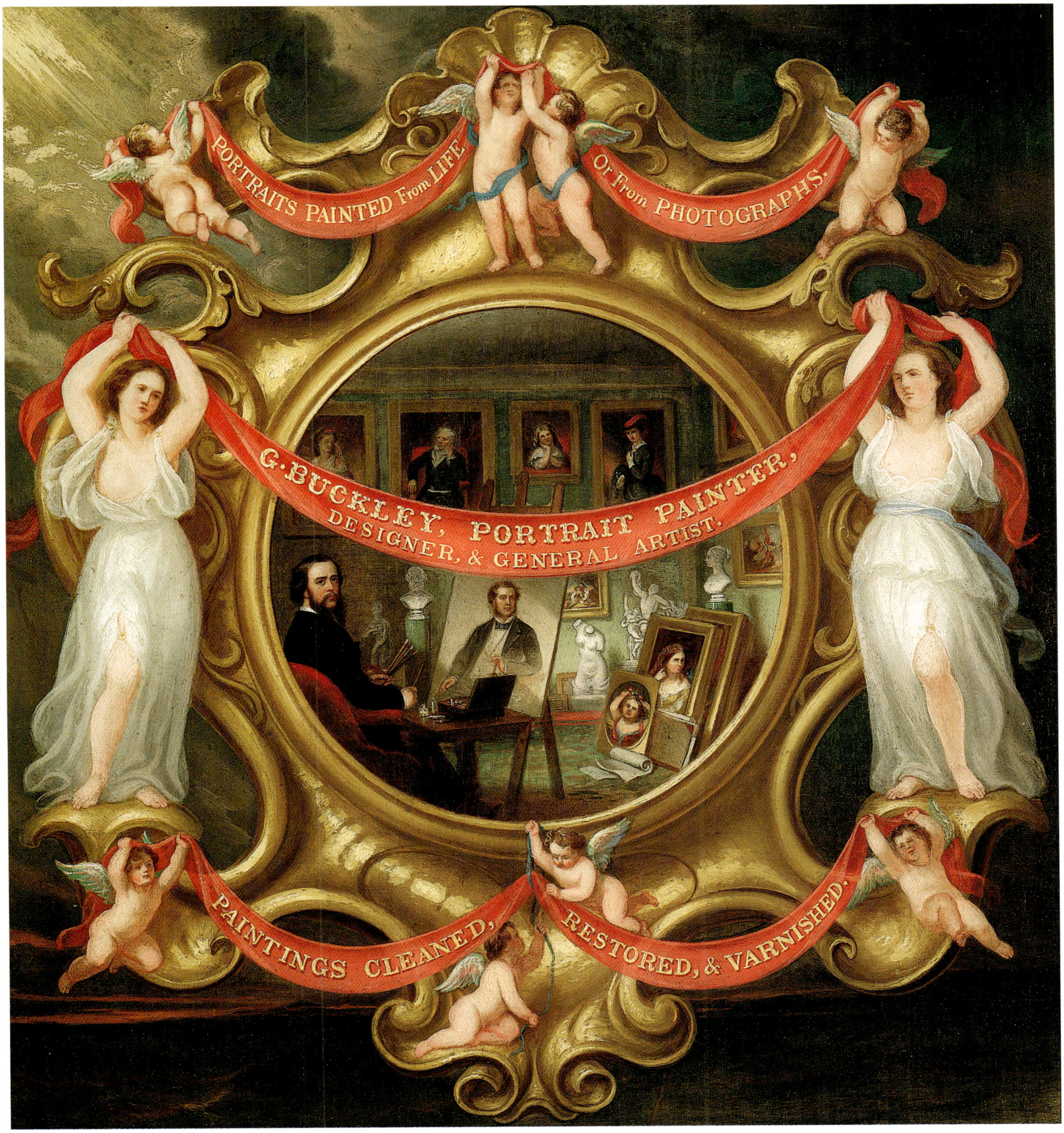
PORTRAITS PAINTED From LIFE
Or From PHOTOGRAPHS.
G. BUCKLEY, PORTRAIT PAINTER,
DESIGNER, & GENERAL ARTIST.
PAINTINGS CLEANED,
RESTORED, & VARNISHED.

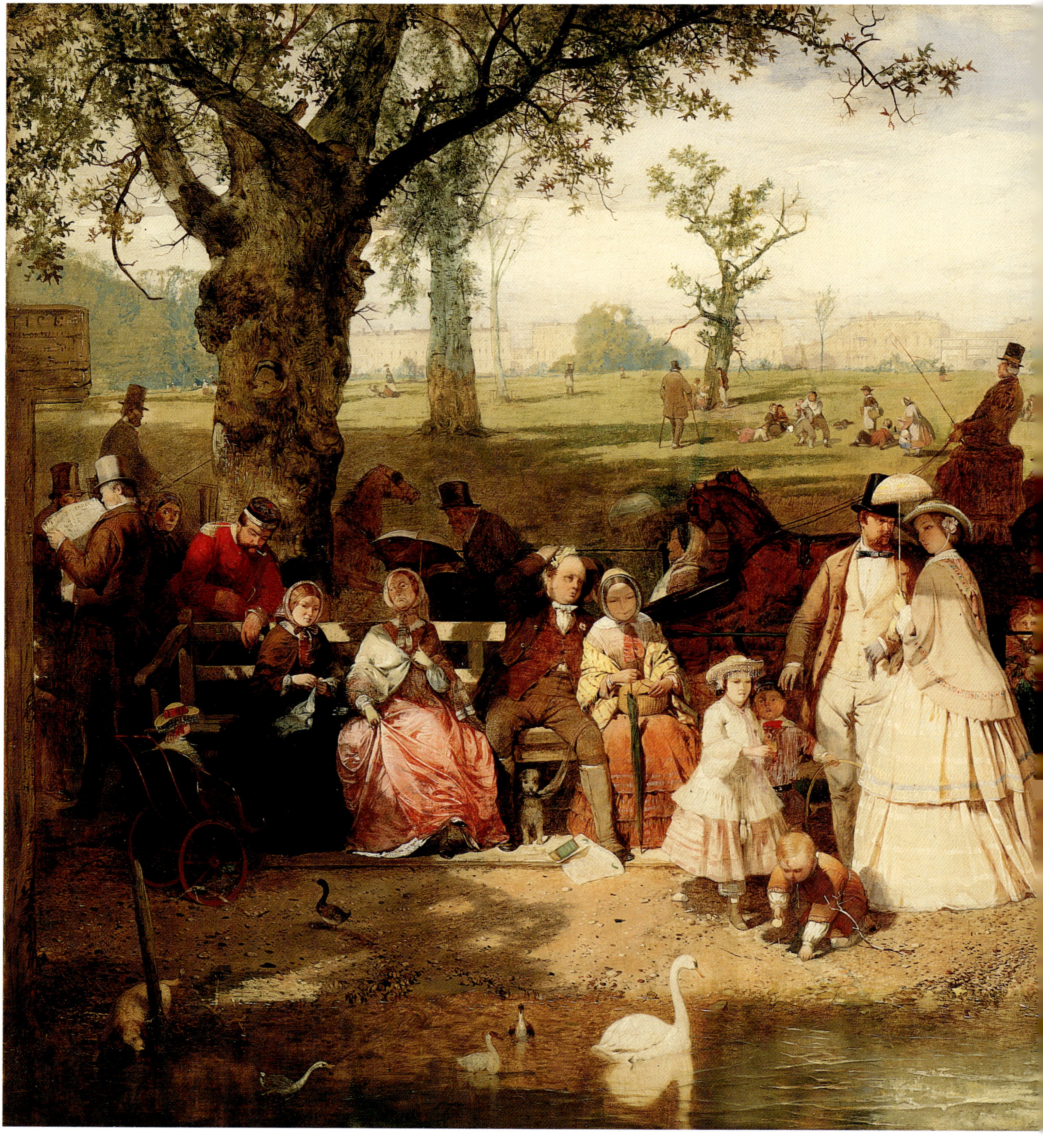

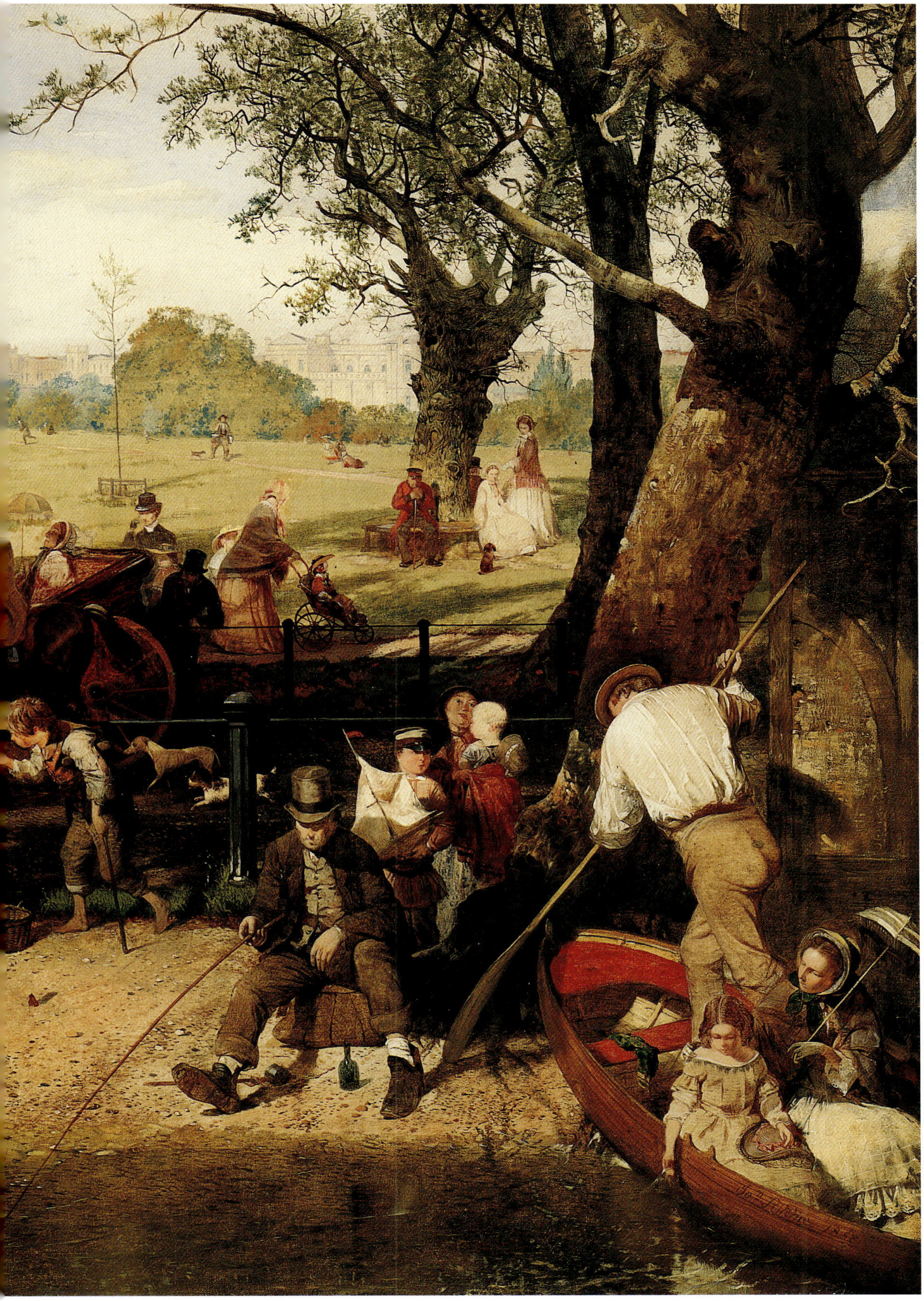

120.
JOHN RITCHIE
(active 1858–75)
A Summer Day in Hyde Park [54.131]
1858
Oil on canvas,
75 x 127.5 cm
Signed and dated bottom right:
Jo^{n}. Ritchie. 1858.

Provenance:
Purchased partly out of the Joicey Trust Fund from Ian MacNicol in 1954.

Bibliography:
Hayes (cat. no. 96).

Exhibited:
British Institution, 1858 (449) under this title, and with a companion picture, *A Winter Day in St James's Park* (281) (see text).

THIS PICTURE, crowded with characters, is in the tradition of William Powell Frith's large genre paintings, and shows an imaginary scene at the north-east corner of the Serpentine on a hot summer's afternoon. Among the figures shown are, from left to right: a gentleman reading a newspaper containing the latest report of the Indian Mutiny; a child in a perambulator; a soldier leaning over the back of a park bench and talking to the child's mother, who is sewing; a lady with her parasol up, sitting next to the mother and evidently severely censorious; a couple up from the country, also seated on the park bench; a man mopping his brow and with a map of London dropped in front of him; three children, one of them with a hoop; a gentleman talking to a lady holding a parasol; three poor children with bare feet, one of them seated on an improvised swing, another walking with a crutch; a man fishing; and another pushing a rowing boat, in which his wife and daughter are seated, away from the shore.

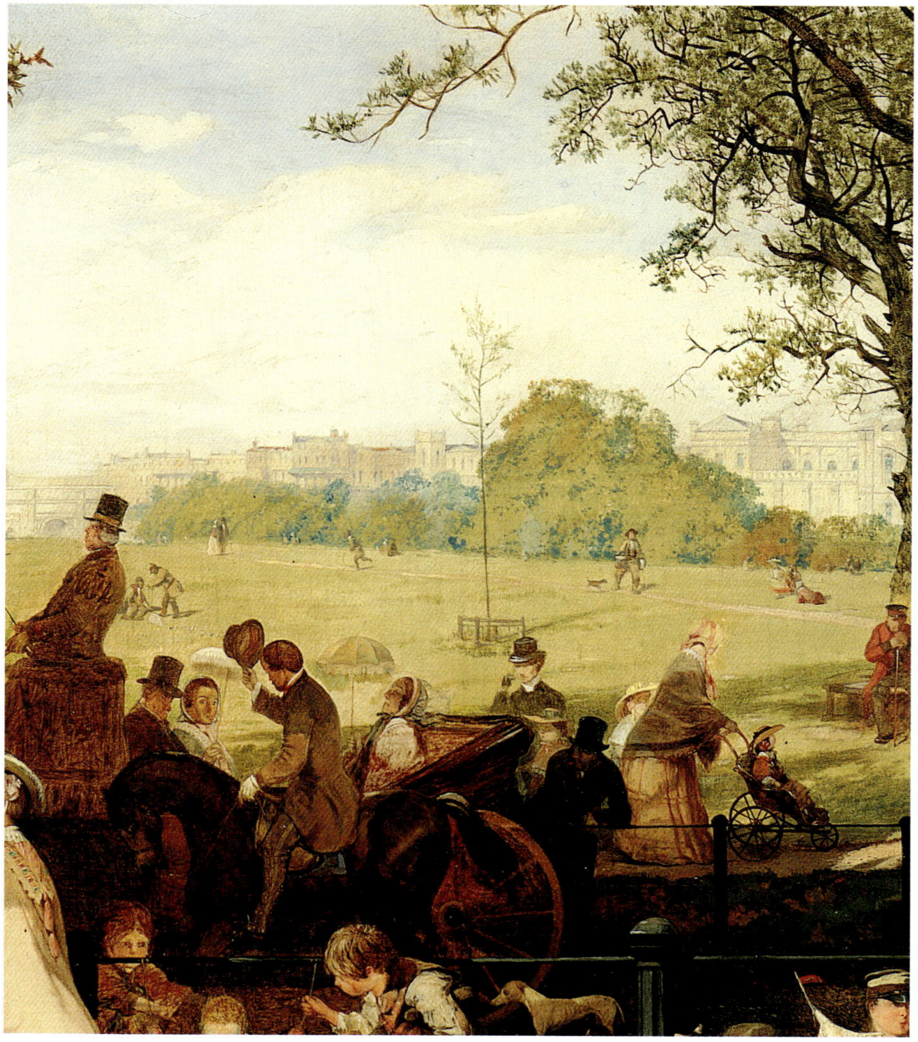

Behind, in the Ring Road, a gentleman on horseback is seen raising his hat to a young lady seated in a passing landau, much to the annoyance of her parents; and other figures are grouped on the grass beyond. In the right middle ground is a Chelsea Pensioner seated on a circular tree bench. Other park activities depicted include kite-flying, bowling a hoop and sailing a model boat. In the distance is Connaught Place, Marble Arch (originally designed by John Nash in 1828 as the gateway into the forecourt of Buckingham Palace, and removed to its present position in 1851), and Park Lane, with the Corinthian screen of the picture gallery attached to Grosvenor House (built by Thomas Cundy in 1827–8) prominent between the trees.

The companion picture, *A Winter Day in St James's Park* (last with the Owen Edgar Gallery, see Terry Friedman, *Great Paintings of Victorian Daily Life*, Leeds City Art Galleries, 1986), highlights the artist's interest in the depiction of the seasons. Unlike the Pre-Raphaelites, who were experimenting with this subject at the time, Ritchie focuses on the social scene rather than the physical manifestations of the weather.

121.

GEORGE HARCOURT SEPHTON
(active 1895–1938)

Portrait of Queen Victoria [60.44/1]
Oil on canvas, 114.4 x 91.7 cm
Inscribed on the back of the canvas in pencil: *painted by/GEORGE SEPHTON/ AFTER WINTERHALTER/1909.*

QUEEN VICTORIA (1819–1901) is shown seated at three-quarter length, facing the spectator, wearing Coronation robes and the crown of state especially made for her coronation; the Imperial State Crown has been placed on a table on the right, and a view of the Houses of Parliament may be seen through a window behind; a column occupies the top left-hand side. This work is a detail (from the central part) of the full-length painting by Francis Xavier Winterhalter (1859) at Buckingham Palace.

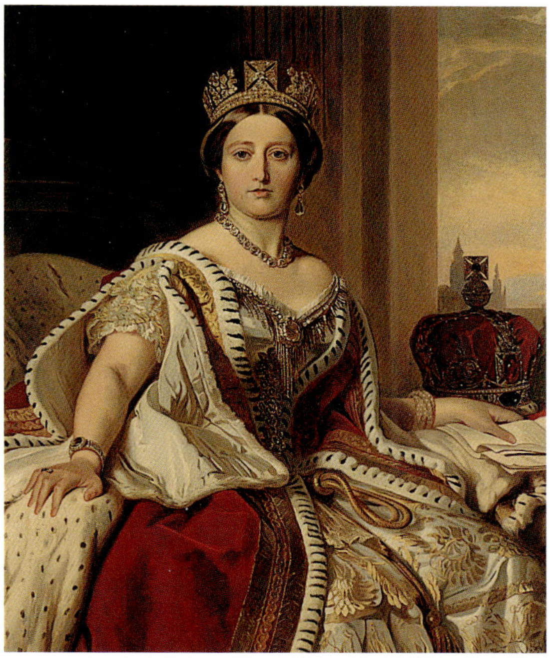

Provenance:
The Marquis of Carisbrooke; presented by Queen Victoria Eugenie of Spain in 1960.

Bibliography:
Hayes (cat. no. 168);
Oliver Millar, *The Victorian Pictures in the Collection of Her Majesty the Queen*, 1992, cat. no. 831.

122.

GEORGE HARCOURT SEPHTON
(active 1895–1938)

Portrait of Prince Albert [60.44/2]
Oil on canvas, 114.7 x 91.7 cm
Inscribed on the back of the canvas in pencil: *1909* and *painted by/George Sephton/ after WINTERHALTER*

PRINCE ALBERT (1819–61) is shown standing, at three-quarter length facing left, with his head turned towards the spectator and wearing a blue uniform; the background is occupied by columns, a curtain, with the partially visible still-life on the right composed of discarded robes and insignia. This work is copied from the upper right part of the full-length painting by Francis Xavier Winterhalter (1859) at Buckingham Palace.

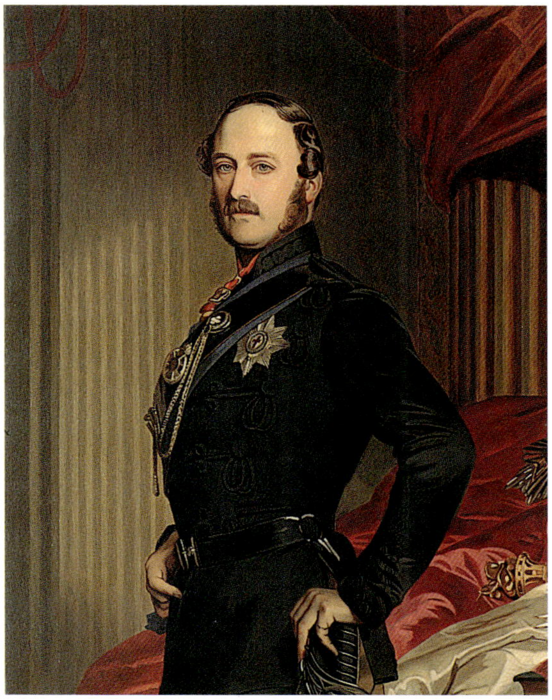

Provenance:
The Marquis of Carisbrooke; presented by Queen Victoria Eugenie of Spain in 1960.

Bibliography:
Hayes (cat. no. 169);
Oliver Millar; *The Victorian Pictures in the Collection of Her Majesty the Queen*, 1992, cat. no. 832.

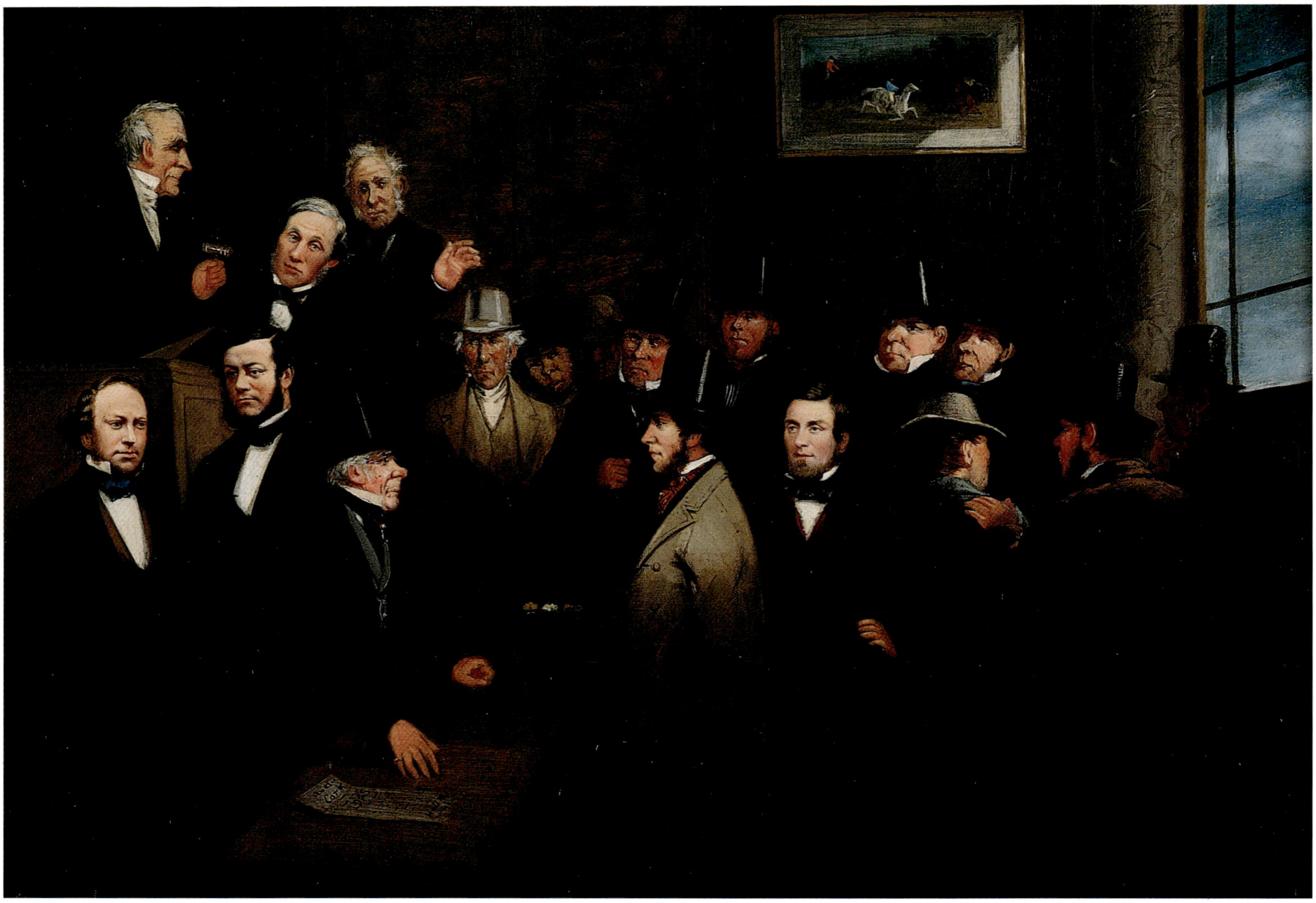

Provenance:
Andrew Barron (1824–74); by descent to Professor W. B. Stevenson, who presented it to the Museum in 1952.

Bibliography:
Hayes (cat. no. 141).

123.
BRITISH SCHOOL
A West Indian Sugar Sale [52.78]
*c.*1860
Oil on canvas, 33 x 48.6 cm
Not signed or dated

AN AUCTIONEER is shown on the rostrum presiding over a sale; on the table are samples of the sugar being sold and a sheet of paper inscribed: Auction/Cork/IDAS/. . . /Hall Esq. (which suggests that the sale depicted was held in Cork). A number of the merchants included are obviously portraits: Andrew Barron, a partner in a London sugar-importing firm and the first owner of the picture, is seen on the extreme left. The costume, and a comparison with photographs of Barron, indicate a date of about 1860.

124.
GEORGE ELGAR HICKS
(1824–1914)

The General Post Office. One Minute to Six
[90.276]
1860
Oil on canvas, 89 x 135 cm
Signed and dated lower right:
G. E. Hicks 1860

THE SCENE is set in the Grand Public Hall at the main entrance of the General Post Office in St Martin's-le-Grand in the City, just before closing time. The painting blends three distinct groups. On the right is 'Newspaper Fair' (held only on Fridays, as described by Sala, below); in the centre is a group of last-minute customers rushing forward carrying (stamped) letters or packages; and on the left is a crowd of spectators who bear witness to the fact that to see people catching the last post had become a tourist attraction in Victorian times. Two contemporary descriptions illuminate the different elements which compose this picture.

> The broad area between the lofty pillars that support the roof is peopled with some hundred or two spectators, come, like ourselves, to observe the multitudinous rush of newspapers and letters . . . Policemen are in attendance to keep a clear passage . . . As closing time approached, and the illuminated dial above points to five minutes to six, the crowd increases . . . [Manby Smith, 1853]

> All day long, newspapers only, stringed or labelled, are thrust into this incision ['a huge longitudinal slit in the panelling'] . . . But as six o'clock approaches (and six o'clock is the irreversably closing time for the departure of newspapers by the current night's mail), they open a tall window above, and the newspapers are no more thrust, but flung in. [Sala, *Twice Round the Clock*]

William M'Connell illustrated the scene for Sala's publication (on p233) and Hicks must have been aware of this work, which bears some resemblance to the right-hand side of his painting (see Allwood, pp11–13).

From the early years of the nineteenth century there had been a steady production of engravings featuring the mail coaches toing and froing from the Post Office. This popular formula was gradually dropped as the development of the railways replaced the mail-coach services. This rare interior view contrasts with previous images: Pugin and Rowlandson for the *Microcosm of London* (1808) showing the Lombard Street premises and Joseph Mead for his *London Interiors* (1841–4). In both these cases the numerous figures, whether working or visiting, are dwarfed by the environment which is recorded in the form of panoramic views. In the Hicks painting the focus has shifted to the users rather than the overpowering dimensions of the building. This compositional formula was the foundation stone of Hicks's preceding work, *Dividend Day. Bank of England*, the success of which he was no doubt trying to repeat. Having mastered the format, he most successfully introduced movement into the painting. The painting that followed, *Billingsgate Market*, still based on a panoramic close up, surprisingly reverts back to a more static approach, perhaps influenced by the stillness and still-life quality of earlier market works (by Peter Angelis, for instance).

The General Post Office (GPO East)

Provenance:
'Coms. by Mr Wallis for £300, but exchanged to Mr Vokins for £350 in mount frame'; sold by Vokins to H. C. McCrea, Halifax; M. Bernard Ltd by 1948; Evelyn Waugh; Sotheby's, 19 October 1971 (61); Richard Green Ltd; purchased in 1990 with help from the MGC/V&A Purchase Grant Fund and the National Art Collections Fund.

Bibliography:
Rosamund Allwood, *George Elgar Hicks,* exhibition catalogue, Geffrye Museum, 1982, no. 22 and pp11-12; Charles Manby Smith, 'The Newsboy's Day' in *Curiosities of London Life*, 1853 (reprinted in 1972 by Frank Cass and Company Ltd.); George Augustus Sala, *Twice Round the Clock*, 1859, pp232–5.

Exhibited:
Royal Academy, 1860 (367).

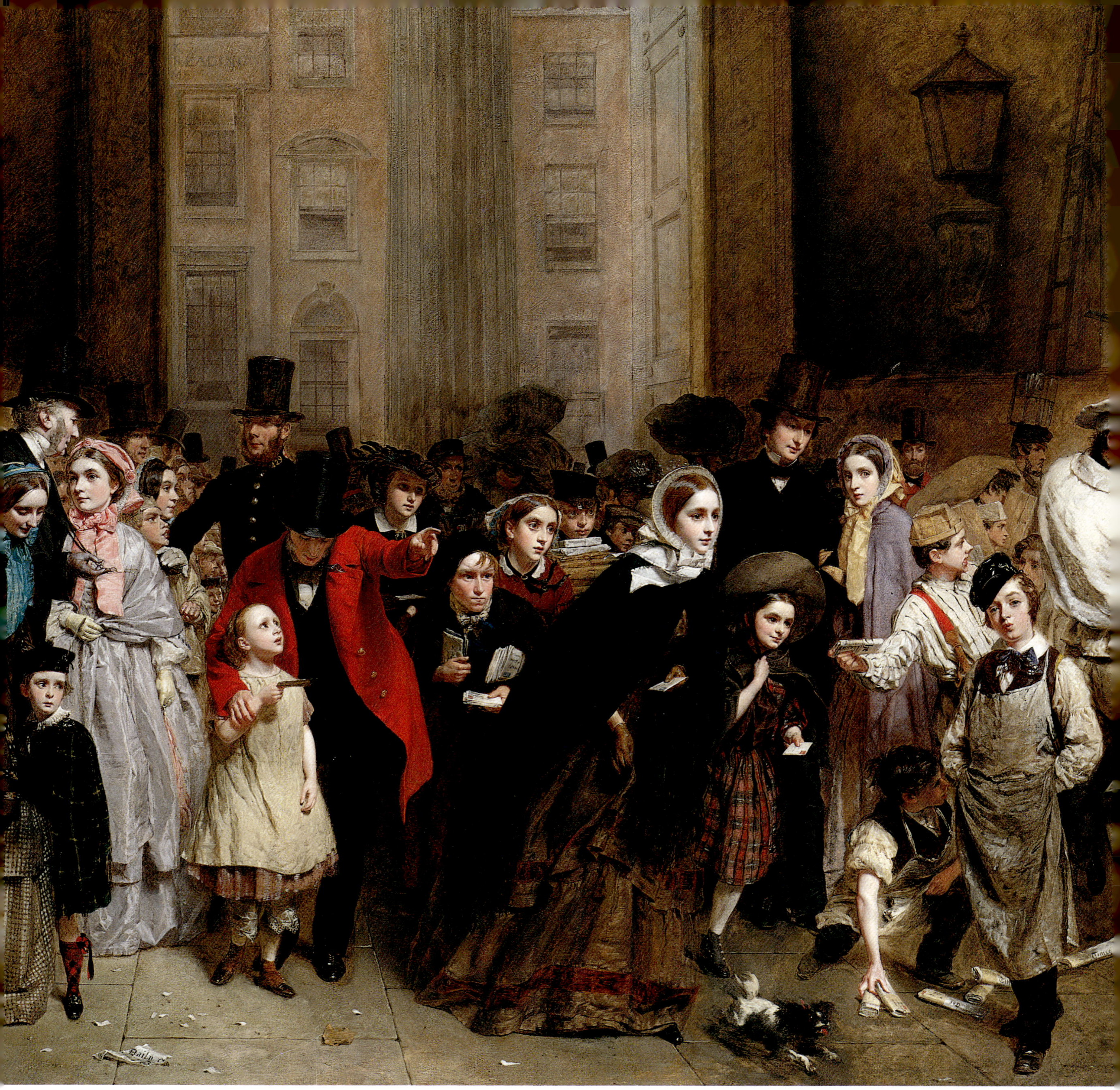

was built by Robert Smirke between 1824 and 1829 and demolished in 1912 after the opening in the 1890s of Henry Tanner's GPO North. Since the introduction of William Docwra's private London Penny Post in 1680, postal services had improved steadily, the cost rising to two pence in 1801 and three pence in 1805. By the 1830s there were still a large number of people who could not afford to send or receive letters (many letters without postage were refused because the receivers

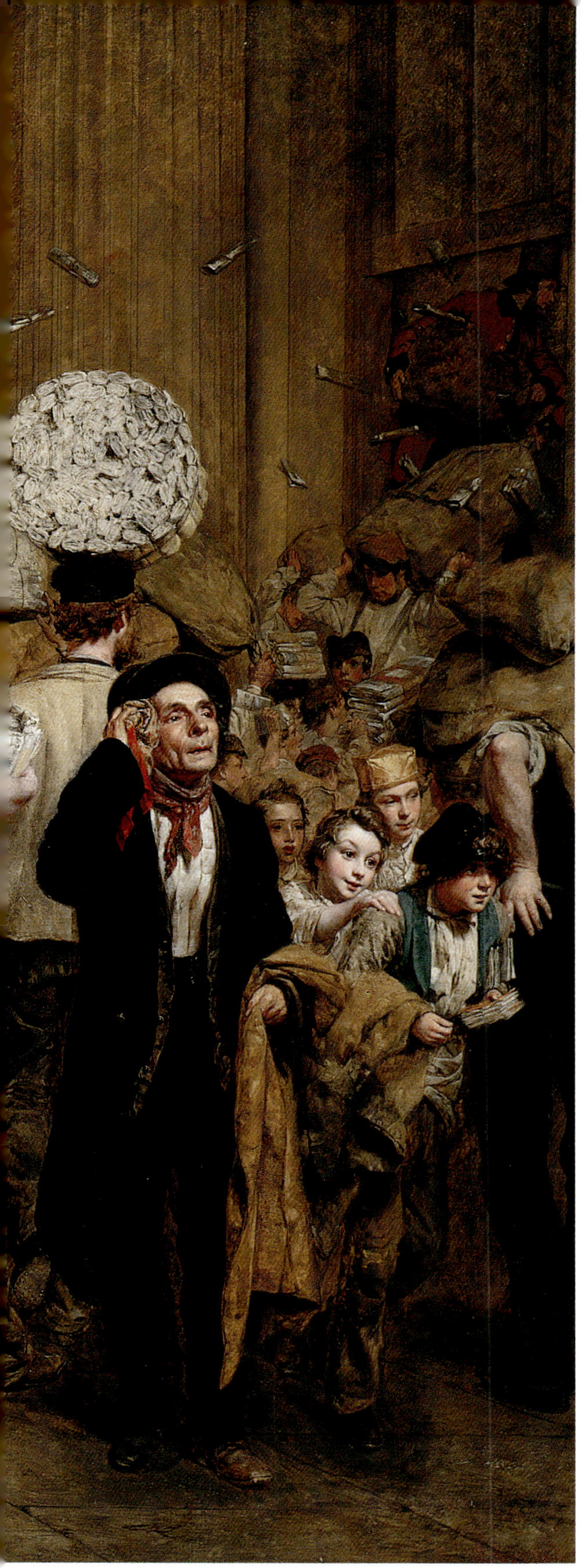

could not pay the postage). A new campaign for Penny Postage was started by Robert Wallace, MP, in 1833. Rowland Hill took up the challenge and on 10 January 1840 a Penny Post was established, followed on 6 May of that year by the world's first adhesive postage stamps.

It should, however, be noted that despite the artist's clear attempt to diversify his crowd – children (male and female), women, men (some very old, others young), the crowd is essentially middle class or 'professional'. Some critics reproached the artist for using 'doll-like' perfection figures, others noted the idealisation of the newsboys. *The Times* deplored the lack of 'grime and printer's ink in their threadbare garments and shapeless headgear'. *Frasers* justly remarked on the one-dimensional quality of the painting: 'a set of persons in good society' with clean, 'pink faced', well-dressed newsboys. These observations are confirmed when we compare the final composition to the preparatory drawing (in the Museum's collection, acc. no. 31.36). The sketch featured a shoe-black on the left-hand side, a London character who was at the very bottom of the social scale. The figure was removed from the painting, thus reinforcing the segregation process based on class and related standards of presentation (see p283).

The painter appears to have used the same model for the two women in the middle of the picture, one standing still and the other running. There are passages treated with great realism found in the background or in some hidden corner, such as the carrier of a large pile of packets in the centre of the picture and the ragged newsboy with 'shapeless headgear' in the right corner.

Hicks produced a version of this painting on panel, also dated 1860 (Christie's, 20 June 1986, Lot 65).

Provenance:
Henry Graves (see label); Mrs Viva King since 1937; bequeathed to April Ashley at her death in 1979; the painting was bought by Christopher Wood and sold to Anthony Brodie in 1979; purchased by the Museum in 1993 via Christopher Wood Gallery with the help of the National Art Collections Fund and the National Heritage Memorial Fund.

Bibliography:
The Times, 27 May 1863; H. Roberts, *British Rebels and Reformers*, 1942, p33; Graham Reynolds, *Painters of the Victorian Scene*, 1953, p84 and plate 63; Georgina Battiscombe, *Shaftesbury*, 1974, p307; Christopher Wood, *Victorian Panorama*, 1976, plate 67; Celina Fox, *Londoners*, 1987, pp216 and 227; Tony Dyson, *Pictures to Print*, 1984; Julian Treuherz, *Hard Times*, exhibition catalogue, Manchester City Art Galleries, 1987, no. 20.

Exhibited:
Royal Academy, 1863 (547).

125.
WILLIAM MACDUFF
(fl.1844–76)

Shaftesbury, or Lost and Found [93.165]
1862
Oil on canvas, 46.7 x 40.5 cm
Signed and dated bottom left:
W. Macduff 1862
One of the labels on the back reads:
the property of Henry Graves Esq.

THE PAINTING shows a young shoe-black, with his arm round the shoulders of a street urchin, gazing into the shop window of the printseller Henry Graves at 6 Pall Mall.

The oldest boy, the shoe-black, points to a portrait engraving of Lord Shaftesbury (1801–85), who was responsible for many improvements to the laws and regulations on housing and labour for the poor, including the Miners Act (1842) and the Lodging House Act (1851). He founded in 1851, with the help of John McGregor, the Shoe-black Brigade, which forms the subject of this painting. The Museum's costume collection holds a doll of 1860–80 wearing the uniform of the London Shoe-black Brigade (acc. no. Z7605).

The artist succeeds in creating an attractive and legible image while illustrating three complex Victorian themes: philanthropy and childhood as well as print publishing in Victorian London.

Lord Shaftesbury was the personification of the philanthropic spirit of the nineteenth century. Philanthropy, a key concept when discussing or assessing the Victorian period, is almost impossible to illustrate graphically. This painting, by juxtaposing the concepts of trade (the printshop), philanthropist (Shaftesbury) and object of philanthropy (the children) succeeds in visualising an intricate set of relationships. It highlights not only the gulf between poverty and capitalism but also what efforts were being made to bridge the gap. Its sentimentality also conveys the character of Victorian philanthropy, harshly described by Carlyle as 'this universal syllabub of philanthropic twaddle'.

The painting offers an archetypal image of ragged Victorian childhood. The earlier archetype of the poor child is well illustrated in this collection by the Cheapside chimneysweeps of *The Curds and Whey Seller* (cat. no. 31). In some ways the shoe-black replaced the sweep as a symbol for deprived childhood in the nineteenth century. In *Lost and Found* the paper on the ground, strategically placed near the shoe-black box, is for a meeting at Exeter Hall of the Ragged School Union, of which Shaftesbury was the chairman for thirty-nine years. This small detail brings into the picture – quite literally – another central social issue for the Victorians: education. Poverty is thus shown to be tackled at its roots and this optimistic painting, which seeks to embody Victorian ideals, implies that it will be eradicated.

Finally the painting is a most vivid record of a large and busy printshop in Victorian times. From 1842 Henry Graves & Company ran their business from 6 Pall Mall. At the time this picture was painted the turnover at Graves's was enormous (see Dyson, p24). Photography had not yet begun to compete, and the engraving trade was indeed flourishing. The painter Landseer noted that Henry Graves was 'the only publisher who consented to give large sums for the loan of important pictures for the purpose of engraving'. All the engravings in the shop window have been identified and their charitable

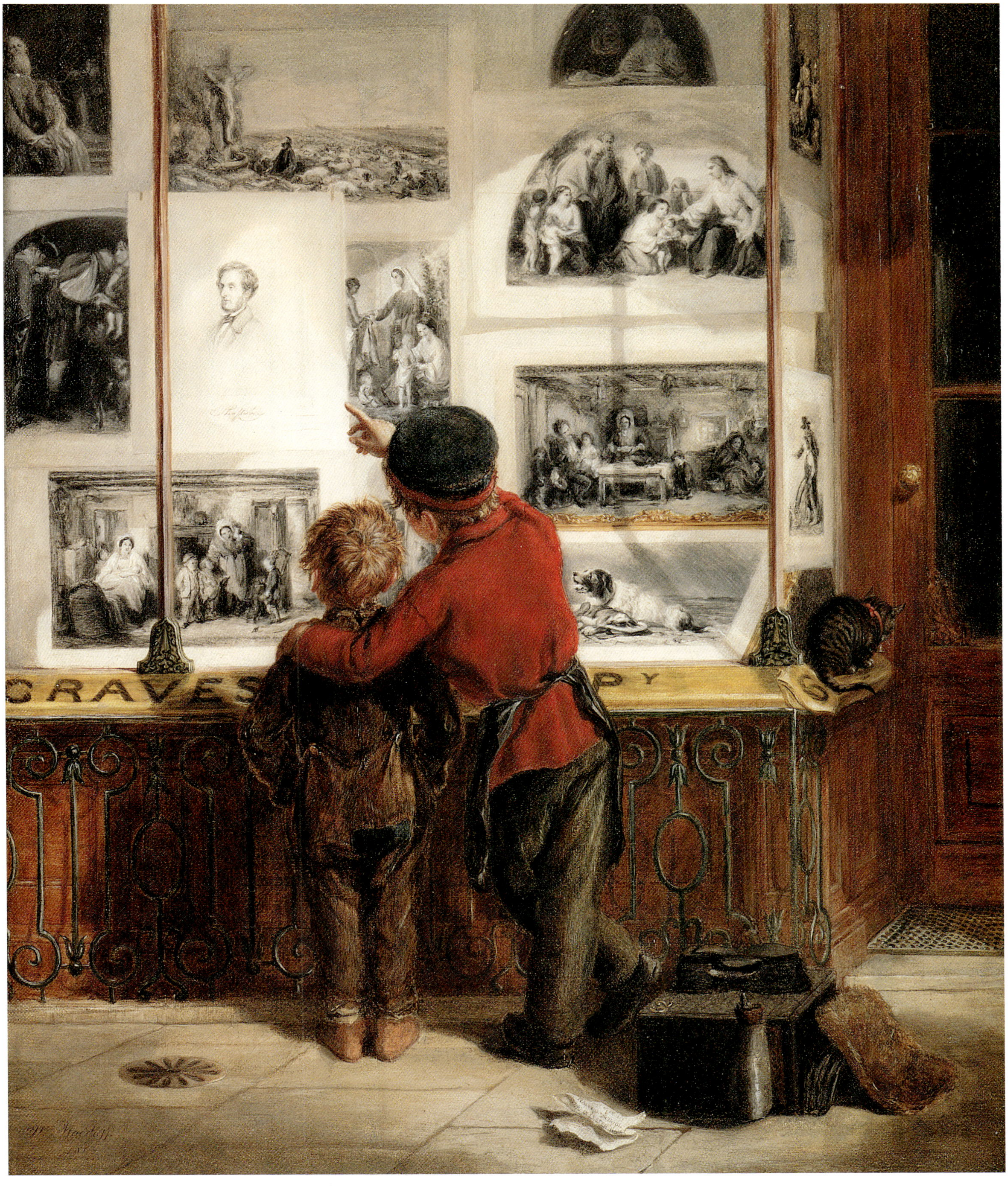
GRAVES

themes echo the main subject of the painting. The engravings are, from left to right starting at the top (the two engravings in the top right-hand corner are unidentified): *The Blind Beggar* after Dyckmans; *The Shepherd's Prayer* after Landseer; *Christ Blessing the Little Children* after James Faed; *The Order of Release* after Millais; *Lord Shaftesbury* after Frederick Sandys; *The Alms Deeds* after Dobson; *Home and the Homeless* after Thomas Faed; *The Plough* after Dobson; *The Mitherless Bairn* after Thomas Faed; and *Saved* after Landseer. A label on the back indicates that this painting belonged to Henry Graves and it may well be the case that the work was also commissioned by Graves, who had it engraved in 1864.

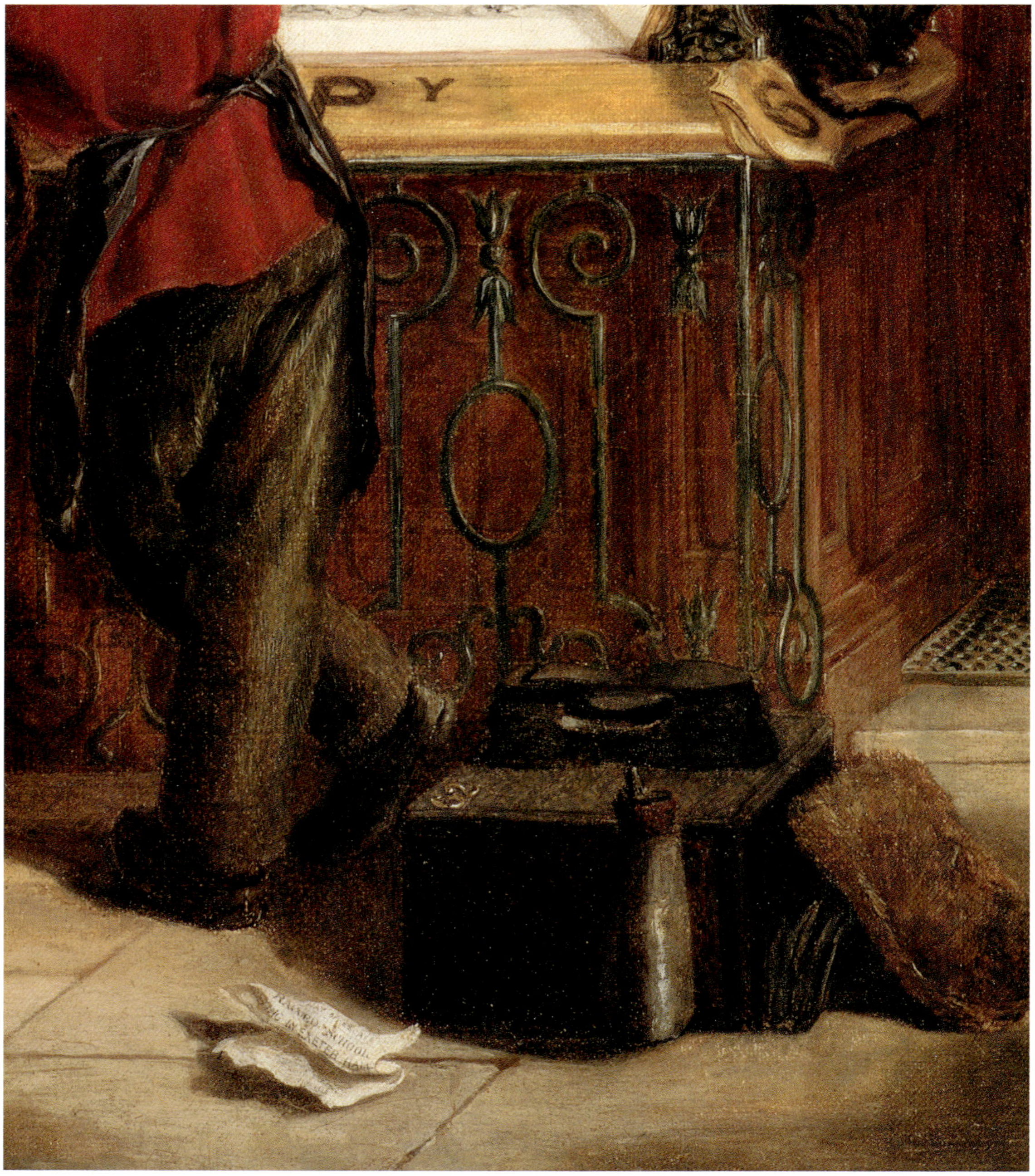

126.

PHOEBUS LEVIN

(active 1855–78)

The Dancing Platform at Cremorne Gardens [A 25327]

1864

Oil on canvas, 66.2 x 107.5 cm

Signed and dated bottom right:

P. Levin 1864

THIS PAINTING showing the crowd on a typical summer's evening represents the south-west corner of Cremorne Gardens, with the dancing platform and its central pagoda where the dance orchestra played. Some of the tables and chairs which were set among trees round the platform can be seen in the foreground, and in the distance are the double tiers of supper boxes.

The 12-acre gardens, which opened in 1846, were situated west of Battersea Bridge between King's Road and the Thames (see cat. no. 93 for the waterside entrance and the history of the site). The principal entrance was in King's Road. Fireworks, balloon ascents, vocal and instrumental concerts, vaudeville, marionettes and dancing were the principal amusements and the charge for entrance was one shilling. The gardens had a circus (on the west side) and a theatre (on the south side), but the most striking feature was the orchestra, depicted here. Brilliantly lit with hundreds of coloured lamps, the pagoda for the orchestra was placed in the middle of a platform said to accommodate four thousand dancers. Dancing took place from 8.30pm until 11.00pm or later.

The main subject of the painting is the character of the crowd. Three distinct groups in the foreground are linked through the gaze of the participants. The two well-dressed ladies in the centre set the tone: one is looking at the gentleman to whom she is being introduced, the other is looking to her right at the Scot in the left-hand group. Close observation of the painting will reveal further 'coupling' scenes: on the left, the lady upstairs is throwing flowers at a gentleman on the ground; on the right a man smoking has just given flowers to a lady provocatively showing her ankles. In the background a woman pokes her parasol into the hat of a man perhaps caught in the act of dancing with a forbidden partner.

The general sense of debauchery is reinforced by excessive drink (the man tipping his glass from the balcony on the left and the scene on the right with a drunken woman). The presence of performing dogs and monkeys parading the grounds suggests cheap fairground entertainment, while a group of businessmen on the left maintains a sense of variety and social panoramic survey. However, the shady goings-on and the presence of roughish characters in the gardens have been considerably attenuated in the painting under review. Two Cremorne drawings by Levin (Christie's, 5 October 1989), one of them closely related to this composition, depict looks, clothing and gestures verging on delinquency and also introduce such controversial social types as a mother breastfeeding, a couple kissing in public and a crippled man begging.

The model for Cremorne was Vauxhall, as regards both amenities and design, though the ironwork was typically early Victorian; overall, it was perhaps more comparable with the Rivoli Gardens in Copenhagen, which opened in 1843.

Provenance:
Jules Singer; Singer sale, Christie's, 1 May 1899 (64), bt Hamilton; G. W. Boorman; Boorman sale, Christie's, 11 December 1922 (83), bt Potter; purchased in 1923.

Bibliography:
Hayes (cat. no. 68); Warwick Wroth, *Cremorne and the Later London Gardens*, 1907; *Illustrated London News*, 22 May 1965, p26; Jean Dethier, *La Ville Moderne en Europe 1870–1996*, exhibition catalogue, Museum of Contemporary Art, Tokyo, pp60–61.

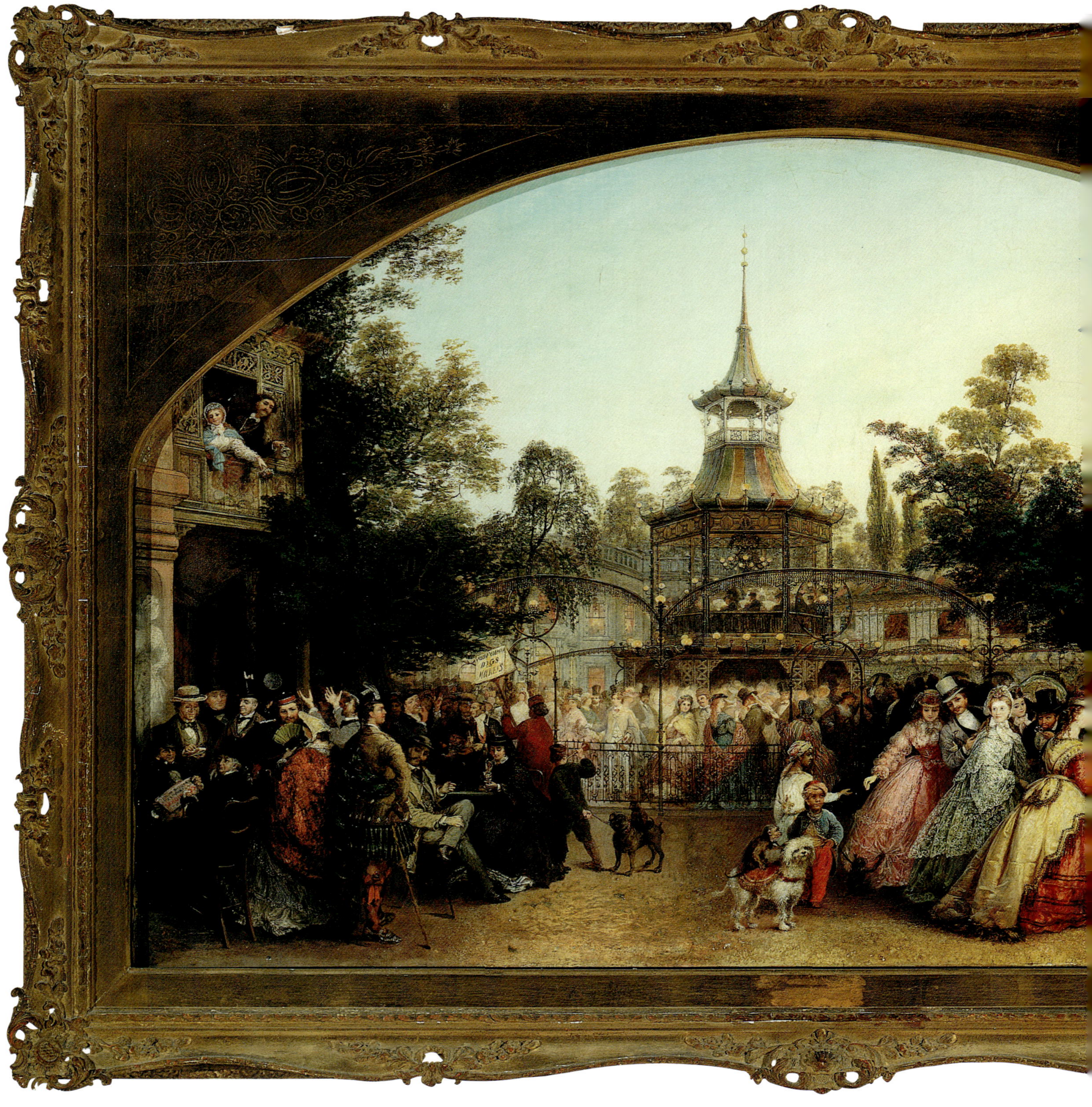

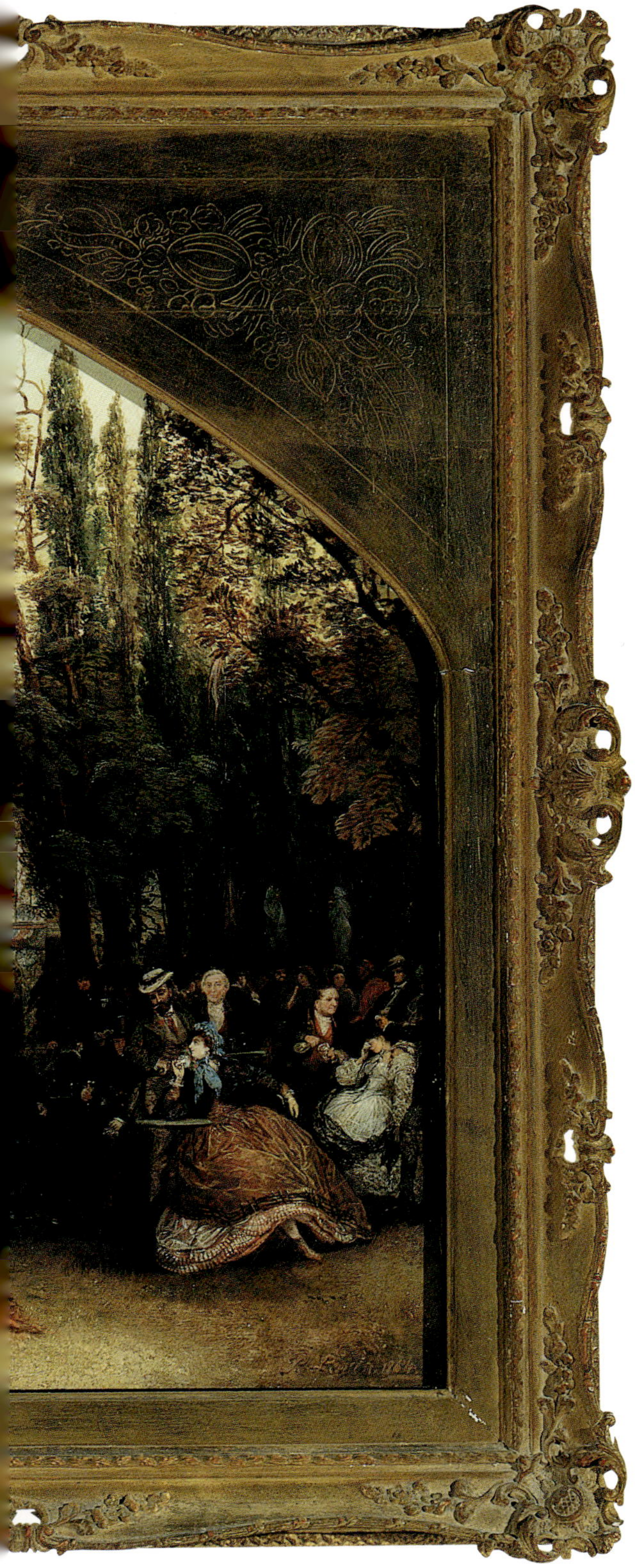

Cremorne was never patronised by fashionable society, as Vauxhall and Ranelagh had been in the eighteenth century, and was frequented more by what were termed 'the lower orders', although close analysis of the costume does not support this. The 'Aristocratic Fête' staged on 9 July 1858, the wettest July day on record, was a disaster which lost Cremorne its chance of grand patronage. A number of riots occurred there in the 1860s, and as a result of the general rowdiness there was considerable opposition to the Gardens from the Chelsea Vestry and the Principal of St Mark's Training College opposite; finally, after a libel action in May 1877, the proprietor decided not to renew his licence.

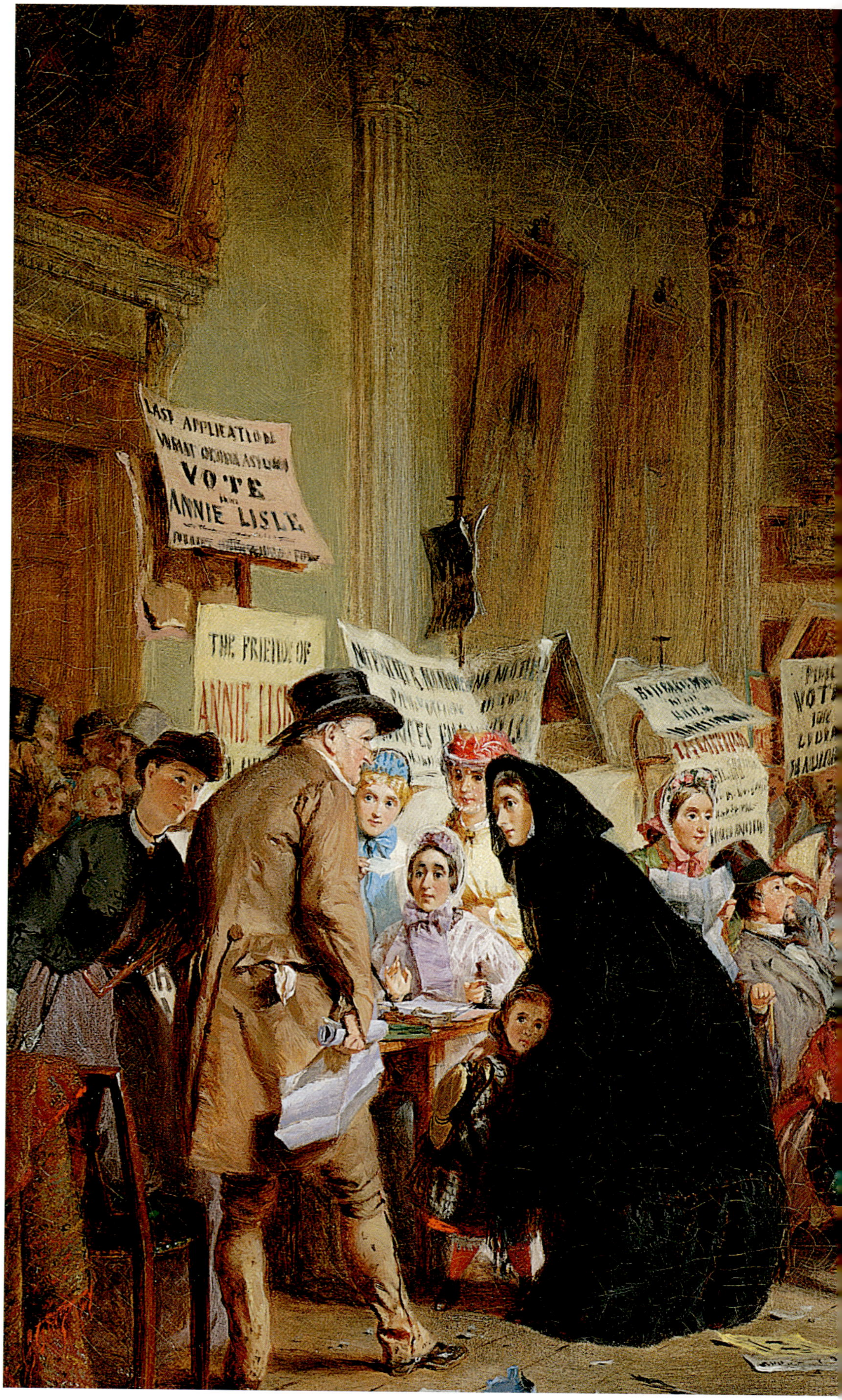
VOTE
ANNIE LISLE
THE FRIENDS OF

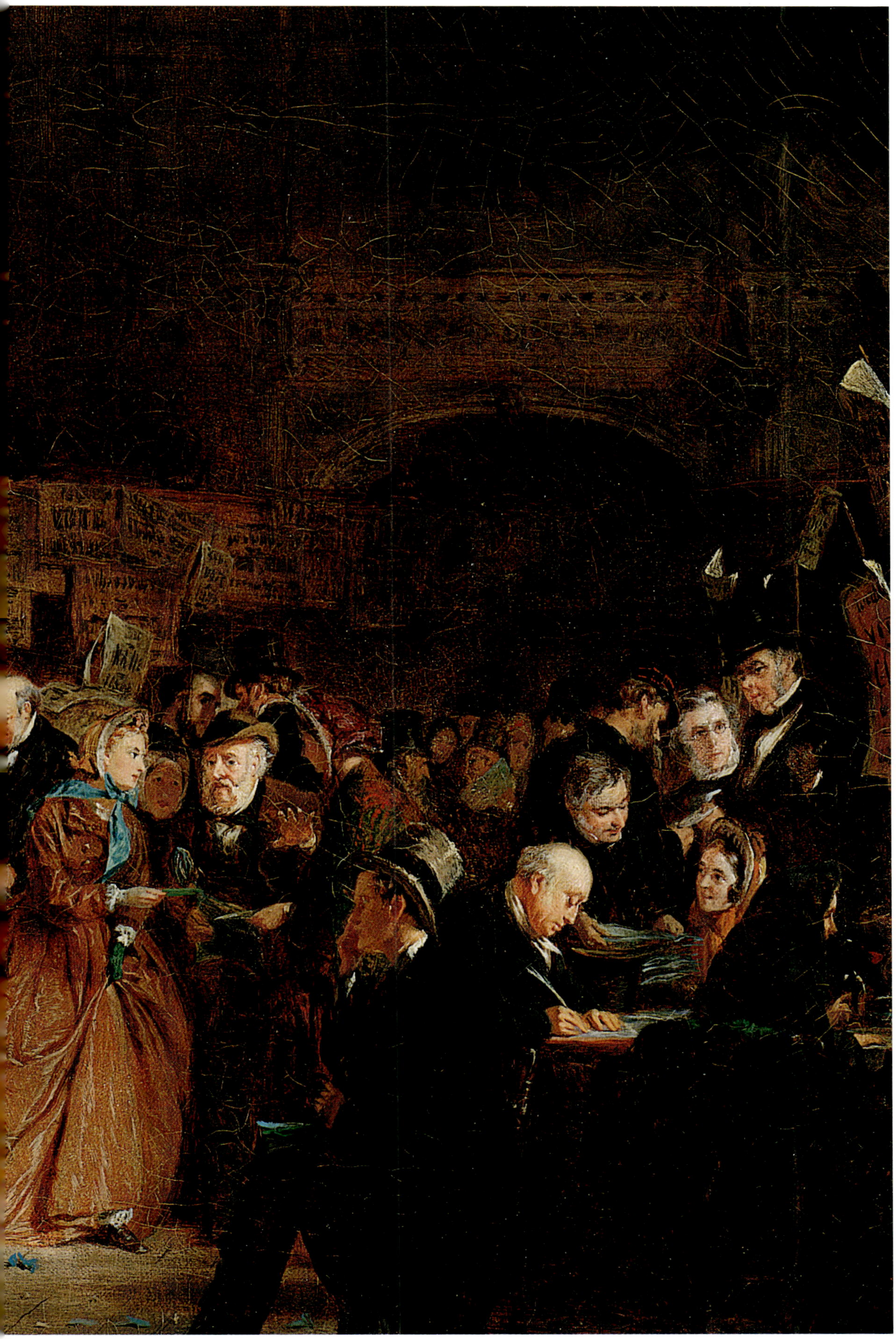

127.
GEORGE ELGAR HICKS
(1824-1914)
An Infant Orphan Election at the London Tavern. 'Polling' [95.523]
1865
Oil on canvas,
46.7 x 61.7 cm
Signed and dated
G. E. Hicks 1865

Provenance:
Exhibited at Scarborough in 1867; sold to Tooth in 1869 (£30); Tennants sale, Aske Hall, 20-22 September 1994 (760); Peter Nahum at the Leicester Galleries; purchased in 1995 with the help of of the National Art Collections Fund, the MGC/V&A Purchase Fund and the Museum's Trust Funds.

Bibliography:
Rosamond Allwood, *George Elgar Hicks*, exhibition catalogue, Geffrye Museum, 1982, pp34-5 and 56; George Augustus Sala, *Twice Round the Clock*, 1859, pp229–32; John Farley, *The London Art of Cookery*, Anne Haly (ed.), 1988, pp1-12.

A CORNER of the grand first floor room at the London Tavern in Bishopsgate has been taken over by a crowd of well-intentioned voters: by subscription they have bought the right to vote for the 'needy' children of their choice in the hope that they may enter the Infant Orphan Asylum at Wanstead. *The Times* of 29 April 1865 made clear that the children were only those whose 'parents were once in prosperous circumstances'. There are many placards around the room and its makeshift enclosure encouraging people to vote for such deserving children as Annie Lisle ('Daughter of a Physician') and Lydia Malvern. However, Joseph Mundy in his diary for 1864 described the principle of such elections, highlighting the fact that they were based not on merit 'but according to the amount of money & votes that A or B can beg or buy for them: the Hospital folks pocketing all receipts with admirable impartiality.' (He was referring to an election of candidates to the Royal Hospital for Incurables.)

Hicks's painting is clearly not intent on criticising such a system and the impartial accuracy of his record was noted by Allwood. The occasion is full of life and bustle and the participants seem filled with the excitement of working for a good cause. Yet the focus of the painting is the figure of the beautiful, sad widow on the left-hand side, anxiously clutching a little girl who is equally anxiously clutching her. The painting is organised, as are many others by this artist, in a horizontal frieze, but the diffused spotlighting of the left-hand side brings out the pathetic case of this mother about to be separated from the child whom she can no longer support after the death of her husband. This, in some way, is far more poignant than a militant painting campaigning to abolish a particular system.

This work is an elaborate sketch for the painting of the same title exhibited at the Royal Academy in 1865 and now in a private collection. It is very interesting to compare the sketch with the finished painting, as it gives insight into the genesis of this image. Hicks made a couple of important adjustments. The romantic figure of the young man seated on the right, who seems to be aware of the widow's drama, was later replaced by the less sympathetic figure of an old man absorbed in the voting process. Hicks also introduced a crawling baby on the extreme right, probably associated with one of the two widows obliviously chatting and unaware of its fate. These changes reinforce the isolation of the widow: she is alone in the realisation of the tragic dimension of this day.

This painting is also a memorable record of the activities of the London Tavern and it is worth emphasising its importance in Georgian and Victorian times. In many ways, it was the Victorian equivalent of the modern-day large-scale conference centre. It could accommodate 355 in its dining room (partially shown in this painting). Its physical appearance in Hicks's painting is confirmed by Sala in his illustrated *Twice Round the Clock* (1859), where a charity dinner is both depicted and discussed. Although many of its activities involved charitable work, the tavern's reputation really stemmed from the excellence of its food. This can still be appreciated today with the reprint of John Farley's *London Art of Cookery* (first published in 1783). John Farley successfully ran the kitchens of the London Tavern in the late eighteenth century. In February 1769, the society of the Supporters of the Bill of Rights was formed there to support the radical politics of John Wilkes. It has been suggested that this association between good dining and radical politics probably caused the chef Beauvilliers to call the restaurant which he opened in Paris in the 1780s La Grande Taverne de Londres.

From Farley's day until 1834, all the hospitality of the East India Company was officially carried out at the London Tavern. Less well known are the Tavern's musical associations: its rooms, let out for concerts, apparently hosted the first public performance in Britain of *Don Giovanni* (17 April 1809) and Beethoven's *Mass in D* (1839), as well as his third and fourth symphonies. The attraction the tavern exercised was perhaps best summed up by Charles Dickens, who mocked the ludicrous pretexts for organising public dinners. In *Nicholas Nickleby* a public meeting is held 'to take into consideration the propriety of petitioning Parliament in favour of the United Metropolitan Improved Hot Muffin and Crumpet Baking and Punctual Delivery Company'.

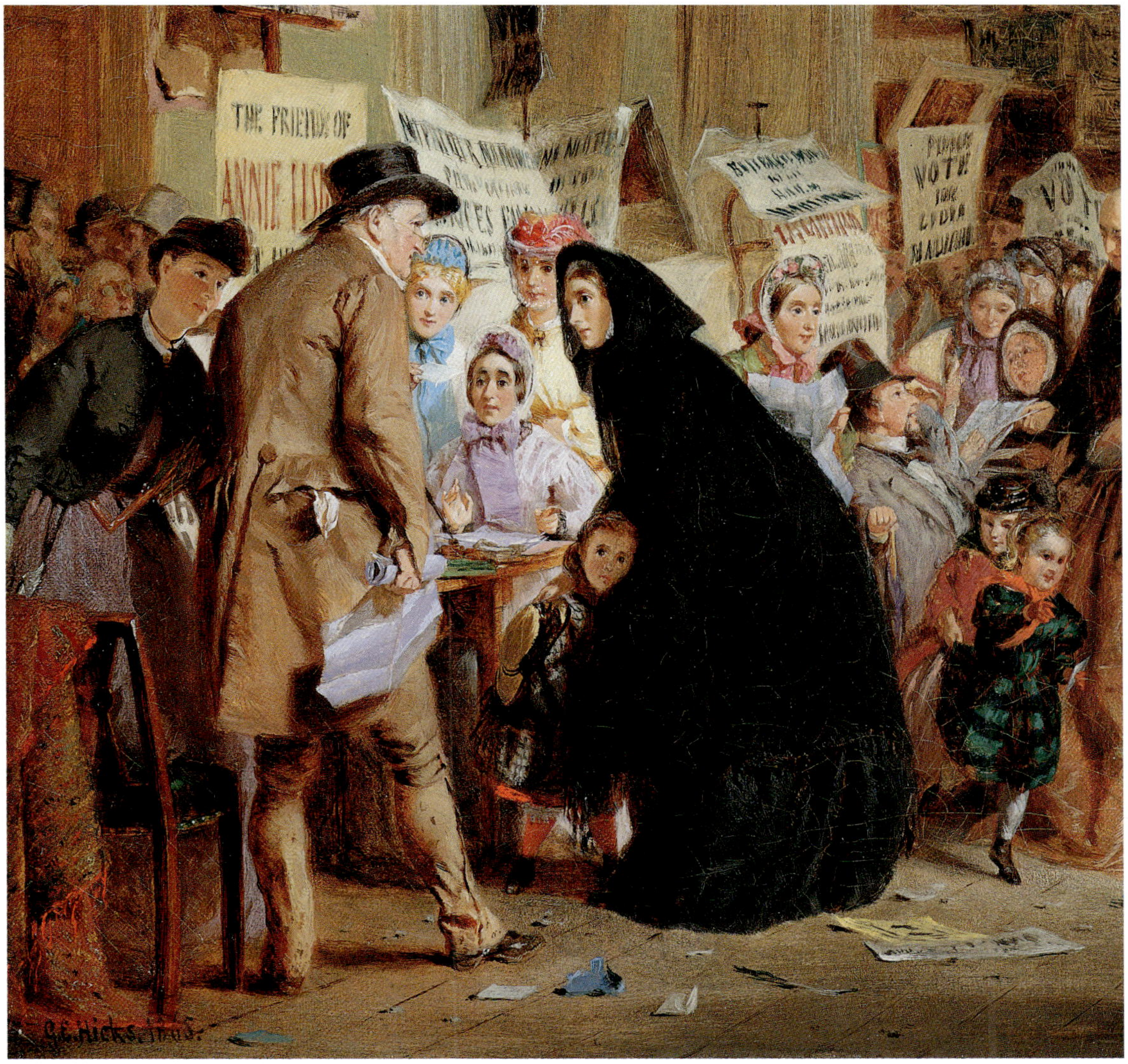

Provenance:
A French private collector (see label); Phillips, 22 March 1988 (23); bt in; purchased by the Museum in 1988 with the help of the MGC/V&A Purchase Grant Fund.

Bibliography:
Henry Mayhew, *London Labour and the London Poor*, 1861, vol. III, pp312–18; Blanchard Jerrold, *London: A Pilgrimage*, 1872; *Gustave Doré 1832–1883*, exhibition catalogue, Musée d'Art Moderne, Strasbourg, 1983; Samuel Clapp, *Gustave Doré 1832–83*, exhibition catalogue, Hazlitt, Gooden and Fox, London, 1983, no. 18; *The Image of London*, exhibition catalogue, Barbican Gallery, 1987, nos 185–215; *La Ville*, Alain Guiheux and Jean Dethier (eds), 1994, p43; Jean Dethier, *La Ville Moderne en Europe 1870–1996*, exhibition catalogue, Museum of Contemporary Art, Tokyo, pp58–59.

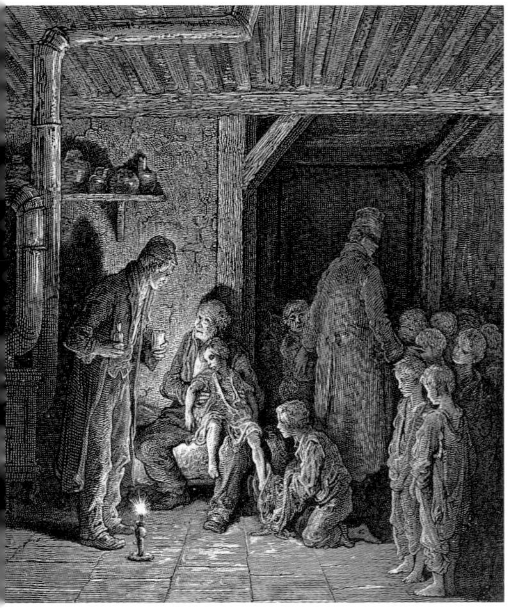

128.
GUSTAVE DORÉ
(1832–83)

A Poor-House [88.60]
*c.*1869
Oil on canvas, 76.5 x 158.5 cm
Signed bottom right: *Gve Doré*
Small label on the back reads:
Atelier Moran [?] Restauration No. 55.80

THE SCENE takes place in a gas-lit basement with a timber rafted ceiling and, on the left-hand side, a timber staircase. It holds around seventy men, women and children, who are massed around the staircase and two tables – a large central one, candle-lit, placed against the back wall and a smaller one on the right-hand side with people playing cards. A man, a child and a dog are in the centre of the room, staring straight out of the painting at the artist. The scene brings to mind Henry Mayhew's account in *London Labour and the London Poor* of his interview with the occupants of a cheap lodging house in the 1850s.

In order to recover the context of this apparently undocumented painting, which does not appear on any of the lists available to us, we should turn to *London: A Pilgrimage*, the book by Blanchard Jerrold which Gustave Doré illustrated. In subject matter and in style this painting bears a close resemblance to the scenes of poverty found in this book. Two engravings in particular make an interesting comparison.

Thieves Gambling (see left), on p137 in the chapter 'Under Lock and Key', recalls several aspects of this painting: the layout and timber fabric of the room seem the same as the arrangement found on the left-hand side of the painting, although viewed from a different angle; the close-up view of

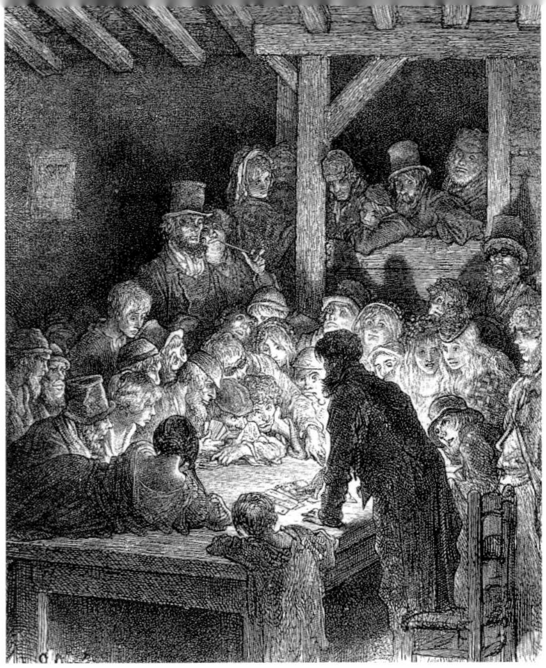

card players at the table also recalls the group on the right-hand side of the painting. However, Doré's expressive powers successfully suggest a gathering of thieves and ruthless individuals in the engraving, while the painting highlights the wretchedness and hopelessness of the participants.

Found in the Street (see above), on p184 in the chapter 'London Charities', shows the receiving room of a night refuge for children. The physical exhaustion of the children recalls that of many of the figures in the painting. The accompanying text with its contemporary statistics also puts in context the existence of poorhouses in London:

> London boasts something like a hundred hospitals, a hundred homes and refuges for the houseless, fifty orphan asylums, over twenty institutions for the blind and deaf, fourteen for the relief of discharged prisoners, eighteen penitentiaries for fallen women, five asylums for incurables, over forty homes and institutions for poor sailors, and twenty for soldiers; twelve charitable institutions for the benefit of poor Jews, and between thirty or forty relief societies for the clergy.

The preparation of *London: A Pilgrimage* was carried out in two stages. In 1869–70, Doré worked up his London album of preparatory drawings which led to the publishing agreement in the spring of 1870 with Grant & Co. The Franco-Prussian war intervened and Doré did not come back to London until July 1871, when he resumed research on the book, this time with his friend Emile Bourdelin. The work was issued in parts from January 1872. This painting may conceivably have been produced during the first campaign, when the discovery of London made its greatest impact on Doré, and before the agreement with Grant & Co was signed, bringing with it the pressure of deadlines which would preclude such elaborate treatment.

Gustave Doré first came to London in 1868 and was rapidly able to develop his career as a painter here. In 1868 Messrs Fairless and Beetforth opened the Doré Gallery, first at 168 and then at 35 New Bond Street. This painting is not listed in any of the catalogues of the Doré Gallery, which mostly displayed religious paintings. While a substantial number of Doré's London drawings survive, this is the only large-scale London painting to have come to light (both the second-hand Whitechapel trader and the flower seller in private collections, as well as the female gin drinker at the Beauvais Museum, are single-figure compositions). The 1869 Doré drawing inscribed by Jerrold, *Gray's Inn Lane – Robbers kitchen* (Strasbourg Museum of Modern Art), bears some similarities with the painting in the Rembrandtesque group around the table, the wooden staircase (but on the wrong side) and a standing (but different) figure staring at us. The drawing seems to stem from the same vision of a dark, ghastly gathering of London poor, but the energy of the figures (even in the slumped bodies of the drunks) contrasts here again with the worn-out look of most of the figures in the painting.

The two most notorious areas of poverty in Victorian London were Whitechapel and Drury Lane, but they were by no means the only places with poorhouses. There is insufficient evidence for identifying with any certainty the location of this work. Most likely, it is not a depiction of a specific poorhouse, but an amalgamation of a number of such institutions that Doré visited. It is worth pointing out that Doré would have painted it in Paris and not in London, where he refused to have a studio.

While the lighting and composition of this work are reminiscent of Doré's *Jesus among the Doctors* (Sète Museum, France), the group of paintings which would have been most relevant for discussion in this context unfortunately does not survive. The series *Paris As It Is* was a group of twelve giant canvases painted between 1854 and 1855, which the artist appears to have destroyed soon after their completion. The critic Paul Lacroix's words are all we have to assess these lost works by Doré and they seem to indicate that this painting was conceived along similar lines: 'Each picture was more frightening than its predecessor, they were so realistic they made one's heart ache.'

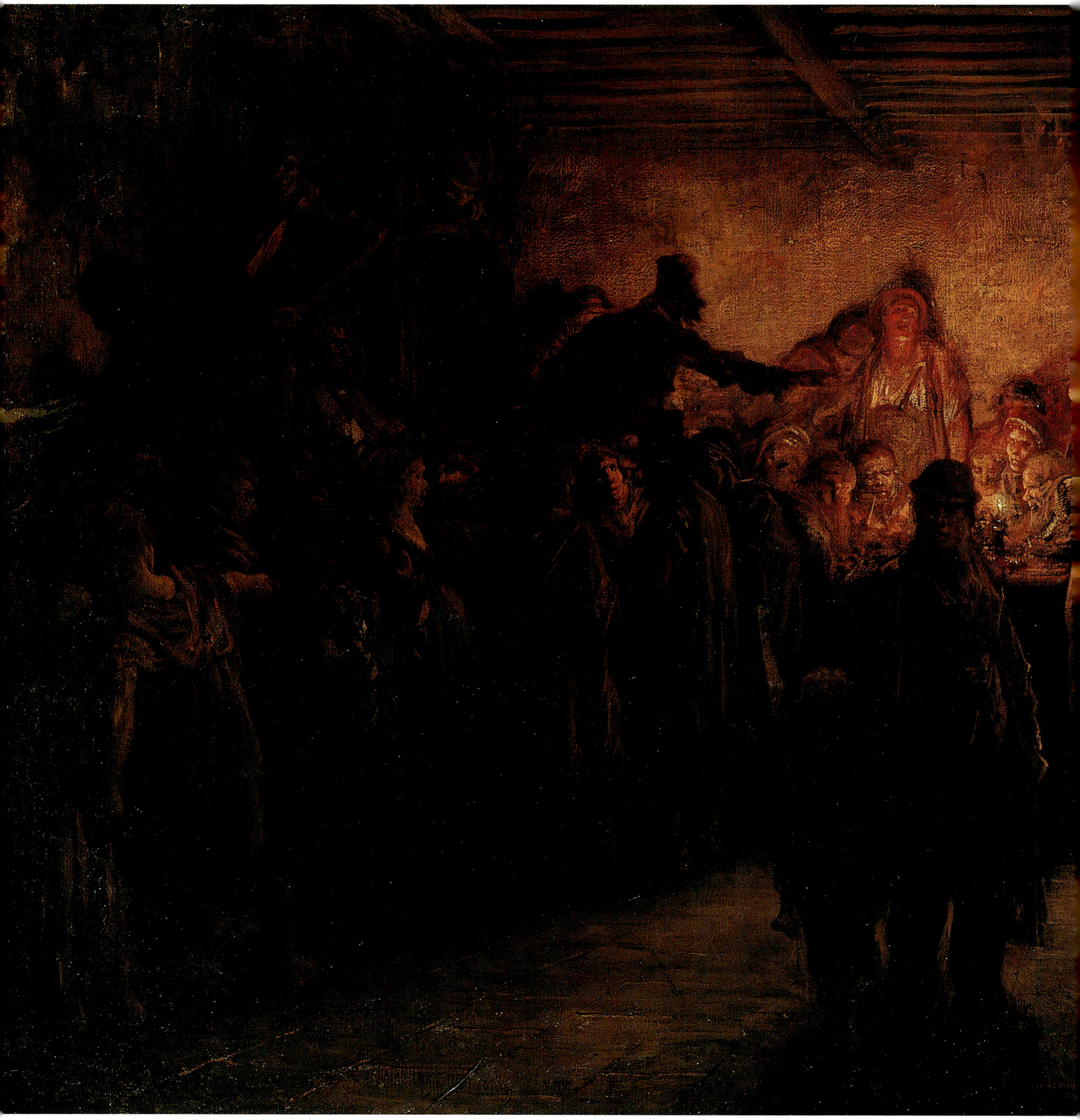

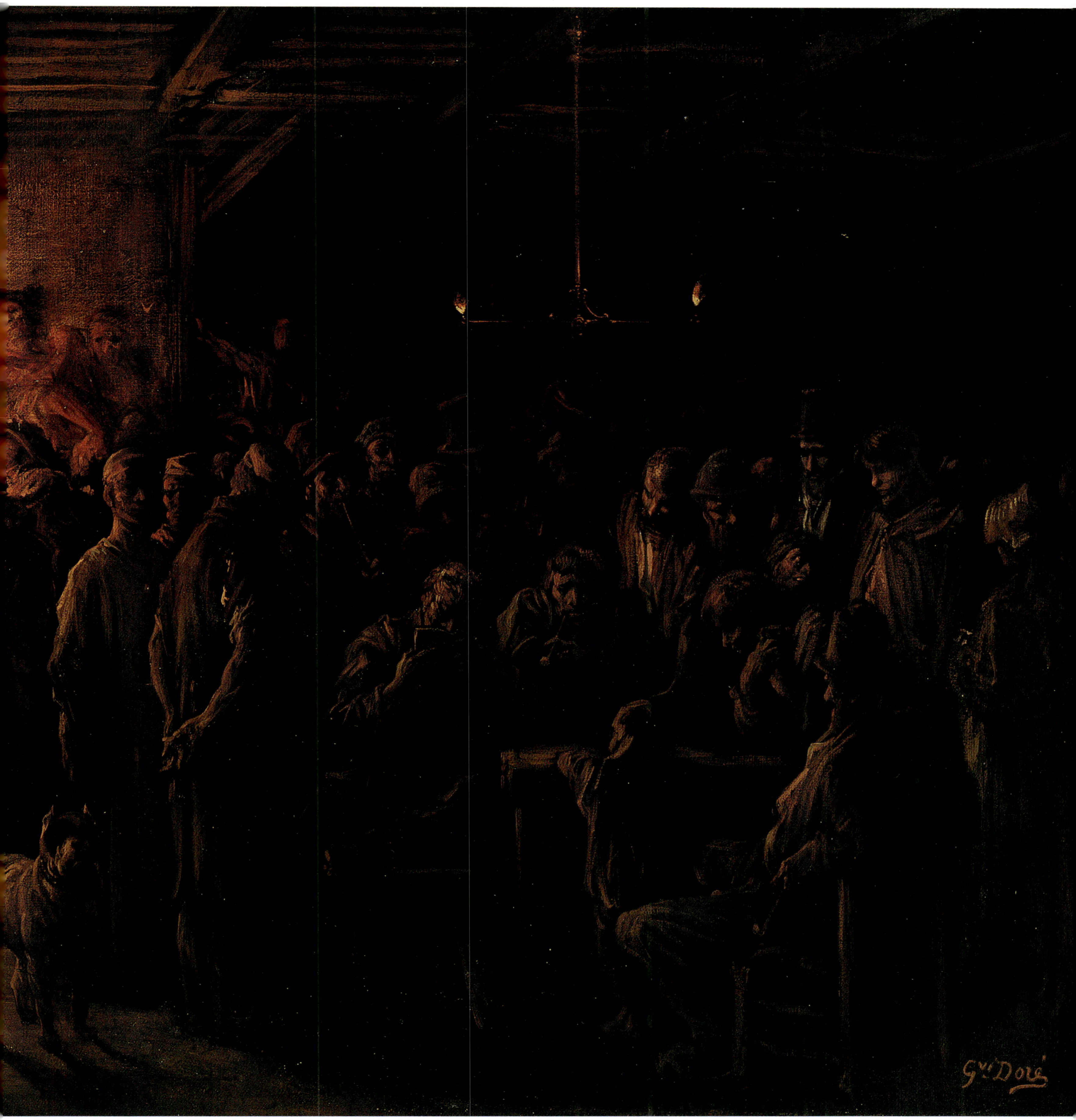
Gve Doré

129.
JAMES ARCHER
(1823–1904)
Sir Henry Irving (1838–1905) as Mathias in *The Bells* [38.41/6]
*c.*1871–2
Oil on canvas, 56.7 x 73.9 cm (oval)
Not signed or dated

Provenance:
The Lyceum Theatre (Beefsteak Room); Weedon Grossmith; Red Cross sale, Christie's, 23 April 1915 (1440) (presented by W. Grossmith), bt Mrs Barton; lent by E. Temple (pseudonym) in 1938 and afterwards presented.

Bibliography:
Hayes (cat. no. 113).

THE ACTOR Henry Irving is shown three-quarter length, seated in an armchair, facing half left, and wearing a reddish-brown suit with a reddish-brown and yellow striped waistcoat.

The part of the burgomaster Mathias in *The Bells*, a man racked by remorse for a murder he had committed many years before, was perhaps Irving's most famous role, and certainly the one he performed most frequently. The scene depicted here is the moment at the end of Act I when Mathias, on the anniversary (to the very hour) of his crime, suddenly hears the bells of the murdered man's sledge ringing in his ears, and sinks back into his chair, transfixed.

The Bells, a play by Leopold Lewis based on a French original, held a place of particular significance in Irving's career, as it was the play which established his reputation on the London stage. The young actor had just joined H. L. Bateman's company at the Lyceum, and things were not going well; he entreated Bateman to try *The Bells*, which would give him the chance to play a tragic role instead of the comic and character parts for which he was actually engaged. Despite the fears of the company, and a thin audience on the opening night, 25 November 1871, Irving's gamble was triumphantly justified; the critics were unanimous in their acclaim, and the play was kept on the bill for six months. In 1892, when Irving's own company wanted to show their affection for their master, they did so by presenting him with a bronze to mark the twenty-first anniversary of his appearance as Mathias.

For the Museum's other portraits of Irving in oils, by Partridge and Eves, see cat. nos 154 and 157. Archer also painted Irving as Charles I (Russell Cotes Art Gallery, Bournemouth).

Costumes worn by Irving as Mathias are in the Museum's collection (nos 24–6 and 31 in the catalogue *Stage Costume and Accessories,* published in 1968). Accessories from the play are also in the collection (nos 27–30 in the same catalogue).

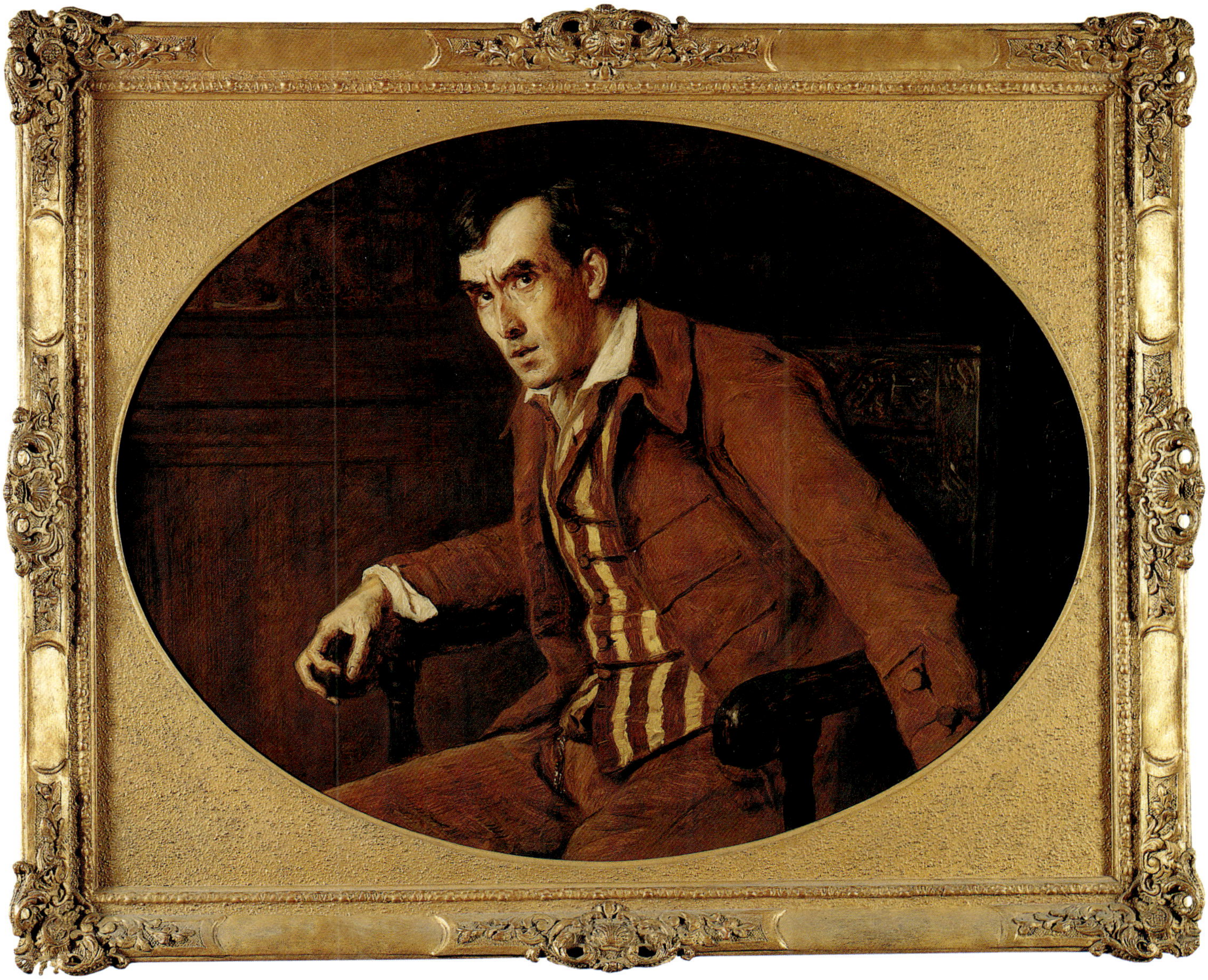

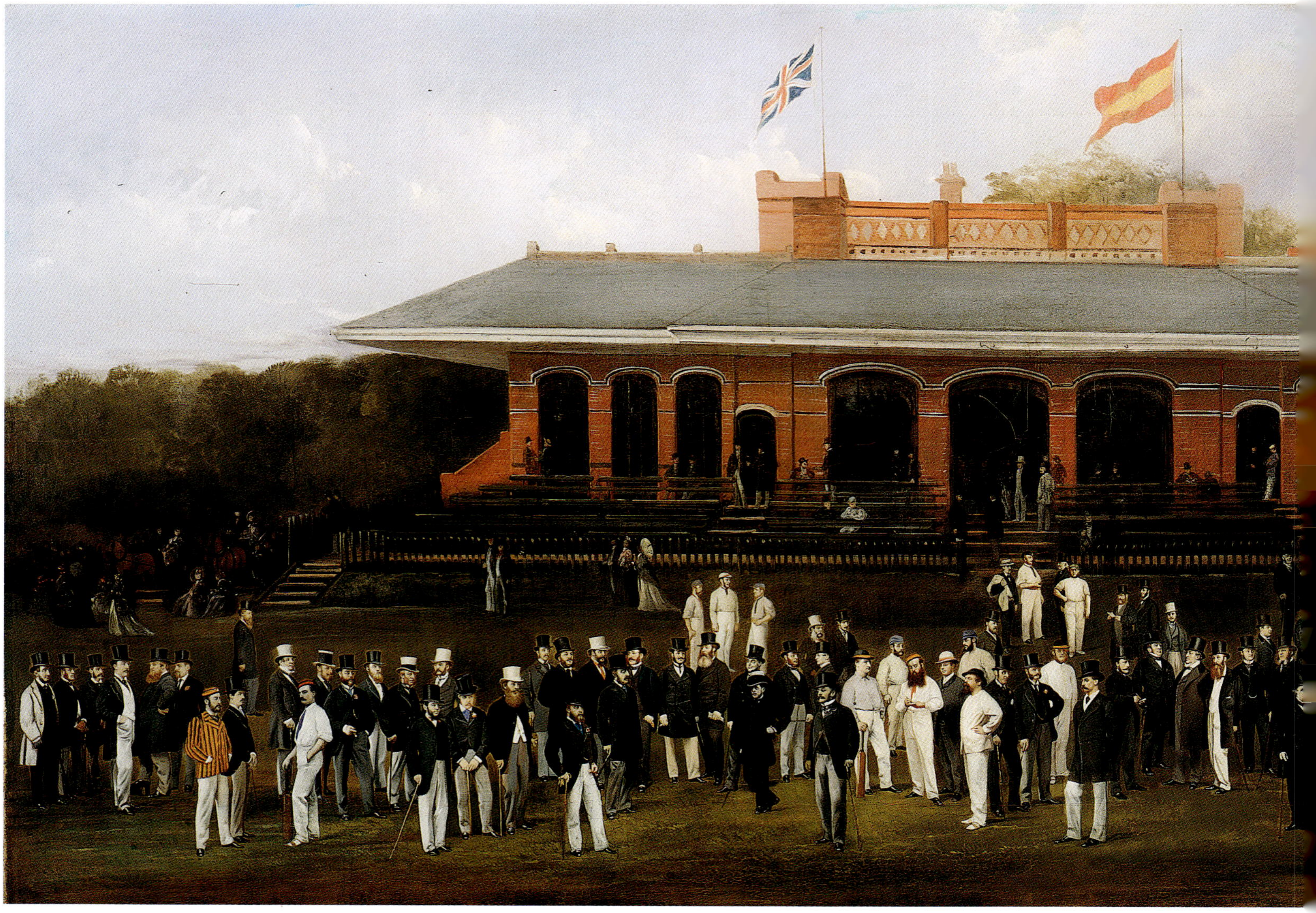

Provenance:
Henry Barraud sale, Christie's, 24 June 1875 (112), bt in; purchased in 1923 (without attribution).

130.

HENRY BARRAUD
(1811–74)

Portrait Group of Members of the Marylebone Cricket Club outside the Pavilion at Lord's [A 25329]
*c.*1870–4
Oil on canvas, 70 x 150 cm
Not signed or dated

ABOUT NINETY members of the Marylebone Cricket Club and well-known patrons of cricket are shown grouped in the foreground, with other figures seen around and outside the Pavilion. Among those who can be identified are Sir Spencer Ponsonby-Fane (fifteenth from the left), the Earl of Darnley (sixteenth from the left), the Prince of Wales, later Edward VII (twenty-first from the left), E. M. Grace (thirty-fifth from the left) R. A. Fitzgerald, then the Hon. Secretary (thirty-sixth from the left), and W. G. Grace (thirty-eighth from the left). The pavilion, which is flying the Union Jack and the MCC flag, is seen as it was when enlarged by H. Newton in 1866; further improvements were carried out in the

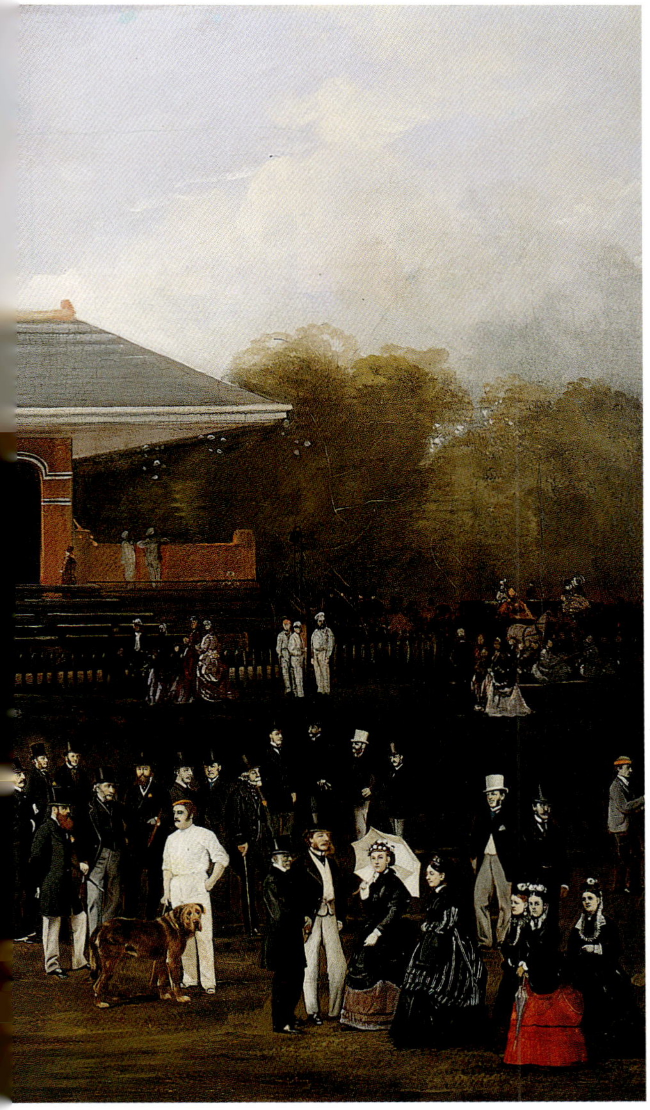

1880s, but the building was soon afterwards demolished, and the present Pavilion, by F. Verity, was built in 1889–90.

In the mid-eighteenth century, cricket matches in London were played first at the Artillery Ground near Finsbury Square in City Road, and then at White Conduit Fields, Islington. The latter, however, was used for amusements of all kinds, which proved a considerable inconvenience and Thomas Lord, one of the employees of the White Conduit Club, was asked to find a new ground. Suitable quarters were found on the site of what is now Dorset Square, the Marylebone Cricket Club was formed, and the first match was played on 31 May 1787. The club moved to its present home in 1814. By the date of this picture, the MCC was well established as the premier club in Britain and the arbiter upon all matters relating to cricket, W. G. Grace was in full career, and the law permitting overarm bowling (which laid the foundations of modern cricket) had been operative for a decade.

The Museum picture, the painting of *The London Season* (set in Hyde Park, see p283) and *The Lobby of the House of Commons* in 1872, both of which were also in the Christie's sale of 1875, were the three canvases by which Barraud was best known to his contemporaries.

The Museum picture is related to two other portrait groups by Barraud, both photographs (in the collection of the Marylebone Cricket Club). The first, which is signed, is substantially the same group, but taken from a different viewpoint, showing more of the ground and with the Pavilion on the right. The second is a different group, but exactly the same background; this was published as an autotype photograph by Barraud and Jerrard on 1 May 1874. In both these groups the foreground figures are separate photographs, and have been stuck on individually.

The costume indicates a date in the early 1870s.

Bibliography:
Hayes (cat. no. 114); E. M. Barraud, 'Artists of the Barraud Family', in *Country Life*, 21 October 1965 (this contains no mention of our painting but has useful information on the artist's background); Robin Simon, *The Art of Cricket*, 1983, no. 8.

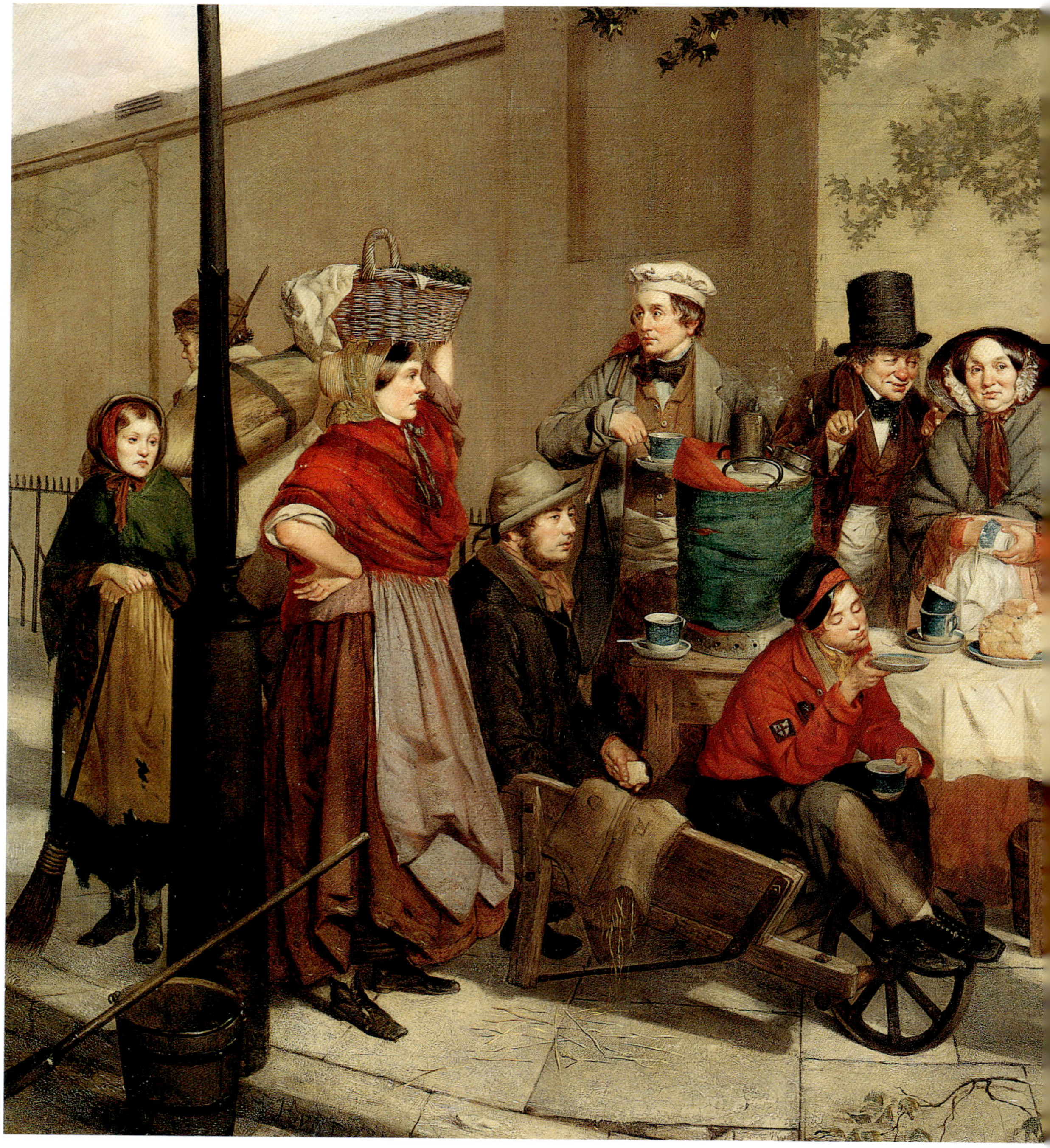

131.

CHARLES HUNT

(1829–1900)

A Coffee Stall [53.28]

1881

Oil on canvas, 60 x 89.7 cm

Signed and dated bottom left:

C. HUNT 1881

AMONG THE many thousand street sellers of all descriptions who thronged Victorian London, the coffee-stall proprietor was one of the most welcome. A baker's man, a boy wearing a City of London badge and seated in a wheelbarrow, and a young lady carrying a band-box are shown with cups of coffee, while the proprietress is washing up (note

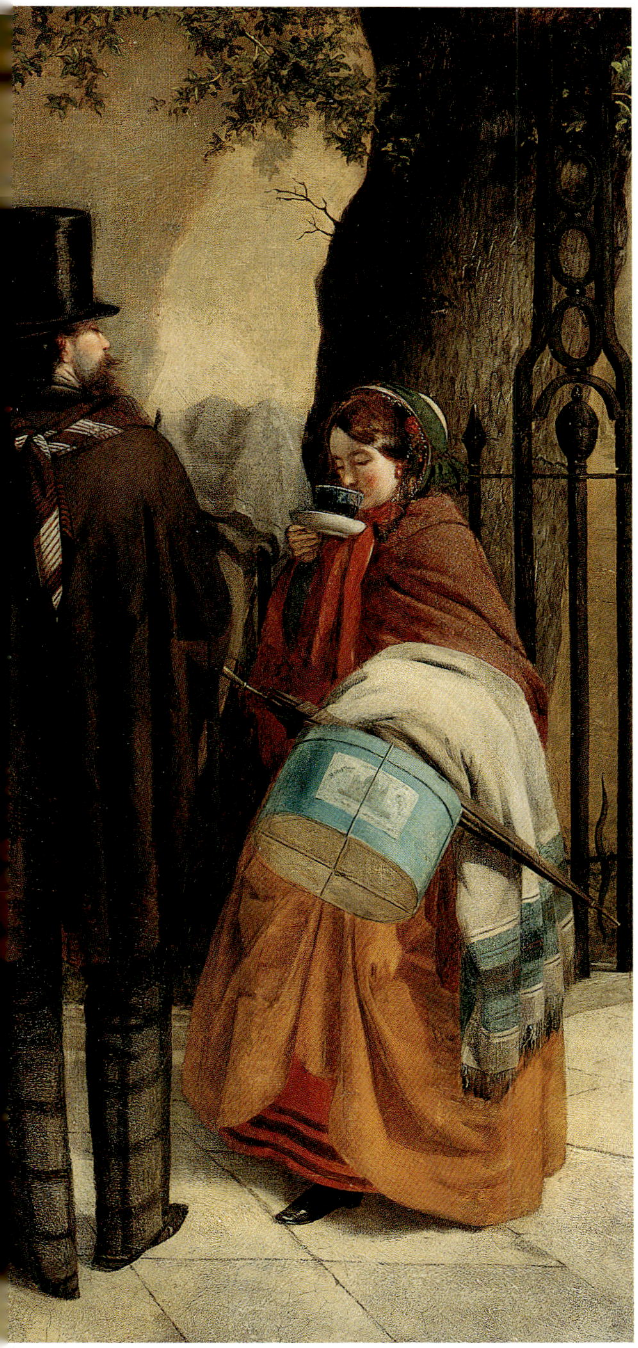

as well as coffee contained tea and sometimes cocoa. The stall is stationary (some were movable) and is a day stall which appears to be situated near a park or square. Like the majority of these stalls, it is run by a woman.

Coffee stalls on London streets were almost unknown in the Regency period. Their appearance was facilitated by the reduction of the tax on coffee in 1824 and the rapid increase in the use of cheap adulteration (mainly chicory, but also other cheaply taxed or even untaxed products). Food as well as drink was often available: 'bread and butter, or currant cake, in slices – ham sandwiches, water cresses and boiled eggs' (Mayhew, 1861).

The costume depicted is of the period 1858–60, so that the picture represents a scene some twenty-odd years earlier than the date of painting. This may have been a deliberate attempt to set the scene at the height of the coffee-stall trade, when London had over three hundred such stalls, and before their number was reduced by what Mayhew encapsulated as 'Two of us are eating one man's bread'.

Provenance:
Robert Frank; purchased out of the Joicey Trust Fund from M. Newman in 1953.

Bibliography:
Hayes (cat. no. 58); Henry Mayhew, *London Labour and the London Poor*, 1861, vol. I, pp65 and 191–6; Graham Reynolds, *Painters of the Victorian Scene*, 1953, p92 and fig. 81.

the bucket under the table). On the left are a ragged girl with broom, evidently a crossing-sweeper, and a woman with a basket on her head.

The stall depicted (a table, not a barrow, and thus stationary) is of modest scope, consisting of a single tin can with a small iron fire-pot underneath; many stalls had two or three (or more rarely four), which

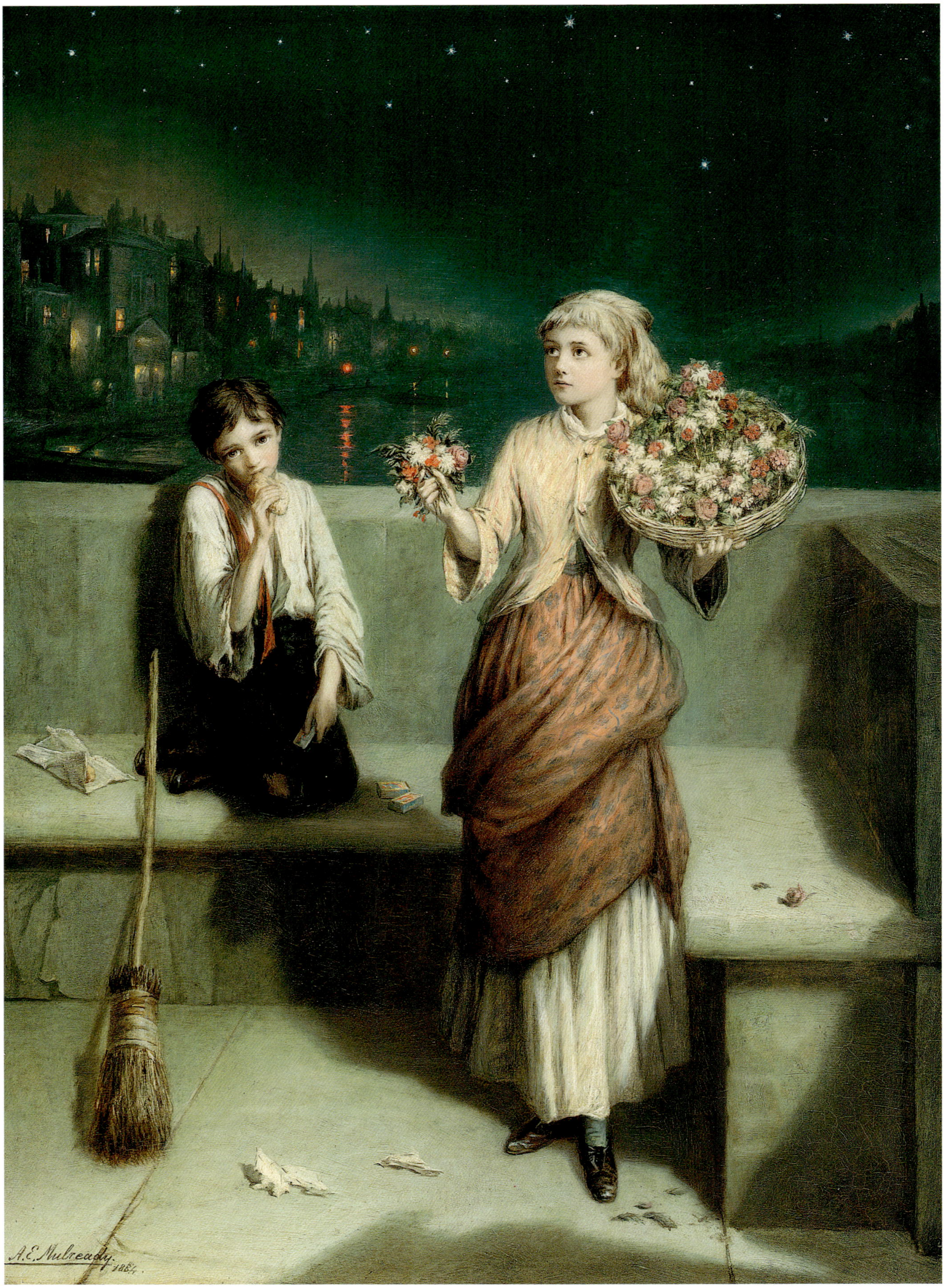

132.

AUGUSTUS E. MULREADY

(1844–1904)

A London Crossing Sweeper and Flower Girl [61.7/1]

1884

Oil on canvas, 97.8 x 50 cm

Signed and dated bottom left: *A. E. Mulready./1884*

Inscribed on the back of the canvas: *London Flower girl and Street Arab/Mutually giving and receiving aid,/They set each other off like light and shade./A. E. Mulready/1884*

IN THIS PICTURE, which over-sentimentalises the London street urchins and suggests nothing of their actual poverty and degradation, the boy, who is resting for a bite to eat, seems also to be engaged in selling matches. The girl has a basket of roses, pinks and carnations. The scene is the north end of Blackfriars Bridge and part of the City waterfront can be seen in the background. The idea for this composition was earlier explored by Gustave Doré in *London: A Pilgrimage* (1872), where a group of poor people and children is depicted huddled in one of the alcoves of a London bridge (ppxii and 179).

Crossing-sweeping was undoubtedly an occupation which absorbed a high proportion of the London poor in Victorian times. It required no capital outlay or risk, and provided ample opportunity for begging. Most adult crossing-sweepers had a regular pitch, for a 'monopoly' of which they sought the protection of the police, and the advantage of this was that they became well-known to those who frequented the district. According to Mayhew's classic survey, *London Labour and the London Poor* (1861), the average takings at this date were between eight pence and a shilling a day. Many children also set up as crossing-sweepers, but they did not normally have a regular pitch and usually moved around after an hour or so in one place.

Flower sellers were mostly female, and mainly between the ages of six and twenty. On a Sunday, which was the best day for trade, four or five hundred girls would be about the streets selling violets, wallflowers, lavender, pinks, roses or mignonette, according to the season. Some flower girls who sold only in the evenings were also prostitutes.

Mulready painted a number of London genre scenes of a similar size, mostly pointing to a moral in more or less overt form. He used the same model in a similar pose for a picture of a flower girl dated 1885 (Christie's sale, 11 July 1969, Lot 63). He also re-used the composition under review (with a flower seller but omitting the crossing-sweeper) in a work he entitled *Violets and May Blossoms* (Sotheby's, 23 November 1982, Lot 85).

Provenance:
Purchased from Abbott and Holder in 1961.

Bibliography:
Hayes (cat. no. 76); Henry Mayhew, *London Labour and the London Poor*, 1861, vol. I, pp494–505, vol. II, pp134–7.

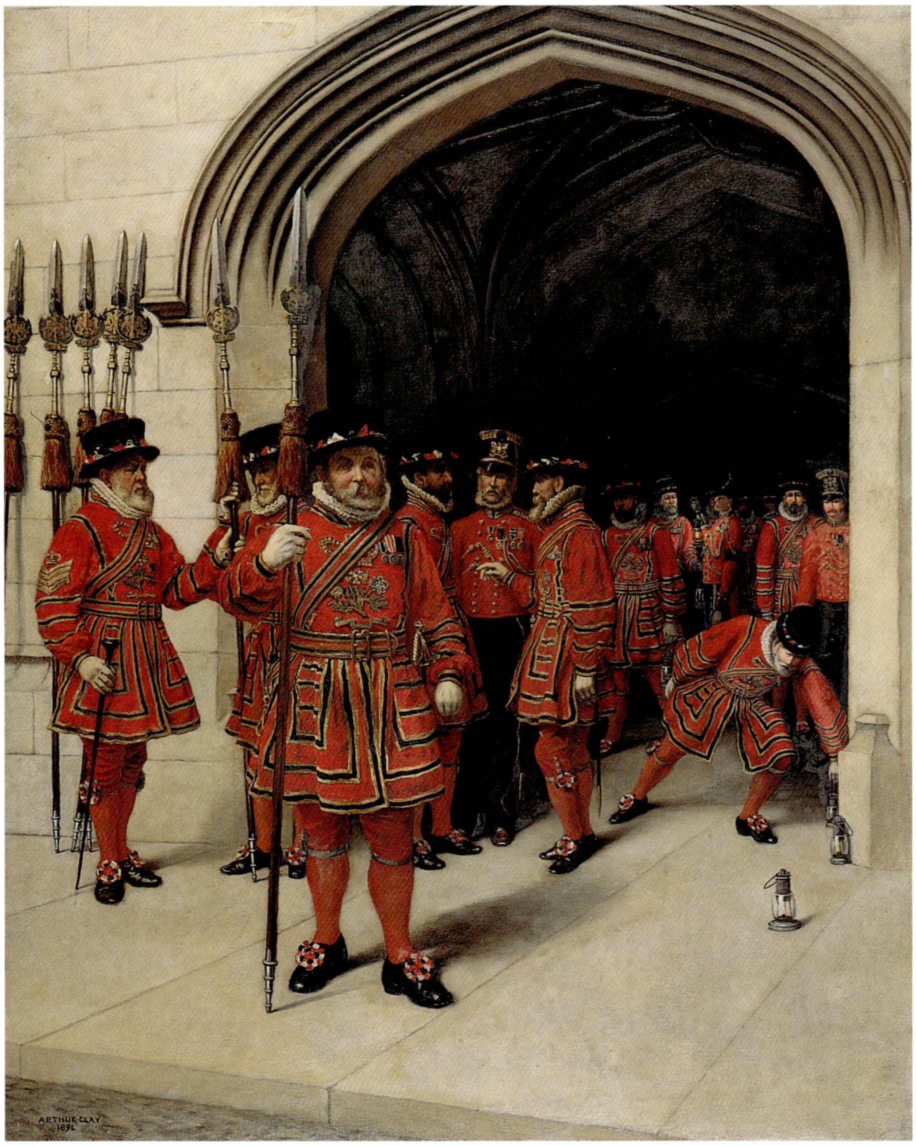

133.
SIR ARTHUR TEMPLE FELIX CLAY, BT
(1842–1928)

The Yeomen of the Guard searching the crypt of the Houses of Parliament
1894
Oil on canvas, 125.3 x 100.6 cm
Signed and dated bottom left:
ARTHUR-CLAY/1894

A PARTY of Yeomen of the Guard – three officers, a sergeant-major and eleven men – are shown searching the crypt of the Houses of Parliament for possible explosives.

This ceremony, which takes place annually at the opening of the Parliamentary session, was initiated after the Gunpowder Plot of 1605, when Guy Fawkes and his fellow conspirators nearly succeeded in blowing up the building with the King, Lords and Commons assembled inside.

The Yeomen of the Guard have been the Sovereign's personal bodyguard since 1485 and they last appeared on a battlefield at Dettingen in 1743. Their uniform, which consists of a red tunic with purple stripes, gold lace and embroidery, a ruff, a partizan (an infantry weapon) with a red and gold tassel, a sword and a crossbelt, has changed little since Tudor times.

Provenance:
Presented by the artist in 1927.

Bibliography:
Hayes (cat. no. 147).

134.

GEORGE WILLIAM JOY

(1844–1925)

The Bayswater Omnibus [29.166]
1895
Oil on canvas, 120.6 x 172.5 cm
Not signed or dated

THIS LATE Victorian painting shows a group of passengers inside an omnibus; among the advertisements above the windows is one for Pears' Soap. The omnibus would have been horse-drawn. Motorised omnibuses did not appear until the early 1900s and came into common use only around 1912–13.

The artist described the characters in the vehicle as follows:

> In the farthest corner sits a poor anxious mother of children, her foot propped on an untidy bundle; beside her, full of kindly thoughts about her, sits a fashionable young woman; next to her the City man, absorbed in his paper; whilst a little milliner, band-box in hand, presses past the blue-eyed, wholesome-looking nurse in the doorway.

The sitters were: the artist's wife (the young mother) and their daughter Rosalind, the donor of the picture (the small girl); a policeman's baby; Miss L'Amy, a friend (the fashionable young woman); Colonel Moutray Read, a cousin (the City man); and the same professional model for the nurse and milliner. Joy also recorded that he borrowed an omnibus from the London General Omnibus Company during his work on the painting. A hansom cab appears in the background, and the omnibus is evidently passing Hyde Park or Kensington Gardens. In *Sketches by Boz* (1835–6) Charles Dickens had highlighted the element of competition between these two forms of transport in 'The Last Cab Driver and the First Omnibus Cad'.

By the time this work was painted the Underground which had been introduced in 1863 was well established and the omnibus was no longer the only form of group transport. This partly explains the general airiness of the composition, in contrast with earlier paintings which depict severely crowded carriages – for instance William Maw Egley's *Omnibus Life in London* (1859, Tate Gallery) or John Morgan's *One of the People – Gladstone in an Omnibus* (1885, Private Collection). However, Joy's compositional formula should be noted for the astute way in which the length of the vehicle is used rather than its cross-section.

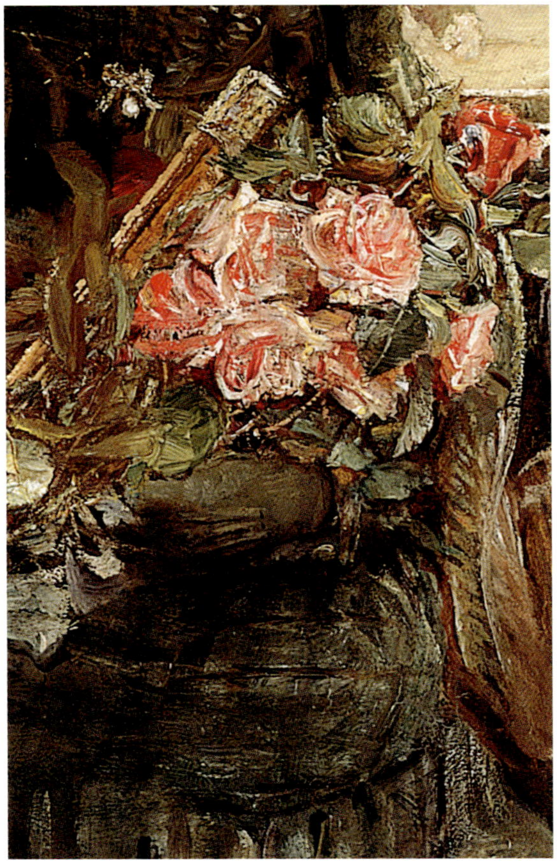

Provenance:
Lent by the artist's widow in 1929; presented by his daughter, Miss Rosalind B. Joy, in 1966.

Bibliography:
Hayes (cat. no. 60); *The Work of George W. Joy*, 1904, pp25–5 and 47, plate 10; Graham Reynolds, *Painters of the Victorian Scene*, 1953, p95, fig. 86; Jeremy Maas, *Victorian Painters*, 1969, p239 and repro. p240; Christopher Wood, *Victorian Panorama*, 1976, pp217–9; Terry Friedman, *Great Paintings of Victorian Daily Life*, exhibition catalogue, Leeds City Art Galleries, 1986; Jean Dethier, *La Ville Moderne en Europe 1870–1996*, exhibition catalogue, Museum of Contemporary Art, Tokyo, pp82–3.

Exhibited:
Royal Academy, 1895 (524) as *The Bayswater 'bus;* Paris Salon, 1896 (1098).

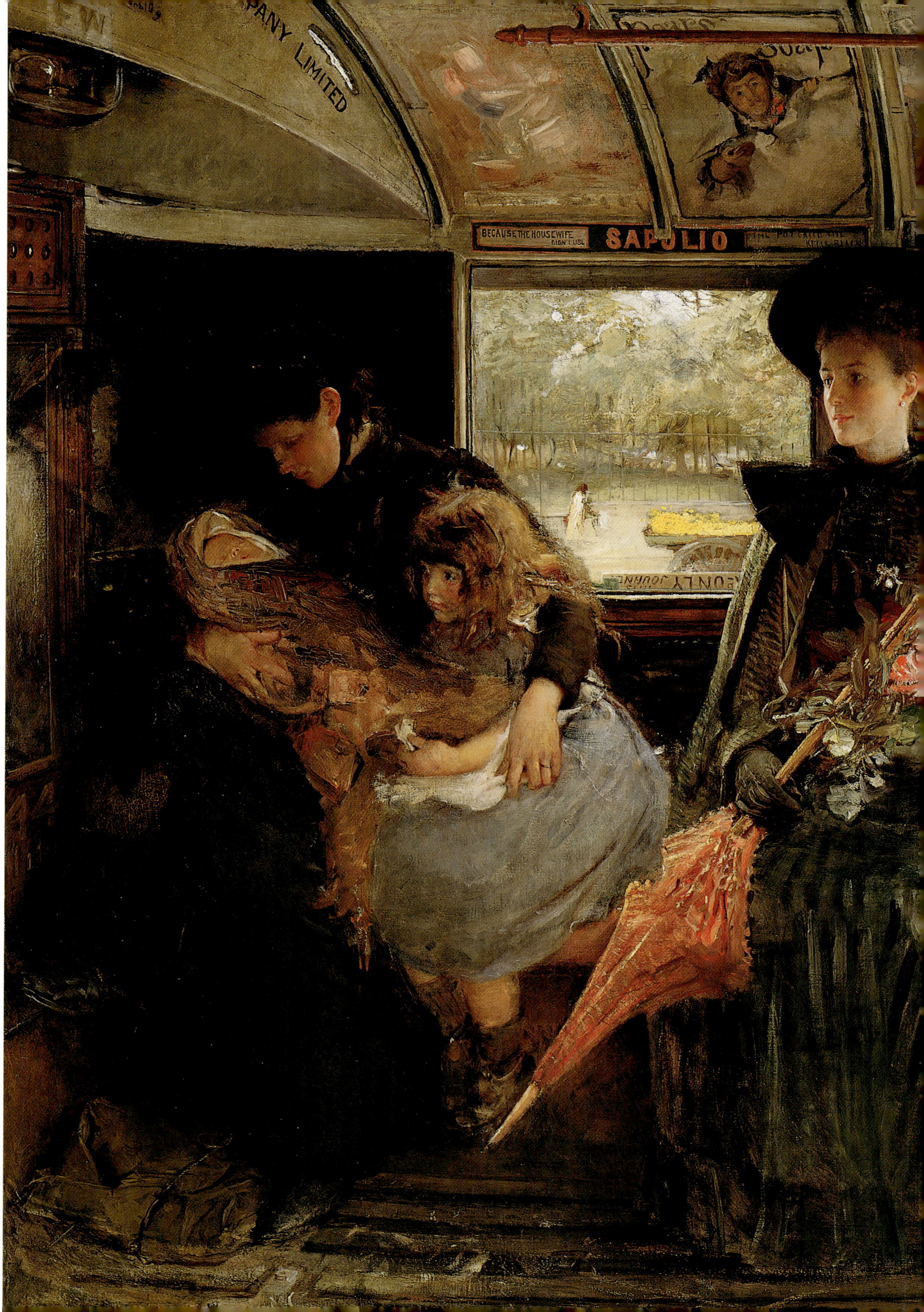
PANY LIMITED
BECAUSE THE HOUSEWIFE
SAPOLIO

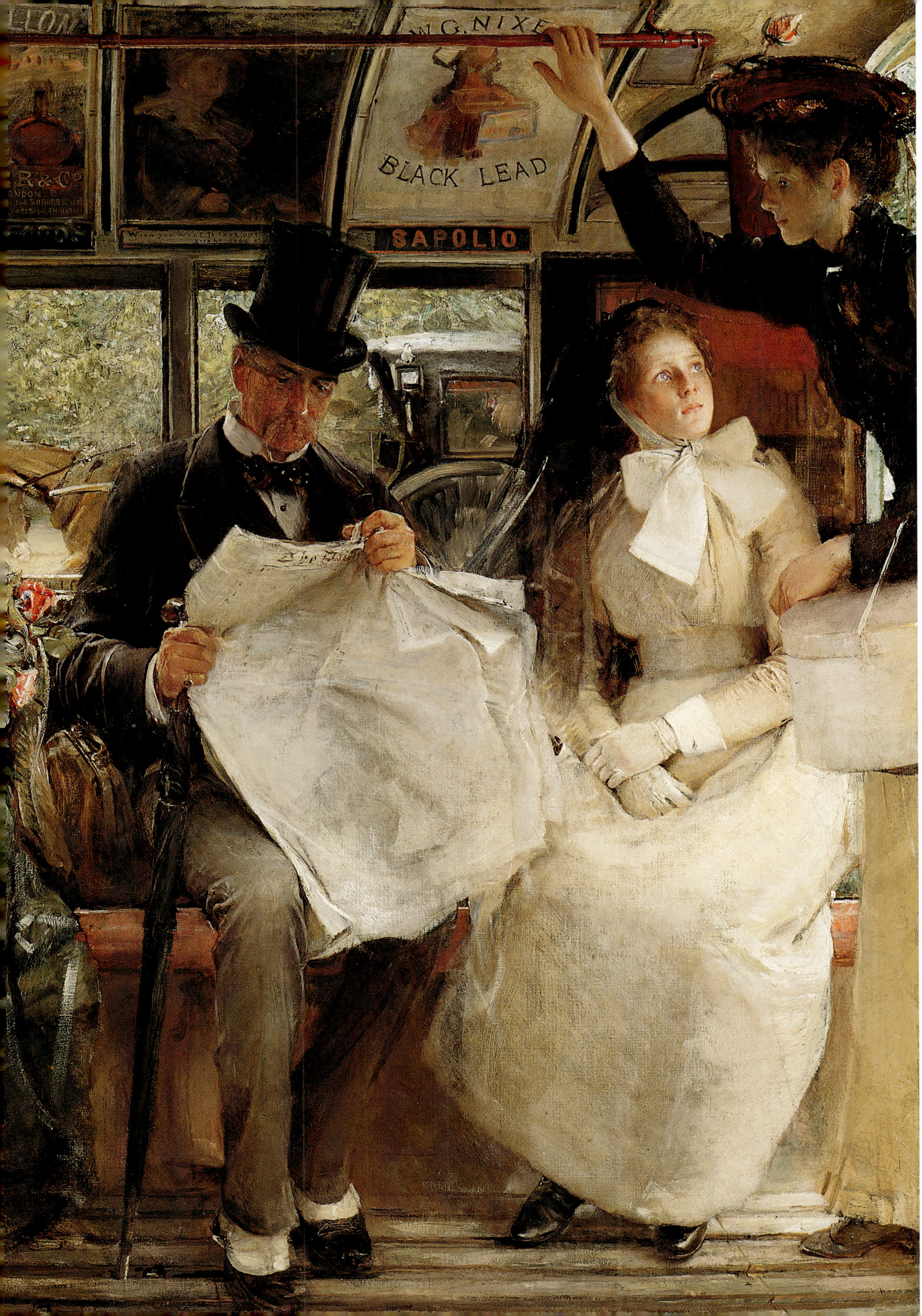
BLACK LEAD
SAPOLIO

Provenance:
Given to Mr Robson (owner of the shop) by the artist; presented by the Misses Robson in 1938.

Bibliography:
Hayes (cat. no. 4); *The New English Art Club*, NEAC centenary exhibition catalogue, Christie's, 1986, no. 116.

135.

CLARE ATWOOD

(1866–1962)

Interior of the Coach-Wheelwright's Shop at 4½ Marshall Street, Soho [38.109/1]
*c.*1897
Oil on canvas, 40.6 x 50 cm
Signed bottom left: *Clare Atwood*

FIVE MEN are seen busily at work in the Marshall Street shop. The man in the left foreground is making spokes while the workers in the middle ground are fitting spokes and fellows to the hubs of wheels. The two smiths at the back are forging iron tyres and shrinking them on to the wheels (this was done by 'shooting' the wheels into cold water). The painting thus records almost a factory process, but places emphasis on the craftsmanship element rather than on the machinery, which has not been recorded here (one would normally expect mechanical saws, for instance).

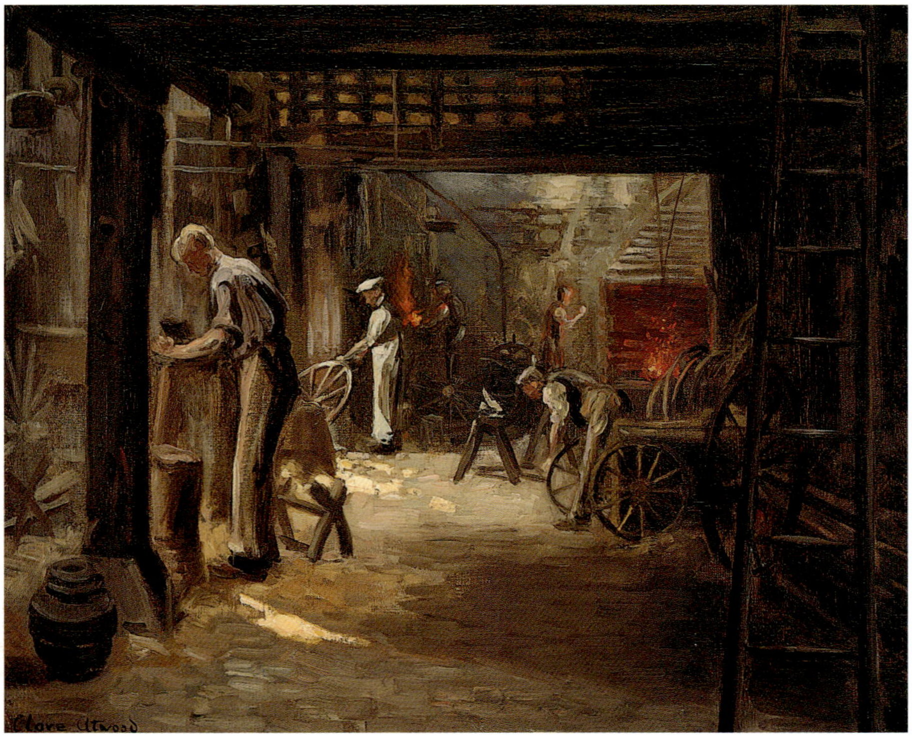

This workshop, owned by George Robson, supplied the wheels for the funeral car of the Duke of Wellington, the household carriages of Queen Victoria, and the state landau of Edward VII, all of which were designed and made by Hooper and Company. Hoopers' had their own small wheelshop in Chelsea, but wheels of greater size than usual were normally ordered from outside wheelmakers, and Robson's name appears frequently in Hoopers' records as a maker and supplier (in this connection, notice the massive hub bottom left). The Marshall Street workshop began to lose its standing and clientele when iron-rimmed wheels were superseded first by solid rubber tyres, and then by pneumatic tyres, and it was finally closed down in 1906. The premises, in use as warehouses until the 1960s, have now been demolished, and a prestige high-rise building, Stirling Court, now stands on the site, but the carriage entrance still exists.

The painting may be compared to the work by the Newlyn painter Albert Chevalier Tayler of *The Shipwright's Workshop*, 1902 (NEAC catalogue, p30).

136.

MARY EDITH DURHAM

(1863–1944)

Queen Victoria's Diamond Jubilee

[A 24382]

1897

Oil on panel, 26.6 x 20.9 cm

Signed and dated bottom left:

ME Durham 97

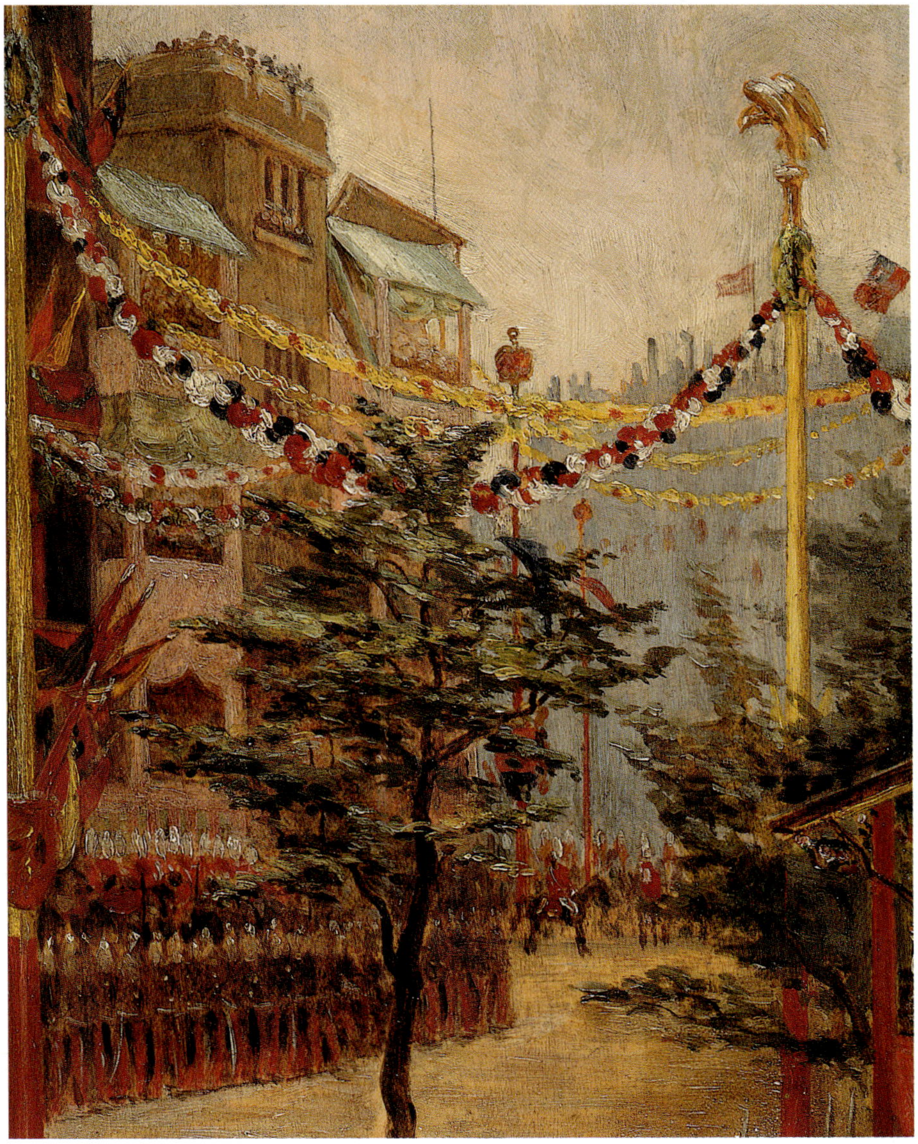

AN IMPRESSION of the decorations along the processional route for Queen Victoria's Diamond Jubilee, 22 June 1897, taken from Borough Road, Lambeth, and looking westwards towards St George's Circus. Examples of the type of stands erected in front of the buildings along the route can be seen on the left, and Life Guards and other troops are shown lining the road, awaiting the procession.

Unlike the Golden Jubilee, to which the crowned heads of Europe were all invited, the Diamond Jubilee was essentially an Imperial occasion. Every Dominion and colony sent a detachment of troops and, as in 1887, the opportunity was taken to hold an Imperial Conference: this was attended by fifteen premiers under the presidency of Joseph Chamberlain. The procession, in which Queen Victoria rode in an open landau, travelled from Buckingham Palace to St Paul's Cathedral for an open-air Thanksgiving Service, and thence past the Mansion House, over London Bridge, and back to the Palace through Southwark and Lambeth. The Queen recorded the occasion in a letter in the following terms: 'A never-to-be-forgotten day. No one ever, I believe, has met with such an ovation as was given to me, passing through those six miles of streets, including Constitution Hill.'

This painting captures some of the energy to which the Queen alludes and is in complete contrast with the official record of this occasion commissioned by her from the painter John Charlton. The latter chose the highlight of the procession, the arrival at St Paul's Cathedral, and incorporated over a hundred figures drawn from life into a work that occupied him for about fourteen months.

Provenance:
Presented by the artist in 1922.

Bibliography:
Hayes (cat. no. 37); Oliver Millar, *The Victorian Pictures in the Collection of Her Majesty The Queen*, 1992, pp47–50.

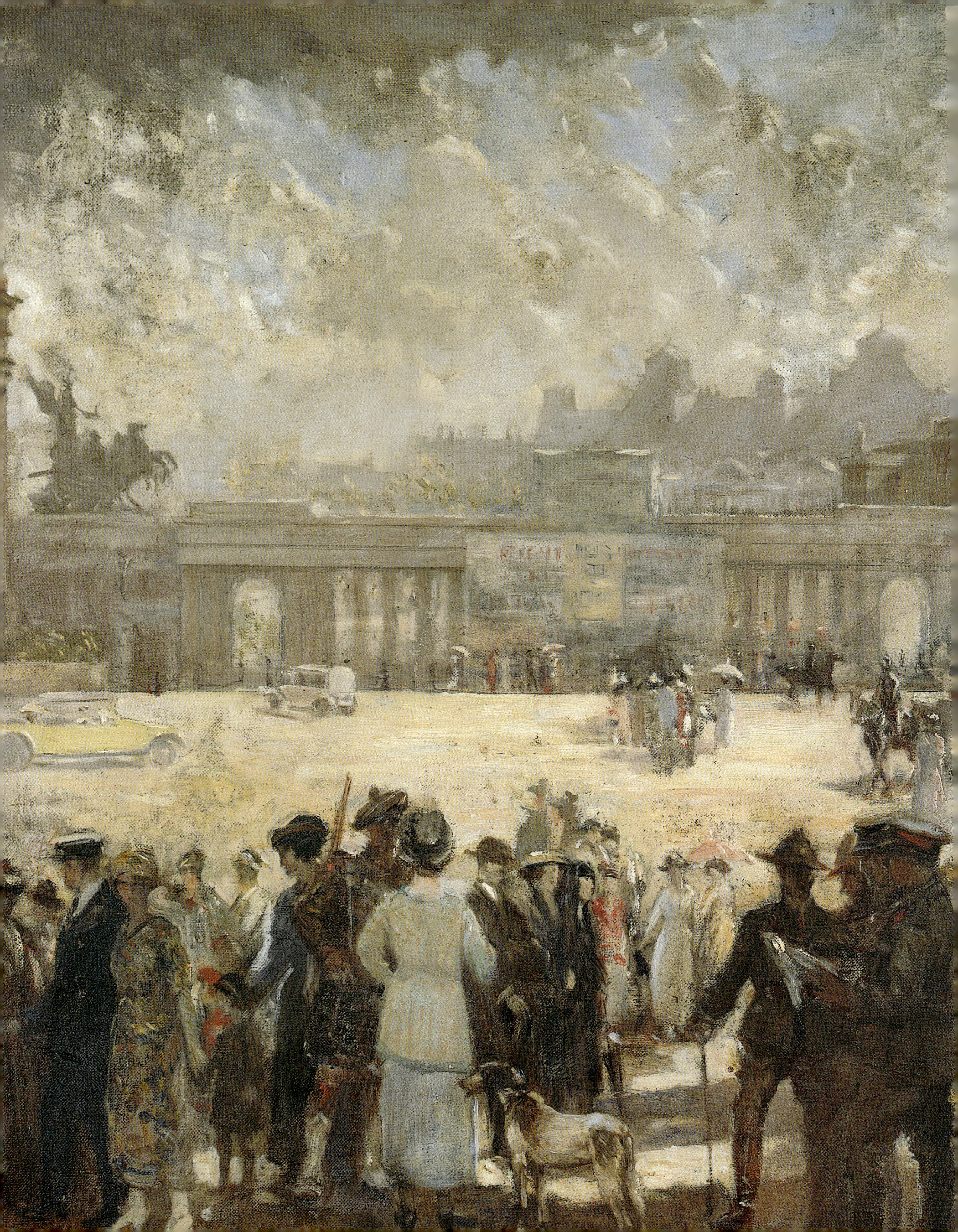

Early Twentieth Century

THE PERIOD dawns in 1901 with glitter and panache under fun-loving Edward VII. Paradoxically, images of London show a more domestic city, reflecting the shift to the suburbs, although there is a continuing interest in night life. The two world wars, which affected the lives of so many Londoners, contrast artistically: the Great War barely makes an impact on representations of the capital, while the bombing of London during the Blitz is exploited over and over again by large numbers of painters attracted by the sublime cityscapes which resulted from this destruction. Between the two wars there is a search among many painters for a more serene image of London, perhaps best illustrated by Algernon Newton, as well as a search for moral ideals, as exemplified by the goals of the Artists' International Association.

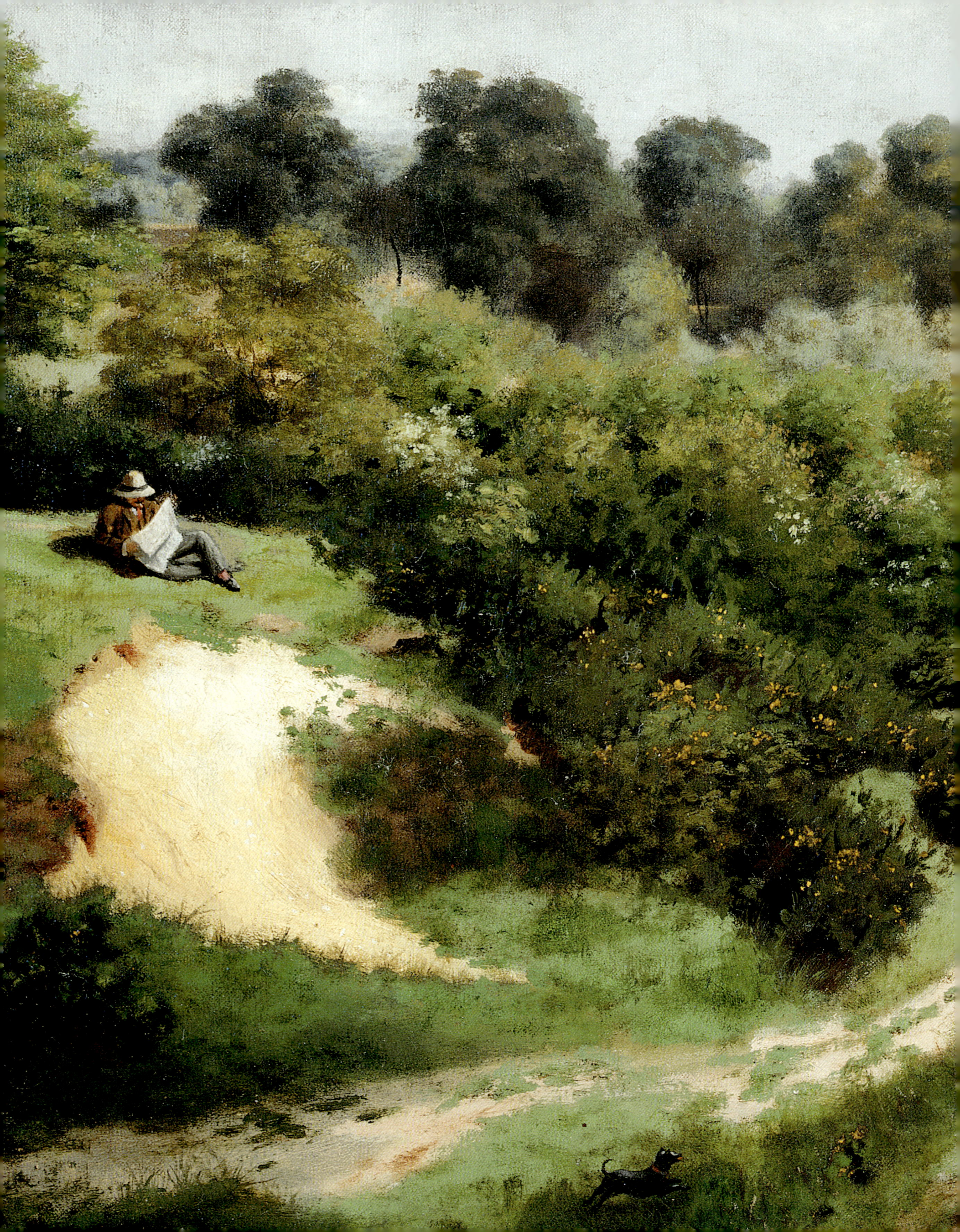

EDWARDIAN LANDSCAPE

THE PAINTINGS which have been grouped under this heading reflect, first, a strong interest in urban *landscape*, ranging from back gardens and residential squares (Gore) to pleasure gardens (Blanche) and parks and commons (Brewtnall and Walker). The varied techniques and approaches to painting they exhibit reflect some of the complexity of the artistic scene at the turn of the century.

Landscape painting in the city

The depiction of London parks and gardens was not exactly a new phenomenon at the turn of the century. The genre is well charted in the Museum's collection, from the earliest painted view of a London garden, that of Old Corney House, in Jacob Knyff's *Chiswick from the River*, to the busy scene of John Ritchie's *Summer Day in Hyde Park*, and includes the rare records of the garden of 10 Downing Street in the eighteenth century and the Regency planting scheme of Leicester Square.

The first generation of the Pre-Raphaelites in the 1850s marked a turning point in the history of London landscape[1] by moving away from the idea of using outdoor settings for social activities – a theme that was born from the fashionable eighteenth-century promenade[2] – and breaking new ground in the depiction of the seasons, the parks and the commons. The French Impressionists gave added impetus to this trend with their advocation of *plein-air* painting. Claude Monet and Camille Pissarro came to London spurred on by the challenge of capturing its atmosphere in paint.[3] The creation of the New English Art Club (NEAC) in 1886 gave a platform to some fifteen artists who had trained or partly trained in France or who were paying formative visits to Paris.[4]

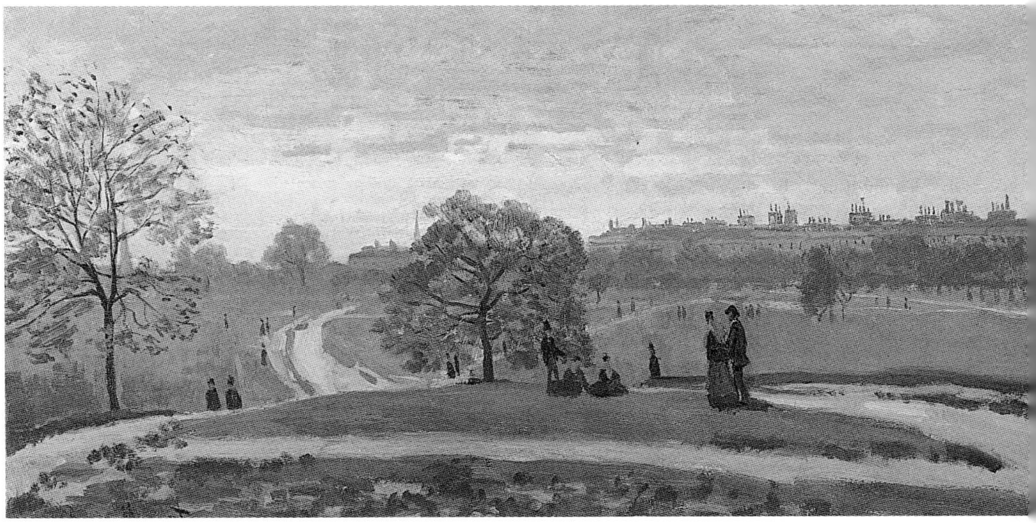

Claude Monet (1840–1926)
Hyde Park, 1871
Oil on canvas
Museum of Art, Rhode Island School of Design; Gift of Mrs Murray S. Danforth.
Photography by Del Bogart.

However, in Edwardian times it still took a courageous (or an amateur) painter to paint landscapes in rather than outside London. Artistic glamour was indeed clearly located elsewhere; the more fashionable contemporaries of Claude Walker (cat. no. 143) or Hamilton Hay (cat. no. 145) had been following the example of the French at Pont Aven and forming artists' colonies - the NEAC in the Wye Valley, and the Newlyn Group in Cornwall. Artists were not alone in their longing for greener pastures. In an age which was witnessing the creation of garden cities, many Londoners themselves were moving out to the peaceful, pollution-free suburbs.

There is therefore a relatively modest group of images, not always oil paintings, of pure landscape associated with London, by those optimistic souls who, based in the capital, still wanted to paint landscape, using parks, squares, commons, any lingering green in the centre and, of course, the suburbs. The Thames continued to be a source of inspiration for many painters. Théodore Roussel's *Battersea Asleep* of around 1905 echoes the work of Whistler,

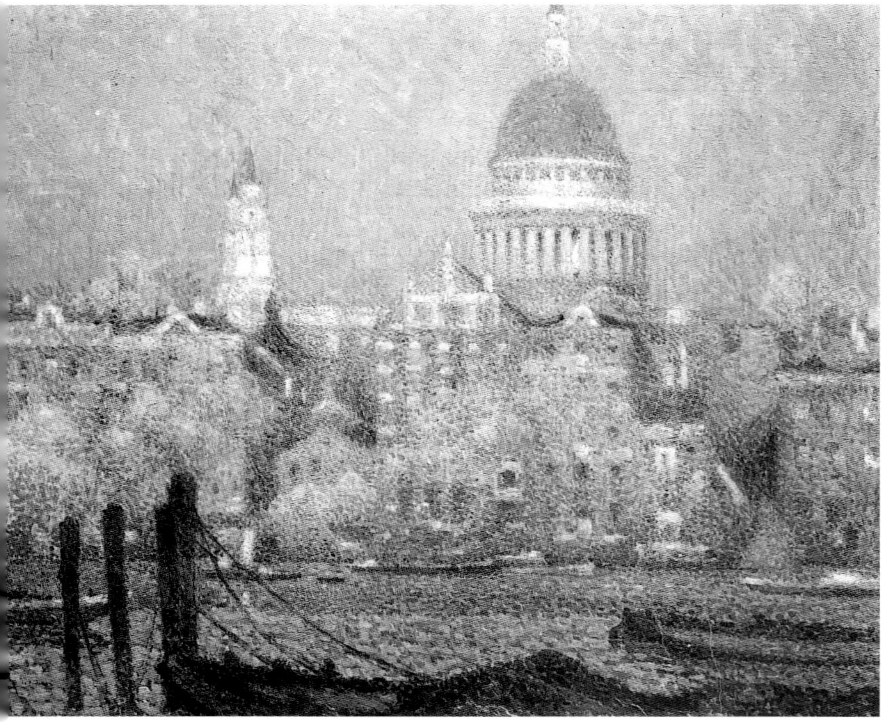

Henri le Sidaner (1862–1939)
*St Paul's from the River, Morning Sun, c.*1906–7
Board of Trustees of the National Museums and Galleries on Merseyside (Walker Art Gallery, Liverpool).

while the paintings of Henri le Sidaner and André Derain explore the brilliant, shimmering colours of the Post-Impressionist palette. Charles Ginner's *London Bridge* (cat. no. 147) is a good, but isolated, example on this subject in the collection.

The London Impressionists

Dominated by the Parisian art scene, London was on the whole a little slow to respond to the French avant-garde. Although the NEAC owed its origins to French inspiration, those artists who from 1889 called themselves the London Impressionists (after the exhibition at the Goupil Gallery in December 1889)[5] worked more in the tradition of the realist Edouard Manet than the Impressionist Claude Monet, and barely adopted the divisionist technique which has come to be identified with Impressionism. (Only very briefly, some twenty years later, was this approach adopted by some of the artists who were to form the Camden Town Group, most notably, perhaps, Spencer Gore. And no sooner was the Impressionist style adopted than it was dropped again in favour of Post-Impressionist techniques.)

Despite the confusion of different styles, schools, groups – either foreign or native – three clearly defined approaches emerge in Edwardian London: the 'atmospheric', the French Impressionist and the Post-Impressionist, the last two merging into one with the Camden Town painters. Both trends of the Camden Town Group are illustrated in the Museum's collection (see cat. nos 144 and 146).

Atmospheric London

This trend among London topographical artists stemmed from a tradition more closely associated with Britain than with France. Atmosphere was, of course, at the centre of the Impressionist movement, but the London atmospheric painters tackled it in a different manner. They were not interested in depicting the ways in which it could break down the fabric of our environment, as in Monet's series on Waterloo bridge or le Sidaner's post-impressionist treatment of *St Paul's from the Thames,* they wanted instead to find a realist and romantic way of rendering atmosphere veiling and embellishing urban structures. In the words of the delightful Yoshio Markino:

> Perhaps the real colours of some buildings in London might be rather crude. But this crude colour is so fascinating in the mists. For instance, that house in front of my window is painted in black and yellow. When I came here last summer I laughed at its ugly colour. But now the winter fogs cover it and the harmony of its colour is most wonderful.[6]

These painters tackled the most visually striking manifestations of atmosphere – sunsets, fog, seasons, night – which can be traced to the first generation of the Pre-Raphaelites. Watercolour was sometimes the most appropriate medium, but oil, though less flexible, was also used (cat. nos 140, 148 and 151). The trend is championed by James McNeill Whistler as well as watercolourists such as Herbert Marshall, Albert Goodwin and Dudley Heath.[7]

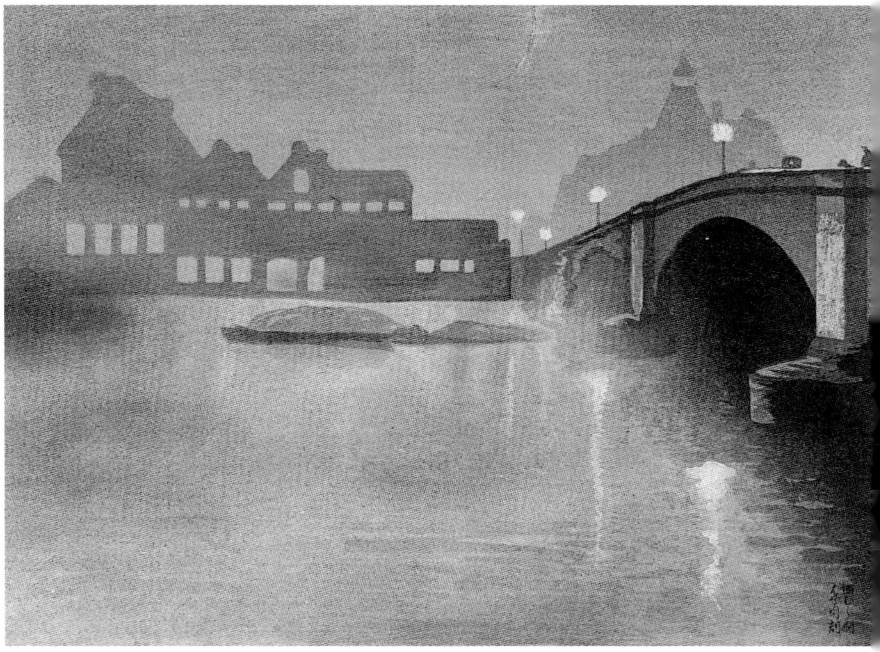

Yoshio Markino (1874–*c.*1938)
Battersea Bridge, 1929
Lithograph
The Museum of London.

The Camden Town painters

The Camden Town Group was short-lived (1911–14) and composed of sixteen artist members.[8] The London art scene in the early years of the century was polarised between the New English Art Club and, from 1907, its avant-garde offshoot led by Walter Sickert, the Fitzroy Group. The latter was grudgingly tolerated by the NEAC until the really subversive show Roger Fry organised on Post-Impressionism in 1910 again provoked outraged reactions. The Camden Town Group, born from the ranks of the Fitzroy Group, was purged of its 'weaker' members, including all the women; Sickert and his friends were now perceived as more able to stage a muscular response to the dominant and stifling conservatism of the NEAC.

Walter Sickert, Spencer Gore, Charles Ginner and Robert Bevan, the four artists represented here, were all founder members of the Camden Town Group and also belonged to the Fitzroy Group. However, the painting scene should not be reduced to the level of political group tactics. Art historians have recognised, beyond these somewhat artificial groupings, the readily shared characteristics of Camden Town painting between 1905 and 1920. As painters struggled to accommodate the strong influence first of French Impressionism, then of Post-Impressionism and even Cubism, their works – such as those in the Museum's collection – reflected to some extent the various 'battles' and stylistic transformations that took place in the early years of the twentieth century. The two works by Spencer Gore illustrate, in one case, his Impressionist phase, in the other his Post-Impressionist approach. The contrast (also perceived as conflict) between Charles Ginner's neo-realism ('The Thickest Painter in London')[9] and Sickert's 'thin' painting can also be observed.

The questions of technique and style which are so often discussed in relation to this period greatly influenced the size and content of paintings. In the Edwardian period paintings are very noticeably smaller in order to capture scenes with greater spontaneity. The rebellion against the great (and artificial) manner of polished Victorian painting in London or Salon painting in France drove artists to choose unassuming domestic subjects – Gore's own back garden or Robert Bevan's street.

Questions of style, composition and palette also gave rise to a dilemma: reality versus art. Monet noted: 'Without the fog London would not be a beautiful city. It is the fog which gives it its magnificent amplitude... How could the English painters of the nineteenth century have painted bricks that they did not see?' The Camden Town painters did not see the fog either, or if they did, they did not paint it, and their vision of London was opposed to that of the 'atmospheric' painters. As a result, our vision of Edwardian London may be warped, and it certainly seems somewhat schizophrenic, but it is also enriched.

1. *London's Pride*, Mireille Galinou (ed.), 1990, pp209–12.
2. Celina Fox, *Londoners*, 1987, pp77–86.
3. *The Impressionists in London*, exhibition catalogue, Arts Council, 1973.
4. *The New English Art Club,* exhibition catalogue, Christie's, 1986. Also see Edward Morris and Amanda McKay, 'British Art Students in Paris 1814–1890: Demand and Supply', in *Apollo*, February 1992.
5. Their names were Francis Bate, Fred Brown, Francis James, Paul Maitland, Théodore Roussel, Bernhard Sickert, Walter Sickert, Sidney Parr, Philip Wilson Steer and George Thomson. See Wendy Baron, *The Camden Town Group*, 1979, p73 (note 3).
6. Yoshio Markino, *A Japanese in London*, 1910, p189
7. Mireille Galinou, 'The Discreet Charm of Edwardian London', in *The Antique Collector*, December 1986.
8. The story of this movement is told by Wendy Baron in *The Camden Town Group,* 1979, and in *The Painters of Camden Town 1905–20*, exhibition catalogue, Christie's, 1988.
9. The phrase was coined by Sickert in the periodical *New Age*, 18 June 1914.

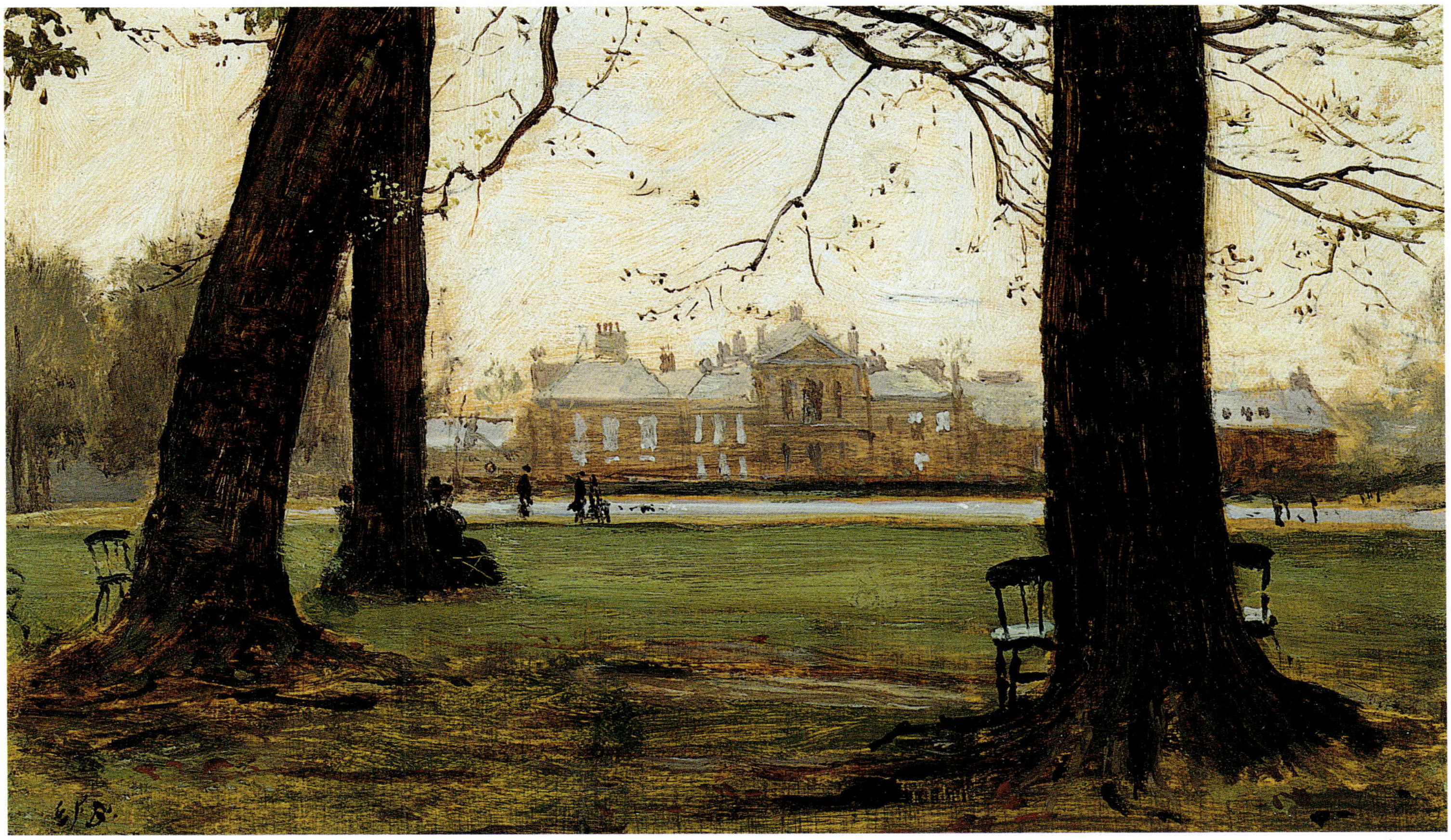

137.

EDWARD FREDERICK BREWTNALL
(1846–1902)

Kensington Palace [68.73]
*c.*1900
Oil on board, 12 x 21 cm
Signed with initials bottom left: *EFB*

THIS SMALL painted sketch (the image above shows it almost full size) showing Kensington Palace from the east was one of a pair and it captures well the soft and tranquil light of early evening on a spring day in London.

Parliament agreed to vote thirty-six thousand pounds for the restoration of Kensington Palace provided that the public was given access to the State Apartments. As a result Queen Victoria announced their proposed opening in January 1898 and the Apartments were opened on 24 May 1899. This may have acted as an incentive on Brewtnall's choice of subject. Between 1912 and 1914 the State Apartments became the home of the newly founded London Museum. (Also see cat. no. 162 for the history of Kensington Gardens.)

Although this painting was probably painted in the last decade of the nineteenth century, it belongs, at least in spirit, to the Edwardian era. With its companion piece on Kensington Gardens (see no. 9 in the *Viewpoints* catalogue) and Brewtnall's *On the Embankment*, exhibited at the Royal Academy in 1899, the work constitutes a rare example of a painting of the city in which the artist lived and worked.

Provenance:
Purchased from the Fine Art Society in 1968.

Bibliography:
Viewpoints: Landscapes by British Artists of the 18th–20th centuries, exhibition catalogue, The Fine Art Society, 1968, no. 10.

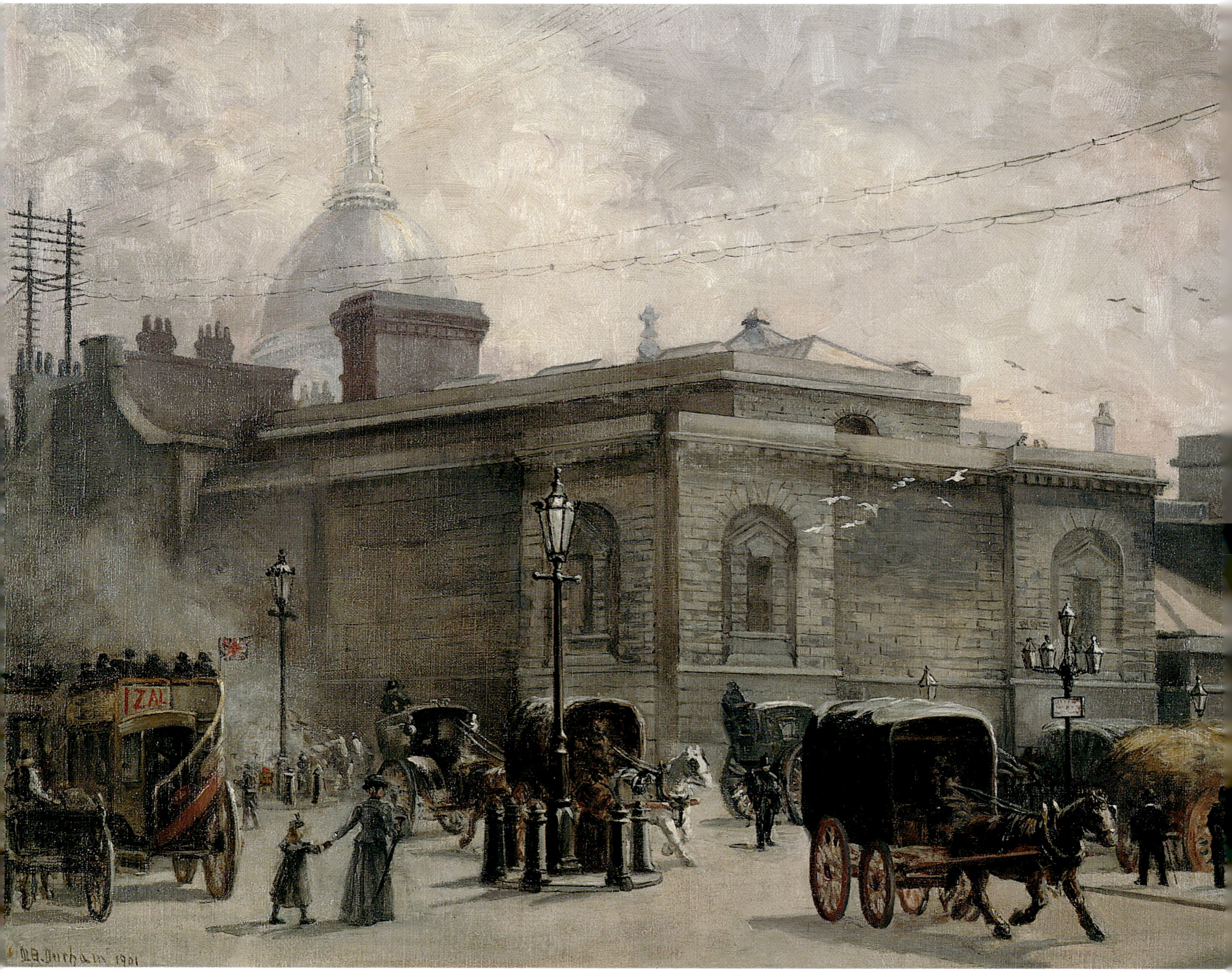
IZAL

138.

MARY EDITH DURHAM

(1863–1944)

Newgate Prison [A 24381]
1901
Oil on canvas, 45.2 x 60.7 cm
Signed and dated bottom left:
ME Durham 1901

THE VIEW is taken from the garden of St Sepulchre's Church. Newgate stood at the intersection of Giltspur Street, Newgate Street (left), Old Bailey and Skinner Street (right), but little of the busy traffic usual at this City crossroads is suggested in the picture; traffic congestion was a problem much in the minds of the authorities in these last years of the horse-drawn vehicle. Two omnibuses, of the garden-seat type, the top deck still open to the elements, are seen on the left, and hansom cabs, covered carts and a hay-cart are among other vehicles. The dome of St Paul's is seen beyond Newgate, and on the left are a couple of early telegraph poles (also see cat. no. 112).

The old Newgate Prison, a gaol for debtors (up to 1815) and for felons, had became so insanitary by the mid-eighteenth century that it was condemned, and the building seen here was designed by George Dance the Younger in 1770–8. It was his first major assignment after succeeding to his father's post as Clerk of the City Works in 1768, and perhaps his greatest work in architecture. The massiveness of the rusticated walls and motifs such as the aedicules set in arched niches, were evidently based on Giulio Romano, whose buildings he would have studied during his sojourn in Italy. The prison was badly damaged during the Gordon Riots of 1780, but later repaired and altered. The first execution held within its walls took place in December 1783, a month after the last to be held at Tyburn. Newgate was demolished in 1902, shortly after this picture was painted, and E. W. Mountford's neo-baroque Central Criminal Court (the Old Bailey) was built on the site.

Provenance:
Presented by the artist in 1922.

Bibliography:
Hayes (cat. no. 39).

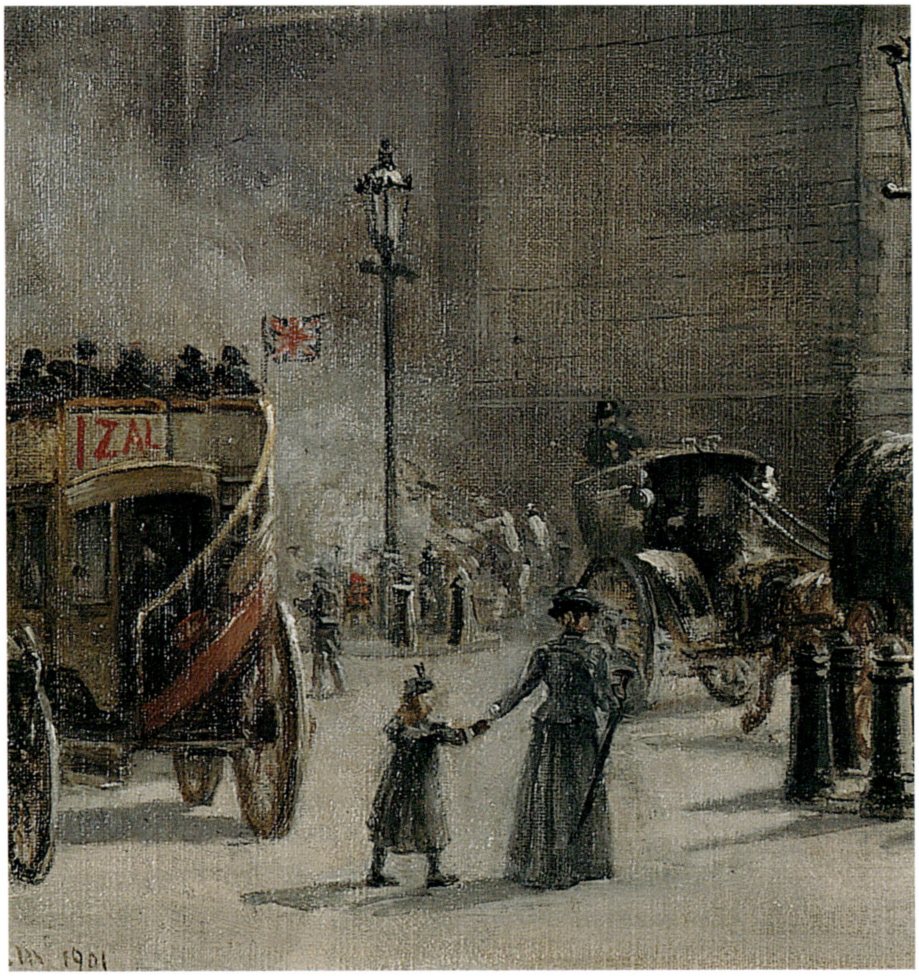

Provenance:
Sotheby's, 26 September 1985 (186), bt Michael Parking; Lady Charlotte Bonham-Carter in March 1986; bequeathed to the Museum in 1990.

Bibliography:
Malcolm Warner, *The Image of London*, exhibition catalogue, Barbican Art Gallery, 1987, nos 225–7; *London's Pride*, Mireille Galinou (ed.), 1990, p156; *The Crystal Palace Sydenham*, auction catalogue, 28 November 1911, Knight, Frank and Rutley (copy in Museum of London Library); Graham Reeves, *Palace of the People*, Bromley Library Service, 1986.

139.
JACQUES EMILE BLANCHE
(1861–1942)

Crystal Palace, Sydenham [90.344/1]
1907
Oil on board, 50 x 63.1 cm
Signed with initials bottom right: *J.E.Bl.*
On the back:
Crystal Palace Sydenham/Juin 1907/J. E. Blanche/William Stout's/Knightsbridge S.W.

THIS VIEW of the Crystal Palace is taken from the south-east, just above the railway station – Crystal Palace Low Level – linked to the main building by a long glass corridor. The circular fountain in the middle ground was one from a pair of water temples which formed part of the spectacular system of fountains at Sydenham. An early motorcar appears to be driving past. By the time the Crystal Palace was sold at auction in 1911 (see bibliography), this had become the standard view; it featured as a photograph on the cover and the frontispiece of the sale publication.

The Crystal Palace, built by Joseph Paxton for the Great Exhibition of 1851 (see cat. no. 90), stood in Hyde Park until 1852 when it was dismantled. It was purchased by a private company (founded by Paxton), transported to a new site in Sydenham (see cat. no. 118) and re-erected. The rebuilt version differed from the Hyde Park structure in three respects: the roof of the nave was now arched rather than flat (and forty feet higher); three transepts (rather than one) were introduced, with recesses in the garden fronts – the north transept (which was destroyed by fire in December 1866), and the central and south transepts visible here; two great Water Towers, shown here, at each end of the building were erected to raise the tanks from which the high jets of the Great Fountains operated.

The new Palace opened on 10 June 1854 and was conceived as a series of Fine Art Courts – Egyptian, Greek, Roman, Alhambra, Byzantine, Romanesque, Medieval, Renaissance, Pompeian and Chinese – said to represent the 'most comprehensive series of Art-illustrations of their kind in the world'. The winter and summer pleasure gardens were fee-paying and the venue for various forms of entertainment, notably fireworks and concerts. The 182-acre grounds included terraces, lakes, fountains and waterfalls, cricket, football and tennis grounds with their pavilions, a maze, a bowling green and bandstands.

The building at Crystal Palace was totally destroyed by fire on the night of 30 November 1936. The twenty-nine prehistoric animals, devised and cast by Waterhouse Hawkins with the help of the biologist Professor Richard Owen, have survived in the gardens.

Jacques Emile Blanche returned to this subject in 1927 when he produced an oil sketch of the Crystal Palace taken from a different viewpoint (Sotheby's, 25 May 1977, Lot 97).

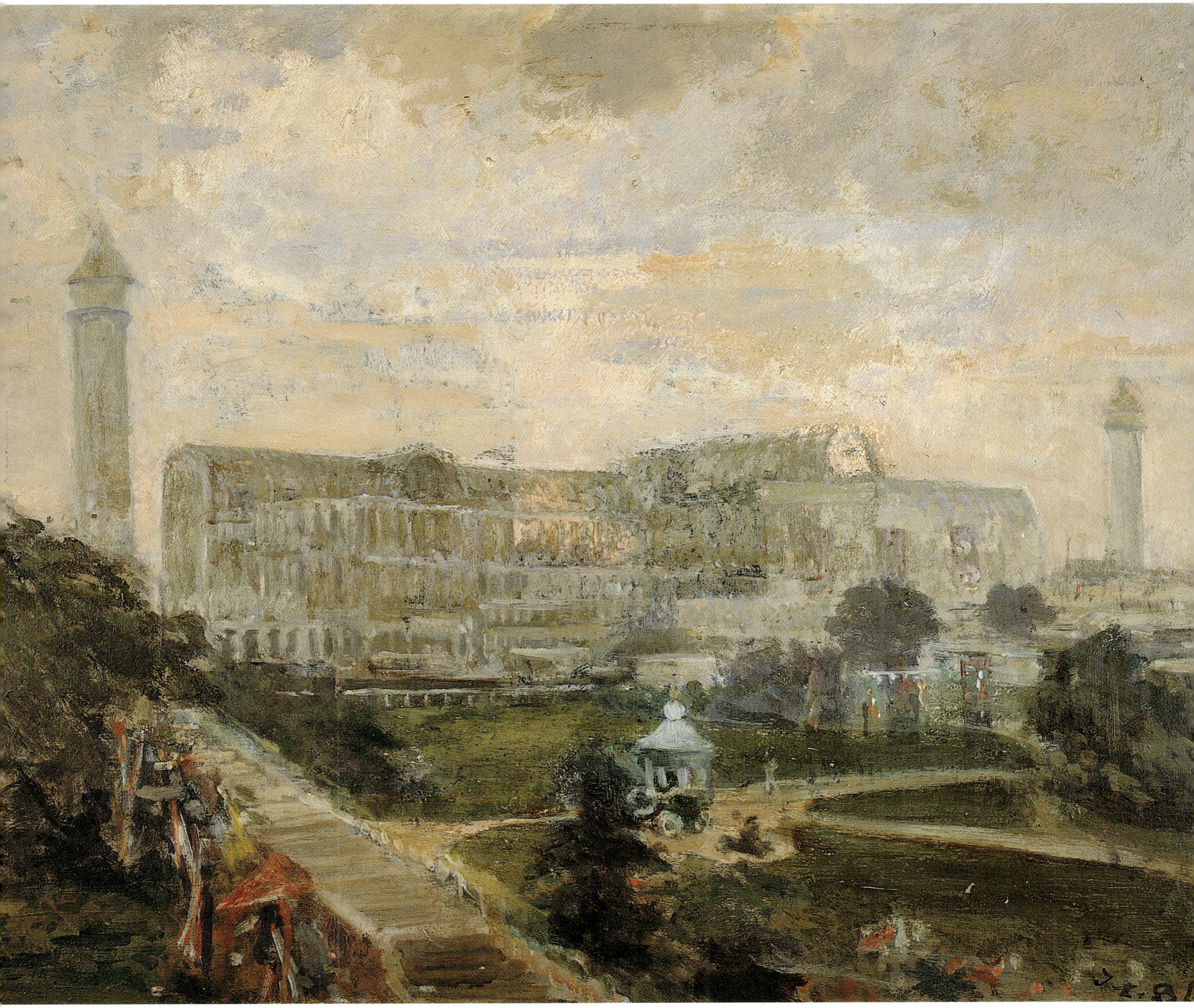

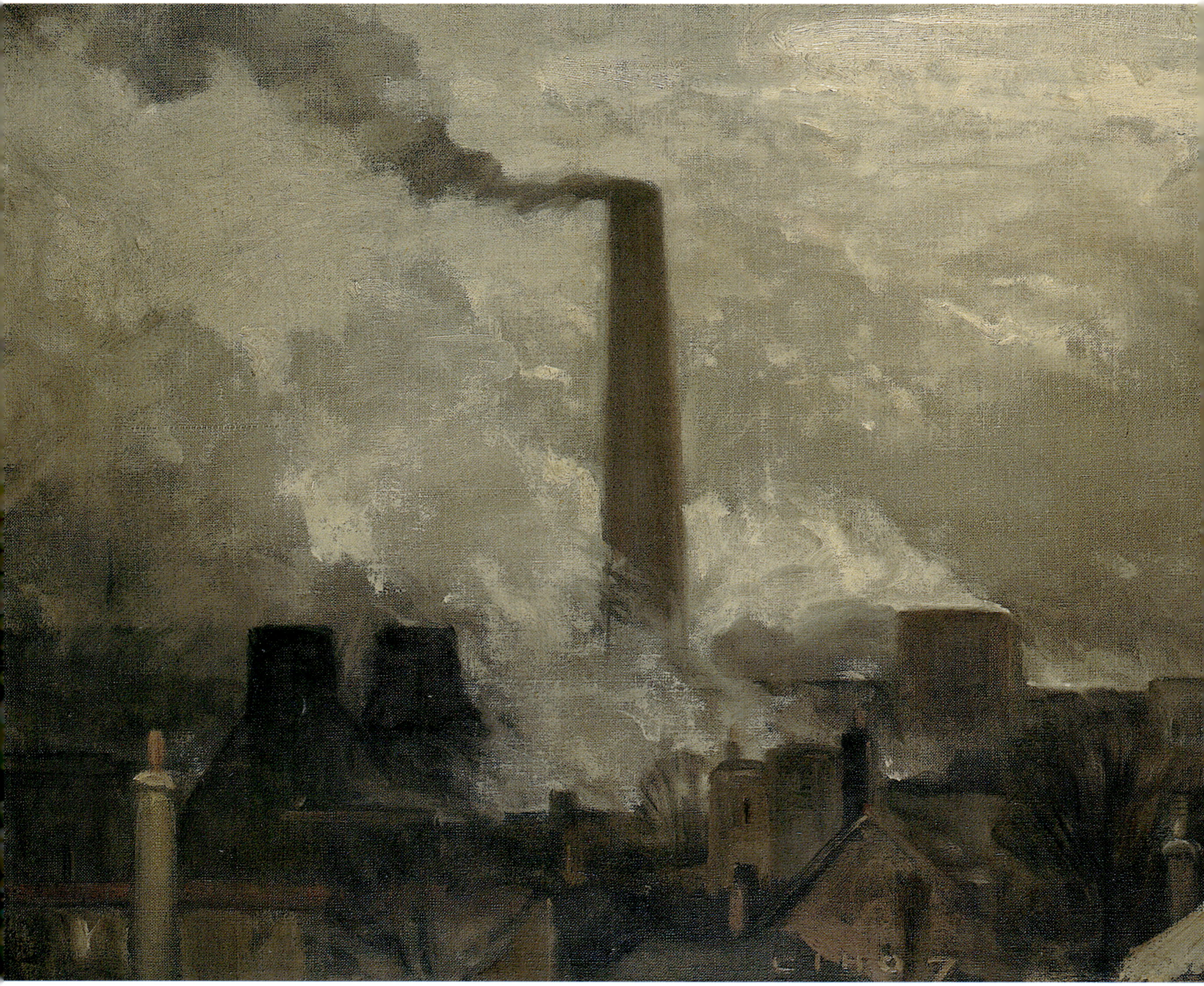

140.

SIR CHARLES JOHN HOLMES
(1868–1936)

The Wood Lane Power Station [37.205]
1907
Oil on canvas, 44.7 x 80 cm
Signed and dated bottom centre: *CJH 07*
Inscribed on the back: *THE POWER STATION. LADBROKE GROVE. 1907.*

THIS VIEW over the rooftops of the power station in Wood Lane, Shepherd's Bush, was taken from the artist's house, 73 Ladbroke Grove. The artist described this painting as his 'first elaborate effort at an Industrial subject', and it was executed at the beginning of what he considered his 'best period', from 1907 to 1913.

Wood Lane Power Station, which supplied electricity to the Kensington area (it was built for the Kensington and Knightsbridge, and the Notting Hill, Electric Light Companies), started operation in 1900. As the earliest generating plant to provide high-voltage, three-phase generation and transmission in this country, it has a place of particular importance in the development of the industry. It was closed down in 1928 and demolished in 1979.

Provenance:
Presented by Lady Holmes in 1937.

Bibliography:
Hayes (cat. no. 54); C. J. Holmes, *Self & Partners*, 1936, p253; R. H. Parsons, *Early Days of the Power Station Industry*, 1939; Gavin Stamp and Glynn Boyde Harte, *Temples of Power*, The Cygnet Press, 1979 (for general background information); *Pictures and Drawings by Professor C. J. Holmes*, exhibition catalogue, Carfax & Co., January 1909 (20).

Provenance:
Red Cross sale, Christie's, 16 April 1915 (730) (presented by the artist), bt Sir Guy Laking for the Museum.

Bibliography:
Hayes (cat. no. 149).

Exhibited:
Royal Glasgow Institute, 1911 (501).

141.
THOMAS CANTRELL DUGDALE
(1880–1952)

A Street Scene in Chelsea [A 17003]
*c.*1907
Oil on canvas, 60.6 x 50.6 cm
Signed bottom left: *T. C. Dugdale*

A BIRD'S-EYE view of the junction of King's Road and Glebe Place, Chelsea, showing the group of early eighteenth-century houses, 213–17 King's Road, which still stands there; the premises on the right are now an antiques shop. The scene is taken from the upper floor of a building on the site of the present Lightfoot Hall (corner of King's Road and Manresa Road) on which stood various houses used as artists' studios. The artist probably painted the view from a friend's studio (Dugdale's studio was at 76 Fulham Road). An open yellow car, a van and an early motor bus, with an open upper deck and serving the number 11 route, are seen in the foreground. The costume indicates a date of about 1907.

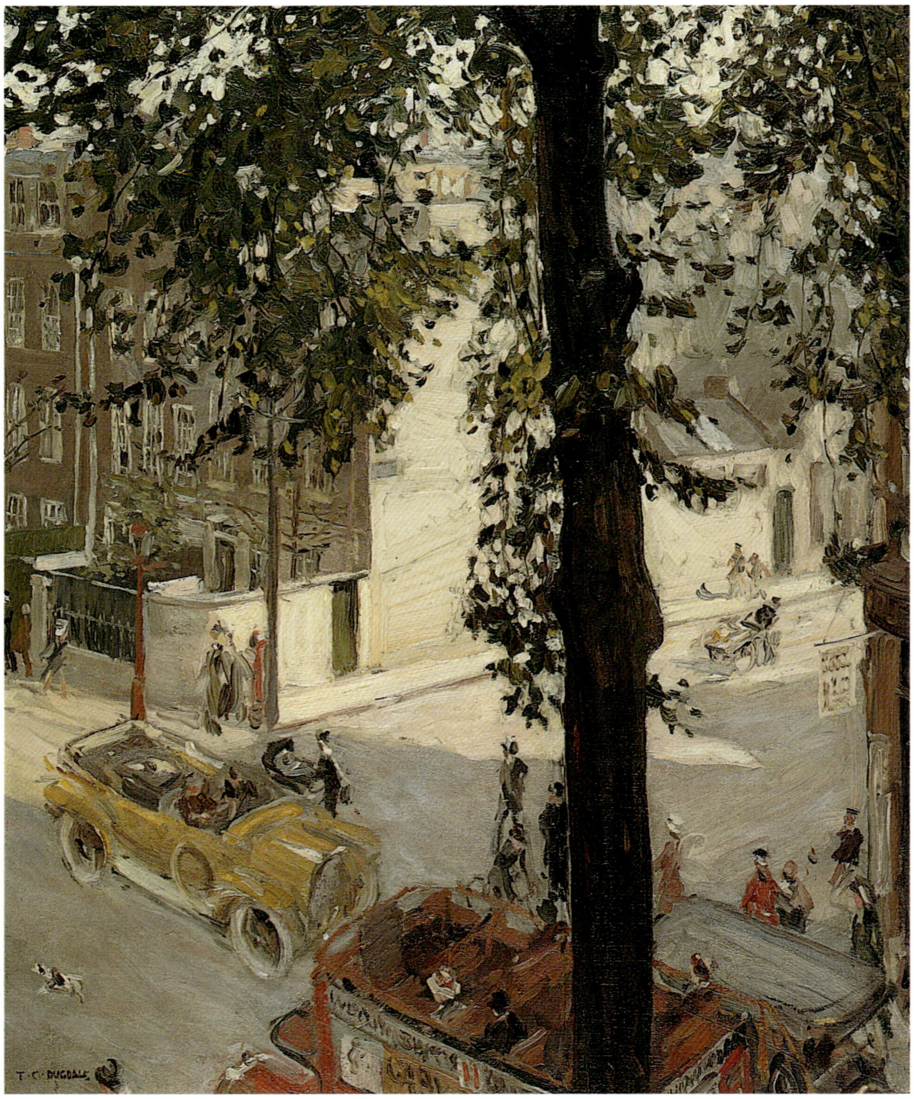

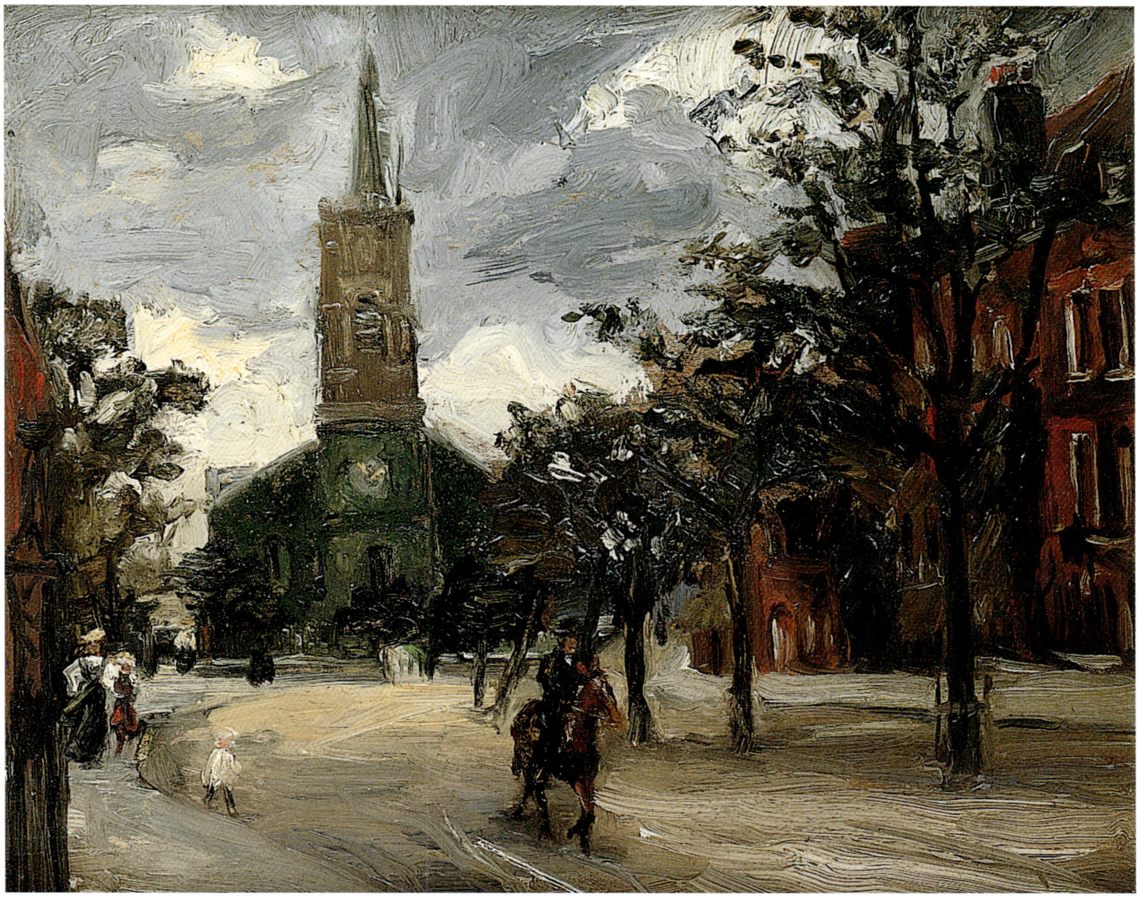

Provenance:
Babington; Sotheby's, 27 July 1960 (141), bt Colnaghi on behalf of the Museum.

Bibliography:
Hayes (cat. no. 66).

142.

SIR JOHN LAVERY
(1856–1941)

The Church of St John, Hampstead
[60.114/1]
*c.*1900–10
Oil on panel, 23.7 x 30 cm
Not signed or dated

AN IMPRESSIONISTIC sketch showing the parish church of St John, Hampstead, taken from Church Row, after the reconstruction of 1878. It was built by John Sanderson in 1745–7. A peculiar feature of the design of this church is that the tower is at the east end, and at the time of planning the alterations of 1878, it was proposed to remove it; this was fortunately opposed by an influential body of opinion, on the grounds that the tower provided an incomparable focal point at the end of Church Row.

Church Row is one of the few streets in London which is still almost entirely early eighteenth-century in character. The houses on the south side are complete, and date from about 1720; those on the north side (some of which are seen here) are less regular in design, and vary a little more in date.

The costume indicates a date of about 1900–10, and there seems no reason to doubt the attribution.

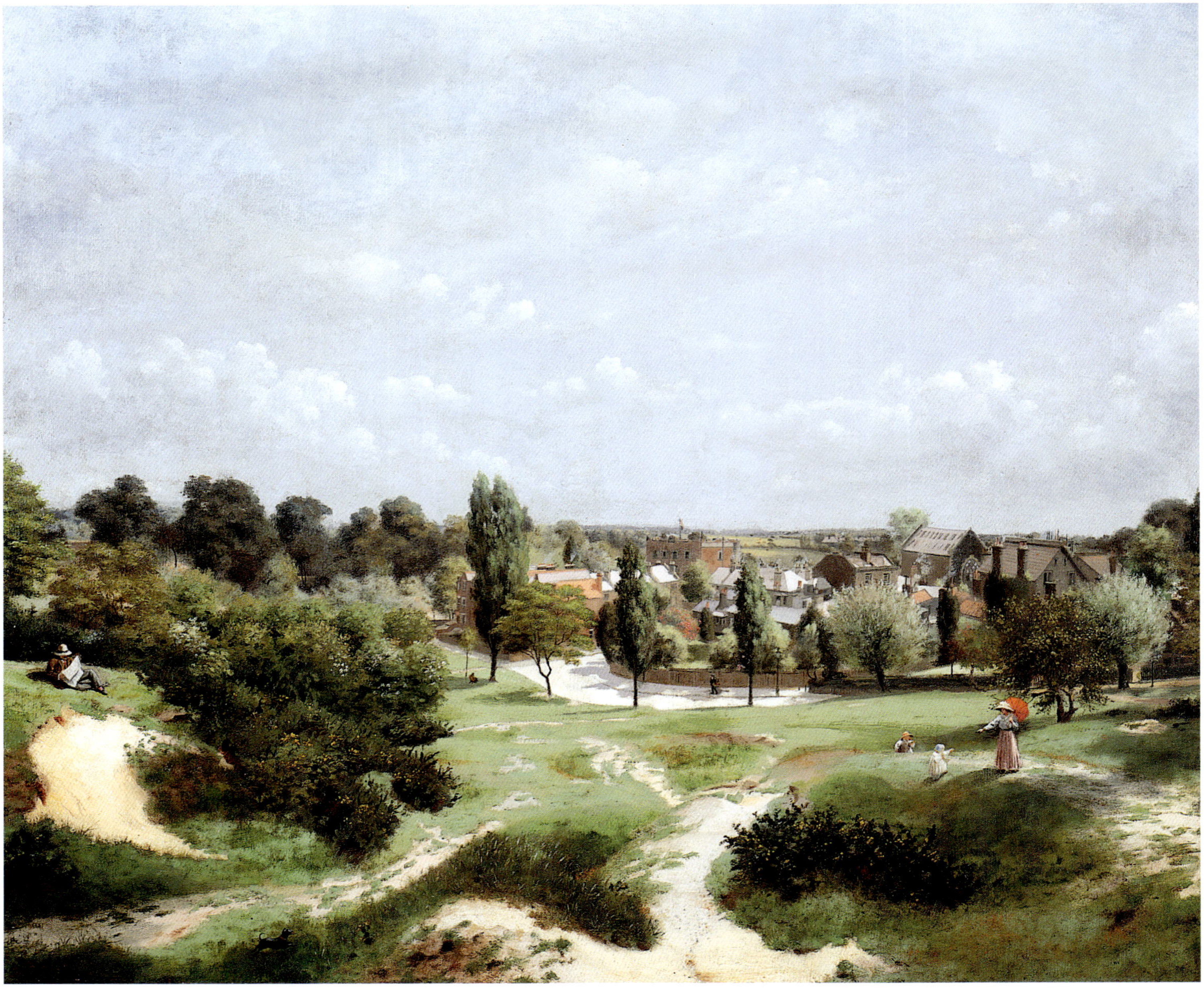

143.
CLAUDE ALFRED PENNINGTON WALKER
(1862–c.1925)

The Vale of Health, Hampstead Heath
[A 28581]
*c.*1910
Oil on canvas, 60.3 x 72.5 cm
Signed bottom left: *C. Walker*

THE VIEW is taken from beneath Jack Straw's Castle, looking east. The road that winds through the village is seen centre and right, and to its left is the walk that leads to the fairground. The Victorian villa whose gables and chimneys appear on the extreme right still stands, adjoining Villas-on-the-Heath, but the building behind has now disappeared: this was the Athenaeum, at first a club, but in use as a gymnasium at the time this picture was painted. It was demolished in 1958 and replaced by a block of flats; the Vale of Health Hotel, seen in the centre, was pulled down in 1964.

The inclusion of a man reading a newspaper and of a mother with her two children highlight the use of the Heath for leisure and fresh air: this is an urban landscape. Stylistically the painting seems untouched by the contemporary movements in landscape painting. It is more attuned to the artistic world of Linnell and Constable.

This part of Hampstead Heath was marshland until the end of the eighteenth century, when it was drained and christened the Vale of Health. A number of tea gardens were soon established, and among the famous people who had houses here were Leigh Hunt, Rowland Hill and Douglas Jerrold. Many of these early villas survive, but for the most part the Vale is now composed of Victorian terrace houses. As well as being a retreat, the Vale was also a centre for laundresses and sweeps in the earlier part of the nineteenth century. The Hampstead Bank Holiday Fair, perhaps the best known of all London's outdoor amusements, takes place annually outside the village.

Although the artistic history of Hampstead Heath begins in earnest in the Regency period with the painters John Constable and John Linnell, the Heath's true identity was forged later out of the fierce battle to preserve it as open space which took place between 1829 and 1889. The artist chose to depict the Vale of Health, the swampy valley drained by the Hampstead Water Company in 1777 and known as Hatches Bottom until about 1800. By the time the poet Leigh Hunt took a cottage there in October 1815, the parish poorhouses had been moved and the area had become socially respectable.

Claude Walker's work as a picture restorer must have hampered the development of his career as a painter since there are only two other known works, both watercolours, dating from the same period as this picture – one taken from Parliament Hill (in the Museum's collection, acc. no. A80889) and the other depicting the Southend Pier (in the Victoria and Albert Museum).

Provenance:
Unknown.

Bibliography:
Hayes (cat. no. 106); John Richardson, *Hampstead One Thousand*, Historical Publications, 1985.

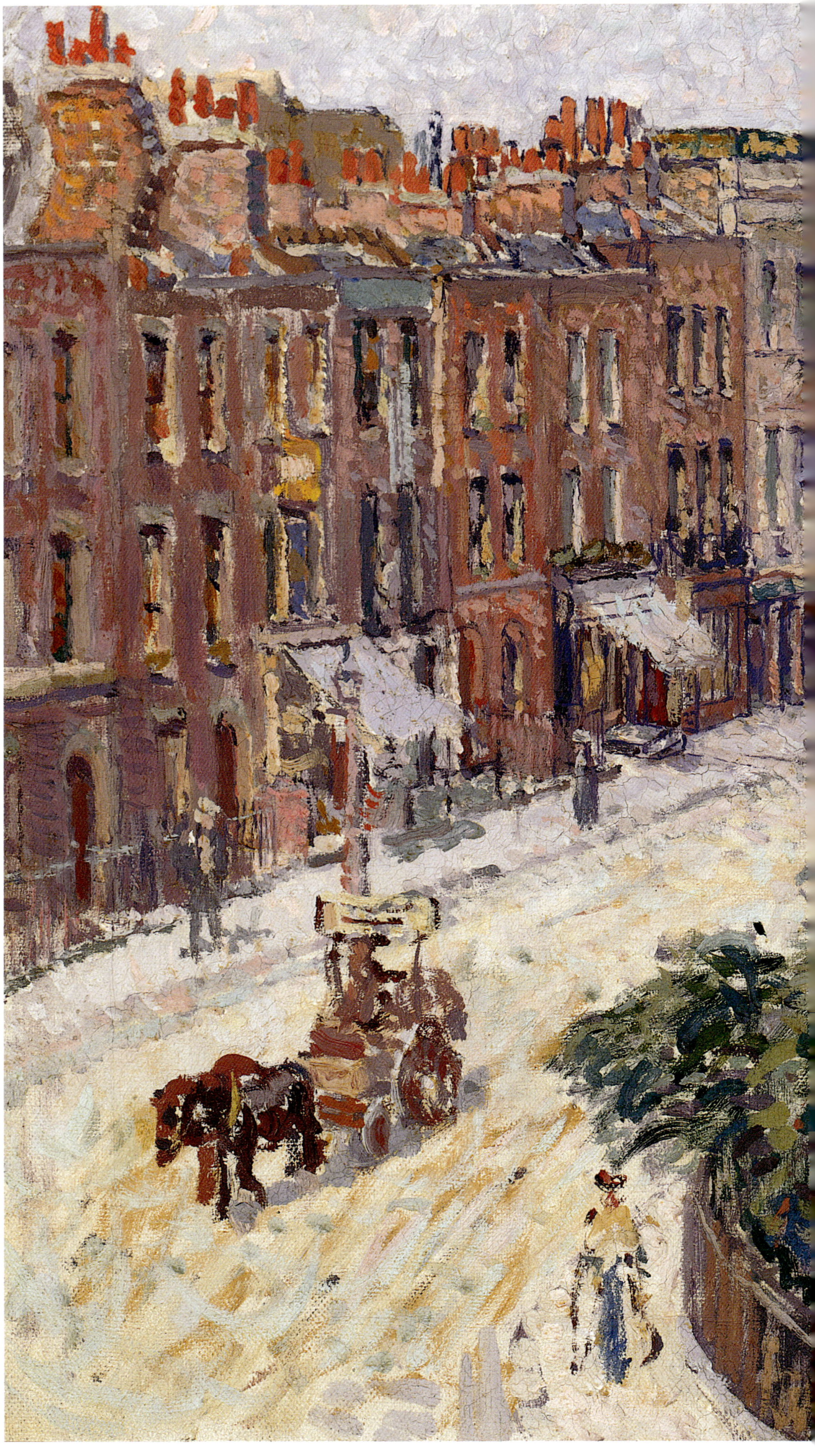

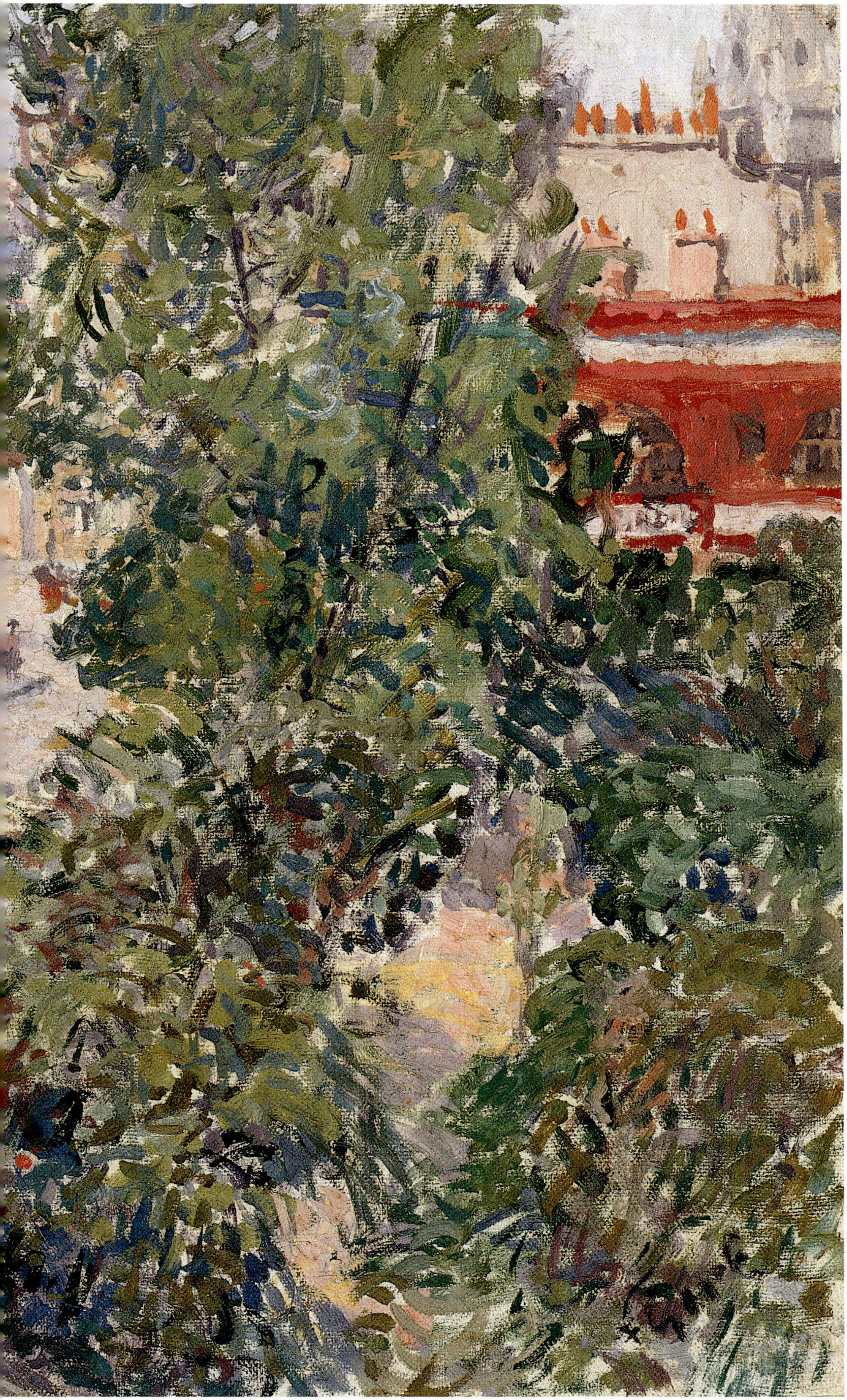

144.

SPENCER GORE

(1878–1914)

Mornington Crescent

[81.323]

1911

Oil on canvas,

40.5 x 50.8 cm

Signed bottom right:

F Gore

Label on the back reads:

Le Bas Collection 1968

(also see cat. no. 156).

Provenance:
From the collection of Edward Le Bas; Christie's, 12 June 1981 (32); purchased Anthony d'Offay on behalf of the Museum with help from the MGC/V&A Purchase Grant Fund.

Bibliography:
A Painter's Collection (Edward Le Bas, RA), exhibition catalogue, Royal Academy, 1963, no. 41; Wendy Baron, *The Camden Town Group*, 1979; *The Painters of Camden Town 1905–20*, exhibition catalogue, Christie's, January 1988.

THE VIEW, taken from the artist's window, is looking north-east, across the Crescent Gardens towards Mornington Crescent Tube Station (which opened on 22 June 1907), with its readily recognisable liver-red tiles. The junction with Camden High Street is visible in the centre of the painting while Arlington Road, hidden from view, would run to the bottom left. The painting of Mornington Crescent in the John Quinn collection (Christie's, 1 July 1993, Lot 100) may have formed a pair with the work under review (see below), since it is also taken from the artist's window, is very similar in technique, and looks in the other direction, with Mornington Place and Terrace clearly depicted.

Spencer Gore rented a room at 31 Mornington Crescent between 1909 and 1912 when, newly married, he moved to Houghton Place (see cat. no. 146). He painted extensively the view from his window in the French Impressionist style that characterised these years. The painter Sickert records how he 'used' the view from his window in June (1911) as if, in premonition, he knew it would be his last summer there. The many paintings he produced, split among a number of public and private collections, recall the concept of 'series' which was first developed by Monet from the 1870s and redefined by Pissarro around the 1900s (see Royal Academy catalogue: *The Impressionist and the city*, 1993). In spirit, Gore's group of Mornington Crescent paintings is close to Pissarro's bird's-eye views, albeit on a domestic scale. He is less concerned with atmosphere (although the painting *The Avenue* pays a moving tribute to morning light) than with finding a pleasing balance between bricks and leaves.

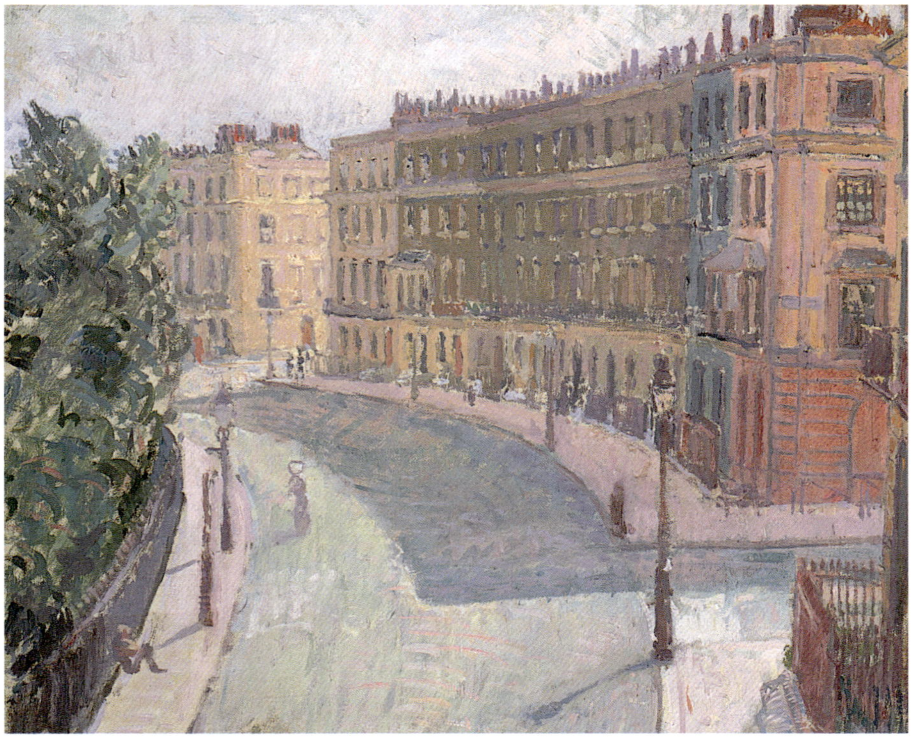

Since its creation in the 1820s, Mornington Crescent has been the home of a number of painters: Clarkson Stanfield (1793–1867) lived at number 36 and Walter Sickert (1860–1942) at number 6, while George Cruikshank (1792–1878) lived at the nearby 48 Mornington Place.

Although much of the residential character of Mornington Crescent has remained unchanged, the opening, in 1928, of the massive Carreras factory (the Black Cat Cigarette Factory) totally transformed the appearance of the neighbourhood. The gardens were obliterated to make way for the dwarfing building, the exterior of which was modelled on an ancient Egyptian temple. The factory was sold in 1959 and the building, still on the site, was converted into offices in 1963. A 1939 drawing by Grace Golden in the Museum's collection (acc. no. 79.427/230) updates this view.

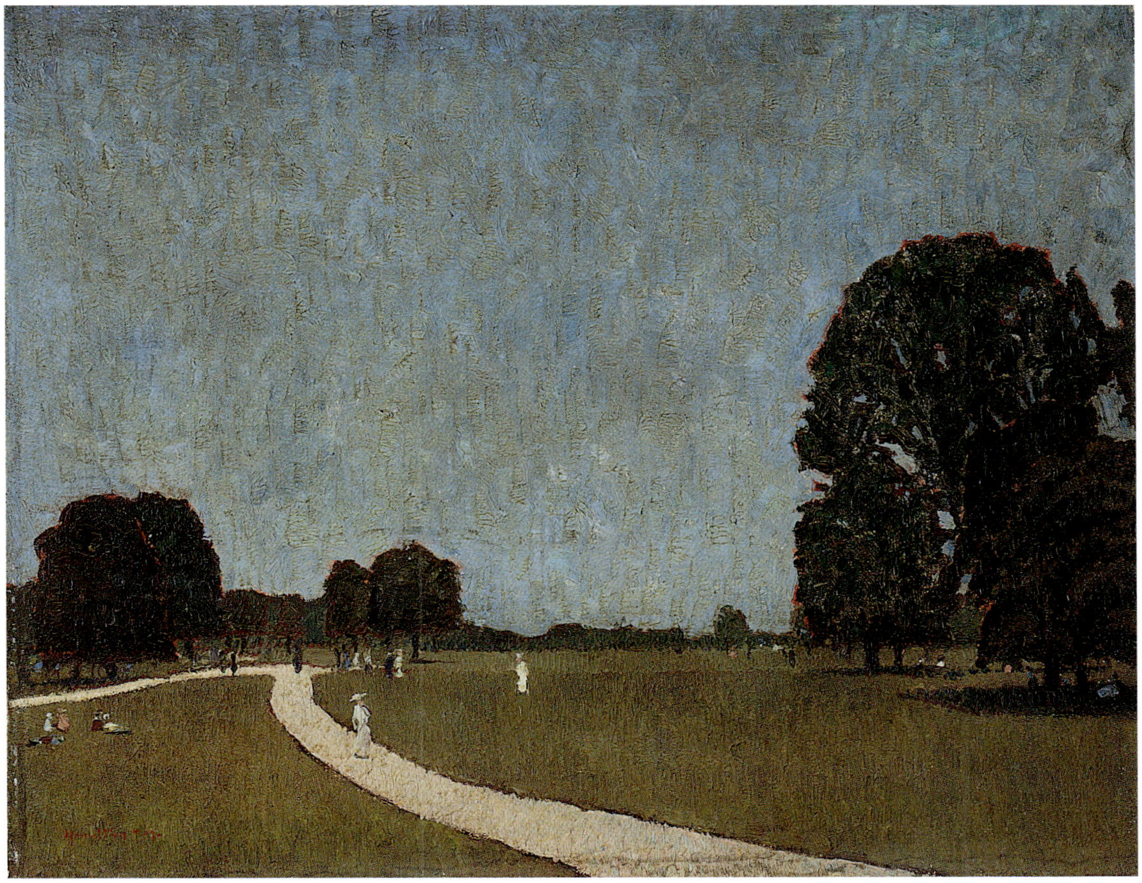

Provenance:
Presented by A. E. Anderson in 1918.

Bibliography:
Hayes (cat. no. 153); *James Hamilton Hay*, exhibition catalogue, Walker Art Gallery, Liverpool, 1973.

Exhibited:
Royal Glasgow Institution, 1911 (505); 'Memorial Exhibition of Works by the late J. Hamilton Hay', Goupil Gallery, March 1917 (85).

145.
JAMES HAMILTON HAY
(1874–1916)
An Evening Scene in Green Park
[A 19841]
*c.*1911
Oil on canvas, 35 x 45cm
Signed bottom left: *Hamilton Hay*

THE LOCATION in Green Park is difficult to determine: the artist, however, is likely to have positioned himself near the middle of the park looking south-west – virtually the only viewpoint which gives one the impression of a park not hemmed in by buildings. A serpentine path goes past large chestnut(?) trees on the right to lead us to a distant clump of trees in the left background. A few figures are scattered throughout, some walking and others seated.

The late work of James Hamilton Hay is principally concerned with London, and more particularly, with its parks and commons (few works survive from the period before he moved to London in about 1912). He produced a body of prints and paintings between 1913 and 1916 featuring Golder's Hill Park (notable was the painting *Silver Birches*), as well as Parliament Hill, Kensington Gardens and Clapham Common.

Although the costume in this work suggests a date of around 1905, the style, consistent with the work of the Camden Town Group, dictates a later date, suggesting that Hay was reworking an earlier picture.

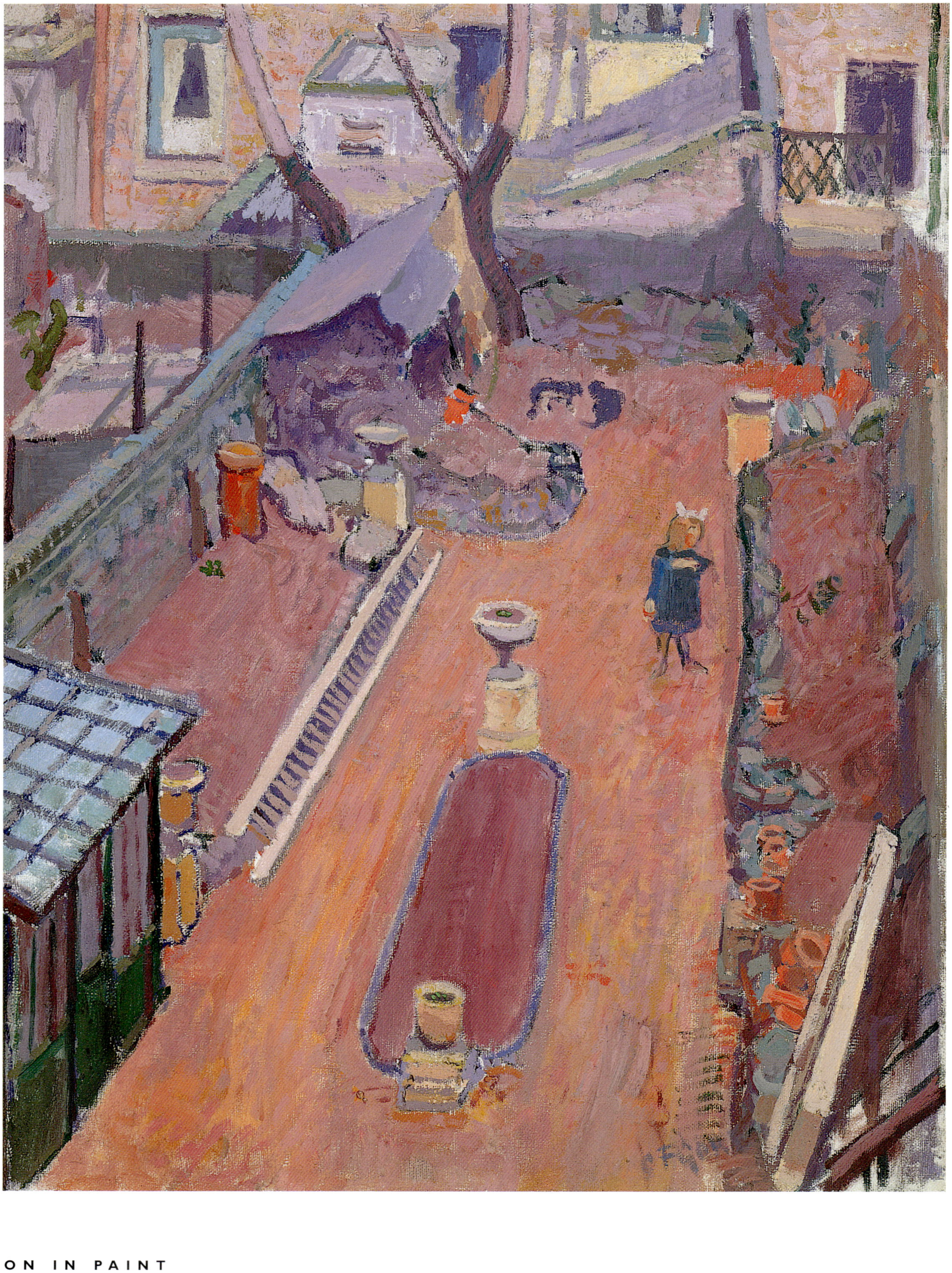

146.

SPENCER GORE

(1878–1914)

Down the Garden [83.360]

1912

Oil on canvas, 51 x 41 cm

Signed bottom right: *SF GORE*

'Gilman' label (see Provenance) on stretcher reads: *painted by S. F. Gore from window up 2 Houghton Place in 1912*/Signed *S. F. Gore/143 (a)*

Also handwritten in ink on stretcher: *S. F. Gore Fitzroy Street Fitzroy Square London W.*

THE ARTIST painted his back garden at 2 Houghton Place, on the south side of Harrington Square, shortly after moving with his wife Mollie Kerr into this temporary rented accommodation at the beginning of 1912.

Among his contemporaries, Gore was probably the least hesitant about depicting ordinary, undramatic subjects. This is the archetypal London back garden, narrow, untidy, with an assortment of accessories ranging from the chicken and potting sheds to tools, pots, raised urns and a discarded ladder. The small oval parterre and plant beds are bare, indicating it is winter – as does the leafless tree at the bottom of the garden.

This painting is not only one of the most unglamorous and severe examples of Camden Town painting, it also marks a change in Gore's style. It is in complete contrast with the divisionist technique which began in 1908 and was used in the series of Mornington Crescent views of 1911 (see cat. no. 144). This must have been partly due to the impact on many artists at that time of the exhibition 'Manet and the Post-Impressionists' organised by Roger Fry at the Grafton Gallery in 1910.

The palette of Gore had been close to that of Gauguin for some time, and the range of colours in his *Ballet Scene from 'On the Sands'* (1910) is identical with *Down the Garden.* His friend, the journalist Ashley Gibson, later summarised it in *Postscript to Adventure* (1930): 'His artist's eyes saw a violet veil drawn of mornings over the chimney-pots, Victorian façades, and grimy plane trees of Camden town, and thus he painted them.'

The second version of this garden view (no. 19 in the Anthony d'Offay catalogue), painted at the beginning of the summer, is still very solid, despite being animated with sunlight and leaves, those flickering elements which gave such a sense of movement to some of the Mornington Crescent views, notably *The Avenue, Mornington Crescent* (private collection).

Provenance:
In the artist's studio at his death (see 'Gilman' label, no. 143a: 143 indicates the chronological sequence, 'a' denotes that after the artist's death Gilman and Mrs Gore considered it an important work); purchased from Anthony d'Offay Gallery in 1983 with help from the MGC/V&A Purchase Grant Fund.

Bibliography:
Wendy Baron, *The Camden Town Group*, 1979, pp100–101; *Spencer Frederick Gore*, exhibition catalogue, Anthony d'Offay, 1983, no. 18.

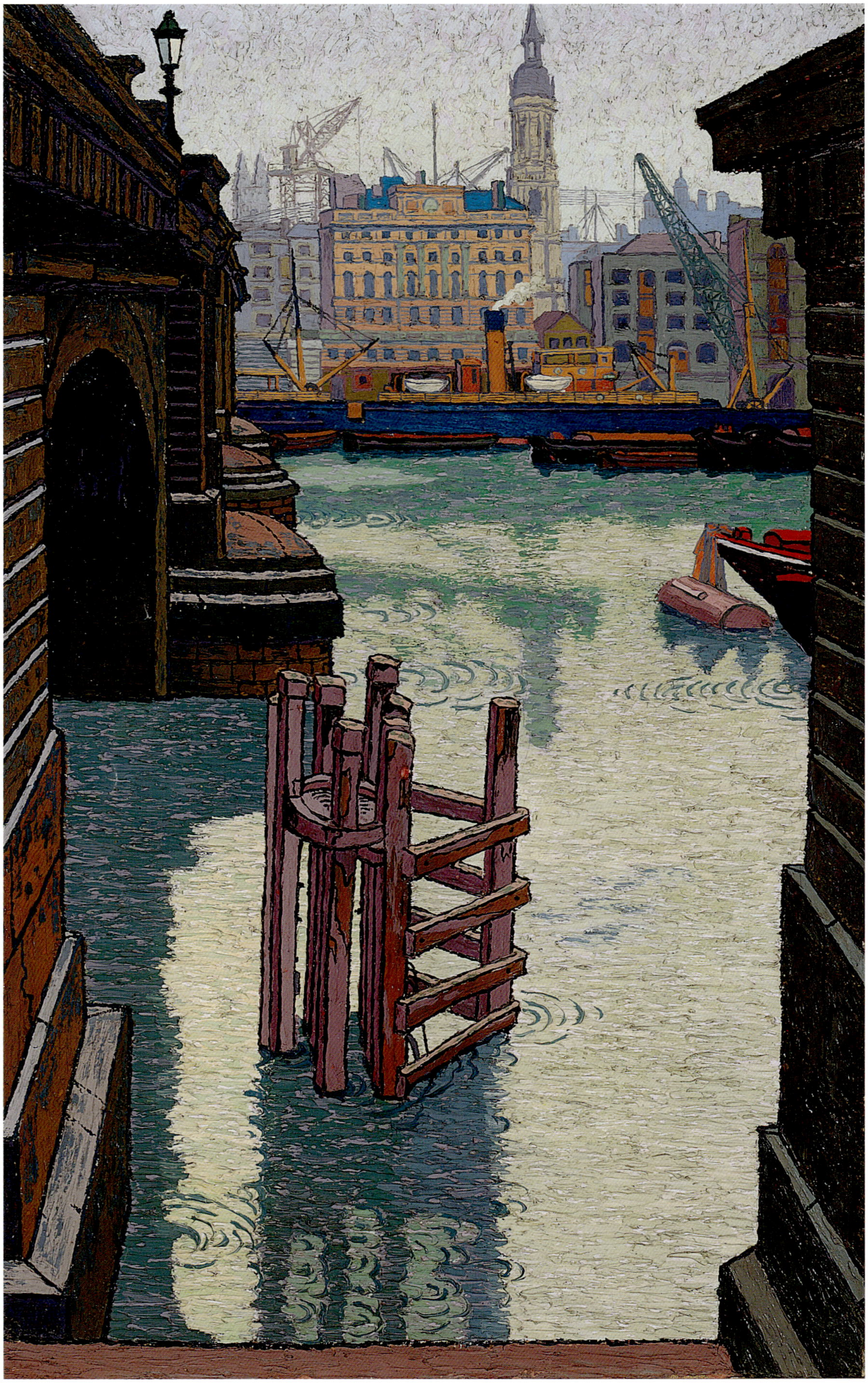

147.
CHARLES GINNER
(1878–1952)

London Bridge: Adelaide House and Fresh Wharf [68.48]

1913

Oil on canvas, 76.2 x 48.4 cm

Signed lower right: *C. Ginner*

THE VIEW is taken from the south-eastern end of London Bridge looking north towards New Fresh Wharf with Adelaide Buildings, which formed part of the reconstruction scheme of London Bridge in the 1830s. The north-east site, opposite Fishmongers' Hall and at the end of King William Street, became known as Adelaide Place in honour of the reigning queen, wife of William IV. Adelaide Buildings are framed on the right by the steeple of St Magnus Church and further north on the left by the tower of St Michael Cornhill. Adelaide Buildings were pulled down in 1920 and replaced by the present taller structure designed by Sir J. Burnet & Partners which, when it was completed in 1924, obscured the view of St Magnus the Martyr.

Misleadingly, the Monument, which should be on the left of St Magnus's steeple, has not been represented. Since this picture was painted, Rennie's elegant bridge, which had been gradually sinking due to the weight of traffic, has been replaced by the present three-span bridge capable of taking six lanes of traffic, which opened in 1973. The painting makes an interesting companion with Marlow's 1762 *Fresh Wharf* (see cat. no. 26).

Ginner's use of impasto is said to have come from the Academy Vitti in Paris, where he trained under the Spanish painter Herman Anglada y Camarasa. The technique seems particularly successful in the treatment of light (as in *The Sunlit Quay, Dieppe*, Walker Art Gallery, Liverpool) and of water, elements which are attractively blended in the painting under review.

An oil sketch for this composition featured in the Christie's sale on 17 November 1978, Lot 33 (wrongly labelled and dated). A drawing entitled *London Bridge* was sold at Christie's on 7 March 1991 (4), for which no oil painting appears to exist. It explores the composition centred on one arch of the bridge with the built-up riverbank beyond, which Ginner fully developed both in *Waterloo Bridge* (painted in 1921 and reproduced in *Apollo*, April 1969, p310) and in *On the Embankment* using Temple Pier as a framing device (Sotheby's, 6 October 1993, Lot 103 and associated woodcut in the Museum of London collection).

Provenance:
Goupil Gallery; bt R. V. Williams in 1920; purchased by the Museum from Thos Agnew & Sons in 1968 (no. 6 in the 'British Paintings' exhibition).

Bibliography:
C. Ginner, *Notebooks*, vol. I, plate lxv; Wendy Baron, *The Camden Town Group*, 1979, p371; *The Painters of Camden Town 1905–20*, exhibition catalogue, Christie's, January 1988, cat. no. 122.

Exhibited:
Allied Artists Association, July 1913 (546); 'English Post-Impressionists and Cubists', Brighton Art Gallery, 1914 (31); Goupil Gallery, 1914 (30); Goupil Gallery, 1915, 'Cumberland Market group' (41).

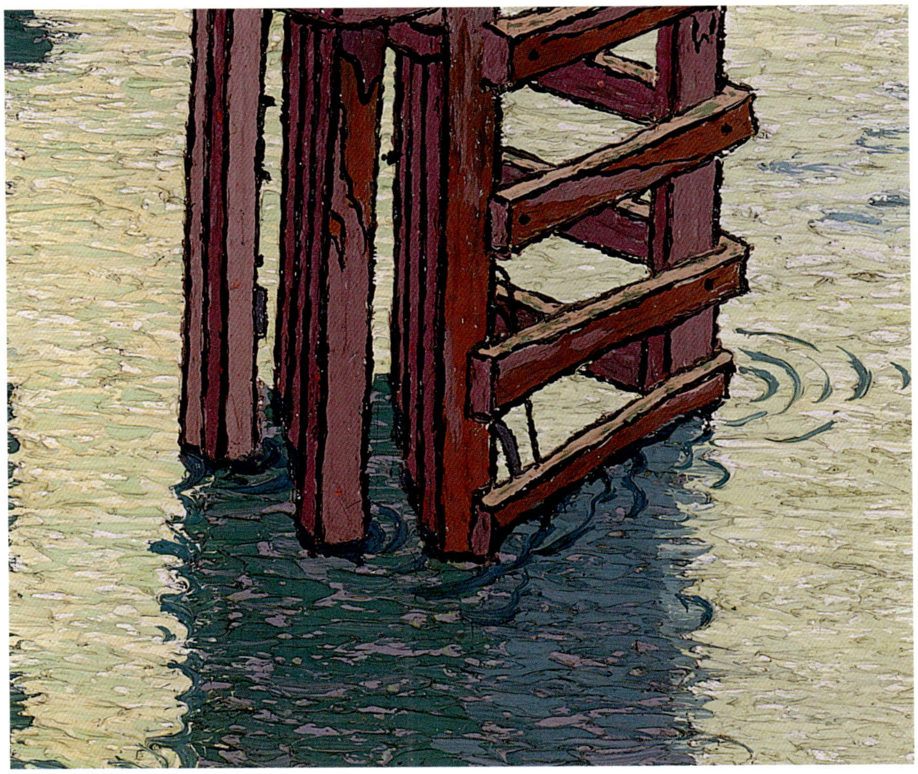

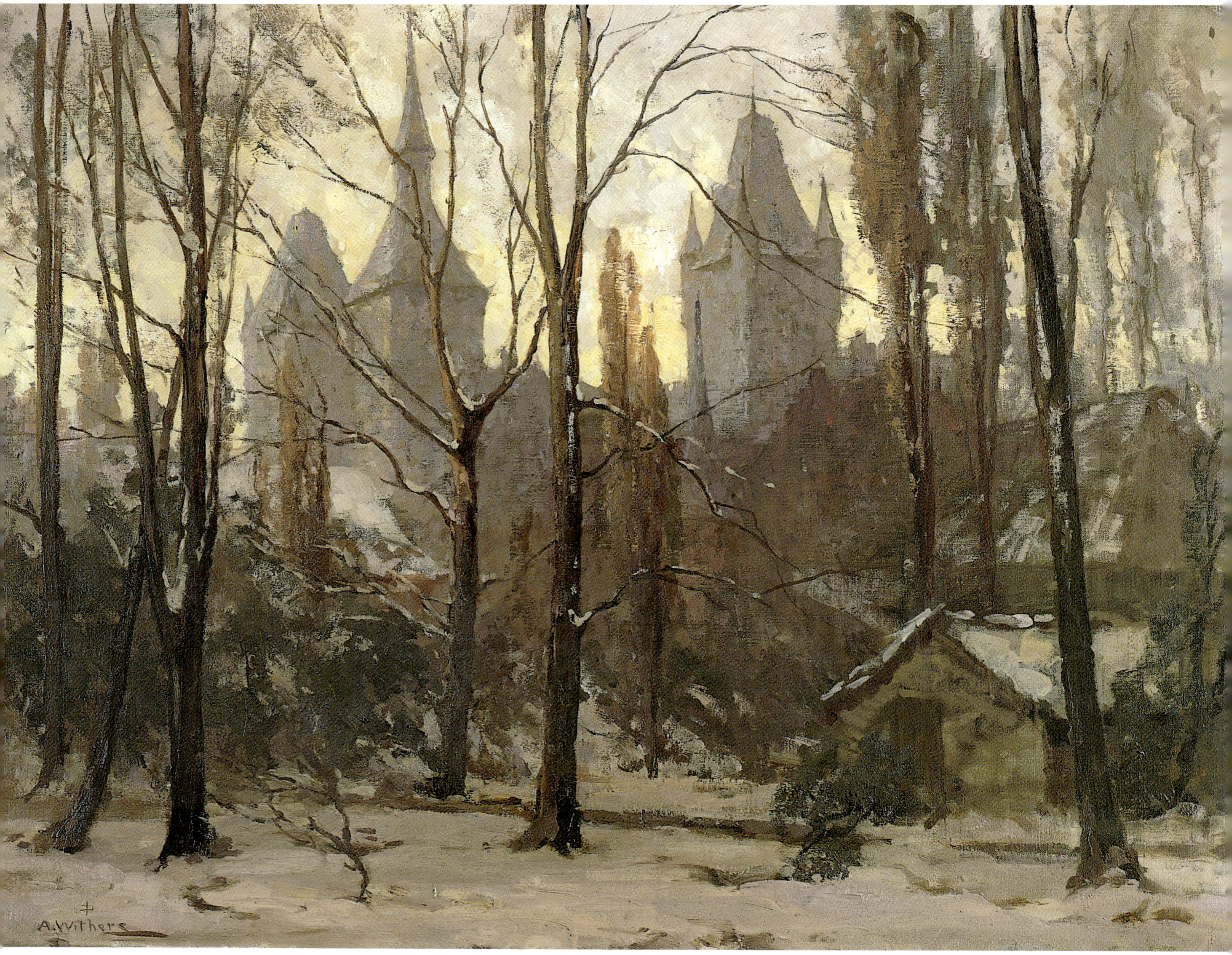
A. Withers

148.

ALFRED WITHERS

(1856–1932)

The Royal Victoria Patriotic Asylum

[84.388/1]

*c.*1915

Oil on canvas, 71 x 96.5 cm

Signed bottom left: *A. Withers* with symbol above

THE CLUSTER of towers visible behind a curtain of trees under snow belongs to the Royal Victoria Patriotic Asylum in Trinity Road, Wandsworth, which was built for the orphaned daughters of soldiers and sailors of the Crimean War (1854–6). A fund was set up under the auspices of the Prince Consort to which all classes of society contributed. The foundation stone was laid by Queen Victoria in 1857, on land which originally formed part of Wandsworth Common. Major Rhode Hawkins designed the building, which he loosely based on Heriot's School in Edinburgh.

When the Asylum was painted by 'Sergeant' Withers during the First World War it was known as the third London Territorial General Hospital and had been taken over by the army unit of the textile firm Hitchcock Williams in 1914. In May 1917 they issued a fact sheet on the hospital: it 'has 2,000 beds and has treated over 30,000 cases since the war broke out'. Paul Kirk, W. R. S. Stott, E. Martin, J. Hodgson Lobley and C. R. W. Nevinson were some of the soldier-artists who depicted the wartime activities at the third London Territorial General Hospital.

During the Second World War the building was used as a debriefing centre for the Secret Service. It was in continual occupation until 1976, its last occupant being a secondary school. Under the ownership of the Greater London Council the building gradually became derelict until in 1981 the New Zealand restaurateur Paul Tutton was able to buy the freehold for one pound. After the building was cleared of four tons of pigeon droppings, it was restored by Dickinson Quarme & Associates and turned into 'a bright community of workshops, studios and flats', including the Academy of Live and Recorded Arts with a professional-standard theatre rehearsal hall.

Provenance:
Presented by Hitchcock Williams in 1984.

Bibliography:
Power Collection (Museum of London), Box no. 56; 'Living in a £1 Gothic Wonder', by Deyan Sudjic, *Sunday Times Magazine,* 29 July 1984.

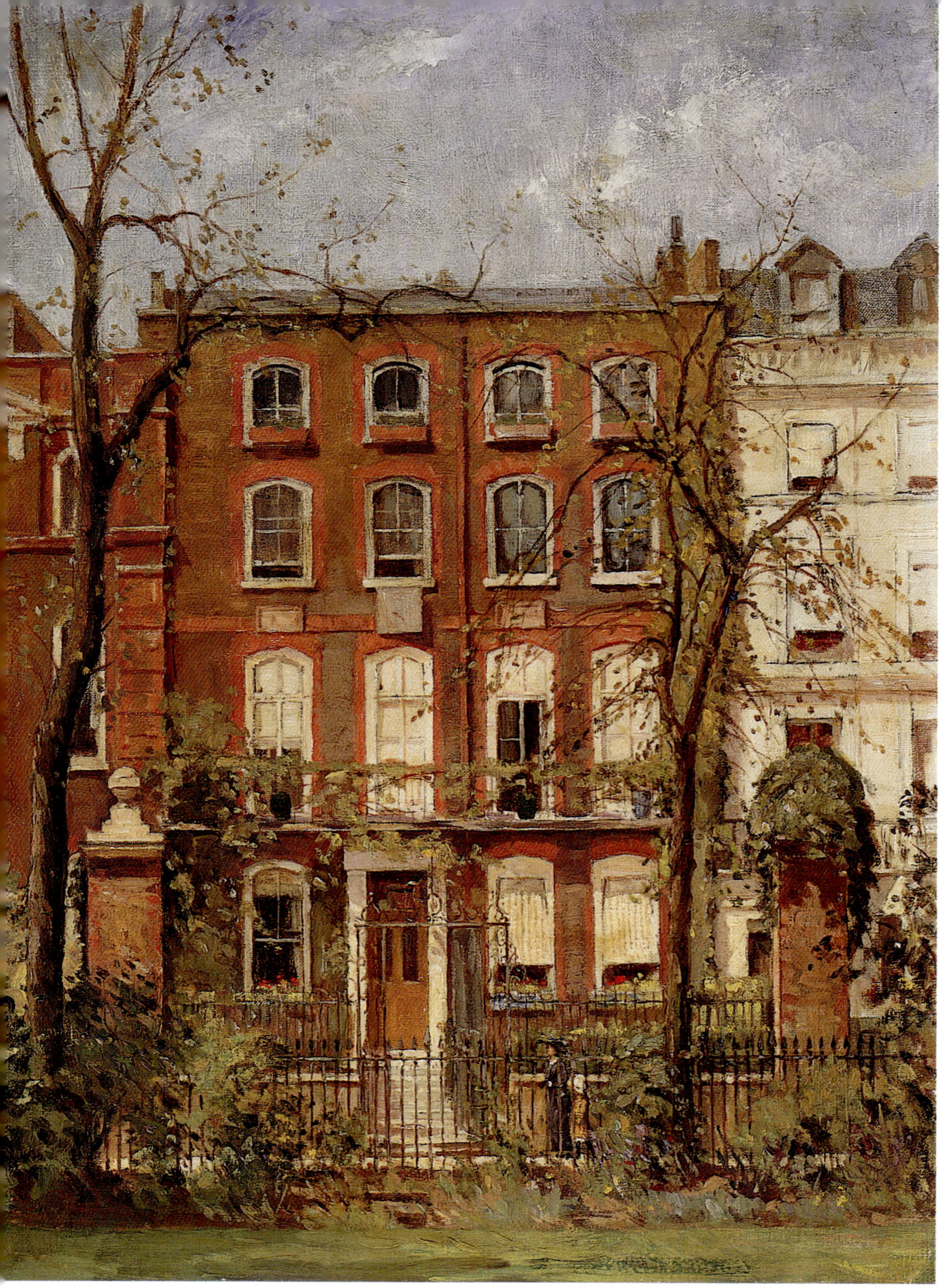

149.

WILLIAM E. FOX

(active 1909–42; d. 1948)

Cheyne Walk, Chelsea* [A 17452]

*c.*1915

Oil on canvas, 55 x 37.7 cm

Signed bottom left: *W. E. Fox*

A VIEW of the facade of 15 Cheyne Walk (at one time called Carlton House), built in 1717, from Chelsea Embankment Gardens. An excellent example of a London terrace house of the Queen Anne period, with arched window heads and the first floor emphasised; the wrought iron work in the gate and railings is of exceptional distinction. The first occupant of the house was Admiral Sir John Balchen (1670–1744); in 1869 it was tenanted by William Lawson whose son, Cecil Gordon Lawson (1851–82), was a well-known Victorian landscape painter, specialising in Chelsea views. The house on the left, only partially visible, is Queen's House, one of the finest in Cheyne Walk, and once the home of Dante Gabriel Rossetti.

Provenance:
Presented by Miss M. C. Ford Smith in 1916.

Bibliography:
Hayes (cat. no. 45).

Exhibited:
Royal Academy 1915 (852).

150.

ROBERT BEVAN

(1865–1925)

A Street Scene in Belsize Park [61.78]

1917

Oil on canvas, 64 x 92 cm

Signed on the bottom left: *Bevan*

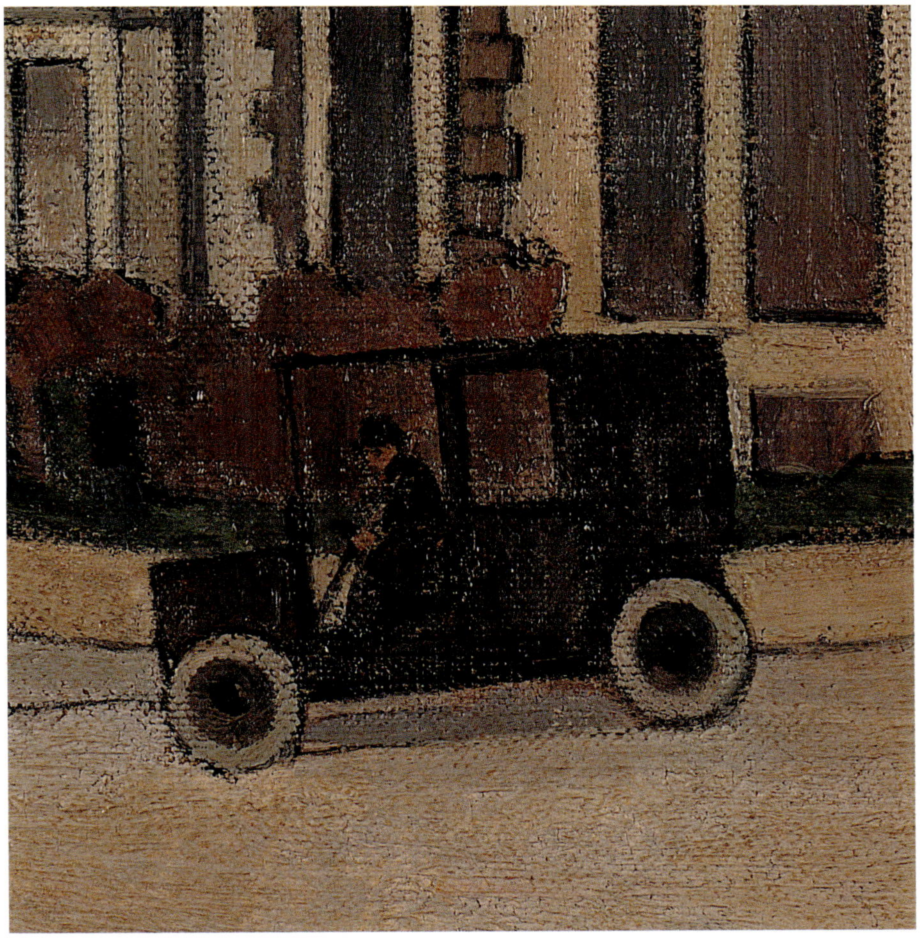

THIS VIEW shows the fork of Buckland Crescent (left) and Belsize Park, and the large house in the centre is the building acquired by the Hall School in 1916 to be used as a preparatory school; the artist's son was a pupil there up to 1913. A motor cab is parked in the street, in contrast to the artist's previous recurrent motif of hansom cabs (which he gave up painting after 1912).

This part of Hampstead was developed in the middle years of the nineteenth century, in the stuccoed Italianate style popular also in Kensington, and, with the exception of the lampposts, which have now been replaced, the scene represented in this painting remains quite unchanged (the modern flats in Belsize Park are on the site of houses which would have appeared beyond, on the right).

This painting is one of a group Bevan executed showing the neighbourhood in which he lived. Bevan married Stanislawa de Karlowska in 1897 (see cat. no. 179); and shortly after the birth of their son in March 1901, the family moved from Cuckfield, Sussex, to 14 Adamson Road in Hampstead. From about 1910, Bevan derived much inspiration from drawing and painting his immediate surroundings. In 1915 and 1916 he painted his own street in *Houses in Sunlight* (artist's family) and *From the Artist's Window* (Leicester), reminiscent of Spencer Gore's views of his back garden (see cat. no. 146). The beginning of this 'N. W. London' period in 1910 was marked by works such as *Adelaide Road in Sunlight* (*c.*1910) and his cab yard studies in Ormonde Yard, St John's Wood, of which a watercolour is in the Museum's collection (acc. no. 81.349).

The single most notable influence on the artist's style was that of the French Post-Impressionist Paul Gauguin, whom he met when he was working in Pont Aven, Brittany, between 1893 and 1894. Consequently the colours in this work are contained within very clear delineated areas.

Provenance:
The artist's family; purchased out of the Mackenzie Bell Trust Fund from Messrs P. & D. Colnaghi in 1961.

Bibliography:
Hayes (cat. no. 8); R. A. Bevan, *Robert Bevan,* 1965, pp21 and 27, plate 59; Wendy Baron, *The Camden Town Group*, 1979; *The Painters of Camden Town 1905–1920,* exhibition catalogue, Christie's, 1988, cat. no. 178.

Exhibited:
London, 'London Group, Peintres Anglais Modernes', April 1917 (35).

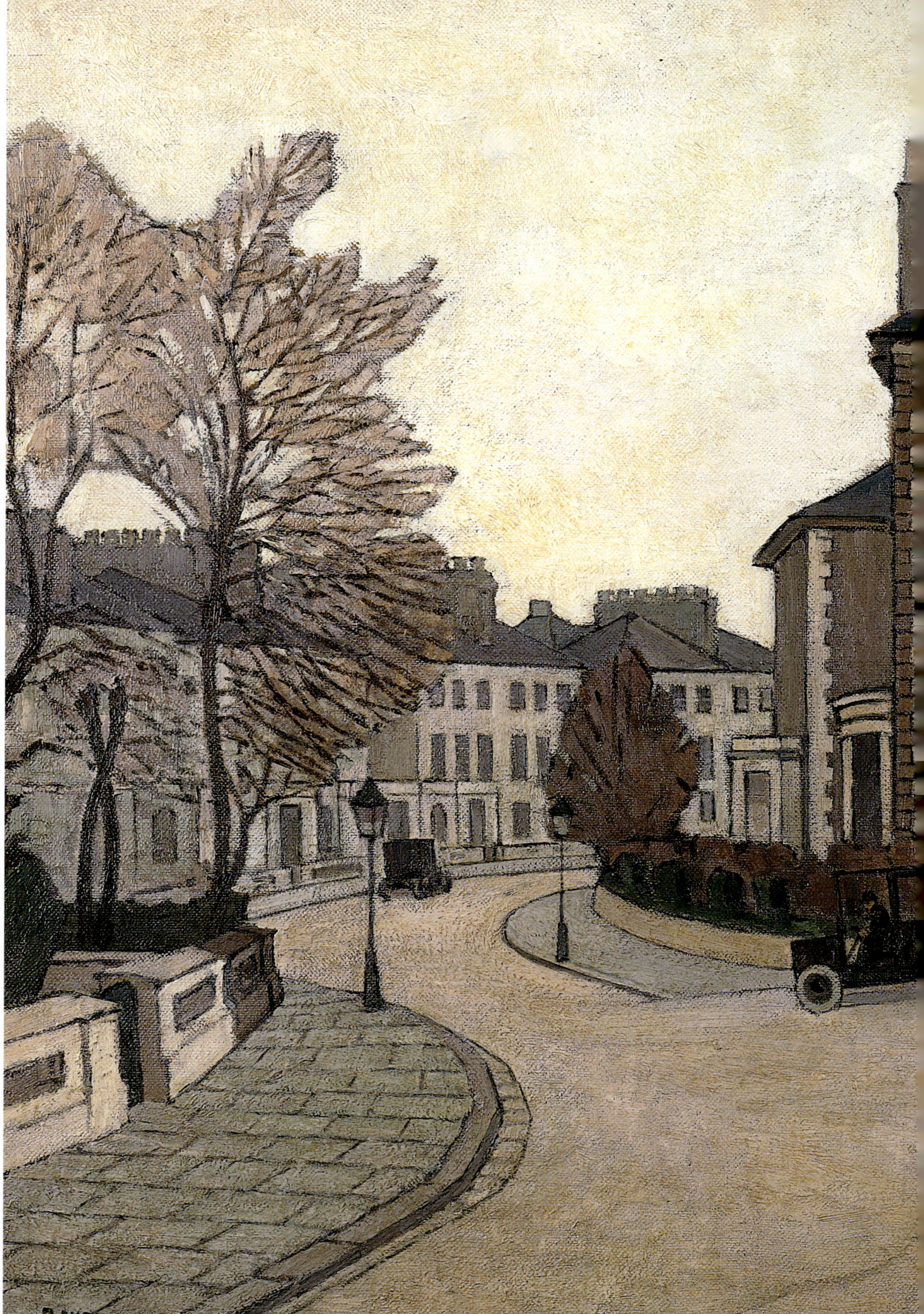
Bevan

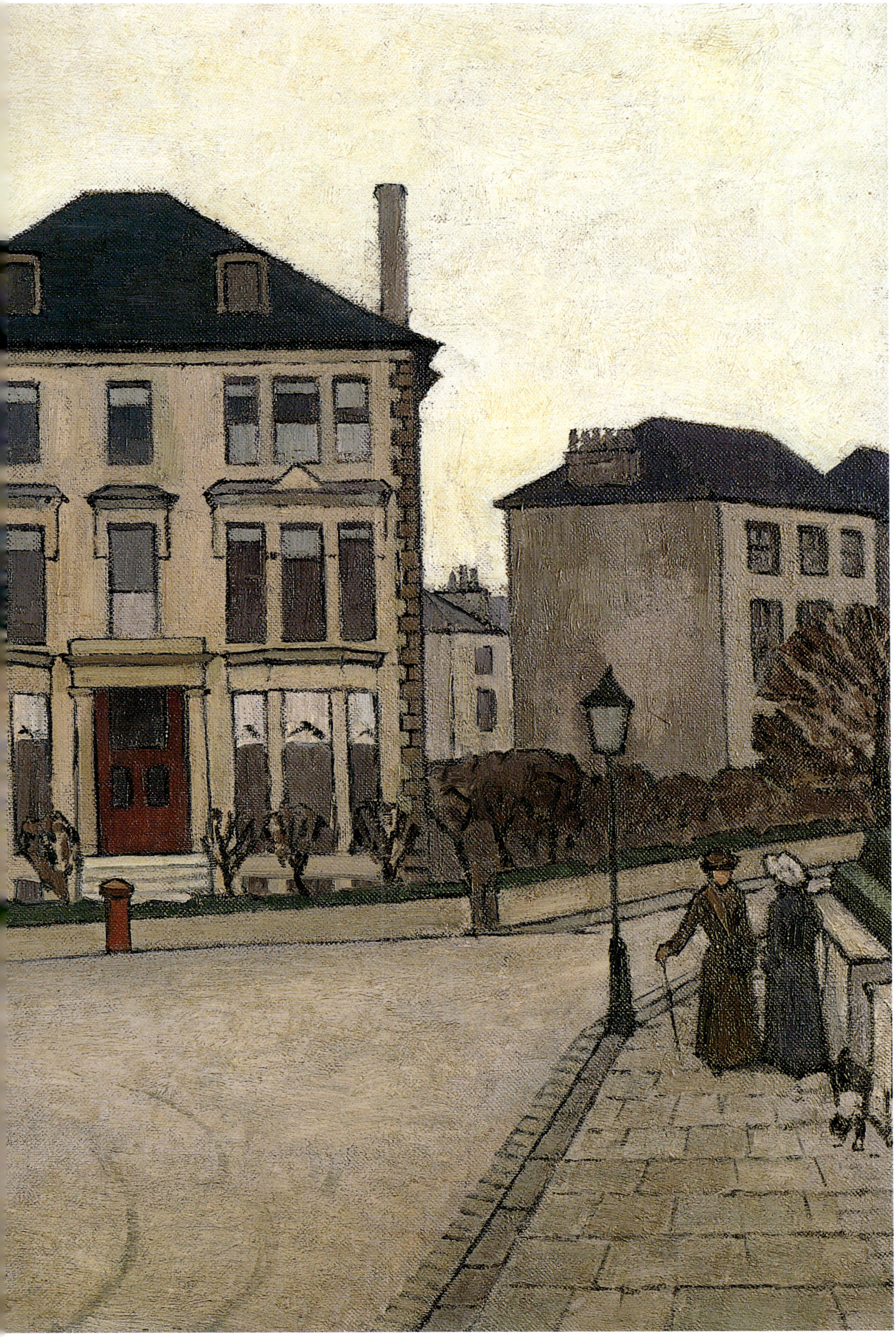

EARLY TWENTIETH CENTURY

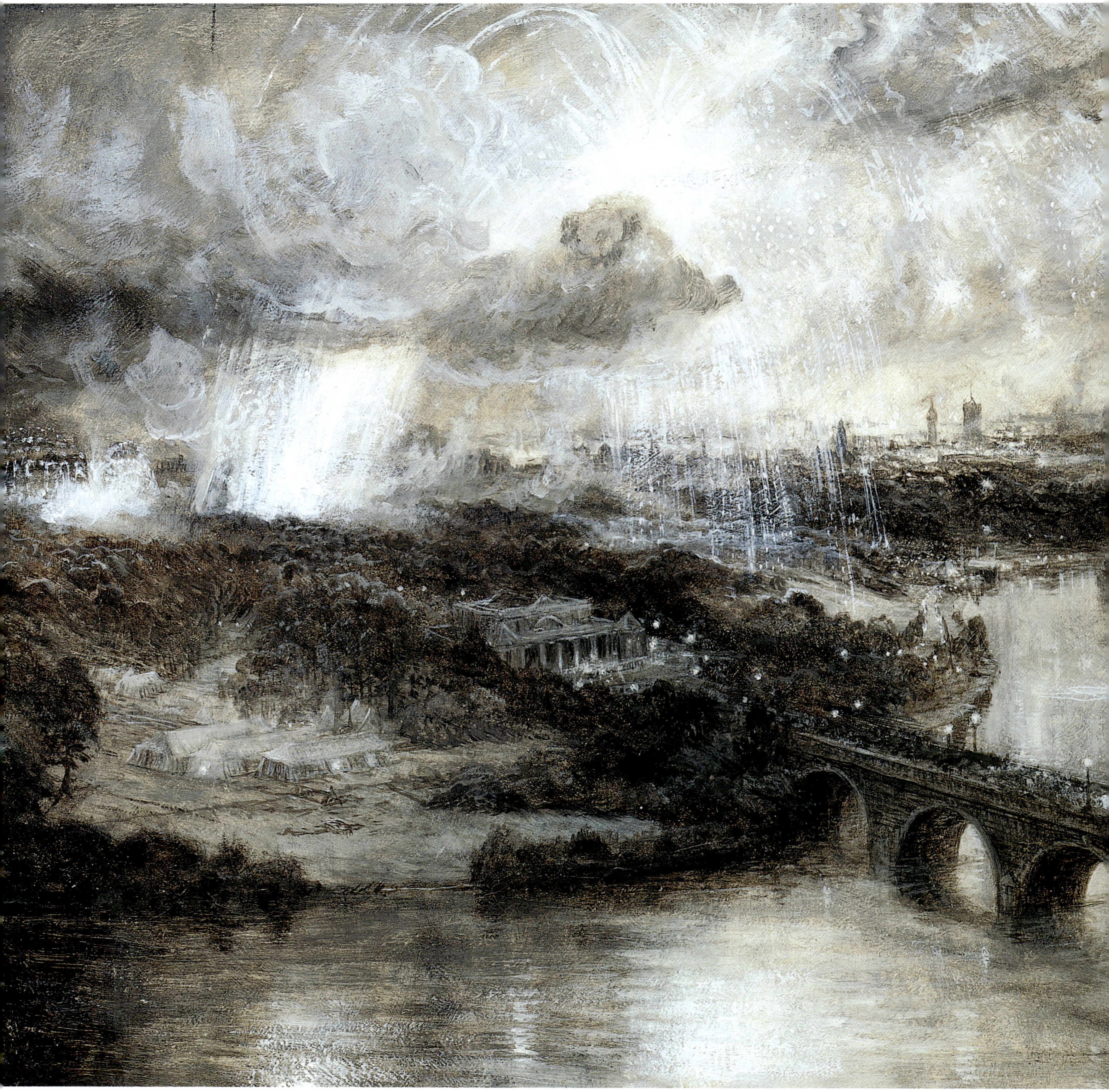

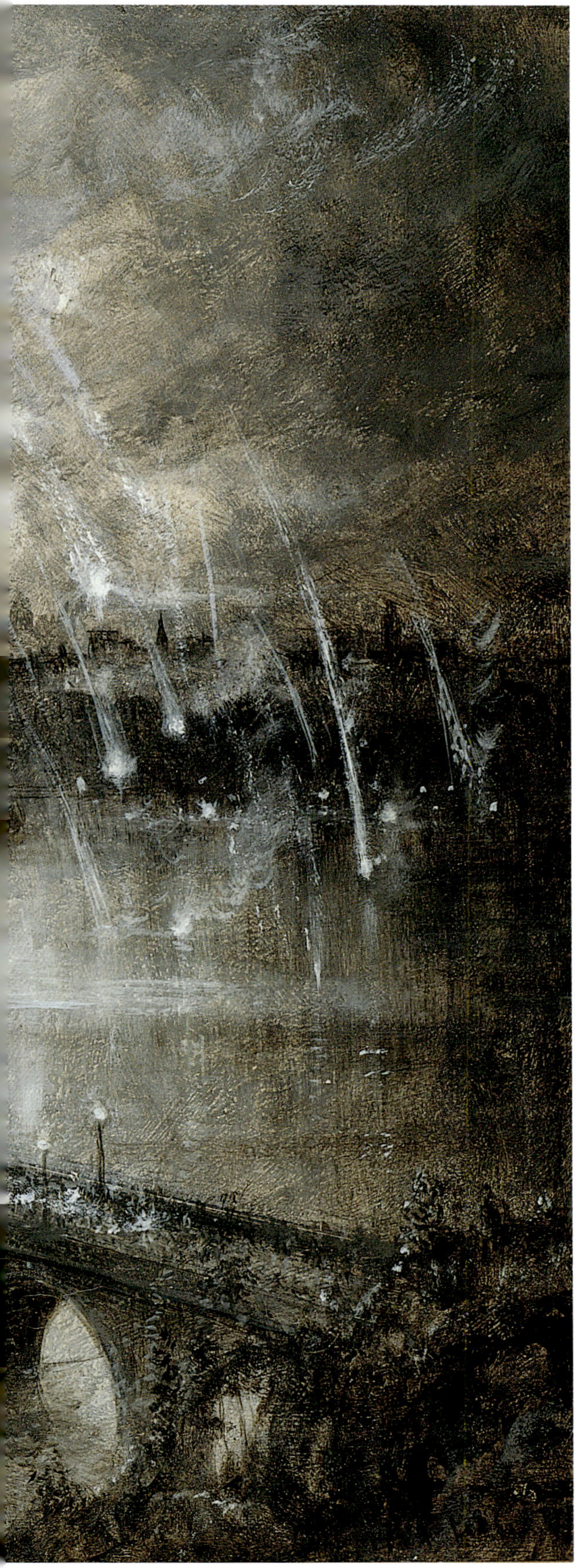

151.

CHARLES WILLIAM WYLLIE

(1859–1923)

Firework Display in Hyde Park [A20681]
1919
Oil on canvas, 40.5 x 60.5 cm
Not signed or dated
Inscribed on the back: *Gift of the Proprietor of the Sphere Original/Painting by C. W. Wyllie*

Provenance:
Gift from Clement Shorter of the *Sphere* in August 1919.

Bibliography:
The *Sphere*, 26 July 1919, pp76, 78–9, 80 and 82.

A 'BLACK and white' vision of the firework display which was held in Hyde Park for the National Peace Celebrations on 19 July 1919. The artist appears to be surveying the scene from a balloon hovering over the south-west corner of the Serpentine Bridge and looking north-east towards Mayfair. The powder magazine (built in 1805) closes the northern perspective of the bridge. On the left-hand side the word 'VICTORY' appears in brightly burning letters (in the area of Lancaster Gate).

The public celebrations in London were carefully planned and consisted of a triumphal peace march (from Albert Gate in Sloane Street to Kennington and back), a drawing of which is in the Museum's collection (A20684, by R. M. Paxton, also published in the *Sphere*) and the Hyde Park fireworks. The latter were set up in a long line parallel with Park Lane and some 10,000 rockets were fired.

This painting was commissioned by the *Sphere* and reproduced in the magazine on 26 July 1919. It contrasts with another work in the Museum's collection, a wash drawing by George Charlton dealing with informal, almost domestic, celebrations on Peace Day and entitled *A Street Tea in the East End* (acc. no. 91.63).

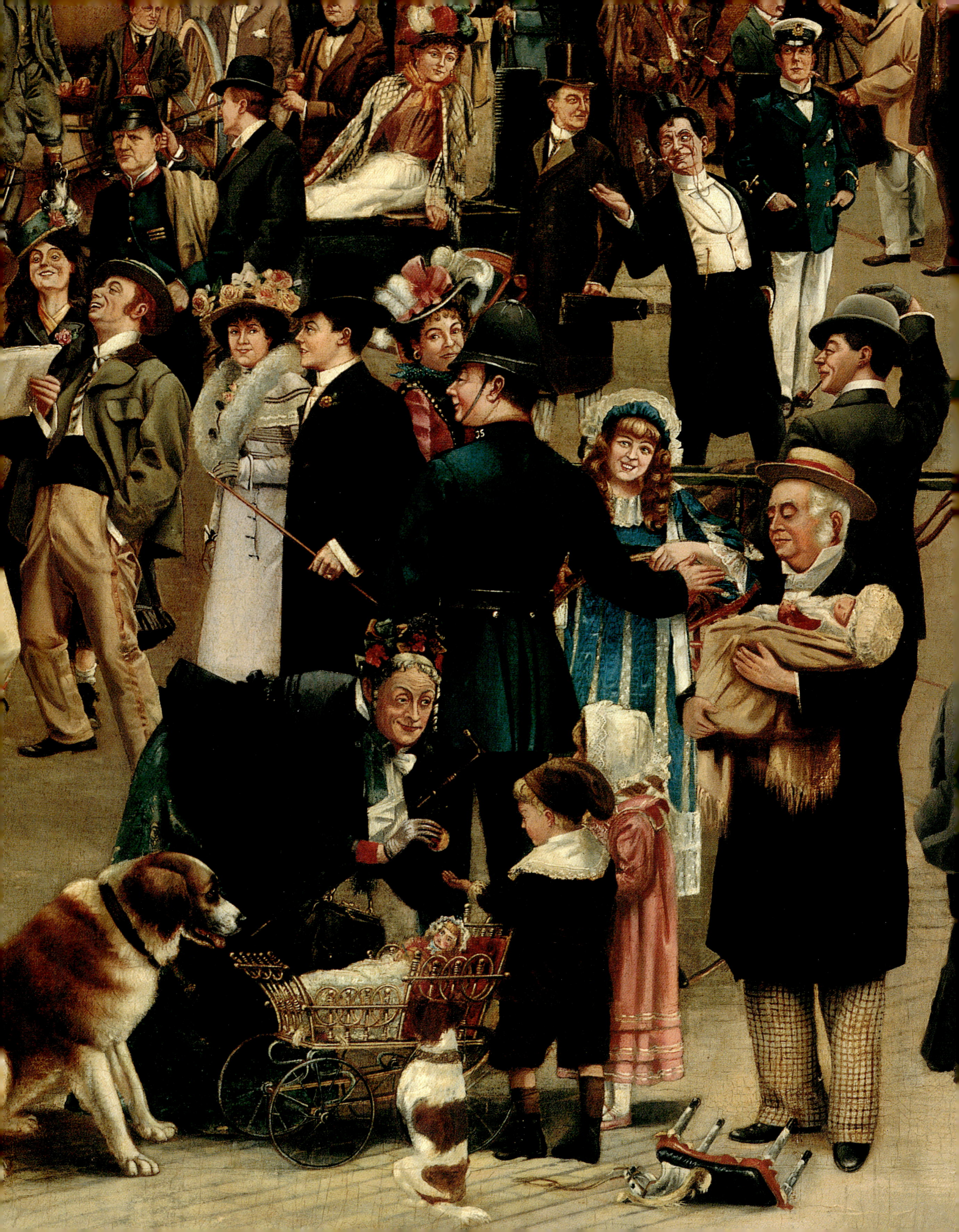

THE EDWARDIAN SOCIAL SCENE

THERE WERE considerable changes to the social scene during the Edwardian period.[1] Queen Victoria had withdrawn her court to Windsor during the latter years of her reign and was rarely seen in public. The Prince of Wales had been at the centre of fashionable society; on ascending the throne in 1901 as Edward VII he at once set to work transforming Buckingham Palace into a centre of glamorous activity ('Get this tomb cleaned up' were his words). At the first Court of the reign, held in March 1902, the live orchestra played Gilbert and Sullivan's overtures and other light pieces chosen by the King against official advice. The London Season – which opened with the Royal Academy Summer Exhibition and ended with the Royal Garden Party in July – was reborn and shone with all the glitter that it had lost during the long years of Victoria's mourning.

Painters took little part in creating this new ethos. Magazine illustrators, on the other hand, played a key role in producing those attractive images of social distinction that we associate with Edwardian London. For instance, the *Sphere* and the *Illustrated London News* glamorised the London Season and developed the concept of the Winter Season, filled with balls, parties, skating (at Prince's in Knightsbridge and from 1914 at Earl's Court), winter promenades in the parks, London lights at night time and supper clubs, of which the most famous, the Lotus, had dance rooms on the ground floor and supper rooms above.[2]

The painters' most memorable contributions to this scene were in portrait painting (particularly John Singer Sargent and John Lavery), while those London social tableaux which had been the hallmark of Victorian art (see Hicks and Joy) seemed to vanish from the painter's repertoire.

The emphasis was on consumption: for the privileged classes at hotels and restaurants such as the Ritz (opened in 1905) and the Savoy (opened in 1880 and extended in 1903–4); for the middle classes at the newly created Lyons tea houses;[3] and for the working classes at the music hall. The early years of the twentieth century also saw the continuation of the late Victorian boom in department stores: the most ambitious, Selfridge's, of Chicago backing and inspiration, opened in March 1909.

The theme of consumption did not seem to interest painters very much. It gave rise to such occasional works as William Strang's 1912 *Bank Holiday* (Tate Gallery), where an ordinary young couple is depicted on a romantic date at a restaurant. The painter Albert Ludovici Jnr (1852–1932), who painted many London scenes, recalled one of the treats of his Edwardian youth in words rather than paint:

> I remember being treated to an ice by old Gatti every time I accompanied my father, who was painting oval panels of life-size figures to decorate the long gallery of the new Monico restaurant and café[4] of which Gatti was the inaugurator; and a very different place he made it from the old fashioned chop-and-steak house one was used to in England. Gatti came to London in the fifties, starting business under one of the arches of the (then) new Charing Cross Bridge, where he baked gauffres [waffles]. . . As time went on he increased his business by turning the arch into a café where comic-songs were sung and eventually it became a music hall.[5]

This ascent from the working-class café to one of London's most fashionable restaurants is interesting because it pinpoints a crossing of class boundaries which is also noticeable in the work of Edwardian painters.

Harold Gilman, for instance, switches from a scene at *The Café Royal*[6] to *Tea in a Bedsitter*[7] or *An Eating-house*[8]. Sickert paints the seedy 'Camden Town murder' series or Mrs Barrett, his charlady, alongside portraits of the wealthy; for Gore it is the refined atmosphere of the art gallery[9] versus *Rinaldo, the Mad Violinist, at the Alhambra*;[10] for Ginner, the Café Royal versus factory scenes. For the first time, it seems, painters looked at the world of the urban working classes without attempting to teach moral lessons. Sickert's paintings of prostitutes[11] are completely removed from the concept of fallen women which had been developed by Victorian artists. The choice of a fish and chip shop, lovingly painted by Stanislawa de Karlowska,[12] no longer carries the disturbing statements found in John Henry Henshall's *Behind the Bar*[13] or Doré's *A Poor-House* (see cat. no. 128).

The Edwardian painter seemed oblivious to the potential clash of class cultures. When in 1908 Brangwyn was commissioned by Lloyd's Register of Shipping to decorate their newly converted committee luncheon room in Fenchurch Street, he chose dockside labour as his theme.

> He thought that such subjects were fitting for Lloyd's and would please his patrons. But he was wrong. When his paintings arrived and the members saw a string of sweating dockers bearing down on them from the ceiling many believed that the subjects could hardly have been less original, less suitable, for a room of Lloyd's where guests were entertained for lunch.[14]

There was a life-force, an energy, in the working classes which painters tried to harness. Perhaps Nevinson's recollections of the Edwardian pleasures of the music hall capture with vividness some of the raw qualities which appealed to so many painters:

> The Bedford Music Hall was our Mecca, not only because it was painted so much by Sickert, but because the twice-nightly performances possessed a vitality, a full-blooded, god blessed vulgarity, that would horrify the BBC fed audiences of today.[15]

Sylvia Pankhurst (1882–1960)
Self Portrait, autumn 1906?
Pastel and charcoal drawing
The Museum of London.

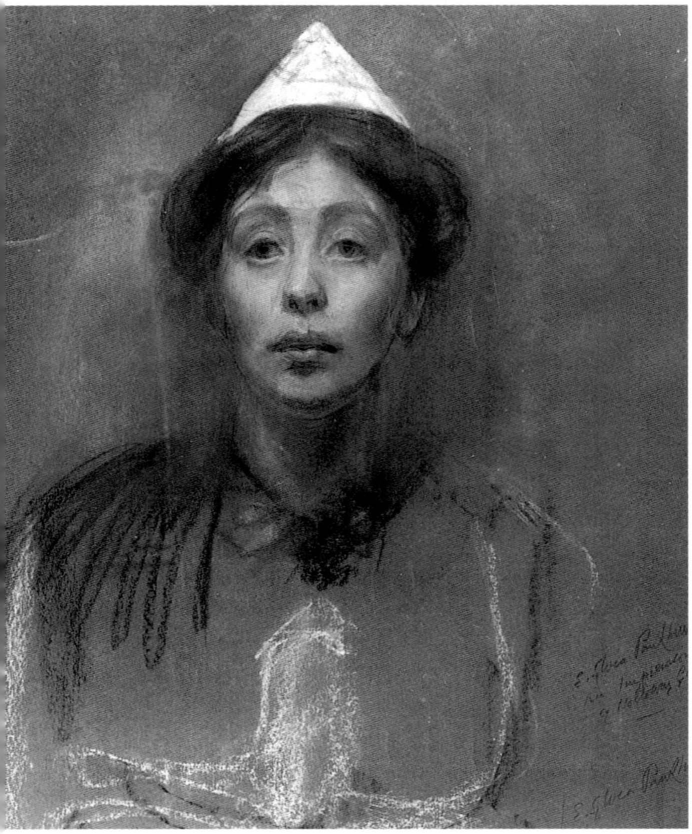

This promiscuity between 'high' and 'low' art finds some echo in the world of theatre. The rise of the 'Theatre of Ideas' which looked at themes of social and domestic conflict and engaged the attention of playwrights as diverse as Pinero, John Galsworthy, Bernard Shaw and Henrik Ibsen offered great contrast to what has been described as 'Theatre Theatrical', a theatre 'resplendent and majestic and enlarged',[16] more mythical and glittering than truly realistic. The modest selection of theatrical paintings below is interesting because it illustrates aspects from the two most important 'institutions' that dominated the theatrical scene in late Victorian and Edwardian times: Henry Irving at the Lyceum and Herbert Beerbohm Tree at His Majesty's.

In equally modest ways this section testifies to the impact of the suffragette movement, one of the most noteworthy and well-studied social phenomena of the Edwardian years.[17] Its impact on painters, however, is not often discussed. Although Sylvia Pankhurst, one of Emmeline's three daughters, trained at the Royal College of Art (1904–6),[18] her career as a painter never really developed. The Museum holds an extraordinary self-portrait executed in pastels and datable to 1906, when she was first incarcerated at Holloway Prison, but most of her creative powers were channelled instead into propaganda design work.

The influence of the suffragette movement may perhaps be detected in the work *A Bloomsbury Family* by William Orpen.[19] The painting has been used to highlight the patriarchal order, with the father figure dominating the composition.[20] However, the mother, relegated to the background, is detached from the family group rather than part of it, a position that may allude to women's new claims for independence.

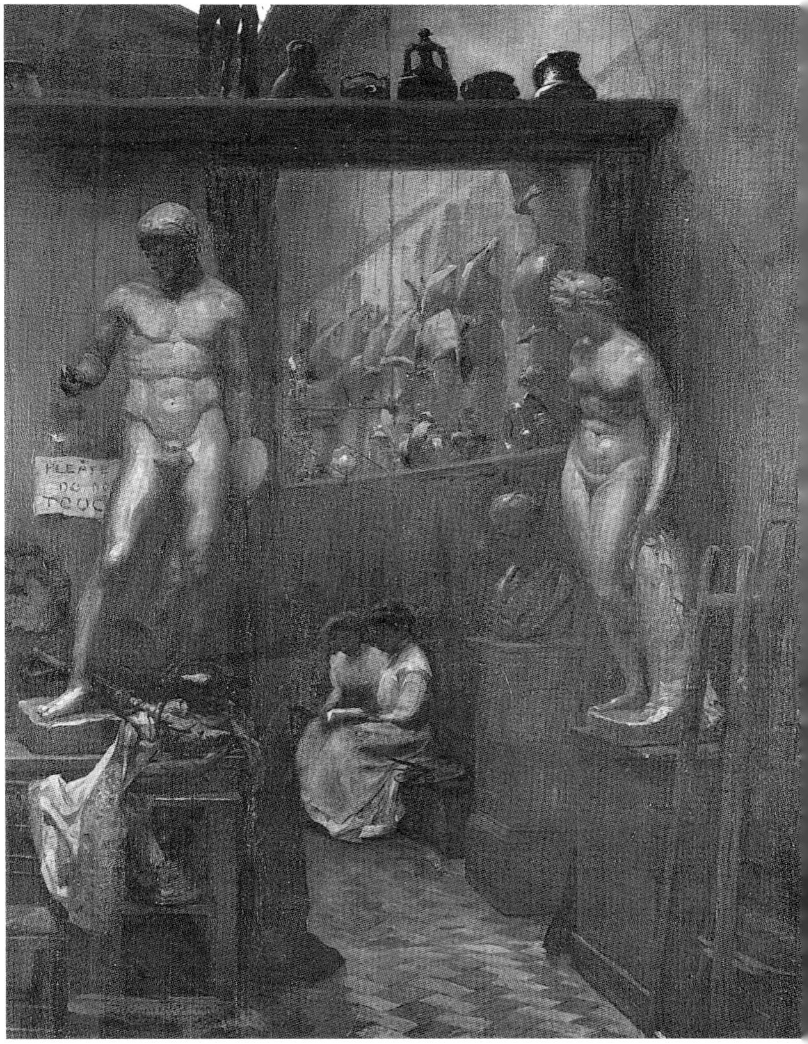

Nellie Joshua (exh. 1902–11)
*Heatherley's Art School, c.*1902
Oil on canvas
Collection: Anissa I El-Helou.

For the first time in this book, the selection below presents the work of a number of female painters: Mary Edith Durham, Stanislawa de Karlowska, and a little later Rosamund Borradaile and Gladys Pinks. The number of women studying and qualifying at the Royal College of Art was substantial. Women's abilities, however, were not recognised and art teaching, one of the natural outlets for art trainees, was virtually closed to them.[21] Around 1902 Nellie Joshua painted Heathersley's Art School,[22] one of the most popular private art schools in London which was open to women. The composition contrasts with the prevalent formula of, for instance, *The Life School* (attributed to Hogarth and in the collection of the Royal Academy): the formal spread of students round a model is replaced here by two lone figures placed in the *background* of a museum-like setting, with all the props vying for attention in the foreground and middle ground. Under the brush of a woman painter, accessories take prominence over the female students themselves.

The declaration of war on 4 August 1914 brought the suffragettes' efforts to a halt and most women rallied round this important new cause. Although the first zeppelin raid over the City killed thirty-nine people when it dropped a bomb near the Guildhall and further nightly raids made the war in London a reality, the success of 'Front' pictures[23] encouraged the trend for artists to be sent across the Channel. Hardly any paintings exist of London at war between 1914 and 1918. The most conspicuous works depict the city at night time with criss-crossing lights in the sky. C. R. W. Nevinson's *Among London Searchlights* is one of the most memorable paintings in this category and was taken from a captive balloon tethered above London Bridge.[24]

Unexpectedly the Royal Victoria Patriotic Asylum in Wandsworth, which had become the third London Territorial General Hospital, became a thriving artistic centre when a plea for help was made by its commandant in the bar of the Chelsea Arts Club: thirty artists joined *en masse*.[25] This interesting First World War episode deserves to be fully researched (see cat. no. 148).

1. See, for instance the recently published *The Edwardian Era*, Jane Beckett and Deborah Cherry (eds.), 1987.
2. 'The Winter Season in London', in the *Sphere*, 24 January 1914.
3. The first teashop opened in Piccadilly in 1894; by 1910 there were ninety-eight of them.
4. At 19 Shaftesbury Avenue.
5. A. Ludovici, *An Artist's Life in London and Paris, 1870–1925*, 1926, p36.
6. *The Painters of Camden Town 1905–20*, exhibition catalogue, Christie's, 1988, no. 133.
7. Ibid, no. 142.
8. Ibid, no. 146.
9. *Gauguins and Connoisseurs at the Stafford Gallery*, private collection, see Wendy Baron, *The Camden Town Group*, 1979, no. 66, pp202–3.
10. Ibid, no. 5, pp116–17.
11. See *Sickert Paintings,* Wendy Baron and Richard Shone (eds.), exhibition catalogue, Royal Academy, 1993, nos 34–42.
12. Tate Gallery, reproduced in Beckett and Cherry (eds.), 1987, p87.
13. Dated 1882, private collection. A watercolour version is in the collection of the Museum of London (acc. no. 82.582).
14. Rodney Brangwyn, *Brangwyn*, 1978, p135.
15. In his 1937 autobiography, *Paint and Prejudice*, p27.
16. J. C. Trewin, *The Edwardian Theatre*, 1976, p3.
17. See Beckett and Cherry (eds.), 1987; Diane Atkinson's *Suffragettes* in the Museum of London's Connection series, 1988; Diane Atkinson, *The Purple, White & Green: Suffragettes in London 1906–14*, 1993; *Kitty Marion: the Autobiography of a Suffragette and Actress*, Diane Atkinson and Viv Gardner (eds.), forthcoming, 1997.
18. See Atkinson, 1988; also Christopher Frayling, *The Royal College of Art*, 1987, pp75–7.
19. 1907, Scottish National Gallery of Modern Art, Edinburgh; reproduced in Beckett and Cherry (eds.), 1987, p98.
20. Ibid, p98.
21. Frayling, 1987, p74.
22. Private collection, reproduced in Beckett and Cherry (eds.), 1987, p40.
23. Meirion and Susie Harris, *The War Artists*, 1983, p3.
24. See *Nevinson War Paintings*, exhibition catalogue, Graves Art Gallery, Sheffield, 1972, no. 32.
25. Harris, 1983, p2.

152.

MARY EDITH DURHAM

(1863–1944)

The Funeral Procession of Queen Victoria

[A24383]

1901

Oil on panel, 26.9 x 20.3 cm

Signed and partially dated bottom left:

Feb[y] ME Durham

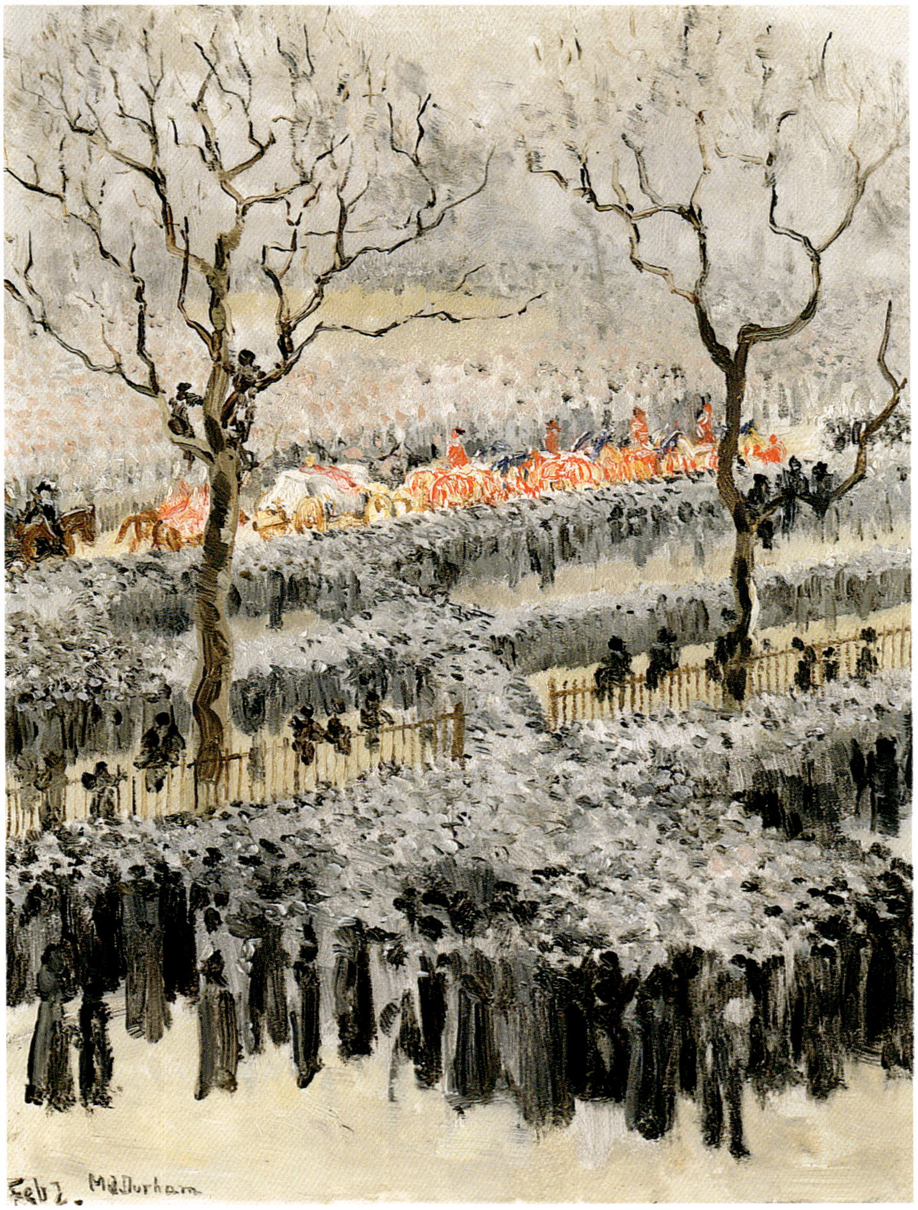

THIS PICTURE was sketched from the roof of a house in Park Lane, and shows the crowds that watched the procession passing through Hyde Park on this February Saturday morning. The gun carriage carrying the body, which was drawn by eight cream-coloured horses, can be seen in the middle distance; the coffin was covered by a pall of white satin and the Royal Standard, upon which rested the Crown, the Regalia and the Insignia of the Order of the Garter.

Queen Victoria died at Osborne House on 22 January 1901, aged eighty-one, having reigned for over sixty-three years. Her body was brought to Gosport on Friday 1 February and by train to London the following morning. The processional route through the metropolis, from Victoria Station to Paddington Station, *en route* for Windsor, passed Buckingham Palace, went down the Mall to St James's Palace, up St James's Street, along Piccadilly to Hyde Park, through the Park to Marble Arch, along Edgware Road and across Praed Street.

Provenance:
Presented by the artist in 1922.

Bibliography:
Hayes (cat. no. 38).

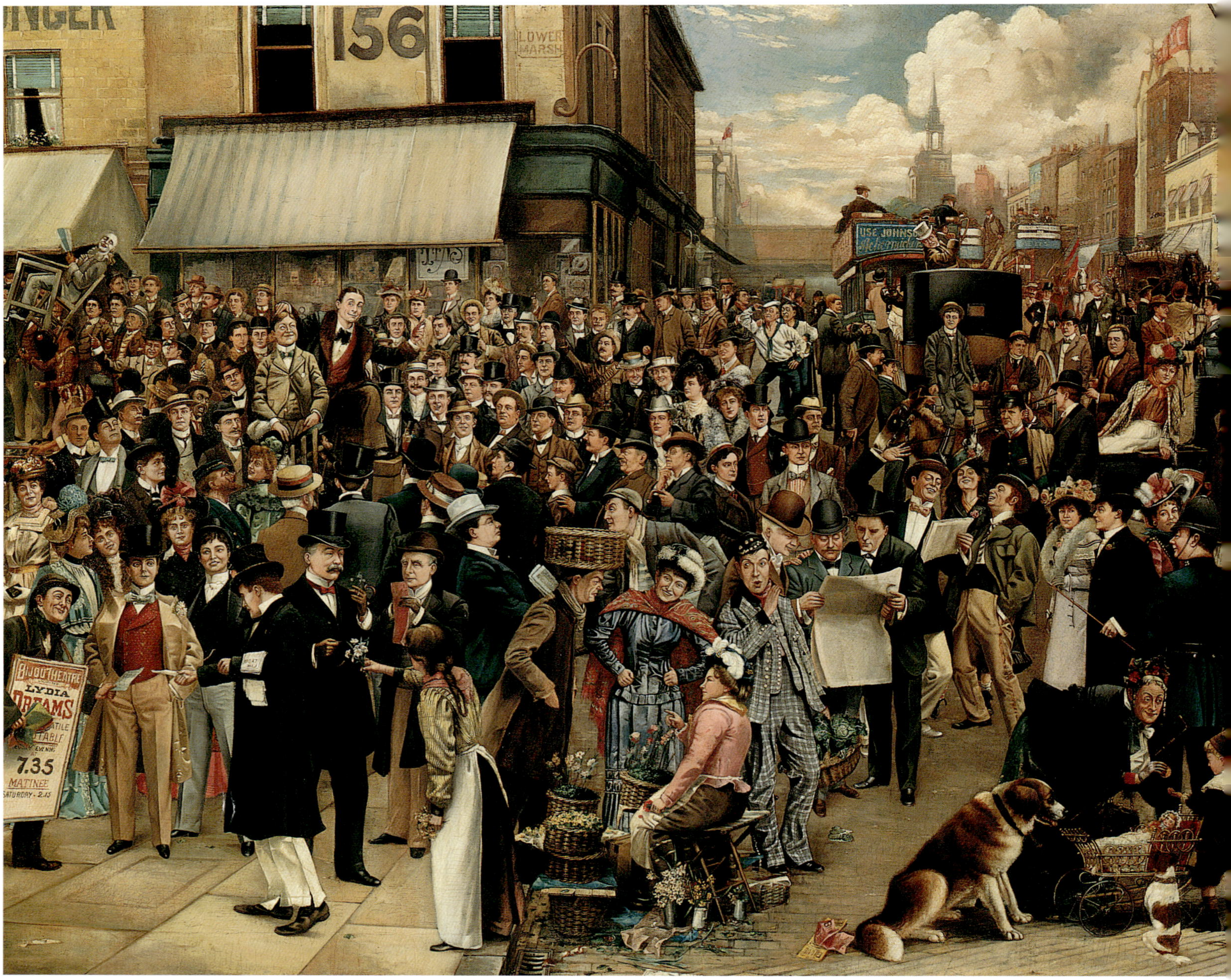

153.

WALTER H. LAMBERT
(1870/1–1950)

Popularity: The Stars of the Edwardian Music Hall [57.114]
1901–3
Oil on canvas, 160 x 375.9 cm
Signed and dated bottom right:
Lydia Dreams. 1901–1903

THIS VAST group portrait of the principal artistes of the Edwardian music hall includes no fewer than 231 performers, among them Harry Champion, Harry Lauder, Dan Leno, Marie Lloyd (on the right of the policeman), George Robey, Little Tich (bowler-hatted in the foreground centre), Vesta Tilley (in male attire in the foreground right) and the artist himself (immediately above the sandwich-board man in the foreground left, in his role as the female impersonator, Lydia Dreams: a self-portrait sketch of the artist signed and dated August 1900 is in

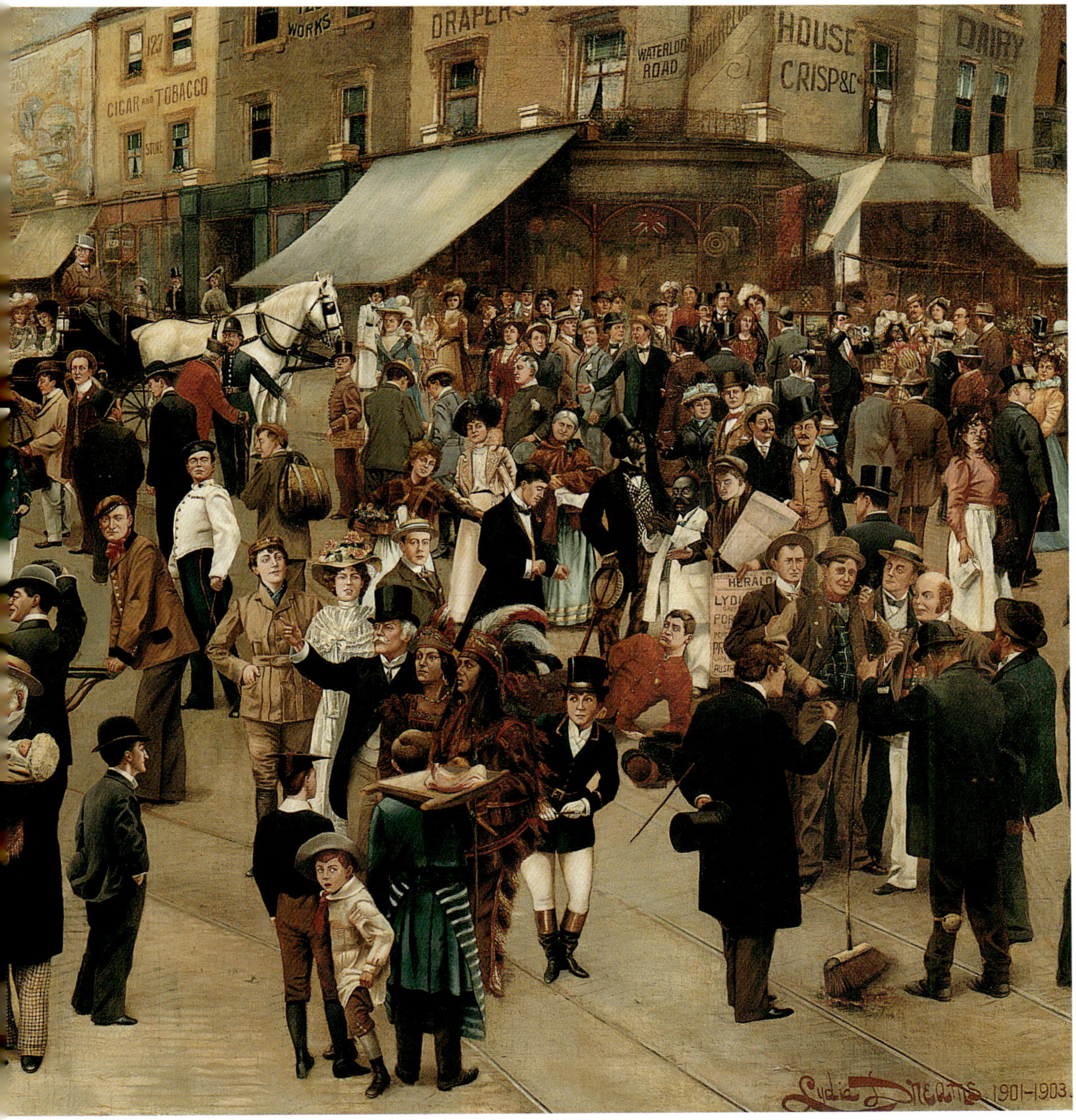

Provenance:
Peter Cannon (see text); A. Squires; A. Coleman, 1934; presented by Bernard Coleman (from the Castle Hotel, Tooting) in 1957.

Bibliography:
Hayes (cat. no. 120).

an autograph book owned by Mr Ellis Ashton). The first owner of the picture, Peter Cannon ('Bijou'), a friend of the artist, is seen with his partner 'Bella' on the left of the policeman, and the artist's son and daughter have also been included as the two little children in the centre foreground.

The scene is the junction of Lower Marsh and the Cut with the Waterloo Road, the traditional meeting place of music hall artistes, and down which a couple of omnibuses, a brougham and an open landau are seen. In the distance is the railway bridge constructed for the extension of the South Eastern Railway from London Bridge to Charing Cross in the early 1860s, and the tower and spire of St John's, Waterloo Road, built in 1822–4. The Old Vic (formerly the Royal Victoria Music Hall) would have appeared just outside the picture, on the right.

A photogravure of the scene was published by the artist on 20 June 1903 with an accompanying key which is

KEY TO

Depicting Well-known

SIZE OF OR

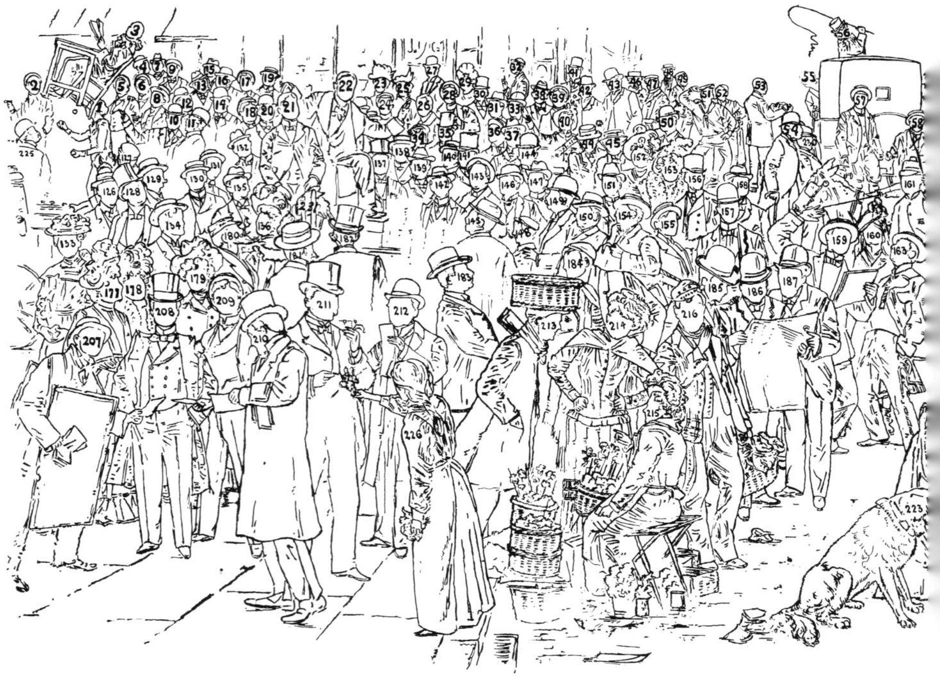

1 Paul Cinquevalli
2 Dan Kelly
3 Griff
4 Allen and Hart
5 Tom Morris
6 T. Morris
7 Harry Nation
8 S. Ethardo
9 Tom Vine
10, 11 Bros. Donaldson
12 Willie Benn
13 Richie Tom
14 James Riley
15 Arthur Harland
16 Albert Rollinson
17 Joe Gee (Burnells)
18 The late Pat Feeney
19 Jimmie Campbell
20 Albert and Edmunds
21 Pimple
22 Dan Leno
23 Nellie Wilson
24 Arthur Forrest
25 Nellie Richards
26 John Lawson
27 Horace White
28 Tom Collins
29 Lilly English
30 George Booker
31 Fred Griffiths
32 Albert Le Fre
33 Joe Griffiths
34 Harry Champion
35 Harry Anderson
36 Harry Blake (2 B's)
37 Bob Leonard
38 Jack Camp
39 Ford and Hanson
40 Fred Millis
41 Hanson
42 Capt. Slingsby
43 Tom McKay
44, 45 Sisters Levy
46 The late Mrs. Florador
47 Florador
48 Harry Lauder
49 Paul Courtenay
50 Frank Coyne
51 Tom Wootwall
52 Nat Clifford
53 Dutch Daly
54 Reid Pinaud
55 Chirgwin
56 Walter Stockwell
57, 58 Two Harvey Boys
59 Rumbo Austin
60 Charles Tempest
61 Johnny Dane
62 Arthur Pearl
63 Jack Rowley
64, 65 Bros. Passmore
66 The late Bessie Bellwood
67 Harry Lester
68 Charlie Edwards
69 Con Fredericks
70 Charles Morton, Esq.
71 Marie Loftus
72 Cissie Loftus
73 Tom Branford
74 Charlie Clark
75 Tom Costello
76 Clarke (Clarke and Glennie)
77 Gus Garrick
78 Jock Bennett
79 Charlie Martell
80 Herbert Darnley
81 Geo. Le Brunn
82 Little Ganty
83 Vene Clements
84 Carrie Laurie
85 Marie Kendall
86 Daisy James
87 Percy Delevine
88 Harry Delevine
89 Lottie Lennox
90 Vosper
91 Billie Barlow
92 George Grey
93 Musical Korries
94 The late Bessie Wer
95 Miss Korrie
96 Sam Glenroy
97 Charlie Fraser
98 Jeff Vendome
99 Mrs. Charlie Fraser
100 Grell and Gray
101 Alice Maydue
102 Jerry Driscoll
103 Bob Allinson
104 Dean Tribune
105 Jean Seul
106 Ernest Rees
107 Douglas Stuart
108 Walter Norman
109 Edna Cragge
110 Ida Heath
111 F. Ayling
112 H. Harris
113, 114 Fish and Warren
115 The late Jolly.John
116 The late Geo. Leybo

reproduced here. The artist's proof for the work was presented to Buckingham Palace on that day.

Music Hall, an essentially popular art form, originated in the early years of Queen Victoria's reign; it started in the taverns and gin palaces of London as an entertainment which accompanied eating and drinking, and the first hall actually built as a music hall was the Canterbury, opened in 1852. The period from 1880 until 1914 was the heyday of the genre, and the principal London theatres in which it played were the Empire, the

LARITY."

the Vaudeville Stage.

y 5ft. 6in.

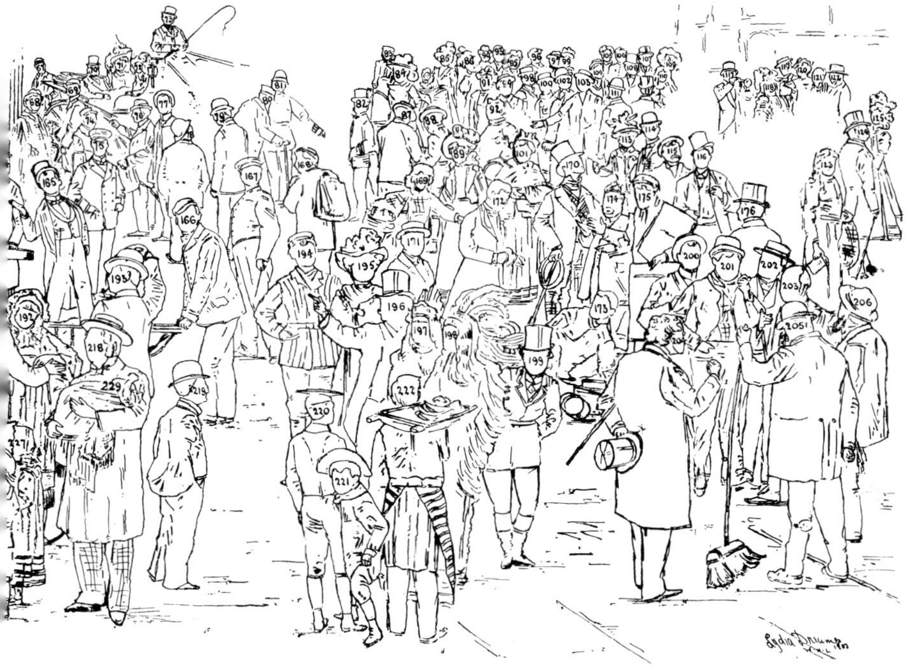

ans
nderson
axwell
a Francis
e Charles Laurie
mbert
e Ada Lundberg
olmes
aradise
Bard
k
e Charles Godfrey
lbini
Norrie
Cornish
issell
Ford
y Williams
ragg
dra Dagmar
e Tom White
Travis
land
Armstrong
Alexander
Randall
Campbell
e Tom O'Brien
ollinson

146 G. W. Hunter
147 Vento
148 Eddy Hanlon
149 Bob Hanlon
150 Teddy Bale
151 George Lashwood
152 Harriet Vernon
153 Jennie Valmore
154 Harry Gee
155 Harry Pleon
156 Harry Freeman
157 Tom Leamore
158 Charles Seel
159 Sam Poluski
160 Ada Cerito
161 Tom Bass
162 Frank Folloy
163 Will Poluski
164 George Mozart
165 Paul Martinetti
166 Alec Hurley
167 Pat Raffety
168 Arthur Lennard
169 Alice Lloyd
170 Eugene Stratton
171 George Robey
172 Jimmie Hall
173 Bill Horne
174 George Le Clercq

175 Chris Horne
176 Charlie Fontaine
177 Lydia Dreams
178 Jessie Preston
179 Georgina Preston
180 H. Missouri
181 J. Sothern
182 Will Oliver
183 Fred Mc'Naughton
184 Tom Mc'Naughton
185 Joe Elvin
186 Jack Lotto
187 Wal Pink
188 Miss Bella } Bella and Bijou
189 Mr. Bijou }
190 Kate Carney
191 James Fawn
192 Marie Lloyd
193 T. E. Dunville
194 Katie Lawrence
195 Vesta Victoria
196 Mr. Leamy
197 } Ara and Vora
198 }
199 Fannie Leslie
200 J. O'Gorman
201 Michael Nolan
202 Joe Tennyson
203 Horace Wheatley

204 Walter Munroe
205 Johnny Dwyer
206 Pat Carey
207 Harry Ford
208 Vesta Tilley
209 The late Bessie Bonehill
210 R. G. Knowles
211 Arthur Lloyd
212 Charles Coborn
213 Gus Elen
214 Jenny Hill
215 Peggy Pryde
216 Albert Chevalier
217 Arthur Rigby
218 Papa Brown
219 Little Tich
220 } Carrie Lorrie's Juveniles
221 }
222 Character
223 Mr. Smith's Dog
224 Dandy George's Dog Rosie
225 T. Beck
226 Artist's late Wife
227 Child of Artist
228 Child of Artist
229 Child of Artist
230 Will Crackles
231 Jack Rich

Palace, and the Coliseum. With the collapse of the Victorian way of life after the Great War, and the coming of the motion picture, music hall declined and the theatres themselves were usually turned into cinemas.

Between 1924 and 1957, *Popularity* was the star attraction of the Castle Hotel, a pub in Tooting High Street, and the story of this establishment, recounted in an undated pamphlet, claims that the reputation of the painting 'spread far beyond the bounds of South London, even to Europe and America!'

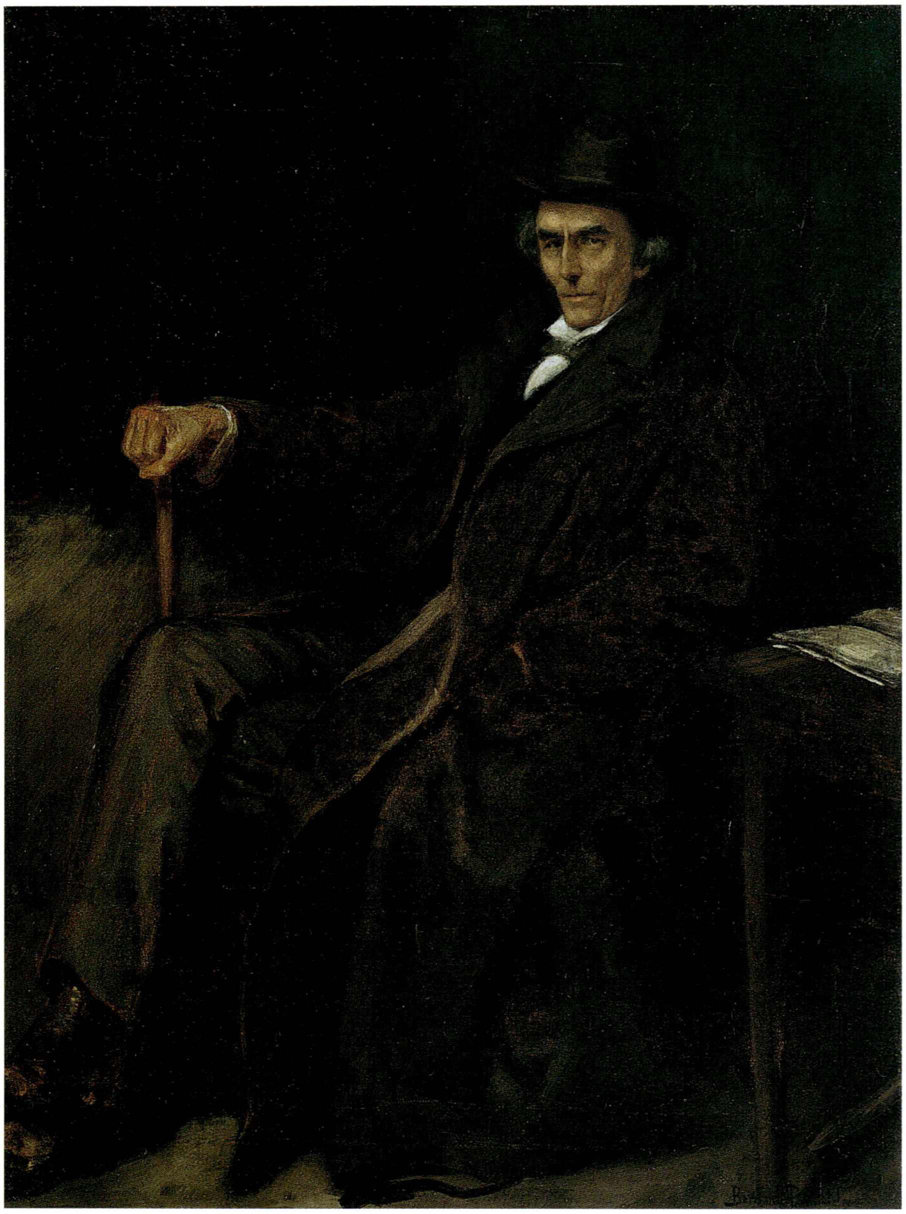

Provenance:
Lent by the artist in 1938; presented by his niece, Mrs Barbara Slater, in 1966.

Bibliography:
Hayes (cat. no. 122).

154.
SIR BERNARD PARTRIDGE
(1861–1945)
Portrait of Sir Henry Irving at Rehearsal
[38.8/1]
*c.*1903
Oil on canvas, 60 x 42.7 cm
Signed bottom right: *Bernard Partridge*

SIR HENRY Irving (1838–1905) is shown here at full length, seated facing left, with his head turned to the spectator, wearing grey trousers, a thick brown overcoat and a felt hat, and clasping a stick in his right hand; he is seated on the stage, with a desk on the right. Irving's arrival in a felt hat was said to presage a long and arduous rehearsal; a top hat, on the other hand, signified that the rehearsal would probably be short.

Irving, whose original name was John Henry Brodribb, began his stage career at the Lyceum Theatre, Sunderland, in 1856. He spent the next ten years in the provinces, playing at the Theatre Royal, Manchester, for five years, and it was not until 1871, after he had joined H. L. Bateman's company at the Lyceum theatre, London, that he began to establish a serious reputation. In 1878 he took over the management of the Lyceum, and for nearly twenty-five years he reigned there, with a policy of alternating Shakespeare and popular melodrama, the acknowledged head of the English stage. Irving's strength as an actor lay in the thought and originality he brought to the parts he played, something entirely new in the Victorian theatre, where playgoers expected a performance to be cast in a traditional mould. Knighted in 1895, he died suddenly in 1905, and was buried in Westminster Abbey.

Partridge appeared as an actor in the early 1890s under the name of Bernard Gould; he was also *persona grata* as an artist at most London theatres, and drew and painted Irving in many of his roles. A pencil sketch for the Museum picture is dated 1903, and this was used for the poster for Irving's farewell seasons in London and on tour.

Other portraits of Irving in oils, by Archer (cat. no. 129) and Eves (cat. no. 157), are in the collection. The Museum of London also holds a large collection of Irving's memorabilia and costume.

155.
CHARLES A. BUCHEL
(active 1901–14)
Lionel Brough as Verges in *Much Ado About Nothing* [56.169/30]
*c.*1905
Oil on canvas, 53.2 x 39 cm
Signed bottom left: *CHAS. A. BUCHEL*

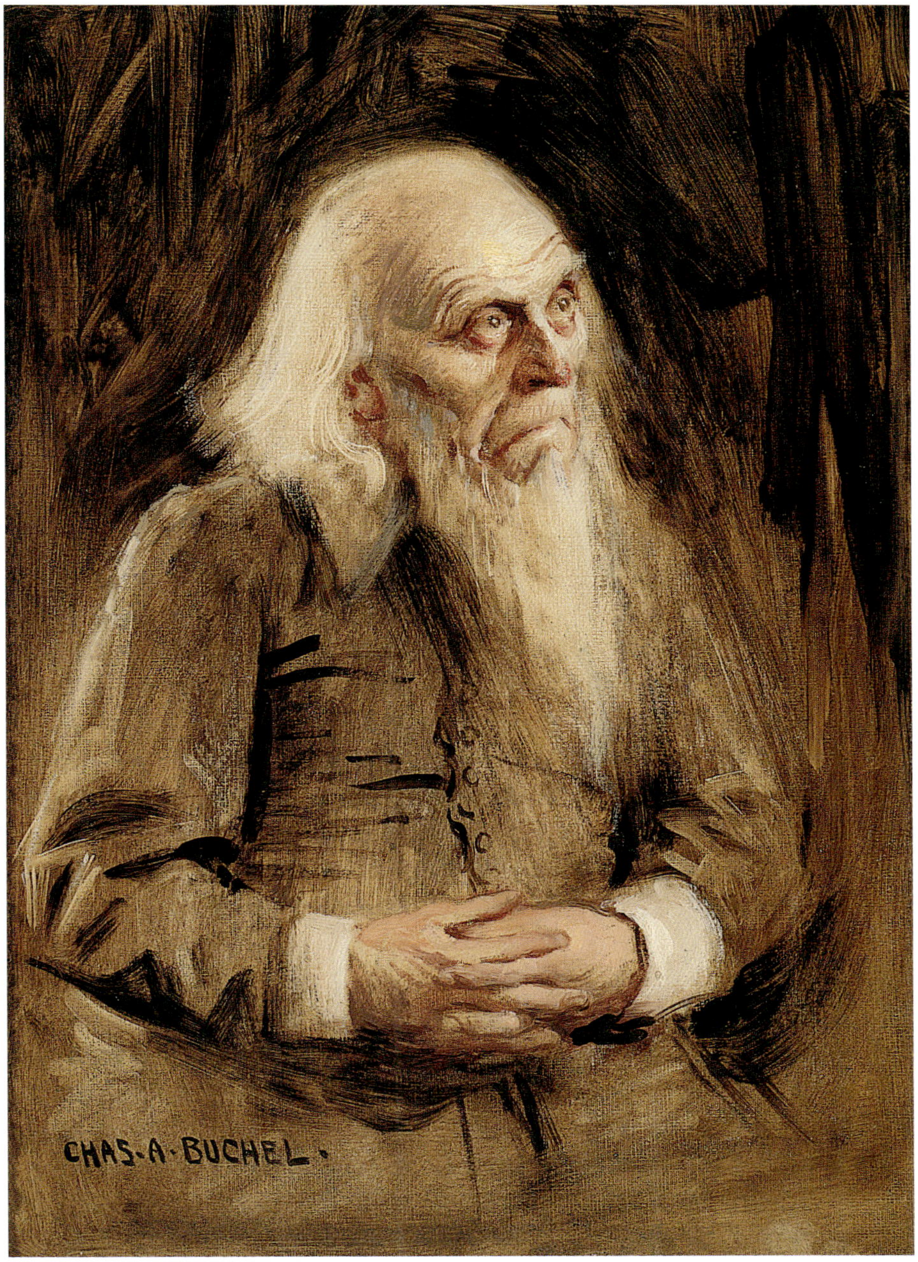

THIS HALF-LENGTH portrait shows Lionel Brough (1836–1909), facing half right and looking upwards, his arms folded in front of him, with a plain background, in the part of Verges in Shakespeare's *Much Ado About Nothing*, which he played at the revival at His Majesty's Theatre, 24 January 1905.

From 1894 till his death in 1909 Brough worked in Herbert Beerbohm Tree's company. The rather intense expression on the actor's face would have appealed to Tree's sense of realism, which at times was very literal. The following anecdote is quoted in relation to his production of *Much Ado About Nothing*: '"Civil as an orange," says Beatrice of Claudio . . . and there at His Majesty's, centre stage, was an orange tree, to ensure that no one lost the point.' (Trewin, 1976).

Lionel Brough made his first appearance on the stage at the Lyceum Theatre, London, in 1854; but he spent much of the next ten years in journalism, and did not begin to make a name for himself as an actor until he appeared in H. J. Byron's *Dearer than Life* in 1868. He was engaged almost exclusively for comic roles, of which the best known was his Tony Lumpkin in *She Stoops to Conquer*, a part he played no less than 777 times.

Provenance:
Presented by R. N. Green-Armytage in 1956.

Bibliography:
Hayes (cat. no. 116); J. C. Trewin, *The Edwardian Theatre*, 1976, p112.

Provenance:
From the collection of Edward Le Bas; Christie's, 3 March 1978 (118); purchased by the Museum with a grant from the National Art Collections Fund.

Bibliography:
A Painter's Collection (Edward Le Bas, RA), Royal Academy, 1963, no. 48; Wendy Baron, *Sickert,* 1973, p344, no. 247; *Sickert Paintings*, Wendy Baron and Richard Shone (eds.), exhibition catalogue, Royal Academy, 1993, no. 86.

156.
WALTER SICKERT
(1860–1942)
Gallery Box at the New Bedford Music Hall [78.155]
*c.*1906–7
Oil on canvas, 50.7 x 41 cm
Signed bottom left: *Sickert*
Label on the back: *Le Bas Collection 1968*
(also see cat. no. 144)

THIS PAINTING of the New Bedford Theatre/Music Hall shows the upper gallery box, which was on the right when facing the stage. Part of the stage curtain is visible on the left-hand side and the presence of the audience suggests that the scene was captured during a performance.

Sickert had first tackled the London music hall scene as early as 1884, when he had produced some etchings of a music hall audience. The first painting on the subject which the artist exhibited was *The Lion Comique* (1887) probably set in the Marylebone Music Hall; it was not until the following year, however, that this new subject in British painting was drawn to public attention with the exhibition of the controversial *Gatti's Hungerford Palace of Varieties: Turn of Miss Katie Lawrence* (see Baron and Shone (eds.), 1993, no. 6).

Sickert, along with a small group of contemporary writers, was keen to champion the artistic qualities of the music hall at a time when many thought that it was a vulgar and degrading pastime. He thus produced a large and unique body of images showing many London music halls, including Sam Collins (Islington Green), Marylebone, Gatti's (off the Strand), Tivoli (in the Strand), the Oxford Music Hall (in the West End) and finally (and most memorably) the Old and New Bedford Music Hall in Camden Town.

Squeezed between Arlington Street and Camden High Street, the old-fashioned Bedford Music Hall was built in 1861 and would probably have gone unrecorded had it not been for Sickert's untiring fascination with it. His first painting of the Old Bedford, *Little Dot Hetherington at the Bedford Music Hall* (in 1888–9, see Baron and Shone (eds.), 1993, no. 8), confirmed the artist's interest in the subject's human element, ranging from the audience to the performers. This very much contrasts with his later paintings of the New Bedford, where the primary focus was given to the interior decoration – as is already the case in this painting.

The theme of the Bedford Music Hall was a haunting one for the artist, who lived in nearby Mornington Crescent. The original music hall burnt down in 1896, then was rebuilt and reopened in 1899, when Sickert lived abroad. There was therefore a time lapse before Sickert produced works showing the New Bedford. The work under review is the first known oil painting by Sickert of the rebuilt music hall.

The artist's output on the New Bedford can be divided into two periods. The first period, which started with the present work, culminated in a painting of about 1908 of which the whereabouts are unknown (see Baron, 1973, p343). Then in 1914 Sickert returned to the theme after he was commissioned by Miss Ethel Sands to produce a decorative scheme for her new house at 15 Vale Avenue in Chelsea. The artist thought that he would be able to develop his earlier studies of the New Bedford – including the painting under review – into an appropriate scheme, but soon realised that more visits to and studies of the Bedford were required.

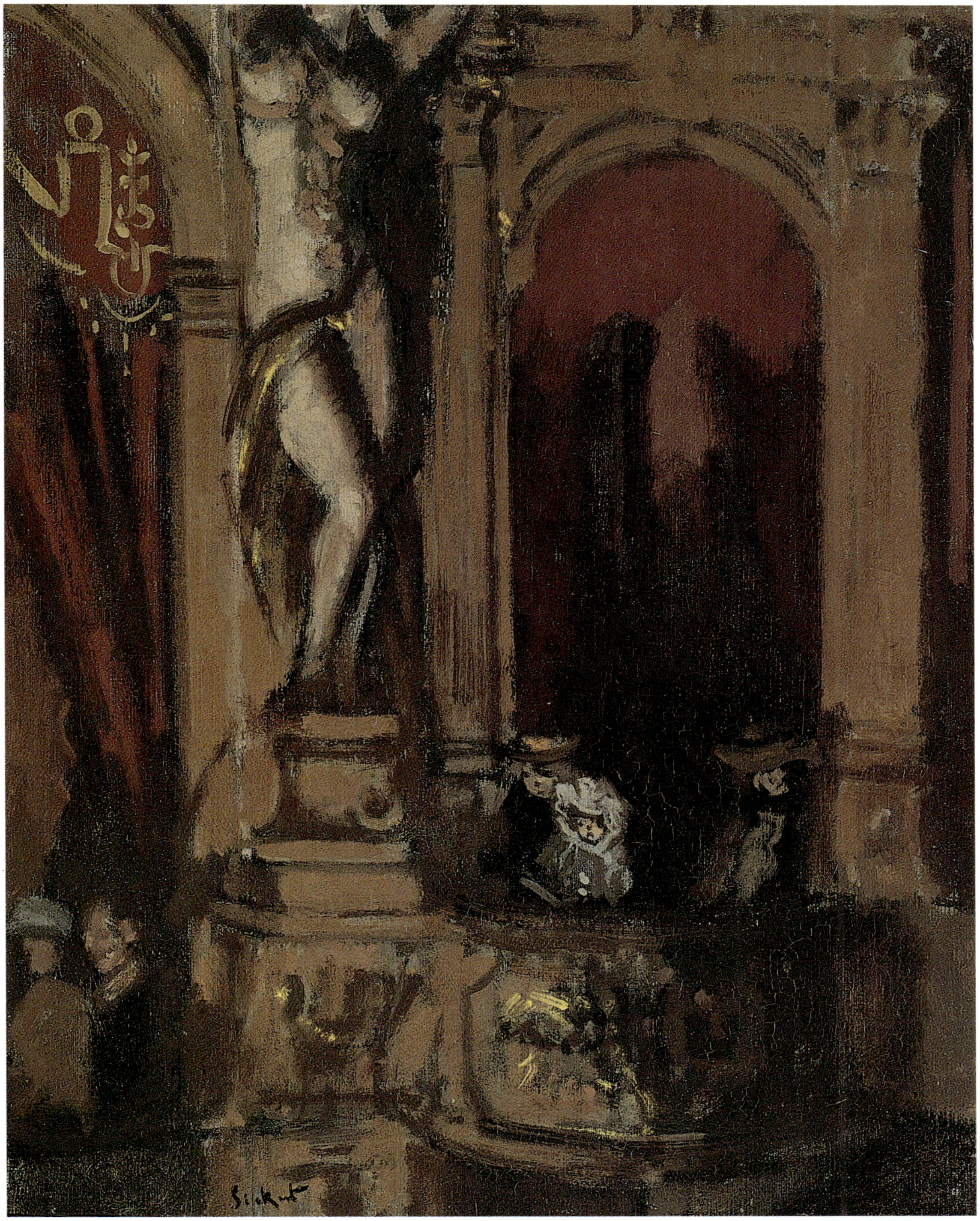

After the last performance at the Bedford Theatre in January 1951, the building lay neglected and vandalised until it was finally demolished in 1969. A drawing by Terence Dalley dated October 1969, 'The End of the Bedford Music Hall Camden Town', is in the Museum's collection (acc. no. 81.595/12).

Sickert showed a drawing of the New Bedford at the New English Art Club in the summer of 1907 (no. 27). It appears to have been related to the painting under review, judging by the thumb-nail sketch found in the Tate Gallery copy of the catalogue for that exhibition. The whereabouts of the drawing are unknown.

Provenance:
Fred Terry; presented by Miss Julia Neilson in 1938.

Bibliography:
Hayes (cat. no. 117).

157.
REGINALD GRANVILLE EVES
(1876–1941)
Portrait of Sir Henry Irving [38.5/9]
*c.*1905–10
Oil on canvas, 60.3 x 50 cm
Signed top right: *R. G. Eves*

SIR HENRY Irving (1838–1905) is shown with his head and shoulders facing slightly to right and with his head turned towards the spectator; the background is plain. This is probably a posthumous portrait of the great actor, based on the photograph by William Crooke taken in Edinburgh in April 1904. For other portraits of Irving, see cat. nos 129 and 154.

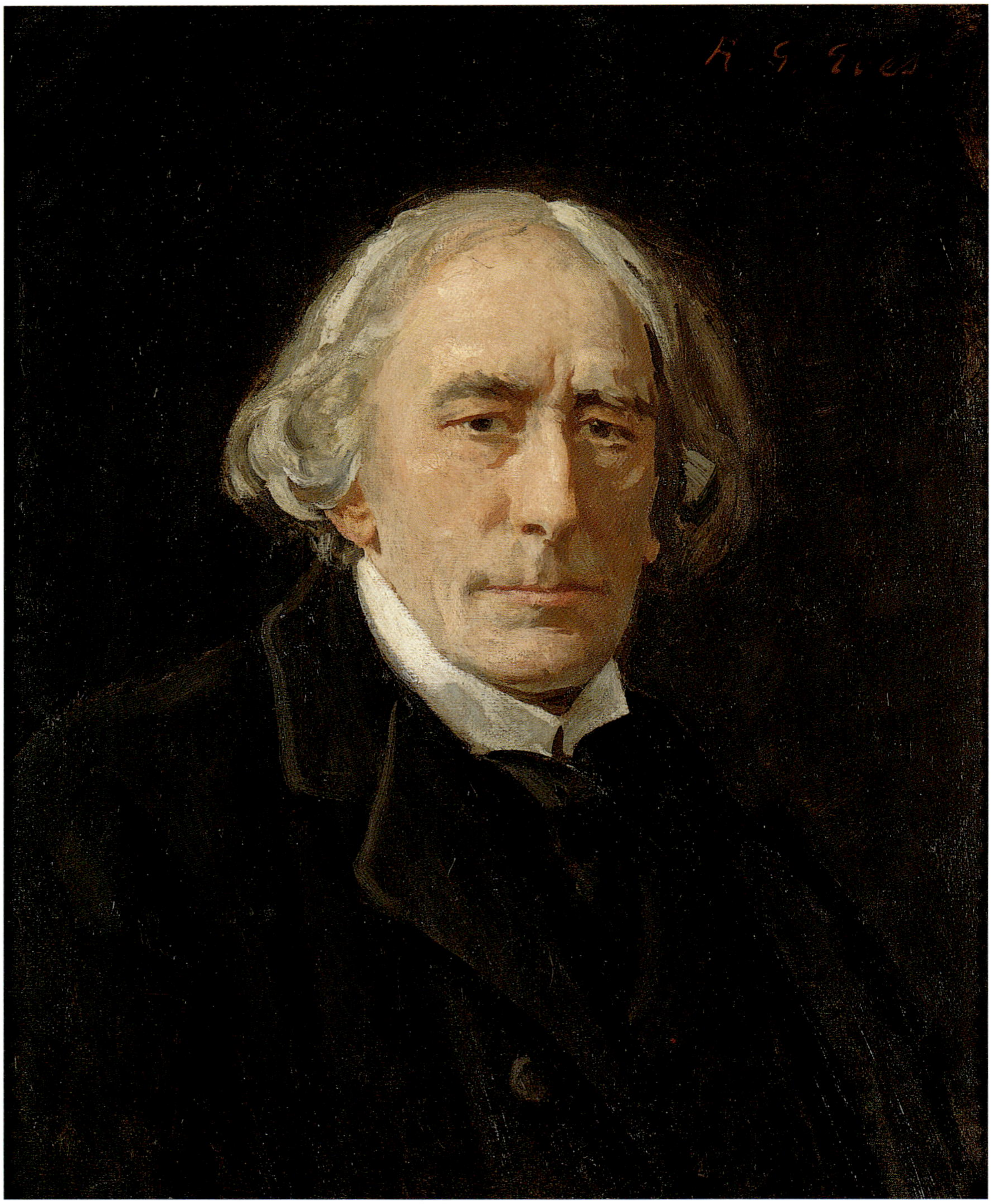

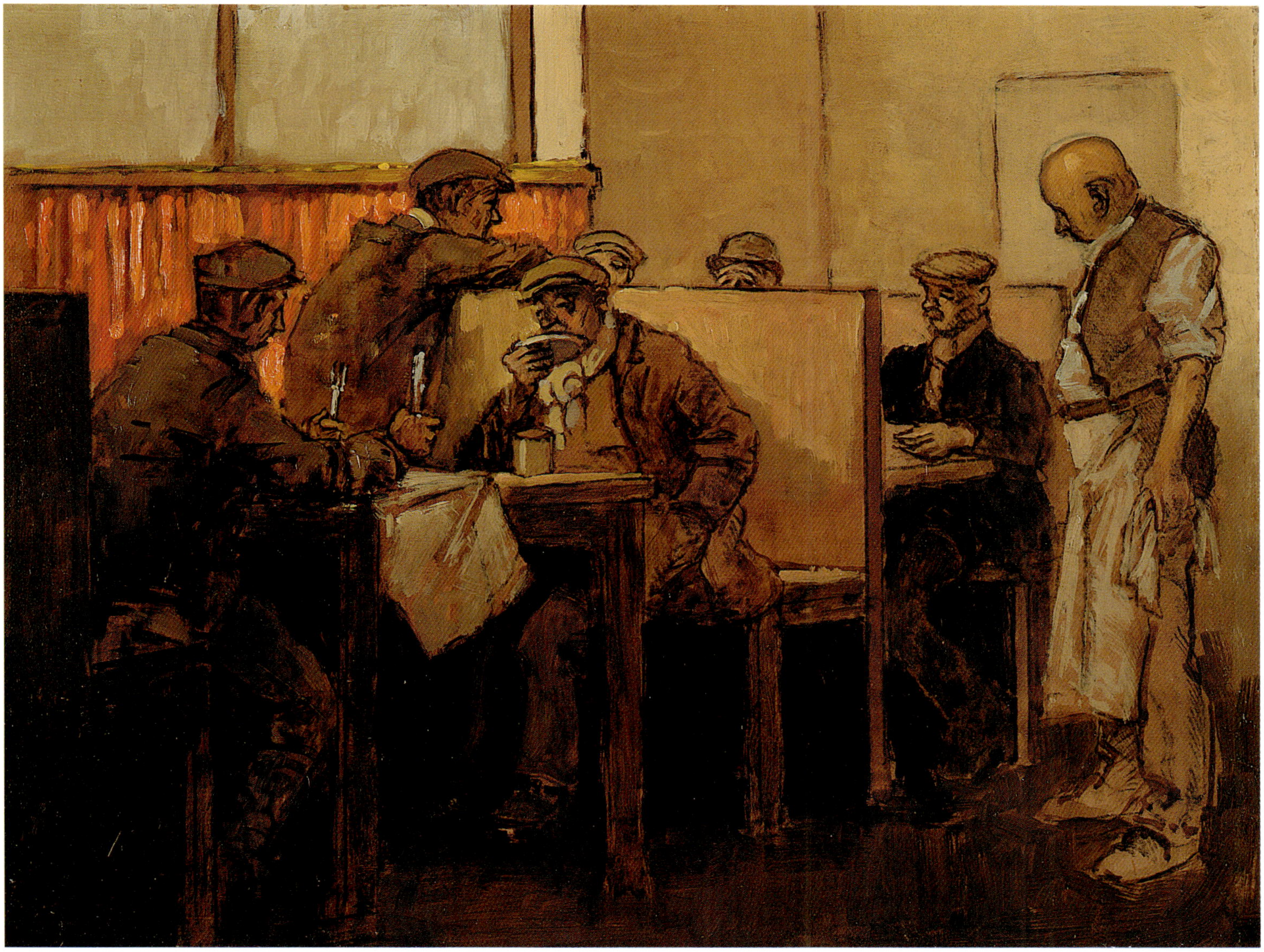

158.

WILLIAM STEWART

(1886–1967)

Interior of a Coffee Shop* [65.96/2]
*c.*1960 (from sketches made between 1900 and 1914)
Oil on board, 30.9 x 41.2 cm
Not signed or dated

SIX MALE customers are shown having a meal in a coffee shop; on the right, a waiter is taking an order. The slogan 'Good pull up for carmen' was usually displayed outside cheap eating houses of this type to attract the trade of drivers of horse vans, lorries and other heavy vehicles. Eating houses like this with their back-to-back seating, were common in Victorian and Edwardian London. Few of them now survive, having been superseded by transport cafés.

By comparison with this work, Harold Gilman's 1914 *Eating House* (see *The Painters of Camden Town* exhibition catalogue, 1988, no. 146) looks positively luxurious, helping us realise how the subject here has been reduced to its stark essentials.

Provenance:
Purchased out of the Mackenzie Bell Trust Fund from the artist in 1965.

Bibliography:
Hayes (cat. no. 175); *William Stewart: London life, past and present*, exhibition pamphlet, Towner Art Gallery, Eastbourne, 1962 (50).

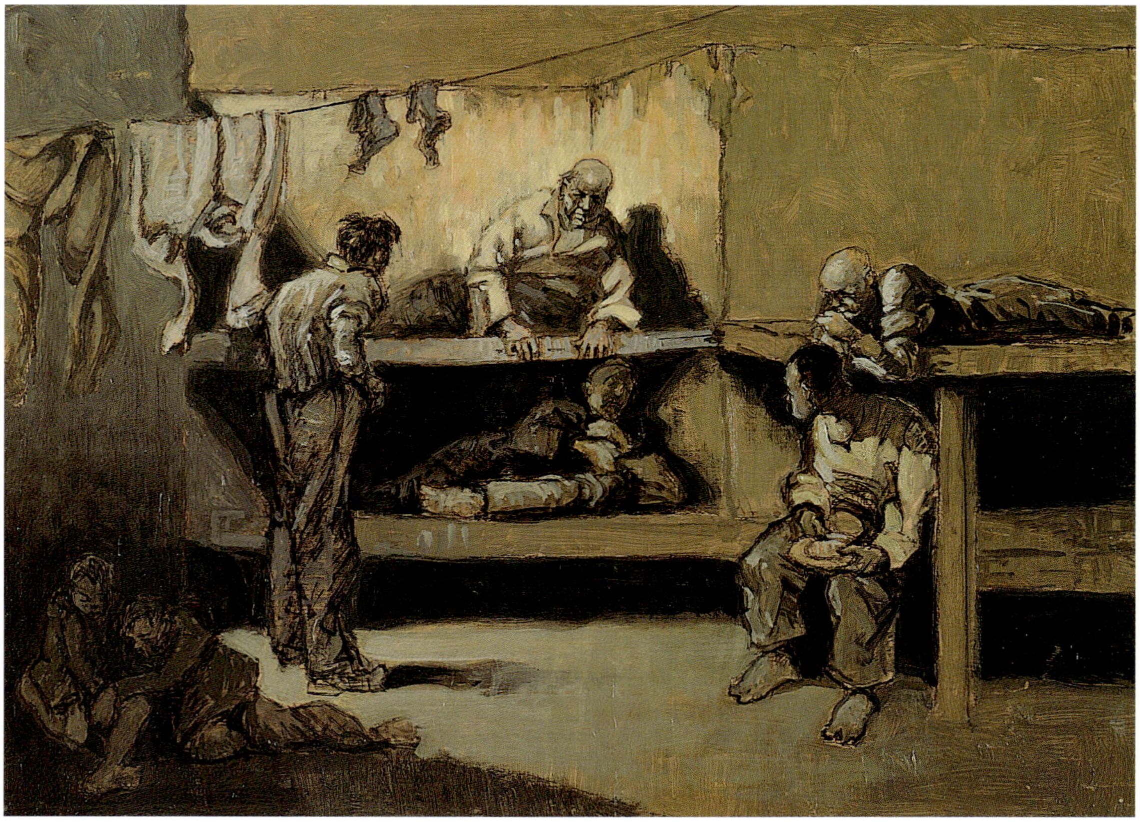

Provenance:
Purchased out of the Mackenzie Bell Trust Fund from the artist in 1965.

Bibliography:
Hayes (cat. no. 176); *William Stewart: London life, past and present*, exhibition pamphlet, Towner Art Gallery, Eastbourne, 1962 (24).

159.

WILLIAM STEWART
(1886–1967)

Interior of a Stepney Doss-House* [65.96/1]
*c.*1960 (from sketches made between 1900 and 1914)
Oil on board, 37.5 x 52.5 cm
Not signed or dated

SEVEN DOWN-AND-OUTS are shown inside a doss-house, where beds could be had for fourpence a night; three of the men are resting on the simple bunks.

Since such a subject has rarely been depicted by artists, it is worth mentioning a Victorian antecedent. A more primitive version of this type of shelter may be found in Jules Vallès's *La Rue à Londres*, 1884 (opposite p68): 'Drury Lane Lodging House – Evening', etched by Auguste Lançon. These basic doss-houses were largely superseded in the Edwardian period by working men's hostels on the Rowton model, the brainchild of Montagu William Lowry, Lord Rowton, who had helped to set up the Guinness Trust. The first Rowton House opened at Vauxhall in 1892, and it housed 430 men in 1995, the same year Maggi Hambling movingly recorded it in her painting *Rowton House*. It was followed by Rowton Houses in King's Cross (1894, now the Mount Pleasant's Hotel), Newington Butts and Hammersmith (1897), Whitechapel (1902) and Camden Town (1905); the largest hostel, Arlington House, was renovated in 1988.

160.

ARTHUR HACKER

(1858–1919)

Sir John Martin-Harvey as Hamlet [50.3]
1916
Oil on canvas, 91.2 x 76.7 cm
Signed and dated bottom right:
Arthur Hacker/1916

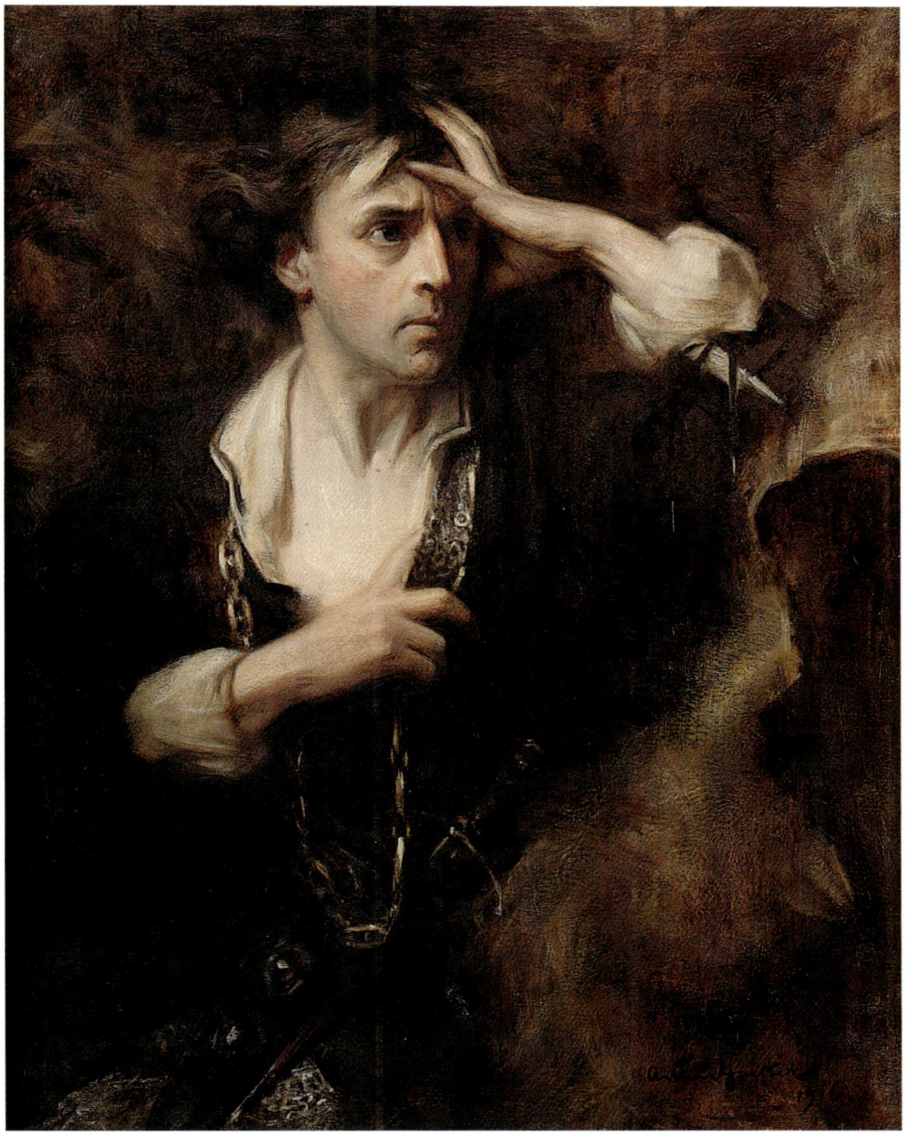

THE ACTOR John Martin-Harvey (1863–1944) is shown half-length facing the spectator, his head turned half right, with his left hand at his brow and his right fingering his doublet. Martin-Harvey first played Hamlet at the Lyric Theatre in 1905, but mounted his own production at His Majesty's Theatre during the Shakespeare tercentenary celebrations of 1916. This picture was painted at the time of the 1916 production and represents the deranged Hamlet, but is probably not illustrative of any particular moment in the play. In this role, Martin-Harvey broke away from the conventional declamatory Shakespeare style; he was a romantic who 'could work himself into a high fever'.

Sir John Martin-Harvey, the distinguished actor-manager, began his career with fourteen years in Sir Henry Irving's company at the Lyceum Theatre, before founding his own company. His best-known production was the play with which he began his career as an actor-manager in 1899, *The Only Way*, an adaptation of Dickens's *A Tale of Two Cities*. He was an early supporter of the idea of founding a national theatre.

Provenance:
Bequeathed by Lady Martin-Harvey in 1950.

Bibliography:
Hayes (cat. no. 118); J. C. Trewin, *The Edwardian Theatre*, 1976, p136.

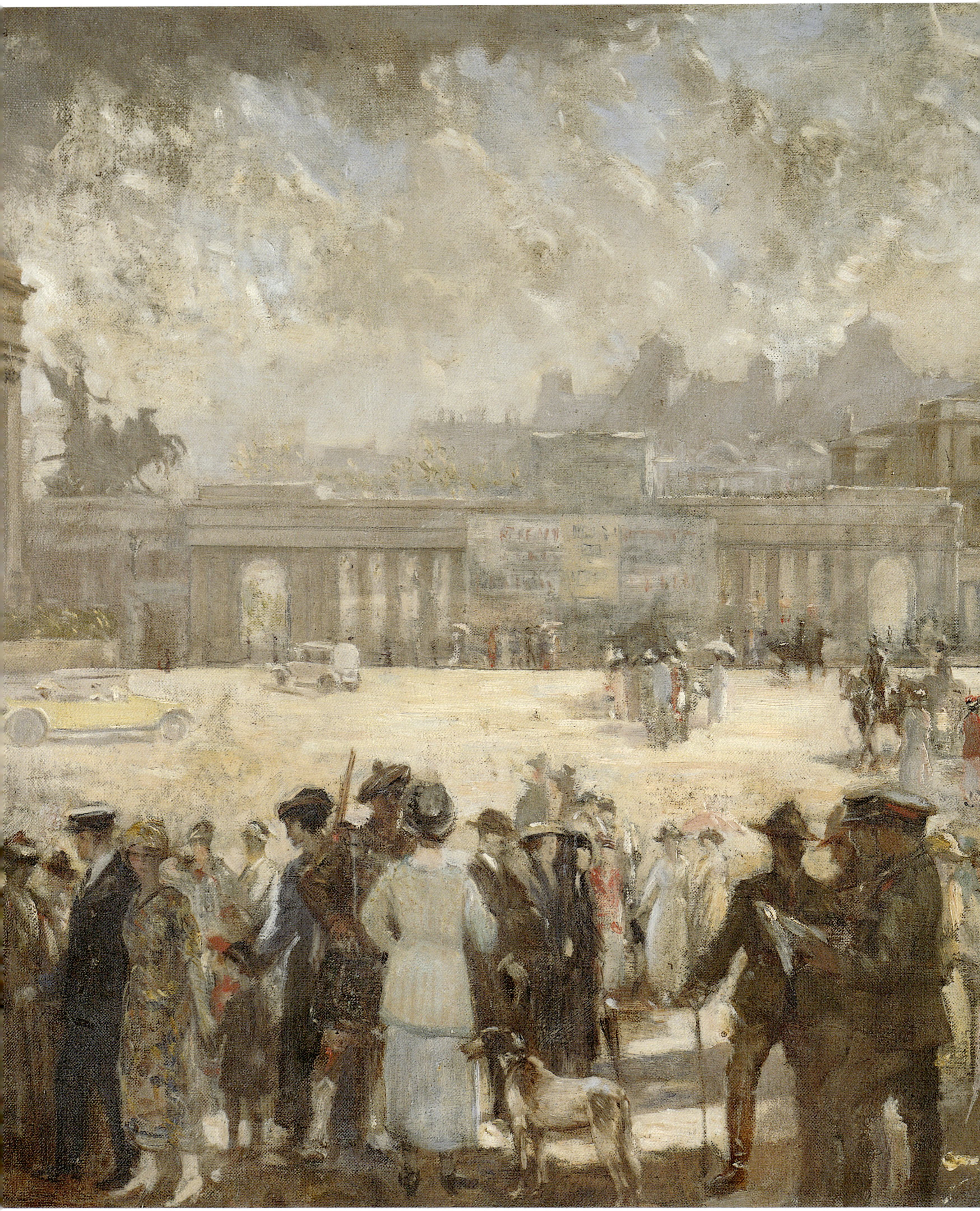

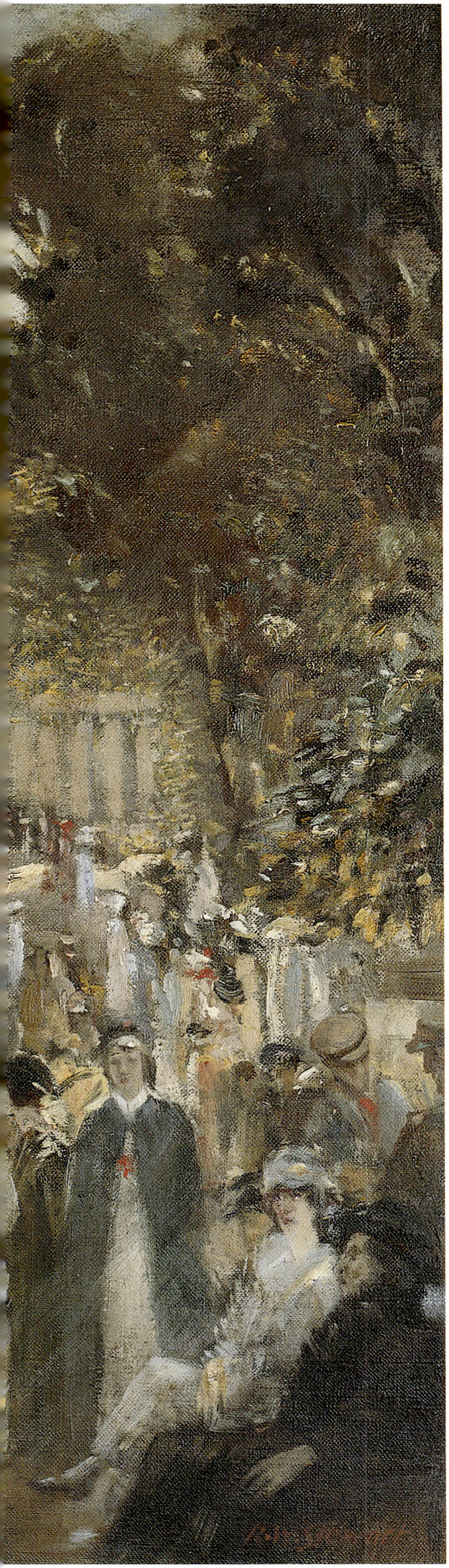

161.

ROBERT WRIGHT STEWART

(?–1950)

Hyde Park Corner, 1918* [66.52]

1918–19

Oil on canvas, 50.3 x 60.3 cm

Signed on bottom right: *R. W. Stewart*

A CROWD of promenaders, including a nurse, soldiers, children and a dog, are depicted in Rotten Row. Behind them the buildings shown are, from left to right: part of Apsley House, the quadriga on Constitution Arch, the Hyde Park Corner screen and St George's Hospital.

Rotten Row became fashionable when, in the 1730s, a new road was built to Kensington, giving the old road a new lease of life. It immediately became fashionable for driving and riding and artists started to depict it from the late eighteenth century onwards. The trend may be seen to culminate in Henry Barraud's *Hyde Park in 1864* (Christie's, 19 November 1976, Lot 92), a portrait painting set in Rotten Row, which succeeded in depicting 164 members of London's fashionable society. At the end of the Victorian era William Nicholson had featured the site as a backdrop to his 'Lady' in the *London Types* series of woodcuts, thus continuing its connection with society. The setting in Wright Stewart's painting is very close to that in Henry Barraud's, although the gathering is considerably more modest and informal. In the middle ground, cars have replaced the horse-drawn carriages of Victorian times. For the continuation of the theme, see cat. no. 172.

The artist returned to this subject and exhibited the following works at the Royal Academy: *Morning in the Row* (1920); *Hyde Park, 1926*; and *London Life: Hyde Park, 1933*.

Provenance:
Lent by the artist in 1919, and given by his sister, Miss Ann Scott Stewart, in 1966.

Bibliography:
Hayes (cat. no. 174); Celina Fox, *Londoners*, 1987, pp89–91.

Exhibited:
Royal Academy, 1919 (454).

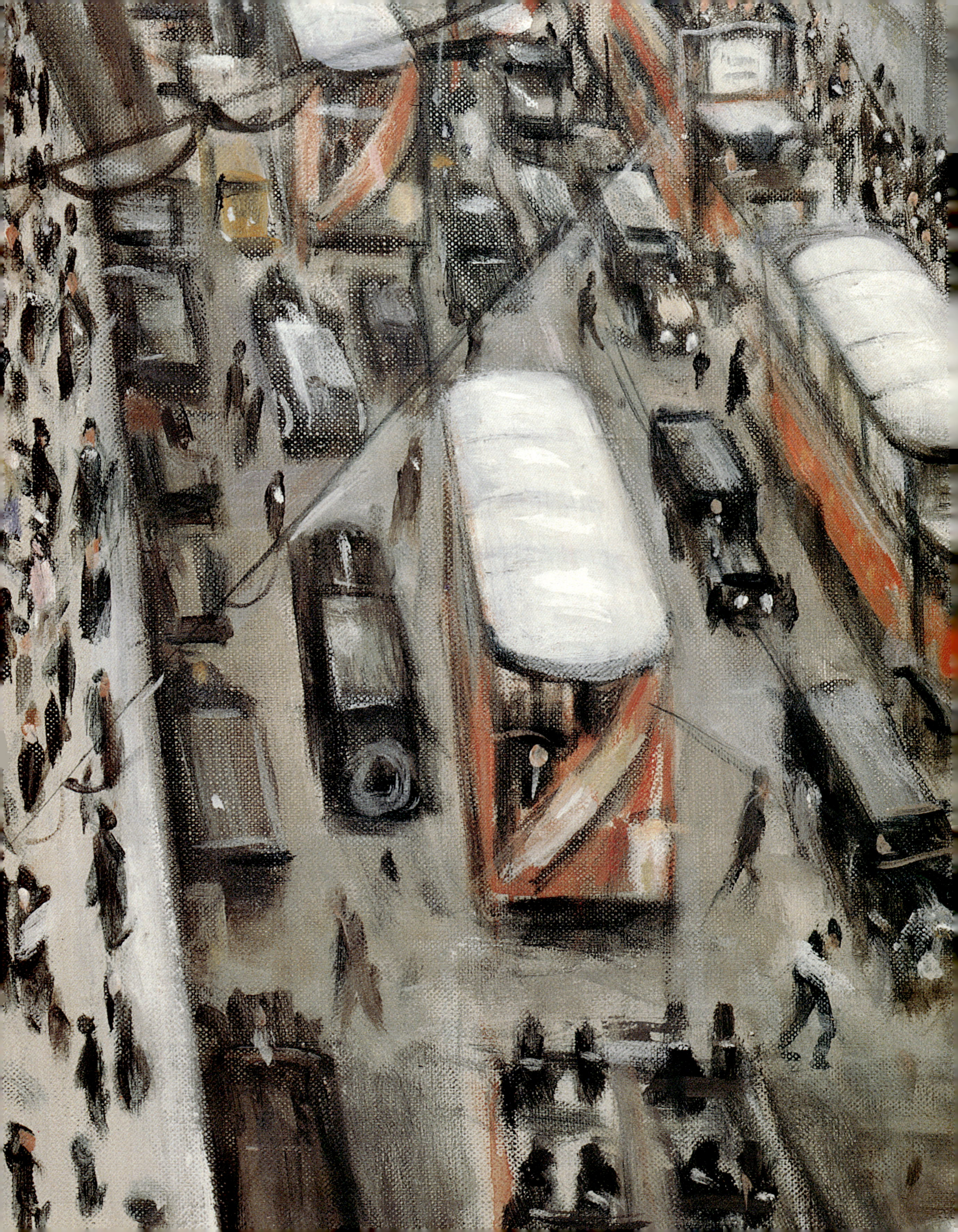

BETWEEN THE WARS

ARTISTS WERE not in general moved to depict scenes of London during the Great War. The criss-crossing of light shafts at night with occasional zeppelins lurking in the dark were all they translated into paint (see p375). But after the war was over, we witness the emergence of a particularly serene image of London, which suggests that artists were consciously rediscovering the city's calm beauty. The once dislocated, futurist style of C. R. W. Nevinson turned dreamy, almost syrupy (particularly cat. no. 165), while Algernon Newton's work presents an 'Arcadian' city bathed in golden light. Harry Bush, too, focuses on the quiet, suburban streets and buildings of his neighbourhood. In 1930 Nevinson wrote of how,

> on the innumerable times that I have arrived back in London, I have been overwhelmed by its peculiar beauty, its exquisite, lingering twilight; the streets, shiny with rain, converted to canals far more romantic than Venice, the scarlet 'buses, more gorgeous than any gondolas, silhouetted against blue mist buildings, more mysterious than any palaces, floating in atmosphere, and obliterating the squatness of English architecture.[1]

This idealistic interlude, however, was short-lived. At the same time as these aspirations for an harmonious world were being expressed, the depression and the socialist movement were taking shape. Cliff Rowe explained: 'Employment for artists was very bad. From 1929 … there would be ten people in front of you for every job. We were all living in poverty; there was no doubt about that.'[2] In order to survive artists gradually moved into commercial art. It is worth noting that the repeated and failed attempts of the Royal College of Art to involve students in the world of industry and design were finally successful under a harsh economic climate.[3] For example, James Boswell, who had trained at the RCA, wrote:

> By 1932 the Great Depression hung over us all. I joined the Communist Party, gave up painting, took to illustration and graphic design and helped found the Artists International Association, which at that time was a mixture of agit prop body, Marxist discussion group, exhibition organiser and anti-war, anti-fascist outfit.[4]

Of all the artists who joined the Artists International Association (AIA) or participated in its activities, Cliff Rowe[5] was the only one to spend some time in Russia. James Fitton asserted: 'Everyone was to the left in those days, what else was there?'[6]

Artists who were less politically minded, such as Grace Golden,[7] faced similar options. Although she did not make the conscious decision of giving up painting, she was gradually steered away from it towards the world of illustration, which provided regular, paid work. For other artists the break was even more dramatic: Clive Branson and Hugh Slater, two talented painters who had trained at the Slade, gave up painting altogether, one to work for the Independent Labour Party, the other for the Communist Party.

In a world increasingly dominated by such economic issues, the AIA enabled artists to pursue more idealistic goals. Their first major success was an exhibition called 'The Social Scene' held in a large shop at 64 Charlotte Street in September/October 1934. The show was criticised for the overall poor quality of the works and for its propagandist approach.

The predominant number of scenes of working life included very few recognisably London paintings, the exceptions being *A London Postman* by Percy Horton and *A Street Meeting in London at Night* by James Lucas.[8]

Since the majority of artists in the 1930s contributed in some way to the work of the AIA, it had a great deal of influence on the London art scene. London as a subject gradually gathered momentum with various converging trends. The quintessentially London work of William Hogarth was re-evaluated in the 1930s (by Klingender and Antal) and a 'Hogarth Group' formed 'because they thought he was the ideal of the socially-conscious British artist'.[9] At the same time Ruskin Spear and his contemporaries at the Royal College were re-examining the Camden Town Group and Sickert in particular, again a London-focused movement. Finally, in 1938, London came into its own when the AIA organised 'London Life in Concrete' at 36 Soho Square, a Peter Peri exhibition of sculptures made from concrete and dealing with Londoners' everyday lives.[10]

That same year another London show was staged by the artists' group which probably contributed most to the subject of London in the 1930s: the short-lived Euston Road School. In the heart of London's West End, an exhibition of '15 Paintings of London' (by fifteen different artists) was held at the Storran Gallery, 5 Albany Court Yard, Piccadilly, between 26 October and 12 November.[11] It was organised by Graham Bell and a copy of the catalogue survives in the Victoria and Albert Museum. As with the AIA, there was some emphasis on making art accessible to the widest public possible, and since the subject was relevant to all Londoners, this included those people who would not normally visit galleries. An unusual device was tried: the organisers sent private-view cards to everyone named Brown (some say Green) in the Post Office Directory.[12]

The term 'Euston Road' was first coined by Clive Bell when he reviewed the '15 Paintings of London' in the *New Statesman and Nation* and it was used again for a show held at the Ashmolean Museum, Oxford, in 1941. The technical achievements of the group have been discussed at length, including the 'dot to dot' method of constructing a painting, but the choice of London subjects has never been investigated as such. The London scene, so evident in many of these works, is taken for granted and the nature of the interpretation of the capital by painters never discussed. This may have led to the absence of Thames paintings in this first 'Euston Road' exhibition, whereas throughout the 1930s and 1940s the river featured high on the painter's agenda.

Artists may have been subconsciously aware of the renewed vitality of the river at that time. The Thames and its large dock system had been managed by the Port of London Authority since 1909 and many improvements had been carried out. By the 1930s the 'First Port of Empire' employed 100,000 people and handled 35,000,000 tons of cargo within its 700 acres of enclosed dock water and at 1,700 riverside wharves.[13] The Museum's collection boasts a fine selection of river paintings for this period, including works by Nevinson and Duncan Grant.

The roots of the Euston Road Group can be easily traced to the preceding decade. The Slade had played a crucial role in the training of artists, not only through the professorship of Henry Tonks between 1917 and 1930, but also through the appointment at the Royal College of Art of an ex-Slade student: William Rothenstein (Principal 1920–35).

The influence of both these men over a generation of artists was considerable and both, unwittingly or unconsciously, promoted the subject of London. After 1919, Tonks had exclaimed: 'The leaders of the London Group have nearly all come from me. What an unholy brood I have raised!'[14]

Rothenstein, on the other hand, unlike his predecessors at the RCA, was driven by the desire to capture 'the real world': 'I was possessed with the faith that if I concerned myself wholly with appearance, something of the mystery of life might creep into my work.'[15] He also appointed artists sympathetic with his views, for instance Percy Horton, who exhorted artists to 'throw away their blinkers and look around them a good bit more'.[16] This rigorous observation of the world around, which for schools sited in London of course meant the city itself, bore its fruit the following decade.

The Euston Road School had started as a small private enterprise at 12 Fitzroy Street in the heart of Bloomsbury, co-founded by Claude Rogers (the prime mover), Victor Pasmore, Graham Bell and William Coldstream in association with Rodrigo Moynihan, Lynton Lamb, Adrian Stokes and Geoffrey Tibble.[17] On 21 February 1938 it had moved to larger premises at 314 Euston Road. The teaching encouraged a realist style expressed in everyday subjects, rather than the socio-political range encountered in the AIA or the commercial approach which had been forced upon art colleges by the Depression. The School's statement is very clear about this last point.[18]

Lawrence Gowing (1918–1991)
Mare Street, Hackney, 1937
Oil on canvas
Shrewsbury College of Arts and Technology
Photograph: the Witt Library, Courtauld Institute of Art.

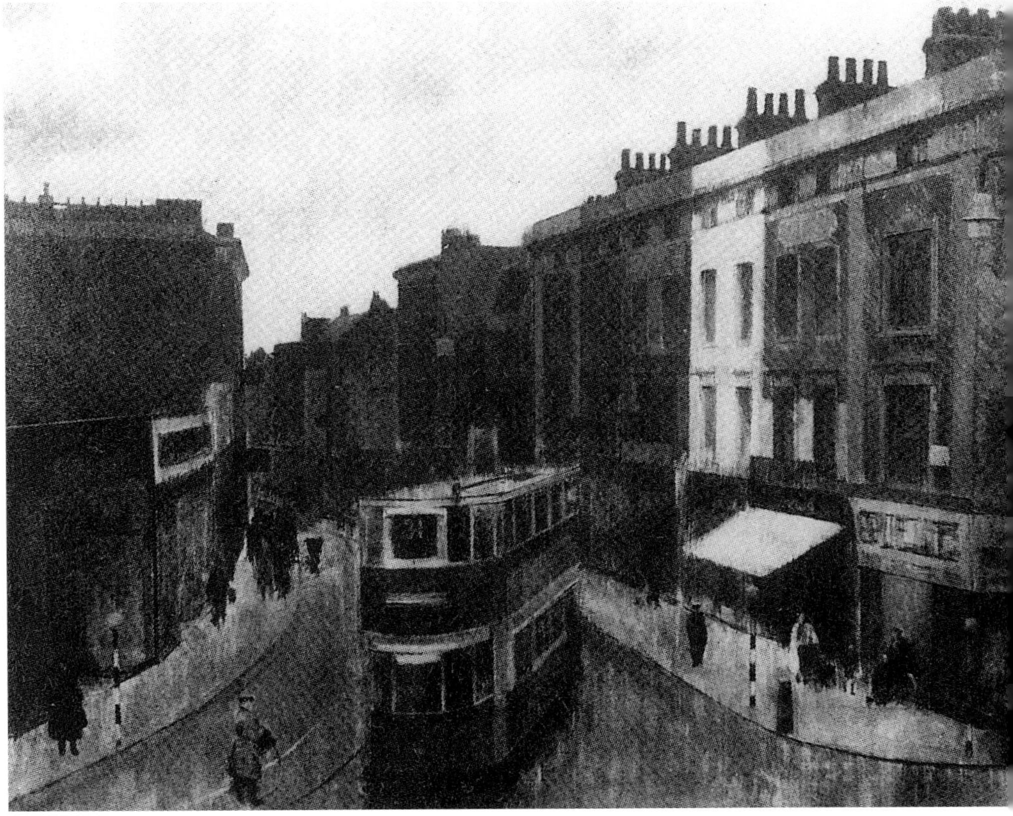

B. A. R. Carter (see cat. nos 195 and 196), Denis Dawnay, Lawrence Gowing, Philip Matthews, Christopher Pinsent and Basil Rocke had all been pupils. The themes many from this group adopted recalled those first investigated by the Camden Town Group, but with a softening of technique and effect displayed, for instance, in Lawrence Gowing's *Mare Street in Hackney* (Shrewsbury Technical College) or Graham Bell's *The Cafe* (Manchester City Gallery); *The Life Room* at Euston Road was depicted by both Adrian Stokes and Victor Pasmore;[19] snow scenes were popular with Claude Rogers, Pasmore and Bell; finally we should mention Pasmore's romantic, misty series on Hammersmith riverside gardens which shows early signs of Pasmore's move towards abstraction.

Initially the Second World War interrupted the activities of the school, but the appointment of many of its teachers and students at the Camberwell School of Arts and Crafts led to the re-creation of the group there – Gowing, Carter, Pasmore, Rogers and Coldstream. The group finally disintegrated after ten years, when Coldstream was appointed Slade Professor of Fine Art in 1949.

1. C. R. W. Nevinson, 'This is what London means to me', in the *Daily Express*, 25 September 1930.
2. Linda Morris and Robert Radford, *AIA: The Story of the Artists International Association 1933–1953*, Museum of Modern Art, Oxford, 1983.
3. See Christopher Frayling, *The Royal College of Art*, 1987.
4. Morris and Radford, 1983, pp9–10.
5. Cliff Rowe is represented in the Museum's collection by a series of drawings, many of which show workers at the Whitefriars glass factory in Harrow.
6. Morris and Radford, 1983, p10.
7. Grace Golden (1904–93) painted in oil, drawing her inspiration from London (see *Free Speech* in the Tate Gallery). The Museum of London holds a large number of her drawings and was bequeathed all the artist's London illustration files at her death (acc. no. 93.15/158).
8. Morris and Radford, 1983, pp13–14. The work by Lucas was praised by T. H. Wintringham in the *Left Review.*
9. Morris and Radford, 1983, p23.
10. Morris and Radford, 1983, p49.
11. Bruce Laughton, *The Euston Road School*, 1986, pp161–5 and 347.
12. Ibid, p161.
13. Chris Ellmers, *The City and the River*, Museum of London booklet, 1989; Chris Ellmers and Alex Werner, *Dockland Life*, 1991.
14. From the London Group, a subsidiary, the London Artists' Association, was born, devised by Roger Fry and based at the Cooling Galleries between 1926 and 1933/4. It offered selected artists an annual income in return for preferential sales to their 'sponsors' – four businessmen led by Maynard Keynes.
15. John Rothenstein, *Modern English Painters*, 1957, p127.
16. Frayling, 1987, p106.
17. See Laughton, 1986; also *Painting the Visible World – Painters at the Euston Road School and at Camberwell School of Arts and Crafts 1930–1960,* exhibition catalogue, Austin/Desmond Fine Art.
18. 'Today there is a tendency in the art schools to concentrate on the teaching of the applied arts, industrial and commercial design, and to relegate to a second position the study of free drawing and painting. It is becoming, therefore, increasingly difficult for those who wish to take up Drawing and Painting as ends in themselves to find a school where they will receive wholehearted encouragement in this subject only, and at the same time obtain direct contact with teachers who are themselves practising painters. This school hopes to supply this want.' (Laughton, 1986, p145.)
19. In 1938; Laughton, 1986, pp173 and 155.

162.

CHARLES SIMS

(1873–1928)

View in Kensington Gardens [65.84]

*c.*1920–5

Oil on fibreboard, 30.2 x 41.5 cm

Signed bottom right: *SIMS*

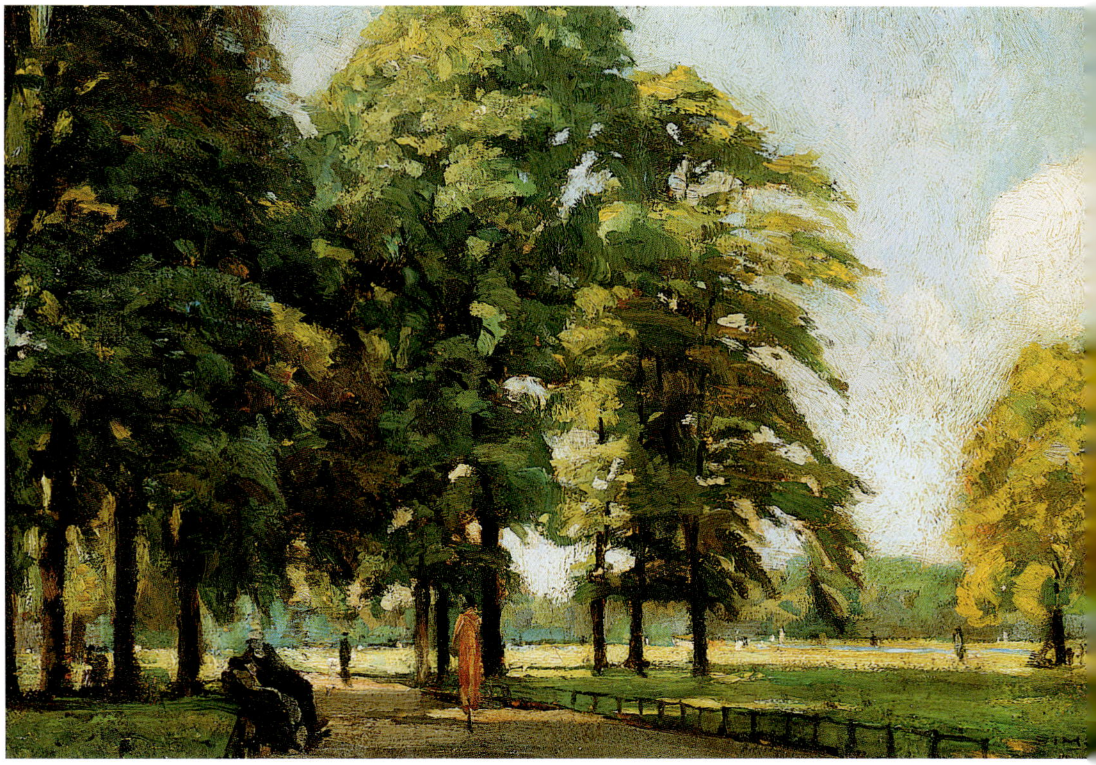

A VIEW in Kensington Gardens looking north-west, and taken from the path which leads diagonally from Queen's Gate to the Broad Walk. The magnificent avenue of elms, cut down in 1953–4, which formerly lined the Broad Walk and masked Kensington Palace, is seen in the distance; on the right is the Round Pond (originally a large octagonal 'bason' completed in 1728). In contrast with Brewtnall's leafless view (see cat. no. 137), Sims captures in this small oil sketch the full glory of the summer season. There are a number of scattered figures.

Kensington Gardens, as we now know them, were laid out between 1726 and 1733, chiefly to designs by Charles Bridgeman. Though they have been much altered since, the Broad Walk, the Round Pond and the avenues which radiate from the Round Pond are all part of the original layout. Once the private grounds of Kensington Palace, the gardens were at first enclosed by a high brick wall, and were open to the public only on Saturdays. From the beginning of the last century, however, they were opened every day, and between 1826 and 1861 the high walls were gradually replaced by low walls surmounted by iron railings. The Round Pond has been a favourite place for sailing model boats for fifty years and more. The shin railings seen in the picture, which formerly lined all the gravel paths, were removed during the Second World War (at the same time the iron railings surmounting the walls were taken down).

Although Charles Sims was born in London and based there until 1906, he made little use of his native surroundings. Many of his works illustrate allegorical or religious themes. The theme of paradise is particularly significant in his output and required imaginary landscapes which the artist presumably grounded in studies such as this one.

Provenance:
Presented by George Fraser in 1965 as *The Round Pond.*

Bibliography:
Hayes (cat. no. 100).

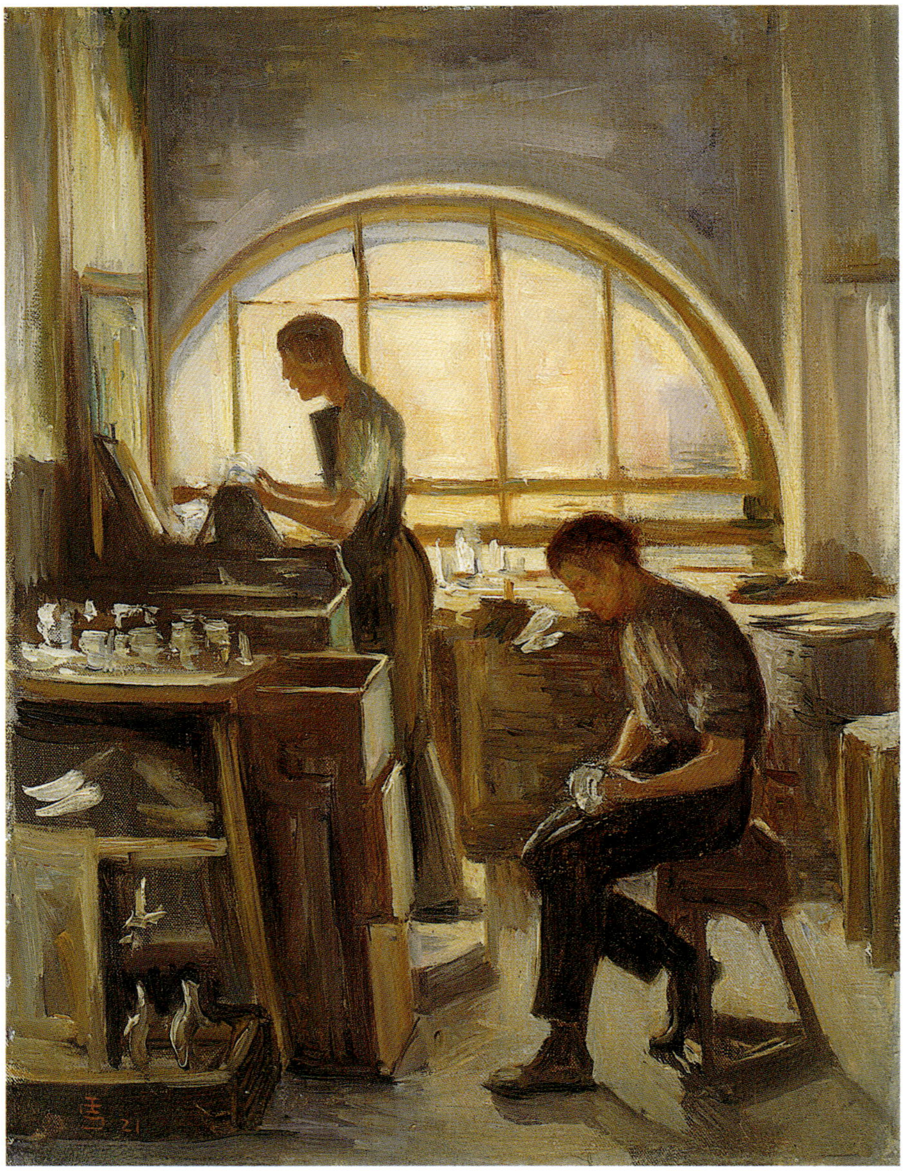

163.

EDGAR SELIGMAN

(active 1920s)

Whitefriars Glass Factory [80.547/1006]
1921
Oil on canvas board, 46 x 35.5 cm
Signed in monogram and dated bottom left:
ES 21
The artist's name, title of this work and its date are inscribed on the back.

SET AGAINST a large semi-circular window, the scene depicts two workers engraving or 'stoppering' glass with the use of a glass engraver's lathe.

This is one from a series of five paintings by this artist on the Whitefriars glassworks in Fleet Street before the factory moved to new premises in Harrow (see Appendix for others in that series).

The move of the Whitefriars glassworks to Harrow in 1923 had been planned shortly after the end of the First World War. Presumably as a consequence of the move, records of production in the 1920s are sparse and this group of paintings therefore constitutes precious documentation: they were clearly intended to record work on the old site before the changes brought about by the move.

Another group of 1960s drawings by Cliff Rowe (acc. no. 82.119) records the workers at the Harrow glassworks, thus making the Museum's visual holdings on this firm extensive. It is interesting to compare the images of the old and the new factory: the scale of the workers versus their environment changes and the atmosphere of a craftsman's workshop becomes that of an industrial factory peopled with 'heroic' workers.

Provenance:
From the Whitefriars Archive (see cat. no. 71).

Bibliography:
Wendy Evans, Catherine Ross and Alex Werner, *Whitefriars Glass*, Museum of London, 1995.

164.

SOLOMON JOSEPH SOLOMON
(1860–1927)

Portrait of Lewis, 1st Viscount Harcourt
[A 28579]
1922–3
Oil on fireboard, 39.4 x 32.2 cm
Signed in monogram bottom right: *SJS*

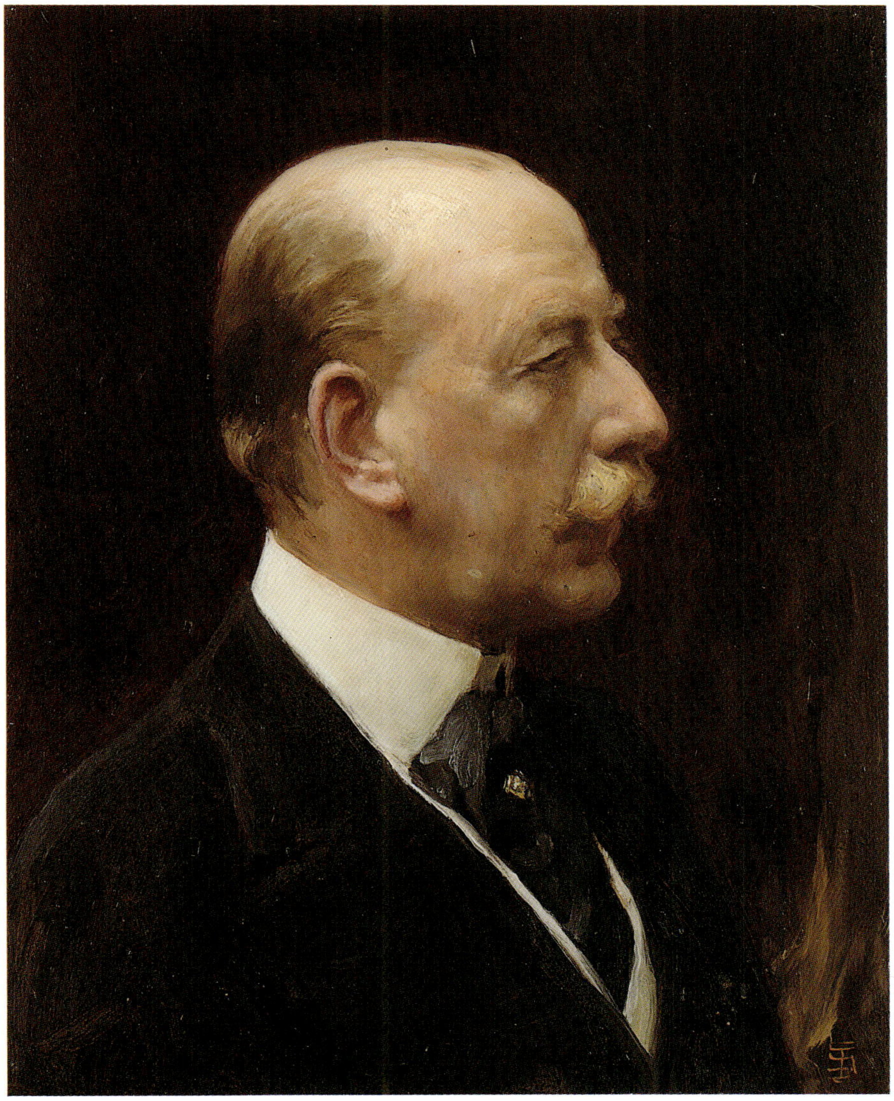

THIS PORTRAIT, painted from a photograph, shows the head and shoulders of Lewis Harcourt (1863–1922) facing right against a plain background. Lewis Harcourt (who was raised to the peerage in 1917) spent his early years as private secretary to his father, Sir William Harcourt; entering Parliament in 1904, he was First Commissioner of Works from 1905 to 1910 and again in 1915–17, and Secretary of State for the Colonies in 1910–15. He was passionately interested in gardening, and made extensive improvements to the London parks while he was at the Office of Works. His other great interests were art and archaeology, and for varying periods he was a Trustee of the British Museum, the Wallace Collection and the National Portrait Gallery. With Reginald, 2nd Viscount Esher (1852–1930), he played a major part in founding the London Museum, which was opened to the public in the State Apartments of Kensington Palace in 1912 and became the Museum of London in 1976. He served as a Trustee until his death in 1922.

Provenance:
Commissioned by the Trustees of the Museum in 1922.

Bibliography:
Hayes (cat. no. 124); Francis Sheppard, *The Treasury of London's Past*, 1991, pp33–5.

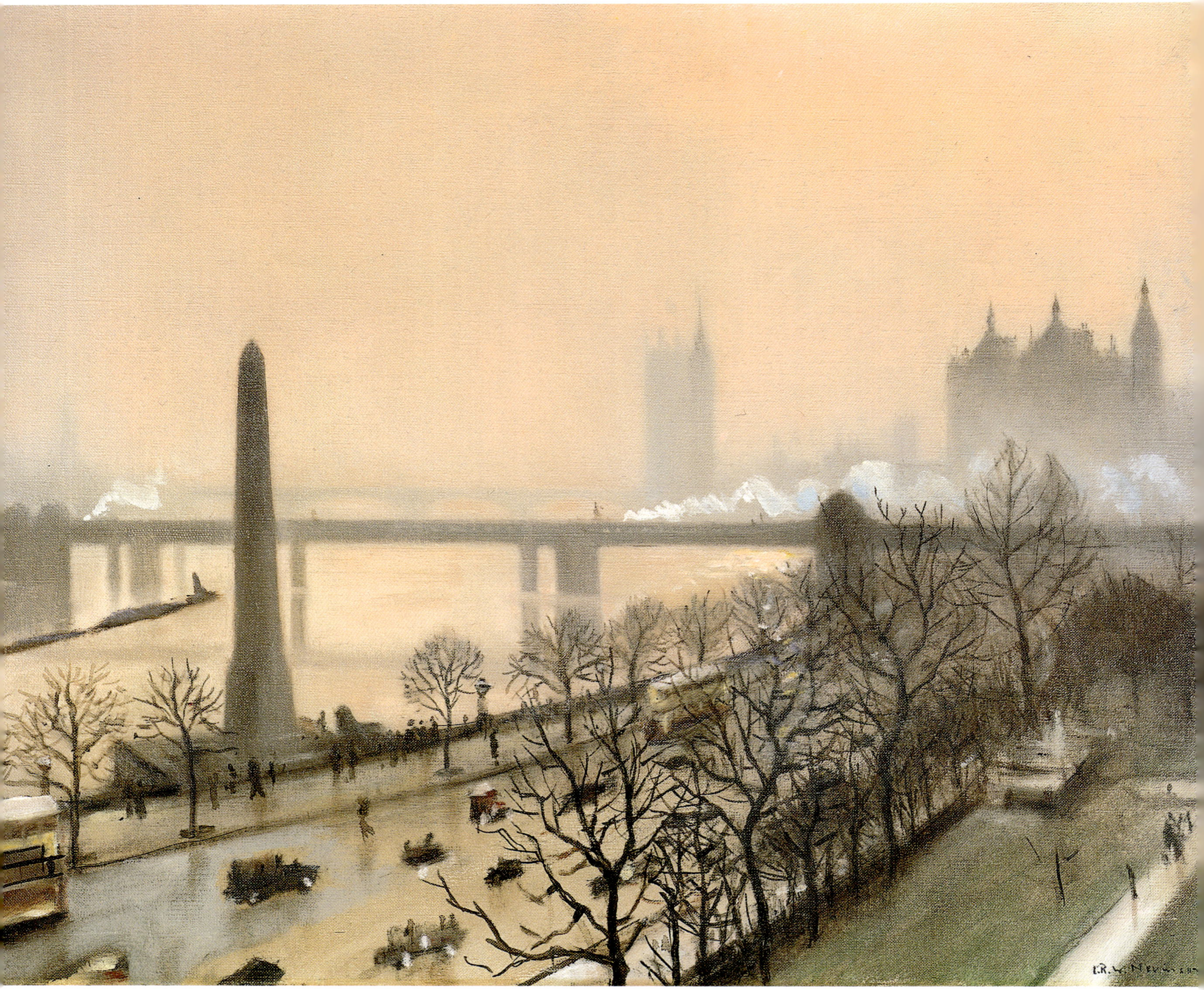

165.

CHRISTOPHER RICHARD WYNNE NEVINSON

(1889–1946)

Victoria Embankment [59.99/140]

*c.*1924

Oil on canvas, 47.2 x 60 cm

Signed bottom right: *C. R. W. Nevinson*

THIS WINTER view of the river looks south-west from an upper window at the Savoy Hotel. In the foreground is Cleopatra's Needle, the obelisk that formerly stood in front of the Temple of Heliopolis. It was shipped from Alexandria at a cost of ten thousand pounds and re-erected on the Victoria Embankment in 1878 (its transportation was recorded in a series of watercolours by the engineer John Dixon which are in the Museum's collection). On the right are the Victoria Embankment Gardens, first opened to the public in 1872. Beyond the Embankment, trains are seen crossing the Charing Cross Railway Bridge (popularly known as Hungerford Bridge), an iron girder bridge built in 1863–4, which replaced Brunel's Hungerford Suspension Bridge (cat. no. 91). The silhouettes of Westminster Bridge, the Houses of Parliament and Whitehall Court are visible in the background.

When in 1872 John O'Connor painted, on a clear, bright summer day, *The Embankment* looking towards the City (see cat. no. 80), he was celebrating the recent completion of a great work of engineering. By contrast, Nevinson's image, painted some fifty years later, celebrates the winter light and atmosphere of London; the subject as well as the viewpoint link the work to the celebrated Hungerford Bridge series by Claude Monet. However, we are no longer dealing with the 'disintegrating' atmosphere of the Impressionists; this is a more solid approach to the representation of structure and light. Cleopatra's Needle, hardly noticeable in Monet's paintings, is a key element in Nevinson's work, while the dark web of bare trees strikingly contrasts with the delicate grey and pink tones of the air, sky and smoke.

Provenance:
Purchased from the Leicester Galleries by A. D. Power in 1924; bequeathed by him through the National Art Collections Fund in 1959.

Bibliography:
Hayes (cat. no. 77).

Exhibited:
'Paintings and Water-colours by C. R. W. Nevinson', Leicester Galleries, March–April 1924 (115).

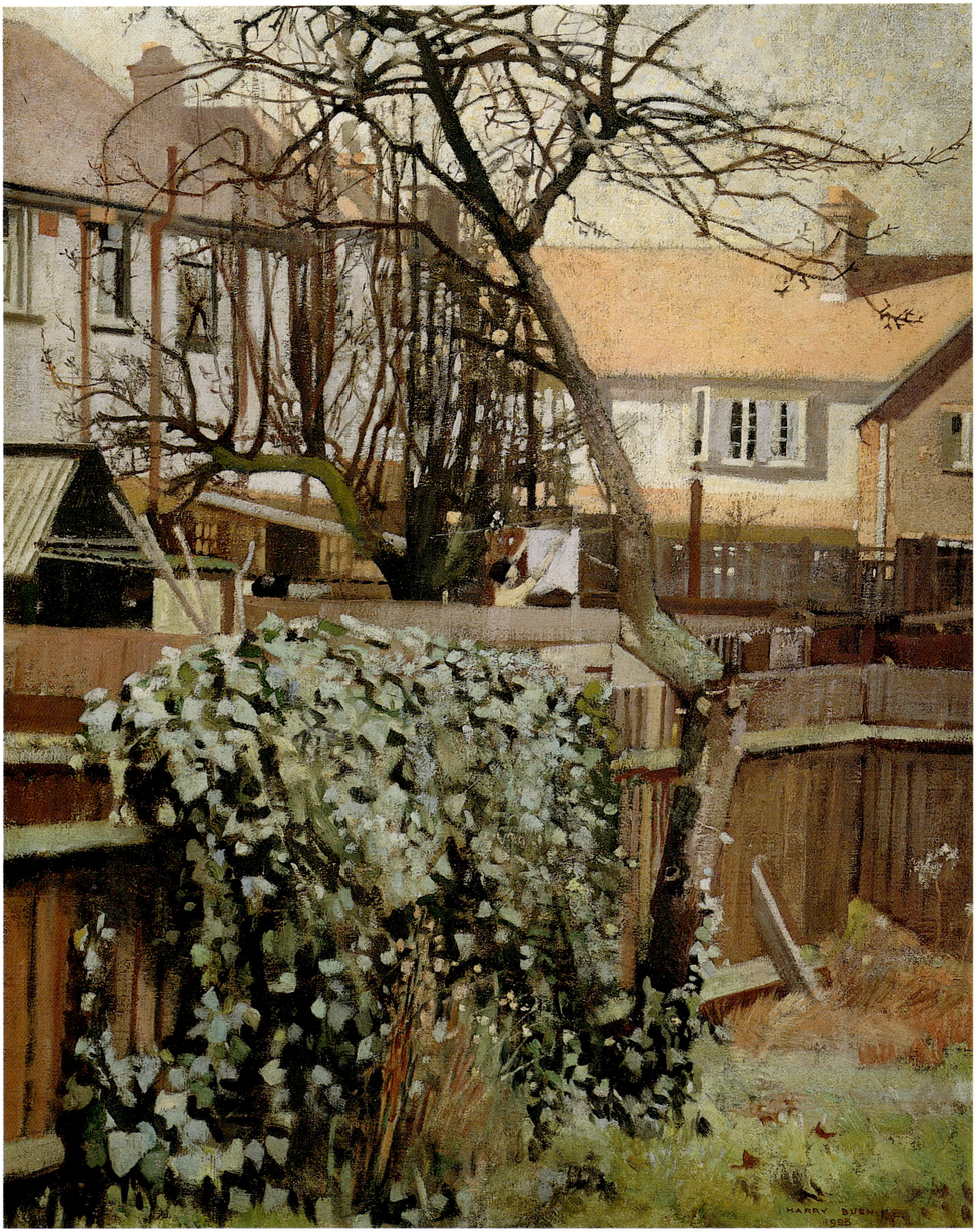
HARRY BUSH

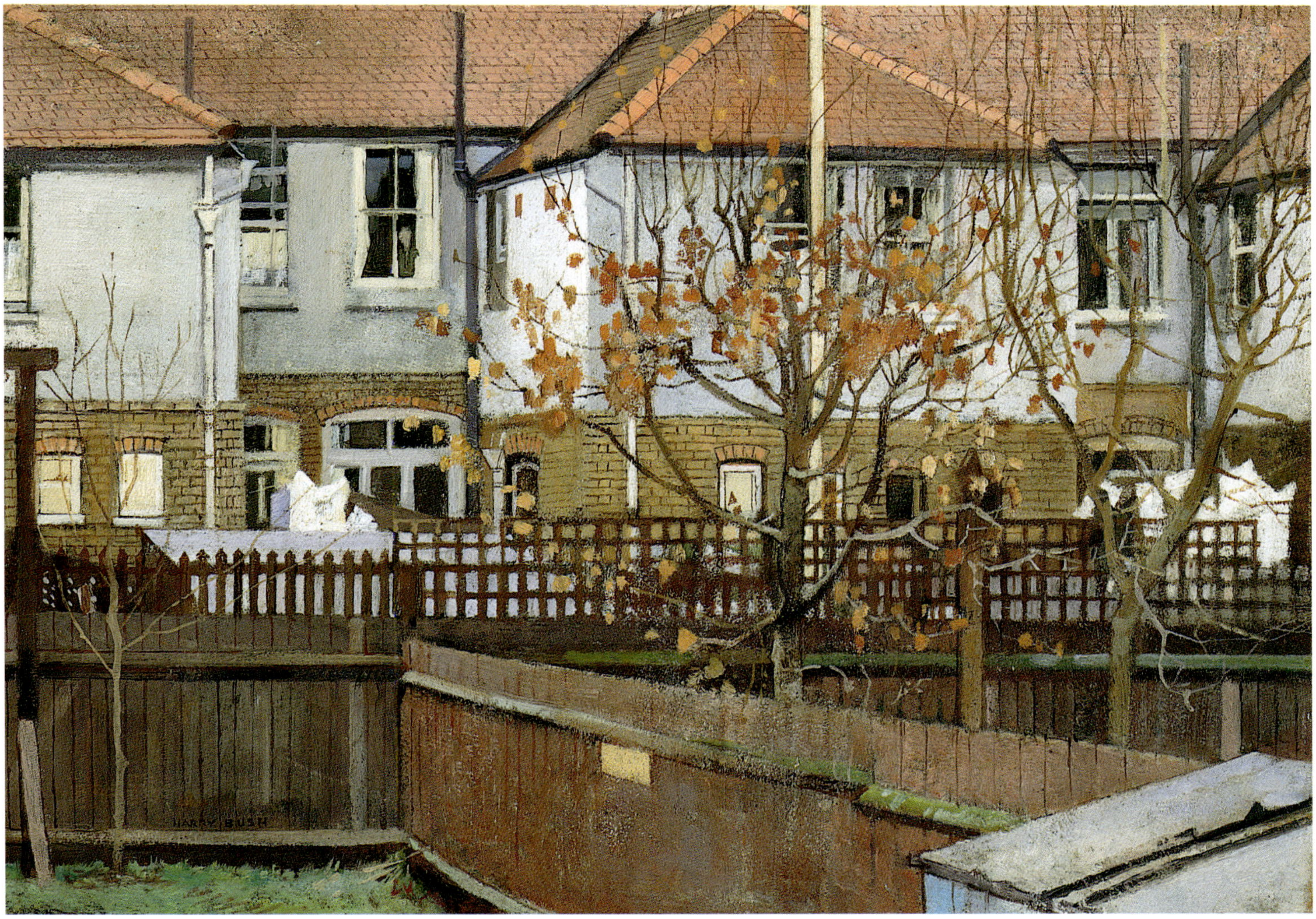

166.

HARRY BUSH

(1883–1957)

December Sunshine [84.346/1]
1925
Oil on canvas, 76 x 60.5 cm
Signed and dated bottom left:
HARRY BUSH 1925

167.

HARRY BUSH

(1883–1957)

Laggard Leaves [84.346/2]
1925
Oil on panel, 35.8 x 25.5 cm
Signed bottom left: *HARRY BUSH*

THESE TWO views were taken from the artist's house at 19 Queensland Avenue, Merton Park, London SW19, and feature the back garden of 19 (*December Sunshine*) and the geometric landscape of the backs of houses from the rear of Bush's home (also see cat. no. 202).

Since much of Harry Bush's output was concerned with the immediate surroundings to his home, he was nicknamed 'the painter of the suburbs'.

Provenance:
Christie's, Artist's studio sale, 28 September 1984 (14 and 17).

Bibliography:
Christie's catalogue, 1984 (see above); also Christie's catalogue, 14 May 1993 (160, as *The Builders*); family records at the V&A National Art Library.

Exhibited:
Royal Academy, 1925.

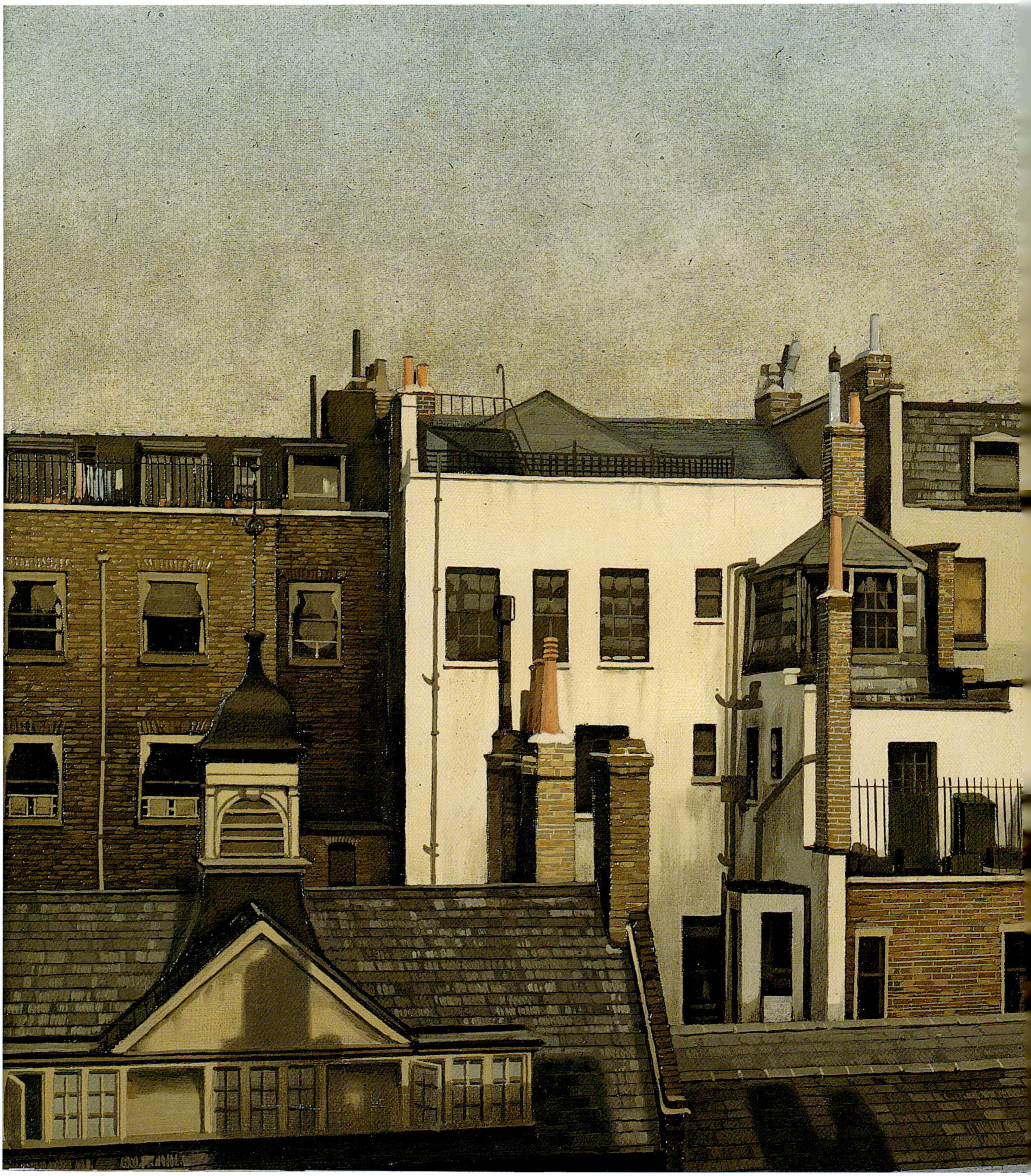

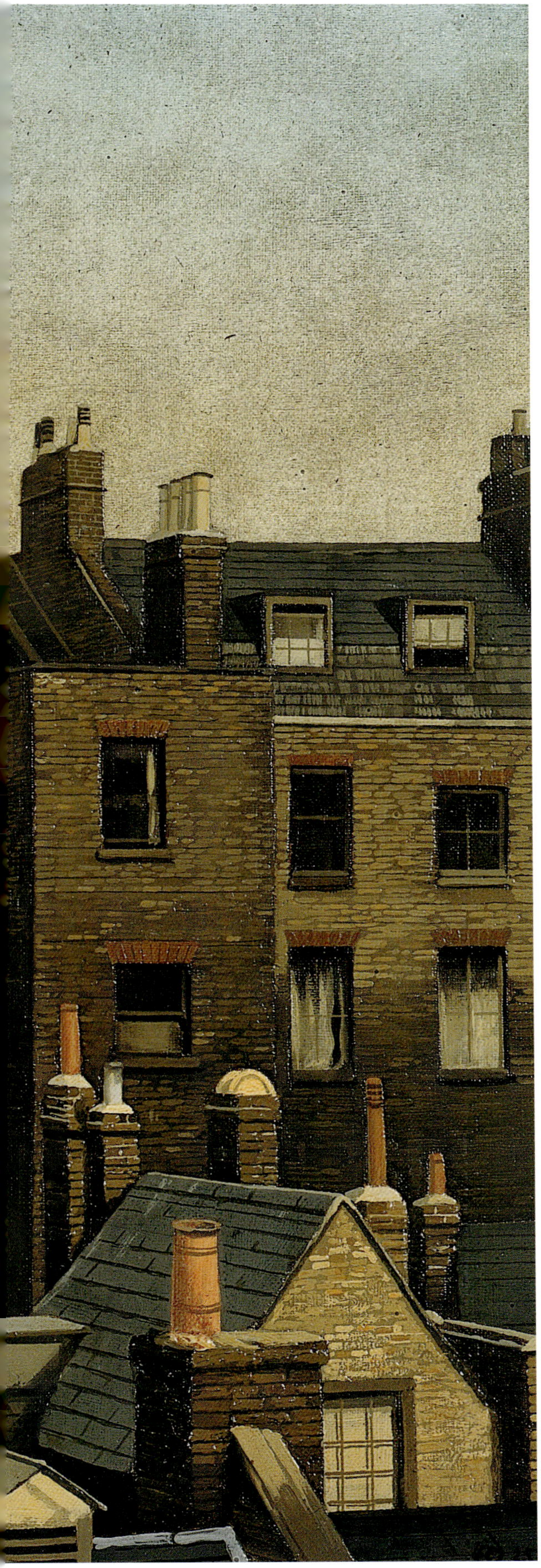

168.

ALGERNON NEWTON

(1880–1968)

The Backs of Houses in Harley Street*

[76.152/1]

1925

Oil on canvas, 39 x 50.8 cm

Signed in monogram and dated bottom right: *AN 1925*

Described on the back: *The backs of houses, Harley Street*

THE VIEW, taken from 10 Wimpole Street, almost opposite Welbeck Way, looks at the backs of houses in Harley Street, probably those of numbers 17–25 of that street. Number 10 was the home of Miss H. A. D. Barlow, who commissioned the painting. Miss Barlow went on to buy a further three or four paintings from Newton. This was the painter's first commission, of which he wrote: 'The view was a very limited one, but I was as pleased as if I had received an order to paint Buckingham Palace.'

Provenance:
Commissioned by Miss H. A. D. Barlow and sold to her in November 1925 (in Newton's account book); bequeathed by her to the Museum in 1976.

Bibliography:
Algernon Newton RA 1880–1968, exhibition catalogue, Graves Art Gallery, Sheffield, 1980, (11); *Like the face of the moon – the art of discovery*, exhibition catalogue, Hayward Gallery, 1991. The Algernon Newton archive is in the Tate Gallery.

Provenance:
Presented by the artist in 1926.

Bibliography:
Hayes (cat. no. 128).

169.

ROSAMUND BORRADAILE
(active 1920s)

George Court, Adelphi [A 28558]
1925
Oil on canvas, 41.9 x 28.1 cm
Signed bottom left: *R. Borradaile*

THE VIEW looks northwards, towards the Strand; two fishmongers are seen at the doorway of a shop in the centre in front of a flight of steps, and the barrels and baskets on the right belong to the greengrocers opposite (cut out from the painting). George Court, the continuation of York Buildings, north of John Adam Street, has now been completely rebuilt, and only the flight of steps leading into the Strand remains.

The site seems to have been popular with artists in the early twentieth century, perhaps stimulated by the notion of 'picturesque London' or 'disappearing London', which the antiquarian topographer Philip Norman had promoted with such passion at the turn of the century (see p 232). F. L. Emanuel had drawn George Court in 1898 and Fred Richards also produced an etching of the site around the time the work under review was painted (acc. no. 35.104/4).

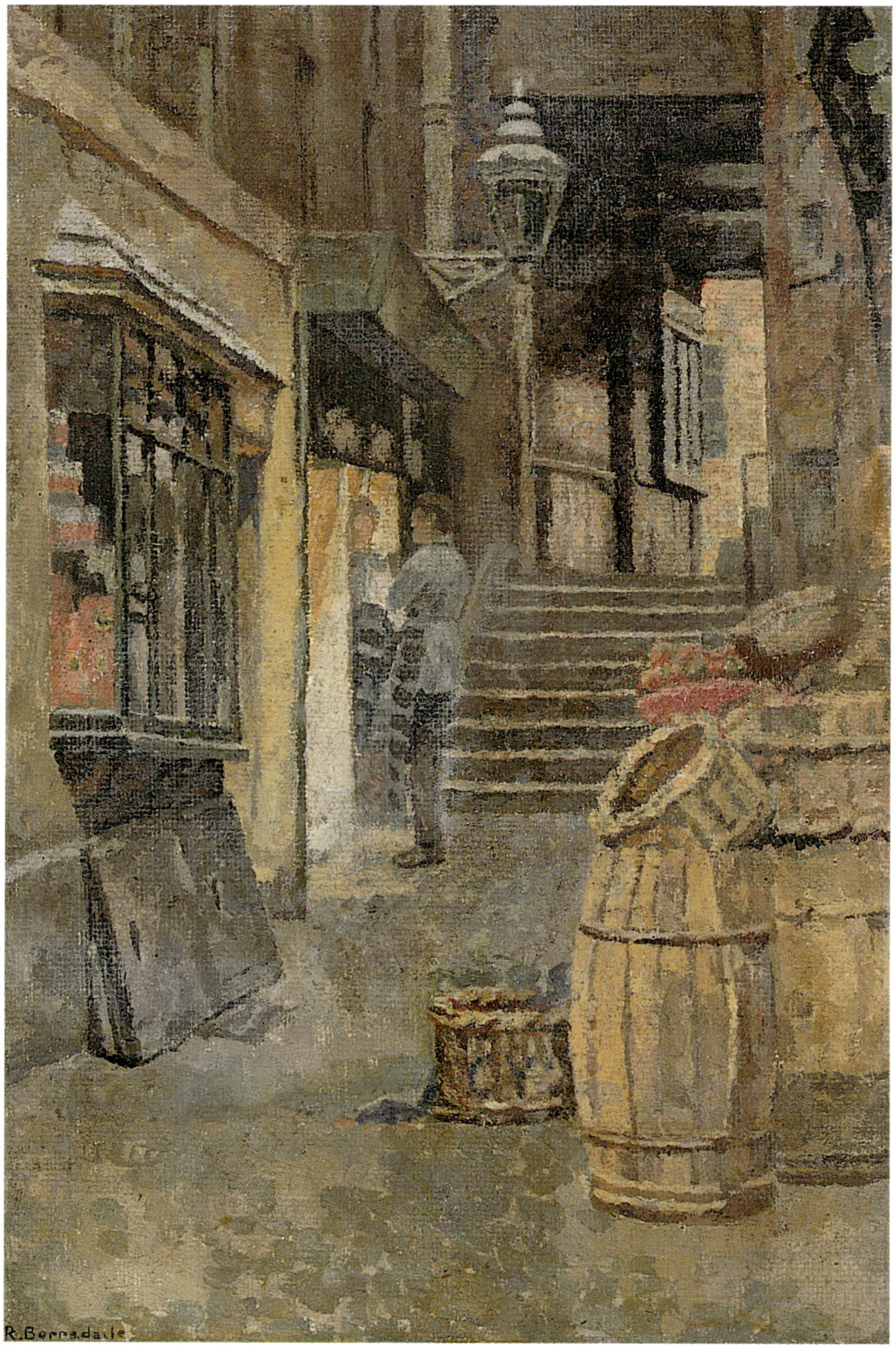

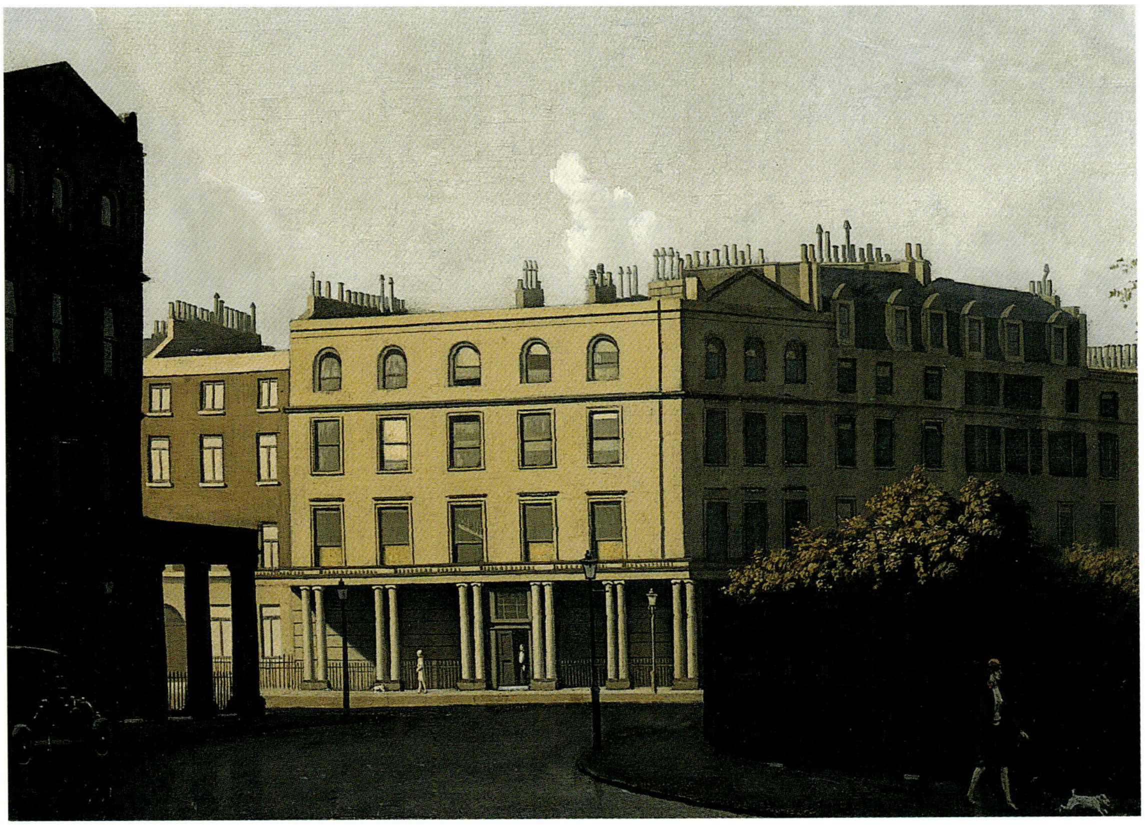

Provenance:
Purchased in 1936 from the Royal Academy by Miss H. A. D. Barlow, who bequeathed it to the Museum in 1976.

Bibliography:
Algernon Newton RA 1880–1968, exhibition catalogue, Graves Art Gallery, Sheffield, 1980 (15); Michael Mansbridge, *John Nash*, Oxford, 1991, p134. The Algernon Newton archive is in the Tate Gallery.

Exhibited:
Royal Academy, 1936 (no. 585, under its present title).

170.
ALGERNON NEWTON
(1880–1968)

Park Crescent* [76.152/2]
1927
Oil on canvas, 39.8 x 55.5 cm
Signed with a symbol (?) and dated '27 bottom left
Described on the back: *Park Crescent, Algernon Newton, 1 Park Hill Studios NW3*

THE VIEW, taken almost at the junction of the west side of Portland Crescent and Euston Road, looks to the end of Portland Place. The Crescent gardens are visible on the right-hand side.

Park Crescent was designed by John Nash and Charles Mayor started building in 1812. The work was interrupted for six years after he went bankrupt but resumed when the builders William Richardson, Samuel Baxter and Henry Peto took over.

The current Park Crescent elevations are modern reconstructions in the original building style which hide modern office developments, a solution adopted after the Second World War when the architecture was extensively damaged. This painting predates these changes and shows the original facade.

The artist's accounts book states for May 1927 that the painting was originally called *Portland Place* and was oval-shaped. Newton changed it to a 'small square' before exhibiting it at the Royal Academy (1936), when it was sold to the donor.

The work is photographed and dated 1927 in the artist's autograph catalogue of paintings (Tate Gallery).

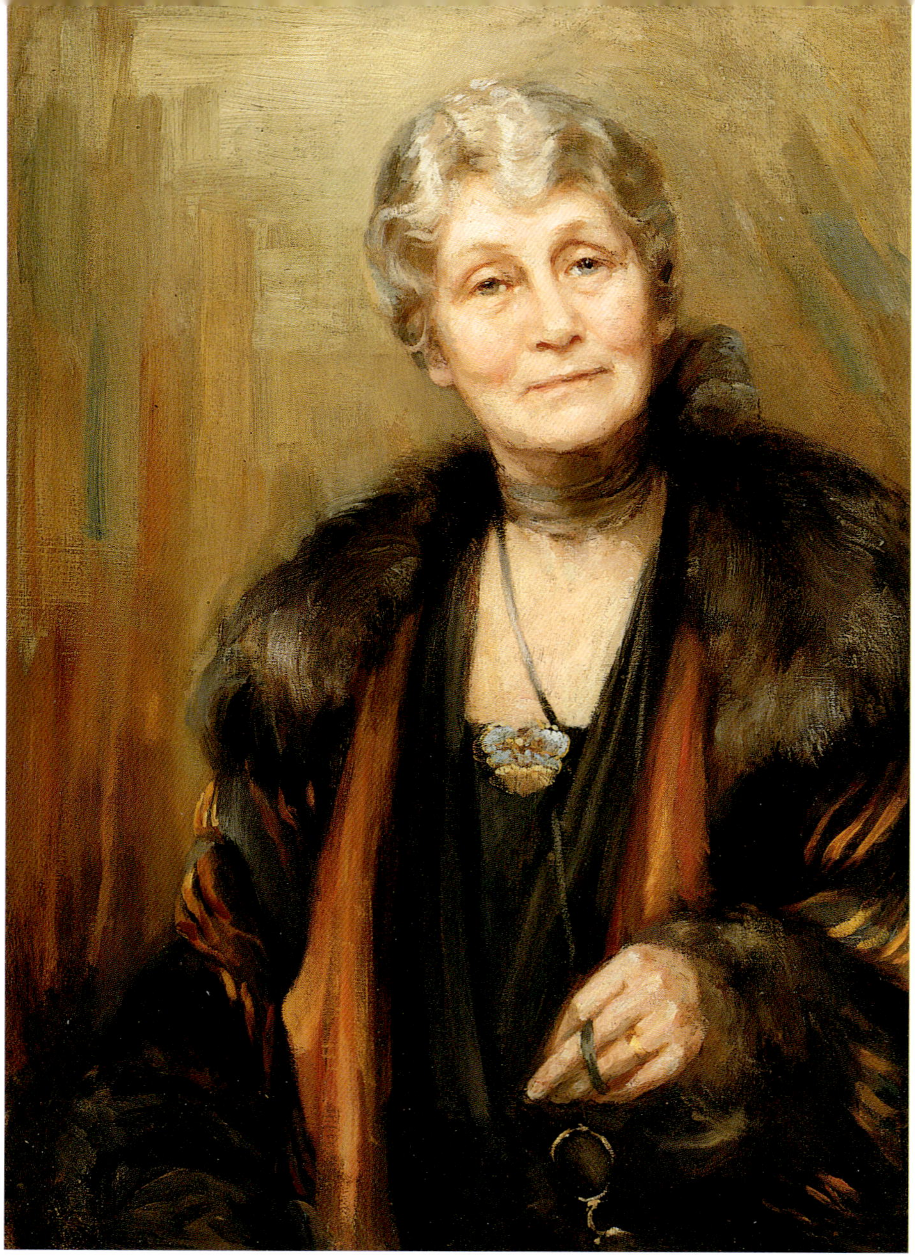

Provenance:
Part of the large collection of relics of the suffragette movement – books, pamphlets, letters, photographs, personal memorabilia and other objects – presented by the Suffragette Fellowship in 1950.

Bibliography:
Hayes (cat. no. 115).

171.

GEORGINA A. BRACKENBURY
(1865–1949)

Portrait of Mrs Richard Marsden Pankhurst, née Emmeline Goulden
[50.82/1486]
*c.*1927
Oil on canvas, 74.7 x 53.7 cm
Not signed or dated

THIS PORTRAIT was painted very shortly before Mrs Pankhurst's death (1858–1928). She is shown at half length, facing the spectator, with her head turned upwards and slightly to right, wearing a black dress and a loose fur-trimmed coat and holding a pair of spectacles in her left hand; the background is plain.

Mrs Pankhurst's husband had been an advocate of women's suffrage long before she knew him and, after marrying, she at once became deeply involved in work for the cause. Successively a member of the Liberal and the Independent Labour parties, neither of which proved sufficiently sympathetic to her aims, she founded the Women's Social and Political Union in 1903. As orthodox political methods achieved no results, she adopted a policy of violence and sensationalism. Arrested and imprisoned several times, and ruining her health by protracted hunger strikes in gaol, Mrs Pankhurst gave up the militant campaign for women's suffrage only with the outbreak of war in 1914. The vote was finally won, largely as a result of the role women had played during the war, by the Acts of 1918 and 1928.

Another, slightly larger, version of this picture is in the National Portrait Gallery (no. 2360), and the artist stated in a letter dated 9 March 1929 (in the NPG archives) that this canvas was painted from life some two years before.

In 1993 the Museum of London acquired an enamelled memorial plaque by Ernestine Mills (1871–1959), commemorating the suffragette activities of Mrs Hilda Brackenbury and her artist daughters, Georgina and Marie, at their home at 2 Campden Hill Square, Notting Hill Gate (acc. no. 93.150). Their house, which became known as 'Mouse Castle', was a nursing home for hunger-striking suffragettes ('mice') released from prison on a special licence under the terms of the 'Cat and Mouse Act'.

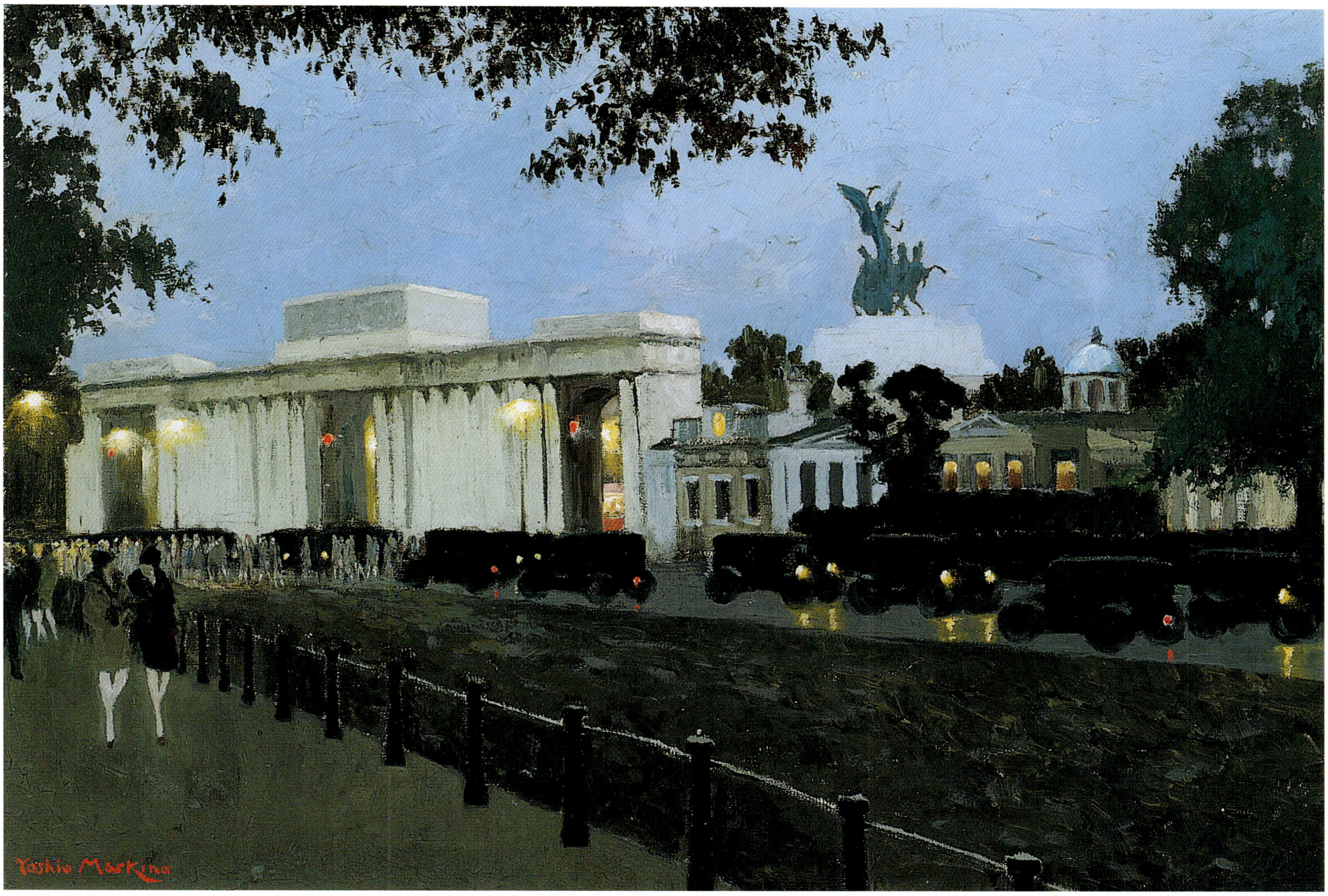

172.
YOSHIO MARKINO
(1874–c.1938)
In the Rotten Row One Evening* [29.73]
1928
Oil on canvas, 50.3 x 75.3 cm
Signed bottom left: *Yoshio Markino*

THE VIEW taken at dusk in Rotten Row, looks at the Hyde Park Corner screen, seen on the left, with the quadriga on Constitution Arch in the middle distance centre; numerous cars and figures are seen in the foreground. Compared with Robert Wright Stewart's depiction of the scene ten years previously (see cat. no. 161), this is the modern Rotten Row, dominated by traffic.

This painting was exhibited in 1929 at the New Studio Gallery, Knightsbridge, where Markino had a one-man show of his oil paintings, the first time he was using the medium. Most of the works were of evening light effects and the *Graphic* reviewer pointed out that Markino's catalogue text read like 'a free verse poem'; the painting on 'Spouters' Corner' was amusingly entitled *Where everyone was freely quacking*.

Provenance:
Presented by the artist in 1929.

Bibliography:
Hayes (cat. no. 160); *Illustrated London News*, 20 April 1929 (this painting is reproduced); *Graphic*, 15 June 1929.

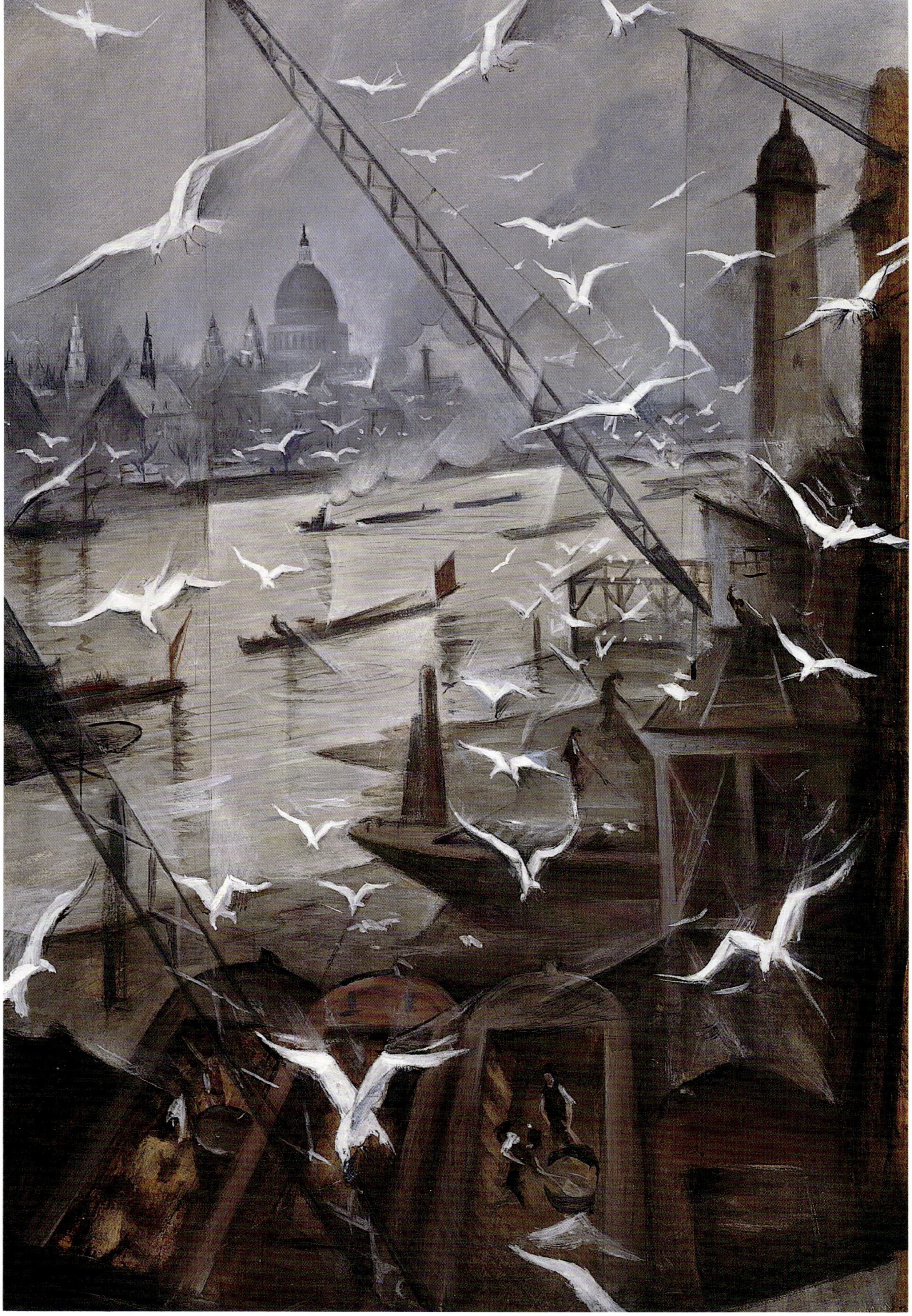

173.
CHRISTOPHER RICHARD WYNNE NEVINSON
(1889–1946)
London, Winter* [28.160]
*c.*1928
Pencil, charcoal and tempera on board, 77.5 x 51.5 cm
Signed bottom right: *C. R. W. Nevinson*

THIS PAINTING, showing the City from the southern end of Waterloo Bridge, succeeds in blending a group of major historic buildings – St Paul's Cathedral, the City of London School (built in 1881–2 by Davis and Emmanuel), the steeple of St Bride's Church, the Monument (which should be seen much farther to the east) and Blackfriars Bridge – with a foreground and middle ground dealing with the contemporary working river, its related industries on the Lambeth riverfront, such as the Shot Tower (built in 1789 by Messrs Watts), its cranes, tugs and craft. The two worlds are made to blend together with seagulls.

In his autobiography, *Paint and Prejudice* (1937), Nevinson rarely discusses the physical appearance of London, but one of his earliest memories is unmistakably linked to this painting: 'The Thames froze over and I was taken to see the ox roasted near Waterloo Bridge. I remember being struck by the great number of seagulls near the Adelphi and being told that this was the first time they had come so far inland.' This recollection probably dates back to the last time the Thames froze over in 1895 (see cat. no. 84), when Nevinson was only six.

Today the elements which compose the foreground of this painting have gone. Except for the Shot Tower (later demolished in 1962), the Lambeth waterfront was cleared for the Festival of Britain in 1951. Richard Rogers's winning architectural scheme for the South Bank should give new life to that part of London.

Another version of this painting is in a private collection.

Provenance:
Purchased from the Leicester Galleries by R. Just Boyd in 1928 and presented through the National Art Collections Fund.

Bibliography:
Hayes (cat. no. 78); *C. R. W. Nevinson*, exhibition catalogue, Kettle's Yard Gallery, Cambridge, 1988, no. 76; C. R. W. Nevinson, *Paint and Prejudice,* 1937, p2.

Exhibited:
'Memorial Exhibition of Pictures by C. R. W. Nevinson', Leicester Galleries, 1947.

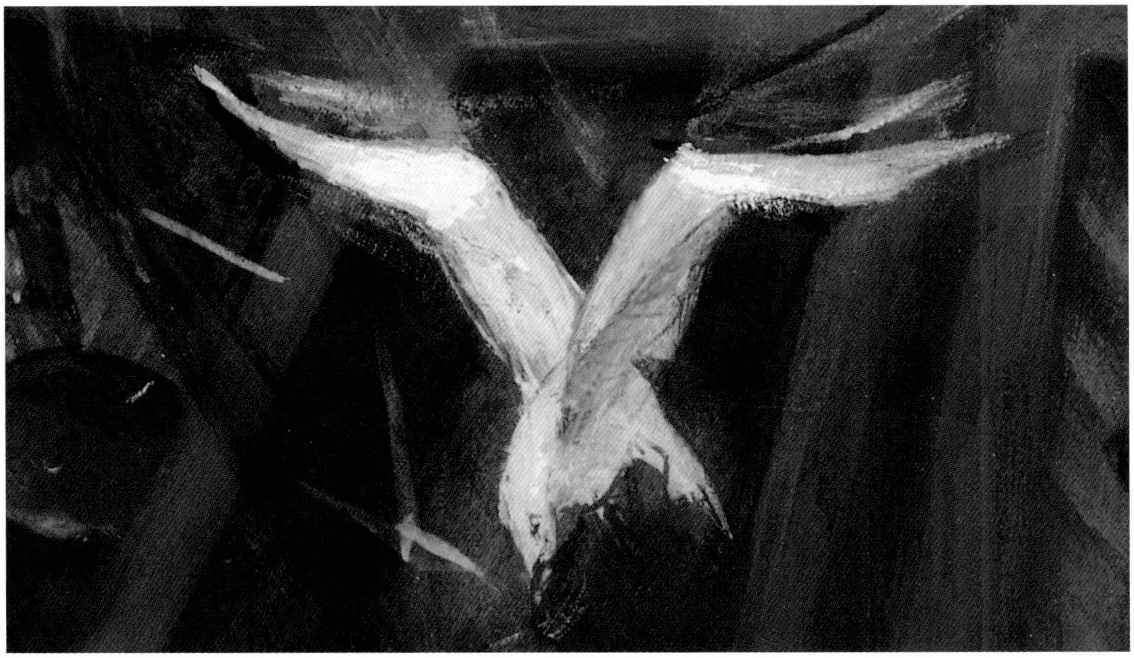

Provenance:
Purchased from the Leicester Galleries in 1930 and presented by an anonymous donor.

Bibliography:
Hayes (cat. no. 79); C. R. W. Nevinson, *Paint and Prejudice*, 1937, pp30 and 191; *C. R. W. Nevinson*, exhibition catalogue, Kettle's Yard Gallery, Cambridge, 1988, no. 77.

Exhibited:
'Paintings, Etchings and Lithographs by C. R. W. Nevinson', Leicester Galleries, October 1930 (43); 'Memorial Exhibition of Pictures by C. R. W. Nevinson', Leicester Galleries, 1947 (35).

174.
CHRISTOPHER RICHARD WYNNE NEVINSON
(1889–1946)

Amongst the Nerves of the World [30.167]
*c.*1930
Tempera on canvas, 76.5 x 50.5 cm
Signed bottom right:
C. R. W. NEVINSON

THIS VIEW of Fleet Street, taken from an upper-storey window at the corner of Shoe Lane, looks east and shows the street crowded with traffic (the buses are seen with the covered tops first introduced in 1925) and pedestrians. In the middle distance a passenger train is shown crossing the Ludgate Hill railway bridge towards Holborn Viaduct Station. Beyond are Wren's church of St Martin's Ludgate, with its tall lead spire, and the dome and west towers of St Paul's Cathedral.

In this picture Nevinson has used telegraph wires and the perspective lines of pavement and ledges as a basis for a system of criss-crossing lines that break up the composition into facets, a method of painting especially characteristic of the Italian futurist Umberto Boccioni (although Nevinson, unlike Boccioni, grounds his 'lines' into reality). Boccioni had first used 'lines of force' in his 1911 painting *Raid*, where they expressed conflict between the crowd and the cavalry, but also notions of atmosphere and noise, as echoed by Nevinson here. It may also be worth noting the similarity of Nevinson's title to those of Boccioni such as *The City Rises, The Street Enters the House* or *The Forces of the Street.*

This vivid image of the buzzing modern city focuses on the Fleet Street of the British press. Nevinson knew that world well: his father was a well-known writer and journalist and a regular correspondent for the *Daily Chronicle*. The artist himself worked as a journalist in his early twenties (see his memoirs, *Paint and Prejudice*, 1937, p30) and was a prolific writer throughout his life.

There have been two major changes to the site depicted since the picture was painted. The newspaper industry started moving out of Fleet Street in 1986, with Rupert Murdoch's News International Ltd transferring four of its main titles to Wapping (*The Times, Sunday Times, Sun* and *News of the World*), the last two of which had been based in Fleet Street. The dispute that followed was the worst in the history of Fleet Street, but every newspaper eventually followed the move to cheaper sites, some going to Docklands (*Associated News* to Surrey Docks, *Guardian* and *Daily Telegraph* to the Isle of Dogs, *Financial Times* to East India Dock), others to Battersea (*Observer*) or Southwark *Express* Newspapers. The second landmark to vanish from this view was Ludgate Hill railway bridge, pulled down in 1990 to make way for the new Thames Link development.

A watercolour version of this painting was sold at Christie's, 7 November 1991 (23).

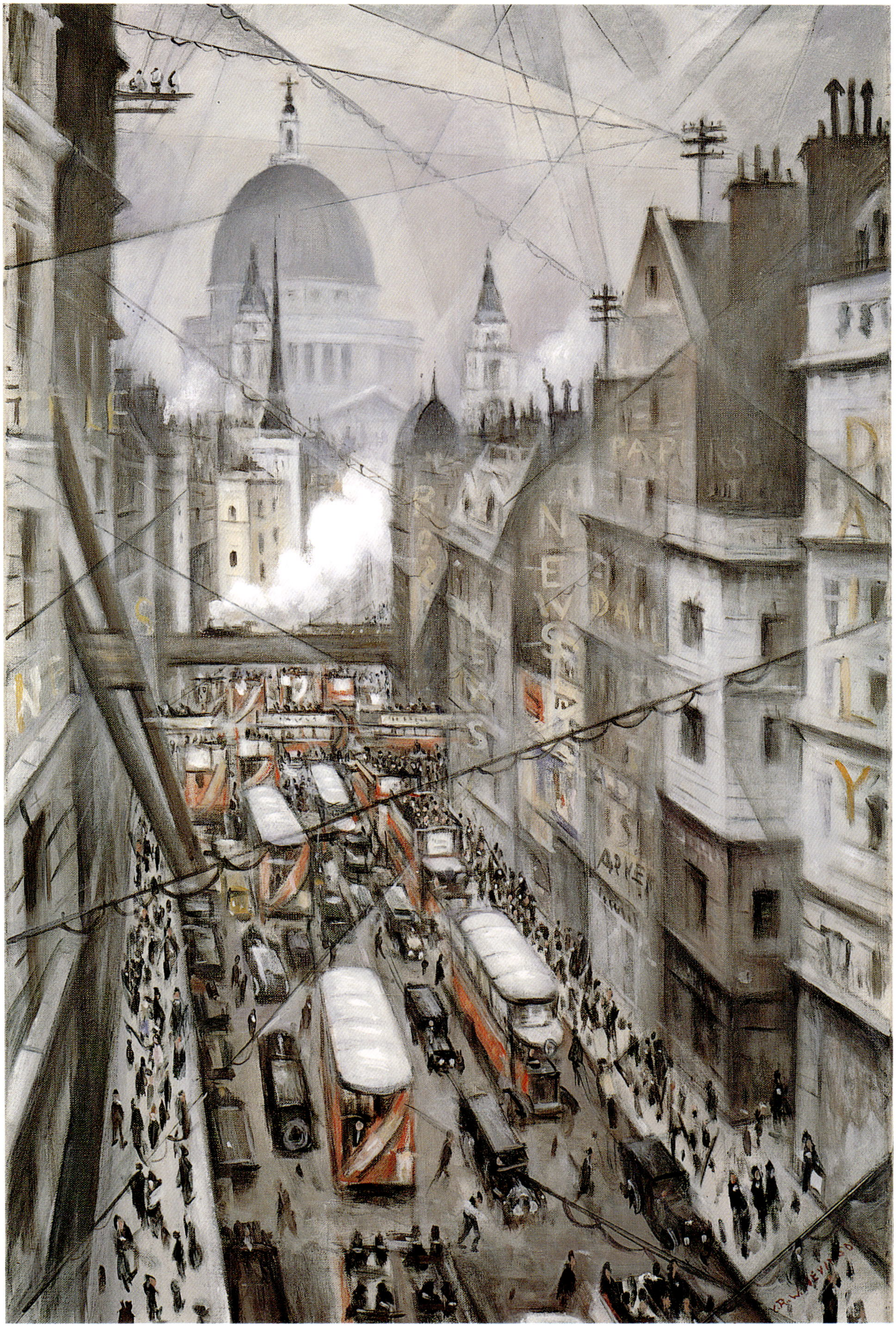

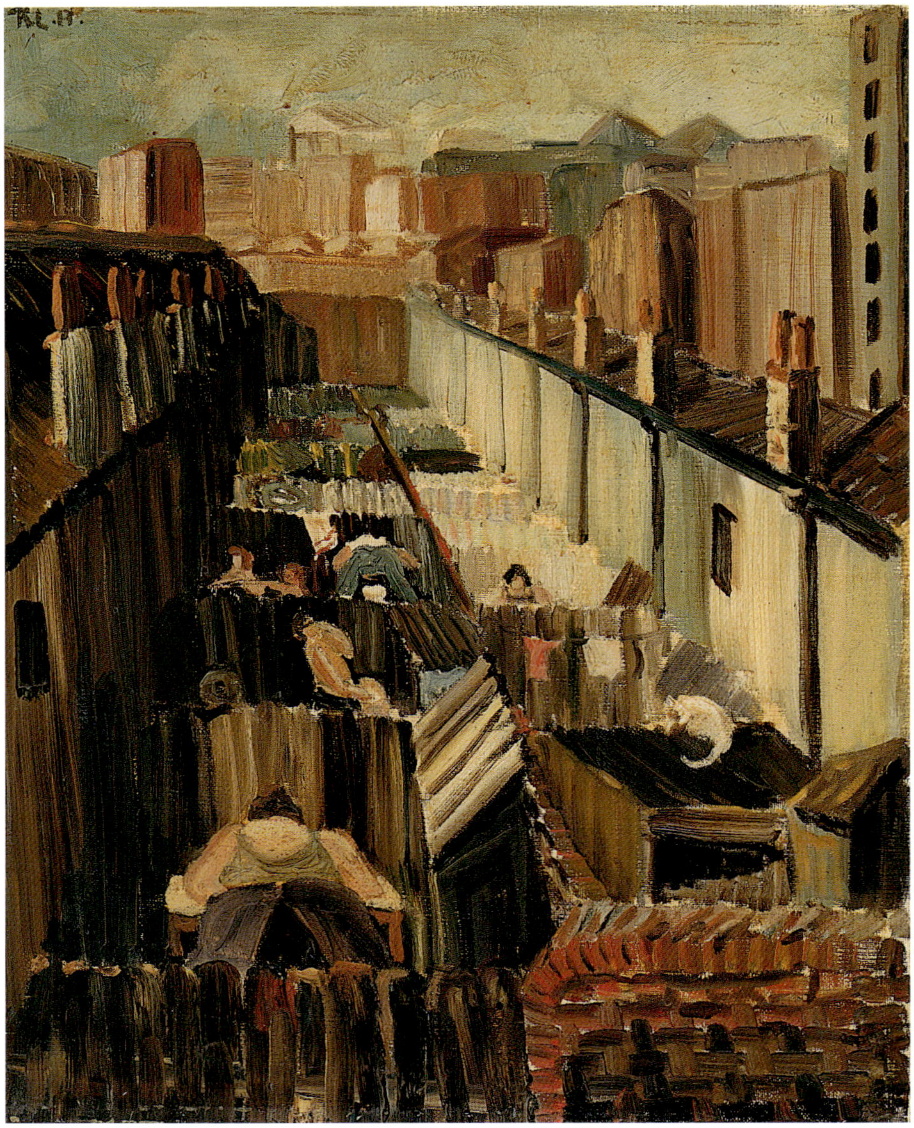

175.

LADY ROSE L. HENRIQUES

(1890–1973)

La Toilette* [47.37/1]

1930

Oil on canvas, 54.4 x 44.4 cm

Signed with initials top left: *R.L.H.*

THE ORIGINAL exhibition catalogue entry (*Stepney in War and Peace*) stated: 'At this period there were shops at the lower end of Berner Street where now Everard & Ellen Houses stand. Potter Clarke's factory was not built.'

Many houses in the poorer parts of Stepney still had little in the way of interior plumbing, even in the period just before the Second World War, and this picture shows four or five women washing in their backyards. The yards, separated by wooden fences, occupy the centre of the canvas, and the backs of the two rows of two-storey terrace houses are seen left and right; taller buildings are seen beyond and to the right.

Provenance:
Purchased from the Whitechapel Art Gallery in 1947.

Bibliography:
Hayes (cat. no. 156); *Stepney in War and Peace*, exhibition catalogue, Whitechapel Art Gallery, June 1947, no. 10; Peter Marcan, *Artists and the East End*, 1986, p33.

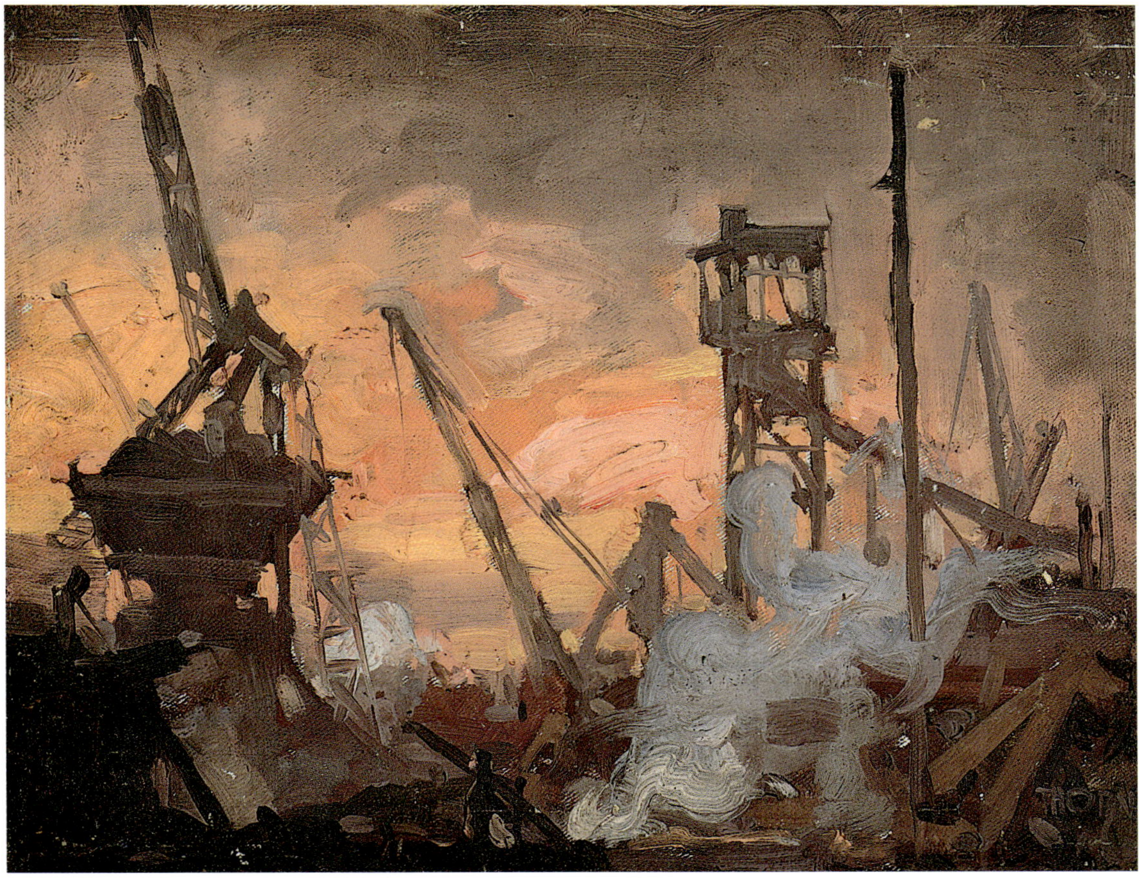

Provenance:
Presented by the artist's son, J. C. Thorn, in 1973.

Bibliography:
Geoffrey Phillips, *Thames Crossings – Bridges, Tunnels and Ferries*, 1981, pp174 and 179.

176.
JOSEPH THORN
(1898–1973)
Laying the Foundations of the New Chiswick Bridge [73.157/32]
1931
Oil on canvas board, 26.4 x 35.3 cm
Signed bottom right: *THORN*
Inscribed on the back: *Laying the foundations of the new Chiswick Bridge. November 1931 – Thorn*

CHISWICK BRIDGE was designed by Alfred Dryland with Sir Herbert Baker as consulting architect, who dealt mainly with cladding the structure with 3,400 tons of Portland stone. Chiswick Bridge takes the Great Chertsey Road over three concrete arches. Work began in September 1930 and the bridge was officially opened on 3 July 1933 by the Prince of Wales.

The royal ceremony disappointed thousands of spectators who had lined the roads between Chiswick and Hampton Court: the Prince was indeed opening three new Thames bridges on that day – Chiswick, Twickenham and Hampton Court. Local papers complained that the visit had been 'cut down to a minimum' and the major ceremony was in any case performed at Hampton Court.

This work is one of many the artist painted of Chiswick and Barnes while living in Hammersmith. It is an early example of the 'crane landscape', which was to become commonplace in the 1990s (see cat. nos 218 and 223).

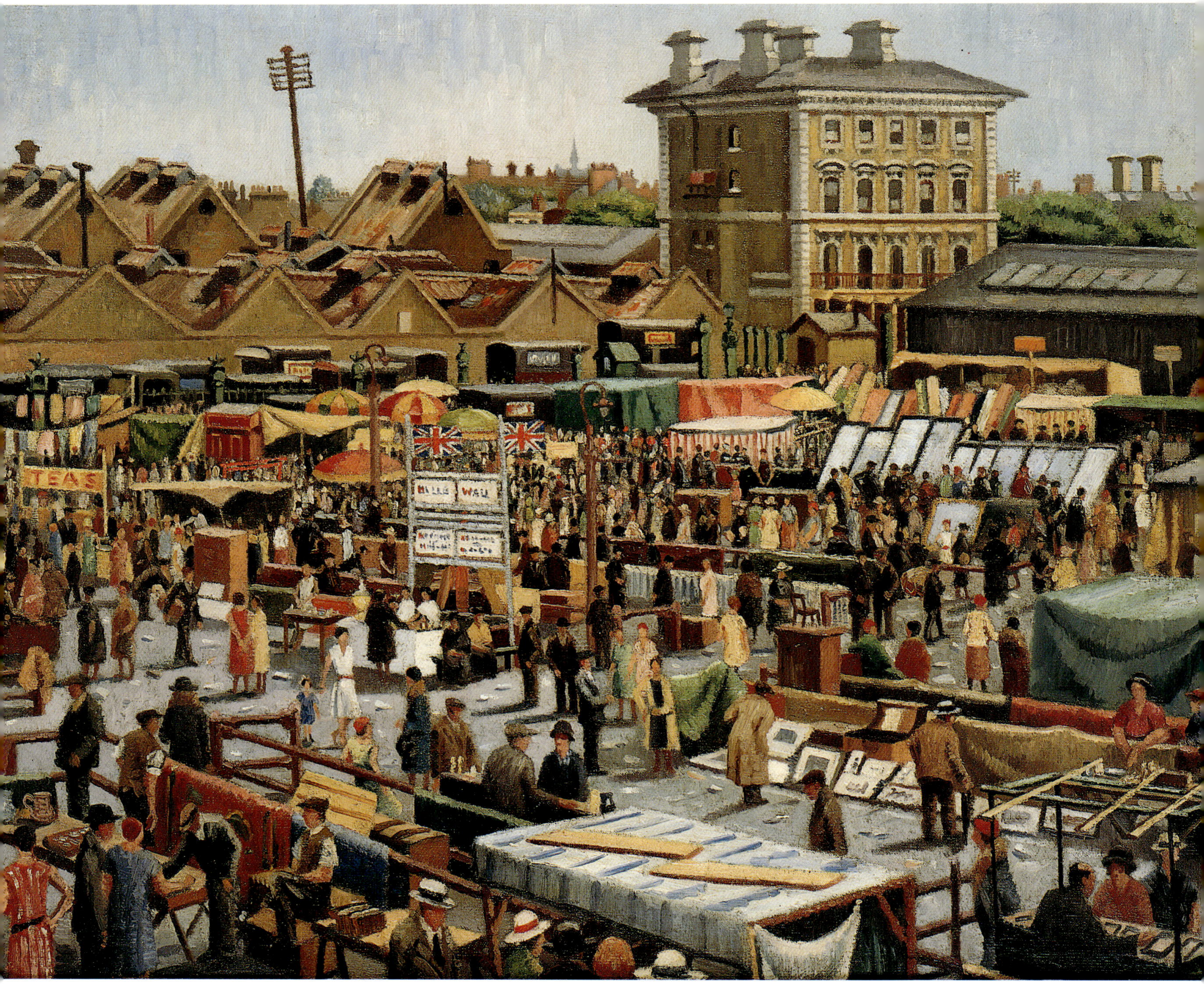
TEAS

177.

CLIFFORD ERIC HALL

(1904–1973)

The Caledonian Market, Copenhagen Fields [51.55]
1933
Oil on canvas, 70.6 x 90.6 cm
Signed and dated bottom right:
Clifford Hall/1933

THIS VIEW of the Caledonian market was taken from the tall central clock tower looking south-east towards the White Horse Tavern. The gabled warehouses are not part of the premises but belong to Caledonian Road railway station, which adjoined the market.

The buildings were originally designed by John Bunning, the architect of the Coal Exchange, for use as the Metropolitan Cattle Market, the livestock market at Smithfield having been demolished in 1851. A large watercolour by William Callow (in the Museum's collection, acc. no. A7739) shows the market in full swing soon after its opening. It was completed in 1855 and officially opened by the Prince Consort. Covering an area of 15 acres, it provided accommodation for some 44,000 animals. The central tower, built on the site of Copenhagen House (a celebrated London tea garden), contained twelve banks and a telegraph office. Two large taverns were erected on the north side of the market, on either side of a fountain, and four smaller taverns at each corner. They were built in a sober style uncharacteristic of contemporary public-house architecture, and perhaps, as Professor Henry-Russell Hitchcock suggests, were piously 'intended to influence for the better the deportment of hard-drinking cattle dealers'.

The cattle market was not in the end a commercial success, and by the beginning of the present century its premises were being used as a vast second-hand market, the equivalent of the *marché aux puces* in Paris. Some impression of its popularity and the variety of stalls is given here. Closed during the Second World War and never reopened, its activities are now carried on south of the river at Bermondsey Square. A housing estate (the Market Estate) has been completed on the north side and the south side has been kept as a park. The central clock tower still stands and three of the four corner taverns remain in business: The Lion, The Lamb and the White Horse Tavern (re-named The Gin Palace).

Hall produced several views of Caledonian market; two of them were sold by the Belgrave Gallery. The Museum also acquired in 1990 a preparatory drawing for this work (acc. no. 90.228/2).

Provenance:
Purchased out of the Joicey Trust Fund from the artist in 1951.

Bibliography:
Hayes (cat. no. 52); *Clifford Hall 1904–1973*, exhibition catalogue, Belgrave Gallery, 1977, nos 9 and 10.

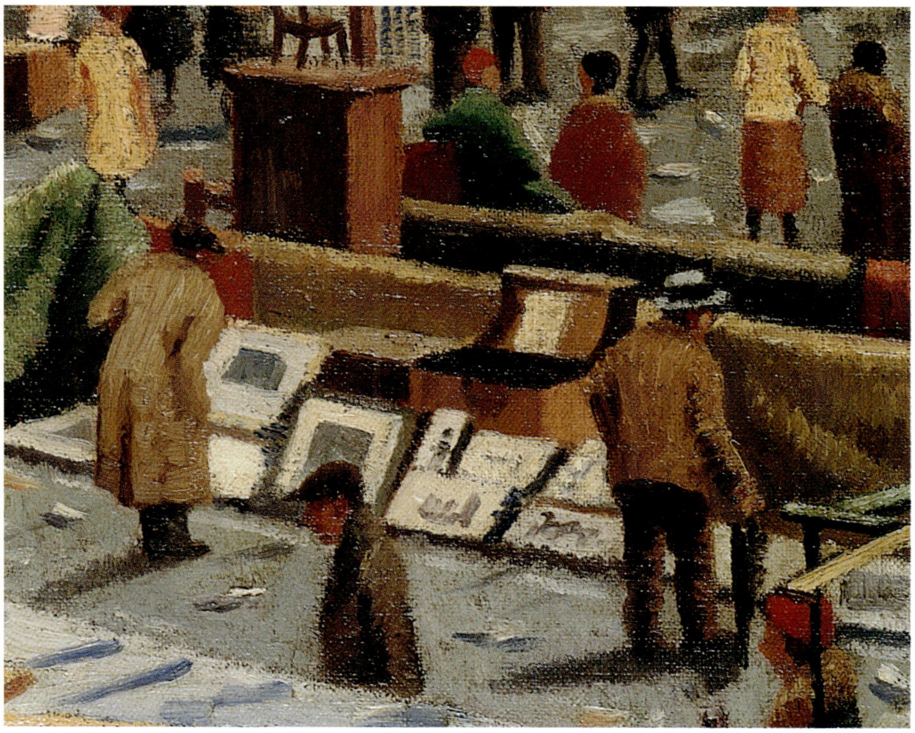

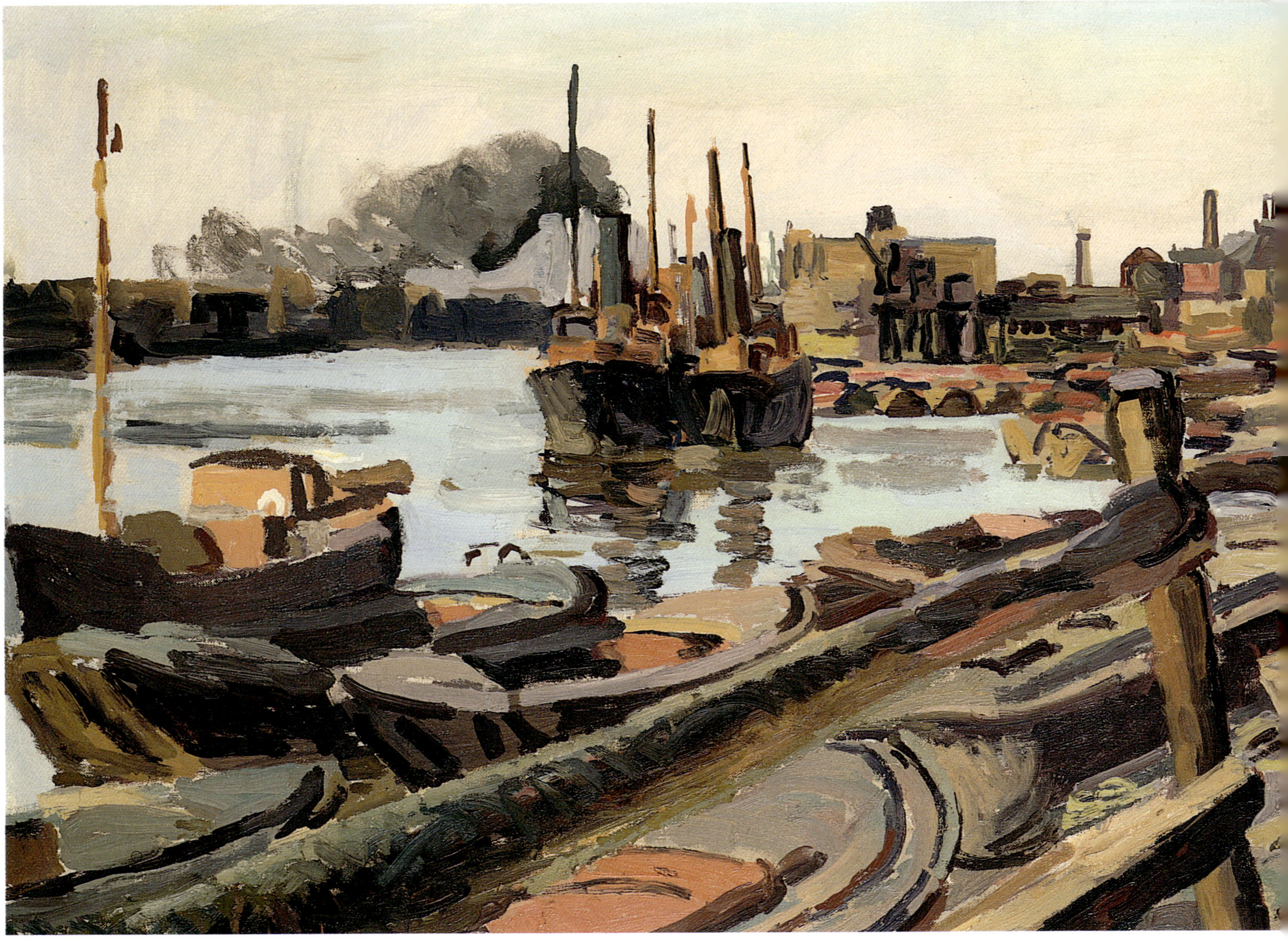

178.
DUNCAN GRANT
(1885–1978)
Rotherhithe [85.220]
1933
Oil on canvas, 51 x 102 cm
Signed and dated top right: *D. Grant 33*

THE ARTIST'S viewpoint was probably from one of the small wharves near the church of St Mary Rotherhithe, perhaps even from the terrace of the Mayflower public house. The scene, looking east, includes barges and lighters lying at low tide alongside the wharves, and a jetty with a crane which may be that of the South Metropolitan Gas Company or Bellamy's Wharf. The highest point in the picture probably shows the late nineteenth-century Thames Tunnel Mills (converted into flats since 1983). The tall building closing the perspective on the riverfront could represent the Globe Wharf warehouses.

The difficulty in identifying the site's topographical landmarks shows that the artist, although anchoring his composition

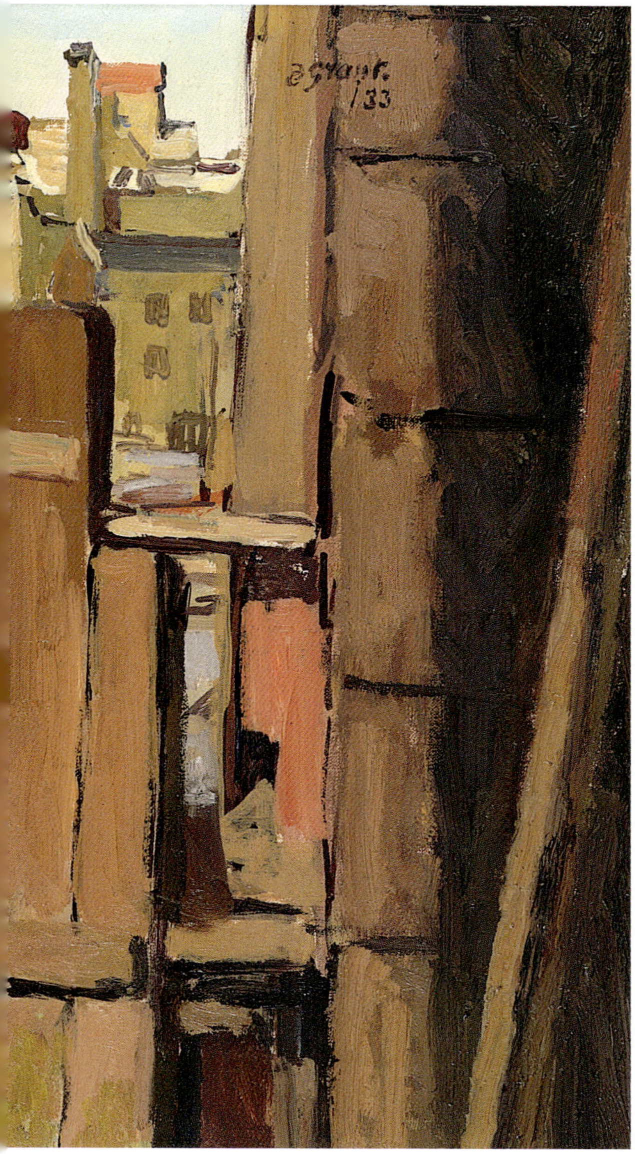

in reality, was pursuing other aims. The oblique viewpoint, the clutter of boats along the bank, the relative flimsiness of the timber structure in the foreground, all convey a sense of the makeshift and precarious which contrasts with the often massive appearance of the warehouses and industrial buildings along the Thames. Some of that scale may be lost when viewing the banks from a distance (see, for instance, Dorothy Belasco's 1915 etching of the oil mills at Surrey Commercial Docks, acc. no. 57.134/4), but here the painter focuses his view and the almost total absence of sky suggests he is pursuing a picturesque jumble of forms rather than a forbidding network of walls.

The bold application of paint and the areas of unpainted canvas (between colours) recall the style of Derain, even though the palette is infinitely more subdued. It gives the painting a shimmering quality, particularly suitable in a maritime context. The inclusion of two steamers, one of which has a smoking funnel, and their projecting shadows on the surface of the Thames, further reinforce the gentle movement of the scene.

The formula chosen by Grant contrasts with that adopted by Whistler in 1860. *Rotherhithe* from his 'Thames Set' is vertical and contains a strong human element.

Provenance:
R. Olag Hambro Esq.; Lady Charlotte Bonham-Carter; purchased in 1985 by private treaty sale through Sotheby's, with the help of the MGC/V&A Purchase Grant Fund.

Bibliography:
Chris Ellmers and Alex Werner, *London's Lost Riverscape*, 1988, pp121–3.

Exhibited:
'British Paintings since Whistler', National Gallery, 1940 (200).

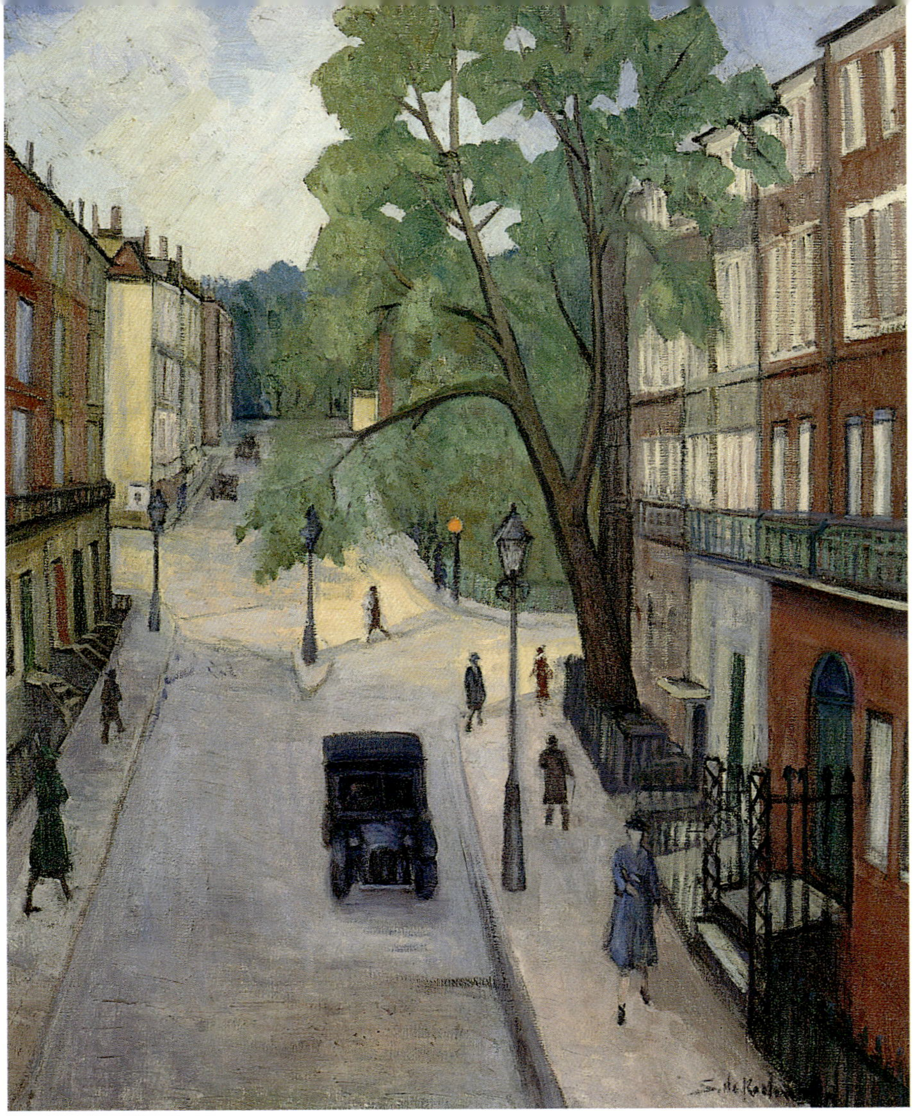

179.
STANISLAWA DE KARLOWSKA
(1876–1952)
Russell Square from Montagu Street
[68.39]
*c.*1935
Oil on canvas, 61 x 50.7 cm
Signed bottom right: *S. de Karlowska*

THE VIEW, taken two-thirds of the way down Montagu Street, past the British Museum, looks towards the western end of Russell Square with Montagu Place on the left-hand side. Characteristically, the artist has placed herself looking at her subject from above.

Perhaps because Russell Square is one of London's largest squares, it has not often been depicted by artists. It was laid out in 1800 by Humphry Repton and the artist was probably unaware that the west side of the square, shown here, is the only side to retain some of James Burton's original houses.

De Karlowska also painted a close-up view of Russell Square (Bevan Collection), taken from within the square. It adopts a similar formula with a bird's-eye view and its cross-path system echoes the road arteries in the painting under review.

Provenance:
Presented by Mrs Charles Baty and her brother R. A. Bevan (the artist's children by Robert Bevan, to whom she was married) in 1968.

Bibliography:
The Painters of Camden Town, 1905–1920, exhibition catalogue, Christie's, 1988.

Exhibited:
'Trends in British Art' (organised by the Art Exhibitions Bureau), Guildhall Art Gallery, 1954; The Polish Library, London, 20 March–1 April 1968 (19).

180.

HUMPHREY JENNINGS

(1907–50)

London in the 17th Century [83.80]
1936
Oil on board, 24.5 x 33.3 cm
Not signed or dated
Inscribed on the back: *H. J. 1936 London in the 17th century.*
A label specifies: *Collection of Charlotte Jennings*

THIS STYLISED view of Lambeth Palace as seen from the Thames is made intriguing by the three-dimensional triangle floating in the sky above it. The choice of subject matter must have been suggested to Jennings by the large body of such views in the early imaging of London. It should, however, be pointed out that, strictly speaking, this type of view belongs more to the eighteenth than to the seventeenth century (see cat. nos 19 and 20). The composition seems unique in the body of surrealist painting because, disorientating as it is, it still retains a strong sense of place.

Jennings was extremely committed to the surrealist movement, as is shown by his 1936 review of the publication *Surrealism*,

Provenance:
From the collection of Charlotte Jennings; presented by the Elephant Trust in 1983.

Bibliography:
Humphrey Jennings Film-Maker/Painter/Poet, Mary-Lou Jennings (ed.), British Film Institute, 1982, pp24–15; *The Humphrey Jennings Film Reader*, Kevin Jackson (ed.), 1993.

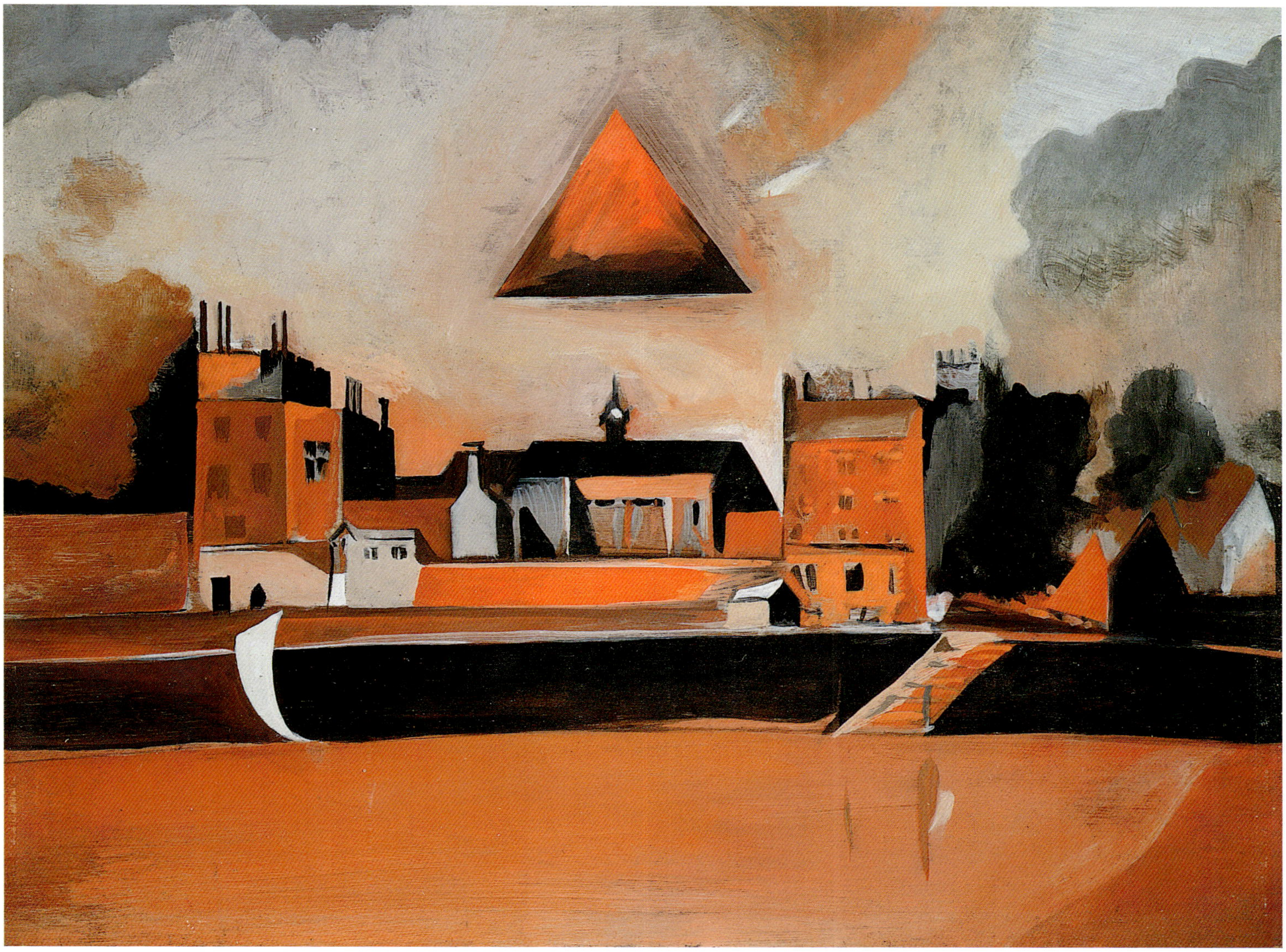

a collection of surrealist essays with an introduction by Herbert Read (see Jackson (ed.), 1993, pp219–21). In 1936, the year this work was painted, he was a member of the Organising Committee of the International Surrealist Exhibition which was shown at the Burlington Galleries for a month that summer.

1936 was also the year when the Mass Observation project was first contemplated by Jennings in collaboration with Stuart Legg, David Gascoyne and Charles Madge.

Perhaps we should turn to Jennings's writings in order to find lines of interpretation for this painting. In 1938 he developed with passion the idea of juxtaposing very ordinary things with something mysterious in an essay on 'Poetry and National Life' (Jackson, pp280–1). That same year, in an essay on Magritte's paintings, he talked about poetry implying a 'bringing together' and with Magritte, he argues, 'the "bringing together" *occurs* in a passive sense in the painter's imagination' (Jackson, p226). But perhaps the closest and most mysterious parallel one could quote comes from a much later poem, 'As I look' (1949, quoted in Jackson, p300):

> . . . As I look into the mist and let my vision dive
> (As Corot in Campagna when the sun descended mixed the paints together)
> I perceive in the grey picture all the colours that were once there
> Not only the simple divisions of the prism
> Brilliant orange icon ore peacock coloured coal
> I perceive also the hues of the men who built the city. . .

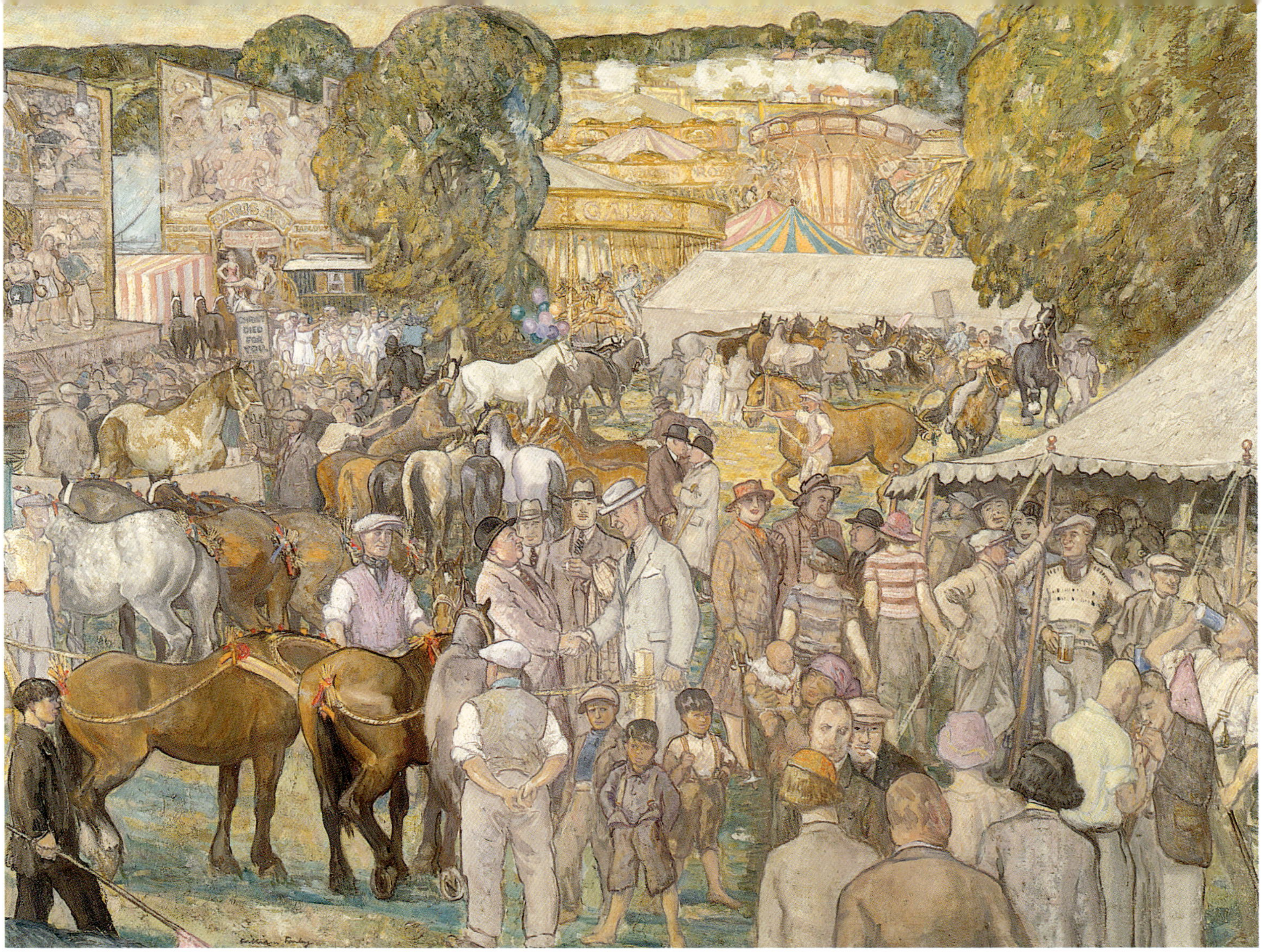

181.
WILLIAM FARLEY
(1893–1964)
Men, Women and Horses: Barnet Fair*
[69.139]
*c.*1937
Oil on canvas, 76.7 x 102 cm
Signed bottom left: *William Farley*

THE ARTIST depicts the horse fair (in the foreground) with a funfair (in the background) which were held on the east side of the Great North Road around the railway station. In the distance can be glimpsed the smoke of a passing train.

The cattle and horse market goes back to medieval times and in 1588 Elizabeth I granted Barnet a charter for its market. Today's September Fair, held in fields off Mays Lane, is still continuing the tradition.

Farley may have been inspired in the subject for this painting by Charles Cundall, who depicted the fair the previous year (Southampton Art Gallery) and also exhibited the *Horse Fair at Stow-on-the-Wold* at the 1932 Royal Academy exhibition. Both artists depict Barnet Fair from the same viewpoint, but Farley, deliberately it seems, has closed in on his subject, also reducing the distance between the funfair and the horse fair.

Provenance:
Purchased from the artist's widow in 1969.

Exhibited:
Royal Academy, 1937 (572).

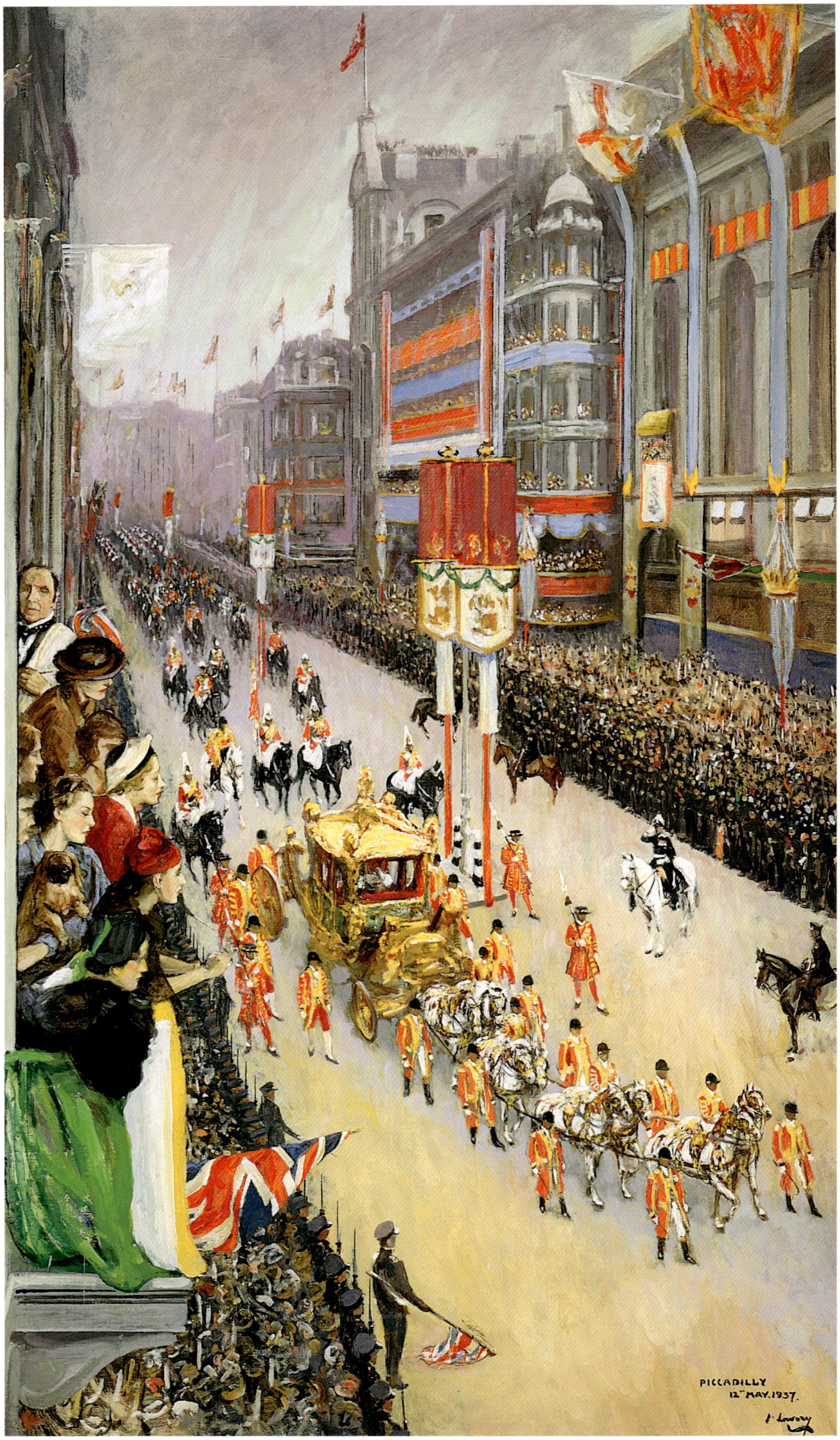
PICCADILLY
12th MAY. 1937.

182.

JOHN LAVERY

(1856–1941)

Piccadilly, 12 May 1937* [70.58]

1937

Oil on canvas 212 x 127.5 cm

Inscribed, signed and dated bottom right:

PICCADILLY 12TH MAY 1937 J. Lavery

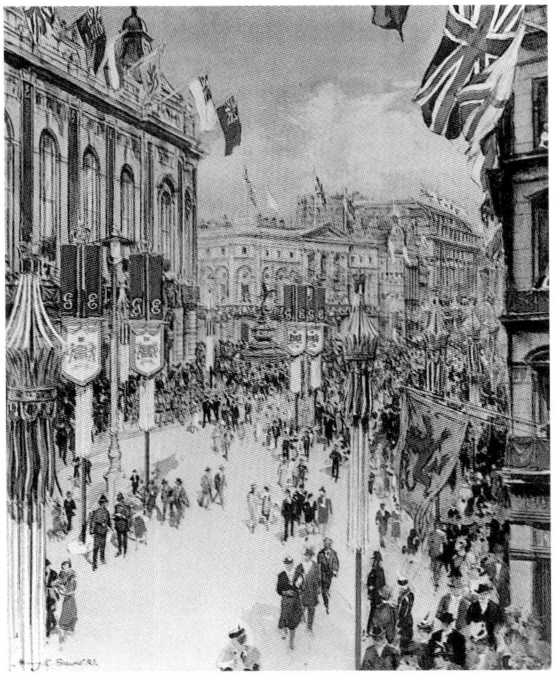

THE STATE coach and Coronation procession of George VI are depicted going along Piccadilly shortly before 3.00pm on 12 May 1937. The gold State coach is accompanied by four Yeomen of the Guard, the Sovereign's escort of the Household Cavalry, grooms in state on either side of the horses and royal dukes on horseback wearing green sashes. The State Coach had left Buckingham Palace at 10.30am that morning and had proceeded along the Mall, down Whitehall to Westminster Abbey. After the crowning ceremony there, the coach left the Abbey at 2.15pm, going down the Victoria Embankment, up Northumberland Avenue, through Trafalgar Square, into Pall Mall, St James's Street and Piccadilly, on to Regent and Oxford Streets and back to Buckingham Palace via Park Lane.

The night before the Coronation, the *Evening Standard* recorded '50,000 sleepers in Hyde Park'. London was lavishly decorated for the occasion. The traffic islands in Piccadilly were decorated with blue, white, gold and red; the pavement masts with red, white and gold; and the buildings with blue and white. The scheme was designed by the architect G. Grey Wornum. At night-time, some of the capital's most important landmarks were illuminated, including 'fairyland' St James's Park (by the Gaslight and Coke Company).

A painting by Henry C. Brewer of the Coronation decorations in Piccadilly was reproduced in the Coronation number of the *Illustrated London News* and this work could almost be seen to complement Lavery's painting. Apart from adopting a similar format, which was dictated by the (identical) viewpoint, the two paintings make a complete tableau, one by looking west (Lavery), down Piccadilly, with the procession coming towards us, the other by looking east (Brewer), towards Piccadilly Circus.

Lavery included a self-portrait in the composition. He stands on the left-hand side of the painting on a balcony overlooking Piccadilly and surrounded by 'a bevy of young women'. Among them were Katherine Fitzgerald, Diana Dickinson and Ann Forbes-Sempill (see McConkey).

The other great society painter, Frank O. Salisbury, commissioned by the prime ministers of Canada, Australia, New Zealand and the Union of South Africa, painted a large number of works related to George VI's coronation (see Christie's 25 September 1985 studio sale).

Provenance:
Presented by Messrs M. Newman Ltd in 1970.

Bibliography:
Illustrated London News, Coronation Number, 1937; Kenneth McConkey, *Sir John Lavery*, Edinburgh, 1993, pp200–202.

Exhibited:
Royal Academy, 1938 (250); 'Memorial Exhibition of the work of Sir John Lavery, RA.' The Leicester Galleries; exhibition celebrating dealers Messrs M. Newman's centenary in 1970 (43a Duke Street).

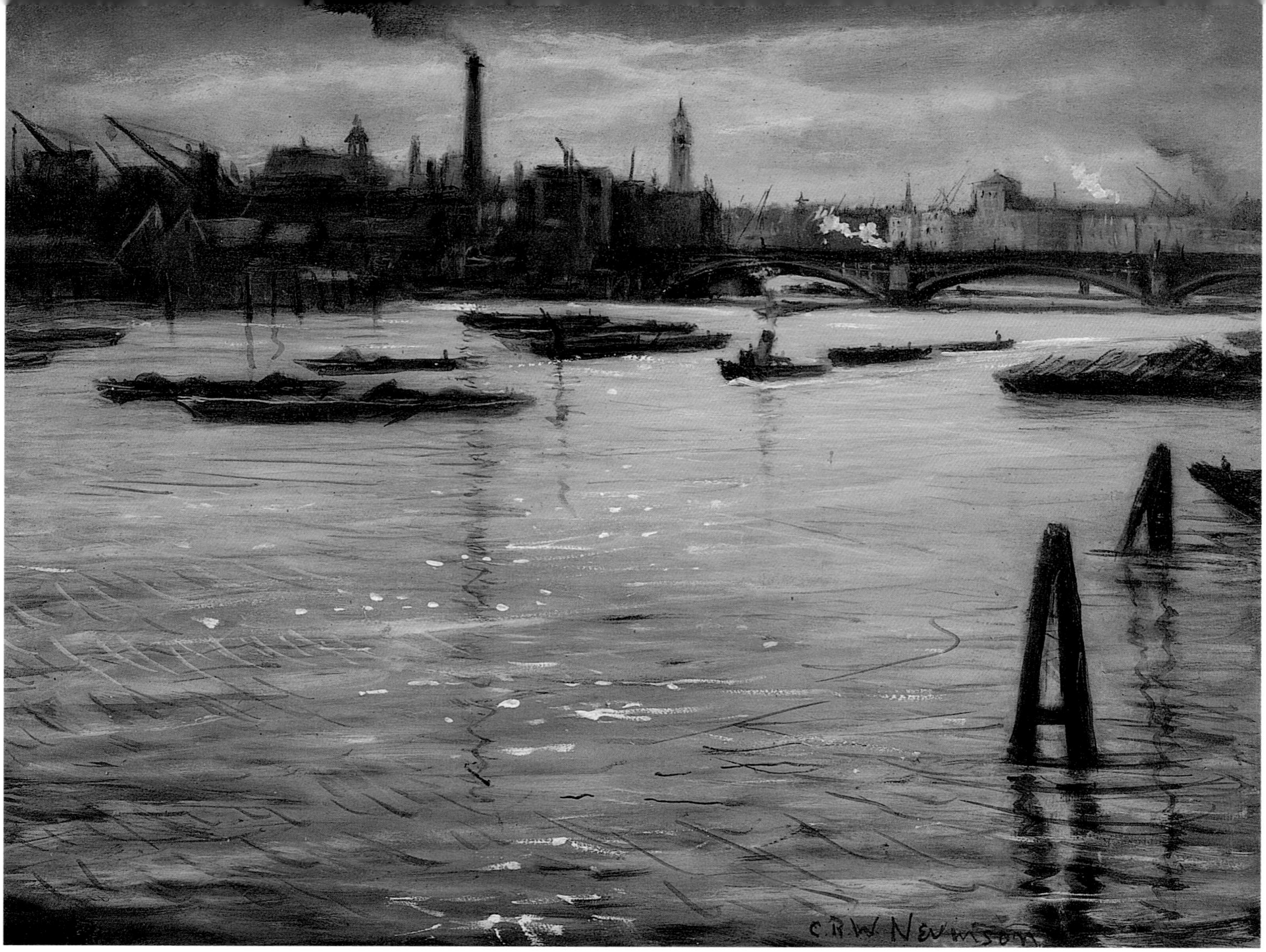

Provenance:
A. D. Power; bequeathed by him through the National Art Collections Fund in 1959.

Bibliography:
Hayes (cat. no. 80).

183.
CHRISTOPHER RICHARD WYNNE NEVINSON
(1889–1946)
The Thames at Southwark [59.99/143]
1938
Oil on panel, 29.7 x 40 cm
Signed bottom right: *C. R. W. Nevinson*

A VIEW of the warehouses of Bankside from Southwark Bridge. Over the rooftops can be seen, from left to right: the hulk of Waterloo Station; the Shot Tower built in 1826, which stood until April 1962 on the west side of Waterloo Bridge; and the Oxo Tower. The iron-girder railway bridge, which was built in the early 1860s immediately next to Blackfriars Bridge to take the London, Chatham and Dover Railway to its new termini on the north bank (first Ludgate Hill, then Holborn Viaduct), is seen to the right; beyond are Big Ben and some of the buildings fronting the Embankment east of Charing Cross, Shell Mex House being the most prominent; the top of Nelson's Column and of the spire of St Martin-in-the-Fields can just be distinguished. A tug and a number of barges are seen on the river.

This oil study and the next two works form a most interesting group, each illustrating a different compositional device, horizontal and vertical, on and off centre. Despite the widely different areas covered (Docklands, City and West End), they form a very tight group concerned with the working river and the industrialisation of its banks.

184.
CHRISTOPHER RICHARD WYNNE NEVINSON
(1889–1946)

The Temporary Waterloo Bridge [59.99/144]
1938
Oil on panel, 40 x 29.7 cm
Signed bottom right: *C. R. W. Nevinson*

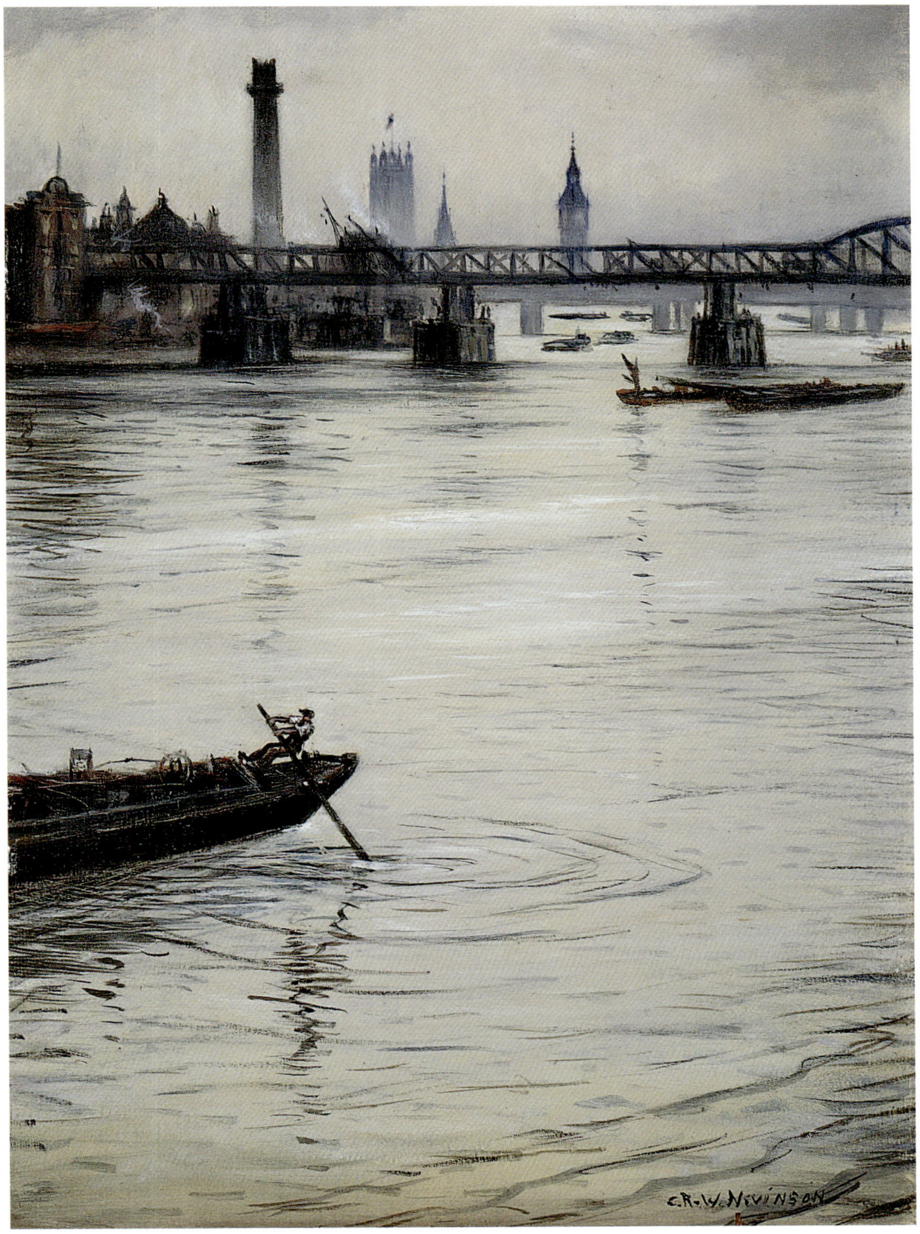

A VIEW of the temporary iron bridge which was erected to replace Rennie's Waterloo Bridge, destroyed in 1936 (see cat. no. 53), pending the construction of the new concrete bridge by Sir Giles Gilbert Scott, finished in 1945. Beyond can be seen the Shot Tower on the south bank (pulled down in 1962), the Victoria Tower, Hungerford Bridge and Big Ben. A barge is being manoeuvred in the foreground.

The scene is depicted from the opposite viewpoint to *London, Winter* (see cat. no. 173) and recurs several times in Nevinson's output, most memorably perhaps in *Waterloo Bridge* (Samuel Hill collection), painted before the erection of the temporary structure shown here.

Provenance:
Purchased from the Leicester Galleries by A. D. Power; bequeathed by him through the National Art Collections Fund in 1959.

Bibliography:
Hayes (cat. no. 81).

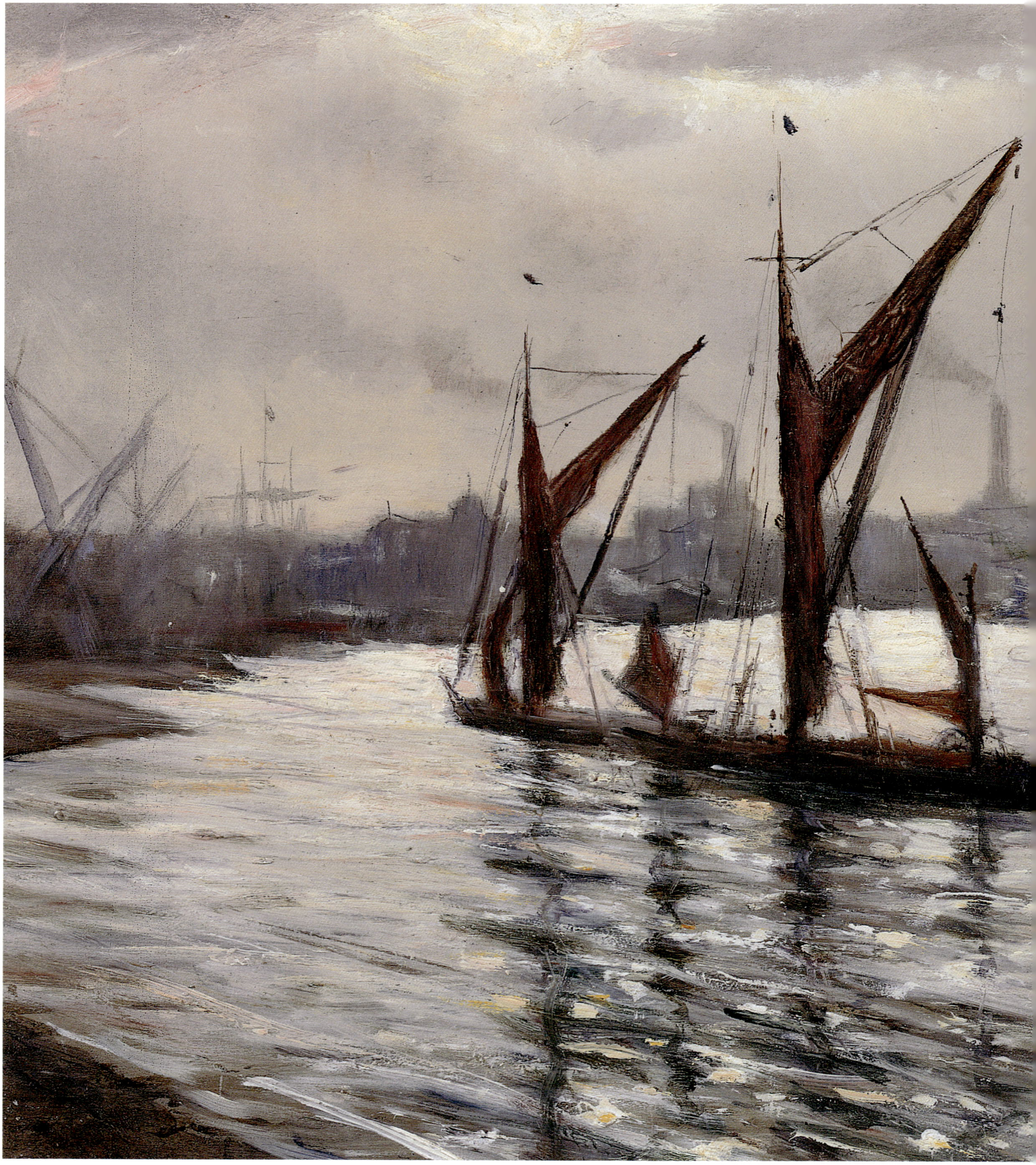

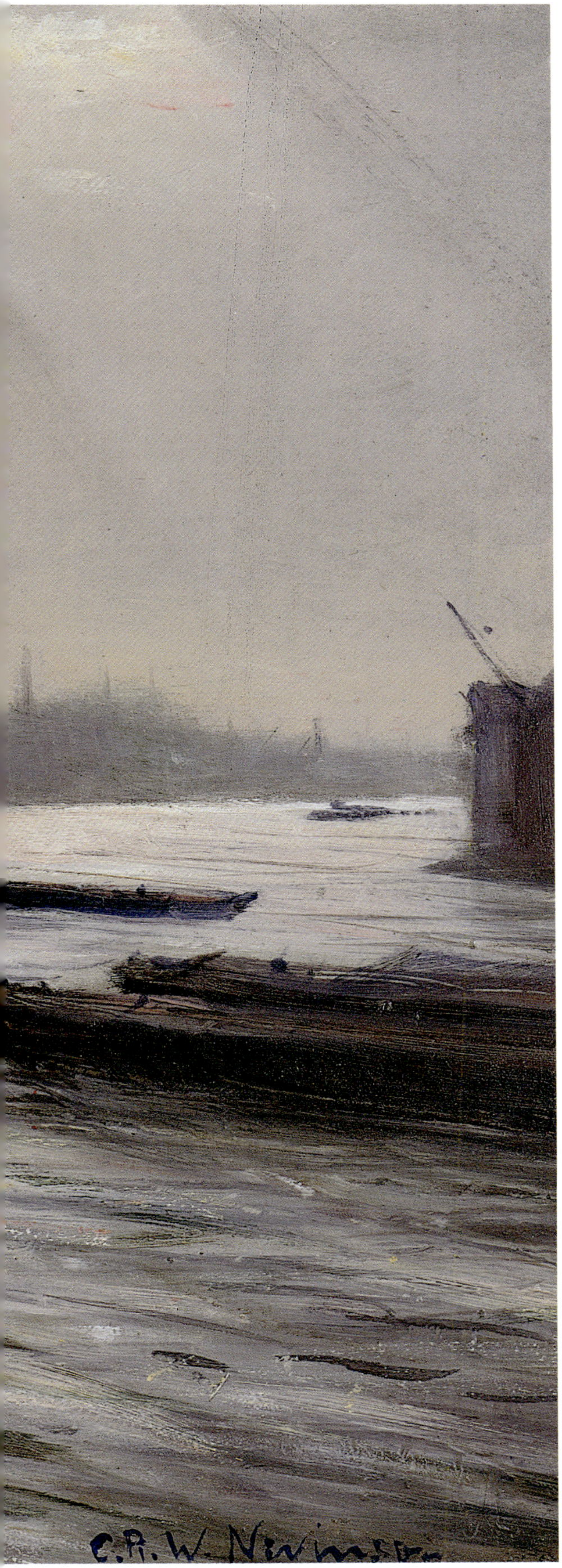

185.

CHRISTOPHER RICHARD WYNNE NEVINSON

(1889–1946)

The Thames at Deptford [59.99/145]
1939
Oil on panel, 35.9 x 45.9 cm
Signed bottom right: *C. R. W. Nevinson*

AN IMPRESSIONISTIC view of the Deptford riverside looking westwards from Greenwich pier, in front of the present berth of the *Cutty Sark*. The opening of Deptford Creek is seen on the left, and in the middle distance are the parish church of St Nicholas's Deptford, destroyed during the Second World War, and the chimneys of Deptford power station (demolished in 1990–91). On the right is part of a warehouse, with a crane, which still stands on the north shore: the Isle of Dogs. A number of barges are seen on the river.

Provenance:
A. D. Power; bequeathed by him through the National Art Collections Fund in 1959.

Bibliography:
Hayes (cat. no. 82).

Exhibited:
'The Recent Paintings of C. R. W. Nevinson', Leicester Galleries, February 1939 (36); 'Memorial Exhibition of Pictures by C. R. W. Nevinson', Leicester Galleries, 1947 (40).

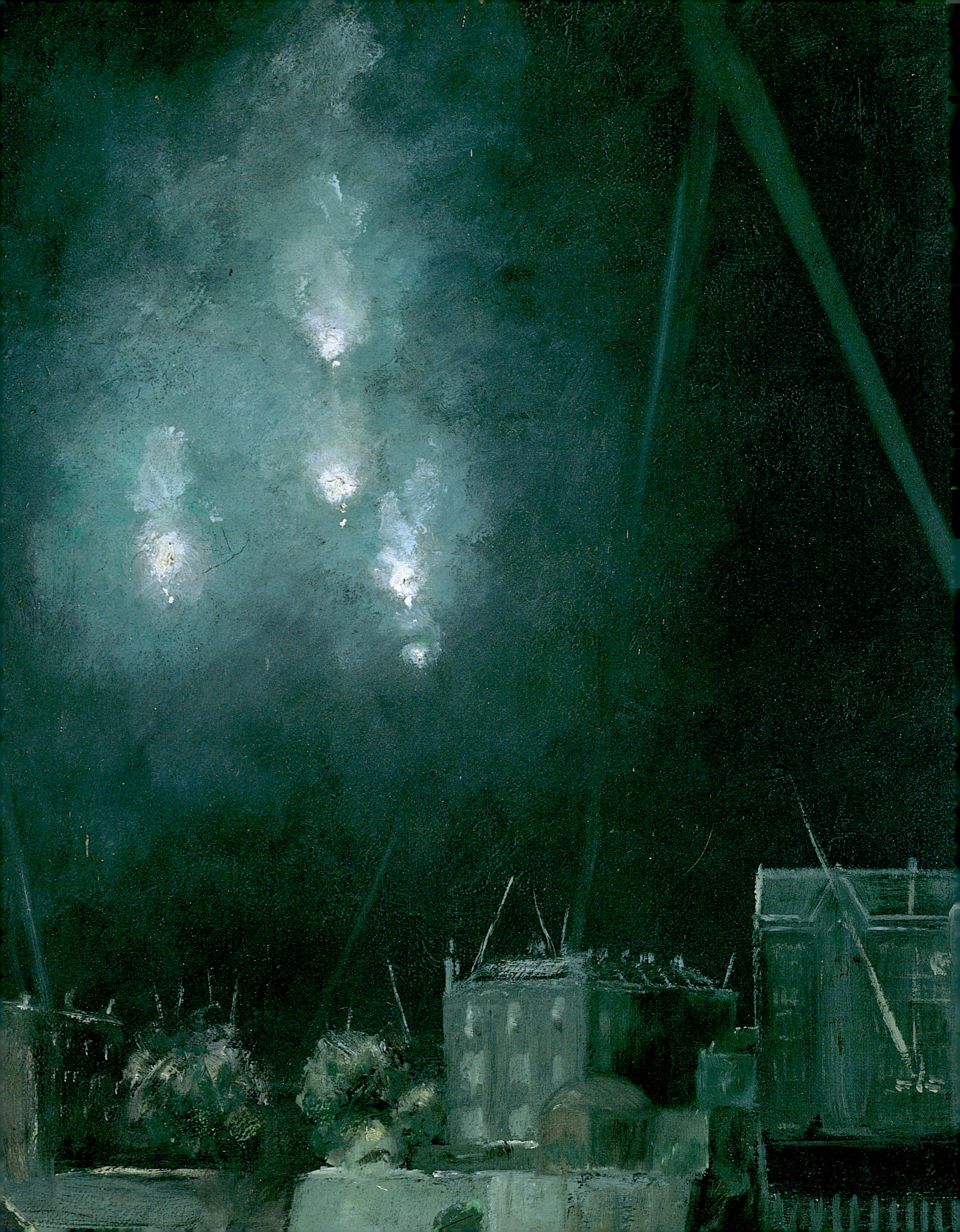

THE SECOND WORLD WAR

THE LANDSCAPE of ruins was the single most popular subject with London artists during the Second World War, ranging from almost literal records of bomb damage in the city, such as Gladys Pinks's *Deserted and Forlorn* (cat. no. 190), to the representation by visionary artists of the 'romantic' gaunt outlines of bombed-out buildings: the work of David Bomberg and of John Piper is represented by two memorable examples.

Some artists strove to capture a panoramic view of the devastation. *A Prospect of the City of London from the South East in the year 1945* was drawn by Cecil Brown[1] as a huge bird's-eye view. It charts in great detail the extensive damage the City of London endured, notably during the blitz, which started on 7 September 1940 and continued until the following May. Three years later Lawrence Wright produced his astonishing 360-degree panoramic view of London seen from the dome of St Paul's Cathedral.[2] The panorama stretches across ten boards. Wright's serene use of the watercolour medium and his impeccable skills as an architectural draughtsman contrast with the spectacle of the extensive bomb damage. The boldest scheme of all, however, was dreamed (rather than executed) by the painter David Bomberg. The execution of *Evening in the City of London*, the artist's only canvas to record the blitzed landscape, inspired him to pursue the idea of a huge panoramic work of the whole of London and not simply of the City (see cat. no. 192). This project, unfortunately never carried out, would have complemented the 'St Paul's work' of Lawrence Wright and could have contributed to the debate of topography versus art, a most relevant but also controversial issue at the heart of the war recording scheme.[3]

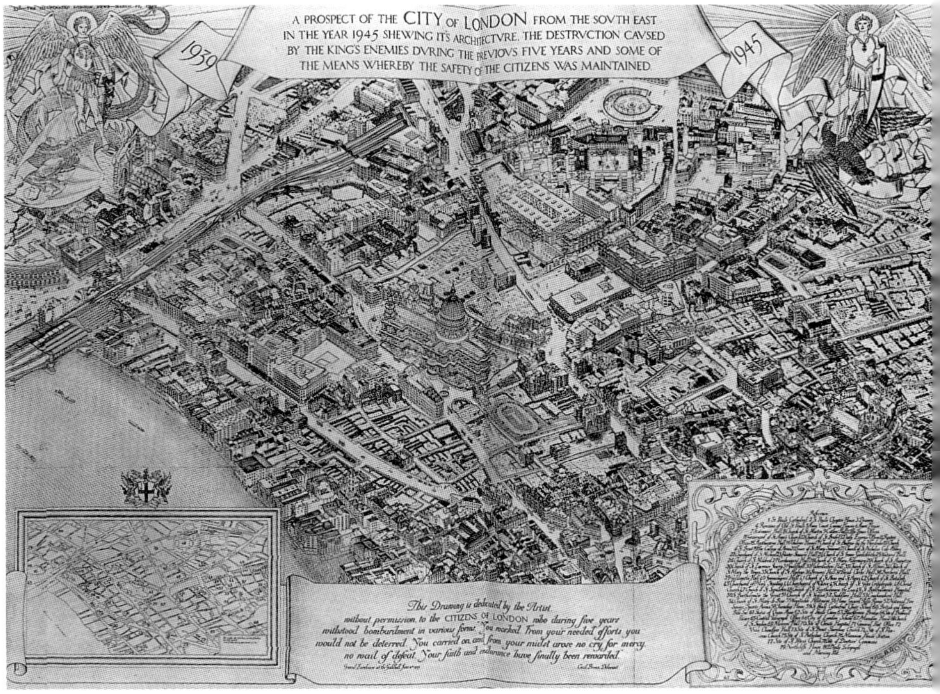

Cecil Brown (1903–1983)
A Prospect of the City of London from the South East in the Year 1945
Reproduced by courtesy of the *Illustrated London News*, 12 March 1949.

Henry Moore's output, although not in oil, should be mentioned, since Moore was one of the very few graphic artists to have tackled the human, rather than the purely physical, dimension of the war.[4] The Museum has one fine example from his extraordinary *Tube Shelter* series (acc. no. 47.26/14). Purists may object to seeing the totally unknown artist Nettie Moon mentioned in the same breath as Henry Moore, but in view of the near absence of the depiction of human suffering, her painting is unusual for the careful balance she gives to devastation versus people; the fact that it was painted over thirty years after the end of the war accounts for this different perception of events (cat. no. 187).

Although it has been argued that the very status of official war artist 'protected' and 'prevented artists from being killed',[5] it was certainly hazardous to be an artist during the war, and not solely because of the bombs. The danger of being taken for a spy gave rise to many stories. On 7 October 1939 the painter and illustrator Grace Golden wrote in her diary:

> Difficulty of sketching in streets now is that interfering busy bodies try to make some fuss. This morning outside Corner House, Tottenham Crt Rd was sketching people waiting for bus, a fat, bald headed, prosperous Jew came up & told me I was drawing a building – it was obvious I was not. I was so angry at his alien look & cheek – kept on in silence – after suggesting he let police interfere. The policeman came up in good time & asked to have a 'decco' – nothing suspicious, so suggested I put it in pocket & took a walk. Meanwhile a crowd had collected – hoping to see me remove to jail. This was not the first time – on Holborn viaduct a woman told a policeman that I didn't look English![6]

The recording of the war by artists was carefully monitored by the Ministry of Information. The War Artists' Advisory Committee was set up under the responsibility of Kenneth Clark (Director of the National Gallery) with E. M. O'Rourke Dickey as secretary; this body eventually assumed general responsibility for all war coverage, including the schemes proposed by the War Office and the Admiralty. The rules for artistic 'record', first devised for the Great War, were re-adapted and the WAAC met for the first time on 23 November 1939, consisting of the following: Muirhead Bone, printmaker (had been a war artist in 1916); P. H. Jowett, Principal of the Royal College of Art; Randolph Schwabe, Slade Professor and Walter Russell, Keeper of the Royal Academy.[7]

Their brief was 'to draw up a list of artists qualified to record the War at home and abroad'. The WAAC was a vast operation which employed thirty full-time artists at any one time; specific commissions were given to an additional 100 artists and the work of a further 200 artists was also bought. The repository for these works was initially the Imperial War Museum, which from March 1946 started allocating them to national public collections. The Museum of London collection represents a good cross-section of the artists who operated during the war: John Piper was employed at irregular intervals by the WAAC, Charles Cundall was a salaried war artist with the rank of honorary Captain, Royal Marines, Paul Dessau and W. S. Haines were firemen artists (see below), while most of the others were 'unofficial'.

The monitoring of artists' work by the WAAC was inevitably cumbersome and this is illustrated by what happened to the painter Eliot Hodgkin, who was almost alone in recording the proliferation of wildlife among the ruins in the City. Ernest Borough Johnson, represented in the collections of the Guildhall Library, produced a few watercolours on this subject. Hodgkin sought to interest Kenneth Clark in his work (in a failed attempt to become a fully fledged home front war artist) and was eventually given a commission in March 1945 to paint a picture of *Flowers among the Bomb Wreckage*. He was required to submit for censorship all his preliminary studies as well as the finished work, and he was asked not to show any of them before they had been passed by the censor.[8] When his artist friend Phyllis Pearsall recorded a fuse factory[9] she was required to ink in certain areas of the drawing so as not to give away certain technical information.

The artistic careers of both Phyllis Pearsall and Eliot Hodgkin were interrupted during the war when they joined the Home Intelligence Division of the Ministry of Information. They were in effect forced to become 'Sunday painters', as a result of which, perhaps, their work had great originality. They were not alone in operating outside the restricting regulations imposed on war artists. The Artists International Association (AIA) was the first exhibiting society to mount an annual members' exhibition under wartime conditions. James Boswell and Patrick Carpenter did produce drawings showing the depressing conditions of the private soldier, poles apart from the world of the official war artists with officer status.[10]

The firemen artists were particularly well organised and their works were highly publicised in the course of touring exhibitions. They held their first exhibition at the Central School of Arts in March 1941. This exhibition was then taken to America and was still touring in 1943. In August 1941 they held their first exhibition at the Royal Academy (attended in one month by 64,000 people); others followed there yearly, as well as touring the provinces and abroad, and showing at other London galleries.[11] All these events were in aid of the Fire Service Benevolent Fund and attracted considerable publicity and interest. The Chief Commander of the London Fire Force, F. W. Jackson, thus explained their origins: 'Firemen train and exercise and keep their apparatus in good order, but they have, when there are no "blitzes", long hours of waiting.'[12] Clearly many chose to develop their painting skills: Leonard Rosoman is one of the most respected names in this field but the work of Paul Dessau (the Auxiliary Fire Service) and W. S. Haines (National Fire Service), both represented in the collection, also deserve to be mentioned. They, more than any other artist, chose to depict the dynamic force of London's fires with dramatic lighting effects rather than images of devastation.

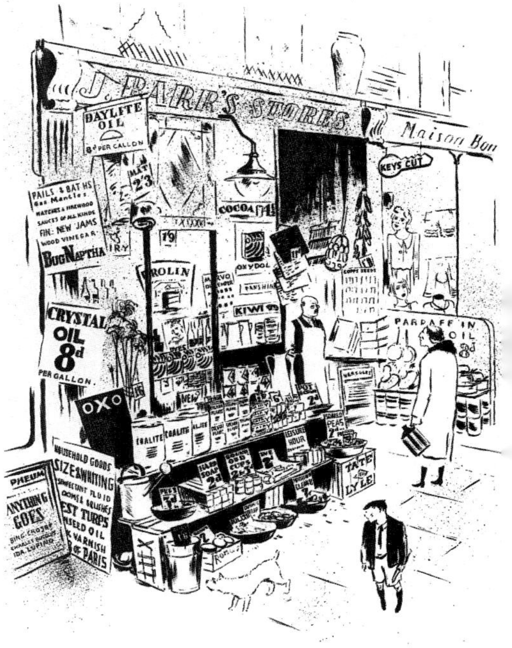

James Boswell (1906–1971)
Parr's Stores, Leather Lane, 1937
Lithograph
The Museum of London.

1. It was exhibited at the Royal Academy in 1946 and reproduced in the *Illustrated London News* on 12 March 1949. The original drawing is in the Guildhall Library. A contemporary facsimile is in the Museum of London print room. Recently, the London Topographical Society has produced a facsimile with notes by Ralph Hyde.
2. In the Museum of London collection (acc. no. 57.7/1–10). Reproduced in the *Illustrated London News*, 10 November 1956, pp800–801.
3. See Meirion and Susie Harries, *The War Artists*, 1983, pp159–63. A brief but excellent summary of the work of the WAAC can also be found in Angela Summerfield, *The Artist at War, Second World War Paintings & Drawings from the Walker Art Gallery's Collection,* 1990.
4. Frances Carey, 'The Shelter Sketchbooks', in *British Museum Society Bulletin*, Autumn 1988. The article also mentions the other 'Shelter' artists.
5. See Summerfield, 1990, p4.
6. Grace Golden (1904–93) diaries for 1939–54, Grace Golden Archive, Museum of London.
7. Both Bone and Schwabe are represented in the Museum's collections.
8. *Eliot Hodgkin (1905–1987)*, exhibition catalogue, Hazlitt, Gooden & Fox, 1990.
9. For *Women at War*, many of the original drawings are in the Museum of London collection. Pearsall's text and most of the accompanying images were finally published in 1990.
10. Linda Morris and Robert Radford, *AIA The Story of the Artists International Association 1933–1953,* Museum of Modern Art, Oxford, 1987, p60.
11. William Sansom, James Gordon, Stephen Spender, *Jim Braidy, The Story of Britain's Firemen*, 1943; see introduction on Firemen Artists opposite title page.
12. *Exhibition of Paintings by Firemen Artists*, exhibition catalogue, Royal Academy, September 1941, foreword (copy seen in Art Department, Imperial War Museum).

Provenance:
Messrs Raphael Tuck & Sons Ltd; purchased from Robin Nordgreen in 1978.

Bibliography:
Firemen Artists, exhibition catalogue, Royal Academy, 1944; William Sansom, James Gordon and Stephen Spender, *Jim Braidy, The Story of Britain's Firemen*, 1943, p15.

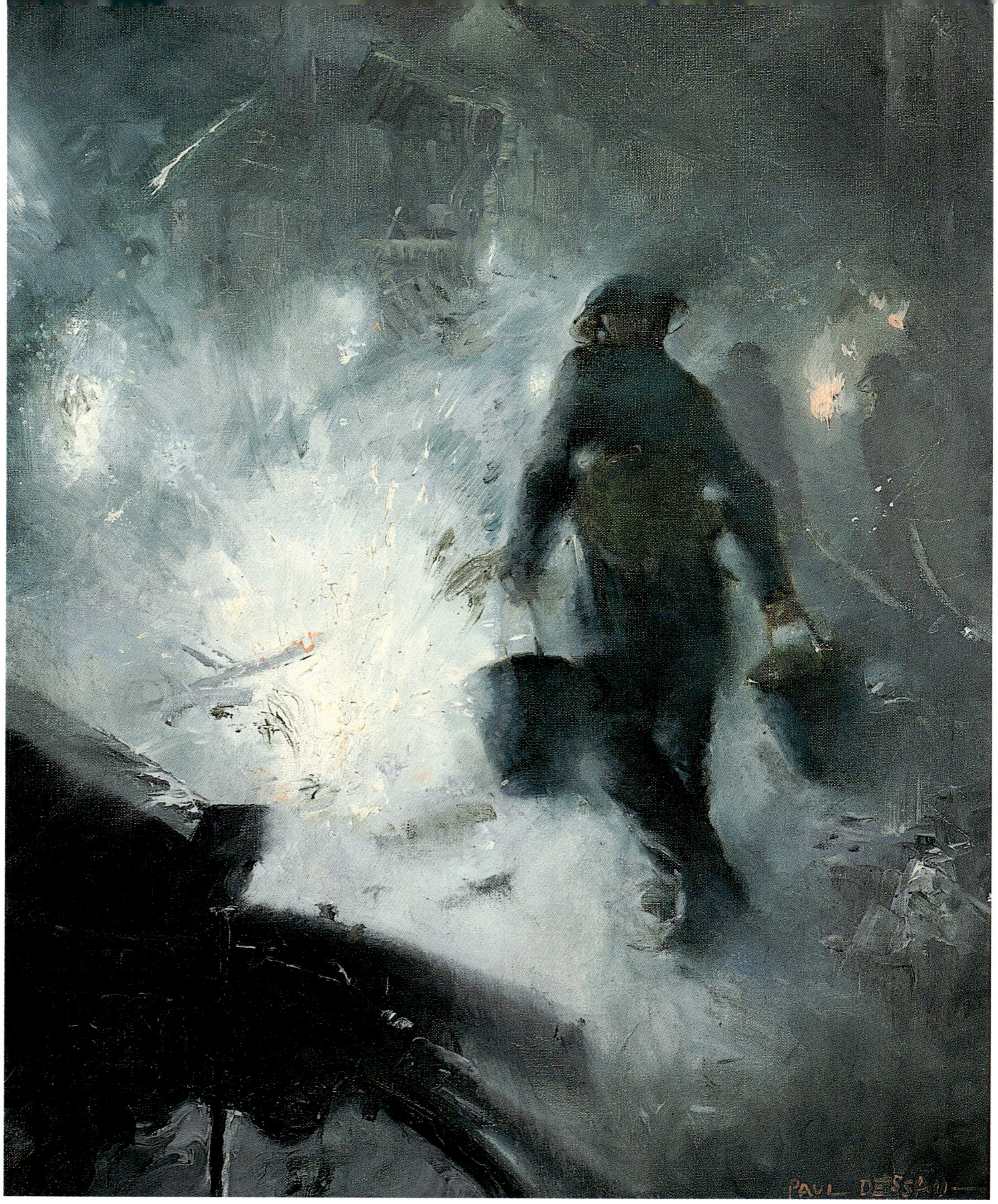

186.
PAUL LUCIEN DESSAU
(born 1909)
Incendiaries* [78.239]
*c.*1941
Oil on canvas, 61 x 50.7 cm
Signed bottom right: *Paul Dessau*

A FIREMAN carrying two buckets of sand is shown from the back trying to extinguish an incendiary fire (with its characteristically magnesium-blue flames).

Most of the war damage to the City was caused by incendiary bombs which fell between September 1940 and May 1941. The intense light and the smoke of the fire obliterate the details of the surroundings. The painting contrasts with Dessau's meticulously painted *And so to Bed*, purchased by the Imperial War Museum, which depicts with great realism and an obsession for detail the uniform worn by Second World War firemen.

187.
NETTIE MOON
(1909–81)

The Spirit of London during the Blitz*
[89.263]
1979
Oil on Rowney canvas board, 50.5 x 60.3 cm
Signed bottom right: *NETTIE MOON*
The name and address of the artist is on the back and the date it was painted. A label on the back reads *The Spirit of London Nettie Moon* (with price). Another title, partly erased, was found underneath: *Generation after Generation.*

AGAINST AN almost apocalyptic setting of rubble and ruined buildings on fire, an air-raid warden directs a woman with two children to the shelter and helps an old man, who is brandishing his cane in the air, to walk. The woman is carrying a baby and a bag packed with all the necessaries to spend the night in a shelter and is holding the hand of a child carrying a gas mask. In the right foreground is a half-demolished house with its door partly unhinged and a bin beside it. In the background the sky is criss-crossed with searchlights and dominated by the dome of St Paul's Cathedral, partly obscured by smoke and buildings.

The painting was entered and shown at the *Spirit of London* competition created and run by the Greater London Council and which in 1986 became the South Bank Picture Show.

Provenance:
Presented by Mrs Freda Elbourne in 1989.

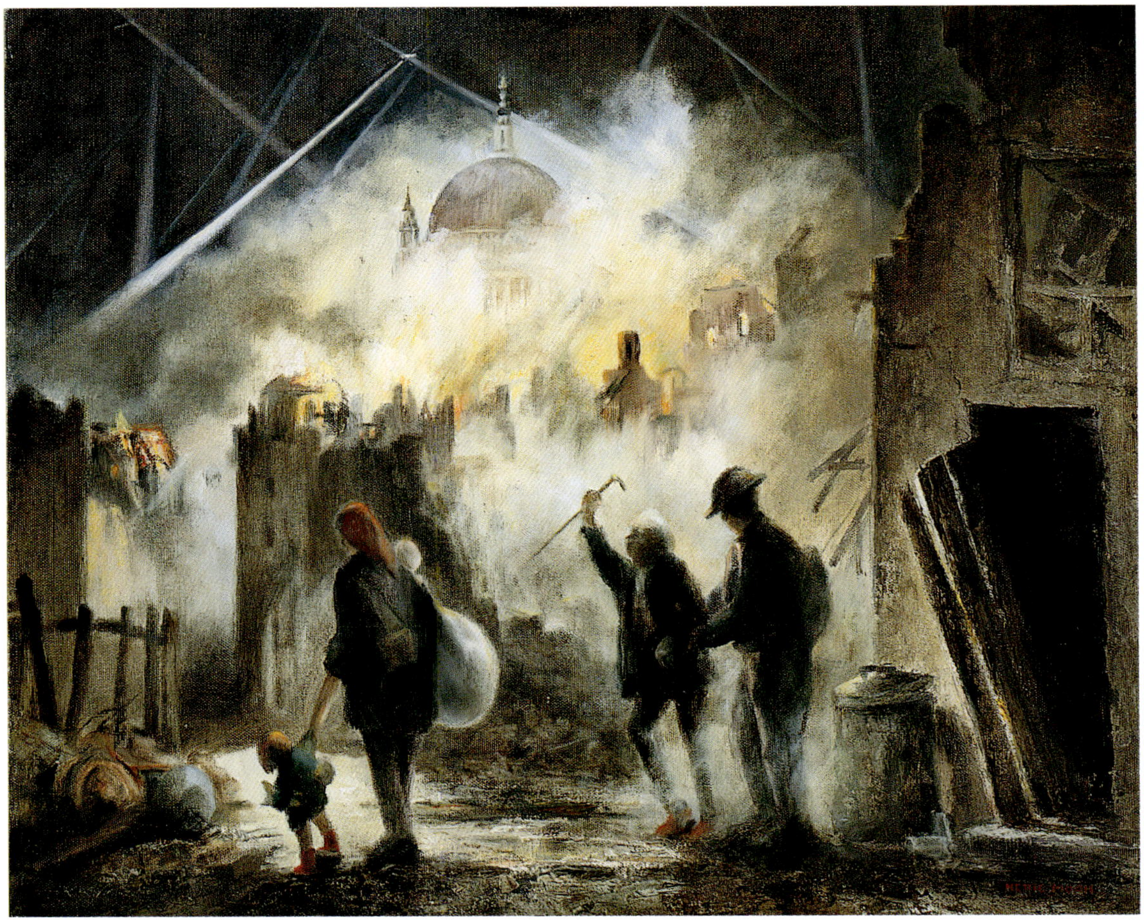

Provenance:
Commissioned by the War Artists' Advisory Committee; presented by HM Government, through the Imperial War Museum, in 1947.

Bibliography:
Hayes (cat. no. 93); J. L. Howgego, *The City of London through Artists' Eyes,* 1969, pp17 and 64; *John Piper,* exhibition catalogue, Tate Gallery, 1993, no. 47.

188.

JOHN PIPER

(1903–92)

Christ Church, Newgate Street, after its Destruction in 1940 [47.26/15]
1941
Oil on canvas, 75.6 x 63.1 cm
Signed bottom right: *John Piper*
Inscribed and dated on the back: *Christ Church, Newgate Street, Jan 1st 1941*

AN IMPRESSION of the east end of the church (built by Sir Christopher Wren 1677–87, on the site of the old Grey Friars church), as it looked from the nave the morning after it had been gutted by incendiary bombs from a Nazi air attack. The first full-scale night raid on London occurred on 29 December 1940, and much of the area north of St Paul's was laid waste in the space of a few short hours. A long succession of night raids then followed, which devastated a great part of the historic city and gutted the majority of Wren's churches.

In accordance with the provisions of the Pastoral Reorganisation Measure 1949, a number of the City parishes were amalgamated and Christ Church, Newgate Street, was merged with St Sepulchre-without-Newgate, where services are now held. Though the steeple, which had also been seriously damaged, was re-erected in 1960 (and the opportunity taken to replace the twelve urns which had been removed as unsafe in the nineteenth century), the church was not restored. The tower has now been refurbished as office space and the nave area tidied up and turned into a rose garden with benches for the public.

This work forms part of the group of paintings Piper produced in December 1940 and January 1941 of bomb-damaged churches in London. It was first exhibited in 'War Pictures at the National Gallery' in October 1941. There is a study for this painting in the British Council collection and a rough pencil drawing, presumably done on the spot, in the 1941 sketchbook in the collection of Brinsley Ford.

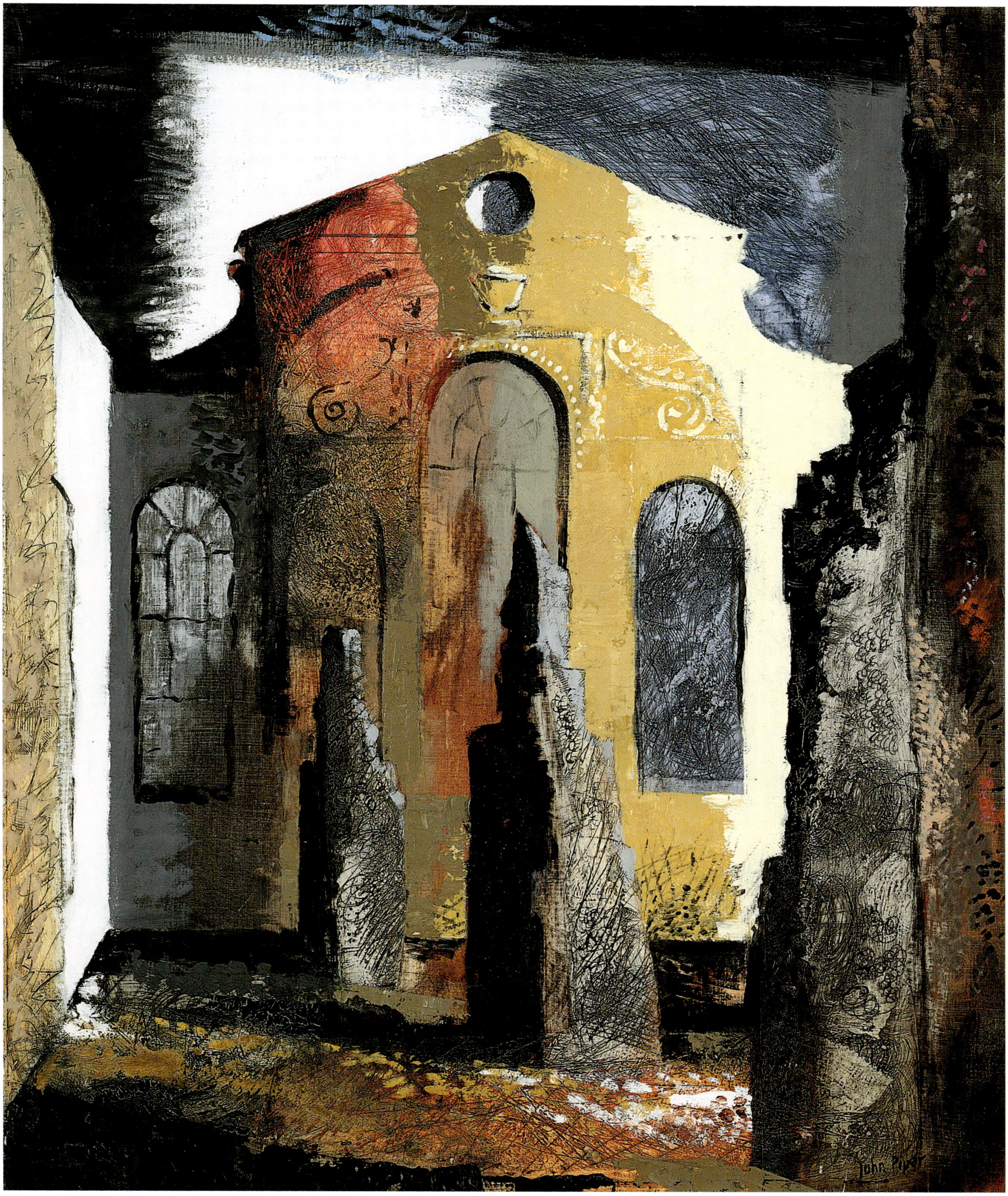

Provenance:
Presented by Mr V. Haines (the artist's brother) through the Imperial War Museum in 1980.

Bibliography:
Chris Ellmers and Alex Werner, *London's Lost Riverscape*, 1988, pp19–22.

189.

WILFRED STANLEY HAINES

(1905–44)

Night Raid over London Docklands

[81.105/2]

*c.*1941

Oil on canvas, 63.3 x 75.8 cm

Not signed or dated

THE VIEW is taken from the barge-building yards of Beard's and Carr's wharves in Rotherhithe on the south bank, with one of the granaries of East India Wharf on the right-hand side. It is looking north towards Wapping, depicting from left to right: Wapping entrance of the London Docks (designed by John Rennie); Wapping Old Stairs with the riverside tavern The Town of Ramsgate; Oliver's Wharf built in 1870 in neo-gothic Victorian style (and the first Docklands' warehouse to be converted into luxury apartments); Orient Wharf; St John's Upper Wharf (built in 1873), known as 'Jack's Hole'; and, finally, Morocco and Eagle Sufferance Wharf. The leaden steeple of St John's Church in Wapping is visible in the middle of the painting.

There are parachute flares in the sky used by the enemy for temporary illumination, four of which, on the left-hand side, are falling towards Wapping entrance. Searchlights are criss-crossing the sky.

This work is one of a pair in the Museum's collection. The other painting depicts an air raid with anti-aircraft shells exploding over Docklands oil tanks (in Appendix).

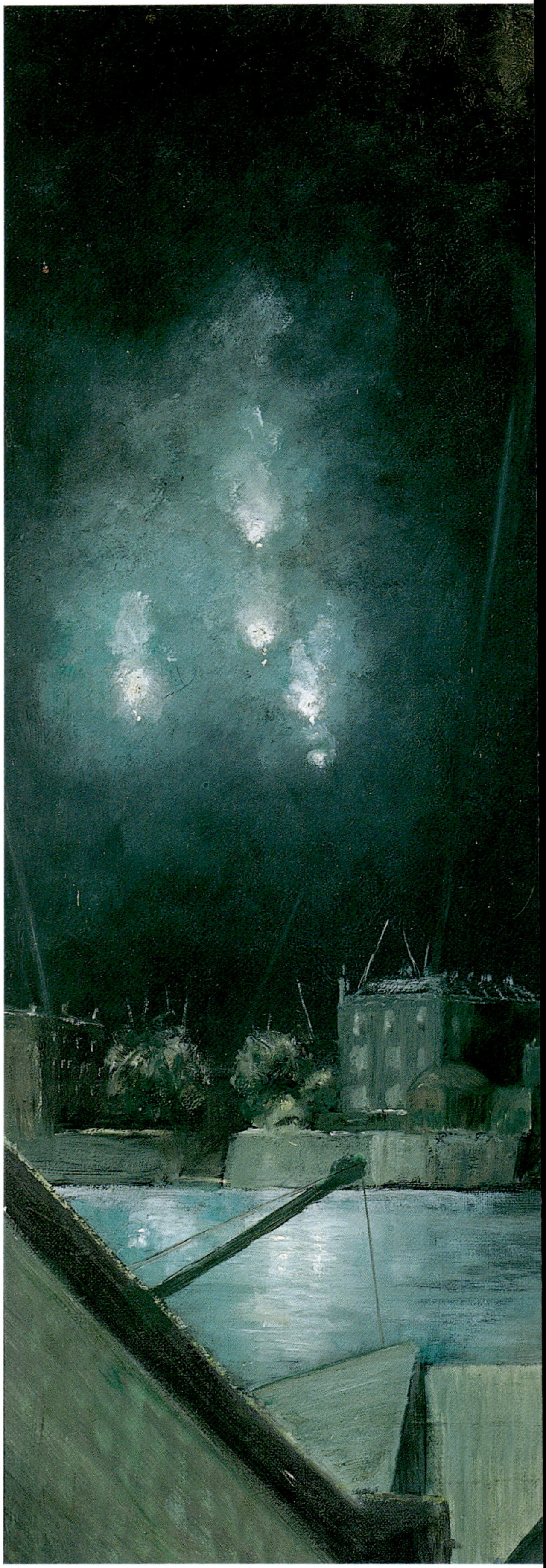

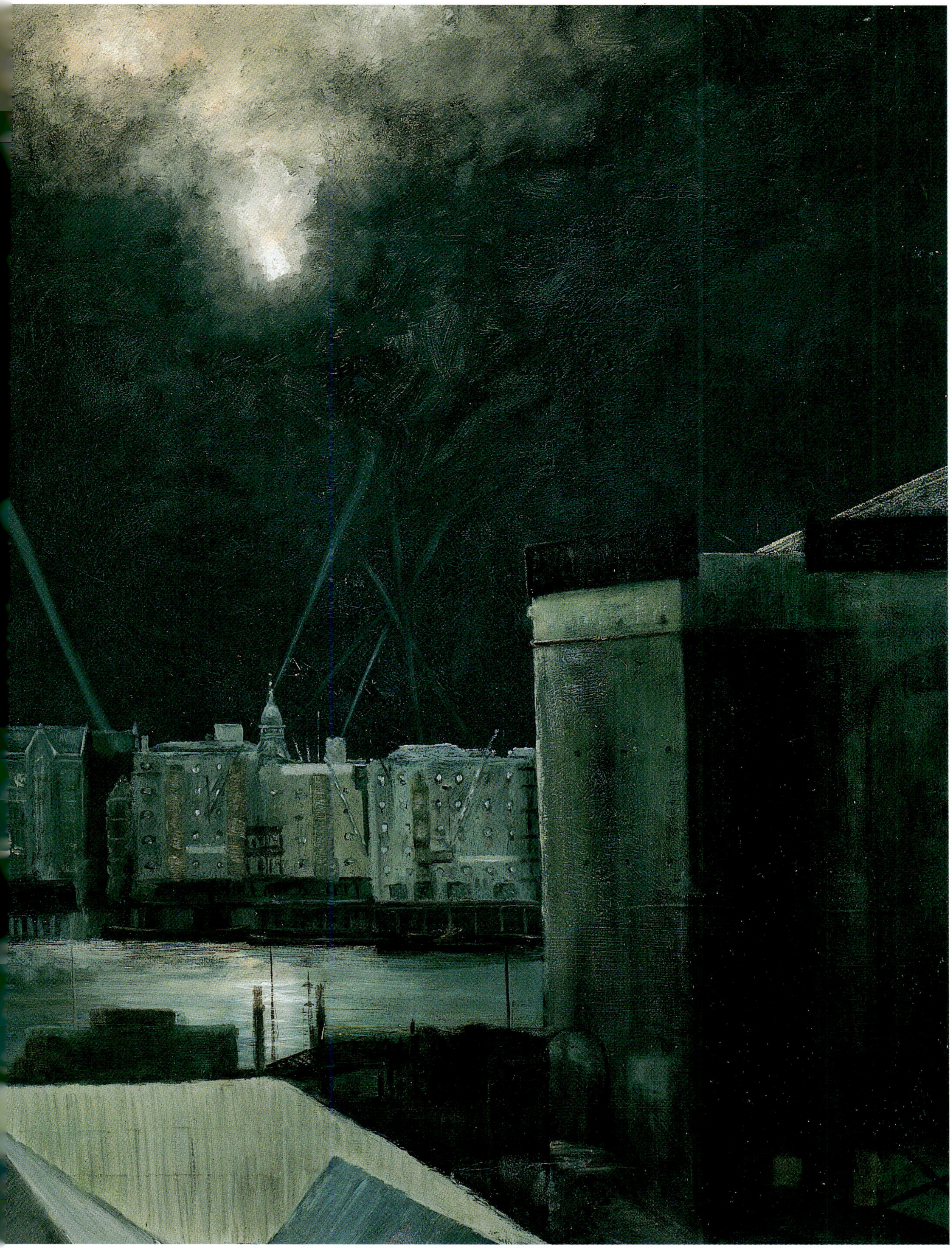

Provenance:
Presented by Nina de Yorke in 1974.

Exhibited:
Royal Academy, 1942 (307); Russell Cotes Gallery, Bournemouth, 1945.

190.

GLADYS A. PINKS
(1890–c.1980)

Deserted and Forlorn* [74.325/1]
1942
Oil on canvas, 90 x 60 cm
Signed and dated lower left:
GA PINKS 1942

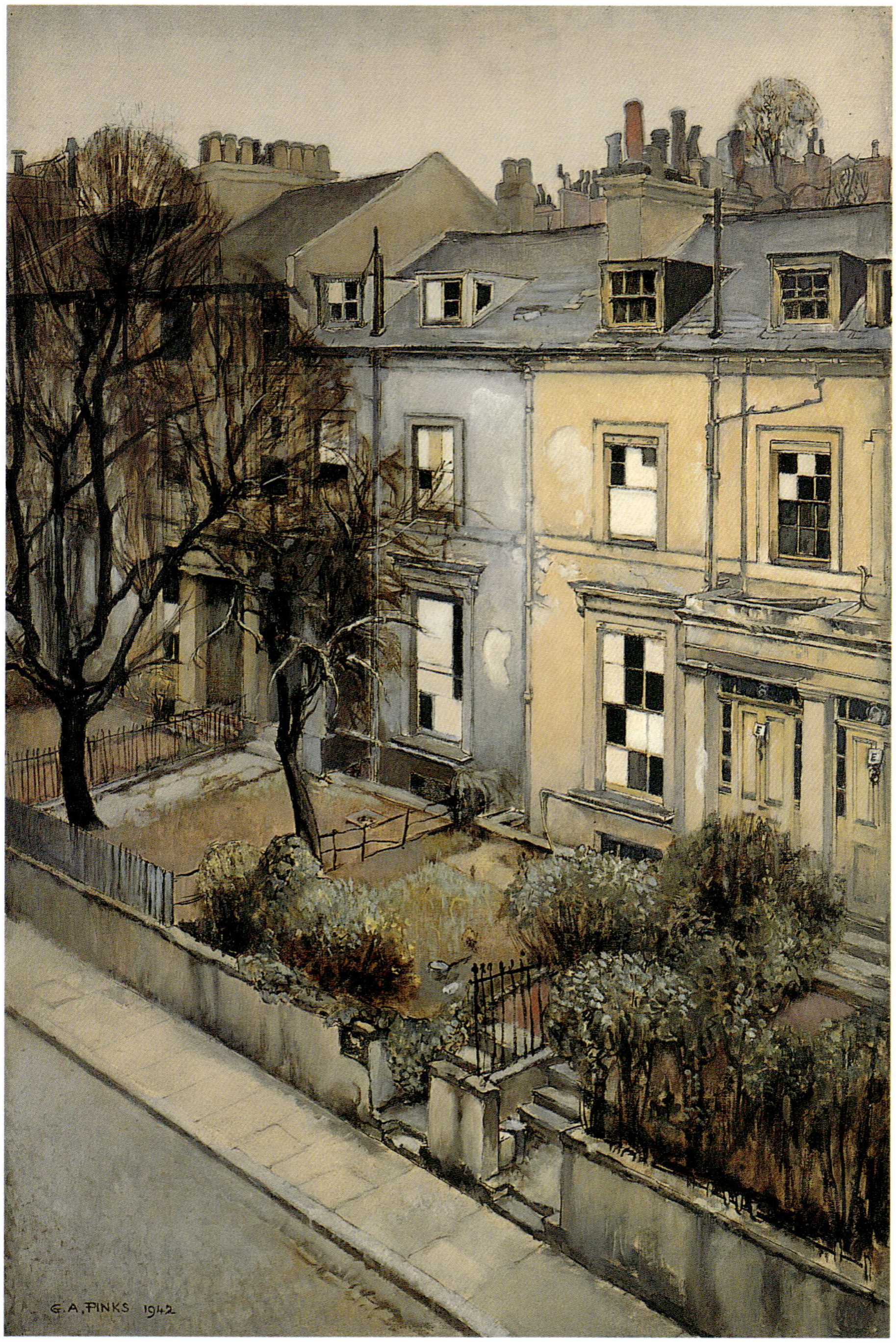

THE PAINTING shows four stuccoed terraced houses with small front gardens in Allen Street (at Phillimore Terrace), taken from the upper window of the artist's studio at 2 Wynnstay Gardens in Kensington. Several windows have been blasted out, the outside paint is flaking and two of the doors have 'E' labels stuck on their knockers for empty or evacuated (it has not been possible to ascertain the exact meaning). It is winter; the sky is grey, the gardens are bare and the trees leafless, thus reinforcing the desolate character of the scene.

Three bomb-damage incidents were recorded in 1940 for Allen Street, one of which, very close to the site depicted, took place on 7 October at the bottom of the Adam & Eve Mews. The only damage reported was to gas mains.

A preparatory drawing for this painting is also in the Museum's collection.

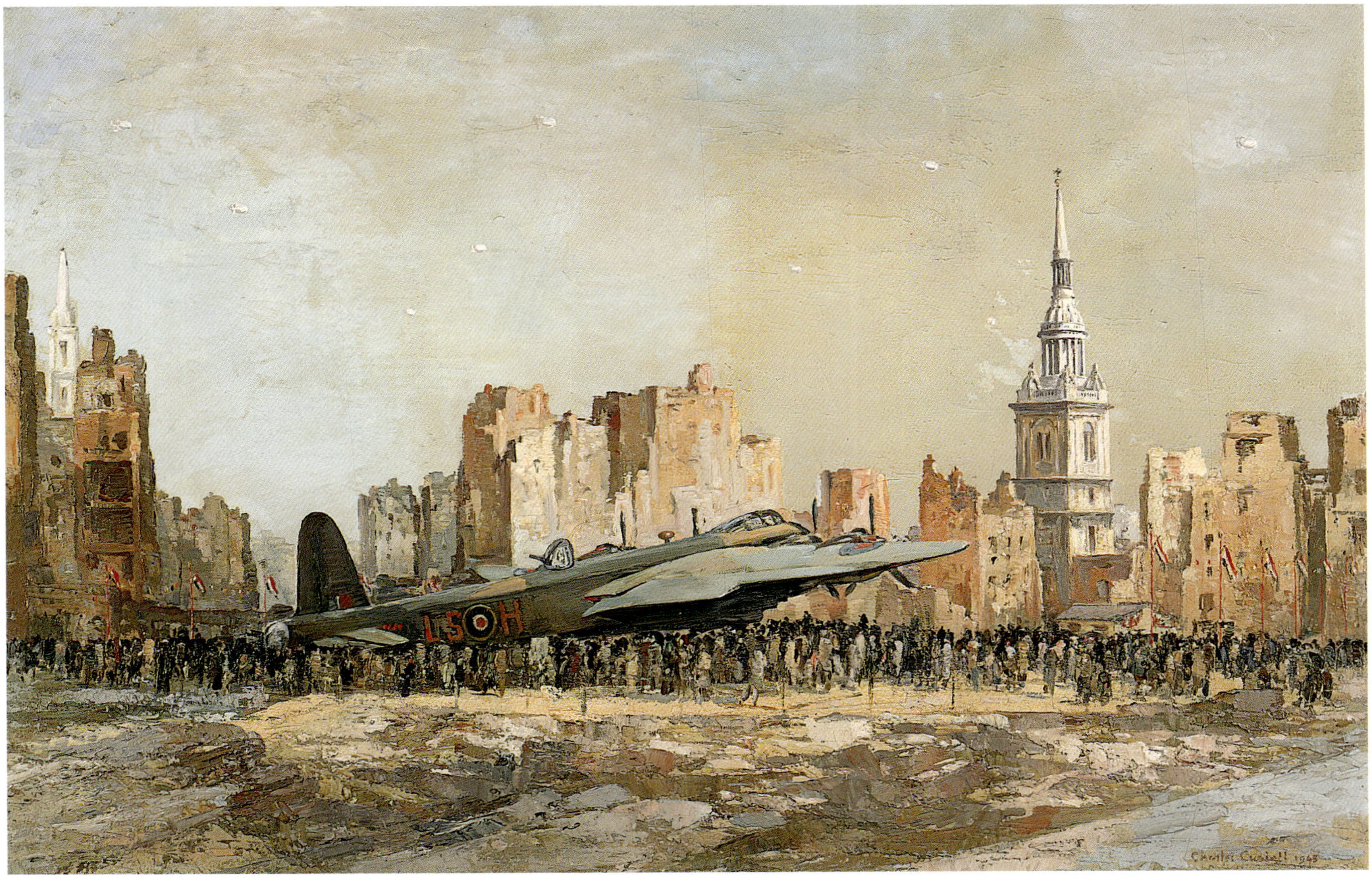

191.
CHARLES ERNEST CUNDALL
(1890–1971)

Bomber by Bow, 1943* [47.26/5]
1943
Oil on canvas, 60 x 94.7 cm
Signed and dated bottom right:
Charles Cundall 1943

THE SITE depicted is the area between the church of St Mary-le-Bow and St Paul's Cathedral, at the east end of which the painter has positioned himself. A Stirling bomber is shown in the foreground centre, surrounded by a crowd of spectators, with ruined buildings behind. The plane would have had to be wheeled there and was used as a focus for fundraising. This whole area, between Cheapside and Cannon Street, was completely devastated by aerial bombardment during the Second World War, mainly in the raids of 29 December 1940 and the nights following. Most of the City churches were gutted, though St Paul's, miraculously, survived almost totally unharmed. The shells of many of the churches remained (see cat. no. 188), and in the distance on the left can be seen the spire of St Vedast's, Foster Lane, and on the right the tower and spire of St Mary-le-Bow.

After the war this large empty space was turned into a grassed stadium which is featured in Cecil Brown's 1945 *Prospect* (see p431). The district is now occupied by the Bank of England extension north of Watling Street and Gateway House on the south side.

Provenance:
Commissioned by the War Artists' Advisory Committee; presented by HM Government, through the Imperial War Museum, in 1947.

Bibliography:
Hayes (cat. no. 32).

Exhibited:
Royal Academy, 1943 (12).

Provenance:
John Rodker (purchased from the artist); Mrs Marianne Rodker; Miss Joan Rodker; Sotheby's, April 1967 (205); Mrs Lilian Bomberg; Mrs Dinora Davies-Rees; Fischer Fine Art; purchased in 1985 with grants from the MGC/V&A purchase fund and the NHMF.

Bibliography:
David Bomberg, A tribute to Lilian Bomberg, exhibition catalogue, Fischer Fine Art, 1985, no. 76; Richard Cork, *David Bomberg*, 1987, pp253–6; Richard Cork, *David Bomberg*, exhibition catalogue, Tate Gallery, 1988, no. 159.

192.
DAVID BOMBERG
(1890–1957)

Evening in the City of London* [85.219]
1944
Oil on canvas, 69.8 x 90.8 cm
Signed and dated bottom right:
Bomberg 44

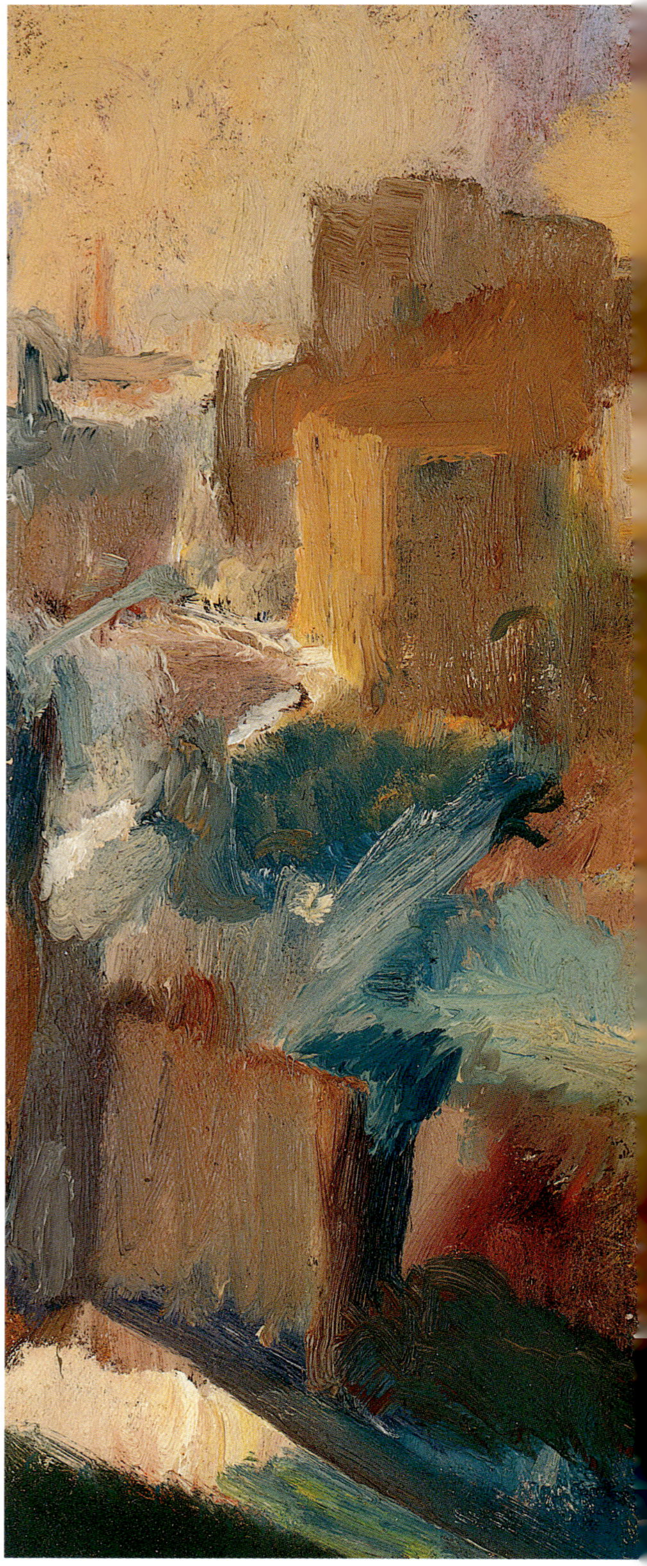

THIS VIEW, painted from the tower of St Mary-le-Bow, stretches from the river on the left to the area north of Cheapside and Newgate Street on the right, with the dome of St Paul's dominating the composition.

The artist's wife, Lilian, explained some of the genesis of this picture: 'He got permission to climb to the top of the church, in Cheapside, I think, and painted St Paul's from its east side. It was done in one go, but he did the drawing first.' This drawing, built in firm geometric units, has been acquired by the Visitors of the Ashmolean Museum in Oxford.

This is the only painting which Bomberg produced of bomb-damaged London. The artist desperately sought involvement in the War Artists' Advisory Committee, but twice his application was rejected. In February 1942 the committee finally invited him to paint the Burton-on-Trent bomb store, but their lack of response before the final works represented for Bomberg a series of humiliations.

This painting is not the result of a commission but is the artist's personal response to the devastated City. St Paul's resilience in spite of deliberate efforts to destroy it became for many a symbol of hope, and perhaps particularly so for Bomberg who had felt so unrecognised as an artist during the war years. Its towering silhouette dominates and shapes the cityscape, with Cheapside acting almost as a 'line of force' into the City, towards St Paul's.

The work on this painting inspired the artist with an even grander panoramic

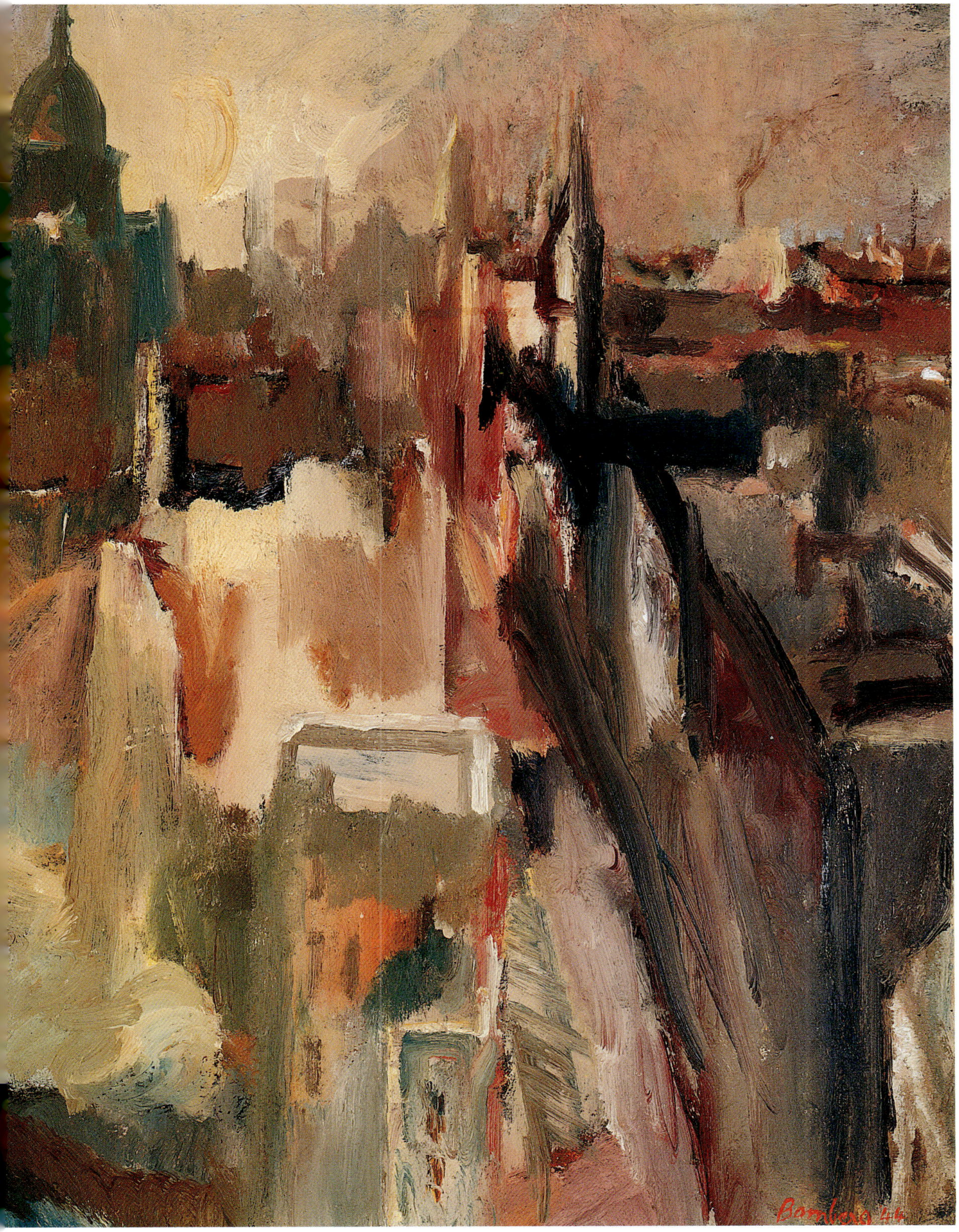

scheme: 'I am working on a series of drawings that will form, when co-ordinated, a panorama of London to be reproduced and published in London.' Although the project came to nothing, it should be mentioned as evidence of the extent to which *Evening in the City of London* fired the imagination of the artist.

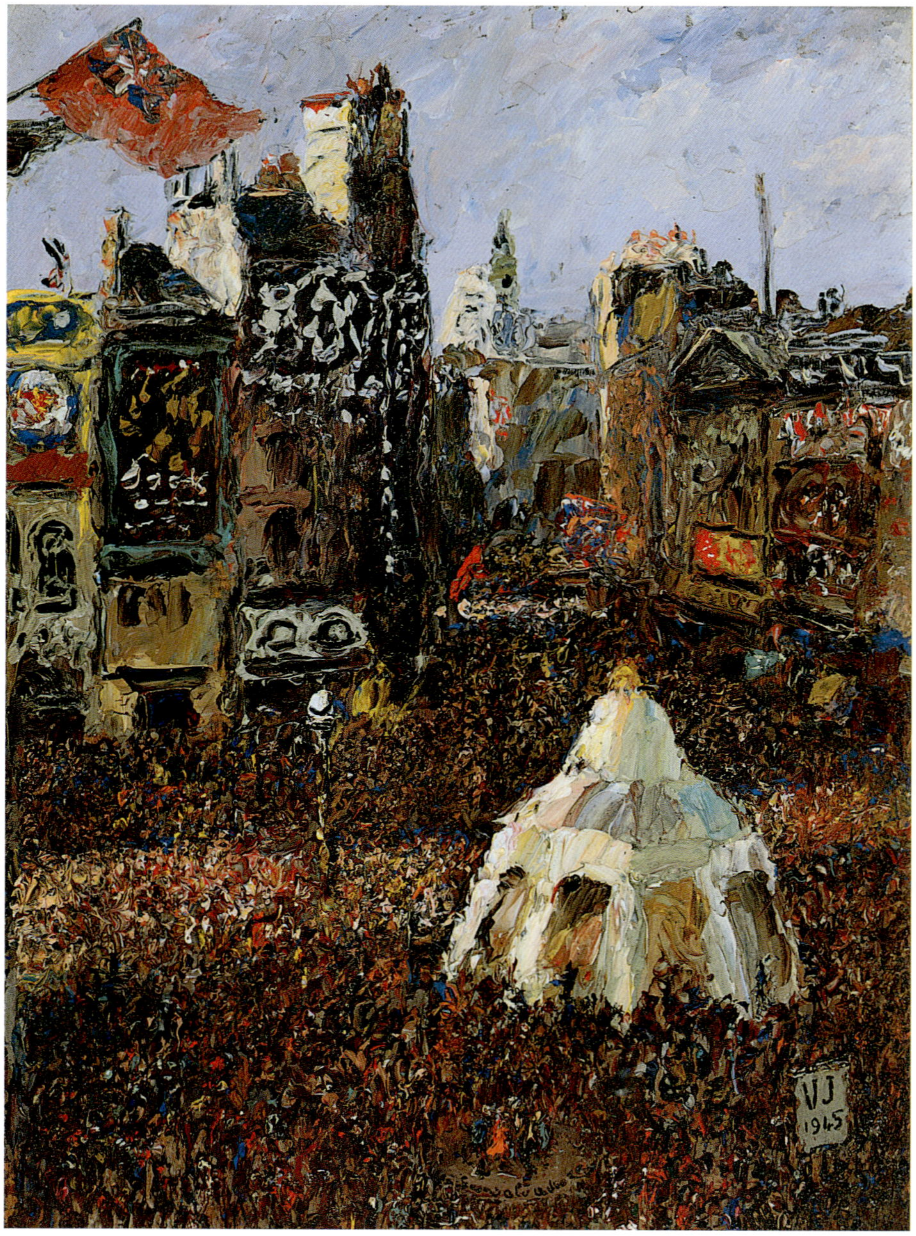

193.

PIERO SANSALVADORE

(1892–1955)

London: VJ Day in Piccadilly Circus*

[81.538]

1945

Oil on thin pine wood, 24.3 x 18.2 cm

Signed bottom centre in a semi-circle: *SANSALVADORE*

Inscribed bottom right: *VJ 1945*

Back: *Piero Sansalvadore London: VJ Day in Piccadilly Circus c97*

THE VIEW, taken from the flat of Hermione Gingold at the south-east corner of Piccadilly, looks down on the Circus. Beyond is Shaftesbury Avenue with the pedimented facade of the London Pavilion on the right. The steeple of the church of St Anne, Soho, is visible in the background. The streets and pavements are thronged with people who are celebrating the end of the Second World War. At the outbreak of the war, the statue of Eros was removed from Piccadilly Circus to Egham and its site boxed in the shape of a polygon as shown here.

Nicknamed in 1953 'The Master of the Little Landscape' by the *Studio,* this artist painted exclusively small works in palette knife on wood. This work, an 'urban' example, was painted on very thin Canadian pine.

Provenance:
Presented by G. M. Reeves in 1981.

Bibliography:
'Sansalvadore paints Le Cinque Terre', in the *Studio*, June 1953, pp202–3; colour reproduction of Sansalvadore's *Waterloo Bridge* in the *Studio*, July 1951.

194.

ROBERT BUHLER

(1916–1989)

Bomb Site in Chelsea [84.138]

*c.*1946

Oil on canvas, 58.5 x 76 cm

Signed bottom right: *Buhler*

THIS BIRD'S-EYE view of an area of Chelsea wasteland sprinkled with snow and hemmed in by three-storey terraced houses was taken from the artist's sixth-floor flat in Nell Gwynn House (built in the late 1930s and still standing) in Draycott Avenue looking towards Rawlings Street. The site depicted, which has since been built over to become Wiltshire Close, is enclosed by Denyer and Rosemoor streets. The terrace of houses in Rawlings Street is still standing.

According to local records, Nell Gwynn House was bomb-damaged on two separate occasions, on 10 September 1940 and on 8 March 1941, but there are no specific records for the adjoining streets. The painting may record the effects of one of these raids on its surroundings.

The artist returned to the idea of 'intersecting' the planes of terrace housing in 1969 in a work entitled *Houses, Pimlico* which makes use of an almost identical run of three-storeyed houses (no. 38 in the Austin/Desmond catalogue on Buhler). The words the painter Rodrigo Moynihan once said of Buhler seem particularly relevant in relation to both paintings: 'His particular strength is the simplification of his given subjects into broad areas of colour – beautifully harmonised. For him tone and colour create reality.'

Provenance:
The artist's studio; Gillian Jason Gallery; purchased by the Museum in 1984.

Bibliography:
Robert Buhler R.A. – Paintings 1937 to 1984, exhibition catalogue, Austin/Desmond Fine Art, 1984; *Painting the Visible World – Painters at the Euston Road School and at Camberwell School of Arts and Crafts 1930–1960*, exhibition catalogue, Austin/Desmond Fine Art, 1988.

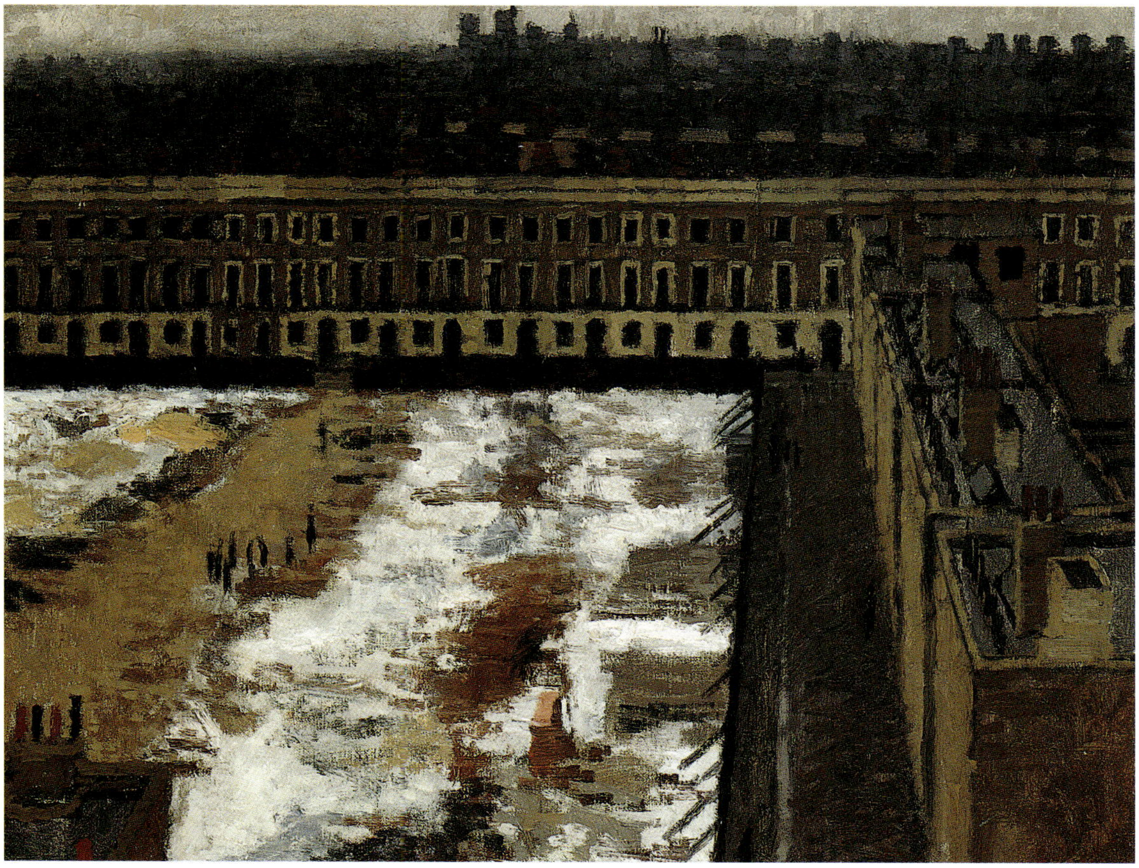

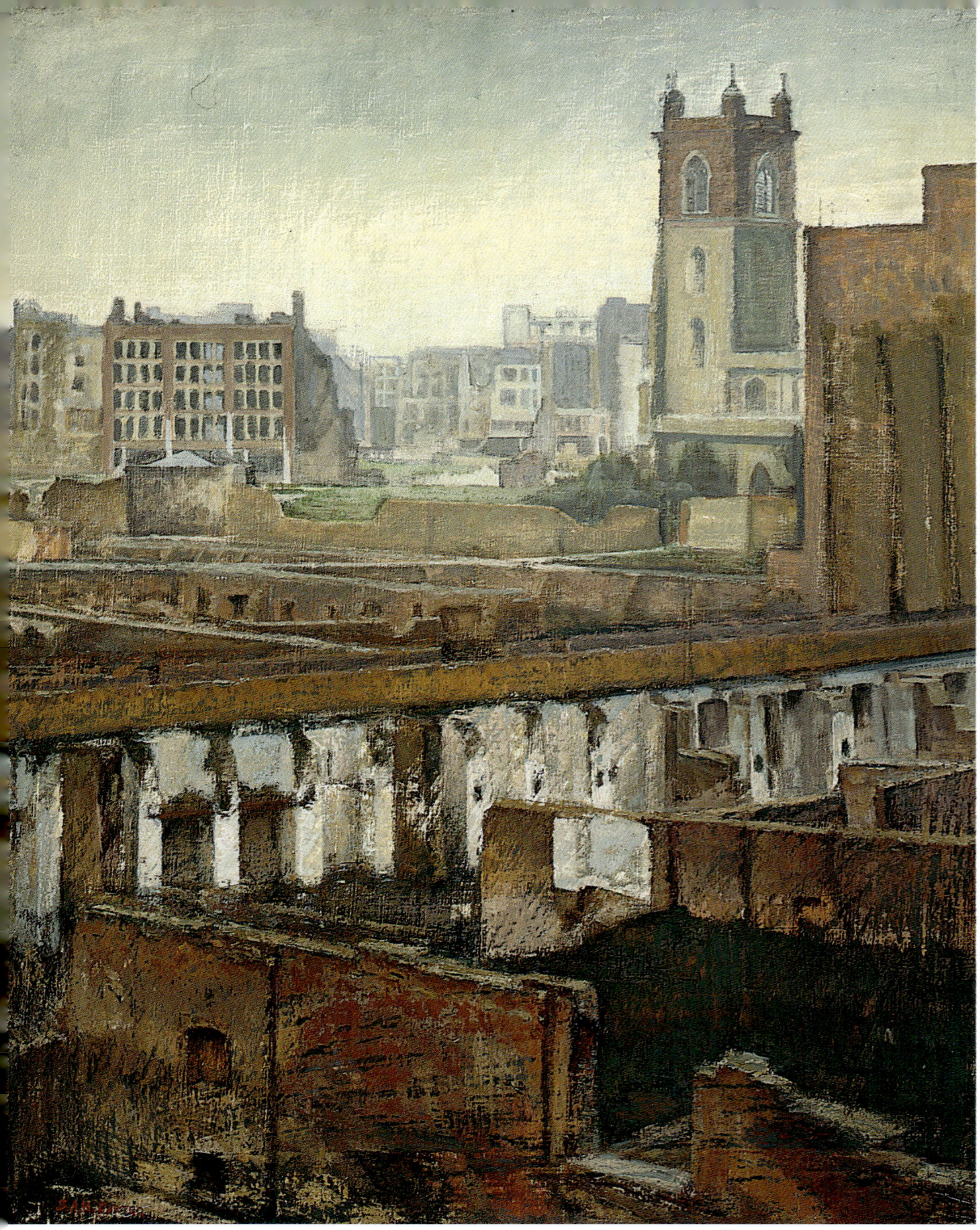

Provenance:
Purchased from the artist in 1974.

Bibliography:
Painting the Visible World – Painters at the Euston Road School and at Camberwell School of Arts and Crafts 1930–1960, exhibition catalogue, Austin/Desmond Fine Art, 1988, p32; Bruce Laughton, *The Euston Road School*, 1986, pp308–11.

195.
B. A. R. (SAM) CARTER
(born 1909)
St Giles Cripplegate [74.31]
1948
Oil on canvas, 76 x 63.5 cm
Signed bottom left: *B. A. R. CARTER*

THIS VIEW of the bombed area around the church of St Giles Cripplegate in the City was taken from Progress House (in London Wall, now demolished), looking north-west. The artist has focused on one of the two most devastated areas in the City (the other was south-west of Cheapside, see cat. no. 191). Cecil Brown recorded with great precision the extent of bomb damage in the City in 1945 (see p431) and we are thus able to ascertain that Carter's painting has been drawn with great accuracy. The criss-crossing of walls from destroyed buildings contrasts with the remaining standing buildings organised in a fringe around the devastated area. The site was recorded by Harold Hussey after it was cleared and before rebuilding began (see cat. no. 210).

This work is one of a number the artist produced of bomb-damaged City churches, including views of St Mary's, Aldermanbury, St Alban's, Wood Street and Bow Church. He painted the site of St Giles Cripplegate four times from the same viewpoint and this painting is the first version. Carter was one of many painters who chose to depict the City wasteland. Both William Townsend and William Coldstream (who, like Carter, were members of the Euston Road School of painting) also addressed this subject. William Coldstream's *St Giles Cripplegate* (Arts Council Collection) should be specially mentioned here: it was started in 1946 and may have influenced the work under review. Although the Ironmongers' Hall viewpoint was at the opposite end to Carter's, and the church purposely placed in the centre of the composition, both Coldstream and Carter set out to exploit the geometrical pattern of the criss-crossing of ruined walls.

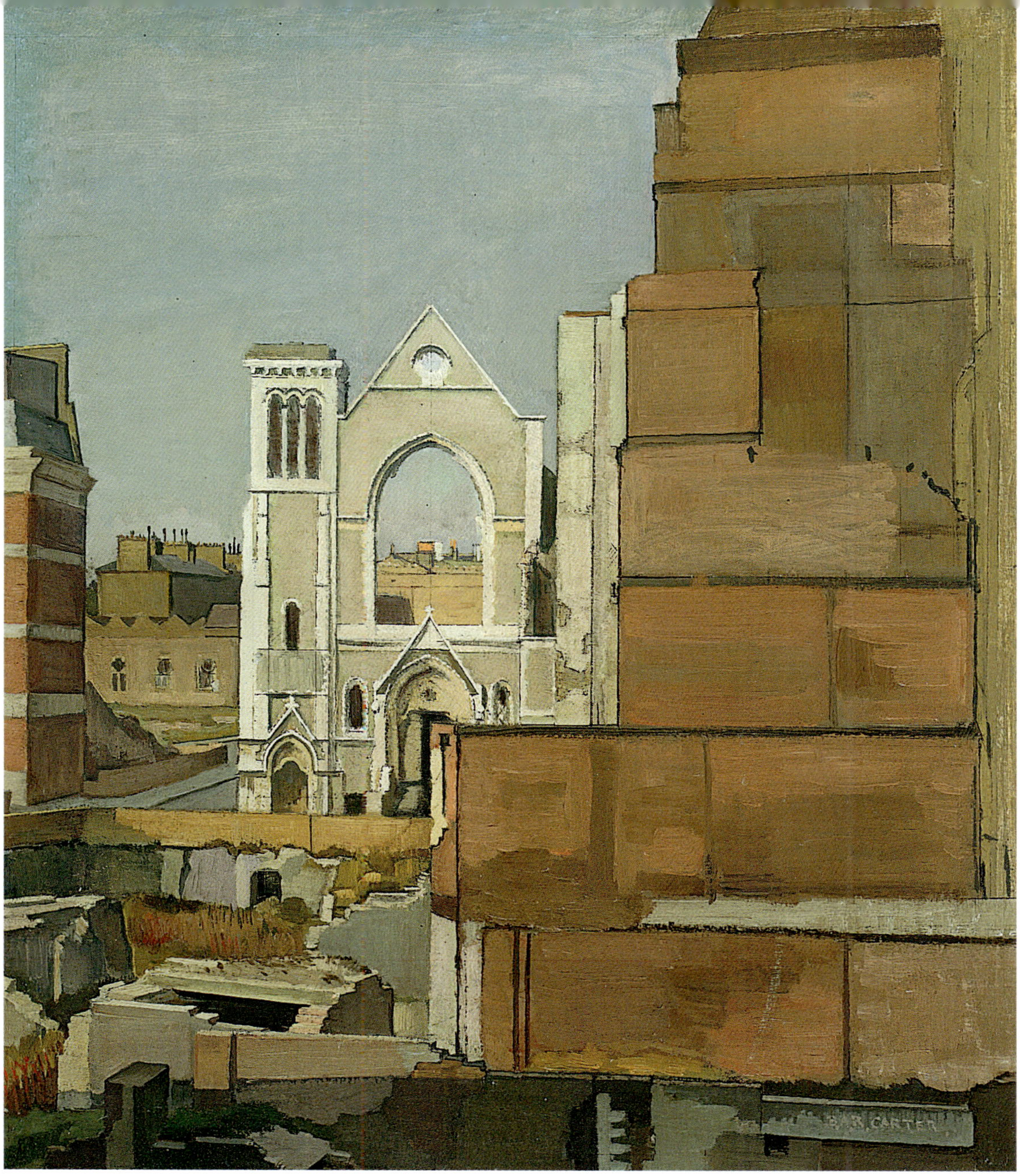

196.

B. A. R. (SAM) CARTER
(born 1909)

The New Jewin Welsh Chapel [94.213]
1948–50
Oil on canvas, 51 x 46 cm
Signed bottom right: *B. A. R. CARTER*

THIS POST-WAR view of the Jewin Welsh Chapel in Fann Street in the City is taken from the middle of a block of buildings situated west of Viscount Street. The composition, based on a pentagon, not only highlights the destruction caused by the war but also strangely evokes Mediterranean shores through the Italianate architecture of the chapel and the limpid blue sky against which it is delineated. It recalls the artist's passion for Piero della Francesca and his academic research into the complex use of perspective in Piero's paintings.

The chapel was demolished and rebuilt shortly afterwards, still adorning the same stretch in Fann Street. Sadly, its 1960s plain 'box architecture' and the proximity of the Golden Lane Estate have eradicated all trace of southern influence.

This work is another example of Sam Carter's painting activities in the City during and after the war (see also cat. no. 195).

Provenance:
Purchased in 1950 by the Contemporary Art Society from the artist (for £85, it was selected by Lord Methuen when shown in a London Group exhibition); gift to the Museum in 1994.

Bibliography:
See cat. no. 195.

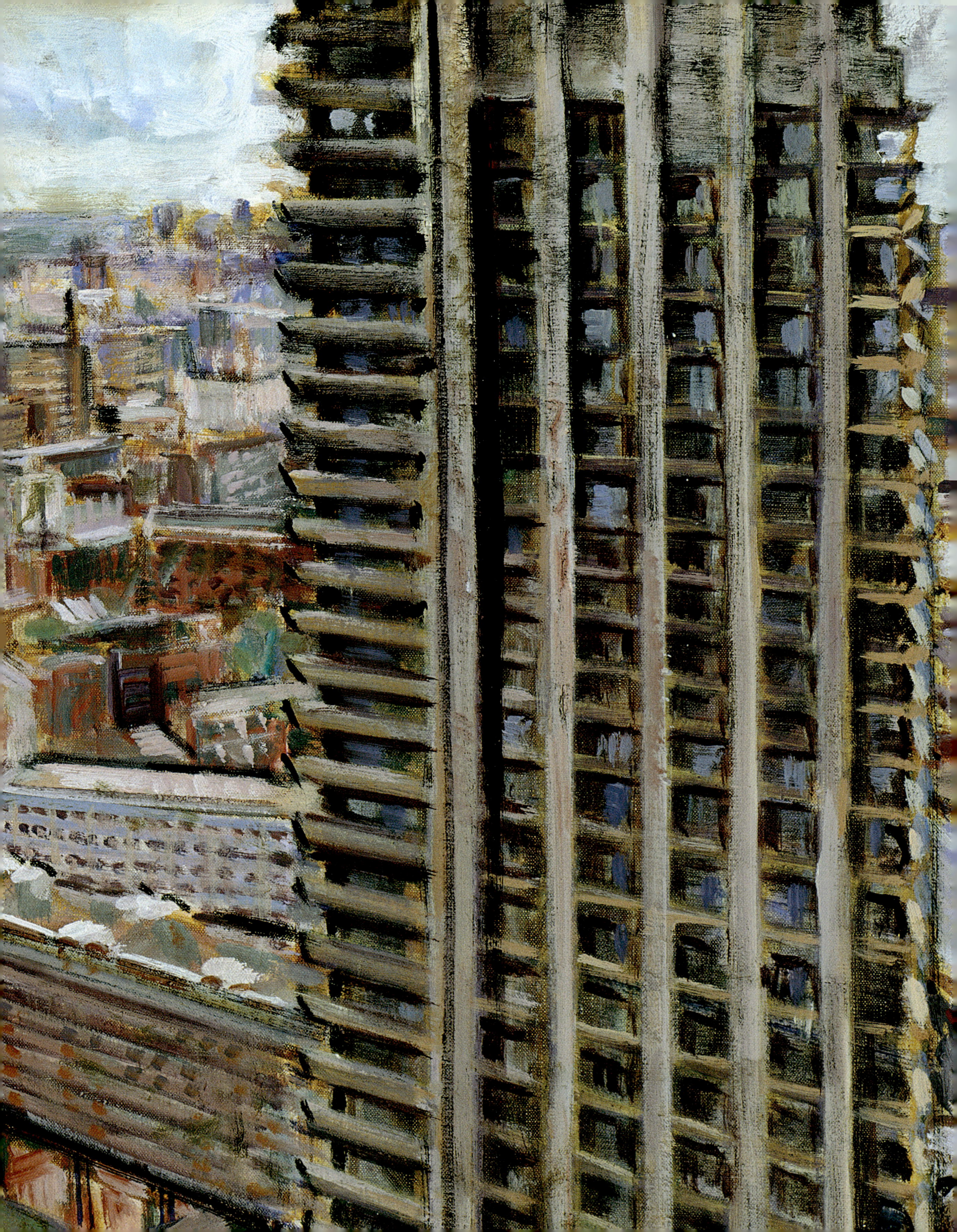

Modern London

FOR MANY painters the reconstruction of London was visually as exciting as its destruction and the idea of capturing the image of a city in transition was very appealing. The cultural euphoria of the 1960s had the ultimate result of turning London into an arts mecca. The astonishing concentration of artists in the capital considerably enriched the urban art scene and the range of subjects and styles is remarkable. The urban poor, a tradition since Hogarth's 'Gin Lane', continue to attract attention in paintings that tackle both human issues and questions of architecture. The juxtaposition of old and new, at Canary Wharf and elsewhere, is also a source of inspiration, sometimes translated as the weight of the old and the excitement of the new.

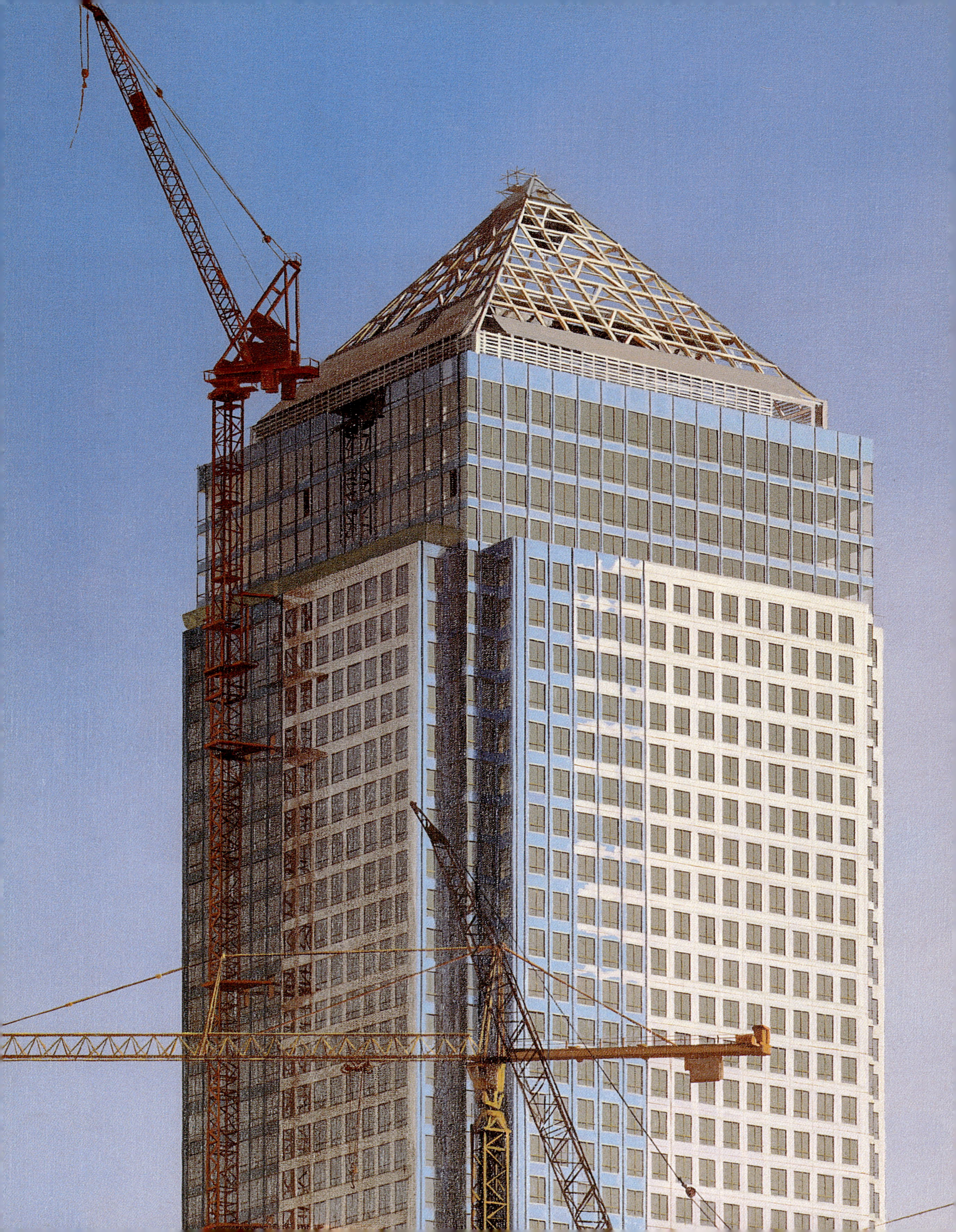

MODERN LONDON

THE SECOND World War caused extensive damage to London's built fabric, but from the rubble a new character emerged. David Tindle was one of many London artists devoted to the painting of the capital who lived through this sometimes painful process of rebirth. He found it so distressing that he eventually moved out of London. He wrote:

> By the end of the 1950s and well into the 1960s I became more interested in the look of open spaces, buildings being pulled down all over the place, dusty shop windows and only fragments left in the empty shops, the reflections of traffic in shop windows all like a fading dream. As the dust settled and the disarray of new buildings appeared, I could no longer find my London by the end of the '60s.[1]

However, the chaos described by Tindle seemed to inspire other artists. The realist movement, which first appeared in 1952,[2] was spearheaded by the Marxist artist and critic John Berger. The series of exhibitions 'Looking Ahead', which he curated in 1952, 1953 and 1956 for the Whitechapel Art Gallery, bracketed such painters as Rodrigo Moynihan, Claude Rogers, the 'Kitchen Sink Painters', Ruskin Spear and Carel Weight, all of whom produced a considerable number of what might be termed London works. In the 1950s Helen Lessore also promoted figurative art at her Beaux Arts Gallery by staging shows of the Kitchen Sink Painters as well as Frank Auerbach and Leon Kossoff, who both painted the capital exclusively. For a figurative painter the city was an inevitable subject. Bryan Ingham's 1960 *Landscape at Peckham* (with the dealer Julian Hartnoll) is a lucid, rather than nostalgic, tribute to the London that was disappearing. Painted in a hyper-realist style, *Landscape at Peckham* shows a row of abandoned houses caught in an area of wasteland between the Lord Lyndhurst pub and Ma's Dining Room, an old-style working café. Ingham's painting is, in retrospect, particularly brave because it was executed at a time when abstraction had established its dominance in Europe and America. The no longer fashionable figurative art was driven underground, superseded by the expression of personal emotions which were not concerned with 'representing' the world.

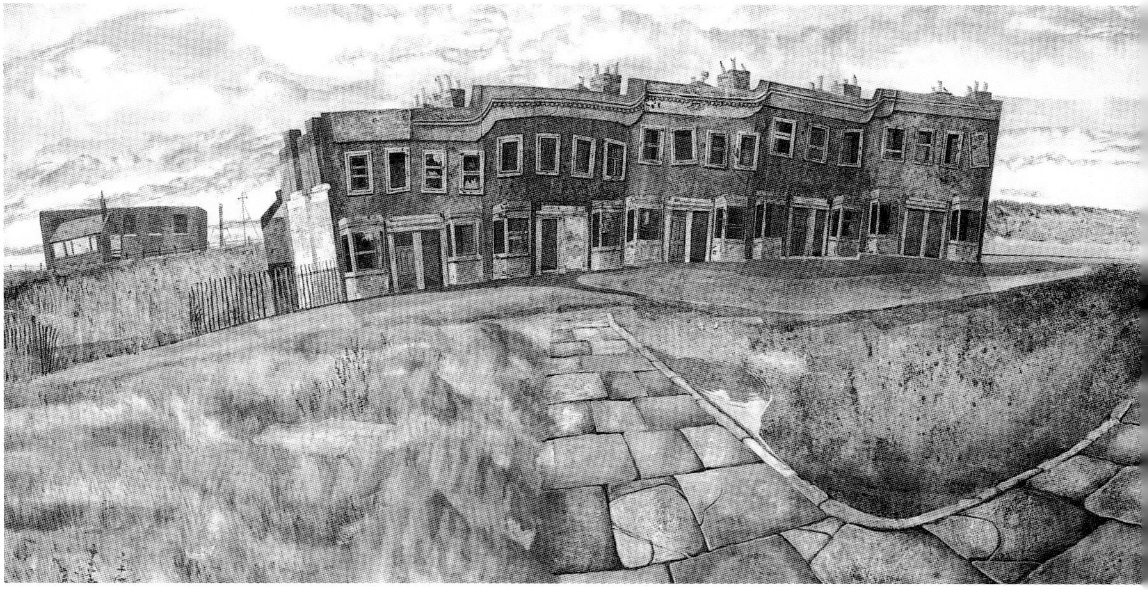

Bryan Ingham (b. 1936)
Landscape at Peckham, late 1950s
Oil on canvas
With Julian Hartnoll, London.

Overshadowed by the Cold War, the realist movement had lost much of its appeal by 1956, when it had become clear it could be linked to left-wing ideology. Abstract painting developed in London with the 1951 creation of the New Vision Group by Denis Bowen, who taught at Hammersmith School of Art. Their first exhibition was held that year, at the Stockpot, a coffee house in Notting Hill Gate, and in 1956 the New Vision Centre Gallery

(NVCG) opened in Marble Arch.[3] For the next ten years it was a point of focus for young abstract artists in this country and abroad.

Both Bryan Ingham and Oliver Bevan, who trained at the Royal College of Art in the early 1960s, became abstract artists, along with many of their contemporaries. The advent of Pop Art in the sixties[4] was not a serious challenge to the appeal of abstraction despite the fact that at one point, as Bryan Ingham explains, one could find three students at the Royal College of Art tackling 'Colgate toothpaste' paintings simultaneously.[5] Even Stephen Willats, who received no formal training, initially embraced abstraction when, drawn to housing issues, he made use of the emergence of high-rise housing (particularly in the Notting Hill area, where he was based in the 1960s) by producing a memorable series of paintings in which geometrical abstract shapes translated visually the units of the housing block.[6]

To the 1960s artist attracted by new modes of expression, conceptual art was a parallel alternative to abstraction. Oliver Bevan, now firmly working in the figurative tradition (see cat. nos 215, 219 and 225), described how in the 1960s he oscillated between conceptual and abstract forms, neither of which had any apparent connection with his vocation as a painter. Stephen Willats, too, turned his back on painting (never to return) and began a series of pieces which distilled in words and photographic images the lives of ordinary, struggling Londoners. His main manifesto, *The New Reality*,[7] describes the world of cities as shaped and controlled by a professional minority and passively experienced by a silent majority. Those unable to adjust to the 'new reality' float at the edges of society and develop their own (sub)cultures, moving into the city's 'no man's lands'.[8] Willats's art is concerned with giving voice and meaning to all those whose lives would normally go unrecorded – the council tenant, the drop-out. The artist charts their thoughts and aspirations in simple, direct interviews and works with his 'subjects' to express the 'new reality' as experienced, or rather endured, by them. His work constitutes a unique document of ordinary London lives.

The image of 'no man's land', so haunting during and immediately after the war, has continued to reappear. In the early 1970s, long before Willats's *Lurky Place* project (see note 8), Lucian Freud was producing his remarkable group of London paintings, thus returning to the theme of city dereliction. For example, *Waste Ground, Paddington* was the subject of three paintings.[9]

Arguably, London has always been central to artists and the world of art. This partly explains why twice since 1945 the term School of London has been coined by artists. First it was Patrick Heron, immediately after the war, who thus described a group of artists who were largely identifiable with the St Ives Group; they now have pride of place in the board rooms and offices of the great 'New Patrons'.[10] The School of London was defined a second time in 1976 by the painter Kitaj in the catalogue of the 'Human Clay' exhibition at the Hayward Gallery. This second School of London was subsequently refined to refer to the painters Francis Bacon, Lucian Freud, Frank Auerbach, Leon Kossoff, Michael Andrews and Kitaj himself.[11] This important group, unlike its predecessor, includes many London works and it is unfortunate that its participants are not at present represented in the collection, except for a series of charcoal drawings by Kossoff.

The 1951 Festival of Britain, held on the South Bank, gave impetus to British culture, but in the arts it drew attention only to the work and vision of already established British artists, such as Henry Moore and John Piper. Kenneth Clark in the official souvenir programme writes, with an apologetic sigh, 'how hard it is to persuade the intelligent foreigner to take an interest in modern English Art'. The number and exuberance of murals may have made some impression on a public who did not normally concern themselves with such matters, but did little to stir the artistic community. The Arts Council initiated the only major painting initiative in the form of 'sixty painters competing for the Arts Council's prize'.

David Mellor pointed out that 'the foundations for the visual mythology of "Swinging London" were laid early on and it was the artists and photographers who first formulated its particular brand of metropolitan romance and modernity'.[12] Although the 1960s did not further the *painted* image of London very much, they did at least put London on the cultural world map. (We are still reaping the benefits of this early wave of enthusiasm: at the time of writing London has arguably become an arts mecca, a model for artists in other European cities with an astonishing concentration of artists and facilities).[13]

The next major opportunity to present itself for assessing the worth, appeal or productivity of London's modern painters was the exhibition 'A New Spirit in Painting' held in 1981 at the Royal Academy. It featured Frank Auerbach as the only artist inspired by a London subject. The selection of a large number of abstract works along with the organisers' wish to find 'common threads which cross national boundaries'[14] somehow missed the emergence of a new force in contemporary art: the city.

In the last twenty years, a new generation of painters has turned to the city for direct inspiration to explore the meaning of our society. The artists are not necessarily aware of one another, but share a common subject matter: London. They could be called the 'Capital Painters', since they boldly tackle many of the issues central to urban living. Their works fall into several general categories.

First there are those artists who have tried to embrace the whole of the city in dazzling panoramic pieces. These, for Timothy Hyman,[15] hark back to Lorenzetti's famous frescos of good and bad government in Siena. Closer to home the trend was 're-invented' by the painter Oskar Kokoshka, whose early heroic panoramic views of the Thames in London were painted in 1926, when he was in London for a year. Another group of these views, very close in spirit to his early explorations of the theme, was painted between the mid-1950s and the early 1960s. Like him, but using different methods, Sharon Beavan (cat. no. 220) and Anthony Lowe[16] naturally adopt the bird's-eye viewpoint to encompass as much of the city as they possibly can.

The theme of council housing has attracted much attention from artists and has been explored in imaginative ways. To Stephen Willats's abstract and conceptual pieces, mentioned above, should be added Keith Coventry's paintings evolved from the plan layouts of housing estates (Karsten Schubert Gallery). David Hepher (cat. no. 214), Julian Perry (cat. no. 221), Gerry Keon and Danny Markey[17] produced further paintings inspired by this theme, ranging from the intimate to the monumental.

Oliver Bevan (cat. no. 225) and Kate Wilson[18] have tackled the theme of transport, so central to late twentieth-century London life, and yet somewhat neglected.

Jock McFadyen[19] and Mandy McCartin[20] have both eloquently addressed the subject of down-and-outs, which may be viewed as a key theme for late twentieth-century urban life.

The decaying fabric of the city had been a traditional subject since the war, but Lucian Freud and Anthony Eyton[21] gave it a new dimension by moving away from war damage to chronic dereliction.

Anthony Green is an exception in his pursuit of 'paradise' in a London home. Although his meticulous paintings are obsessively personal, they also document with great optimism domestic life in the capital in comfortable detached housing.

The following (incomplete, but growing) selection gives a flavour of the range of painting since the Second World War and bears witness to the extraordinary renaissance of serious and committed London-inspired art.

1. In a letter addressed to the Museum and dated 21 April 1992.
2. Margaret Garlake, *New Vision 56–66*, Warwick Arts Trust, 1986.
3. Ibid.
4. *Pop Art*, Royal Academy, 1992.
5. In a letter to the Museum.
6. All in private collections. The artist has photographs of them.
7. Orchard Gallery, Londonderry, 1982.
8. *The Lurky Place*, exhibition catalogue, Lisson Gallery, 1978.
9. Reproduced in Lawrence Gowing's *Lucian Freud,* nos 133, 136 and 137.
10. Garlake, 1986, p12; *The New Patrons*, exhibition catalogue by the NACF at Christie's, 1992.
11. Alastair Hicks, *The School of London,* 1989.
12. David Mellor, *The Sixties Art Scene in London*, 1993, p43.
13. A conference entitled 'London – Arts Mecca', organised by the Museum of London, Leicester Urban History Centre and The Whitechapel Art Gallery, was held at the Museum on 21 September 1996. The papers for this conference will be published in 1997.
14. *A New Spirit in Painting*, exhibition catalogue, Royal Academy, 1981, p12.
15. *Timothy Hyman, Recent Work*, exhibition catalogue, Austin/Desmond Fine Art, 1990.
16. Antony Lowe in *A Several World*, exhibition leaflet, Cleveland Gallery, 1991. Joint exhibition with Julian Perry which featured cityscapes other than London. Lowe has also produced panoramic views of both the City and Westminster.
17. Francis Kyle Gallery for G. Keon and Redfern Gallery, London, for D. Markey.
18. Exhibition at the Keppler Gallery, Brixton, 1992.
19. See William Jackson Gallery catalogues.
20. *Witnesses and Dreamers,* exhibition catalogue, various venues (including the Museum of London), 1993–4, From the Street, paintings & drawings by *Mandy McCartin*, with an introduction by *Cherry Smyth*, 1996.
21. *Anthony Eyton*, retrospective exhibition, South London Art Gallery, 1980.

197.

KATHLEEN ALLEN

(1906–83)

Roof Garden from High Holborn*

[84.142/1]

1944

Oil on canvas, 25.2 x 17.5 cm

Signed and dated bottom right: *Allen 44*

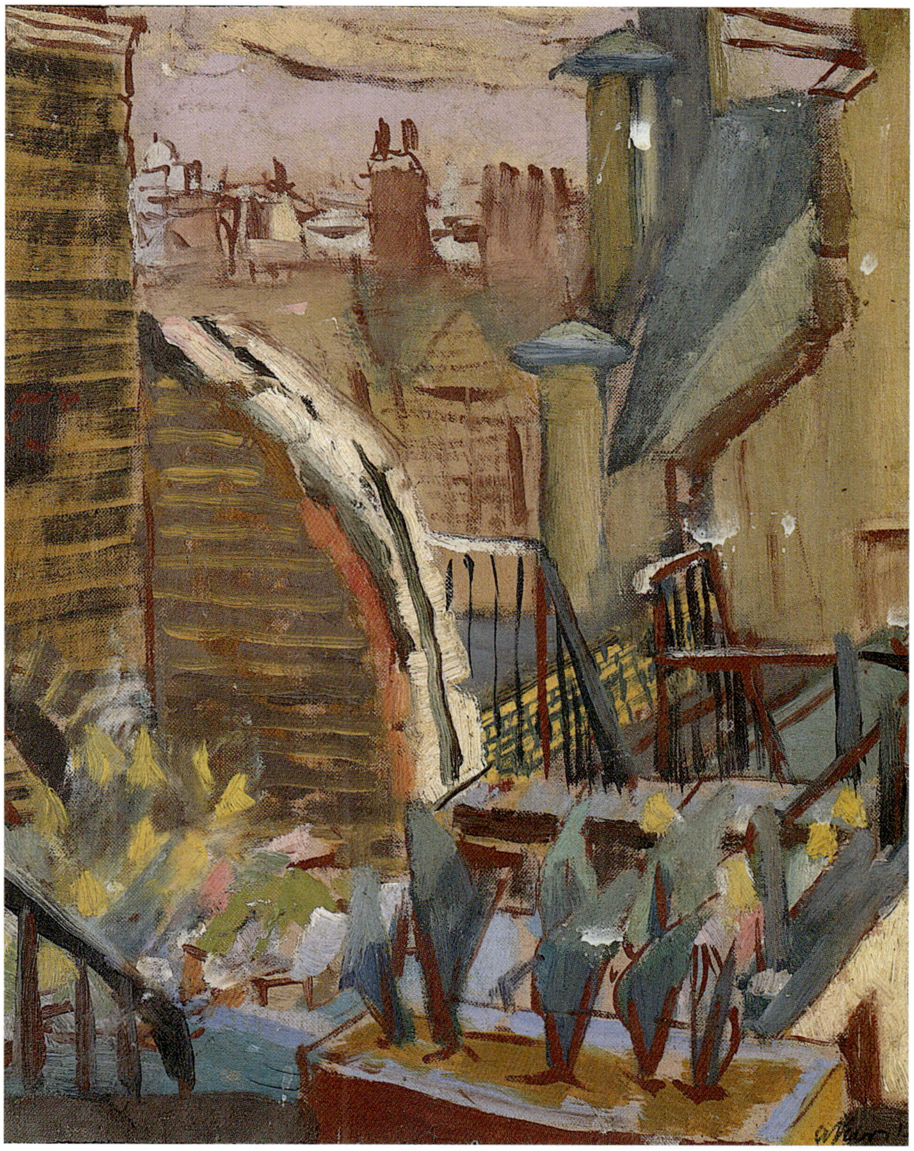

THE UNPRETENTIOUS subject matter, almost a still life, presents the windowbox as a roof-top 'garden' in an urbanised context. The work illustrates the view from the artist's window: she moved to 30 High Holborn in 1941 when her Fetter Lane studio (15 Stokes Court) was bombed and all her early works destroyed. It is springtime, with tulips and daffodils brightening up the roof-tops.

Provenance:
Purchased through the agency of Sarah Hosking from the artist's studio in 1984.

Bibliography:
Kathleen Allen, a Retrospective Exhibition, exhibition catalogue, South London Art Gallery, 1983, no. 20.

Provenance:
Zwemmer Gallery, where it was purchased by private collector in 1954; Christie's, 5 June 1992 (92), bt Museum of London.

Bibliography:
The Kitchen Sink Painters, exhibition catalogue, The Mayor Gallery (with Julian Hartnoll), 1991.

198.

JOHN BRATBY

(1928–92)

Blackheath [92.94]

1953

Oil on canvas, 91.6 x 121.8 cm

Signed bottom right: *John Bratby*

On the back, written in biro: *View looking NE from Greenwich end of Blackheath. St Paul's Cathedral just not visible at top R. corner. bought at Zwemmer Gallery Sept. 1954*

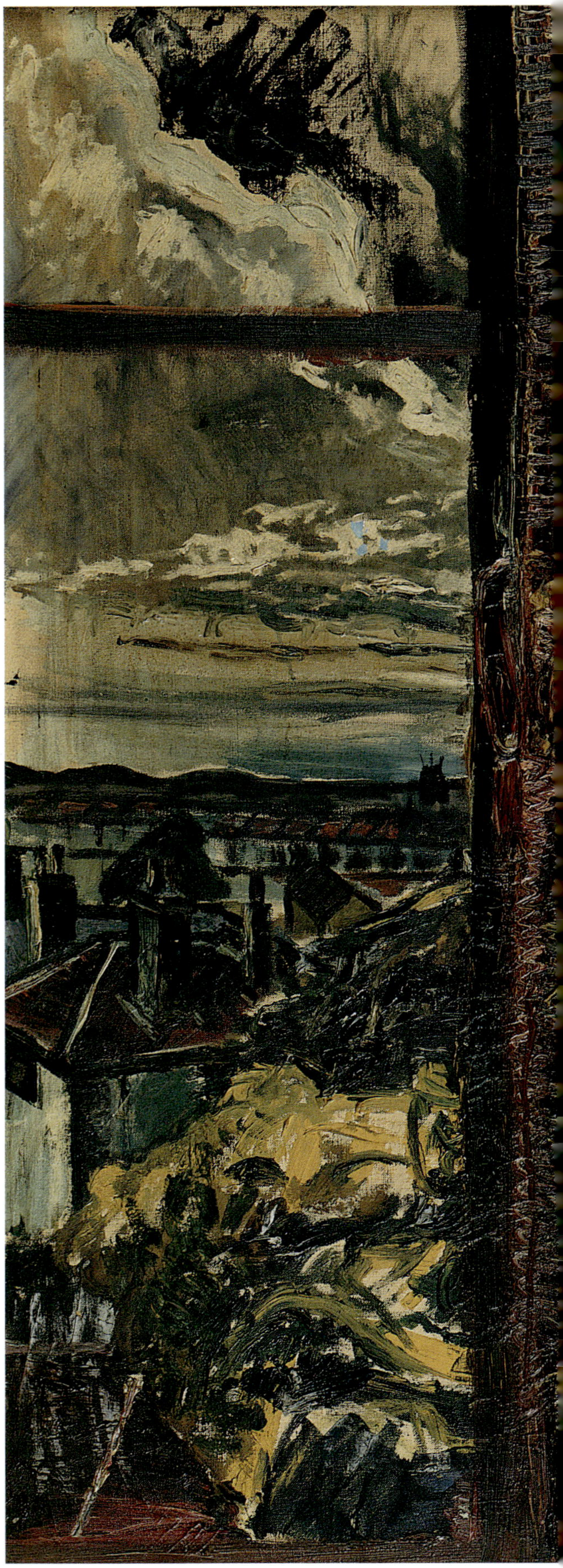

THIS VIEW, taken from the top of Blackheath Hill, is from the artist's window when he lived at 42 Dartmouth Row.

This London landscape, a good example of the artist's work, captures the light and landscape of the capital with great originality. The sky in particular is powerfully rendered, in the tradition of Van Gogh. Bratby's colours, however, are subdued dark browns, greens and greys, in this case perfectly suited to the mood of London.

A few months before his death the artist brought the attention of Julian Hartnoll, his dealer, to the Christie's sale (see provenance) which also featured one of the painter's kitchen interiors (see cat. no. 200). Bratby sent him a note on letter paper strikingly decorated with a border of large corn cobs, which was donated to the Museum by Mr Hartnoll.

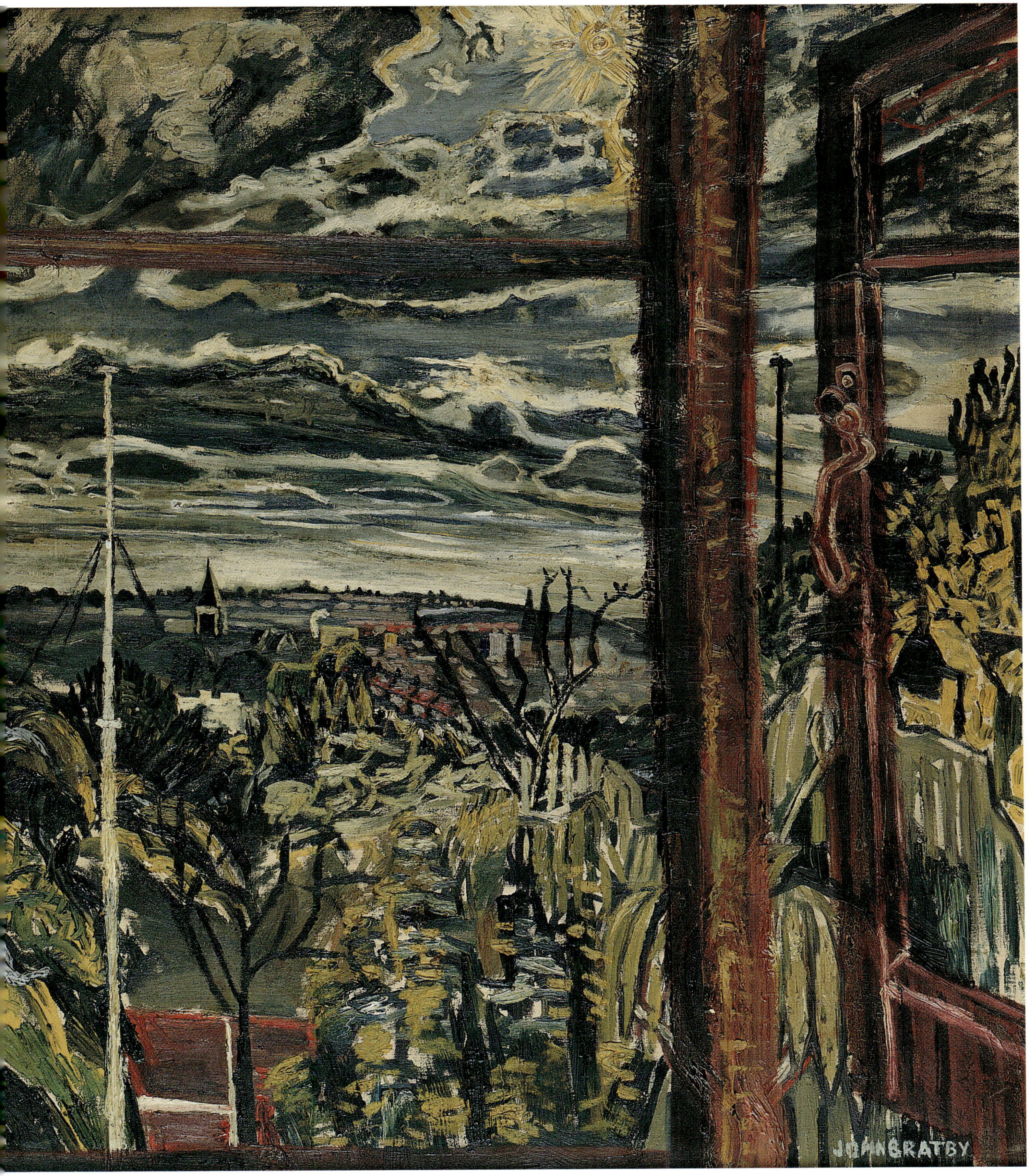
JOHNBRATBY

Provenance:
Purchased out of the Mackenzie Bell Trust Fund from the artist in 1965.

Bibliography:
Hayes (cat. no. 50); Nick Wates, *The Battle for Tolmers Square,* 1976.

199.

CHRISTOPHER HALL
(born 1930)

Tolmers Square, St Pancras [65.93]
1954
Oil on fibreboard, 64.2 x 42.6 cm
Signed and dated bottom left:
C. Hall/May/1954

THIS VIEW is taken looking south and shows 14 and 15 Tolmers Square; on the left is the alleyway which leads into Gower Street, and on the right the back of the Tolmers cinema.

Tolmers Square lies just north of the Euston Road, between Hampstead Road and Gower Street. Now completely rebuilt, it was developed in the early 1860s on the site of the reservoir belonging to the New River Company, which had been removed in 1860. William Sawyer built four-storey Italianate terraced houses between 1861 and 1864. The Gothic Congregational Church, which occupied the whole of the centre of the square, was built at the same time and opened in 1863. It closed soon after the First World War and was converted into the Tolmers cinema, which opened in 1923 (and closed in 1972).

The recent history of Tolmers Square has been turbulent and contrasts with the subdued and peaceful scene depicted here. There is a door lintel in the Museum's collection (acc. no. 83.44) which dates from around 1914 and was discovered above a shop door in Tolmers Square. Its rough hand-painted inscription reads 'The Owner is a British subject'. At the outbreak of the First World War, many shops run by Londoners with German names were attacked and looted. Some attempted to protect themselves by stressing that they were British.

The Tolmers Square Tenants Association was formed following the Rent Act in 1957. Between 1959 and 1963 they fiercely opposed various plans for redeveloping the site as an office/ commercial concern along the lines of the near-by Euston Centre developed by Joe Levy in the 1960s, on the corner of Hampstead and Euston roads. From 1962 for the next thirteen years Stock Conversion bought land in Tolmers Square for development and their policy of emptying and if possible demolishing properties met with increasing opposition and the formation of the Tolmers Village Association (in August 1973). Eventually Camden Council bought and developed Stock Conversion's property and the actual Tolmers Square land was developed as a housing estate, the arrangement of which around a central green area recalls the original layout. If the painting was updated, the tall block of RTB House on the corner of Gower Street and Euston Road would now dominate its background.

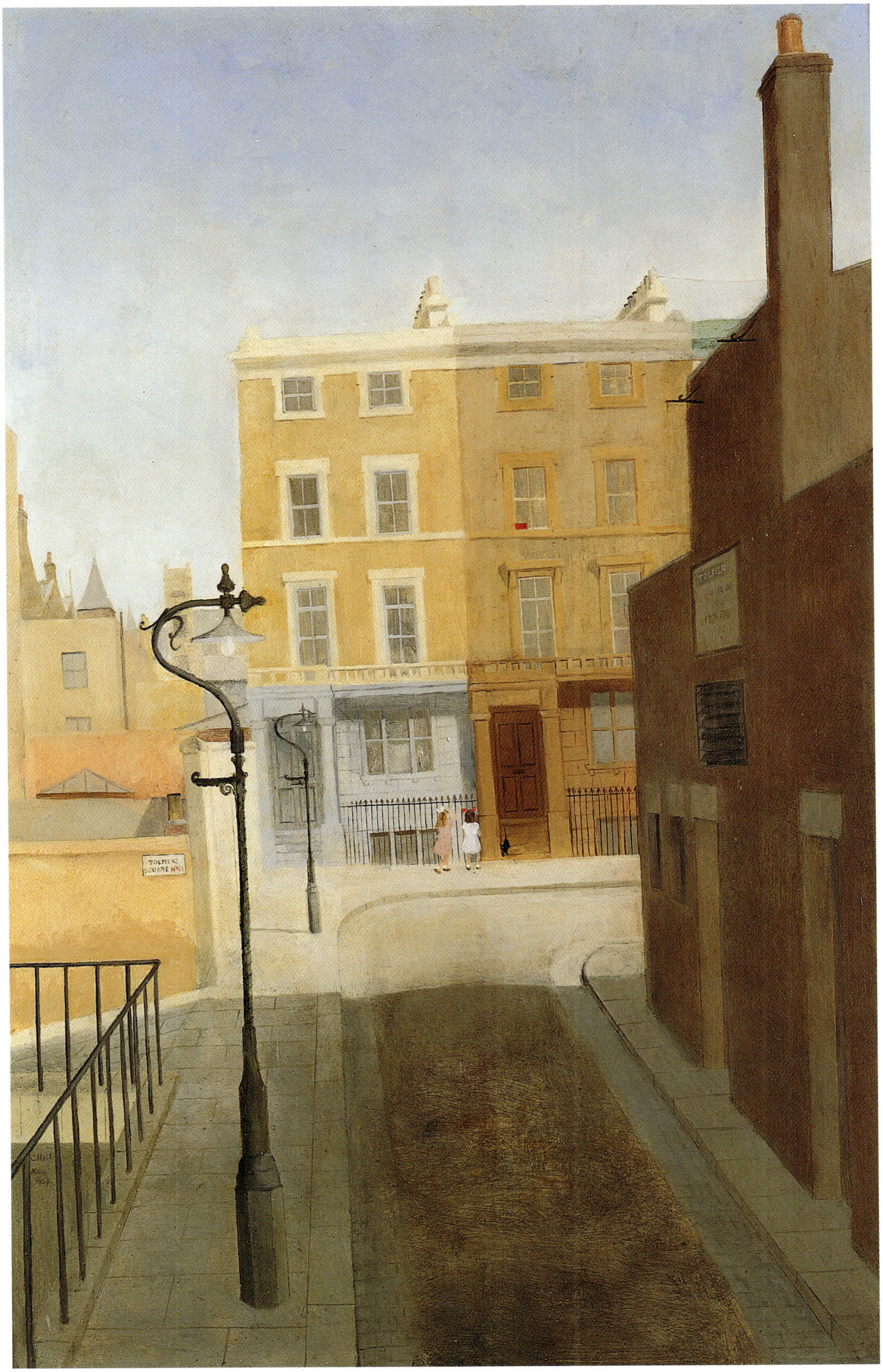
TOLMERS
SQUARE

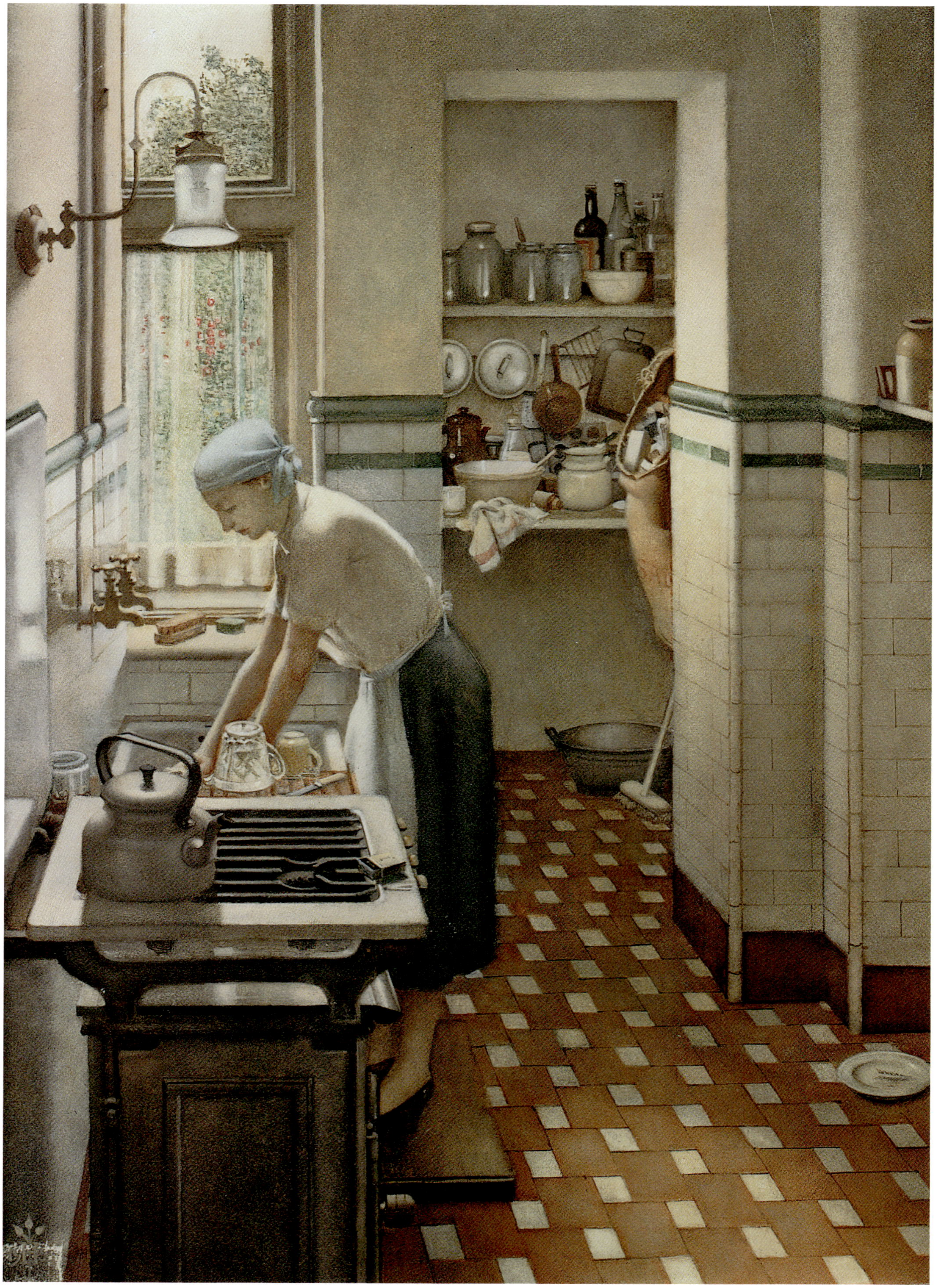

200.

HARRY BUSH
(1883–1957)

The Tiled Kitchen [84.346/3]
1954
Oil on panel, 38.5 x 50.8 cm
Signed and dated with monogram bottom left: *H* (surmounted by a three-branched finial)

THE ARTIST'S daughter, Janet Bush (born in 1922 and later Mrs Locke), is shown washing up in the kitchen of the family home at 19 Queensland Avenue, Merton Park, London SW19. The kitchen is the archetypal 1930s adjunct to a suburban house, with its distinctive floor and wall tiling and such appliances as the ceramic sink, nobbly taps and gas light fitting. The friendly clutter of pots and pans on the shelves next to the window includes the ubiquitous brown mixing bowl, a bain-marie and a range of jars and bottles which suggest 'home-made' products.

The preparatory pencil drawing for this work is also in the Museum's collection (acc. no. 90.291).

John Bratby painted *Kitchen Interior, Carlisle* the same year (see Christie's, 5 June 1992, Lot 94), and although stylistically the two works could not be more apart, one should note the common theme and the similarities in composition.

Provenance:
The artist's studio sale, Christie's, 28 September 1984 (76), bt Museum of London.

Bibliography:
Christie's sale catalogue, 28 September 1984; family records deposited at the V&A National Art Library.

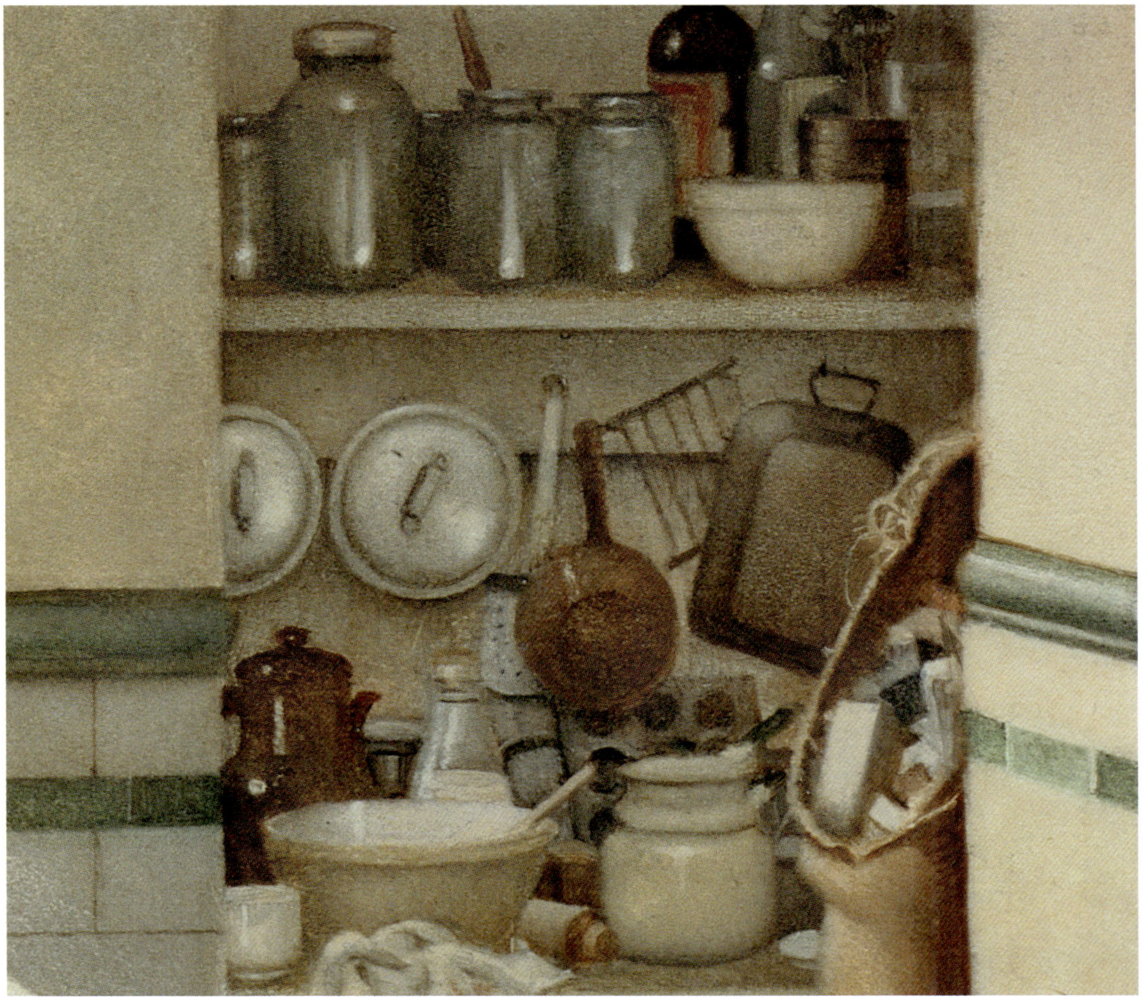

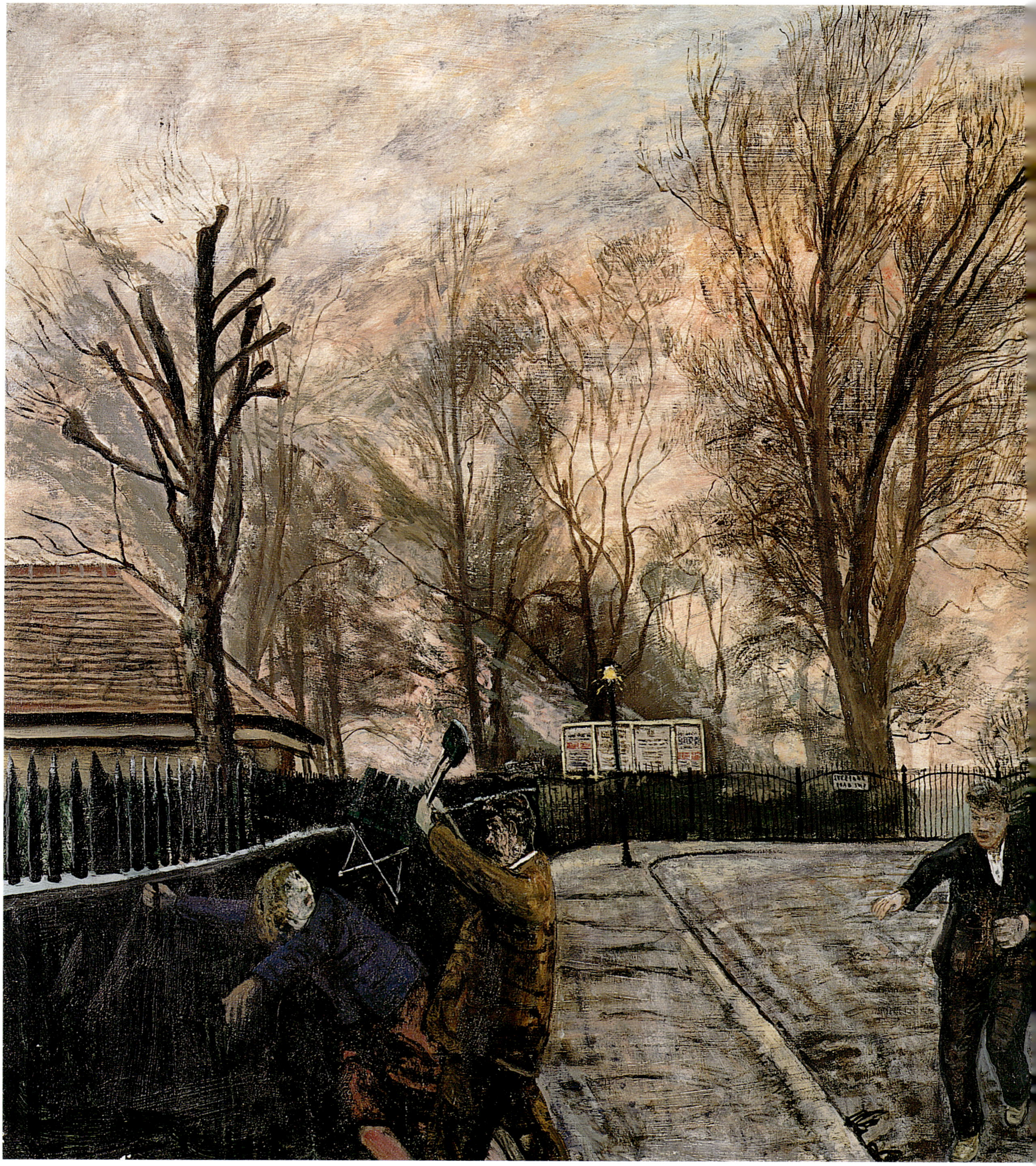

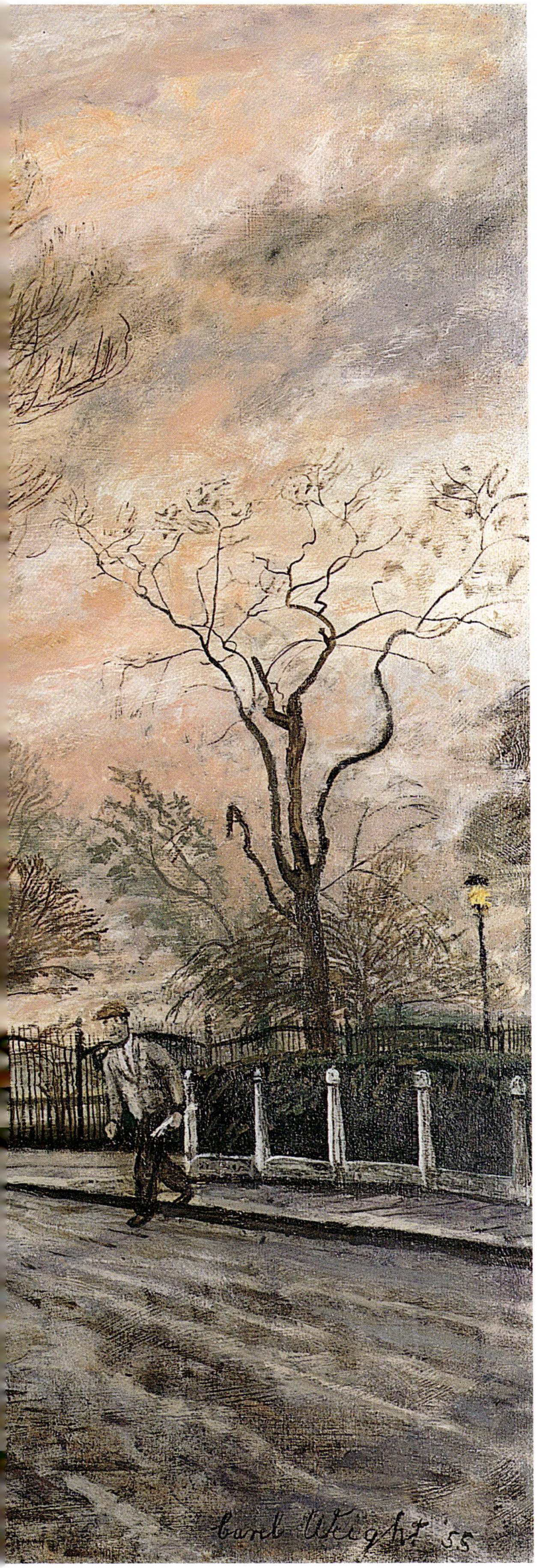

201.

CAREL WEIGHT

(born 1908)

Anger* [96.76]
1955
Oil on canvas, 91.5 x 122 cm
Signed and dated bottom right:
Carel Weight '55

THE SCENE is set just outside Fulham's Bishop's Park, at the junction of Bishop's Park and Stevenage roads, a setting which the artist used on a number of occasions. The incident depicted – a man attacking a woman with a chair – is characteristic of the haunted world of Carel Weight: he has developed a body of work on suburban London which revolves on the themes of public and domestic outbursts of violence, as well as ghosts.

Although this strange pictorial vocabulary may at first glance appear excessive and idyosyncratic, it is probably the nearest thing Britain has to the American blockbusters of *ET, Close Encounters of the Third Kind* or *Halloween*. The real subject is the clash between the soft and gentle living of the middle classes, in 'respectable' neighbourhoods, and a subversive unexpected dimension – the less familiar the interference, the more effective its impact. Into the world of peaceful suburbia the artist introduces the 'unreal' (ghosts) or in this case the 'hyper-real'– unrestrained personal violence. The universe of bourgeois comfort threatens to crumble, and to reinforce the clash, Carel Weight uses the insidious beauty of a sunset in a park.

Actually, I suppose I am rather a passive individual but I love the scaring sensation of going up in an aeroplane

Provenance:
Collection of Lord Chandos; Crane Kalman Gallery; private collector; Austin Desmond Gallery; purchased by the Museum in 1996 with the help of the National Art Collections Fund.

Bibliography:
Carel Weight RA., A Retrospective Exhibition, exhibition catalogue, Royal Academy, 1982; R. V. Weight, *Carel Weight – A Haunted Imagination*, 1994.

Exhibited:
Royal Academy 1956 (illustrated); 'Carel Weight', Leicester Galleries, 1962.

> because the 'blood courses in one's veins'. It is this sort of sensation that I like to create in my pictures. I like to create what seems to be the normal world but I like to make it as though some magical thing had happened. [*Carel Weight, RA, A Retrospective Exhibition*, 1982, p14]

The artist remembers well the genesis of this picture. One late afternoon, he was wandering the streets around the park and enjoying the striking effect of the sunset when he heard a scream, a female scream. He never discovered the reason for this but this is how he translated the incident into paint.

The imagery of walls is extremely striking in the work of Carel Weight and we are thus invited to reflect on their various meanings. His quiet domestic pieces show people in the protected environment of a walled garden (for example, *The Silence* or *Departing Angel),* but here the natural world is separate and contained within the park fences. All the protagonists are outside, almost 'out in the cold'. Despite the sense of apparent spaciousness, the woman is trapped within the pictorial space, as if in a cage, and this is accentuated by the choice of a visual cul-de-sac. The all-male cast, except for the victim, reinforces the sense of danger – will the other two men join in or effect a rescue? The theme of personal safety, so paramount to life on the streets these days, particularly in relation to women, is handled with strident effect. With recent events highlighting the increasing outbursts of individual and public violence, the work is particularly poignant.

Paintings of the London suburban scene are rare. A few years ago the Museum was fortunate in acquiring three works by the little known Harry Bush, who spent his life painting his adopted Merton (cat. nos 166, 167 and 200). What is unique with Carel Weight is to have this suburban art disrupted (some would say subverted) by fears usually associated with inner-city areas, almost as if no place was safe. This makes for a very different statement from the image of suburbia as a protected, almost paradisiac place, which started being 'sold' to Londoners at the turn of the century and found a contemporary echo in the 'Come to Milton Keynes' advertising campaign. They are two sides of the same coin and both sides of suburban life should duly be represented in the Museum's collection.

Stylistically and in mood the painting is close to works such as *The Presence* (1955, private collection) or *The Moment* (1955, Nottingham Castle Museum). However, the artist, oblivious to issues of site and type of incident, links this work to another (in a private collection) entitled *Day of Doom*. It shows people fleeing a fire in a suburban area (the sky is red with flames). This incident was based on a real-life event and was the closest the artist could get to painting people's great fear of the atom bomb. The two works unexpectedly connect through the stark world of fear.

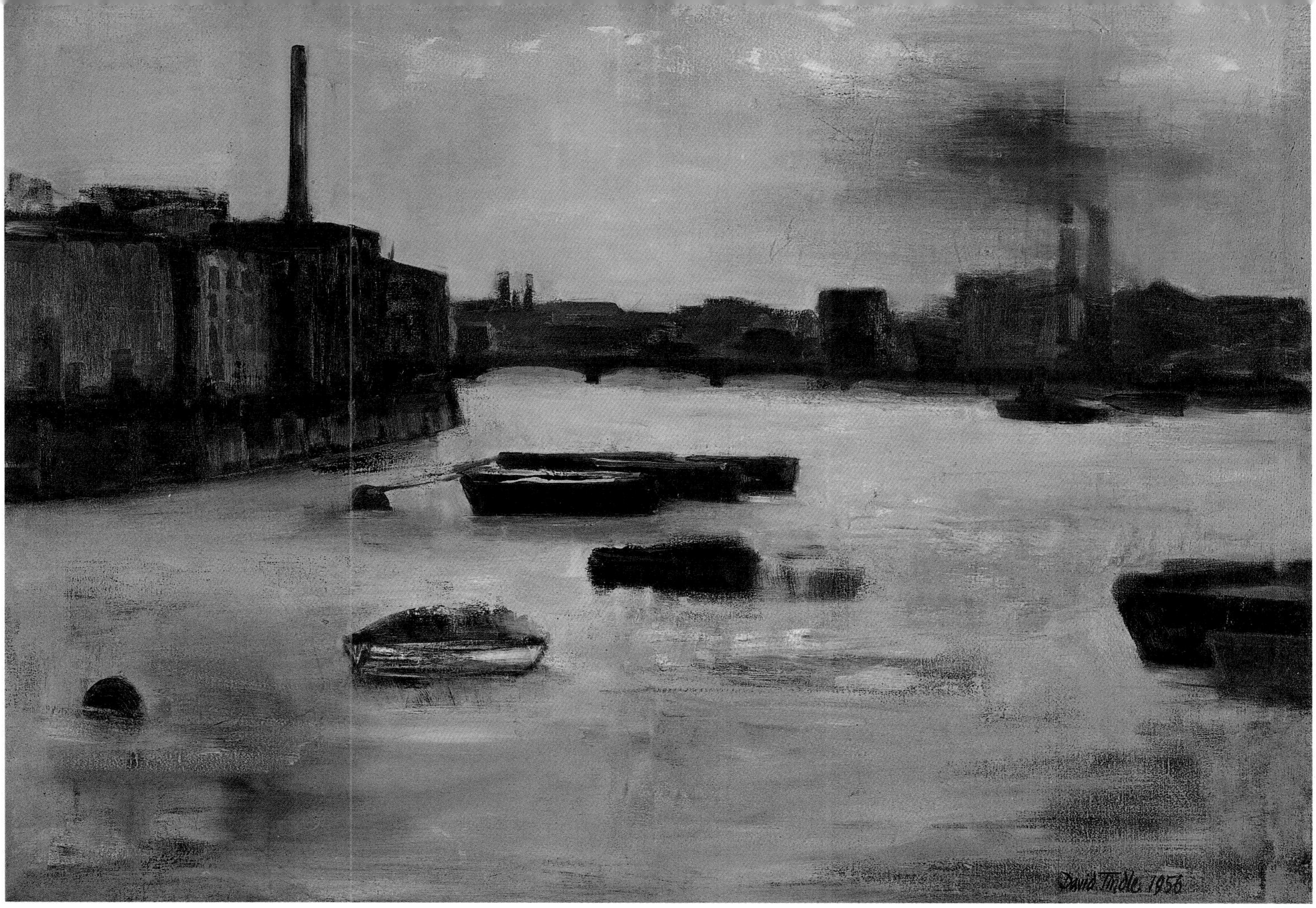

202.
DAVID TINDLE
(born 1932)
Battersea Reach 1956* [63.145]
1956
Oil on canvas, 81.4 x 115.6 cm
Signed and dated bottom right:
David Tindle 1956

THIS VIEW of Battersea Reach and the railway bridge, taken from Battersea Bridge, conveys all the greyness of the London atmosphere on a winter's day. On the left are some of the Victorian warehouses that line the Battersea shore. In the distance is the railway bridge built for the Southern Railway and at the time of its construction the widest railway bridge in the world; beyond this is the Fulham power station. On the right is the Lots Road power station, used for London Transport underground railways, situated just to the west of the Chelsea Flour Mills and at the extreme end of Cheyne Walk. A number of barges are seen on the river.

In a letter he wrote to the Museum in 1992, the artist comments:

> My Thames paintings started in 1952–3 and went on to the end of the 50s... Further to the painting *Battersea Reach 1956*, I lived for a short time in Beaufort St – very near the bridge for *Battersea Reach*. This period was very monochromatic, at that time buildings had not been cleaned as they are now, the water was very oily and so caught the sun in an odd way.

It is interesting to compare this painting with the work by Jesse Dale Cast (see cat. no. 204). Both works are contemporary, but their perceptions of the Thames could not be further apart.

Provenance:
Purchased from the Piccadilly Gallery in 1963.

Bibliography:
Hayes (cat. no. 104).

Provenance:
Purchased through the agency of Sarah Hosking from the artist's studio in 1984.

Bibliography:
Kathleen Allen, a Retrospective Exhibition, exhibition catalogue, South London Art Gallery, 1983, no. 24.

203.

KATHLEEN ALLEN

(1906–83)

The Prudential Remembers* [84.142/2]
1958
Oil on canvas, 27.5 x 22.5 cm
Signed and dated bottom right: *Allen 58*

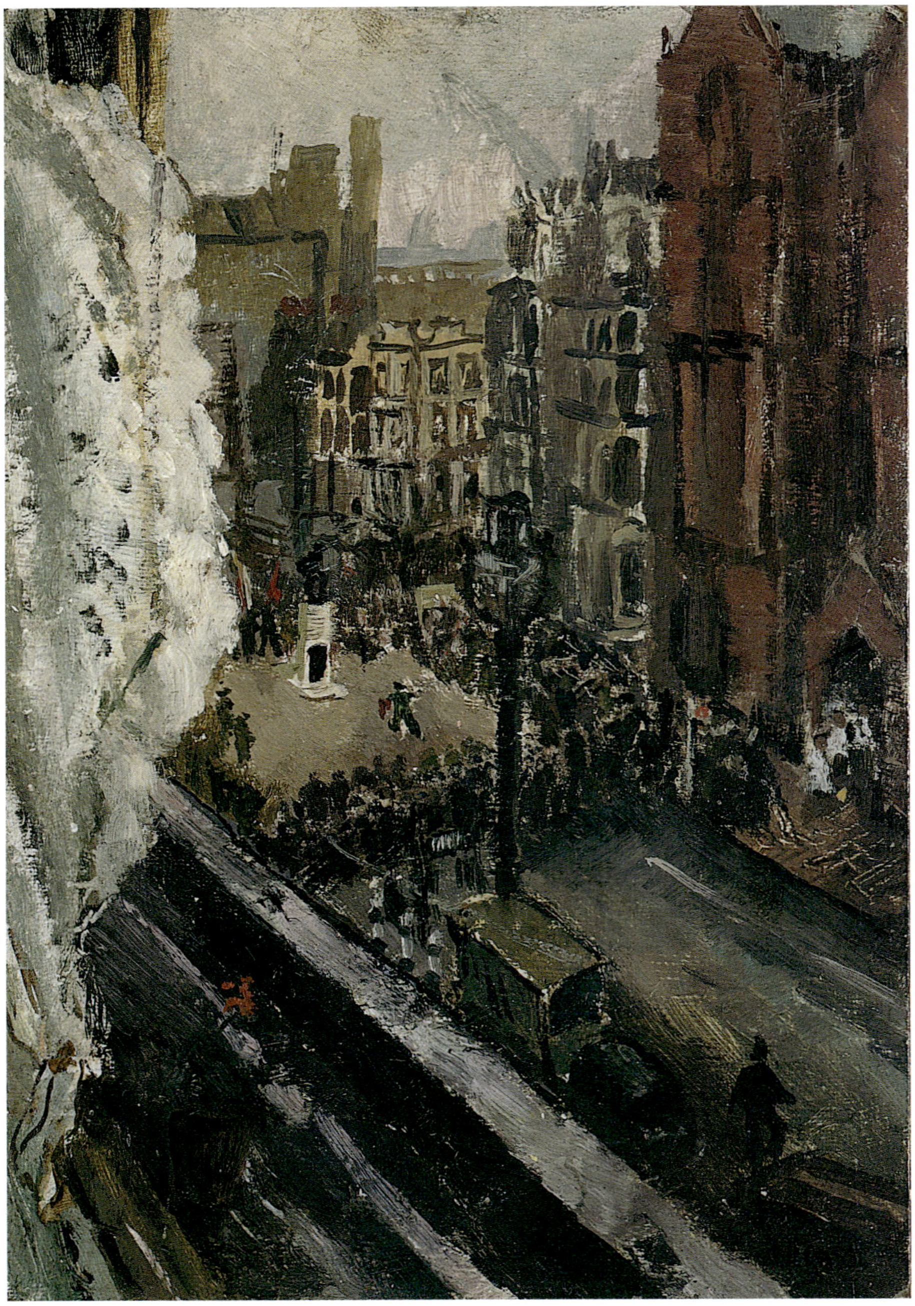

THE ARTIST depicts a bird's-eye view of a memorial service on Remembrance Sunday at Holborn Bars, around the war memorial to the 22,000 Royal Fusiliers (City of London Regiment) 'who fell in the Great War 1914–18 and to the Royal Fusiliers who fell in the World War 1939–45'. The memorial was erected in 1924 by the sculptor Alfred Toft (1862–1949). The scene is taken from the curtained window of the artist's flat, at the top of 30 High Holborn (south side, now Buchanan House) next to Barnard's Inn and across the road from the Prudential Assurance Building. From 1919 the Prudential had held a ceremony of remembrance each year on 11 November, in the internal courtyard of their building. However, despite its title (given by the artist), the event depicted has no connection with the Prudential other than proximity.

On a more prosaic note, the painting also features the railings and air vent (the green-painted cabin) attached to the underground public toilets which were commissioned by the City in 1906, two years after those installed in Guildhall Yard (which are now closed). These toilets were recently refurbished and modernised and the Museum of London salvaged some of the original fittings for its collections.

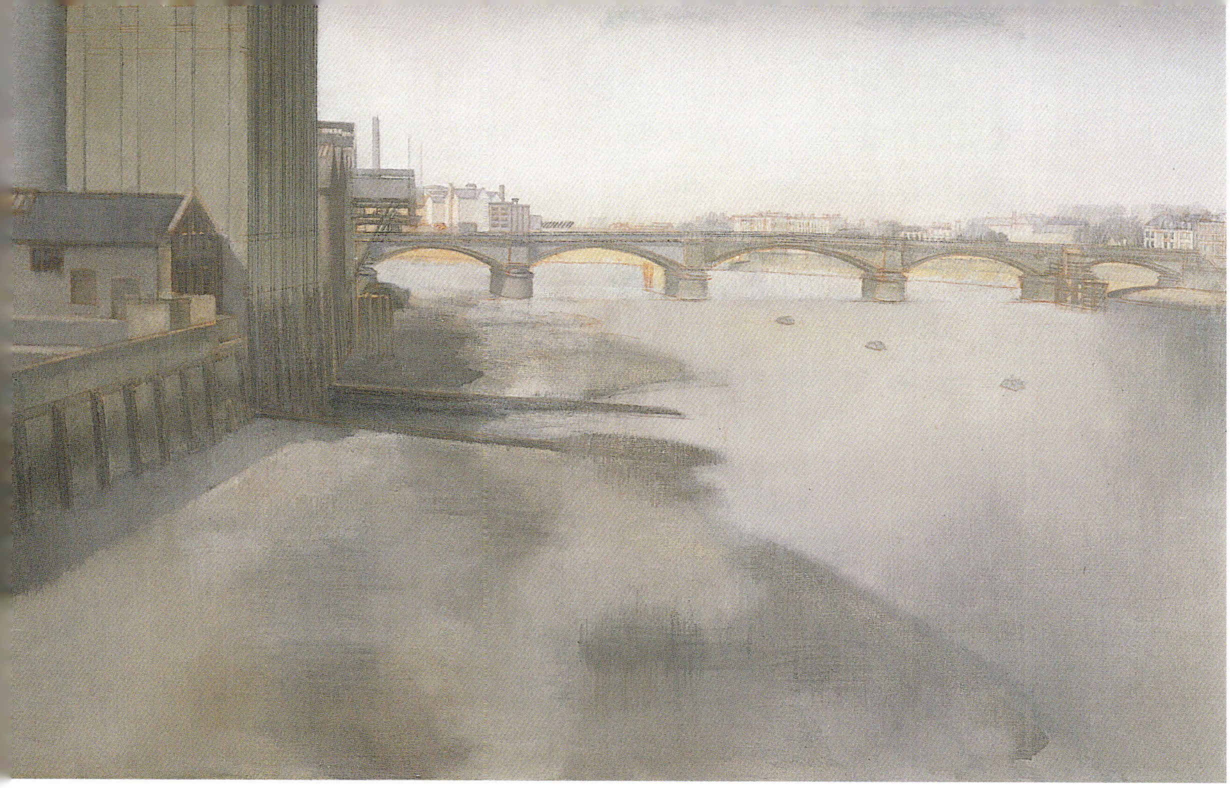

Provenance:
Purchased from Jason & Rhodes in 1995.

Bibliography:
Jesse Dale Cast 1900–1976, exhibition catalogue, South London Art Gallery, 1980, nos 49–53; David Cast, *Jesse Dale Cast*, exhibition catalogue, The Strang Print Room, University College, 1994.

204.

JESSE DALE CAST

(1900–76)

Battersea Bridge from the Albert Bridge
[95.254]
1950s
Oil on canvas, 55.5 x 91.3 cm
Not signed or dated

THIS VIEW of the Thames between Albert and Battersea bridges is taken at low tide. In the background can be seen the mass of Lots Road power station on the left and the white facade of Lindsay House near the northern end of Battersea Bridge. On the left, the entrance to Ransome's Dock is visible, but in developing the idea for his composition, the artist has placed it underneath the large square tower belonging to Albert Bridge Flour Mills (the correct topography is recorded in the Museum's preparatory drawing for this painting, acc. no. 82.487/2). On the western side of Ransome's Dock, abutting Battersea Bridge, was the second main industrial landmark along this stretch, the paper warehouse of Phillips Mills & Co. This stretch of the Thames was recently redeveloped to become Riverside Apartments and the offices of Sir Norman Foster's architectural practice. Nowadays the cluster of tower blocks at World's End on the north bank dominates the skyline.

This painting is one of a series the artist painted of this scene in the 1950s when he was living near by in Battersea on the Albert Bridge Road. In the late 1920s, when he was travelling in Europe, he had done a number of river or sea views of Ghent and Bruges, as well as Soller, Majorca. After he returned to England in the 1930s, he painted many Thames scenes: Surrey Docks, Lambeth (private collection, London), Hillock's Wharf, Greenwich (Brinsley Ford collection) and the Greenwich jetty. These earlier works are the closest to the Battersea series.

The combining of such a carefully constructed composition with a beautiful and delicate brown and silvery palette gives the painting a sense of peace and poetry which contrasts with the bleak version of a similar scene made by David Tindle during the same decade (see cat. no. 202).

Provenance:
Presented to the Museum by W. G. M. Angliss, the last owner of the fish shop, in 1983.

205.
IAN RIBBONS
(born 1924)
Interior of Burkett's Fish Shop, 114 Brompton Road [83.850]
1959
Oil on canvas, 101.5 x 101.5 cm
Signed and dated bottom left:
Ian Ribbons 59

THE VIEW, taken from the entrance, shows the length of the fishmonger's shop, with a lavish display of fish on the right-hand side: lobsters, scallops, Dublin Bay prawns, sea crayfish, haddock, kippers, red mullet, trout etc. In the middle ground on the left is the work area where the fish are weighed, cleaned and wrapped. The back of the shop is fitted with a conservatory.

The presence of poultry in a fish shop (pheasants hanging from hooks and chickens next to the fish) requires some explanation. Some fishmongers began to sell poultry to enliven business on days when the sale of fish was slow. The practice was not, however, generally followed, because many fishmongers were reluctant to allocate space and labour to the selecting and plucking of stock. A licence was required for the sale of game.

In one of his letters to the Museum the donor of the painting recounted the following anecdote:

> As it happens, my father – William Angliss – owned the freeholds of a number of shops in Roehampton High Street, one of which was occupied by his own fish shop, Rudman. A neighbouring butcher's shop, Hartshorn, held a lease from him 'to engage in the trade of butcher'. During the 1939–45 War poultry was unrationed, so that Hartshorn not unreasonably started to sell poultry to supplement his trade in rationed butcher's meat. When the lease was due for renewal, *c.*1954, my father asked him to resume trade solely as butcher (he was, after all, competing with us in the next door shop!). The case went to the High Court and judgment was given in favour of Hartshorn, so that hereafter any butcher could legitimately claim that the sale of poultry was part of his trade.

Around 1880 Lawrence Josephus Burkett started a fish shop at 145 Brompton Road and when this was demolished to make way for Harrods around 1902/3, Burkett took a forty-and-a-half year lease (in the Museum's collection) at number 114, opposite Hans Road, which now runs along the south-west side of Harrods. The new premises had been those of a florist's and the conservatory was a leftover from the shop's previous function.

At Burkett's death, the business passed to his partner Harry Webb (*c.*1919). Some two years after Webb's death in 1929 it was bought from his estate by Charles and William Angliss (the donor's father), proprietors of Rudman & Co., fishmongers of Putney (which was also painted by Ian Ribbons). The freehold of the shop was purchased in 1949. The painting shows the premises before rebuilding work was carried out at the back of the shop and the adjoining 16/17 Montpelier Mews. The conservatory, which had survived both World Wars, was removed in 1964 when a new roof was installed. Two years later, the front of the shop was completely rebuilt. The shop in its modern guise went on trading for another ten years, after which the freehold was sold, in 1977, and the

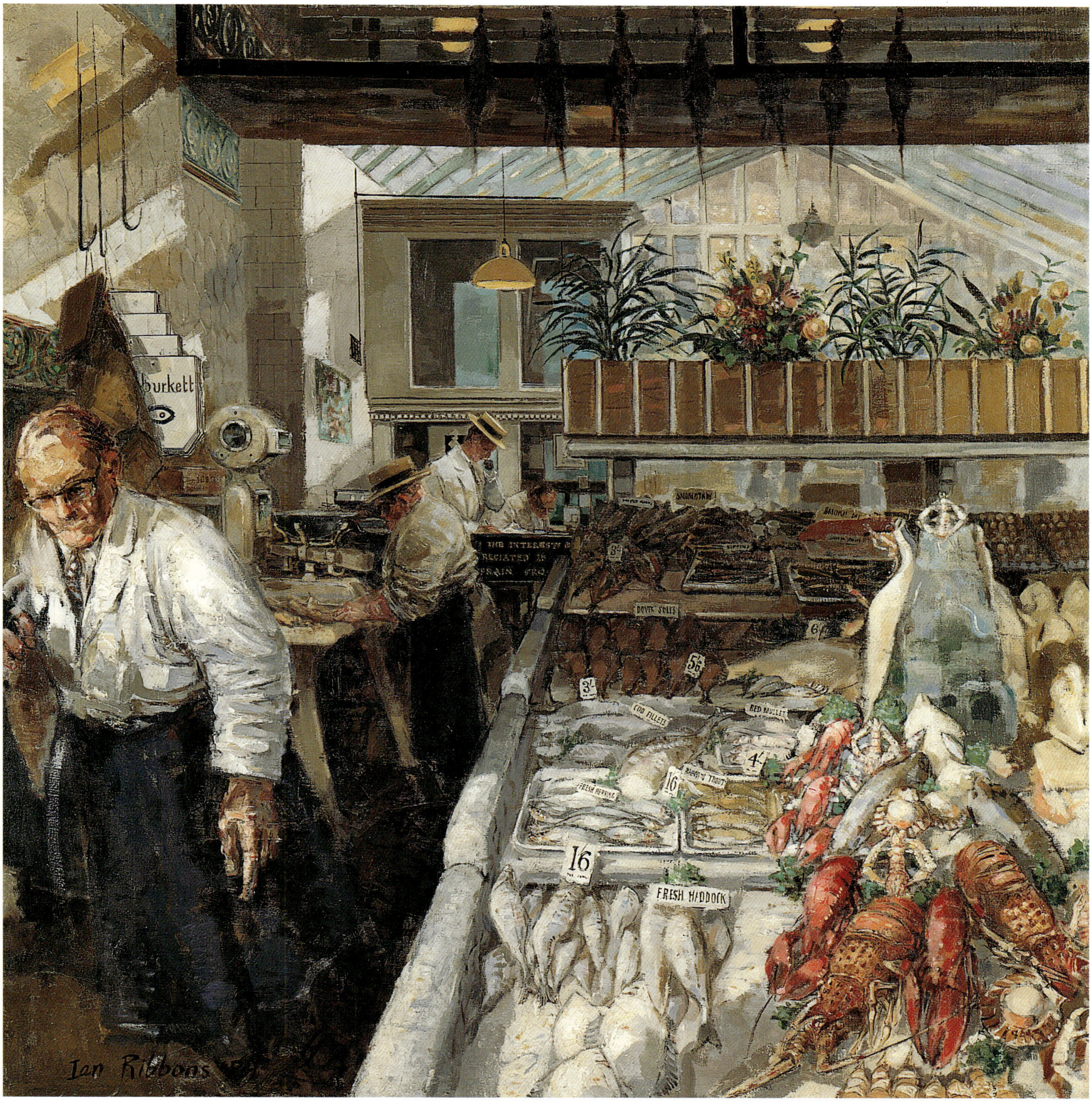

company placed in voluntary liquidation. The site has now been rebuilt and the Sanderson Gallery is at number 114.

The people portrayed in the painting are: W. G. Christie, shop manager (in the foreground); H. Carini, fishblockman, in the middle ground; Jeremy Angliss, co-owner (with donor), in the middle background; and E. R. Worboys, head clerk, in the background. Christie, Carini and Worboys were all with the firm for more than thirty years.

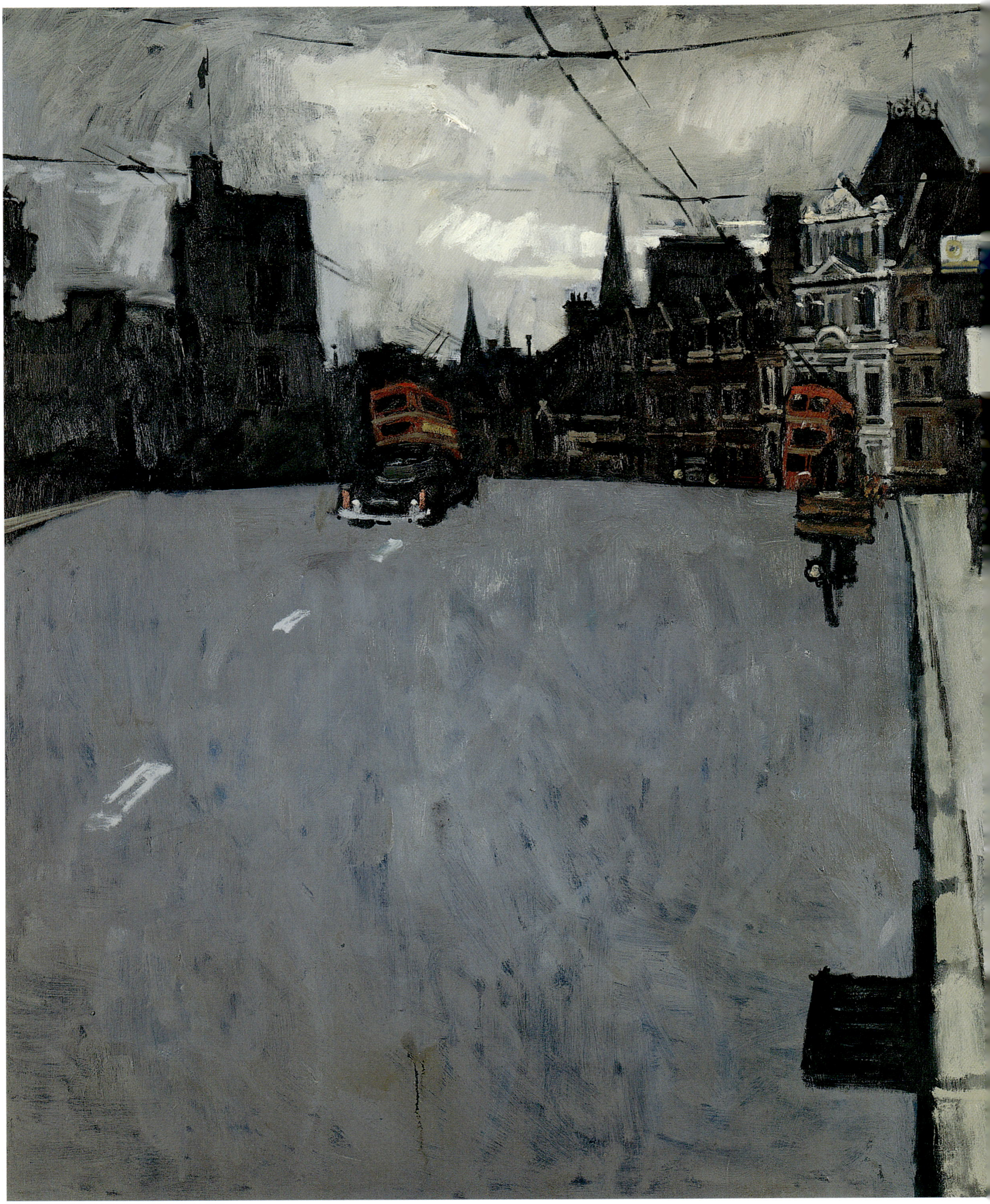

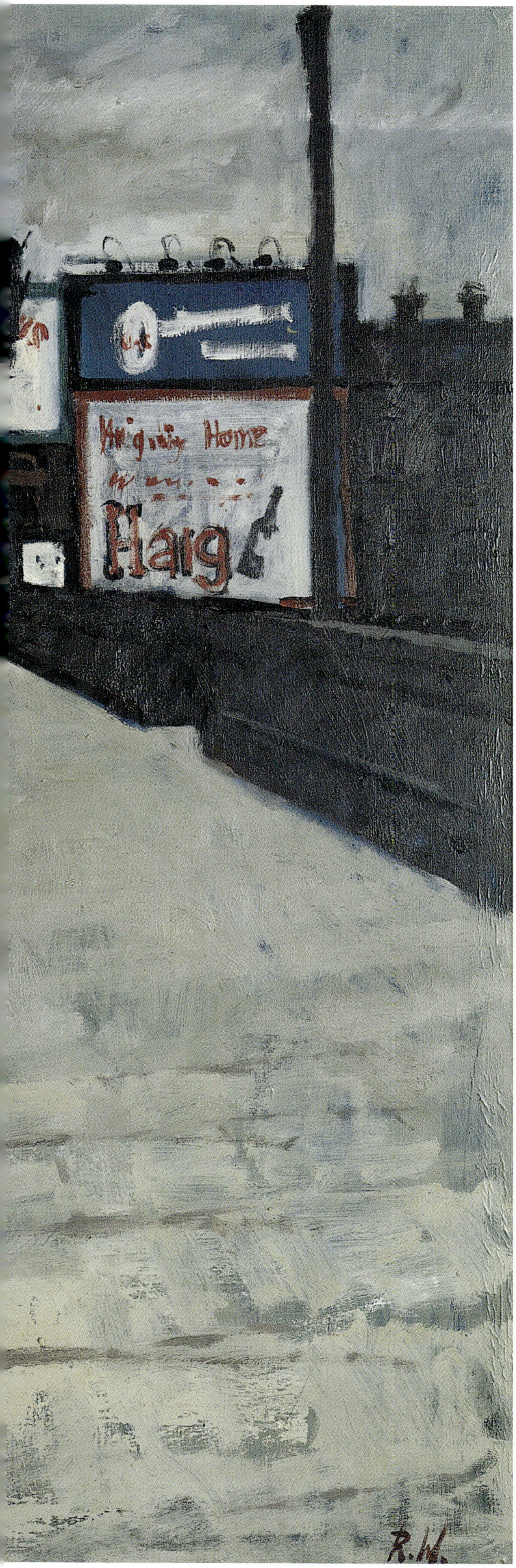

206.

RAYMOND WYLIE
(active 1960s)

On Putney Bridge [74.84/3]
*c.*1960
Oil on canvas, 101.5 x 126.7 cm
Signed with initials bottom right: *R.W.*

Provenance:
Presented by Peter Alward in 1974.

THE ARTIST has positioned himself on Putney Bridge and is looking south towards Putney. The row of Victorian houses in the right and centre of the picture has remained unchanged to this day, but the tall public house behind the cyclist, which opened in 1887 as The White Lion, is now rechristened The Slug and Lettuce. The two steeples featured in the painting would appear to belong to High Street buildings, now demolished: the one shown in the centre situated at the corner of Weimar Street was burnt down in the 1970s; the one on the left belonged to The Bull and Star on the corner of Felsham Road and was demolished between 1965 and 1970. The distant steeple to the right of the latter may belong to St John's Church (in St John's Avenue). On the left-hand side of the painting is the tower of the church of St Mary. The traffic is reduced to one double decker and one car travelling in each direction, as well as a bicycle coming towards the painter. One should also note trolleybus wires criss-crossing the sky, as well as the poles clearly delineated above the roof-top on the right. The mood of the work is close to that of David Tindle's river scene of the same period (see cat. no. 202), but its asymmetric composition recalls the unexpected compositions of French *Nouvelle Vague* Cinéma Vérité.

Provenance:
Presented by Peter Alward in 1974.

207.

RAYMOND WYLIE

(active 1960s)

Boxing Match at Albert Hall [74.84/4]

*c.*1960

Oil on board, 36.3 x 31 cm

Signed with initials bottom right: *R.W.*

IT IS not possible to identify the particular fight depicted here, but the work is a rare post-war painted record of the Albert Hall's sporting activities.

Prince Albert had first suggested the building of a hall to inspire 'the moral improvement of the people' in 1853. However, the foundation stone was not laid until 1867 (by the Queen in mourning) and the opening came only in 1871. At first the hall was strictly used for artistic and scientific events, as its charter specified, but in 1886 an additional charter increased the uses allowed and soon political and religious meetings and balls were staged there. The Chelsea Arts Ball was held at the Albert Hall between 1910 and 1985, as well as trade fairs, basketball championships, clairvoyance demonstrations and, from 1941, The Proms. On Boxing Day 1919 the first 'big fight' was staged at the hall (which had been used for boxing since 1886) when Ted 'Kid' Lewis stopped Matt Wells in twelve rounds. Boxing took a firm hold at the Albert Hall after this event.

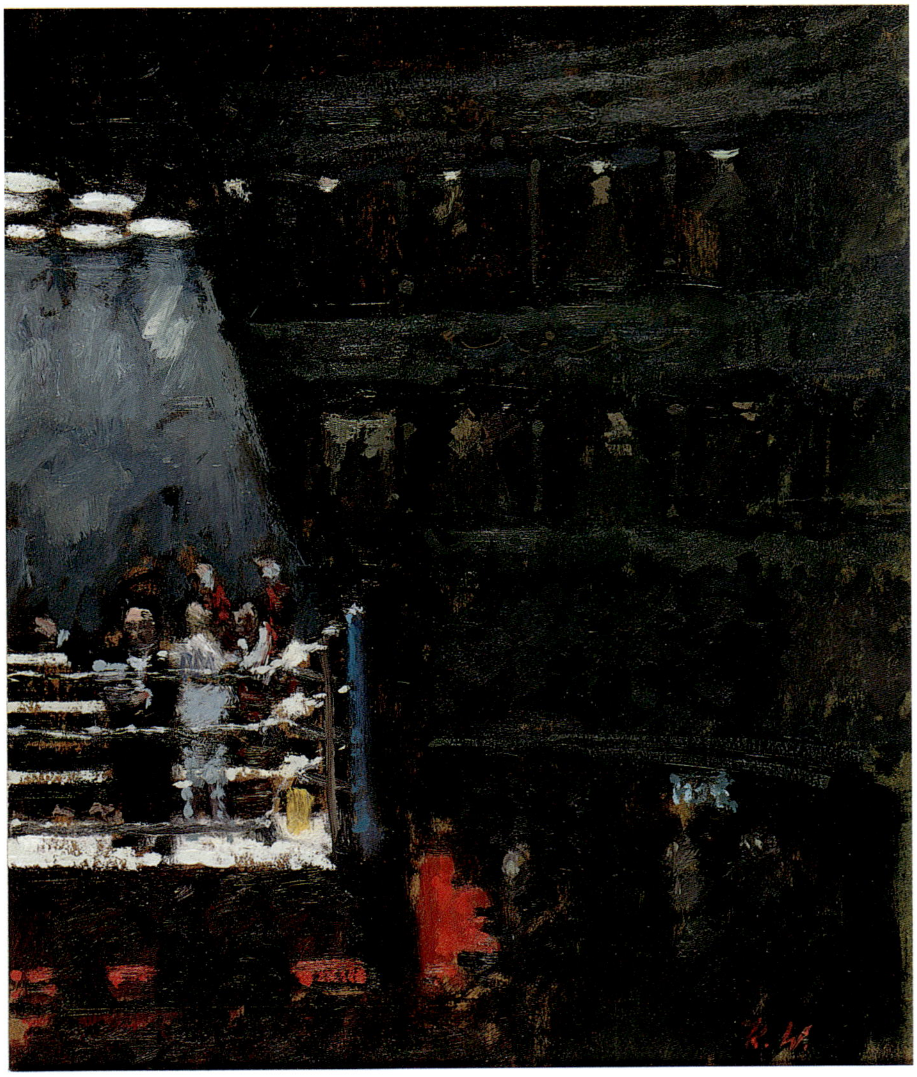

208.
NOEL SPENCER
(1901–86)
Bayswater* [81.36/3]
1960
Tempera painting, 76.6 x 50.6 cm
Signed and dated bottom right:
NOEL SPENCER 1960
A label on the back gives the artist's address in Norwich, the date (Aug–Sept 1960) and title.

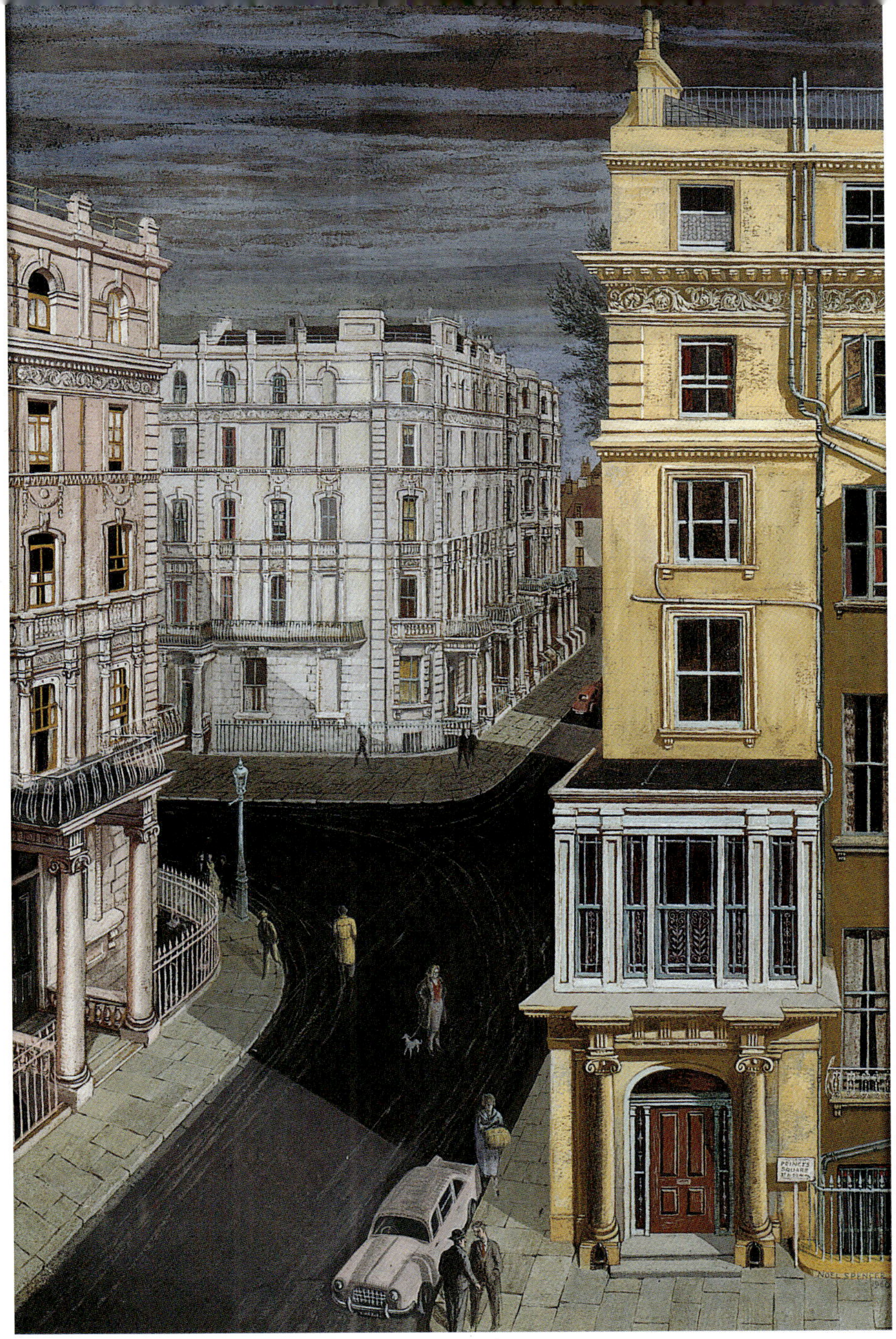

THE PAINTING shows a view of Princes Square taken from a window in Leinster Square, Bayswater. It is looking south down Garway Road with Porchester Gardens on the left-hand side.

The development of Bayswater began in the early nineteenth century, with Tyburnia, or the Hyde Park Estate, just east of the area shown in the painting. The arrival of the Great Western Railway in the 1830s stimulated development further. The introduction of four- and five-storey buildings (as opposed to just three in the early Connaught Street area), with colonnaded entrances and attractive plasterwork decoration, dates from that time onwards.

A preliminary pencil study for this work, dated 1955, is in the Museum's collection (acc. no. 73.101/104). Spencer was Principal of the Norwich School of Art between 1946 and 1964, but throughout the 1950s he produced a series of pencil drawings of the Bayswater area where he usually stayed when in London.

This work belongs to a group of five tempera paintings which the artist gave to the Museum. The other four show views of Clink Street, Pickle Herring Street, the church of St Ethelburga and Kensal Green Cemetery (see Appendix). In subject and technique *Kensal Green Cemetery* recalls the work of the artist Eliot Hodgkin (1905-87), who exhibited his *Painswick Churchyard I* and *II* at the Royal Academy in 1948. The revival of the tempera technique followed the publication in 1930 of Maxwell Armfield's *Manual of Tempera Painting* and subsequently the flourishing of the Society of Painters in Tempera between 1957 and 1975 (see their year-book, *Tempera*). Eliot Hodgkin had been practising tempera painting since about 1937 and he described his particularly accomplished technique in *Tempera* in 1967.

Provenance:
Presented by the artist in 1981.

Provenance:
Purchased from the artist in 1962.

Bibliography:
Hayes (cat. no. 36).

Exhibited:
Royal Academy, 1962 (421).

209.

BERNARD DUNSTAN
(born 1920)

Hyde Park Corner, 1961* [62.118]
1961
Oil on hardboard, 105.5 x 86.7 cm
Signed with initials bottom left: *BD*

THE UNDERPASS at Hyde Park Corner, which connects Knightsbridge with Piccadilly, was opened in 1962, the first improvement of this kind to be planned as an integral part of London's street system (the subway under the Strand connecting Kingsway and the Thames Embankment, built in the 1900s, having been designed solely for tramways). It formed part of the Marble Arch–Park Lane–Hyde Park Corner improvements, themselves only one element in a concerted programme initiated by Ernest Marples, then Minister of Transport, for easing the traffic congestion which was choking the arteries of central London. The introduction of parking meters in business areas to restrict the number of private vehicles brought into town, and of one-way streets to facilitate the flow of traffic, were other features of an energetic policy which has had successful results wherever it has been applied, making it possible for vehicles to move reasonably freely in the central area.

The view is taken looking eastwards, and beyond the massive girders and the group of cranes and lorries can be seen the Hyde Park Corner screen and Apsley House (see also cat. no. 65).

The artist later described the scene as an 'impossible subject'. He was attracted by the rich and varied geometrical framework formed by the cranes and the shadows, which would give his picture the kind of solid structure adopted by painters such as Claude Rogers. The scene must indeed have been 'irresistible', in the words of the artist, since Charles Cundall (1890–1971) was also, unbeknown to Dunstan, attracted to the scene which he painted from a different angle; his own *Hyde Park Corner 1961* was exhibited the same year at the Royal Academy.

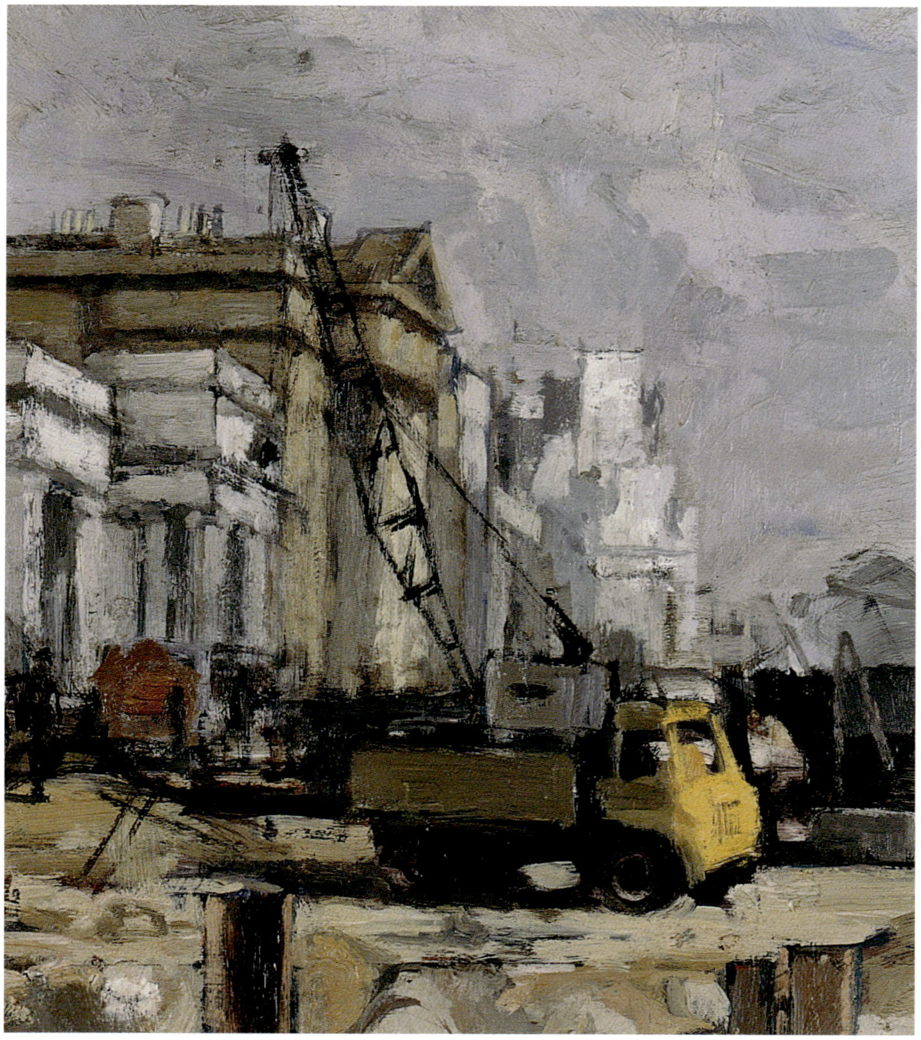

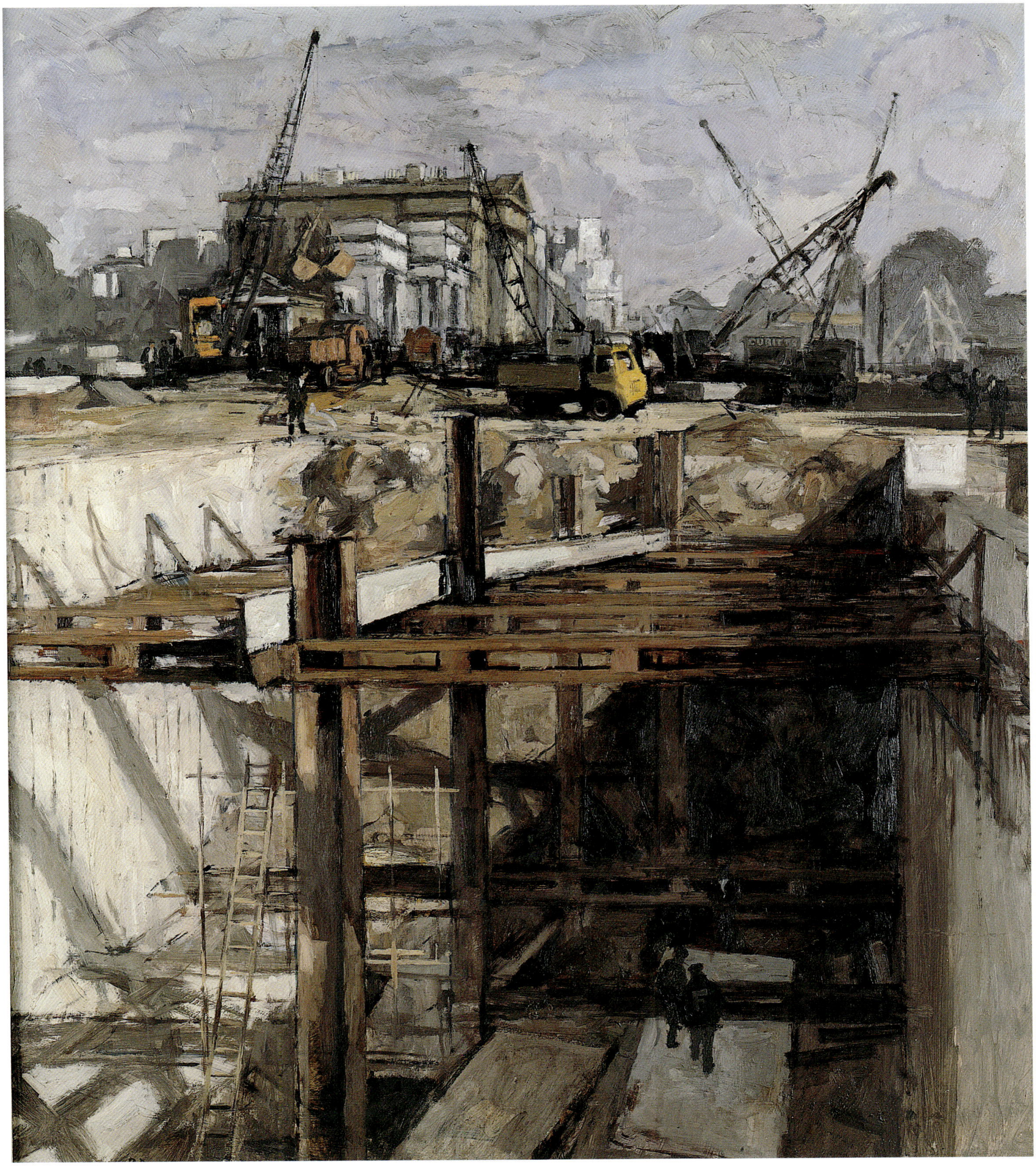

Provenance:
Purchased from the artist in 1978.

Bibliography:
Jennifer Clarke, *The Barbican – Sitting on History*, 1990.

210.

HAROLD HUSSEY

(born 1912)

Barbican Site [78.166]
1962
Oil on canvas, 61.5 x 101 cm
Signed and dated bottom left:
Harold Hussey–62

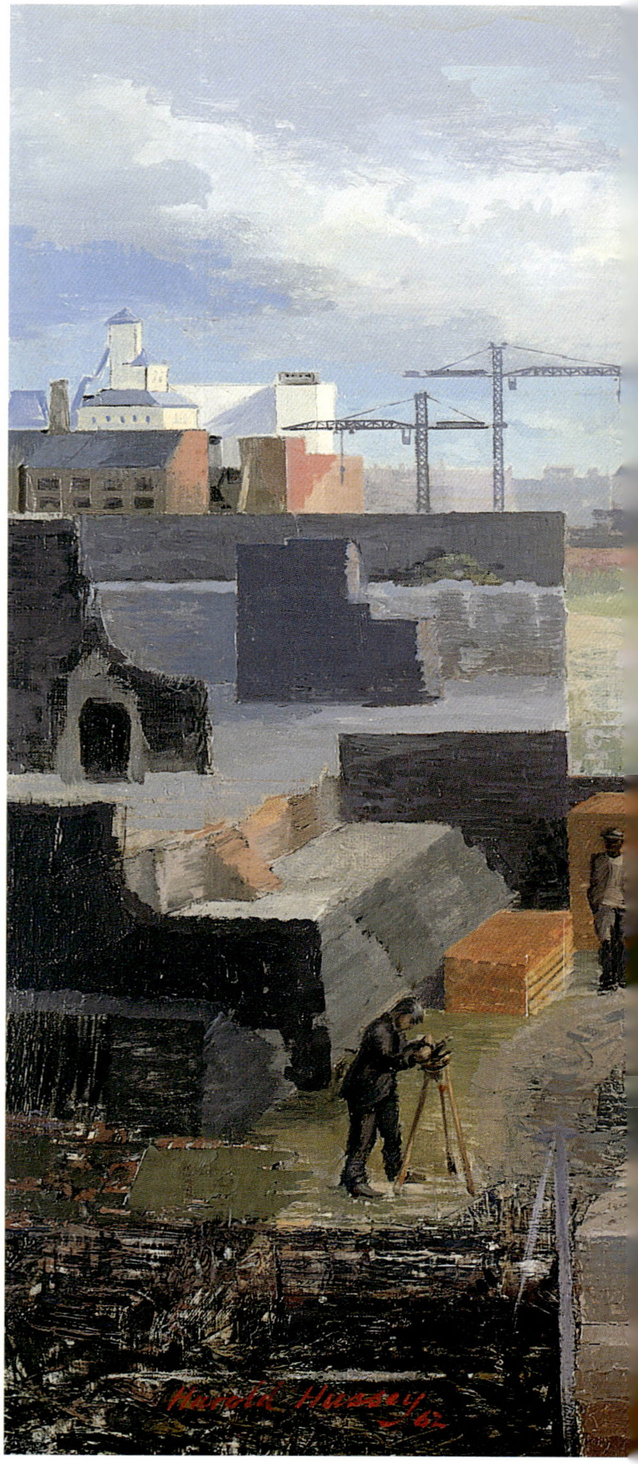

THIS PAINTING records the appearance of the Barbican site before the building of the Barbican Estate between 1959 and 1982 and soon after the building of the Golden Lane Estate between 1954 and 1959. The view is taken from the north-east, near the junction of Aldersgate Street and Old Street. In the background the following buildings are identifiable, from left to right: the tower structure of Whitbread's Brewery; the Red Cross Street Fire Brigade Station; the church of St Giles Cripplegate; and three London Wall office blocks (the now demolished Lee House, St Alphage House and Moor House). The dome of St Paul's is just visible on the extreme right. In the middle ground a temporary car park is visible.

In May 1956 the architects Chamberlin, Powell & Bon produced a model and a feasibility study for a residential scheme on the 35 acres of Barbican land which had been bombed out during the war. After some debate on the implications of adopting such a project on London's most expensive land, the final scheme was ready in 1959 and building began shortly afterwards. The first block of flats to be completed was Speed House (1968). The City of London School for Girls followed (1968); then the Museum of London (1976), the Guildhall School of Music and Drama (1977), and the Barbican Arts Centre (1982). The dream of Duncan Sandys, Minister of Housing in the 1950s, had come true: he had urged the Lord Mayor to create 'a genuine residential neighbourhood incorporating schools, shops, open spaces and amenities even if this means foregoing a more remunerative return on the land'.

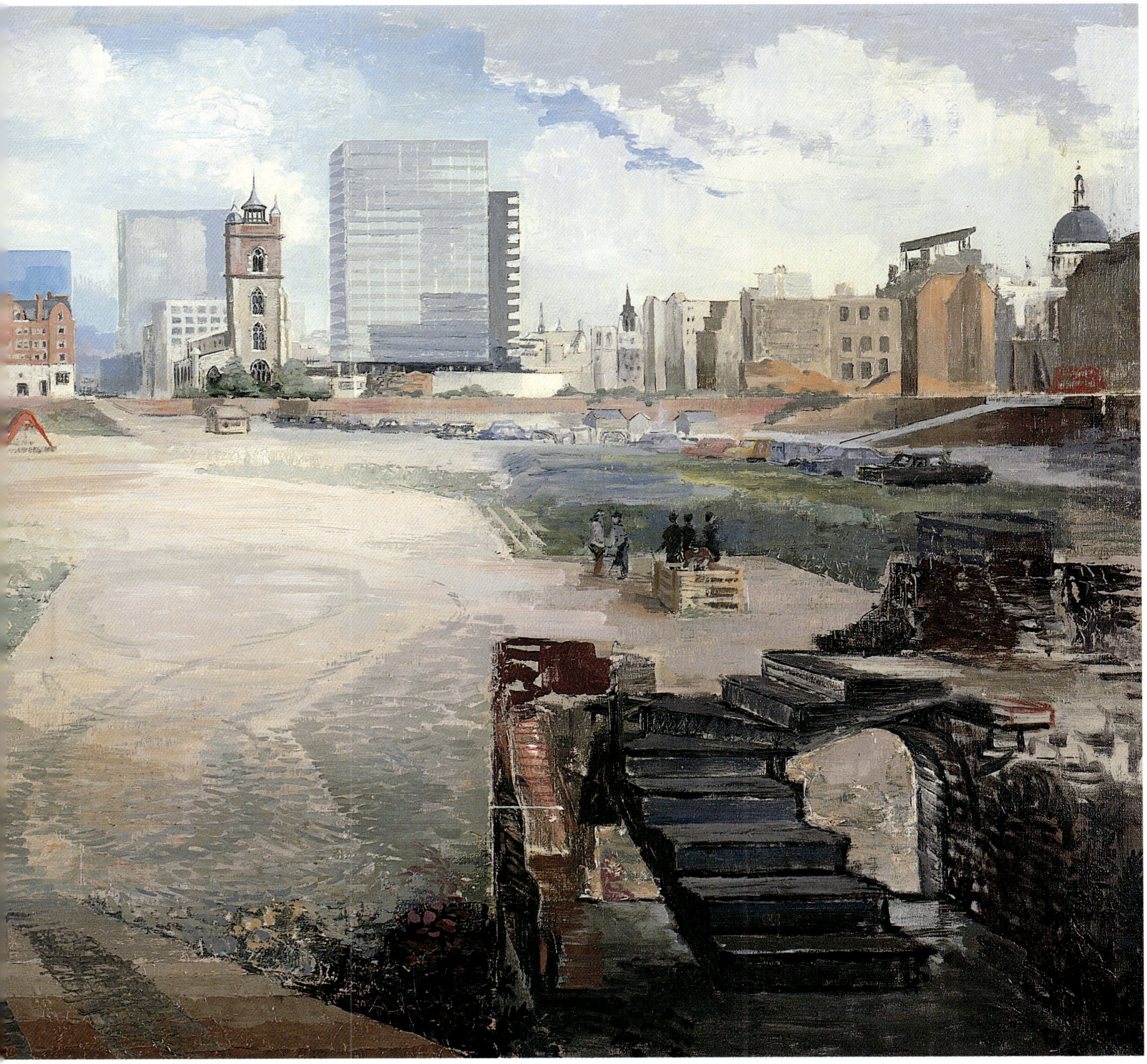

For the appearance of the St Giles Cripplegate area shortly after the end of the Second World War, see the painting by B. A. R. Carter (cat. no. 195), and for the appearance of the area as it is today, see the painting by Richard Walker (next entry).

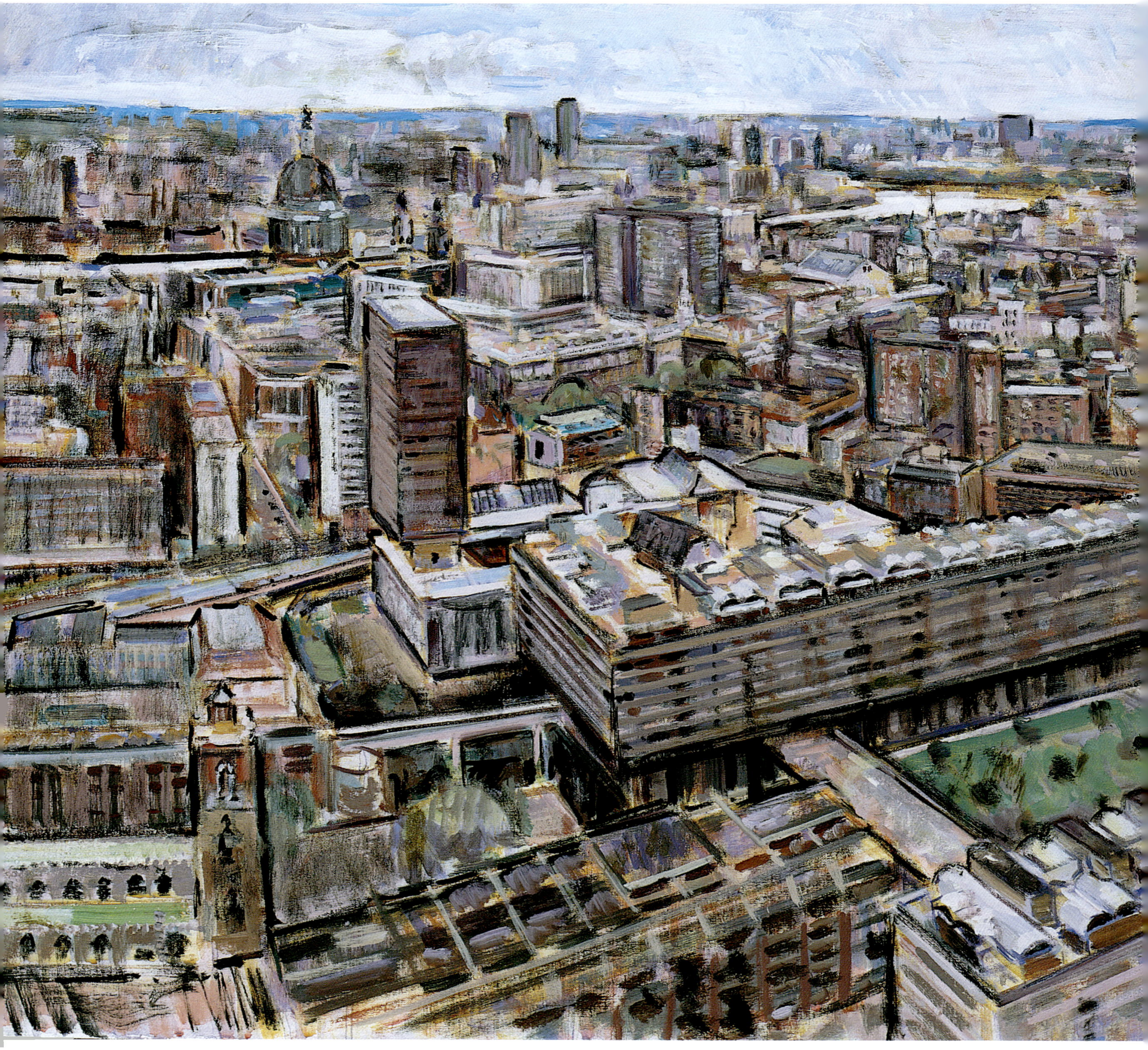

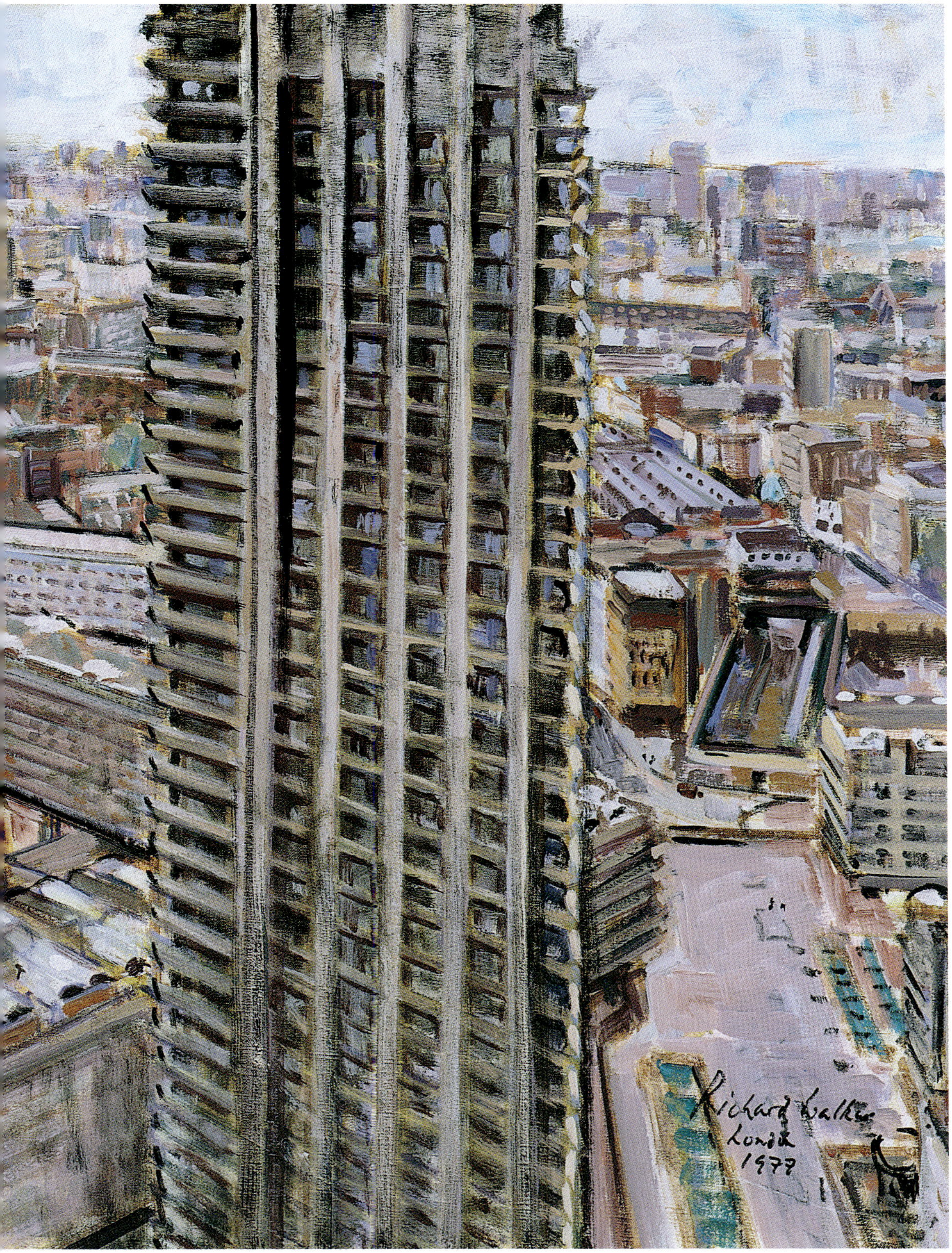

211.

RICHARD I. B. WALKER

(born 1925)

London from Cromwell Tower, Barbican

[78.158]

1977

Oil on canvas,

61.5 x 121.8 cm

Signed and dated bottom right: *Richard Walker/London/1977*

Provenance:
Purchased from the artist in 1978.

THIS PANORAMIC view of the City is taken from a 'small and rather precarious balcony' on the top floor of Cromwell Tower, Barbican Estate, looking south-west. The artist, who is afraid of heights, explains: 'at first [I] strapped the easel, etc., plus, I think, myself, and ominously-flapping canvas, to my available anchorages'. The following landmarks are clearly identifiable: the Barbican Estate in the bottom half of the painting with Shakespeare Tower on the right and the church of St Giles Cripplegate in the bottom left corner. Above the church tower and slightly to the right is Bastion House, next to it, the Museum of London (with its pitched glass roof) and the green roof of St Botolph's Aldersgate. Beyond is the General Post Office and, just discernible, the spire of Christ Church, Newgate. Farther to the right may be seen the green dome of the Old Bailey. The dome of St Paul's Cathedral is placed above Bastion House, but slightly to the left, with the river running across (the bend of the river at Waterloo Bridge is clearly visible). On the right-hand side the Barbican tube station and the railway tracks of the Circle and Metropolitan Lines are clearly shown.

This painting contrasts with the other two views of the Barbican site in the Museum's collection (see previous entry, and cat. no. 195). All three paintings provide a lucid chronicle of the development of this area in the second half of the twentieth century.

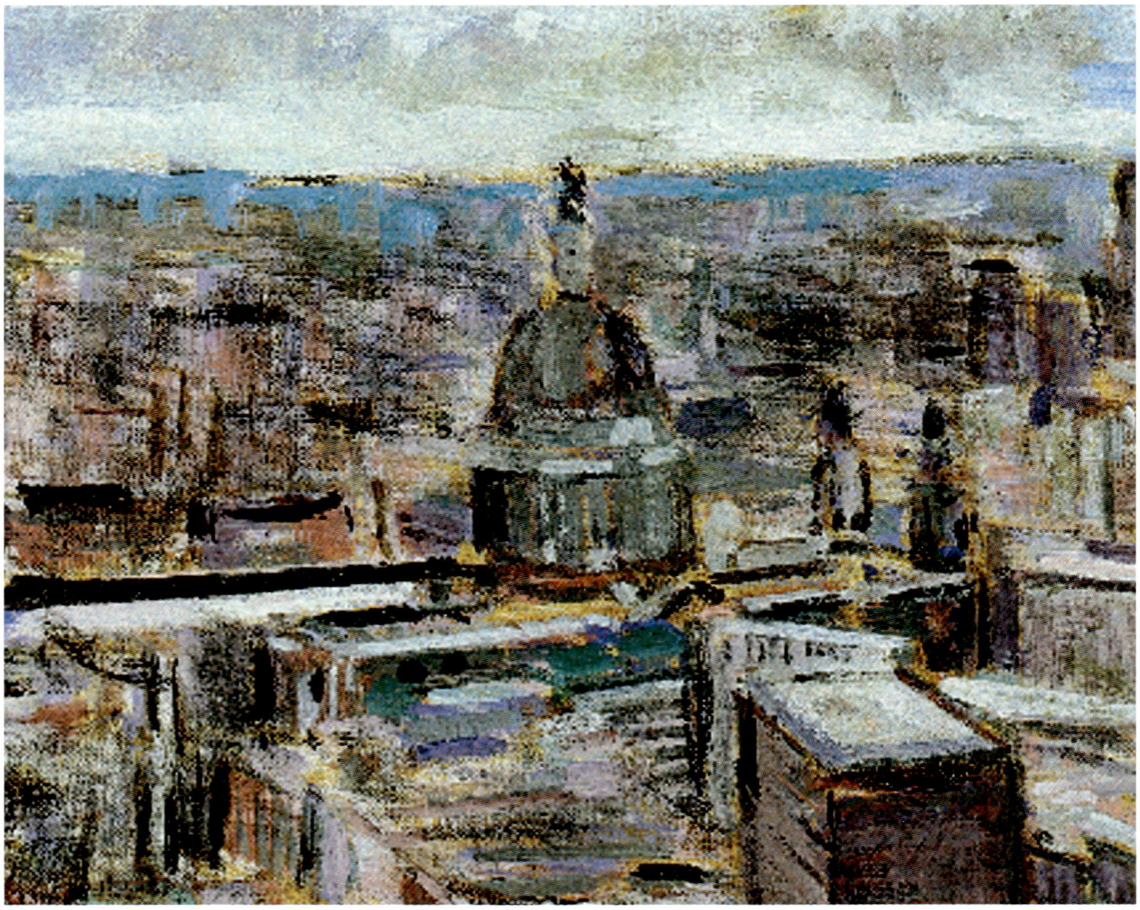

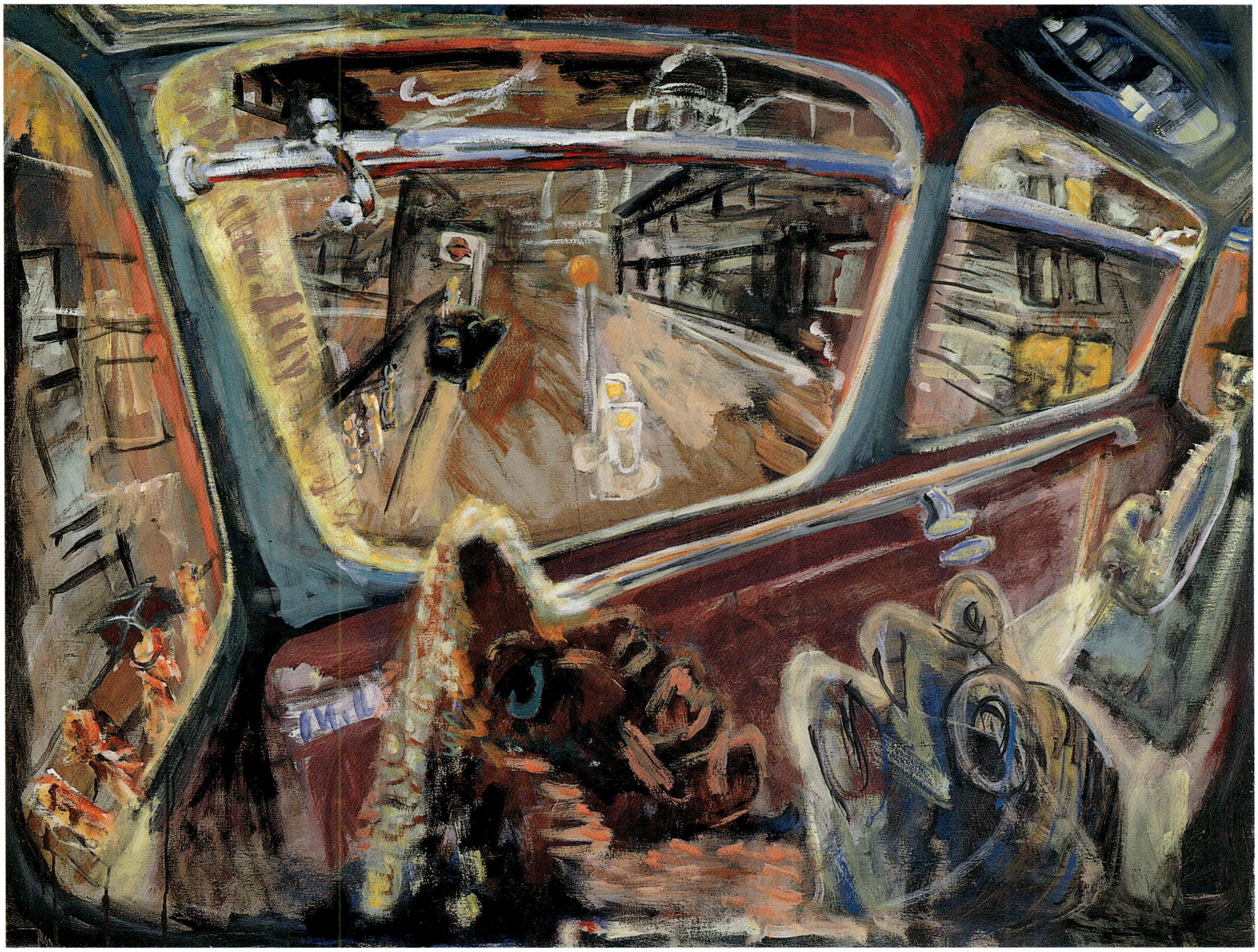

212.
TIMOTHY HYMAN
(born 1946)
Night Bus* [94.165/1]
1981–5
Oil on canvas, 91.2 x 121.5 cm
Not signed or dated

213.
TIMOTHY HYMAN
(born 1946)
At Barbican Station* [94.165/2]
1991–3
Oil on board, 59 x 45.5 cm
Not signed or dated

BOTH WORKS developed from the time when the artist commuted between his studio in the Barbican and Soho, where he lived, often by bus or using the Barbican tube station. Both offer a reflection on public transport in London: the vision of a piece of pure landscape in the romantic light of the moon, or the buzz of a speedy ride in the artificial glow of the capital. Although the two paintings were conceived at around the same time, the ten-year gap between the two works is due to the difficulty the artist had with the Barbican tube station work. He has thus described the two paintings:

Provenance:
Purchased from the artist in 1994.

Bibliography:
Timothy Hyman, Recent Work, exhibition catalogue, Austin/Desmond Fine Art, 1990, no. 23.

Night Bus

This was among the first pictures I began, on moving back into London, after an eleven-year stint in a Sussex village. But I grew up in London and all my life I've loved the powerful spatial sensations on the top of the bus: the sense of being uncontrollably lurched forward (no driver visible) as though entirely in the hands of headlong fate. (AMOR FATI could be a subtitle.)

Rushing often between the Barbican studio and a Soho flat, I was often struck by the imprint of St Paul's dome through the picture-window. I also made small drawings of street furniture (lamps, bus-stops) and figures as they rushed past. And the picture became about my new relationship with Judith (we are the foreground figures) and the sense of participating together in some hilarious/infernal nocturnal adventure – with fear and laughter combined (our shared relish for London has been a component in our marriage).

I thought it complete in 1982, but reworked it sporadically in subsequent years, finally completing the frame in 1985.

It was exhibited briefly at Blond, and again at Austin/Desmond in 1990 (where it was illustrated in the catalogue).

At Barbican Station

The experience that generated the picture dates from 1985. I was then working at Barbican Arts Group Studios. One evening, going a little further along the platform than usual, I was astonished by the saw-edged towers rising up, and started to draw. Half an hour (and several tube trains) later, the moon appeared.

But although the idea seemed urgent and real, the small horizontal canvas I made based on those drawings never quite took fire. Eventually (about 1990) I destroyed it. But a few months later, rediscovering those first drawings, I felt impelled to make another attempt – this time on a vertical board, which would give more emphasis to the verticality of the towers and the cross-like fluorescent light above.

Many more 'problems' remained – I returned again and again to the various areas of blue sky, which seemed to make their own unexpected demands if they were to be read at all. The figure (a kind of self) was also a problem – I didn't want it to be sentimental. I had to make the angle of the left hand platform steeper. And so on. Eventually I 'completed' it near the end of November 1993, and took it out to India (where it was framed) to be first exhibited in Bombay in Jan 1994.

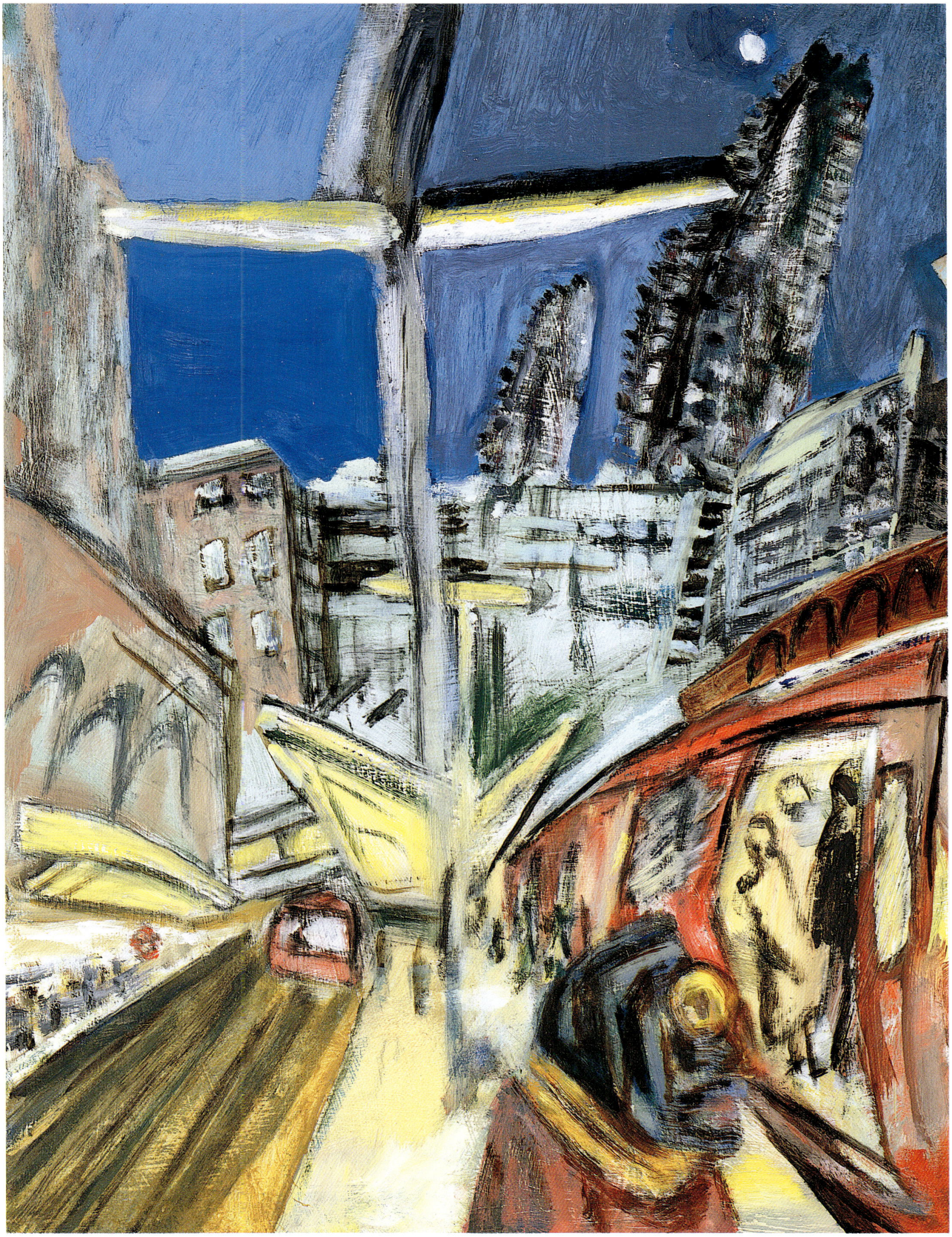

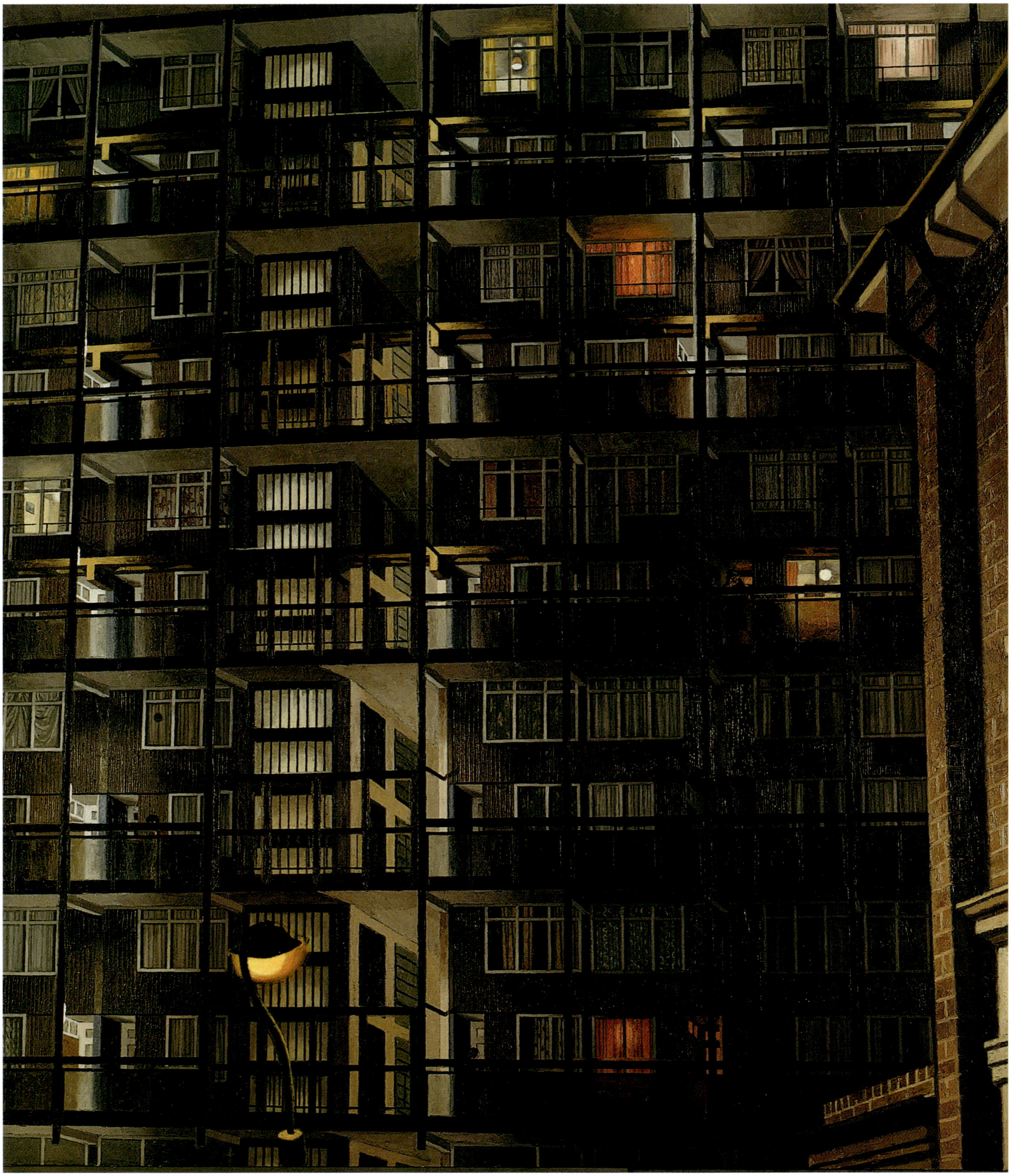

214.

DAVID HEPHER
(born 1935)

Camberwell Nocturne* [92.2]
1984
Oil on canvas, 242.3 x 212 cm
Not signed or dated. Title written on the stretcher on the back

THIS PAINTING is a close-up view of Habington block on the Elmington Estate. The view is taken from Sears Street, Camberwell Green, at night-time. It forms part of a series which evolved between 1983/4 and 1986/9 and which culminated in works based on Piranesi's *Carceri d'Invenzioni*, blending tower blocks and medieval-style prisons:

> When I paint the blocks, I do not see them as prisons, any more than I do Piranesi's etchings. I cannot escape the irony of what they represent, but to me they can be curiously beautiful. Powerful and menacing, like the north face of the Eiger by day; transformed, a mass of coloured lights against a velvet sky by night.

Camberwell Nocturne is such a night view. The combination of the close-up view and the artificial lighting silhouetting the intricate lines of the housing block makes for a strikingly beautiful and heroic image.

The architecture of the tower block is made to come to life and the artist's vision challenges the usual perception of flat, undifferentiated surfaces.

> The English have never understood true metropolitan apartment living in the European sense, where such concepts were born. And many critics seem unable to divorce the consequence of that failure in human terms from a purely aesthetic judgement based on a building's individual merits and atmosphere.

The theme of housing estates is recurrent in the work of many contemporary artists. The low-life back-to-backs of the Victorian era were replaced by the dream of the vertical village, until the 1968 Ronan Point disaster helped to alert planners to the dangers of high-rise living as well as to hostile public opinion. On 18 May 1968, at 6.00am, a violent gas explosion on the eighteenth floor of the twenty-three storey block in Newham completely tore down one side of the building, killing four people and making eighty families homeless. Subsequent structural and fire tests revealed that Ronan Point and other 'sister' tower blocks built on the same principles were unsafe. In 1984 about 600 residents living in eight tower blocks had to be rehoused. Ronan Point was finally demolished in 1986. By contrast, the blocks on the Elmington Estate were refurbished a few years ago and 1996-7 is the first year that the estate is managed by the Council, under contract, which was won through a tendering process against a private company.

When tackling this theme, artists have on one hand reinforced the idea of inhuman housing conditions and on the other been attracted to the striking plastic qualities of the tower block (also see cat. no. 221).

Provenance:
Purchased from the Flowers East Gallery in 1992 with a grant from the National Art Collections Fund.

Bibliography:
Piranesi's Prisons, A Perspective, exhibition catalogue, Graves Art Gallery, 1988, pp18–19; *David Hepher New Paintings*, exhibition catalogue, Flowers East, 1989; Edward Lucie-Smith, *David Hepher*, 1996.

Exhibited:
Graves Art Gallery and Flowers East (see above); *The Subjective City*, Barbican Centre, 1991; *Streets in the Sky, the Paintings of David Hepher*, Museum of London, 1996.

Provenance:
Purchased from the artist in 1985.

Bibliography:
Oliver Bevan – The Farringdon Paintings, exhibition catalogue, Rochdale Art Gallery, 1983; *Witnesses and Dreamers*, exhibition catalogue, various venues (including the Museum of London), 1993.

Exhibited:
'Oliver Bevan: Inner City Paintings', Odette Gilbert Gallery, 1984.

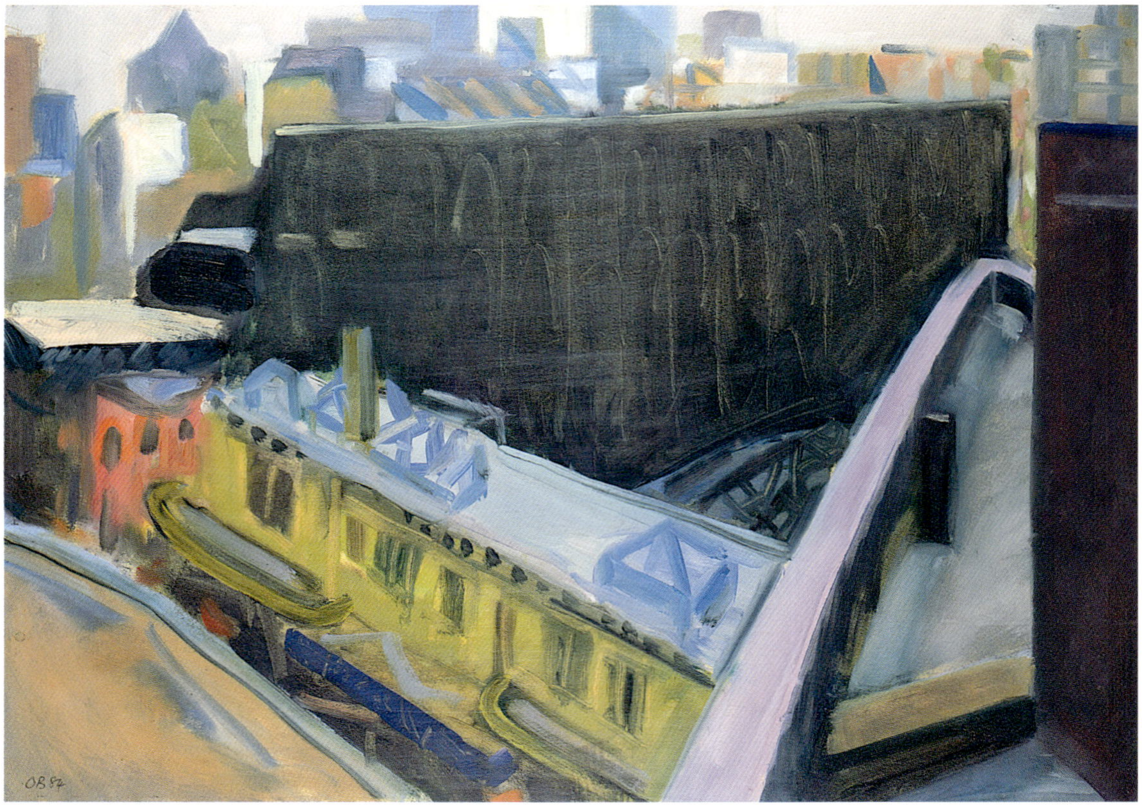

215.

OLIVER BEVAN

(born 1941)

Station Facade [85.38]
1984
Oil on paper, 46.4 x 65.5 cm
Initialed and dated bottom left: *OB84*

THIS BIRD'S-EYE view of Farringdon Station was taken from the artist's fourth-floor studio (above an ironmonger's shop) at 62 Cowcross Street. The rail tracks can be seen behind and below the yellow brick building which is the station's main entrance; at the back is the wall of a derelict railway building which used to flank the east side of Farringdon Road, replaced in the 1980s by an office building.

In 1979, when the artist returned to London after spending two years in Canada, he wrote:

> I seemed to see the city for the first time – I had lived there for seventeen years – it was unimaginably dense, energetic and strange. I used a camera to record weird window displays, front gardens, holes in the road . . . before eventually taking a lease on a studio high above Farringdon Station. It felt like the centre of the universe, so intense was the activity down below. Within months the first of my city paintings emerged, an awkward stew of features derived from views from the studio windows assembled like a collage because I was trying to hang on to my first love – abstraction.

During the period in which *Station Facade* was completed, the artist achieved a greater degree of clarity and fought less against the realism which was to become a feature of the later paintings (see below).

216.

PETER SNOW

(born 1927)

The Passing World [95.538]

1985

Oil on Sundeala (Swedish board),

136.8 x 122 cm

Not signed or dated

THIS NIGHT view of Cleaver Square in South London, seen beyond Kennington Park Road (in the foreground), is taken from the artist's window. The painting shows the domestic cosiness of people's lit windows and by contrast the blue, cold, even dangerous beauty of the streets beyond. It also contrasts the reassurance of the main road, busy with traffic, with the remote eeriness of the residential streets behind. The use of space reinforces the presence of two worlds, one warm, alive and safe which is near; the other, at some distance, is attractive, but inert and mysterious.

Provenance:
Purchased from the artist in 1995.

Bibliography:
Peter Snow – Retrospective, exhibition catalogue, Morley Gallery, 1995.

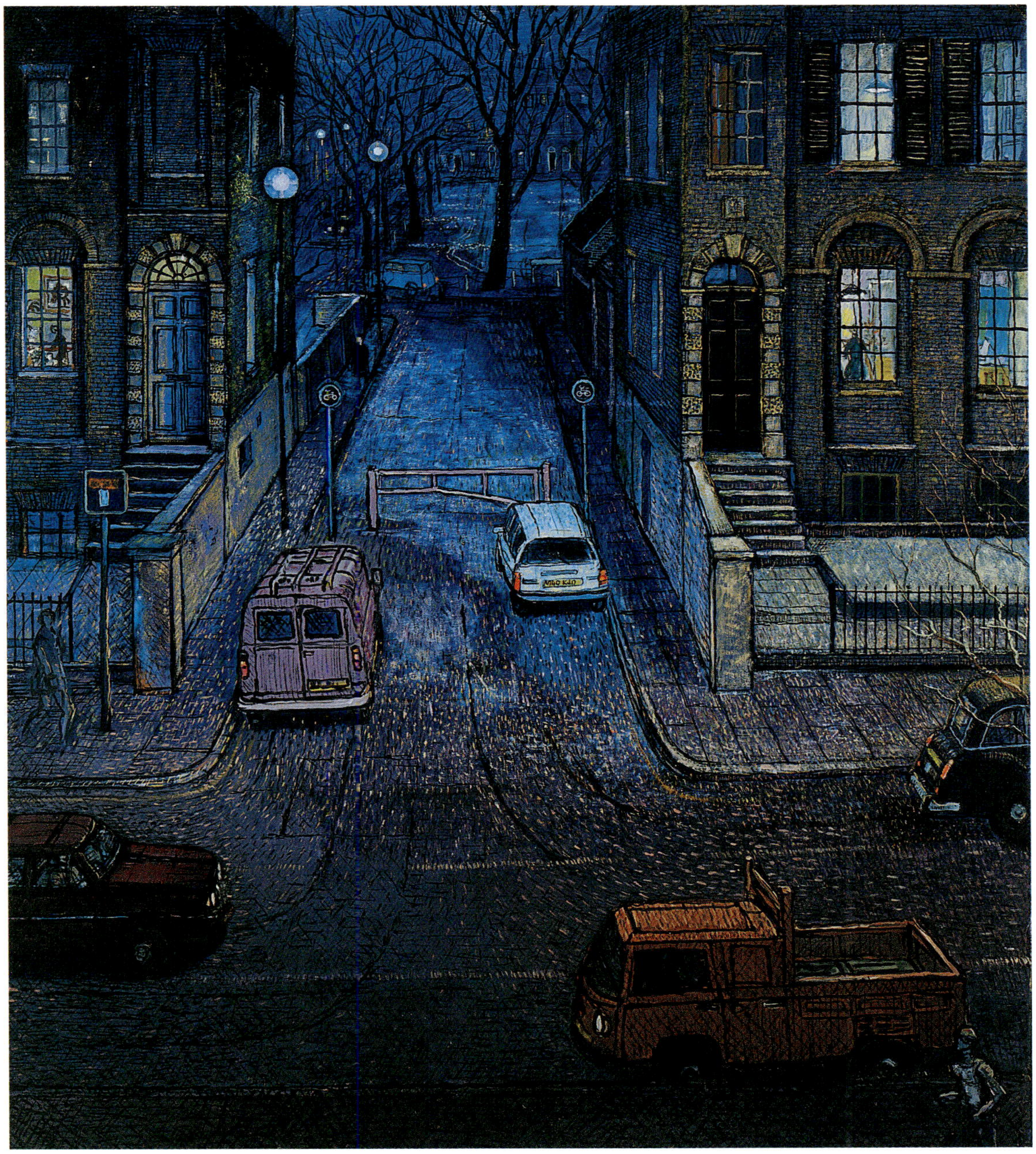

By some apt coincidence the artist lives just across the road from the City & Guilds of London Art School (on the right). The school occupies a complete terrace of six eighteenth-century houses and is rather undistinguishable from its residential neighbours. This art school was created by the City & Guilds of London Institute in 1879 as an extension of the Lambeth School of Art. In 1971 the City & Guilds of London Institute stopped its financial support and the school subsequently became independent with charitable status.

In the painting the traffic, often nose-to-tail during rush hour, is fluid. The vehicles depicted are for the most part very utilitarian – a taxi, three vans in all, an estate car. This particular corner of London is rich in traffic signals (more utilitarian detail), the very things one would leave out of a photograph, given half a chance: a dead-end sign, two cyclist signs, a 'no-entry' barrier, yellow lines. Yet the scene glitters, as if touched by magic – the million and one paint strokes of ochre, white, yellow, mauve and green shimmer against the blue-purple night. Two factors unify this environment, which could potentially be viewed as an accumulation of disparate fragments: the strong spatial composition of the painting (the all-encompassing aerial view and the strong vertical and horizontal axes) as well as the light.

Peter Snow has written to the Museum explaining the original impulse behind painting the scene, as well as exploring some of the art historical connections the painter of London can make with the rest of the world:

> The picture was painted, because I was excited by the light at night-time on the bricks and houses in Kennington Park Rd and the dark square (Cleaver Square) beyond. There is neon and electricity and ordinary lamplight from the interior of the houses and art school . . . I particularly love Vermeer and the Japanese print makers – Utamaro, Hiroshige, Kunisada, Hokusai etc of Edo (Old Tokyo), where their prints were especially famous and popular. These are a sort of a dream of an area (a pleasure district). Much life is going on in the street – puppet sellers, prostitutes, geisha girls, sellers of goods etc. It is *moving* city life and we can watch what is going on in the street and in the houses like voyeurs. Similarly I love Dutch painting (like that of Pieter de Hooch) with its interlinked rooms. I often visit Utrecht, Amsterdam and the Hague. One watches what is happening inside, yet all is kept out by windows of glass, walls, fences, railings, manners! The name of this experience is UKIYOIE. I have in my studio a print of Vermeer's painting of Delft in which the bricks, doorways and windows make a surface which is 'alive' (curiously it reminds me too of Mondrian). I think that most painting, whether figurative or non-figurative, is abstract. That is, the process generally includes a taking apart and putting together again in order to form an organised, emotional and structural aesthetic.

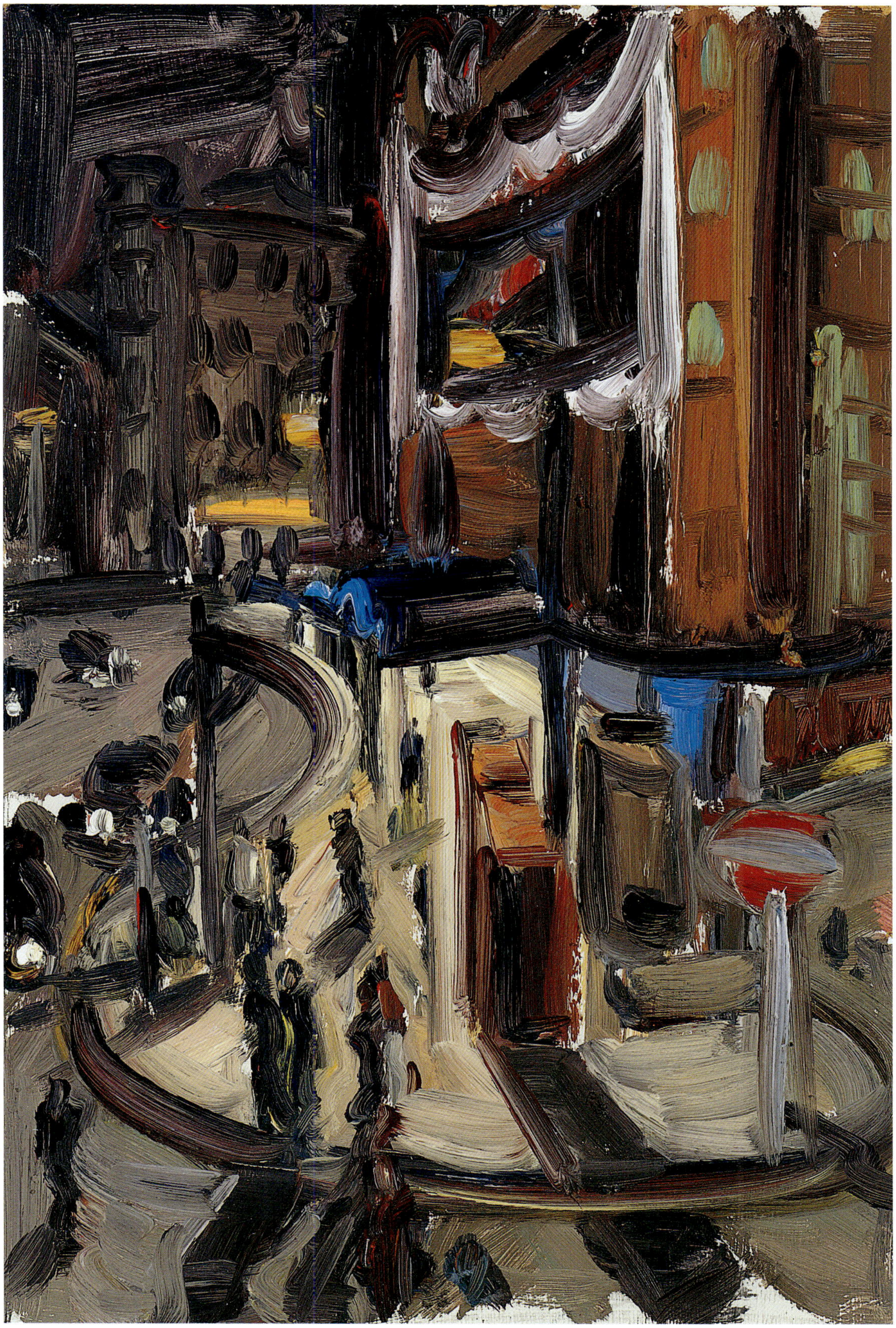

217.
PETER SAUNDERS
(born 1940)
Cambridge Circus [93.4]
1987
Oil on board,
40 x 27.2 cm
Not signed or dated
Label on reverse gives artist's address in Deptford

Provenance:
Purchased from the artist in 1993.

Exhibited:
One-man show at Cadogan Contemporaries in 1990; the 1990 South Bank Show.

THIS PAINTING of the Palace Theatre at Cambridge Circus was done from drawings taken from the first-floor window of the pub opposite, The Cambridge, revealing the gracious way in which the pavement lines used to echo the sweeping curve of the facade. The pavement subsequently lost this aesthetic refinement after being redesigned to accommodate a greater number of pedestrians. The painting, by night, is most evocative of London's theatreland and conveys the excitement and the lights of theatre-going in the West End.

London by night is a recurrent theme in the work of Peter Saunders. He has also painted Blackheath and Soho at night-time.

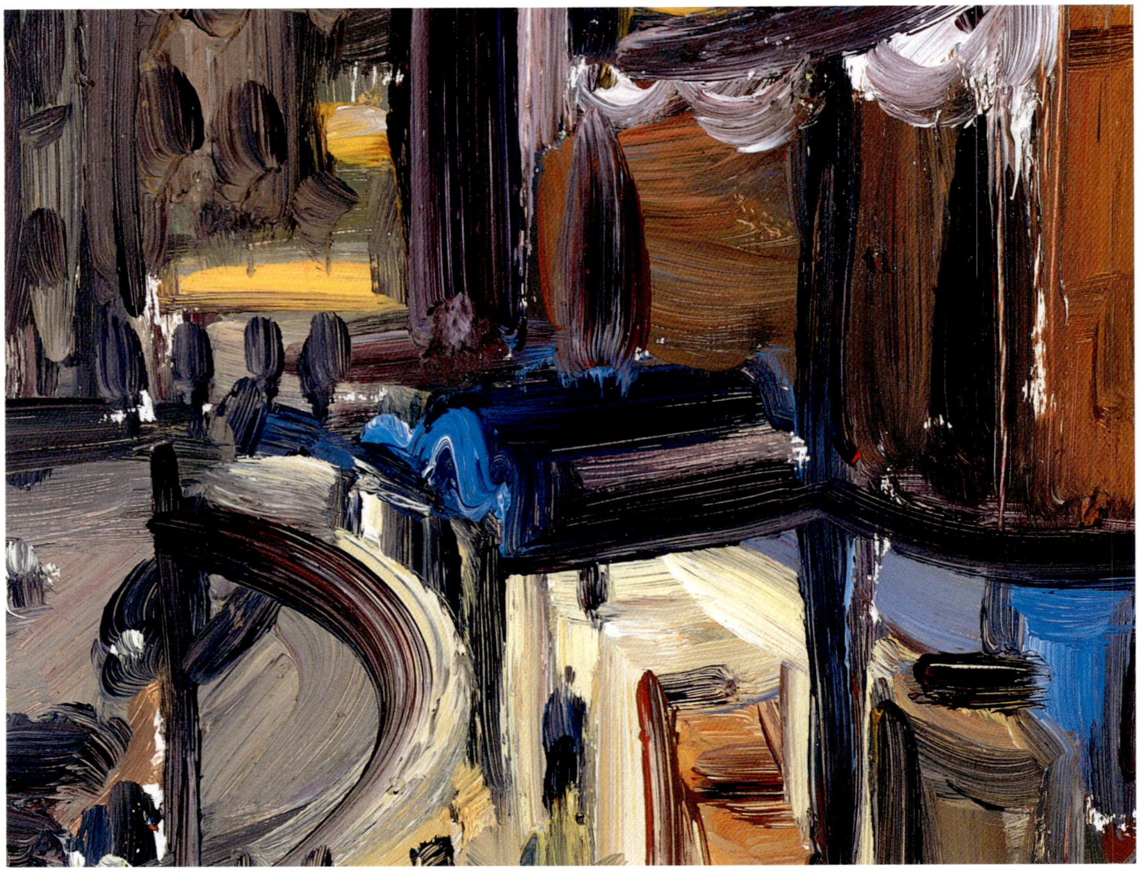

218.

BRIAN YALE

(born 1936)

The Monument [96.52]

1987

Acrylic on canvas, 139 x 88.7 cm

Signed and dated bottom right:

BRIAN YALE 1987

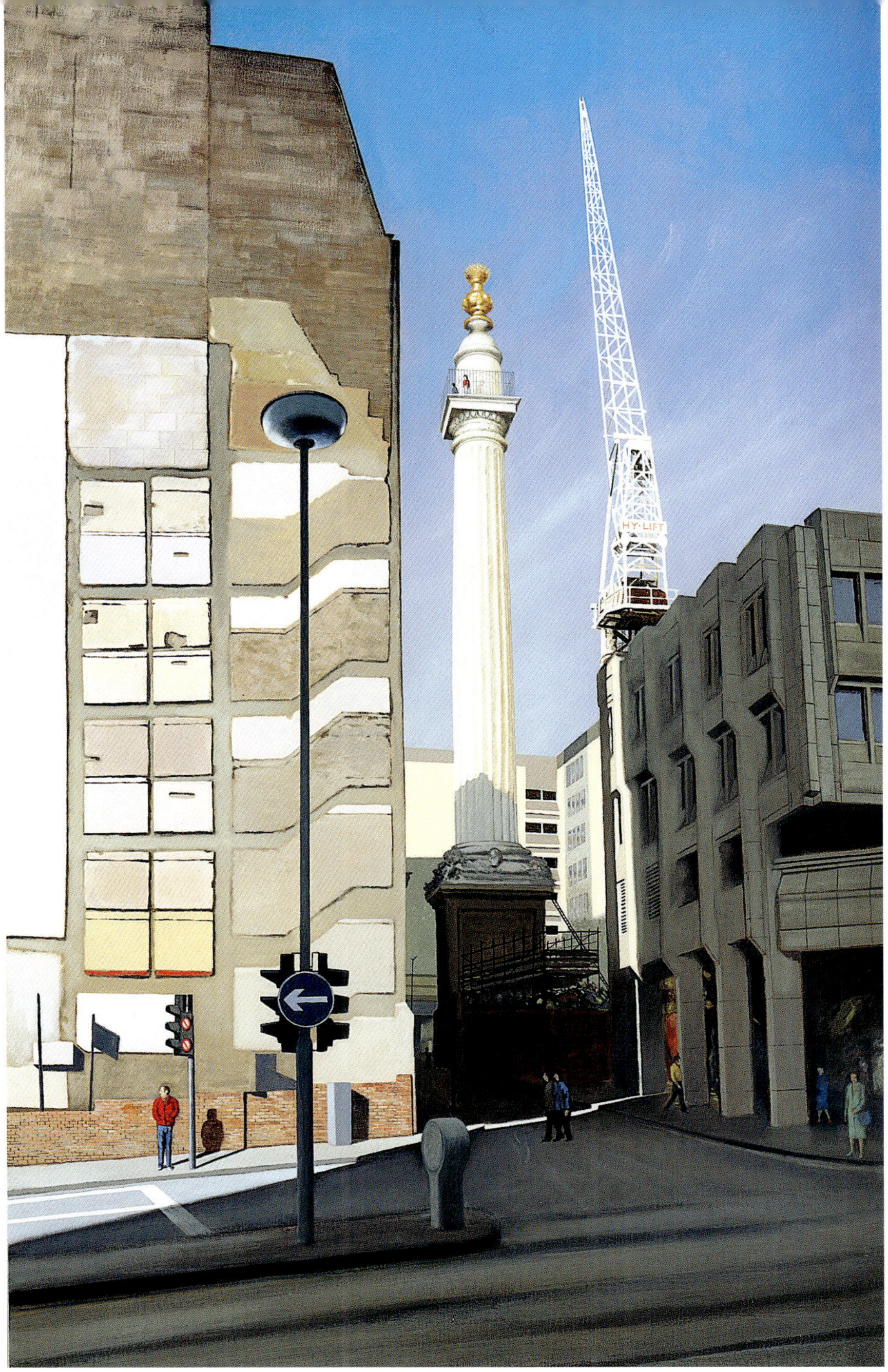

THE VIEW, taken from Lower Thames Street, shows Fish Street Hill leading up to the Monument. The painter was attracted by the contrast between old and new architecture as well as the juxtaposition of a derelict site and a crane with one of London's most famous landmarks. He chose a quiet weekend to depict the scene.

The Monument was erected after a design by Christopher Wren, between 1671 and 1677, by Act of Parliament, to commemorate the Great Fire of London. Constructed of Portland stone, it measures 202 feet and is the tallest single stone column in the world. A gilt-bronze urn with burning flames crowns its summit and the balcony beneath is reached by a spiral staircase of 311 steps. Despite his great fear, James Boswell visited the Monument in 1762, only to find that he was horrified by such great height. This painting is a poignant reminder of the dramatic change of scale in the twentieth century. This tallest of all columns appears dwarfed on the left by a derelict building and on the right by a crane.

The grey block on the right is Centurion House, while the crane behind it occupies the site of the office block which has now become 24 Monument Street. The bomb-damaged building on the left abutted a large block known as Regis House (built in the 1930s) with its main frontage on King William Street (a *c.*1970 photograph in the Guildhall Library shows Regis House and the position of the derelict building, ref. A335/11). Regis House was bomb-damaged during the war and later refurbished.

Since 1974 when planning permission was granted, the City of London Real Property Co Ltd has been trying to redevelop the site as a complex of offices, shops and licensed premises. The scheme, however, was only able to proceed recently (around 1995) and is a thriving building site at the time of writing (1996).

Provenance:
Presented by the artist in 1996.

Bibliography:
Hazel Harrison, *The Encyclopedia of Acrylic Techniques*, Australia, 1994.

Exhibited:
Thackeray Gallery, London, 1987; The Ogle Gallery, Cheltenham, showed it at the London Contemporary Art Fair in 1990.

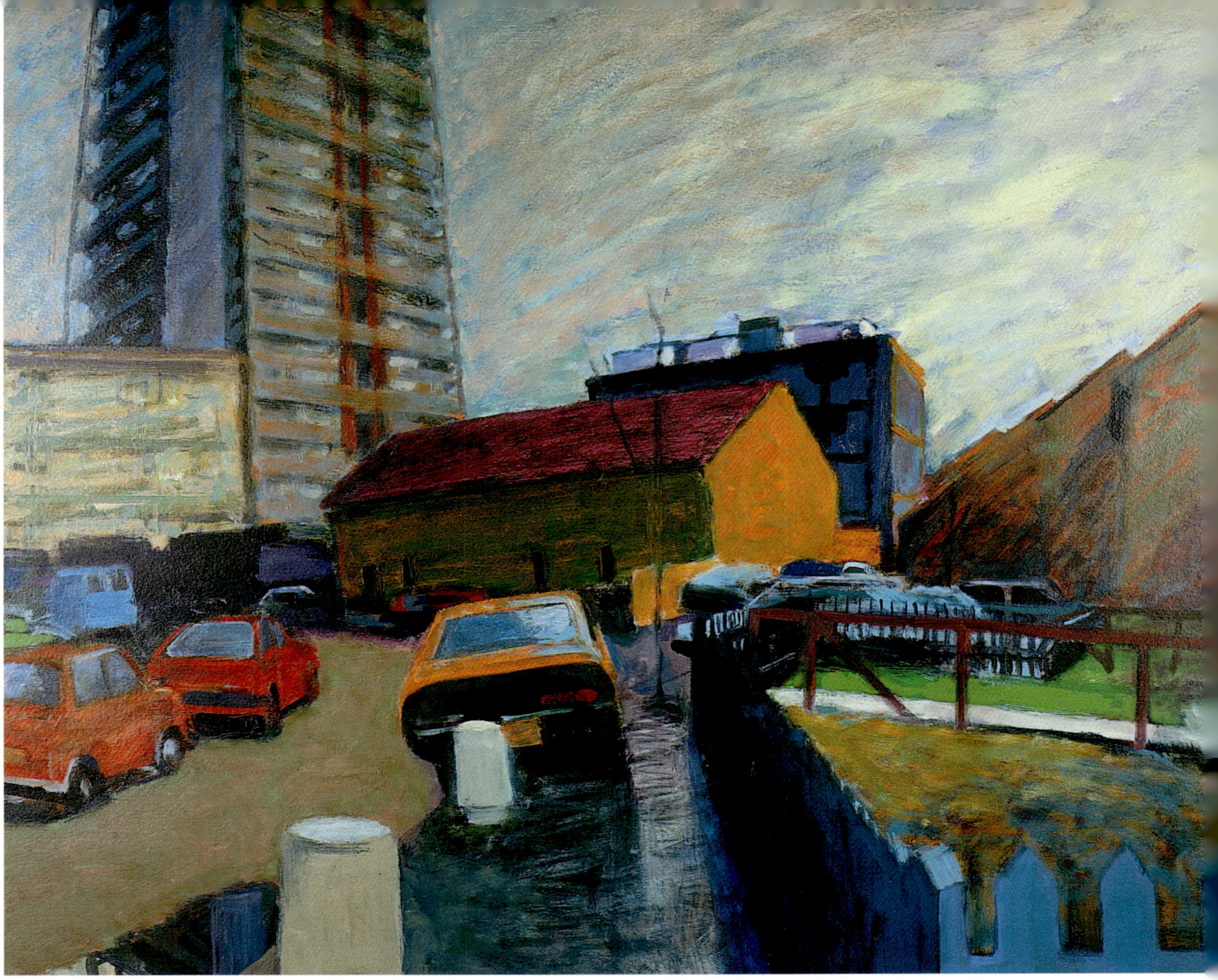

Provenance:
Purchased from the artist in 1989.

219.

OLIVER BEVAN

(born 1941)

Elephant and Castle: High Rise, '88* [89.47/1]
1988
Oil on canvas, 75.8 x 101.8 cm
Not signed or dated

THIS VIEW was taken on the Draper Estate near Hampton Street, at the Elephant and Castle. The painter has positioned himself in Howell Walk with Clock Place behind him and is looking at Draper House, the twenty-five-storey tower block (and the tallest block of flats in London at the time of its construction), with a medium-sized block on the left, Sherston Court, and single-storey accommodation on the right.

The Draper Estate, designed by Hubert Bennett and Kenneth J. Campbell, was built by Wates Ltd and formed an intrinsic part of the Elephant and Castle redevelopment in the 1960s, dubbed 'Piccadilly Circus at the Elephant' by the *Evening Standard* on 21 March 1947. In July 1958 the LCC Town Planning and Housing Committee had approved proposals for stage one of the estate envisaged to provide 194 dwellings (the tower block shown here contained eighty-eight maisonettes and fifty-two flats); the 'topping out' ceremony of Draper House took place in December 1963 and tenants started occupying the flats in February 1964. Oliver Bevan writes:

> I was attracted by the red columns that run right up through the building forming a landmark visible for miles around, and by the idea of taking in a very wide angle of view and all the distortion that it entails. When David Hepher painted that same building [*Walworth Flats,* 1977], he accounted meticulously for every detail. I wanted to answer him with a more expressive, more atmospheric version.

220.

SHARON BEAVAN

(born 1956)

Angel [91.182]

1989

Oil on canvas, 101 x 131 cm

Not signed or dated

THIS VIEW is taken from above Wakley Street looking down the junction of City Road and Goswell Road with the Angel tube station on the right (being redeveloped) and Pentonville Road stretching beyond. *Angel* captures late twentieth-century life, the colours and the energy of the street in a central London borough. The scene echoes the 1823 aerial lithograph of Cheapside in the collection, a classic display of vehicles and their impact in the street (acc. no. A18153 by Duryer/Baynes). Some 170 years on, *Angel* not only conjures up the state of traffic in the capital, but also its relationship to the fabric of London, in the extraordinary mixture of Victorian buildings and modern office blocks, with the familiar building site, complete with a forest of cranes, foundations and scaffolding.

Provenance:
Purchased from Le Chat Noir Gallery, Covent Garden, in 1991.

Bibliography:
On the Streets – A View of the Urban Landscape, exhibition catalogue, Ipswich Borough Museums & Galleries, 1991.

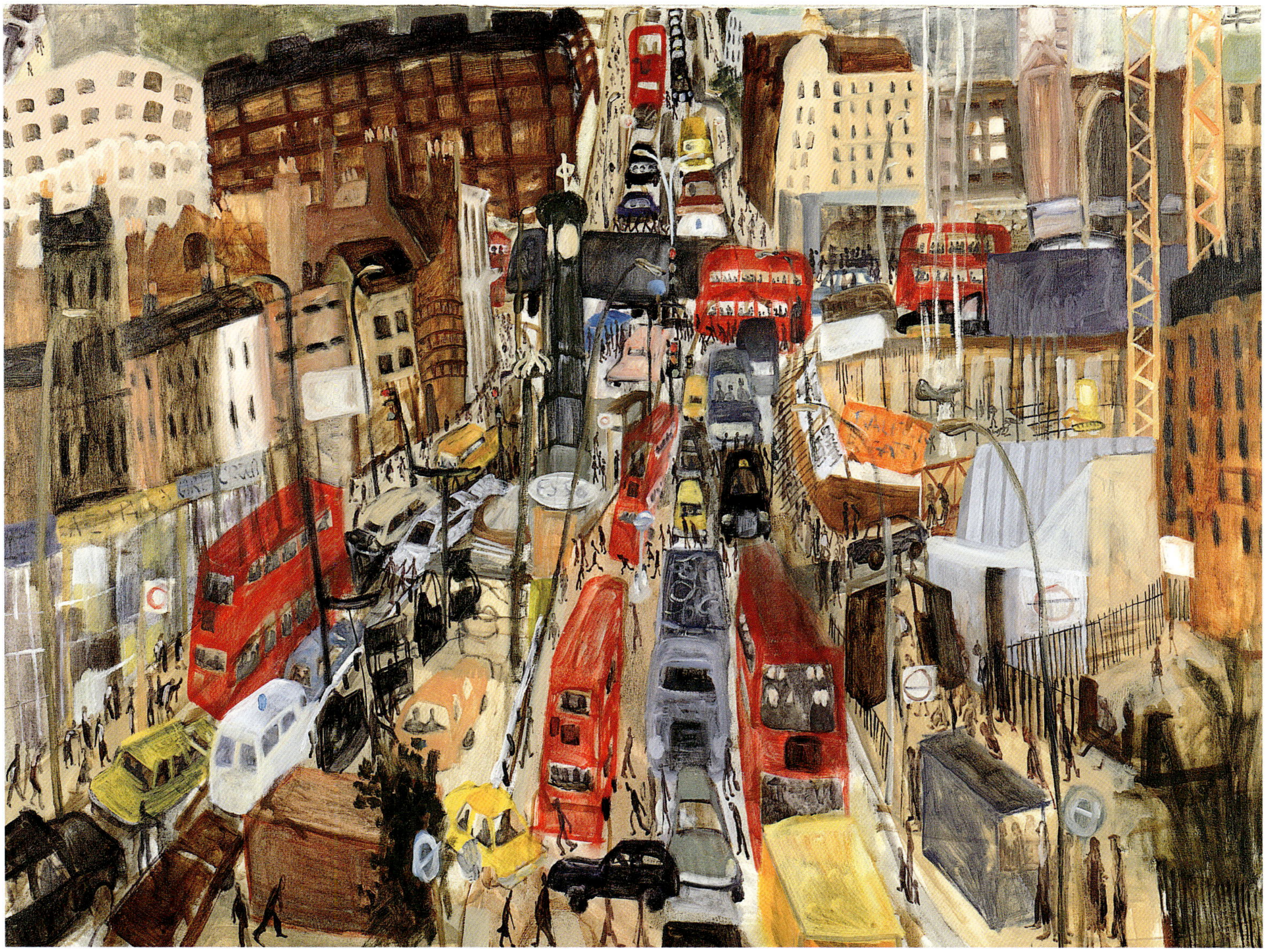

Provenance:
Purchased from the artist in 1992 with help from the MGC/V&A Purchase Grant Fund.

Bibliography:
A Several World, Paintings and Drawings by Julian Perry and Anthony Lowe, exhibition leaflet, Cleveland Gallery, 1991; *A walk through the Marshes, Paintings by Julian Perry*, exhibition leaflet, Austin/Desmond Fine Art, 1996.

221.

JULIAN PERRY

(born 1960)

The Enchanted Castle* [92.91]
1990
Oil on canvas, 146.7 x 107.3 cm
Not signed or dated
On the back: title, artist and telephone number

PERRY SETS out to do an almost impossible task – to make an exciting, positive and even enthusiastic image of a desolate housing block in east London. The result, *The Enchanted Castle*, is indeed a bold and romantic rendering of a composite Hackney council tower block at Clapton Park, London E5.

The context for this painting is the housing scene after 1950. The building of high-rise flats by local authorities was a new departure in the 1950s. It started slowly and between 1953 and 1959 accounted for only nine per cent of local authority building, but in 1966 it reached a peak of twenty-six per cent. High-rise building used in a housing context had come under growing criticism since the early 1960s, and in 1967 the additional subsidy for storeys above six was abolished. These concerns became unmistakably real with the 1968 Ronan Point disaster (see cat. no. 214), which became a symbol for the rejection of tower-block living by both the residents and the architectural profession.

While Julian Perry links his works to some of the great masterpieces from the past (the present title is an 'ironic' reference to the work by Claude Lorrain in the National Gallery and the name of Constable is mentioned several times in the catalogue of his Cleveland Gallery show), what is so striking is the rendering of light, both sensitive and dynamic, and the modernity of Perry's vision.

The artist succeeds in animating the drab vertical lines of the tower block and then the desolate horizontal lines of the surrounding wasteland with both light and wind. The wind is not strong enough to challenge the verticality of the painting, so the trees stand as straight as the buildings they adorn, but the sky, on the other hand, is mottled with large woolly clouds and one can almost feel the wind pushing them through the canvas. Strips of light and shadow, those of the tower and those of the trees, cut across the emptiness of the grass area in the foreground to bring almost organic life to the painting.

The artist sees the work 'raising questions' about the paradox between romanticism and reality. *The Enchanted Castle* is the culmination of a series Perry painted between 1989 and 1991 when, housed by ACME, his studio was in Leytonstone.

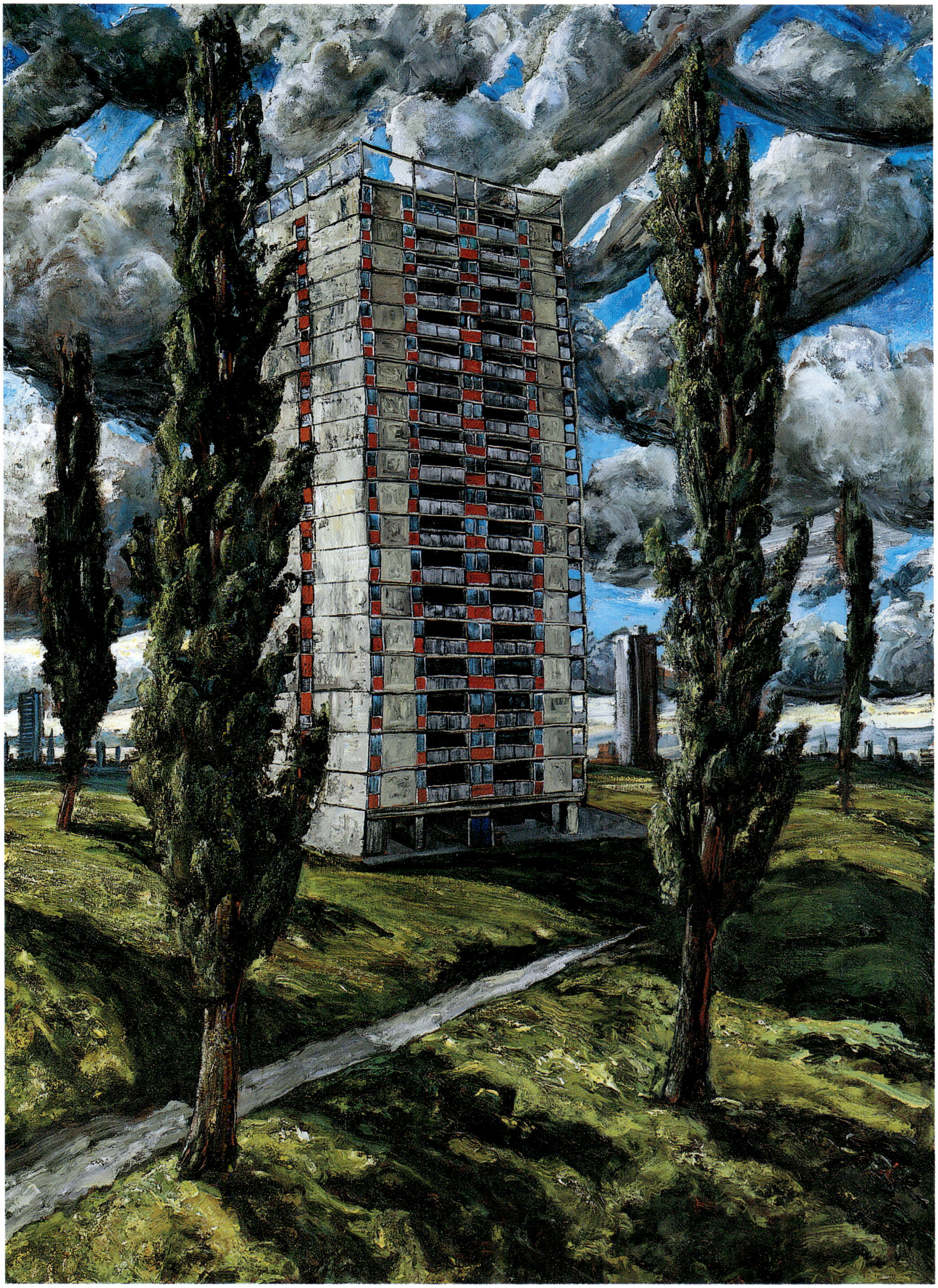

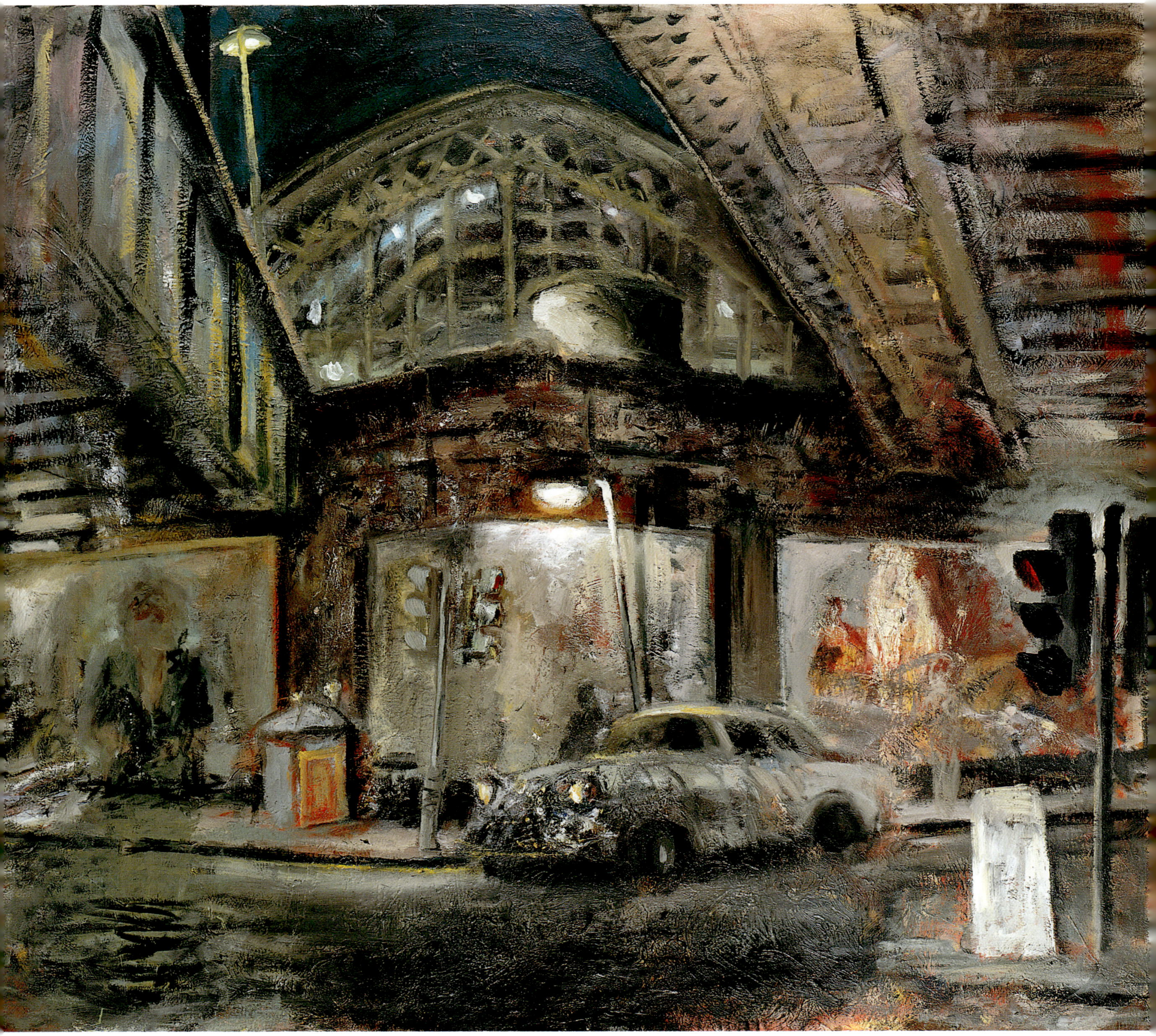

222.
DICK FRENCH
(born 1946)
Under the Bridges [93.41]
1991
Oil on canvas, 152.5 x 183.5 cm
Signed and dated on the back:
Dick French '91

THIS DEEPLY atmospheric night painting features two of the railway bridges over St Pancras Road (Midland Road is on the right) as they converge on the Victorian Gothic gantry of St Pancras Station. A large car, waiting at the lights, is in the centre of a complex transport network of roads and rail tracks; the split-level presentation focuses on the threatening sub-world of life in the shadow of the great station and its bridges.

The work forcefully conveys the 'fallen' energy and seediness of the King's Cross area. Night-time is depicted as an extraordinary mixture of rich and dazzling lights – blue, orange and red, as well as glaring white – which, jewel-like, are set against the dominant infrastructure of the King's Cross/St Pancras complex. The artist blends pseudo-medieval and industrial structures, reminiscent of both American *film noir* and Victorian England. As a result, this London scene can be viewed as an emblematic image of the twentieth-century city.

French went on to paint a series about striptease, perhaps a logical follow-up to the red-light district of *Under the Bridges.* (A painting from this series was highly commended at the 1995 Hunting Art Prizes competition and in 1996 another London painting, *The Waltzer at Hampstead Fair,* won the Hunting Travel Prize.) The artist is drawn to the vitality of crowds – fairgrounds, street markets (Brick Lane) and restaurants. *Under the Bridges*, however, stands out for its absence of people. In a related painting, *Goods Way*, French painted a prostitute, a client and a car (very similar to the one shown here against a gloomy wooden fence). The composition under review initially included a woman on the left-hand side, but she was eventually painted over, the top half of her body incorporated into one of the hoardings. The absence of a figure in *Under the Bridges* prompts the viewer to consider the beauty of a dark, deserted street corner of London in an area noted for its vice patrols and high police presence.

Provenance:
Art Now (Eirlys Tynan), with help from the MGC/V&A Purchase Grant Fund.

Bibliography:
David Lee, 'Dick French' in the *Art Review*, May 1993.

Provenance:
Purchased from the artist in 1992.

Bibliography:
'Poplar, Blackwall and the Isle of Dogs', in *The Survey of London,* vols XLIII and XLIV, 1994; Jeremy Dixon, 'Carl Laubin Portrait', in *Archives d'Architecture Moderne*, no. 40, Brussels, 1989; Kenneth Powell, 'Getting behind the facade', in *Country Life*, 27 June 1991; Roger White, 'Dreamscapes', in *House and Garden*, September 1992.

223.
CARL LAUBIN
(born 1947)
Canary Wharf [92.167]
1991
Oil on canvas, 200 x 150 cm
Not signed or dated

THIS METICULOUSLY painted work shows the unfinished Canary Wharf Tower (Canada House), the second tallest building in Europe and London's landmark for the year 2000. Its walls still partly bear the protective blue plastic sheeting which would be peeled off when the work was finished. Canary Wharf has rapidly become a visual reference point for the capital, in the same league as St Paul's and the Houses of Parliament, symbolising London's change from being church-dominated, to State-ruled, before finally drawing its life force from public commercial enterprise, as was first typified by the Post Office/Telecom Tower.

The viewpoint is taken from the Westferry platform of the Docklands Light Railway (DLR) station. In the foreground the Limehouse link (which opened in April 1993) runs underneath the waste ground. The partly demolished wall is all that remains of a brass foundry and warehouse building (1846–7) which was gutted by fire in 1986. Next is a line of Dock Constable houses (1819) built to house the private police force of the West India Dock Company. On its left is Greig House (originally the annexe of the Scandinavian Sailors Temperance Home) and the West India Dock Excise Office (1807), which became the Jamaica Tavern in 1845, and then in 1926 the Dock Superintendent's Office. In the middle ground on the right is Riverside House, a Salvation Army hostel. There are plans to demolish it. Next to it we have number 1 and number 2 warehouses on the north quay of West India Docks. The oldest surviving dock warehouse buildings in London, they were built by George Gwilt and Son from 1802. Between 1981 and 1987, the Museum of London hoped that they could be secured for their Museum in Docklands.

Unlike most of the images of this grandiose scheme, this painting does not glorify its subject by choosing the perfect viewpoint, but its tight composition shows the dwarfing effect of the scheme on its surroundings while also capturing London's late twentieth-century 'cranomania'.

The artist writes of the birth of his painting:

> I felt that the tallest building in Europe deserved the sort of commemorative treatment that was once common with great architectural and engineering projects such as the construction of Westminster and Blackfriars Bridges. That is why I chose to portray the buildings under construction and in a monumental composition.
> [Letter, June 1992]

> It seemed, and time would appear to have borne this out, that Canary Wharf was the last big fling of the eighties property boom, a very specific time and situation to record, the end of an era... I searched everywhere for 'my' viewpoint, climbing the surrounding half-finished buildings, but without success. I gave up, returned to the light railway and left. But I took the wrong line and had to change at Westferry to go back. When I stepped on to the platform, there was 'my' view, with the added benefit of the warehouses and Customs House which I had not foreseen!
> [Letter, 20 October, 1992]

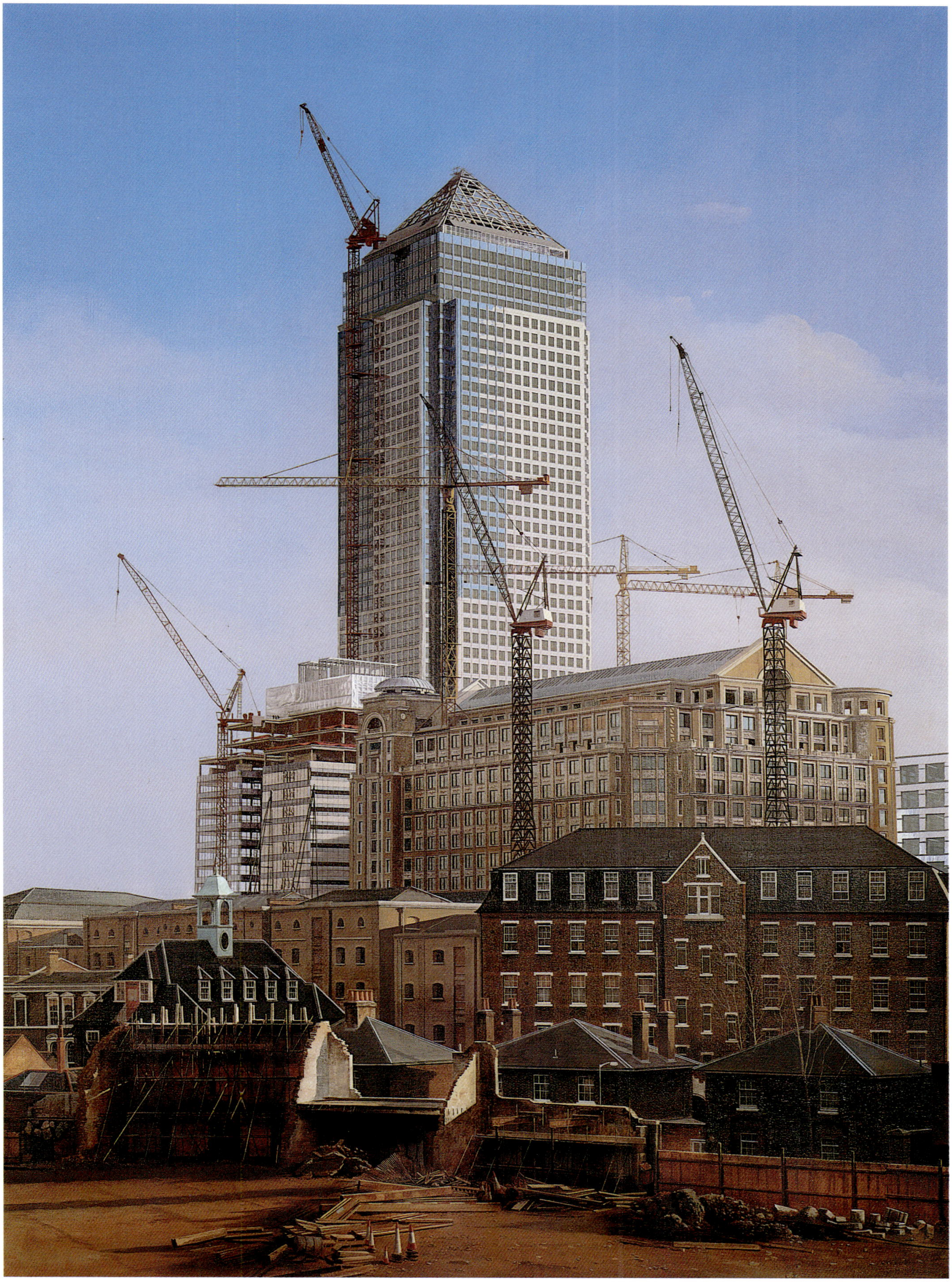

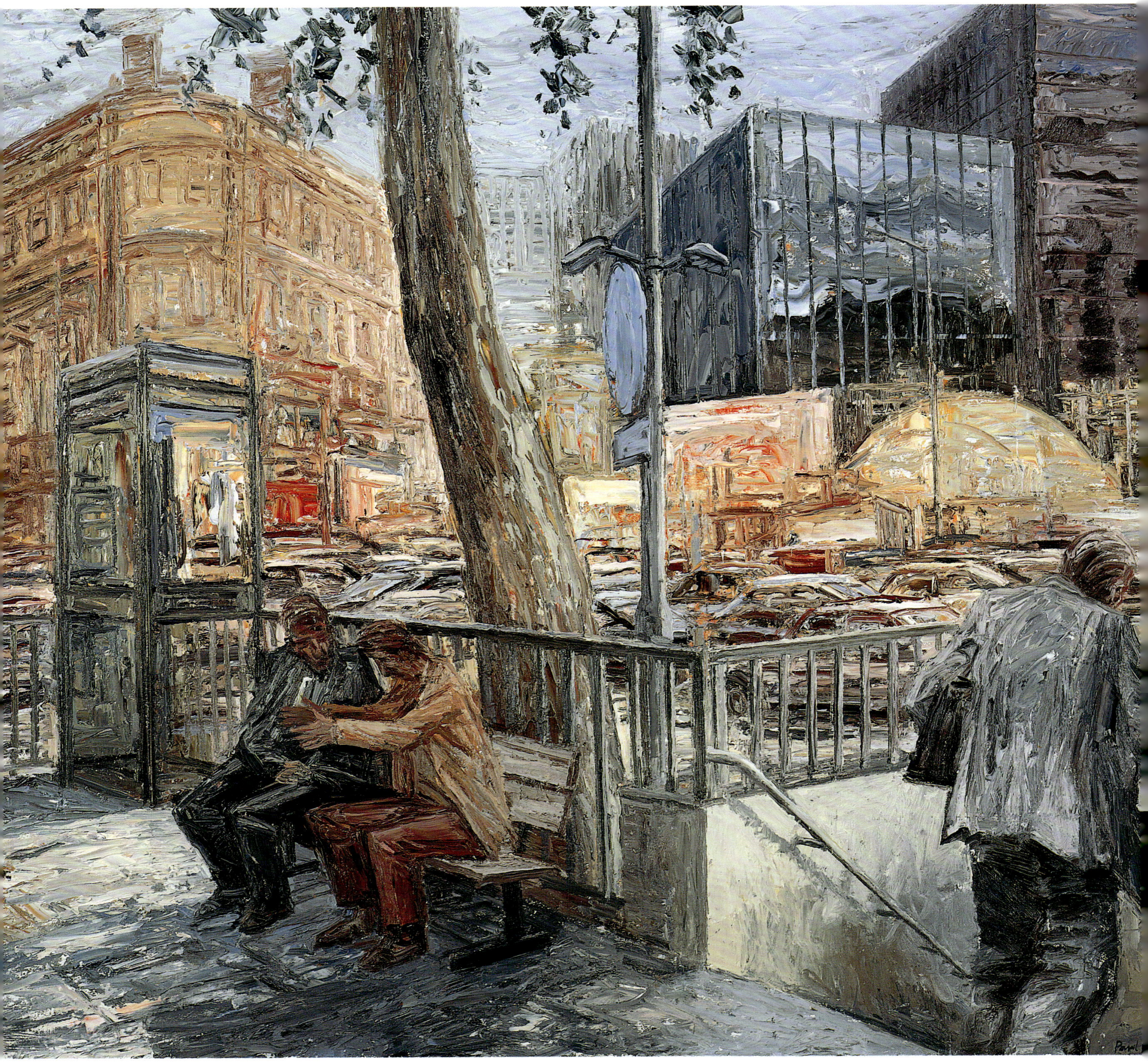

224.

PAUL BUTLER

(born 1947)

Heart to Heart (Hammersmith)* [92.96]
1991
Oil on board, 121.1 x 138.5 cm
Signed and dated bottom right:
Paul Butler '91
On the back: title and artist's name/*Small Mansion Arts Centre, Gunnersbury Park* (where the artist has his studio).

PLANS FOR the redevelopment of Hammersmith Broadway were in the offing for about thirty years. Delays of all kinds, including radical changes of mind, account for this lengthy gestation period, to which many attribute the temporary deterioration of a once-thriving London village.

The view is taken from the junction of King Street and Beadon Road looking east towards the Broadway and Hammersmith Road. The artist worked out his composition on the pavement outside a friendly Victorian pub, The Clarendon. Butler presents us with the new environment at Hammersmith Broadway: the glittering mirror-like Hammersmith International Centre in the background contrasts on the right with the stark, dark Commonwealth House and on the left, the Victorian block of shops and flats screening the convent school of the Sacred Heart from the busy thoroughfare. The new British Telecom 'phone box and underground entrance and newish-looking benches and railings confirm the sense that Hammersmith is a modern, comfortable and even exciting thoroughfare. The familiar but run-down group of buildings on the island (bus garage, post office and assorted shops) are gone, while on the right, the ubiquitous sight of cranes and scaffolding heralds the arrival of the contemporary mix of shops and offices, London's magic formula for redevelopment with the promise of revenue. In the middle ground is thick, rush-hour traffic. Traffic congestion at Hammersmith Broadway is a reality and it is also a theme of crucial importance in relation to London as a whole. Although it is hidden in this view, Ralph Erskine's building project, The Ark, has also added excitement to the new look of Hammersmith.

There is something Mediterranean about the light and the comfortable way in which people blend with their surroundings, sitting in the shade of a single tree or casually disappearing underground. Butler has captured the changing London climate, perhaps linked to the 'greenhouse effect', with its blisteringly hot summers which in the last few years have altered the character of street life in London and our use of the outdoors.

The fact that this painting captures the changing fabric, traffic and atmosphere of the capital through the changing character of one of its 'villages' is thrown into focus if we compare this work with its 1953 equivalent, *Hammersmith Broadway, Rush Hour* by Ruskin Spear (Christie's, 6 November 1992, 131). Dangerously positioning himself in the middle of the roundabout, Spear painted a London which no longer exists. How peaceful his rush hour, how dark and Victorian his Hammersmith. Both artists, however, have captured, forty years apart, the spirit of Hammersmith with its street life dominated by traffic arteries.

Provenance:
Purchased from the artist in 1992.

Bibliography:
Witnesses and Dreamers, exhibition catalogue, various venues (including the Museum of London, 1993); *Paul Butler – Oil Paintings*, exhibition catalogue, Montpelier Sandelson Gallery, 1996.

Exhibited:
'Passers-by': Paintings and Drawings of London by Paul Butler, Small Mansion Arts Centre, October 1992.

Provenance:
Purchased from the artist in 1992.

Bibliography:
Witnesses and Dreamers, exhibition catalogue, 1993, various venues (including the Museum of London).

225.
OLIVER BEVAN
(born 1941)

Traffic [92.170/1–5]
1992
Oil sketches on board and paper
All inscribed in pencil: *OB92*

THE ARTIST'S titles for these works are: *Full Stretch* [bus]/*Sierra* [cars]/*Passenger* [Green Coat]/*Steady Progress* [taxi]/*Cyclist*. These are oil studies for a large-scale series which the artist describes as:

> ...a set of paintings of the same format to be hung together like an altarpiece. They originated in a series of photographs I took in Hammersmith in the autumn of 1990...There is no narrative intended and the events shown are as much a mystery to me as they are to the spectator. The pictures have a certain coolness, a balance between the expressiveness of the paint and the remoteness of figures half hidden behind glass. I like the idea of something that transient being presented as a monument.

The subject of modern road transport is a key theme in post-war urban landscape. These paintings contrast with the thick, colourful, nose-to-tail mass of traffic in Paul Butler's Hammersmith scene (see cat. no. 224). Butler's perception of traffic is removed, seen from the friendly terrace of a corner pub. Bevan tackles the theme of traffic from 'within', in close ups depicting the visual experience of being caught in a traffic jam. Here he paints anonymous drivers at the wheel, sometimes seen through an open window, sometimes deformed by glass reflections; he captures, too, the frustration of confined spaces on slow-moving roads: a biker zipping through the traffic, a woman riskily getting off a bus.

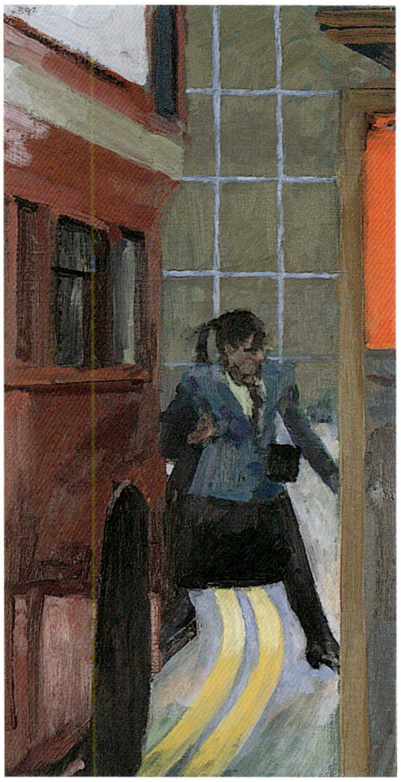
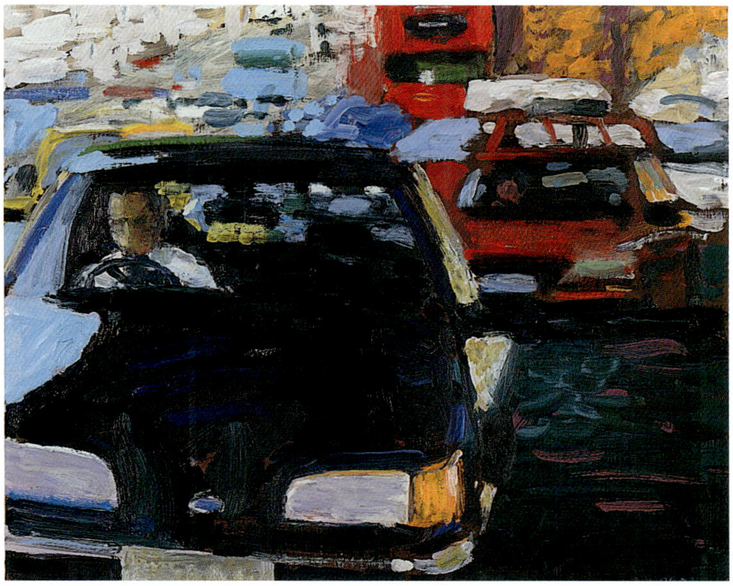
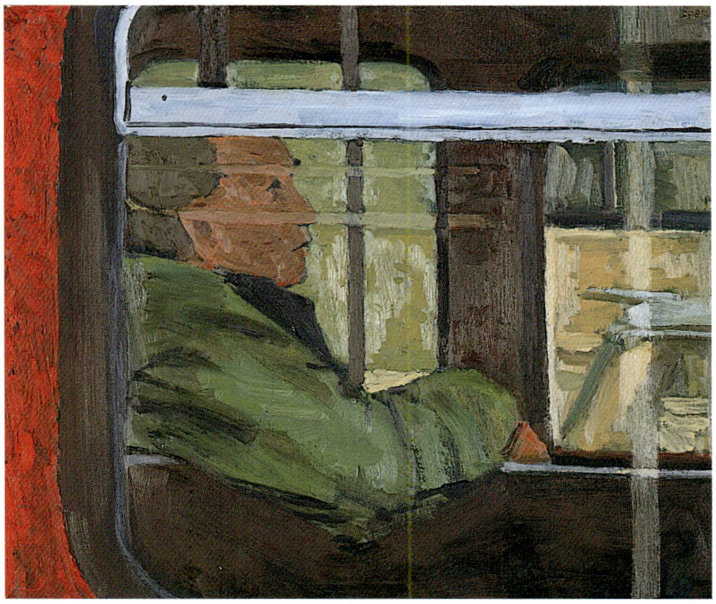
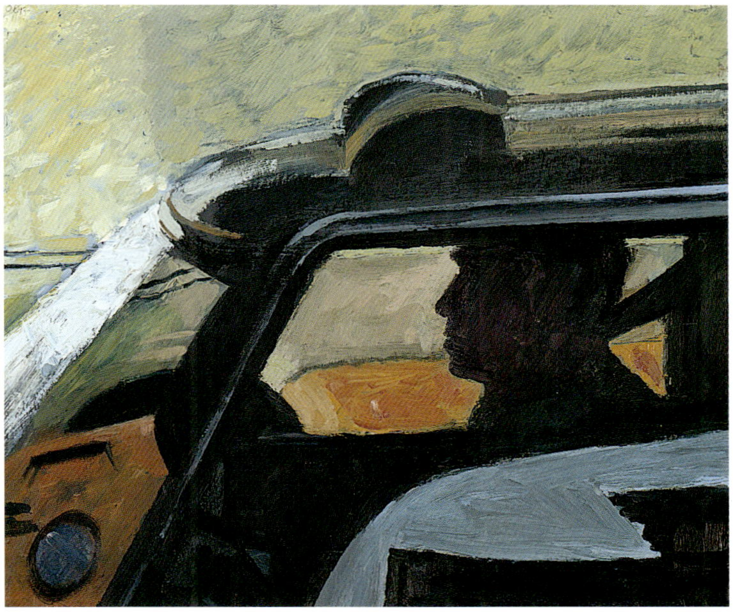
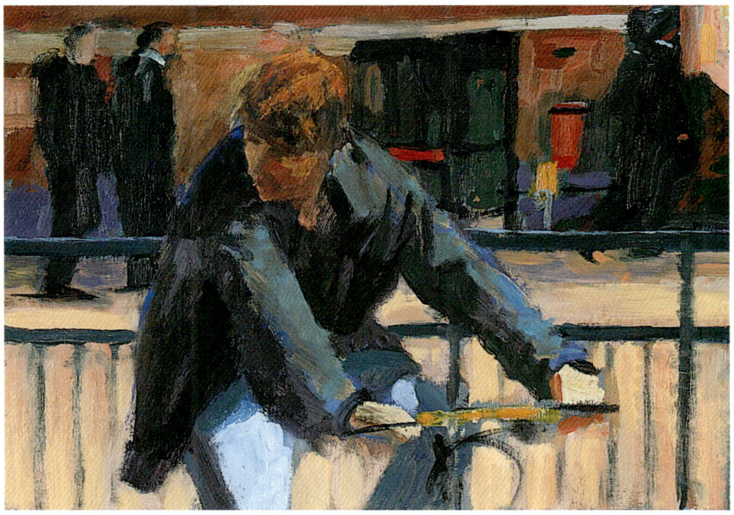

Provenance:
Presented by the artist at the close of his residency at the Museum in 1993.

226.
MAO WEN BIAO
(born 1950)
Islands and Sea* [93.19/1]
1993
Oil on canvas, 91 x 101 cm
Signed and dated lower left: *Mao 93*

THIS IS one of five paintings the artist produced during his residency at the Museum of London in January 1993. His brief was the link between the past and the present, drawing inspiration from the Museum's exhibits and the response they prompted in the visitor. The residency lasted a month, during which time Mao divided his hours between the Museum's galleries (see Appendix) and a studio in the Education Department.

His first bout of inspiration was for this painting and he was first seen sketching outside the Museum, in cold and wet weather. The 'islands' are the thick brown impastos of remnants from the past: portions of the City wall and ruined church towers. The 'sea' is represented by the mass of modern buildings, glazed office blocks which absorb the blue (or grey) of the sky. The Museum of London, a low modern building which makes the synthesis between past and present, is clearly labelled.

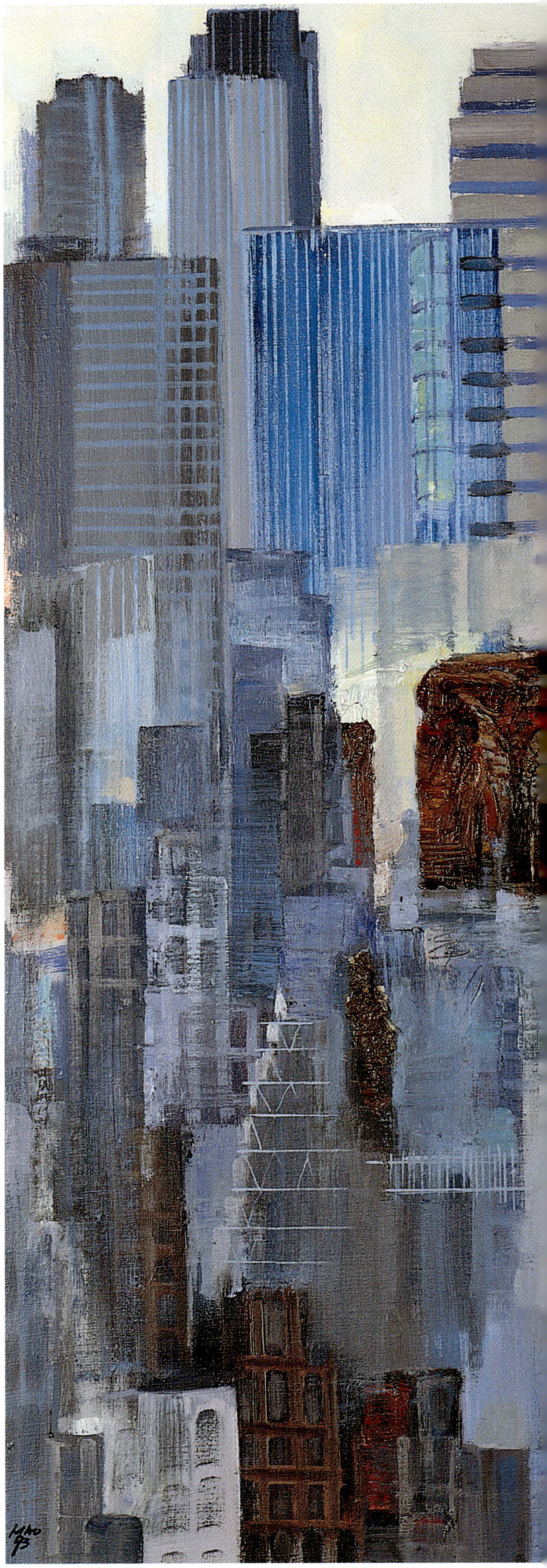

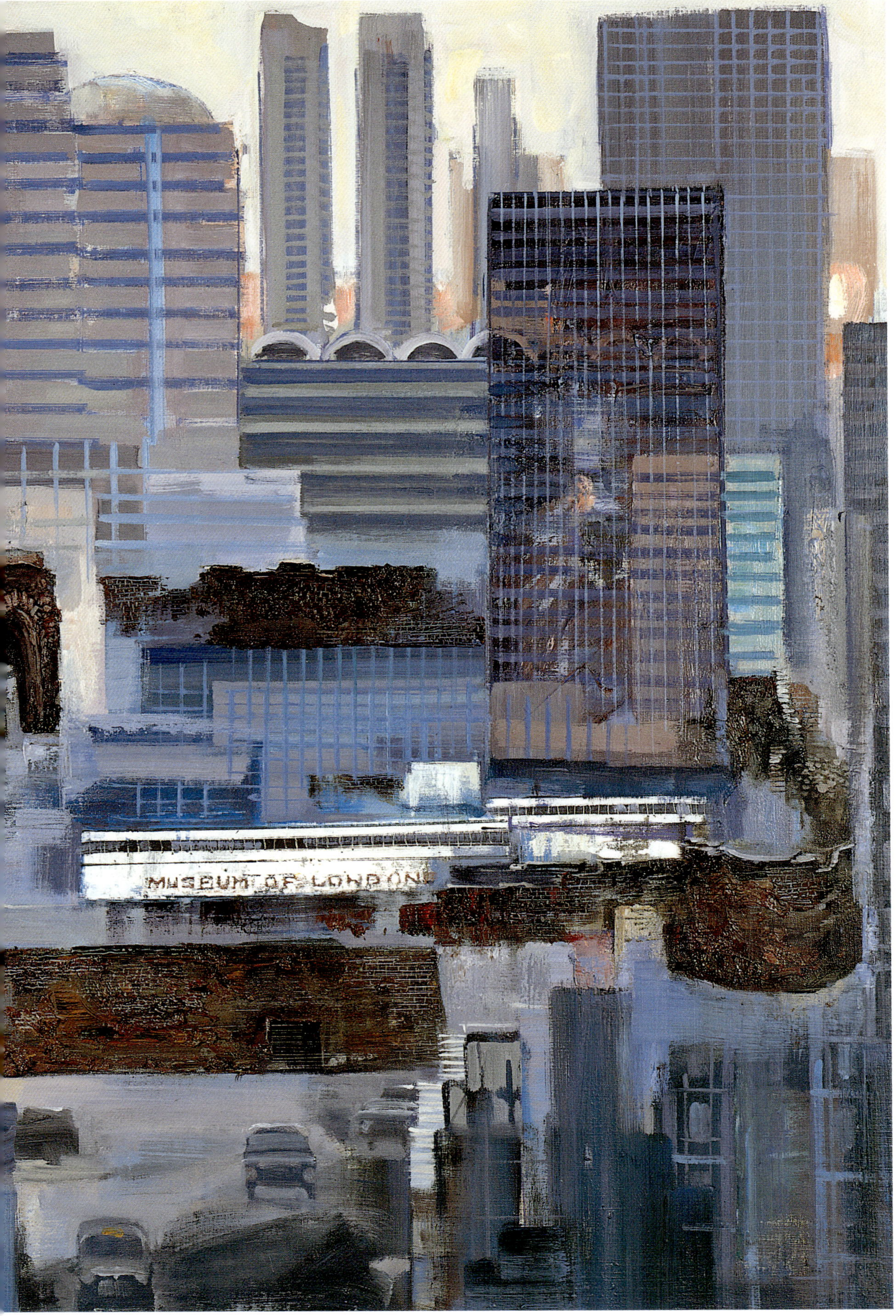
MUSEUM OF LONDON

Provenance:
Purchased from the artist in 1995.

227.
JOCK McFADYEN

(born 1950)

Canal Lovers* [95.532]
1993-4
Oil on canvas laid on board, 90 x 73.4 cm
Signed on verso: *McFADYEN*

THE PAINTING shows a young couple kissing by the side of a canal. The scene is set at the Grand Union Canal at Salmon Lane, London E3, not far from Limehouse Basin at the point where the railway line is carried over the canal. The contrast between the dark rail structure covered with graffiti and the limpid blue of the sky and water is striking.

Jock McFadyen mostly paints London's seedy side and this work is unusual for the harmonious relationship between figures and landscape, however ephemeral the nature of this harmony. The genesis for this painting tells a harder tale:

> The picture started life as a glue sniffer who I saw on the towpath. He had a red anorak with the hood pulled down to conceal his face. Only his lips protruded, and they were clamped on to a Tesco plastic bag which was expanding and contracting like a lung as he breathed the glue in and out. He cut a striking figure. I saw him three or four times after that and realised that he was sleeping rough and was completely off his head.

The painter had to abandon the figure of the glue sniffer because he could not bring it to life.

This painting constitutes a transitional work in the oeuvre of the artist, who made a spectacular change of direction as a result of his collaboration with Kenneth McMillan on the production of the ballet *The Judas Tree* in 1990. McFadyen based his set designs on the East End with Canary Wharf dominating the composition. The enforced role of painting a place but leaving out its characters, suddenly made the artist realise that despite his emphasis on character, it was places that really interested him and had done so all along. From then on, the figures in his work started shrinking, giving the setting centre stage. In *Canal Lovers*, the figures are quite small by comparison with those in earlier works. Soon after this they disappear altogether.

This painting is a rare moment of equilibrium and even peace between figures and cityscape. The lovers, despite being 'cheaply' dressed seem to transcend momentarily the world of grim reality which McFadyen has elected to paint. The equation between bleak cityscape and cheap love often meant that previous paintings made valid but depressing statements about the city. The artist's reworking of the female figure showed that he wanted the couple to blend with the landscape rather than display signs of carnal passion: he substituted the lean, fluid lines of the present figure for the fleshy, vivacious and provocative curves of his first version. It is also interesting to compare this work with C. R. W. Nevinson's famous *Towpath, Camden Town, by Night* (*c.*1912): there is almost a middle-class solidity and permanence to the Nevinson couple which is singularly missing from McFadyen's rather fragile moment of fusion.

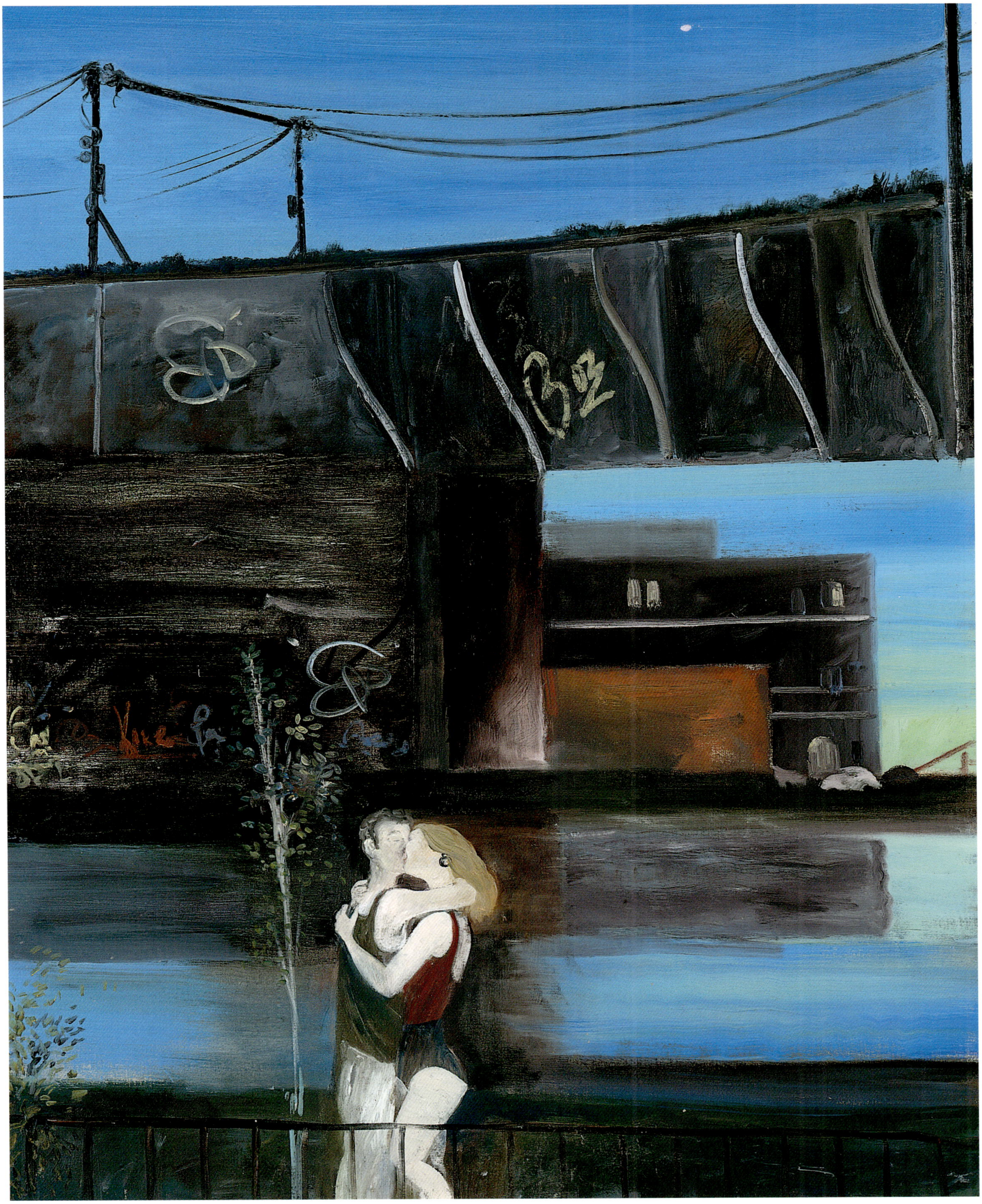

Provenance:
Presented by the artist at the end of his three-month residency at the Museum of London in 1994.

228.
TIMO LEHTONEN
(born 1953)
The New Union Club (after George Cruikshank)* [94.76]
1994
Oil on canvas, 122.3 x 91.5 cm
Title, signed and dated on the back

IN THE course of his residency at the Museum of London, Timo Lehtonen was asked to respond to the exhibition 'The Peopling of London' held in 1993-4 and which addressed the theme of fifteen thousand years of settlement from overseas. This painting is the culmination of a series of works based on George Cruikshank's 1819 etching 'The New Union Club' which, in the exhibition, hung in the section 'Early Black and South Asian Presence'.

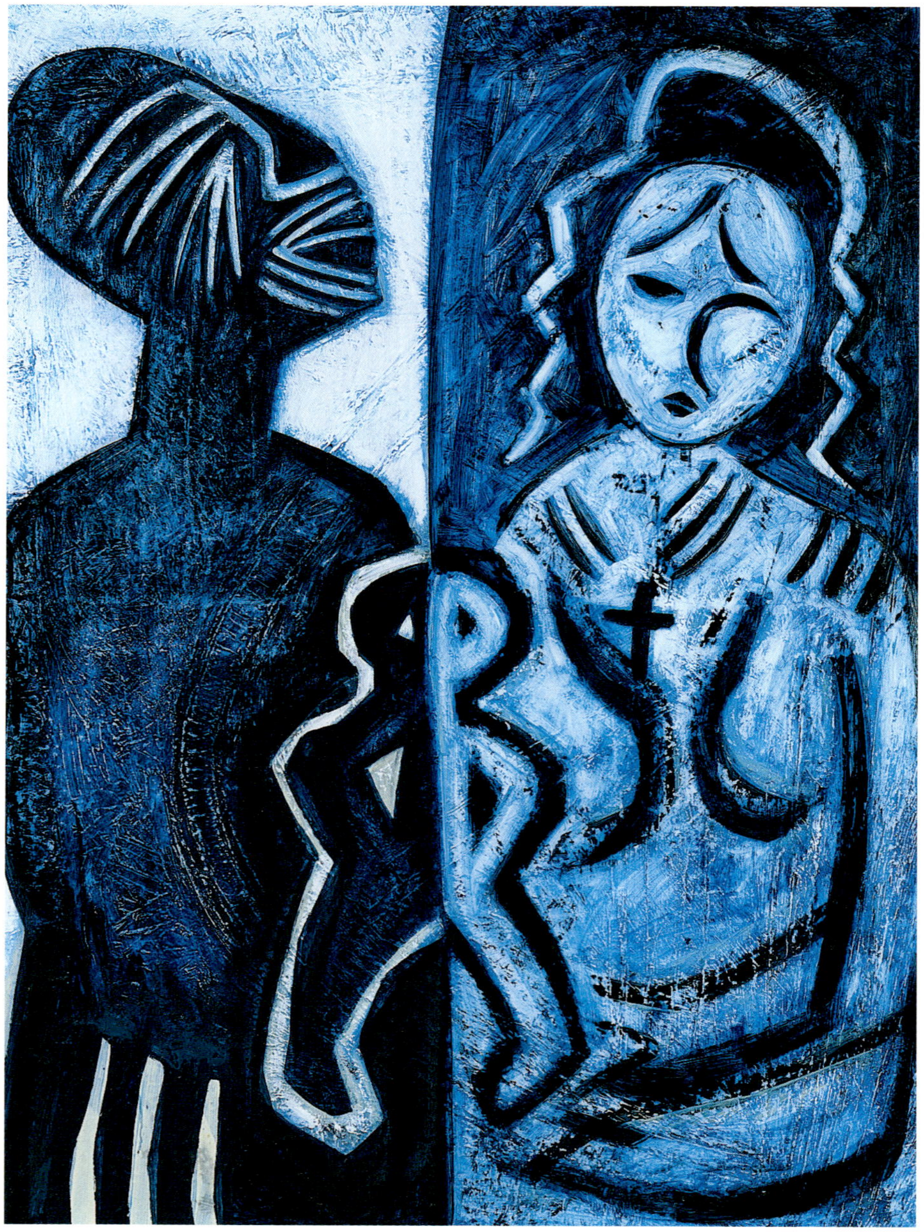

James Gillray's *The Union Club*, published in 1801, had mocked the union with Ireland (1801) by presenting the fraternisation of the English and Irish as a drunken riot. Cruikshank's design follows the same principle, updating the reconciled parties to English and Blacks. His print was a severe attack on the anti-slavery movement and notably contained a detail showing a black man and a white woman whose matrimonial union resulted in a child who was quite literally half black and half white. This is the theme which Lehtonen chose to develop.

The stylised half-length figures of a black male (left) and white female (right) are depicted side by side, each set against its opposite 'colour' (dark blue background for the white female and white background for the black male). Between them is the fruit of their union, a small child cut in two, one half black and the other white. The gap between the two races is accentuated by the woman's wearing of a Christian cross.

The artist's investigation cannot be dissociated from his own multi-cultural status: his mother is Finnish, his father Nigerian; his education and training English and his current daily experience based on London. His reflection, however, articulates the experience of the many Londoners with foreign roots who through the centuries have settled in the capital and struggled with ensuing issues of racial and/or cultural identity.

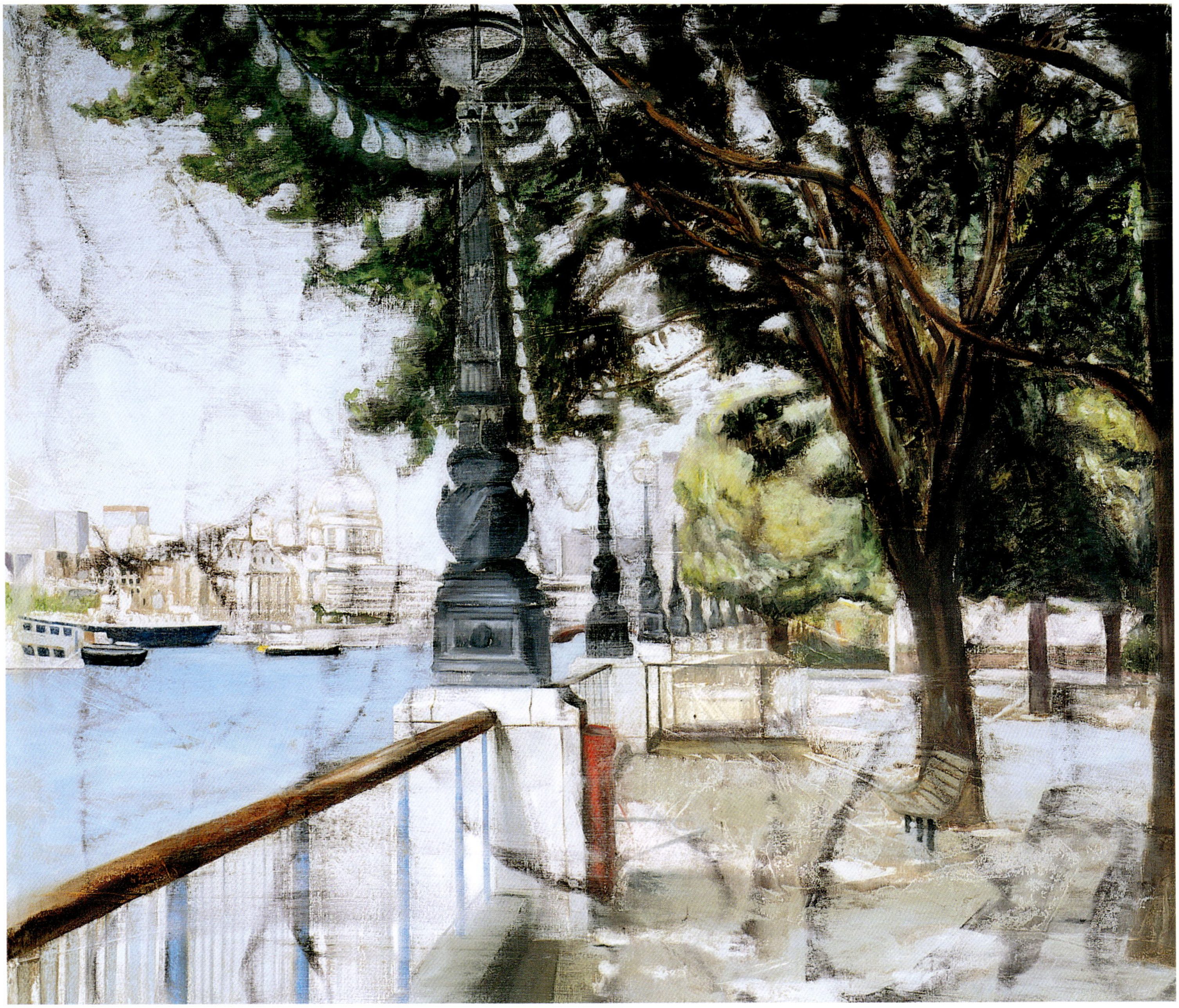

229.
ARTURO DI STEFANO
(born 1955)
South Bank* [95.169]
1994
Oil on canvas, 181.8 x 213.2 cm
Signed and dated on the reverse:
A. Di Stefano 1994

THIS BEAUTIFULLY balanced composition is taken outside the National Theatre on the South Bank looking east towards the City, which is dominated by the dome of St Paul's. The painter achieves an almost magic equilibrium between plant life, water and architecture. The use of dark trails over the surface of the painting suggests the folds of a veil and the experience of a momentary vision. This is reinforced by the softening of the colours

Provenance:
Purchased from Purdy Hicks Gallery in 1995.

Bibliography:
Arturo Di Stefano, exhibition catalogue, Purdy Hicks, 1995, cat. no. 4.

of the City (note that St Paul's grey dome has turned white, an actual fact which the painter has exaggerated) and the light, abstract treatment of London's modern buildings, all melting into the very pale sky. One is irresistibly reminded of William Morris's own visionary lines about London from *The Earthly Paradise* (1868–70):

> Forget six counties overhung with smoke,
> Forget the snorting steam and piston stroke,
> Forget the spreading of the hideous town;
> Think rather of the pack-horse on the down,
> And dream of London, small, and white, and clean,
> The clear Thames bordered by its gardens green.

This is the view that moved Nevinson to paint *London, Winter* (see cat. no. 173). The continuing presence of the London School for Boys building and St Paul's create a sense of timelessness despite the astonishing changes that have taken place on the South Bank since that time.

For much of the twentieth century, however, this stretch of the riverbank remained untamed. The construction of the Albert, Victoria and Chelsea embankments in Victorian times had been co-ordinated and supervised by Sir Joseph Bazalgette between 1868 and 1874 and each was received with enthusiasm when it finally opened. The Albert Embankment (1869), west of the site we are considering, was personally financed by the builder Thomas Cubitt and displays the hallmarks of a Bazalgette scheme: solid retaining walls, rows of plane trees and dolphin-based lamps of cast iron. The task of co-ordinating the continuation of the embankment on the South Bank was taken up by the GLC and in the Victorian style adopted for the Albert Embankment. The stretch between Hungerford Bridge and Gabriel's Wharf became part of the 1977 Silver Jubilee celebrations and was later named Queen's Walk (which extends to Tower Bridge). A granite stone outside Coin Street Gardens commemorates its official opening by the Queen on 7 December 1988.

The painter Richard Gilbert was commissioned by Clifford Chance Solicitors to produce a large painting of the South Bank. His interpretation of the scene is completely different and focuses on the popularity of this stretch of the river with Londoners. His people-centred composition contrasts greatly with this work, which chooses instead to bring out the harmony of London's structures.

230.

MARK CAZALET

(born 1964)

Half Light* [95.311]

1994–5

Oil on canvas, 76 x 127 cm

Title, signed and dated on the back:

Oct 94–Feb/95 MJ Cazalet

THE WESTWAY, carrying the A40(M) and Britain's longest elevated motorway, is shown at Royal Oak in Paddington. The view is taken from Torquay Street (north of the Westway) looking south-east to Royal Oak tube station (not visible) and Bishops' Bridge (the semi-circular metal bridge in the background on the right). The painting focuses on the infrastructure of the Westway and is totally devoid of traffic and people.

The Westway has been described as London's 'most dramatic work of engineering' and was the outcome of the GLC's Highways Programme. The idea of urban motorways was first mooted by Le Corbusier in the 1920s and was adopted in Britain in the 1950s. Although plans for the Westway were published in 1951, funding for this project was approved only in 1961. There was fierce local opposition to it, as a result of which a range of amenities for the communities affected by this ambitious scheme were secured and urban motorways disappeared from the GLC's agenda. This local success story reminds us of the Coin Street scenario which is, at the time of writing, still vivid in Londoners' minds. The Westway spearheaded a twenty-year programme of road improvements known as the Ringways – the M25 being the only 'survivor' of the proposed schemes.

The manipulation of light and proportions in this painting enables the artist to fill the structure with organic life. The supporting pillars, rather squat in reality, have been elongated and it is no longer the cars that move along the structure but the structure that moves, caterpillar-like, along the earth. The choice of night-time creates spectacular effects on the sky and gives the painter a free hand with artificial lighting. The painting evokes a forest of concrete pillars, with pure darkness in the middle ground – fear? – and (angelic) light in the background – hope?

A number of artists have been attracted to the subject of urban motorways. Robert Soden in watercolour and Oliver Bevan in oil have produced complete series of paintings on this theme (Soden in northern England and Oliver Bevan in London, see his *Westway* catalogue, 1992). Berlin-based artist Hans Stein painted *Autobahn-dreieck Funkturm* in 1973 (see *La Ville, art et architecture en Europe, 1870–1993*; exhibition catalogue, Pompidou Centre) in a triptych which may be compared to Oliver Bevan's *Westway Triptych* (1987). These concrete monsters have not said their last word.

Provenance:
Purchased from East West Gallery in 1995.

Bibliography:
Intangible Worlds, exhibition catalogue, East West Gallery, 1995; *Strangely Familiar, narratives of architecture in the city*, Iain Borden, Joe Kerr, Alicia Pivaro and Jane Rendell (eds), 1996, pp38-40.

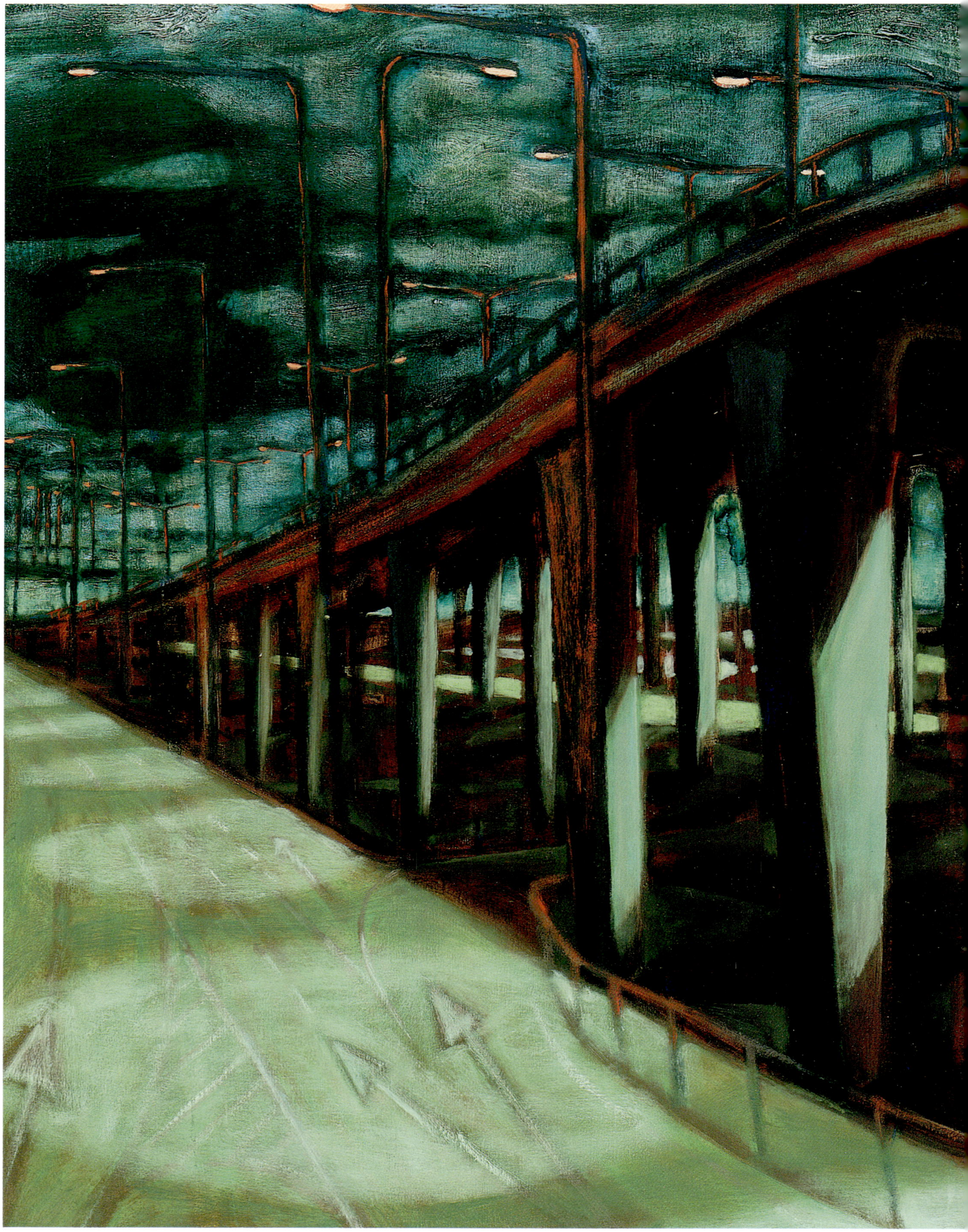

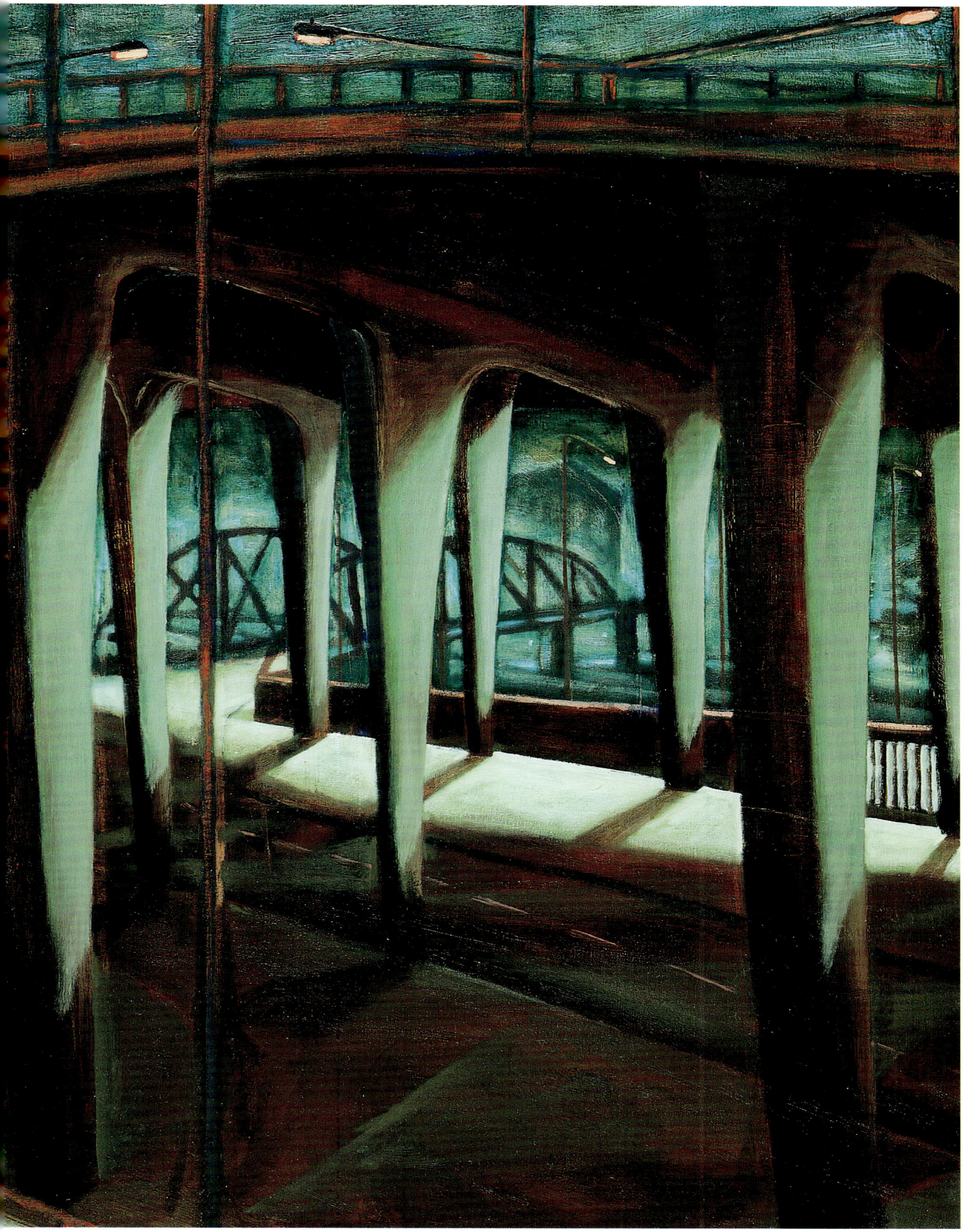

Appendix

Paintings in the Museum's collection without detailed catalogue entries
The entries are organised in chronological order

The Appendix may be considered by some as the category reserved for duplicates and second rate or irrelevant paintings. This may indeed be the case with a few of the works below, but I prefer to think of this section as some kind of Pandora's box. I took great pleasure in rediscovering and re-evaluating some of the paintings cursorily catalogued in John Hayes's 'Reserve Collections' in the Museum's 1970 catalogue (in particular cat. nos 9, 161, 172 in this publication). I feel sure that my successors will take equal delight in re-evaluating the works found here, some of which, particularly in the Stuart period, are only placed in this category because they do not fit the theme of this volume – *London in Paint.*

M. G.

Stuart London

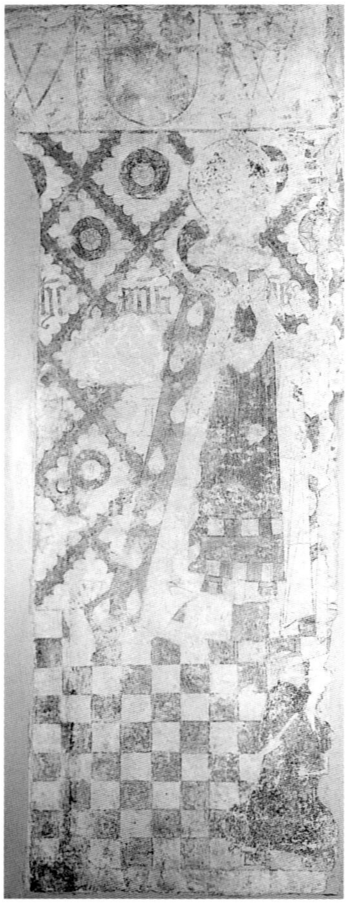

ENGLISH SCHOOL
St Peter and a Kneeling Cleric
[56.167]
fifteenth or sixteenth century
Distemper on plaster,
293.7 x 95 to 111.2 cm
Hayes (cat. no. 41);
Source: Presented by the London County Council in 1956, at the time of the demolition of Brooke House, Hackney.

ENGLISH SCHOOL
Jonah Cast Overboard and Swallowed by a Whale
[A7928)
Sixteenth century
Distemper on plaster,
94.3 x 183.1 cm
Hayes (cat. no. 42);
Source: Part of the decoration of a house on the south side of High Bridge Street, Waltham Abbey, discovered in 1892 at the time of its demolition; presented by Charles Welch in 1912.

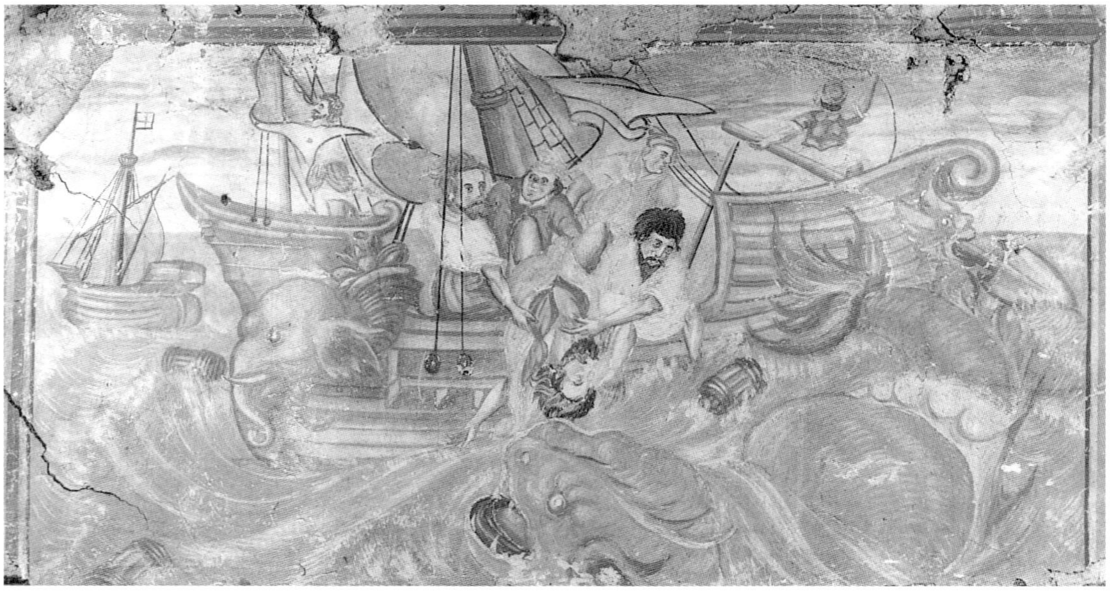

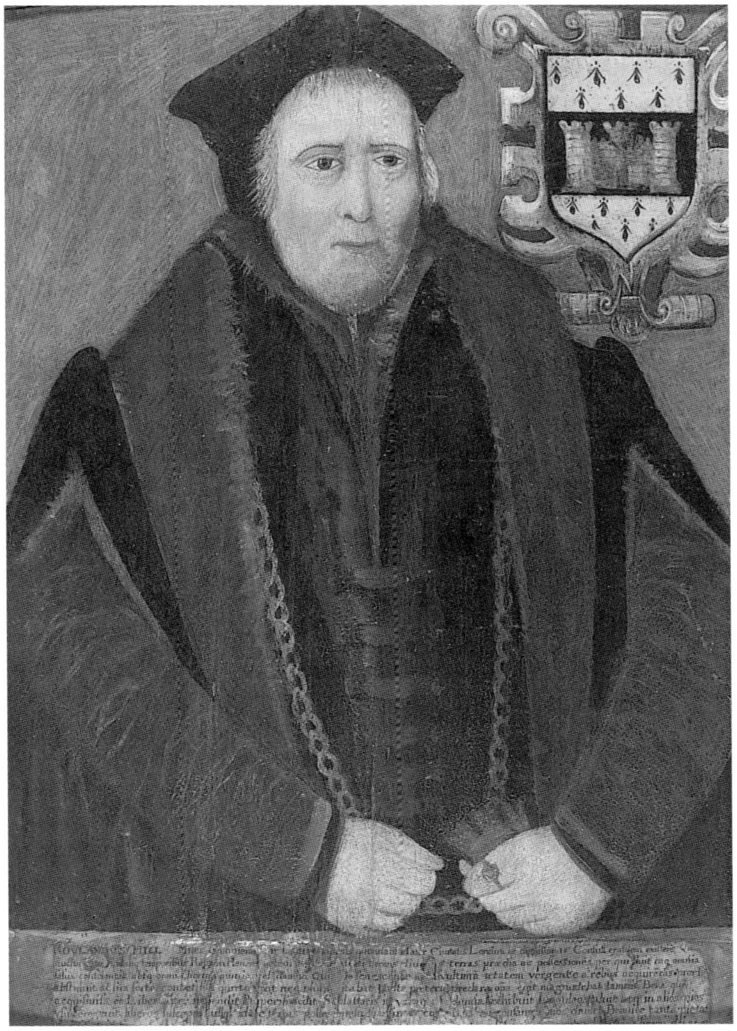

ENGLISH SCHOOL

Portrait of Sir Rowland Hill (?1492–1561) [51.67]
Sixteenth century.
Oil on panel,
63.75 x 45.6 cm
Hayes (cat. no. 150);
Source: Bequeathed by Miss Mildred Aldrich Cotton in 1951.

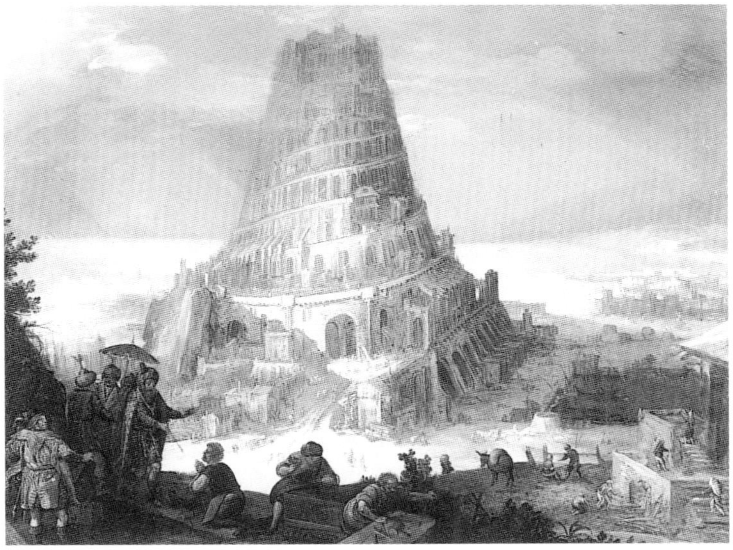

MARTIN VAN VALCKENBORGH
(1535–1612)

The Tower of Babel [62.75]
(painted on reverse of one of the two surviving Copperplate Map plates – North Side, *c.*1560)
*c.*1595
37 x 49.5 cm
Source: Purchased from Paul Larsen in 1962.

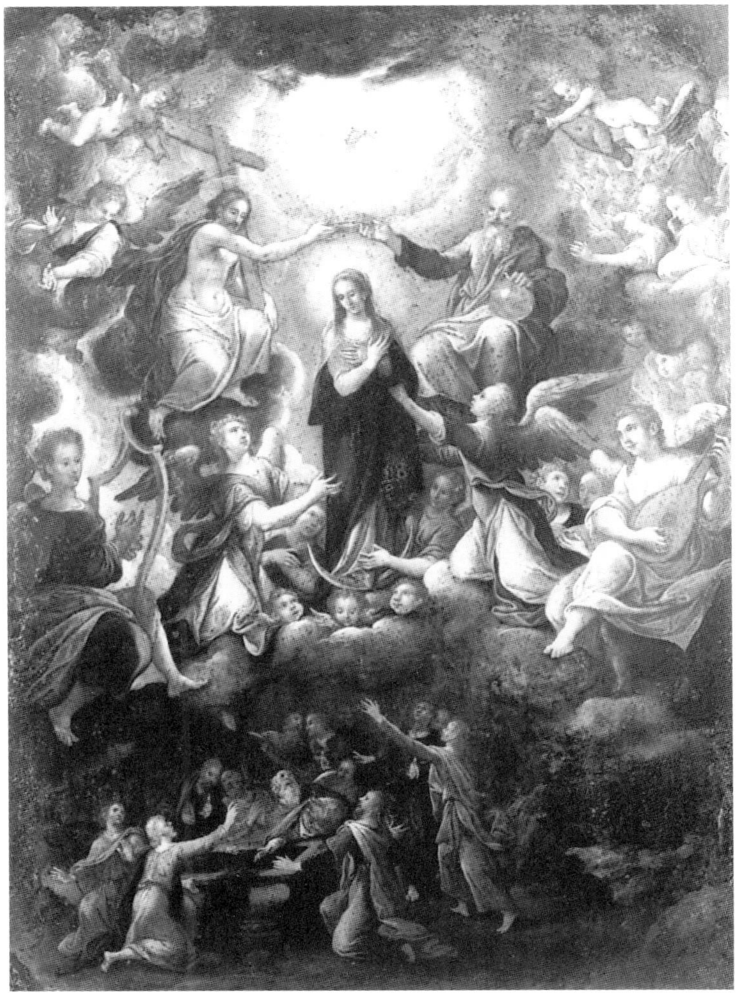

ATTR. CIRCLE OF FRANS FRANKEN
(1542–1616)

The Assumption of the Virgin
(painted on reverse of one of the two surviving Copperplate Map plates – South Side, *c.*1560)
*c.*1620
37 x 49.5 cm
Source: Purchased from Bernard Quaritch Ltd.

AFTER JAN GRIFFIER THE ELDER (c.1645/?52–1718)
The Great Fire of London, 1666 [27.69]
Oil on canvas,
88.75 x 123.1 cm
Hayes (cat. no. 151);
Source: Presented by Reginald, 2nd Viscount Esher in 1927 (without attribution).

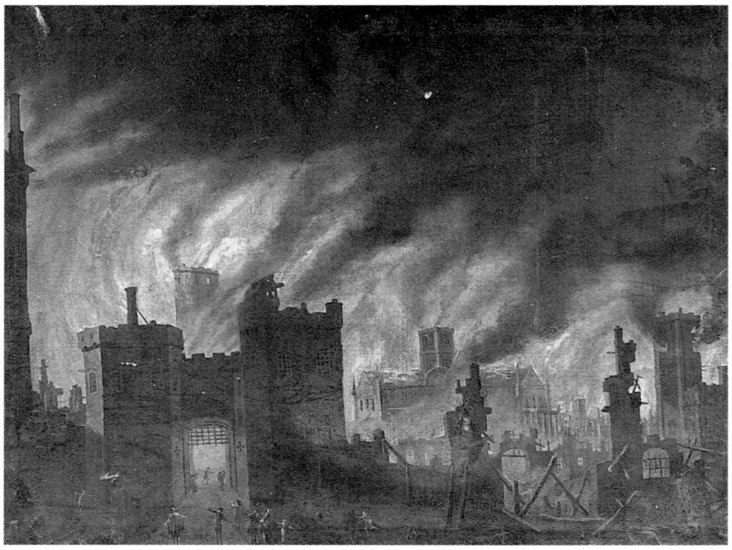

BRITISH SCHOOL
Allegory of Summer [64.77]
Late seventeenth century
Oil on plaster,
285 x 315 cm (oval)
Hayes (cat. no. 12);
Source: Part of the decoration of 15 Buckingham Street, Strand, removed from the premises at the time of its demolition in November 1961; presented by the Royal National Pension Fund for Nurses in 1964.

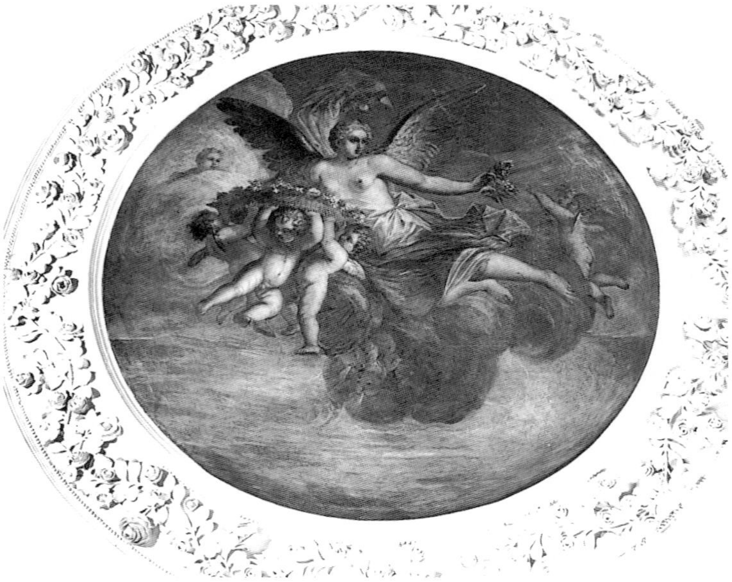

TANGYE COLLECTION
[46.78]
Collection of Cromwelliana gathered by Sir Richard Tangye (1833–1906) and presented by his son Sir Harold Lincoln Tangye in 1913. The collection of paintings is largely made up of Victorian interpretations of the Civil War (see, for instance, cat. no. 116), but also contains a few contemporary paintings (see cat. nos 4, 5 and 6). The collection of images has not been fully catalogued and awaits re-evaluation.

Georgian Era

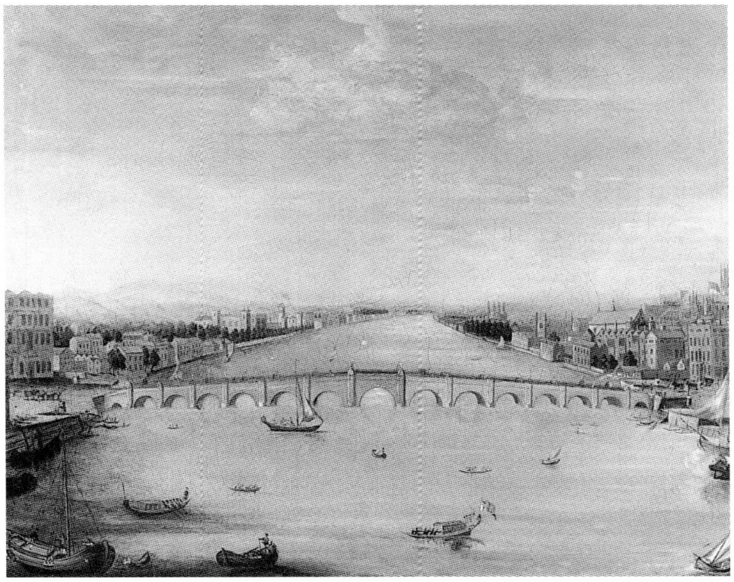

BRITISH SCHOOL
Westminster Bridge from the River, looking South
[A24667]
Oil on canvas,
63.5 x 76.5 cm
Hayes (cat. no. 131);
Source: Purchased in 1922
(as after Scott).

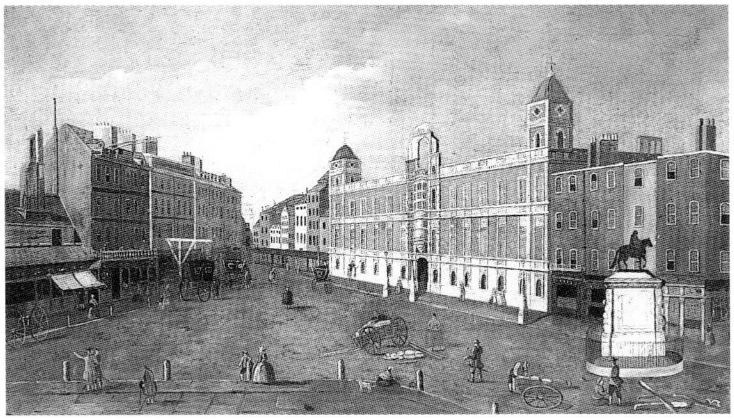

BRITISH SCHOOL
Charing Cross and Northumberland House
[30.70]
Post-1753
Oil on canvas, 60 x 102.5 cm
Hayes (cat. no. 129);
Source: Presented by
Miss Grace Baker in 1930.

JOHN PAUL (1804–87)
Charing Cross and Northumberland House
[C2389]
Post–1753
Oil on canvas,
93.75 x 97.4 cm
Hayes (cat. no. 164);
Source: J. G. Joicey bequest,
1919.

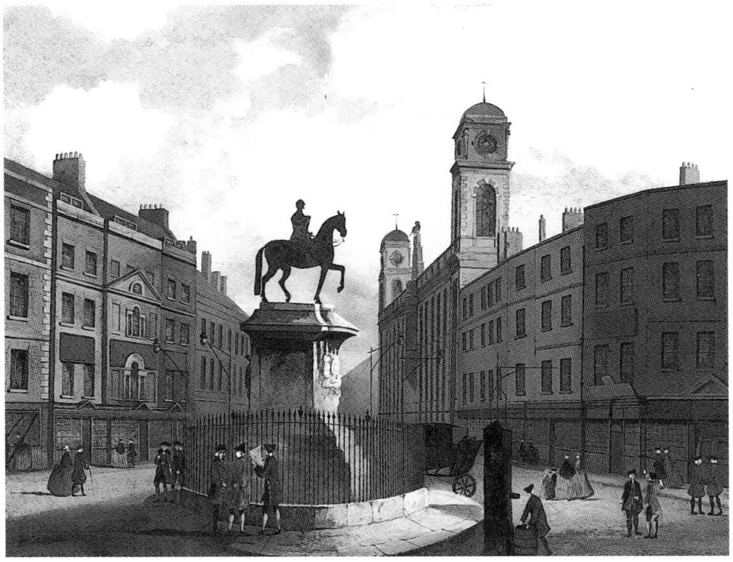

Regency London

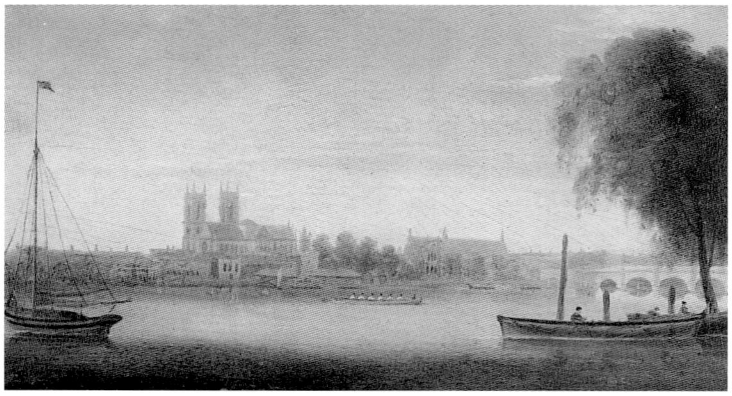

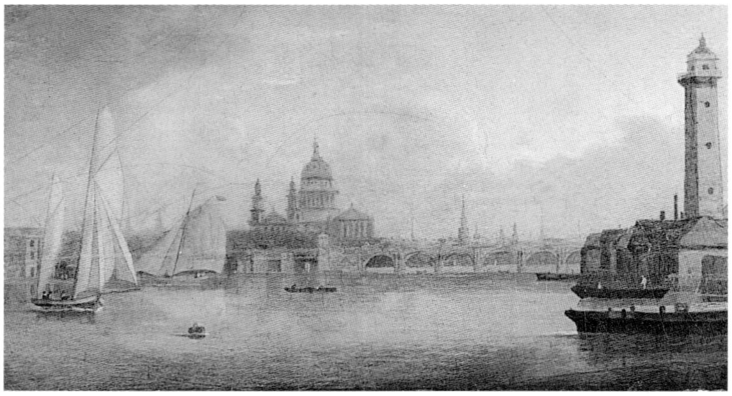

J. W. EDGE
Westminster and Westminster Bridge from Lambeth [A8074]
Early 19th century?
Oil on panel, 17.2 x 32.2 cm
Source: Purchased from Leggatt Brothers in 1912.

J. W. EDGE
St Paul's Cathedral and Blackfriars Bridge [A8075]
Early 19th century?
Oil on panel, 17.2 x 32.2 cm
Source: Purchased from Leggatt Brothers in 1912.

AFTER DANIEL TURNER (active 1782–1806)
The Adelphi and the City from the River, with the Funeral Procession of Lord Nelson [27.5]
1806
Oil on canvas (laid down on panel), 39.7 x 55.9 cm
Hayes (cat. no. 179);
Source: Presented by the Rev. Sydney W. Wheatley in 1927 (without attribution).

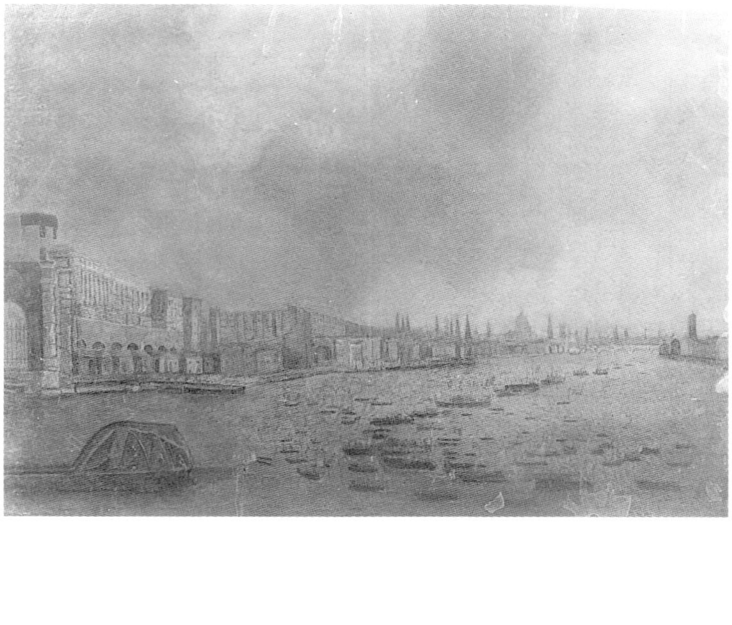

DANIEL TURNER
(active 1782–1806)
Blackfriars Bridge and St Paul's from the River
[A8082]
*c.*1800–10
Oil on panel, 15.8 x 23 cm
Hayes (cat. no. 178);
Source: Purchased from Leggatt Brothers in 1912.

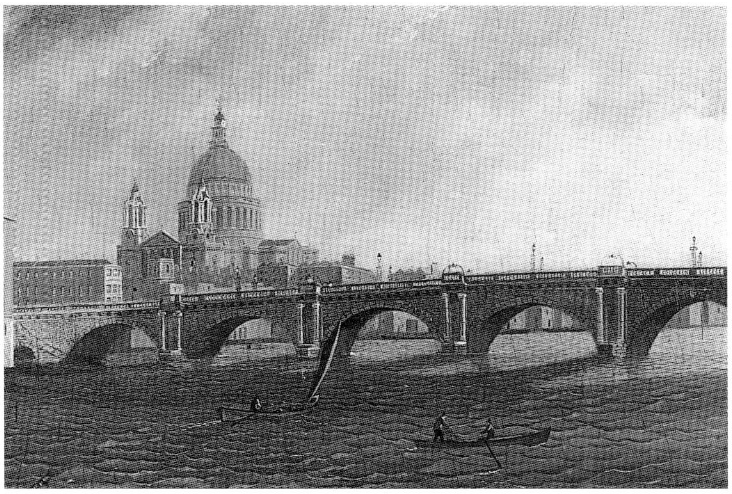

J. CORDREY
(active 1799–1822)
The London to Dartford Stage Coach [A20710]
1813
Oil on canvas,
50.8 x 76.2 cm
Hayes (cat. no. 31);
Source: Presented by an anonymous donor in 1919.

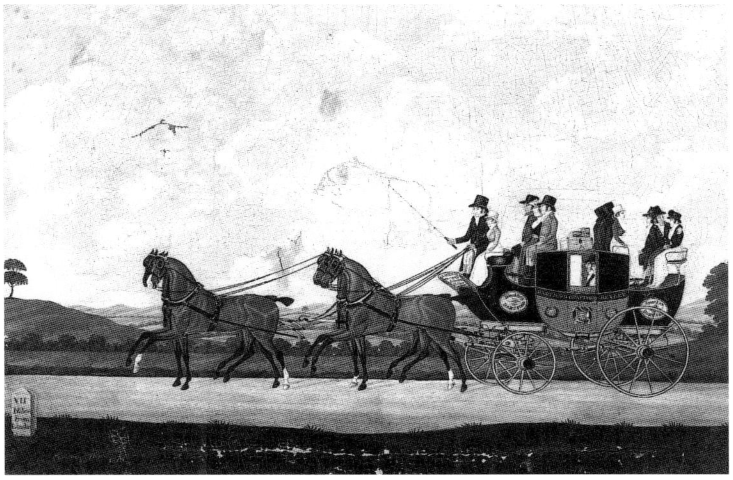

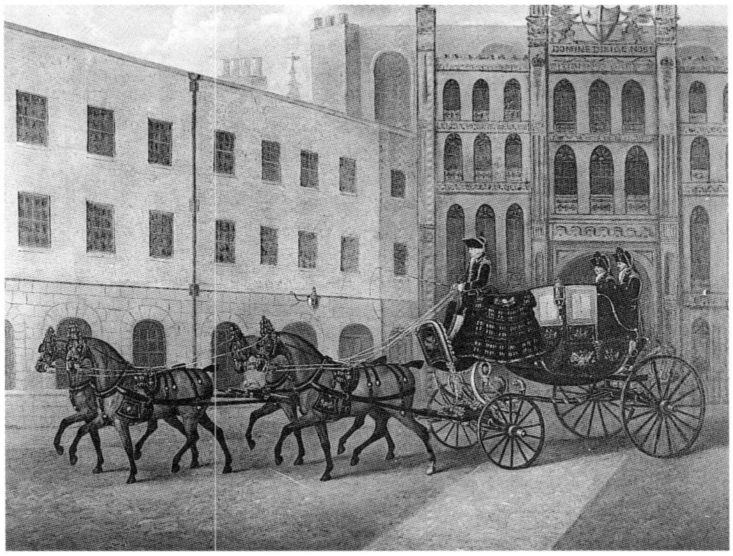

JOHN NOST SARTORIUS (1759–1828)
The Dress Chariot of the Sheriff of the City of London in the Courtyard of Guildhall
[A16492]
1807
Oil on canvas,
82.2 x 88.3 cm
Hayes (cat. no. 98);
Source: Presented by J. G. Joicey in 1915.

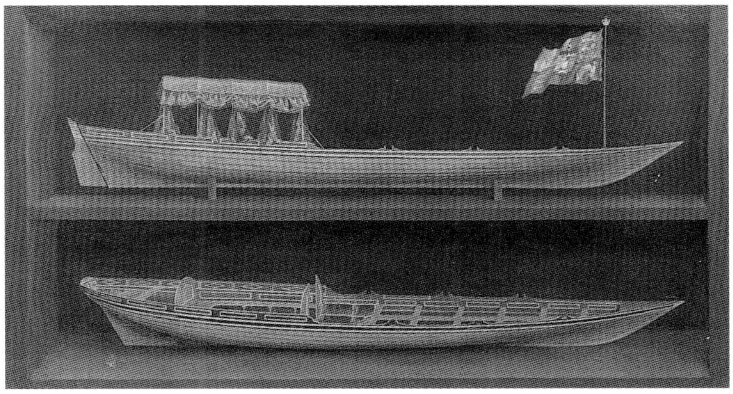

S. B. CULL ...
(active early nineteenth century)
The State Barge of George IV
[A27043]
*c.*1820–30
Oil on canvas, 37.5 x 63.75 cm
Hayes (cat. no. 148);
Source: Presented by A. T. Barber in 1924 (without attribution).

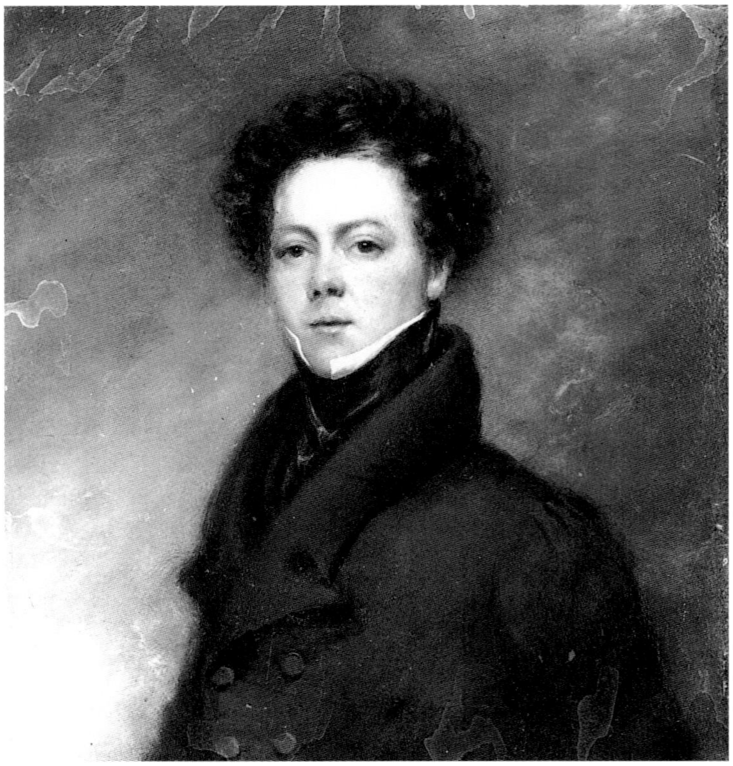

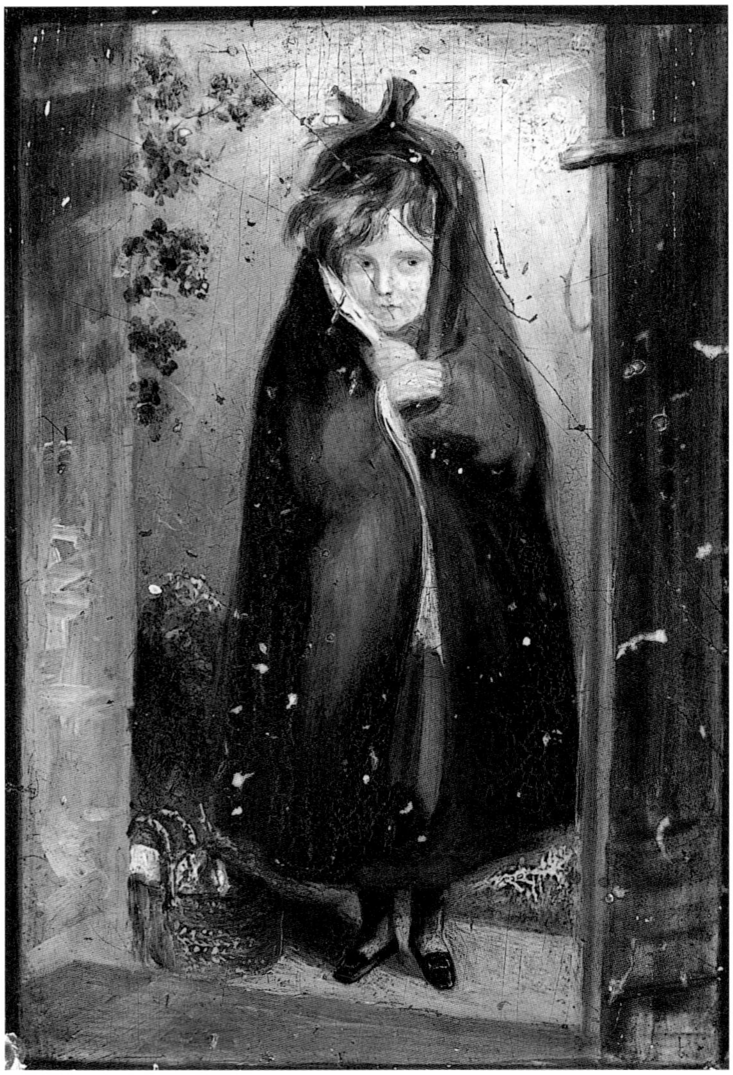

BRITISH SCHOOL

Portrait of an Unknown Man

[A7462]

*c.*1830–5

Oil on panel, 24.1 x 22.5 cm

Hayes (cat. no. 140);

Source: Purchased in 1912 (as a portrait of John Liston, the actor, by Roberts).

AFTER SIR EDWIN HENRY LANDSEER

(1802–73)

Little Red Riding Hood

[77.168/5]

(labelled 'Louisa Ducrow as a child')

Oil on panel,

22.9 x 16.1 cm

Source: Presented by Mrs S. E. Sutherland.

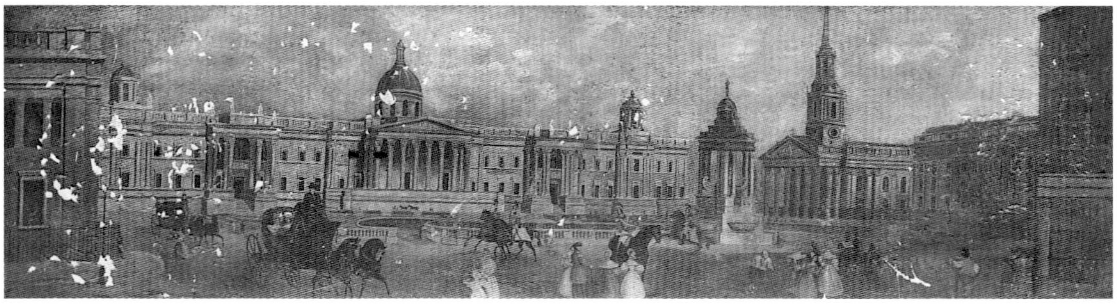

THOMAS WATERS

(active mid-nineteenth century)

Trafalgar Square from Spring Gardens [29.132]

*c.*1835

Oil on canvas, 48.1 x 177.5 cm

Hayes (cat. no. 180);

Source: Unknown.

Victoria's Reign

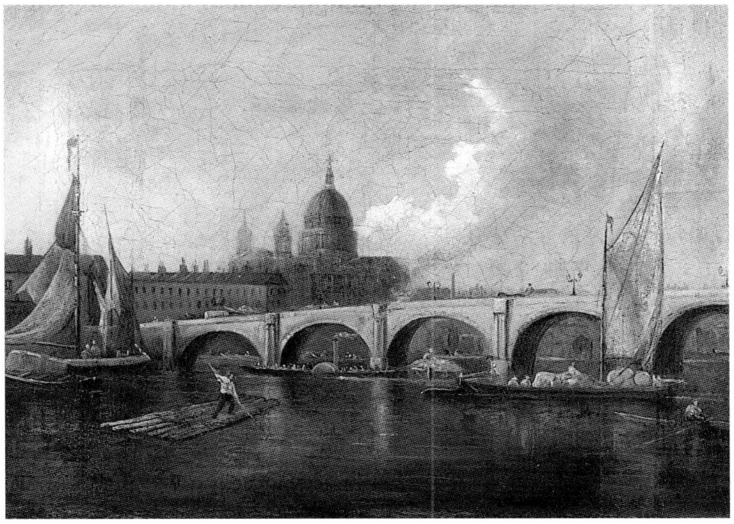

BRITISH SCHOOL
Blackfriars Bridge and St Paul's from the River [A22242]
*c.*1800–50
Oil on canvas, 26.25 x 39.4 cm
Hayes (cat. no. 132);
Source: Presented by Queen Mary in 1921 (as Sir A.W. Callcott).

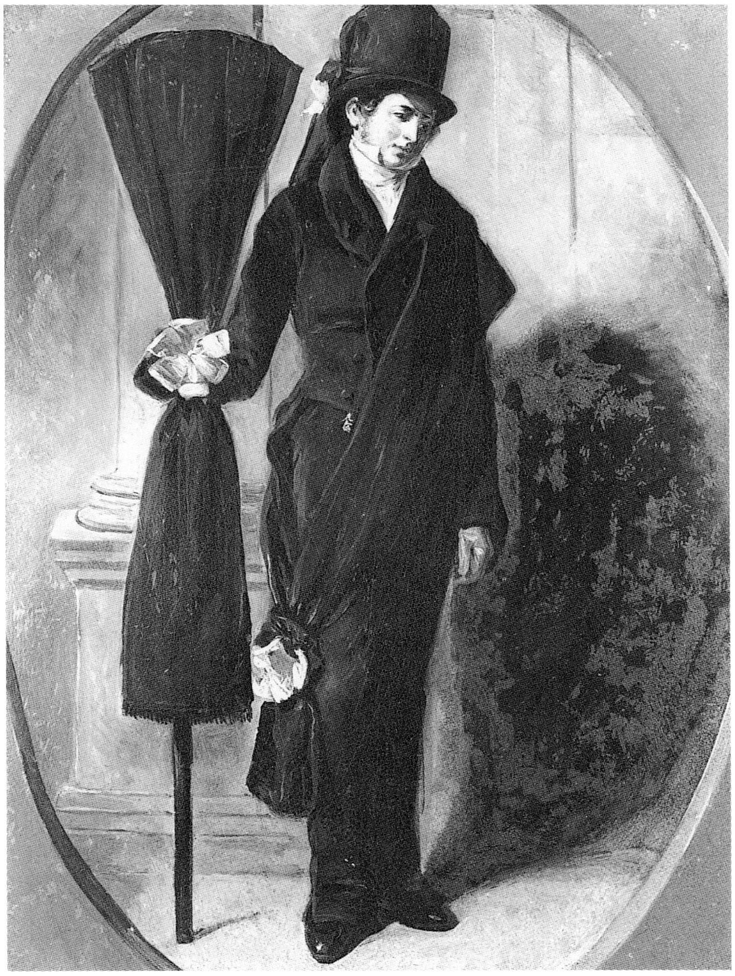

ROBERT WILLIAM BUSS (1804–74)
A Funeral Bearer [A9251]
*c.*1830–40
Oil on tinplate, 36.25 x 27.5 cm
Hayes (cat. no. 143);
Source: Presented by Gerald M. Burn in 1912 (without attribution).

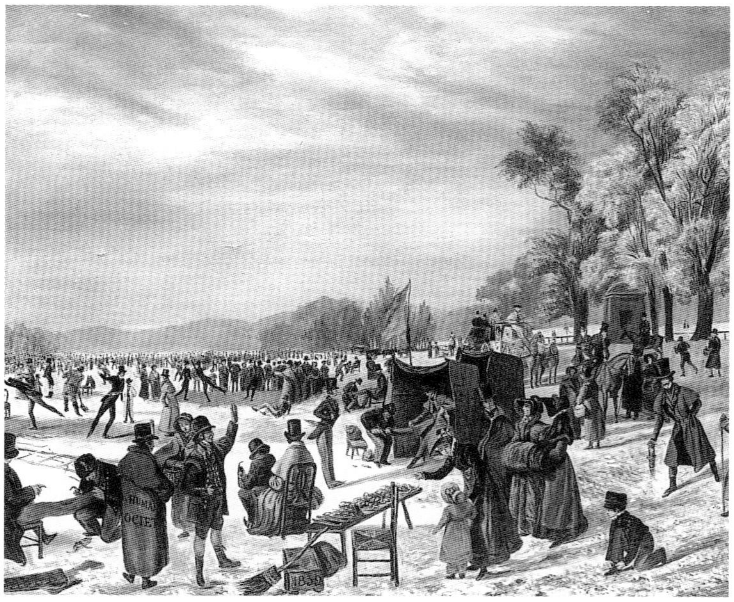

J. BABER
(active early nineteenth century)
Skating on the Serpentine
(A8076)
1839 (copy of a picture by John Chalon painted in 1823)
Oil on canvas, 45.3 x 55.5 cm
Hayes (cat. no. 5);
Source: Purchased from Leggatt Brothers in 1912.

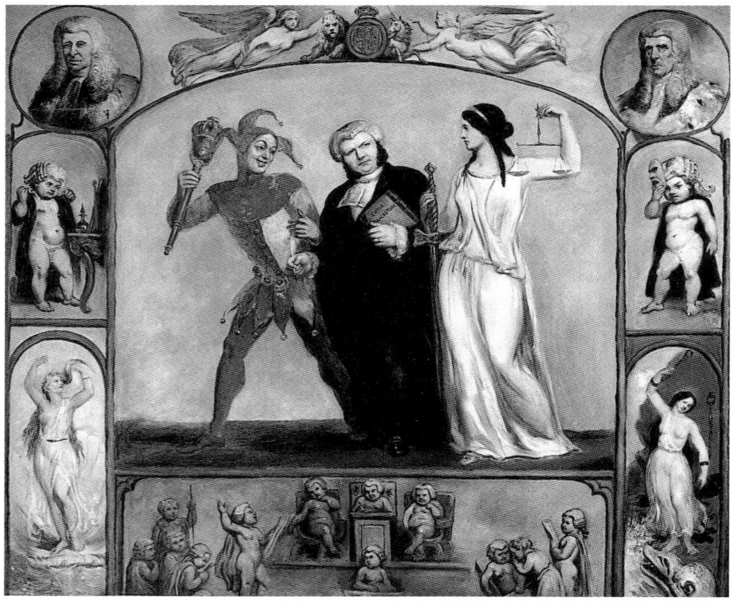

ARCHIBALD HENNING
(active second quarter of nineteenth century)
Portrait of Renton Nicholson (1809–61) with allegorical scenes and figures [34.272]
*c.*1841–61
Oil on canvas, 89.7 x 110 cm
Hayes (cat. no. 155);
Source: Presented by C. Reginald Grundy through the National Art Collections Fund in 1934.

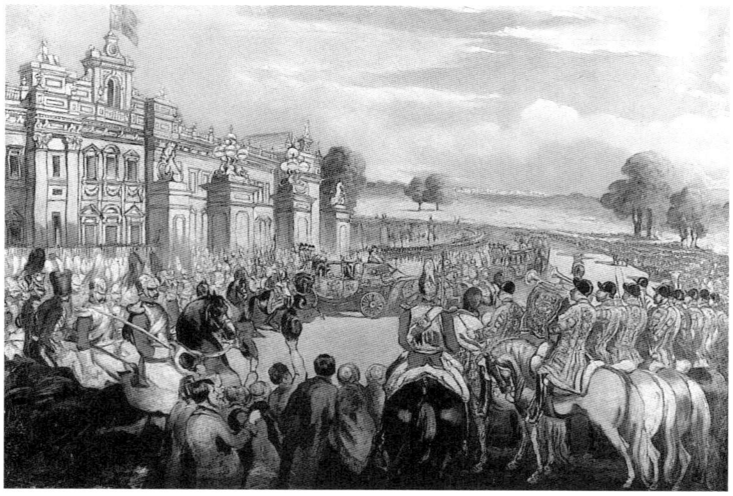

BRITISH SCHOOL
The Christening Procession of the Prince of Wales leaving Buckingham Palace [A23092a]
1842
Oil on canvas, 58.75 x 76.25 cm
Hayes (cat. no. 135);
Source: Presented by Alan F. Hooke in 1920 (as Henry Bright).

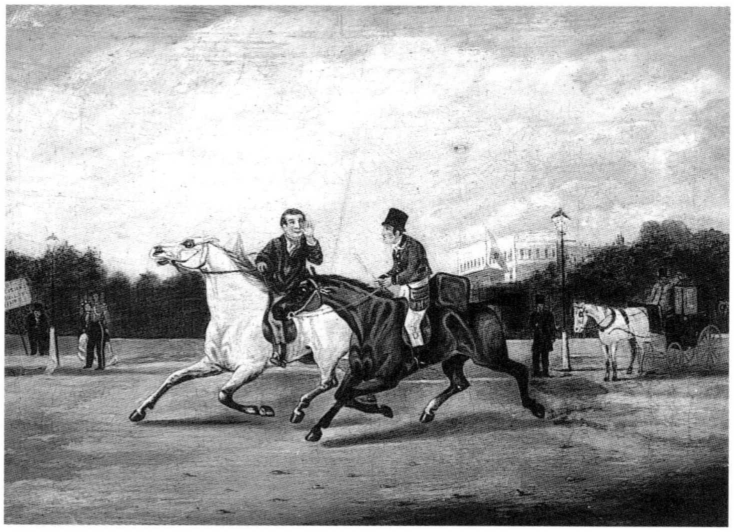

BRITISH SCHOOL
A Butcher's Boy racing with a Postman in the Mall [31.38]
*c.*1845–55
Oil on canvas, 40.6 x 57.5 cm
Hayes (cat. no. 134);
Source: Presented by Messrs Pawsey and Payne in 1931.

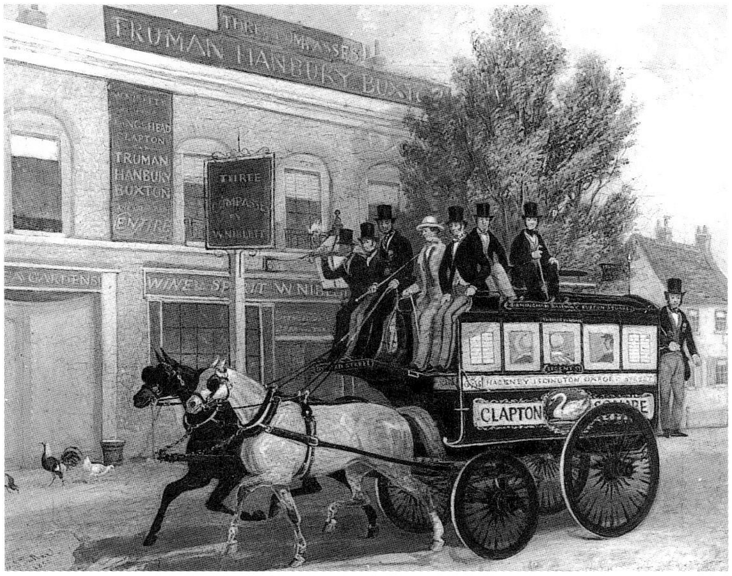

JAMES POLLARD
(1792–1867)
The Omnibus passing the Three Compasses Inn, Clapton
[A6392]
1850
Oil on canvas, 35 x 45 cm
Hayes (cat. no. 95);
Source: Purchased in 1913.

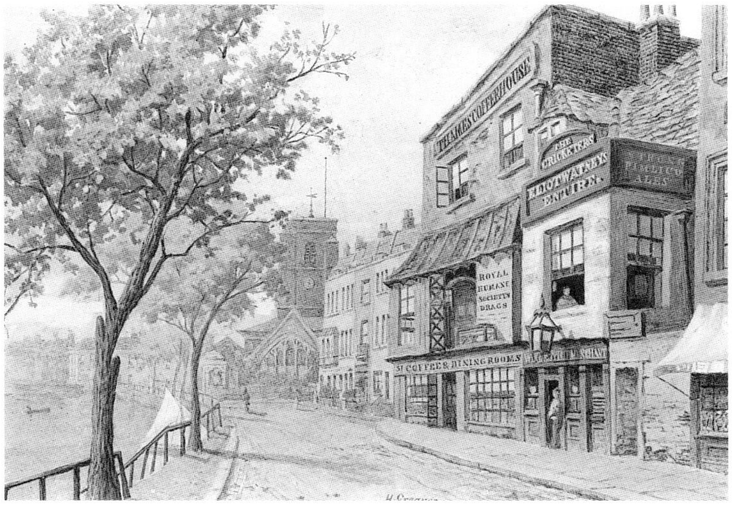

HENRY GREAVES
(1844—1904)
Cheyne Walk and Chelsea Old Church [60.58/2]
1857
Oil on cardboard, 23.75 x 34.35 cm
Hayes (cat. no. 46);
Source: Purchased from P. & D. Colnaghi in 1960.

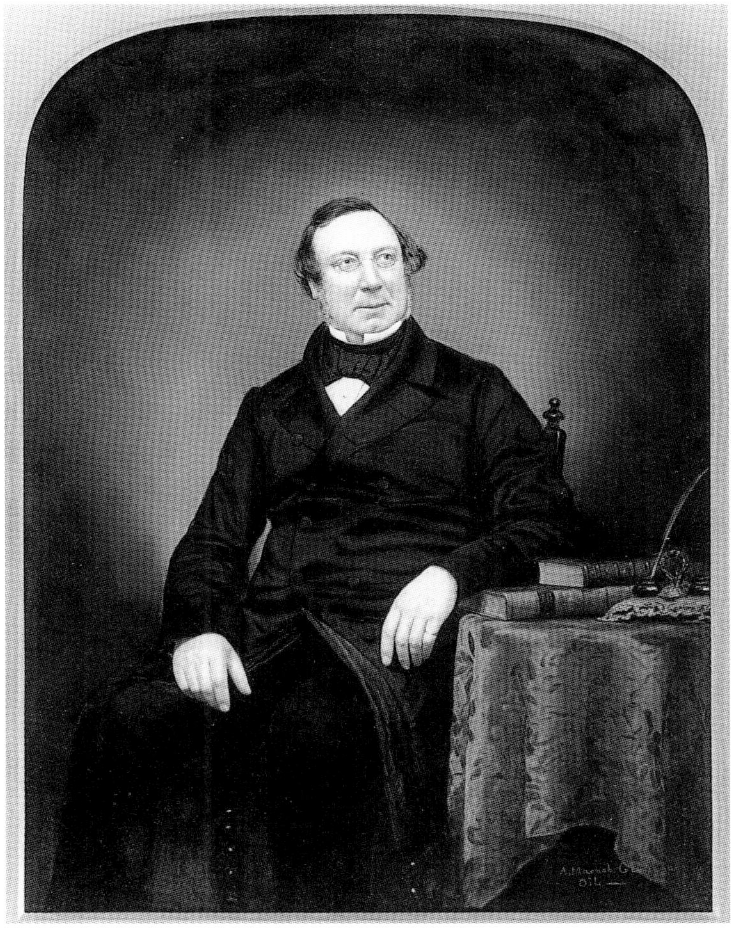

A. MACNAB
Portrait of an Unknown Man
[56.194/43]
*c.*1860
32.5 x 26.5 cm
Signed and dated bottom right: *A. Macnab Glasgow. Oil*
Source: Bequeathed by Mrs Mackenzie Bell in 1956.

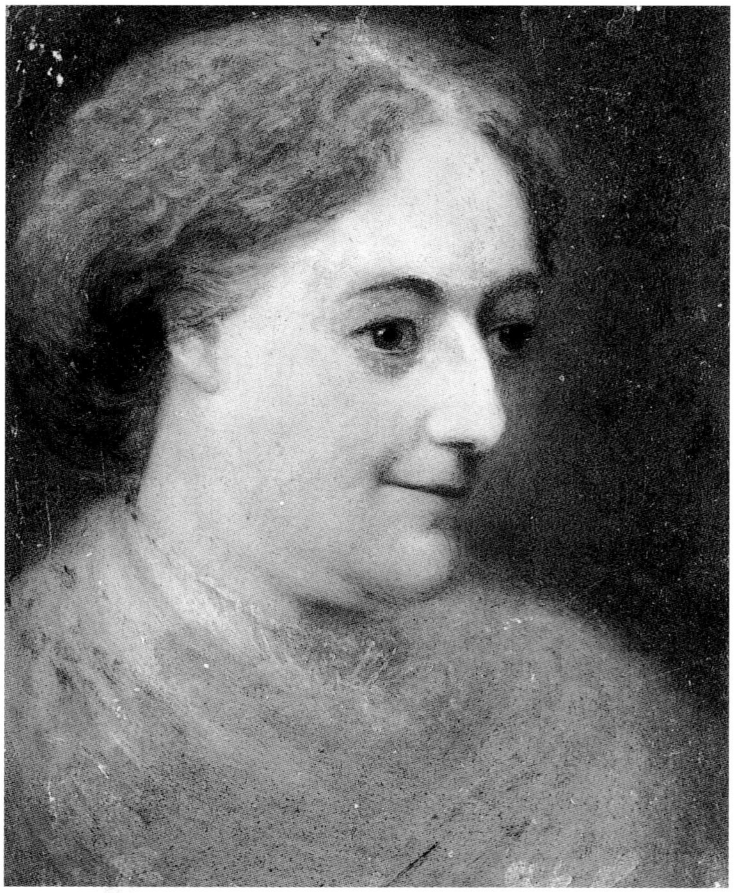

M. J. RORSNIGER
(active late nineteenth century)
Portrait of Mrs Fanny Stirling (1813–95), née Anne Mary Kehl [56.169/31]
*c.*1860–70
Oil on fibreboard, 30 x 25 cm
Hayes (cat. no. 167);
Source: Presented by R. N. Green-Armytage in 1956.

E. L. LAURIE
(active late nineteenth century)
The Coldstream Guards marching out of the Tower of London 3 April 1875 [A25332]
Oil on canvas, 66.3 x 101.25 cm
Hayes (cat. no. 65);
Source: Purchased in 1923.

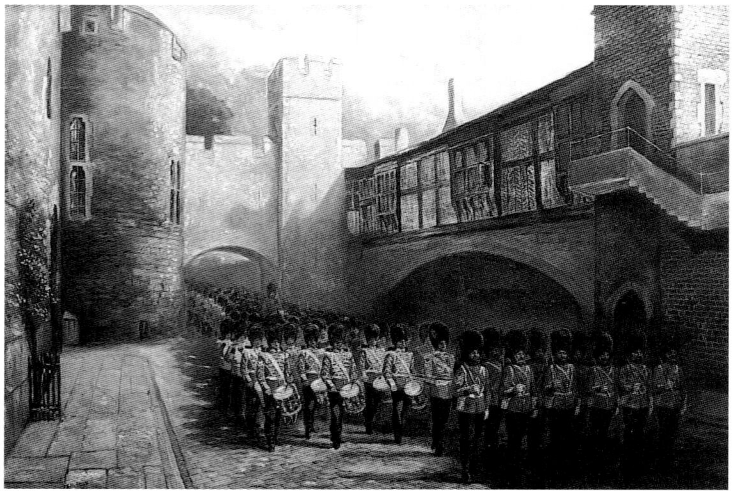

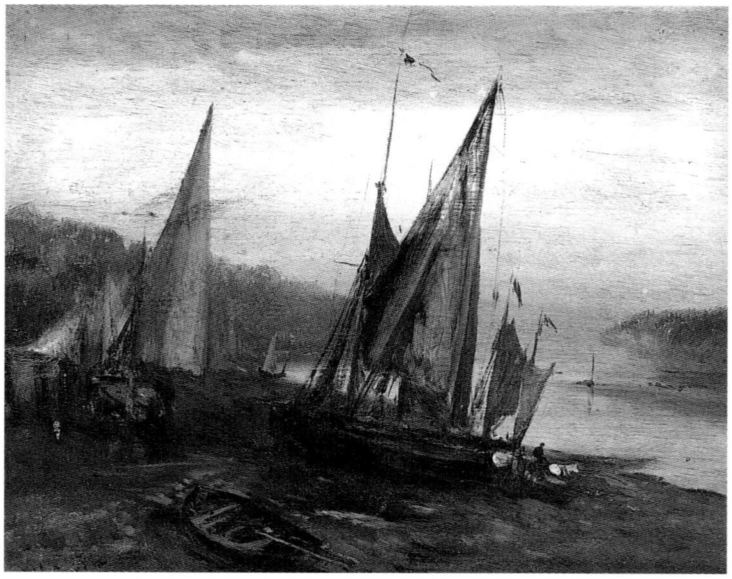

W. J. CALLCOTT
(active late nineteenth century)
Barges on the Thames [28.100/1]
1875–1900
Oil on canvas, 17.5 x 22.5 cm
Hayes (cat. no. 145);
Source: Presented by Herbert K. Rooke in 1928.

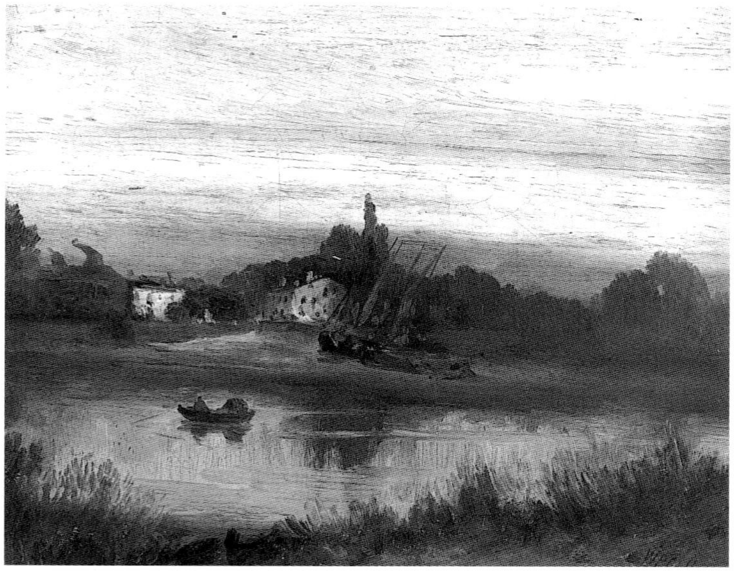

W. J. CALLCOTT
(active late nineteenth century)
The Crab Tree Inn, Fulham, from the Surrey Shore [28.100/2]
1875–1900
Oil on canvas, 17.5 x 22.5 cm
Hayes (cat. no. 146);
Source: Presented by Herbert K. Rooke in 1928.

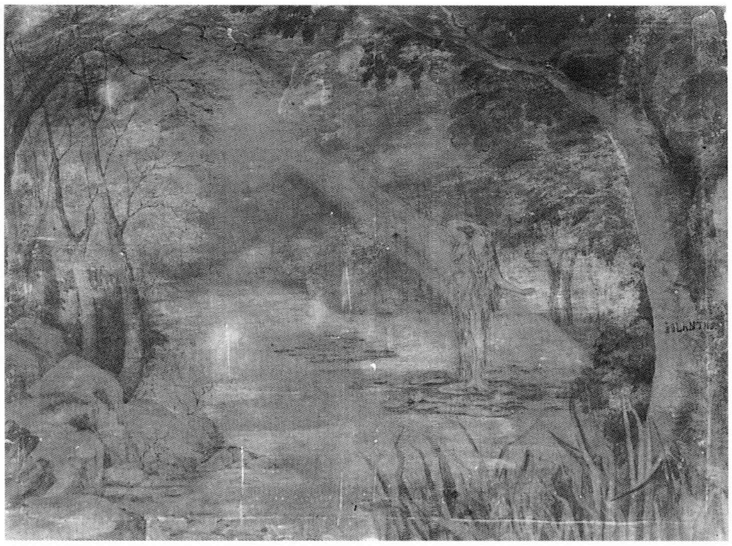

BRITISH SCHOOL
Jessie Bond as Iolanthe rising from the Stream [64.84]
*c.*1882
Oil on canvas, 86.4 x 117.5 cm
Hayes (cat. no. 133);
Source: Presented by Ernest J. Tytler in 1960.

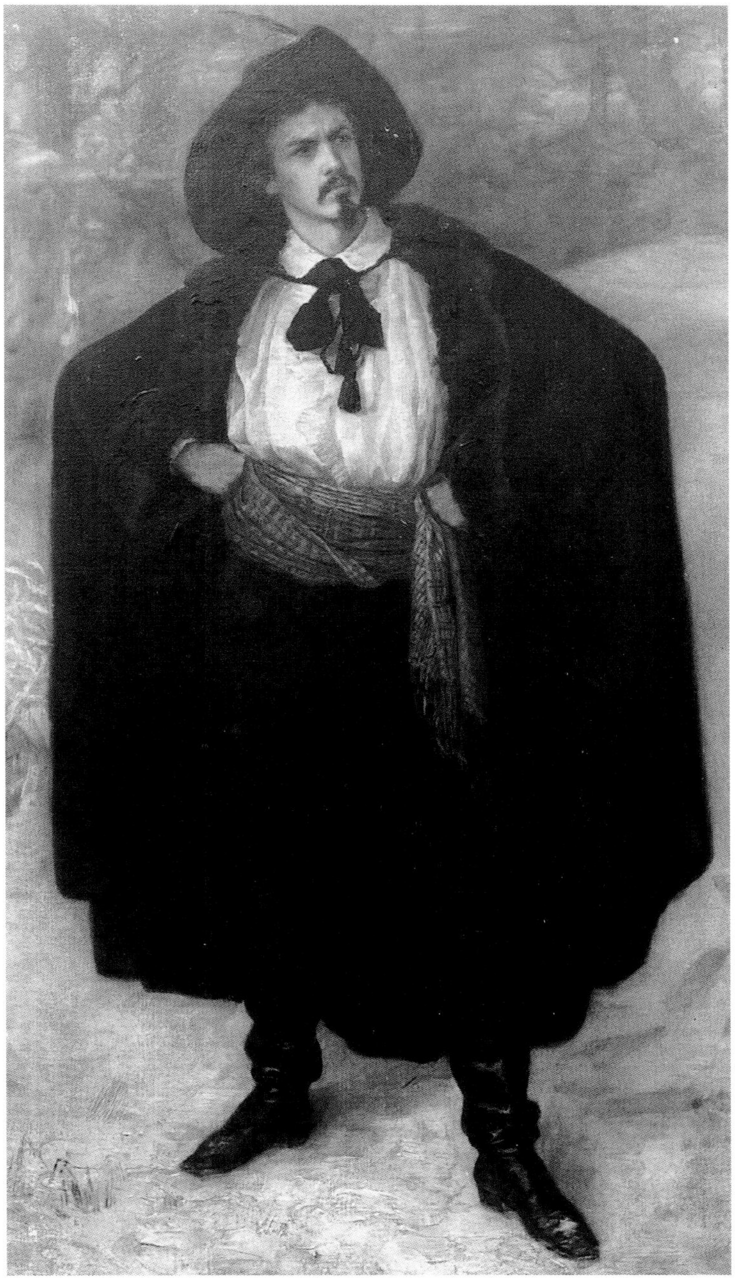

FRANK MARKHAM SKIPWORTH (d.1929)
An Unknown Man dressed as Fabien dei Franchi in The Corsican Brothers [A 28582]
1883
Oil on canvas, 75 x 43.3 cm
Hayes (cat. no. 172);
Source: Unknown.

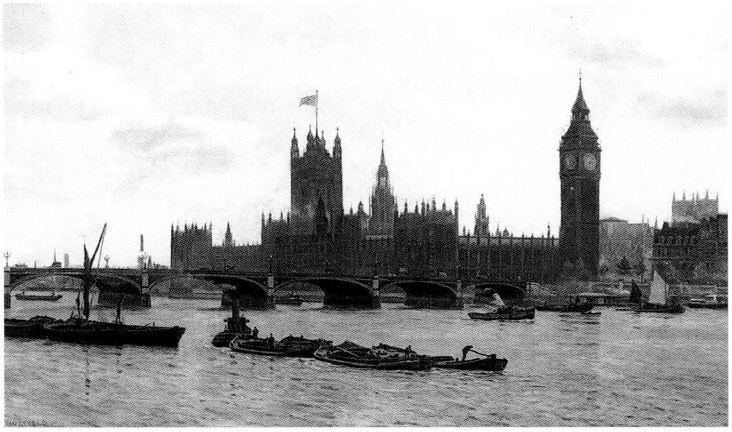

FREDERICK A. WINKFIELD
(active 1873–1904, d.1920)
Westminster Bridge and the Houses of Parliament from the River [61.142/1]
*c.*1890
Oil on canvas, 35.3 x 60 cm
Hayes (cat. no. 109);
Source: Purchased from the Piccadilly Gallery in 1961.

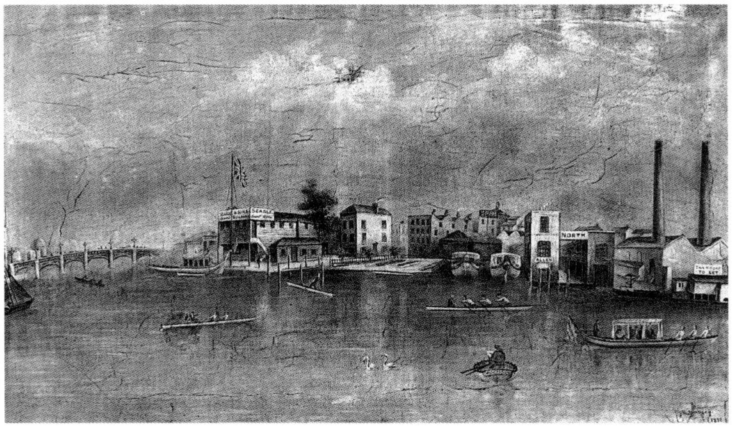

R. PEMBERY
(active second half nineteenth century)
Searle's Boat Building Yard, Lambeth, from the River [B732]
1890
Oil on canvas, 60.6 x 105.6 cm
Hayes (cat. no. 165);
Source: Purchased from the executors of Theodore Lumley in 1923.

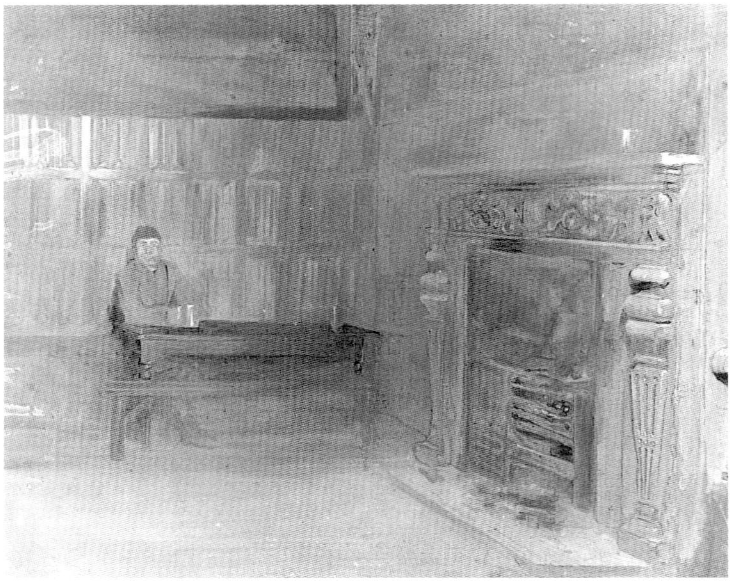

FREDERICK ROE
(1864–1947)
The Tap Room of the Baptist's Head Inn, Clerkenwell [A25674]
1891
Oil on canvas, 45 x 52.2 cm
Hayes (cat. no. 166);
Source: Presented by Frederick Gordon Roe (the artist's son) in 1923.

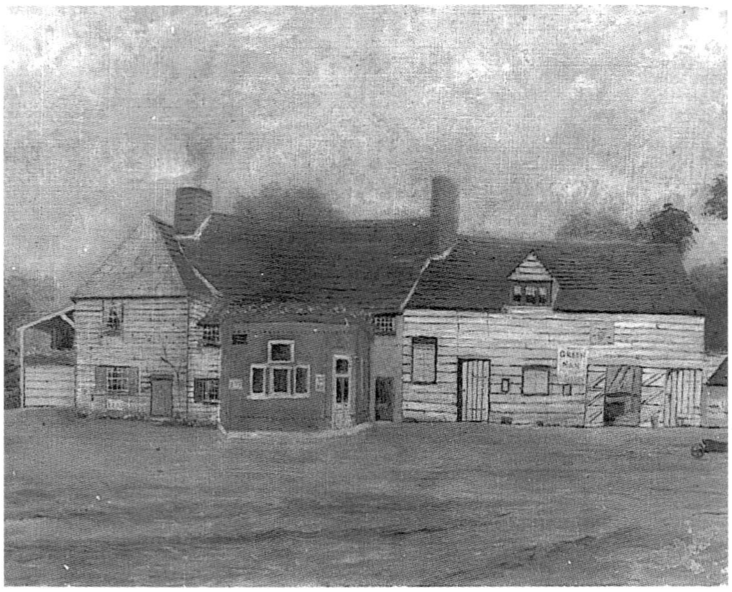

KIRBY WATFORD
(active late nineteenth century)
The Green Man Inn, Wembley
[53.137]
1899
Oil on canvas, 25 x 47 cm
Hayes (cat. no. 181);
Source: Presented by C. Burgin in 1953.

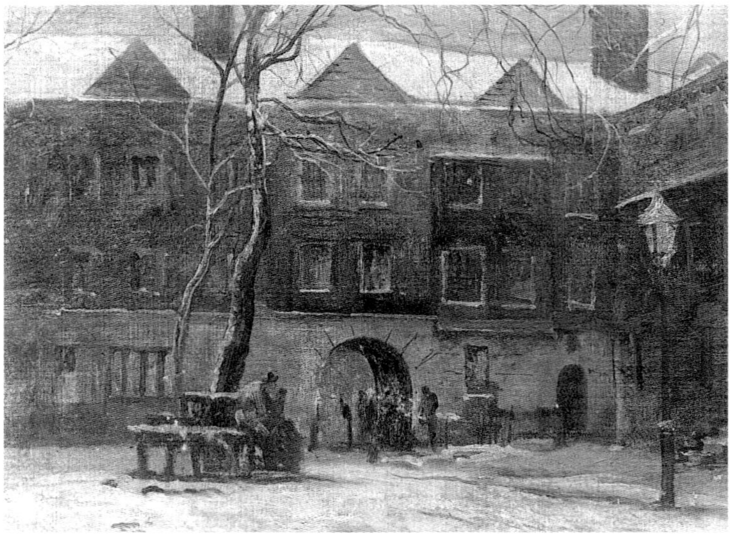

TOM HESLEWOOD
(1868–1959)
The Quadrangle of Staple Inn
[38.209/1]
*c.*1900
Oil on canvas board,
27.7 x 37.7 cm
Hayes (cat. no. 157);
Source: Presented by the artist in 1938.

BRITISH SCHOOL
Portrait of William Shakespeare
[64.61/1]
Date uncertain
Oil on panel, 26.7 x 20.6 cm
Hayes (cat. no. 138);
Source: Presented by Mrs D. Brooke-Booth in 1964.

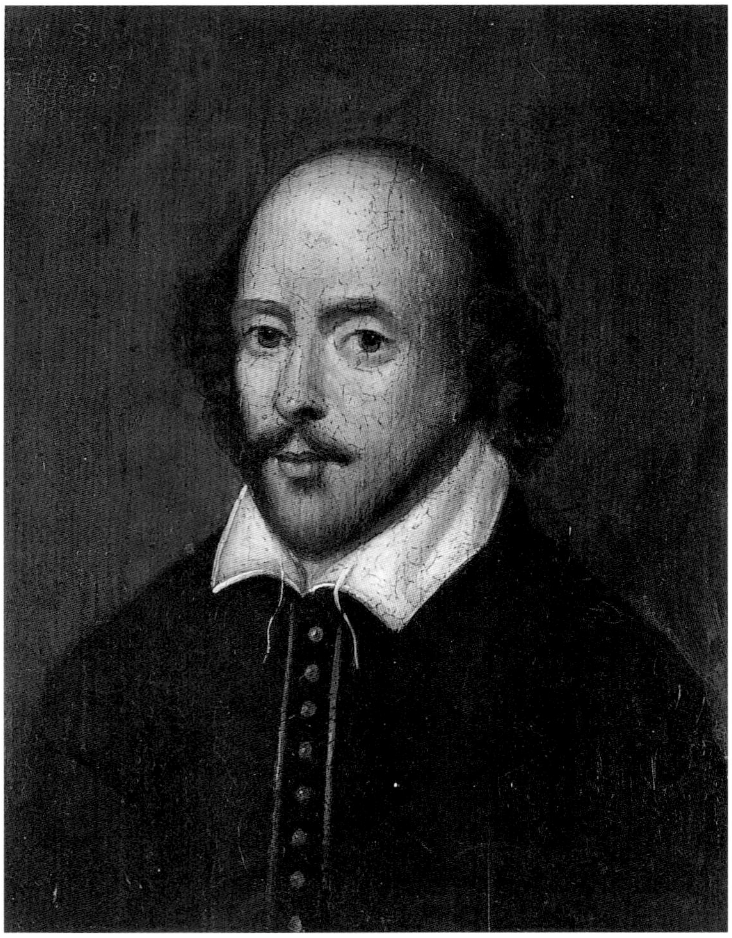

Early Twentieth Century

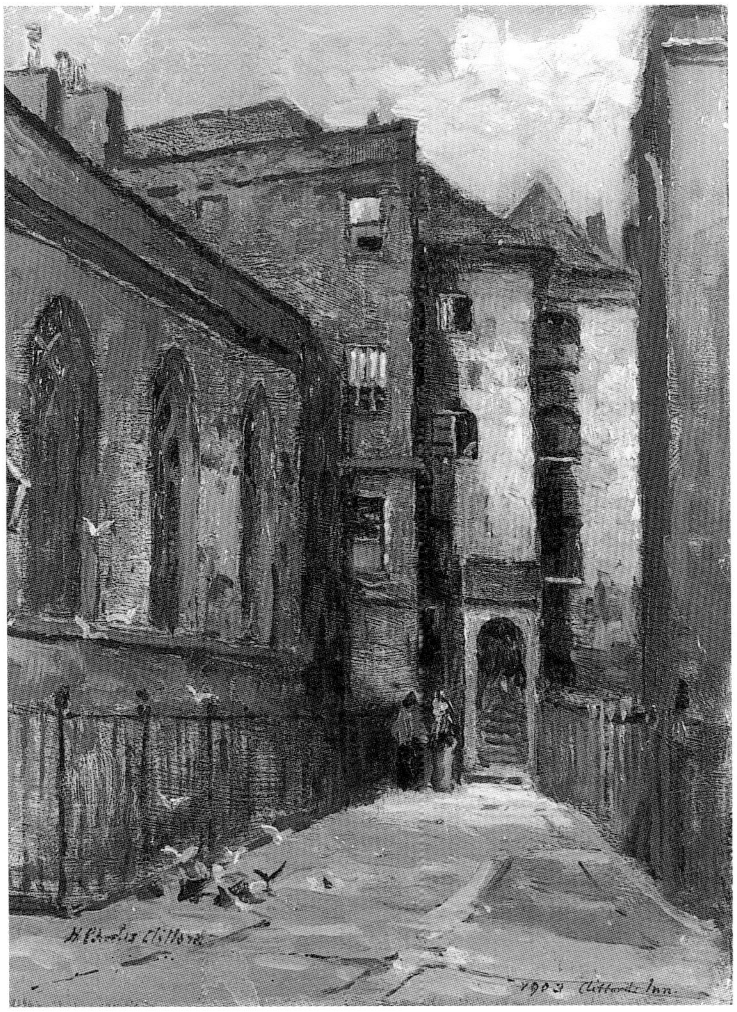

HENRY CHARLES CLIFFORD (1861–1947)
No. 8 Clifford's Inn, with part of the Hall [A23976]
1903
Oil on canvas board,
23.1 x 17.2 cm
Hayes (cat. no. 28);
Source: Purchased in 1921.

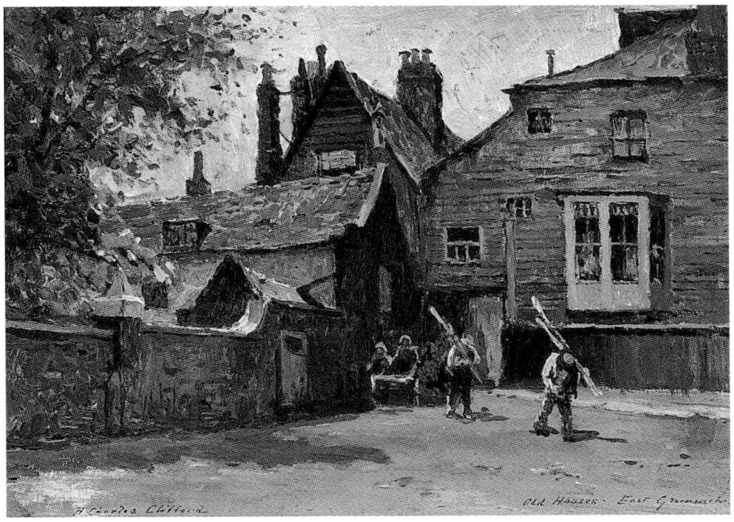

HENRY CHARLES CLIFFORD (1861–1947)
A Scene in East Greenwich
[A24289]
1903
Oil on board,
19.7 x 28.6 cm
Hayes (cat. no. 29);
Source: Purchased in 1921.

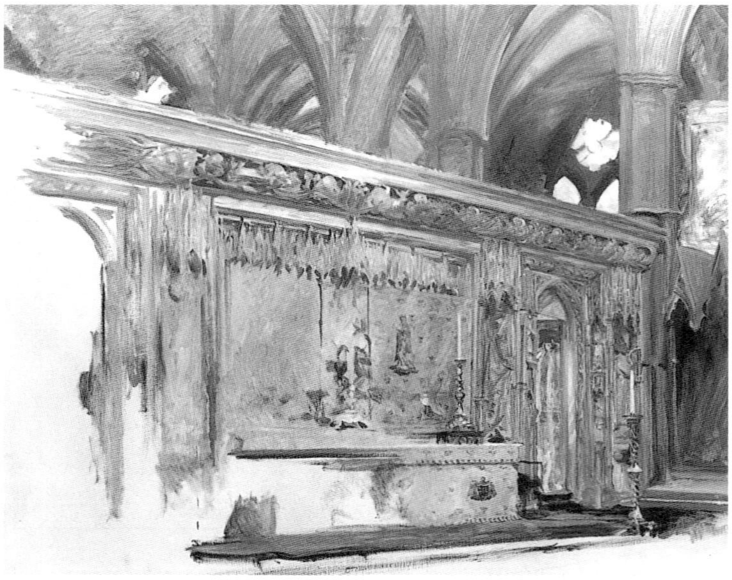

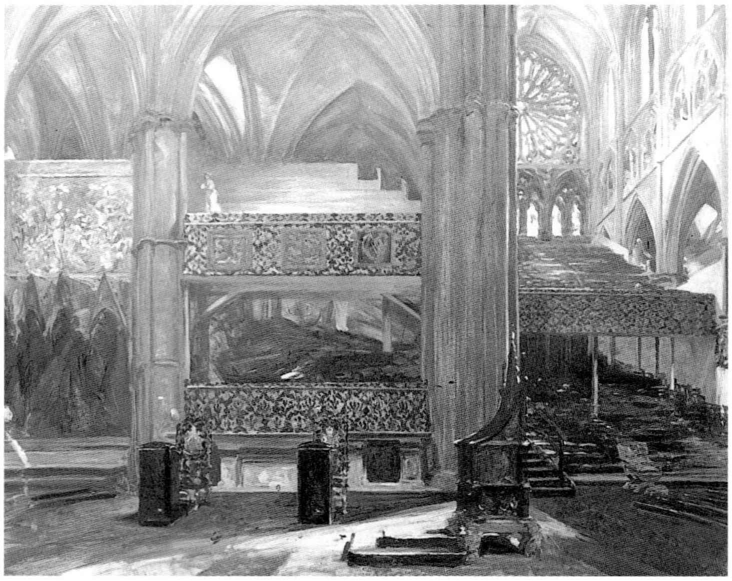

JOHN HENRY FREDERICK BACON
(1865–1914)
Unfinished sketches for part of the large canvas of the coronation of King George V and Queen Mary:

Interior of Westminster Abbey, showing the high altar
[A13264]
1914
Oil on canvas, 100 x 124.6 cm
Hayes (cat. no. 6);
Source: Christie's, 27 April 1914 (60).

Interior of Westminster Abbey, looking into the S. Transept
[A13265]
1914
Oil on canvas, 100 x 124.6 cm
Hayes (cat. no. 7);
Source: Christie's, 27 April 1914 (60).

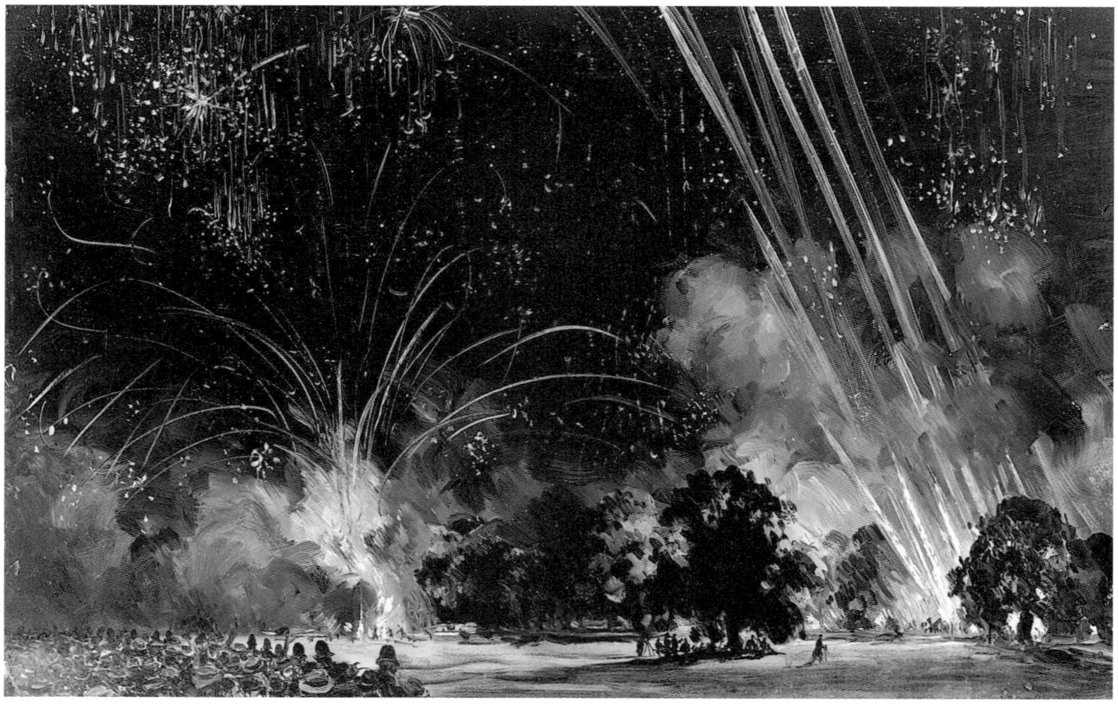

A. SIMPSON
(active 1910s and '20s)
Fireworks in Hyde Park on Peace Night [A20683]
1919
Oil on board, 38.8 x 61.8 cm
Signed bottom right
Source: Presented by the *Illustrated London News* in 1919.

EDGAR SELIGMAN
(active 1920s)

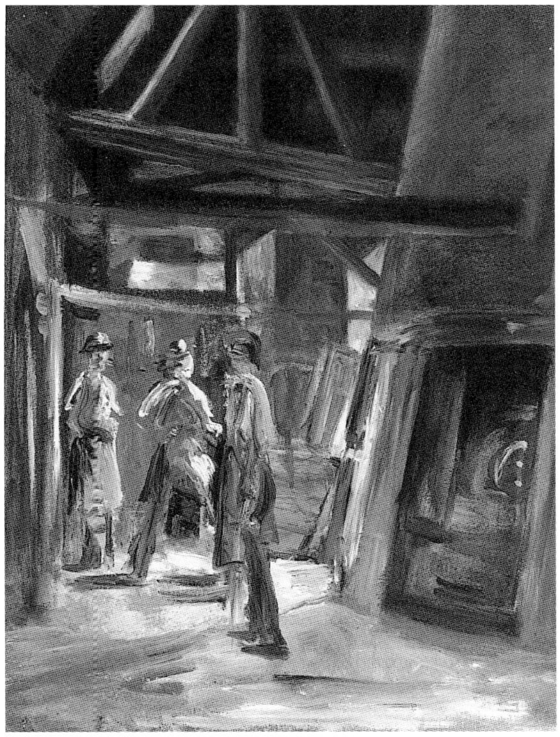

Whitefriars Glass Works: the glass house
[80.547/1004]
1920
Oil on canvas board,
46.0 x 36.0 cm
Source: Whitefriars Archive
(see cat. no. 71).

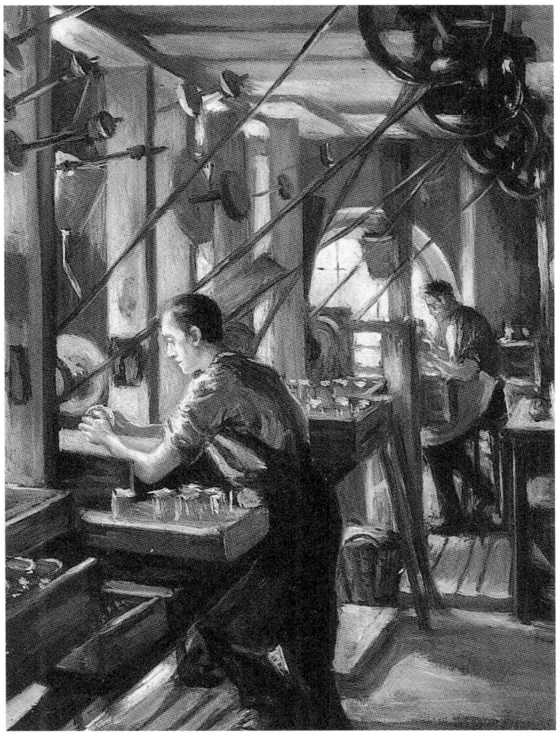

Whitefriars Glass Works: cutting shop using belt driven lathes
[80.547/1005]
1920
Oil on canvas board,
46.5 x 35.3 cm
Source: Whitefriars Archive
(see cat. no. 71).

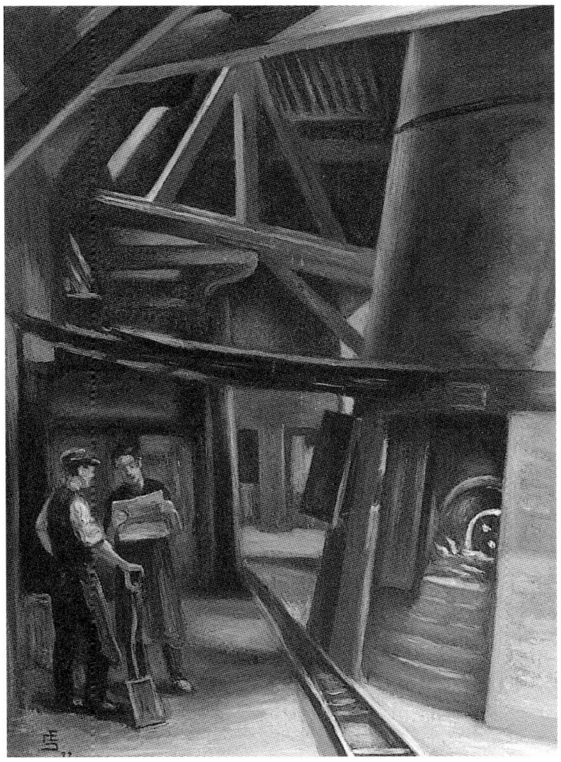

Whitefriars Glass Works: the glass house
[80.547/1001]
1922
Oil on canvas board,
46.0 x 35.4 cm
Source: Whitefriars Archive
(see cat. no. 71).

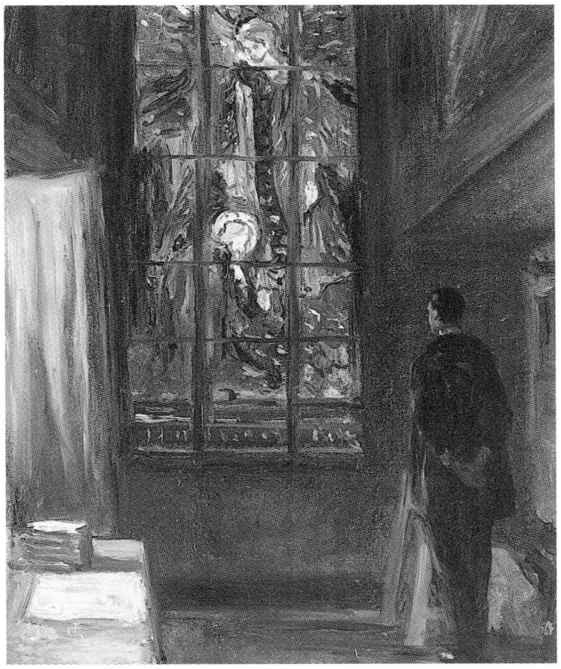

Whitefriars Glass Works: man viewing completed stained glass window, 1922
[80.547/1002]
Oil on canvas board,
42.0 x 35.4 cm
Source: Whitefriars Archive
(see cat. no. 71).

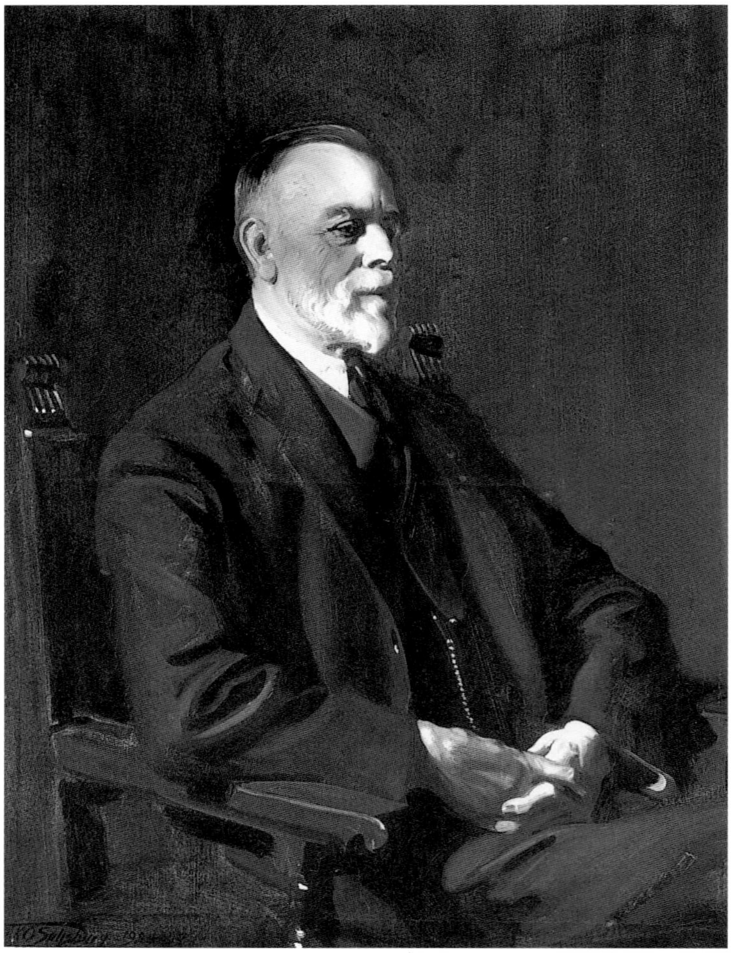

FRANK O. SALISBURY
(1874–1962)
Portrait of a member of the Powell Family who ran the Whitefriars Glass Works
[80.547/1008]
1924?
Oil on canvas, 112.5 x 87.5 cm
Source: Whitefriars Archive (see cat. no.71).

ERNEST STAMP
(1869–1942)
Perrin's Court, Hampstead
[37.212]
1931
Oil on panel, 42.8 x 30 cm
Hayes (cat. no. 173);
Source: Presented by the artist in 1937.

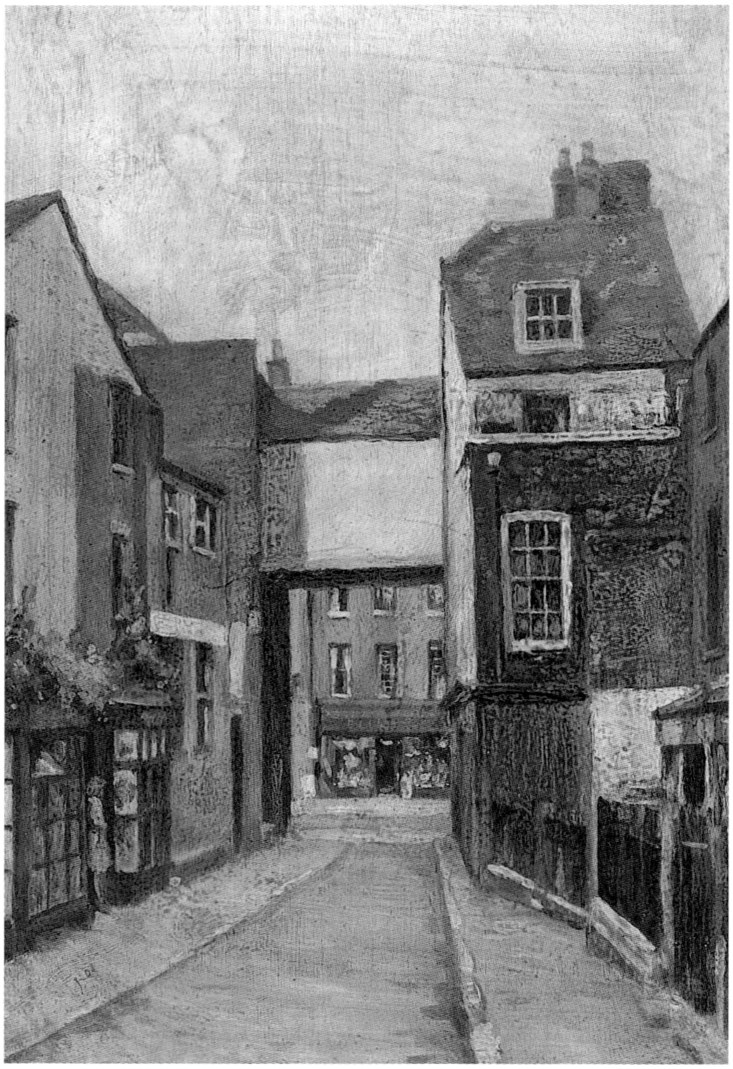

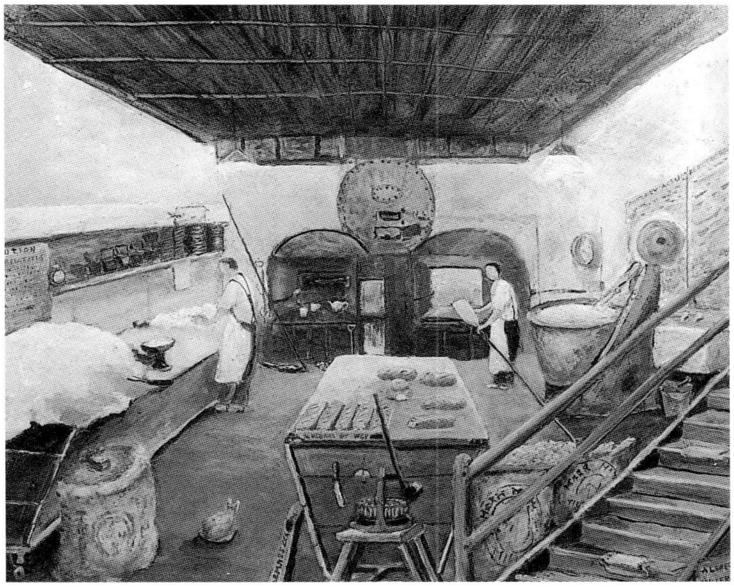

ALFRED MILLER
(active mid-twentieth century)
A Bakery in Floral Street, Covent Garden [59.53]
1959 (retrospective work – subject: 1934)
Oil on fibreboard, 47.5 x 60.3 cm
Hayes (cat. no. 161);
Source: Presented by the artist in 1959.

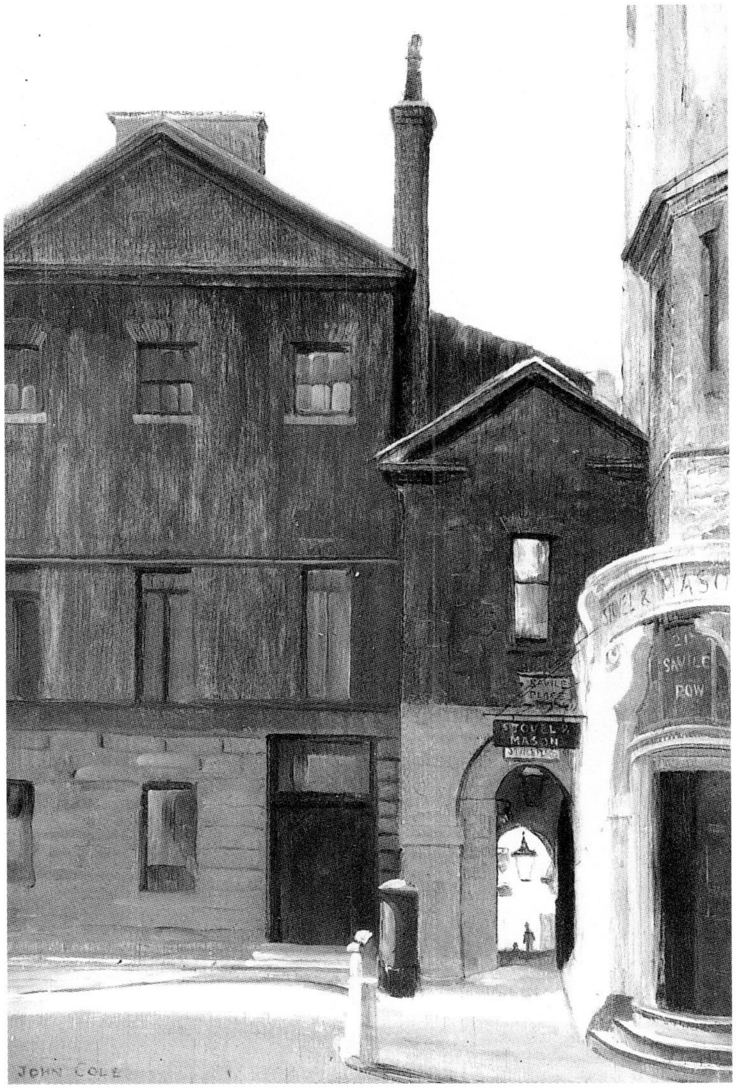

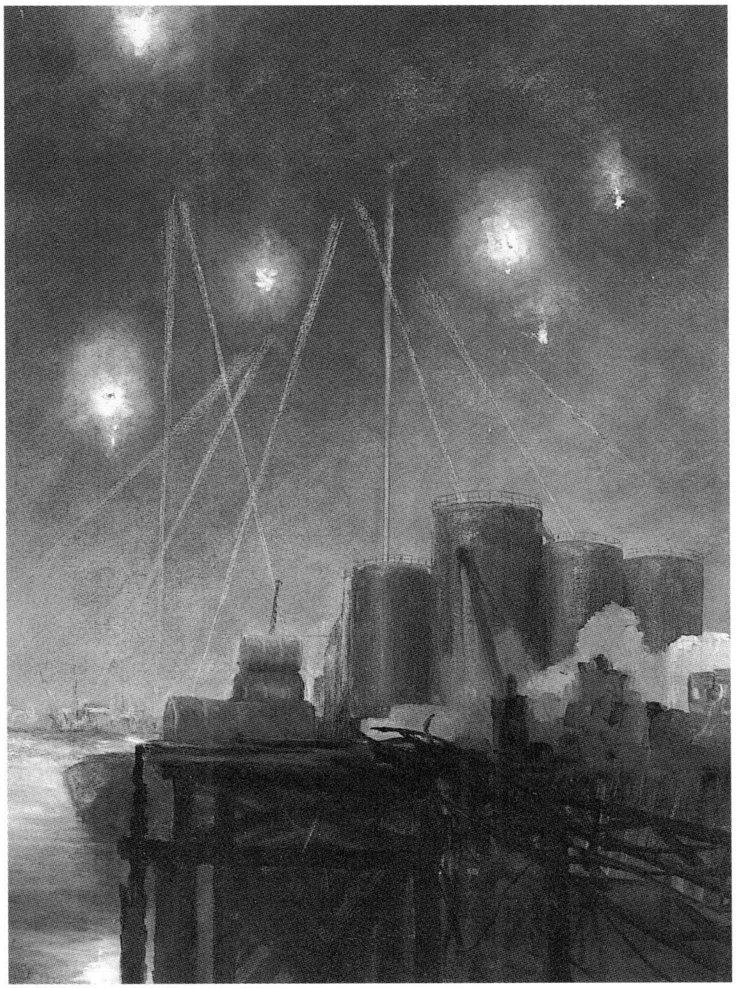

JOHN VICAT COLE
(born 1903)
View of former Alpine Club and passage from Savile Row leading to Conduit Street
[76.152/5]
Late 1930s
Oil on panel, 27.3 x 37 cm
Source: bequeathed by Miss H. A. D. Barlow in 1976.

W. S. HAINES (1905–1944)
Night Air Raid with Anti-aircraft Shells exploding over Oil Tanks [81.105/1]
*c.*1941
Oil on canvas, 60.8 x 46 cm
Source: Presented by Mr V. Haines (the artist's brother) through the Imperial War Museum in 1980.

Modern London

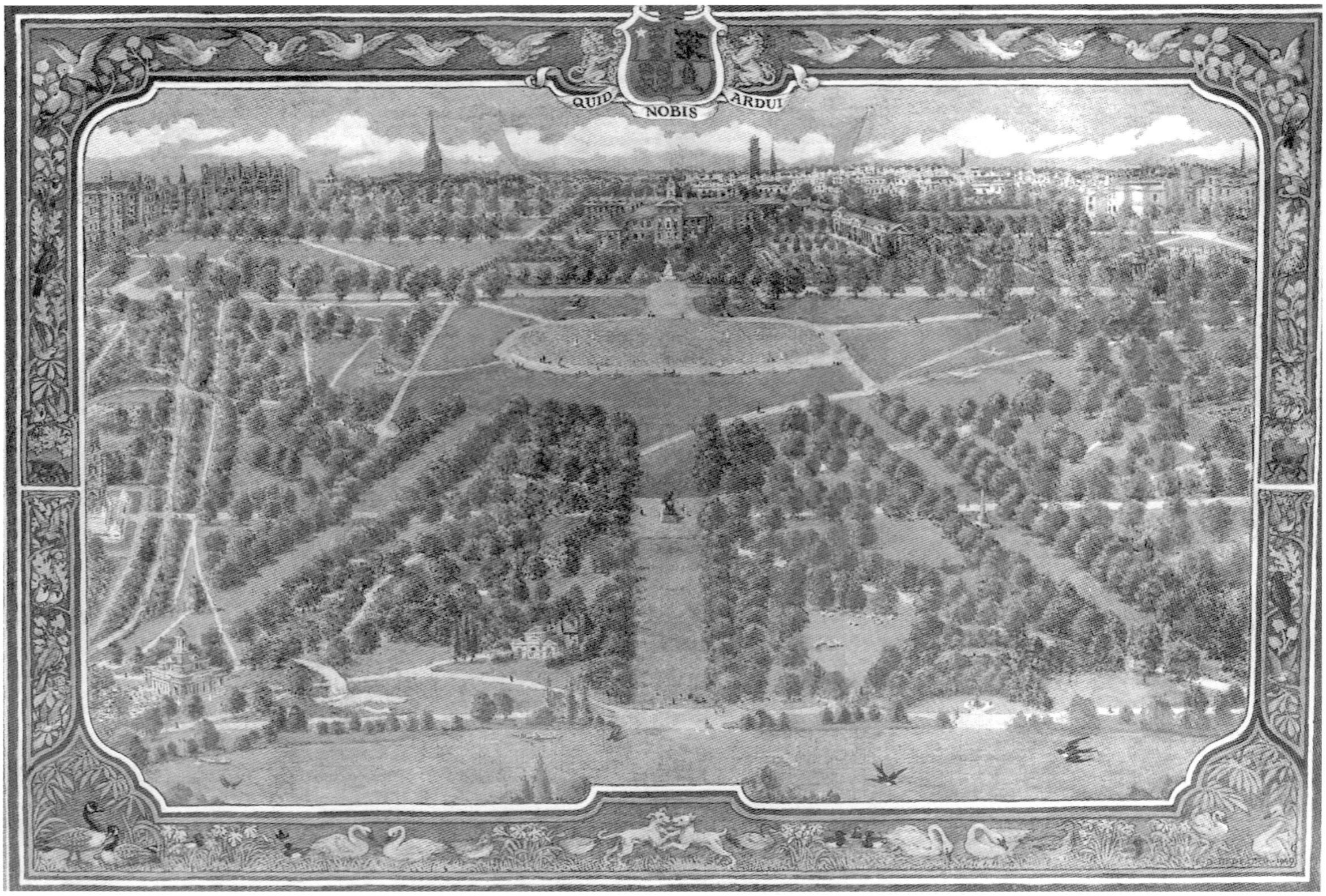

FRANCIS DONKIN BEDFORD (1864–?)
Bird's Eye View of Kensington Palace and Gardens from above the Serpentine [64.155]
Mid-twentieth century

Tempera on canvas,
49.1 x 72.8 cm
Hayes (cat. no. 127);
Source: Presented by
A. D. Royce in 1964.

NOEL SPENCER (1901–1986)

Facade of the Church of St Ethelburga, Bishopsgate
[81.36/4]
1955
Tempera, on board,
57.2 x 26.5 cm
Source: Gift from the artist in 1981.

Kensal Green Cemetery
[81.36/5]
1960
Tempera on board,
38.5 x 34.5 cm
Source: Gift from the artist in 1981.

Looking down Clink Street from Southwark Cathedral
[81.36/1]
1961
Tempera on board,
74.2 x 27.4 cm
Source: Gift from the artist in 1981.

Pickle Herring Street
[81.36/2]
1961
Tempera on board,
74 x 31.2 cm
Source: Gift from the artist in 1981.

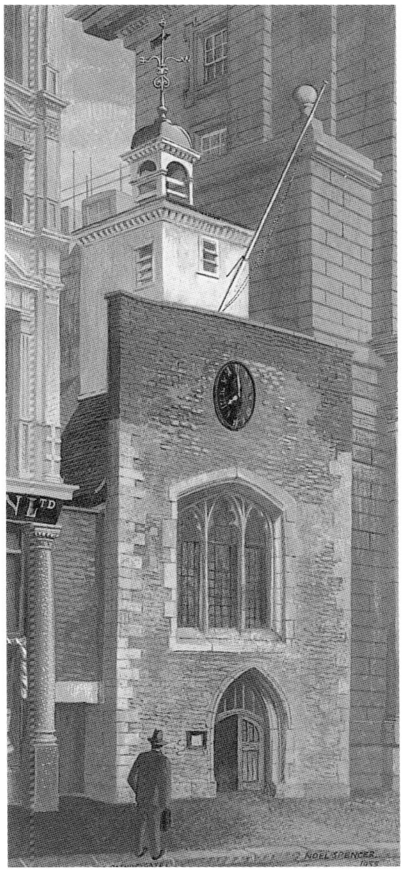

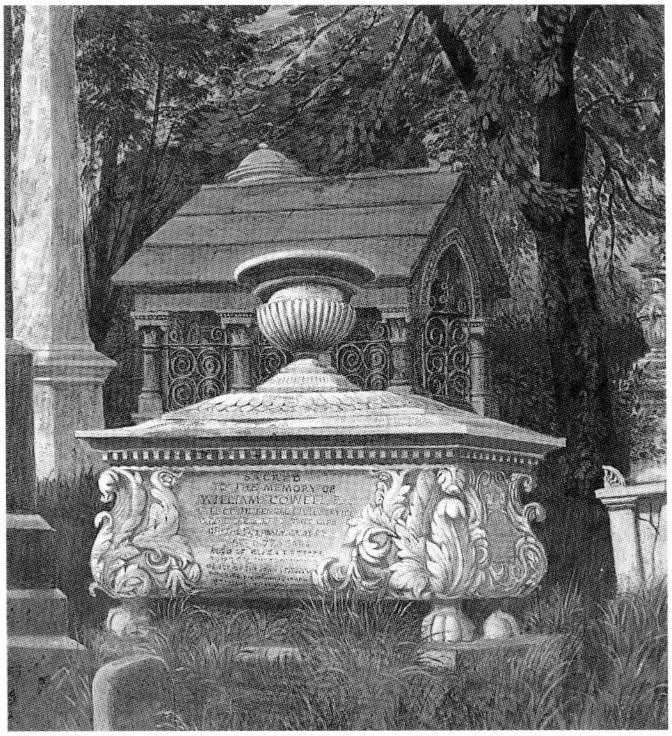

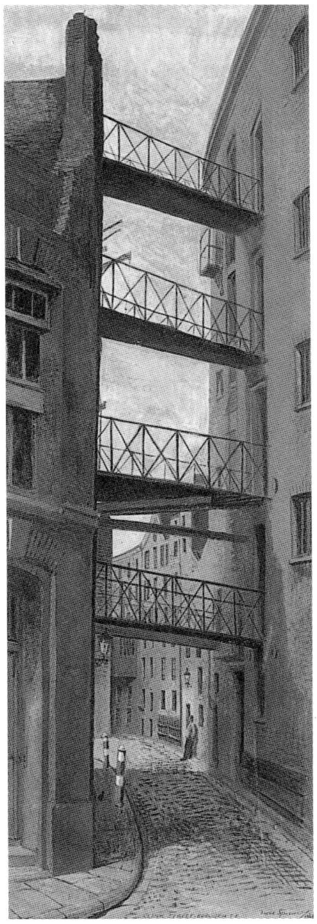

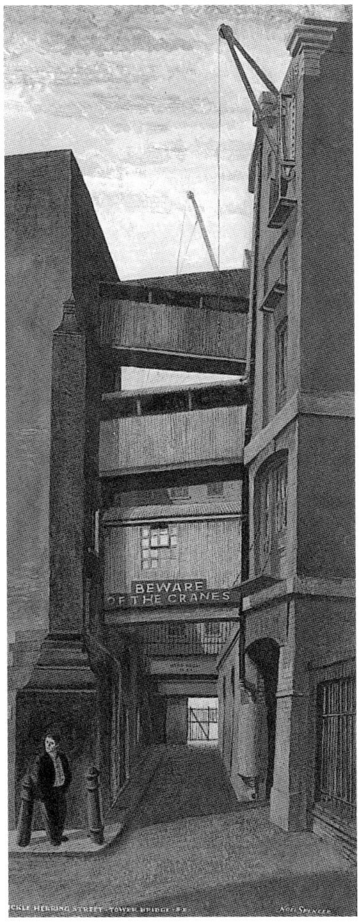

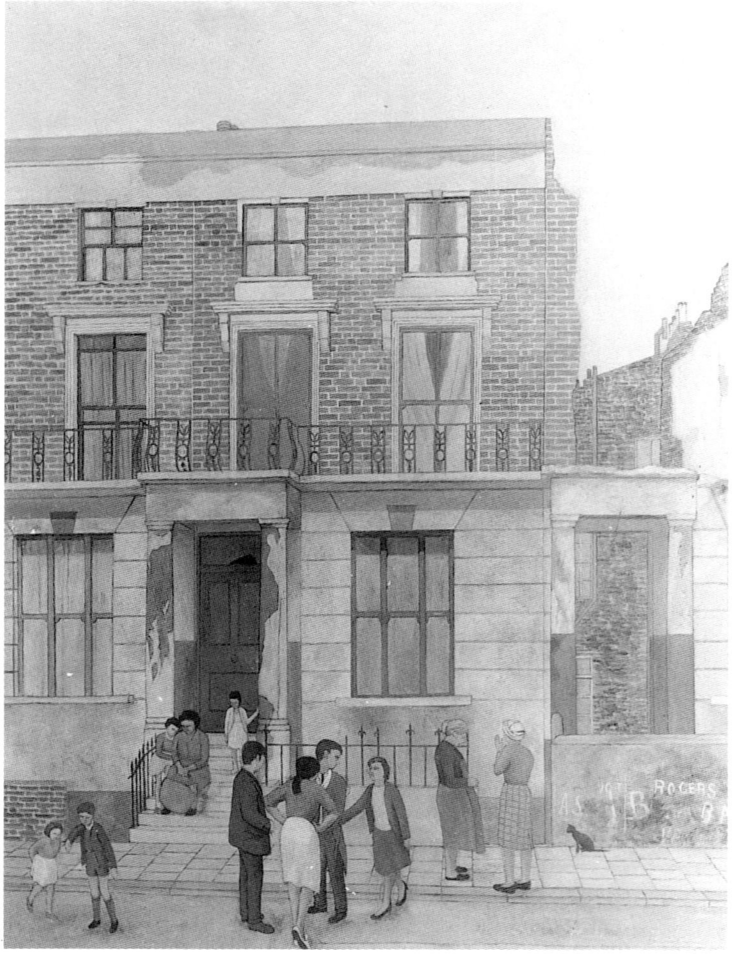

CHRISTOPHER HALL
(born 1930)
A Scene in Southam Street, N. Kensington [61.62]
1959
Oil on fibreboard, 51.25 x 40 cm
Hayes (cat. no. 51);
Source: Purchased from Arthur Jeffress Gallery in 1961.

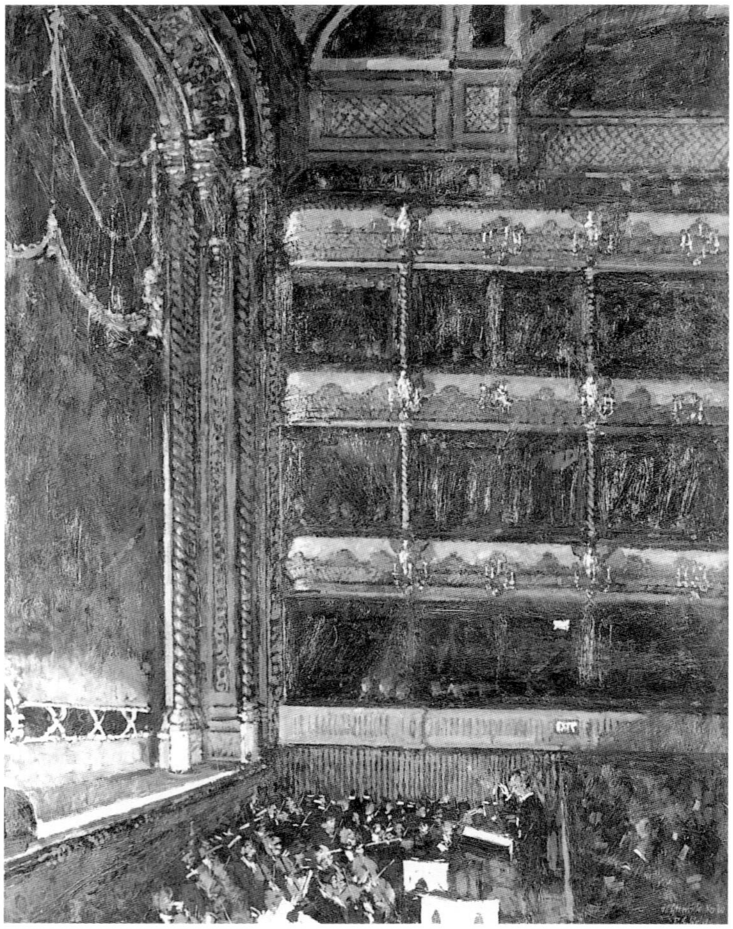

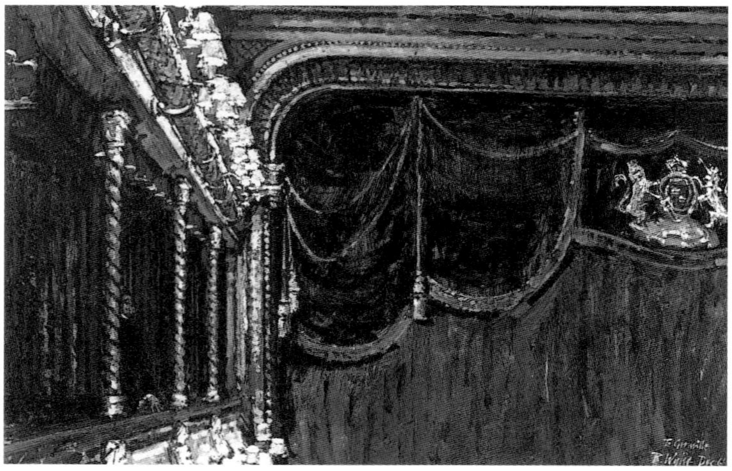

RAYMOND WYLIE
(active 1960s)
Covent Garden Opera House
[74.84/2]
1961
Oil on canvas, 127 x 101 cm
Source: Gift from Peter Alward in 1974.

Covent Garden Opera House
[74.84/1]
1961
Oil on canvas, 51.5 x 77 cm
Source: Gift from Peter Alward in 1974.

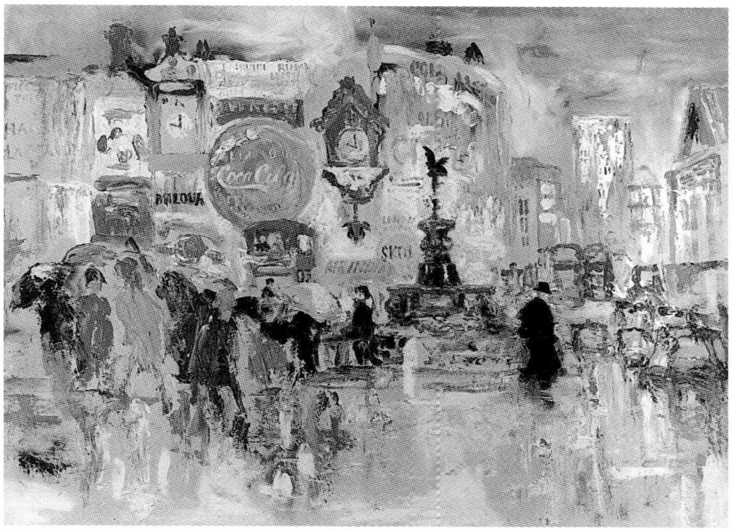

CHARLES POTTER
(active 1960s)
Piccadilly Circus
[77.169/14]
1960s
Oil on board, 38 x 43 cm
Source: Presented by the artist in 1977.

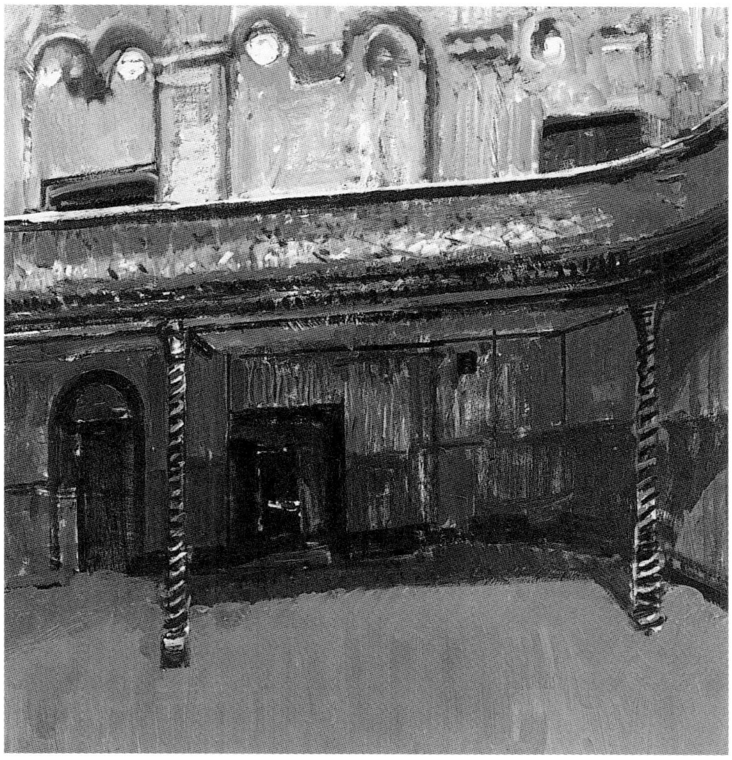

DAVID GRAHAM
(born 1926)
Wilton's Music Hall [80.448]
1970
Oil on canvas, 61 x 60 cm
Source: Purchased from Leonie Jonleigh Studio, Guildford, Surrey in 1980.

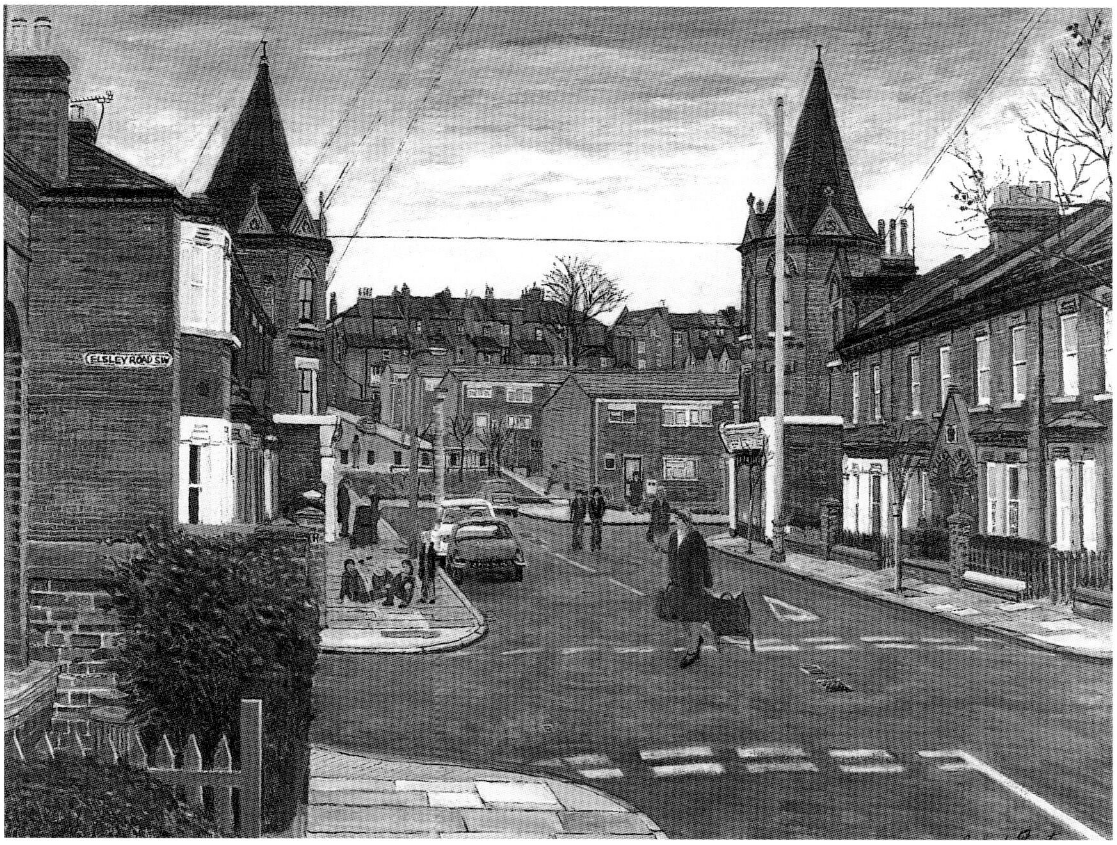

ROBERT POWTER
Grayshott Road, Battersea
[80.162]
1978–9
Oil on canvas, 76 x 101.5 cm
Source: Purchased from Fieldborne Galleries in 1980.

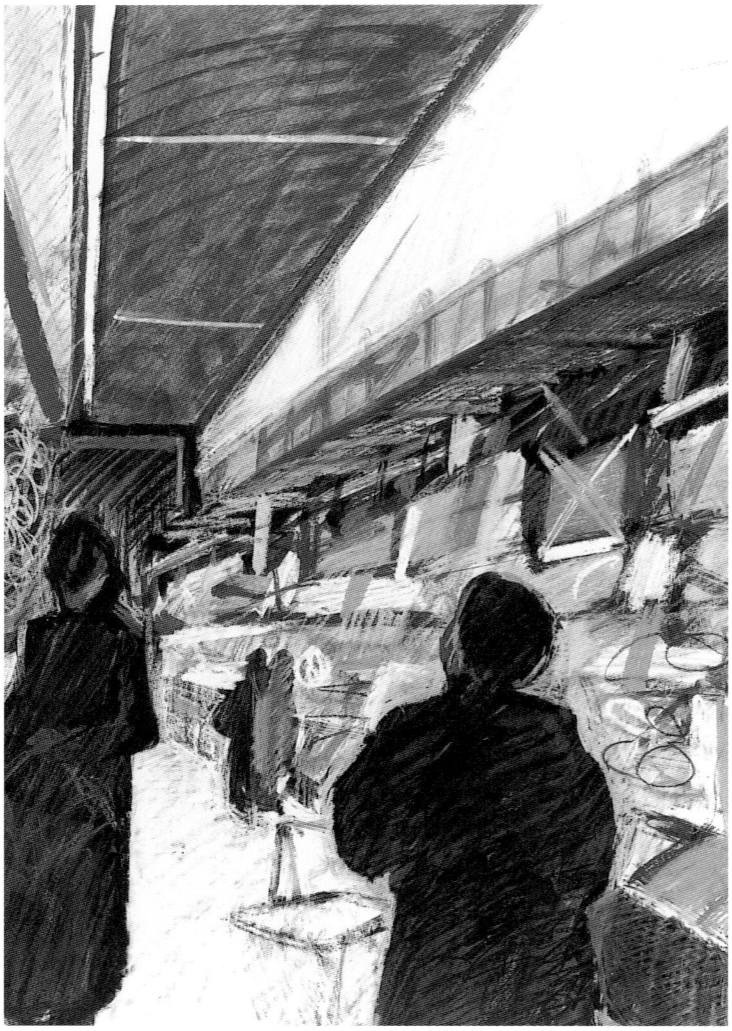

OLIVER BEVAN
(born 1941)
Supermarket [89.47/2]
1985
Oil on paper, 59.4 x 49.8 cm
Source: Purchased from the artist in 1989.

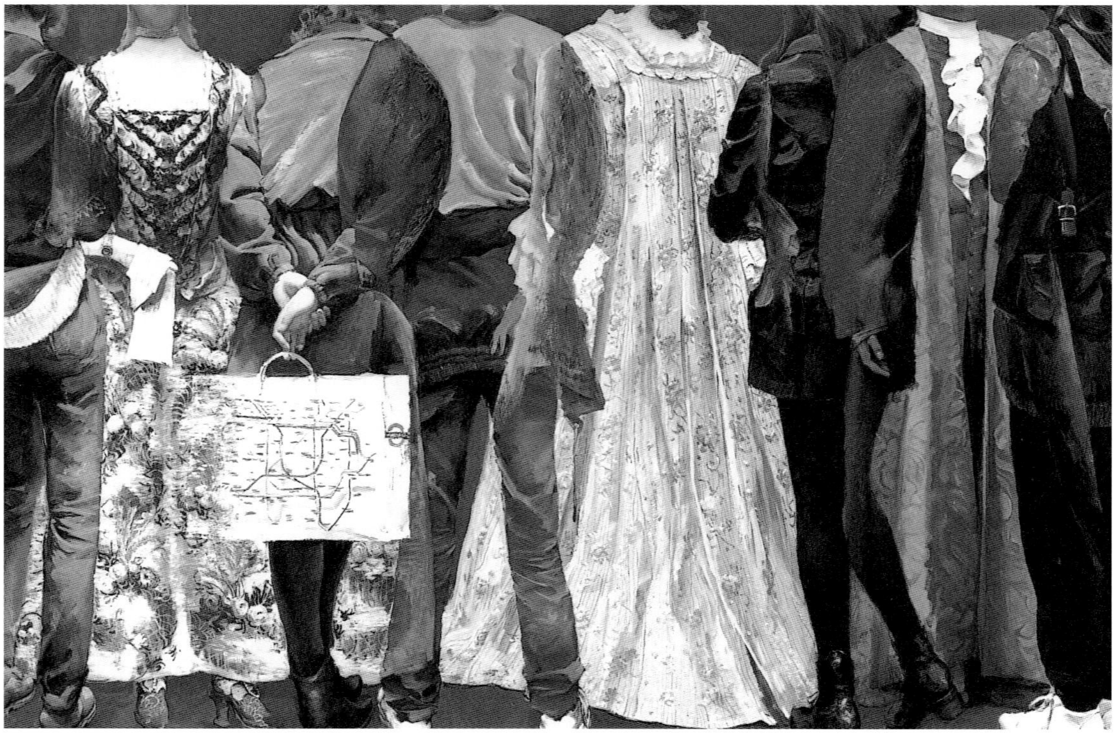

MAO WEN BIAO
(born 1950)
The costume case in the Museum of London's eighteenth-century gallery
[93.19/2]
1993
Oil on canvas, 95 x 147 cm
Source: Gift from the artist following his residency at the Museum (1993).

Artists' biographies

Abbreviations

AIA	Artists' International Association
ARA	Associate of the Royal Academy
BI	British Institution, 1806–1867
NEAC	New English Art Club
RA	Royal Academy
RCA	Royal College of Art
RP	Royal Society of Portrait Painters
RBA	Royal Society of British Artists
RSA	Royal Scottish Academy
RWS	Royal Society of Painters in Water Colours

JOSEPH VAN AKEN (*c.*1699–1749)
Painter of market scenes, interiors and conversation pieces; but from about 1735 best known as a drapery painter to most of the leading portraitists of the day. Probably born in Antwerp. He died in London and according to George Vertue, he was 'aged about 50' and 'had been 30 years or more in England'.
Cat. no. 39. See also 'The Covent Garden Group' on p118–19

KATHLEEN ALLEN (1906–83)
Painter of genre and urban scenes. Born in Acton, trained at the RCA (between 1924–8) and the Slade. Left London to teach art and paint murals in schools (1935–8). Returned in 1936 and studied at Slade (1936–7). Her Fetter Lane studio was bombed in 1941 destroying all early work. Involved in AIA, member of Society of Industrial Design (1945–59), taught at Goldsmiths College (1946–66). Retrospective exhibition at the South London Art Gallery in 1983. Member of the Painter-Stainers Company.
Cat. nos 197, 203

ROBERT ALLEN (active second quarter of the nineteenth century)
Sign-painter and amateur artist.
Cat. no. 87

JOHN ANDERSON (1835–1919)
Topographical and landscape painter. Born in Annan in Dumfriesshire, he trained at the Department of Science and Art, South Kensington. He was headmaster of the Coventry School of Art between 1863 and 1906. He exhibited at the RA (1858–84), at Suffolk Street and the BI. He also exhibited eighteen works at the Royal Birmingham Society of Artists. Painted several views of Westminster, of which two were exhibited at the BI.
Cat. no. 78

WILLIAM ANDERSON (1757–1837)
Marine artist. Born in Scotland, he was a shipwright by trade. He had moved to London by 1787, when he first exhibited at the RA. He was a friend of J. C. Ibbetson and between 1793 and 1796, both artists lived in Bell Street, Paddington.
Cat. no. 53

JAMES ARCHER (1823–1904)
Portrait, history and genre painter. Born in Edinburgh, the son of a dentist. Studied at the Edinburgh Trustees Academy. ARSA (1850); RSA (1858). Settled in London in 1862, and lived in Kensington; spent his last years at Haslemere.
Cat. no. 129

CLARE ATWOOD (1866–1962)
Painter of landscapes, industrial life, portraits, interiors and still lifes. Born in Richmond, the daughter of an architect. Studied at the Westminster School of Art and the Slade School. Member of the NEAC (1912). Lived in Chelsea, Covent Garden and Tenterden, Kent, where she died.
Cat. no. 135

J. BABER (active early nineteenth century)
Possibly the architect of this name who exhibited at the RA 1806–12.
Appendix

JOHN HENRY FREDERICK BACON (1865–1914)
Genre, ceremonial and portrait painter, best known for his painting of the Coronation of George V and Queen Mary. Studied at the Westminster Art and RA Schools. ARA (1903). Lived in St John's Wood and South Kensington.
Appendix

HENRY BARRAUD (1811–74)
Portrait and animal painter of Huguenot descent (came from a family of seventeen: see 'Artists of the Barraud Family', *Country Life*, 21 October 1965), best known for his large group portraits, for which his brother, William Barraud (1810–50), sometimes painted the backgrounds. Pupil of J. J. Middleton. Lived first in Camberwell, and afterwards in Mayfair and St Marylebone.
Cat. no. 130

SHARON BEAVAN (born 1956)
Urban painter. Born in London, she trained at the Hertfordshire College of Art and Design (1974–6), Falmouth School of Art (1976–9) and the RCA (1981–4). Since 1990 the artist has been working on an extensive panorama of London, an ambitious summary of her vision of the city.
Cat. no. 220

FRANCIS DONKIN BEDFORD (1864– ?)
Book illustrator. Born in London, the son of a solicitor. Studied at South Kensington, and the RA Architectural Schools; articled to Sir Arthur Blomfield. Lived in Wimbledon.
Appendix

OLIVER BEVAN (born 1941)
Landscape and cityscape painter. Born in Peterborough, the artist trained at the RCA between 1960 and 1964. As well as regularly exhibiting his work, he also curates exhibitions, particularly with the aim of promoting the work of urban artists. Two of his shows, *The Subjective City* (1988 and 1990) and *Witnesses and Dreamers* (1993) are particularly eloquent in this respect. Four of his paintings were commissioned by BAA for Gatwick Airport and Bevan also contributed to the 'Art on the Underground' scheme.
Cat. nos 215, 219, 225, Appendix (Modern)

ROBERT POLHILL BEVAN (1865–1925)
Painter of horses, landscapes and London scenes. Born at Hove, Sussex. Pupil of Alfred Pearce and studied at the Westminster School of Art and the Académie Julian in Paris; worked in Pont Aven in 1893–4, where he met Gauguin. Settled in Hampstead in 1910. Original member of the Camden Town Group (1911), the London Group (1913) and the Cumberland Market Group (1915); member of the NEAC (1922).
Cat. no. 150. See also 'The Camden Town Painters' on p343

ALFRED S. BISHOP (active 1874–89)
Nothing is known about this painter, and hardly any of his pictures are recorded; a portrait of the 4th Marquess of Salisbury on horseback, signed and dated 1874, is at Hatfield.
Cat. no. 102

JACQUES EMILE BLANCHE (1861–1942)
Portrait and landscape painter. Born in Paris, Blanche studied under Gervex and Humbert. He was an anglophile and his family house in Dieppe was a meeting point for many English artists, including Sickert. Early member of the NEAC (1887). Unlike other French Impressionists who concentrated on open spaces, much of his London output dealt with Central London.
Cat. no. 139

DAVID BOMBERG (1890–1957)
Born in Birmingham of a Jewish family and brought up in Whitechapel. Trained at the City and Guilds Institute, the Westminster School of Art and the Slade (1911–13). Founder member of the London Group (1913). His main London work features scenes of life in the East End. His teaching was influential and two of his most noted pupils were Frank Auerbach and Leon Kossoff, both specialising in London work.
Cat. no. 192

I. F. BORGNIS (active mid-nineteenth century)
Nothing is known about this painter, who was presumably an amateur.
Cat. no. 88

ROSAMUND BORRADAILE (active 1920s)
Very little is known about this artist: apart from the Museum painting, which dates from the 1920s, we know that she later became the secretary to the Society of Painters in Tempera.
Cat. no. 169

GEORGINA A. BRACKENBURY (1865–1949)
Miniature and portrait painter. The artist trained at the Slade between 1888 and 1890 and gave up her artistic career for seven years to work for the Women's Social and Political Union (WSPU), with her sister Marie, a landscape painter. Lived in Chelsea and Kensington.
Cat. no. 171

JOHN BRATBY (1928–92)
Born in Wimbledon, he trained at Kingston School of Art (1949–50) and the RCA (1951–4). He painted canvases for the film *The Horse's Mouth* (1958) which, set in London's Chelsea, is a study of an obsessive painter and a social outcast. After widely exhibiting his work and publishing novels, he was elected RA in 1971, had his *30 Years Retrospective* exhibition at the Sandford Gallery in London (1980) and a major show at the National Portrait Gallery (1991). He became known as one of the 'Kitchen Sink Painters' from 1954, because of his predilection for domestic subjects.
Cat. no. 198

ANTONY DE BREE (1855–1921)
Little is known about this Dutch artist who came to England around 1876. He was supposed to have been discovered in London practically destitute by the 6th Earl of Mayo and employed by him as a copyist; he painted animals and copies for Edward VII (a painting of a horse executed in 1893 survives in the royal collection). There may have been two different artists answering to that name: A. de Bree represented in the Royal Collection and Arnoldus de Bree from Antwerp. However, the artist represented here appears to be Anthony, who apparently changed the spelling of his name Brie to Bree in the early 1890s.
Cat. no. 98

EDWARD FREDERICK BREWTNALL (1846–1902)
Brewtnall was both landscape painter and illustrator. He was an early contributor to the *Graphic* and the *Illustrated London News*, specialising in narrative scenes, many of which are reminiscent of the work of Gustave Doré.
Cat. no. 137

CHARLES A. BUCHEL (active 1901–14)
Painter of nudes and portraits, chiefly theatrical portraits. Lived in Bloomsbury and Hampstead.
Cat. no. 155

GEORGE BUCKLEY (1823/4–70)
Everything that is known about this artist can be found under cat. no. 119.

ROBERT BUHLER (1916–89)
Born of Swiss parents and educated in Switzerland. Trained at St Martin's School of Art (1934–6) and RCA (1935) where he later taught. Member of the NEAC (1946), RA (1956). He produced a large number of London works, for instance the series of townscapes he executed of his area when living at Carlyle Square.
Cat. no. 194

HARRY BUSH (1883–1957)
'Painter of the Suburbs', as he is sometimes known. Bush moved from Brighton (where he was born) to Clapham in 1898. Joined Chelsea's Carlton Studios in 1904, where he worked under the artist Fred Taylor. Studied at Regent Street Polytechnic. After he married the painter Noel Nisbet from Clapham in 1910, the couple moved to Battersea Park Road, then Walham Green and from 1914 to the end of their lives they lived at their Merton address.
Cat. nos 166, 167, 200

ROBERT WILLIAM BUSS (1804–74)
Genre and topographical painter. Born in London, the son of the engraver and enameller, William Church Buss, and pupil of George Clint. This well-known genre and humorous painter had ten children (five of whom died in infancy) and lived in Camden Town. Editor of the *Fine Art Almanach* and *English Graphic Satire*, which was illustrated with his etchings.
Cat. no. 114, Appendix (Victorian)

PAUL BUTLER (born 1947)
Trained at Kingston College of Art (1966–9), with regular one-man shows since 1980. His London work includes a substantial group of works on Hammersmith and a number of murals in Shepherd's Bush, where he lives and works, as well as the large-scale mural in Cable Street, East End (with Ray Walker and Desmond Rochford). Powerful draughtsmanship best expressed in his charcoal drawings.
Cat. no. 224

WILLIAM J. CALLCOTT (active 1844–79)
Painter of coastal and river scenes who lived in various parts of London. Exhibited at RBA between 1844 and 1879.
Appendix (Victorian)

GIOVANNI ANTONIO CANAL called CANALETTO (1697–1768)
Landscape and topographical painter and etcher; best known for his views of Venice. Born in Venice. Trained as a scene painer with his father, but, under the influence of Carlevaris, soon turned to topographical painting. Worked chiefly for visiting Englishmen on the Grand Tour, and for Joseph Smith, the English Consul in Venice, who sold his large collection of Canalettos to George III in 1762. Visited London 1746–55, and the subjects he painted there were much imitated by English artists over the following decades. Between 1746 and 1749, he painted around eighteen paintings, twelve of which were London views. Member of the Venetian Academy of Painting (1763).
Cat. no. 33

B. A. R. (Sam) CARTER (born 1909)
After training for languages at Grenoble and Innsbruck Universities, Carter attended Trinity Hall, Cambridge (1929–32). He subsequently attended classes at Central School of Art (under Bernard Meninski); there he met Duncan Grant, who introduced him to the Euston Road School. Taught at Camberwell (1945–8), the Slade (1949–75) and was professor of perspective at the RA (1975–83). His fascination with questions of perspective led him to research the work of Piero della Francesca and to 'construct' his London views (and also his nudes and still lifes) in terms of strong geometry.
Cat. no. 195, 196

JESSE DALE CAST (1900–76)
Portrait and landscape painter who trained at Camberwell School of Art and Crafts under Albert Rutherston (1920–22) and at the Slade under Henry Tonks (1922–6). Regularly exhibited at the NEAC and RA during the 1930s. In 1944 his London home at Prince of Wales Drive was bombed, killing his wife and destroying many of his paintings. After the war he taught at Harrow School of Art and the

Central School of Art and Design before accepting a full-time appointment at Hornsey College of Art where he remained for the rest of his teaching career. From 1954 he exhibited regularly at the RP, of which he was made a member in 1957.
Cat. no. 204

MARK CAZALET (born 1964)
Painter born in London on 1 May 1964. He trained at Chelsea School of Art (1982–83) and Falmouth School of Art (1983–87). His awards and residencies have taken him to Paris (1986–87) and Baroda University in Western India (1988–89). Discouraged by the lack of interest in religious painting, his natural subject, he recently turned to painting the city which, to him, offers similar potential for carrying a spiritual message.
Cat. no. 230

SIR ARTHUR TEMPLE FELIX CLAY, BT (1842–1928)
Painter of portraits, landscapes and genre. Painter who exhibited at the RA between 1874 and 1890. Lived in Shere in Surrey until 1892, when he moved to Hyde Park Gate in Kensington. Member of the Literary Society.
Cat. no. 133

HENRY CHARLES CLIFFORD (1861–1947)
Landscape and topographical painter, best known for his views of disappearing London. Born in Greenwich, the son of an engineer. Studied in Paris under Bouguereau, Fleury and Benjamin Constant. Lived in Chelsea and Kensington; retired to Pulborough. RBA (1912).
Appendix (Victorian)

JOHN VICAT COLE (born 1903)
Landscape painter and stained glass designer. Born in a London family of painters, son of Rex Vicat Cole (1870–1940) and grandson of George Vicat Cole (1833–93). All produced paintings of London. Became a member of of the NEAC in 1965.
Appendix (Early Twentieth Century)

JOHN COLLET (1725–80)
Painter of narrative, genre and London views, best known for his scenes of London life, especially low life, derived from Hogarth. Born into London, the son of an official. Studied at the St Martin's Lane Academy. Lived in Chelsea. There was a considerable demand for his genre pictures, and many of them were engraved by Goldar.
Cat. nos 34, 41. See also 'The Covent Garden Group' on p118–19

J. CORDREY (active 1799–1822)
Coaching and sporting painter; specialised in 'portraits' of stagecoaches, with landscape setting, and his *oeuvre* provides useful visual documention of the network of services in England in the early nineteenth century.
Appendix (Regency)

S. B. CULL … (active early nineteenth century)
Appendix (Regency)

CHARLES ERNEST CUNDALL (1890–1971)
Topographical and townscape painter. Born at Stretford, Lancashire. Began designing pottery and stained glass for Pilkington's Pottery Company. Studied at the Manchester School of Art, obtaining a scholarship to the RCA in 1912; returned to the RCA in 1918 after war service (wounded, he had to learn to paint with his left hand), studied at the Slade School (1919–20), and afterwards in Paris. Member of the NEAC (1924); ARA (1937); RA (1944). Official War Artist with the Royal Navy and Royal Air Force (1940–4). Lived in Chelsea.
Cat. no. 191

CHARLES DEANE (active 1815–51)
Topographical and landscape painter, best known for his views of the Thames in and around London. Lived chiefly in St Marylebone.
Cat. no. 54

PAUL DESSAU (born 1909)
Portrait painter and illustrator. Educated in London, he trained at Hornsey and St Martin's Schools of Art. He joined the Auxiliary Fire Service (AFS) in 1940 and was an Auxiliary fireman at sub-station 61U, Magdalen Street, off Tooley Street, Southwark. He thus became one of London's Firemen Artists and regularly exhibited at the RA from 1942.
Cat. no. 186

THOMAS COLMAN DIBDIN (1810–93)
Topographical, scene painter and book illustrator, best known for his watercolours and pencil drawings of London views. Born in Betchworth, Surrey. At first apprenticed to a chemist, he secured an appointment in the Post Office at the age of sixteen. Apparently self-taught in painting and drawing. Worked as a scene painter for the Olympic and City Theatres, and at Sadler's Wells. Lived in various parts of London.
Cat. no. 90

JOHN CHARLES DOLLMAN (1851–1934)
Genre and animal painter. Born in Hove, the son of a bookseller. Studied at the South Kensington and RA Schools. Lived in Bedford Park.
Cat. no. 101

GUSTAVE DORÉ (1832–83)
French painter and illustrator who also produced sculpted works. First came to London in 1868 and visited the capital yearly after that date. His success in this country came mostly from his biblical paintings and in his day he was considered the greatest contemporary French artist. A Doré Gallery was opened that year in London by Messrs Fairless and Beetforth (1868). He is now best remembered for the extraordinary illustrations to Blanchard Jerrold's *London a Pilgrimage* (1872), published in France in 1876 as Ennault's *Londres*. He was presented to Queen Victoria by the Prince of Wales in 1875.
Cat. no. 128

THOMAS CANTRELL DUGDALE (1880–1952)
Portrait, topographical and genre painter. Born at Blackburn, Lancashire, the son of an engineer. Studied at the Manchester

School of Art, the RCA, the City and Guilds School, Kennington, the Académie Julian and the Atelier Colarossi in Paris. Married the painter Amy K. Browning (1916). ARA (1936); RA (1943). Lived in Chelsea.
Cat. no. 141

BERNARD DUNSTAN (born 1920)
Now better known as a painter of nudes, he also paints interiors and townscenes. Studied at the Byam Shaw and Slade Schools. Born in Teddington, the son of a scientist. Member of the NEAC (1946), ARA (1959), RA (1968). He is married to the painter Diana Armfield and lives in Kew. He has been regularly exhibiting at Agnew's since 1973.
Cat. no. 209

MARY EDITH DURHAM (1863–1944)
Portrait, genre and topographical painter and book illustrator. Born in London, the daughter of a surgeon. Studied at the RA Schools. Lived in various parts of London.
Cat. nos 136, 138, 152

REGINALD GRANVILLE EVES (1876–1941)
Portrait, topographical and landscape painter. Born in Holborn, the son of a Justice of the Peace. Protégé of John Singer Sargent. Studied at the Slade School (1891–5). In Yorkshire between 1895–1900, then settled in London as a portrait painter in 1901, and painted many of the most prominent people in public life. Lived in Bloomsbury and St John's Wood. ARA (1933); RA (1939).
Cat. no. 157

WILLIAM FARLEY (1893–1964)
Self-taught artist. Born in Northampton, his father had a shoe-making factory, but Farley's passion was for painting and horses and he joined the Canadian cavalry when World War I broke out. He settled in Suffolk when he married and exhibited sporting paintings and landscapes at the RA between 1936 and 1951. Later in life he worked in Paris and northern France.
Cat. no. 181

FRANCIS L. M. FORSTER (d.1916)
Painter of landscapes, portraits, genre and theatrical scenes. Pupil of Sickert. Member of the NEAC. Lived in Chelsea and Belgravia. Killed in the First World War.
Cat. no. 112

WILLIAM E. FOX (active Early Twentieth Century)
Flower and topographical painter. Lived in Kensington.
Cat. no. 149

DICK FRENCH (born 1946)
Trained at the RCA (1967–70) and widely exhibited in Britain, both in the commercial and public sectors (Piccadilly and Redfern galleries in London, Wolverhampton Gallery and South Hill Park Arts Centre) as well as in Europe. He illustrated J. G. Ballard's *Drowned World* (1981) by setting in London apocalyptic scenes of jungles and dying civilisations.
Cat. no. 222

CHARLES GINNER (1878–1952)
Painter of rural and urban landscapes much influenced by Van Gogh. Born and educated in France. Trained in Paris and moved to London in 1910, when he joined the Fitzroy Street Group, then the Camden Town Group (1911); later the London Group (1913) and the Cumberland Market Group (1914). Member of the NEAC (1920), ARA (1942).
Cat. no. 147. See also 'The Camden Town Painters' on p343

SPENCER GORE (1878–1914)
Painter of urban and rural scenes much influenced by Gauguin. Born at Epsom, Surrey and educated at Harrow. He trained at the Slade (1896–9). Friend of Harold Gilman, Sickert and Wyndham Lewis, he first joined the Fitzroy Group before becoming a key figure of the Camden Town Group (1911).
Cat. nos 144, 146. See also 'The Camden Town Painters' on p343

DAVID GRAHAM (born 1926)
Born in London, Graham trained at the Hammersmith School of Art (1939–43), St Martin's School of Art (1943–4) and the RCA (1948–51). Won twice *The Spirit of London* competition (1978 and 1979). His teaching career started at the Wimbledon School of Art in 1951 and he taught at John Cass College between 1962 and 1989.
Appendix (Modern)

DUNCAN GRANT (1885–1978)
Landscape, portrait and decorative painter. Born in Rothiemurchus, Invernessshire, but spent most of his life in England, most famously at Charleston Farm, Sussex, with Vanessa Bell. Educated St Paul's School and trained at Westminster School of Art (1902–5), with Jacques Emile Blanche in Paris (1906–7), in Italy and at the Slade (1907–8). Member of the Camden Town Group (1911) and the London Group (1919). Became a director of Roger Fry's Omega Workshops. Retrospective exhibition of his work at the Tate in 1959.
Cat. no. 178

HENRY GREAVES (1844–1904)
Topographical painter, best known for his views of Chelsea. Born in Chelsea, the son of a waterman and boatbuilder and Walter's brother (see below). Both were pupils and studio assistants of Whistler from about 1863. Both brothers greatly admired their master. Lived in Chelsea.
Appendix (Victorian)

WALTER GREAVES (1846–1930)
Topographical, genre, and portrait painter, best known for his views of Chelsea. Born in Chelsea, the son of a waterman and boatbuilder. Pupil and studio assistant of Whistler from about 1863. Walter came under the total influence of Whistler to the point of copying not only his painting style, but also his dress and manner. Lived in Chelsea.
Cat. nos 93, 109

JAN GRIFFIER THE ELDER (*c.*1645/52?–1718)
Painter of landscapes and topographical views. Born in Amsterdam, he trained with Roghman in Rotterdam. According to George Vertue, Griffier came to London soon after the Great Fire and produced several versions of the city on fire. He became a Painter-Stainer in 1677 and

although he returned to Holland (*c.*1695–*c.*1705) he died in London.
Cat. nos 9, 10. Also see cat. no. 19

ARTHUR HACKER (1858–1919)
Painter of portraits, religious subjects, nudes and genre; also painted several views of London at night. Born in London, the son of an engraver. Studied at the RA Schools (1876–80), and in Paris at the Atelier Bonnat (1880–1). ARA (1894); RA (1910). Lived in St Pancras, St Marylebone and Kensington.
Cat. no. 160

WILFRED STANLEY HAINES (1905–44)
London fireman artist. Born in Wimbledon in April 1905, Haines, who came from a family of weavers, was initially a textile designer (the V&A holds some of his designs). He became a fireman during the war and his paintings were regularly exhibited with those of firemen artists (see p433). He lived at 10 Berkeley Court, Tulse Hill and was buried at Wimbledon Cemetery after he was killed by a flying bomb.
Cat. no. 189, Appendix (Early Twentieth Century)

CHRISTOPHER HALL (born 1930)
Landscape and topographical painter, sometimes nicknamed 'the painter of back streets'. Studied at the Slade School (1950–4). Regular exhibitor at the RA Schools. Lives in Newbury.
Cat. no. 199, Appendix (Modern)

CLIFFORD ERIC HALL (1904–73)
Painter of landscapes, townscapes, interiors and portraits. Born in London, the son of a newspaper manager. Studied at Richmond and Putney Art Schools respectively under Charles Wheeler and Stanley Anderson (1922–5), the RA Schools under Charles Sims and Walter Sickert (1926–7), and with André Lhôte in Paris (1928). Lived in Paddington. After his death the Belgrave Gallery staged several shows of his works (with accompanying catalogues 1977, 1982, 1989).
Cat. no. 177

JAMES HAMILTON HAY (1874–1916)
Landscape and marine painter, and etcher. Born in Birkenhead, he trained in Birkenhead and Liverpool before attending Julius Olsson's painting classes at St Yves (late 1890s) and returning to Liverpool where he was taught by David Muirhead and Augustus John. Although Hay exhibited with the NEAC in 1909, he only moved to London late 1911 or early 1912. Joined the London Group in 1915.
Cat. no. 145

FRANCIS HAYMAN (1708–76)
Painter of history, portraits, conversation pieces, interiors, theatrical scenes and genre; and book illustrator. Best known for the large decorative canvases with genre subjects that he painted for Vauxhall Gardens during the 1730s and 1740s. Born at Exeter. Studied with Robert Brown, an Exeter portrait painter; came to London at an early age, and worked as a scene painter at Drury Lane Theatre. Played a leading part in forming the Society of Artists of Great Britain in 1760, and became its President 1766–8. Founder member of the RA (1768); appointed Librarian in 1771.
Cat. no. 43

ERNEST DUDLEY HEATH (active *c.*1886–1940)
Painter of portraits and genre, and book illustrator. Son of Henry Charles Heath, Miniature Painter to Queen Victoria. Studied at the RA Schools and was lecturer in art for the University of London extension between 1803–8. Principal of the Hampstead Garden Suburb School of Arts and Crafts (1914–26) and lecturer on Principles of Art Teaching at the RCA (1927). Lived in Hendon.
Cat. no. 111

CHARLES NAPIER HEMY (1841–1917)
Landscape and seascape painter who studied at Newcastle Art School. His lifelong passion for the sea started when the family emigrated to Australia in 1850, to return two years later. After much travelling Hemy was in London in 1865. Went to study under Baron Leys in Antwerp (1867). Returned August 1869 and lived at Myrtle Lodge, North End, Fulham. He settled in London for the next eleven years and regularly exhibited at the Grosvenor Gallery. He was notably influenced by the Pre-Raphaelites, Whistler and Tissot and by the foreign painters Leys and Legros.
Cat. no. 77

ARCHIBALD S. HENNING (active second quarter of the nineteenth century, d.1864)
Comic illustrator and genre painter. A 'Bohemian' artist who lived in Tulse Hill and Belgravia. He designed *Punch's* first wrapper and was a prolific wood engraver.
Appendix (Victorian)

LADY ROSE L. HENRIQUES (1890–1973)
Self-taught artist. Specialised in views of Stepney and scenes of Stepney life. Warden of the Bernhard St George's Jewish Settlement 1914–48.
Cat. no. 175

DAVID HEPHER (born 1935)
Born in Surrey, Hepher trained at the Camberwell School of Art and the Slade (1955–61). He says of himself that he is a landscape artist who happens to be based in a city. While he uncomprisingly tackles the most urban manifestations of capital life (for instance tower blocks), his output is mainly architectural and devoid of figures.
Cat. no. 214

TOM HESLEWOOD (1868–1959)
Amateur artist.
Appendix (Victorian)

GEORGE ELGAR HICKS (1824–1914)
Genre, religious and portrait painter. Although Hicks had trained to be a doctor, he changed his mind and entered the RA Schools in 1844. The success of *Dividend Day at the Bank* encouraged him to paint further London contemporary genre scenes on the model of W. P. Frith.
Cat. no. 124, 127

WILLIAM HODGES (1744–97)
Landscape painter. Trained at the Shipleys' Academy and under Richard Wilson. RA (1787). Now best remembered for his exotic

scenery paintings, which he first started producing when he joined Captain Cook's second expedition to the South Pacific (1772–5). He produced work for Boydell's Shakespeare Gallery. Gave up painting for banking in 1795 but went bankrupt.
Cat. no. 37

JAMES HOLLAND (1799–1870)
Flower and topographical painter, best known for his views of Venice; painted several views of Greenwich. Born at Burslem, Staffordshire. Worked for seven years as a flower painter at the John Davenport porcelain factory, as there was no vacancy for him at the family-run Hill Top pottery, before coming to London in 1819, and continued to exhibit flower paintings at the RA until 1838. Lived in various parts of London. RWS.
Cat. no. 65

SIR CHARLES JOHN HOLMES (1868–1936)
Painter and etcher of landscapes, topographical and industrial scenes. Born at Preston, Lancashire. Self-taught in painting, but studied etching under William Strang. Member of the NEAC (1904). Slade Professor at Oxford (1904–10). Director of the National Portrait Gallery (1909–16). Director of the National Gallery (1916–28). Lived in Kensington.
Cat. no. 140

EDWIN FREDERICK HOLT (1830–1912)
Portrait and landscape painter born in Hampstead. Holt trained at the Royal Academy School of Art and had a studio in Camden Town. In 1854 he won the RA silver medal for the best Painting from the Life. Exhibited at the RA, BI and RBA. Holt spent most of his adult life in Dunstable, where he settled in the early 1860s with his wife Elizabeth Bunker. After an escapade with a French lady he met in Paris, Holt returned to his wife and painted local scenes.
Cat. no. 92

ABRAHAM HONDIUS (*c.*1625/30–91)
Painter of religious, mythological and topographical subjects, interiors and hunting scenes, but specialised in animals and birds. Born in Rotterdam, the son of the city stonemason. Settled in England by 1674. Lived first on Ludgate Hill, and later in the parish of St Dunstan-in-the-West. Died in London.
Cat. nos 15, 16

CHARLES HUNT (1829–1900)
Genre painter of modern life, son of the carver and gilder Richard Hunt. Lived in various parts of south-west London (Chelsea, Parson's Green, Fulham Broadway and Wandsworth).
Cat. no. 131

HAROLD HUSSEY (born 1912)
Trained at the RCA and the Shell-Mex Studios. Lived in Kew for his 'London period', and now lives at Henley-on-Thames.
Cat. no. 210

TIMOTHY HYMAN (born 1946)
Painter born in Hove, Sussex and brought up in London. He trained at the Slade between 1963 and 1967. He started writing art criticism in 1977 for the *London Magazine* and is now arts correspondent with the *Times Literary Supplement*. He courageously curated the exhibition *Narrative Painting* for the Arnolfini Gallery in Bristol at a time when figurative painting was at its lowest ebb. He wove links with painters and the art scene in India while he was Visiting Professor at the University of Baroda in Western India (1980–1). A committed and prolific painter, he combines his love for London, religious subjects and for his wife in vibrant compositions ranging from the very small to the very large.
Cat. nos. 212, 213

JULIUS CAESAR IBBETSON (1759–1817)
Painter of landscapes, topographical subjects, portraits and genre. Born at Farnley Moor, Yorkshire, the son of a cloth merchant. Apprenticed to John Fletcher, a ship painter in Hull in about 1771; broke his articles and ran away to London in 1777, where he worked for a picture restorer. Lived in London until 1798, chiefly in Kilburn and Paddington; then moved to the north, finally settling in Masham in 1805.
Cat. no. 46

HUMPHREY JENNINGS (1907–50)
Film director, painter, poet. Born in East Anglia, educated at Cambridge, Jennings moved to London in 1934. His subsequent work for the GPO Film Unit and his interest in domestic anthropology (he founded with others the Mass Observation Movement) are the foundation stones for the documentary movement in Britain. This perhaps contrasts with his passion for poetry and surrealism. Memorial exhibition of paintings held at the ICA in 1951.
Cat. no. 180

GEORGE WILLIAM JOY (1844–1925)
Painter of historical and religious subjects, portraits, fancy pictures, nudes and genre. Born in Dublin, the son of a doctor. Studied under Millais, Leighton and Watts, at the RCA and the RA Schools, and in Paris with Jalabert (1868) and at the Atelier Bonnat. Lived in Bayswater.
Cat. no. 134

STANISLAWA DE KARLOWSKA (1876–1952)
Painter of urban and rural landscape. Born at Szeliwy near Lowicz in Russian Poland. Trained at the Académie Julian in Paris. Married Robert Bevan in 1899, who influenced her style considerably. Founder member of the London Group (1913).
Cat. no. 179

WILLIAM KIDD (1790?–1863)
Scottish genre painter born in Edinburgh who was influenced by the work of David Wilkie and Alxander Carse. He was first apprenticed to a house painter and then came to London. He exhibited at the RA, BI and SS between 1817 and 1853. After 1849, when he was elected an honorary member of the Royal Scottish Academy, he increasingly exhibited his work in Edinburgh. He lived in poverty towards the end of his life and died in London in 1863, on Christmas Eve.
Cat. no. 73

JACOB KNYFF (1639–81)
Topographical painter. Born in Haarlem, the son of Wouter Knyff, the painter. Studied with his father. Travelled to Paris in 1672, and working in England by 1673. He died in London.
Cat. no. 13

E. F. LAMBERT (active 1823–1846)
Painter of portraits and literary subjects, who lived in various parts of London.
Cat. no. 74

WALTER H. LAMBERT (1870/1–1950)
Amateur painter of historical and genre pictures. Born in Jarrow. Studied at Harrogate Art School. Worked professionally on the stage as a female impersonator, under the name of Lydia Dreams. He is buried at Streatham Park Cemetery.
Cat. no. 153

CARL LAUBIN (born 1947)
Born in New York, Laubin trained as an architect at Cornell University. Moved to London in 1973 working for architectural practices. In 1986, produced architectural paintings for Jeremy Dixon of the Royal Opera House project and housing in Docklands. In 1987 left architectural practice to paint full time. Lives in Hitchin.
Cat. no. 223

E. L. LAURIE (active late nineteenth century)
Nothing is known about this artist.
Appendix (Victorian)

SIR JOHN LAVERY (1856–1941)
Portrait, genre and landscape painter whose London views are rather exceptional. Born in Belfast. Studied at the Haldane Academy in Glasgow (1876), Heatherley's School in London (1879), and from 1881 at the Académie Julian and the Atelier Colarossi in Paris. Settled in London in 1896, and lived in South Kensington. NEAC (1890–2); ARA (1911); RA (1921).
Cat. nos 142, 182

SIR THOMAS LAWRENCE (1769–1830)
Portrait painter. Born in Bristol, self-taught before coming to London in 1787, when he attended the RA Schools for three months. He first exhibited there that same year. In 1792 he succeeded Reynolds as Painter in Ordinary. His fame became European after the large-scale project of the Waterloo Chamber portraits at Windsor.
Cat. no. 48

TIMO LEHTONEN (born 1953)
Painter and printmaker. Born in Helsinki, trained at Sheffield City Polytechnic and at the RCA (1976–9). His training was in printmaking but access to printmaking equipment became such a strain that Lehtonen gradually turned to painting. Teaches at West Surrey College of Art and Polytechnic of Central London (Harrow School of Art). Early images of architectural London have been replaced by a more symbolic and abstract mode of expression which is still very much focused on the capital.
Cat. no. 228

PHOEBUS LEVIN (active 1855–78)
Painter of historical and religious subjects, and genre. Born in Berlin. Studied at the Berlin Academy (1836–44). Worked in Rome (1845–7), and settled in London 1855–78. Lived first in Bond Street, and afterwards in Kensington.
Cat. nos 95, 228

JAMES ISAIAH LEWIS (1861–1934)
Although he began his career as photographer's assistant, he is first listed as 'artist' in Richmond in an 1887 trade directory. He produced a great many versions of local popular scenes, but also worked from life when he was especially commissioned. The Museum of Richmond organised an exhibition of his works in 1994 and the Orleans House Gallery holds some of his paintings.
Cat. no. 60

JOHN LINNELL (1792–1882)
Painter of landscapes, portraits and religious subjects. Born in London, the son of a carver and gilder. Studied with John Varley and at the RA Schools (1805–6). Became an intimate friend of William Blake. Lived in Bloomsbury, Bayswater, Hampstead and (from 1851) Redhill.
Cat. no. 64

THOMAS LUNY (1759–1837)
Marine painter; painted a number of London river scenes in the style of Marlow, which are dated betwen 1793 and 1806. Born in London. Studied under Francis Holman. Served at sea for varying periods up to 1810. Lived in Ratcliffe and the City, but retired to Teignmouth in 1810, where he lived as an invalid, suffering from arthritis.
Cat. nos 50, 66, 68

WILLIAM MACDUFF (active 1844–76)
Genre painter. Nothing is known about his life. His genre scenes tend to be set in country settings, but his best known painting is that in the Museum's collection.
Cat. no. 125

JOCK MCFADYEN (born 1950)
Painter and sculptor born in Paisley, Scotland. Trained at Chelsea School of Art between 1973 and 1977. He was artist-in-residence at the National Gallery in 1981. The artist's prime source of inspiration is the seedy side of the East End, where he lives. His collaboration with Kenneth McMillan for the ballet *The Judas Tree* at Covent Garden (1990) led McFadyen to a change of direction, moving away from painting people to concentrate instead on built structures.
Cat. no. 227

MAO WEN BIAO (born 1950)
Mao trained in Bejing, Wimbledon School of Art and the RCA. In his native China, he painted political and historical murals in a strongly figurative style. He came to London to find new ways of communicating and has succeeded in developing an effective semi-abstract formula, of which cat. no. 226 is an excellent example.
Cat. no. 226, Appendix (Modern)

YOSHIO MARKINO (1874–*c.*1938)
Painter of genre scenes, and specialised in illustrations of British life. Born in Koromo, Mikawa. Came to London in 1897, and lived in Fulham. Early autobiographical material may be found in his book *A Japanese artist in London* (published in 1910).
Cat. no. 172

WILLIAM MARLOW (1740–1813)
Landscape and topographical painter; painted a number of views of the Thames in and around London. Born in Southwark. Pupil of Samuel Scott from about 1756 to 1761. Travelled in France and Italy 1765–8. Member of the Society of Artists of Great Britain, of which he became Vice-President in 1778. Lived in Leicester Square until about 1783, when he retired to Twickenham.
Cat. nos 26, 27, 38

HENRY MILBOURNE (1781–*c.*1826)
Landscape, topographical, marine and animal painter who lived in various parts of north London. Perhaps the son of the painter John Milbourne. He was thirty-five when he entered the RA Schools.
Cat. no. 62

ALFRED MILLER (active mid-twentieth century)
Amateur artist.
Appendix (Early Twentieth Century)

NETTY MOON (1909–81)
Photographer and amateur painter. She started her professional life as a designer of fabrics but soon turned to photography. She worked for and became a Partner in Dorretts, the firm of commercial photographic printers. After being the Secretary of the Surrey Centre of the Institute of British Photographers, she became the first lady president of the Institute of Incorporated Photographers in 1954–5. She took up painting late in life.
Cat. no. 187

AUGUSTUS E. MULREADY (1844–1904)
Genre painter who specialised in London characters. Lived in various parts of London. Died in University College Hospital on 8 March 1904, when he was listed as living at 191 Vauxhall Bridge Road.
Cat. no. 132

CHRISTOPHER RICHARD WYNNE NEVINSON (1889–1946)
Landscape, topographical, genre and figure painter, etcher and lithographer; best known for his war paintings and townscapes. Born in Hampstead, the son of the journalist and essayist Henry Wood Nevinson. Studied at the St John's Wood School of Art, the Slade (1908–12), and in Paris at the Académie Julian and the *Cercle Russe* (1912–13), sharing a studio with Modigliani. Foundation member of the London Group (1913). Associated with the Futurist Movement, and published the manifesto *Vital English Art* with Marinetti (1914). Became an official war artist in 1917. Member of the NEAC (1929); ARA (1939).
Cat. nos 165, 173, 174, 183, 184, 185

ALGERNON NEWTON (1880–1968)
Born in Hampstead, Newton trained at the Frank Calderon School of Animal Painting (*c.*1900–03), at the Slade (non degree classes), at the London School of Art in Kensington (*c.*1906–7). After extensive travels and then the war, he settled in Cornwall. Lived in London between 1919–37 and *c.*1947–68. ARA (1936); RA (1943). The artist's papers relating to his work have been deposited at the Tate Gallery (Archives).
Cat. nos 168, 170

EDMUND JOHN NIEMANN (1813–76)
Landscape and topographical painter. Born in Islington, the son of a German underwriter at Lloyd's. A clerk at Lloyd's from the age of thirteen, he did not take up painting until 1839. Lived at High Wycombe, and from 1848 in various parts of London.
Cat. no. 91

W. R. NOBLE (active mid-nineteenth century)
Amateur artist.
Cat. no. 76

PHILIP NORMAN (1842–1931)
Watercolour painter, principally of London buildings. Born in Bromley, the son of the Governor of the Bank of England (G. W. Norman). Studied at the Slade School from 1872. Vice-President of the London Topographical Society 1906–31. Chairman and Editor of the Survey of London Committee from 1907 until his death. Lived at 45 Evelyn Gardens and in South Kensington. Philip Norman dedicated himself to recording sites and buildings threatened with demolition. Some of this work was published in his book *London Vanished and Vanishing* (1905).
Cat. nos. 96, 97

JOHN O'CONNOR (1830–89)
Topographical and scene painter. Born in Londonderry, into a family connected with the stage. Had no formal training, and as a boy assisted in scene painting at theatres in Belfast and Dublin; came to London in 1848, where he worked first at Drury Lane and later, as principal scene painter at the Haymarket Theatre 1863–78. Drawing master to the London and South-Western Literary and Scientific Institution (1855–8). ARHA (1883). Drew numerous royal ceremonies, including the Jubilee service in Westminster Abbey, 1887. Lived chiefly in St John's Wood.
Cat. nos 79, 80, 99

JAMES LYNWOOD PALMER (1868–1941)
Painter of horses, coaches and equestrian portraits. Born in Linwood, Lincolnshire, the son of a clergyman. Educated at King's College, London. Self-taught artist. Lived at Heston, Middlesex.
Cat. no. 104

SIR BERNARD PARTRIDGE (1861–1945)
Magazine and book illustrator and portrait painter; stained glass designer and decorative painter (1880–4). Born in London, the son of a distinguished surgeon. Joined the staff of *Punch* in 1891 and was principal cartoonist between 1909 and 1945. Lived in West Kensington.
Cat. no. 154

JOHN PAUL (1804–87)
Topographical painter, and copyist.
Cat. no. 56, 59, Appendix (Georgian)

ROBERT PEAKE THE ELDER (*c.*1551–1619)
Portrait painter. On the staff of the Office of the Revels (1576–8). Serjeant Painter to the King (with John de Critz) from 1607 and Picturemaker to Henry, Prince of Wales until 1612.
Cat. no. 1

R. PEMBERY (active second half of the nineteenth century)
Landscape and topographical painter. An amateur artist, whose known pictures all suffer from extensive cracking.
Appendix (Victorian)

EDWARD PENNY (1714–91)
Genre and portrait painter. Born in Knutsford, Cheshire, he studied with Hudson and later in Rome. Exhibited at the RSA from 1862 and was a founder member of the RA. He became its first Professor of Painting (1769–83). Died in Chiswick.
Cat. no. 35

JULIAN PERRY (born 1960)
Urban painter. Born in Worcester and trained at Bristol Polytechnic (1978–81). He regularly exhibited from 1983. Started living in London in 1984 when the city became exclusively his source of inspiration. Until 1989 his first London studio was in Leyton (an ACME Studio) and then in Southwark. Dealer: Austin Desmond.
Cat. no. 221

HENRY PETHER (1800–80)
Topographical painter, best known for his moonlight pictures. Son of the painter Abraham Pether (1756–1812) who was already known as 'moonlight Pether'. Lived in various parts of London.
Cat. nos 105, 106, 107

GLADYS A. PINKS (1890–*c.*1980)
Studied art at Grosvenor Studio under Walter Donne (1909–12) and in Paris under Lucien Simon (1909–12). Lived at 51a Marloes Road (with Richard Arthur Pinks) in 1930; at 2 Wynnstay Gardens, W8 during the war; then had a Garden Studio at 77 Bedford Gardens, W8 between 1945 and 1963.
Cat. no. 190

JOHN PIPER (1903–92)
Landscape, topographical and abstract painter, and theatrical designer. Born at Epsom, the son of a solicitor. Student at the Richmond and Kingston Schools of Art, and the RCA (1928–9). Member of the London Group (1933). Official War Artist (1940–2). Supervised the design of the Battersea Pleasure Gardens (with Osbert Lancaster) in 1951. Lived near Henley.
Cat. no. 188

JAMES POLLARD (1792–1867)
Painter of coaching and sporting subjects, best known for his views of the famous London coaching inns. Born in London, the son of the engraver and publisher, Robert Pollard (1755–1838); Received help and advice from Thomas Bewick and started painting coaching scenes in 1820. Lived in Holloway.
Cat. no. 89, Appendix (Victorian)

IAN RIBBONS (born 1924)
Painter illustrator. Trained at the RCA (1947–51). His fourth year was spent in the Design School and he worked as a student assistant on a mural for the Festival of Britain. Lives and works in London, where he teaches at St Martin's School of Art. His London work is extensive and includes a series on Billingsgate Market.
Cat. no. 205

THOMAS MILES RICHARDSON (1784–1848)
Newcastle painter and watercolourist who principally painted views in the north-east of England as well as Continental scenes (after other people's drawings). There also exists a small body of London work. Richardson was a cabinet maker until 1806 when he became Master of St Andrews School. He exhibited at the RA between 1814 and 1845 and was very active in promoting artistic outlets for the north east. Several of his sons chose to become painters.
Cat. no. 55

JOHN RITCHIE (active 1858–75)
Genre painter who specialised in imaginary scenes set in sixteenth- and seventeenth-century costume; hardly anything is known about his life. Lived in various parts of London and exhibited at the RA and RBA.
Cat. no. 120

FREDERICK ROE (1864–1947)
Painter of portraits, landscapes, historical subjects and genre. Born in London, the son of an engraver. Studied at Heatherley's School, London. Lived in various parts of London.
Appendix (Victorian)

M. J. RORSNIGER (active late nineteenth century)
Nothing is known about this painter, who was presumably an amateur.
Appendix (Victorian)

FRANK O. SALISBURY (1874–1962)
Portrait and ceremonial painter. Born at Harpenden. Trained at Heatherley's School of Art under John Crompton, at the RA Schools and in France, Germany and Italy. Painted portraits of royalty and celebrities of his day, including Americans.
Appendix (Early Twentieth Century)

PIERO SANSALVADORE (1892–1955)
The artist was born in Turin and first came to England in 1931. After he gave up work as an insurance salesman around 1938, he became a full time artist in London living on his savings. At the outbreak of the war he joined the BBC Foreign department broadcasting anti-Mussolini propaganda to Italy. He exhibited with the Parsons Gallery and had a one-man show there in 1953. At that time his studio was at 91a Peel Street, W8. He died in Italy. The Guildhall Art Gallery has seven of his London paintings.
Cat. no. 193

JOHN NOST SARTORIUS (1759–1828)
Sporting painter. Born in London, the son of Francis Sartorius, also a sporting painter. Lived in Soho and Covent Garden.
Appendix (Regency)

PETER SAUNDERS (born 1940)
For almost thirty years, the work of Peter Saunders has been entirely devoted to the London scene and three times in the 1980s he won the GLC *Spirit of London* competition. Saunders notably produced a series of paintings on roller-skating underneath the Royal Festival Hall and on the French pub in Soho, for decades a pub-club which has acted as a meeting point for artists and literati. Contributed to 'Art on the Underground' scheme.
Cat. no. 217

SAMUEL SCOTT (1702–72)
Marine and topographical painter; specialising in London views. Worked chiefly as a marine painter until the mid–1740s, when, as a result of the enhanced demand for London views stimulated by the arrival of Canaletto in this country in 1746, he added this genre to his other activities. Painted several versions of his most popular subjects, and was much copied. Lived in Covent Garden until 1758, when he retired to a house he had bought in Twickenham in 1748; left London in 1765 and spent his last years in Ludlow and Bath.
Cat. no. 40

EDGAR SELIGMAN (active 1920s)
Nothing is known about this artist, who may have been on the staff of the Whitefriars glasshouse.
Cat. no. 163, Appendix (Early Twentieth Century)

GEORGE HARCOURT SEPHTON (active 1895–1938)
Painter of portraits, landscapes and genre. Lived in Bloomsbury, Campden Hill and later West Kensington.
Cat. nos 121, 122

THOMAS FREDERICK MASON SHEARD (1866–1921)
Painter of landscapes, portraits and genre, best known for his Oriental subjects. Born in Oxford. Studied in Paris under Courtois and others. Professor of Art at Queen's College, London, from 1915. Lived in Chelsea and Kensington.
Cat. no. 103

FREDERICK P. SHUCKARD (active early twentieth century)
Painter of portraits, topographical subjects and genre. Lived chiefly in Peckham.
Cat. no. 113

WALTER R. SICKERT (1860–1942)
Born in Munich, Sickert settled in London in 1868. Studied at the Slade (1881–2). Became a pupil of Whistler and fell under the influence of Degas from 1885. Member of the NEAC from 1887. Organised and participated in the London Impressionist Show in 1889. Founded the Fitzroy Group (1907) and the Camden Town Group (1911). His influence was enormous and his output dominated by the cityscapes of London, Dieppe and Venice.
Cat. no. 156

A. SIMPSON (active 1910s and '20s)
Perhaps A. Brantingham Simpson, the watercolour painter who exhibited at the Royal Institute of Painters in Watercolours? (See Grant Waters's Dictionary).
Appendix (Early Twentieth Century)

CHARLES SIMS (1873–1928)
Portrait, religious, figure, genre, landscape and decorative painter. Born in Islington, the son of a costume manufacturer. Studied at the RCA (1890), the Académie Julian, Paris, (1891–2), and the RA Schools (1892–5). ARA (1908); RA (1916); Was an official war artist; later Keeper of the RA (1920–5). Painted the large mural of *King John confronted by his Barons* for St Stephen's Hall, Westminster, in 1924. Lived in various parts of London, and after 1906, at Fittleworth, Sussex.
Cat. no. 162

FRANK MARKHAM SKIPWORTH (d.1929)
Painter of genre, portrait and historical subjects. Exhibited at the RA between 1882 and 1916. Lived in Chelsea.
Appendix (Victorian)

F. W. SMITH (active late seventeenth century)
Nothing is known about this artist.
Cat. no. 18

SOLOMON JOSEPH SOLOMON (1860–1927)
Painter of portraits, classical and religious paintings, genre and nudes. Born in Southwark, the son of a leather merchant. Studied at Heatherley's School (1876), the RA Schools (1877–80), and with Capanel at the Ecole des Beaux Arts in Paris (1880 and 1882–3). ARA (1896); RA (1906). Executed the murals in the Royal Exchange. Lived chiefly in West Kensington.
Cat. no. 164

PETER SNOW (born 1927)
Painter born in Catford. Trained at Goldsmith's College of Art (1946) and at the Slade (1948–53). He joined the staff of the Slade in 1957 and on his retirement was made Honorary Visiting Professor and Fellow of UCL (1996). He is, in the words of Peter Hall, 'a painter in love with the theatre' who has worked with Joan Littlewood and Peter Hall and taught Yolanda Sonnabend and Derek Jarman. He has always held a fascination for night subjects.
Cat. no. 216

NOEL SPENCER (1901–86)
Born and brought up in Lancashire where he went to Ashton-under-Lyne art school for four years. Trained at the RCA (1923–6), where he met his wife Vera Wheeler. His teaching career (1926–64) ranged from Birmingham's College of Art & Crafts to Sheffield, Huddersfield and finally Norwich School of Art (1946–64). His studies and sketches of London (many of the Thames and a number in the collection of the Museum of London) were made from student days until about 1957.
Cat. no. 208, Appendix (Modern)

P. STAHL (active late nineteeth century)
Nothing is known about this artist.
Cat. no. 110

ERNEST STAMP (1869–1942)
Portrait painter and mezzotint engraver. Born at Sowerby, Yorkshire, the son of a leather merchant. Studied under Sir Hubert Herkomer. Lived at Bushey, and later in Hampstead. He exhibited at the RA from 1892.
Appendix (Early Twentieth Century)

CALEB ROBERT STANLEY (1795–1868)
Topographical and landscape painter. Honorary exhibitor at the RA (1816–63) but mainly exhibited at the BI (87 works) and elsewhere. Lived in Mayfair. His studio sale was held at Christie's 19 March 1869.
Cat. no. 63

ARTURO DI STEFANO (born 1955)
Painter born of Italian parents. Trained at Goldsmiths' College (1974–7), the RCA (1978–81) and the Accademia Albertina in Turin (1985–86). Initially he painted interiors, followed by a series of histroric portraits (often literary figures). Around 1990, his subject matter changed completely and he started painting London, where he lives and works. These images are totally devoid of people. At the time of writing Di Stefano has just started on a series of etchings of London scenes.
Cat. no. 229

ROBERT WRIGHT STEWART (?–1950)
Painter and etcher. Trained at the Edinburgh School of Art (*c.*1906), at the RCA in 1908, and in Paris. Lived in Chelsea. Taught at the RCA in 1926.
Cat. no. 161

WILLIAM STEWART (1886–1967)
Press artist, illustrator and scene-painter. Born in Greenwich, the son of a journalist. Studied at the Lambeth Art School and lived in Stockwell. For over forty years he was a scenic artist, starting at the old Elephant and Castle in 1910 and later working for Drury Lane, the Lyceum, the Queen's and the King's, Hammersmith. He retired to Jointure Cottage, Ditchling, Sussex, also the home of Frank Brangwyn. He worked in the studio of Brangwyn and stayed on after the latter's death in 1967. Stewart's figure style shows the influence of this artist. He is the author of *Characters of Bygone London*, 1960.
Cat. nos 158, 159

DIRCK (RODERIGO) STOOP (*c.*1618–86?)
Dutch painter and etcher who specialised in horse pictures. Probably born at Utrecht. He was appointed official painter to the court of Portugal and came to England in 1662 when Catherine of Braganza married Charles II. He may have remained in London until 1665.
Cat. no. 7

W. THOMSON (active early nineteenth century)
Genre painter; nothing is known about his life.
Cat. no. 72

JOSEPH JOHNSTON THORN (1898–1973)
Born Harold Vincent Woodfield Johnson in Leicester and changed his name in 1931. He moved to Hammersmith about 1920 where he lived until the end of his life. After his family (in the Leicester boot industry) lost all their money, the artist was apprenticed to a sign-writer and trained at Leicester art school. He served in the Royal Artillery, Third Army, in France as Gunner Johnson and was wounded in 1918. Painted murals at the 1924 Wembley exhibition. During World War II served in the Civil Defence in Hammersmith. Had a nervous breakdown after the war from which he never recovered.
Cat. no. 176

DAVID TINDLE (born 1932)
Landscape, topographical and abstract painter. Born in Huddersfield. Studied at Coventry Art School. Taught at Hornsey College of Art, and lived in Islington. Now lives in France and paints still lifes and interiors.
Cat. no. 202

DANIEL TURNER (active 1782–1806)
Landscape, marine and portrait painter and engraver; best known for his views of London's riverside. Pupil of John Jones, the mezzotint engraver. Lived in Millbank. Sometimes known as David Turner.
Cat. nos 49, 51, 52, Appendix (Regency)

CLAUDE ALFRED PENNINGTON WALKER (1862–*c.*1925)
Picture restorer and topographical painter. Born in Cheltenham, the son of a mathematician. Studied at the South Kensington schools. Lived first in Primrose Hill and Belsize Park, and afterwards in Fulham.
Cat. no. 143

RICHARD I. B. WALKER (born 1925)
Painter (mainly portraits) and illustrator (music books). Born and based in Croydon. Trained at Croydon Art School (1948–53) and later at the Slade. Extensive travels. Now runs his own teaching studio. Has a special interest in architectural painting.
Cat. no. 211

THOMAS WATERS (active mid-nineteenth century)
Amateur artist.
Appendix (Victorian)

KIRBY WATFORD (active late nineteenth century)
Amateur artist.
Appendix (Victorian)

CHARLES JOHN WATSON (1846–1927)
Topographical painter, etcher and lithographer. Born in Norwich, the son of a printseller, carver and gilder. Prevented from studying in London by his father's death, and carried on the family business. Left Norwich in 1888, and lived first in Chelsea and afterwards in Hammersmith.
Cat. no. 100

JAMES WEBB (1825–95)
Marine and landscape painter. He was born in a family of artists (Archibald and Byron, also based at the same address, exhibited at the RA). Lived at Trafalgar Lodge, Chelsea.
Cat. no. 81

CAREL WEIGHT (born 1908)
Painter born in London. Trained at Hammersmith School of Art and Goldsmiths' College and first exhibited at the RA in 1931. He was a war artist and joined the staff of the RCA soon after, in 1947. He was Head of Painting at the RCA between 1955 and 1973 and was elected RA in 1965. His principal source of inspiration has been South London, where he lives, and many of his suburban scenes are disrupted by ghosts and violent incidents.
Cat. no. 201

C. WELLS (active mid-nineteenth century)
Nothing is known about this artist.
Cat. no. 118

SAMUEL DE WILDE (*c.*1751–1832)
Painter of theatrical portraits and scenes. Born in Holland. Apprenticed to a carver in Soho. Student at the RA Schools 1769. Pupil of Zoffany. His theatrical portraits began in 1790 and were first exhibited at the RA in 1795. Portrayed nearly every leading actor and actress of the day in their principal roles; many of these portraits were acquired by the collector, Charles Mathews, and purchased for the Garrick Club in 1835. Lived chiefly in Covent Garden.
Cat. no. 45

FREDERICK A. WINKFIELD (active 1873–1904, d.1920)
Landscape and marine painter. Lived in Fulham.
Cat. nos 82, 83, Appendix (Victorian)

ALFRED WITHERS (1856–1932)
Painter of rural and urban scenes. Exhibited at the RA from 1882. Member and Secretary of the Society of Twenty-five English Painters formed in 1906.
Cat. no. 148

RAYMOND WYLIE (active 1960s)
Nothing is known about this artist.
Cat. nos 206, 207, Appendix (Modern)

CHARLES WILLIAM WYLLIE (1859–1923)
Landscape and marine painter, brother of William Lionel W. Trained at Leigh's School of Art and the RA Schools. Exhibited at the RA from 1872.
Cat. no. 151

BRIAN YALE (born 1936)
Painter and sculptor born in Staffordshire. Trained at Stourbridge School of Art (1952–6) and the RCA (1958–62). He was a founder member of the Group One Four dedicated to promoting art to a wider public and responsible for more than eighty exhibitions (1965–71). Between 1968 and 1986 he was artist/environmental designer in the Architectural Department of the Greater London Council. In 1988 and 1991 he received two major commissions from the London Docklands Development Corporation, one for sculptures on the theme of nature (Beckton) and the other for a huge free-standing frieze on the history of the docks (Prince Regent Station). The latter was erected in 1995 and the artist presented the Museum with the preparatory drawings for this work.
Cat. no. 218

List of donors

GIFTS AND BEQUESTS

Acworth, Angus Whiteford   cat. no. 22   1981
Alice, HRH Princess   cat. no. 14   1960
Alward, Peter   cat. nos 206, 207, Appendix (Modern)   1983
Anderson, A. E.   cat. no. 145   1918
Anglis, W. G. M.   cat. no. 205   1983

Baker, Miss Grace   Appendix (Georgian)   1930
Barber, A.T.   Appendix (Regency)   1924
Barlow, Miss H. A. D.   cat. nos 168, 170,
Appendix (Early Twentieth Century)   1976
Baty, Charles   cat. no. 179   1968
Bevan, R. A.   cat. no. 179   1968
Bonham-Carter, Lady Charlotte   cat. nos 12, 139   1990
Bonney, Mrs Victor   cat. no. 105   1957
Borradaile, Rosamund   cat. no. 169   1926
Boyd, R. Just   cat. no. 173   1928
Brooke-Bootes, Mrs   Appendix (Victorian)   1964
Buckley Slater, Graham   cat. no. 119   1987
Burgin, C.   Appendix (Victorian)   1953
Burn, Gerald M.   cat. no. 114, Appendix (Victorian)   1912
Byers, Norman J.   cat. no. 117   1917

Clay, Arthur   cat. no. 133   1927
Coleman, Bernard (The Castle, Tooting)   cat. no. 153   1957
Contemporary Art Society   cat. no. 196   1994
Cook, Ernest E.   cat. no. 41   1955
Cotton, Miss Mildred Aldrich   Appendix (Stuart)   1951
Crossley, Gordon Y.   cat. no. 118   1972

Dowson, S. H.   cat. no. 100   1939
Durham, Mary Edith   cat. nos 136, 138, 152   1922

Elbourne, Mrs Freda   cat. no. 187   1989
Elephant Trust, The   cat. no. 180   1983
Ellam, Miss Ruth   cat. no. 53   1985
Esher, Oliver, 3rd Viscount   cat. no. 92   1919
Esher, Reginald, 2nd Viscount   Appendix (Stuart)   1927

Fitzgerald, Sir Arthur   cat. no. 21   1966
Ford Smith, M. C.   cat. no. 149   1916
Forster, Miss Evelyn   cat. no. 112   1926
Fownes, Misses   cat. no. 104   1944
Fraser, George   cat. no. 162   1965

Granard, Bernard, 8th Earl of   cat. no. 70   1938
Green-Armytage, R. N.   cat. nos 44, 48, 155,
Appendix (Victorian)   1956
Grundy, Reginald C.   Appendix (Victorian)   1934

Haines, Mr. V.   cat. no. 189,
Appendix (Early Twentieth Century)   1980
Harmsworth, Cecil B.   cat. no. 33   1919
Heath, Ernest Dudley   cat. no. 111   1941
Herrick Collins, Mr L.   cat. no. 52   1987
Heslewood, Tom   Appendix (Victorian)   1938
Hitchcock Williams   cat. no. 148   1984
Holmes, Lady   cat. no. 140   1937
Hooke, Alan F.   Appendix (Victorian)   1920

Joicey, J. G.   Appendix (Regency)   1915
cat nos 57, 58   1916
cat. nos 56, 89,   Appendix (Georgian)   1919
cat. no. 1   1920
Jones, William   cat. no. 9   1927
Joy, Rosalind B.   cat. no. 134   1966

Leggatt Brothers cat. no. 88, Appendix (Regency) 1912
London County Council Appendix (Stuart) 1956
Lumley, Theodore cat. no. 59 1914

Mackenzie Bell, Mrs Appendix (Victorian) 1956
Mao Wen Biao cat. no. 226, Appendix (Modern) 1993
Markino, Yoshio cat. no. 172 1929
Martin-Harvey, Lady cat. no. 160 1950
Mayo, Dermot, 7th Earl of cat. no. 98 1923
MGC/V&A Purchase Grant Fund
cat. no. 144 1981
cat. no. 31 1982
cat. no. 38, 146 1983
cat. no. 34 1984
cat. no. 178 1985
cat. nos 35, 128 1988
cat. no. 124 1990
cat. no. 3 1991
cat. no. 127 1995
Montmorency, G. S. M. de cat. no. 84 1953

National Art Collections Fund
cat. no. 33 1919
cat. nos 54, 173 1928
cat. no. 17, Appendix (Victorian) 1934
cat. no. 15 1935
cat. no. 10 1951
cat. no. 41 1955
cat. no. 8 1957
cat. nos 165, 183, 184, 185 1959
cat. no. 13 1962
cat. no. 2 1964
cat. no. 156 1978
cat. no. 7 1979
cat. no. 80 1985
cat. no. 124 1990
cat. no. 125 1993
cat. no. 127 1995
National Heritage Memorial Fund cat. no. 125 1993
Neilson, Julia cat. no. 157 1938
Newman Ltd, Messrs M. cat. no. 182 1970
Nicholson, A. L. cat. no. 54 1928

Pawsey and Payne, Messrs Appendix (Victorian) 1931
Phillips, P. A. S. cat. no. 78 1923
Pierpont Morgan Jr, J. cat. no. 27 1923
Power, A. D. cat. nos 183, 184, 185 1959
Queen Victoria Eugenie of Spain cat. nos 121, 122 1960

Reeves, G. M. cat. no. 193 1981
Robson, Misses cat. no. 135 1938
Roe, Frederick Gordon Appendix (Victorian) 1923
Rooke, Herbert K. Appendix (Victorian), 2 paintings 1928
Royal National Pension Fund for Nurses Appendix (Stuart) 1964
Royce, A. D. Appendix (Modern) 1964

Samuel, Marcus R. cat. nos 23, 24 1942
Science Museum cat. nos 71, 163,
Appendix (Early Twentieth Century) 1980
cat. no. 115 (PRISM Fund) 1995
Scott Stewart, Ann cat. no. 161 1966
Scrimgeour, John cat. no. 101 1928
Shorter, Clement (the *Sphere*) cat. no. 151 1919
Shuckard, F. P. cat. no. 113 1923
Slater, Mrs Barbara cat. no. 154 1966
Smith, Owen H. cat. no. 15 1935
Spencer, Noel cat. no. 208 and Appendix (Modern) 1981
Stamp. Ernest Appendix (Early Twentieth Century) 1937
Stephenson, Professor W. B. cat. no. 123 1952
Suffragette Fellowship cat. no. 171 1950
Sutherland, Mrs S. E. Appendix (Regency) 1977

Tangye, Sir Harold Lincoln cat. nos 4, 5, 6, 116 1913
Temple, E. (pseudonym) cat. no. 129 1938
Thorn, J. C. cat. no. 176 1973
Tytler, Ernest J. Appendix (Victorian) 1960

Welch, Charles Appendix (Stuart) 1912
Wheatley, Sydney W. Appendix (Regency) 1927
Wood, Miss Emily J. (to the National Gallery)
cat. no.65 1897 and 1957

Yakovleff, Alexandre cat. no. 76 1938
Yale, Brian cat. no. 218 1996
Yorke, Nina de cat. no. 190 1974

Zeal, Messrs cat. nos 71, 163,
Appendix (Between the Wars) 1980

Bibliography

The single most quoted publication in this volume is John Hayes's *Catalogue of the Oil Paintings in the London Museum*, published by HMSO in 1970. This has been out of print since around 1980 but constitutes an important basic reference work for *London in Paint*. All catalogue entries previously published by John Hayes have been noted under the 'bibliography' of the individual painting as Hayes (cat. no…). In a number of cases the text has been used without alteration, but many of the entries have been revised or updated. Catalogue entries without this reference are for works acquired after the Hayes catalogue had gone to press.

This bibliography, although far from exhaustive, is not simply the total of the works mentioned throughout the text. It has been expanded to be used as a reference tool.

The A to Z of Elizabethan London, compiled by Adrian Prockter and Robert Taylor, with introductory notes by John Fisher, London Topographical Society, 1979

The A to Z of Georgian London, with notes by Ralph Hyde, London Topographical Society, 1982

The A to Z of Regency London, with an introduction by Paul Laxton and Joseph Wisdom, London Topographical Society, 1985

The A to Z of Victorian London, with notes by Ralph Hyde,London Topographical Society, 1987

Adams, Bernard: *London Illustrated* 1604–1851, 1983

[Agasse] *Jacques Laurent Agasse*, exhibition catalogue, Tate Gallery, 1989

Allen, Brian: *Francis Hayman*, Yale Center for British Art, New Haven, 1987

[Allen] *Kathleen Allen, a retrospective exhibition*, exhibition catalogue, South London Art Gallery, 1983

Allwood, Rosamund: *George Elgar Hicks*, exhibition catalogue, Geffrye Museum, 1982

Altick, Richard: *The Shows of London*, Massachusetts and London, 1978

Archer, Ian with Barron, Caroline and Harding, Vanessa: *Hugh Alley's Caveat: the Markets of London in 1598*, London Topographical Society, 1988

Atkinson, Diane: *Suffragettes* (London Connection series), Museum of London, 1988

Atkinson, Diane: *Purple White and Green: Suffragettes in London 1906–14*, Museum of London, 1993

Atkinson, Diane and Gardner, Viv (eds): *Kitty Marion: The Autobiography of a Suffragette and Actress*, Museum of London, forthcoming 1997

Ayres, James: *The Artist's Craft*, 1985

Barker, Felix and Jackson, Peter: *London 2000 years of a city and its people*, 1974

Barker, Felix and Hyde, Ralph: *London as it Might Have Been*, 1982

Barker, Felix and Jackson, Peter: *The History of London in Maps*, 1990

Baron, Wendy: *The Camden Town Group*, 1979

Baron, Wendy: *Sickert*, 1973

Baron, Wendy and Shone, Richard (eds) *Sickert Paintings*, exhibition catalogue, Royal Academy, 1993

Baron, Xavier (ed.): *London 1066–1914 Literary Sources & Documents*, 2 vols, publ. Helm Information, 1996

Battiscombe, Georgina: *Shaftesbury*, 1974

Beckett, Jane and Cherry, Deborah: *The Edwardian Era*, Barbican Art Gallery, 1987

Bell, Walter G.: *The Great Fire of London*, 1920

Bénézit, E.: *Dictionnaire des Peintres, Sculpteurs, Dessinateurs et Graveurs*, 8 vols, first publ. 1948

Beresford Chancellor, E.: *Lost London*, 1926

Beresford Ellis, John: *The Great Fire of London*, 1976

[Bevan] *Oliver Bevan – The Farringdon Paintings*, exhibition catalogue, Rochdale Art Gallery, 1983
Bevan, Oliver: *Witnesses and Dreamers*, exhibition catalogue for touring exhibition, 1993
Bevan, R. A.: *Robert Bevan*, 1965
[Bomberg] *David Bomberg, A tribute to Lilian Bomberg*, exhibition catalogue, Fischer Fine Art, 1985
Booth, Charles: *Life and Labour of the People of London*, 17 vols, 1892–7, reprinted AMS Press, New York, 1970
Borden, Iain; Kerr, Joe; Pivaro, Alicia and Rendell, Jane (eds): *Strangely Familiar, narratives of architecture in the city*, 1996
Brailey, E. W. and Britton, John: *The History of the Ancient Palace & late Houses of Parliament at Westminster*, 1836
Brailey, E. W.: *A Topographical History of Surrey*, 5 vols, 1841
Brangwyn, Rodney: *Brangwyn*, 1978
Brazell, J. H.: *London Weather*, 1968
Brettell, Richard and Pissarro, Joachim: *The Impressionist and the City, Pissarro's Series Paintings*, exhibition catalogue, Royal Academy, 1992
Bryan's *Dictionary of Painters and Engravers*, 5 vols, 1910–13
[Buhler] *Robert Buhler R.A. – Paintings 1937 to 1984*, exhibition catalogue, Austin/Desmond Fine Art, 1985

[Canaletto] *Canaletto and his Influence on London Artists*, exhibition catalogue, Guildhall Art Gallery, 1965
Carey, Frances: 'The Shelter Sketchbooks', *British Museum Society Bulletin*, Autumn 1988
Mr Cartwright's Pictures, A Seventeenth Century Collection, exhibition catalogue, Dulwich Picture Gallery, 1988
Casanova: *The Memoirs of Jacques Casanova de Seingalt*, privately printed for the Navarre Society, 1922
[Cazalet, Mark] *Intangible Worlds*, exhibition catalogue, East West Gallery, 1995
[Christies] *Painters of Camden Town 1905–20, The*, Wendy Baron and Francis Farmar, exhibition catalogue, Christie's, 1988
The City's Pictures, exhibition catalogue, Barbican Art Gallery, 1984
Clapp, Samuel: *Gustave Doré 1832–1883*, exhibition catalogue, Hazlitt, Gooden and Fox, London, 1983
Clark, John: 'Trinovantum – the evolution of a legend', in *Journal of Medieval History* 7, 1981
Clay, Rotha Mary: *Julius Caesar Ibbetson 1759–1817*, 1948
Coke, David: *The Muse's Bower, Vauxhall Gardens 1728–1786*, exhibition catalogue, Gainsborough's House, 1978
Constable, W. G. (revised J. G. Links), *Canaletto*, 1989
Cork, Richard: *David Bomberg*, 1987
Cork, Richard: *David Bomberg*, exhibition catalogue, Tate Gallery, 1988
Crouan, Katharine: *John Linnell*, exhibition catalogue, Martyn Gregory Gallery, 1982
Crouan, Katharine: *John Linnell*, exhibition catalogue, Fitzwilliam Museum, Cambridge, 1982
Cruikshank, Dan and Burton, Neil: *Life in the Georgian city*, 1990

Dabydeen, David: *Hogarth's Blacks*, 1985
Dacey, Jane: 'A note on Canaletto's Views of Greenwich', in *The Burlington Magazine*, 1981
Daniels, Jeffery: 'C. R. Leslie: A Rediscovery', in *Art and Artists*, January 1977
Dawson, Alfred: *The Life of Henry Dawson, Landscape Painter*, 1891
Denvir, Bernard (ed.): *The Impressionists at first hand*, 1987
Derby Day 200, exhibition catalogue compiled by Patricia Connor and Lionel Lambourne, Royal Academy of Arts, 1979
Dethier, Jean and Guiheux, Alain (eds): *La ville, art et architecture en Europe, 1870–1993*, Pompidou Centre, Paris, 1994
Deuchar, Stephen: *Paintings, Politics and Porter*, exhibition catalogue, publ. Whitbread & Co, 1984
Dictionary of National Biography, 63 vols, 1885–1900
Dodd, George: *Days at the Factory*, 1843
[Doré] *Gustave Doré 1832–1883*, exhibition catalogue, Musée d'Art Moderne, Strasbourg, 1983
Dorment, Richard and MacDonald, Margaret F.: *James McNeill Whistler*, exhibition catalogue, Tate Gallery, 1994
Dyos, H. J. and Woolf, M. (eds): *The Victorian City: images and realities*, 2 vols, 1976
Dyson, Tony: *Pictures to Print*, 1984

Edmond, Mary: 'Limners and Picture Makers – New light on the lives of miniaturists and large-scale portrait painters working in London in the sixteenth and seventeenth centuries', in *Walpole Society*, 1978–1980
Einberg, Elizabeth and Egerton, Judy: *The Age of Hogarth, British Painters born 1675–1709*, Tate Gallery, 1988
Eitner, Lorenz E. A.: *Géricault, his Life and Work*, 1983
Ellmers, Chris and Werner, Alex: *London's Lost Riverscape*, 1988
Ellmers, Chris and Werner, Alex: *Dockland Life: A Pictorial History of London's Docks 1860–1970*, 1991, reprinted 1995
Elmes, James and Shepherd, Thomas: Hosmer: *Metropolitan Improvements: London in the nineteenth century*, 2 vols, London, 1827–30
Emden, C.: *Picturesque Westminster*, 1902
[Euston Road School] *Painting the Visible World – Painters at the Euston Road School and at Camberwell School of Arts and Crafts 1930–1960*, exhibition catalogue, Austin/Desmond Fine Art, 1988
Evans, Wendy, Ross, Catherine and Werner, Alex: *Whitefriars Glass*, Museum of London, 1996
Eyre, Karen and Galinou, Mireille: *Picnics*, (London Connections series), Museum of London, 1988
[Eyton] *Anthony Eyton, retrospective exhibition*, South London Art Gallery, 1980

Farington, Joseph: *The Diary of Joseph Farington*, Kenneth Garlick and Angus McIntyre (eds), Yale University Press, Newhaven and London, vols, I–VI, 1978–9, vols, VII–XI, Kathryn Cave (ed.), 1982–3
Farr, Denis: *English Art 1870–1940*, Oxford, 1978
Feret, C. J.: *Fulham Old and New*, 3 vols, 1900
Finberg, Hilda F.: 'Pictures of Covent Garden in the Duke of Bedford's collection' in *Country Life*, 10 September 1921
Fox, Celina and Ribero, Aileen: *Masquerade*, (London Connections series), Museum of London, 1983
Fox, Celina: *Londoners*, 1987
Fox, Celina: 'Hogarth's Southwark Fair', in Notes, *Print Quarterly*, vol. IV, no. 4, December 1987
Fox, Celina: 'Géricault's Lithographs of the London Poor', in *Print Quarterly*, vol. V, 1988

Fox, Celina: 'Introduction to *Specimens of Genius truly English*, an exhibition of 18th century designs for London signboards from the collection of the late Lord Clark', exhibition catalogue, The Clarendon Gallery and Niall Hobhouse, 1984
Fox, Celina (ed.): *London – World City 1800–1840*, Yale University Press, Newhaven and London, 1992 (separate index available, publ. 1995)
Frayling, Christopher: *The Royal College of Art*, 1987
Friedman, Terry: *Great Paintings of Victorian Daily Life*, exhibition catalogue, Leeds City Art Galleries, 1986
Frith, William: *My Autobiography and Reminiscences*, 1888
From London [Bacon, Freud, Kossoff, Andrews, Auerbach, Kitaj], exhibition catalogue, British Council, 1995

Galinou, Mireille: 'Adam Lee's Drawings of St Stephen's Chapel, Westminster – Antiquarianism and showmanship in early 19th century London', in *Transactions of the London and Middlesex Archaeological Society*, vol. 34, 1983
Galinou, Mireille: 'The Discreet Charm of Edwardian London' in *The Antique Collector*, December, 1986
Galinou, Mireille: 'Palace on Paper' [Adam Lee], in *Country Life*, 3 November 1988
Galinou, Mireille: 'Green Finger Painting', [James Tissot], *Country Life*, 13 July 1989
Galinou, Mireille (ed.): *London's Pride – The Glorious History of the Capital's Gardens*, 1990
Galinou, Mireille: 'Acquisition in focus', in *Apollo*, vol. 140, 1994
Garlick, Kenneth: *Sir Thomas Lawrence*, 1989

Gaunt, William: *The Restless Century, Painting in Britain 1800–1900*, 1972
George, Dorothy: *London Life in the XVIIIth century*, 1925
Getting London in Perspective, exhibition catalogue, Barbican Art Gallery, 1984
Gibbs-Smith, C. H.: *The Great Exhibition of 1851*, exhibition catalogue, Victoria and Albert Museum, 1981
A Gift to the Nation: The Fine And Decorative Art Collections of Ernest E. Cook, exhibition catalogue, Holburne Museum, Bath, 1991
Goldwater, R. and Treves, M. (eds): *Artists on Art*, 1976
Gordon, C.: *Old Time Aldwych, Kingsway & Neighbourhood*, *c.*1904
[Gore] *Spencer Frederick Gore*, exhibition catalogue, Anthony d'Offay, 1983
Gowing, Lawrence: *Lucian Freud*, 1982
Graves, Algernon: *The Royal Academy Exhibitors 1769–1904*, 1905–06
Graves, Algernon: *The Society of Artists 1760–1791, The Free Society of Artists 1761–1783*, 1907
[Greaves] *Walter Greaves*, exhibition catalogue, Leighton House
[Greaves] *Walter Greaves and the Nocturne*, exhibition catalogue, Parkin Gallery, 1974
Griffiths, Anthony and Kesnerova, Gabriela: *Wenceslaus Hollar*, British Museum, 1983
[Grimshaw] *Atkinson Grimshaw*, exhibition catalogue, Leeds City Art Gallery, 1979
[Grimshaw] *Atkinson Grimshaw*, exhibition catalogue, Richard Green and Christopher Wood, 1990
Groenveld, Simon and Wintle, Michael (eds): 'The Exchange of Ideas', in *Britain and the Netherlands*, Zutphen, Netherlands, 1994, vol. XI
[Guildhall Art Gallery]*1666 and other London Fires*, exhibition catalogue, Guildhall Art Gallery, 1966
Guiterman, Helen and Llewelyn, Briony: *David Roberts*, exhibition catalogue, Barbican Art Gallery, 1986

Harben, Henry A.: *A Dictionary of London*, 1918
Harley, R. D.: *Artists's Pigments 1600–1835*, 2nd ed., 1982
Hardwick, Arthur: *Memorable Fires*, 1926
Harris, John: *The Artist and the Country House*, 1979
Harris, John: *The Artist and the Country House – From the fifteenth century to the present day*, exhibition catalogue, Sotheby's, 1996
Harris, Susie and Meirion: *The War Artists*, 1983
Haskell, Francis: *Past and Present in Art and Taste*, Yale University Press, New Haven and London, 1987
Hassell, Geoff: *Camberwell School of Arts and Crafts, its students & teachers 1943–1960*, Antique Collectors' Club, 1995
[Hay] *James Hamilton Hay*, exhibition catalogue, Walker Art Gallery, Liverpool, 1973
Haydon, Benjamin: *The Diaries of Benjamin Haydon*, John Joliffe (ed.), 1990
Hayes, John: 'Claude de Jongh', in *The Burlington Magazine*, no. 634, vol. XCVIII, January 1956
Hayes, John: *Catalogue of the Oil Paintings in the London Museum*, 1970
Hearn, Karen (ed.): *Dynasties*, exhibition catalogue, Tate Gallery, 1995
Hearsay, John E. N.: *London and the Great Fire*, 1965
[Hemy] *Charles Napier Hemy R.A. 1841–1917*, exhibition catalogue, Laing Art Gallery, Tyne and Wear, 1984
[Hepher] *David Hepher New Paintings*, exhibition catalogue, Flowers East, 1989
Hibbert, Christopher: *London the Biography of a City*, 1969
Hicks, Alistair: *The School of London*, Oxford, 1989
Hobhouse, Hermione: *Prince Albert His Life and Work*, 1983
Hobhouse, Hermione: 'Ninety Years of The Survey of London', in *Transactions of the Ancient Monuments Society*, vol. 31, 1987
Hobhouse, Hermione and Saunders, Ann (eds): *Good and Proper Materials: The Fabric of London since the Great Fire*, publ. London Topographical Society, 1989
[Hodgkin] *Eliot Hodgkin (1905–1987)*, exhibition catalogue, Hazlitt, Gooden & Fox, 1990
Hollis, Marianne (ed.): *Late Sickert*, exhibition catalogue, Arts Council, 1981
Hunting, Penelope: *Royal Westminster*, 1981
Hunting, Penelope: *St Paul's Vista*, commissioned by Lep Group plc to mark the development of the Sunlight Wharf Site, 1988
Hutchings: *London Town Past and Present*, 1909
Huxley, Paul (ed.): *Exhibition Road – Painters at the Royal College of Art*, 1988
Hyde, Ralph: *A Prospect of Britain – The Town Panoramas of Samuel and Nathaniel Buck*, 1994
Hyde, Ralph: *Gilded Scenes and Shining Prospects*, exhibition catalogue, Yale Center for British Art, New Haven, 1985
[Hyman] *Timothy Hyman, Recent Work*, exhibition catalogue, Austin/Desmond Fine Art, 1990

[Ibbetson] *Julius Caesar Ibbetson*, exhibition catalogue, Iveagh Bequest, Kenwood, 1957
The Impressionists in London, exhibition catalogue, Arts Council, 1973

'The Inventories and Valuations of the King's Goods 1649–1651', in *Walpole Society*, no. 43
[Ipswich] *On the Streets – A View of the Urban Landscape*, exhibition catalogue, Ipswich Borough Museums and Galleries, 1991

Jackson, Kevin (ed.): *The Humphrey Jennings Film Reader*, 1993
Jackson, Peter: *George Scharf's London*, 1987
Jennings, Mary-Lou (ed.): *Humphrey Jennings Film-Maker/Painter/ Poet*, British Film Institute, 1982
Jerrold, Blanchard: *London: A Pilgrimage*, 1872
Johnson, J. and Greutzner, A.: *British Artists 1880–1940*, Antique Collectors' Club, 1994 (first publ. 1976)
Johnson, Jane: *Works exhibited at the Royal Society of British Artists 1824–1893 and the New English Art Club 1888–1917*, Antique Collectors' Club, 1993 (first publ. 1975)
[Joy] *The Work of George W. Joy*, Cassell & Co, 1904

Kingzett, Richard: 'A Catalogue of the Works of Samuel Scott', in *Walpole Society*, vol. 48
The Kitchen Sink Painters, exhibition catalogue, The Mayor Gallery with Julian Hartnoll, 1991
Knight, Vivien: *The Works of Art of the Corporation of London*, 1986
Knight, Vivien: 'Luke Clennell at the Guildhall', in *Apollo*, October 1993
[Kokoschka] *Oscar Kokoschka: London Views, British Landscapes*, 1972

Latham, Robert and Mathews, William (eds): *The Diary of Samuel Pepys*, 1971
[Laubin] 'Carl Laubin. Portrait', Jeremy Dixon, in *Archives d'Architecture Moderne*, no. 40, Brussels, 1989
Laughton, Bruce: *The Euston Road School*, 1986
Le Bas, E.: *A Painter's Collection*, exhibition catalogue, Royal Academy, 1963
Links, J. G.: 'Canaletto and old Westminster', in *Apollo*, May 1992
Liversidge, Michael and Farrington, Jane (eds): *Canaletto & England*, exhibition catalogue, Birmingham Art Gallery, 1993
Lucie-Smith, Edward: *David Hepher*, 1996
Ludovici, A.: *An Artist's Life in London and Paris, 1870–1925*, 1926

Maas, Jeremy: *The Prince of Wales Wedding*, 1977
Maas, Jeremy: *Victorian Painters*, 1969
McConkey, Kenneth: *Sir John Lavery*, Edinburgh, 1993
McConkey, Kenneth: *Impressionism in Britain*, exhibition catalogue, Barbican Art Gallery, 1995
[McFadyen, Jock] *Canal*, exhibition catalogue, William Jackson Gallery, 1991; 'Jock McFadyen: towards the edge of a reality', *Art Line International*, vol. 5, no. 7, Spring 1992
Mackintosh, Iain and Ashton, Geoffrey: *The Georgian Playhouse*, exhibition catalogue, Arts Council, 1975
Manners and Morals – Hogarth and British Painting 1700–1760, exhibition catalogue, Tate Gallery, 1987
Marcan, Peter: *Artists and the East End*. Peter Marcan Publications, 1986
Markino, Yoshio: *A Japanese in London*, 1910
Maré, Eric de: *London 1851, The Year of the Great Exhibition*, 1973
Masters, Betty R.: *The Public Markets of the City of London surveyed by William Leybourn in 1677*, publ. London Topographical Society, 1974
Matyjaszkiewitcz, Krystyna (ed.): *James Tissot*, exhibition catalogue, Barbican Art Gallery, 1984
Mayhew, Henry: *London Labour and the London Poor*, 2nd ed. 1861–2, reprinted in 4 vols, Dover, New York, 1968
Mellor, David: *The Sixties Art Scene in London*, Barbican Art Gallery, 1993
Merriman, Nick (ed): *The Peopling of London: 15,000 Years of Settlement from Overseas*, Museum of London, 1993
Millar, Oliver and Whinney, Margaret: *English Art 1625–1714*, Oxford, 1957
Millar, Oliver: *The Tudor, Stuart and Early Georgian Pictures in the collection of Her Majesty the Queen*, 2 vols, 1963
Millar, Oliver: *The Later Georgian Pictures in the collection of Her Majesty the Queen*, 2 vols, 1969
Millar, Oliver: *The Age of Charles I*, exhibition catalogue, Tate Gallery, 1972
Millar, Oliver: *Sir Peter Lely 1618–80*, exhibition catalogue, National Portrait Gallery, 1978
Millar, Oliver: *The Victorian Pictures in the Collection of Her Majesty the Queen*, Cambridge, 1992
Milne, Gustav: *The Great Fire of London*, 1986
Montias, Michael J.: *Artists and Artisans in Delft*, Princeton, New Jersey, 1982
Montias, Michael J.: 'Cost and value in seventeeth century art', in *Art History*, vol. 10, December 1987
Moore, Andrew W.: *Dutch and Flemish Paintings in Norfolk*, 1988,
Mordaunt Crook, J.: *The Dilemma of Style*, 1987
Morris, Edward and Milner, Frank: *When did you last see your Father?* exhibition catalogue, Walker Art Gallery, Liverpool, 1993
Morris, Edward and McKay, Amanda: 'British Art Students in Paris 1814–1890, Demand and Supply', in *Apollo*, February 1992
Morris, Linda and Radford, Robert: *AIA The Story of the Artists International Association 1933–1953*, Museum of Modern Art, Oxford, 1983

[National Art Collections Fund] *The New Patrons*, exhibition catalogue by the NACF, Christie's, 1992
Nadell, I. B. and Schwarzbach, F. S. (eds): *Victorian Artists and the City*, 1980
Nevinson, C. R. W.: *Paint and Prejudice*, 1937
[Nevinson] *Nevinson War Paintings*, exhibition catalogue, Graves Art Gallery, Sheffield, 1972
[Nevinson] *C.R.W. Nevinson*, exhibition catalogue, Kettle's Yard, Cambridge, 1988
Nevinson, John: 'The Dress of the Citizens of London 1540–1640' in *Collectanea Londiniensia*, London and Middlesex Archaeological Society, 1978
[New English Art Club] *The Early Years of the New English Art Club*, exhibition catalogue, Fine Art Society, 1968
[New English Art Club] *The New English Art Club*, centenary exhibition, Christie's, 1986
Newall, Christopher: *The Grosvenor Gallery Exhibitions*, Cambridge, 1995
[Newton] *Algernon Newton R.A. 1880–1968*, exhibition catalogue, Graves Art Gallery, Sheffield, 1980
Noakes, A.: *William Frith, Extraordinary Victorian Painter*, 1978

Norman, Philip: *London Vanished and Vanishing*, 1905

Ogilvy, F.: *Reliques and Memorials of London Town*, 1901
Olsen, Donald: *The City as a Work of Art: London. Paris. Vienna*, Yale University Press, New Haven and London, 1986

Panoramania!, exhibition catalogue, Barbican Art Gallery, 1988
Paul, R.: *Vanishing London*, 1894
Paulson, Ronald: *Hogarth's Graphic Works*, 3rd revised ed., 1989
Pearce, David: *London Mansions*, 1986
Pears, Ian: *The Discovery of Painting*, 1988
Pfautz, Harold (ed.): *Charles Booth on the City: Physical Pattern and Social Structure*, Chicago, 1967
Piper, David: *Artists' London*, 1982
Piper, David: 'The contemporary portraits of Oliver Cromwell' in *Walpole Society*, vol. XXXIV, 1958
[Piper] *John Piper*, exhibition catalogue, Tate Gallery, 1993
Phillips, J. F .C.: *Shepherd's London*, 1976
Phillips, Hugh: *The Thames around 1750*, 1951
Phillips, Hugh: *Mid Georgian London*, 1964
Pointon, Marcia: *William Mulready*, exhibition catalogue, Victoria and Albert Museum, 1986
Porter, Roy: *London*, 1994
Pragnell, H. J.: *The London Panoramas of Robert Barker and Thomas Girtin c.1800*, London Topographical Society, 1968
[Pre-Raphaelites] *The Pre-Raphaelites*, exhibition catalogue, Tate Gallery, 1984
Pyne, W. H.: *The Costume of Great Britain*, 1808

Quarm, Roger and Wyllie, John: *W. L. Wyllie Marine Artist (1851–1931)*, Chris Beetles, 1981
Quiet Conquest: The, The Huguenots 1585–1985, Tessa Murdoch (ed.), exhibition catalogue, Museum of London, 1985

Raines, Robert: *Marcellus Lauron*, 1967
Reynolds, Graham: *Turner*, 1969
Reynolds, Graham: *Painters of the Victorian Scene*, 1953
Ribero, Aileen: *The Dress Worn at Masquerades in England 1730–90 and its relationship to fancy dress in portraiture*, New York, 1984 (originally presented as the author's PhD thesis in 1975)
[Richardson] *Art for Newcastle, Thomas Miles Richardson and the Newcastle Exhibitions 1822–1843*, Tyne and Wear County Council Museums, 1984
Rosenfeld, S.: *Theatre of the London Fairs in the 18th century*, Cambridge, 1960
Rothenstein, John: *Modern English Painters*, 1957
[Royal Academy] *Exhibition of Paintings by Firemen Artists*, Royal Academy, September 1941, catalogue foreword (copy seen in Art Department, Imperial War Museum)
Royal Academy Directory of Membership, from the foundation in 1768 to 1995, compiled by Gabriele Popp and Helen Valentine, 1996
Royal Academy exhibitors 1905–1970, 6 vols, 1973–82
[Royal College of Art] *An American Passion*, The Susan Summer and Robert D. Summer Collection of Contemporary British Painting, exhibition catalogue, Royal College of Art, 1994
Royal Opera House Retrospective 1732–1982, exhibition catalogue, Royal Academy, 1983

Sala, G. A.: *Twice Round the Clock*, 1859
Saunders, Ann: *The Art and Architecture of London*, Oxford, 1984
Saunders, Ann: *Regent's Park: a study of the development of the area from 1086 to the present day*, New York, 1969
Saussure, César de: *A foreign view of England in the reigns of George I and George II*, transl. and ed. Madame Van Muyden, London, 1902
Schofield, John (ed.): *The London Surveys of Ralph Treswell*, London Topographical Society, 1987
Schofield, John: *The Building of London from the Conquest to the Great Fire*, 2nd ed., 1993
Scouloudi, Irene: *Panoramic Views of London 1600–1666*, Guildhall Library, 1953
Scouloudi, Irene: 'Return of Strangers.in the Metropolis, 1593, 1627, 1635, 1639', in *Quarto Series of the Huguenot Society*, vol. LVII 1985
Sheppard, Francis: *The Treasury of London's Past*, Museum of London, 1991
[Sidaner] *Henri le Sidaner (1862–1939)*, exhibition catalogue, Musée Marmottan, Paris, 1989
Smith, Charles Manby: *Curiosities of London Life*, first publ. 1853, reprinted 1972 by Frank Cass & Co Ltd
Smith, John Thomas: *Vagabondiana*, 1817
Snodin, Michael (ed.): *Rococo Art & Design in Hogarth's England*, exhibition catalogue, Victoria and Albert Museum, 1984
Solender, Katherine: *Dreadful Fire! Burning of the Houses of Parliament*, exhibition catalogue, The Cleveland Museum of Art, 1984
Solkin, David H.: *Painting for Money – The Visual Arts and the Public Sphere in Eighteenth-Century England*, 1993
Spalding, Frances: *20th Century Painters and Sculptors*, The Antique Collectors' Club, 1990
[Stanfield] *The spectacular carreer of Clarkson Stanfield*, exhibition catalogue, Tyne and Wear Council Museums, 1979
[Stewart] *William Stewart: London Life, past and present*, exhibition pamphlet, Towner Art Gallery, Eastbourne, 1962
Strong, Sir Roy: *Tudor & Jacobean Portraits in the National Portrait Gallery*, 2 vols, 1969
Strong, Sir Roy: *When did you last see your father?*, 1978
Summerfield, Angela: *The Artist at War, Second World War Paintings & Drawings from the Walker Art Gallery's Collection*, Liverpool, 1990
Survey of London, 44 vols, 1900–94
Sutton, Denys: *Nocturne; The Art of James McNeill Whistler*, Country Life publications, 1963
Sykes, Christopher Simon: *Life in the Great London Houses*, 1985

Tangye Collection: *Catalogue of the Cromwellian collection in the possession of Sir Richard Tangye*, privately printed, 1905, (copy in the Museum of London Library)
[Tate Gallery] *Concise Catalogue of the Tate Gallery Collection*, first publ. 1967, 9th ed. 1991
Thomson, E.P. and Yeo, Eileen: *The Unknown Mayhew: Selections from the Morning Chronicle 1849–1850*, first publ. 1971, Penguin 1984
Treuherz, Julian: *Hard Times*, exhibition catalogue, Manchester City Art Galleries, 1987
Trewin, J. C.: *The Edwardian Theatre*, 1976
Tristan, Flora: *London Journal, 1840*, 1980
[Turner] *Turner 1775–1851*, exhibition catalogue, compiled by Butlin,

Martin; Wilton, Andrew and Gage, John: Tate Gallery, 1974

Vallès, Jules: *La Rue à Londres*, 1884
Vertue, G.: 'Note Books', in *Walpole Society*, 1930–55

Walford, Edward: *Frost Fairs on the Thames*, 1887 (privately printed)
Walker, R. J. B.: *Old Westminster Bridge: the Bridge of Fools*, 1979
Walkley, Giles: *Artists' Houses in London 1764–1914*, 1994
Ward, Ned: *The London Spy*, first publ. 1698, republ. 1927
Warner, Malcolm: *The Image of London – Views by Travellers and Emigrés 1550–1920*, exhibition catalogue, Barbican Art Gallery, 1987
Waterfield, Giles: *Palaces of Art*, exhibition catalogue, Dulwich Picture Gallery, 1992
Waterfield, Giles (ed.): *Art for the People – Culture in the Slums of late Victorian Britain*, exhibition catalogue, Dulwich Picture Gallery, 1994
Waterhouse, Ellis: *Painting in Britain, 1530 to 1790*, Oxford, 1953
Waterhouse, Ellis: *The Dictionary of British 18th Century Painters in oils and crayons*, Antique Collectors' Club, 1981
Waterhouse, Ellis: *The Dictionary of 16th & 17th Century British Painters*, Antique Collectors' Club, 1988
Waters, Grant M.: *Dictionary of British Artists working 1900–1950*, Eastbourne Fine Art, 1975
Way, T. R.: *Reliques of Old London*, 1897
Webster, Mary: *Johann Zoffany*, exhibition catalogue, National Portrait Gallery, 1976
Weightman, Gavin and Humphries, Steve: *The Making of Modern London, 1815–1914*, 1983
Weinreb, Ben and Hibbert, Christopher (eds): *The London Encyclopaedia*, 1983
Wentworth, Michael: *James Tissot*, Oxford, 1984
[Wilde] *The De Wildes*, exhibition catalogue, Northampton Central Art Gallery, 1971
Wilkinson, Robert: *Londina Illustrata*, 2 vols, 1819–34
[Whistler] *The Paintings of James McNeill Whistler*, Yale University Press, London and Newhaven, 1980
Whitley, William T.: *Artists and their Friends in England 1700–1799*, 2 vols, 1928
[Willats, Stephen] *The Lurky Place*, exhibition catalogue, Lisson Gallery, 1978
[Willats, Stephen] *The New Reality*, exhibition catalogue, Orchard Gallery,
Londonderry, 1982
Wood, Christopher: *Victorian Panorama*, 1976
Wood, Christopher: *Victorian Painters*, 1995, 2 vols, Antique Collectors' Club, 1995
[Wright] *The King's Painter, John Michael Wright*, exhibition catalogue, Scottish National Portrait Gallery, September 1982
Wroth, Warwick: *Cremorne and the later London Gardens*, 1907

Yung, K. K.: *National Portrait Gallery – Complete Illustrated Catalogue*, 1981

Index

Page numbers in *italics* refer to illustrations
(k) following page number indicates key to illustration

Churches are grouped under heading 'churches'
Chapels are under heading 'chapels'